DK EYEWITNESS
France
D0101585

Project Editor Rosemary Bailey
Art Editor Janis Utton
Editors Tanya Colbourne, Fiona Morgan, Anna Streiffert, Celia Woolfrey
Designers Joy FitzSimmons, Erika Lang, Clare Sullivan
Map Co-ordinators
Simon Farbrother, David Pugh
Researcher
Philippa Richmond
Main Contributors
John Ardagh, Rosemary Bailey, Judith Fayard, Lisa Gerard-Sharp, Colin Jones, Alister Kershaw, Alec Lobrano, Anthony Roberts, Alan Tillier, Nigel Tisdall
Photographers
Max Alexander, Neil Lukas, John Parker, Kim Sayer
Illustrators
Stephen Conlin, John Lawrence, Maltings Partnership, John Woodcock

Printed and bound in China

First published in Great Britain in 1994 by Dorling Kindersley Limited
80 Strand, London, WC2R 0RL, UK

18 19 20 21 10 9 8 7 6 5 4 3 2 1

Reprinted with revisions 1995, 1996, 1997, 1999, 2000, 2001, 2002, 2003, 2004, 2006, 2008, 2010, 2012, 2014, 2016, 2018

A CIP catalogue record is available from the British Library.

ISBN 978-0-2413-0612-3

Floors are referred to throughout in accordance with French usage; ie the "first floor" is the floor above ground level.

MIX
Paper from responsible sources
FSC™ C018179

Introducing France

Eiffel Tower, Paris

Paris and Ile-de-France

Lavender field near Gordes, Provence

The information in this DK Eyewitness Travel Guide is checked regularly.
Every effort has been made to ensure that this book is as up-to-date as possible at the time of going to press. Some details, however, such as telephone numbers, opening hours, prices, gallery hanging arrangements and travel information, are liable to change. The publishers cannot accept responsibility for any consequences arising from the use of this book, nor for any material on third-party websites, and cannot guarantee that any website address in this book will be a suitable source of travel information. We value the views and suggestions of our readers very highly. Please write to: Publisher, DK Eyewitness Travel Guides, Dorling Kindersley, 80 Strand, London WC2R 0RL, Great Britain, or email: travelguides@dk.com.

◀ **Title page** The stunning cliffs at Etretat, famous for their naturally formed archways and pointed "needle" **Front cover image** Semur-en-Auxois town with the River Armançon, Burgundy **Back cover image** The Mont-Blanc Massif, the French Alps

Contents

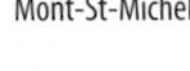

Mont-St-Michel

HOW TO USE THIS GUIDE

This guide helps you to get the most from your visit to France. It provides both expert recommendations and detailed practical information. *Introducing France* maps the country and sets it in its historical and cultural context. The 15 regional chapters, plus *Paris and Ile-de-France*, describe important sights, with maps, pictures and illustrations. Throughout, features cover topics from food and wine to culture and beaches. Restaurant and hotel recommendations can be found in *Travellers' Needs*. The *Survival Guide* has tips on everything from the French telephone system to transport.

Paris and Ile-de-France

The centre of Paris has been divided into five sightseeing areas. Each has its own chapter, which opens with a list of the sights described. A further section covers the Ile-de-France. All sights are numbered and plotted on an area map. The detailed information for each sight follows the map's numerical order, making sights easy to locate within the chapter.

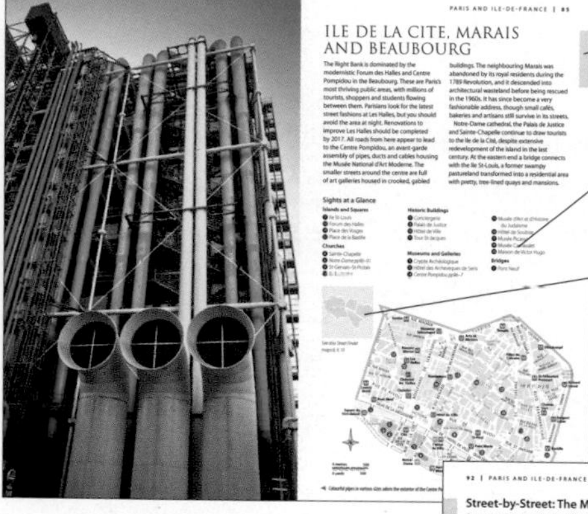

All pages relating to Paris and Ile-de-France have green thumb tabs.

Sights at a Glance lists the chapter's sights by category: Churches; Museums and Galleries; Historic Buildings; Squares and Gardens.

A locator map shows where you are in relation to other areas of the city centre.

1 Area Map For easy reference, the sights are numbered and located on a map. Sights in the city centre are also shown on the Paris Street Finder on pages 160–73.

A suggested route for a walk is shown in red.

Stars indicate the sights that no visitor should miss.

2 Street-by-Street Map This gives a bird's-eye view of the key areas in each chapter.

3 Detailed information The sights in Paris and the Ile-de-France are described individually. Addresses, telephone numbers, opening hours and information on admission charges and wheelchair access are also provided for each entry.

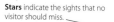

France Area by Area

Apart from Paris and Ile-de-France, the country has been divided into 15 regions, each of which has a separate chapter. The most interesting towns and places to visit have been numbered on a *Regional Map*.

1 Introduction The landscape, history and character of each region is described here, showing how the area has developed over the centuries and what it offers to the visitor today.

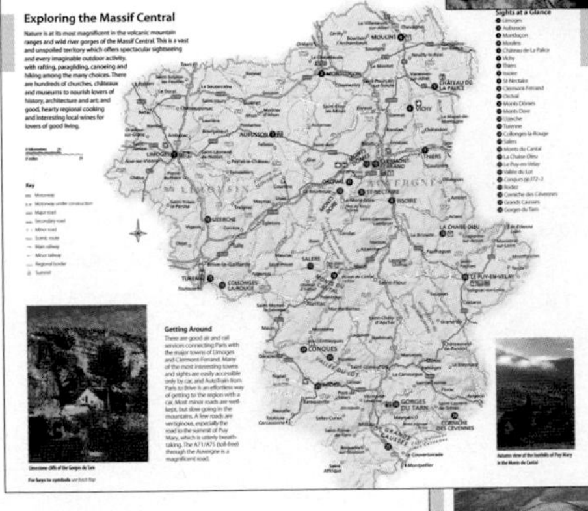

Each area of France can be quickly identified by its colour coding, shown on the inside front cover.

2 Regional Map This shows the road network and gives an illustrated overview of the whole region. All interesting places to visit are numbered and there are also useful tips on getting around the region by car and train.

3 Detailed information All the important towns and other places to visit are described individually. They are listed in order, following the numbering on the Regional Map. Within each town or city, there is detailed information on important buildings and other sights.

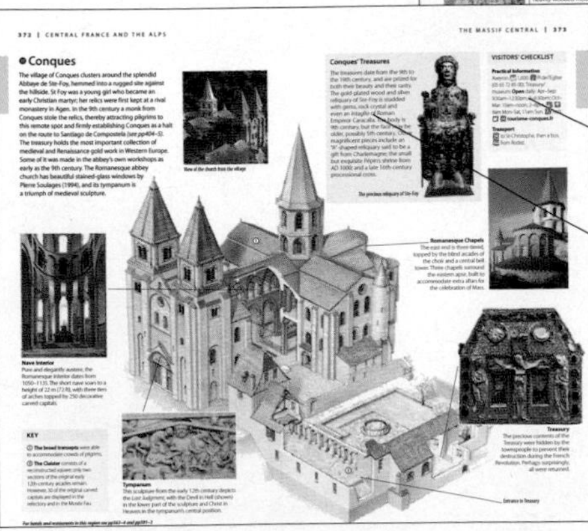

For all the top sights, a Visitors' Checklist provides the practical information you will need to plan your visit.

Story boxes highlight noteworthy features of the top sights.

4 France's top sights These are given two or more full pages. Historic buildings are dissected to reveal their interiors. The most interesting towns or city centres are shown in a bird'seye view, with sights picked out and described.

INTRODUCING FRANCE

DISCOVERING FRANCE

The following tours have been designed to take in as many of the country's highlights as possible, while keeping long-distance travel to a minimum. First comes a two-day visit to France's unmissable heart, Paris. Next is a one-week tour of the greatest architectural monuments near the capital – Versailles, Loire châteaux and great Gothic cathedrals. Two more seven-day tours cover Northern France and the Rhône Valley and the Southwest. These can be combined to make a superb two-week tour. Finally, two seven-day routes focus on regions legendary for fine wines and food – Burgundy, Périgord and Bordeaux – and the beauties of the Mediterranean coast. Suggestions are provided for those who want to extend their stay, so pick and combine your favourite tours, or simply be inspired.

A One-Week Tour of Great Architectural Sites

- Take in the extravagance of **Versailles** and explore Le Nôtre's magnificent gardens.
- Trace the stories told by the stunning stained-glass windows at **Chartres** Cathedral.
- View the famous châteaux of **Chenonceau** and **Villandry**.
- Marvel at the skills of medieval stonemasons at **Reims**, **Laon** and **Amiens**.

English Channel
HAUTE-NORMANDIE
Bayeux
Trouville
Honfleur
Deauville
Caen
Giverny
BASSE-NORMANDIE
St-Malo
Cancale
Dinard
Mont-St-Michel
Chartres
BRETAGNE
Rennes
Vitré
Le Mans
Blois
Chambord
PAYS DE LA LOIRE
Tours
Amboise
Loire
Villandry
Fontevraud
Chinon
Loches
POITOU-CHARENTES
Bay of Biscay
Cognac
Pauillac
Médoc
Bordeaux
Périgueux
Saint-Emilion
Sarlat
Dordogne Valley
Domme
Graves
Sauternes
AQUITAINE
Garonne
Mont-de-Marsan
Toulouse
MIDI-PYRENEES

A Week in Northern France

- Admire the vibrant colours of Monet's garden at **Giverny**.
- Linger over dinner beside the old harbour of **Honfleur**.
- Take in the fascinating details of the **Bayeux Tapestry**.
- Go to the **Normandy beaches** where the 1944 D-Day landings took place.
- Wonder at the majesty of **Mont-St-Michel**, rising up out of the sea.
- Follow the Loire Valley from Gothic **Tours** to Renaissance **Chambord**.
- Visit the historic centre of **Dijon**, once home to the grand Burgundian court.

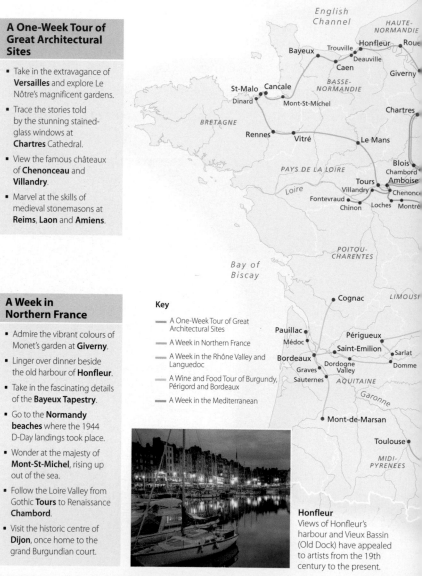

Key

- A One-Week Tour of Great Architectural Sites
- A Week in Northern France
- A Week in the Rhône Valley and Languedoc
- A Wine and Food Tour of Burgundy, Périgord and Bordeaux
- A Week in the Mediterranean

Honfleur
Views of Honfleur's harbour and Vieux Bassin (Old Dock) have appealed to artists from the 19th century to the present.

◀ *The Quai du Louvre* (1867), by Claude Monet

Versailles
In 1668, Louis XIV began work on enlargements to his father's old hunting lodge just outside Paris. Over the course of the next century, the château was transformed into one of the finest palaces in the world.

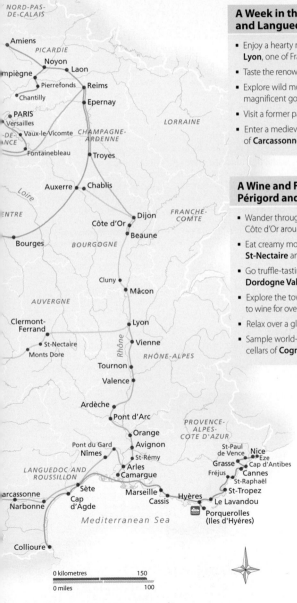

A Week in the Rhône Valley and Languedoc

- Enjoy a hearty meal in a traditional restaurant in **Lyon**, one of France's culinary capitals.
- Taste the renowned wines of the **Côtes du Rhône**.
- Explore wild mountain landscapes around the magnificent gorges of the **Ardèche**.
- Visit a former papal palace in historic **Avignon**.
- Enter a medieval fantasy in the walled city of **Carcassonne**.

A Wine and Food Tour of Burgundy, Périgord and Bordeaux

- Wander through beautiful vineyards along the Côte d'Or around **Beaune**.
- Eat creamy mountain cheeses such as **St-Nectaire** and **Cantal** in the Auvergne.
- Go truffle-tasting in pretty villages along the **Dordogne Valley**.
- Explore the town of **Saint-Emilion**, dedicated to wine for over 10 centuries.
- Relax over a glass of fine wine in **Bordeaux**.
- Sample world-famous brandy in the historic cellars of **Cognac**.

A Week in the Mediterranean

- Delight in work by a great 20th-century artist at the **Musée Matisse** in **Nice**.
- Take in breathtaking views of the coast from the clifftop village of **Eze**.
- Join the rich and famous in the harbour at **St-Tropez**.
- Discover perfect pine ringed beaches on the **Iles d'Hyères**.
- Taste the local seafood in the lively harbour restaurants of **Sète**.

The great glass pyramid entrance to the Musée du Louvre, viewed from across the fountain pool

Two Days in Paris

With its great art, glorious architecture, chic shopping, gourmet food and unique street life, the French capital offers an array of attractions.

- **Arriving** Charles-de-Gaulle international airport is about 30 km (18 miles) from the city. RER Line B trains run frequently to central Paris (40 mins). International trains arrive at seven Paris stations, all with connections to the city Métro network.
- **Booking ahead** It is wise to book tickets for the Eiffel Tower in advance.

Day 1

Morning There is so much to see and do in Paris that a two-day visit can only be a taster, but for a first dose of Parisian atmosphere begin with a café breakfast on the riverside quays of **Ile St-Louis** *(p89)*, for a fabulous view of the Seine and the buttresses of **Notre-Dame cathedral** *(pp90–91)*. Then stroll across to the Ile de la Cité to visit the cathedral itself and see the Gothic jewel of **Sainte-Chapelle** *(p88)*. Cross to the Left Bank on the **Pont Neuf** *(p87)* and walk along the quays to the **Musée d'Orsay** *(pp124–5)*. Allow about 2 hours, and don't miss the Impressionist masterpieces and stunning paintings by van Gogh and Toulouse Lautrec. Then cross back to the Right Bank for a rest and lunch in one of the **Louvre**'s courtyard restaurants.

Afternoon Give at least 2 to 3 hours to the **Musée du Louvre** *(pp104–7)*. The display of historic art is vast and awe-inspiring. Be sure to see the *Mona Lisa* and the Greek and Roman sculptures. Then take a break in the **Jardin des Tuileries** *(pp102–3)* and wander up to **Place de la Concorde** *(p102)* for majestic vistas. From there, take a taxi or bus along the **Champs-Elysées** *(pp110–12)* to the **Arc de Triomphe** *(p111)*, and go to the top to watch the chaotic traffic below. Return to the centre for dinner, stopping to browse chic fashion shops on **rue St-Honoré** and irresistable food shops in **Place de la Madeleine** *(p101)*.

Day 2

Morning Explore the bohemian Left Bank, beginning at the **Panthéon** *(p129)* and **La Sorbonne** *(p127)* in the old **Latin Quarter** *(pp128–9)*. Wander through the district towards the river, perhaps with a stop at **Musée de Cluny** *(pp126–7)* for Roman baths and medieval art, then head west to **St-Germain-des-Prés** *(p126)*, past lively rue de Buci with its street market. Stop for coffee in one of the classic intellectual cafés, Café de Flore or the Deux Magots. Then cross the Seine through the Ile de la Cité and head right to enter the **Marais** *(pp92–3)* district for lunch on **Place des Vosges** *(p95)*, arguably Paris's most attractive square.

The iconic Eiffel Tower, from across the River Seine

Afternoon Stroll around the 17th-century streets of the Marais, with their trendy shops, cafés and historic Jewish Quarter. Return to modern Paris at the **Centre Pompidou** *(pp96–7)*; (2 hours), to see works by Picasso, Matisse and other 20th-century masters, and the views from the tube-like escalators. Then take the Métro or a cab – or walk part of the way along the river – to the **Eiffel Tower** *(p117)*, and get to the top in time for the views at sunset. Dine in one of the Tower restaurants, or, for less view but more Parisian colour, head to boulevard du Montparnasse to eat in one of its classic 1920s brasseries.

To extend your trip...
Spend a day in the **Luxembourg Quarter** *(pp130–31)* and window-shop on **rue du Faubourg-St-Honoré**.

For practical information on travelling around France, see pp632–41

A One-Week Tour of Great Architectural Sites

Within a short distance of Paris, discover an extraordinary range of famous buildings – Gothic, Renaissance and Baroque.

- **Airports** Arrive and depart from Paris.
- **Transport** A rental car is essential for the full route, but many places can be visited by train on day trips from Paris.
- **Booking ahead** Advisable at Versailles in July and August.

Day 1: Versailles, Vaux-le-Vicomte, Fontainebleau

Louis XIV's palace of **Versailles** *(pp178–81)* is the epitome of regal grandeur. Take time to walk through the equally magnificent gardens to the Trianon palaces and Marie Antoinette's village. Rest for lunch, then drive south to more discreet **Vaux-le-Vicomte** *(pp182–3)*, model of French 17th-century mansion style, and Napoleon's favourite palace at **Fontainebleau** *(pp184–5)*. Relax after châteaux-visiting in the lovely surrounding forest.

Day 2: Chartres to the Loire Valley

Head west to **Chartres** *(p310)* to the most intact of all medieval **cathedrals** *(pp312–15)*. The stories and images in its stunning stained glass are fascinating to trace. Move on to Renaissance architecture at **Blois** *(pp308–9)*, one of the first royal châteaux. Explore the old town before a short hop east to François I's vast palace at **Chambord** *(pp306–7)*, surrounded by a delightful wooded park.

Day 3: The Loire: Amboise to Chinon

Looming over the tiny town, the royal château of **Amboise** *(p305)* has a dramatic history, and a few streets away is the Clos-Lucé mansion, where Leonardo da Vinci lived just before his death. Nearby, **Chenonceau** *(pp302–3)* and its gardens typify the grand life of the Loire Valley châteaux. For one of the loveliest French gardens, stop at **Château de Villandry** *(p300)*. A very different château is **Chinon** *(pp298–9)*, a 12th-century fortress built for Henry II of England, in a medieval town known for fine wines.

Day 4: Fontevraud to Bourges

The Benedictine **Abbaye Royale de Fontevraud** *(p298)* reflects the deep spirituality of the Middle Ages. To the east, the rugged ruined keep at **Loches** *(p304)* is one of the oldest Loire castles, set in an exquisite walled town. Nearby is idyllic **Montrésor** *(p305)* with its 15th-century castle. In the afternoon head to **Bourges** *(p317)*, a little-known gem with a giant cathedral and a Gothic merchant mansion, the Palais Jacques Coeur.

Stained-glass window at Chartres Cathedral in the Loire Valley

Day 5: Into Champagne

Northeast from Bourges, in Burgundy, **Auxerre** *(pp334–5)* is famed for the cathedral and its fine stained glass. Champagne and Picardy contain several great Gothic monuments. Ancient **Troyes** *(p220)* has a wonderful old centre of Gothic churches and half-timbered houses. Carry on north through green hills and vineyards to **Epernay** *(p215)*, home of Champagne, and visit at least one cellar for a tasting.

Day 6: Reims to Amiens

Explore **Reims** *(pp214–15)* and its magnificent **cathedral** *(pp216–17)*, site of the coronations of French kings. To the northeast in Picardy are a number of astonishing Gothic cathedrals: **Laon** *(p209)*, with its curious carvings, harmonious **Noyon** *(p205)* and glorious **Amiens** *(p204)*, with a façade that has been called "the Bible in stone".

Day 7: Royal Compiègne and Chantilly

The château and forest at **Compiègne** *(p205)* were a royal hunting estate for centuries. Napoleon III's own Neo-Gothic castle, **Château de Pierrefonds** *(p205)*, is nearby. To the south, visit the Musée Conde inside the **Château de Chantilly** *(pp208–9)*. Don't miss the *Très Riches Heures du Duc de Berry*, one of the world's finest medieval manuscripts.

Champagne vineyards at Ville-Dommange, near Reims

A Week in Northern France

- **Airports** Arrive and depart from Paris.
- **Transport** A rental car is essential for the full route, but many places can be visited by train on separate trips from Paris.
- **Booking ahead** Advisable at Champagne cellars on the weekends.

Day 1: Giverny, Rouen and Honfleur

Travel to **Giverny** *(p270)* in time for the 9:30am opening of Claude Monet's house (Apr–Oct only), and enjoy the stunning colours of the artist's garden with the fewest crowds. In the afternoon, continue down the Seine Valley to lively **Rouen** *(pp268–9)* and its three great Gothic jewels: the churches of St-Ouen and St-Maclou, and the magnificent cathedral, painted many times by Monet. Finish the day with dinner beside the quaint harbour at **Honfleur** *(p266)*.

Day 2: Heart of Normandy

Living up to its name, the **Côte Fleurie** (Flowery Coast); *(p259)*, west of Honfleur, contains attractive beach resorts including the bohemian Trouville and elegant Deauville. Just inland is Normandy's most exuberantly lush green countryside, in the cider farms of the **Pays d'Auge** *(p259)*. Linger there, or go on to **Caen** *(pp257–8)* to visit the two great abbeys built by William the Conqueror and his queen. From there it's a short drive to **Bayeux** *(pp256–7)*, where the unmissable tapestry portrays the vivid details of William's invasion of England. Bayeux is also an ideal base for visiting the coast nearby at Arromanches and **Omaha Beach** *(p255)*, which witnessed the dramatic events of the June 1944 Allied invasion.

Day 3: Mont-St-Michel and St-Malo

Soaring up out of the sea, **Mont-St-Michel** *(pp260–65)* is one of France's greatest sights, a magical monument to medieval ambition. It dominates the view as you continue west around the giant bay, past charming **Cancale** *(p287)*, towards **St-Malo** *(p286)* and its fascinating walled city. Relax on the city's beaches or across the river at **Dinard** *(p285)*, a classic Breton seaside resort.

Day 4: Rennes to Tours

Turn inland to visit Brittany's capital, **Rennes** *(pp288–9)*, with its half-timbered houses, and on the way west don't miss **Vitré** *(p289)*, a picture-book medieval walled town. Stop for lunch in **Le Mans** *(p295)*, famed for motor racing but also for its fascinating ancient city and Roman walls. Join the Loire Valley at **Tours** *(pp300–1)* and visit the soaring Gothic cathedral and atmospheric riverside old quarter.

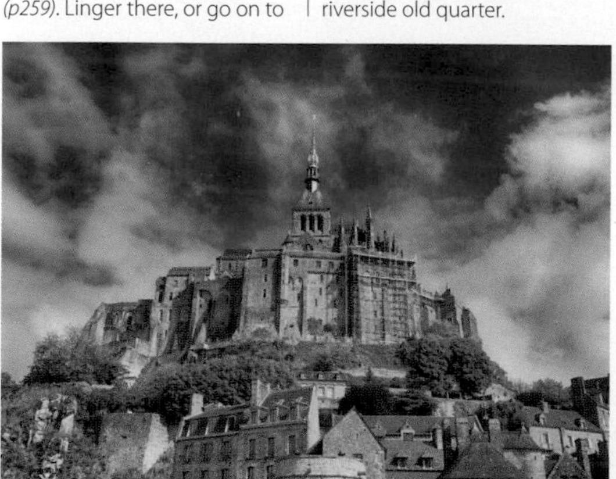

Normandy's Mont-St-Michel, one of the most enchanting sights in France

Day 5: Loire Valley Highlights

The Loire is famously studded with magnificent mansions. Be sure to see luxurious **Chenonceau** *(pp302–3)*, regal **Amboise** *(p305)* and majestic **Chambord** *(pp306–7)*. Then cross the river north to **Chartres** *(pp311–15)*, and stay in the town to enjoy the spectacular light show around the cathedral (mid-Apr–mid-Sep only).

The imposing façade of the cathedral at Reims

Day 6: Reims and Champagne Country

Start early and drive east around Paris on the outer-ring roads to **Reims** *(pp216–17)* and its sumptuous cathedral. Relax after the drive by visiting some of the famous Champagne houses in Reims and in the soft green countryside towards **Epernay** *(p215)*. Continue on to **Troyes** *(pp220–21)*, with another fine Gothic cathedral and a delightfully preserved old city.

Day 7: Into Burgundy

Burgundy's capital **Dijon** *(pp344–6)* has a particular grandeur inherited from the days when the region's dukes were a great power in the medieval world. To the south, some of the world's most celebrated vineyards, many open to visitors, extend along the **Côte d'Or** *(p348)* down to the delightful old wine town of **Beaune** *(p348)*, with its superb **Hôtel-Dieu** *(pp350–51)*.

To extend your trip...
Continue through the southern Côte d'Or to **Lyon** *(pp382–5)* or head east to **Besançon** *(p354)*.

For practical information on travelling around France, see pp632–41

The famous medieval fortified town of Carcassonne

A Week in the Rhône Valley and Languedoc

- **Airports** Arrive at Lyon and depart from Toulouse airport, or arrive and depart from Paris and take trains to Lyon (2 hours) and back from Toulouse (5 and a half hours).
- **Transport** A rental car is essential to tour the route after Vienne.

Day 1: Lyon
France's sophisticated second city, **Lyon** *(pp382–5)* has an array of attractions, from Roman amphitheatres and a lovely old quarter to trendy shops and a variety of museums. It's also one of France's culinary capitals, so be sure to sample *cuisine lyonnaise* in a *bouchon* or traditional restaurant.

Day 2: Vienne and the Côtes du Rhône
Take the train or rent a car and make the short journey south to **Vienne** *(p386)*, a charming town with an extraordinary concentration of Roman relics as well as a Gothic cathedral. In the afternoon, drive down the Rhône Valley to **Valence** *(p388)*, with detours east near **Tournon-sur-Rhône** *(p388)* to taste robust red Côtes du Rhône wines in the village of Tain l'Hermitage.

Day 3: The Ardèche
The rugged rocky hills west of the Rhône contain dramatic scenery around the spectacular gorges of the fast-flowing **Ardèche** *(pp388–9)* river. Make a detour to wander among captivating hill villages and enjoy stunning views, ending up at the fabulous natural bridge Pont d'Arc, near Vallon-Pont d'Arc.

Day 4: Orange and Avignon
Return to the Rhône and head for **Orange** *(p506)*, with its Roman Theatre and Arc de Triomphe. Nearby, the vineyards of **Châteauneuf-du-Pape** *(pp506–7)* are famed for their powerful red wines. **Avignon** *(pp507–9)* is perhaps the archetypal southern French city, with its golden stone walls, relaxing squares and warm sunlight, plus the 14th-century **Palais des Papes** *(pp508–9)*, 12th- century bridge and vibrant summer arts festival.

Day 5: Arles to the Camargue
Little **St-Rémy-de-Provence** *(p511)* is where Vincent van Gogh produced many of his famous paintings. He is also associated with **Arles** *(pp512–13)*, where many places he painted are easy to recognize. Don't miss the Roman Amphitheatre. The misty flat landscape of the **Camargue** *(pp514–15)* also begins just outside town. Head back north to the astonishing Roman aqueduct **Pont du Gard** *(pp498–9)* before arriving in Nîmes for the night.

Diners in Lyon enjoying traditional cuisine at a small bistro known as a *bouchon*

Day 6: Nîmes to Narbonne
Ancient **Nîmes** *(pp500–1)* has France's most complete Roman monuments in the Maison Carrée, the giant Arènes amphitheatre and more. Spend much of the day there, or head southwest along the coast for lunch in the great Mediterranean port of **Sète** *(p496)*. Take a walk along the harbour and then continue to **Narbonne** *(pp490–91)*. See the Gothic cathedral and cloisters, before ending the day in Carcassonne.

Day 7: Carcassonne and Toulouse
Carcassonne *(pp492–3)*, a carefully restored medieval city of stone walls and winding alleys, stuns everyone who sees it. Visitors who stay overnight can explore before the crowds arrive towards midday. From there it's a short distance to **Toulouse** *(pp450–51)*, with at its heart a charming old town and historic buildings such as the Jacobins church and Musée des Augustins, housed around an exquisite Gothic cloister.

To extend your trip...
Drive west from Toulouse to the university town of **Pau** *(p462)*; (2 hours) or to the Atlantic surf beaches around **Biarritz** *(p456)*; (3 hours).

The River Dordogne, viewed from the village of Trémolat, near Sarlat

A Wine and Food Tour of Burgundy, Périgord and Bordeaux

This tour takes you to some of France's classic regions for fine wines and food, focusing on local specialities along the way.

- **Airports** Arrive at Paris, and depart from there or Bordeaux. Rent a car in Paris or take trains to Auxerre (2 hours) and back from Bordeaux (just over 3 hours).
- **Transport** A rental car is essential.
- **Booking ahead** Required at larger Burgundy vineyards and the châteaux wine estates near Bordeaux.

Day 1: Chablis to the Côte d'Or
Burgundy's northernmost wine district is found just east of **Auxerre** *(pp334–5)* around the pleasant village of **Chablis** *(p335)*, famed for delicious whites. Make a brief stop in **Dijon** *(pp344–6)* before reaching one of the most famous and beautiful wine regions in the world along the **Côte d'Or** *(p348)*. The roads here are lined with village names magnetic to any wine lover – Nuits-St-Georges, Gevrey-Chambertin – and there are plenty of great opportunities for tasting. End the day in lovely **Beaune** *(p348)*, which has a wine museum in a Gothic palace as well as the famous Hôtel-Dieu hospital.

Day 2: Beaune to Beaujolais
Continue down the southern half of the Côte d'Or, and for a change from wines stop to visit the impressive ruins of **Cluny Abbey** *(p349)*. In the afternoon, leave the main routes south of Mâcon to explore the charming villages and vineyards of the **Beaujolais** *(p381)* district. Stay the night in **Lyon** *(pp382–5)*, and enjoy some of the city's famous cuisine.

Day 3: The Auvergne
To the west, beyond Clermont-Ferrand and the extinct volcanoes the **Monts Dore** *(p366)*, the mountains of the Auvergne are known for fine soft cheeses such as **Cantal** *(p367)* and **St-Nectaire** *(p364)*. Driving westwards through rugged landscapes, be sure to explore the enticing displays of local produce in village shops and markets, reaching the borders of Périgord in the evening.

Vineyards and fields in the wine district around Chablis

Day 4: Périgord and the Dordogne
The Périgord region and Dordogne Valley are equally famed for beautiful scenery and delicious foods. Window-shop and learn about truffles in the capital **Périgueux** *(p435)*, and be sure to catch the spectacular market in **Sarlat** *(pp436–7)*. Try the Périgord's famed specialities – truffles, duck, *foie gras* – in the restaurants of the many pretty villages along the Dordogne, notably **Domme** *(p439)*.

Day 5: Saint-Emilion to Bordeaux
Saint-Emilion *(pp426–7)* has been producing wine since Roman times, and its winding streets are full of historic buildings and early medieval churches. Visit famous estates in the village of **Figeac** *(p427)*, and in nearby Libourne and Pomerol. Then head into Bordeaux to end the day with a relaxing drink in the city's Maison du Vin wine centre.

Day 6: Bordeaux and Graves
The centre of **Bordeaux** *(pp424–7)* retains its 18th-century grandeur. Admire the huge Neo-Classical **Grand Théâtre** *(p426)*, and stroll along the quays beside the River Garonne. Later, explore the southern areas of Bordeaux's wine region around Graves and Sauternes, known for sweet dessert wines or, if you have time, head south to **Mont-de-Marsan** *(p429)*, home of Armagnac.

Day 7: Médoc and Cognac
The grandest Bordeaux wines – Château Mouton-Rothschild, Château Latour – all come from the Médoc district north of the city around **Pauillac** *(p427)*, from estates presided over by grand châteaux that provide a luxurious setting for tasting. If there's time, return to Bordeaux and head north to **Cognac** *(pp422–3)* for a sample of its famous brandy.

To extend your trip...
Relax on the beaches and sample seafood at **La Rochelle** *(p420)* and the **Ile d'Oléron** *(p421)*.

For practical information on travelling around France, see pp632–41

A Week in the Mediterranean

This tour visits some of the finest beaches and beauty spots of France's celebrated south coast.

- **Airports** Arrive and depart from Nice, Toulouse or Paris. Return to Nice (6 and a half hours) or Paris (5–6 hours) by train from Perpignan.
- **Transport** Several parts of the trip can be made by train, but for others a car is essential.
- **Booking ahead** Pre-book boat trips from Cassis to the Calanques in July and August.

Bright sun and Mediterranean colours seen from the perched village of Eze

Day 1: Nice
Capital of the Côte d'Azur, **Nice** *(pp530–31)* has superb restaurants and an elegant seafront. Don't miss the Musée Matisse, with stunning works by the painter who celebrated Mediterranean colours more than any other artist. In the afternoon, rent a car to visit the exquisite coastline east of the city, at **Cap Ferrat** *(p532)* and especially the clifftop village of **Eze** *(p533)*, for unforget-table views over the Riviera.

Day 2: St-Paul de Vence to Cannes
Take a car and drive inland to **St-Paul de Vence** *(pp528–9)*, an artists' mecca full of echoes of Picasso and Chagall, and the perfume capital of **Grasse** *(p521)*, ringed by fields of lavender and jasmine. Drop down to the sea again for a look at the opulent **Cap d'Antibes** *(p525)* before ending the day in ever-fashionable **Cannes** *(p524)*.

Day 3: West to St-Tropez
All along the winding coast road west from Cannes there are magnificent views and seascapes. The road runs into **St-Raphaël** *(p521)* and **Fréjus** *(p521)*, two pleasant, relaxed resorts with long beaches. Further west again, **St-Tropez** *(p520)* has been the chicest spot on the Riviera since Brigitte Bardot arrived in the 1950s. Watch the fashion parade around the harbour, and count the luxury yachts.

Day 4: Island Beaches
The coast road west through Le Lavandou to the charming harbour of **Hyères** *(p518)* is one of the loveliest on the Côte d'Azur, but there is also a faster inland road. From Hyères take a boat to Porquerolles, the largest of the **Iles d'Hyères** *(p519)*, with turquoise seas and perfect beaches that are easily explored by rented bicycle. Return to Hyères to stay for the night.

To extend your trip...
Stay overnight to enjoy Porquerolles' beaches to the full, or spend a day exploring **Marseille** *(pp516–17)*.

Day 5: Cassis and the Calanques
Cassis *(p517)* is one of the most vibrant small towns on the Provençal coast, with a lively café-lined fishing harbour. The surrounding coast is magnificently wild and rocky, and boats run regularly to the **Calanques** *(p517)*, jagged inlets accessible only by sea that are fabulous for swimming and known for an abundance of birds and wild flowers.

Day 6: Sète and Cap d'Agde
Leave your car in Marseille and take an early train to **Sète** *(p496)*; (2 hours) to transfer to a very different Mediterranean coast, in Languedoc. Sète is an atmospheric old port town, with superb, no-frills seafood restaurants along its canalside quays. Walk or take a train or bus beside the endless sandy beaches south towards **Cap d'Agde** *(p491)*, and watch the colourful sails running in the wind at one of Europe's foremost windsurfing and kitesurfing locations.

Day 7: Collioure
Take another train down the coast to **Collioure** *(p487)*, a classic small Mediterranean harbour loved by artists such as Matisse and Derain. Explore the old port and medieval Catalan castle, then lie back on the beaches with a superb view of the town's imposing stone church.

To extend your trip...
Catch a boat or plane to **Corsica** *(pp536–47)* for some of France's purest Mediterranean beaches.

Rocky coastline and the narrow inlet of Calanque d'En-Vau near the Bouches-du-Rhône

Putting France on the Map

France, one of the largest countries in Europe, has airline connections with most cities in the world. Paris is the major transport hub, with two international airports; others include Bordeaux, Lille, Lyon, Nice and Toulouse. There are good, high-speed rail links with the rest of Europe, and a network of efficient motorways. A number of ferry routes cross the Mediterranean to Corsica and beyond. Cross-Channel ferries serve several ports, with the Channel Tunnel providing an alternative link by rail.

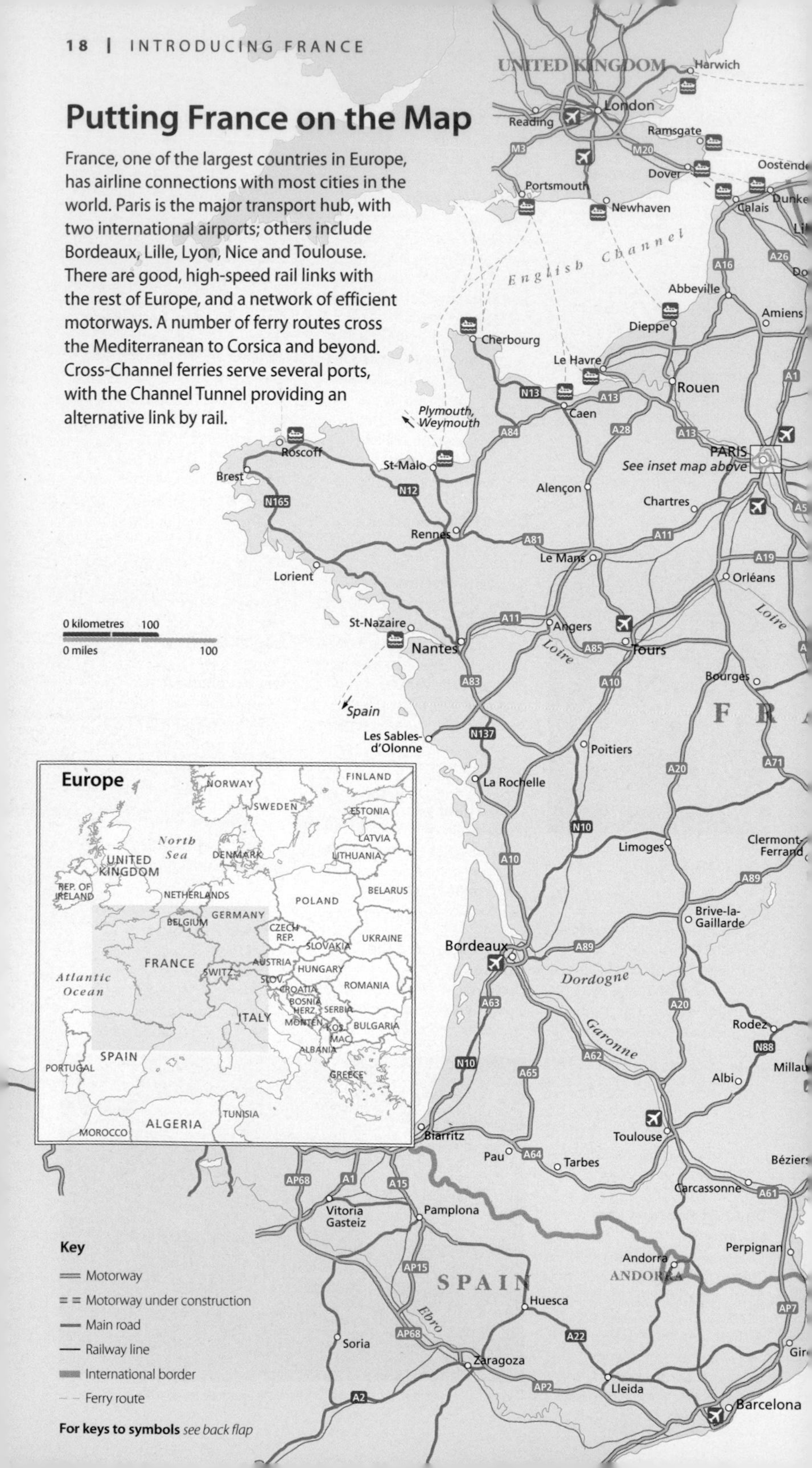

0 kilometres 100

0 miles 100

Europe

Key

- Motorway
- Motorway under construction
- Main road
- Railway line
- International border
- Ferry route

For keys to symbols *see back flap*

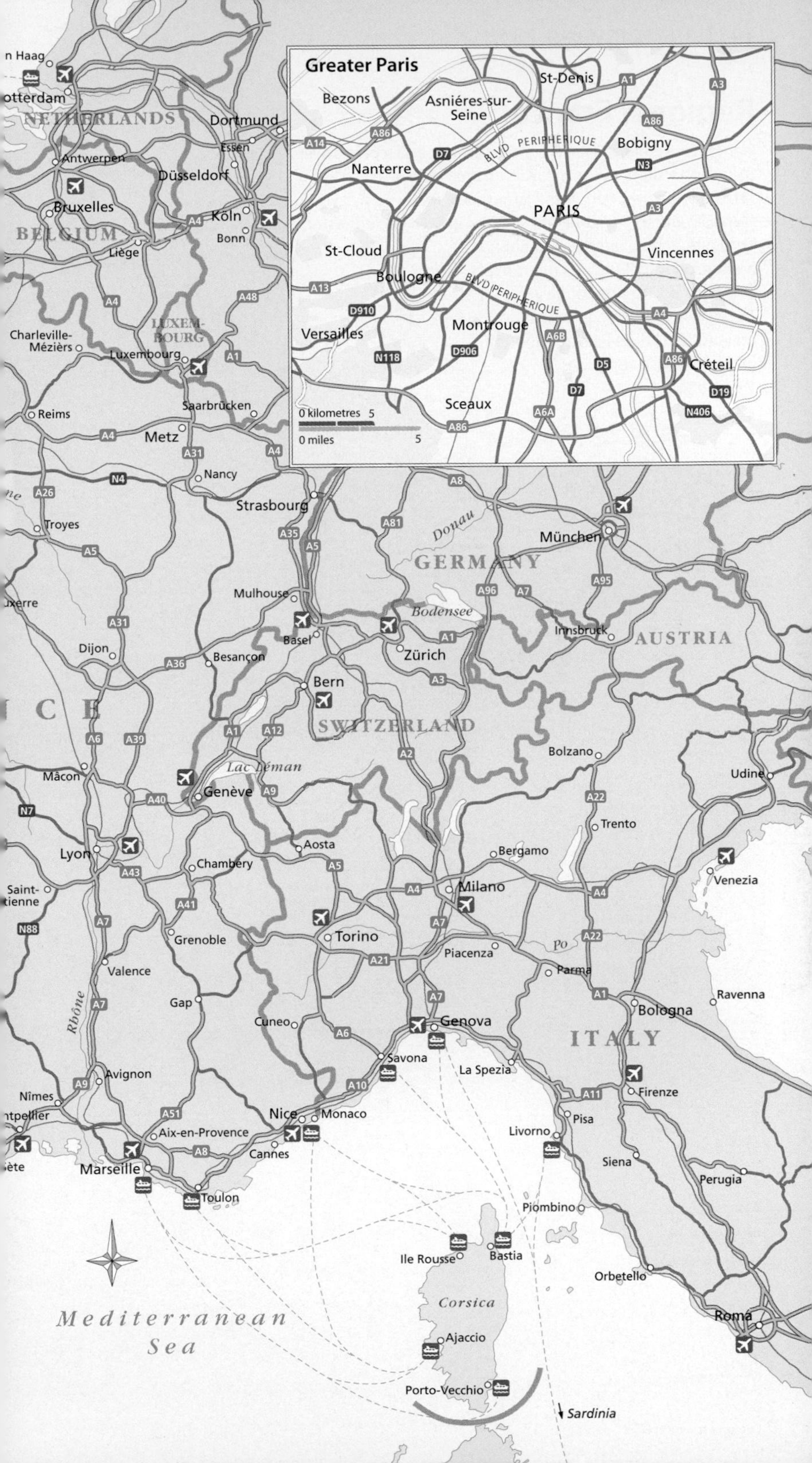
Greater Paris
St-Denis
A1
A3
Bezons
Asniéres-sur-Seine
A86
A14
BLVD PERIPHERIQUE
Bobigny
D7
Nanterre
N3
PARIS
A3
St-Cloud
Vincennes
Boulogne
A13
BLVD PERIPHERIQUE
D910
Versailles
Montrouge
A4
A6B
N118
D906
A86
Créteil
D5
D19
D7
Sceaux
A6A
N406
A86
0 kilometres 5
0 miles 5
n Haag
otterdam
NETHERLANDS
Dortmund
Essen
Antwerpen
Düsseldorf
Bruxelles
Köln
A4
BELGIUM
Bonn
Liège
A48
A4
LUXEMBOURG
Charleville-Méziers
Luxembourg
A1
Saarbrücken
Reims
A4
Metz
A31
A4
Nancy
N4
A26
Strasbourg
Troyes
A35
A81
A8
Donau
A5
München
A5
GERMANY
A95
A96
A7
Mulhouse
Bodensee
uxerre
A31
Basel
A1
Innsbruck
AUSTRIA
Zürich
Dijon
A36
Besançon
Bern
A3
C E
SWITZERLAND
A1
A12
A6
A39
A2
Bolzano
Mâcon
Lac Léman
Udine
Genève
A9
A22
N7
A40
Trento
Aosta
Lyon
Bergamo
A43
Chambery
A5
Milano
Saint-étienne
A41
A4
A4
Venezia
N88
A7
A7
Torino
A22
Grenoble
Po
Piacenza
A21
Parma
Valence
A7
A1
Ravenna
Bologna
Gap
Rhône
A7
Cuneo
Genova
A6
ITALY
Savona
La Spezia
Avignon
A9
Nîmes
A10
A11
Firenze
A51
Nice
Monaco
ntpellier
Pisa
Aix-en-Provence
Livorno
A8
Cannes
Siena
ète
Marseille
Perugia
Toulon
Piombino
Ile Rousse
Bastia
Orbetello
Corsica
Mediterranean Sea
Roma
Ajaccio
Porto-Vecchio
Sardinia

Regional France

France has a population of around 66 million, and receives over 85 million visitors a year. It covers an area of 543,965 sq km (210,025 sq miles). Paris is the largest city, followed by Lyon, Marseille and the conurbation of Lille-Lens-Valenciennes. The Loire, Seine, Garonne and Rhône are the longest of France's many rivers. This book divides the country into 15 regions, plus a separate section for Paris and Ile-de-France, although officially France comprises 13 *régions*.

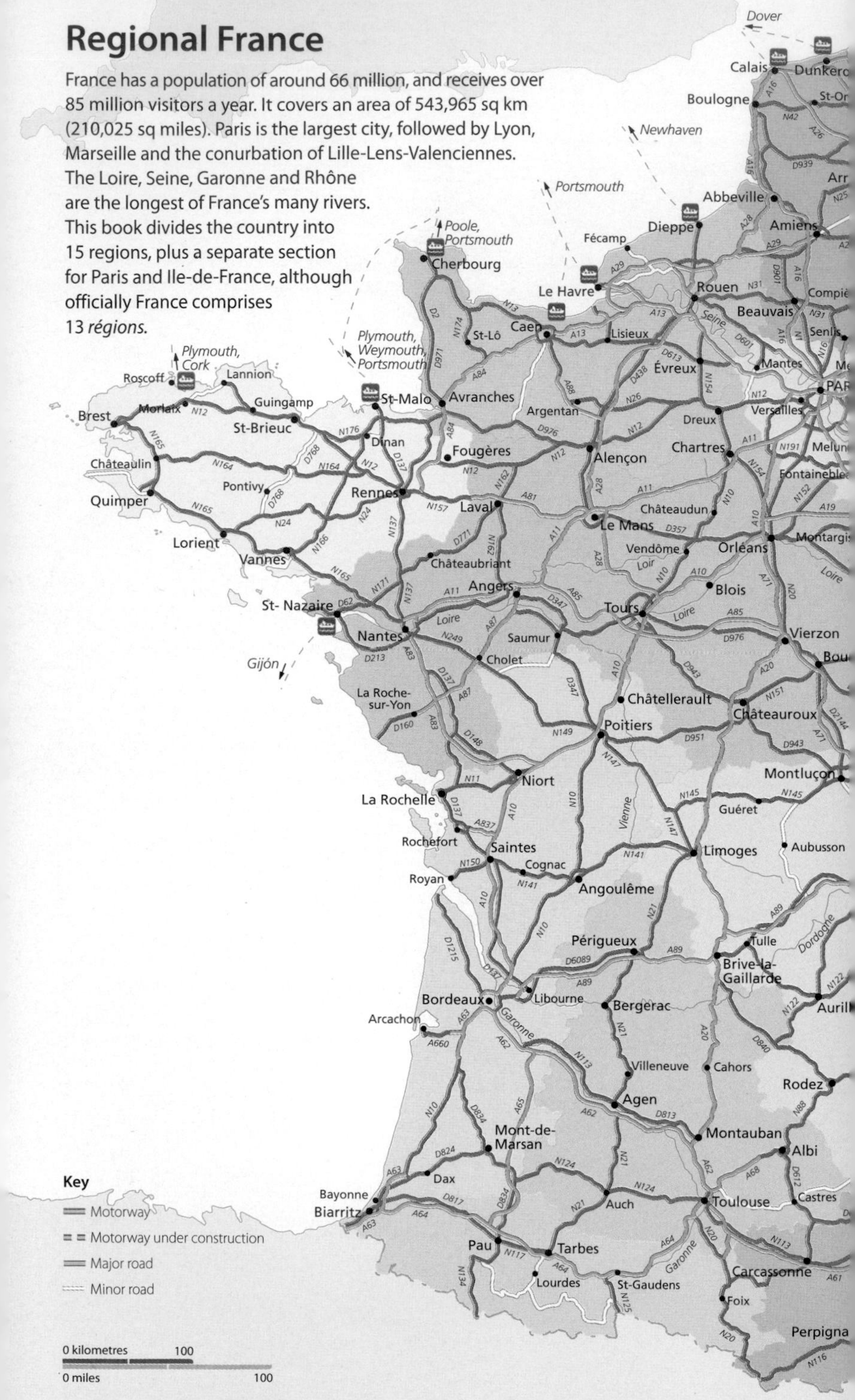

Key

Motorway

Motorway under construction

Major road

Minor road

0 kilometres 100

0 miles 100

For keys to symbols *see back flap*

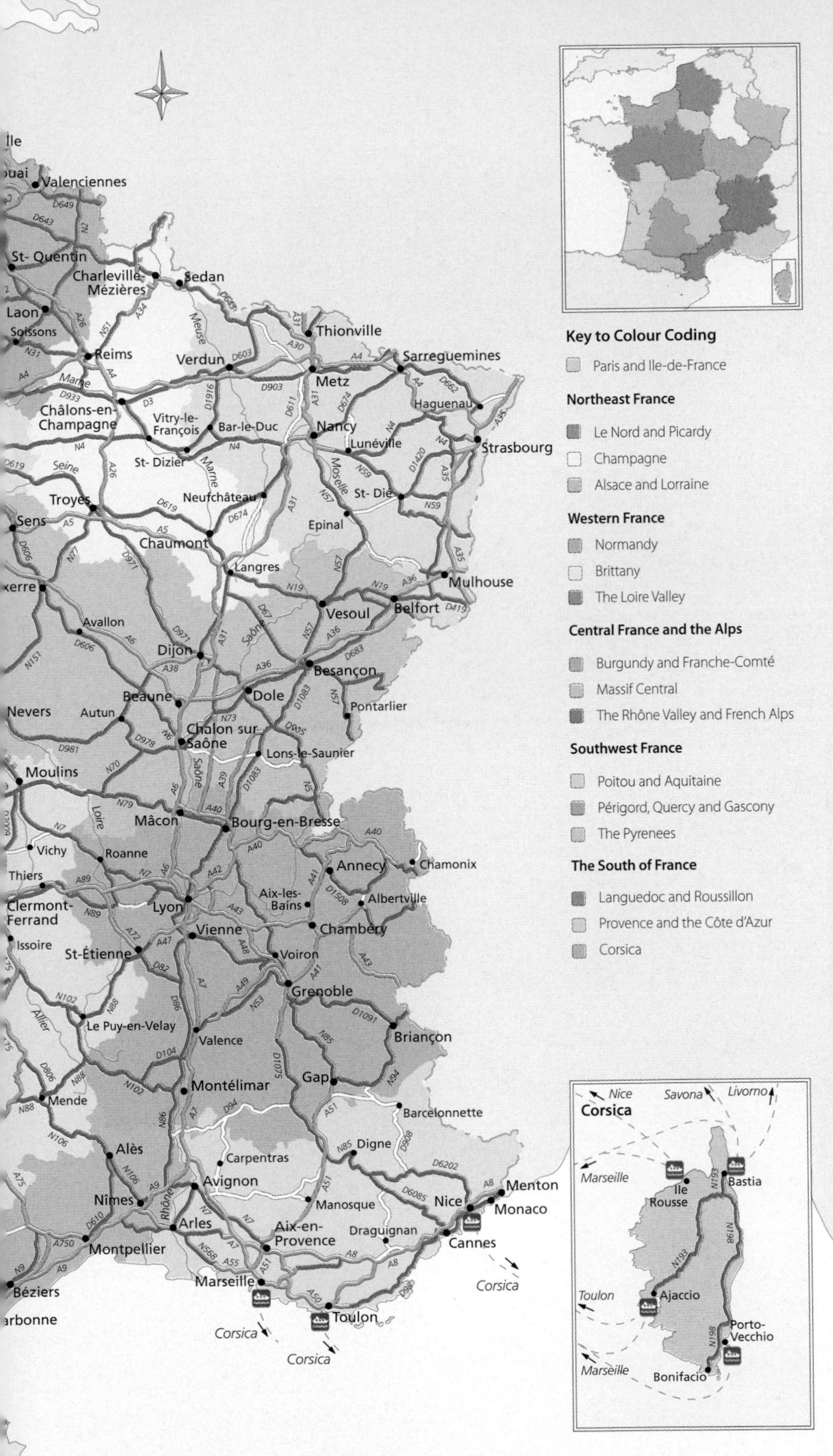
Key to Colour Coding
Paris and Ile-de-France
Northeast France
Le Nord and Picardy
Champagne
Alsace and Lorraine
Western France
Normandy
Brittany
The Loire Valley
Central France and the Alps
Burgundy and Franche-Comté
Massif Central
The Rhône Valley and French Alps
Southwest France
Poitou and Aquitaine
Périgord, Quercy and Gascony
The Pyrenees
The South of France
Languedoc and Roussillon
Provence and the Côte d'Azur
Corsica
Valenciennes
St- Quentin
Charleville-Mézières
Sedan
Laon
Soissons
Reims
Verdun
Thionville
Sarreguemines
Metz
Haguenau
Châlons-en-Champagne
Vitry-le-François
Bar-le-Duc
Nancy
Lunéville
Strasbourg
St- Dizier
Troyes
Neufchâteau
St- Dié
Sens
Epinal
Chaumont
Langres
Mulhouse
Vesoul
Belfort
Avallon
Dijon
Besançon
Beaune
Dole
Pontarlier
Nevers
Autun
Chalon sur Saône
Lons-le-Saunier
Moulins
Mâcon
Bourg-en-Bresse
Vichy
Roanne
Annecy
Chamonix
Thiers
Clermont-Ferrand
Lyon
Aix-les-Bains
Albertville
Vienne
Chambéry
Issoire
St-Étienne
Voiron
Grenoble
Le Puy-en-Velay
Briançon
Valence
Montélimar
Gap
Mende
Barcelonnette
Alès
Digne
Carpentras
Avignon
Menton
Nîmes
Manosque
Nice
Monaco
Arles
Aix-en-Provence
Draguignan
Cannes
Montpellier
Marseille
Béziers
Toulon
Corsica
Seine
Marne
Meuse
Moselle
Saône
Loire
Allier
Rhône
Nice
Savona
Livorno
Marseille
Ile Rousse
Bastia
Ajaccio
Toulon
Porto-Vecchio
Bonifacio

A PORTRAIT OF FRANCE

The French are convinced that their way of life is best, and that their country is the most civilized on earth. Many millions of visitors agree with them. The food and wine are justly celebrated. French culture, literature, art, cinema and architecture can be both profound and provocative. Whether cerebral, sensual or sportive, France is a country where anyone might feel at home.

France's landscape ranges from mountain plateaux to lush farmland, traditional villages to chic boulevards. Its regional identities are equally diverse. The country belongs to both northern and southern Europe, and encompasses Brittany with its Celtic maritime heritage, the Mediterranean sunbelt, Germanic Alsace-Lorraine, and the hardy mountain regions of the Auvergne and the Pyrenees. Paris remains the lynchpin, with its famously brusque citizens and intense tempo. Other cities range from the industrial conglomeration of Lille in the north, to Marseille, the biggest port on the Mediterranean. The differences between north and south, country and city are well-entrenched, indeed cherished. The TGV (high-speed train), internet and mobile phone technology have reduced distance (both physical and emotional) yet have simultaneously provoked an opposite reaction: as life in France becomes more city-based and industrialized, so the desire grows to safeguard the old, traditional ways and to value rural life.

The idea of life in the country – *douceur de vivre* (the good life) is as seductive as ever for residents and visitors alike. Nevertheless, the rural way of life has been changing. Whereas in 1945 one person in three worked in farming, today it is only one in 35. France's main exports used to be luxury goods such as perfumes and Cognac; these have largely been overtaken by cars, aircraft, nuclear power stations and telecommunications equipment.

Château de Saumur, one of the Loire's most romantic and complete castles

◀ Glass pyramid entrance to the Musée du Louvre, Paris

People remain firmly committed to their roots, and often retain a place in the country for holidays or retirement. On average, more French people have second homes than any other nationality; and in many areas, such as Provence, dying villages have found new life as chic summer residences for Parisians. Many artists and artisans now live and work in the country, and entrepreneurs have set up factory workshops there.

The scooter, ever popular in France

The decline in the influence of the Catholic Church has resulted in social changes. Today only 5 per cent of people attend Mass regularly. Many couples live together before marriage, and are allowed the same tax status as married couples. Abortion is now legal, and, since 2013, same-sex couples can legally marry.

Feminism in France has quite a different look than in Anglo-Saxon countries. French feminists are unwilling to condemn frivolous sex appeal. As EU citizens, women in France have legal equality with men, but French attitudes remain traditional. It may have seemed like a milestone in 1991, when Edith Cresson became France's first woman prime minister, but her unpopularity and the 1999 corruption case against her arguably held back women's equality in French politics. Ségolène Royal re-established a prominent political role for women when she won 47 per cent of the vote in the 2007 presidential elections, as did Martine Aubry in 2008, when she became head of the French Socialist Party.

The May 1968 disturbances, a catalyst for profound change in France

Another female role model is Christine Lagarde, who in 2011 became the first woman to lead the International Monetary Fund (IMF). Anne Hidalgo, the first female mayor of Paris, has been pushing a progressive, eco-friendly agenda since her election in 2014.

Social Customs and Politics

French social life, except between close friends, has always been marked by formality – hand-shaking, the use of titles, the preference for the formal *vous* rather than the intimate *tu*. However, this is changing among the younger generation, who now tend to call you by your first name. Known for their stylishness, the French have been influenced by globalisation and evolving trends. Fashion is much more functional than before, with young fashionistas making a simple pair of jeans and tee shirt look chic.

Formality lingers on, however, and France remains very legalistic – whether you are buying a house or exporting an

Farming in Alsace-Lorraine

antique. But the French are insouciant about their famous red tape. Rules and laws are there to be ingeniously evaded, twisted or made more human. This sport of avoiding cumbersome bureaucracy has a name of its own, *le système D*, to be accompanied with a shrug and a smile.

After the end of the Cold War, the sharp Left/Right divisions in French society were replaced by pragmatic centrism. For 14 years, President François Mitterrand – elected in 1981 as head of a Socialist–Communist coalition – steadily moved towards a more central-focused political agenda. In 1995, he was replaced by Jacques Chirac, who promised right-wing policies; he too moved to the centre. By 2002, immigration and security fears, broken electoral promises and political corruption had caused widespread disenchantment and a swing to the Front National. The result was the elimination of Socialist Lionel Jospin in the first round of the presidential elections and the election of Chirac by default in the second round. Further electoral discontent was revealed by the rejection of the European Constitution in 2005.

Charles de Gaulle

In 2007, Chirac's Deputy Prime Minister, Nicolas Sarkozy, won the presidency by addressing public fears and promising an end to corruption. He forged a closer relationship with the US, re-engaged France in the European Union and opened up his government to ministers from the Left. But his popularity waned in 2010, after his plans to raise the retirement age provoked strikes, and deportation of gypsies drew criticism from other European states.

In 2012, François Hollande was elected France's second Socialist president. Early reforms included increasing the income tax rate on high earnings (this was later rejected) and supporting same-sex marriage. He also sent French troops to curtail Islamic extremists in Mali. However, with a rise in unemployment figures and a slump in economic growth, Hollande's presidency reached historic levels of unpopularity. France dealt with particularly troubling times with the terrorist attacks by Islamic extremists in 2015 and 2016. With the election of centrist president Emmanuel Macron in 2017, the country hopes to move forward to understand its role in this ever-changing world.

Traditional Breton costumes, worn for festivals and *pardons*

Culture and the Arts

Culture is taken seriously in France, and writers, intellectuals, artists and fashion designers are held in high social esteem. As a result, the state finances a large network of provincial arts centres and has traditionally given subsidies that allow experimentation in art and design. The French remain justly proud of their own cinematic tradition and are determined to defend it against pressures from Hollywood. Other activities – from the music industry to the French language itself – are subject to the same protectionist attitudes.

Avant-garde art and literature and modern architecture all enjoy strong patronage in France. Some of the more exciting architectural projects range from the striking modern buildings in Paris – the Fondation Louis Vuitton and the Philarmonie de Paris – to the Post-Modern housing developments of Nîmes, Montpellier and Marseille in the south.

Modern Life

While one half of the French were heralding the new millennium in true Gallic style, the other half were plunged into darkness caused by some of the worst storms ever to hit Europe. This is an extreme illustration of French ambivalence towards modernism. France's agro-business is one of the most advanced in the world, but the peasant farmer is deeply revered. France hankers after a leading role in the world, yet the country effectively closes down for the whole of August, when the French take to the roads and coastal resorts of France. However, two factors have forced a change of pace: the internet, which France embraced keenly, and the euro, which, in one fell swoop, swept away Europe's oldest decimalized currency, the franc.

The French are enthusiastic, discerning consumers. Even small towns have stylish

The ultra-modern Philarmonie de Paris

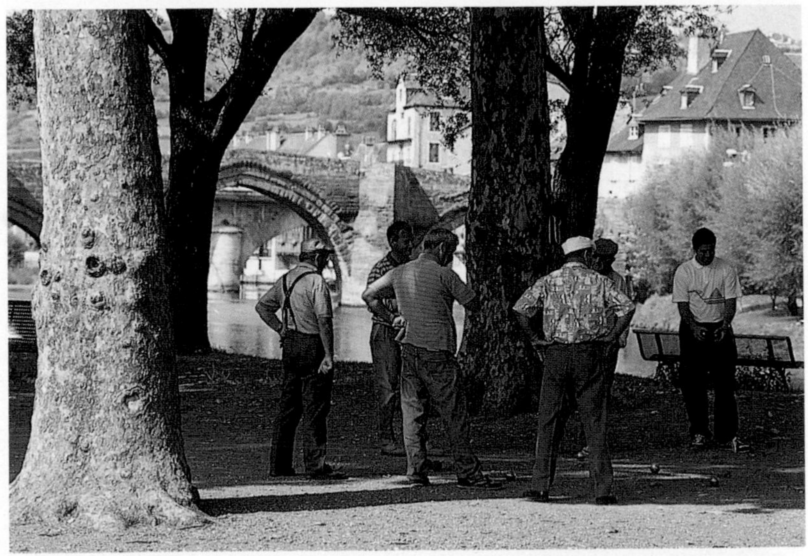

The traditional game of *boules* or *pétanque,* still extremely popular – especially in the south

clothes shops and street markets with the best of local produce. France also has Europe's largest hypermarkets, which have been steadily ousting the local grocery or corner shop. These are remarkably French in what they sell: a long delicatessen counter may display 100 or so French cheeses and types of *charcuterie,* while the range of fresh vegetables and fruit is a tribute to their role in French cuisine.

Southern produce: melons, peaches, and apricots

However, modern pressures have been changing eating habits in a curious way. The French used to eat well daily as a matter of course. Today many are in a hurry, and for most, meals during the working week are simple – either a quick steak or pasta dish at home, or a snack in town (hence the wave of fast-food places that have sprung up, in defiance of French tradition). But meals still remain an important part of French culture – not just for the food and wines, but also for the pleasure of lengthy meals and good conversation around a table of family or friends. They will reserve their gastronomy for the once- or-twice-a-week special occasion, or the big family Sunday lunch, an important French ritual. It is at these times that the French zest for life really comes into its own.

Remote farm – a nostalgic reminder of rural life

Areas of Natural Beauty

France has some of the most memorable and diverse landscapes in Europe. While often pushed to the background in favour of fairytale towns or majestic castles, the natural landscape is hardly less impressive. Two dramatically different coastlines feature in the north and south, with prominent mountain ranges towering in the east, south and west. In between there are lush marshes, plunging gorges and ancient volcanos. Mix in a diverse range of flora and fauna, and France is a nature-lover's haven. Every region has some natural wonder to discover.

Etretat Cliffs
These famous cliffs in Normandy overlook the English Channel where the coastline draws summer crowds.

Côte de Granit Rose
The north of France along the English Channel has its share of beautiful locations. These pink-hued beaches in Brittany are not least among them.

Loire Valley
Most travellers come here for the châteaux, but the Loire Valley is also known for the wildlife that royalty used to hunt here. Today, the paths lining the river are popular with cyclists.

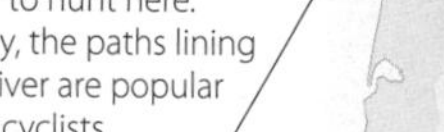

Marais Poitevin
The "Green Venice" of France includes miles of canals through the marshland carved by monks centuries ago, and is populated with a rich variety of wildlife.

Cirque de Gavarnie (The Pyrenees)
In the southwest of France, this soaring natural amphitheatre is part of the natural wonders hewn through the mountains and hills by glaciers over the past millennia.

Auvergne
The most wilderness-like region of France, complete with former volcanoes, the Auvergne attracts hikers, nature lovers and sports enthusiasts to its Massif Central.

Burgundy
Rolling vineyards and stone formations make up the landscapes that get even better with a few glasses of the local wine.

Trois Vallées
These stunning mountains and valleys are best known for their wintertime skiing, when France's elite hit the slopes, but summertime hiking reveals equally beautiful views through the mountain passes.

Gorges du Verdon
Cut by the Verdon River millions of years ago, this breathtaking gorge is nowadays a popular route for kayakers who paddle through the limestone structures.

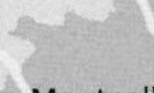

Corsica
The Scandola Nature Reserve surrounding the Golfe de Porto is just one of seemingly endless natural wonders to explore on the island of Corsica, which boasts 1000 km (620 miles) of pristine coastline.

The Camargue
Sandy beaches and marshland are home to flocks of rosy flamingoes which share the landscape with white horses and black bulls in this Mediterranean marvel.

Calanques
The Calanques, stunning cliffs and islets surrounded by the blue Mediterranean, are best explored by boat while visiting Marseille or Cassis.

The Wines of France

Winemaking in France dates back to pre-Roman times, although it was the Romans who disseminated the culture of the vine and the practice of winemaking throughout the country. The range, quality and reputation of the fine wines of Bordeaux, Burgundy, the Rhône and Champagne in particular have made them role models the world over. France's everyday wines can be highly enjoyable too, with plenty of good-value ones now emerging from the southern regions.

Traditional vineyard cultivation

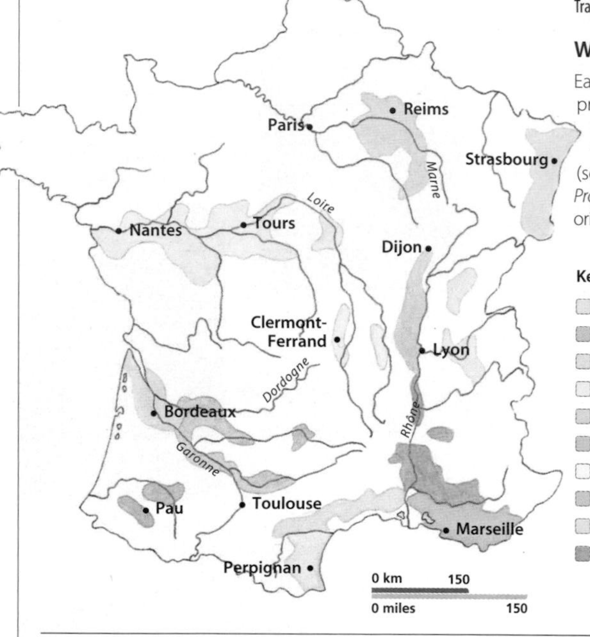

Wine Regions

Each of the ten principal wine-producing regions has its own identity, based on grape varieties, climate and *terroir* (soil). *Appellation d'Origine Protégée* laws guarantee a wine's origins and production methods.

Key

- Bordeaux
- Burgundy
- Champagne
- Alsace
- Loire
- Provence
- Jura and Savoie
- The Southwest
- Languedoc and Roussillon
- Rhône

How to Read a Wine Label

Even the simplest label will identify the wine and provide a key to its quality. It will bear the name of the wine and its producer, its vintage, if there is one, and whether it comes from a strictly defined area (*Appellation d'Origine Protégée*), or is a more general *IGP* (*Indication Géographique Protégée*) wine or *vin de France*. It may also have a regional grading, as with the *crus classés* in Bordeaux. The shape and colour of the bottle is also a guide to the kind of wine it contains. Green glass is often used, since this helps to protect the wine from light.

How Wine is Made

Wine is the product of the juice of freshly picked grapes, after natural or cultured yeasts have converted the grape sugars into alcohol during the fermentation process. The yeasts, or lees, are normally filtered out before bottling.

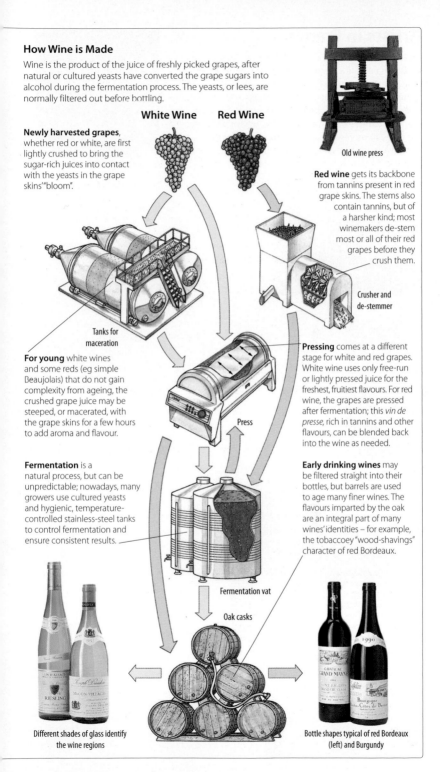

White Wine **Red Wine**

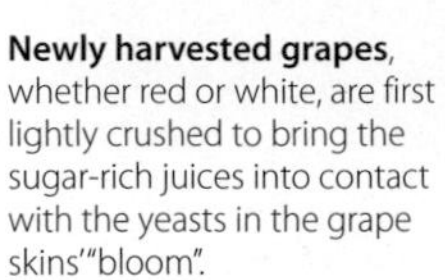

Newly harvested grapes, whether red or white, are first lightly crushed to bring the sugar-rich juices into contact with the yeasts in the grape skins' "bloom".

Old wine press

Red wine gets its backbone from tannins present in red grape skins. The stems also contain tannins, but of a harsher kind; most winemakers de-stem most or all of their red grapes before they crush them.

Crusher and de-stemmer

Tanks for maceration

For young white wines and some reds (eg simple Beaujolais) that do not gain complexity from ageing, the crushed grape juice may be steeped, or macerated, with the grape skins for a few hours to add aroma and flavour.

Pressing comes at a different stage for white and red grapes. White wine uses only free-run or lightly pressed juice for the freshest, fruitiest flavours. For red wine, the grapes are pressed after fermentation; this *vin de presse,* rich in tannins and other flavours, can be blended back into the wine as needed.

Press

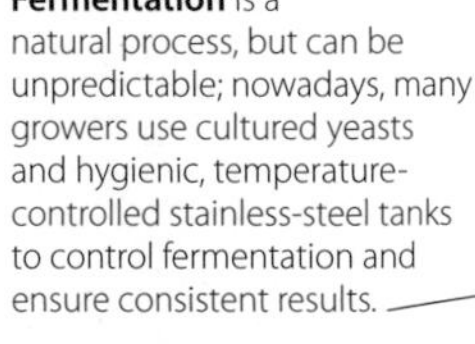

Fermentation is a natural process, but can be unpredictable; nowadays, many growers use cultured yeasts and hygienic, temperature-controlled stainless-steel tanks to control fermentation and ensure consistent results.

Early drinking wines may be filtered straight into their bottles, but barrels are used to age many finer wines. The flavours imparted by the oak are an integral part of many wines' identities – for example, the tobaccoey "wood-shavings" character of red Bordeaux.

Fermentation vat

Oak casks

Different shades of glass identify the wine regions

Bottle shapes typical of red Bordeaux (left) and Burgundy

Artists in France

Artists have always been inspired by France, especially since landscape became a legitimate subject for art in the 19th century. Art and tourism have been closely linked for over a century, when the establishment of artists' colonies in the forest of Fontainebleau, Brittany and the south of France did much to make these areas attractive to visitors. Today, one of the pleasures of touring the countryside is the recognition of landscapes made famous in paintings.

A few months before his tragic death in July 1890, Vincent van Gogh painted *The Church at Auvers*. He noted that the building "appears to have a violet-hued blue colour; pure cobalt".

Gustave Courbet, socialist and leader of the Realist School of painting, captured this famous coastal town in *The Cliffs at Etretat after a Storm* (1870).

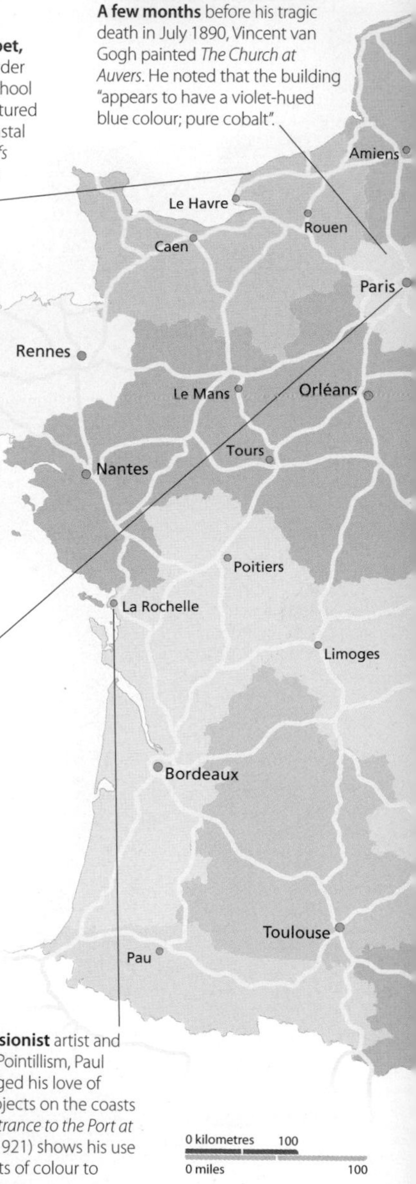

Emile Bernard was fascinated by the wild, almost primitive character of the Breton landscape and the individuality of its inhabitants. He was one of the community of artists based in Pont Aven. His *La Ronde Bretonne* (1892) portrays local Celtic customs.

In his *Eiffel Tower* (1926) Robert Delaunay investigated the abstract qualities of colour. His wife, artist Sonia Delaunay, said, "The Eiffel Tower and the Universe were one and the same to him".

Neo-Impressionist artist and exponent of Pointillism, Paul Signac indulged his love of maritime subjects on the coasts of France. *Entrance to the Port at La Rochelle* (1921) shows his use of myriad dots of colour to represent nature.

Amiens
Le Havre
Rouen
Caen
Paris
Rennes
Le Mans
Orléans
Tours
Nantes
Poitiers
La Rochelle
Limoges
Bordeaux
Toulouse
Pau

0 kilometres 100
0 miles 100

Follower of the French Classical tradition of landscape painting, Jean-Baptiste-Camille Corot recorded *The Belfry of Douai* (1871).

Scenes from everyday life were realistically rendered by Gustave Courbet, as here in *Young Ladies of the Village Giving Alms to a Cow Girl in a Valley near Ornans* (1851–2).

Maurice Utrillo painted this village scene, *The Church of St Bernard, Ain, in Summer* (1924), while staying at his mother's home. The sombre tone and emptiness reflect his unhappy life.

Théodore Rousseau, the leading light of the Barbizon School *(see p185)* of landscape painters, visited the Auvergne in 1830. It was here that he began to paint "en plein air" (in the open air). The results are seen in this sensitively observed scene, *Sunset, Auvergne* (c.1830).

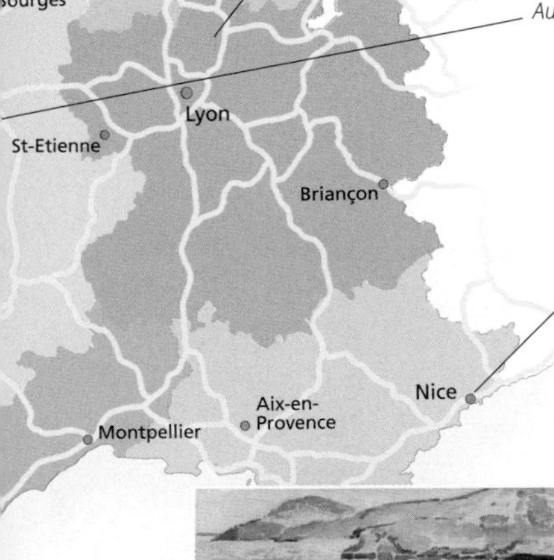

The French Riviera attracted many artists *(see pp476–7)*. Raoul Dufy particularly appreciated its pleasures, seen in this typical scene of blue skies and palm trees, *The Pier and Promenade at Nice* (1924).

Landscape at Collioure (1905) depicts the vivid colours of this little Catalan fishing village. It was here that Henri Matisse founded the art movement of the Fauves, or "Wild Beasts", who used exceptionally bright, expressive colours.

Writers in France

Writers and intellectuals traditionally enjoy high prestige in France. One of the most august of French institutions is the Académie Française, whose 40 members, most of them writers, have pronounced on national events and, on occasion, held public office.

The work of many French novelists is deeply rooted in their native area, ranging from the Normandy of Gustave Flaubert to Jean Giono's Provence. In addition to their literary merit, these novels provide a unique guide to France's regional identities.

The Novel

The farmland of the Beauce, where Zola based his novel *La Terre*

The most renowned Renaissance French writer was Rabelais, in the 16th century, a boisterous, life-affirming satirist *(see p299)*. Many writers in the Age of Enlightenment that followed emphasized the tradition of reason, clarity and objectivity in their work. The 19th century was the golden age of the French humanist novel, producing Balzac, with his vast fresco of contemporary society; Stendhal, a critic of the frailties of ambition in *Scarlet and Black*; and Victor Hugo, known for epics such as *Les Misérables*. George Sand broke ground with her novels such as *The Devil's Pool*, which depicted peasant life, albeit in an idealized way. In the same century, Flaubert produced his masterwork *Madame Bovary*, a study of provincialism and misplaced romanticism. In contrast, Zola wrote *Germinal*, *La Terre* and other studies of lower-class life.

Marcel Proust, author of *Remembrance of Things Past*

Marcel Proust combined a poetic evocation of his boyhood with a portrait of high society in his epic novel *Remembrance of Things Past*. Others have also written poetically about their childhood, such as Alain-Fournier in *Le Grand Meaulnes* and Colette in *My Mother's House*.

Colette's house in Burgundy

A new kind of novel emerged after World War I. Jean Giono's *Joy of Man's Desiring*, and François Mauriac's masterly *Thérèse Desqueyroux*, explored the impact of landscape upon human character. Mauriac, and also George Bernanos in his *Diary of a Country Priest*, used lone spiritual struggle as a theme. The free thinker André Gide was another leading writer of the inter-war years with his *Strait is the Gate* and the autobiographical *If it Die*.

In the 1960s Alain Robbe-Grillet and others experimented with the Nouveau Roman, which subordinated character and plot to detailed physical description. Critics held it in part responsible for the decline of the novel. Acclaimed best-selling contemporary writers include Michel Houllebecq and Catherine Cusset, while Mark Levy's many novels include *If Only It Were True*, which was made into a film by Steven Spielberg in 2005.

Hugo's novel *Les Misérables*, made into a musical in the 1980s

Theatre

The three classic playwrights of French literature, Racine, Molière and Corneille, lived in the 17th century. Molière's comedies satirized the vanities and foibles of human nature. Corneille and Racine wrote noble verse tragedies. They were followed in the 18th century by Marivaux, writer of romantic comedies, and Beaumarchais, whose *Barber of Seville* and *Marriage of Figaro* later became operas. Victor Hugo's dramas were the most vigorous product of the 19th century. The exceptional dramatists of the 20th century range from Jean Anouilh, author of urbane philosophical comedies, to Jean Genet, ex-convict critic of the establishment. In the 1960s, Eugéne Ionesco from Romania and Samuel Beckett from Ireland were among the pioneers of a new genre, the "theatre of the absurd". Since then, no major playwrights have emerged, but experimental work flourishes in state-subsidized theatre companies.

Molière, the 17th-century dramatist

Poetry

The greatest of early French poets was Ronsard, who wrote sonnets about nature and love in the 16th century. Lamartine, a major poet of the early 19th century, also took nature as one of his themes (his poem *Le Lac* laments a lost love). Later the same century, Baudelaire *(Les Fleurs du mal)* and Rimbaud *(Le Bateau Ivre)* were judged to be provocative in their day. Nobel prizewinner in 1904, Frédéric Mistral wrote in his native Provençal tongue. The greatest poet of the 20th century is considered to be Paul Valéry, whose work is profoundly philosophical.

Philosophy

France has produced a large number of major philosophers in the European humanist tradition. One of the first was Montaigne, in the 16th century, an inspired moralist. Then came Descartes, the master of logic, and Pascal. The 18th century produced Voltaire, the supreme liberal, and Rousseau, who preached the harmonizing influence of living close to nature.

In the 20th century, Sartre, de Beauvoir and Camus used the novel as a philosophical vehicle. Sartre led the existentialist movement in Paris in the early 1940s with his novel *Nausea* and his treatise *Being and Nothingness*. Camus's novel *The Outsider* was equally influential.

The 1970s and 1980s brought the structuralists, such as Foucault and Barthes, with their radical ideas. Post-structuralism took this rationalist approach into the 1990s, with Derrida, Kristeva, Deleuze and Lyotard. At the start of the 21st century, Alain Badiou, known for his political ideas, is considered to be one of France's key philosophers.

Sartre and de Beauvoir in La Coupole restaurant in Paris, 1969

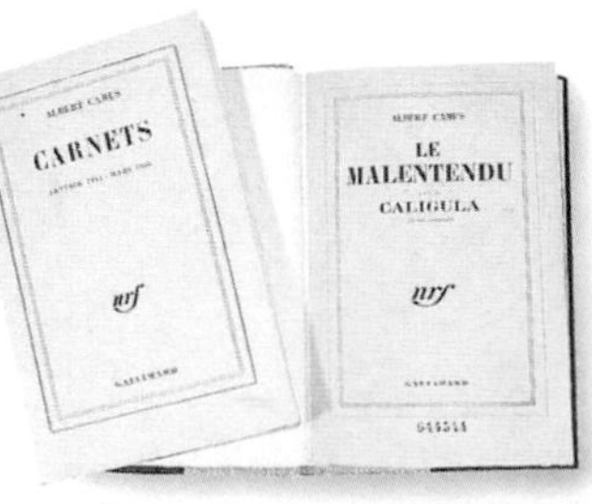

Novels by Albert Camus, who won the Nobel Prize in 1957

Foreign Writers

Many foreign writers have visited and been inspired by France, from Petrarch in 14th-century Avignon to Goethe in Alsace in 1770–71. In the 20th century the Riviera attracted novelists Somerset Maugham, Katherine Mansfield, Ernest Hemingway and Graham Greene. In 1919 the American Sylvia Beach opened Paris's first Shakespeare and Company bookshop, which became a cultural centre for expatriate writers. In 1922 she was the first to publish James Joyce's masterwork, *Ulysses*.

Hemingway with Sylvia Beach and friends, Paris 1923

Romanesque and Gothic Architecture in France

France is rich in medieval architecture, ranging from small Romanesque churches to great Gothic cathedrals. As the country emerged from the Dark Ages in the 11th century, there was a surge in Romanesque building, based on the Roman model of thick walls, round arches and heavy vaults. French architects improved this basic structure, leading to the flowering of Gothic in the 13th century. Pointed arches and flying buttresses were the key inventions that allowed for much taller buildings with larger windows.

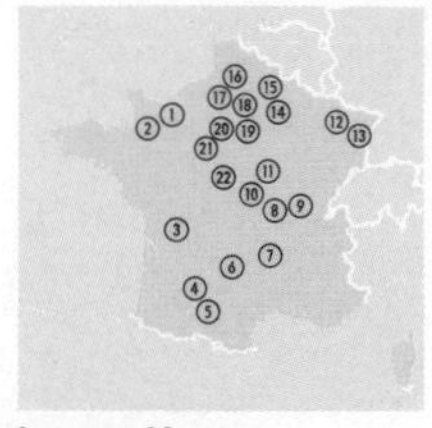

Locator Map

① *Romanesque abbeys and churches*

⑬ *Gothic cathedrals*

Romanesque Features

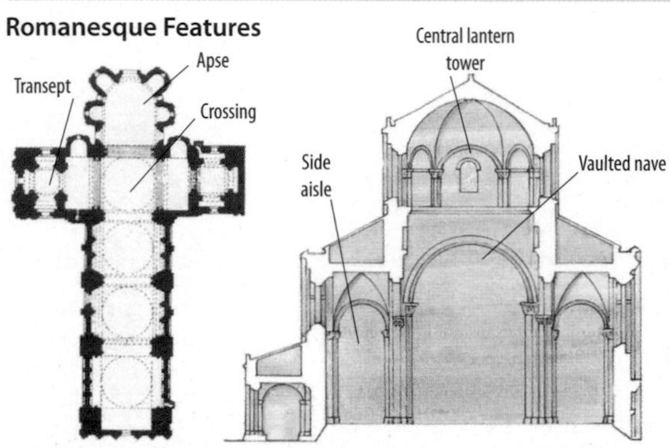

The plan of Angoulême shows the cross shape and the rounded eastern apse typical of Romanesque architecture.

A section of Le Puy reveals a high barrel-vaulted nave with round arches and low side aisles. Light could enter through windows in the side aisles and the central lantern tower.

The massive walls of the nave bays of St-Etienne support a three-storey structure of arcades, a gallery and clerestory.

Gothic Features

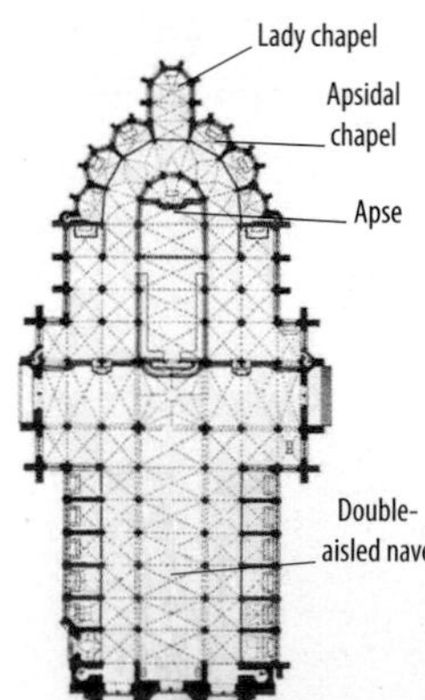

The plan of Amiens shows the nave and apse flanked by a continuous row of chapels.

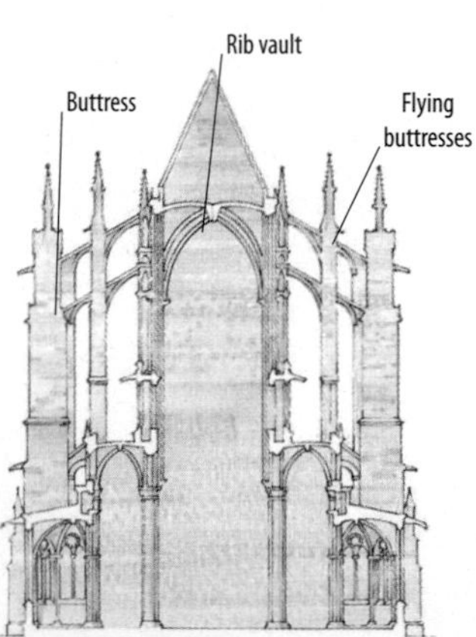

A section of Beauvais shows how the nave could be raised to staggering heights thanks to exterior support from flying buttresses.

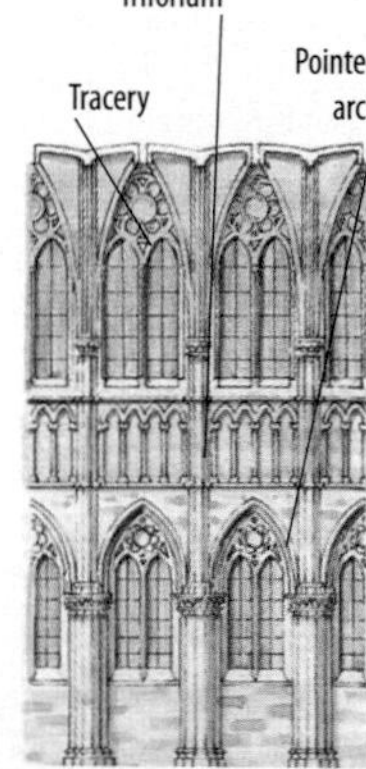

Pointed arches withstood greater stress, permitting larger windows as in the nave at Reims.

Where to find Romanesque Architecture

① St-Etienne, Caen *p258*
② Mont-St-Michel, Normandy *pp260–63*
③ St-Pierre, Angoulême *p423*
④ Notre-Dame, Le Puy *p369*
⑤ St-Pierre, Moissac *pp446–7*
⑥ St-Sernin, Toulouse *p451*
⑦ Ste-Foy, Conques *pp372–3*
⑧ Sacré-Coeur, Paray-le-Monial *p349*
⑨ St-Philibert, Tournus *pp348–9*
⑩ St-Etienne, Nevers *p342*
⑪ Ste-Madeleine, Vézelay *pp340–41*
⑫ Marmoutier, Saverne *p237*

Where to find Gothic Architecture

⑬ Notre-Dame, Strasbourg *p234*
⑭ Notre-Dame, Reims *pp216–17*
⑮ Notre-Dame, Laon *p209*
⑯ Notre-Dame, Amiens *pp206–7*
⑰ St-Pierre, Beauvais *p204*
⑱ St-Denis, Ile-de-France *pp176–7*
⑲ Sainte-Chapelle, Paris *pp88–9*
⑳ Notre-Dame, Paris *pp90–91*
㉑ Notre-Dame, Chartres *pp312–15*
㉒ St-Etienne, Bourges *p317*

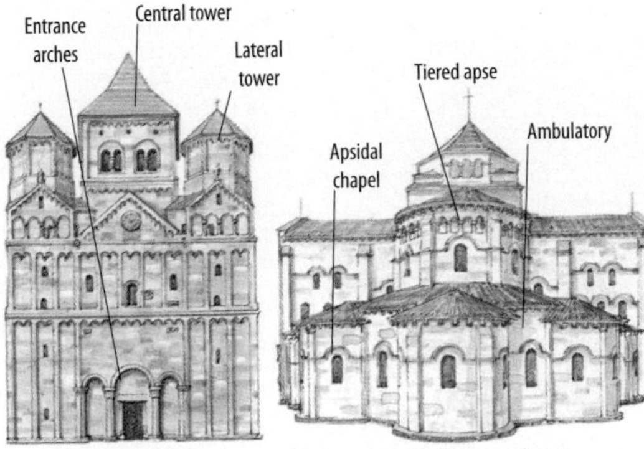

The west façade of Marmoutier Abbey with its towers, narrow windows and small portal give it a fortified appearance.

The east end of Nevers has a rounded apse surrounded by a semi circular ambulatory and radiating chapels. The chapels were added to provide space for altars.

The west façade of Laon has decorative, sculpted portals and a rose window characteristic of Gothic style.

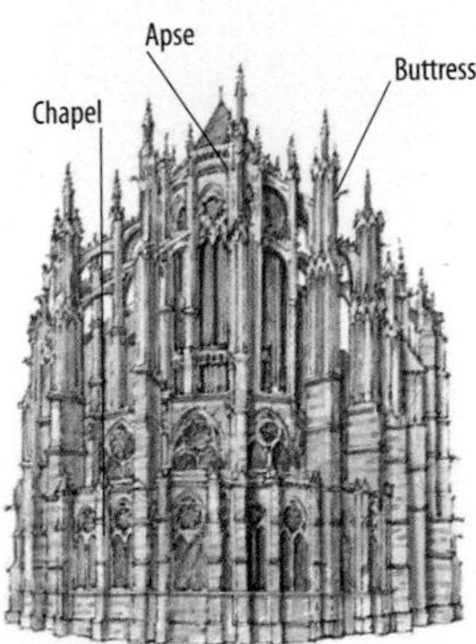

The east end of Beauvais, with its delicate buttresses topped by pinnacles, is the culmination of High Gothic.

Terms Used in this Guide

Basilica: Early church with two aisles and nave lit from above by clerestory windows.

Clerestory: A row of windows illuminating the nave from above the aisle roof.

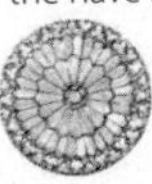

Rose: Circular window, often stained glass.

Buttress: Mass of masonry built to support a wall.

Flying buttress: An arched support transmitting thrust of the weight downwards.

Portal: Monumental entrance to a building, often decorated.

Tympanum: Decorated space, often carved, over a door or window lintel.

Vault: Arched stone ceiling.

Transept: Two wings of a cruciform church at right angles to the nave.

Crossing: Centre of cruciform, where transept crosses nave.

Lantern: Turret with windows to illuminate the interior, often with cupola (domed ceiling).

Triforium: Middle storey between arcades and the clerestory.

Apse: Termination of the church, often rounded.

Ambulatory: Aisle running round the east end, passing behind the sanctuary.

Arcade: Set of arches and supporting columns.

Rib vault: Vault supported by projecting ribs of stone.

Gargoyle: Carved grotesque figure, often a water spout.

Tracery: Ornamental carved stone pattern within Gothic window.

Flamboyant Gothic: Carved stone tracery resembling flames.

Capital: The top of a column, usually carved.

Rural Architecture

French farmhouses are entirely products of the soil, built of stone, clay or wood, depending on what materials are found locally. As the topography changes, so does the architecture, from the steeply sloped roofs covered in flat tiles in the north to the broad canal-tiled roofs of the south.

Despite this rich regional diversity, French farmhouses fall into three basic categories: the *maison bloc,* where house and outbuildings share the same roof; the high house, with living quarters upstairs and livestock or wine cellar below; and courtyard farmsteads, with their buildings set around a central court.

Shuttered window in Alsace

The chalet is typical of the Jura, Alps and Vosges mountains. The *maison bloc* housed both family and livestock throughout the winter. Gaps between the gable planks allowed air to circulate around crops stored in the loft, and an earth ramp behind gave wagons access. Many lofts also had a threshing floor.

Half-timbered houses are typical of Normandy, Alsace, Champagne, Picardy, the Landes and Basque country. The filling between the timbers was wattle and daub or in some cases brick, but it is the arrangement of the smaller posts, different in each region, that best expresses the local style.

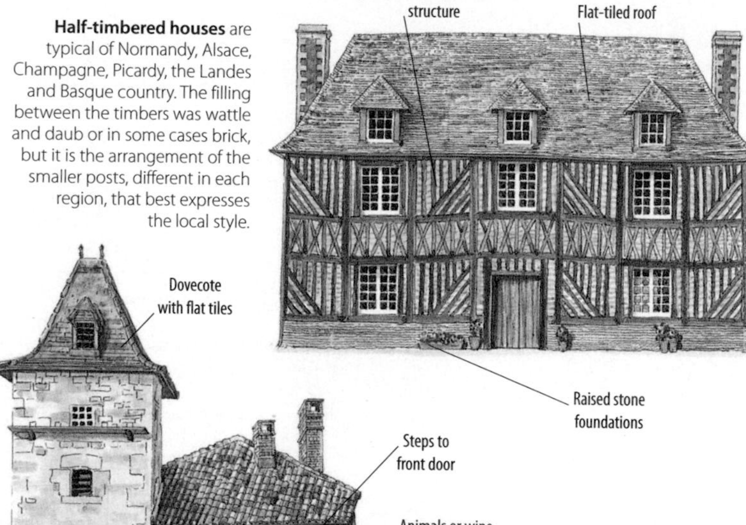

The high house is most prominent in the southeast, and is normally built of stone with an exterior stone staircase and upstairs porch. Wine growers' barrels could be stored on the ground floor without hoisting, or livestock could be stabled there. High houses in the Lot Valley often boast a dovecote.

The longhouse is the oldest form of *maison bloc*, with family and livestock at opposite ends of the building – originally one room. In this Breton version, separate doorways lead to house and stable. A dividing wall only became common in the 19th century.

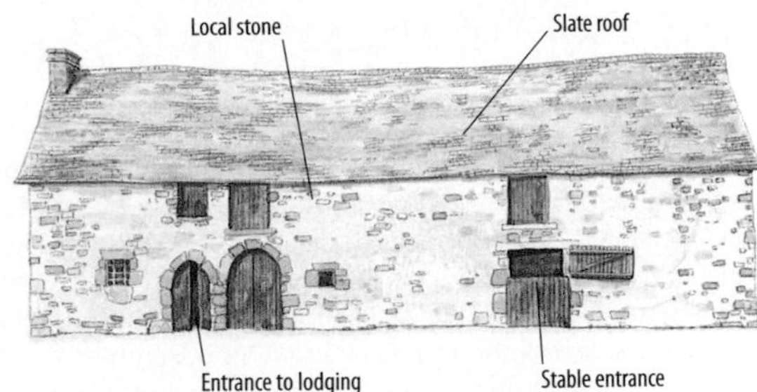

The word *"mas"* generally refers to any Provençal farmhouse. In the Camargue and the Crau, it is a farmstead for large-scale sheep farming built in an "agglomerated" style: the outbuildings, although attached to one another, are of different heights. Often, a dovecote is included.

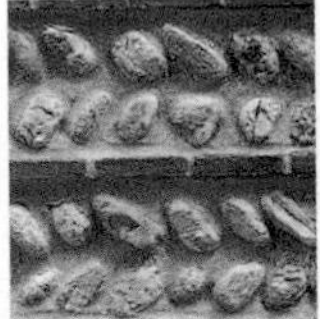
Pebble-and-brick wall

Half-timber and brick

Compressed cob: *pisé*

Sun-dried adobe bricks

Pebbles in lime mortar

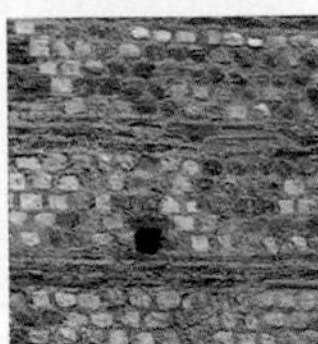
Brick, flint and chalk

Walls

Limestone, granite, sandstone and pebbles were all used for building walls. But if no stone was available, clay was dug for infilling half-timbered houses, as wattle and daub. The alternative was to use a cob mixture *(pisé)*, pressed into blocks in a process called *banchange*. Adobe (sun-dried brick) was also used but fired brick was fairly rare as it was expensive to bake. However, brick was sometimes used as trim or combined with chalk or pebbles in a "composite" walling. Walls were generally rendered with mortar.

Flat terracotta tiles in colours of local sand

Pantiles, used in Flanders and Picardy

Canal clay tiles typical of the south

Roofing

Two roof styles distinguish the north and south. Northern roofs are steeply pitched, so that any rainwater runs off easily. In the south, roofs are covered with canal clay tiles, and more gently sloped to prevent the tiles sliding off.

FRANCE THROUGH THE YEAR

The French, with their farming roots, are deeply aware of the changing seasons, and the mild climate means that they can celebrate outdoors most of the year. History and tradition are honoured with *fêtes*, such as Bastille Day (14 July). For culture lovers, thousands of arts festivals are held throughout France, ranging from the huge Avignon Theatre Festival down to small village affairs. Large national sports events, such as the Tour de France cycle race, are a key feature in the calendar. Throughout the year, festivals take place celebrating every kind of food and wine. In high summer, the cities empty, and French and foreign visitors flock to the beaches and countryside.

Spring

France's outdoor life resumes in spring, terrace-cafés filling up in the sunshine. Easter is a time of Catholic processions, and concerts of sacred music. The Cannes Film Festival in May is the best known of the season's many conventions and trade fairs.

March

International Half Marathon, Paris, beginning and ending at Château de Vincennes.
Six Nations Rugby Tournament, Stade de France, Paris.
Tinta' Mars *(fortnight)*, Langres. Cabaret and musical evenings at various venues.
Babel Med Music, Marseille *(mid-Mar)*. Three-day international music festival.
Europa Jazz Festival *(mid-Mar–mid-May)*, Le Mans. International jazz festival.

La Bravade procession honouring St Torpès (the resort's namesake) in St-Tropez

Formula One racing at the Monaco Grand Prix

Banlieues Bleues Jazz Festival *(late Mar–early Apr)*, St-Denis. Jazz music.
Les Détours de Babel *(late Mar–early Apr)*, Grenoble. Festival of contemporary world music.

April

Festival de Pâques *(2 weeks)*, Deauville. Chamber music.
Feria Pascale *(Easter week)*, Arles. Start of the bullfighting season *(see pp512–13)*.
Lourdes Pilgrimage *(Palm Sun to Oct, see pp462–3)*.
Floréal Musical d'Epinal *(early Apr–mid-May)*, Epinal. Multi-genre music festival.
Bourges Spring Festival *(end Apr/early May, see p317)*. Modern music.
Joan of Arc Festival *(end Apr–early May)* Orléans. Pageant and cathedral service *(see p316)*.
Paris International Marathon Competitors run 42 km (26 miles) through the city, from place de la Concorde to avenue Foch.

May

Asparagus harvest, notably in the Loire.
International Grand Prix de Monaco *(Ascension weekend, see p534)*.

International Sailing Week *(first half of May)*, La Rochelle.
La Bravade *(16–18 May)*, St-Tropez *(see p520)*.
Cannes Film Festival *(second and third week, see p524)*.
Gypsy Pilgrimage *(late May)*, Stes-Maries-de-la-Mer *(see p514)*.
Fête de la Transhumance *(end May)*. Herds are taken up to summer pastures.
International Garden Festival *(May–mid-Oct)*, Chaumont sur Loire.
Nîmes Feria *(Pentecost)*. Bullfights and street music *(see pp500–1)*.
Grandes Eaux Musicales *(Apr–Oct: Sat & Sun; mid-May–Jun: Tue)*, Versailles. Fountain jets set to classical music in the grounds of the château.
Puy du Fou Pageant *(May–Sep)*. Actors, audio guides and horse stunts make a "living pageant", which evokes local life through the ages *(see p294)*.
Football Cup Final *(second week)*, Stade de France, Paris.

Traditional transhumance of animals to summer pastures

Summer

The French holiday season begins in mid-July, with the return to work and school *(la rentrée)* in early September. Beaches, marinas and camp sites are all full to bursting. Each village has its *fête* and there are festivals, sporting events and flea markets.

June

French Tennis Open *(last week May–first week Jun)*, Stade Roland Garros, Paris.
Le Mans 24-Hour Automobile Race *(second or third weekend, see p295)*. The world's oldest endurance sports car race.
Fête de la Musique *(21 Jun)*. Numerous music events are held all over France.
La Marche des Fiertés Lesbiennes, Gaies, Bi et Trans *(late June/early Jul)*. LGBT march in Paris.
Fête de St-Jean *(24 Jun)*. Music and fireworks all over France.
Le Printemps des Arts *(late Jun)*, Nantes area. Baroque dance and music.
Des Rives et Des Notes *(1 week late Jun)*, Oloron-Ste-Marie (near Pau). Jazz festival.
Tarasque Festival *(last weekend)*, Tarascon *(see p511)*.

July

Festival d'Art Lyrique *(Jun–Jul)*, Aix-en-Provence. International classical music festival.
Avignon Theatre Festival *(all month, see p507)*.
Troménie *(Sun Jul)*, Locronan. Penitents' procession *(see p277)*.

Bullfighting in Mont-de-Marsan

Tombées de la Nuit *(first week)*, Rennes. Arts festival.
Jazz Vienne *(first 2 weeks)*, Vienne *(see p386)*.
Tour de France cycle race *(first 3 weeks)*. The grand finale takes place on the Champs-Elysées, Paris.
Francofolies *(mid-Jul)*. Music festival at La Rochelle.
Paris-Plage *(mid-Jul–mid-Aug)*. Paris and other cities get an annual temporary beach.
Mont-de-Marsan Feria *(third or fourth weekend)*. Bullfights and music *(see p429)*.
International Jazz Festival *(second half)*, Antibes and Juan-les-Pins *(see p525)*.
Nice Jazz Festival *(late Jul)*.
Comminges Music Festival *(Jul–end Aug, see p466)*.
Pablo Casals Festival *(end Jul–mid-Aug)*, Prades *(see p484)*.

Cyclists competing in the famous Tour de France cycle race

Holiday-makers on a crowded beach in Cannes on the Côte d'Azur

August
Mimos *(first week)*, Périgueux. World-famous international mime festival.
Fête du Jasmin *(first weekend)*, Grasse. Floats, music and dancing in town.
Foire aux Sorciers *(first Sun)*, Bué (near Bourges). Costumed witch and wizard festival and folk groups.
Parade of Lavender Floats *(first or second weekend)*, Digne *(see p521)*.
Fête de la Véraison *(first or second weekend)*, Châteauneuf-du-Pape *(see pp506–7)*. Medieval celebration of thanks-giving for the fruit harvest.
Interceltic Festival *(second week)*, Lorient. Celtic arts and music.
Feria – Bullfight *(mid-Aug)*, Dax *(see p429)*.
St-Jean-Pied-de-Port-Basque Fête *(mid-Aug, see p458)*. Celebration of Basque culture with music and dancing.
Fête de St-Louis *(around 25 Aug)*, Sète *(see p496)*.
Les Rendezvous de l'Erdre *(last weekend)*, Nantes. Jazz and river-boats.

Autumn

In wine regions, the grape harvest is the occasion for much jollity, and every wine village has its wine festival. When the new wine is ready in November, there are more festivities. The hunting season begins – everywhere there is game shooting. In the southwest, migrating birds are trapped.

September
Deauville American Film Festival *(first fortnight)*.
Le Puy "Roi de l'Oiseau", *(second week)*. Renaissance-style festival *(see pp368–9)*.
Grape harvest, wine regions throughout France.
Biennale de Lyon *(mid-Sep–Dec)*. Dance festival and art festival alternate years.
Journées du Patrimoine, *(third weekend)*. Over 14,000 historical buildings can be visited, many not normally open.
Musica *(late Sep–early Oct)*, Strasbourg. International music festival.

Ceremony for the Induction of new Chevaliers at the Hospice de Beaune at the Wine Auctions

October
Dinard British Film Festival *(first week,)*.
Prix de l'Arc de Triomphe *(first Sun)*, Horse racing at Longchamp, Paris.
Jazz Pulsations *(mid-Oct)*, Nancy. International jazz fest.
Espelette Pepper Festival *(last weekend, see p457)*.
Festival de Lanvellec and Trégor *(mid-Oct)*. Baroque music festival.
Les Castagnades *(Oct–Nov)*. Chestnut festival throughout the Ardéche.

November
Dijon International Food and Wine Festival *(first 2 weeks)*. Traditional gastronomic fair.
Wine Auctions and Les Trois Glorieuses *(third weekend)*, Beaune *(see p350)*.
Truffle season *(until Mar)*, Périgord, Quercy and Provence.

Winter

At Christmas, traditional nativity plays are held in churches and there are fairs and markets throughout France. In the Alps and the Pyrenees, and even the Vosges and Massif Central, the ski slopes are crowded. In Flanders and Nice, carnivals take place before Lent.

December

Feast of St Nicolas *(weekend in early Dec)*, Nancy. A celebration with parades, concerts, floats and a fireworks display.
Critérium International de la Première Neige *(early Dec)*, Val d'Isère. First skiing competition of the season.
Festival of Lights *(early Dec)*, Lyon. The city's architecture – buildings, streets, squares and parks – provides the backdrop for a contemporary light show.

Downhill skier on the slopes in the French Alps

The Taj Mahal re-created at the Lemon Festival in Menton

Habits de Lumière *(weekend in mid-Dec)*, Epernay. This three-day event along the famous avenue de Champagne offers street theatre, concerts and exhibitions, plus Champagne tastings and a vintage car parade.

January

Monte-Carlo Rally *(usually mid-Jan, see p534)*.
Limoux Carnival *(until Mar)*. Street festival held since the Middle Ages.
Fashion shows, Paris. Summer collections.
Festival du Cirque *(end)*, Monaco. International event.
Festival de la Bande Dessinée *(last weekend)*. International strip cartoon festival, Angoulême.

February

Lemon Festival *(mid-Feb–Mar)*, Menton *(see p533)*.
Nice Carnival and the Battle of Flowers *(late Feb–early Mar, see p530)*.
Paris Carnaval, *(date varies, check)*, Quartier St-Fargeau.
Fête de Mimosa, *(third Sun)*, Bormes-les-Mimosas.

Bastille Day parade past the Arc de Triomphe

Public Holidays

New Year's Day (1 Jan)
Easter Sunday and Monday
Ascension Day (sixth Thursday after Easter)
Whit Monday (second Monday after Ascension)
Labour Day (1 May)
VE Day (8 May)
Bastille Day (14 Jul)
Assumption Day (15 Aug)
All Saints' Day (1 Nov)
Remembrance Day (11 Nov)
Christmas Day (25 Dec)

The Climate of France

Set on Europe's western edge, France has a varied, temperate climate. An Atlantic influence prevails in the northwest, with westerly sea winds bringing humidity and warm winters. The east experiences Continental temperature extremes with frosty, clear winters and often stormy summers. The south enjoys a Mediterranean climate with hot, dry summers and mild winters, punctuated by violent winds.

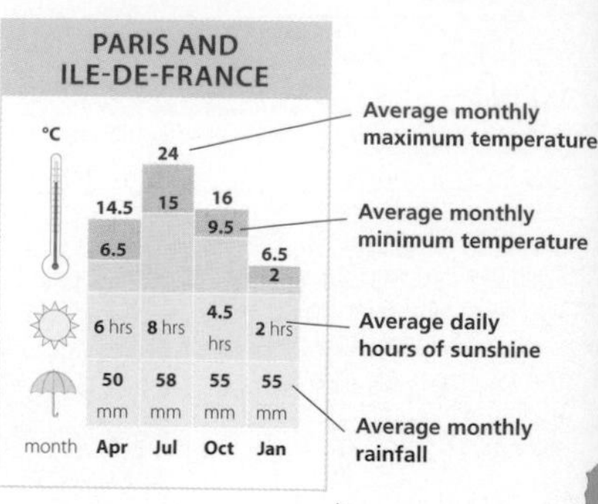

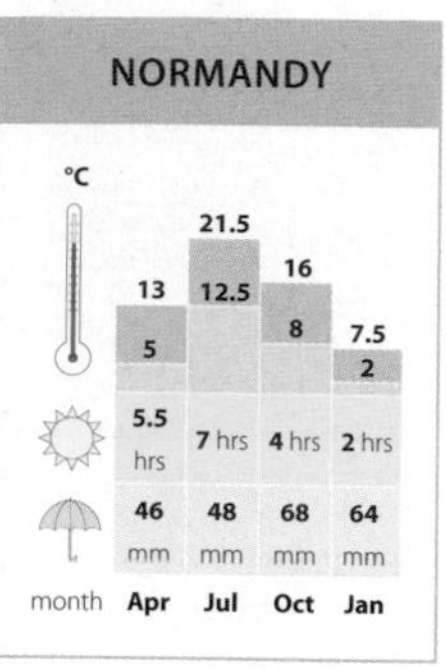

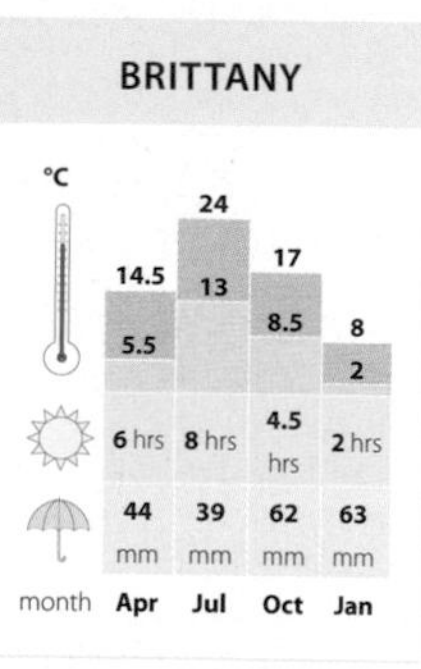

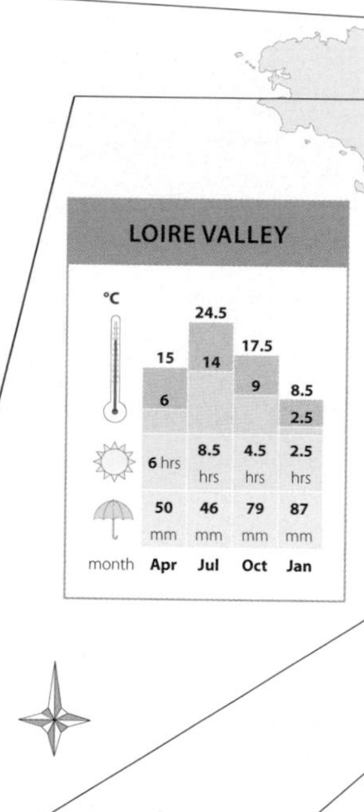

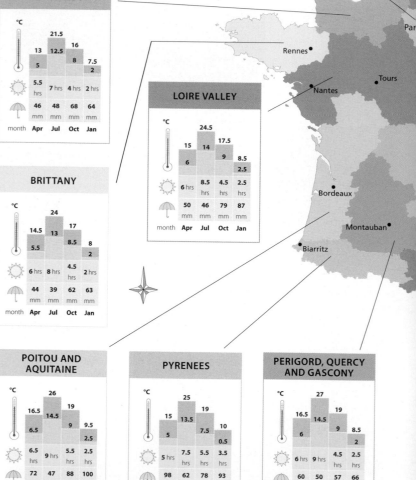

Le Havre
Par
Rennes
Nantes
Tours
Bordeaux
Montauban
Biarritz

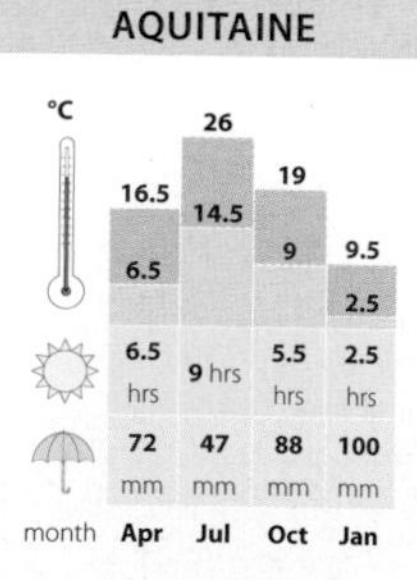

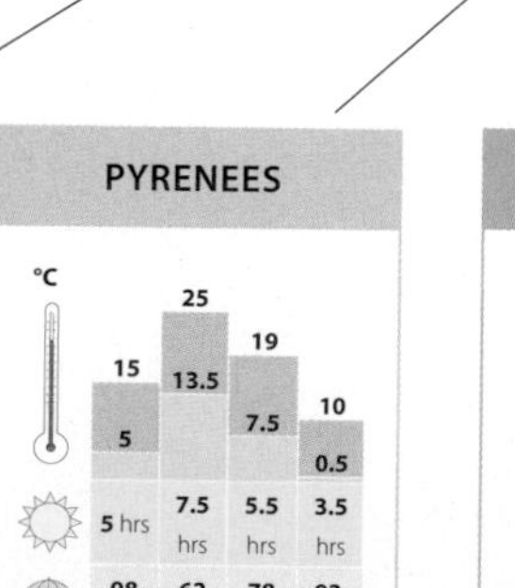

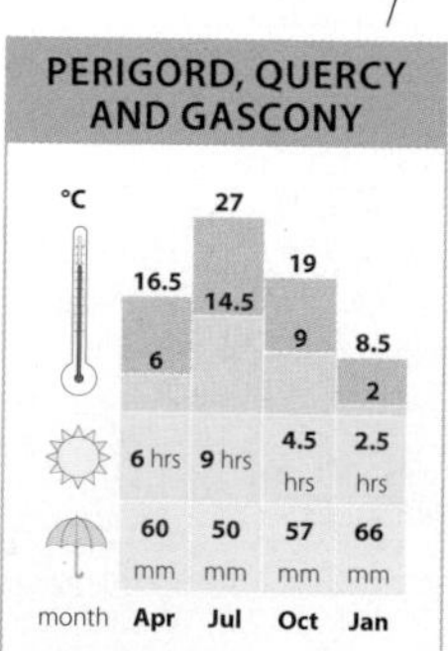

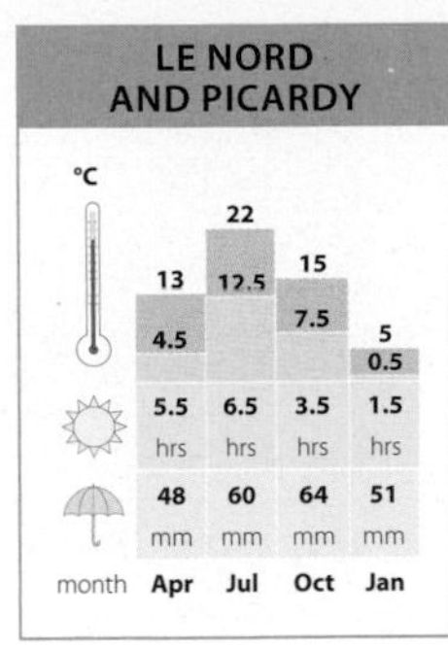

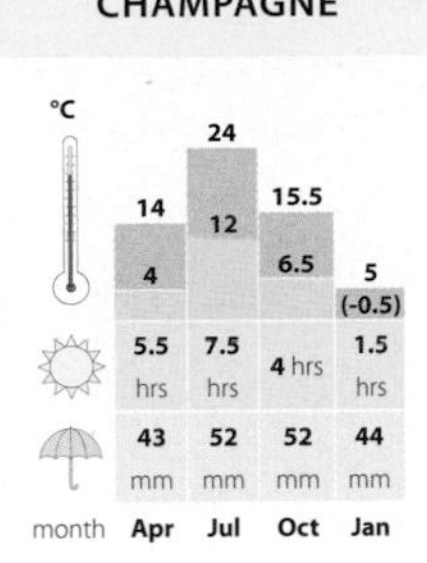

ALSACE AND LORRAINE

month	Apr	Jul	Oct	Jan
°C	14.5	25	15	3.5
	4.5	13.5	6.5	(-1.5)
	5.5 hrs	7.5 hrs	3 hrs	1.5 hrs
	48 mm	57 mm	43 mm	33 mm

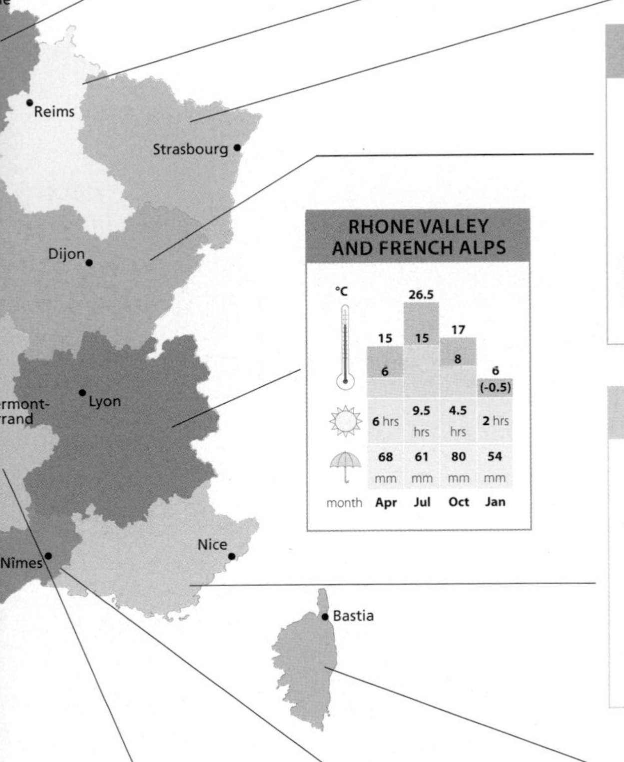

BURGUNDY AND FRANCHE-COMTE

month	Apr	Jul	Oct	Jan
°C	14.5	25.5	15.5	4
	5	14	9	(-1)
	6 hrs	8.5 hrs	4 hrs	1.5 hrs
	52 mm	51 mm	58 mm	59 mm

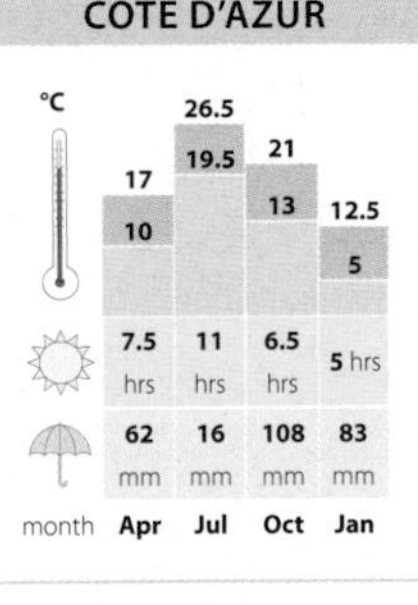

PROVENCE AND COTE D'AZUR

month	Apr	Jul	Oct	Jan
°C	17	26.5	21	12.5
	10	19.5	13	5
	7.5 hrs	11 hrs	6.5 hrs	5 hrs
	62 mm	16 mm	108 mm	83 mm

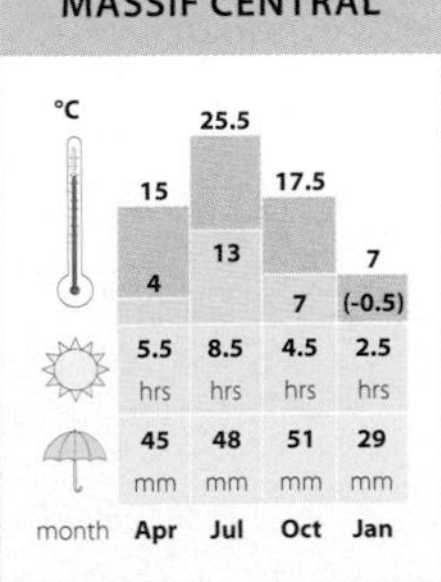

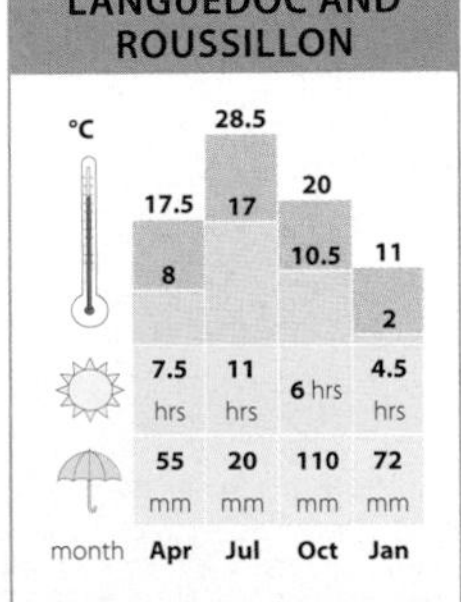

CORSICA

month	Apr	Jul	Oct	Jan
°C	17.5	28.5	21.5	13.5
	8.5	18	12.5	5
	7 hrs	11 hrs	6.5 hrs	4.5 hrs
	66 mm	15 mm	107 mm	62 mm

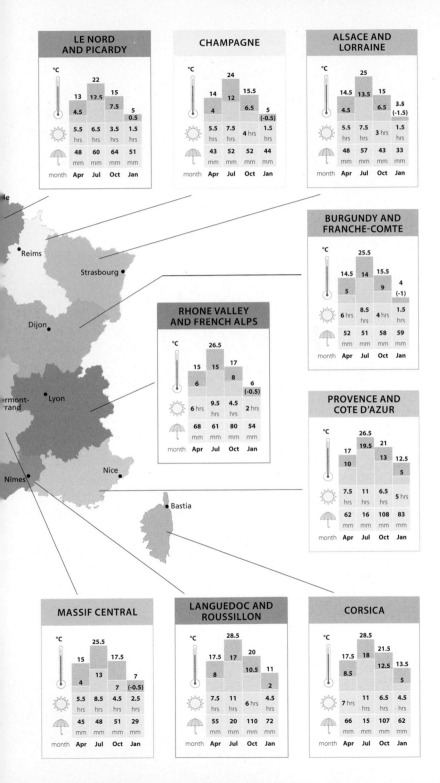

THE HISTORY OF FRANCE

The only European country facing both the North Sea and the Mediterranean, France has been subject to a particularly rich variety of cultural influences. Though famous for the rootedness of its peasant population, it has also been a European melting pot, even before the arrival of the Celtic Gauls in the centuries before Christ, through to the Mediterranean immigrations of the 20th century. Roman conquest by Julius Caesar had an enduring impact, but from the 4th and 5th centuries AD, waves of Barbarian invaders destroyed much of the Roman legacy. The Germanic Franks provided political leadership in the following centuries, but when their line died out in the late 10th century, France was socially and politically fragmented.

The Formation of France

The Capetian dynasty gradually pieced France together over the Middle Ages, a period of great economic prosperity and cultural vitality. The Black Death and the Hundred Years' War brought setbacks, and the dynasty's power was seriously threatened by the rival Burgundian dukes. France recovered and despite the wars of religion flourished during the Renaissance, followed by the grandeur of Louis XIV's reign. During the Enlightenment, in the 18th century, French culture was the envy of Europe.

The Revolution of 1789 ended the absolute monarchy and introduced major social and institutional reforms, many of which were endorsed and consolidated by Napoleon. Yet the Revolution also inaugurated the instability that remained a hallmark of French politics until de Gaulle and the Fifth Republic: since 1789, France has known five republics, two empires and three brands of royal power, plus the Vichy government in World War II.

Modernization in the 19th and 20th centuries proved a slow process. Railways, the military service and radical educational reforms were crucial in forming a sense of French identity among the citizens.

Rivalry with Germany dominated French politics for most of the late 19th and early 20th century. The population losses in World War I were traumatic for France, while during 1940 to 1944 the country was occupied by Germany. Yet, today, together with Germany, France forms the backbone of the European Union.

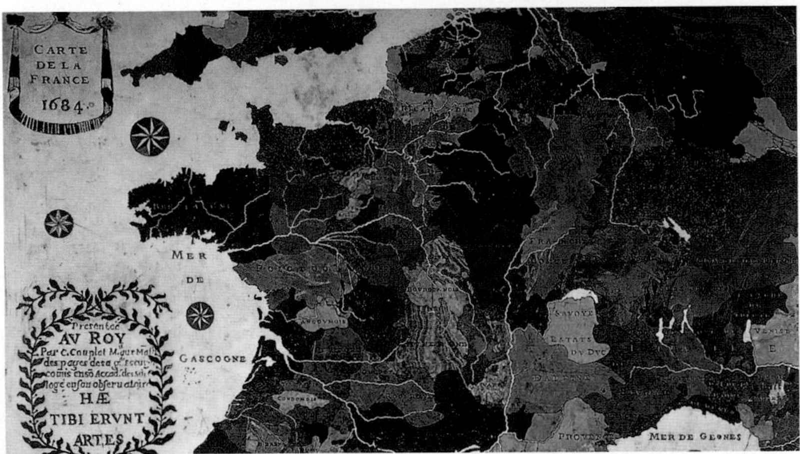

Inlaid marble table top showing the map of France in 1684

◀ *La République*, painted by Charles Landelle in 1848

Kings and Emperors of France

Following the break-up of the Roman Empire, the Frankish king Clovis consolidated the Merovingian dynasty. It was followed by the Carolingians, and from the 10th century by Capetian rulers. The Capetians established royal power, which passed to the Valois branch in the 14th century, and then to the Bourbons in the late 16th century, following the Wars of Religion. The Revolution of 1789 seemed to end the Bourbon dynasty, but it made a brief comeback in 1814–30. The 19th century was dominated by the Bonapartes, Napoleon I and Napoleon III. Since the overthrow of Napoleon III in 1870, France has been a republic.

768–814 Charlemagne

447–458 Merovich

458–482 Childéric I

558–562 Clothaire I

566–584 Chilpéric I

628–637 Dagobert I

655–668 Clothaire III

674–691 Thierry III

695–711 Childebert II

716–721 Chilpéric II

743–751 Childéric III

840–877 Charles I, the Bald

879–882 Louis III

884–888 Charles III, the Fat

898–929 Charles III, the Simple

954–986 Lothaire

987–996 Hugh Capet

1031–60 Henri I

1060–1108 Philippe I

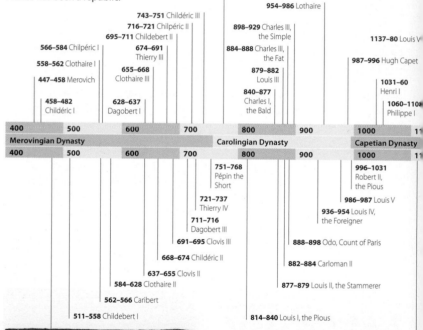

1137–80 Louis V

400 | 500 | 600 | 700 | 800 | 900 | 1000 | 1

Merovingian Dynasty | Carolingian Dynasty | Capetian Dynasty

400 | 500 | 600 | 700 | 800 | 900 | 1000 | 1

751–768 Pépin the Short

721–737 Thierry IV

711–716 Dagobert III

691–695 Clovis III

668–674 Childéric II

637–655 Clovis II

584–628 Clothaire II

562–566 Caribert

511–558 Childebert I

996–1031 Robert II, the Pious

986–987 Louis V

936–954 Louis IV, the Foreigner

888–898 Odo, Count of Paris

882–884 Carloman II

877–879 Louis II, the Stammerer

814–840 Louis I, the Pious

482–511 Clovis I

1108–37 Louis VI, the Fat

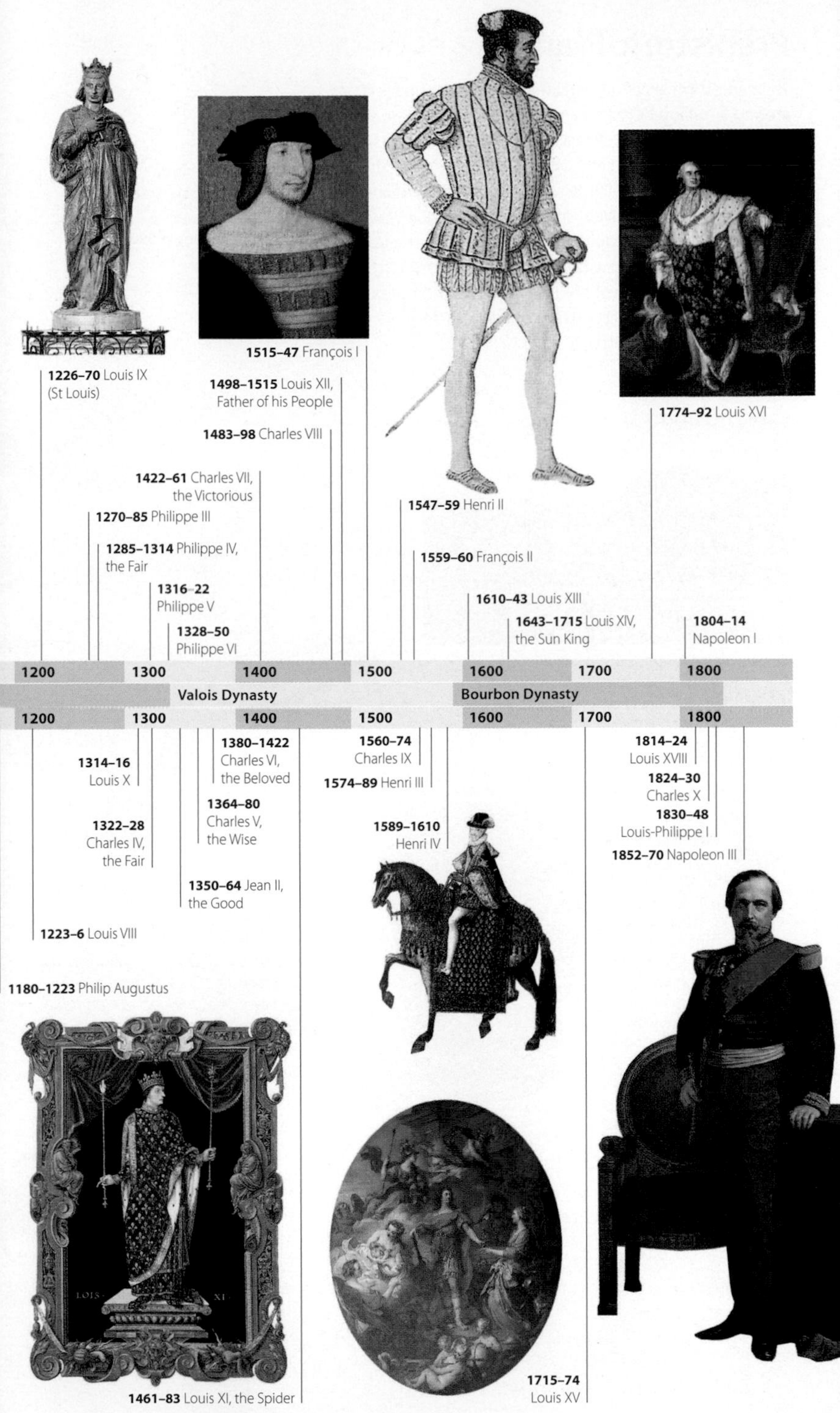
1226–70 Louis IX (St Louis)
1515–47 François I
1498–1515 Louis XII, Father of his People
1483–98 Charles VIII
1422–61 Charles VII, the Victorious
1270–85 Philippe III
1285–1314 Philippe IV, the Fair
1316–22 Philippe V
1328–50 Philippe VI
1547–59 Henri II
1559–60 François II
1610–43 Louis XIII
1643–1715 Louis XIV, the Sun King
1774–92 Louis XVI
1804–14 Napoleon I
1200
1300
1400
1500
1600
1700
1800
Valois Dynasty
Bourbon Dynasty
1314–16 Louis X
1380–1422 Charles VI, the Beloved
1364–80 Charles V, the Wise
1322–28 Charles IV, the Fair
1350–64 Jean II, the Good
1223–6 Louis VIII
1180–1223 Philip Augustus
1560–74 Charles IX
1574–89 Henri III
1589–1610 Henri IV
1814–24 Louis XVIII
1824–30 Charles X
1830–48 Louis-Philippe I
1852–70 Napoleon III
LOIS XI
1461–83 Louis XI, the Spider
1715–74 Louis XV

Prehistoric France

The earliest traces of human life in France date back to around 2 million BC. From around 40,000 BC, *Homo sapiens* lived an itinerant existence as hunters and gatherers. Around 6000 BC, following the end of the Ice Age, a major shift in lifestyle occurred, as people settled down to herd animals and cultivate crops. The advent of metal working allowed more effective tools and weapons to be developed. The Iron Age is associated particularly with the Celts, who arrived from the east during the first millennium BC. A more complex social hierarchy developed, consisting of warriors, farmers, artisans and druids (Celtic priests).

France in 8000 BC

Former coastline

Present-day land mass

Carnac Stone Alignments (4500–4000 BC)
The purpose of the extensive networks of megaliths around Carnac *(see pp282–3)* remains obscure. They possibly served in pagan rituals or as an astronomical calendar.

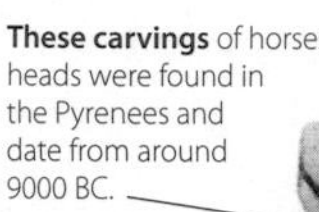

These carvings of horses' heads were found in the Pyrenees and date from around 9000 BC.

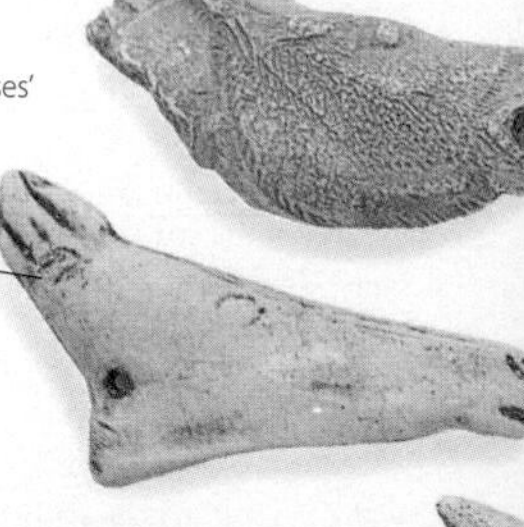

The mammoth, here carved from animal bone, was a thick-coated giant who died out after the end of the Ice Age.

Cro-Magnon Man
This skull, dating to c.28,000 BC, was discovered at Cro-Magnon in the Dordogne in 1868. In comparison with most of his predecessors, Cro-Magnon man was tall, robust, and had a large head. He differed only marginally from us.

Prehistoric Art

The rich deposits of cave art in France have only been recognized as authentic for just over a century. They include wall paintings and daubings but also various engraved objects. Venus figurines, carved with flint tools, probably had ritual and religious rather than erotic purposes.

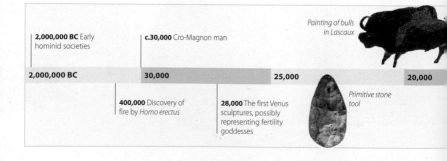

2,000,000 BC Early hominid societies

c.30,000 Cro-Magnon man

Painting of bulls in Lascaux

2,000,000 BC | **30,000** | **25,000** | **20,000**

400,000 Discovery of fire by *Homo erectus*

28,000 The first Venus sculptures, possibly representing fertility goddesses

Primitive stone tool

Doorway, Roquepertuse
Religion was an important part of Celtic life. The Celts made a cult of severed heads – presumably of their enemies – as seen in this sanctuary doorway dating from the 3rd century BC.

The prehistoric hunter's quarry is here represented by a flock of chamois carved on a piece of bone.

This carved bone, found in Laugerie-Basse in the Dordogne, shows a bison chased by a man with a spear.

This highly stylized female figure, a Venus figurine found in southwest France, was carved from mammoth tusk in around 20,000 BC.

Where to See Prehistoric France

The Lascaux cave paintings in Périgord *(see p438)* are among the best in the world. Further cave decoration is found around Les Eyzies *(pp438–9)*, at the Vallée des Merveilles near Tendes in the Alpes-Maritimes *(p533)* and in the Grotte du Pech Merle in the Lot Valley *(p442)*. The intriguing menhirs at Filitosa in Corsica *(pp546–7)* are about 4,000 years old.

The Lascaux cave paintings, dating from 16,000–14,000 BC, include images of bulls and mammoths.

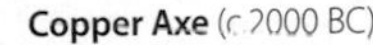

Copper Axe (c.2000 BC)
Copper tools preceded the arrival of the stronger and more malleable bronze alloy. Iron was to prove the toughest and most useful metal of all.

Bronze Armour
Bronze and Iron Age people were highly warlike. The Celtic Gauls were feared even by Romans. Their protective armour, such as this breastplate dating from 750–475 BC, was light but reasonably effective.

15,000 Hunters live on wandering herds of mammoth, rhinoceros and reindeer. Art includes the Lascaux caves and Val Camonica/Mont Bego engravings

7000–4500 Neolithic revolution: farming, megaliths and menhir stone sculptures

600 Greek colony at Marseille. Mediterranean luxury goods exchanged for tin, copper, iron, and slaves. Early urban development

15,000 | **10,000** | **5,000**

10,000 End of Ice Age. More regions become inhabitable

10,000–6000 Mammoth herds disappear and hunters must rely on animals of the forest, including wild boar and aurochs

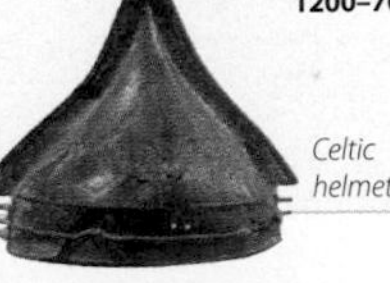

Celtic helmet

1200–700 Arrival of the Celts during the Bronze and Iron Ages

500 Celtic nobles bury their dead with riches such as the Vix treasure *(see p338)*

Roman Gaul

The Romans had annexed the southern fringe of France by 125–121 BC. Julius Caesar brought the rest of Gaul under Roman control in the Gallic Wars (58–51 BC). The province of Gaul prospered: it developed good communications, a network of cities crammed with public buildings and leisure facilities such as baths and amphitheatres, while in the countryside large villas were established. By the 3rd century AD, however, barbarian raids from Germany were causing increasing havoc. From the 5th century barbarians began to settle throughout Gaul.

France in 58 BC

▢ Roman Gaul

Roman Dolce Vita
The Romans brought material comfort and luxury, and wine growing became widespread. This 19th-century painting by Couture conveys a contemporary view of Roman decadence.

Emperor Augustus, who was considered a living God, was worshipped at this altar.

Vercingetorix
The Celtic chieftain Vercingetorix was Julius Caesar's greatest military opponent. This bronze statue is at Alise-Ste-Reine *(see p338)*, the Gauls' final stand in 51 BC.

La Turbie

This impressive monument near Monaco was erected in 6 BC by the Roman Senate. It celebrates Augustus's victory over the Alpine tribes in 14–13 BC. Badly pillaged for its stone, restoration only began in the 1920s.

125–121 BC Roman colonization of Southern Gaul

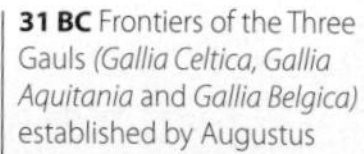

31 BC Frontiers of the Three Gauls *(Gallia Celtica, Gallia Aquitania* and *Gallia Belgica)* established by Augustus

Augustus

200 BC | 100 | 0 | AD 100

Julius Caesar

58–51 BC Julius Caesar's Gallic Wars result in establishment of Roman Gaul

52–51 BC Vercingetorix revolt

16 BC Maison Carrée built in Nîmes *(see pp500–1)*

AD 43 Lugdunum (Lyon) established as capital of the Three Gauls

Dancing Girl
Celtic art continued uninfluenced by Roman naturalistic ideals. This bronze statuette of a young woman dates from the 1st–2nd century AD.

A statue of Augustus was placed at the top of the original monument.

Enamelled Brooch
This decorative Gallo-Roman brooch dates from the second half of the 1st century BC.

Where to See Gallo-Roman France

Gallo-Roman remains are to be found all over France, many of them in Provence. In addition to La Turbie *(see p533)*, there is the Roman amphitheatre in Arles *(p512 13)* and the theatre and triumphal arch in Orange *(p506)*. Elsewhere, there are ruins at Autun in Burgundy *(p343)*, the Temple d'Auguste et Livie in Vienne *(p386)*, Les Arènes at Nîmes *(pp500–1)* and fragments of Vesunna in Périgueux *(p435)*.

Les Arènes in Nîmes, built at the end of the 1st century AD, is still in use today.

The Claudian Tables
In AD 48, Emperor Claudius persuaded the Senate to allow Gauls full Roman citizenship. The grateful Gauls recorded the event on stone tables found at Lyon.

The 44 tribes subjugated by Augustus are listed on an inscription, with a dedication to the emperor.

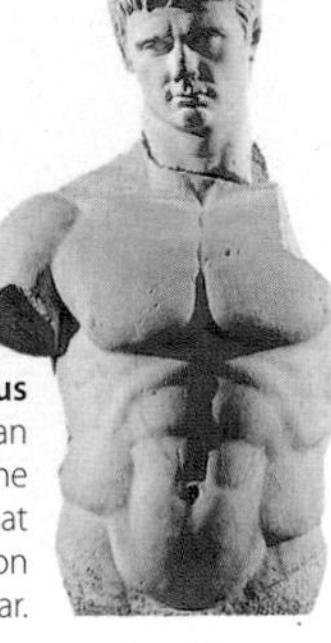

Emperor Augustus
Augustus, the first Roman Emperor (27 BC–AD 14), upheld the Pax Romana, an enforced peace that allowed the Gauls to concentrate on culture rather than war.

AD 177 First execution of Christian martyrs, Lyon. St Blandine is thrown to the lions, who refuse to harm her

St Blandine

360 Julian, prefect of Gaul, proclaimed Roman emperor. Lutetia changes name to Paris

200 | 300 | 400

275 First Barbarian raids

313 Christianity officially recognized as religion under the rule of Constantine, the first Christian emperor

406 Barbarian invasion from the east. Settlement of the Franks and Germanic tribes

476 Overthrow of the last Roman emperor leads to end of the western Roman Empire

The Monastic Realm

The collapse of the Roman Empire led to a period of instability and invasions. Both the Frankish Merovingian dynasty (486–751) and the Carolingians (751–987) were unable to bring more than spasmodic periods of political calm. Throughout this turbulent period, the Church provided an element of continuity. As centres for Christian scholars and artists, the monasteries helped to restore the values of the ancient world. They also developed farming and viticulture and some became extremely powerful, dominating the country economically as well as spiritually.

France in 751

Carolingian Empire

Charlemagne (742–814)
The greatest of Carolingian rulers, Charlemagne created an empire based on strictly autocratic rule. Powerful and charismatic, he could neither read nor write.

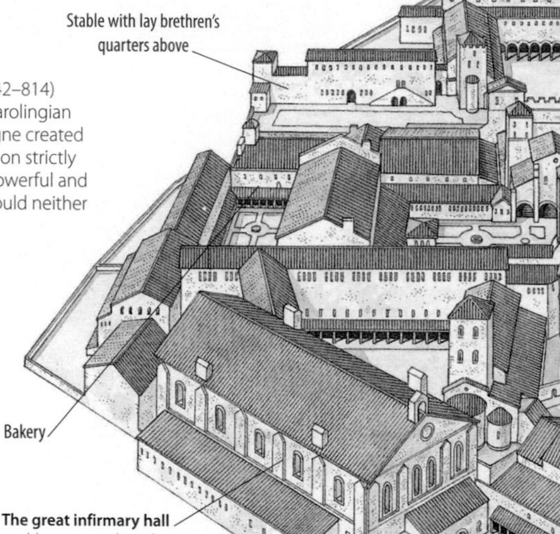
Stable with lay brethren's quarters above
Bakery
The great infirmary hall could accommodate about 100 patients. It was flanked by the Lady Chapel.

Cluny Monastery

The Benedictine abbey of Cluny (see p349) was founded in 910 with the aim of major monastic reforms. This major religious centre, here shown as a reconstruction (after Conant), had great influence over hundreds of monasteries throughout Europe.

St Benedict
This Italian-born saint established the Benedictine rule: monks were to divide their time between work and prayer.

482 Clovis the Frank becomes first Merovingian king

496 Conversion of Clovis, king of the Franks, to Christianity

508 Paris made capital of the Frankish kingdom

500

c.590 St Colombanus introduces Irish monasticism to France

600

629–37 Dagobert I, the last effective ruler of the Merovingian dynasty, brings temporary unity to the Frankish kingdom

Dagobert I

700

732 Battle of Poitiers: Charles Martel repulses Arab invasion

751 Pepin becomes first king of the Carolingian dynasty

Baptism of Clovis
The Frankish chieftain Clovis was the first barbarian ruler to convert to Christianity. He was baptized in Reims in 496.

Where to See Monastic France

Cluny capitals

The monastic realm has survived in austere Cistercian abbeys in Burgundy, such as Fontenay *(see pp336–7)*. Little remains of Cluny, but some of the superb capitals can still be admired *(p349)*. The best way to experience monastic France might be to retrace the steps of medieval pilgrims and visit the monastic centres on the route to Santiago de Compostela *(pp404–5)*, such as Vézelay *(pp340–41)*, Le Puy *(pp368–9)*, Conques *(pp372–3)*, Moissac *(pp446–7)* and St-Sernin in Toulouse *(pp450–51)*.

The abbey church, begun in 1088, was the largest church in Europe before St Peter's was built in Rome in the 16th century.

Cemetery chapel

Monastic Arts
In scriptoriums, talented artists dedicated their time to the meticulous art of illuminating and copying manuscripts for the libraries.

Monastic Labour
Monks of the Cistercian rule were renowned for their commitment to manual labour such as cultivating the land and producing wine and liqueurs.

Carolingian soldiers

800

800 Coronation of Charlemagne as Holy Roman Emperor

843 Treaty of Verdun: division of the Carolingian Empire into three parts including West Francia

900

910 Foundation of the Benedictine monastery of Cluny

987 Hugh Capet, first Capetian ruler

1000

1066 Conquest of England by the Normans

1077 Bayeux tapestry

1096 First Crusade

William the Conqueror steering his ship on the Bayeux tapestry

Gothic France

The Gothic style, epitomized by soaring cathedrals *(see pp36–7)*, emerged in the 12th century at a time of growing prosperity and scholarship, crusades and an increasingly dominant monarchy. The rival French and Burgundian courts *(see p347)* became models of fashion and etiquette for all of Europe. *Chansons de gestes* (epic poems) performed by troubadours celebrated the code of chivalry.

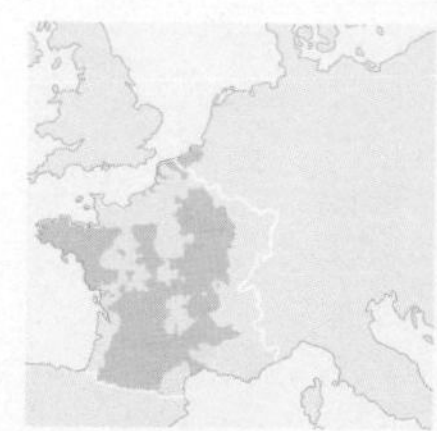

France in 1270

Royal territory

Other fiefs

Ciborium of Alpais
Alpais, a renowned 12th-century goldsmith in Limoges, made this superb ciborium used to hold wafers for the Holy Communion.

Courtly Love
According to the code of chivalry, knights dedicated their service to an ideal but unapproachable lady. Courtesy and romance were introduced in art and music.

Winch to lift up stone sections

The king supervised the building of the cathedral, accompanied by the architect.

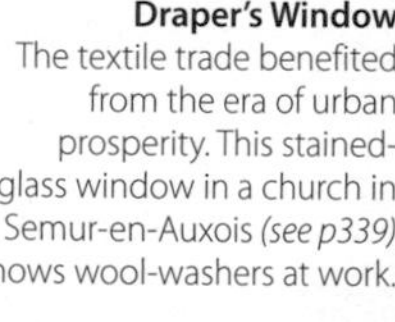

Draper's Window
The textile trade benefited from the era of urban prosperity. This stained-glass window in a church in Semur-en-Auxois *(see p339)* shows wool-washers at work.

c.1100 First edition of the epic poem *Chanson de Roland*

1117 Secret marriage of the scholar Abelard and his student Héloise. Her uncle, canon Filibert, does not approve and forces him to become a monk, while she retires as a nun

1154 Angevin Empire created by Anglo-Norman dynasty starting with Henry Plantagenet, count of Anjou and king of England (as Henry II)

1100 | 1125 | 1150 | 1175

1115 St Bernard founds the Cistercian abbey at Clairvaux

1120 Rebuilding of the abbey of St-Denis; birth of the Gothic style

King Philip Augustus, who adopted the fleur-de-lys emblem

1180–1223 Reign of Philip Augustus

The Crusades
In an attempt to win back the Holy Land from the Turks, Philip Augustus set out on the Third Crusade (1189) alongside England's Richard the Lionheart and Holy Roman Emperor Frederick Barbarossa.

Eleanor of Aquitaine

Strong-willed and vivacious Eleanor, duchess of independent Aquitaine, contributed to the conflict between France and England. In 1137 she married the pious Louis VII of France. Returning from a Crusade, Louis found that their marriage had broken down. After the annulment in 1152, Eleanor married Henry of Anjou, taking her duchy with her. Two years later Henry successfully claimed the throne of England. Aquitaine came under English rule, and thus the Angevin Empire began.

Eleanor of Aquitaine and Henry II are buried in Fontevraud *(p298)*.

Lace-like sculpture adorned the façades of the Gothic cathedrals.

Stonemasons cut stones on site.

St Bernard (1090–1153) Key figure of the Cistercian rule and counsellor to the pope, St Bernard preached rigorous simplicity of life.

Holy Relic
Throughout the Middle Ages most churches could boast at least one saint's relic. The cult of relics brought pilgrims and more riches.

The Building of a Cathedral

In affluent, mercantile towns, skilled masons constructed towering Gothic cathedrals of revolutionary design, such as Chartres (see pp312–15) *and Amiens* (pp206–7). *With their improbable height and lightness, these buildings were a testimony to both faith and prosperity.*

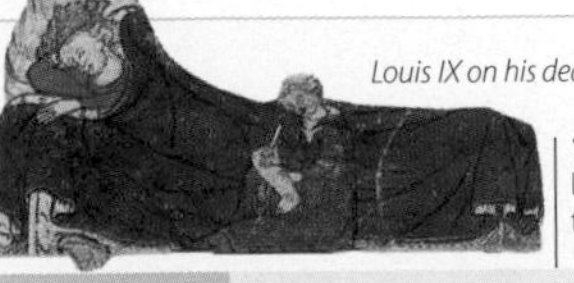

Louis IX on his deathbed

1200 | **1225** | **1250** | **1275** | **1300**

1214 Battle of Bouvines. Philip Augustus begins to drive the English out of France

1226 Louis IX crowned king

1259 Normandy, Maine, Anjou and Poitou acquired from England

1270 Death of Louis IX at Tunis in the Eighth Crusade

1285 Philip the Fair crowned

1297 Louis IX is canonized, becoming St Louis

1305 Papacy established in Avignon

The Hundred Years' War

The Hundred Years' War (1337–1453), pitting England against France for control of French land, had devastating effects. The damage of warfare was amplified by frequent famines and the ravages of bubonic plague in the wake of the Black Death in 1348. France came close to being permanently partitioned by the king of England and the duke of Burgundy. In 1429–30 the young Joan of Arc helped rally France's fortunes, and within a generation the English had been driven out of France.

Men of War
One of the reasons men enlisted as soldiers was hope for plunder. Both the French and English armies lived off the land, at the expense of the peasantry.

Angels with trumpets announce the Last Judgment.

The elect, springing resurrected from their graves, are ushered into Heaven.

The Black Death
The plague of 1348–52 caused 4–5 million deaths, about 25 per cent of the French population. For want of medicines, people had to put their faith in prayers and holy processions.

14th-century flame-thrower

1325

1328 Philip VI, first Valois monarch

1337 Start of the Hundred Years' War

1346 Battle of Crécy: French defeated by English

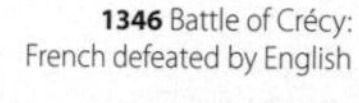

Plague victims

1350

1348–52 The Black Death

1356 French defeat at the Battle of Poitiers

1358 Bourgeois uprising in Paris led by Etienne Marcel. The Jacquerie peasant uprising in Northern France

1375

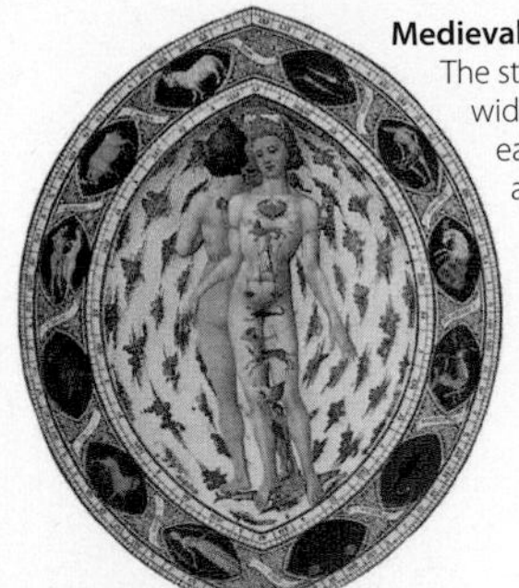

Medieval Medicine
The state of the heavens was widely held to influence earthly conditions, such as health, and a diagnosis based on the zodiac was considered reliable. The standby cure for all sorts of ailments was blood-letting.

English Longbow
The king's troops fought against England, but the individual French duchies supported whichever side seemed more favourable. In the confused battles, English bowmen excelled. Their longbows caused chaos among the hordes of mounted French cavalry.

Christ as Supreme Judge is flanked by angels bearing the instruments of the Passion.

Archangel Michael, resplendent with peacock wings, holds the judgment scales. The weight of sinners outbalances the elect.

John the Baptist is accompanied by the 12 apostles and the Virgin Mary, dressed in blue.

The damned, with hideously twisted faces, fall into Hell.

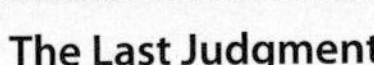

The Last Judgment

With war, plague and famine as constant visitors, many people feared that the end of the world was nigh. Religious paintings, such as the great 15th-century altar screen by Rogier van der Weyden in the Hôtel-Dieu in Beaune (see pp350–51)*, reflected the moral fervour of the time.*

Attack on Heresy
The general anxiety spilled over into anti-Semitic pogroms and attacks on alleged heretics, who were burned at the stake.

1400 — **1425** — **1450**

1411 *Les Très Riches Heures du Duc du Berry* prayer book, by Paul and Jean de Limbourg *(see pp208–9)*

1415 Battle of Agincourt. French defeat by Henry V of England

1419 Charles VI of France makes Henry V of England his heir

1429 Intervention of Joan of Arc: Charles VII crowned king

1431 Joan of Arc burned at stake as witch by the English

1453 End of the Hundred Years' War. Only Calais remains in English hands

Joan of Arc

Renaissance France

As a result of the French invasion of Italy in 1494, the ideals and aesthetic of the Italian Renaissance spread to France, reaching their height during the reign of François I. Known as a true Renaissance prince, he was skilled in letters and art as well as sports and war. He invited Italian artists, such as Leonardo and Cellini, to his court and enjoyed Rabelais's bawdy stories. Another highly influential Italian was Catherine de' Medici (1519–89). Widow of Henri II, she virtually ruled France through her sons, François II, Charles IX and Henri III. She was also one of the major players in the Wars of Religion (1562–93) between Catholics and Protestants, which divided the nobility and tore the country to pieces.

France in 1527

Royal territory

Other fiefs

Galerie François I, Fontainebleau
The artists of the School of Fontainebleau blended late Italian Renaissance style with French elements.

Power Behind the Throne
Catherine de' Medici dominated French politics from 1559 to 1589.

The corner towers are a Gothic feature transformed by Italian lightness of touch into pure decoration.

Azay-le-Rideau

One of the loveliest of the Loire châteaux, Azay was begun in 1518 (see p300). *Italian influences are visible and it is clear that this is a dwelling meant for pleasure rather than defence.*

1470 First printing presses established in France

Prototype tank by Leonardo da Vinci

1477 Final defeat of the dukes of Burgundy, who sought to establish a middle kingdom between France and Germany

1494–1559 France and Austria fight over Italian territories in the Italian Wars

1515 Reign of François I begins

1519 Leonardo da Vinci dies in the arms of François I at the French court in Amboise

1536 Calvin's *Institutes of the Christian Religion* leads to a new form of Protestantism

1470 | 1480 | 1490 | 1500 | 1510 | 1520 | 1530

Golden coin showing the fleur-de-lys and the salamander of François I

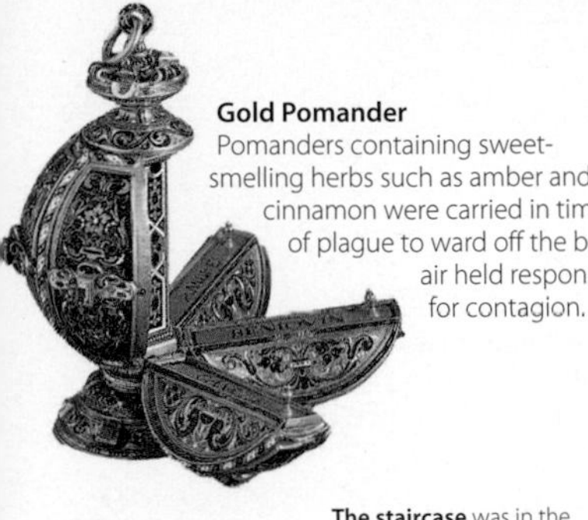

Gold Pomander
Pomanders containing sweet-smelling herbs such as amber and cinnamon were carried in time of plague to ward off the bad air held responsible for contagion.

Ballroom with Flemish tapestries
The staircase was in the new Italian fashion with double flights of steps rather than a spiral.
The Red Room

Where to See Renaissance France

In Paris, many churches and the impressive place des Vosges *(see p95)* date from the Renaissance. There are countless 16th-century châteaux in the Loire and Burgundy. Among the finest are Chenonceau *(pp302–3)* and Tanlay *(p335)*.
Salers *(p367)* is a virtually intact Renaissance town. The historic centre of Toulouse *(pp450–51)* has many elegant Renaissance palaces.

This fireplace stands in François I's room in the Château de Chenonceau.

François I and the Italian Influence
François I, here receiving Raphael's painting *The Holy Family* in 1518, collected Italian art at Fontainebleau. Among the favoured painters were Michelangelo, Leonardo and Titian.

New France
French expansion and quest for colonies started with Cartier's expedition to Canada in 1534 *(see p286)*.

1559 Treaty of Cateau–Cambrésis ends the Italian Wars

1572 Massacre of Protestants on St Bartholomew's Eve in Paris

1589 Henry III murdered. The Huguenot Henry IV becomes first Bourbon king of France

1598 Edict of Nantes: tolerance for Protestantism

1608 Foundation of Quebec

1540 | 1550 | 1560 | 1570 | 1580 | 1590 | 1600

[1]539 Edict of Villers Cotterets [m]akes French the official [la]nguage of state

1562 Wars of Religion between Catholics and Protestants start

St Bartholomew's Day Massacre

1593 Henry IV converts to Catholicism and ends the Wars of Religion

The Grand Siècle

The end of the Religious Wars heralded a period of exceptional French influence and power. The cardinal ministers Richelieu and Mazarin paved the way for Louis XIV's absolute monarchy. Political development was matched by artistic styles of unprecedented brilliance: enormous Baroque edifices, the drama of Molière and Racine and the music of Lully. Versailles *(see pp178–81)*, built under the supervision of Louis's capable finance minister Colbert, was the glory of Europe, but its cost and Louis XIV's endless wars proved expensive for the French state and led to widespread misery by the end of his reign.

France in 1661

- Royal territory
- Avignon (papal enclave)

OEUVRES
DE
MOLIERE.
NOUVELLE EDITION.
TOME PREMIER.
A AMSTERDAM ET A LEIPZIG,

Molière (1622–73)
Actor-playwright Molière performed many plays for Louis XIV and his court, though some of his satires were banned. After his death, his company became the basis of the French state theatre, the Comédie Française.

Madame de Maintenon
In 1683, following the death of his first wife Marie-Thérèse, Louis secretly married his mistress Madame de Maintenon, then aged 49.

The Sun King and his Family

Claiming to be monarch by divine right, Louis XIV commanded court painter Jean Nocret to devise this allegorical scene in 1665. Surrounded by his family, the king appears as the sun god Apollo.

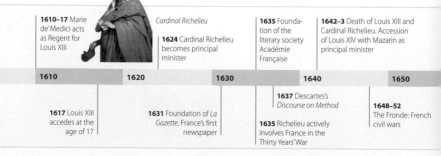

Cardinal Richelieu

1610–17 Marie de' Medici acts as Regent for Louis XIII

1617 Louis XIII accedes at the age of 17

1624 Cardinal Richelieu becomes principal minister

1631 Foundation of *La Gazette*, France's first newspaper

1635 Foundation of the literary society Académie Française

1635 Richelieu actively involves France in the Thirty Years' War

1637 Descartes's *Discourse on Method*

1642–3 Death of Louis XIII and Cardinal Richelieu. Accession of Louis XIV with Mazarin as principal minister

1648–52 The Fronde: French civil wars

1610 | 1620 | 1630 | 1640 | 1650

Louis XIV's Book of Hours
After a lively and libertine youth, Louis became increasingly religious. His *Book of Hours* (1688–93) is in Musée Condé *(see p209)*.

Royal Wedding
Louis XIII and Anne of Austria were married in 1615. After his death, Anne became regent for the young Louis XIV with Cardinal Mazarin as minister.

Baroque Figurine
The royal glory was reflected in the arts. This objet d'art features Christ made of jasper on a pedestal decorated with gilded cherubs and rich enamelling.

Where to See Architecture of the Grand Siècle

Paris boasts many imposing Grand Siècle buildings, such as the Hôtel des Invalides *(see p118)*, the Dôme church *(p119)* and the Palais du Luxembourg *(pp130–31)*, but the Château de Versailles *(pp178–81)* is the ultimate example of the flamboyance of the period. Reminders of this glory include the sumptuous Palais Lascaris in Nice *(p530)* and the Corderie Royale in Rochefort *(p421)*. At the same time, military architect Vauban constructed mighty citadels, such as Neuf-Brisach *(see pp230–31)*.

Versailles's interior is a typical example of the gilded Baroque style.

Playwright Jean Racine (1639–99)

1660

1661 Death of Mazarin: Louis XIV becomes his own principal minister

1662 Colbert, finance minister, reforms finances and the economy

1670

1680

1680 Creation of the theatre Comédie Française

1682 Royal court moves to Versailles

1685 Revocation of the Edict of Nantes of 1598: Protestantism banned

1686 Opening of the Café Procope (first coffeehouse in Paris)

1689 Major wars of Louis XIV begin

1690

1700

1709 Last great famine in French history

17th-century cannon

Enlightenment and Revolution

In the 18th century, Enlightenment philosophers such as Voltaire and Rousseau redefined man's place within a framework of natural principles, thus challenging the old aristocratic order. Their essays were read across Europe and even in the American colonies. But although France exported worldly items as well as ideas, the state's increasing debts brought social turmoil, triggering the 1789 Revolution. Under the motto "Liberty, Equality, Fraternity", the new Republic and its reforms had a far-reaching impact on the rest of Europe.

France in 1789

Royal France

Avignon (papal enclave)

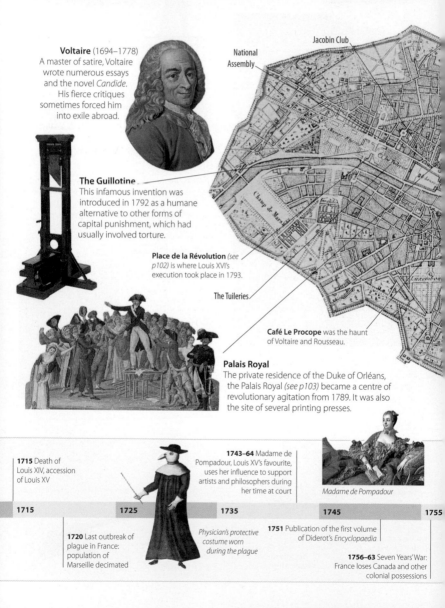

Voltaire (1694–1778)
A master of satire, Voltaire wrote numerous essays and the novel *Candide*. His fierce critiques sometimes forced him into exile abroad.

Jacobin Club

National Assembly

The Guillotine
This infamous invention was introduced in 1792 as a humane alternative to other forms of capital punishment, which had usually involved torture.

Place de la Révolution *(see p102)* is where Louis XVI's execution took place in 1793.

The Tuileries

Café Le Procope was the haunt of Voltaire and Rousseau.

Palais Royal
The private residence of the Duke of Orléans, the Palais Royal *(see p103)* became a centre of revolutionary agitation from 1789. It was also the site of several printing presses.

Madame de Pompadour

1715 Death of Louis XIV, accession of Louis XV

1720 Last outbreak of plague in France: population of Marseille decimated

Physician's protective costume worn during the plague

1743–64 Madame de Pompadour, Louis XV's favourite, uses her influence to support artists and philosophers during her time at court

1751 Publication of the first volume of Diderot's *Encyclopaedia*

1756–63 Seven Years' War: France loses Canada and other colonial possessions

1715 | 1725 | 1735 | 1745 | 1755

Revolutionary Symbols
The motifs of the Revolution such as the blue, white and red of the tricolour even appeared on wallpaper in the 1790s.

Queen Marie Antoinette
Marie Antoinette's frivolous behaviour helped to discredit the monarchy. She was held in the Conciergerie and brought to the guillotine in 1793.

The Marais, earlier an aristocratic area, fell into decay as a result of the Revolution.

Bastille

Revolutionary Paris

From 1789, Paris housed numerous political clubs, such as the left-wing Jacobins, and many revolutionary newspapers. The war tune La Marseillaise, *introduced by volunteers from the south, was soon heard everywhere.*

Where to See 18th-Century France

The Palais de l'Elysée, built in 1718 *(see p112)*, is an outstanding example of 18th-century Parisian architecture. Examples across France include the curious Saline Royale in Arc-et-Senans *(p354)*, the Grand Théâtre in Bordeaux *(p426)*, the elegant mansions in Condom *(p444)* and the merchants' houses in Ciboure *(p457)*. The Château de Laàs in Sauveterre de Béarn is a feast of 18th-century art and furniture *(p458)*.

The Grand Théâtre in Bordeaux is an excellent example of elegant 18th-century architecture.

Revolutionary Calendar
A new calendar was introduced, the months named after seasonal events. This engraving shows Messidor, the month of harvest.

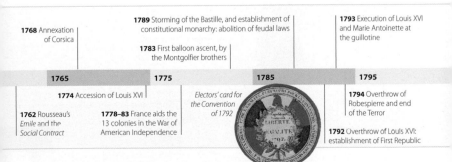

1762 Rousseau's *Emile and the Social Contract*

1765

1768 Annexation of Corsica

1774 Accession of Louis XVI

1775

1778–83 France aids the 13 colonies in the War of American Independence

1783 First balloon ascent, by the Montgolfier brothers

1785

1789 Storming of the Bastille, and establishment of constitutional monarchy: abolition of feudal laws

1792 Overthrow of Louis XVI: establishment of First Republic

1793 Execution of Louis XVI and Marie Antoinette at the guillotine

1794 Overthrow of Robespierre and end of the Terror

1795

Electors' card for the Convention of 1792

Napoleonic France

Two generations of Napoleons dominated France from 1800 to 1870. Napoleon Bonaparte took the title of Emperor Napoleon I. He extended his empire throughout most of Western Europe, placing his brothers and sisters on the thrones of conquered countries. Defeated in 1814 and replaced by the restored Bourbon dynasty, followed by the 1830 Revolution and the so-called July Monarchy, the Napoleonic clan made a comeback after 1848. Napoleon I's nephew, Louis Napoleon, became President of the Second Republic, then made himself emperor as Napoleon III. During his reign Paris was modernized and the industrial transformation of France began.

Europe in 1812
Napoleonic rule
Dependent states

Musée du Louvre
The museum had opened in 1792, but it flourished during Napoleon's reign. He took a personal interest in both the acquisitions and organization.

The Laurel, crown of the Roman emperors

Napoleon, as First Consul, is crowned by Chronos, the God of Time.

The revolutionary tricolour flag was kept throughout the empire.

Légion d'Honneur medal

Imperial Insignia
Napoleon I created a new titled aristocracy, who were allowed coats of arms. Only his, however, was permitted a crown. The eagle symbol was adopted in 1800, an evocation of Imperial Rome.

1800 Establishment of the Bank of France

1802 Treaty of Amiens brings temporary peace to Europe

1802 Establishment of the Légion d'Honneur

1803 Resumption of wars to create the Napoleonic Empire

1804 Napoleon crowned as Emperor. Napoleonic Civil Code established

Josephine's bed at Malmaison

1806 Arc de Triomphe commissioned

1809 Josephine and Napoleon divorce. She retains the Château de Malmaison *(see p177)*

1800 | 1810 | 1820

1814 Defeat of Napoleon by the Allies (England, Russia, Austria and Prussia). Napoleon exiled to Elba

1815 The "Hundred Days": Napoleon returns from Elba, is defeated at Waterloo and exiled to St-Helena

July Revolution
Three days of street fighting in July 1830 ended unpopular Bourbon rule.

The Napoleons
This imaginary group portrait depicts Napoleon I (seated), his son "Napoleon II" *(right)* – who never ruled – Napoleon's nephew Louis Napoleon (Napoleon III) and the latter's infant son.

The Civil Code, created by Napoleon, is here shown as a tablet.

Napoleonic Glory

Though professing himself a true revolutionary, Napoleon developed a taste for imperial pomp. However, he also achieved some long-lasting reforms such as the Civil Code, the new school system and the Bank of France.

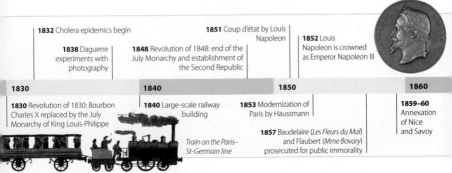

Napoleon on Campaign
A dashing general in the late 1790s, Napoleon remained a remarkable military commander throughout his reign.

Empire Fashion

Greek and Roman ideals were evident in architecture, furniture, design and fashion. Women wore light, Classical tunics, the most daring with one shoulder or more bare. David and Gérard were the most fashionable portraitists, while Delacroix and Géricault created many Romantic masterpieces.

Madame Récamier held a popular salon and was renowned for her beauty and wit. David painted her in 1800.

1832 Cholera epidemics begin

1838 Daguerre experiments with photography

1848 Revolution of 1848: end of the July Monarchy and establishment of the Second Republic

1851 Coup d'état by Louis Napoleon

1852 Louis Napoleon is crowned as Emperor Napoleon III

1830 | **1840** | **1850** | **1860**

1830 Revolution of 1830: Bourbon Charles X replaced by the July Monarchy of King Louis-Philippe

1840 Large-scale railway building

Train on the Paris–St-Germain line

1853 Modernization of Paris by Haussmann

1857 Baudelaire (*Les Fleurs du Mal*) and Flaubert (*Mme Bovary*) prosecuted for public immorality

1859–60 Annexation of Nice and Savoy

The Belle Epoque

The decades before World War I became the *belle époque* for the French, remembered as a golden era forever past. Nevertheless, this was a politically turbulent time, with working-class militancy, organized socialist movements, and the Dreyfus Affair polarizing the country between Left and anti-Semitic Right. New inventions such as electricity and vaccination against disease made life easier at all social levels. The cultural scene thrived and took new forms with Impressionism and Art Nouveau, the Realist novels of Gustave Flaubert and Emile Zola, cabaret and cancan and, in 1895, the birth of the cinema.

France in 1871

Under Third Republic

Alsace and Lorraine

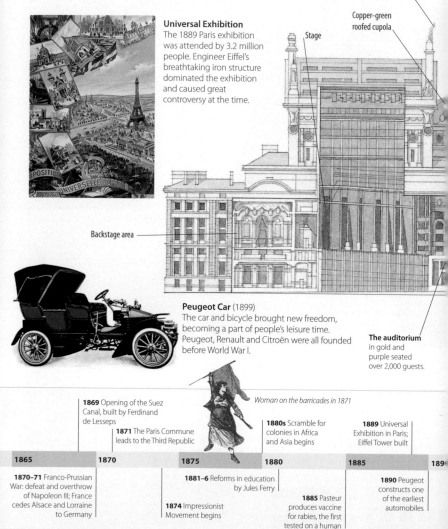

Universal Exhibition
The 1889 Paris exhibition was attended by 3.2 million people. Engineer Eiffel's breathtaking iron structure dominated the exhibition and caused great controversy at the time.

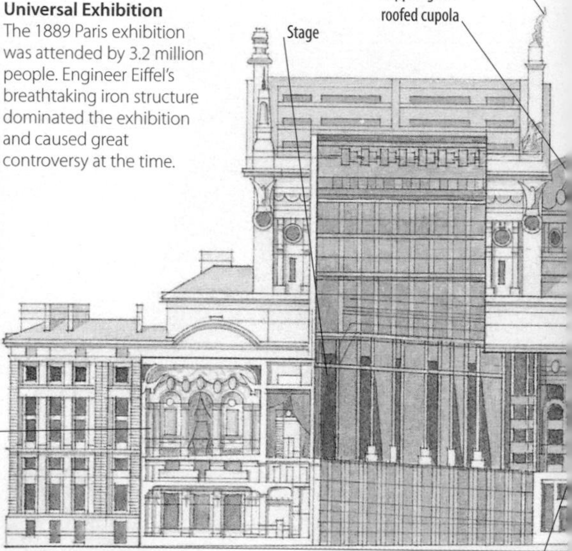

Statue of Apollo by Aimé Millet

Copper-green roofed cupola

Stage

Backstage area

The auditorium in gold and purple seated over 2,000 guests.

Peugeot Car (1899)
The car and bicycle brought new freedom, becoming a part of people's leisure time. Peugeot, Renault and Citroën were all founded before World War I.

Woman on the barricades in 1871

1865	1870	1875	1880	1885	189

1869 Opening of the Suez Canal, built by Ferdinand de Lesseps

1870–71 Franco-Prussian War: defeat and overthrow of Napoleon III; France cedes Alsace and Lorraine to Germany

1871 The Paris Commune leads to the Third Republic

1874 Impressionist Movement begins

1880s Scramble for colonies in Africa and Asia begins

1881–6 Reforms in education by Jules Ferry

1885 Pasteur produces vaccine for rabies, the first tested on a human

1889 Universal Exhibition in Paris; Eiffel Tower built

1890 Peugeot constructs one of the earliest automobiles

Poster Art
The poster was revolutionized by Art Nouveau, with designs by Alphonse Mucha particularly popular. This one from 1897 is for beer, the beverage of the lost Alsace and Lorraine, which became a "patriotic" drink.

Staircase at the Opera
The grand staircase had coloured marble columns and a frescoed ceiling. As this painting by Béroud from 1877 shows, it soon became a showcase for high society.

Where to See the Belle Epoque

Belle époque buildings include the Negresco Hotel, Nice *(see p530)*, the Grand Casino in Monte Carlo *(p534)* and the Palais Hotel in Biarritz *(p456)*. The Musée d'Orsay in Paris *(pp124–5)* exhibits Art Nouveau objects and furniture.

Guimard's Métro entrance is a typical example of the elegant, swirling lines of Art Nouveau.

Emperor's pavilion

Grand staircase

Grand Foyer with balconies and lavishly decorated ceiling

Opéra National Garnier

Founded by Napoleon III in 1862, the new opera was opened to great public acclaim in 1875 and became a focus of belle époque *social life. Designed by Charles Garnier, its extravagant exterior was matched by its sumptuous interior decor.*

The Divine Sarah
Actress Sarah Bernhardt (1844–1923) worked in all theatrical genres, dominating the Paris stage.

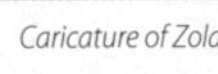
Caricature of Zola

1894–1906 The alleged treason of Dreyfus sparks the Dreyfus Affair, involving the author Zola among others

1895 First public cinema by the Lumière brothers

1898 Marie and Pierre Curie discover radium

1905 Official separation of Church and State

1909 Blériot flies the Channel

1913 Publication of Proust's first volume of *Remembrance of Things Past*

1914 World War I breaks out

1916 Battle of Verdun

1917 Mutinies in the army suppressed by Pétain

1918 Germany asks for armistice to end war

1919 Treaty of Versailles

French recruit, 1916

1895 | 1900 | 1905 | 1910 | 1915

Avant-Garde France

Despite the devastation wrought by two world wars, France retained its international renown as a centre for the avant garde. Paris in particular was a magnet for experimental writers, artists and musicians. The cafés were full of American authors and jazz musicians, French Surrealists and film-makers. The French Riviera also attracted colonies of artists and writers, from Matisse and Picasso to Hemingway and F. Scott Fitzgerald, along with the wealthy industrialists and aristocrats arriving in automobiles or by the famous Train Bleu. And from 1936 paid holidays meant that the working classes could also enjoy the new fashion for sunbathing.

France in 1919

French territory

Art Deco 1925
The International Exhibition in Paris in 1925 launched the Art Deco style: characterized by geometrical shapes and utilitarian designs, adapted for mass production.

The costumes and scenery by the Cubist Léger were striking and made to look partly mechanical.

The Jazz Age
Paris welcomed American jazz musicians, such as Sidney Bechet in 1925 and Dizzy Gillespie *(left)*, co-founder of bebop in the 1940s.

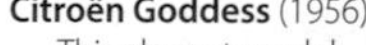

Citroën Goddess (1956)
This elegant model became an icon of the new French consumerism evident in the 1950s and 1960s.

Air France aircraft, 1937

1920 French Communist Party founded. Publication of Tristan Tzara's Dada Manifesto

1928 Premiere of *Un Chien Andalou* by Luis Buñuel and Salvador Dalí

1933 Air France begins operation

1937 Premiere of *La Grande Illusion* by Jean Renoir

1920

1930

1924 Olympic Games in Paris. André Breton publishes the *Surrealist Manifesto*

Poster for the 1924 Olympics

1929–39
The Depression

1936–38 The "Popular Front": radical social programme introduced, including paid holidays

1938 Munich Conference: height of appeasement

Coco Chanel (1883–1971)
Chanel, photographed here by Man Ray, revolutionized fashion in the 1920s with her elegant but comfortable clothes.

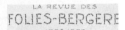

Par Avion
France pioneered the use of airmail, starting in 1927.

First Man and Woman

World War II

Following the collapse of the Third Republic in 1940, Paris and the north and west parts of France were occupied by the Germans until the Liberation in 1944. Southeast France formed the collaborationist Vichy state, led by Marshal Pétain and Pierre Laval. Meanwhile, the Free French movement was led by Charles de Gaulle, with Jean Moulin coordinating the operations of the many different Resistance factions.

German soldiers liked to pose in front of the Eiffel Tower during the occupation of Paris.

Josephine Baker (1906–75)
The music hall flourished in the 1920s with Mistinguett and Josephine Baker as its undisputed queens.

La Création du Monde (1923)

Artistic experimentation thrived in the early 20th century. La Création du Monde *by Les Ballets Suédois had costumes by Léger and music by Milhaud. Diaghilev's Ballets Russes also competed for avant-garde artists including Picabia, Cocteau, Satie and Sonia Delaunay.*

The African theme was based on text by Blaise Cendrars.

1939 Declaration of World War II

1940 The Fall of France. Vichy government led by Pétain. De Gaulle fights on from London

1942 The whole of France controlled by Germany

1944 D-Day: Allied landings in Normandy (June). Liberation of Paris (August)

1945 End of the war. Fourth Republic begins. Votes for women

1946 Sartre establishes *Les Temps Modernes*. First Cannes Film Festival

1949 Establishment of NATO. Founding of the Council of Europe

1940

1950

1954 France withdraws from Indochina after Battle of Dien Bien Phu. Start of Algerian insurrection

1956 Late in her career, Edith Piaf crowns her success at Carnegie Hall, New York

1958 Fifth Republic begins under President de Gaulle

Edith Piaf

Modern France

After the 1950s, the traditional foundations of French society changed: the number of peasant farmers plummeted, old industries decayed, and jobs in the service sector and high-technology industries grew dramatically. High-profile projects, such as Concorde, TGV, La Défense and the Centre Pompidou, brought international acclaim. Prestigious building projects in the 21st century include the Tour D2 at La Défense, Fondation Louis Vuitton and Philarmonie de Paris. The turn of the century brought more social change as France legalized same-sex marriage and emerged as a leader in environmental issues.

France Today

- France
- European Union

Centre Pompidou (1977)
The Centre Pompidou's controversial building changed the aspect of the historic quarter of Beaubourg. A major arts centre, it has revitalized the formerly rundown area *(see pp96–7)*.

21st-Century Film
Among the successes of 21st-century films are *Amélie* (2001) and *The Artist* (2011), which won acclaim for their heartwarming stories.

Gleaming white "sails" composed of glass panels encase the building, giving it an appearance of a sailboat or a huge bird.

Fondation Louis Vuitton
Opened in 2014 in the Bois de Boulogne, Frank Geh structure is one of France's most daring architectur feats. It features eleven exhibition spaces housing contemporary art and temporary exhibitions, but the building is enough of a draw in itself.

1960

- **1960** First French atomic bomb. Decolonization of black Africa
- **1962** Evian agreements lead to Algerian independence
- **1963** First French nuclear power station
- **1967** Common Agricultural Policy, subsidizing Europe's farmers
- **1968** May student riots

1970

- **1969** Pompidou replaces de Gaulle as president
- **1973** Extension of the Common Market (EU) from six to nine states
- **1974** Giscard d'Estaing elected president
- **1976** Concorde's first commercial flight

The Concorde's maiden take-off

- **1977** Jacques Chirac first mayor of Paris since 1871. Opening of the Centre Pompidou

1980

- **1980** Giverny, Monet's garden, opens to the public *(see p270)*
- **1981** Socialist Mitterrand becomes president for 14 years
- **1987** Mitterrand and Thatcher sign agreement for Channel Tunnel. Trial in Lyon of ex-SS Officer Klaus Barbie
- **1989** Bicentenn celebratic of the Frenc Revolutic

François Mitterra

EU Flag
France has been one of the leading forces in the European Union ever since the move toward closer European collaboration began in the 1950s.

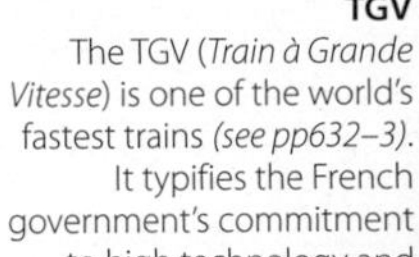

TGV
The TGV (*Train à Grande Vitesse*) is one of the world's fastest trains *(see pp632–3)*. It typifies the French government's commitment to high technology and improved communications.

Fashion by Saint Laurent
Despite less demand for haute couture, Paris is still a major fashion centre. The designs shown on the catwalk, here by Saint Laurent, remain proof of the world-renowned skills of French labels and designers.

A stepped water fountain is located under the building.

Charlie Hebdo

Following the terrorist attacks at the satirical magazine *Charlie Hebdo* in 2015, the world showed solidarity with the French people and journalistic freedom through the social media hashtag #jesuischarlie. The paper continues today despite losing many of its prominent contributors and cartoonists, defying those who challenge the right to free speech in France.

Charlie Hebdo, a French weekly satirical magazine, featuring cartoons, reports and jokes

Prince Albert II

1994 Channel Tunnel opens

2002 National Front defeat Socialists in first round of presidential campaign. France re-elects Jacques Chirac

2010 The head of France's King Henry IV is found after it was lost in 1793

2012 Socialist candidate François Hollande is elected as president

2013 Legalization of same-sex marriage

2000 | 2010 | 2020

991 Edith resson is nade France's rst woman rime minister

1995 Jacques Chirac is elected president

2002 Euro replaces franc as legal tender

2005 Prince Rainier III of Monaco dies and is succeeded by his only son, Prince Albert II

2007 Centre-right Nicolas Sarkozy is elected president

2008 Jean-Marie Gustave Le Clézio wins the Nobel Prize for literature

2017 Emmanuel Macron becomes the youngest president in French history

PARIS AND ILE-DE-FRANCE

Introducing Paris and Ile-de-France

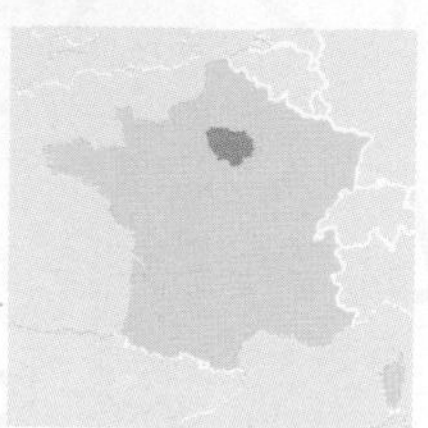

The French capital is rich in museums, art galleries and monuments. The Louvre, Eiffel Tower and Centre Pompidou are among the most popular sights.

Surrounding Paris, the Ile-de-France takes in 12,000 sq km (4,600 sq miles) of busy suburbs and commuter towns punctuated by châteaux, the most celebrated being Versailles. Further out, suburbia gives way to farmland, forests and the magnificent palace of Fontainebleau.

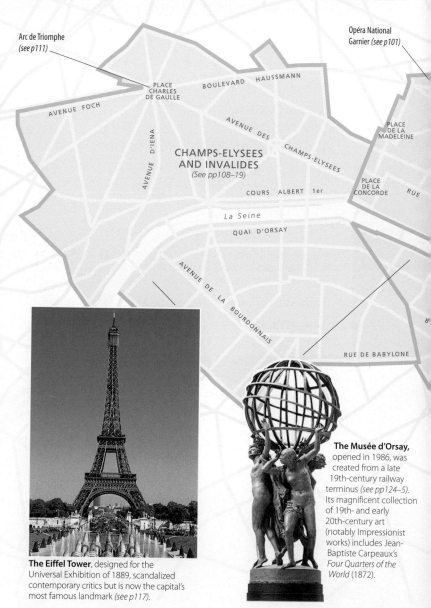

Arc de Triomphe *(see p111)*

Opéra National Garnier *(see p101)*

PLACE CHARLES DE GAULLE

BOULEVARD HAUSSMANN

AVENUE FOCH

AVENUE D'IENA

AVENUE DES CHAMPS-ELYSEES

PLACE DE LA MADELEINE

CHAMPS-ELYSEES AND INVALIDES

(See pp108–19)

PLACE DE LA CONCORDE

RUE

COURS ALBERT 1er

La Seine

QUAI D'ORSAY

AVENUE DE LA BOURDONNAIS

B

RUE DE BABYLONE

The Eiffel Tower, designed for the Universal Exhibition of 1889, scandalized contemporary critics but is now the capital's most famous landmark *(see p117)*.

The Musée d'Orsay, opened in 1986, was created from a late 19th-century railway terminus *(see pp124–5)*. Its magnificent collection of 19th- and early 20th-century art (notably Impressionist works) includes Jean-Baptiste Carpeaux's *Four Quarters of the World* (1872).

◀ The iconic Eiffel Tower, viewed from below

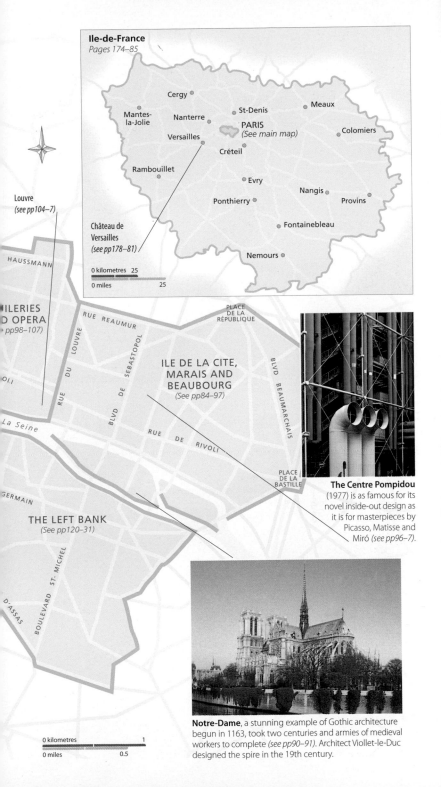

Ile-de-France
Pages 174–85

Cergy
Mantes-la-Jolie
Nanterre
St-Denis
Meaux
PARIS
(See main map)
Colomiers
Versailles
Créteil
Rambouillet
Evry
Nangis
Provins
Ponthierry
Fontainebleau
Nemours
0 kilometres 25
0 miles 25

Louvre
(see pp104–7)

Château de Versailles
(see pp178–81)

HAUSSMANN
RUE REAUMUR
PLACE DE LA RÉPUBLIQUE
RUE DU LOUVRE
BLVD DE SEBASTOPOL
BLVD BEAUMARCHAIS
RUE DE RIVOLI
La Seine
PLACE DE LA BASTILLE
GERMAIN
BOULEVARD ST-MICHEL
D'ASSAS

ILERIES
D OPERA
pp98–107)

ILE DE LA CITE, MARAIS AND BEAUBOURG
(See pp84–97)

THE LEFT BANK
(See pp120–31)

The Centre Pompidou (1977) is as famous for its novel inside-out design as it is for masterpieces by Picasso, Matisse and Miró *(see pp96–7)*.

Notre-Dame, a stunning example of Gothic architecture begun in 1163, took two centuries and armies of medieval workers to complete *(see pp90–91)*. Architect Viollet-le-Duc designed the spire in the 19th century.

0 kilometres 1
0 miles 0.5

A RIVER VIEW OF PARIS

The remarkable French music-hall star Mistinguett described the Seine as a "pretty blonde with laughing eyes". The river most certainly has a beguiling quality, but the relationship that exists between it and the city of Paris is far more than one of flirtation.

No other European city defines itself by its river in the same way as Paris. The Seine is the essential point of reference to the city: distances are measured from it, street numbers determined by it and it divides the capital into two distinct areas: the Right Bank on the north side of the river and the Left Bank on the south side. These are as well defined as any of the official boundaries. The city is also divided historically: the east is linked to the city's ancient roots and the west to the 19th–20th centuries. Many of the most notable buildings in Paris are either along the river bank or within a stone's throw of it. The quays are lined by bourgeois apartments, magnificent town houses, world-renowned museums and striking monuments.

Above all, the river is very much alive. For centuries, fleets of small boats used it. Today, the river is busy with commercial barges and massive *Bâteaux-Mouches* (pleasure boats) carrying sightseers. Initiatives have been put in place to restrict motorized traffic along the Seine and both river banks in the city centre are largely pedestrianized.

The Berges de Seine is a river promenade on the Left Bank running from the Musée d'Orsay to Pont de l'Alma. It has sport and leisure facilities along with numerous cafés.

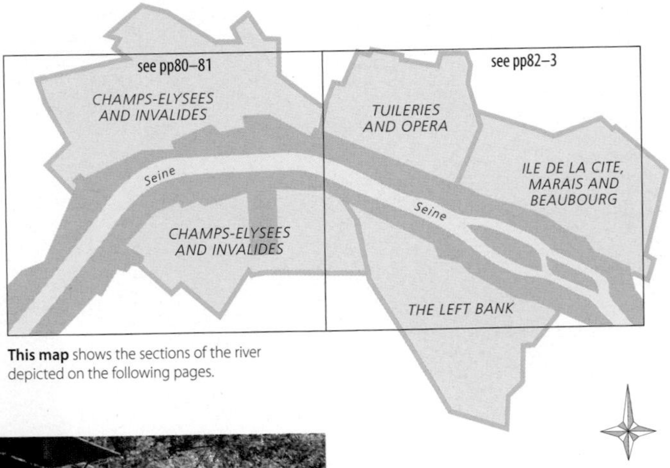

see pp80–81

CHAMPS-ELYSEES AND INVALIDES

see pp82–3

TUILERIES AND OPERA

Seine

ILE DE LA CITE, MARAIS AND BEAUBOURG

Seine

CHAMPS-ELYSEES AND INVALIDES

THE LEFT BANK

This map shows the sections of the river depicted on the following pages.

0 kilometres 2

0 miles 1

Key

Illustrated area

Les Bouquinistes, the bookstalls on the river banks, are treasure troves of second-hand books and prints, and perfect for an afternoon's browsing.

◀ River view of Paris from the height of the Eiffel Tower

From Pont de Grenelle to Pont de la Concorde

The grand monuments along this stretch of the river are remnants of the Napoleonic era and the Industrial Revolution. The elegance of the Eiffel Tower, the Petit Palais and the Grand Palais is matched by more recent buildings, such as the Palais de Chaillot and the Musée du Quai Branly.

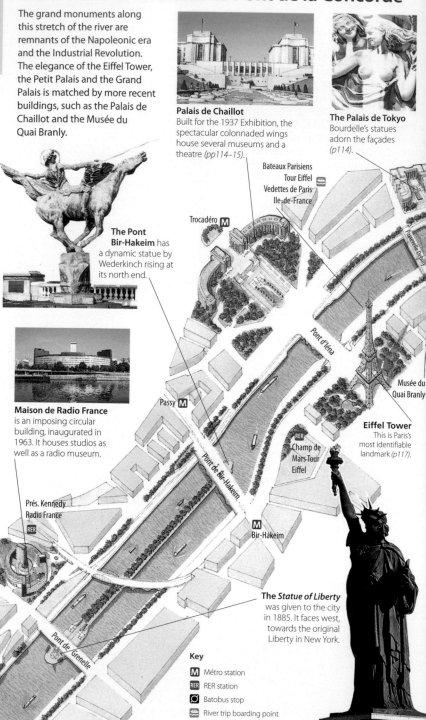

Palais de Chaillot
Built for the 1937 Exhibition, the spectacular colonnaded wings house several museums and a theatre *(pp114–15)*.

The Palais de Tokyo
Bourdelle's statues adorn the façades *(p114)*.

The Pont Bir-Hakeim has a dynamic statue by Wederkinch rising at its north end.

Maison de Radio France is an imposing circular building, inaugurated in 1963. It houses studios as well as a radio museum.

Eiffel Tower
This is Paris's most identifiable landmark *(p117)*.

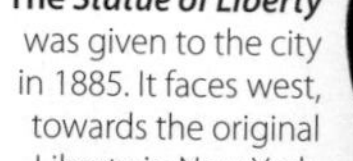

The *Statue of Liberty* was given to the city in 1885. It faces west, towards the original Liberty in New York.

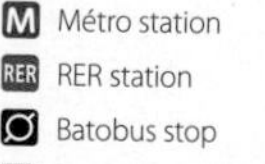

Key

- Métro station
- RER station
- Batobus stop
- River trip boarding point

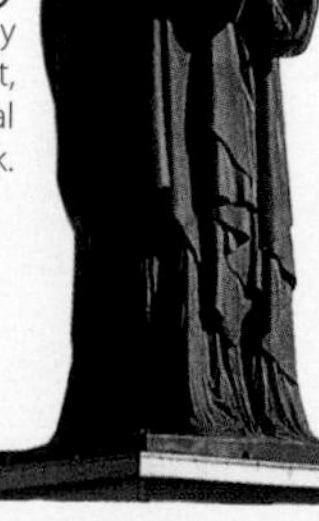

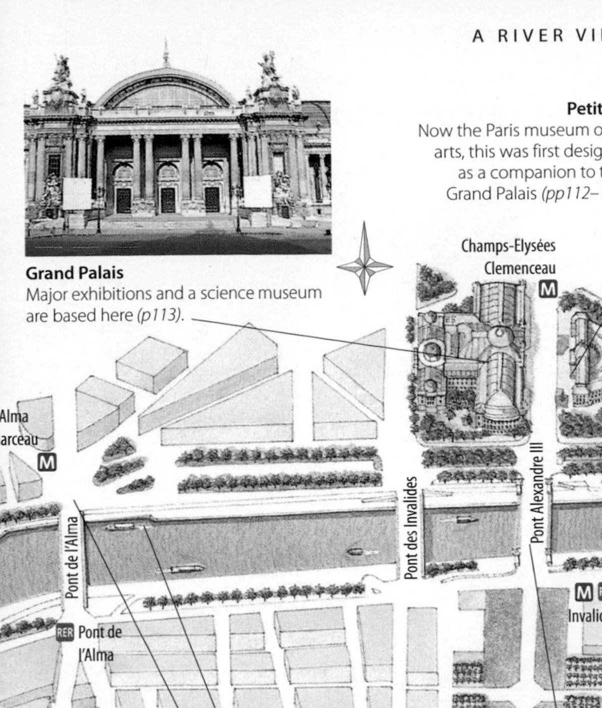

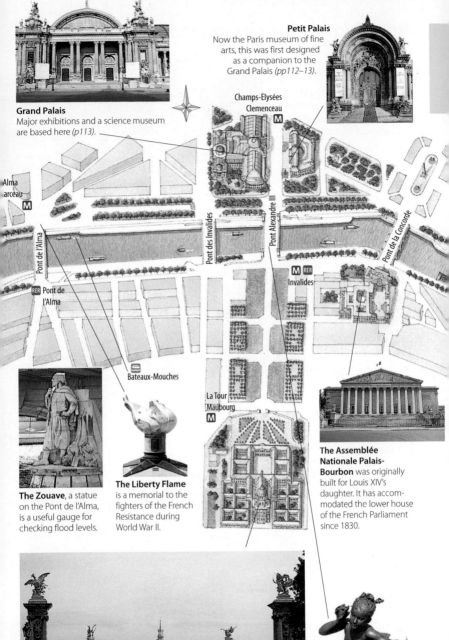

Grand Palais
Major exhibitions and a science museum are based here *(p113)*.

Petit Palais
Now the Paris museum of fine arts, this was first designed as a companion to the Grand Palais *(pp112–13)*.

Pont de la Concorde

Invalides

Bateaux-Mouches

The Zouave, a statue on the Pont de l'Alma, is a useful gauge for checking flood levels.

The Liberty Flame is a memorial to the fighters of the French Resistance during World War II.

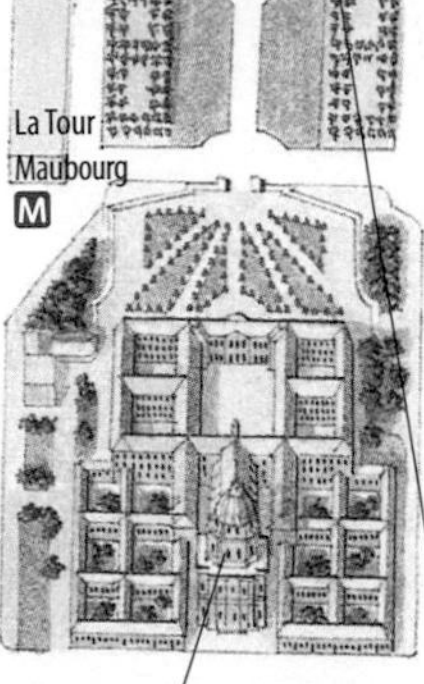

The Assemblée Nationale Palais-Bourbon was originally built for Louis XIV's daughter. It has accommodated the lower house of the French Parliament since 1830.

Dôme des Invalides
The majestic dome *(p119)*, now used as a burial site for many of France's war heroes, is here seen from Pont Alexandre III. Napoleon's tomb is in the crypt.

Pont Alexandre III
Flamboyant statuary decorates Paris's most ornate bridge *(p113)*.

From Pont de la Concorde to Pont de Sully

The historic heart of Paris lies on the banks and islands of the east river. At its center is the Ile de la Cité, a natural stepping stone across the Seine and the cultural core of medieval Paris. Today it is still vital to Parisian life.

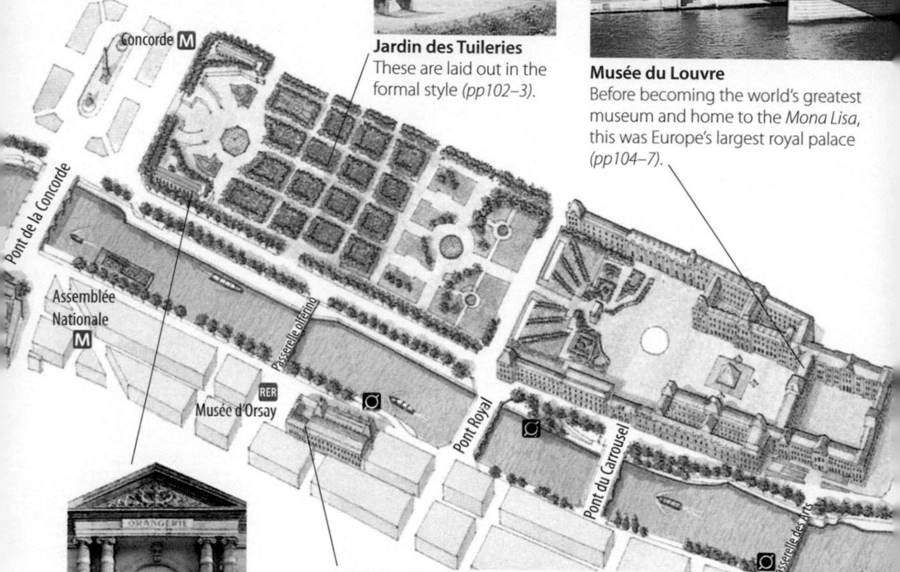

Jardin des Tuileries
These are laid out in the formal style *(pp102–3)*.

Musée du Louvre
Before becoming the world's greatest museum and home to the *Mona Lisa*, this was Europe's largest royal palace *(pp104–7)*.

Concorde M

Pont de la Concorde

Passerelle Solferino

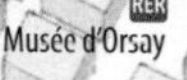

Pont Royal

Pont du Carrousel

Passerelle des Arts

Musée de l'Orangerie
An important collection of 19th-century paintings is on display here *(p102)*.

Musée d'Orsay
This converted railway station houses Paris's outstanding collection of Impressionist art *(pp124–5)*.

Vedettes du Pont-Neuf

Batobus cruises

The boarding points are: **Eiffel Tower. Map** 6 D3. M Bir-Hakeim. **Champs-Elysées. Map** 7 B1. M Champs-Elysées-Clemenceau or Concorde. **Musée d'Orsay. Map** 8 D2. M Assemblée Nationale. **Louvre. Map** 8 E2. M Palais Royal-Musée du Louvre. **Hôtel de Ville. Map** 9 B4. M Hôtel de Ville. **Notre-Dame. Map** 9 B4. M St-Michel or Maubert-Mutualité. **St-Germain-des-Prés. Map** 8 E4. M St-Germain des Prés. **Jardin des Plantes. Map** 13 C1. M Jussieu or Cardinal-Lemoines. ***Departures*** *early Sep–early Apr: 10am–7pm (every 25 mins); early Apr–early Sep: 10am–9:30pm (every 20 mins)*. **Tel** 08 25 05 01 01. W **batobus.com**

Passerelle des Arts
This steel reconstruction of Paris's first cast-iron bridge (1804) was inaugurated in 1984.

Monnaie de Paris, the Mint, built in 1778, has an extensive coin and medallion collection in its old milling halls and features a restaurant by famed chef Guy Savoy.

How to Take a Seine Cruise

Vedettes du Pont-Neuf
Boarding point: **Square du Vert-Galant** (Pont Neuf). **Map** 8 F3. **Tel** 01 46 33 98 38. Ⓜ Pont Neuf. RER Châtelet/St-Michel. 🚌 27, 58, 67, 70, 72, 74, 75. **Departures** Mar 15–Oct 31: 10:30 am, 11:15am, noon, 1:30–10:30pm (every 30 mins) daily; Nov–Mar 14: 10:30am, 11:15am, noon, 2–6:30pm (every 45 mins), 8pm, 10pm Mon–Thu, 10:30am, 11:15am, noon, 2–6:30pm (every 30 mins), 8pm, 9pm, 10pm Fri–Sun. **Duration** 1 hr. Snacks available. **W vedettesdupontneuf.com**

Bateaux-Mouches
Boarding point: **Pont de l'Alma. Map** 6 E2. **Tel** 01 76 64 79 12 Ⓜ Alma-Marceau. RER Pont de l'Alma. 🚌 28, 42, 63, 72, 80, 81, 92. **Departures** Apr–Sep: 10:15am–10:30pm daily (every 20–45 mins); Oct–Mar: 11am–9:20pm Mon–Fri, 10:15am–9:20pm Sat & Sun (every 30–60 mins). **Duration** 1hr 10 mins. **Lunch cruise** 1pm Sat, Sun, bank hols (boards 12:15pm). **Dinner cruise** 8:30pm daily (boards 7:30–8:15pm). **Duration** 2 hrs 15 mins. Jacket and tie. **W bateaux-mouches.fr**

Vedettes de Paris Ile-de-France
Boarding point: **Port du Suffren. Map** 6 D3. **Tel** 01 44 18 19 50. Ⓜ Trocadéro, Bir-Hakeim. RER Champ-de-Mars–Tour Eiffel. 🚌 22, 30, 32, 42, 44, 63, 69, 72, 82, 87. **Departures** mid-Feb–Oct 10:30am–9pm (Apr–Sep: to 11pm; Oct: 10pm) (every 45 mins); Nov–mid-Feb: 11:15am–9pm Mon–Fri, 10:30am–10pm Sat & Sun (every 20–45 mins). **Duration** 1hr. **Champagne cruise** 6pm Thu–Sat (May–Aug: 6:30pm daily). **Duration** 1hr. **Dinner cruise** 9:15pm daily. **Duration** 2 hrs 30 mins. **W vedettesdeparis.com**

Bateaux Parisiens Tour Eiffel
Boarding point: **Port de la Bordonnais** (foot of Eiffel Tower). **Map** 6 D2. **Tel** 08 25 01 01 01. Ⓜ Trocadéro, Bir-Hakeim. RER Champ-de-Mars–Tour Eiffel. 🚌 42, 82. **Departures** Apr–Sep: 10am–10:30pm (Jun–Aug: to 11pm); Oct–Mar: 10:30am–10pm (every 30 mins). **Duration** 1 hr. **Lunch cruise** 12:30pm daily (duration 2 hrs). **Dinner cruises** 6pm (boards 5–6pm, duration 1 hr, 30 mins) & 8:30pm (boards 7:15–8:15pm, duration 2 hrs, 30 mins) daily. Jacket and tie. **W bateauxparisiens.com**

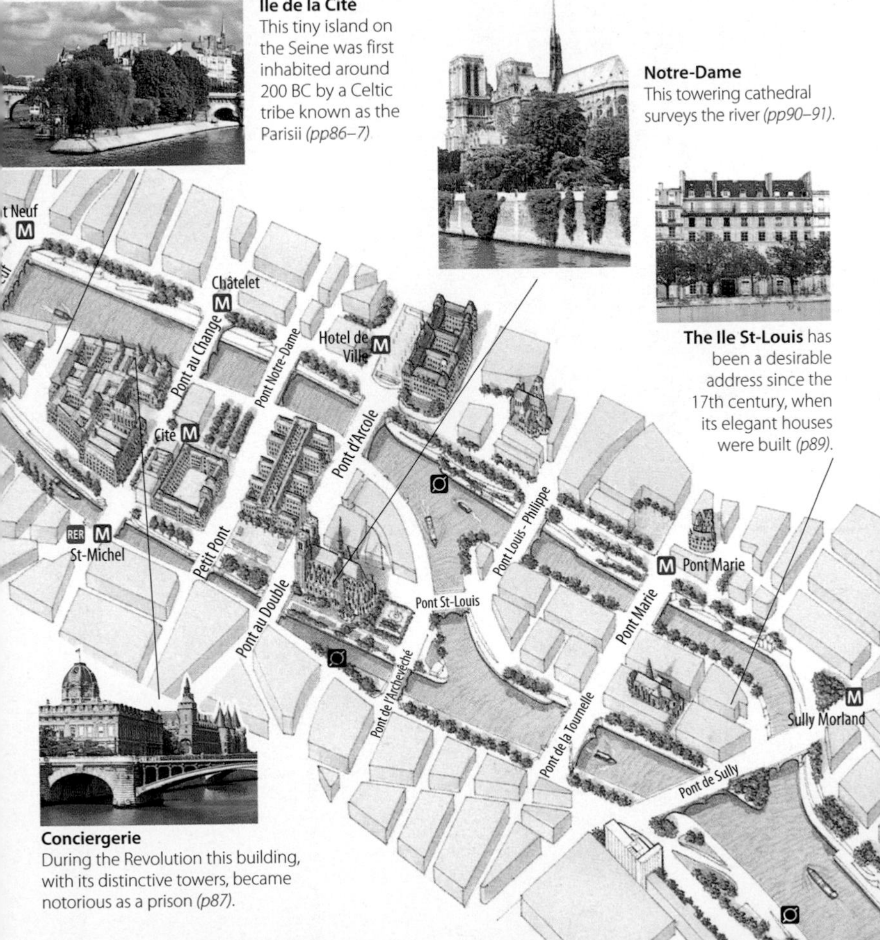

Ile de la Cité
This tiny island on the Seine was first inhabited around 200 BC by a Celtic tribe known as the Parisii *(pp86–7)*.

Notre-Dame
This towering cathedral surveys the river *(pp90–91)*.

The Ile St-Louis has been a desirable address since the 17th century, when its elegant houses were built *(p89)*.

Conciergerie
During the Revolution this building, with its distinctive towers, became notorious as a prison *(p87)*.

ILE DE LA CITE, MARAIS AND BEAUBOURG

The Right Bank is dominated by the modernistic Forum des Halles and Centre Pompidou in the Beaubourg. These are Paris's most thriving public areas, with millions of tourists, shoppers and students flowing between them. Parisians look for the latest street fashions and designer boutiques in the underground shopping complex at Les Halles, with its huge undulating glass-and-steel roof known as "The Canopy". All roads from here appear to lead to the Centre Pompidou, an avant-garde assembly of pipes, ducts and cables housing the Musée National d'Art Moderne. The smaller streets around the centre are full of art galleries housed in crooked, gabled buildings. The neighbouring Marais was abandoned by its royal residents during the 1789 Revolution, and it descended into an architectural wasteland before being rescued in the 1960s. It has since become a very fashionable address, peppered with boutiques, hip restaurants, small cafés and artisan bakeries.

Notre-Dame cathedral, the Palais de Justice and Sainte-Chapelle draw tourists to the Ile de la Cité. At the eastern end, a bridge connects with the Ile St-Louis, a former swampy pastureland transformed into a residential area with pretty, tree-lined quays and mansions.

Sights at a Glance

Islands and Squares

7 Ile St-Louis
13 Forum des Halles
19 Place des Vosges
21 Place de la Bastille

Churches

4 Sainte-Chapelle
6 *Notre-Dame pp90–91*
9 St-Gervais–St-Protais
12 St-Eustache

Historic Buildings

2 Conciergerie
3 Palais de Justice
10 Hôtel de Ville
11 Tour St-Jacques

Museums and Galleries

5 Crypte Archéologique
8 Hôtel des Archeveques de Sens
14 *Centre Pompidou pp96–7*
15 Musée d'Art et d'Histoire du Judaïsme
16 Hôtel de Soubise
17 Musée Picasso
18 Musée Carnavalet
20 Maison de Victor Hugo

Bridges

1 Pont Neuf

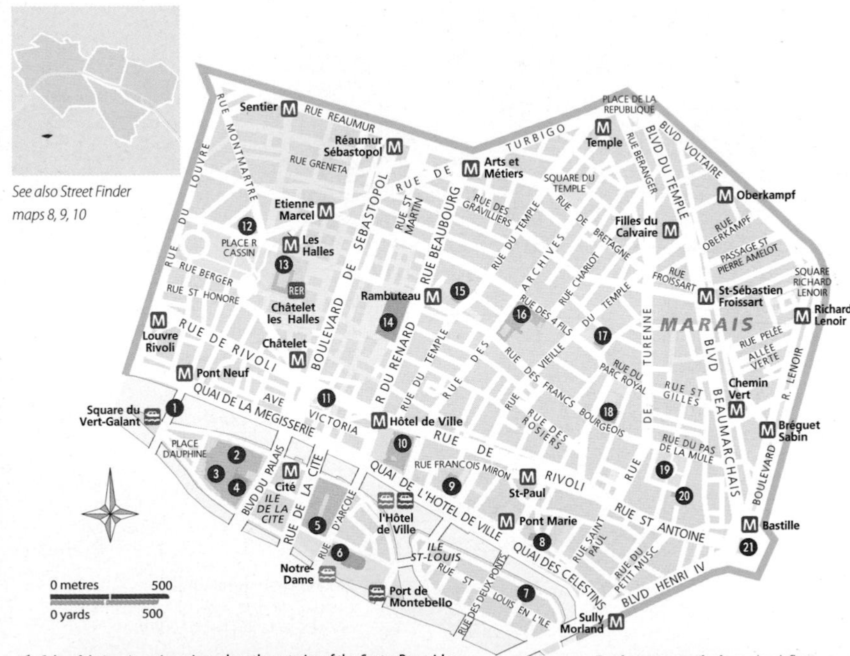

◀ Colourful pipes in various sizes adorn the exterior of the Centre Pompidou

For keys to symbols *see back flap*

Street-by-Street: Ile de la Cité

The origins of Paris are on the Ile de la Cité, the boat-shaped island on the Seine first inhabited by Celtic tribes in the 3rd century BC. One tribe, the Parisii, eventually gave its name to the city. The island offered a convenient river crossing on the route between northern and southern Gaul and was easily defended. In later centuries the settlement was expanded by the Romans, the Franks and the Capetian kings to form the nucleus of today's city.

Remains of the first buildings can still be seen today in the archeological crypt of the great medieval cathedral of Notre-Dame. At the other end of the island is Sainte-Chapelle, another Gothic masterpiece.

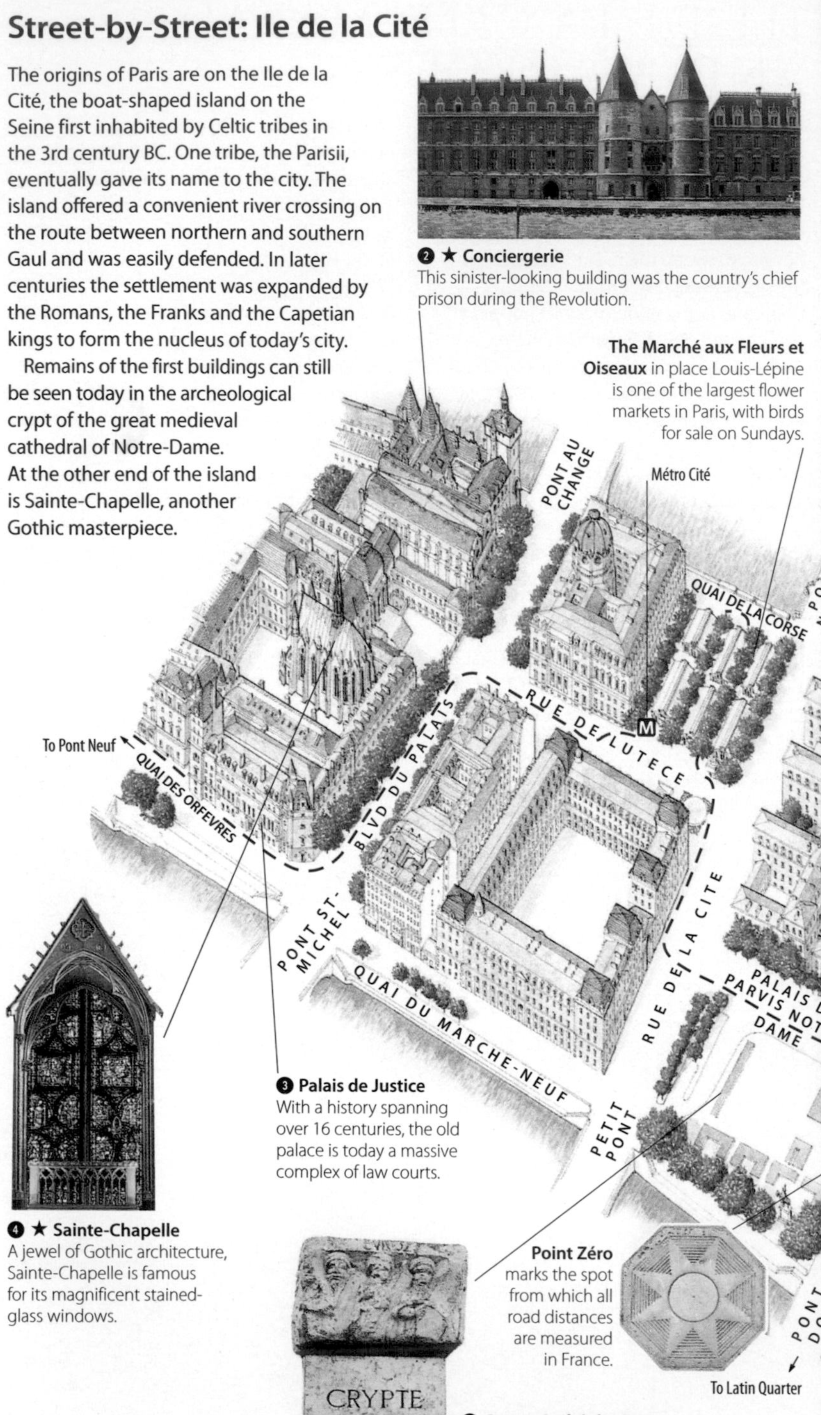

2 ★ Conciergerie
This sinister-looking building was the country's chief prison during the Revolution.

The Marché aux Fleurs et Oiseaux in place Louis-Lépine is one of the largest flower markets in Paris, with birds for sale on Sundays.

3 Palais de Justice
With a history spanning over 16 centuries, the old palace is today a massive complex of law courts.

4 ★ Sainte-Chapelle
A jewel of Gothic architecture, Sainte-Chapelle is famous for its magnificent stained-glass windows.

Point Zéro marks the spot from which all road distances are measured in France.

5 Crypte Archéologique
Deep under the square lie remnants of houses dating back 2,000 years.

Key

— Suggested route

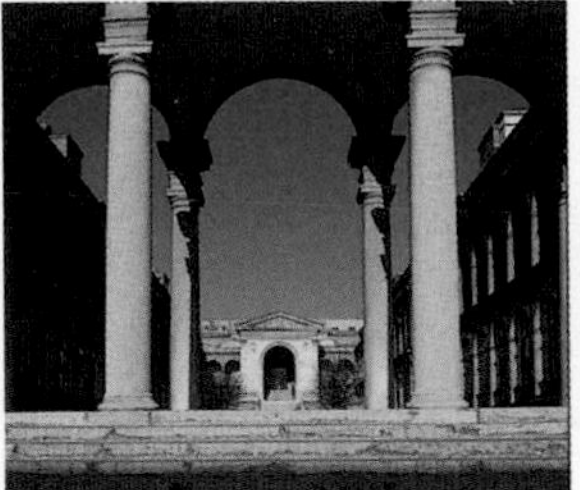

Hôtel Dieu, the oldest hospital in Paris, was founded in AD 651 by St Landry, Bishop of Paris.

TUILERIES AND OPERA
ILE DE LA CITE, MARAIS AND BEAUBOURG
THE LEFT BANK
Seine

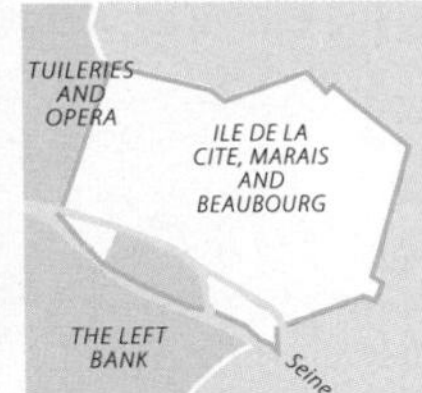

Locator Map
See Street Finder maps 9, 10

❻ ★ Notre-Dame
This cathedral, with its magnificent south-facing rose window and impressive array of gargoyles, is one of the finest examples of French Gothic architecture.

PONT D'ARCOLE
RUE D'ARCOLE
RUE CHANOINESSE
RUE DU CLOITRE-NOTRE-DAME
SQ JEAN-XXIII
0 metres 100
0 yards 100

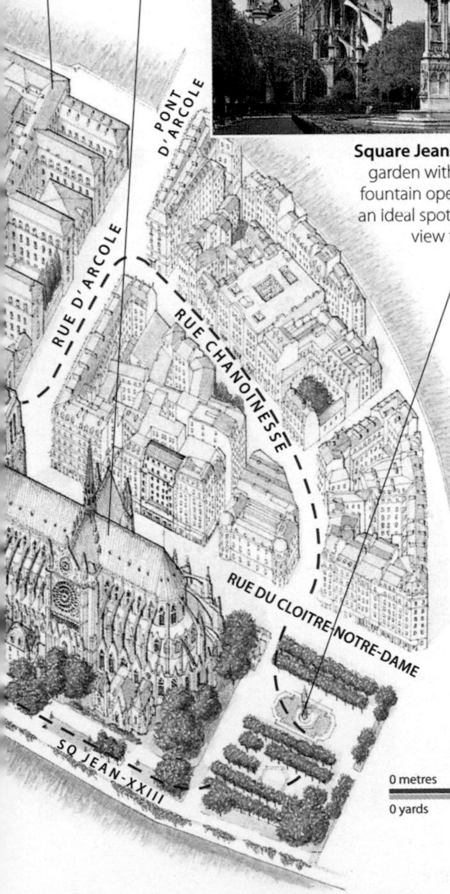

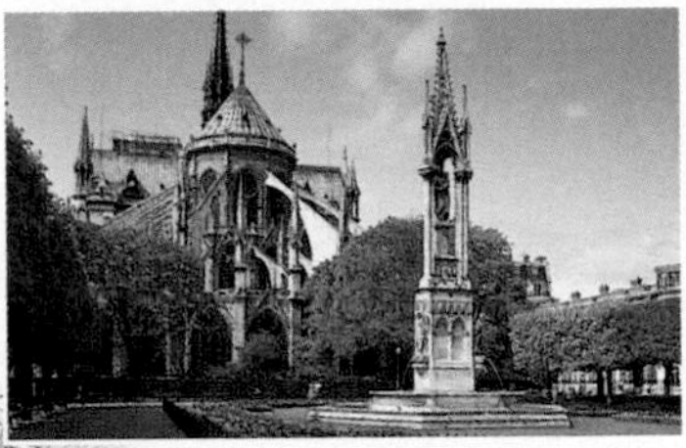

Square Jean-XXIII, a formal garden with a Neo-Gothic fountain opened in 1844, is an ideal spot from which to view the east end of the cathedral.

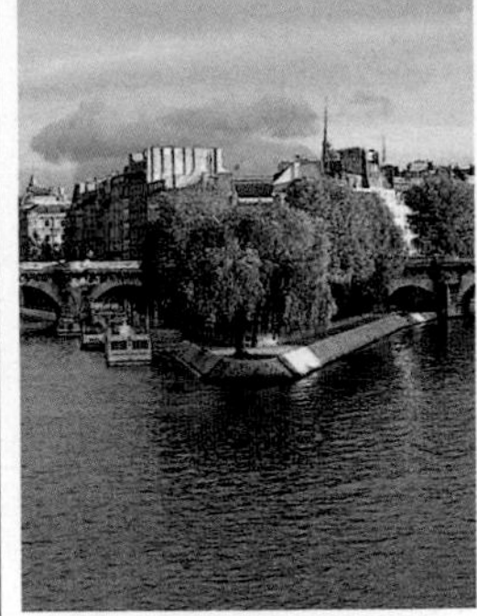

Pont Neuf, the city's oldest bridge

❶ Pont Neuf

75001. **Map** 8 F3. Ⓜ Pont Neuf, Cité.

Despite its name (New Bridge), this bridge is the oldest in Paris and has been immortalized by major literary and artistic figures. The first stone was laid by Henri III in 1578, but it was Henri IV (whose statue stands at the centre) who inaugurated it and gave it its name in 1607.

❷ Conciergerie

2 bd du Palais 75001. **Map** 9 A3. **Tel** 01 53 40 60 80. Ⓜ Cité. **Open** 9:30am–6pm daily (last adm: 30 mins before closing). **Closed** 1 Jan, 1 May, 25 Dec. Combined ticket with Sainte-Chapelle *(see p88)* available. phone to check. **W conciergerie.monuments-nationaux.fr**

Forming part of the huge Palais de Justice, the historic Conciergerie served as a prison from 1391 to 1914. Henri IV's assassin, François Ravaillac, was imprisoned and tortured here in 1610.

During the Revolution the building was packed with over 4,000 prisoners. Its most celebrated inmate was Marie Antoinette, who was held in a tiny cell until her execution in 1793. Others included Charlotte Corday, who stabbed Revolutionary leader Marat.

The Conciergerie has a superb four-aisled Gothic hall, where guards of the royal household once lived. Renovated during the 19th century, the building retains its 11th-century torture chamber and 14th-century clock tower.

A sculptured relief on the Palais de Justice

❸ Palais de Justice

4 bd du Palais (entrance at 8 bd du Palais) 75001. **Map** 9 A3. **Tel** 01 44 32 52 52. Ⓜ Cité. **Open** 8:30am–6pm Mon–Fri. **Closed** public hols & Aug recess. **W ca-paris.justice.fr**

This huge block of buildings making up the law courts of Paris stretches the entire width of the Ile de la Cité. It is a splendid sight with its Gothic towers lining the quays. The site has been occupied since Roman times, when it was the governors' residence. It was the seat of royal power, until Charles V moved the court to the Marais following a bloody revolt in 1358. In April 1793 the notorious Revolutionary Tribunal began dispensing justice from the Première Chambre Civile, or first civil chamber. Today the site embodies Napoleon's great legacy – the French judicial system.

❺ Crypte Archéologique

Parvis Notre-Dame–7 pl Jean-Paul II 75004. **Map** 9 A4. **Tel** 01 55 42 50 10. Ⓜ Cité. **Open** 10am–6pm Tue–Sun (last adm: 30 mins before closing). **Closed** 1 Jan, 1 & 8 May, 15 Aug, 25 Dec & religious hols. **W crypte.paris.fr**

Situated beneath the *parvis* (main square) of Notre-Dame and stretching 120 m (393 ft) underground, the crypt was opened in 1980.

There are Gallo-Roman streets and houses with an underground heating system, sections of Lutetia's 3rd-century-BC wall and remains of the cathedral. Models explain the development of Paris from a settlement of the Parisii, the Celtic tribe who inhabited the island 2,000 years ago.

❻ Notre-Dame

See pp90–91.

❹ Sainte-Chapelle

8 bd du Palais 75001. **Map** 9 A3. **Tel** 01 53 40 60 80. Ⓜ Cité. **Open** Jan–Mar: 9am–5pm; Apr–mid-May: 9am–7pm; mid-May–mid-Sep: 9am–9:30pm; mid-Sep–end Sep: 9am–7pm; Oct–Dec: 9am–5pm. **Closed** 1 Jan, 1 May, 25 Dec. Combined ticket with Conciergerie *(see p87)* available. No sharp objects permitted. **W sainte-chapelle.fr**

Ethereal and magical, Sainte-Chapelle has been hailed as one of the greatest architectural masterpieces of the Western world. In the Middle Ages the devout likened this church to "a gateway to heaven". Today no visitor can fail to be transported by the blaze of light created by the 15 magnificent stained-glass windows, separated by pencil-like columns soaring 15 m (50 ft) to the star-studded roof. The windows portray more than 1,000 biblical scenes in a kaleidoscope of red, gold, green and blue. Starting from the left near the entrance and proceeding clockwise, you can trace the scriptures from Genesis to the Crucifixion and the Apocalypse.

The chapel was completed in 1248 by Louis IX to house what was believed to be Christ's Crown of Thorns and fragments of the True Cross (now in the treasury at Notre-Dame). The king, who was canonized for his good works, purchased the relics from the Emperor of Constantinople, paying three times more for them than for the entire construction of Sainte-Chapelle.

The building actually consists of two separate chapels. The sombre lower chapel was used by servants and lower court officials, while the exquisite upper chapel, reached via a narrow spiral staircase, was reserved for the royal family and its courtiers. A discreetly placed window enabled the king to take part in the celebrations unobserved.

During the Revolution the building was badly damaged and became a warehouse. It was renovated a century later by Félix Duban and Jean-Baptiste Lassus.

Today, evening concerts of classical music are held regularly in the chapel, taking advantage of its superb acoustics.

The magnificent interior of Sainte-Chapelle

7 Ile St-Louis

75004. **Map** 9 C4. M Pont Marie, Sully Morland. St-Louis-en-l'Ile 19 rue St-Louis en l'Ile: **Tel** 01 46 34 11 60. **Open** 9:30am–1pm, 2–7:30pm daily (7pm Sun, public hols). 6:45pm Mon–Fri, 6:30pm Sat, 11am Sun. Concerts W **saintlouisenlile.catholique.fr**

Across Pont St-Louis from Ile de la Cité, Ile St-Louis is a little haven of quiet streets and riverside quays. The luxurious restaurants and shops include the famous ice-cream maker Berthillon. Almost everything on the Ile was built in Classical style in the 17th century. The church of **St-Louis-en-l'Ile**, with its marble-and-gilt Baroque interior, was completed in 1726 from plans by royal architect Louis de Vau. Note the 1741 iron clock at the church entrance, the pierced iron spire and a plaque given in 1926 by St Louis, Missouri. The church is twinned with Carthage Cathedral in Tunisia, where St Louis is buried.

The interior of St-Louis-en-l'Ile

8 Hôtel des Archeveques de Sens

1 rue du Figuier 75004. **Map** 9 C4. **Tel** 01 42 78 14 60. M Pont-Marie. **Open** 10am–7:30pm Wed, Thu (from 1pm Tue, Fri, Sat). **Closed** public hols.

One of only a handful of medieval buildings still standing in Paris, the Hôtel de Sens is home to the Forney arts library. During the period of the Catholic League in the 16th century, it was turned into a fortified mansion and occupied by the Bourbons, the Guises and Cardinal de Pellevé.

9 St-Gervais–St-Protais

Pl St-Gervais 75004. **Map** 9 B3. **Tel** 01 48 87 32 02. M Hôtel de Ville. **Open** 5:30am–9pm daily. Organ concerts.

Named after Gervase and Protase, two Roman soldiers martyred by the Emperor Nero, this church has magnificent origins, which go to the 6th century. It boasts the earliest Classical façade in Paris, dating from 1621, with a triple-tiered arrangement of Doric, Ionic and Corinthian columns.

Behind the façade lies a late Gothic church renowned for its association with religious music. François Couperin (1668–1733) composed his two Masses for this church's organ.

Upper Chapel Windows

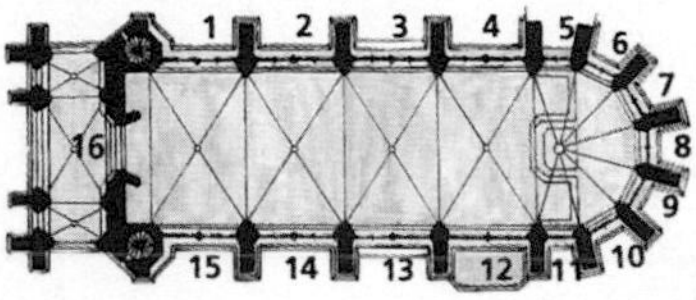

1 Genesis
2 Exodus
3 Numbers
4 Deuteronomy: Joshua
5 Judges
6 *left* Isaiah *right* Rod of Jesse
7 *left* St John the Evangelist *right* Childhood of Christ
8 Christ's Passion
9 *left* St John the Baptist *right* Story of Daniel
10 Ezekiel
11 *left* Jeremiah *right* Tobias
12 Judith and Job
13 Esther
14 Book of Kings
15 Story of the Relics
16 Rose Window: The Apocalypse

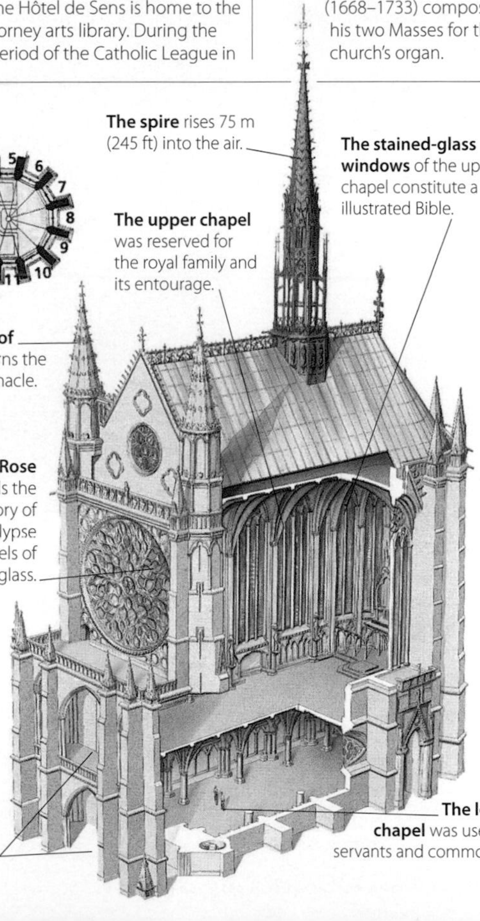

The spire rises 75 m (245 ft) into the air.

The stained-glass windows of the upper chapel constitute a vast illustrated Bible.

The upper chapel was reserved for the royal family and its entourage.

The Crown of Thorns adorns the chapel's pinnacle.

The Rose Window tells the biblical story of the Apocalypse in 86 panels of stained glass.

Main portals

The lower chapel was used by servants and commoners.

6 Notre-Dame

No other building epitomizes the history of Paris more than Notre-Dame. Built on the site of a Roman temple, the cathedral was commissioned by Bishop de Sully in 1159. The first stone was laid in 1163, marking the start of two centuries of toil by armies of Gothic architects and medieval craftsmen. It has been witness to great events of French history, including the coronations of Henry VI in 1422 and Napoleon Bonaparte in 1804. During the Revolution it was desecrated and rechristened the Temple of Reason. Extensive renovations (including the addition of the spire and gargoyles) were carried out in the 19th century by architect Viollet-le-Duc (1814–79). Notre Dame received a new set of bells in 2012 to celebrate its 850th anniversary.

★ West Façade
The beautifully proportioned west façade is a masterpiece of French Gothic architecture.

★ Galerie des Chimères
The cathedral's legendary gargoyles *(chimères)* gaze menacingly from the cathedral's ledge.

KEY

① **The Kings' Gallery** features 28 stone images of the kings of Judah.

② **West Rose Window** depicts the Virgin in a medallion of rich reds and blues.

③ **Some 387 steps** lead to the top of the south tower, where the famous Emmanuel bell is housed.

④ **The spire**, designed by Viollet-le-Duc, soars to a height of 96 m (315 ft).

⑤ **The treasury** houses the cathedral's religious treasures, including ancient manuscripts and reliquaries.

⑥ **The transept** was built at the start of Philippe-Auguste's reign, in the 13th century.

Portal of the Virgin
The Virgin surrounded by saints and kings is a fine composition of 13th-century statues.

For hotels and restaurants in this region see pp554–5 and pp576–9

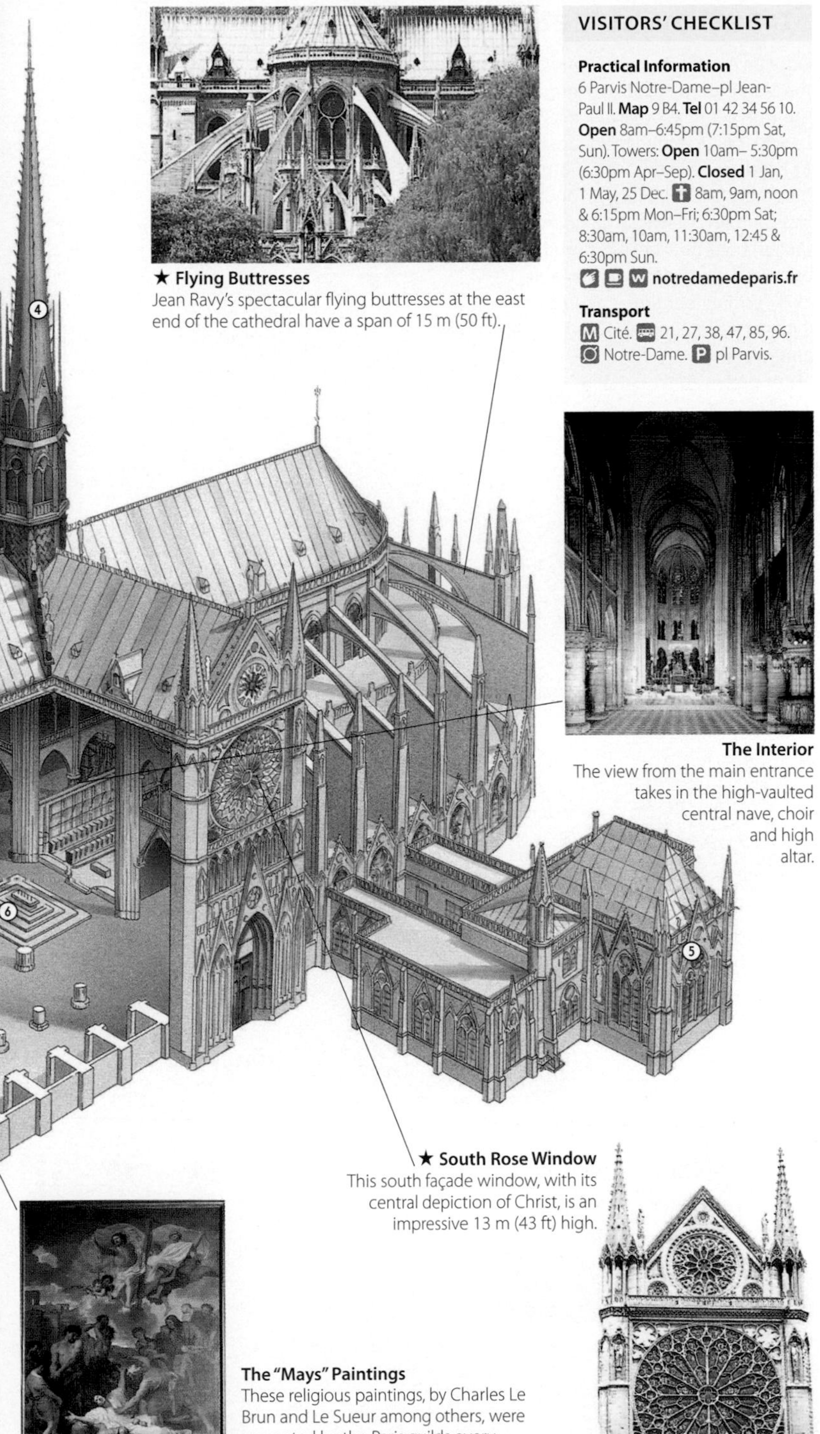

★ Flying Buttresses
Jean Ravy's spectacular flying buttresses at the east end of the cathedral have a span of 15 m (50 ft).

VISITORS' CHECKLIST

Practical Information
6 Parvis Notre-Dame–pl Jean-Paul II. **Map** 9 B4. **Tel** 01 42 34 56 10. **Open** 8am–6:45pm (7:15pm Sat, Sun). Towers: **Open** 10am– 5:30pm (6:30pm Apr–Sep). **Closed** 1 Jan, 1 May, 25 Dec. 8am, 9am, noon & 6:15pm Mon–Fri; 6:30pm Sat; 8:30am, 10am, 11:30am, 12:45 & 6:30pm Sun.
notredamedeparis.fr

Transport
Cité. 21, 27, 38, 47, 85, 96. Notre-Dame. pl Parvis.

The Interior
The view from the main entrance takes in the high-vaulted central nave, choir and high altar.

★ South Rose Window
This south façade window, with its central depiction of Christ, is an impressive 13 m (43 ft) high.

The "Mays" Paintings
These religious paintings, by Charles Le Brun and Le Sueur among others, were presented by the Paris guilds every 1 May from 1630 to 1707.

Street-by-Street: The Marais

Once an area of marshland (*marais* means "swamp"), the Marais grew steadily in importance from the 14th century, by virtue of its proximity to the Louvre, the preferred residence of Charles V. Its heyday was in the 17th century, when it became a fashionable area for the monied classes, many of whose grand mansions (*hôtels*) have now been restored as museums. Once again fashionable, chic designer boutiques alternate with small restaurants and stores.

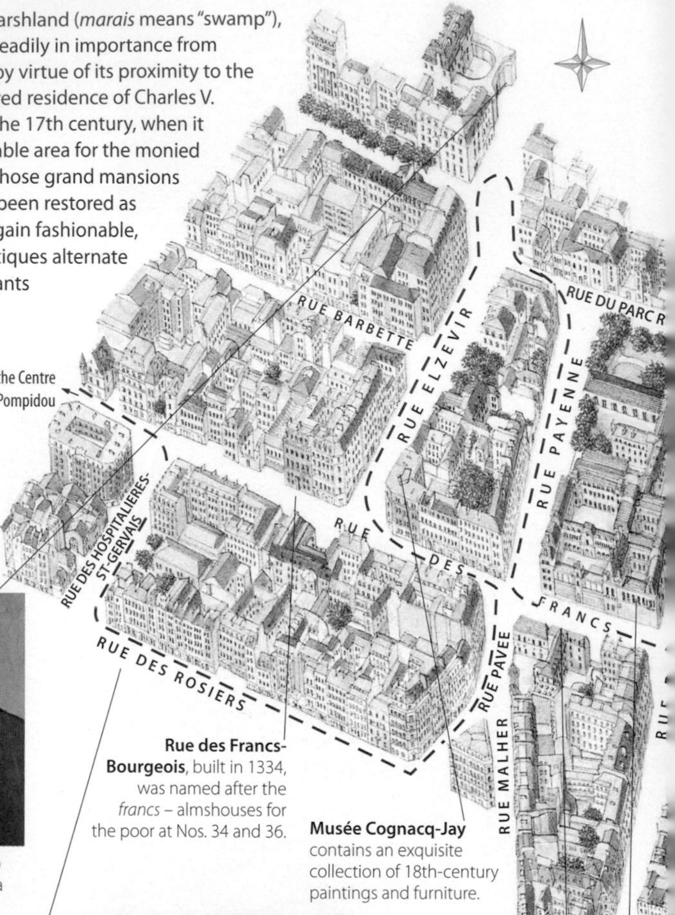

To the Centre Pompidou

RUE BARBETTE

RUE ELZEVIR

RUE DU PARC R

RUE PAYENNE

RUE DES HOSPITALIERES-ST-GERVAIS

RUE DES FRANCS

RUE DES ROSIERS

RUE PAVEE

RUE MALHER

⓱ ★ Musée Picasso
The palatial home of a 17th-century salt-tax collector houses the most extensive collection of Picassos in the world.

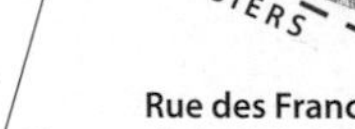

Rue des Francs-Bourgeois, built in 1334, was named after the *francs* – almshouses for the poor at Nos. 34 and 36.

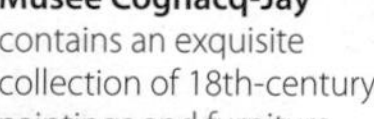

Musée Cognacq-Jay contains an exquisite collection of 18th-century paintings and furniture.

Hôtel de Lamoignon was built in 1584 and houses Paris's historical library.

Rue des Rosiers, heart of the city's oldest Jewish quarter, is lined with 18th-century houses, stores and cafés serving dishes such as hot pastrami and borscht.

⓲ ★ Musée Carnavalet
Occupying two large mansions, this museum covers the history of Paris from Prehistoric and Gallo-Roman times.

Key

— Suggested route

0 metres 100

0 yards 100

For hotels and restaurants in this region see pp554–5 and pp576–9

⑲ ★ Place des Vosges
This enchanting square is an oasis of peace and tranquillity.

Locator Map
See Street Finder maps 9, 10

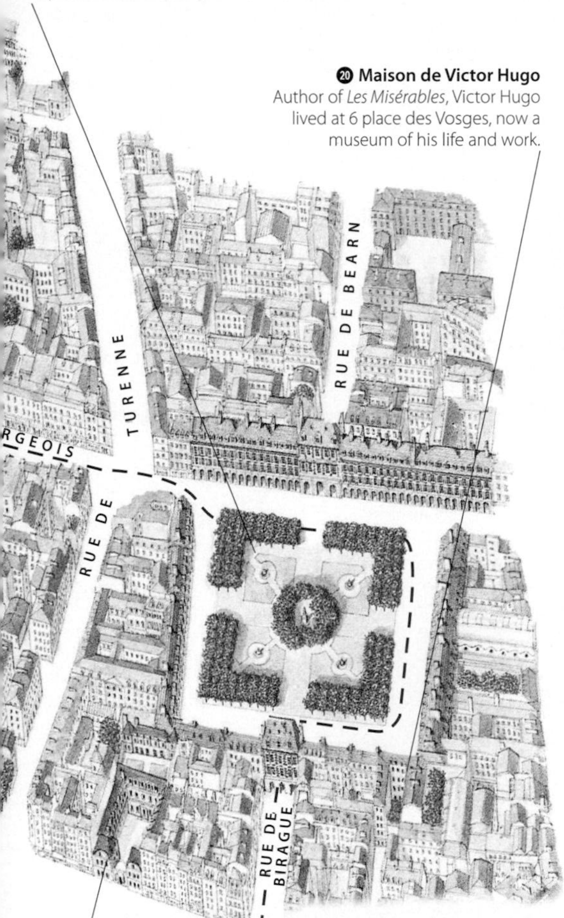

⑳ Maison de Victor Hugo
Author of *Les Misérables*, Victor Hugo lived at 6 place des Vosges, now a museum of his life and work.

RUE DE BEARN

TURENNE

RGEOIS

RUE DE

RUE DE BIRAGUE

To Métro Sully Morland

Hôtel de Sully, with its orangery and courtyard, is an elegant Renaissance mansion.

⑩ Hôtel de Ville

Pl de l'Hôtel de Ville, 29 rue de Rivoli 75004. **Map** 9 B3. **Tel** 01 42 76 40 40. Ⓜ Hôtel-de-Ville. **Open** Groups: phone 2 months in advance (01 42 76 54 04). Individuals: days/hours vary, phone to reserve (01 42 76 43 43). **Closed** public hols, and for official functions (phone to check).

The home of the city council is a 19th-century reconstruction of the 17th-century town hall burned down by insurgents of the Paris Commune in 1871. It is a highly ornate example of Third Republic architecture, with turrets and statues overlooking a pedestrianized square.

The 16th-century Tour St-Jacques

⑪ Tour St-Jacques

Sq de la Tour St-Jacques 75004. **Map** 9 A3. Ⓜ Châtelet. **Open** Jun–late Oct: 10am–5pm Fri–Sun. www.desmotsetdesarts.com (01 83 961505). Gardens open year-round.

This imposing late Gothic tower, dating from 1523, is all that remains of a church used as a rendezvous by pilgrims setting out for Compostela in Spain. The building was destroyed by revolutionaries in 1797.

Earlier, Blaise Pascal, 17th-century philosopher, mathematician, physicist and writer, used the tower for barometric experiments. His statue stands at the base of the tower, now used as a meteorological station.

⑫ St-Eustache

2 impasse St-Eustache 75001. **Map** 9 A1. **Tel** 01 42 36 31 05. Ⓜ Les Halles. RER Châtelet-Les-Halles. **Open** 9:30am–7pm Mon–Fri, 10am–7pm Sat, 9am–7pm Sun. ✝ 12:30pm Mon–Fri, 6pm Sat, 11am, 6pm Sun. Concerts. W **saint-eustache.org**

With its Gothic plan and Renaissance decoration, St-Eustache is one of Paris's most beautiful churches. Its massive interior is modelled on Notre-Dame, with five naves and side and radial chapels. The 105 years (1532–1637) it took to complete the church saw the flowering of the Renaissance style, which is evident in the magnificent arches, pillars and columns.

St-Eustache has hosted many ceremonial events, including the baptisms of Cardinal Richelieu and Madame de Pompadour, and the funerals of fabulist La Fontaine, Colbert (prime minister to Louis XIV), 17th-century dramatist Molière and the revolutionary orator Mirabeau. It was here that Berlioz first performed his *Te Deum* in 1855. Today talented choir groups perform regularly, and organ recitals are often held here.

⑬ Forum des Halles

101 Porte Bergére 75001. **Map** 13 A2. **Tel** 01 44 76 87 08. Ⓜ Les Halles. RER Châtelet-Les-Halles. **Open** 10am–8pm Mon–Sat, 11am–7pm Sun (cinemas/restaurants: 9:30am–11pm). Le Forum des Images: 2 rue du Cinéma. **Tel** 01 44 76 63 00. **Open** 12:30–9pm Tue–Fri, 2–9pm Sat & Sun. W **forumdeshalles.com** W **forumdesimages.fr**

Known simply as Les Halles and built amid controversy on the site of a famous fruit-and-vegetable market, the large underground complex is covered by an undulating glass-and-steel roof, known as "The Canopy", unveiled in 2016. Shops and restaurants abound, and there are two multi-screen cinemas, a cinema resource centre (the **Forum des Images**) and a gym and swimming pool. Above ground are gardens, pergolas and mini-pavilions.

St-Eustache and sculptured head, *L'Ecoute*, by Henri de Miller

⑭ Centre Pompidou

See pp96–7.

⑮ Musée d'Art et d'Histoire du Judaïsme

Hôtel de St-Aignan, 71 rue du Temple 75003. **Map** 9 C2. **Tel** 01 53 01 86 60. Ⓜ Rambuteau. **Open** 11am–6pm Mon–Fri, 10am–6pm Sun. **Closed** Jewish hols. W **mahj.org**

This museum in a Marais mansion, the elegant Hôtel de St-Aignan, brings together collections formerly scattered around the city, and commemorates the culture of French Jewry from medieval times to the present. Visitors learn that there has been a sizable Jewish community in France since Roman times, and some of the world's greatest Jewish scholars – Rashi, Rabenu Tam, the Tosafists – were French. Much exquisite craftsmanship is displayed, with elaborate silverware, Torah covers, fabrics, and items of fine Judaica and religious objects for use both in the synagogue and in the home. There are also photographs, paintings, and cartoons and historical documents, including some on the anti-Semitic Dreyfus Affair around the turn of the 20th century.

⑯ Hôtel de Soubise

60 rue des Francs-Bourgeois 75003. **Map** 9 C2. **Tel** 01 40 27 60 96 (guided tours: 01 40 27 60 29). Ⓜ Rambuteau. **Open** 10am–5:30pm Mon, Wed–Fri, 2–5:30pm Sat & Sun. **Closed** public hols. 1st Sat of month.

This imposing mansion, built from 1705 to 1709 for the Princesse de Rohan, houses the Musée des Archives Nationales. It boasts a majestic courtyard and 18th-century interior decoration by some of the best-known artists of the time.

Notable items held here include Natoire's *rocaille* work in the princess's bedchamber and Napoleon's will. Some of the rooms are accessible only to researchers, by appointment. Concerts and special events also take place here.

⑰ Musée Picasso

Hôtel Salé, 5 rue de Thorigny 75003. **Map** 10 D2. **Tel** 01 85 56 00 36. Ⓜ St-Sébastien Froissart. **Open** 11:30am–6pm Tue–Fri (from 9:30am Sat, Sun & hols; to 9pm 3rd Fri of month). **Closed** 1 Jan, 1 May, 25 Dec. groups by appointment only. W **museepicassoparis.fr**

On the death of the Spanish-born artist Pablo Picasso (1881–1973), who lived most of his life in France, the French State inherited one quarter of his works in lieu of death duties. In 1986, it used them to create

Woman Reading (1932) by Pablo Picasso

For hotels and restaurants in this region see pp554–5 and pp576–9

the Musée Picasso in the beautifully restored Hôtel Salé, one of the loveliest buildings in the Marais. It was built in 1656 for Aubert de Fontenay, collector of the dreaded salt tax (*salé* means "salty").

Comprising 5,000 works, including over 200 paintings, 158 sculptures, 88 ceramic works and some 3,000 sketches and engravings, this unique collection shows the enormous range and variety of Picasso's work, including examples from his Blue, Pink and Cubist periods.

Highlights include his Blue period *Self-portrait*, painted at age 20; *Still Life with Caned Chair*, which introduced collage to Cubism; the Neo-Classical *Pipes of Pan;* and *The Crucifixion*.

The museum frequently loans canvases for special exhibitions elsewhere, so some works will be on show in other galleries.

⓲ Musée Carnavalet

16 rue des Francs-Bourgeois 75003. **Map** 10 D3. **Tel** 01 44 59 58 58. Ⓜ St-Paul, Chemin Vert. **Closed** for major renovations until 2020.
W carnavalet.paris.fr

Devoted to the history of Paris since prehistoric times, this vast museum in two adjoining mansions is currently closed for major renovations until 2020. The interiors include entire decorated rooms with gilded panelling, furniture and objets d'art; many works of art, such as paintings and sculptures of prominent personalities; and engravings showing Paris being built.

The main building is the Hôtel Carnavalet, which was built as a town house in 1548 by Nicolas Dupuis. The literary hostess Madame de Sévigné lived here between 1677 and 1696, entertaining the intelligentsia of the day and writing her celebrated *Lettres*. Many of her possessions are in the first-floor exhibition covering the Louis XIV era.

The 17th-century Hôtel le Peletier, opened in 1989, features reonstructions of early 20th-century interiors and artifacts from the Revolution and Napoleonic era. The Orangery houses a section devoted to Prehistory and Gallo-Roman Paris. The collection includes pirogues discovered in 1992, during an archaeological dig in the Parc de Bercy, which unearthed a Neolitich village.

Magnificent 17th-century ceiling painting by Charles Le Brun, Musée Carnavalet

⓳ Place des Vosges

75003, 75004. **Map** 10 D3. Ⓜ Bastille, St-Paul.

This perfectly symmetrical square, laid out in 1605 by Henri IV, is considered among the most beautiful in the world. Thirty-six houses, nine on each side, are built over arcades that today accommodate antiques shops and fashionable cafés. The square has been the scene of many historical events over the centuries, including a three-day tournament in celebration of the marriage of Louis XIII to Anne of Austria in 1615.

⓴ Maison de Victor Hugo

6 pl des Vosges 75004. **Map** 10 D3. **Tel** 01 42 72 10 16. Ⓜ Bastille. **Open** 10am–6pm Tue–Sun. **Closed** public hols. Library
W maisonvictorhugo.paris.fr

The French poet, dramatist and novelist lived on the second floor of the former Hôtel de Rohan-Guéménée, the largest house on the square, from 1832 to 1848. It was here that he wrote most of *Les Misérables*. On display are reconstructions of some of the rooms in which he lived, complete with his desk, his drawings and mementos from key periods of his life, from his childhood to his exile between 1852 and 1870. There are also regular temporary exhibitions.

㉑ Place de la Bastille

75004. **Map** 10 E4. Ⓜ Bastille.

Nothing remains of the infamous prison stormed by the revolutionary mob on 14 July 1789, the event that sparked the French Revolution.

The 50-m (164-ft) Colonne de Juillet stands in the middle of the traffic-clogged square to honour the victims of the July Revolution of 1830. On the south side of the square (at 120 rue de Lyon) is the 2,700-seat **Opéra National de Paris Bastille**, completed in 1989, the bicentennial of the French Revolution.

To the south of the square is **Bassin de l'Arsenal** marina, with pleasure boats, bars, restaurants and art galleries, and the small **Jardin de l'Arsenal**. Just east of the Opéra Bastille is the start of the **Promenade Plantée**, a 4.5-km (2.8-mile) elevated walking trail along a disused railway line.

The "genius of liberty" statue on top of the Colonne de Juillet, Place de la Bastille

⑭ Centre Pompidou

The Centre Pompidou is like a building turned inside out: escalators, lifts, air and water ducts and even the massive steel struts that make up the building's skeleton are all on the outside. This allowed the architects, Richard Rogers, Renzo Piano and Gianfranco Franchini, to create a flexible exhibition space. Among the artists featured in the Musée National d'Art Moderne (MNAM) inside are Matisse, Picasso, Miró and Pollock, representing such schools as Fauvism, Cubism and Surrealism. The Centre Pompidou also keeps abreast of the Paris art scene with frequently changing temporary exhibitions. Outside in the piazza, crowds gather to watch street performers.

Key

Exhibition space

Non-exhibition space

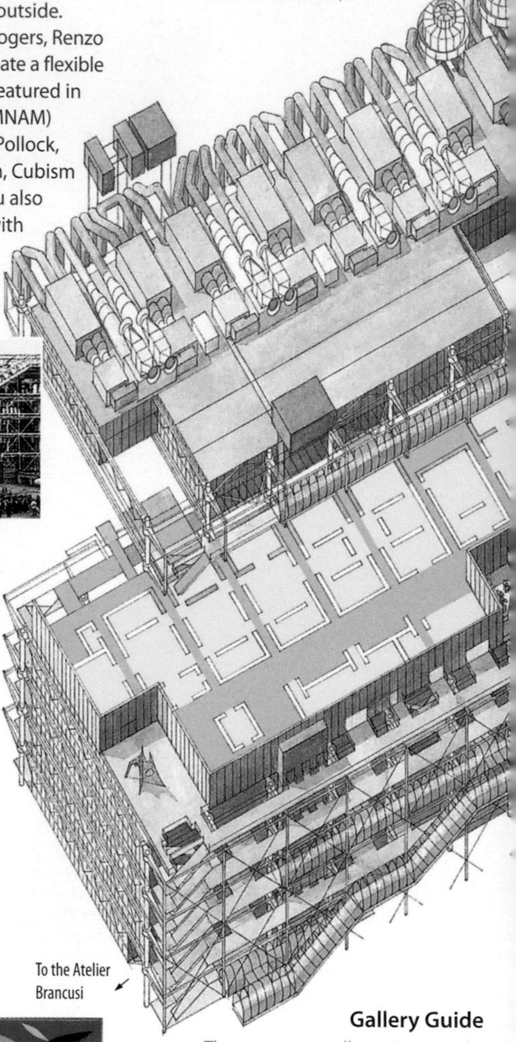

This riotous jumble of glass and steel, known as Beaubourg, is Paris's top tourist attraction, built in 1977 and drawing over 7 million visitors a year.

Mobile on Two Planes (1955)
The 20th-century American artist Alexander Calder introduced the mobile as an art form.

To the Atelier Brancusi

Gallery Guide

The permanent collections are on the fourth, fifth and sixth levels: works from 1905 to 1960 are on the former, contemporary art on the latter. The first and sixth levels also showcase temporary exhibitions; the second and third house a library. The lower levels make up "The Forum", the focal public area, with a performance centre, a cinema, shops and a children's workshop.

Sorrow of the King (1952)
This collage was created by Matisse using gouache-painted paper cut-outs.

For hotels and restaurants in this region see pp554–5 and pp576–9

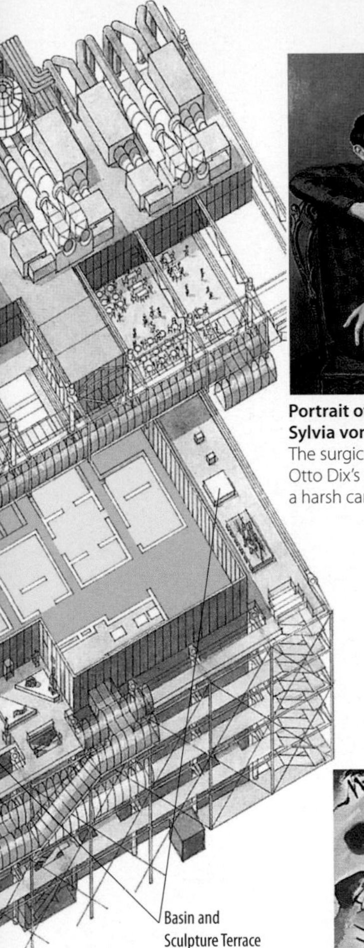

Portrait of the Journalist Sylvia von Harden (1926)
The surgical precision of Otto Dix's style makes this a harsh caricature.

VISITORS' CHECKLIST

Practical Information
Centre d'Art et de Culture Georges Pompidou, pl G Pompidou 75004.
Map 9 B2. **Tel** 01 44 78 12 33.
Open 11am–10pm Wed–Mon (to 11pm Thu) (ticket office: to 8pm); MNAM: 11am–9pm; Atelier Brancusi: 2–6pm; Library: noon–10pm (from 11am Sat & Sun).
(free 1st Sun of month & for under-18s.)
centrepompidou.fr

Transport
M Rambuteau, Châtelet, Hôtel de Ville. 21, 29, 38, 47, 58, 69, 70, 72, 74, 75, 76, 81, 85, 96. RER Châtelet-Les-Halles. P Centre G Pompidou.

Le Duo (1937)
Georges Braque, like Picasso, developed the Cubist technique of representing different views of a subject in a single picture.

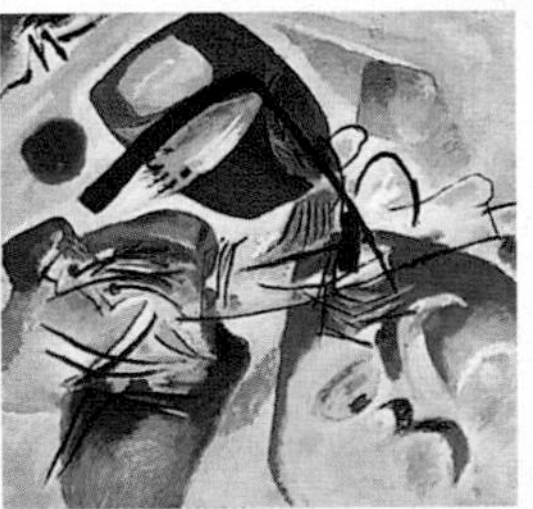

With the Black Arc (1912)
The transition to Abstraction, one of the major art forms of the 20th century, can be seen in the works of Wassily Kandinsky.

Stravinsky Fountain
This fountain, which was inaugurated in 1983, is in the place Igor Stravinsky near the Centre Pompidou. It was designed by sculptors Jean Tinguely and Niki de Saint Phalle, both of whom are represented in the Centre Pompidou.

Brancusi Workshop

The Atelier Brancusi, on the rue Rambuteau side of the piazza, is a reconstruction of the workshop of the Romanian-born artist Constantin Brancusi (1876–1957), who lived and worked in Paris. He bequeathed his entire collection of works to the French state on condition that his workshop be rebuilt as it was. The collection includes over 200 sculptures and plinths, 1,600 photographs, exhibited in rotation, and tools that Brancusi used to create his works. Also featured are some of his more personal items, such as documents, pieces of furniture and his book collection.

Interior of the Brancusi workshop, designed by Renzo Piano

TUILERIES AND OPERA

The 19th-century grandeur of Baron Haussmann's *grands boulevards* offsets the bustle of bankers, theatre-goers, sightseers and shoppers who frequent the area around the Opéra. A profusion of shops and department stores, ranging from the exclusively expensive to the popular, draws the crowds. Much of the area's older character is found in the early 19th-century shopping arcades, with elaborate steel-and-glass roofs. They are known as *galeries* or *passages*, and were restored to their former glory in the 1970s. Galerie Vivienne, which is the smartest, has an elaborate, patterned mosaic floor. The passage des Panoramas, passage Verdeau and tiny passage des Princes are more old-style Parisian. These streets abound with curious stores of all kinds, from mouthwatering food shops, to antiquarian bookshops and stamp collectors' havens.

The Tuileries area lies between the Opéra and the river, bounded by the vast place de la Concorde in the west and the Louvre to the east. The Louvre palace combines one of the world's greatest art collections with I M Pei's avant-garde glass pyramid. Elegant squares and formal gardens give the area its special character. Monuments to monarchy and the arts coexist with modern luxury at its most ostentatious. Place Vendôme, home to exquisite jewellery shops and the luxurious Ritz Hotel, is a heady mix of the wealthy and the chic. Parallel to the Jardin des Tuileries are two of Paris's foremost shopping streets, rue de Rivoli and rue St-Honoré, full of expensive boutiques, bookshops and deluxe hotels.

Sights at a Glance

Museums and Galleries

3 Musée Grévin
6 Galerie Nationale du Jeu de Paume
8 Musée de l'Orangerie
11 Musée des Arts Décoratifs
14 *Musée du Louvre pp104–7*

Squares, Parks and Gardens

5 Place Vendôme
7 Place de la Concorde
9 Jardin des Tuileries

Monuments

12 Arc de Triomphe du Carrousel

Historic Buildings

2 Opéra National de Paris Garnier
13 Palais Royal

Churches

1 La Madeleine
10 St-Roch

Shops

4 Les Passages

See also Street Finder maps 3, 4, 7, 8

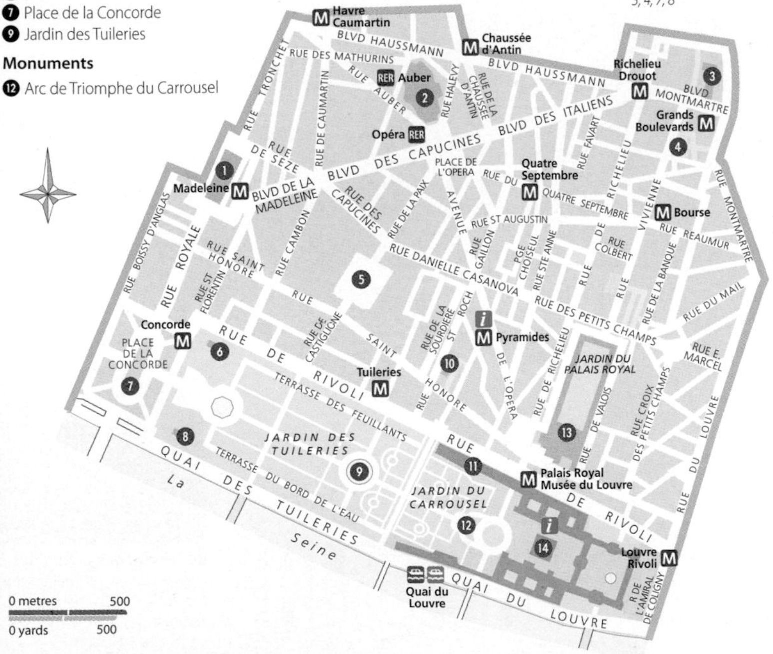

◀ Ceiling in the Grand Foyer at the Opéra National de Paris Garnier

For keys to symbols *see back flap*

Street-by-Street: Opéra Quarter

It has been said that the whole world will pass you by if you sit for long enough at the Café de la Paix (opposite the Opéra National de Paris Garnier). During the day, the area is a centre of commerce, tourism and shopping, with mammoth department stores lining the adjacent *grands boulevards*. In the evening, the clubs and theatres in this area attract a totally different crowd, and the cafés along boulevard des Capucines throb with life.

2 ★ Opéra National de Paris Garnier
Dating from 1875, the grandiose opera house has come to symbolize the opulence of the Second Empire.

Statue by Gumery on the Opéra

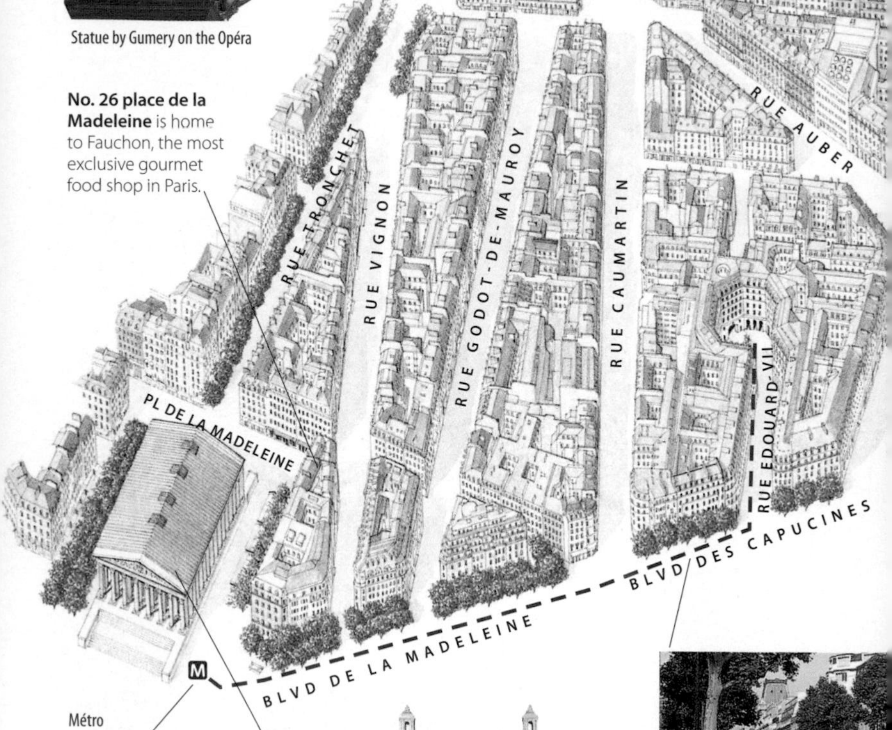

No. 26 place de la Madeleine is home to Fauchon, the most exclusive gourmet food shop in Paris.

Métro Madeleine

1 ★ La Madeleine
The original model of the Madeleine can be seen at the Musée Carnavalet *(see p95)*.

Boulevard des Capucines (No. 14) is where the Lumière brothers staged the first public screening of a movie on 28 December 1895.

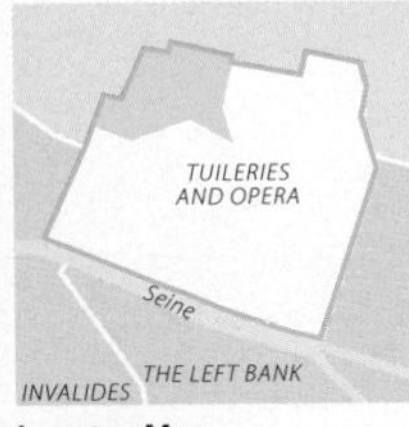

Locator Map
See Street Finder maps 3, 4

Bibliothèque and Musée de l'Opéra contains the scores of every ballet and opera performed at the Opéra, and memorabilia from Nijinsky's dancing shoes to Pavlova's tiara.

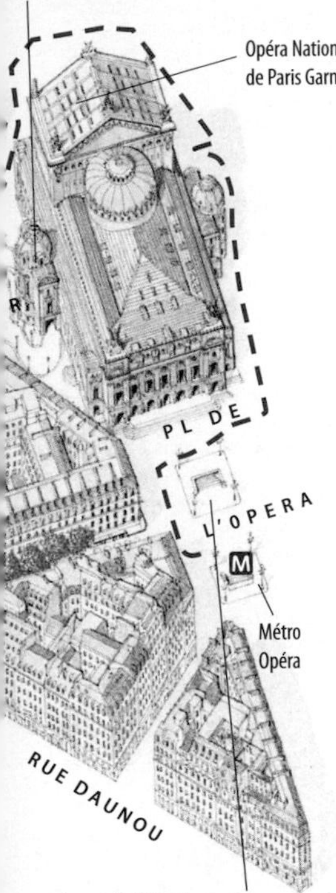

Place de l'Opéra was designed by Baron Haussmann and is one of Paris's busiest intersections.

Key

— Suggested route

0 metres 100
0 yards 100

Marochetti's *Mary Magdalene Ascending to Heaven* in La Madeleine

❶ La Madeleine

Pl de la Madeleine 75008. **Map** 3 C5. **Tel** 01 44 51 69 00. Ⓜ Madeleine. **Open** 9:30am–7pm daily. ✝ 12:30pm Mon–Fri, 6:30pm Tue–Fri, 6pm Sat, 9:30am, 11am, 6pm Sun. Concerts
W **eglise-lamadeleine.com**

Modelled after a Greek temple, La Madeleine was begun in 1764 but not consecrated until 1845. Before that, there were proposals to turn it into a stock exchange, a bank or a theatre.

Corinthian columns encircle the building, supporting a sculptured frieze. Three ceiling domes crown the inside, which is richly decorated with sculptures, rose marble and gilt.

❷ Opéra National de Paris Garnier

Pl de l'Opéra 75009. **Map** 4 E4. **Tel** 08 92 89 90 90 or 01 75 25 24 23 (from abroad); 08 25 05 44 05 (bookings). Ⓜ Opéra. **Open** 10am–4:30pm daily (until 5:30pm mid-Jul–late Aug). **Closed** 1 Jan, 1 May & special events. (Wed, Sat & Sun in English).
W **visitpalaisgarnier.fr**

Sometimes compared to a giant wedding cake, this lavish building was designed by Charles Garnier for Napoleon III in 1862. The Prussian War and the 1871 uprising delayed the opening until 1875.

The interior is famous for its Grand Staircase made of white Carrara marble, topped by a huge chandelier, as well as for its auditorium bedecked in red velvet and gold, with a false ceiling painted by Chagall in 1964. It is primarily used for dance, but shares operatic productions with the Opéra National de Paris Bastille *(see p157)*.

❸ Musée Grévin

10 bd Montmartre 75009. **Map** 4 F4. **Tel** 01 47 70 85 05. Ⓜ Grands Boulevards. **Open** 10am–6pm Mon–Fri, 9:30am–7pm Sat, Sun & school hols.
W **grevin.com**

Sign outside the Grévin

Founded in 1882, this is a Paris landmark, on a par with Madame Tussauds. The historical scenes include Louis XIV at Versailles and the arrest of Louis XVI. Notable figures from the worlds of art, politics, film and sport are also on display. On the first floor is a holography museum devoted to optical tricks. The museum also houses a 320-seat theatre.

❹ Les Passages

75002. **Map** 4 F5. Ⓜ Bourse.

The early 19th-century glass-roofed shopping arcades (known as *galeries* or *passages*) are to be found mainly between boulevard Montmartre and rue St-Marc. They house an eclectic mixture of small stores selling anything from designer jewellery to rare books and art supplies. One of the most charming is the Galerie Vivienne (off rue Vivienne or rue des Petits Champs) with its mosaic floor and excellent wine bar.

❺ Place Vendôme

75001. **Map** 8 D1. Ⓜ Tuileries.

Perhaps the best example of 18th-century elegance in the city, the architect Jules Hardouin-Mansart's royal square was begun in 1698. The original plan was to house academies and embassies behind its arcaded façades, but instead bankers moved in and created sumptuous mansions for themselves. The square's most famous residents include Frédéric Chopin, who died here in 1849 at No. 12, and César Ritz, who established his famous hotel at No. 15 in 1898.

Monet's *Waterlilies (Nymphéas)* on display in the Musée de l'Orangerie

❻ Galerie Nationale du Jeu de Paume

Jardin des Tuileries, 1 place de la Concorde 75008. **Map** 7 C1. **Tel** 01 47 03 12 50. Ⓜ Concorde. **Open** 11am–9pm Tue, 11am–7pm Wed–Sun. **Closed** 1 Jan, 1 May, 25 Dec. **jeudepaume.org**

The Jeu de Paume – literally "game of the palm" – was built as two royal tennis courts by Napoleon III in 1851 on the north side of the Tuileries Gardens. The courts were later converted into an art gallery and exhibition space. The Jeu de Paume now has rotating exhibitions of photography, video and film.

❼ Place de la Concorde

75008. **Map** 7 C1. Ⓜ Concorde.

One of Europe's most magnificent and historic squares, the Place de la Concorde was a swamp until the mid-18th century. It became the Place Louis XV in 1775, when royal architect Jacques-Ange Gabriel was asked by the king to design a suitable grand setting for an equestrian statue of himself. The monument, which lasted here less than 20 years, was replaced by the guillotine (the Black Widow, as it came to be known), and the square was renamed Place de la Révolution. On 21 January 1793 Louis XVI was beheaded, followed by over 1,300 other victims, including Marie Antoinette, Madame du Barry, Charlotte Corday (Marat's assassin) and revolutionary leaders Danton and Robespierre.

The blood-soaked square was optimistically renamed Place de la Concorde, after the Reign of Terror finally came to an end in 1794. In the 19th century a 3,300-year-old Luxor obelisk was presented to King Louis-Philippe as a gift from the viceroy of Egypt (who also donated Cleopatra's Needle in London), and two fountains and eight statues personifying French cities were added to the square.

Flanking rue Royale on the north side of the square are two of Gabriel's Neo-Classical mansions, the Hôtel de la Marine and the exclusive Hôtel Crillon.

The 3,300-year-old obelisk from Luxor

❽ Musée de l'Orangerie

Jardin des Tuileries, place de la Concorde 75001. **Map** 7 C1. **Tel** 01 44 77 80 07. Ⓜ Concorde. **Open** 9am–6pm Wed–Mon. **Closed** 1 May, 25 Dec. by appt. **musee-orangerie.fr**

Paintings from Claude Monet's crowning work, representing part of his waterlily series, fill the two oval upper floor rooms. Known as the *Nymphéas*, most of the canvases were painted between 1899 and 1921.

This superb work is complemented by the Walter-Guillaume collection, including 27 Renoirs, notably *Young Girls at the Piano,* works by Soutine and 14 Cézannes, including *The Red Rock*. Picasso is represented by works including *The Female Bathers*, and Rousseau by nine paintings, notably *The Wedding*. Other works are by Matisse, Derain, Utrillo and Modigliani.

❾ Jardin des Tuileries

75001. **Map** 8 D1. Ⓜ Tuileries, Concorde. **Open** Apr–May: 7am–9pm; Jun–Aug: 7am–11pm; Sep: 7am–9pm; Oct–Mar: 7:30am–7:30pm.

These Neo-Classical gardens once belonged to the Palais des Tuileries, which the Communards razed to the ground in 1871. They were laid out in the 17th century

For hotels and restaurants in this region see pp554–5 and pp576–9

by André Le Nôtre, who created the broad central avenue and geometric topiary. Ongoing restoration has created a new garden with lime and chestnut trees, and modern sculptures.

⑩ St-Roch

296 rue St-Honoré 75001. **Map** 8 E1. **Tel** 01 42 44 13 20. Ⓜ Tuileries, Pyramides. **Open** 8:30am–7pm daily. **Closed** non-religious public hols. ✝ 12:30pm, 6:30pm Mon, Wed–Fri, 6:30pm Tue & Sat, 11am, 12:15pm, 6:30pm Sun. Concerts.

This huge church was designed by Jacques Lemercier, architect of the Louvre, and its foundation stone was laid by Louis XIV in 1653. It is a treasure house of religious art, much of it from now-vanished churches and monasteries, and contains the tombs of the playwright Pierre Corneille, the royal gardener André Le Nôtre and the philosopher Denis Diderot.

Vien's *St Denis Preaching to the Gauls* (1767) in St-Roch

⑪ Musée des Arts Décoratifs

Palais du Louvre, 107–111 rue de Rivoli 75001. **Map** 8 E2. **Tel** 01 44 55 57 50. Ⓜ Palais Royal, Tuileries. **Open** 11am–6pm Tue–Sun (to 9pm Thu). **Closed** public hols. Library: **Tel** 01 44 55 59 36. **Open** 1–7pm Mon, 10am–7pm Tue, 10am–6pm Wed–Fri. **Closed** public hols. **W** **lesartsdecoratifs.fr**

Occupying the northwest wing of the Palais du Louvre (along with the Musée de la Publicité and the Musée de la Mode et du Textile), this museum offers an eclectic mix of decorative art and domestic design from the Middle Ages to the present day. The Art Nouveau and Art Deco rooms include a reconstruction of the home of couturier Jeanne Lanvin. Other floors show Louis XIV, XV and XVI styles of decoration and furniture. Contemporary designers are also represented. The restaurant has breathtaking views over the Tuileries Gardens.

The Buren Columns in the main courtyard of the Palais Royal

⑫ Arc de Triomphe du Carrousel

Pl du Carrousel 75001. **Map** 8 E2. Ⓜ Palais Royal.

This rose-marble arch was built by Napoleon to celebrate various military triumphs, notably the Battle of Austerlitz in 1805. The crowning statues, added in 1828, are copies of the famous Horses of St Mark's, which Napoleon had stolen from Venice and was subsequently forced to return after his defeat at Waterloo in 1815.

⑬ Palais Royal

Pl du Palais Royal 75001. Gardens: 6 rue de Montpensier. **Map** 8 E1. **Tel** 01 47 03 92 16. Ⓜ Palais Royal. Gardens and court: **Open** Apr–Sep: 8am–10:30pm daily; Oct–Mar: 8am–8:30pm daily. **W** **palais-royal.monuments-nationaux.fr**

This former royal palace, built by Cardinal Richelieu in the early 17th century, passed to the Crown on his death and became the childhood home of Louis XIV. Under the 18th-century royal dukes of Orléans, it became the epicentre of brilliant gatherings, interspersed with periods of gambling and debauchery. It was from here that the clarion call to revolution roused the mobs to storm the Bastille on 14 July 1789.

Today the south section of the building houses the Councils of State and the Ministry of Culture. Just to the west is the Comédie Française, established by Louis XIV in 1680. At the back of the palace are luxury shops where artists such as Colette and Cocteau once lived.

The Arc de Triomphe du Carrousel crowned by Victory riding a chariot

⑭ Musée du Louvre

The Musée du Louvre, containing one of the most important art collections in the world, has a history dating back to medieval times. First built as a fortress in 1190 by King Philippe-Auguste to protect Paris against Viking raids, it lost its keep in the reign of François I, who replaced it with a Renaissance-style building. Thereafter, four centuries of kings and emperors improved and enlarged it. Visitors should request a schedule of room closures from the information point, as not all rooms are open on any given day.

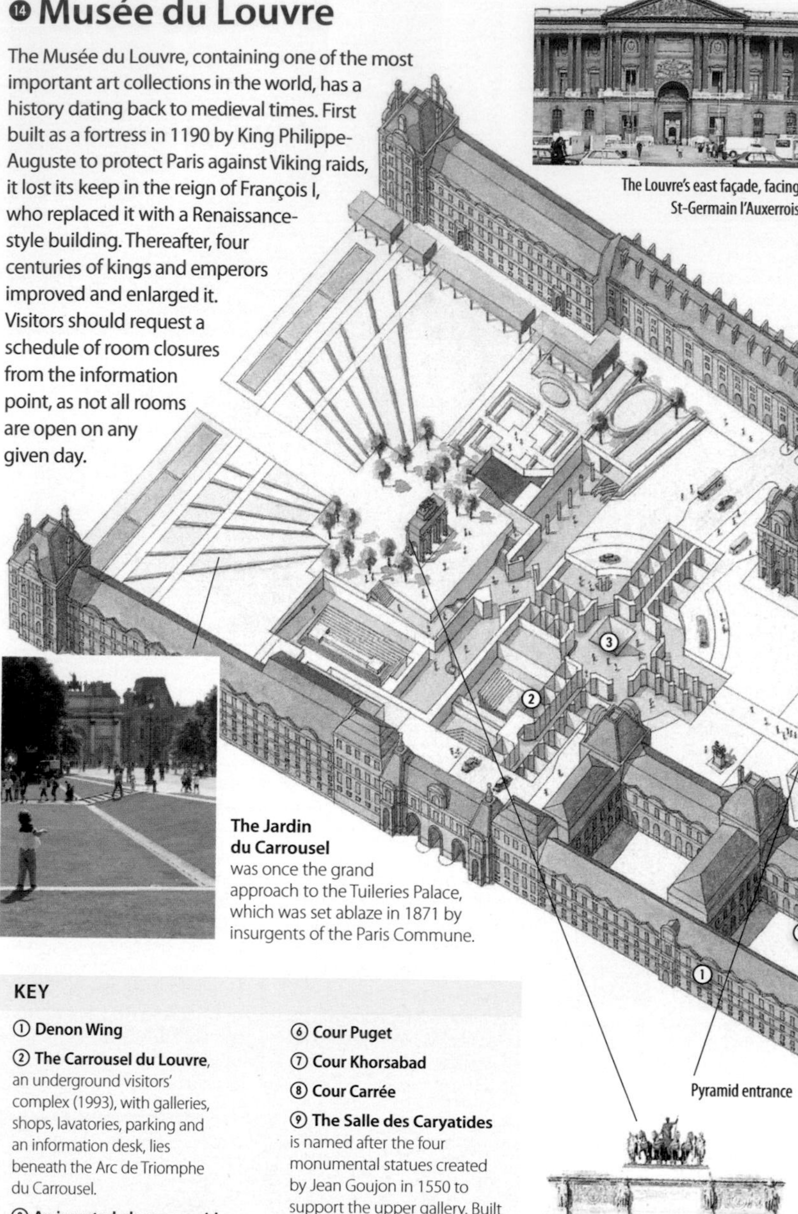

The Louvre's east façade, facing St-Germain l'Auxerrois

The Jardin du Carrousel was once the grand approach to the Tuileries Palace, which was set ablaze in 1871 by insurgents of the Paris Commune.

Pyramid entrance

KEY

① **Denon Wing**

② **The Carrousel du Louvre**, an underground visitors' complex (1993), with galleries, shops, lavatories, parking and an information desk, lies beneath the Arc de Triomphe du Carrousel.

③ **An inverted glass pyramid** brings light to the subterranean complex, echoing the museum's main entrance in the Cour Napoléon.

④ **Cour Marly** is the glass-roofed courtyard that now houses the *Marly Horses* *(see p107)*.

⑤ **Richelieu Wing**

⑥ **Cour Puget**

⑦ **Cour Khorsabad**

⑧ **Cour Carrée**

⑨ **The Salle des Caryatides** is named after the four monumental statues created by Jean Goujon in 1550 to support the upper gallery. Built for Henri II, it is the oldest room in the palace.

⑩ **Sully Wing**

⑪ **Cour Napoléon**

⑫ **Hall Napoléon** is situated under the pyramid.

⑬ **Cour Visconti** houses Islamic art: over 3,000 objects from the 7th to the 19th centuries.

★ Arc de Triomphe du Carrousel
This triumphal arch was built to celebrate Napoleon's military victories in 1805.

The Glass Pyramid

Plans for the modernization and expansion of the Louvre were first conceived in 1981. They included the transfer of the Ministry of Finance from the Richelieu Wing of the Louvre to new offices elsewhere, as well as a new main entrance designed by architect I M Pei in 1989. Made of metal and glass, the pyramid enables the visitor to see the buildings around the palace, while allowing light down into the underground visitors' reception area.

VISITORS' CHECKLIST

Practical Information
Main entrance: 99 rue de Rivoli, Pyramid Cours Napoléon. **Map** 8 E2. P Carrousel du Louvre (entrance via av du Général Lemonnier); pl du Louvre. **Open** 9am–6pm Wed–Mon (9:45pm Wed & Fri). **Closed** 1 Jan, 1 May, 25 Dec. (free 1st Sun of month, but with some restrictions Oct–Mar, for under-18s & 18- to 26-year-old EU nationals). Switchboard 01 40 20 50 50, reception 01 40 20 53 17.
W **louvre.fr** Advance bookings: W **ticketweb.com**; W **fnac.com**

Transport
M Palais Royal, Musée du Louvre. 21, 24, 27, 39, 48, 68, 69, 72, 81, 95. RER Châtelet-Les-Halles. Louvre.

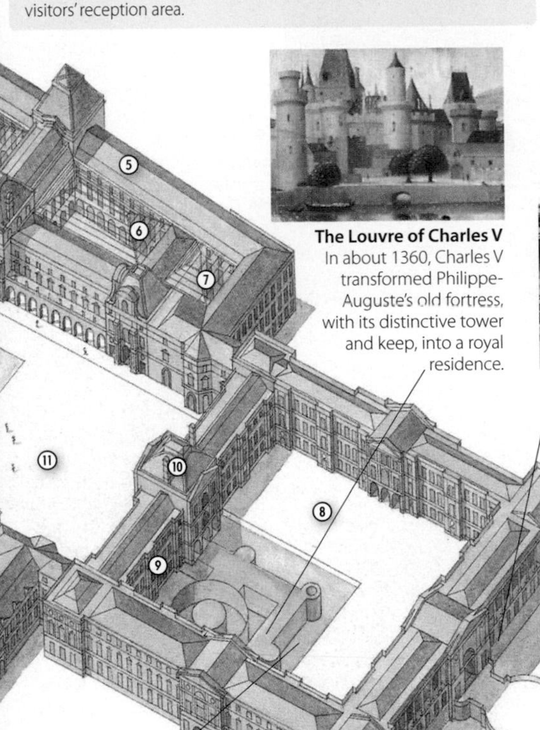

The Louvre of Charles V
In about 1360, Charles V transformed Philippe-Auguste's old fortress, with its distinctive tower and keep, into a royal residence.

★ Perrault's Colonnade
The east façade, with its majestic rows of columns, was built by Claude Perrault, who worked on the Louvre with Louis Le Vau in the mid-17th century.

★ Medieval Moats
The base of the twin towers and the drawbridge support of Philippe-Auguste's fortress can be seen in the excavated area.

Building the Louvre

Over many centuries the Louvre was enlarged by royalty, leaders and architects, shown below with their dates.

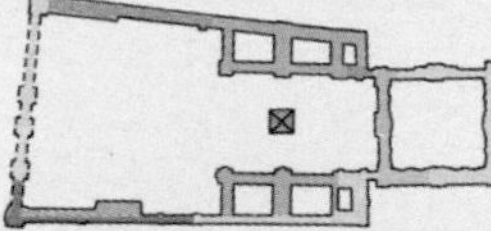

Major Alterations

- Reign of François I (1515–47)
- Catherine de' Medici (about 1560)
- Reign of Henri IV (1589–1610)
- Reign of Louis XIII (1610–43)
- Reign of Louis XIV (1643–1715)
- Reign of Napoleon I (1804–15)
- Reign of Napoleon III (1852–70)
- I M Pei (1989) (architect)

Exploring the Louvre's Collection

Owing to the vast size of the Louvre's collection, it is useful to set a few viewing priorities before starting. The collection of European paintings (1200–1848) is comprehensive, with over half the works by French artists. The departments of Oriental, Egyptian, Greek, Etruscan, and Roman antiquities feature numerous acquisitions and rare treasures. The varied display of objets d'art includes furniture and jewelry.

The Raft of the Medusa (1819) by Théodore Géricault

European Painting: 1200 to 1848

Painting from northern Europe (Flemish, Dutch, German, and English) is well covered. One of the earliest Flemish works is Jan van Eyck's *Madonna of the Chancellor Rolin* (about 1435), showing the Chancellor of Burgundy kneeling in prayer before the Virgin and Child. Hieronymus Bosch's *Ship of Fools* (c.1500) is a satirical account of the futility of human existence. In the fine Dutch collection, Rembrandt's *Self-Portrait*, his *Disciples at Emmaus* (1648), and *Bathsheba* (1654) are examples of the artist's genius.

Mona Lisa (c.1503–19) by Leonardo da Vinci

The three major German painters of the 15th and 16th centuries are represented by important works. There is a youthful *Self-Portrait* (1493) by Albrecht Dürer, a *Venus* (1529) by Lucas Cranach, and a portrait of the great humanist scholar Erasmus by Hans Holbein.

The impressive collection of Italian paintings is arranged in chronological order from 1200 to 1800. The father figures of the early Renaissance, Cimabue and Giotto, are here, as is Fra Angelico, with his *Coronation of the Virgin* (1430–32), and Raphaël, with his stately portrait of Count Baldassare Castiglione (1514–15). Several paintings by Leonardo da Vinci are on display; for instance, the *Virgin with the Infant Jesus and St Anne*, which is as enchanting as his *Mona Lisa*.

The Louvre's fine collection of French painting ranges from the 14th century to 1848. Paintings after this date are housed in the Musée d'Orsay *(see pp124–5)*. Outstanding is Jean Fouquet's portrait of Charles VII (1450–55). The great 18th-century painter of melancholy, J A Watteau, is represented, as is J H Fragonard, master of the Rococo, whose delightfully frivolous subjects are evident in *The Bathers* from 1770.

European Sculpture: 1100 to 1848

Early Flemish and German sculpture in the collection has many masterpieces such as Tilman Riemenschneider's *Virgin of the Annunciation* from the end of the 15th century, and a life-size nude figure of the penitent Mary Magdalene by Gregor Erhart (early 16th century). An important work of Flemish sculpture is Adrian de Vries's long-limbed *Mercury and Psyche* (1593), which was originally made for the court of Rudolph II in Prague.

The French section opens with early Romanesque works, such as the figure of Christ by a 12th-century Burgundian sculptor, and a head of St. Peter. With its eight black-hooded mourners, the late 15th-century tomb of Philippe Pot (a high-ranking official in Burgundy) is one of the more unusual pieces. Diane de Poitiers, Henri II's mistress, had a large figure of her namesake Diana, goddess of the hunt, installed in the courtyard of her castle west of Paris. It is now in the Louvre.

The tomb of Philippe Pot (late 15th century) by Antoine le Moiturier

The celebrated *Marly Horses* (1745) by Guillaume Coustou

The works of French sculptor Pierre Puget (1620–94) have been assembled in the Cour Puget. They include a figure of Milo of Crotona, the Greek athlete who got his hands caught in the cleft of a tree stump and was eaten by a lion. The wild horses of Marly now stand in the Cour Marly, surrounded by other masterpieces of French sculpture, including Jean-Antoine Houdon's early 19th-century busts of luminaries including Diderot and Voltaire.

The collection of Italian sculpture includes such splendid exhibits as Michelangelo's *Slaves* and Benvenuto Cellini's Fontainebleau *Nymph*.

Oriental, Egyptian, Greek, Etruscan, and Roman Antiquities

The Louvre's collection of antiquities ranges from the Neolithic period to the fall of the Roman Empire. Among the exhibits are Greek and Roman glassware dating from the 6th century BC. Important works of Mesopotamian art include one of the world's oldest legal documents, a basalt block bearing the code of the Babylonian King Hammurabi, dating from about 1700 BC.

The warlike Assyrians are represented by delicate carvings and a spectacular reconstruction of part of Sargon II's (722–705 BC) palace with its winged bulls. A fine example of Persian art is the enameled brickwork depicting the king of Persia's personal guard of archers (5th century BC). Most Egyptian art was made for the dead, who were provided with the things they would need for the afterlife. Examples include the lifelike funeral portraits, such as the *Squatting Scribe* and everal sculptures of married couples.

The departments of Greek, Roman, and Etruscan antiquities contain a vast array of fragments, among them some exceptional pieces. There is a geometric head from the Cyclades (2700 BC) and an elegant swan-necked bowl hammered out of a gold sheet (2500 BC). The two most famous Greek marble statues, the *Winged Victory of Samothrace* and the *Venus de Milo*, both belong to the Hellenistic period (late 3rd to 2nd century BC), when more natural-looking human forms were produced.

Venus de Milo (Greece, late 3rd–early 2nd century BC)

The undisputed star of the Etruscan collection is the terracotta sarcophagus of a married couple, who look as though they are attending an eternal banquet, while the highlight of the Roman section is a 2nd-century bronze head of the Emperor Hadrian.

Squatting Scribe (about 2500 BC), a lifelike Egyptian funeral sculpture

Objets d'Art

The catch-all term objets d'art (art objects) covers a vast range of items: jewelry, furniture, clocks, watches, sundials, tapestries, miniatures, silver and glassware, cutlery, Byzantine and Parisian carved ivory, Limoges enamels, porcelain, French and Italian stoneware, rugs, snuffboxes, scientific instruments and armour. The Louvre has well over 8,000 pieces, from many ages and regions.

Many of these precious objects came from the Abbey of St-Denis, where the kings of France were crowned. The treasures include a serpentine stone plate from the 1st century AD with a 9th-century border of gold and precious stones, a porphyry vase that Suger, Abbot of St-Denis, had mounted in gold in the shape of an eagle, and the golden sceptre made for King Charles V in about 1380.

The French crown jewels include the coronation crowns of Louis XV and Napoleon, scepters, swords, and other accessories of the coronation ceremonies. On view also is the Regent, one of the purest diamonds in the world, which Louis XV wore at his coronation in 1722.

One whole room is taken up with a series of tapestries called the *Hunts of Maximilian*, originally executed for Emperor Charles V in 1530. The large collection of French furniture ranges from the 16th to the 19th centuries. The 18th-century furniture rooms are assembled by period, from Louis XIV to Marie Antoinette. On display are pieces by such prominent furniture-makers as André-Charles Boulle, Louis XIV's cabinet-maker, who worked at the Louvre in the late 17th to mid-18th centuries.

CHAMPS-ELYSEES AND INVALIDES

The River Seine bisects this area, much of which is built on a monumental scale, from the imposing 18th-century buildings of Les Invalides to the Art Nouveau avenues surrounding the Eiffel Tower. Two of Paris's grandest avenues dominate the neighbourhood to the north of the Seine: the Champs-Elysées has many smart hotels and shops but today is more mainstream, while the more chic rue du Faubourg St-Honoré has the heavily guarded Palais de l'Elysée. The village of Chaillot was absorbed into the city in the 19th century, and many of its opulent Second Empire mansions are now embassies or company headquarters. Streets around Place du Trocadéro and Palais de Chaillot are packed full of museums and elegant cafés.

Sights at a Glance

Historic Buildings and Streets

2 Avenue des Champs-Elysées
3 Palais de l'Elysée
14 Les Egouts
17 No. 29 Avenue Rapp
18 Parc du Champ-de-Mars
19 Ecole Militaire
21 Hôtel des Invalides

Museums and Galleries

4 Petit Palais
5 Grand Palais
7 Musée d'Art Moderne de la Ville de Paris
8 Palais Galliera
9 Musée National des Arts Asiatiques Guimet
10 Cité de l'Architecture et du Patrimoine
11 Musée Dapper
13 Palais de Chaillot
15 Musée du Quai Branly
22 Musée de l'Armée
25 Musée Rodin
27 Musée Maillol

Churches

23 Cathedral of St-Louis-des-Invalides
24 Eglise du Dôme
26 Sainte-Clotilde

Monuments and Fountains

1 Arc de Triomphe
16 *Eiffel Tower p117*

Modern Architecture

20 UNESCO

Gardens

12 Jardins du Trocadéro

Bridges

6 Pont Alexandre III

See also Street Finder maps 1, 2, 3, 5, 6, 7, 8

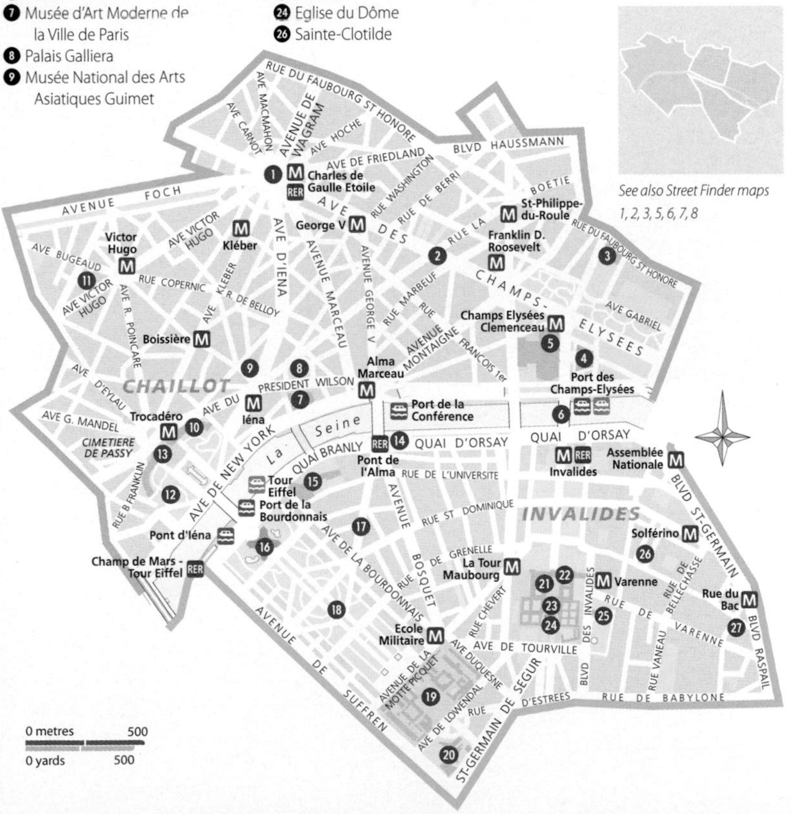

0 metres 500
0 yards 500

Street-by-Street: Champs-Elysées

The formal gardens that line the Champs-Elysées from place de la Concorde to the Rond-Point have changed little since they were laid out by the architect Jacques Hittorff in 1838. The gardens were used as the setting for the World Fair of 1855, which included the Palais de l'Industrie, Paris's response to London's Crystal Palace. The Palais was later replaced by the Grand Palais and by the Petit Palais, which was created as a showpiece of the Third Republic for the Universal Exhibition of 1900. They sit on either side of an impressive vista that stretches from the place Clémenceau across the elegant curve of the Pont Alexandre III, with its four strong anchoring columns, to the Invalides.

Théâtre du Rond Point, an original Champs-Elysées building, presents the work of active authors.

❷ ★ **Avenue des Champs-Elysées**
This was the setting for the victory parades following the two World Wars.

❺ ★ **Grand Palais**
Designed by Charles Girault, and built between 1897 and 1900, this elaborate exhibition hall with its splendid glass dome is frequently used for major exhibitions.

The Lasserre restaurant is decorated in the style of a luxury ocean liner dating from the 1930s.

Palais de la Découverte, a museum of scientific discovery, was originally opened in the Grand Palais for the World Fair of 1937.

0 metres 100
0 yards 100

Key

— Suggested route

The Jardins des Champs-Elysées, with their fountains, flowerbeds and pleasure pavilions, have been a popular spot since the 19th century.

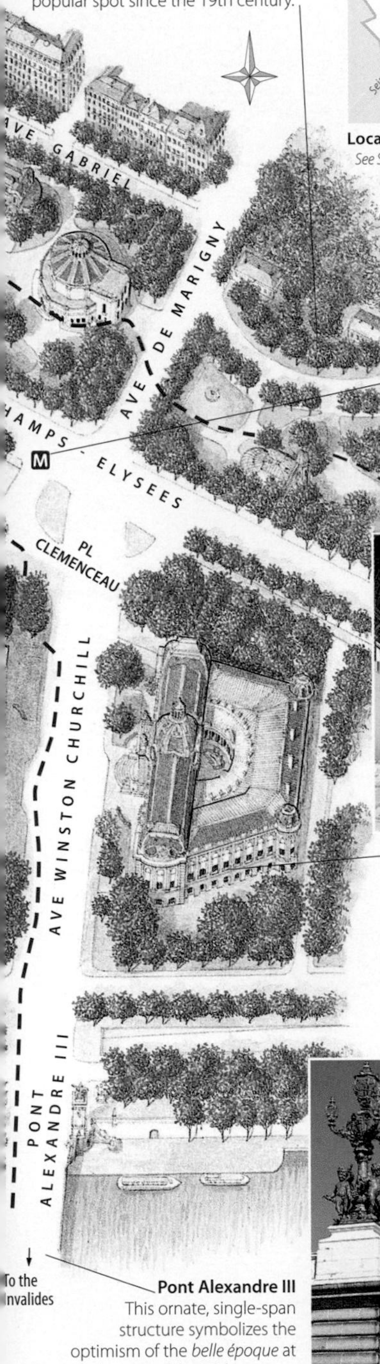

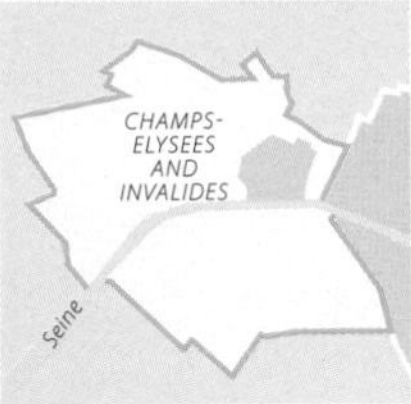

Locator Map
See Street Finder maps 3, 7

Métro Champs-Elysées-Clémenceau

To place de la Concorde

4 ★ Petit Palais
The art collections of the city of Paris are housed here. They contain 19th-century works from objets d'art to paintings by the Barbizon School.

To the Invalides

Pont Alexandre III
This ornate, single-span structure symbolizes the optimism of the *belle époque* at the turn of the 20th century.

The east façade of the Arc de Triomphe

1 Arc de Triomphe

Place Charles de Gaulle 75008. **Map** 2 D4. Ⓜ Charles de Gaulle-Etoile. **Tel** 01 55 37 73 77. **Open** Apr–Sep: 10am–11pm daily; Oct–Mar: 10am–10.30pm daily (last adm: 30 mins earlier); 8 May, 14 Jul, 11 Nov: am only (last adm: 45 mins before closing). **Closed** 1 Jan, 1 May, 25 Dec. **arc-de-triomphe.monuments-nationaux.fr**

After his greatest victory, the Battle of Austerlitz in 1805, Napoleon promised his men they would "go home beneath triumphal arches". The first stone of the world's most famous triumphal arch was laid in 1806, but disruptions to architect Jean Chalgrin's plans and the demise of Napoleonic power delayed completion. Standing 50 m (164 ft) high, the Arc is encrusted with reliefs, sculptures and shields, and offers splendid views.

The body of the Unknown Soldier was placed beneath the arch in 1921 to commemorate the dead of World War I. The tomb's eternal flame is lit every evening at 6:30pm.

High relief by J P Corot, celebrating the Triumph of Napoleon

Baron Haussmann

A lawyer by training and civil servant by profession, Georges-Eugène Haussmann (1809–91) was appointed Prefect of the Seine in 1853 by Napoleon III. For 17 years Haussmann was responsible for the urban modernization of Paris. With a team of the best architects and engineers of the day, he demolished the crowded, insanitary streets of the medieval city and created a well-ventilated and ordered capital within a geometrical grid. The new scheme involved redesigning the area at one end of the Champs-Elysées and creating a star of 12 avenues, which were centred on the new Arc de Triomphe.

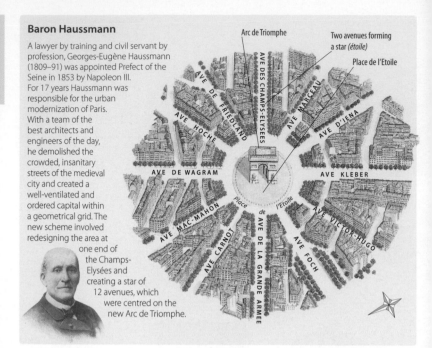

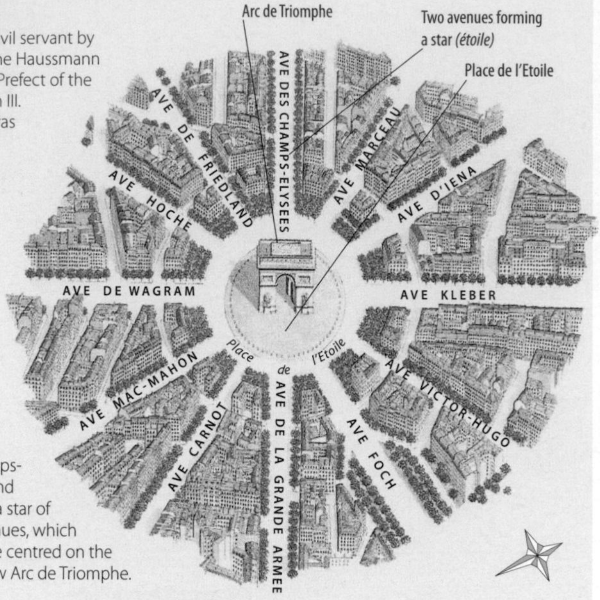

❷ Avenue des Champs-Elysées

75008. **Map** 3 A5. Ⓜ Charles de Gaulle-Etoile, George V, Franklin D. Roosevelt, Champs-Elysées-Clemenceau, Concorde.

The majestic tree-lined avenue "of the Elysian Fields" (the mythical Greek heaven for heroes), first laid out in the 1660s by the landscape designer André Le Nôtre, forms a 3-km (2-mile) straight line from the huge place de la Concorde to the Arc de Triomphe. The 19th century saw it transformed into an elegant boulevard, lined with cafés and restaurants. The Champs-Elysées keeps a special place in the French heart. National parades are held here, the finish of the annual Tour de France cycle race is always on the Champs-Elysées and it is the site of the city's largest Christmas market. Above all, ever since the homecoming of Napoleon's body from St Helena in 1840, it has been the place where Parisians congregate at times of major national celebration.

❸ Palais de l'Elysée

55 rue du Faubourg-St-Honoré 75008. **Map** 3 B5. Ⓜ St-Philippe-du-Roule. **Closed** to the public.

Built in 1718 amid splendid gardens, the Elysée Palace has been the official residence of the French President since 1848. Several occupants left their mark. Louis XV's mistress, Madame de Pompadour, had the whole site enlarged. After the Revolution, it became a dance hall. In the 19th century, it was home to Napoleon's sister, Caroline Murat, and his wife Empress Josephine. The President's Apartments are today on the first floor.

❹ Petit Palais

Av Winston Churchill 75008. **Map** 7 B1. **Tel** 01 53 43 40 00. Ⓜ Champs-Elysées-Clemenceau. **Open** 10am–6pm Tue–Sun (to 9pm Fri for temporary exhibitions). **Closed** public hols. for exhibitions. **petitpalais.paris.fr**

Built for the Universal Exhibition in 1900, this jewel of a building houses the **Musée des Beaux-Arts de la Ville de Paris**. The architect, Charles Girault, arranged the palace around a semicircular courtyard and garden. Permanent exhibits, housed on the Champs-Elysées side, include the Dutuit

Grand Palais

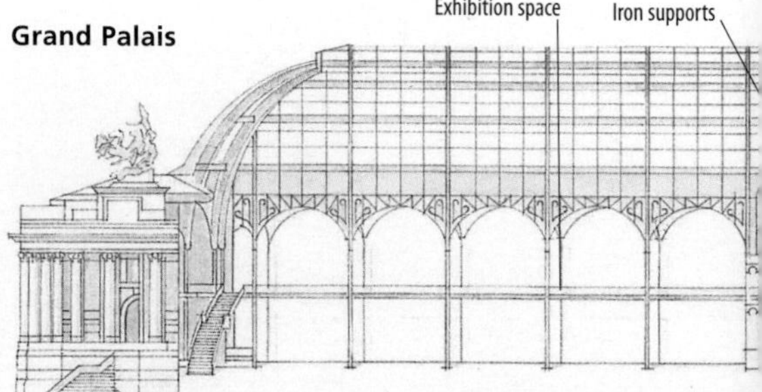

For hotels and restaurants in this region see pp554–5 and pp576–9

Pont Alexandre III, built 1896–1900 and inaugurated at the Universal Exhibition

Collection of medieval and Renaissance objets d'art, paintings and drawings; the Tuck Collection of 18th-century furniture and objets d'art; and the City of Paris collection, with work by Ingres, Delacroix and Courbet, and the landscape painters of the Barbizon School. Temporary exhibitions are housed in the Cours de la Reine wing.

Entrance to the Petit Palais

❺ Grand Palais

Porte A, 3 av Général Eisenhower 75008. **Map** 7 A1. **Tel** 01 44 13 17 17. Ⓜ Champs-Elysées-Clemenceau. Galeries Nationales: pl Clemenceau; sq Jean Perrin, Champs-Elysées; av Winston Churchill. **Open** for temporary exhibitions only, usually 10am–10pm Wed–Mon (to 8pm Sun & Mon). **Closed** 1 May, 25 Dec. **W grandpalais.fr**
Palais de la Decouverte: av Franklin D Roosevelt 75008. **Tel** 01 44 43 20 20. Ⓜ Franklin D. Roosevelt. **Open** 9:30am–6pm Tue–Sat, 10am–7pm Sun. **Closed** 1 Jan, 1 May, 14 Jul, 25 Dec. **W palais-decouverte.fr**

Built at the same time as the Petit Palais opposite, this huge, glass-roofed palace housing the Galeries Nationales has a fine Classical façade adorned with statuary and Art Nouveau ironwork. Bronze flying horses and chariots stand at the four corners. The Great Hall and the glass cupola can be admired during the palace's superb exhibitions. The **Palais de la Découverte**, on the west side of the building, is an imaginative child-oriented science museum.

❻ Pont Alexandre III

75008. **Map** 7 A1. Ⓜ Champs-Elysées-Clemenceau.

This is Paris's prettiest bridge, with exuberant Art Nouveau decoration of gilt and bronze lamps, cupids and cherubs, nymphs and winged horses at either end. It was built between 1896 and 1900 to commemorate the 1892 French–Russian alliance, and in time for the Universal Exhibition of 1900. Pont Alexandre III was named after Tsar Alexander III (father of Nicholas II), who laid the foundation stone in October 1896.

The style of the bridge reflects that of the Grand Palais, to which it leads on the Right Bank. The construction of the bridge is a marvel of 19th-century engineering. It consists of a 6-m- (18-ft-) high single-span steel arch across the Seine. The design was subject to strict controls that prevented the bridge from obscuring the view of the Champs-Elysées or the Invalides, so today you can still enjoy the magnificent views from here.

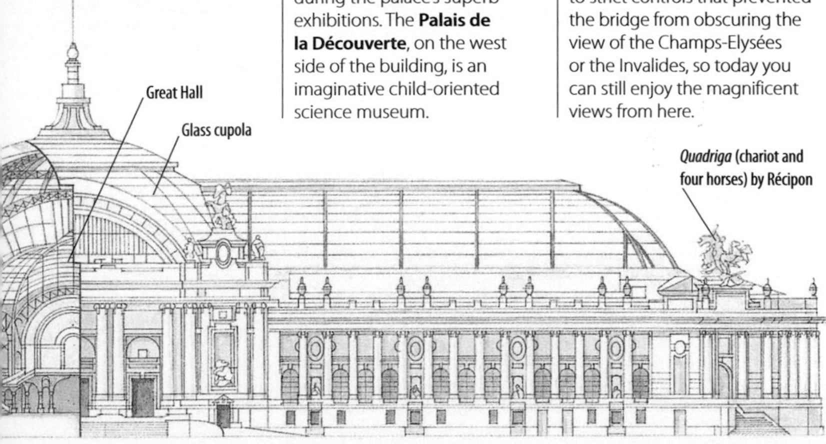

7 Musée d'Art Moderne de la Ville de Paris

Palais de Tokyo, 11 av du Président-Wilson 75016. **Map** 6 E1. **Tel** 01 53 67 40 00. Iéna, Alma-Marceau. **Open** 10am–6pm Tue–Sun (until 10pm Thu for temporary exhibitions). **Closed** public hols. for temporary exhibitions. **mam.paris.fr**

This museum covers trends in 20th-century art and is located in the east wing of the Palais de Tokyo. The Fauves and Cubists are well represented here. Highlights include Raoul Dufy's gigantic mural, *The Electricity Fairy* (created for the 1937 World Fair), and Matisse's *The Dance* (1931–3). There is also a collection of Art Deco furniture.

8 Palais Galliera

10 av Pierre 1er de Serbie 75116. **Map** 6 D1. **Tel** 01 56 52 86 00. Iéna, Alma–Marceau. **Open** 10am–6pm Tue–Sun (to 9pm Thu). **Closed** some public hols (check website). Children's room. **galliera.paris.fr**

Devoted to the evolution of fashion, this museum, also known as the Musée de la Mode de la Ville de Paris, is housed in the Renaissance-style palace built for the Duchesse Maria de Ferrari Galliera in 1892. The collection includes more than 250,000 outfits, fashion accessories, pieces of underwear, drawings and prints, from the 18th century to the present day. Donations have been made by such fashionable women as Baronne Hélène de Rothschild and Princess Grace of Monaco. Eminent couturiers such as Balmain and Balenciaga have donated their designs.

Due to their fragility, the collections are not on permanent display. Pieces are shown in two or three temporary major exhibitions each year. The museum is closed between exhibitions.

Trocadéro fountains in front of the Palais de Chaillot

11 Musée Dapper

35bis rue Paul-Valéry, 75016. **Map** 1 B5. **Tel** 01 45 00 91 75. Victor-Hugo. **Open** 11am–7pm Wed, Fri–Mon. **dapper.com.fr**

A world-class ethnographic research centre, this is one of France's premier showcases of African and Caribbean art and culture. Located in an attractive building with an "African" garden, it is a treasure house of colour and powerful, evocative work. The focus is on pre-colonial folk arts, with sculpture, carvings and tribal work, but there is later art on display, too. The highlight is tribal masks, with a dazzling array of richly carved religious, ritual and funerary masks, as well as theatrical ones used for comic, magical or symbolic performances.

12 Jardins du Trocadéro

75016. **Map** 6 D2. Trocadéro. Cinéaqua: **Tel** 01 40 69 23 23. **Open** 24 hours daily.

The centrepiece of these beautiful gardens is a long rectangular ornamental pool, bordered by stone and bronze-gilt statues, and it looks spectacular at night, when the fountains are illuminated. The statues include *Woman* by Georges Braque and *Horse* by Georges Lucien Guyot. On either side of the pool, the slopes of the Chaillot hill lead gently down to the Seine and the Pont d'Iéna. Cinéaqua, the high-tech aquarium here, has over 25 sharks and a petting pool for children.

13 Palais de Chaillot

Pl du Trocadéro 75016. **Map** 5 C2. Trocadéro. Théâtre National de Chaillot: **Tel** 01 53 65 30 00. **theatre-chaillot.fr**
Musée de l'Homme: **Tel** 01 44 05 72 72. **Open** 10am–6pm Wed–Mon. **museedelhomme.fr**
Musée National de la Marine: **Tel** 01 53 65 69 53. **Closed** for renovation until 2021. **musee-marine.fr**

The Palais, with its huge, curved, colonnaded wings each culminating in a vast pavilion, has three museums and a theatre. Designed in Neo-Classical style for the 1937 Paris Exhibition by Azéma, Louis-Auguste Boileau and Jacques Carlu, it is adorned with sculptures and bas-reliefs; inside, the gold inscriptions on the walls were written by the poet and essayist Paul Valéry.

For hotels and restaurants in this region see pp554–5 and pp576–9

Buddha head from the Musée Guimet

9 Musée National des Arts Asiatiques Guimet

6 pl d'Iéna 75016. **Map** 6 D1. **Tel** 01 56 52 53 00. Iéna. **Open** 10am–6pm Wed–Mon. Panthéon Bouddhique, 19 av d'Iéna. **Tel** 01 40 73 88 00. **Open** 10am–5:45pm Wed–Mon (phone ahead), garden to 5pm. **Closed** 1 Jan, 1 May, 25 Dec. **guimet.fr**

One of the world's leading museums of Asian art, the Guimet has a fine collection of Cambodian (Khmer) art. It was set up in Lyon in 1889 by Emile Guimet, and later moved to Paris. It includes a comprehensive Asian research centre.

10 Cité de l'Architecture et du Patrimoine

Palais de Chaillot, pl du Trocadéro 75016. **Map** 5 C2. **Tel** 01 58 51 52 00. Trocadéro. **Open** 11am–7pm Wed–Sun (until 9pm Thu). **Closed** 1 Jan, 1 May, 25 Dec. **citechaillot.fr**

This museum charts French architecture through the ages and includes models of great French cathedrals, such as Chartres *(see pp311–15)*. There is also a reconstruction of an apartment designed by Le Corbusier.

Palais de Chaillot

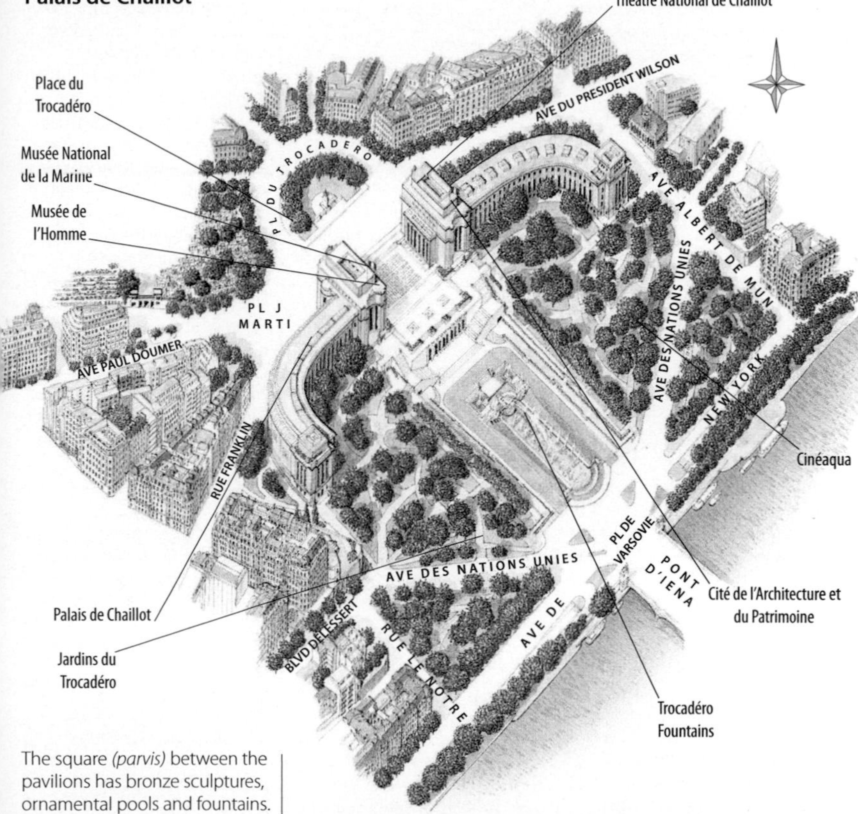

Théâtre National de Chaillot
Place du Trocadéro
Musée National de la Marine
Musée de l'Homme
Cinéaqua
Palais de Chaillot
Cité de l'Architecture et du Patrimoine
Jardins du Trocadéro
Trocadéro Fountains
AVE DU PRESIDENT WILSON
PL DU TROCADERO
AVE ALBERT DE MUN
AVE DES NATIONS UNIES
PL J MARTI
AVE PAUL DOUMER
NEW YORK
RUE FRANKLIN
PL DE VARSOVIE
PONT D'IENA
AVE DES NATIONS UNIES
BLVD DELESSERT
RUE LE NOTRE
AVE DE

The square *(parvis)* between the pavilions has bronze sculptures, ornamental pools and fountains. Steps lead down from the terrace to the **Théatre National de Chaillot**, offering an experimental approach to all genres.

The **Musée de l'Homme**, in the west wing, is an anthropological and ethnographic museum that traces the history of human evolution. Next door is the **Musée National de la Marine**, devoted to French naval history and aspects of the modern-day navy. This is closed due to extensive renovations until 2021. The east wing of the palais contains the vast **Cité de l'Architecture et du Patrimoine** *(see above)*.

⓮ Les Egouts

Pont d'Álma, opposite 93 quai d'Orsay 75007. **Map** 6 F2. **Tel** 01 53 68 27 81 (in English). M Alma-Marceau. RER Pont-de-l'Alma. **Open** 11am–5pm (6pm in summer) Sat–Wed. **Closed** last 2 wks Jan.

One of Baron Haussmann's finest achievements, most of Paris's sewers (*égouts*) date from the Second Empire. If laid end to end, the 2,400 km (1,490 miles) of sewers would stretch from Paris to Istanbul. One-hour walking tours of this attraction have been limited to an area around the quai d'Orsay entrance. Visiting the sewers without a guide can be dangerous, and is against the law. Visitors can discover the mysteries of underground Paris in the sewer museum and learn how the machinery used has changed over the years.

⓯ Musée du Quai Branly

37 quai Branly 75007, or 206/218 rue de l'Université. **Map** 6 E2. **Tel** 01 56 61 70 00. M Alma-Marceau. RER Pont-de-l'Alma. **Open** 11am–7pm Tue, Wed, Sun, 11am–9pm Thu–Sat. **Closed** 1 May, 25 Dec. free 1st Sun of month & for 18–25s after 6pm Sat. Exhibitions, theatre, film, library. **W quaibranly.fr**

Built to give the arts of Africa, Asia, Oceania and the Americas a platform as shining as that for Western art in the city, this museum has a massive collection of more than 300,000 objects. It is particularly strong on Africa, with stone, wooden and ivory masks, as well as ceremonial tools. The Jean-Nouvel-designed building, which is raised on stilts, is a worthwhile sight in itself, while the ingenious use of glass in its construction allows the surrounding greenery to act as a natural backdrop.

Aztec mask, Musée du Quai Branly

⓰ Eiffel Tower

See p117.

Original Art Nouveau doorway at No. 29 avenue Rapp

⓱ No. 29 Avenue Rapp

75005. **Map** 6 E3. M Alma-Marceau. RER Pont-de-l'Alma.

A prime example of Art Nouveau architecture, No. 29 avenue Rapp won its designer, Jules Lavirotte, first prize at the Concours des Façades de la Ville de Paris in 1901. Its ceramics and brickwork are decorated with animal and flower motifs intermingling with female figures. These are superimposed on a multicoloured sandstone base to produce a façade that is deliberately erotic, and was certainly subversive in its day. Another Lavirotte building worth visiting nearby is No. 3 square Rapp, an apartment building complete with a watchtower.

⓲ Parc du Champ-de-Mars

75007. **Map** 6 E3. M Ecole-Militaire. RER Champ-de-Mars–Tour-Eiffel.

The vast gardens stretching from the Eiffel Tower to the Ecole Militaire (Military School) were originally a parade ground for young officer cadets. The area has since been used for horse racing, balloon ascents and mass ceremonies to celebrate the anniversary of the Revolution on 14 July. The first ceremony was held in 1790, in the presence of a glum, captive, Louis XVI.

Mammoth exhibitions were held here in the late 19th century, among them the 1889 World Fair for which the Eiffel Tower was erected.

Today, this is a popular park, with playgrounds and a café.

⓳ Ecole Militaire

1/21 pl Joffre 75007. **Map** 6 F4. **Tel** 01 80 50 14 00. M Ecole-Militaire: Open to the public during European Heritage Days in September.

The Royal Military Academy of Louis XV was founded in 1751 to educate 500 sons of impoverished officers. Louis XV and Madame de Pompadour commissioned architect Jacques-Ange Gabriel to design a building that would rival Louis XIV's Hôtel des Invalides. Financing the building became a problem, so a lottery was authorized and a tax was raised on playing cards. One of the main features is the central pavilion – a magnificent example of the French Classical style, with ten Corinthian columns and a quadrangular dome. Four figures adorn the entablature frieze, symbolizing France, Victory, Force and Peace.

An early cadet at the academy was Napoleon, whose passing-out report stated that "he could go far if the circumstances are right".

A 1751 engraving showing the planning of the Ecole Militaire

16 Eiffel Tower

Built for the Universal Exhibition of 1889, and to commemorate the centennial of the Revolution, the 324-m (1,063-ft) Eiffel Tower (Tour Eiffel) was meant to be a temporary addition to Paris's skyline. Designed by Gustave Eiffel, and fiercely decried by 19th-century aesthetes, it was the world's tallest building until 1930, when New York's Chrysler Building was completed. The Eiffel Tower draws as many as 7 million visitors a year, and its first floor houses a modern, fully accessible visitor centre.

VISITORS' CHECKLIST

Practical Information
Quai Branly and Champ-de-Mars, 75007. **Map** 6 D3. **Tel** 08 92 70 12 39. **Open** 9:30am–11:45pm (mid-Jun–early Sep: 9am–12:45am). Last lift: 45 mins before closure. (Access to top limited in bad weather.) **toureiffel.paris**

Transport
M Bir-Hakeim. 42, 69, 72, 82, 87 to Champ-de-Mars. RER Champ-de-Mars. Tour Eiffel.

Daring Feats

The tower has always inspired crazy stunts. In 1912, Reichelt, a Parisian tailor, attempted to fly from the parapet with only a cape for wings. He plunged to his death in front of a large crowd.

Stuntman Reichelt

The third level, 276 m (905 ft) above the ground, can hold 400 people at a time. Gustave Eiffel's office is located here, plus a champagne bar.

★ Viewing Gallery
On a clear day it is possible to see for 72 km (45 miles), including a distant view of Chartres Cathedral.

The double-decker lifts have a limited capacity, and there can be long waits. Queuing for the lifts requires patience and a good head for heights. Book your tickets online ahead of your visit.

The second level is at 115 m (380 ft), separated from the first level by 359 steps or a few minutes in the lift. Food outlets and souvenir shops can be found here.

Pavillon Ferié
Multimedia displays and touch screens illustrate the history of the tower.

The Jules Verne restaurant is rated highly in Paris, offering not only superb food, but a breath-taking panoramic view.

★ Eiffel Bust
The achievement of Eiffel (1832–1923) was honoured by Antoine Bourdelle, who placed this bust under the tower in 1929.

The first level, 57 m (187 ft) high, is reached by lift or by 345 steps. The glass floors let visitors see right down to the ground.

Les Invalides

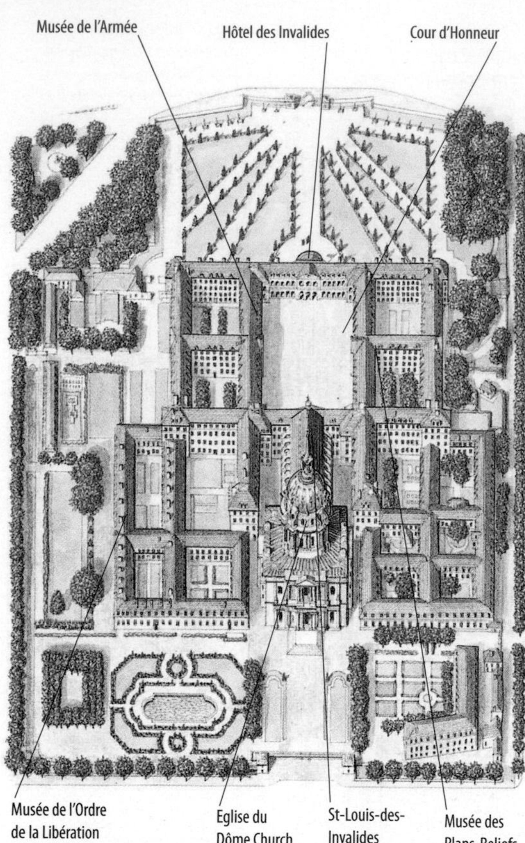

⓴ UNESCO

7 pl de Fontenoy 75007. **Map** 6 F5. **Tel** 01 45 68 10 00. Ⓜ Ségur, Cambronne. **Open** for guided tours only: 10am & 3pm Tue–Fri (reservations essential, email visits@unesco.org). **Closed** public hols. **W** **unesco.org**

This is the headquarters of the United Nations Educational, Scientific and Cultural Organization (UNESCO). Its aim is to contribute to international peace through education, science and culture.

UNESCO is a treasure trove of modern art, including an enormous mural by Picasso, ceramics by Joan Miró and sculptures by Henry Moore, and the calm Japanese garden by Nogushi. Exhibitions and films are also held here.

㉑ Hôtel des Invalides

6 bd des Invalides 75007. **Map** 7 A3. **Tel** 08 10 11 33 99. Ⓜ La Tour Maubourg, Invalides, Varenne. **Open** 7:30am–7pm daily (Apr–Sep: to 9pm Tue). **Closed** 1 Jan, 1 May, 25 Dec. good for admission to all attractions. book ahead online. **W** **musee-armee.fr**

This imposing building, from which the area takes its name, was commissioned by Louis XIV in 1670 for his wounded and homeless veterans. Designed by Libéral Bruand, it was completed in 1676 by Jules Hardouin-Mansart. He later incorporated the Eglise du Dôme, with its golden roof, which was built as Louis XIV's private chapel. Nearly 6,000 soldiers once lived here. Today there are fewer than 100.

The harmonious Classical façade is one of the most impressive sights in Paris. The building houses the Musée de l'Armée and the Musée de l'Ordre de la Libération, set up to honour feats of heroism during World War II under the leadership of Charles de Gaulle. The story is told using film, photographs and mementos. The Musée des Plans-Reliefs also houses a large collection of military models of French forts.

㉒ Musée de l'Armée

129 rue Grenelle 75007 (also 6 bd des Invalides). **Map** 7 A3. **Tel** 08 10 11 33 99. Ⓜ Varenne, La Tour Maubourg, Invalides. RER Invalides. **Open** 10am–6pm daily (to 9pm Tue; to 5pm Nov–Mar; to 5:30pm school hols). **Closed** 1st Mon of month Oct–Jun, 1 Jan, 1 May, 25 Dec. for admission to all attractions. **W** **musee-armee.fr**

One of the most comprehensive museums of military history in the world is housed in two galleries on either side of the magnificent courtyard of the Hôtel des Invalides. The "Priests' Wing" holds the World War II galleries.

A major exhibit of France's victories and defeats, dedicated mainly to the Napoleonic era, includes the emperor's death mask and stuffed horse, Vizier. Also on display are François I's ivory hunting horns and a model of the 1944 Normandy landing.

The façade of the Musée de l'Armée

For hotels and restaurants in this region see pp554–5 and pp576–9

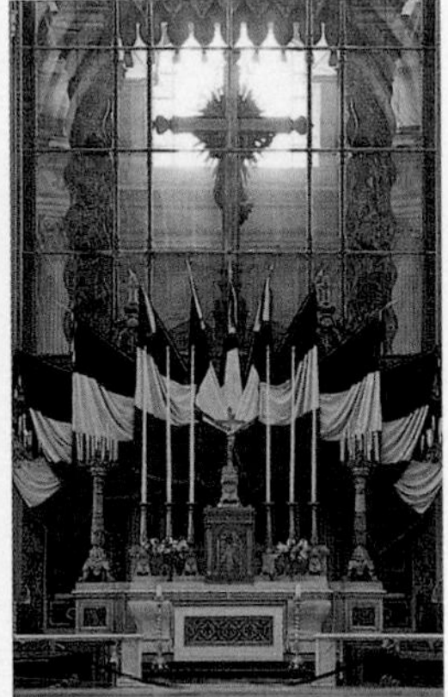

Altar of St-Louis-des-Invalides with banners seized in battle

㉓ Cathedral of St-Louis-des-Invalides

6 bd des Invalides, Hôtel des Invalides 75007. **Map** 7 A3. M Invalides, La Tour Maubourg, Varenne. **Tel** 08 10 11 33 99. **Open** 10am–6pm daily (Jul–Aug: to 7pm; Apr–Sep: to 9pm Tue). W **musee-armee.fr**

Also known as the "soldiers' church", this is the chapel of the Hôtel des Invalides. It was built from 1679 to 1708 by Jules Hardouin-Mansart, to Bruand's design. The stark Neo-Classical interior is well-proportioned, designed in the shape of a Greek cross.

There is a fine 17th-century organ, on which the first performance of Berlioz's *Requiem* was given on 5 December 1837, with more than 200 musicians and choristers participating.

㉔ Eglise du Dôme

6 bd des Invalides, Hôtel des Invalides, 129 rue de Grenelle, 75007. **Map** 7 A4. **Tel** 08 10 11 33 99. M La Tour Maubourg, Varenne, Invalides. 82, 92 to Les Invalides. RER Invalides. Tour Eiffel. **Open** 10am–6pm daily (Apr–Sep: to 9pm Tue; Jul–Aug: to 7pm). **Closed** 1st Mon of month, 1 Jan, 1 May, 25 Dec. restaurant. W **musee-armee.fr**

Jules Hardouin-Mansart was asked in 1676 by the Sun King, Louis XIV, to build the Eglise du Dôme to complement the existing buildings of the Invalides military refuge, designed by Libéral Bruand. The Dôme was to be reserved for the exclusive use of the Sun King and as the location of royal tombs.

The resulting masterpiece is one of the greatest examples of 17th-century French architecture, the period known as the *grand siècle*. After Louis XIV's death, plans to bury the royal family in the church were abandoned.

The main attraction is the tomb of Napoleon; 20 years after his death on the island of St Helena, his body was returned to France and installed in this magnificent crypt, encased in six coffins in a vast red porphyry sarcophagus.

Eglise du Dôme with cupola, first gilded in 1715

㉕ Musée Rodin

79 rue de Varenne 75007. **Map** 7 B3. **Tel** 01 44 18 61 10. M Varenne. **Open** 10am–5:45pm Tue–Sun (to 8:45pm Wed). **Closed** 1 Jan, 1 May, 25 Dec. free 1st Sun of month & for 18–25s after 6pm Sat. restricted. W **musee-rodin.fr**

Auguste Rodin (1840–1917), regarded as one of the greatest French sculptors, lived and worked in the Hôtel Biron, an elegant 18th-century mansion, from 1908 until his death. In return for a state-owned flat and studio, Rodin left his work to the nation, and it is now exhibited here. Some of his most celebrated sculptures are on display in the garden: *The Burghers of Calais, The Thinker, The Gates of Hell* *(see p124)* and *Balzac*.

The indoor exhibits are arranged in chronological order, spanning the whole of Rodin's career. Highlights include *The Kiss* and *Eve*.

Rodin's *The Thinker* in museum garden

㉖ Sainte-Clotilde

23bis rue Las Cases 75007. **Map** 7 B3. **Tel** 01 44 18 62 60. M Solférino, Varenne, Invalides. **Open** 9am–7:30pm Mon–Fri, 10am–8pm Sat & Sun (to 7pm daily in summer). **Closed** Mon (Aug), non-religious pub hols. Concerts.

Designed by the German-born architect Franz Christian Gau and built in 1846–56, this Neo-Gothic church was inspired by the 19th-century enthusiasm for the Middle Ages, popularized by such writers as Victor Hugo.

Inside are wall paintings by James Pradier and stained-glass windows with scenes relating to the patron saint of the church. The composer César Franck was organist here from 1858 to 1890.

㉗ Musée Maillol

61 rue de Grenelle 75007. **Map** 7 C4. **Tel** 01 42 22 59 58. M Rue du Bac, Sèvres-Babylone. **Open** 10:30am–6:30pm daily during exhibitions (to 9:30pm Fri). W **museemaillol.com**

This museum was created by Dina Vierny, muse to Aristide Maillol. His work is exhibited here in all its diverse forms: drawings, engravings, paintings, sculpture and decorative objects. The museum also plays host to two major temporary exhibitions a year. Allegorical figures of the city of Paris and the four seasons adorn Bouchardon's fountain outside.

THE LEFT BANK

The Left Bank has long been associated with poets, philosophers, artists and radical thinkers of all kinds. It still has its share of bohemian street life and pavement cafés, but the smart set has moved in, patronizing Yves Saint-Laurent and the exclusive interior design shops in rue Jacob.

The Latin Quarter is the ancient area lying between the Seine and the Luxembourg Gardens, and is today filled with bookshops, art galleries and cafés. Boulevard St-Michel, bordering the Latin Quarter and St-Germain-des-Prés, has slowly given way to commerce, and is full of fast-food outlets and cheap shops. The surrounding maze of narrow, cobbled streets has retained its character, with ethnic shops and avant-garde theatres dominated by the façade of the Sorbonne, France's first university, built in 1253. Many Parisians dream of living near the Luxembourg Gardens, a quiet area with charming old streets, gateways, and elaborate gardens full of paths, lawns and tree-lined avenues. Students come here to chat, and on warm days Parisian men still meet underneath the chestnut trees to play chess or the traditional French game of *boules*.

Sights at a Glance

Churches

- 5 St-Germain-des-Prés
- 9 St-Séverin
- 10 St-Julien-le-Pauvre
- 12 St-Etienne-du-Mont
- 13 Panthéon
- 15 St-Sulpice
- 17 Val-de-Grâce

Museums and Galleries

- 1 *Musée d'Orsay pp124–5*
- 6 Musée Eugène Delacroix
- 8 Musée de Cluny

Historic Buildings and Streets

- 2 Boulevard St-Germain
- 3 Quai Voltaire
- 4 Ecole Nationale Supérieure des Beaux-Arts
- 7 Rue de l'Odéon
- 11 La Sorbonne
- 14 Palais du Luxembourg

Fountains

- 16 Fontaine de l'Observatoire

See also Street Finder maps 7, 8, 9, 12, 13

◀ La Fontaine de l'Observatoire, in the Luxembourg Gardens

Street-by-Street: St-Germain-des-Prés

After World War II, St-Germain des-Prés became synonymous with intellectual life centred on bars and cafés. Philosophers, writers, actors and musicians mingled in the cellar nightspots and brasseries, where existentialist philosophy coexisted with American jazz. The area is now smarter than in the heyday of Jean-Paul Sartre and Simone de Beauvoir, the enigmatic singer Juliette Greco and the New Wave film-makers. However, the writers are still around, enjoying the pleasures of sitting in Les Deux Magots, Café de Flore and other haunts. The 17th-century buildings have survived, but signs of change are evident in the affluent shops dealing in antiques, books and fashion.

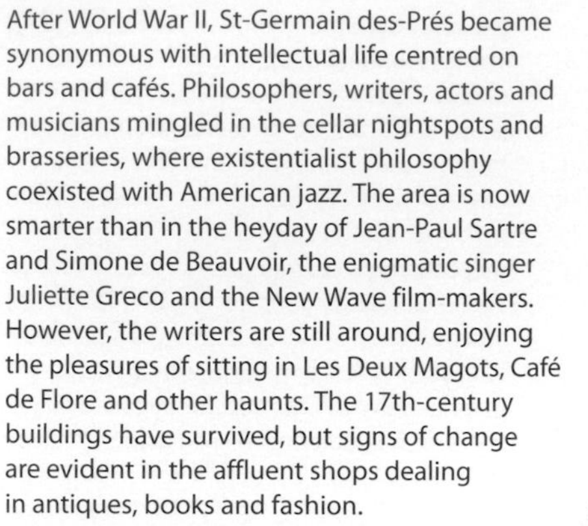

Les Deux Magots became a focus of bohemian and literary activity in the 1920s.

Café de Flore, the former favourite haunt of Jean-Paul Sartre, Simone de Beauvoir and other French intellectuals, still has a classic Art Deco interior.

Métro St-Germain-des-Prés

Brasserie Lipp, decorated with colourful ceramics, is a renowned brasserie frequented by politicians.

❺ ★ St-Germain-des-Prés
The philosopher René Descartes is among the notables buried here in Paris's oldest church.

❷ ★ Boulevard St-Germain
Café terraces, boutiques, cinemas, restaurants and bookshops characterize the central section of the Left Bank's main street.

For hotels and restaurants in this region see pp554–5 and pp576–9

Key

▬ Suggested route

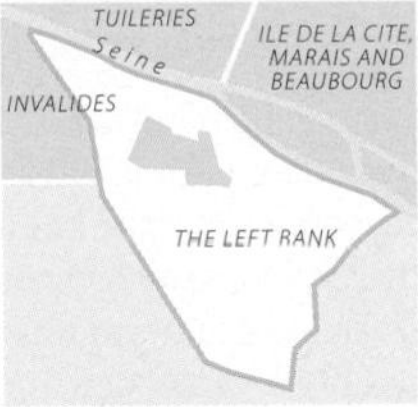

Locator Map

See Street Finder map 8

❻ ★ Musée Eugène Delacroix The home of the Romantic painter Eugène Delacroix (1798–1863) is now a museum devoted to his art.

Palais Abbatial de St-Germain-des-Prés was the residence of abbots from 1586 till the 1789 Revolution.

Rue de Buci was for centuries an important street and the site of some real tennis courts. It now holds a lively market.

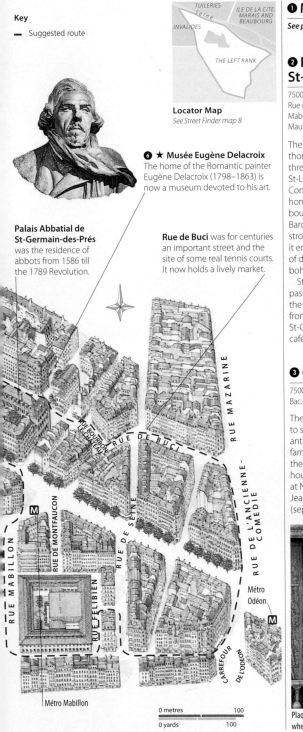

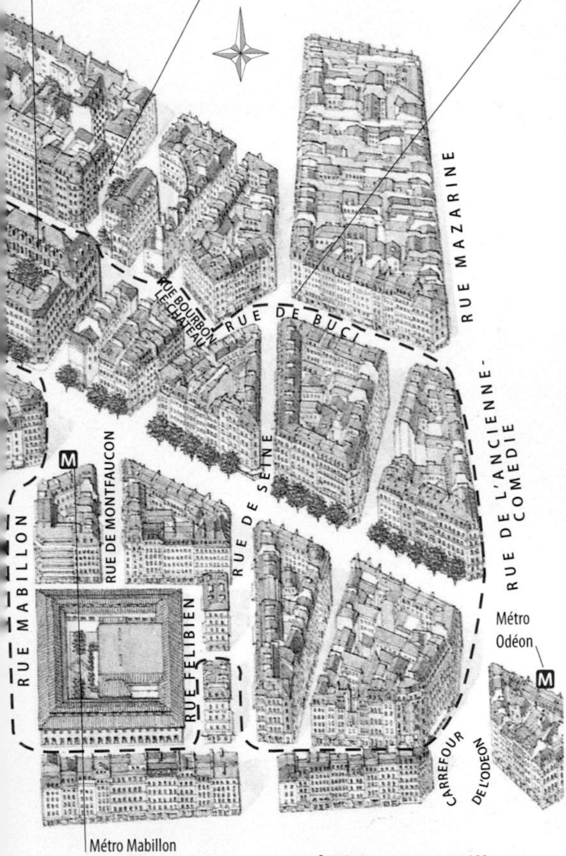

Métro Mabillon

Métro Odéon

0 metres 100

0 yards 100

❶ Musée d'Orsay

See pp124–5.

❷ Boulevard St-Germain

75006, 75007. **Map** 8 D3. Ⓜ Solférino, Rue du Bac, St-Germain-des-Prés, Mabillon, Odéon, Cluny-La Sorbonne, Maubert-Mutualité.

The Left Bank's most celebrated thoroughfare slinks across three districts from the Ile St-Louis to the Pont de la Concorde. The architecture is homogeneous, because the boulevard was another of Baron Haussmann's bold strokes of urban planning, but it encompasses a wide range of different lifestyles, from bohemian to bourgeois.

Starting from the east, it passes the Musée de Cluny and the Sorbonne. It is most lively from boulevard St-Michel to St-Germain-des-Prés, with its café culture.

❸ Quai Voltaire

75006, 75007. **Map** 8 D3. Ⓜ Rue du Bac. RER Museé d'Orsay.

The quai Voltaire is now home to some of the most important antiques dealers in Paris. Many famous people have lived in the attractive 18th-century houses; among others, Voltaire at No. 27 and Richard Wagner, Jean Sibelius and Oscar Wilde (separately) at No. 19.

VOLTAIRE
NÉ A PARIS
LE 21 NOVEMBRE 1694
EST MORT
DANS CETTE MAISON
LE 30 MAI 1778

Plaque marking the house in quai Voltaire where Voltaire died in 1778

❶ Musée d'Orsay

In 1986, 47 years after it had closed as a mainline railroad station, Victor Laloux's turn-of-the-century building reopened as the Musée d'Orsay. Built as the Orléans railway terminus in the heart of Paris, it narrowly avoided demolition in the 1970s. In the conversion to a museum, much of the original architecture was retained. The museum presents the rich diversity of visual arts from 1848 to 1914, featuring mainly the Impressionist, Post-Impressionist and Art Nouveau movements, and explains the social and technological context in which the works were created. Exhibits include paintings, sculptures, furniture and decorative objects. The museum also has a programme of classical music concerts. Exhibits are subject to change.

The Gates of Hell (1880–1917)
Rodin included figures that he had already created, such as *The Thinker* and *The Kiss*, in this famous gateway.

Dance at the Moulin de la Galette (1876)
Renoir painted this picture outside to capture the light as it filtered through the trees.

The Dance (1865–9)
Carpeaux's dynamic sculpture caused a scandal when it was first unveiled in 1869.

Key to Floorplan

- Architecture and Decorative Arts
- Sculpture
- Painting before 1870
- Impressionism
- Neo-Impressionism and Post-Impressionism
- Naturalism and Symbolism
- Art Nouveau
- Temporary exhibitions
- Nonexhibition space

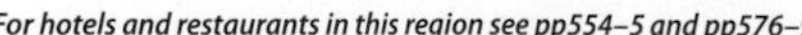

For hotels and restaurants in this region see pp554–5 and pp576–9

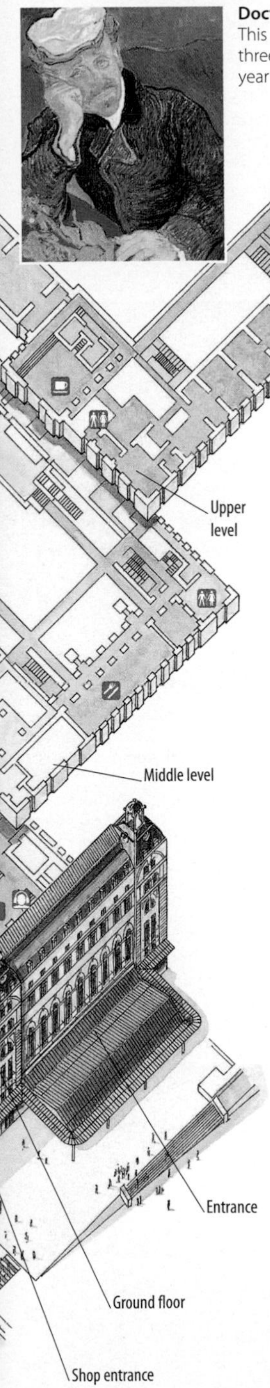

Doctor Paul Gachet (1890)
This portrait by van Gogh is one of three and was painted the same year that the artist died.

Gallery Guide

The ground floor has works from the mid- to late 19th century. The middle level features Art Nouveau, decorative art, and late 19th- to early 20th-century paintings and sculptures. The upper level showcases the celebrated Impressionists, as well as temporary exhibitions.

VISITORS' CHECKLIST

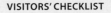

Practical Information
Quai A France/rue de la Légion d'Honneur 75007. **Map** 8 D2. **Tel** 01 40 49 48 14. Carrousel du Louvre/Bac Montalembert.
Open 9:30am–6pm Tue–Sun (to 9:45pm Thu; last entry 1 hr before closing). **Closed** Jan 1, May 1, Dec 25. Events: call 01 53 63 04 63. **musee-orsay.fr**

Transport
Solférino. 24, 68, 69, 84 to quai A France; 73 to rue de la Légion d'Honneur; 63, 83, 84, 94 to bd St-Germain.
RER Musée d'Orsay.

Exploring the Musée d'Orsay

Many of the paintings in the Musée d'Orsay came from the Louvre and the Impressionist collection once in the Jeu de Paume. Paintings from before 1870 are on the ground floor, presided over by Thomas Couture's massive *Romans of the Decadence*. Neo-Classical masterpieces, such as Ingres's *La Source*, hang near Romantic works including Delacroix's turbulent *Tiger Hunt*. These exotic visions contrast with Realist works by artists such as Courbet and early canvases by Degas and Manet, including the latter's famous *Olympia*.

The museum's central aisle overflows with sculpture, from Daumier's satirical busts of members of parliament to Carpeaux's exuberant *The Dance* and Rodin's *The Gates of Hell*. Decorative arts and architecture are on the middle level, where there is also a display of Art Nouveau – sinuous lines characterize Lalique's jewelry and glassware and the designs of Hector Guimard, who produced the characteristic curvy entrances of the Paris Métro.

Blue Waterlilies (1916–19) by Claude Monet

Among the many highlights of the Impressionist rooms are Monet's *Rouen Cathedral* series *(see p271)* and Renoir's joyful *Dance at the Moulin de la Galette*. The Post-Impressionist collection on the middle level includes the *Eglise d'Auvers* by van Gogh, Seurat's Pointillist compositions such as *Le Cirque*, Gauguin's highly coloured Symbolist works, and Toulouse-Lautrec's depictions of Parisian night-life. Among the highlights of the post-1900 display is Matisse's *Luxe, Calme et Volupté*.

Le Déjeuner sur l'Herbe (1863) by Edouard Manet

The façade of the Ecole Nationale Supérieure des Beaux-Arts

❹ Ecole Nationale Supérieure des Beaux-Arts

14 rue Bonaparte 75006. **Map** 8 E3. **Tel** 01 47 03 50 00. Ⓜ St-Germain-des-Prés. **Open** from 10am Mon–Fri for guided visits only (01 42 46 92 02 to book). Library. **W** **beauxartsparis.com**

The main French school of fine arts has an enviable position at the corner of rue Bonaparte and the riverside quai Malaquais. It is housed in several buildings, the most imposing being the 19th-century Palais des Etudes. A host of budding French and foreign painters and architects have crossed the courtyard, which contains a 17th-century chapel, to learn in the ateliers of the school. Many American architects have studied here.

❺ St-Germain-des-Prés

3 pl St-Germain-des-Prés 75006. **Map** 8 E4. **Tel** 01 55 42 81 10. Ⓜ St-Germain-des-Prés. **Open** 8am–7:45pm Mon–Sat, 9am–8pm Sun. 3pm Tue, Thu & 3rd Sun of month (call 01 55 42 81 18). Concerts: 8pm (usually Thu & Fri). **W** **eglise-sgp.org**

The oldest church in Paris originated in 542 as a basilica to house holy relics. It became a powerful Benedictine abbey, rebuilt in the 11th century, but most of it was destroyed by fire in 1794. Major restoration took place in the 1800s. One of the three original towers survives, housing one of France's oldest belfries. The interior is a mix of styles, with 6th-century marble columns, Gothic vaulting, Romanesque arches and 19th-century frescos. Famous tombs include that of 17th-century philosopher René Descartes.

❻ Musée Eugène Delacroix

6 rue de Fürstenberg 75006. **Map** 8 E4. **Tel** 01 44 41 86 50. Ⓜ St-Germain-des-Prés. **Open** 9:30am–5:30pm Wed–Mon. **Closed** 1 Jan, 1 May, 25 Dec. free 1st Sun of month & for 18–25s (EU residents). **W** **musee-delacroix.fr**

The leading Romantic painter Eugène Delacroix lived and worked here from 1857 till his death in 1863. Here he painted *The Entombment of Christ* and *The Way to Calvary* (which hang in the museum). He also created murals for the Chapel of the Holy Angels in the nearby St-Sulpice church *(see p131)*.

The apartment and studio has a portrait of George Sand, and Delacroix self-portraits.

Jacob Wrestling with the Angel by Delacroix, in St-Sulpice *(see p131)*

❼ Rue de l'Odéon

75006. **Map** 8 F5. Ⓜ Odéon.

Opened in 1779 to improve access to the Odéon theatre, this was the first street in Paris to have pavements with gutters and it still has many 18th-century houses.

Sylvia Beach's bookshop, the original Shakespeare & Company, stood at No. 12 from 1921 to 1940. It was a magnet for writers such as James Joyce, Ezra Pound and Hemingway.

❽ Musée de Cluny

6 pl Paul-Painlevé, 75005. **Map** 9 A5. **Tel** 01 53 73 78 16/00. Ⓜ St-Michel, Odéon, Cluny. RER St-Michel. **Open** 9:15am–5:45pm Wed–Mon. **Closed** 1 Jan, 1 May, 25 Dec. Concerts: **W** **musee-moyenage.fr**

The museum (officially the Musée National du Moyen Age) is a unique combination of Gallo-Roman ruins, incorporated

Stone heads of the Kings of Judah carved around 1220

❾ St-Séverin

1 rue-des-Prêtres-St-Séverin 75005. **Map** 9 A4. **Tel** 01 42 34 93 50. Ⓜ St-Michel. **Open** 11am–7:30pm Mon–Sat, 9am–8:30pm Sun. **W** **saint-severin.com**

St-Séverin, one of the finest churches in Paris, is named after a 6th-century hermit who lived locally. It is a perfect example of the Flamboyant Gothic style. Begun in the 13th century and finished in the early 16th, it includes a double aisle encircling the chancel. In the garden is the church's medieval gable-roofed charnel house.

Gargoyles adorning the gables of the Flamboyant Gothic St-Séverin

The School woodcarving (English, early 16th century)

into a medieval mansion (in newly created medieval gardens), and one of the world's finest collections of medieval art and crafts. Its name comes from Pierre de Chalus, Abbot of Cluny, who bought the ruins in 1330. The present building dates from 1485–98. Among the star exhibits are the tapestries, remarkable for their quality, age and state of preservation. The highlight of the sculpture section is the Gallery of the Kings, while one of Cluny's most precious items, the Golden Rose of Basel from 1330, is found in the collection of jewellery and metalwork. Other treasures include stained glass, woodcarvings and books of hours.

Lady with the Unicorn Tapestries

These six outstanding tapestries are fine examples of the *millefleurs* style. Developed in the 15th and early 16th centuries, the style is noted for its graceful depiction of animals and people and its fresh and harmonious colours.

The poetic elegance of a unicorn on the sixth tapestry

⑩ St-Julien-le-Pauvre

79 rue Galande 75005. **Map** 9 A4. **Tel** 01 43 54 52 16. M St-Michel. **Open** 9:30am–1pm, 3–6:30pm daily. ✝ 12:15pm Tue & Thu; 10am, 11am & 6pm Sun. Concerts. W **sjlpmelkites.fr**

The church is one of the oldest in Paris, dating from between 1165 and 1220. The university held its official meetings in the church until 1524, when a student protest created so much damage that they were barred from the church by parliament. It has belonged to the Melchite sect of the Greek Orthodox Church since 1889 and is now the setting for classical and religious concerts.

⑪ La Sorbonne

1 rue Victor Cousin 75005. **Map** 9 A5. **Tel** 01 40 46 22 11. M Cluny-La Sorbonne, Maubert-Mutualité. Mon–Fri & 1 Sat a month, by appt. Email visites.sorbonnes@ac-paris.fr. W **paris-sorbonne.fr**

The Sorbonne, one of the oldest universities in the world, was established in 1253 by Robert de Sorbon, confessor to Louis IX, for 16 poor scholars to study theology. It went on to become the centre of scholastic theology. In 1469, three printing presses were brought from Mainz, and the first printing house in France was founded. The college's opposition to liberal 18th-century philosophical ideas led to its suppression during the Revolution. It was re-established by Napoleon in 1806, and the 17th-century buildings replaced. In 1969, the Sorbonne split into 13 separate universities, but the building still holds some lectures.

⑫ St-Etienne-du-Mont

Pl Ste-Geneviève 75005. **Map** 13 A1. **Tel** 01 43 54 11 79. M Cardinal Lemoine. **Open** 6:30pm–7:30pm Mon, 8:45am–7:45pm Tue–Thu (to 10pm Wed), 8:45am–noon & 2 7:45pm Sat & Sun. ✝ 6:45pm daily, plus 12:15pm Tue–Fri, 11am Sat, 9 & 11am Sun. monthly. W **saintetiennedumont.fr**

Part Gothic and part Renaissance, this church houses the shrine of Paris's patron saint, Geneviève, and remains of literary figures Racine and Pascal.

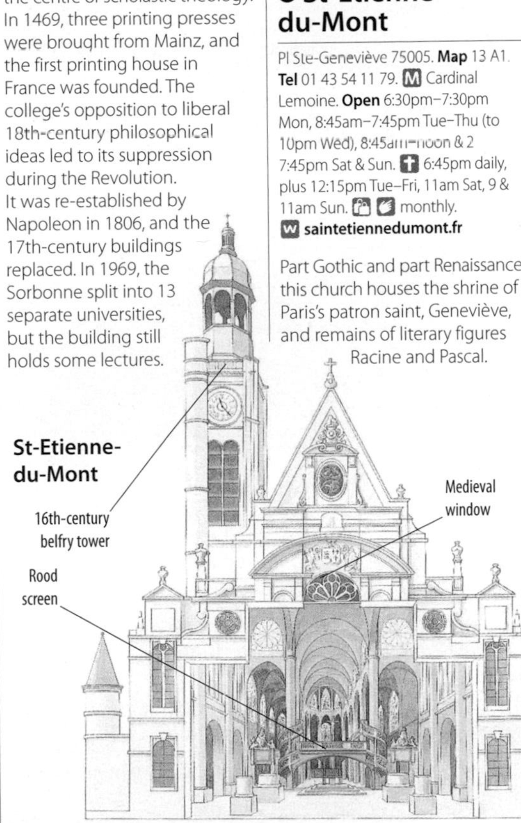

Street-by-Street: Latin Quarter

Since the Middle Ages this riverside quarter has been dominated by the Sorbonne, and acquired its name from the early Latin-speaking students. It dates back to the Roman town across from the Ile de la Cité; at that time rue St-Jacques was one of the main roads out of Paris. The area is generally associated with artists, intellectuals and a bohemian way of life; it also has a history of political unrest. In 1871, place St-Michel became the centre of the Paris Commune, and in May 1968 it was a site of student uprisings. Today the eastern half has become sufficiently chic, however, to house members of the Establishment.

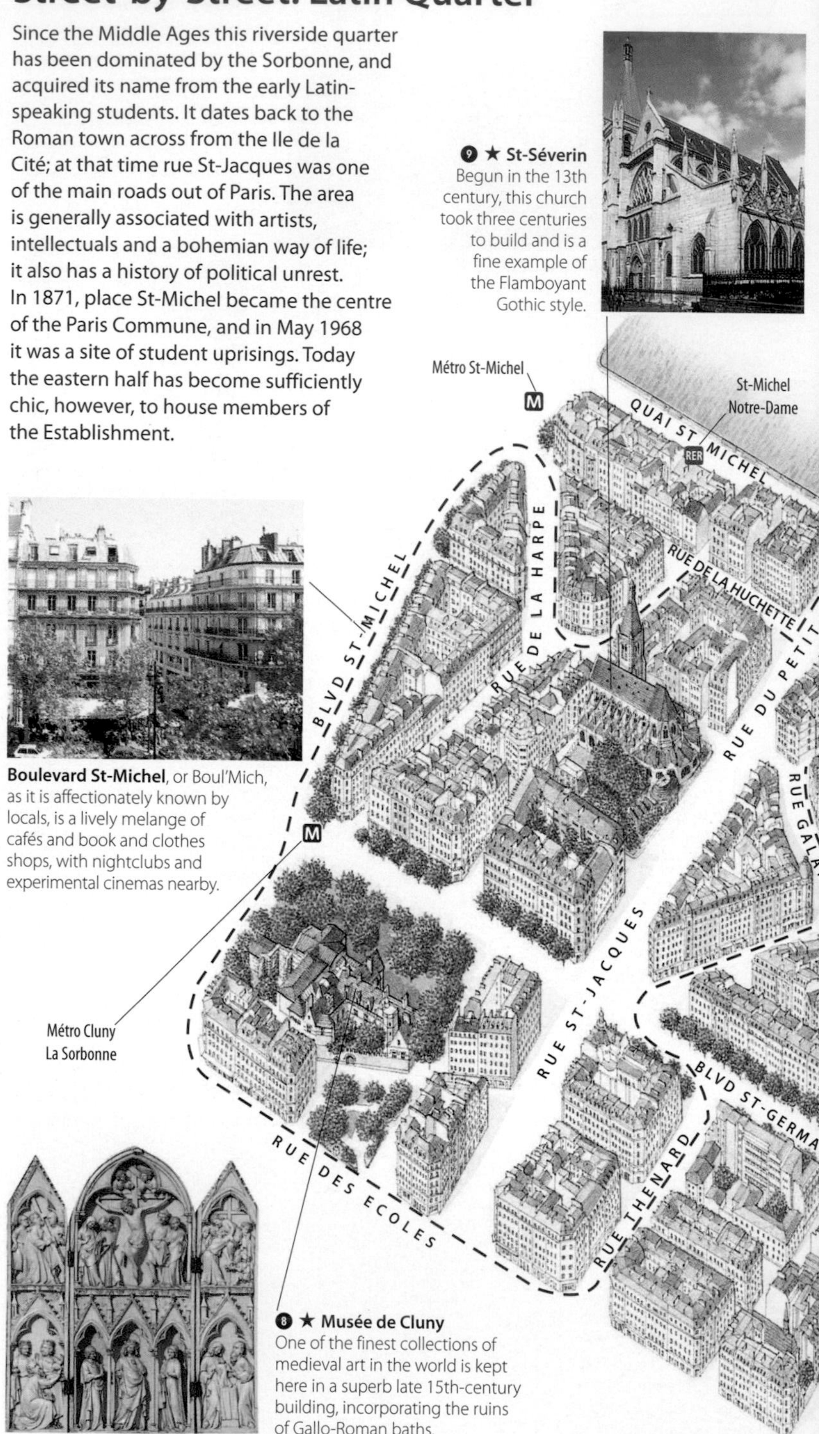

9 ★ St-Séverin
Begun in the 13th century, this church took three centuries to build and is a fine example of the Flamboyant Gothic style.

Boulevard St-Michel, or Boul'Mich, as it is affectionately known by locals, is a lively melange of cafés and book and clothes shops, with nightclubs and experimental cinemas nearby.

8 ★ Musée de Cluny
One of the finest collections of medieval art in the world is kept here in a superb late 15th-century building, incorporating the ruins of Gallo-Roman baths.

Locator Map
See Street Finder maps 8, 9

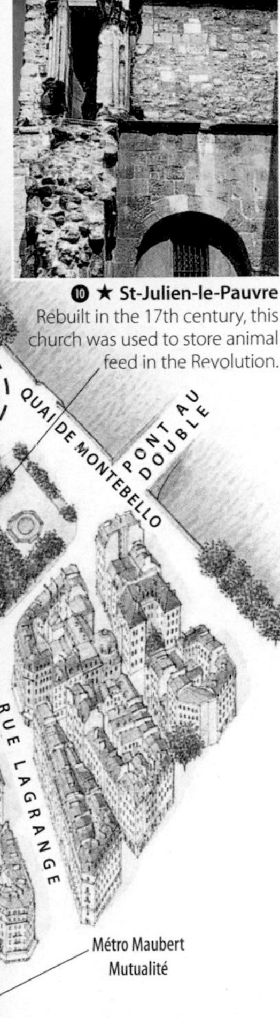

⑩ ★ St-Julien-le-Pauvre
Rebuilt in the 17th century, this church was used to store animal feed in the Revolution.

0 metres 100
0 yards 100

Key

▬ Suggested route

⑬ Panthéon

Pl du Panthéon 75005. **Map** 13 A1. **Tel** 01 44 32 18 00. Ⓜ Maubert-Mutualité, Cardinal-Lemoine. RER Luxembourg. **Open** Apr–Sep: 10am–6:30pm daily; Oct–Mar: 10am–6pm daily (last adm: 45 mins before closing). **Closed** 1 Jan, 1 May, 25 Dec. **pantheon.monuments-nationaux.fr**

When Louis XV recovered from illness in 1744, he was so grateful that he conceived a magnificent church to honour Ste Geneviève, the patron saint of Paris. The French architect Jacques-Germain Soufflot planned the church in Neo-Classical style. Work began in 1764 and was completed in 1790 under the control of Guillaume Rondelet. But with the Revolution under way, the church was soon turned into a pantheon – a monument housing the tombs of France's great heroes. Napoleon returned it to the Church in 1806, but it was secularized and then desecularized once more, before finally being made a civic building in 1885.

The façade, inspired by the Rome Pantheon, has a pediment relief depicting the mother country granting laurels to her great men. Those resting here include Voltaire, Rousseau and Zola, and the ashes of Pierre and Marie Curie and André Malraux.

The Panthéon Interior
The interior has four aisles arranged in the shape of a Greek cross, from the centre of which the great dome rises.

Iron-Framed Dome
The fresco in the dome's stone cupola represents the *Glorification of Sainte Geneviève*, commissioned by Napoleon in 1811.

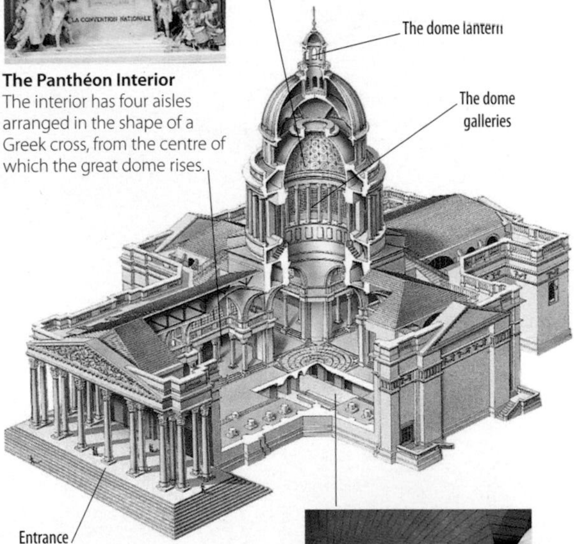

The dome lantern

The dome galleries

Entrance

Crypt
Under the building, the vast crypt divides into galleries flanked by Doric columns. Many French notables rest here, including Voltaire and Emile Zola.

Street-by-Street: Luxembourg Quarter

Situated only a few steps from the bustle of St-Germain-des-Prés, this graceful and historic area offers a peaceful haven in the heart of a modern city. The Jardin du Luxembourg and Palais du Luxembourg dominate the surroundings. The gardens became fully open to the public in the 19th century under the ownership of the Comte de Provence (later to become Louis XVIII), when for a small fee visitors could come in and feast on fruit from the orchard. Today the gardens, palace and old houses on the streets to the north remain unspoiled and attract many visitors.

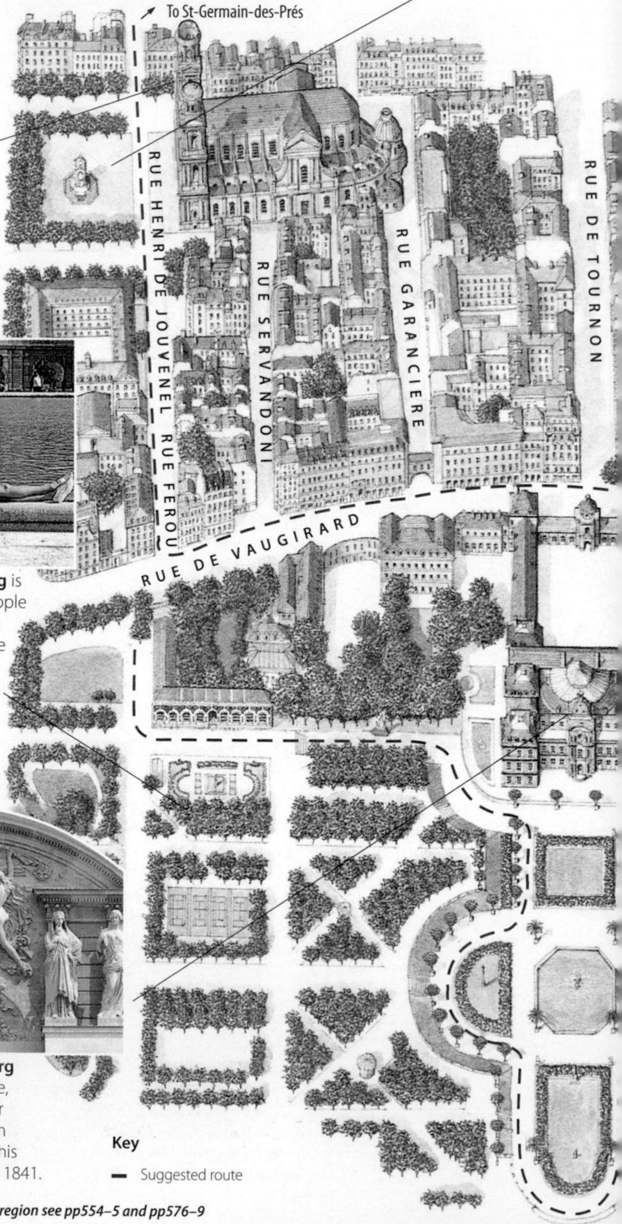

Place St-Sulpice, ringed by flowering chestnut trees, was begun in 1754.

To St-Germain-des-Prés

RUE HENRI DE JOUVENEL

RUE SERVANDONI

RUE GARANCIERE

RUE DE TOURNON

RUE FEROU

RUE DE VAUGIRARD

⓯ ★ St-Sulpice
This huge Neo-Classical church, by six different architects, took more than a century to build. Highlights include murals by Delacroix.

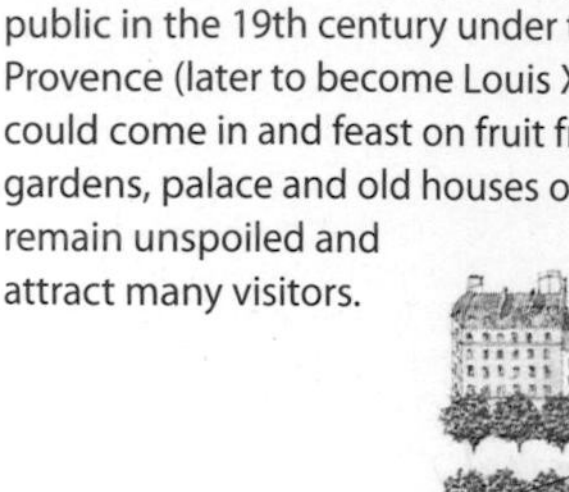

The Jardin du Luxembourg is a popular garden where people come to relax, sunbathe, sail boats on the pond or admire the many beautiful statues erected in the 19th century.

0 metres 100

0 yards 100

⓮ ★ Palais du Luxembourg
First built as a royal residence, the palace has been used for various purposes from prison to Luftwaffe headquarters. This garden façade was added in 1841.

Key

— Suggested route

For hotels and restaurants in this region see pp554–5 and pp576–9

Locator Map
See Street Finder maps 8, 12

Fontaine Médicis is a 17th-century fountain in the style of an Italian grotto. It is thought to have been designed by Salomon de Brosse.

Ste Geneviève, patron saint of Paris, whose prayers saved Paris from the Huns in AD 451, is honoured by this statue by Michel-Louis Victor in 1845.

⓮ Palais du Luxembourg

15 rue de Vaugirard 75006. **Map** 8 E5. **Tel** 01 42 34 20 00. Ⓜ Odéon. RER Luxembourg. groups: Mon, Fri, Sat (apply 3 months in advance: 01 42 34 20 60); indiv: email visites@senat.fr for sponsorship. **W senat.fr/visite** Museum: **Tel** 01 40 13 62 00. **Open** 10am–7pm daily (to 10pm Mon) during exhibitions. **Closed** 1 May. **W museeduluxembourg.fr**

Now home to the French Senate, this palace was built to remind Marie de' Medici, widow of Henri IV, of her native Florence. It was designed by Salomon de Brosse in the style of Florence's Pitti Palace. By the time it was finished (1631), Marie had been banished from Paris, but it remained a royal palace until the Revolution. In World War II it became the Luftwaffe headquarters. The Musée du Luxembourg in the east gallery hosts art exhibitions.

⓯ St-Sulpice

2 rue Palatine, pl St-Sulpice 75006. **Map** 8 E5. **Tel** 01 42 34 59 98. Ⓜ St-Sulpice. **Open** 7:30am–7:30pm daily. call 01 43 25 03 10; for tours of the crypt (3:30pm, 2nd & 4th Sun of month), 01 42 34 59 98. Concerts. **W paroisse-saint-sulpice-paris.org**

This imposing church, started in 1646, took more than 100 years to finish. Its simple façade has two tiers of elegant columns and two mismatched towers at the ends. Large windows fill the interior with light. The side chapel to the right has murals by Eugène Delacroix, including *Jacob Wrestling with the Angel (see p126)*.

The Classical two-storey west front of St-Sulpice with its two towers

Carpeaux's fountain sculpture

⓰ Fontaine de l'Observatoire

Pl Ernest Denis, av de l'Observatoire 75006. **Map** 12 E2. RER Port Royal.

Situated at the southern tip of the Jardin du Luxembourg, this is one of the finest fountains in Paris. The central sculpture, by Jean-Baptiste Carpeaux, was erected in 1873. Made of bronze, it has four women holding aloft a globe representing four continents – the fifth, Oceania, was left out for reasons of symmetry. There are some subsidiary figures, including dolphins, horses and a turtle.

⓱ Val-de-Grâce

1 pl Alphonse-Laveran 75005. **Map** 12 F2. **Tel** 01 40 51 51 92. Ⓜ Gobelins. RER Port Royal. **Open** 2–6pm Tue–Thu, noon,–6pm Sat & Sun. **Closed** Aug. ✝ 11am Sun. except for nave. **W valdegrace.org**

This is one of the most beautiful churches in France, and forms part of a military hospital complex. Built for Anne of Austria (wife of Louis XIII) in gratitude for the birth of her son, young Louis XIV himself laid the first stone in 1645.

The church is noted for its dome. In the cupola is Pierre Mignard's enormous fresco, with over 200 triple-life-size figures. The six huge marble columns framing the altar are similar to ones in St Peter's in Rome.

FURTHER AFIELD

Many of Paris's famous sights are slightly out of the city centre. Montmartre, long a mecca for artists and writers, still retains much of its bohemian atmosphere, and Montparnasse is full of bustling cafés and theatre crowds. The famous Cimetière du Père Lachaise numbers Chopin, Oscar Wilde and Jim Morrison among its dead and, along with the parks and gardens, provides a tranquil escape from sightseeing. Modern architecture can be seen at Fondation Louis Vuitton, Fondation Le Corbusier and La Défense, and there is a huge selection of museums to visit. To the northeast, the science museum at La Villette provides an educational family day out.

Sights at a Glance

Museums and Galleries

3 Fondation Louis Vuitton
6 Musée Marmottan Monet
9 Musée Gustave Moreau
16 *Cité des Sciences et de l'Industrie pp140–41*
21 Cité Nationale de l'Histoire de l'Immigration
25 Musée National d'Histoire Naturelle

Churches and Mosques

7 St-Alexandre-Nevsky
11 Sacré-Coeur
28 Grande Mosquée de Paris

Parks and Gardens

2 Bois de Boulogne
8 Parc Monceau
18 Parc des Buttes-Chaumont
24 Parc Montsouris
26 Jardin des Plantes
29 Parc André Citroën

Cemeteries

13 Cimetière de Montmartre
19 Cimetière du Père-Lachaise
31 Cimetière du Montparnasse

Historic Districts

10 *Montmartre pp136–7*
17 Canal St-Martin
30 Montparnasse

Historic Buildings and Streets

5 Rue La Fontaine
12 Moulin Rouge
22 Château de Vincennes
32 Catacombes

Modern Architecture

1 La Défense
4 Fondation Le Corbusier
20 Bercy
23 Bibliothèque Nationale de France
27 Institut du Monde Arabe

Markets

14 Marché aux Puces de St-Ouen

Key

Main sightseeing area
Motorway
Main road
Other road
Railway

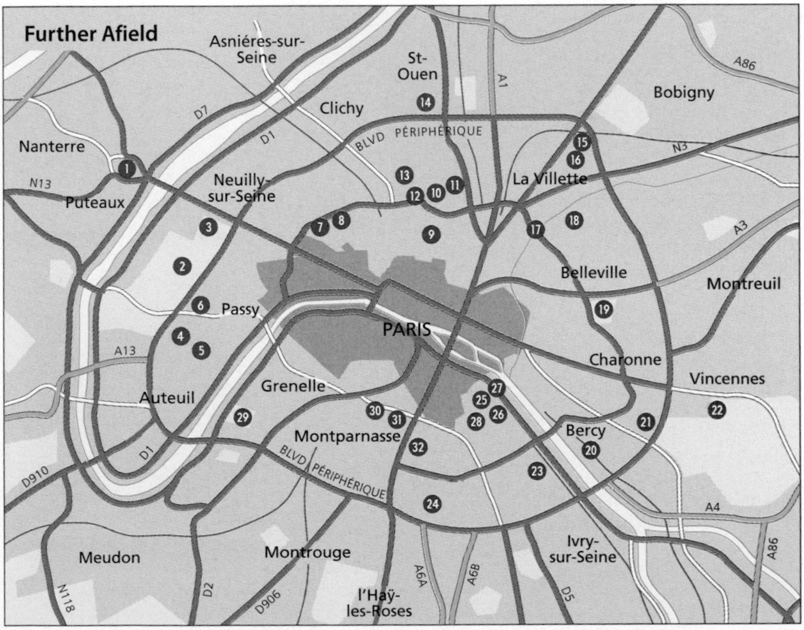

0 kilometres 4
0 miles 2

◀ La Grande Arche at La Défense

West of the City

❶ La Défense

La Grande Arche. **Tel** 01 49 07 27 55. RER La Défense. **Open** 10am–7pm daily (to 8pm Apr–Aug). Rooftop: **Closed** for renovation; phone for information. **w grandearche.com**

This skyscraper business city on the western edge of Paris is the largest office development in Europe. La Grande Arche is an enormous hollow cube large enough to contain Notre-Dame cathedral. Designed by Danish architect Otto von Spreckelsen in the late 1980s, the arch houses a gallery, conference centre, computer museum and video-game museum and has superb views.

La Grande Arche in La Défense

❷ Bois de Boulogne

75016. M Porte Maillot, Porte Dauphine, Porte d'Auteuil, Sablons. **Open** 24 hrs daily. to specialist gardens and museum.

The 8.5-sq-km (3.3-sq-mile) Bois de Boulogne, located between the western edges of Paris and the River Seine, offers a vast belt of greenery for strolling, cycling, riding, boating, picnicking or spending a day at the races. The Bois de Boulogne was once part of the immense Forêt du Rouvre. In the mid-19th century Napoleon III had the Bois designed and landscaped by Baron Haussmann, along the lines of Hyde Park in London. Several self-contained parks within the forest include the Jardin d'Acclimatation, a fun park for children, Pré Catalan and the Bagatelle gardens, with architectural follies and an 18th-century villa famous for its rose garden. The villa was built in just 64 days after a bet between the Comte d'Artois and Marie Antoinette.

By day the Bois is busy with families, joggers and walkers, but after dark it is notoriously seedy – and best avoided.

Rose garden in the Bois de Boulogne

❸ Fondation Louis Vuitton

8 av du Mahatma Gandhi, Bois de Boulogne, 75116. **Open** hours vary according to exhibitions. **w fondationlouisvuitton.fr**

Located close to the Jardin d'Acclimatation in the Bois de Boulogne, Frank Gehry's dramatic glass structure consisting of twelve glass "sails" is a thrilling example of modern architecture. It contains a gallery and event space hosting contemporary art exhibitions and events. A shuttle to the arts centre leaves Place Charles de Gaulle every 15 minutes.

❹ Fondation Le Corbusier

8–10 sq du Docteur-Blanche 75016. Villa La Roche: **Tel** 01 42 88 75 72. M Jasmin. **Open** 1:30–6pm Mon, 10am–6pm Tue–Sat. **Closed** public hols. in English 2pm Tue (and Fri during summer). Films, videos. Maison Jeanneret: **Tel** 01 42 88 41 53. **w fondationlecorbusier.fr**

In a quiet corner of Auteuil stand the villas La Roche and Jeanneret, the first two Parisian houses built by the influential 20th-century architect Charles-Edouard Jeanneret, better known as Le Corbusier. Built at the start of the 1920s, they demonstrate his revolutionary use of white concrete in Cubist forms. Rooms flow into each other, allowing maximum light and volume, and the houses stand on stilts with windows along their entire length.

Today, the villas hold lectures on Le Corbusier and his work.

❺ Rue la Fontaine

75016. **Map** 5 A4. M Michel-Ange-Auteuil, Jasmin. RER Radio-France.

Rue la Fontaine and the surrounding streets act as a showcase for some of the most exciting early 20th-century Art Nouveau architecture, featuring sinuous decorative detail. At No. 14 stands the Castel

An Art Nouveau window in rue la Fontaine

For hotels and restaurants in this region see pp554–5 and pp576–9

Béranger, a stunning apartment block made from cheap building materials to keep costs low, yet featuring stained glass, convoluted ironwork, balconies and mosaics. It established the reputation of architect Hector Guimard, who went on to design the city's Art Nouveau Métro entrances. Other examples of his work can be seen further along the street, such as the Hôtel Mezzara at No. 60.

6 Musée Marmottan Monet

2 rue Louis Boilly 75016. **Tel** 01 44 96 50 33. M Muette. **Open** 10am–6pm Tue–Sun (to 9pm Thu). **Closed** 1 Jan, 1 May, 25 Dec.
marmottan.fr

This museum was created in the 19th-century mansion of the famous art historian Paul Marmottan, in 1932. He bequeathed his house, plus his Renaissance, Consular and First Empire paintings and furniture, to the Institut de France.

In 1966 the museum acquired a fabulous collection of work by Impressionist painter Claude Monet, the bequest of his son, Michel. Some of Monet's most famous paintings are here, including *Impression – Sunrise* (hence the term "Impressionist"), a painting of Rouen Cathedral *(see p271)*, and the *Waterlilies* series *(see p102)*. Also here is the work painted at Giverny during the last years of Monet's life. This includes *The Japanese Bridge* and *The Weeping Willow*. The iridescent colours and daring brushstrokes make these some of the museum's most powerful works.

Part of Monet's personal art collection was passed on to the museum, including work by fellow Impressionists Camille Pissarro, Pierre-Auguste Renoir, Edgar Degas, Paul Gauguin and Alfred Sisley. The museum also displays medieval illuminated manuscripts and 16th-century Burgundian tapestries. Piano and chamber music concerts are held here on occasion.

Colonnade beside the *naumachia* basin in Parc Monceau

North of the City

St-Alexandre-Nevsky Cathedral

7 St-Alexandre-Nevsky

12 rue Daru 75008. **Map** 2 F3. **Tel** 01 42 27 37 34. M Courcelles, Ternes. **Open** 3–5pm Tue, Fri, Sun. by appt, call 03 86 91 97 88. 6pm Sat, 10:30am Sun.

This imposing Russian Orthodox cathedral with its five golden-copper domes signals the presence of a large Russian community in Paris. Designed by members of the St Petersburg Fine Arts Academy and financed jointly by Tsar Alexander II and the local Russian community, it was completed in 1861.

Inside, a wall of icons divides the church in two. The Greek-cross plan and the rich mosaics and frescoes decorating the interior are Neo-Byzantine, while the exterior and gilt domes are traditional Russian Orthodox.

8 Parc Monceau

Bd de Courcelles 75017. **Map** 3 A3. **Tel** 01 42 27 08 64. M Monceau. **Open** 7am–8pm daily (10pm summer). by appt.

This green haven dates back to 1778, when the Duc de Chartres commissioned the painter-writer and amateur landscape designer Louis Carmontelle to create a magnificent garden. The result was an exotic landscape full of architectural follies in the English and German style.

In 1852 the garden became a chic public park. A few original features remain, among them the *naumachia* basin – an ornamental version of a Roman pool that was used for simulating naval battles.

9 Musée Gustave Moreau

14 rue de la Rochefoucauld 75009. **Map** 4 E3. **Tel** 01 48 74 38 50. M Trinité. **Open** 10am–5:15pm Wed–Mon. **Closed** 12:45–2pm Mon, Wed & Thu.
musee-moreau.fr

The Symbolist painter Gustave Moreau (1826–98), known for his symbolic works depicting biblical and mythological fantasies, lived and worked in this handsome town house. *Jupiter and Semele*, one of the artist's outstanding works, is displayed here, along with other major paintings, and some of the collection's 7,000 drawings and 1,000 oils and watercolours.

⑩ Montmartre

The steep *butte* (hill) of Montmartre has been associated with artists for 200 years. Théodore Géricault and Camille Corot came here at the start of the 19th century, and in the 20th century Maurice Utrillo immortalized the streets in his works. Today, street artists thrive predominantly on the tourist trade, but much of the area still preserves its rather louche, villagey prewar atmosphere. The name of the area is ascribed to martyrs who were tortured and killed in the area around AD 250, hence *mons martyrium.*

Clos Montmartre
This is one of the last Parisian vineyards. The harvest is celebrated on the first Saturday in October.

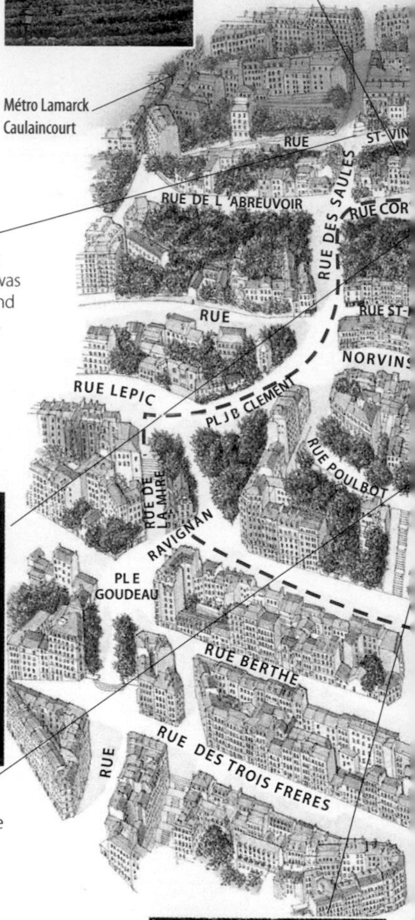

Métro Lamarck Caulaincourt

Au Lapin Agile
"The Agile Rabbit" is a famous cabaret that was popular with artists and poets such as Picasso, Renoir, Apollinaire and Paul Verlaine.

Musée de Montmartre
Changing Montmartre-related exhibitions usually include works by artists who lived here, such as this *Portrait of a Woman* (1918) by Amedeo Modigliani.

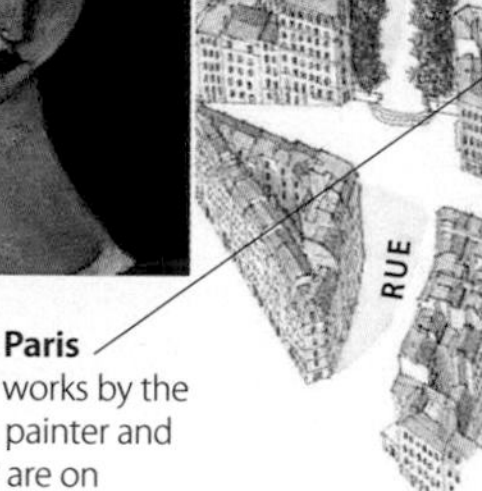

Espace Dalí Paris
Some 330 works by the Surrealist painter and sculptor are on display here.

Place du Tertre
The tourist centre of Montmartre is full of portraitists. Artists first exhibited in the square in the 19th century.

Key

— Suggested route

0 metres 100
0 yards 100

La Mère Catherine
This was a favourite French restaurant of Russian cossacks. They would shout "Bistro!" (meaning "quick") – which gave the bistro its name.

Locator Map
See Street Finder map 4

⓫ Sacré-Coeur
This Neo-Romanesque church, started in the 1870s and completed in 1914, contains many treasures, such as this figure of the *Virgin Mary and Child* (1896) by P Brunet.

St-Pierre de Montmartre
This is an early Parisian church with origins dating back to the 6th century.

The *funiculaire*, or cable railway, at the end of rue Foyatier takes you to the foot of the basilica of the Sacré-Coeur. Métro tickets are valid for it.

Square Willette lies below the forecourt of the Sacré-Coeur. It is laid out on the side of the hill in a series of descending terraces with lawns, shrubs, trees and flowerbeds.

Musée de la Halle Saint Pierre
Exhibitions here showcase Outsider Art and Art Brut, such as this piece by S Feleggakis.

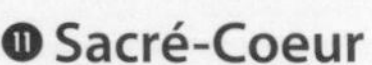

⓫ Sacré-Coeur

33–35 rue du Chevalier-de-la-Barre 75018. **Map** 4 F1. **Tel** 01 53 41 89 00. M Abbesses (then *funiculaire* to steps of Sacré-Coeur), Anvers, Jules Joffrin, Pigalle. 30, 31, 80, 85. Basilica: **Open** 6am–10:30pm daily. Dome: **Open** 9am–6pm daily. 3–4 times a day (call for hours). Vespers 4pm Sun. W **sacre-coeur-montmartre.com**

The Sacré-Coeur basilica, dedicated to the Sacred Heart of Christ and consecrated in 1919, was built as a result of a private religious vow made at the outbreak of the Franco-Prussian war. Two Catholic businessmen, Alexandre Legentil and Hubert Rohault de Fleury, promised to finance the basilica should France be spared from assault. Despite the war and the Siege of Paris, invasion was averted and work began in 1875 to Paul Abadie's designs. Never considered very graceful, the basilica is vast and impressive, and one of France's most important Roman Catholic buildings.

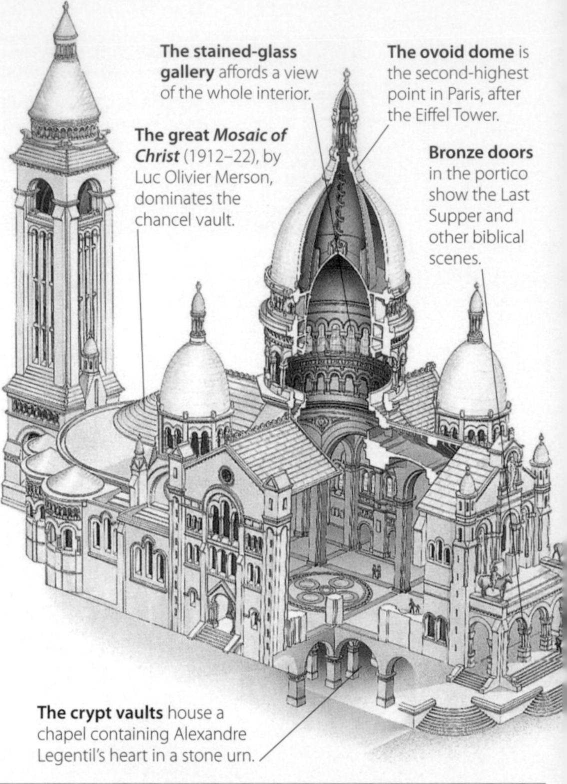

The stained-glass gallery affords a view of the whole interior.
The ovoid dome is the second-highest point in Paris, after the Eiffel Tower.
The great *Mosaic of Christ* (1912–22), by Luc Olivier Merson, dominates the chancel vault.
Bronze doors in the portico show the Last Supper and other biblical scenes.
The crypt vaults house a chapel containing Alexandre Legentil's heart in a stone urn.

⓬ Moulin Rouge

82 bd de Clichy 75018. **Map** 4 E1. **Tel** 01 53 09 82 82. M Blanche. Dinner: 7pm. Shows: 9pm & 11pm daily. W **moulinrouge.com**

Built in 1885, the Moulin Rouge was turned into a dance hall as early as 1900. Henri de Toulouse-Lautrec immortalized the wild and colourful cancan shows here in his posters and drawings of famous dancers such as Jane Avril. The high-kicking routines continue today in glitzy, Las-Vegas-style revues.

⓭ Cimetière de Montmartre

20 av Rachel 75018. **Map** 4 D1. **Tel** 01 53 42 36 30. M Place de Clichy. **Open** 8am–6pm Mon–Fri (from 8:30am Sat, from 9am Sun).

This has been the resting place for many luminaries of the creative arts since the beginning of the 19th century. The composers Hector Berlioz and Jacques Offenbach (who wrote the renowned cancan tune), Russian dancer Vaslav Nijinsky and film director François Truffaut are just a few of the famous people who have been buried here over the years.

There is also a Montmartre cemetery near square Roland-Dorgelès, known as the St-Vincent cemetery. This is where the French painter Maurice Utrillo is buried.

African stall in the Marché aux Puces de St-Ouen

⓮ Marché aux Puces de St-Ouen

Rue des Rosiers, St-Ouen 93406. M Porte-de-Clignancourt, Garibaldi. **Open** 9am–6pm Sat, 10am–6pm Sun, 10am–5pm Mon (reduced hours in summer). *See Markets p153.* W **marcheauxpuces-saintouen.com**

The oldest and largest Paris flea market spans 6 ha (15 acres) near the Porte de Clignancourt. In the 19th century, rag merchants and tramps would gather outside the fortifications that marked the city limits and offer their wares for sale. Today the area is divided into separate markets, and is well-known for its heavy Second Empire furniture and ornaments.

⓯ Parc de la Villette

211 av Jean Jaurés, 75109. **Tel** 01 40 03 75 75. **Open** daily. M Porte de la Villette, Porte de Pantin.

Straddling the canal in the city's northeast corner, this park houses the Cité des Sciences et de l'Industrie, as well as a popular children's outdoor playground. It's also home to Jean Nouvel's Philharmonie de Paris, a shimmering modern concert hall inaugurated in 2015.

⑯ Cité des Sciences et de l'Industrie

See pp140–41.

⑰ Canal St-Martin

Ⓜ Jaurès, J Bonsergent, Goncourt.

A walk along the quays on either side of the Canal St-Martin gives a glimpse of how this thriving, industrial, working-class area of the city looked at the end of the 19th century. The 5-km (3-mile) canal, opened in 1825, provided a shortcut for river traffic between loops of the Seine. A smattering of brick-and-iron factories and warehouses survive from this time along quai de Jemmapes. Here, too, is the legendary Hôtel du Nord, from Marcel Carné's 1930s film of the same name. Around it are tree-lined quays with quirky shops and cafés, iron footbridges and public gardens. At Jaurès, it meets the Canal de l'Ourcq, which offers a pleasant stroll to Parc de la Villette *(see p140)*.

⑱ Parc des Buttes-Chaumont

Pl Armand Carrel 75019. No phone. Ⓜ Botzaris, Buttes-Chaumont. **Open** May–Sep: 7am–10pm daily; Oct–Apr: 7am–8pm daily.

Urban planner Baron Haussmann converted the hilly site from a rubbish dump and quarry with gallows at the foot, to English-style gardens in the 1860s. His colleague was landscape architect Adolphe Alphand, who was responsible for a vast 1860s programme to provide new pavement-lined Parisian avenues *(see p112)* with benches, street-lights, kiosks and urinals.

Others involved in the creation of this highly praised park were the engineer Darcel and the landscape gardener Barillet-Deschamps. They created a lake, made an island with real and artificial rocks, gave it a Roman-style temple, and added a waterfall, streams and footbridges leading to the island. Today, in summer, visitors will also find donkey rides and a puppet (*guignol*) theatre for the kids, and beautiful lawns.

Boats moored at Port de l'Arsenal

East of the City

⑲ Cimetière du Père-Lachaise

16 rue du Repos 75020. **Tel** 01 55 25 82 10. Ⓜ Père Lachaise, A Dumas. 🚌 60, 69, 102 to pl Gambetta. 🅿 Pl Gambetta. **Open** 8am–5:30pm daily (to 6pm Apr–Nov; from 8:30am Sat, from 9am Sun & hols).

Paris's most prestigious cemetery is set on a wooded hill overlooking the city. The land was once owned by Père de la Chaise, Louis XIV's confessor, but it was bought by order of Napoleon in 1803. The cemetery became so popular that the boundaries were extended six times in the 19th century. Here are buried celebrities such as writer Honoré de Balzac and composer Frédéric Chopin, singer Jim Morrison and actors Yves Montand and Simone Signoret.

⑳ Bercy

75012. Ⓜ Bercy, Cour St-Emilion. 🚌 24, 64, 87. Cinémathèque Française: 51 rue de Bercy. **Tel** 01 71 19 33 33. Museum: **Open** noon–7pm Wed–Mon (Library: till 8pm).

This former wine-trading quarter just east of the city centre, with its riverside warehouses and pavilions, has been transformed into an ultra modern district. An automatic Métro line (Line 14) links it to the heart of the city.

The centrepiece is the AccorHotels Arena, which is the city centre's principal concert venue, as well as its premier sports stadium. The vast pyramidal structure, its sides clad with real lawns, has become a landmark for the eastern part of central Paris.

Other architecturally adventurous buildings dominate the skyline, notably Chemetov's Ministry of Finance building, and Frank Gehry's American Center, which houses the **Cinémathèque Française**, a cinema museum with film screenings, a library and retrospectives on directors.

At the foot of these structures, the Parc de Bercy provides a welcome green space.

Cinématique Française (former American Center), designed by Frank Gehry, Bercy

⑯ Cité des Sciences et de l'Industrie

This hugely popular science and technology museum occupies the largest of the old Villette slaughterhouses, which now form part of a massive urban park. Architect Adrien Fainsilber has created an imaginative interplay of light, vegetation and water in the high-tech, five-storey building, which soars 40 m (133 ft) high. At the museum's heart is the Explora exhibit, a fascinating guide to the worlds of science and technology. Visitors can take part in computerized games on space, the earth and ocean, computers and sound. On other levels there are a children's science city, cinemas, a science newsroom, a library and shops.

Planetarium
In this 260-seat auditorium you can watch eclipses and fly over Martian landscapes, thanks to their 3-D video system.

Le Nautile
This full-scale model of the *Nautile*, France's technologically advanced exploration submarine, represents one of the most sophisticated machines in the world.

KEY

① **The moat** was designed by Fainsilber, so that natural light could penetrate into the lower levels of the building.

② **The main hall** is vast, with a soaring network of shafts, bridges, escalators and balconies, and has a cathedral-like atmosphere.

③ **The greenhouse** is a square hothouse, 32 m (105 ft) high and wide.

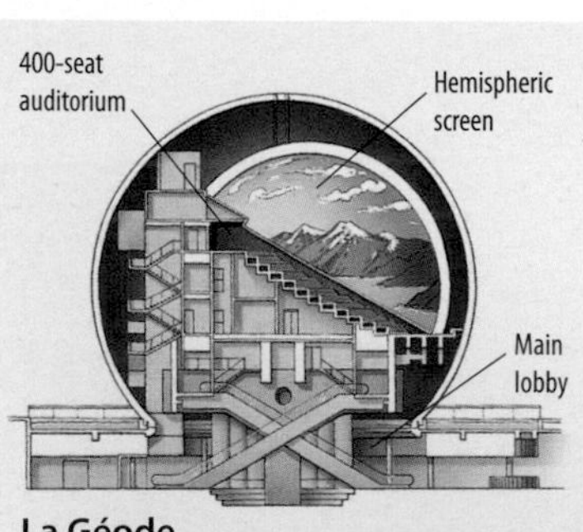

La Géode

This giant entertainment sphere houses a huge hemispherical cinema screen, 1,000 sq m (11,000 sq ft), showing IMAX films on nature, travel, history and space.

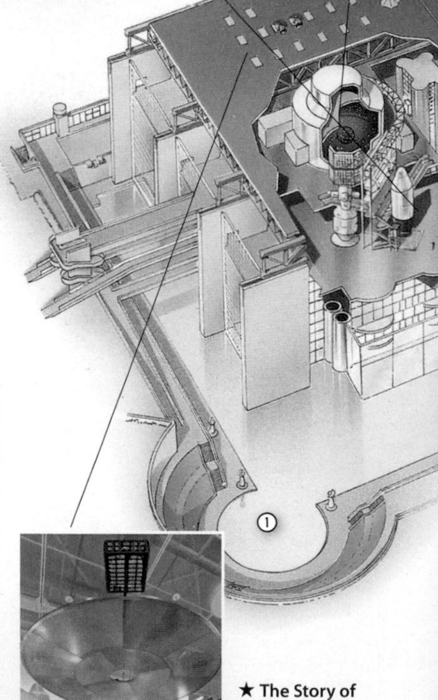

★ The Story of the Universe
An exploration of the birth of the universe, this exhibit takes you back 13.7 billion years to the creation of the first atom.

For hotels and restaurants in this region see pp554–5 and pp576–9

Cupolas
The two glazed domes, 17 m (56 ft) in diameter, filter the flow of natural light into the main hall.

VISITORS' CHECKLIST

Practical Information
30 av Corentin-Cariou 75019.
Tel 01 40 05 80 00. **Open** 10am–6pm Tue–Sun (to 7pm Sun).
Closed 1 Jan, 1 May, 25 Dec. Shows, films, videos, library, conference centre. **cite-sciences.fr**

Transport
M Porte de la Villette. 139, 150, 152, 249, 375, PC2.

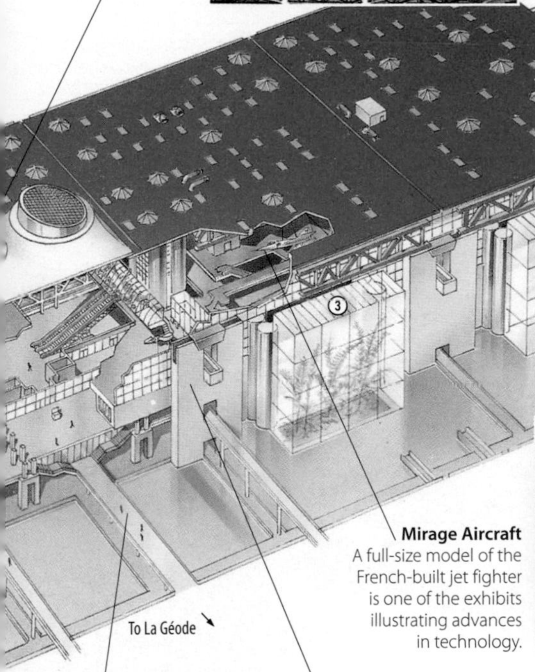

3

To La Géode

Mirage Aircraft
A full-size model of the French-built jet fighter is one of the exhibits illustrating advances in technology.

Walkways
The walkways cross the encircling moat to link the various floors of the museum to the Géode and the park.

★ Children's City
In this lively, extensive area, children can experiment and play with machines that show how scientific principles work.

Bibliothèque Nationale de France

㉑ Cité Nationale de l'Histoire de l'Immigration

293 av Daumesnil 75012. **Tel** 01 53 59 58 60. Ⓜ Porte Dorée. **Open** 10am–5:30pm Tue–Fri (7pm Sat & Sun). **Closed** 1 Jan, 1 May, 14 Jul, 25 Dec. restricted. **histoire-immigration.fr**

Housed in the Palais de la Porte Dorée, this museum is devoted to immigration in France. The palace is an Art Deco building designed by Albert Laprade and Léon Jaussely for the city's grand colonial exhibition in 1931.

The cellar also contains tropical fish collections, along with tortoises and crocodiles.

㉒ Château de Vincennes

Av de Paris 94300 Vincennes. **Tel** 01 48 08 31 20. Ⓜ Château de Vincennes. RER Vincennes. **Open** 10am–5pm daily (6pm mid-May–Sep). **Closed** 1 Jan, 1 May, 1 & 11 Nov, 25 Dec. Chapel & donjon: **Tel** 01 40 74 19 12. **chateau-vincennes.fr**

The Château de Vincennes was the permanent royal residence until the 17th century, before the court moved to Versailles. The donjon, the tallest fortified medieval building in Europe, the Gothic chapel, 17th-century pavilions and moat are all worth seeing.

Beyond lies the Bois de Vincennes. Once a royal hunting ground, it is now a landscaped forest with ornamental lakes and a racecourse.

㉓ Bibliothèque Nationale de France

Quai François-Mauriac 75013. **Tel** 01 53 79 59 59. Ⓜ Bibliothèque François-Mitterrand. **Open** 10am–8pm Tue–Sat, 1–7pm Sun. **Closed** public hols, 1 week Sep. **bnf.fr**

These four great book-shaped towers house 10 million volumes. The libraries offer more than 400,000 titles. Other resources include digitized illustrations and sound archives. There are also frequent temporary exhibitions.

South of the City

㉔ Parc Montsouris

2 rue Gazan, bd Jourdan 75014. **Tel** 01 40 71 75 60. Ⓜ Pte d'Orléans. RER Cité Universitaire, Glacière. **Open** 9am–9:30pm (to 5:30pm in winter) daily, but times vary, so call ahead.

This English-style park, the second largest in Paris, was laid out by Adolphe Alphand from 1865 to 1878. Its restaurant, lawns and lake – home to a variety of birds – are enduringly popular.

Skull of the reptile dimetrodon

㉕ Musée National d'Histoire Naturelle

36 rue Geoffroy Saint-Hilaire 75006. **Map** 13 C2. **Tel** 01 40 79 54 79/56. Ⓜ Jussieu, Austerlitz. **Open** 10am–6pm Wed–Mon. **Closed** 1 May. Library. **mnhn.fr**

The highlight of the museum is the Grande Galerie de l'Evolution. There are also four other departments: palaeontology, featuring skeletons, casts of various animals and an exhibition showing the evolution of the vertebrate skeleton; palaeobotany, devoted to plant fossils; mineralogy, including gemstones; and entomology, with some of the oldest fossilized insects on earth. The bookstore is in the house that was occupied by the naturalist Buffon, from 1772 until his death in 1788.

㉖ Jardin des Plantes

57 rue Cuvier 75005. **Map** 13 C1. **Tel** 01 40 79 56 01 or 01 40 79 54 79. Ⓜ Jussieu, Austerlitz. **Open** 7:30am–8pm daily (8am–5:30pm winter). **jardindesplantes.net** Parc Zoologique: av Daumesnil & rt de la Ceinture du Lac. **Tel** 08 11 22 41 22. **Open** daily. **parczoologiquedeparis.fr**

The botanical gardens were established in 1626, when Jean Hérouard and Guy de la Brosse, Louis XIII's physicians, founded a royal medicinal herb garden. A school of botany, natural history and pharmacy followed. The garden, which opened to the public in 1640, houses a natural history museum, botanical school and zoo.

As well as vistas and walkways flanked by ancient statues, the park has an alpine garden with plants from Corsica, Morocco, the Alps and the Himalayas, and an unrivalled display of herbaceous and wild plants. The Cedar of Lebanon here, originally from Britain's Kew Gardens, was the first to be planted in France.

Rue Mouffetard, one of several markets near the Jardin des Plantes

For hotels and restaurants in this region see pp554–5 and pp576–9

㉗ Institut du Monde Arabe

1 rue des Fossés St-Bernard, pl Mohammed V 75005. **Map** 9 C5. **Tel** 01 40 51 38 38. Ⓜ Jussieu, Cardinal-Lemoine. Museum & temp exhibs: **Open** 10am–6pm Tue–Sun (to 7pm Sat & Sun). **Closed** 1 May. **W imarabe.org**

This magnificent contemporary building was designed by French architect Jean Nouvel, and cleverly combines high-tech details with the spirit of traditional Arab architecture. From the fourth to seventh floors there is a comprehensive display of Islamic art from the 9th to 19th centuries, including glassware, ceramics and sculpture. The museum's highlight is its collection of astrolabes, the much-prized tool used by ancient Arab astronomers.

㉘ Grande Mosquée de Paris

2 bis pl du Puits de l'Ermite 75005. **Tel** 01 45 35 97 33. Ⓜ Place Monge. **Open** 9am–noon, 2–6pm Sat–Thu (till 7pm in summer). **Closed** Muslim hols. Library. **W mosqueedeparis.net**

Built in the 1920s in the Hispano-Moorish style, these buildings are the centre for Paris's Muslim community. Once used solely by scholars, the mosque has expanded over the years and now houses some rather salubrious but fun Turkish baths, a fine restaurant and a beautiful *salon de thé*.

Tour Montparnasse

Institut du Monde Arabe, covered with photosensitive lightscreens

㉙ Parc André Citroën

2 rue Cauchy, Quai André Citroën 75015. **Tel** 01 40 71 75 60. Ⓜ Balard. **Open** May–Sep: 8am–8:30 pm daily; Oct–Apr: 8am–7pm daily (from 9am Sat & Sun).

This park, built on the site of a former automobile manufacturing plant, is a fascinating blend of styles, ranging from wild-flower meadow in the north to monochrome mineral and sculpture gardens in the southern section. Modern water sculptures dot the park, and there is also a chance to take a hot-air balloon ride.

㉚ Montparnasse

75014 & 75015. **Map** 11 & 12. Ⓜ Montparnasse, Vavin, Raspail, Edgar Quinet. Tour Montparnasse: 33 av du Maine. **Tel** 01 45 38 52 56. **Open** Apr–Sep: 9:30am–11:30pm; Oct–Mar: 9:30am–10:30pm (to 11pm Fri, Sat & hols). **W tourmontparnasse56.com**

The name Montparnasse was first used ironically, when 17th-century arts students performed on a "mount" of rubble left over from quarrying. In ancient Greece, Mount Parnassus was dedicated to poetry and music. By the 19th century, crowds were drawn to the local cabarets and bars by duty-free prices. The mixture of art and high living was especially potent in the 1920s and 1930s, when Hemingway, Picasso, Cocteau, Giacometti, Matisse and Modigliani were residents here. The modern *quartier* is dominated by the much-hated **Tour Montparnasse**, although the view from the top (the 56th floor) is spectacular.

㉛ Cimetière du Montparnasse

3 bd Edgar Quinet 75014. **Map** 12 D3. **Tel** 01 44 10 86 50. Ⓜ Edgar Quinet. **Open** mid-Mar–Nov: 8am–6pm Mon–Fri, 8:30am–6pm Sat, 9am–6pm Sun; Dec–mid-Mar: closes 5:30pm. 01 40 33 85 85

Montparnasse cemetery opened in 1824. Among those buried here are Serge Gainsbourg, Charles Baudelaire, Jean-Paul Sartre and Simone de Beauvoir, and Guy de Maupassant.

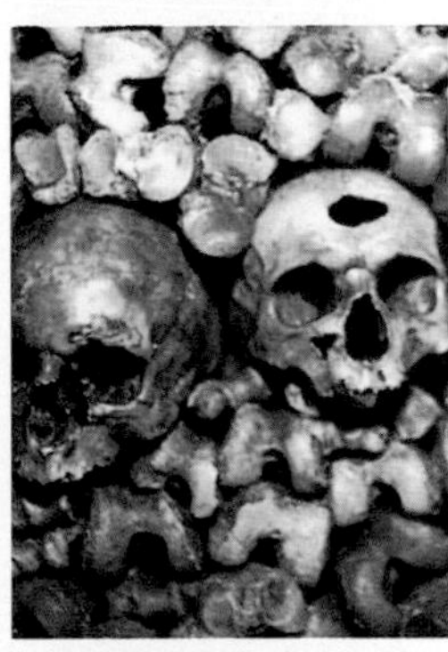

Skulls and bones stored in the Catacombes

㉜ Catacombes

1 av du Colonel Henri Rol-Tanguy 75014. **Map** 12 E4. **Tel** 01 43 22 47 63. Ⓜ Denfert-Rochereau. **Open** 10am–8:30pm Tue–Sun (ticket office closes 7:30pm). **Closed** public hols. **W catacombes.paris.fr**

A long series of quarry tunnels built in the 13th century, the catacombs are lined with ancient bones and skulls. Thousands of rotting corpses were transported here in the 1780s to absorb the excess from the insanitary Les Halles cemetery.

SHOPS AND MARKETS

For many people, Paris epitomizes luxury and good living. Exquisitely dressed men and women sip wine by the banks of the Seine against the backdrop of splendid French architecture, or browse at small specialist shops. The least expensive way of joining the chic set is to create French style with accessories or costume jewellery. Alternatively, try shopping in the January or July sales. If your budget allows, take the opportunity to buy world-famous Paris fashions, or feast on the wonderful gourmet delicacies displayed with consummate artistry. Parisian shopping streets and markets are the ideal place to indulge in the French custom of strolling for the express purpose of seeing and being seen. For up-to-the-minute high fashion, rue du Faubourg-St-Honoré, with its exquisite couture window displays, is hard to beat. Browsing around the bookstalls along the Seine is another favourite French pastime. A survey of some of the best and most famous places to shop follows.

Shopping on avenue Montaigne

Opening Hours

Shops are usually open from 10am to 7pm, Monday to Saturday, but hours can vary. Many department stores stay open late on Thursdays, while boutiques may shut for an hour or two at midday. Markets and local neighbourhood shops usually close on Mondays. Large department stores, supermarkets and many shops in the main shopping areas are open on Sundays. Some places shut for the summer, usually in August.

Payment and VAT

Cash is readily available from the ATMs in most banks, which accept both credit and bank debit cards. Visa and MasterCard are the most widely accepted credit cards.

A sales tax (TVA) from 5.5 to 20 per cent is imposed on most goods and services in EU countries. Non-EU residents shopping in France are entitled to a refund of this if they spend a minimum of €175 in one shop in one day. You must have been resident in France for less than six months and either carry the goods with you out of the country within three months of purchase, or get the shop to forward them to you. Larger shops will generally supply a form *(bordereau de détaxe* or *bordereau de vente)* and help you to fill it in. When you leave France or the EU you present the form to Customs, who either permit you to be reimbursed straight away, or forward your claim to the place where you purchased the merchandise; the shop eventually sends you a refund.

The Chanel logo, recognized worldwide

Sales

The main sales *(soldes)* are held in January and July, although more and more you can find good deals throughout the year. If you see goods labelled *Stock*, it means that they are stock items that have been reduced for clearance. *Dégriffé* means designer labels, (with the label cut out) marked down, frequently from the previous year's collections. *Fripes* indicates that the clothes are second-hand.

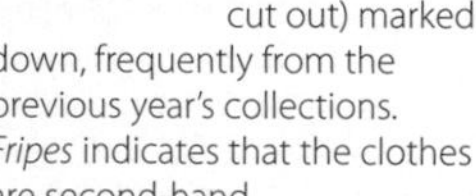

The Centre of Paris Couture

The couture houses are concentrated on the Right Bank, around rue du Faubourg-St-Honoré and avenue Montaigne.

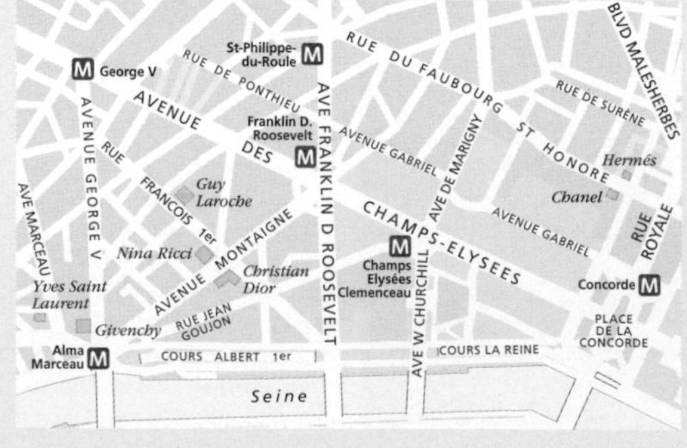

Department Stores

Much of the pleasure of shopping in Paris is derived from going to the small specialist shops. But if time is short, try the *grands magasins* (department stores) or the mall at **Beaugrenelle**, which offers a wide range of shops at all price levels, including a FNAC and a Marks & Spencer, plus a cinema and a restaurant court. Some stores still operate a ticket system for selling goods. The shop assistant writes up a ticket for goods from their own boutique. You take the ticket to one of the cashiers, and then return with the validated ticket to pick up your purchase. This can be time-consuming, so go early in the morning and don't shop on Saturdays, unless you enjoy a crush. The French do not pay much attention to queues, so be assertive! One peculiarity of a visit is that the security guards may ask to inspect your bags as you leave. These are random checks and should not be taken as an implication of theft.

All department stores have places to eat, although the stores themselves tend to have different emphases. **Au Printemps** is noted for its exciting and innovative household goods section, vast cosmetic range and large menswear store. The clothes departments for women and children are well-stocked. Fashion shows are held at 10am on Tuesdays (and each Friday from April to October: by invitation only). The lovely domed restaurant in the cupola often hosts chic after-hours parties, which are private, but a visit to the restaurant during shopping hours is worthwhile.

Kenzo designerwear in place des Victoires

The 1865 façade of Au Printemps department store

BHV (Le Bazar de l'Hôtel de Ville) is a DIY enthusiast's paradise, and sells a host of other items, such as fashion decor. The Left Bank's **Le Bon Marché** was Paris's first department store and today is its chicest. The designer clothing sections are well sourced, the high-end accessories are excellent and the own-brand linen has a good quality-to-price ratio. The prepared food and gourmet grocery sections serve restaurant-quality fare to take away.

Galeries Lafayette is perhaps the best-known department store and has a wide range of clothes available at all price levels. Its first-floor trends section plays host to lots of innovative designers. Galeries Lafayette Gourmet, the food court, sells a range of French and international delicacies. Across the road is the store's homeware building, which stocks a good selection of kitchenware.

FNAC specializes in CDs, books (foreign editions can be found at Les Halles) and electronic equipment, while **FNAC Beaugrenelle** sells a wide range of the latest technological equipment. **Gibert Joseph** has an impressive selection of books, CDs and DVDs.

DIRECTORY

Department Stores

Au Printemps
64 bd Haussmann 75009.
Map 4 D4.
Tel 01 42 82 50 00.
W printemps.com

Beaugrenelle
12 rue Linois 75015.
Map 5 B5.
Tel 01 53 95 24 00.
W beaugrenelle-paris.com

BHV
52 rue de Rivoli 75004.
Map 9 B3.
Tel 09 77 40 14 00.
W bhv.fr

Le Bon Marché
24 rue de Sèvres 75007.
Map 7 C5.
Tel 01 44 39 80 00.
W lebonmarche.com

FNAC
Forum des Halles, 1/7 rue Pierre Lescot 75001.
Map 9 A2.
Tel 0825 020 020.
W fnac.com

FNAC Beaugrenelle
5 rue Linois 75015.
Map 5 B5.
Tel 0825 020 020.
W fnac.com

Galeries Lafayette
40 bd Haussmann 75009.
Map 4 E4.
Tel 01 42 82 34 56.
W galerieslafayette.com

Gibert Joseph
5 rue Pierre Sarrazin 75006.
Map 8 F5.
Tel 01 44 41 88 88.
W gibertjoseph.com

Clothes and Accessories

For many people Paris is synonymous with fashion, and Parisian style is the ultimate in chic. More than anywhere else in the world, women in Paris seem to be in tune with current trends and when a new season arrives appear, as one, to don the look. Though less trend-conscious generally, Parisian men are aware of style, and mix and match patterns and colours with *élan*. Finding the right clothes at the right price means knowing where to shop. For every luxury boutique on the avenue Montaigne, there are ten young designers' shops waiting to become the next Jean-Paul Gaultier – and hundreds more selling imitations.

Haute Couture

Paris is the home of haute couture. The original couture garments, as opposed to the imitations and adaptations, are one-off creations, designed by one of the nine haute couture houses listed with the Fédération Française de la Couture. The rules for being classified are fairly strict, and many of the top designers are not included. Astronomical prices put haute couture beyond the reach of all but a few immensely deep pockets, but it is still the lifeblood of the fashion industry providing inspiration for the mass market.

Women's Clothes

Most couture houses are found on or near the rue du Faubourg St-Honoré and avenue Montaigne: **Christian Dior**, **Pierre Cardin**, **Chanel**, **Christian Lacroix**, **Versace**, **Givenchy**, **Nina Ricci**, **Giorgio Armani** and **Yves Saint Laurent**.

Hermès has classic country chic. **MaxMara**'s Italian elegance is popular in France, and no one can resist a Giorgio Armani suit. The legendary **Prada** store has stuck to the Right Bank, but many fashion houses prefer the Left Bank.

Many designers have a Left Bank branch in addition to their Right Bank bastions, and most have ready-to-wear shops here. For sheer quality there's **Georges Rech**, and **Jil Sander** for exquisite tailoring. Try **Sonia Rykiel** for knitwear, and **Barbara Bui** for soft, feminine clothes. **Comptoir des Cotonniers** and **Anne Fontaine** have branches throughout Paris and stock excellent basics, and **Vanessa Bruno** is extremely popular for feminine flair.

For ready-to-wear, head to Japanese designers **Kenzo** and **Comme des Garçons**, with quirky fashion for both sexes. In nearby rue du Jour, find the timeless elegance of **Agnès B**.

The Marais is a haven for up-and-coming designers. One of the best streets is rue des Rosiers, which includes the wonderful **L'Eclaireur**. Daring designer **Azzedine Alaïa** is just around the corner.

The Bastille area has trendy boutiques, as well as established names, including **Paul and Jo** and high-street stores such as **Petit Bateau**. **Isabel Marant's** boutique is renowned for original designs.

Young designers' creations are found at **Stella Cadente** and **Zadig & Voltaire**.

Children's Clothes

Lots of options for children exist in various styles and many price ranges. Many top designers of adult clothes also have boutiques for children. These include **Kenzo**, Baby Dior and **Agnès B**. Ready-to-wear shops such as **Jacadi** and **Du Pareil au Même** are serviceable and wide ranging, and **Tartine et Chocolat**'s best-selling garments are overalls. **Bonpoint** stocks adorably chic clothing for mini-Parisians. **Petit Bateau** is coveted as much by grown-ups as it is by children. The inevitable has finally happened – children now have their own concept store in **Bonton**.

For little feet, **Froment-Leroyer** probably offers the best all-round classics.

Men's Clothes

Paris has plenty of clothing stores that cater to style-conscious men. On the Right Bank, there's **Giorgio Armani**, **Pierre Cardin** and **Lanvin** (also good for accessories). On the Left Bank, **Yves Saint Laurent** and **Michel Axel** are known for their ties. **Francesco Smalto**'s elegant creations are worn by some of the world's leading movie stars. Yohji Yamamoto's clothes in **Y3 No. 42** are for those who are intent on making a serious fashion statement, while **Gianni Versace** is classic, suave and Italian in style. **Sauver le Monde des Hommes** has stylish shirts, jeans, T-shirts and accessories.

The ultimate in Parisian elegance for men, however, is a suit, custom-made shirt or silk tie from **Charvet**.

Vintage and Second-Hand Stores

The vintage craze hit Paris some time back, and there are some wonderful shops to plunder for a retro look. The best of the bunch is **Didier Ludot**, where an Aladdin's cave of chic haute couture is elegantly displayed. The **Depôt-Vente de Buci-Bourbon** is another good place to bargain-hunt. A cheaper option is to head for one of the second-hand consignment stores. Chic Parisians discard their outfits with the seasons, so it is very easy to pick up some quality items, often in top condition, from places such as **Réciproque** in Passy or **Emmaus Alternatives** in the Marais.

A cheaper option for sample pieces and sale stock can be found at **Le Mouton à Cinq Pattes**.

Jewellery

The couture houses probably stock some of the best jewellery and scarves. **Chanel**'s jewels are classics and those of **Christian Lacroix** are fun. Boutique YSL is a great place for accessories.

Among the main expensive Paris jewellery outlets are **Boucheron**, **Mauboussin** and **Poiray**. They are for the serious jewellery buyer. Other top retailers include **Harry Winston** and **Cartier**. **Dinh Van** has some quirky pieces, while **Mikimoto** is a must for pearls and **H Stern** has some innovative designs using semi-precious and precious stones. For a range of more unusual jewellery and accessories, try the **Swarovski Boutique**, which is owned by the Swarovksi crystal family.

Shoes and Bags

For both classic and wild footwear designs, you can't beat **Miu Miu**. **Rodolphe Ménudier** and **Christian Louboutin** are mainstays for sexy stilettos. **Carel** stocks smart basics and **Jonak** is a must for good imitations of designer footwear.

For ladies' handbags, nothing beats **Chanel** or Dior at the top end of the scale, although **Goyard** comes close. Mid-range bags from **Furla** are a great compromise. Fabric bags from **Jamin Puech** or **Vanessa Bruno** are a feature in every chic Parisian closet. For those with tighter purse strings, cheap, cheerful and stylish bags can be found at **Lollipops**.

Lingerie

For modern lingerie go to **Fifi Chachnil**, whose shop is filled with colourful underwear. **La Boîte à Bas** sells fine French stockings, whereas **Princesse Tam Tam** offers quality items at reasonable prices, and divine designer underwear can be found at cult store **Sabbia Rosa**. The ultimate in Parisian lingerie can be bought off the peg or made to order at **Cadolle**, the store that invented the bra.

DIRECTORY

Women's Clothes

Agnès B.
6 rue du Jour 75001. **Map** 9 A1. **Tel** 01 45 08 56 56. **W agnesb.fr**
One of several branches.

Anne Fontaine
24 rue Boissy d'Anglas 75008. **Map** 3 C5. **Tel** 01 42 68 04 95. **W annefontaine.fr**
One of several branches.

Azzedine Alaïa
7 rue de Moussy 75004. **Map** 9 C3. **Tel** 01 42 72 30 69. **W alaia.fr**

Barbara Bui
62 rue du Faubourg St-Honoré 75008. **Map** 3 B5. **Tel** 01 42 66 05 87. **W barbarabui.com**
One of several branches.

Chanel
51 av Montaigne 75008. **Map** 3 A5. **Tel** 01 44 50 73 00. **W chanel.com**
One of several branches.

Christian Dior
30 av Montaigne 75008. **Map** 6 F1. **Tel** 01 40 73 73 73. **W dior.com**

Christian Lacroix
2–4, Pl St-Sulpice 75006. **Map** 8 E4. **Tel** 01 46 33 48 95. **W christian-lacroix.fr**

Comme des Garçons
54 rue du Faubourg St-Honoré 75008. **Map** 2 E3. **Tel** 01 53 30 27 27.

Comptoir des Cotonniers
12 pl St-Sulpice 75006. **Map** 8 E4. **Tel** 01 46 33 42 37.

L'Eclaireur
40 rue de Sévigné 75003. **Map** 10 D3. **Tel** 01 48 87 10 22. **W leclaireur.com**

Georges Rech
190 blvd St-Germain 75006. **Map** 8 D4. **Tel** 01 45 44 36 26. **W georges-rech.fr**
One of several branches.

Giorgio Armani
2 av Montaigne 75008. **Map** 6 F1. **Tel** 01 56 62 12 16. **W armani.com**

Givenchy
36 av Montaigne 75008. **Map** 6 F1. **Tel** 01 44 43 99 90. **W givenchy.com**

Hermès
24 rue du Faubourg St-Honoré 75008. **Map** 3 C5. **Tel** 01 40 17 46 00. **W hermes.com**
One of several branches.

Isabel Marant
16 rue de Charonne 75011. **Map** 10 F4. **Tel** 01 49 29 71 55. **W isabelmarant.com**

Jil Sander
56 av Montaigne 75008. **Map** 6 F1. **Tel** 01 44 95 06 70. **W jilsander.com**

Kenzo
51 av George V 75008. **Map** 2 E5. **Tel** 01 47 23 33 49. **W kenzo.com**
One of several branches.

MaxMara
31 av Montaigne 75008. **Map** 6 F1. **Tel** 01 47 20 61 13. **W maxmara.com**
One of several branches.

Nina Ricci
39 av Montaigne 75008. **Map** 6 F1. **Tel** 01 83 97 72 12. **W ninaricci.fr**

Paul and Jo
64–66, rue des Saints Pères, 75007. **Map** 8 D4. **Tel** 01 42 22 47 01. **W paulandjoe.com**

Pierre Cardin
59 Faubourg St-Honoré 75008. **Map** 3 B5. **Tel** 01 42 66 92 25. **W pierrecardin.com**

Prada
10 av Montaigne 75008. **Map** 6 F1. **Tel** 01 53 23 99 40. **W prada.com**

Sonia Rykiel
175 bd St-Germain 75006. **Map** 8 D4. **Tel** 01 49 54 60 60. **W soniarykiel.com**
One of several branches.

Stella Cadente
6 rue Alfred Roll 75017. **Map** 2 E1. **Tel** 09 51 26 06 38. **W stella-cadente.com**

Vanessa Bruno
25 rue St-Sulpice 75006. **Map** 8 E5. **Tel** 01 43 54 41 04. **W vanessabruno.com**

Versace
45 av Montaigne 75008. **Map** 3 A5. **Tel** 01 47 42 88 02. **W versace.com**

Yves Saint Laurent
38 rue du Faubourg St-Honoré 75008. **Map** 3 C5. **Tel** 01 42 65 74 59. **W ysl.com**
One of several branches.

Zadig & Voltaire
9 rue du 29 Juillet 75001. **Map** 8 D1. **Tel** 01 42 92 00 61. **W zadig-et-voltaire.com**
One of several branches.

DIRECTORY

Children's Clothes

Bonpoint
320 rue St-Honoré 75001. **Map** 9 A2. **Tel** 01 49 27 94 82. **W** bonpoint.com

Bonton
82 rue de Grenelle 75007. **Map** 6 F3. **Tel** 01 44 39 09 20. **W** bonton.fr

Du Pareil au Même
1 rue St-Denis 75001. **Map** 9 B3. **Tel** 01 42 36 07 57. **W** dpam.com

Froment-Leroyer
7 rue Vavin 75006. **Map** 12 E1. **Tel** 01 43 54 33 15. **W** froment-leroyer.fr

Jacadi
17 rue Tronchet 75008. **Map** 3 C5. **Tel** 01 42 65 84 98. **W** jacadi.com

Petit Bateau
116 av des Champs-Elysées 75008. **Map** 2 E4. **Tel** 01 40 74 02 03. **W** petit-bateau.com

Tartine et Chocolat
84 rue du Faubourg St-Honoré 75008. **Map** 3 B5. **Tel** 01 45 62 44 04. **W** tartine-et-chocolat.fr

Men's Clothes

Charvet
28 pl Vendôme 75001. **Map** 4 D5. **Tel** 01 42 60 30 70. **W** charvet.com

Francesco Smalto
44 rue François 1er 75008. **Map** 2 F5. **Tel** 01 47 20 70 63. **W** smalto.com

Gianni Versace
45 av Montaigne 75008. **Map** 6 F1. **Tel** 01 47 42 88 02. **W** versace.com

Giorgio Armani
18 av Montaigne 75008. **Map** 6 F1. **W** armani.com

Kenzo
(see p147).

Lanvin
22 rue du Faubourg St-Honoré 75008. **Map** 10 F4. **Tel** 01 44 71 33 33. **W** lanvin.com

Michel Axel
44 rue du Dragon 75006. **Map** 8 E4. **Tel** 01 42 84 13 86. **W** michelaxel.com

Pierre Cardin
(see p147).

Sauver le Monde des Hommes
8 rue Beaurepaire 75010 **Map** 10 E2. **Tel** 09 83 84 60 88

Y3 (No. 42)
42 rue de Sevigné 75003. **Map** 10 D3. **Tel** 01 44 61 78 11. **W** y-3.com

Yves Saint Laurent
6 pl St-Sulpice 75006. **Map** 8 E5. **Tel** 01 43 29 43 00. **W** ysl.com

Vintage and Second-Hand Stores

Depôt-Vente de Buci-Bourbon
4–6 rue de Bourbon-le-Château 75006. **Map** 8 E4. **Tel** 01 46 34 28 28.

Didier Ludot
24 Galerie de Montpensier 75001. **Map** 8 E1. **Tel** 01 42 96 06 56. **W** didierludot.fr

Emmaus Alternatives
35 rue Quincampoix 75004. **Map** 9 B2. **Tel** 01 44 61 69 19.

Le Mouton à Cinq Pattes
8/18 rue St-Placide 75006. **Map** 8 D5. **Tel** 01 45 48 86 26 or 01 42 84 25 11. **W** moutonacinqpattesparis.com

Réciproque
89–101 rue de la Pompe 75016. **Map** 5 A1. **Tel** 01 47 04 30 28. **W** reciproque.fr

Jewellery

Boucheron
26 pl Vendôme 75001. **Map** 4 D5. **Tel** 01 42 61 58 16. **W** boucheron.com

Cartier
13 rue de la Paix 75002. **Map** 4 D5. **Tel** 01 58 18 23 00. **W** cartier.fr

Dinh Van
16 rue de la Paix 75002. **Map** 4 D5. **Tel** 01 42 61 74 49. **W** dinhvan.com

H Stern
3 rue Castiglione 75001. **Map** 8 D1. **Tel** 01 42 60 22 27. **W** hstern.net

Harry Winston
29 av Montaigne 75008. **Map** 6 F1. **Tel** 01 47 20 03 09. **W** harrywinston.com

Mauboussin
15 rue de la Paix 75002. **Map** 4 D5. **Tel** 01 80 18 15 90. **W** mauboussin.fr

Mikimoto
8 pl Vendôme 75001. **Map** 4 D5. **Tel** 01 42 60 33 55. **W** mikimoto.fr

Poiray
17 rue de la Paix 75002. **Map** 4 D5. **Tel** 01 40 41 94 91. **W** poiray.com

Swarovski Boutique
146 av des Champs-Elysées 75008. **Map** 2 E4. **Tel** 01 45 61 13 80. **W** swarovski.com

Shoes and Bags

Carel
2 rue Tronchet 75008. **Map** 4 D4. **Tel** 01 42 66 21 58. **W** carel.fr

Christian Louboutin
38–40 rue de Grenelle 75007. **Map** 6 F3. **Tel** 08 00 94 58 04. **W** christianlouboutin.com

Furla
74 av des Champs-Elysées 75008. **Map** 2 F5. **Tel** 01 40 75 02 40. **W** furla.com

Goyard
233 rue St-Honoré 75001. **Map** 8 D1. **Tel** 01 42 60 57 04. **W** goyard.com

Jamin Puech
43 rue Madame 75006. **Map** 8 E5. **Tel** 01 45 48 14 85. **W** jamin-puech.com

Jonak
70 rue de Rennes 75006. **Map** 12 D1. **Tel** 01 45 48 27 11. **W** jonak.fr

Lollipops
Les Halles, 1 rue Pierre Lescot 75001. **Map** 9 A2. **Tel** 01 40 26 32 95. **W** lollipopsparis.fr

Miu Miu
219 rue St-Honoré 75001. **Map** 8 D1. **Tel** 01 58 62 53 20. **W** miumiu.com

Rodolphe Ménudier
14 rue de Castiglione 75001. **Map** 8 D1. **Tel** 06 07 02 81 91. **W** rodolphmenudier.com

Vanessa Bruno
(see p147).

Lingerie

La Boîte à Bas
27 rue Boissy-d'Anglas 75008. **Map** 3 C5. **Tel** 01 42 66 26 85.

Cadolle
4 rue Cambon 75001. **Map** 4 D5. **Tel** 01 42 60 94 22. **W** cadolle.com

Fifi Chachnil
231 rue St-Honoré 75001. **Map** 8 D1. **Tel** 01 42 61 21 83. **W** fifichachnil.com

Princesse Tam Tam
52 bd St-Michel 75006. **Map** 8 F5. **Tel** 01 40 51 72 99. **W** princessetamtam.com

Sabbia Rosa
73 rue des Sts-Pères 75006. **Map** 8 D4. **Tel** 01 45 48 88 37.

Gifts and Souvenirs

Paris has a wealth of stylish gift options, from designer accessories to Eiffel Tower paperweights. Shops on rue de Rivoli and around major tourist attractions offer a range of cheap holiday paraphernalia, or for something more quirky go to one of the specialist stores such as **Les Drapeaux de France.**

Perfume

Many shops advertise discounted perfume. They include **Eiffel Shopping** near the Eiffel Tower. The **Sephora** chain has a big selection, or try the department stores for a range of beauty brands that are hard to find elsewhere.

Parfums Caron has many scents created at the turn of the 19th century, and unavailable elsewhere. Beautifully packaged perfumes made from natural essences are available from **Annick Goutal**. **Guerlain** has the ultimate in beauty care, while the elegant shops of **L'Artisan Parfumeur** specialize in exquisitely packaged scents evoking specific memories.

Household Goods

It is difficult to ignore some of the world's most elegant tableware. Luxury homeware stores line rue Royale. **Lalique**'s Art Nouveau and Art Deco glass sculptures are collected all over the world. Impeccable silverware comes from **Christofle**.

For beautiful porcelain tableware and crystal, go to French specialists **Villeroy & Boch** or **Baccarat**.

La Chaise Longue has a selection of fun gift ideas to suit most tastes, while **BoConcept** has an extensive range of contemporary goods to add a new lease of life to any home.

Books

Some department stores have a books section, and there are several English language bookshops such as **W H Smith** and **Brentano's**. **Shakespeare and Company** and **Librairie Galignani** (the first English bookshop in Continental Europe) are good for convivial browsing among expats. French-language bookshops include **La Hune**, specializing in art, cinema, fashion and photography, and **Gibert Joseph**, for academic books.

Specialist Shops

A La Civette is perhaps Paris's most beautiful tobacconist's, stocking a vast range of cigars. **La Boîte à Joujoux** is one of the largest dollhouse boutiques in Paris, while the name **Cassegrain** is synonymous with high-quality stationery and paper products. **Les Drapeaux de France** sells miniatures and toy tin soldiers.

DIRECTORY

Perfume

Annick Goutal
16 rue de Bellechasse 75007. **Map** 7 C3. **Tel** 01 45 51 36 13. **W** annickgoutal.com

L'Artisan Parfumeur
24 bd Raspail 75007. **Map** 12 D1. **Tel** 01 42 22 23 32. **W** artisanparfumeur.com
One of several branches.

Eiffel Shopping
9 av de Suffren 75007. **Map** 6 D3. **Tel** 01 45 66 55 30.

Guerlain
68 av des Champs-Elysées 75008. **Map** 2 F5. **Tel** 01 45 62 52 57. **W** guerlain.com

Parfums Caron
34 av Montaigne 75008. **Map** 6 F1. **Tel** 01 47 23 40 82. **W** parfumscaron.com

Sephora
70–72 av des Champs-Elysées 75008. **Map** 7 B1. **Tel** 01 53 93 22 50. **W** sephora.fr

Household Goods

Baccarat
11 pl des Etats-Unis 75116. **Map** 2 D5. **Tel** 01 40 22 11 22. **W** baccarat.fr

BoConcept
8 bd de Sebastopol 75004. **Map** 9 A3. **Tel** 01 42 78 66 66. **W** boconcept.fr

La Chaise Longue
30 rue Croix-des-Petits-Champs 75001. **Map** 8 F1. **Tel** 01 42 96 32 14. **W** lachaiselongue.fr

Christofle
24 rue de la Paix 75002. **Map** 4 D5. **Tel** 01 42 65 62 43. **W** christofle.com

Lalique
11 rue Royale 75008. **Map** 3 C5. **Tel** 01 53 05 12 81. **W** lalique.com

Villeroy & Boch
94 bd de Montparnasse 75014. **Map** 12 D2. **Tel** 01 56 54 10 00. **W** villeroy-boch.fr

Books

Brentano's
37 av de l'Opéra 75002. **Map** 4 E5. **Tel** 01 42 60 87 37.

Gibert Joseph
26–34 bd St-Michel 75006. **Map** 8 F5. **Tel** 01 44 41 88 88. **W** gibertjoseph.com

La Hune
16–18 rue de l'Abbaye 75006. **Map** 8 D4. **Tel** 01 42 01 43 55.

Librairie Galignani
224 rue de Rivoli 75001. **Tel** 01 42 60 76 07. **W** galignani.com

Shakespeare and Company
37 rue de la Bûcherie 75005. **Map** 9 A4. **Tel** 01 43 25 40 93. **W** shakespeareandcompany.com

W H Smith
248 rue de Rivoli 75001. **Map** 7 C1. **Tel** 01 44 77 88 99. **W** whsmith.fr

Specialist Shops

A La Civette
157 rue St-Honoré 75001. **Map** 8 F2. **Tel** 01 42 96 04 99.

La Boîte à Joujoux
41–43 passage Jouffroy 75009. **Tel** 01 48 24 58 37. **W** joujoux.com

Cassegrain
109 bd Haussman 75008. **Map** 3 B4. **Tel** 01 42 60 20 08. **W** cassegrain.fr

Les Drapeaux de France
1 pl Colette 75001. **Map** 8 E1. **Tel** 01 40 20 00 11. **W** lesdrapeauxdefrance.com

Food and Drink

Paris is arguably more famous for food than for fashion. Gastronomic treats include *foie gras*, cold meats from the *charcuterie*, cheese and wine. Certain streets are so overflowing with food shops that you can put together a picnic for 20 in no time: try rue Montorgueil *(see Map 9 A1)*. Rue Rambuteau, running on either side of the Centre Pompidou, has a marvellous row of fishmongers and delicatessens.

Bread and Cakes

There is a vast range of breads and pastries in France's capital. The *baguette* is often translated as "French bread", a *bâtard* is similar but thicker, while a *ficelle* is thinner. A *fougasse* is a crusty, flat loaf often filled with onions, cheese, herbs or spices.

Croissants can be bought *ordinaire* or *au beurre* – the latter is flakier and more buttery. *Pain au chocolat* is a chocolate-filled pastry eaten for breakfast, and *chausson aux pommes* is filled with apples. There are also pear, plum and rhubarb variations. A *pain aux raisins* is a bread-like wheel filled with custard and raisins.

Poilâne sells perhaps the only bread in Paris known by the name of its baker (the late Lionel, brother of Max) and his hearty whole-wheat loaves are tremendously popular.

Many think **Ganachaud** bakes the best bread in Paris. Thirty different kinds, with ingredients such as walnuts and fruit, are made in the old-fashioned ovens.

Maison Kayser, a high-end chain bakery, produces a variety of artisan breads including *pain aux céréale* (multi-grain bread) and *pain d'amande* (almond bread), the owner's favourite.

The Jewish delicatessens have the best ryes and the only pumpernickels in town. One of the best is **Sacha Finkelsztajn**.

Le Moulin de la Vierge uses a wood fire to bake organic breads and rich pound cakes. **Boulanger et Pâtisserie Secco** is known for madeleines and "Paris–Brest" (*choux* pastry filled with hazelnut praline buttercream, in honour of the famous bicycle race).

Pierre Hermé is to cakes what Chanel is to fashion, while **Ladurée**'s macaroons are legendary.

Chocolate

Like all food in France, chocolate is to be savoured. **Un Dimanche à Paris** is a concept store dedicated to cocoa. The chocolate theme continues in the adjacent restaurant. **Dalloyau** makes all types of chocolate and is not too expensive (it is also known for its pâtisserie and cold meats). **Fauchon** is world-famous for its luxury food products. Its chocolates are excellent, as is the pâtisserie. Robert Linxe at **La Maison du Chocolat** is constantly inventing fresh, rich chocolates with mouthwatering exotic ingredients. **Edwart** offers an array of ganaches and pralines with fragrant flavours from all over the world.

Cheese

Although Camembert is undoubtedly a favourite, there is an overwhelming range of cheeses available and a friendly *fromager* will always help you choose. **Marie-Anne Cantin** is one of the leading figures in the fight to protect traditional production methods, and her fine cheeses are available from the store that she inherited from her father. Some say that **Alléosse** is the best cheese delicatessen in Paris – all the cheeses are made according to traditional methods. **Fromagerie Quatrehomme** sells farm-made cheeses, many of which are in danger of becoming extinct. These include a rare and delicious truffle Brie (when in season). **Le Jardin Fromager** is one of the best shops in Paris for all types of cheese – the *chèvre* (goat's cheese) is particularly good, as are the *camemberts au lait cru* (cheese made with unpasteurized milk), which ooze over the plate. **Laurent Dubois**, medalled cheese maker in the boulevard St-Germain, is known for his marinated goat's cheese.

Androuët is a Parisian institution with several branches across the city. Try a pungent Munster or a really ripe Brie. A charming cheese shop, **La Fermette** offers a dazzling array of dairy products, which the staff will encase in plastic for the journey home – imperative when bringing cheese through customs.

Well-heeled locals queue in the street to buy oozing *livarot* and sharp *chèvre* from **La Fromagerie d'Auteuil**.

Other Gourmet Foods

Charcuteries often sell cheese, snails, truffles, smoked salmon, caviar and wine as well as cold meats. **Fauchon** has a good grocery, as does the department store **Le Bon Marché – La Grande Epicerie de Paris**. **Hédiard** is a luxury shop similar to Fauchon, and **Maison de la Truffe** sells *foie gras* and sausages as well as truffles. For Beluga caviar, Georgian tea and Russian vodka, go to **Petrossian**.

Award-winning *charcutier* **Gilles Verot**'s delicacies are internationally renowned. His shops are a feast for the eyes as well as the stomach. **Maison Pou** is a sparklingly clean and popular store selling *pâté en croute* (pâté baked in pastry), *boudins* (black and white puddings), Lyonnais sausages, ham and *foie gras*. Just off the Champs-Elysées, **Vignon** has superb *foie gras* and Lyonnais sausages as well as popular prepared food.

Together with truffles and caviar, *foie gras* is the ultimate in gourmet food. Though most specialist food shops sell *foie gras*, you can be sure of quality at **Comtesse du Barry**, which has six outlets in Paris. **Divay** is relatively inexpensive and will ship overseas. **Lafitte** has a wide range of *foie gras* and wines, including gift boxes suitable for giving as presents.

Wine

The chain store that has practically cornered the everyday tippling market is **Nicolas** – there is a branch in every neighbourhood that can provide a range of wines to suit all pockets. As a rule, the salespeople at Nicolas are knowledgeable and helpful. Try the charming **Legrand Filles et Fils** for a carefully chosen selection of high-end champagnes. **Caves Taillevent** on rue du Faubourg St-Honoré is well worth a sightseeing tour. It is an enormous, overwhelming cellar with some of the most expensive wine available.

Cave Péret on rue Daguerre has a vast selection of wines, and staff can offer personal advice to help you with your purchase. The beautiful **Ryst-Dupeyron**, in the St-Germain quarter, displays whiskies, wines, ports and Monsieur Ryst's own Armagnac. On request, he will even personalize a bottle for that special occasion.

Other great wine stores in Paris include **Lavinia**, which is the largest in Europe. The staff in **Les Caves Augé** are also very knowledgeable and friendly.

DIRECTORY

Bread and Cakes

Boulangerie Flute Gana by Ganachaud
226 rue des Pyrénées 75020. **Tel** 01 43 58 42 62.

Boulangerie et Pâtisserie Secco
75 bd de Grenelle 75015. **Map** 6 D5.

Ladurée
75 av des Champs-Elysées 75008. **Map** 2 F5. **Tel** 01 40 75 08 75. **W laduree.fr**

Maison Kayser
8 rue Monge 75005. **Map** 9 B5. **Tel** 01 44 07 01 42. **W maison-kayser.com**

Le Moulin de la Vierge
105 rue Vercingétorix 75014. **Map** 11 A4. **Tel** 01 45 43 09 84. **W lavierge.com**

Pierre Hermé
72 rue Bonaparte 75006. **Map** 8 E4. **Tel** 01 43 54 47 77. **W pierreherme.com**

Poilâne
8 rue du Cherche-Midi 75006. **Map** 8 D4. **Tel** 01 45 48 42 59. **W poilane.com**

Sacha Finkelsztajn
27 rue des Rosiers 75004. **Map** 9 C3. **Tel** 01 42 72 78 91. **W finkelsztajn.com**

Chocolate

Dalloyau
101 rue du Faubourg-St-Honoré 75008. **Map** 3 B5. **Tel** 01 42 99 90 00. **W dalloyau.fr**

Edwart
17 rue Vieille du Temple 75004. **Map** 10 D2. **Tel** 01 42 78 48 92. **W edwart.fr**

Fauchon
24–26, 30 pl de la Madeleine 75008. **Map** 3 C5. **Tel** 01 70 39 38 00/02. **W fauchon.fr**

La Maison du Chocolat
225 rue du Faubourg St-Honoré 75008. **Map** 2 E3. **Tel** 01 42 27 39 44. **W lamaisonduchocolat.com**

Un Dimanche à Paris
4-6-8 Cour du Commerce Saint André. **Map** 8 F4. **Tel** 01 56 81 18 18.

Cheese

Alléosse
13 rue Poncelet 75017. **Map** 2 E3. **Tel** 01 46 22 50 45. **W fromage-alleosse.com**

Androuët
134 rue Mouffetard 75005. **Map** 13 B1. **Tel** 01 45 87 85 05. **W androuet.com**

La Fermette
86 rue Montorgeuil 75002. **Map** 9 A1. **Tel** 01 42 36 70 96.

La Fromagerie d'Auteuil
58 rue d'Auteuil 75016. **Map** 5 A5. **Tel** 01 45 25 07 10. **W lafromageriedauteuil.fr**

Fromagerie Quatrehomme
62 rue de Sèvres 75007. **Map** 7 C5. **Tel** 01 47 34 33 45. **W quatrehomme.fr**

Le Jardin Fromager
53 rue Oberkampf 75011. **Map** 10 E1. **Tel** 01 48 05 19 96.

Laurent Dubois
47ter bd St-Germain 75007. **Map** 9 A5. **Tel** 01 43 54 50 93. **W fromageslaurentdubois.fr**

Marie-Anne Cantin
12 rue du Champ-de-Mars 75007. **Map** 6 F3. **Tel** 01 45 50 43 94. **W cantin.fr**

Other Gourmet Foods

Le Bon Marché – La Grande Epicerie de Paris
24 rue de Sèvres 75007. **Map** 7 C5. **Tel** 01 44 39 80 00. **W lagrandeepicerie.com**

Comtesse du Barry
1 rue de Sèvres 75006. **Map** 8 D4. **Tel** 01 45 48 32 04. **W comtessedubarry.com**

Divay
4 rue Bayen 75017. **Map** 2 D2. **Tel** 01 43 80 16 97. **W foie-gras-divay.com**

Gilles Verot
7 rue Lecourbe 75015. **Map** 11 1A. **Tel** 01 47 34 01 03. **W verot-charcuterie.fr**

Hédiard
21 pl de la Madeleine 75008. **Map** 3 C5. **Tel** 01 43 12 88 88. **W hediard.com**

Lafitte
Ile St-Louis, 8 rue Jean du Bellay 75004. **Map** 9 B4. **Tel** 01 43 26 08 63. **W lafitte.fr**

Maison de la Truffe
19 pl de la Madeleine 75008. **Map** 3 C5. **Tel** 01 42 65 53 22. **W maison-de-la-truffe.com**

Maison Pou
16 av des Ternes 75017. **Map** 2 D3. **Tel** 01 43 80 19 24. **W maisonpou.com**

Petrossian
18 bd de la Tour-Maubourg 75007. **Map** 7 A2. **Tel** 01 44 11 32 22. **W petrossian.fr**

Vignon
13 rue Clément-Marot 75008. **Map** 2 E5. **Tel** 01 47 20 10 01.

Wine

Cave Péret
6 rue Daguerre 75014. **Map** 12 D4. **Tel** 01 43 22 57 05. **W maisonperet.com**

Les Caves Augé
116 bd Haussman 75008. **Map** 3 C4. **Tel** 01 45 22 16 97. **W cavesauge.com**

Caves Taillevent
228 rue du Faubourg St-Honoré 75008. **Map** 2 F3. **Tel** 01 45 61 14 09. **W taillevent.com**

Lavinia
3–5 bd de la Madeleine 75008. **Map** 4 D5. **Tel** 01 42 97 20 20. **W lavinia.fr**

Legrand Filles et Fils
1 rue de la Banque 75002. **Map** 8 F1. **Tel** 01 42 60 07 12. **W caves-legrand.com**

Nicolas
35 bd Malesherbes 75008. **Map** 3 C5. **Tel** 01 42 65 00 85. **W nicolas.com**

Ryst-Dupeyron
79 rue du Bac 75007. **Map** 8 D3. **Tel** 09 54 39 72 78. **W vintageandco.com**

Arts and Antiques

In Paris you can buy art and antiques either from shops and galleries with established reputations, or from flea markets and avant-garde galleries. Many of the prestigious antiques shops and galleries are located around rue du Faubourg St-Honoré and are worth a visit even if you can't afford to buy. On the Left Bank is Le Carré Rive Gauche, an organization of 30 antiques dealers.

Exporting

Objets d'art over 50 years old, worth more than a given amount, will require a *Certificat pour un bien culturel* to be exported (provided by the vendor), plus a *licence d'exportation* for non-EU countries. Seek professional advice from the large antiques shops. The **Centre des Renseignements des Douanes** has a booklet, *Bulletin Officiel des Douanes*, with all the details.

Antiques

If you wish to buy antiques, you might like to stroll around the areas that boast the most galleries – in Le Carré Rive Gauche around quai Malaquais, try **L'Arc en Seine** and **Anne-Sophie Duval** for Art Nouveau and Art Deco. Rue Jacob is still one of the best places to seek beautiful objects, antique or modern. Close to the Louvre, the **Louvre des Antiquaires** comprises 250 shops selling mainly expensive, quality furniture. Many of the prestigious antiques stores are near rue du Faubourg St-Honoré, including **Didier Aaron**, expert on furniture from the 17th and 18th centuries. **Village St-Paul** is the most charming group of antiques shops and is also open on Sundays. In the south of the city, **Le Village Suisse** also groups many art and antiques dealers.

Art Galleries

Most established art galleries are located on or around avenue Montaigne. However, the **Fondation Cartier** can be found in the 14th *arrondissement*. Set in a glass building, it houses modern exhibits in a range of media, from sculpture to performance art.

On the Left Bank **Galerie Maeght** has a tremendous stock of paintings at prices to suit most budgets; it also publishes fine art books. Under the Eiffel Tower is **Millésime Gallery**, which displays works by new artists.

Rue Louise-Weiss, known as Scène Est, has become the area for cutting-edge creativity and innovation. The **Air de Paris** gallery is popular.

In the Marais try **Yvon Lambert** and **Galerie du Jour Agnès B.**; in the Bastille, try **Arts Factory**, also a fashionable place to buy catalogues on new artists, if not their works.

Auction Houses

The great Paris auction centre, in operation since 1858, is **Drouot**. Bidding can be intimidating, since most of it is done by dealers. Beware of the auctioneer's high-speed patter. *La Gazette Drouot* tells you what auctions are coming up when. Drouot also has its own auction catalogue. The house only accepts cash and French cheques, but there is an exchange desk in-house. A 10–15 per cent commission to the house is charged, so remember to add it on to any price you hear. You may view from 11am to 6pm on the day before the sale, and from 11am to noon on the morning of the sale.

DIRECTORY

Exporting

Centre des Renseignements des Douanes
Tel 08 11 20 44 44 or 01 72 40 78 40.
W **douane.gouv.fr**

Antiques

Anne-Sophie Duval
5 quai Malaquais 75006. **Map** 8 E3. **Tel** 01 43 54 51 16. W **annesophieduval.com**

L'Arc en Seine
31 rue de Seine 75006. **Map** 8 E3. **Tel** 01 43 29 11 02. W **arcenseine.com**

Didier Aaron
152 bd Haussmann 75008. **Map** 3 A4. **Tel** 01 47 42 47 34.
W **didieraaron.com**

Louvre des Antiquaires
2 pl du Palais Royal 75001. **Map** 8 E2. **Tel** 01 42 97 27 27. W **louvre-antiquaires.com**

Village St-Paul
Between rues St-Paul, Ava Maria, Charlemagne and Jardins St-Paul 75004. **Map** 9 C4. W **levillagesaintpaul.com**

Le Village Suisse
78 av de Suffren 75015. **Map** 6 E4. **Tel** 01 73 79 15 41. W **villagesuisse.com**

Art Galleries

Air de Paris
32 rue Louise-Weiss 75013. **Map** 14 E4. **Tel** 01 44 23 02 77. W **airdeparis.com**

Arts Factory
27 rue de Charonne 75011. **Map** 10 F4. **Tel** 06 22 85 35 86. W **artsfactory.net**

Fondation Cartier
261 bd Raspail 75014. **Map** 12 E3. **Tel** 01 42 18 56 50. W **fondation.cartier.com**

Galerie du Jour Agnès B.
44 rue Quincampoix 75004. **Map** 9 B2. **Tel** 01 44 54 55 90. W **galeriedujour.com**

Galerie Maeght
42 rue du Bac 75007. **Map** 8 D3. **Tel** 01 45 48 45 15.
W **maeght.com/galeries**

Millésime Gallery
41 av de la Bourdonnais 75007. **Map** 6 E3. **Tel** 06 82 55 57 96. W **millesime-gallery.com**

Yvon Lambert
108 rue Vieille-du-Temple 75003. **Map** 10 D2. **Tel** 01 42 71 89 05.
W **yvon-lambert.com**

Auction Houses

Drouot
9 rue Drouot 75009. **Map** 4 F4. **Tel** 01 48 00 20 20. W **drouot.fr**

Markets

For eye-catching displays of wonderful food, or a lively shopping atmosphere, there is no better place than a Paris market. There are large covered food markets, markets where stalls change regularly and permanent street markets. Some of the more famous venues, with approximate opening times, follow. While you are enjoying browsing round the stalls, remember to keep an eye on your valuables and be prepared to bargain.

Food Markets

The French still shop daily, hence food markets are always packed. Most fruit-and-vegetable markets are open from around 8am to 1pm and from 4 to 7pm Tuesday to Saturday, and from 9am to 1pm Sunday. Watch out for rotten goods – buy produce loose, not in boxes. A little language is useful for specifying *pas trop mûr* (not too ripe), or *pour manger ce soir* (to be eaten tonight).

Marché d'Aligre

Pl d'Aligre 75012. **Map** *10 F5.* M *Ledru-Rollin.* **Open** *9am–1pm, 4–7:30pm Tue–Sat, 9am–1:30pm Sun.* W **marchedaligre.free.fr**

Reminiscent of a Moroccan bazaar, this must be the cheapest and liveliest market in the city. Traders hawk ingredients such as North African olives, groundnuts and hot peppers, and there are even a few halal butchers. Stalls on the square sell mostly second-hand clothes and bric-a-brac. This is a less affluent area of town with only a few tourists and many Parisians.

Marché des Enfants Rouges

39 rue de Bretagne 75003. **Map** *10 D2.* M *Temple, Filles-du-Calvaire.* **Open** *8:30am–1pm, 4–7:30pm Tue–Sat, 8:30am–2pm Sun.*

This part-covered fruit-and-vegetable market is the oldest covered market in Paris and dates from 1620. Famous for the freshness of its produce, on Sunday mornings street singers and accordionists enliven the proceedings.

Marché Raspail

Between blvd Raspail, rue Cherche-Midi and rue de Rennes, 75006. **Map** *8 D4.* M *Rennes.* **Open** *7am–2:30pm Tue & Fri, 9am–2pm Sun.*

Conveniently sited between Montparnasse and St-Germain, this market sells fresh produce during the week and organic-only produce on Sundays.

Marché St-Germain

4–86 rue Lobineau 75006. **Map** *8 E4.* M *Mabillon.* **Open** *8am–1pm, 4–8pm Mon–Sat, 8am–1:30pm Sun.*

St-Germain is one of the few covered markets left in Paris. Here you can buy Italian, Mexican, Greek, Asian and organic produce.

Rue Montorgueil

75001 & 75002. **Map** *9 A1.* M *Les Halles.* **Open** *10am–6pm Mon–Sat, Sun am only (subject to change).*

The paved rue Montorgueil is what remains of the old Les Halles market. Here you can buy exotic fruit and vegetables from green bananas to yams, or sample offerings from the delicatessens. Expect high prices.

Rue Mouffetard

75005. **Map** *13 B2.* M *Pl Monge.* **Open** *8am–1pm Tue–Sun.*

This is one of the oldest market streets in Paris, and, although it has become touristy, it is still a charming winding street full of quality fresh food.

Rue Poncelet

75017. **Map** *2 E3.* M *Ternes.* **Open** *8am–1pm, 3–7:30pm Tue–Sat, 8am–1pm Sun.*

Situated away from the main tourist areas, this market street is worth visiting for its authentic French atmosphere. Choose from many bakeries, patisseries and *charcuteries*.

Flea Markets

It is often said that you can no longer find bargains at the Paris flea markets. Though this may be true, it is still worth going to one for the sheer fun of browsing. Whether you pick up any real bargains has as much to do with luck as with judgement. Often the sellers themselves have little or no idea of the true value of their goods – which can work either for or against you. The biggest and most famous market, incorporating several smaller ones, is the Marché aux Puces de St-Ouen. Keep an eye on your wallet, as pickpockets frequent these markets.

Marché aux Puces de la Porte de Vanves

Av Georges-Lafenestre & av Marc-Sangnier 75014. M *Porte-de-Vanves.* **Open** *7am–2 or 5pm Sat & Sun.* W **pucesdevanves.fr**

Porte de Vanves is a small market selling good-quality bric-a-brac and junk as well as some second-hand furniture. It's best to get to the market early on Saturday morning for the best choice of wares. Artists exhibit nearby.

Marché aux Puces de Montreuil

Porte de Montreuil, 93 Montreuil 75020. M *Porte-de-Montreuil.* **Open** *7am–7:30pm Sat–Mon.*

Go early to the Porte de Montreuil flea market for a better chance of picking up a bargain. The substantial second-hand clothes section attracts many young people. Stalls sell everything from used bicycles to bric-a-brac and exotic spices.

Marché aux Puces de St-Ouen

(See p138).

This is the most well-known, the most crowded and the most expensive of all the flea markets. Here you'll find a range of markets, locals dealing from their car boots, and large buildings packed with stalls. Some of them are very upmarket; others sell junk. *A Guide des Puces* (guide to the flea markets) can be obtained from the information kiosk in the Marché Biron on rue des Rosiers.

Marché Couvert Saint Quentin

85 bis, Blvd Magenta 75010. **Open** *8am–8pm Tue–Sat, 8am–1:30pm Sun.* **Tel** *01 48 85 93 30.*

Located steps from the Gare du Nord, this 19th-century covered market is the perfect place to stock up on last-minute cheese and charcuterie before boarding the Eurostar. The dozens of vendors also sell flowers, local beers, breads and pastries, and a variety of other delicacies.

ENTERTAINMENT IN PARIS

Whether your preference is for classical drama, avant-garde theatre, ballet, opera, jazz, cinema or dancing the night away, Paris has it all. There is plenty of free entertainment, too, from the street performers outside the Centre Pompidou to musicians busking all over town and in the metros.

Parisians themselves like nothing better than strolling along the boulevards or sitting at a pavement café nursing a drink as they watch the world go by. If, however, you're looking for the ultimate "Oh la-la!" experience, you can take in any of the celebrated nightclubs.

For fans of spectator sports there is tennis, the Tour de France or horse racing. Recreation centres and gyms cater to the more active. And for those disposed to more leisurely pursuits, there is always a quiet game of *boules* to be played in the park.

The glass façade of the Bastille Opéra

Booking Tickets

Depending on the event, tickets can be bought at the door, but for popular events it is wiser to check online for availability and purchase tickets in advance at one of the **FNAC** stores or at **Carrefour Spectacles**. Theatre box offices open daily from about 11am to 7pm. Credit cards are accepted for bookings online or by telephone.

Theatre

From the grandeur of the **Comédie Française** to slapstick farce and avant-garde drama, theatre is flourishing, both in Paris and in its suburbs. Founded in 1680 by royal decree, the Comédie Française is the bastion of French theatre, aiming to keep classical drama in the public eye and to perform works by the best modern playwrights. Formerly the second theatre of the Comédie Française, the **Odéon Théâtre de l'Europe** now specializes in plays from other countries, performed in their original languages. In an underground auditorium in the Art Deco Palais de Chaillot, the **Théâtre National de Chaillot** is famed for staging some very lively productions of European classics. The **Théâtre National de la Colline** specializes in contemporary drama.

Among the most important of the serious independents is the **Comédie des Champs-Elysées**, while for over 100 years the **Théâtre du Palais Royal** has been known as the temple of risqué farce. The café theatres such as **Théâtre d'Edgar** and **Le Point Virgule** are always good venues for seeing the best of the emerging new talent. In the summer, street theatre thrives in tourist areas such as the Centre Pompidou, Les Halles and St-Germain-des-Prés. Open-air performances of Shakespeare and classic French plays are given at the Shakespeare Garden in the Bois de Boulogne.

Classical Music

Paris has many first-class venues with an excellent range of opera, classical and contemporary music productions. Opened in 1989, the stylish, 2,700-seat **Opéra National de Paris Bastille** stages classic and modern operas. The beautifully renovated **Opéra National de Paris Garnier** puts on mostly ballets as well as some operas.

The **Philharmonie de Paris** in the Cité de la Musique – Parc de la Villette is Paris's principal concert hall and one of its most vibrant. It houses the Orchestre de Paris and Radio France's Philharmonic Orchestra. The venue is renowned for its eclectic music programmes and workshops, while the museum charts the history of music and exhibits over 4,000 instruments Both the **Théâtre des Champs-**

Listings Magazines

Pariscope and *L'Officiel des Spectacles* are the best listings magazines in Paris. Published every Wednesday, you can pick them up at any newsstand. *Le Figaro* also has a good listings section on Wednesdays. *Time Out Paris* online or *Premier* online are also handy websites for up-to-date events listings.

The famous silhouette of the Moulin Rouge nightclub

Elysées and the **Théâtre du Châtelet** (closed till 2019) are recommended for their varied high-quality programmes. Venues for chamber music include the **Salle Gaveau** and the **Théâtre de la Ville**. .

Dance

The opulent **Opéra National de Paris Garnier** has space for 450 artists and is home to the Ballet de l'Opéra de Paris, which has earned a reputation as one of the best classical ballet companies in the world. Government support has helped the **Théâtre de la Ville** to become Paris's most important venue for modern dance, with subsidies keeping ticket costs relatively low.

The **Maison des Arts de Créteil** stages famous overseas companies, as well as its own much-praised productions.

Clubs and Cabaret

Music in Paris clubs tends to follow the trends set in the US and Britain. Only a few clubs such as **Balajo**, once frequented by Edith Piaf, and the ultra-hip **Showcase**, under Alexandre III bridge, are genuinely up-to-the-minute with their music.

Manko Cabaret is a trendy nightspot, attracting people from the fashion world and from showbusiness. For comedy in English, try **La Java**. The stage of this club, where Edith Piaf once performed, now showcases British and American comedians.

When it comes to picking a cabaret, the rule of thumb is simple: the better-known places are best. The **Folies-Bergère** is the oldest music hall in Paris and probably the most famous in the world. It is closely rivalled by the **Lido** and the **Moulin Rouge**, birthplace of the cancan. **Paradis Latin** is the most "French" cabaret in the city. It shows variety acts with sketches enlivened by remarkable special effects and scenery.

Rock, Jazz and World Music

The top international acts are usually to be found at the enormous arenas such as the **AccorHotels Arena** or the **Zénith**. The Art Deco **Salle Pleyel**, which formerly hosted classical music, is now a venue for rock, pop and jazz concerts. For a more intimate atmosphere, the legendary **Olympia** has assigned seating and good acoustics. To hear indigenous rock groups such as Les Négresses Vertes and Mano Negra, go to **La Cigale** or **Elysée-Montmartre** in the Pigalle area.

Jazz-crazy Paris has innumerable packed clubs, where the best talent in the world can be heard on any evening. All the great jazz musicians have performed at **New Morning**, which also hosts African, Brazilian and other sounds. For Dixieland, go to **Le Petit Journal St-Michel**.

World music and jazz lovers alike can see top acts and dance until dawn at the excellent **Chapelle des Lombards**.

The spectacular façade of the Opéra National de Paris Garnier

Cinema

Paris is the world's capital of film appreciation. It was the cradle of the cinematograph in the 1890s. Then in the late 1950s and early 1960s the city nurtured that very Parisian vanguard movement, the New Wave, when film directors such as François Truffaut and Jean-Luc Godard revolutionized the way films were made and perceived.

There are now more than 370 screens within the city limits, distributed among over 100 cinemas. Most are concentrated in cinema belts, which enjoy the added appeal of nearby restaurants and shops. The Champs-Elysées has the densest cinema strip in town, where you can see the latest Hollywood smash or French *auteur* triumph, as well as some classic re-issues.

In the vicinity of the Opéra de Paris Garnier, the cinemas in the Grands Boulevards include two notable landmarks: the 2,800-seat **Le Grand Rex**, with its Baroque decor, and the **Max Linder Panorama**, which was completely refurbished in the 1980s. Place de Clichy is the last Parisian stronghold of Pathé, while the hub of Right Bank cinema is in the Forum des Halles mall. France's largest screen is at **La Géode**.

On the Left Bank, Odéon-St-Germain-des-Prés has taken over from the Latin Quarter as the city's heartland for art and repertory cinemas. The new, and huge, **MK2 Bibliothèque** points to the future with its collection of 14 screens, a bar, shops and exhibition space.

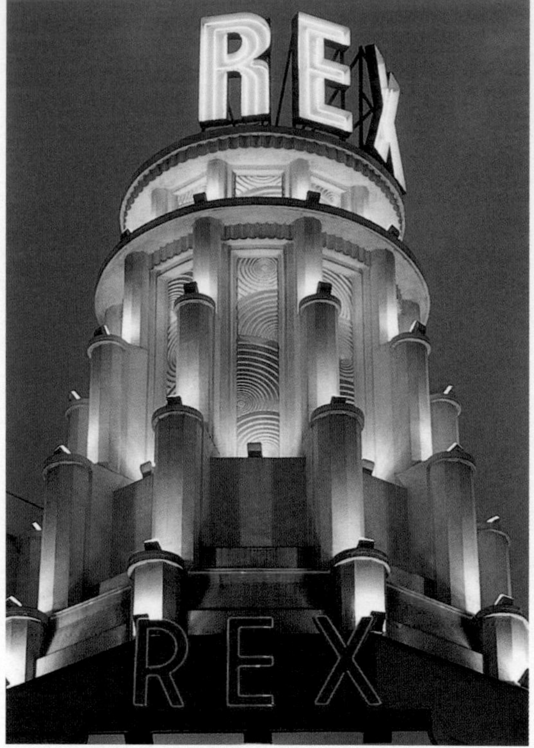

The dome of the 2,800-seat Le Grand Rex cinema

Sport

Paris is host to some of the foremost sporting events in the world. City-wide frenzy sweeps Paris, when the Tour de France bicycle race finishes there in July. From late May to mid-June Parisians live and breathe tennis during the **Roland Garros** national tennis championship. The Prix de l'Arc de Triomphe, held at the **Hippodrome de Longchamp** on the first Sunday in October, provides the opportunity to see the rich in all their finery, as well as first-class flat racing.

The **AccorHotels Arena** is the venue for a vast range of events, including the Paris tennis open and rock concerts, as is the new **Stade de France** at St-Denis. **Parc des Princes** is home to Paris's top football team, Paris St-Germain.

The Celebrated Cafés of Paris

One of the most enduring images of Paris is the Left Bank café scene, where great artists, writers and eminent intellectuals consorted. Before World War I, hordes of Russian revolutionaries, including Lenin and Trotsky, whiled away their days in the Rotonde and the Dôme in Montparnasse. In the 1920s, Surrealists dominated café life. Later came the American writers led by Ernest Hemingway and Scott Fitzgerald, whose haunts included La Coupole. After World War II, Jean-Paul Sartre and other Existentialists shifted the cultural scene northwards slightly to St-Germain.

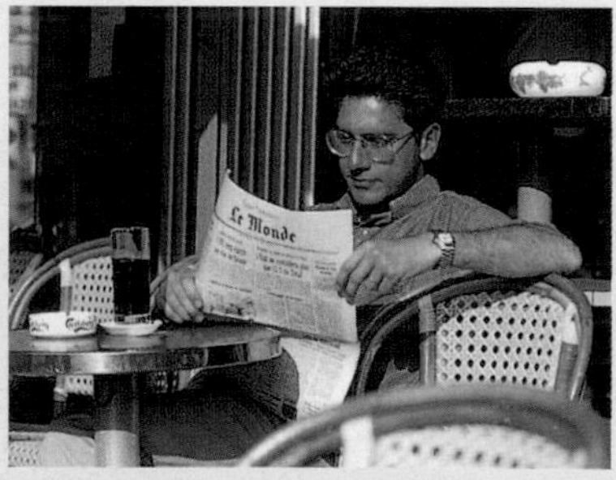

Newspaper reading remains a typical café pastime

DIRECTORY

Booking Tickets

Carrefour Spectacles
29 rue du Pont Neuf 75001. **Map** 9 A2. **W** carrefour.fr

FNAC
26–30 av des Ternes 75017. **Map** 2 D3. **Tel** 0825 020 020. Forum Les Halles, 1 rue Pierre Lescot 75001. **Map** 9 A2. **Tel** 0825 020 020. **W** fnac.com

Theatre

Comédie des Champs-Elysées
15 av Montaigne 75008. **Map** 6 F1. **Tel** 01 53 23 99 19. **W** comediedeschampselysees

Comédie Française
1 pl Colette 75001. **Map** 8 E1. **Tel** 08 25 10 16 80. **W** comedie-francaise.fr

Odéon Théâtre de l'Europe
Place de l'Odéon 75006. **Map** 12 F5. **Tel** 01 44 85 40 40. **W** theatre-odeon.eu

Le Point Virgule
7 rue Ste-Croix de la Bretonnerie 75004. **Map** 9 C3. **Tel** 01 42 78 67 03. **W** lepointvirgule.com

Théâtre d'Edgar
58 bd Edgar-Quinet 75014. **Map** 12 D2. **Tel** 01 42 79 97 97. **W** theatre-edgar.com

Théâtre National de Chaillot
Pl du Trocadéro 75016. **Map** 5 C2. **Tel** 01 53 65 30 00. **W** theatre-chaillot.fr

Théâtre National de la Colline
15 rue Malte-Brun 75020. **Tel** 01 44 62 52 52. **W** colline.fr

Théâtre du Palais Royal
38 rue Montpensier 75001. **Map** 8 E1. **Tel** 01 42 97 40 00. **W** theatrepalaisroyal.com

Classical Music

Cité de la Musique
221 av Jean-Jaurès 75019. **Tel** 01 44 84 44 84. **W** citedelamusique.fr

Opéra National de Paris Bastille
Pl de la Bastille, 120 rue de Lyon 75012. **Map** 10 E4. **Tel** 08 92 89 90 90. **W** operadeparis.fr

Opéra National de Paris Garnier
Pl de l'Opera 75009. **Map** 4 E4. **Tel** 08 92 89 90 90. **W** operadeparis.fr

Philarmonie de Paris
Cité de la Musique, 221 av Jean-Jaurès 75019. **W** philarmoniedeparis.fr

Salle Gaveau
45–47 rue la Boétie 75008. **Map** 3 B4. **Tel** 01 49 53 05 07. **W** sallegaveau.com

Théâtre des Champs-Elysées
15 av Montaigne 75008. **Map** 6 F1. **Tel** 01 49 52 50 50. **W** theatrechampselysees.fr

Théâtre du Châtelet
2 rue Edouard Colonne 75001. **Map** 9 A3. **Tel** 01 40 28 28 40. **W** chatelet-theatre.com

Théâtre de la Ville
2 pl du Châtelet 75004. **Map** 9 A3. **Tel** 01 42 74 22 77. **W** theatredelaville-paris.com

Dance

Maison des Arts de Créteil
Pl Salvador Allende 94000 Créteil. **Tel** 01 45 13 19 19. **W** maccreteil.com

Opéra National de Paris Garnier
(See Classical Music.)

Théâtre de la Ville
(See Classical Music.)

Clubs and Cabaret

Balajo
9 rue de Lappe 75011. **Map** 10 E4. **Tel** 01 47 00 07 87. **W** balajo.fr

Folies-Bergère
32 rue Richer 75009. **Tel** 08 92 68 16 50. **W** foliesbergere.com

La Java
105 rue du Faubourg-du-Temple 75010. **Tel** 01 42 02 20 52. **W** la-java.fr

Lido
116bis av des Champs-Elysées 75008. **Map** 2 E4. **Tel** 01 40 76 56 10. **W** lido.fr

Manko Cabaret
15 av Montaigne 75008. **Map** 6 F1. **Tel** 06 49 07 20 54. **W** manko-paris.com

Moulin Rouge
82 bd de Clichy 75018. **Map** 4 E1. **Tel** 01 53 09 82 82. **W** moulinrouge.fr

Paradis Latin
28 rue du Cardinal-Lemoine 75008. **Map** 9 B5. **Tel** 01 43 25 28 28. **W** paradislatin.com

Showcase
Under Pont Alexandre III. Porte des Champs-Elysées 75008. **Map** 7 A1. **Tel** 01 45 61 25 43. **W** showcase.fr

Rock, Jazz and World Music

AccorHotels Arena
8 bd de Bercy 75012. **Map** 14 F2. **Tel** 01 75 44 04 00. **W** accorhotels-arena.com

Chapelle des Lombards
19 rue de Lappe 75011. **Map** 10 F4. **Tel** 01 43 57 24 24. **W** la-chapelle-des-lombards.com

La Cigale
120 bd de Rochechouart 75018. **Map** 4 F2. **Tel** 01 49 25 89 99. **W** lacigale.fr

Elysée-Montmartre
72 bd de Rochechouart 75018. **Map** 4 F2. **Tel** 01 44 92 78 00.

New Morning
7–9 rue des Petites-Ecuries 75010. **Tel** 01 45 23 51 41. **W** newmorning.com

Olympia
28 bd des Capucines 75009. **Map** 4 D5. **Tel** 08 92 68 33 68. **W** olympiahall.com

Le Petit Journal St-Michel
71 bd St-Michel 75005. **Map** 12 F1. **Tel** 01 43 26 28 59. **W** petitjournalsaintmichel.fr

Salle Pleyel
252 rue du Faubourg St-Honoré 75008. **Map** 2 E3. **Tel** 01 42 56 13 13. **W** sallepleyel.fr

Zénith
Parc de Villette, 211 av de Jean-Jaurès 75019. **Tel** 01 44 52 54 56. **W** zenith-paris.com

Cinema

La Géode
26 av Corentin-Cariou 75019. **Tel** 08 92 68 45 40. **W** lageode.fr

Le Grand Rex
1 bd Poissonnière 75002. **Tel** 01 45 08 93 89. **W** legrandrex.com

Max Linder Panorama
24 bd Poissonnière 75009. **Tel** 01 48 00 90 24. **W** maxlinder.cine.allucine

MK2 Bibliothèque
128–162 av de France 75013. **Tel** 08 92 69 84 84. **W** mk2.com

Sport

AccorHotels Arena
(See Rock section.)

Hippodrome de Longchamp
Rte des Tribunes 75016. **Tel** 01 44 30 75 00.

Parc des Princes
20 av du Parc des Princes 75016. **Tel** 3275. **W** leparcdesprinces.fr

Stade de France
Saint-Denis 93200. **Tel** 01 55 93 00 00. **W** stadedefrance.com

Stade Roland Garros
2 av Gordon-Bennett 75016. **Tel** 01 47 43 51 11. **W** rolandgarros.com

PARIS STREET FINDER

The map references given with sights, shops and entertainment venues described in the Paris section of the guide refer to the maps on the following pages. Map references are also given for Paris hotels *(see pp554–5)* and restaurants *(pp576–9)*, and for useful addresses in the *Travellers' Needs* and *Survival Guide* sections at the back of the book. The maps include not only the main sightseeing areas but also the most important districts for hotels, restaurants, shopping and entertainment venues. The key map below shows the area of Paris covered by the *Street Finder*, with the *arrondissement* numbers for the various districts shown in green. The symbols used for sights and other features on the *Street Finder* maps are listed opposite.

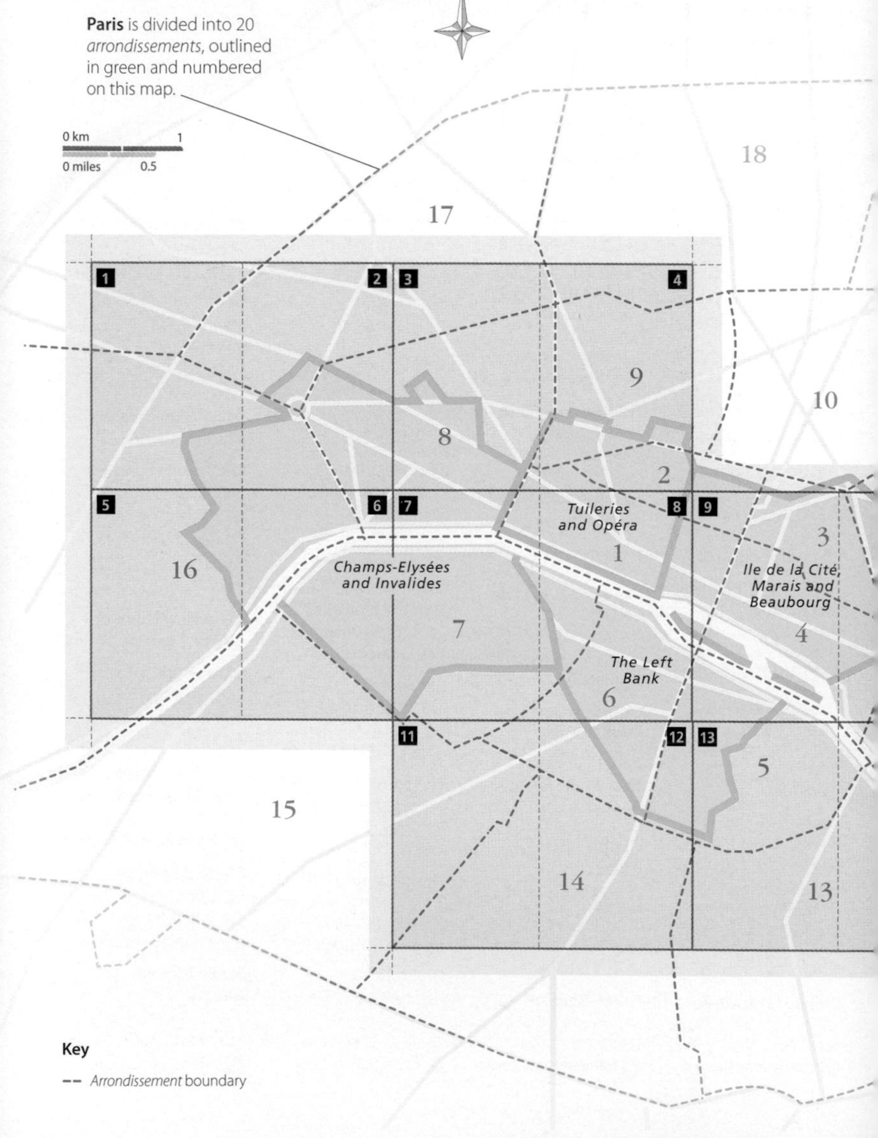

Key

-- *Arrondissement* boundary

How the Map References Work

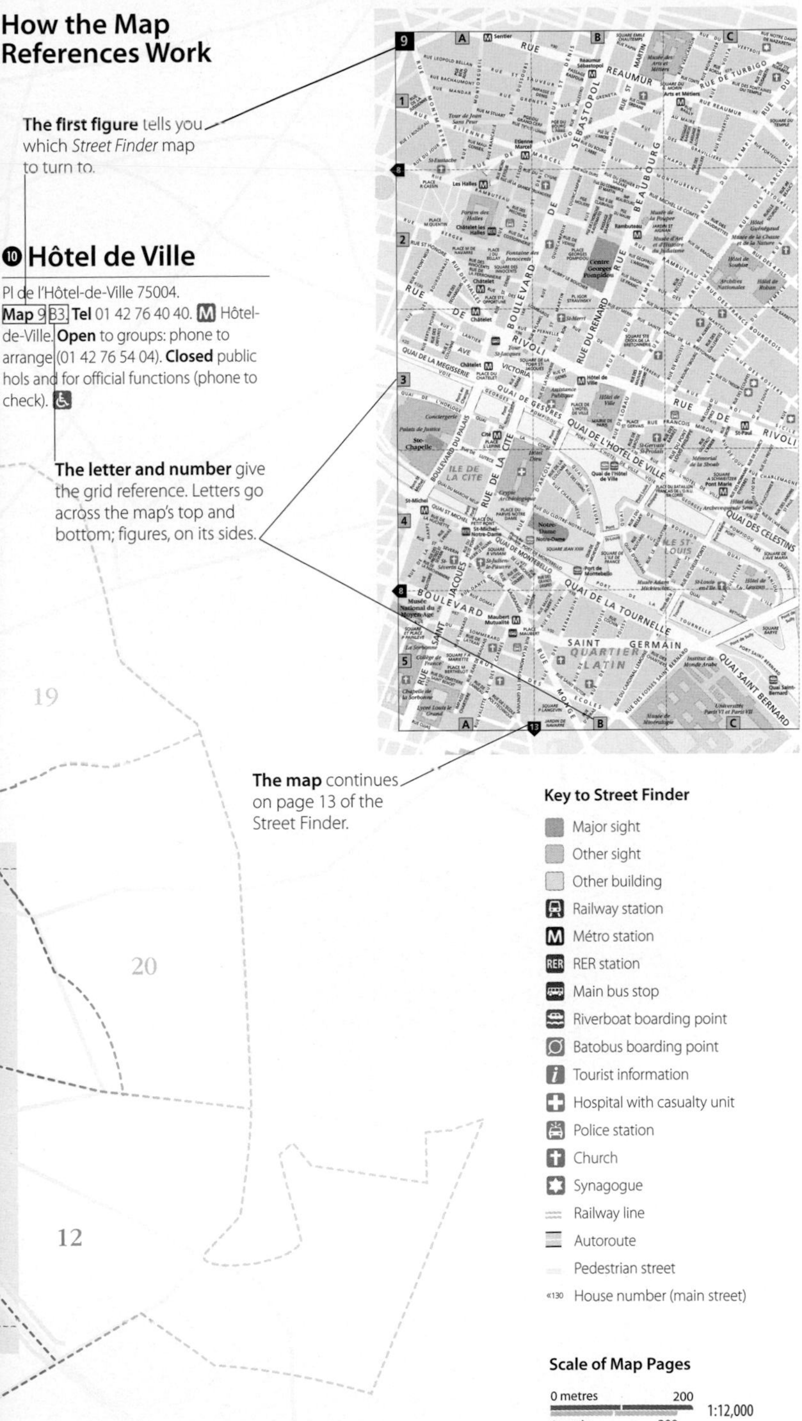

The first figure tells you which *Street Finder* map to turn to.

⓾ Hôtel de Ville

Pl de l'Hôtel-de-Ville 75004.
Map 9 B3. **Tel** 01 42 76 40 40. Ⓜ Hôtel-de-Ville. **Open** to groups: phone to arrange (01 42 76 54 04). **Closed** public hols and for official functions (phone to check).

The letter and number give the grid reference. Letters go across the map's top and bottom; figures, on its sides.

The map continues on page 13 of the Street Finder.

Key to Street Finder

- Major sight
- Other sight
- Other building
- Railway station
- Métro station
- RER station
- Main bus stop
- Riverboat boarding point
- Batobus boarding point
- Tourist information
- Hospital with casualty unit
- Police station
- Church
- Synagogue
- Railway line
- Autoroute
- Pedestrian street
- «130 House number (main street)

Scale of Map Pages

0 metres 200
0 yards 200
1:12,000

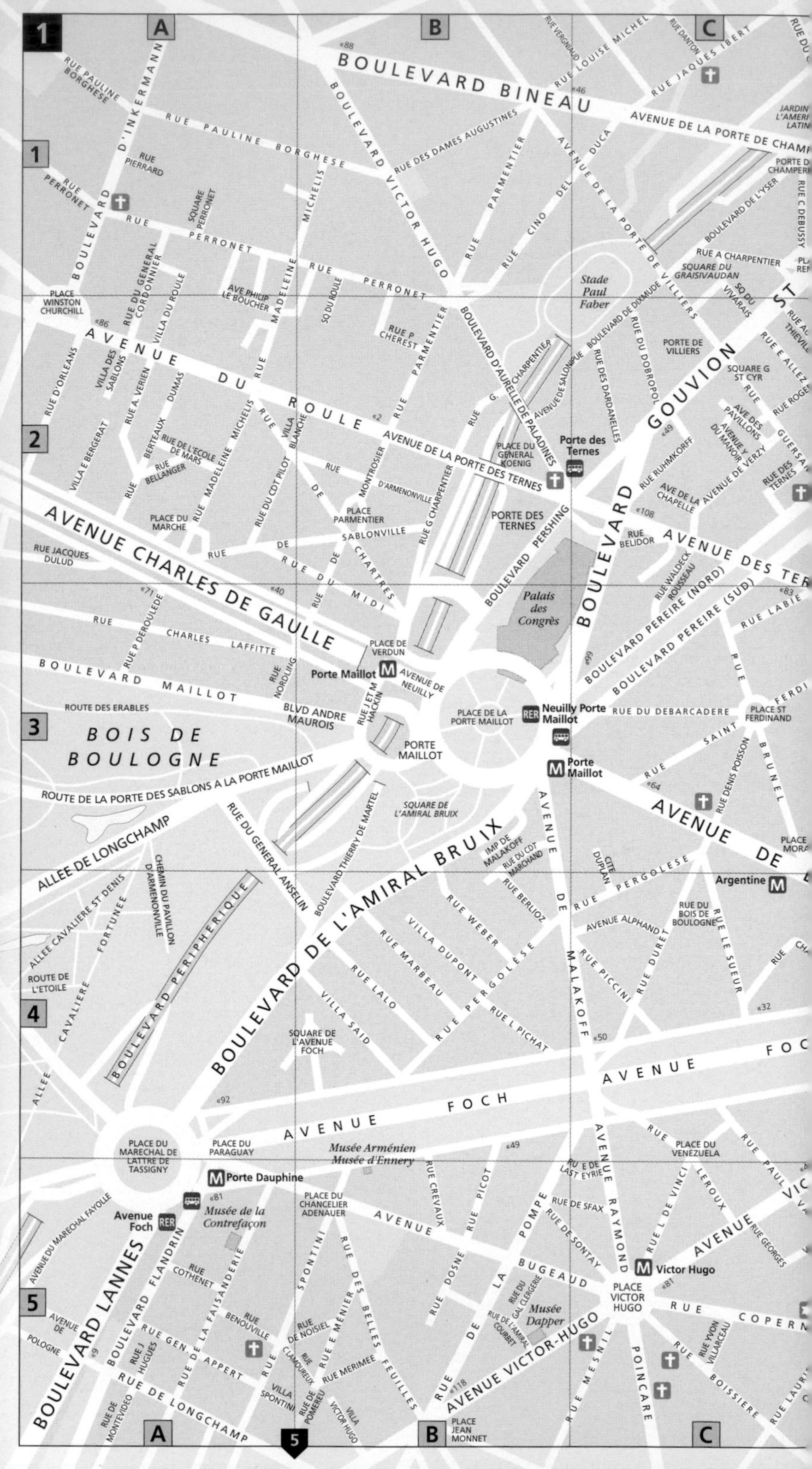
A
B
C
1
2
3
4
5
BOULEVARD BINEAU
BOULEVARD D'INKERMANN
RUE PAULINE BORGHESE
RUE PIERRARD
RUE PERRONET
SQUARE PERRONET
BOULEVARD VICTOR HUGO
RUE DES DAMES AUGUSTINES
RUE PARMENTIER
RUE CINO DEL DUCA
AVENUE DE LA PORTE DE VILLIERS
RUE LOUISE MICHEL
RUE VERGNIAUD
RUE DANTON
RUE JACQUES IBERT
AVENUE DE LA PORTE DE CHAMPERRET
JARDIN L'AMERI LATIN
PORTE DE CHAMPERRET
BOULEVARD DE L'YSER
RUE C DEBUSSY
RUE A CHARPENTIER
SQUARE DU GRAISIVAUDAN
SQ DU VIVARAIS
Stade Paul Faber
PLACE WINSTON CHURCHILL
RUE DU GENERAL CORDONNIER
VILLA DU ROULE
AVE PHILIP LE BOUCHER
RUE MADELEINE MICHELIS
SQ DU ROULE
RUE P CHEREST
BOULEVARD D'AURELLE DE PALADINES
RUE G. CHARPENTIER
AVENUE DE SALONIQUE
BOULEVARD DE DIXMUDE
RUE DES DARDANELLES
RUE DU DOBROPOL
PORTE DE VILLIERS
BOULEVARD GOUVION ST CYR
SQUARE G ST CYR
AVE DES PAVILLONS
AVENUE Y DU MANOIR
RUE ROGER
AVENUE DU ROULE
RUE D'ORLEANS
VILLA DES SABLONS
RUE A. VERIEN
RUE DUMAS
VILLA E BERGERAT
RUE BERTEAUX
RUE DE L'ECOLE DE MARS
RUE BELLANGER
AVENUE DE LA PORTE DES TERNES
VILLA BLANCHE
RUE DU CDT PILOT
RUE D'ARMENONVILLE
RUE MONTROSIER
PLACE DU GENERAL KOENIG
Porte des Ternes
RUE RUHMKORFF
AVE DE LA CHAPELLE
AVENUE DE VERZY
RUE DES TERNES
PLACE DU MARCHE
PLACE PARMENTIER
RUE DE SABLONVILLE
RUE DE CHARTRES
RUE G CHARPENTIER
PORTE DES TERNES
BOULEVARD PERSHING
RUE BELIDOR
AVENUE DES TERNES
AVENUE CHARLES DE GAULLE
RUE JACQUES DULUD
RUE DU MIDI
Palais des Congrès
RUE WALDECK ROUSSEAU
BOULEVARD PEREIRE (NORD)
BOULEVARD PEREIRE (SUD)
RUE LABIE
RUE CHARLES LAFFITTE
RUE P DEROULEDE
PLACE DE VERDUN
RUE NORDLING
Porte Maillot
AVENUE DE NEUILLY
BOULEVARD MAILLOT
ROUTE DES ERABLES
BLVD ANDRE MAUROIS
RUE J ET M HACKIN
PLACE DE LA PORTE MAILLOT
Neuilly Porte Maillot
RER
RUE DU DEBARCADERE
PLACE ST FERDINAND
BOIS DE BOULOGNE
PORTE MAILLOT
Porte Maillot
RUE SAINT FERDINAND
RUE DENIS POISSON
RUE BRUNEL
ROUTE DE LA PORTE DES SABLONS A LA PORTE MAILLOT
RUE DU GENERAL ANSELIN
BOULEVARD THIERRY DE MARTEL
SQUARE DE L'AMIRAL BRUIX
AVENUE DE LA GRANDE ARMEE
ALLEE DE LONGCHAMP
CHEMIN DU PAVILLON D'ARMENONVILLE
BOULEVARD DE L'AMIRAL BRUIX
IMP DE MALAKOFF
RUE DU CDT MARCHAND
AVENUE DE MALAKOFF
CITE DUPLAN
RUE PERGOLESE
Argentine
ALLEE CAVALIERE ST DENIS
FORTUNEE
BOULEVARD PERIPHERIQUE
RUE WEBER
RUE BERLIOZ
AVENUE ALPHAND
RUE DU BOIS DE BOULOGNE
RUE LE SUEUR
ROUTE DE L'ETOILE
VILLA DUPONT
RUE MARBEAU
RUE PICCINI
RUE DURET
RUE LALO
VILLA SAID
RUE L PICHAT
SQUARE DE L'AVENUE FOCH
AVENUE FOCH
PLACE DU MARECHAL DE LATTRE DE TASSIGNY
PLACE DU PARAGUAY
Musée Arménien
Musée d'Ennery
RUE CREVAUX
RUE PICOT
RUE DE LAST EYRIE
AVENUE RAYMOND POINCARE
PLACE DU VENEZUELA
RUE PAUL VALERY
Porte Dauphine
Avenue Foch
Musée de la Contrefaçon
PLACE DU CHANCELIER ADENAUER
AVENUE BUGEAUD
RUE DE SFAX
RUE DE SONTAY
RUE L DE VINCI
RUE LEROUX
AVENUE VICTOR HUGO
RUE GEORGES
AVENUE DU MARECHAL FAYOLLE
BOULEVARD LANNES
BOULEVARD FLANDRIN
RUE COTHENET
RUE DE LA FAISANDERIE
RUE SPONTINI
RUE DES BELLES FEUILLES
RUE DOSNE
RUE DE LA POMPE
RUE DU GAL CLERGERIE
RUE DE L'AMIRAL COURBET
Musée Dapper
Victor Hugo
PLACE VICTOR HUGO
RUE COPERNIC
AVENUE DE POLOGNE
RUE J HUGUES
RUE GEN. APPERT
RUE BENOUVILLE
RUE DE NOISIEL
RUE E MENIER
RUE CLAMOUREUX
RUE MERIMEE
VILLA SPONTINI
RUE DE POMEREU
VILLA VICTOR HUGO
RUE DE LONGCHAMP
RUE DE MONTEVIDEO
PLACE JEAN MONNET
AVENUE VICTOR-HUGO
RUE MESNIL
RUE YVON VILLARCEAU
RUE BOISSIERE
RUE LAURISTON

5

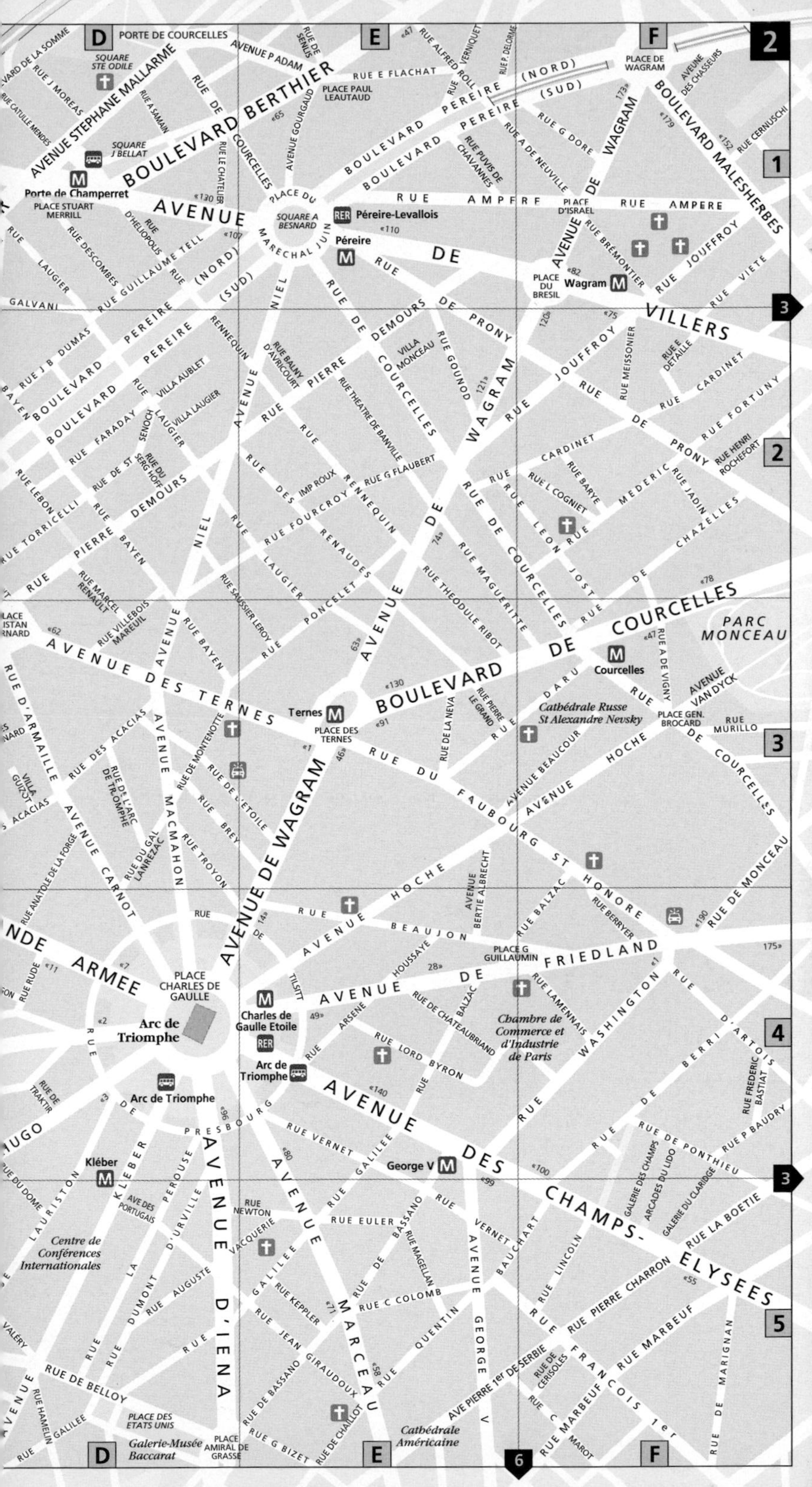

D
E
F
2
1
2
3
4
5
3
3
6
PORTE DE COURCELLES
SQUARE STE ODILE
AVENUE STEPHANE MALLARME
SQUARE J BELLAT
Porte de Champerret
PLACE STUART MERRILL
BOULEVARD BERTHIER
AVENUE P ADAM
RUE E FLACHAT
PLACE PAUL LEAUTAUD
AVENUE GOURGAUD
RUE ALFRED ROLL
RUE VERNIQUET
RUE P. DELORME
PLACE DE WAGRAM
AVENUE DES CHASSEURS
BOULEVARD MALESHERBES
RUE CERNUSCHI
BOULEVARD PEREIRE (NORD)
BOULEVARD PEREIRE (SUD)
RUE G DORE
RUE PUVIS DE CHAVANNES
RUE A DE NEUVILLE
AVENUE DE WAGRAM
RUE AMPERE
PLACE D'ISRAEL
PLACE DU MARECHAL JUIN
SQUARE A BESNARD
Péreire-Levallois
Péreire
RUE DE PRONY
RUE BRÉMONTIER
RUE JOUFFROY
PLACE DU BRESIL
Wagram
RUE VIETE
RUE DE VILLIERS
AVENUE DE VILLIERS
RUE DE COURCELLES
RUE LE CHATELIER
RUE D'HELIOPOLIS
RUE DESCOMBES
RUE LAUGIER
RUE GUILLAUME TELL
RUE GALVANI
RUE J B DUMAS
RUE BAYEN
RUE RENNEQUIN
AVENUE NIEL
RUE BALNY D'AVRICOURT
RUE PIERRE DEMOURS
VILLA MONCEAU
RUE GOUNOD
RUE THEATRE DE BANVILLE
RUE MEISSONIER
RUE E DETAILLE
RUE CARDINET
RUE FORTUNY
RUE HENRI ROCHEFORT
VILLA AUBLET
VILLA LAUGIER
RUE FARADAY
RUE SENOCH
RUE DU SERG HOFF
RUE DE ST SENOCH
RUE LEBON
RUE TORRICELLI
IMP ROUX
RUE G FLAUBERT
RUE FOURCROY
RUE DES RENAUDES
RUE L COGNIET
RUE BARYE
RUE MEDERIC
RUE JADIN
RUE DE CHAZELLES
RUE LEON JOST
RUE MAGUERITTE
RUE THEODULE RIBOT
RUE SAUSSIER LEROY
RUE PONCELET
RUE MARCEL RENAULT
RUE VILLEBOIS MAREUIL
AVENUE DES TERNES
BOULEVARD DE COURCELLES
PARC MONCEAU
Courcelles
RUE A DE VIGNY
AVENUE VAN DYCK
RUE DARU
Cathédrale Russe St Alexandre Nevsky
RUE PIERRE LE GRAND
RUE DE LA NEVA
Ternes
PLACE DES TERNES
PLACE GEN. BROCARD
RUE MURILLO
RUE D'ARMAILLE
RUE DES ACACIAS
VILLA GUIZOT
RUE DE L'ARC DE TRIOMPHE
AVENUE MACMAHON
RUE DE MONTENOTTE
RUE DE L'ETOILE
RUE BREY
RUE DU GAL LANREZAC
RUE TROYON
AVENUE CARNOT
RUE ANATOLE DE LA FORGE
RUE DU FAUBOURG ST HONORE
AVENUE BEAUCOUR
AVENUE HOCHE
AVENUE BERTIE ALBRECHT
RUE BALZAC
RUE BERRYER
RUE DE MONCEAU
AVENUE DE LA GRANDE ARMEE
RUE RUDE
PLACE CHARLES DE GAULLE
Arc de Triomphe
Charles de Gaulle Etoile
RUE DE TILSITT
RUE BEAUJON
PLACE G GUILLAUMIN
AVENUE DE FRIEDLAND
AVENUE HOUSSAYE
RUE ARSENE
RUE DE CHATEAUBRIAND
RUE LAMENNAIS
Chambre de Commerce et d'Industrie de Paris
RUE WASHINGTON
RUE LORD BYRON
RUE D'ARTOIS
RUE DE BERRI
RUE FREDERIC BASTIAT
RUE P BAUDRY
AVENUE DES CHAMPS-ELYSEES
AVENUE D'IENA
AVENUE KLEBER
RUE DE PRESBOURG
AVENUE VICTOR HUGO
RUE DE TRAKTIR
RUE DU DOME
RUE LAURISTON
Kléber
Centre de Conférences Internationales
RUE LA PEROUSE
AVE DES PORTUGAIS
RUE D'URVILLE
RUE DUMONT D'URVILLE
RUE AUGUSTE VACQUERIE
RUE NEWTON
RUE EULER
RUE VERNET
RUE GALILEE
AVENUE MARCEAU
George V
RUE DE BASSANO
RUE MAGELLAN
RUE C COLOMB
RUE QUENTIN BAUCHART
AVENUE GEORGE V
RUE DE PONTHIEU
GALERIE DES CHAMPS
ARCADES DU LIDO
GALERIE DU CLARIDGE
RUE LA BOETIE
RUE LINCOLN
RUE PIERRE CHARRON
RUE MARBEUF
RUE FRANCOIS 1er
RUE DE MARIGNAN
RUE KEPPLER
RUE JEAN GIRAUDOUX
RUE DE CHAILLOT
AVE PIERRE 1er DE SERBIE
RUE DE CERISOLES
RUE C MAROT
Cathédrale Américaine
RUE DE BELLOY
RUE HAMELIN
RUE GALILEE
PLACE DES ETATS UNIS
Galerie-Musée Baccarat
PLACE AMIRAL DE GRASSE
RUE G BIZET

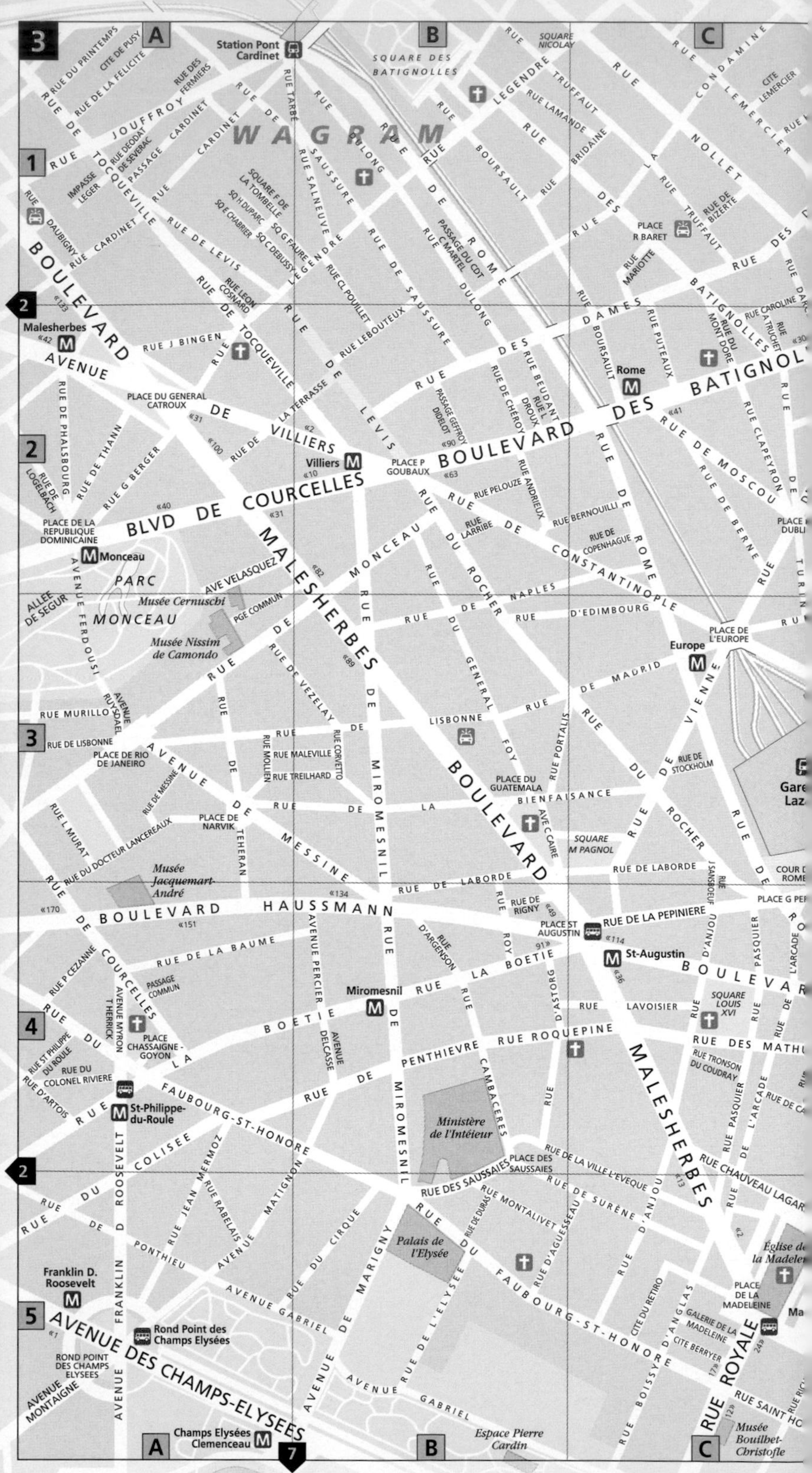

3
A
B
C
1
2
3
4
5
2
7
Station Pont Cardinet
SQUARE DES BATIGNOLLES
SQUARE NICOLAY
WAGRAM
RUE DU PRINTEMPS
CITE DE PUSY
RUE DE LA FELICITE
RUE DES FERMIERS
JOUFFROY
RUE DEODAT DE SEVERAC
PASSAGE CARDINET
IMPASSE LEGER
RUE DE TOCQUEVILLE
RUE CARDINET
RUE DAUBIGNY
RUE TARBE
RUE DE SAUSSURE
RUE SALNEUVE
RUE DULONG
SQUARE F DE LA TOMBELLE
SQ H DUPARC
SQ E CHABRIER
SQ G FAURE
SQ C DEBUSSY
RUE DE LEVIS
RUE LEGENDRE
RUE CL POUILLET
RUE LEON COSNARD
RUE LEBOUTEUX
PASSAGE DU CDT C MARTEL
RUE DE ROME
RUE BOURSAULT
RUE LAMANDE
RUE TRUFFAUT
RUE BRIDAINE
RUE NOLLET
RUE LEMERCIER
CITE LEMERCIER
RUE CONDAMINE
RUE DE LA
PLACE R BARET
RUE DE BIZERTE
RUE MARIOTTE
RUE DES DAMES
RUE PUTEAUX
RUE DU MONT DORE
RUE CAROLINE
RUE LA TRUCHET
Malesherbes
RUE J BINGEN
AVENUE DE VILLIERS
Rome
BOULEVARD DES BATIGNOLLES
PLACE DU GENERAL CATROUX
RUE DE LA TERRASSE
PASSAGE GEFFROY DIDELOT
RUE DE CHEROY
RUE BEAUDANT
RUE L DROUX
RUE DE PHALSBOURG
RUE DE THANN
RUE G BERGER
RUE DE LOGELBACH
Villiers
PLACE P GOUBAUX
BOULEVARD DE COURCELLES
RUE ANDRIEUX
RUE PELOUZE
RUE DE MOSCOU
RUE CLAPEYRON
PLACE DE LA REPUBLIQUE DOMINICAINE
BLVD DE COURCELLES
Monceau
BOULEVARD MALESHERBES
RUE LARRIBE
RUE DE CONSTANTINOPLE
RUE BERNOUILLI
RUE DE COPENHAGUE
RUE DE BERNE
PARC MONCEAU
AVE VELASQUEZ
Musée Cernuschi
ALLEE DE SEGUR
AVENUE FERDOUSI
RUE DE MONCEAU
RUE DU ROCHER
RUE DE NAPLES
RUE D'EDIMBOURG
PGE COMMUN
Musée Nissim de Camondo
PLACE DE L'EUROPE
Europe
RUE DE VEZELAY
RUE DU GENERAL FOY
RUE DE MADRID
RUE DE VIENNE
RUE MURILLO
AVENUE RUYSDAEL
RUE DE LISBONNE
RUE MALEVILLE
RUE CORVETTO
RUE MOLLIEN
RUE TREILHARD
RUE PORTALIS
RUE DE STOCKHOLM
RUE DE MIROMESNIL
PLACE DE RIO DE JANEIRO
AVENUE DE MESSINE
RUE DE MESSINE
RUE DE TEHERAN
PLACE DU GUATEMALA
RUE DE LA BIENFAISANCE
Gare
RUE L MURAT
PLACE DE NARVIK
AVE CAIRE
SQUARE M PAGNOL
RUE DU DOCTEUR LANCEREAUX
RUE DE LABORDE
RUE J SANSBOEUF
Musée Jacquemart-André
COUR DE ROME
RUE DE COURCELLES
BOULEVARD HAUSSMANN
RUE DE RIGNY
RUE ROY
PLACE G PEREIRE
PLACE ST AUGUSTIN
RUE DE LA PEPINIERE
RUE D'ARGENSON
RUE DE LA BAUME
AVENUE PERCIER
RUE D'ANJOU
RUE PASQUIER
RUE DE L'ARCADE
St-Augustin
BOULEVARD
RUE P CEZANNE
PASSAGE COMMUN
RUE LA BOETIE
RUE D'ASTORG
Miromesnil
RUE LAVOISIER
SQUARE LOUIS XVI
AVENUE MYRON T HERRICK
PLACE CHASSAIGNE - GOYON
AVENUE DELCASSE
RUE ROQUEPINE
RUE DES MATHURINS
RUE ST PHILIPPE DU ROULE
RUE DU COLONEL RIVIERE
RUE D'ARTOIS
RUE DE PENTHIEVRE
RUE CAMBACERES
RUE TRONSON DU COUDRAY
RUE DU FAUBOURG-ST-HONORE
St-Philippe-du-Roule
Ministère de l'Intéieur
RUE DE CAUMARTIN
RUE DU COLISEE
RUE JEAN MERMOZ
AVENUE MATIGNON
RUE DES SAUSSAIES
PLACE DES SAUSSAIES
RUE DE LA VILLE L'EVEQUE
RUE CHAUVEAU LAGARDE
RUE DE PONTHIEU
RUE RABELAIS
RUE DU CIRQUE
RUE MONTALIVET
RUE DE DURAS
RUE DE SURENE
Palais de l'Elysée
RUE D'AGUESSEAU
Église de la Madeleine
Franklin D. Roosevelt
AVENUE FRANKLIN D ROOSEVELT
AVENUE GABRIEL
AVENUE DE MARIGNY
RUE DE L'ELYSEE
CITE DU RETIRO
PLACE DE LA MADELEINE
Rond Point des Champs Elysées
GALERIE DE LA MADELEINE
CITE BERRYER
RUE D'ANGLAS
RUE BOISSY D'ANGLAS
RUE ROYALE
ROND POINT DES CHAMPS ELYSEES
AVENUE MONTAIGNE
AVENUE DES CHAMPS-ELYSEES
RUE SAINT HONORE
Champs Elysées Clemenceau
Espace Pierre Cardin
Musée Bouilhet-Christofle

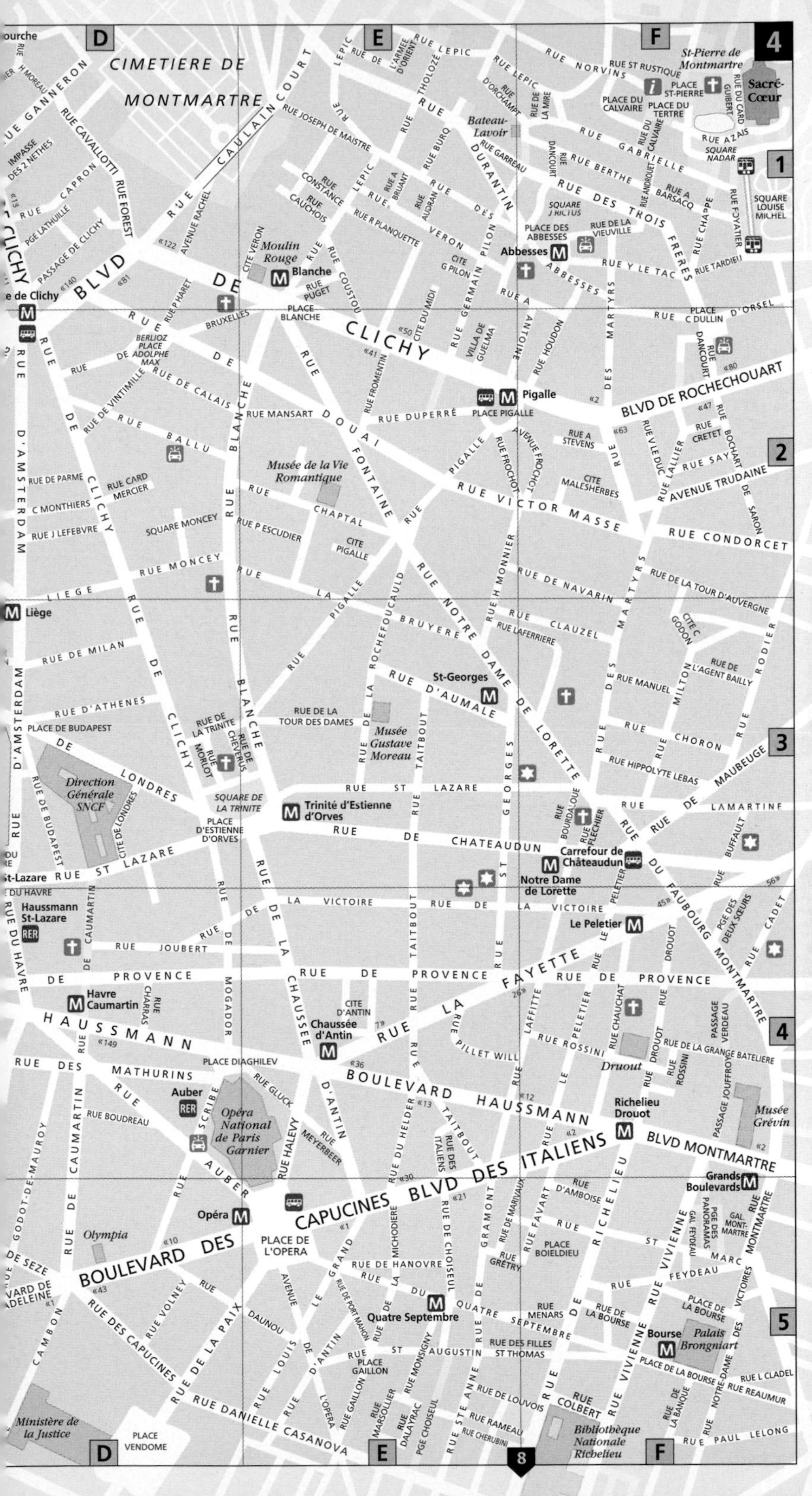

D
E
F
4
CIMETIERE DE MONTMARTRE
St-Pierre de Montmartre
Sacré-Cœur
RUE LEPIC
RUE DE L'ARMEE D'ORIENT
RUE NORVINS
RUE ST RUSTIQUE
PLACE ST-PIERRE
PLACE DU CALVAIRE
PLACE DU TERTRE
RUE GUIBERT
RUE DU CARD
RUE AZAIS
SQUARE NADAR
1
SQUARE LOUISE MICHEL
RUE FOYATIER
RUE TARDIEU
RUE GANNERON
RUE CAVALLOTTI
IMPASSE DES 2 NETHES
RUE CAPRON
RUE FOREST
PGE LATHUILLE
PASSAGE DE CLICHY
RUE CAULAINCOURT
AVENUE RACHEL
RUE JOSEPH DE MAISTRE
RUE THOLOZÉ
Bateau-Lavoir
RUE D'ORCHAMPT
RUE DE LA MIRE
RUE GARREAU
RUE DURANTIN
RUE GABRIELLE
RUE BERTHE
RUE DU CALVAIRE
RUE ANDROUET
RUE A BARSACQ
RUE CHAPPE
RUE DES TROIS FRERES
RUE DANCOURT
SQUARE J RICTUS
PLACE DES ABBESSES
RUE DE LA VIEUVILLE
Abbesses
RUE DES ABBESSES
RUE Y LE TAC
RUE CONSTANCE
RUE CAUCHOIS
RUE A BRUANT
RUE BURQ
RUE AUDRAN
RUE VERON
RUE R PLANQUETTE
CITE G PILON
RUE GERMAIN PILON
CITE VERON
Moulin Rouge
Blanche
RUE PUGET
RUE COUSTOU
PLACE BLANCHE
BLVD DE CLICHY
Place de Clichy
RUE P HARET
RUE DE BRUXELLES
BERLIOZ
PLACE DE ADOLPHE MAX
CITE DU MIDI
VILLA DE GUELMA
RUE ANTOINE
RUE HOUDON
PLACE C DULLIN
RUE D'ORSEL
RUE DANCOURT
Pigalle
PLACE PIGALLE
BLVD DE ROCHECHOUART
RUE DE CALAIS
RUE DE VINTIMILLE
RUE MANSART
RUE DE DOUAI
RUE FROMENTIN
RUE DUPERRÉ
AVENUE FROCHOT
RUE FROCHOT
RUE A STEVENS
RUE BOCHART
RUE CRETET
RUE SAY
2
RUE BALLU
RUE PIGALLE
RUE VICTOR MASSE
CITE MALESHERBES
RUE LALLIER
RUE VLE DUC
AVENUE TRUDAINE
RUE DE SARON
Musée de la Vie Romantique
RUE DE PARME
RUE CARD MERCIER
C MONTHIERS
RUE J LEFEBVRE
SQUARE MONCEY
RUE P ESCUDIER
RUE CHAPTAL
CITE PIGALLE
RUE FONTAINE
RUE CONDORCET
RUE D'AMSTERDAM
RUE DE CLICHY
RUE BLANCHE
RUE MONCEY
RUE H MONNIER
RUE DE NAVARIN
RUE DES MARTYRS
RUE DE LA TOUR D'AUVERGNE
RUE DE LIEGE
Liège
RUE DE LA BRUYERE
RUE DE LA ROCHEFOUCAULD
RUE NOTRE DAME DE LORETTE
RUE CLAUZEL
RUE LAFERRIERE
CITE C GODON
RUE RODIER
RUE DE MILAN
St-Georges
RUE D'AUMALE
RUE MANUEL
RUE MILTON
RUE DE L'AGENT BAILLY
RUE D'ATHENES
PLACE DE BUDAPEST
RUE DE LA TRINITE
RUE DE CHEVREUX
RUE MORLOT
RUE DE LA TOUR DES DAMES
Musée Gustave Moreau
RUE TAITBOUT
RUE ST GEORGES
RUE CHORON
RUE HIPPOLYTE LEBAS
3
RUE DE LONDRES
Direction Générale SNCF
RUE DE BUDAPEST
CITE DE LONDRES
SQUARE DE LA TRINITE
RUE ST LAZARE
Trinité d'Estienne d'Orves
PLACE D'ESTIENNE D'ORVES
RUE DE CHATEAUDUN
RUE BOURDALOUE
RUE FLECHIER
Carrefour de Châteaudun
Notre Dame de Lorette
RUE DE MAUBEUGE
RUE LAMARTINE
RUE BUFFAULT
St-Lazare
RUE DU HAVRE
Haussmann St-Lazare
RUE CAUMARTIN
RUE DE LA VICTOIRE
RUE DE MOGADOR
RUE DE LA CHAUSSEE D'ANTIN
RUE JOUBERT
Le Peletier
RUE LE PELETIER
RUE DROUOT
RUE DU FAUBOURG MONTMARTRE
PGE DES DEUX SOEURS
RUE CADET
RUE DE PROVENCE
Havre Caumartin
RUE CHARRAS
CITE D'ANTIN
Chaussée d'Antin
RUE LA FAYETTE
RUE LAFFITTE
RUE PILLET WILL
RUE ROSSINI
RUE CHAUCHAT
PASSAGE VERDEAU
4
BOULEVARD HAUSSMANN
RUE DE LA GRANGE BATELIERE
RUE DES MATHURINS
PLACE DIAGHILEV
Auber
RUE SCRIBE
RUE GLUCK
Opéra National de Paris Garnier
RUE HALEVY
RUE MEYERBEER
RUE DE LA CHAUSSEE D'ANTIN
RUE DU HELDER
RUE DES ITALIENS
Drouot
Richelieu Drouot
PASSAGE JOUFFROY
Musée Grévin
BLVD MONTMARTRE
RUE BOUDREAU
RUE GODOT-DE-MAUROY
RUE AUBER
Opéra
BLVD DES ITALIENS
BOULEVARD DES CAPUCINES
PLACE DE L'OPERA
RUE DE LA MICHODIERE
RUE DE CHOISEUL
RUE DE GRAMONT
RUE DE MARIVAUX
RUE FAVART
RUE D'AMBOISE
PLACE BOIELDIEU
RUE GRETRY
RUE DE RICHELIEU
RUE ST MARC
Grands Boulevards
GAL FEYDEAU
PGE DES PANORAMAS
GAL MONTMARTRE
RUE MONTMARTRE
Olympia
RUE DE SEZE
BLVD DE LA MADELEINE
RUE DE HANOVRE
RUE DU QUATRE SEPTEMBRE
Quatre Septembre
RUE MENARS
RUE DE LA BOURSE
RUE FEYDEAU
RUE VIVIENNE
PLACE DE LA BOURSE
RUE DES VICTOIRES
5
Bourse
Palais Brongniart
RUE CAMBON
RUE DES CAPUCINES
RUE VOLNEY
RUE DAUNOU
RUE DE LA PAIX
AVENUE DE L'OPERA
RUE LOUIS LE GRAND
RUE DE PORT MAHON
RUE D'ANTIN
RUE ST AUGUSTIN
PLACE GAILLON
RUE DES FILLES ST THOMAS
RUE NOTRE DAME DES VICTOIRES
RUE L CLADEL
RUE REAUMUR
RUE DE LA BANQUE
RUE DANIELLE CASANOVA
RUE GAILLON
RUE MARSOLLIER
RUE DALAYRAC
PGE CHOISEUL
RUE MONSIGNY
RUE STE ANNE
RUE DE LOUVOIS
RUE RAMEAU
RUE CHERUBINI
RUE COLBERT
Bibliothèque Nationale Richelieu
RUE PAUL LELONG
Ministère de la Justice
PLACE VENDOME
8

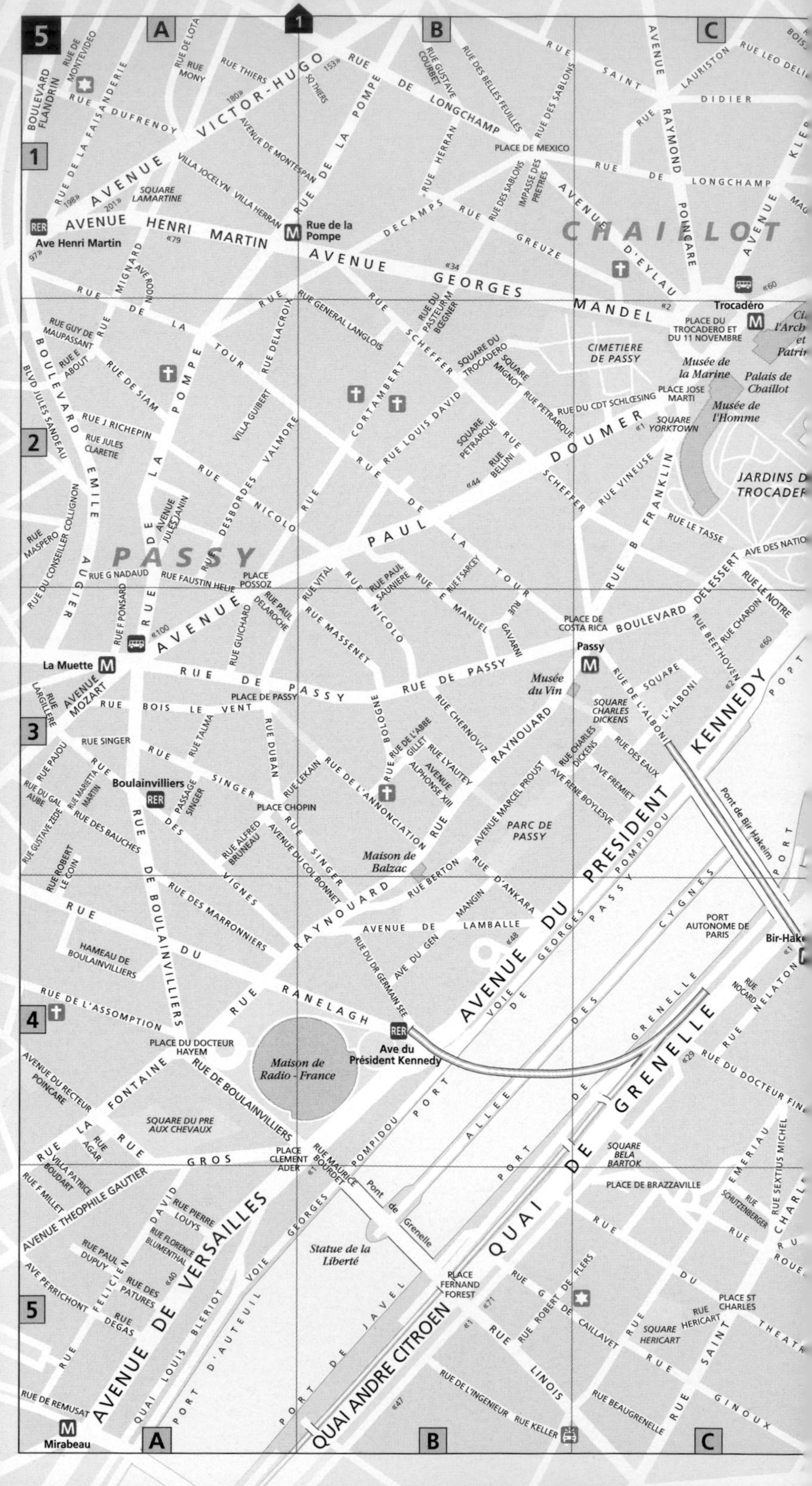
5
A
B
C
1
2
3
4
5
BOULEVARD FLANDRIN
RUE DE MONTEVIDEO
RUE DE LA FAISANDERIE
RUE DUFRENOY
RUE DE LOTA
RUE MONY
RUE THIERS
AVENUE VICTOR-HUGO
SQ THIERS
RUE DE LA POMPE
RUE DE LONGCHAMP
RUE GUSTAVE COURBET
RUE DES BELLES FEUILLES
RUE DES SABLONS
RUE SAINT DIDIER
AVENUE RAYMOND POINCARE
RUE LAURISTON
RUE LEO DELIBES
AVENUE DE MONTESPAN
VILLA JOCELYN
VILLA HERRAN
SQUARE LAMARTINE
RUE HERRAN
PLACE DE MEXICO
IMPASSE DES PRETRES
AVENUE D'EYLAU
AVENUE KLEBER
RUE DE LONGCHAMP
RER
Ave Henri Martin
AVENUE HENRI MARTIN
Rue de la Pompe
RUE DECAMPS
RUE GREUZE
CHAILLOT
AVENUE GEORGES MANDEL
Trocadéro
PLACE DU TROCADERO ET DU 11 NOVEMBRE
RUE MIGNARD
AVE RODIN
RUE DE LA TOUR
RUE GUY DE MAUPASSANT
RUE E ABOUT
BOULEVARD EMILE AUGIER
BLVD JULES SANDEAU
RUE DE SIAM
RUE J RICHEPIN
RUE JULES CLARETIE
RUE DELACROIX
RUE GENERAL LANGLOIS
RUE SCHEFFER
RUE DU PASTEUR M BOEGNER
SQUARE DU TROCADERO
SQUARE MIGNOT
CIMETIERE DE PASSY
Musée de la Marine
Palais de Chaillot
Musée de l'Homme
PLACE JOSE MARTI
RUE DU CDT SCHLŒSING
RUE PETRARQUE
SQUARE YORKTOWN
RUE CORTAMBERT
RUE LOUIS DAVID
SQUARE PETRARQUE
RUE BELLINI
AVENUE PAUL DOUMER
VILLA GUIBERT
RUE VALMORE
RUE DESBORDES
RUE NICOLO
AVENUE JULES JANIN
RUE VINEUSE
RUE FRANKLIN
JARDINS DU TROCADERO
RUE LE TASSE
AVE DES NATIONS
RUE MASPERO
RUE DU CONSEILLER COLLIGNON
PASSY
RUE G NADAUD
RUE FAUSTIN HELIE
PLACE POSSOZ
RUE VITAL
RUE PAUL SAUNIERE
RUE E MANUEL
RUE F SARCEY
RUE GAVARNI
BOULEVARD DELESSERT
RUE LE NOTRE
RUE CHARDIN
RUE BEETHOVEN
PLACE DE COSTA RICA
RUE F PONSARD
AVENUE MOZART
RUE GUICHARD
RUE PAUL DELAROCHE
RUE MASSENET
Passy
La Muette
RUE DE PASSY
PLACE DE PASSY
Musée du Vin
RUE DE L'ALBONI
SQUARE L'ALBONI
SQUARE CHARLES DICKENS
RUE LARGILLIERE
RUE BOIS LE VENT
RUE SINGER
RUE TALMA
RUE DUBAN
RUE BOLOGNE
RUE DE L'ABBE GILLET
RUE LYAUTEY
AVENUE ALPHONSE XIII
RUE CHERNOVIZ
RUE RAYNOUARD
RUE CHARLES DICKENS
RUE DES EAUX
AVE FREMIET
AVENUE DU PRESIDENT KENNEDY
Pont de Bir Hakeim
RUE PAJOU
RUE MARIETTA MARTIN
RUE DU GAL AUBE
Boulainvilliers
PASSAGE SINGER
PLACE CHOPIN
RUE LEKAIN
RUE DE L'ANNONCIATION
AVENUE MARCEL PROUST
AVE RENE BOYLESVE
PARC DE PASSY
RUE GUSTAVE ZEDE
RUE DES BAUCHES
RUE DES VIGNES
RUE ALFRED BRUNEAU
AVENUE DU COL BONNET
Maison de Balzac
RUE BERTON
RUE D'ANKARA
RUE ROBERT LE COIN
RUE DES MARRONNIERS
RUE DE BOULAINVILLIERS
RUE MANGIN
AVENUE DE LAMBALLE
VOIE DE GEORGES POMPIDOU
PORT DE PASSY
ALLEE DES CYGNES
PORT AUTONOME DE PARIS
Bir-Hakeim
HAMEAU DE BOULAINVILLIERS
RUE DU RANELAGH
RUE DU DR GERMAIN SEE
AVE DU GEN MANGIN
RUE DE L'ASSOMPTION
RER
Ave du Président Kennedy
RUE NOCARD
RUE NELATON
PLACE DU DOCTEUR HAYEM
Maison de Radio - France
AVENUE DU RECTEUR POINCARE
RUE LA FONTAINE
RUE DU DOCTEUR FINLAY
QUAI DE GRENELLE
SQUARE DU PRE AUX CHEVAUX
RUE AGAR
RUE GROS
PLACE CLEMENT ADER
RUE MAURICE BOURDET
PORT DE GRENELLE
SQUARE BELA BARTOK
RUE EMERIAU
RUE SEXTIUS MICHEL
VILLA PATRICE BOUDART
AVENUE THEOPHILE GAUTIER
PLACE DE BRAZZAVILLE
RUE SCHUTZENBERGER
RUE F MILLET
RUE DAVID
RUE PIERRE LOUYS
Pont de Grenelle
RUE CHARLES
RUE FLORENCE BLUMENTHAL
RUE PAUL DUPUY
AVENUE DE VERSAILLES
Statue de la Liberté
RUE DU THEATRE
RUE DE ROUELLE
AVE PERRICHONT
RUE FELICIEN DAVID
RUE DES PATURES
RUE DEGAS
PLACE FERNAND FOREST
RUE ROBERT DE FLERS
RUE G DE CAILLAVET
PLACE ST CHARLES
RUE HERICART
SQUARE HERICART
QUAI LOUIS BLERIOT
PORT D'AUTEUIL
VOIE GEORGES POMPIDOU
PORT DE JAVEL
QUAI ANDRE CITROEN
RUE LINOIS
RUE SAINT CHARLES
RUE DE L'INGENIEUR
RUE KELLER
RUE BEAUGRENELLE
RUE GINOUX
RUE DE REMUSAT
Mirabeau

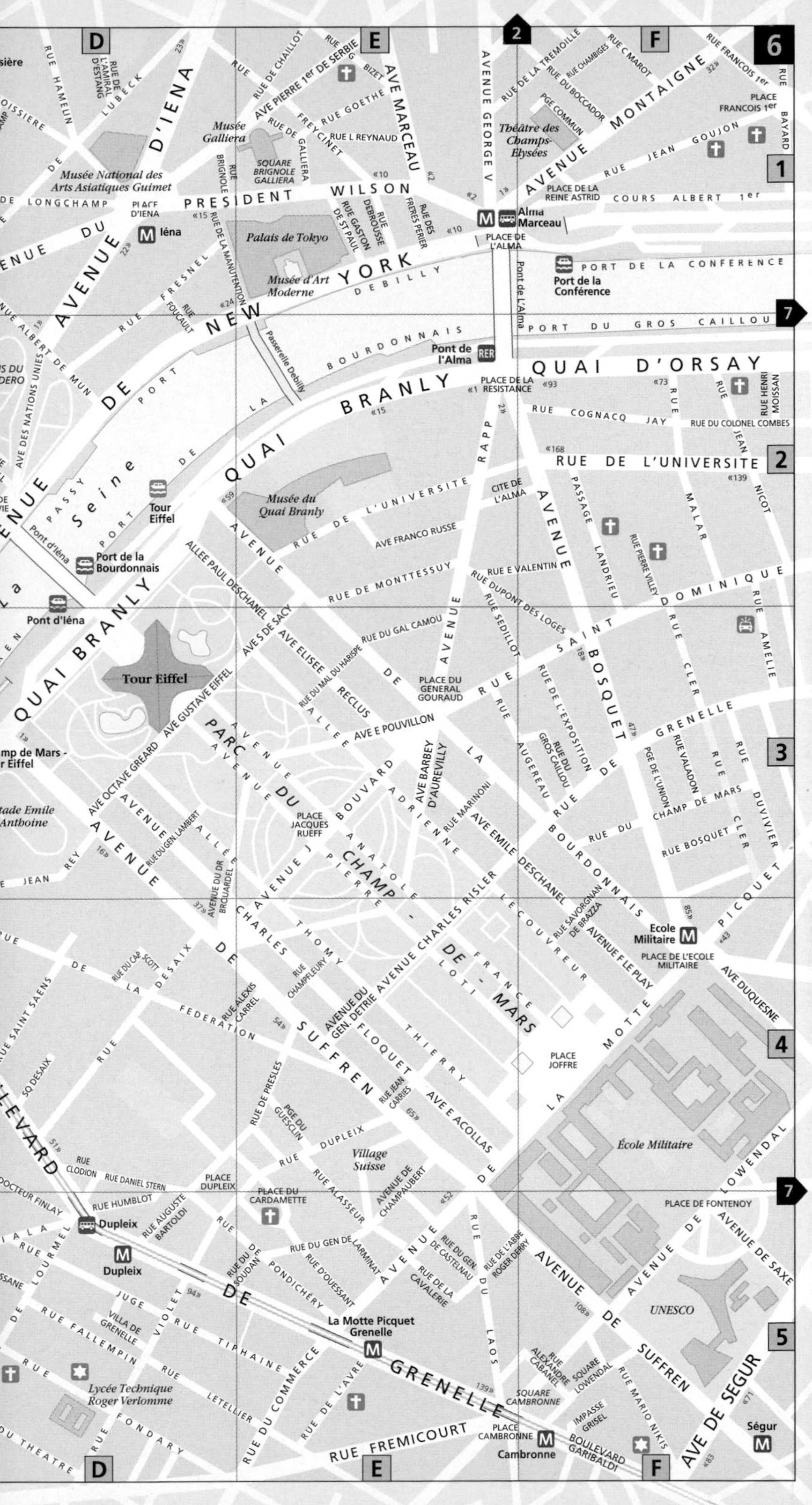

D
E
F
2
6
1
2
3
4
5
7
Musée Galliera
Musée National des Arts Asiatiques Guimet
Palais de Tokyo
Musée d'Art Moderne
Théâtre des Champs-Elysées
Iéna
Alma Marceau
PLACE DE L'ALMA
Port de la Conférence
PORT DE LA CONFERENCE
PORT DU GROS CAILLOU
Pont de l'Alma
AVENUE GEORGE V
AVENUE MONTAIGNE
AVE MARCEAU
AVENUE D'IENA
AVENUE DU PRESIDENT WILSON
AVENUE DE NEW YORK
PLACE D'IENA
PLACE DE LA REINE ASTRID
COURS ALBERT 1er
RUE JEAN GOUJON
PLACE FRANCOIS 1er
RUE FRANCOIS 1er
RUE BAYARD
RUE DE LA TREMOILLE
RUE DU BOCCADOR
RUE CHAMBIGES
RUE C MAROT
PGE COMMUN
RUE DE CHAILLOT
AVE PIERRE 1er DE SERBIE
RUE GOETHE
RUE BIZET
RUE DE GALLIERA
RUE L REYNAUD
RUE FREYCINET
SQUARE BRIGNOLE GALLIERA
RUE BRIGNOLE
RUE DE LA MANUTENTION
RUE GASTON DE ST PAUL
RUE DEBROUSSE
RUE DES FRERES PERIER
RUE HAMELIN
RUE DE L'AMIRAL D'ESTAING
RUE DE LUBECK
RUE DE LONGCHAMP
RUE FRESNEL
RUE FOUCAULT
AVENUE ALBERT DE MUN
AVE DES NATIONS UNIES
Passerelle Debilly
PORT DEBILLY
PORT DE LA BOURDONNAIS
Pont de l'Alma
PLACE DE LA RESISTANCE
QUAI D'ORSAY
QUAI BRANLY
PORT DE PASSY
Seine
Tour Eiffel
Port de la Bourdonnais
Pont d'Iéna
Pont d'Iéna
Musée du Quai Branly
RUE COGNACQ JAY
RUE DU COLONEL COMBES
RUE JEAN NICOT
RUE HENRI MOISSAN
RUE DE L'UNIVERSITE
CITE DE L'ALMA
AVENUE RAPP
AVENUE BOSQUET
PASSAGE LANDRIEU
RUE MALAR
RUE PIERRE VILLEY
AVE FRANCO RUSSE
RUE E VALENTIN
RUE DE MONTTESSUY
RUE DUPONT DES LOGES
RUE SEDILLOT
RUE SAINT DOMINIQUE
RUE CLER
RUE AMELIE
ALLEE PAUL DESCHANEL
AVE S DE SACY
AVE ELISEE RECLUS
RUE DU GAL CAMOU
RUE DU MAL DU HARISPE
PLACE DU GENERAL GOURAUD
AVENUE DE LA BOURDONNAIS
RUE DE L'EXPOSITION
RUE DU GROS CAILLOU
RUE AUGEREAU
RUE DE GRENELLE
RUE VALADON
PGE DE L'UNION
RUE DU CHAMP DE MARS
RUE DUVIVIER
RUE BOSQUET
AVE E POUVILLON
Tour Eiffel
AVE GUSTAVE EIFFEL
AVE OCTAVE GREARD
PARC DU CHAMP-DE-MARS
PLACE JACQUES RUEFF
ALLEE ADRIENNE LECOUVREUR
AVE BARBEY D'AUREVILLY
RUE MARINONI
AVE EMILE DESCHANEL
RUE SAVORGNAN DE BRAZZA
AVENUE F LE PLAY
AVENUE DE LA MOTTE PICQUET
Ecole Militaire
PLACE DE L'ECOLE MILITAIRE
AVE DUQUESNE
Champ de Mars - Tour Eiffel
Stade Emile Antoine
AVENUE DE SUFFREN
RUE DU GEN. LAMBERT
ALLEE THOMY THIERRY
AVENUE DU DR BROUARDEL
RUE JEAN REY
AVENUE J BOUVARD
AVENUE ANATOLE FRANCE
AVENUE PIERRE LOTI
AVENUE CHARLES RISLER
AVENUE CHARLES FLOQUET
AVENUE DU GEN. DETRIE
RUE CHAMPFLEURY
RUE DESAIX
RUE DU CAP SCOTT
RUE DE LA FEDERATION
RUE ALEXIS CARREL
PLACE JOFFRE
École Militaire
AVENUE DE LOWENDAL
RUE SAINT SAENS
SQ DESAIX
BOULEVARD DE GRENELLE
RUE DE PRESLES
PGE DU GUESCLIN
RUE DUPLEIX
Village Suisse
RUE JEAN CARRIES
AVE E ACOLLAS
AVENUE DE CHAMPAUBERT
RUE CLODION
RUE DANIEL STERN
RUE DU DOCTEUR FINLAY
PLACE DUPLEIX
PLACE DU CARDAMETTE
RUE HUMBLOT
RUE AUGUSTE BARTOLDI
Dupleix
RUE ALASSEUR
RUE DU LAOS
PLACE DE FONTENOY
AVENUE DE SAXE
RUE DE LOURMEL
RUE DE PONDICHERY
RUE DU SOUDAN
RUE DU GEN DE LARMINAT
RUE D'OUESSANT
RUE DU GEN. DE CASTELNAU
RUE DE LA CAVALERIE
RUE DE L'ABBE ROGER DERRY
UNESCO
RUE DE LA JUGE
RUE VIOLET
VILLA DE GRENELLE
RUE FALLEMPIN
RUE TIPHAINE
La Motte Picquet Grenelle
RUE DU COMMERCE
RUE DE L'AVRE
RUE ALEXANDRE CABANEL
SQUARE LOWENDAL
SQUARE CAMBRONNE
RUE MARIO NIKIS
AVE DE SEGUR
Lycée Technique Roger Verlomme
RUE LETELLIER
RUE FONDARY
RUE DU THEATRE
RUE FREMICOURT
PLACE CAMBRONNE
Cambronne
BOULEVARD GARIBALDI
IMPASSE GRISEL
Ségur

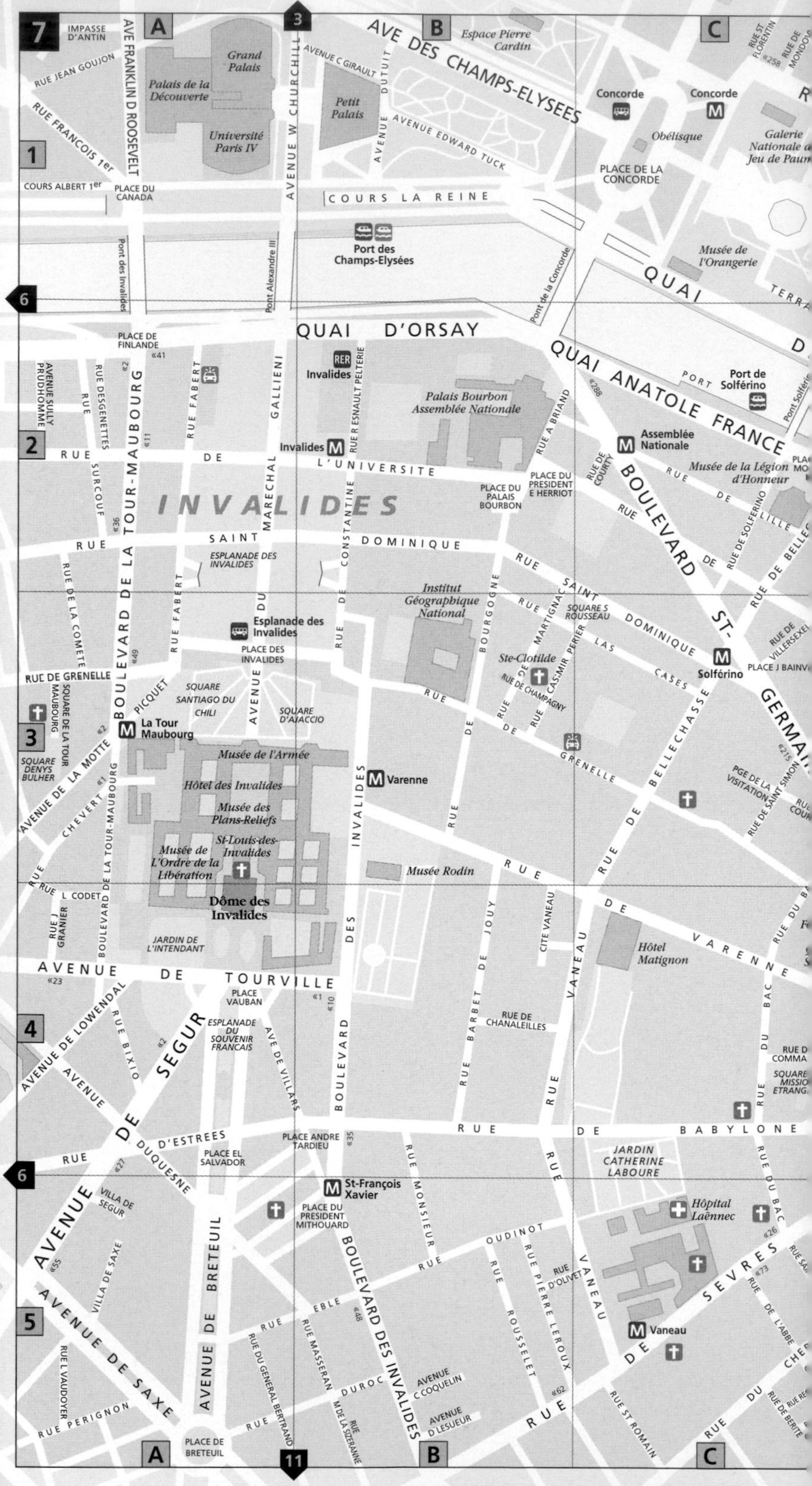

7
A
B
C
1
2
3
4
5
6
11
AVE DES CHAMPS-ELYSEES
Grand Palais
Palais de la Découverte
Université Paris IV
Petit Palais
Espace Pierre Cardin
Concorde
Obélisque
PLACE DE LA CONCORDE
Galerie Nationale du Jeu de Paume
Musée de l'Orangerie
COURS LA REINE
Port des Champs-Elysées
QUAI D'ORSAY
QUAI ANATOLE FRANCE
Port de Solférino
Invalides
Palais Bourbon Assemblée Nationale
Assemblée Nationale
Musée de la Légion d'Honneur
INVALIDES
BOULEVARD ST-GERMAIN
BOULEVARD DE LA TOUR-MAUBOURG
Esplanade des Invalides
Institut Géographique National
Ste-Clotilde
Solférino
La Tour Maubourg
Musée de l'Armée
Hôtel des Invalides
Musée des Plans-Reliefs
St-Louis-des-Invalides
Musée de L'Ordre de la Libération
Dôme des Invalides
Varenne
Musée Rodin
Hôtel Matignon
AVENUE DE TOURVILLE
AVENUE DE SEGUR
RUE DE BABYLONE
JARDIN CATHERINE LABOURE
St-François Xavier
Hôpital Laënnec
Vaneau
BOULEVARD DES INVALIDES
AVENUE DE SAXE
AVENUE DE BRETEUIL
PLACE DE BRETEUIL
RUE DE SEVRES

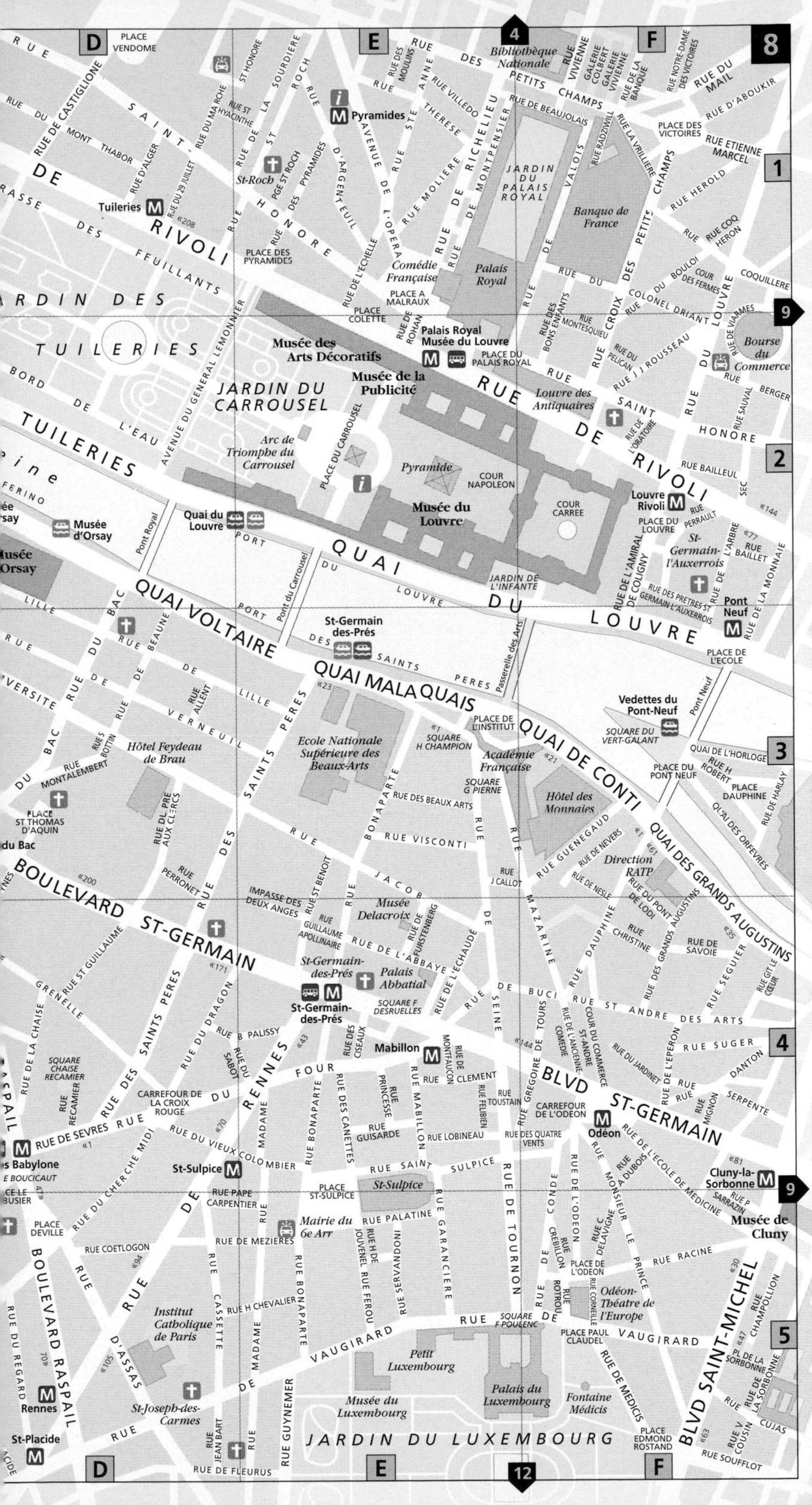
8
D
E
F
4
12
1
2
3
4
5
9
Place Vendome
Bibliothèque Nationale
Pyramides
St-Roch
Tuileries
Rue de Rivoli
Jardin des Tuileries
Jardin du Palais Royal
Banque de France
Comédie Française
Palais Royal
Palais Royal Musée du Louvre
Musée des Arts Décoratifs
Musée de la Publicité
Jardin du Carrousel
Arc de Triomphe du Carrousel
Pyramide
Cour Napoleon
Musée du Louvre
Cour Carree
Louvre des Antiquaires
Louvre Rivoli
St-Germain-l'Auxerrois
Bourse du Commerce
Musée d'Orsay
Quai du Louvre
Quai Voltaire
Quai Malaquais
Quai de Conti
Quai des Grands Augustins
Pont Neuf
Vedettes du Pont-Neuf
Square du Vert-Galant
Place Dauphine
Ecole Nationale Supérieure des Beaux-Arts
Académie Française
Hôtel des Monnaies
Hôtel Feydeau de Brau
Direction RATP
Musée Delacroix
Boulevard St-Germain
St-Germain-des-Prés
Palais Abbatial
Mabillon
Odéon
Cluny-la-Sorbonne
Musée de Cluny
St-Sulpice
Mairie du 6e Arr
Odéon-Théatre de l'Europe
Institut Catholique de Paris
Petit Luxembourg
Palais du Luxembourg
Musée du Luxembourg
Fontaine Médicis
St-Joseph-des-Carmes
Jardin du Luxembourg
Rennes
St-Placide
Boulevard Raspail
Blvd Saint-Michel
Rue de Vaugirard
Rue de Rennes
Rue de Tournon

9
A
B
C
1
2
3
4
5
8
8
13
Sentier
Réaumur Sébastopol
Arts et Métiers
Etienne Marcel
Les Halles
Châtelet les Halles
Châtelet
Rambuteau
Hôtel de Ville
St-Paul
Cité
St-Michel
St-Michel–Notre-Dame
Pont Marie
Maubert Mutualité
RUE REAUMUR
BOULEVARD DE SEBASTOPOL
RUE DE TURBIGO
RUE ETIENNE MARCEL
RUE MONTMARTRE
RUE LEOPOLD BELLAN
RUE BACHAUMONT
RUE MANDAR
RUE MONTORGUEIL
RUE ST SAUVEUR
RUE DUSSOUBS
RUE GRENETA
RUE ST DENIS
RUE DE PALESTRO
PASSAGE BASFOUR
IMPASSE ST DENIS
PGE DU GRAND CERF
RUE TIQUETONNE
PGE DU BOURG L'ABBE
RUE M STUART
Tour de Jean Sans Peur
RUE DE LA JUSSIENNE
RUE J J ROUSSEAU
RUE DU JOUR
RUE MAUCONSEIL
RUE FRANCAISE
St-Eustache
PLACE R CASSIN
RUE MONDETOUR
RUE PIERRE LESCOT
RUE DU CYGNE
RUE DE LA GRANDE TRUANDERIE
RUE RAMBUTEAU
Forum des Halles
RUE DES PRECHEURS
RUE BERGER
PLACE M QUENTIN
RUE ST HONORE
RUE DE LA COSSONNERIE
PLACE M DE NAVARRE
PLACE J DU BELLAY
Fontaine des Innocents
RUE DES INNOCENTS
SQUARE DES INNOCENTS
RUE DE LA FERRONNERIE
RUE DU PONT NEUF
RUE BOURDONNAIS
RUE DES HALLES
RUE DES DECHARGEURS
PLACE STE OPPORTUNE
RUE DE RIVOLI
BOULEVARD DE SEBASTOPOL
RUE DES LOMBARDS
RUE BERTIN POIREE
RUE DES ORFEVRES
RUE J LANTIER
RUE DE LA COLONNE
AVE VICTORIA
QUAI DE LA MEGISSERIE
VOIE GEORGES POMPIDOU
PLACE DU CHATELET
Tour St-Jacques
SQUARE DE LA TOUR ST-JACQUES
RUE ST MARTIN
RUE QUINCAMPOIX
RUE DE VENISE
PLACE GEORGES POMPIDOU
Centre Georges Pompidou
RUE AUBRY LE BOUCHER
PL IGOR STRAVINSKY
St-Merri
RUE N FLAMEL
RUE PERNELLE
RUE ST BON
RUE DE LA TACHERIE
RUE ST DENIS
Assistance Publique
Hôtel de Ville
PLACE DE L'HOTEL DE VILLE
MAIRIE DE PARIS
RUE DE LOBAU
RUE AUX OURS
RUE DU GRENIER ST LAZARE
PGE DU COMMERCE ST MARTIN
PGE MOLIERE
RUE B DE CLAIRVAUX
IMP BEAUBOURG
PGE DU MAURE
PGE DE L'HORLOGE A AUTOMATES
PASSAGE BRANTOME
RUE BEAUBOURG
RUE DU RENARD
RUE GEOFFROY L'ANGEVIN
RUE SIMON LE FRANC
RUE ST MERRI
RUE SAINTE CROIX DE LA BRETONNERIE
SQUARE STE CROIX DE LA BRETONNERIE
RUE DE LA VERRERIE
RUE DES MAUVAIS GARCONS
RUE DU TEMPLE
RUE DU PLATRE
RUE DES ARCHIVES
RUE MICHEL LE COMTE
RUE DES HAUDRIETTES
Musée de la Poupee
JARDIN ST AIGNAN
Musée d'Art et d'Histoire du Judaïsme
RUE DE BRAQUE
RUE PECQUAY
RUE DES BLANCS MANTEAUX
RUE DES FRANCS-BOURGEOIS
Hôtel de Soubise
Archives Nationales
Hôtel de Rohan
Hôtel Guénégaud
Musée de la Chasse et de la Nature
RUE AUBRIOT
RUE DES GUILLEMITES
RUE VIEILLE DU TEMPLE
RUE DE MOUSSY
RUE DU BOURG TIBOURG
RUE DU ROI DE SICILE
RUE DU TRESOR
RUE DES ECOUFFES
RUE DES ROSIERS
RUE F DUVAL
RUE DE RIVOLI
RUE FRANCOIS MIRON
RUE CLOCHE PERCE
RUE TIRON
PLACE ST GERVAIS
RUE DE BROSSE
RUE DES BARRES
St-Gervais St-Protais
RUE DU PONT LOUIS PHILIPPE
RUE GEOFFROY L'ASNIER
Mémorial de la Shoah
RUE DE JOUY
RUE DE FOURCY
RUE DU PREVOT
RUE CHARLEMAGNE
RUE DES NONNAINS D'HYERES
RUE DU FIGUIER
RUE DU FAUCONNIER
SQUARE A SCHWEITZER
Hôtel des Archeveques de Sens
QUAI DES CELESTINS
RUE DE L'AVE MARIA
RUE VIEILLE DU TEMPLE
RUE DES FONTAINES DU TEMPLE
RUE DU VERTBOIS
RUE VOLTA
RUE DE BORDA
RUE MONTGOLFIER
RUE VAUCANSON
RUE CONTE
RUE STE ELISABETH
SQUARE EMILE CHAUTEMPS
RUE PAPIN
Musée des Arts et Métiers
SQUARE DU G. MORIN
RUE CUNIN GRIDAINE
RUE BAILLY
RUE AU MAIRE
PASSAGE BARROIS
PASSAGE ALOMBERT
RUE DES VERTUS
RUE DES GRAVILLIERS
PGE DES GRAVILLIERS
RUE CHAPON
RUE DE MONTMORENCY
RUE PORTEFOIN
RUE DE PASTOURELLE
RUELLE SOURDIS
PGE DE L'ANCRE
RUE DU BOURG L'ABBE
Pont au Change
Pont Notre-Dame
QUAI DE GESVRES
QUAI DE L'HORLOGE
Conciergerie
Palais de Justice
Ste-Chapelle
BOULEVARD DU PALAIS
QUAI DE LA CORSE
RUE DE LUTECE
PLACE L LEPINE
ILE DE LA CITE
RUE DE LA CITE
Hôtel Dieu
Pont d'Arcole
QUAI DE L'HOTEL DE VILLE
PORT DE L'HOTEL DE VILLE
Quai de l'Hôtel de Ville
VOIE GEORGES POMPIDOU
RUE D'ARCOLE
RUE DE LA COLOMBE
RUE DES URSINS
QUAI AUX FLEURS
RUE CHANOINESSE
RUE DU CLOITRE-NOTRE-DAME
Crypte Archéologique
PLACE DU PARVIS NOTRE-DAME
Notre-Dame
SQUARE JEAN-XXIII
QUAI DE L'ARCHEVECHE
SQUARE DE L'ILE DE FRANCE
Pont St-Louis
Pont Louis Philippe
PLACE DU BATAILLON FRANCAIS DE L'O.N.U. EN COREE
QUAI DE BOURBON
RUE J DU BELLAY
RUE BOUTAREL
QUAI D'ORLEANS
RUE LE REGRATTIER
ILE ST-LOUIS
RUE BUDE
RUE ST LOUIS EN L'ILE
RUE DES DEUX PONTS
St-Louis-en-l'Ile
Pont Marie
PORT DES CELESTINS
QUAI D'ANJOU
SQUARE DE L'AVE MARIA
Hôtel de Lauzun
QUAI DE BETHUNE
RUE POULLETIER
Pont de la Tournelle
QUAI DU MARCHE-NEUF
Pont St-Michel
Petit Pont
QUAI ST MICHEL
PLACE DU PETIT PONT
RUE DE LA HUCHETTE
RUE X PRIVAS
RUE DE LA HARPE
RUE ST SEVERIN
RUE DES PRETRES ST SEVERIN
RUE DE LA PARCHEMINERIE
RUE BOUTEBRIE
St-Séverin
RUE DU PETIT PONT
RUE ST JULIEN LE PAUVRE
SQUARE R VIVIANI
St-Julien-le-Pauvre
QUAI DE MONTEBELLO
Pont au Double
PORT DE MONTEBELLO
Port de Montebello
RUE DE LA BUCHERIE
RUE DE L'HOTEL COLBERT
RUE GALANDE
RUE DES GRANDS DEGRES
RUE DANTE
RUE LAGRANGE
RUE DOMAT
RUE F SAUTON
RUE MAITRE ALBERT
RUE DE BIEVRE
QUAI DE LA TOURNELLE
PORT DE LA TOURNELLE
Musée Adam Mickiewicz
BOULEVARD SAINT-GERMAIN
RUE SAINT-JACQUES
Musée de Cluny
RUE DU SOMMERARD
SQUARE ET PLACE P PAINLEVE
RUE THENARD
RUE DE LATRAN
PLACE MAUBERT
RUE DES BERNARDINS
RUE DE PONTOISE
RUE COCHIN
RUE DE POISSY
La Sorbonne
Collège de France
SQUARE F A MARIETTE
PLACE M BERTHELOT
RUE JEAN DE BEAUVAIS
RUE DES CARMES
RUE DE LA MONTAGNE STE GENEVIEVE
RUE MONGE
QUARTIER LATIN
RUE DES ECOLES
RUE DU CARDINAL LEMOINE
RUE DES CHANTIERS
RUE DES FOSSES SAINT BERNARD
Institut du Monde Arabe
QUAI SAINT BERNARD
PORT SAINT BERNARD
Pont de Sully
SQUARE BARYE
RUE ST VICTOR
RUE DU CIMETIERE SAINT BENOIT
RUE DE LANNEAU
RUE DE L'ECOLE POLYTECHNIQUE
RUE VALETTE
IMPASSE CHARTIERE
Chapelle de la Sorbonne
Lyceé Louis le Grand
RUE CUJAS
SQUARE P LANGEVIN
JARDIN DE NAVARRE
RUE D'ARRAS
Musée de Minéralogie
Universités Paris VI et Paris VII

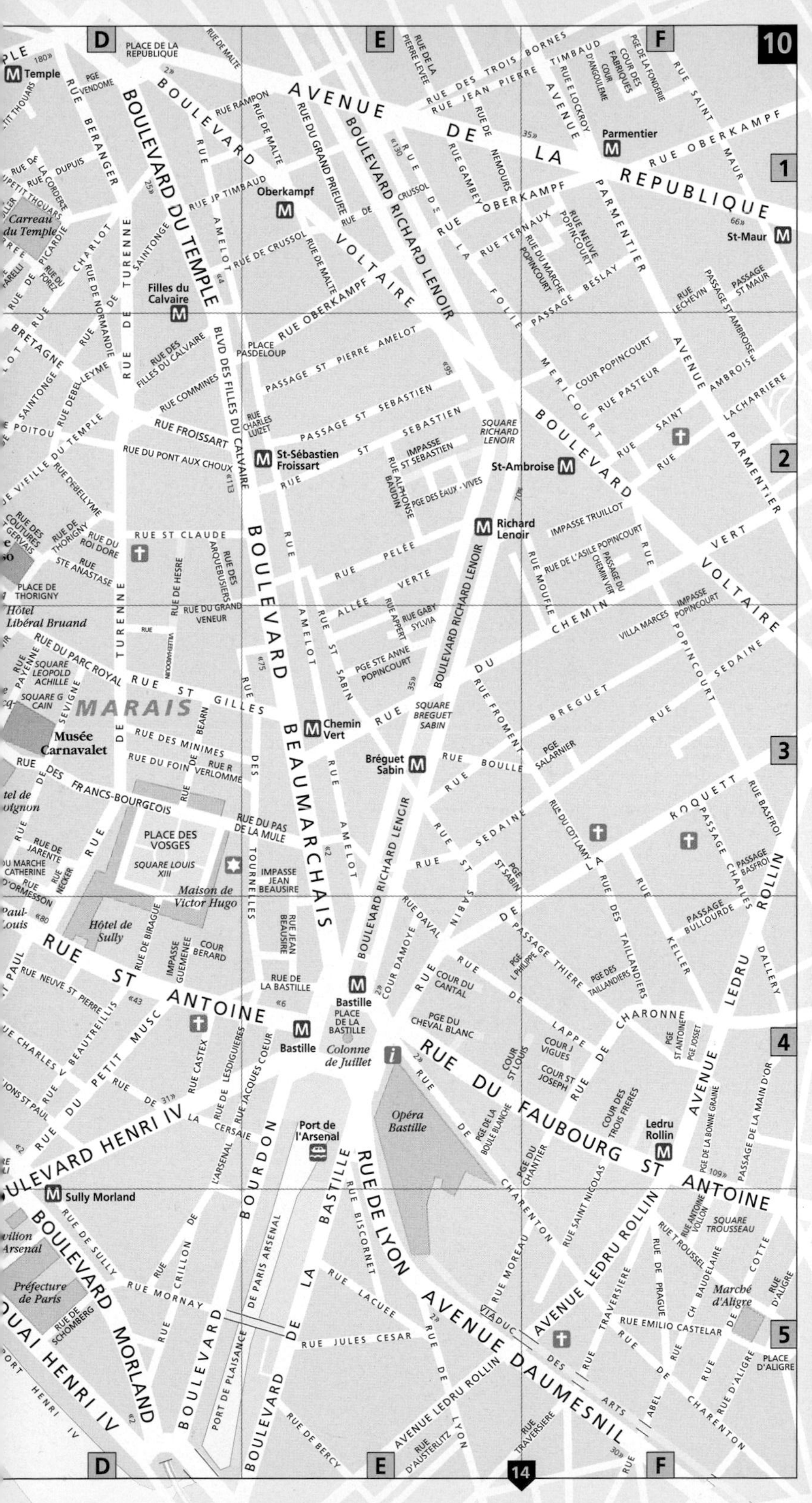
D
E
F
1
2
3
4
5
PLACE DE LA REPUBLIQUE
Temple
Parmentier
Oberkampf
St-Maur
Filles du Calvaire
St-Sébastien Froissart
St-Ambroise
Richard Lenoir
Chemin Vert
Bréguet Sabin
Bastille
Ledru Rollin
Sully Morland
Port de l'Arsenal
AVENUE DE LA REPUBLIQUE
BOULEVARD DU TEMPLE
BOULEVARD VOLTAIRE
BOULEVARD RICHARD LENOIR
BOULEVARD BEAUMARCHAIS
BLVD DES FILLES DU CALVAIRE
BOULEVARD HENRI IV
BOULEVARD MORLAND
BOULEVARD BOURDON
BOULEVARD DE LA BASTILLE
QUAI HENRI IV
RUE DE LYON
AVENUE DAUMESNIL
AVENUE LEDRU ROLLIN
RUE DU FAUBOURG ST ANTOINE
RUE ST ANTOINE
RUE DE LA ROQUETTE
RUE DE CHARONNE
RUE DU CHEMIN VERT
RUE OBERKAMPF
RUE PARMENTIER
RUE DE TURENNE
RUE AMELOT
RUE ST GILLES
RUE DES FRANCS-BOURGEOIS
RUE FROISSART
RUE DU PONT AUX CHOUX
RUE ST CLAUDE
RUE DE CRUSSOL
RUE JP TIMBAUD
RUE DE MALTE
RUE SEDAINE
RUE BREGUET
RUE DE CHARENTON
RUE DE LA FOLIE MERICOURT
RUE SAINT AMBROISE
RUE DES TAILLANDIERS
RUE KELLER
RUE SAINT NICOLAS
RUE CRILLON
RUE MORNAY
RUE DE SULLY
RUE JULES CESAR
RUE DE BERCY
RUE BISCORNET
RUE LACUEE
RUE TRAVERSIERE
RUE EMILIO CASTELAR
RUE D'ALIGRE
PLACE D'ALIGRE
Marché d'Aligre
SQUARE TROUSSEAU
PLACE DES VOSGES
SQUARE LOUIS XIII
Maison de Victor Hugo
Hôtel de Sully
MARAIS
Musée Carnavalet
Hôtel Libéral Bruand
PLACE DE THORIGNY
Carreau du Temple
PLACE PASDELOUP
SQUARE RICHARD LENOIR
SQUARE BREGUET SABIN
PLACE DE LA BASTILLE
Colonne de Juillet
Opéra Bastille
Préfecture de Paris
Pavilion Arsenal
PORT DE PLAISANCE
VIADUC DES ARTS

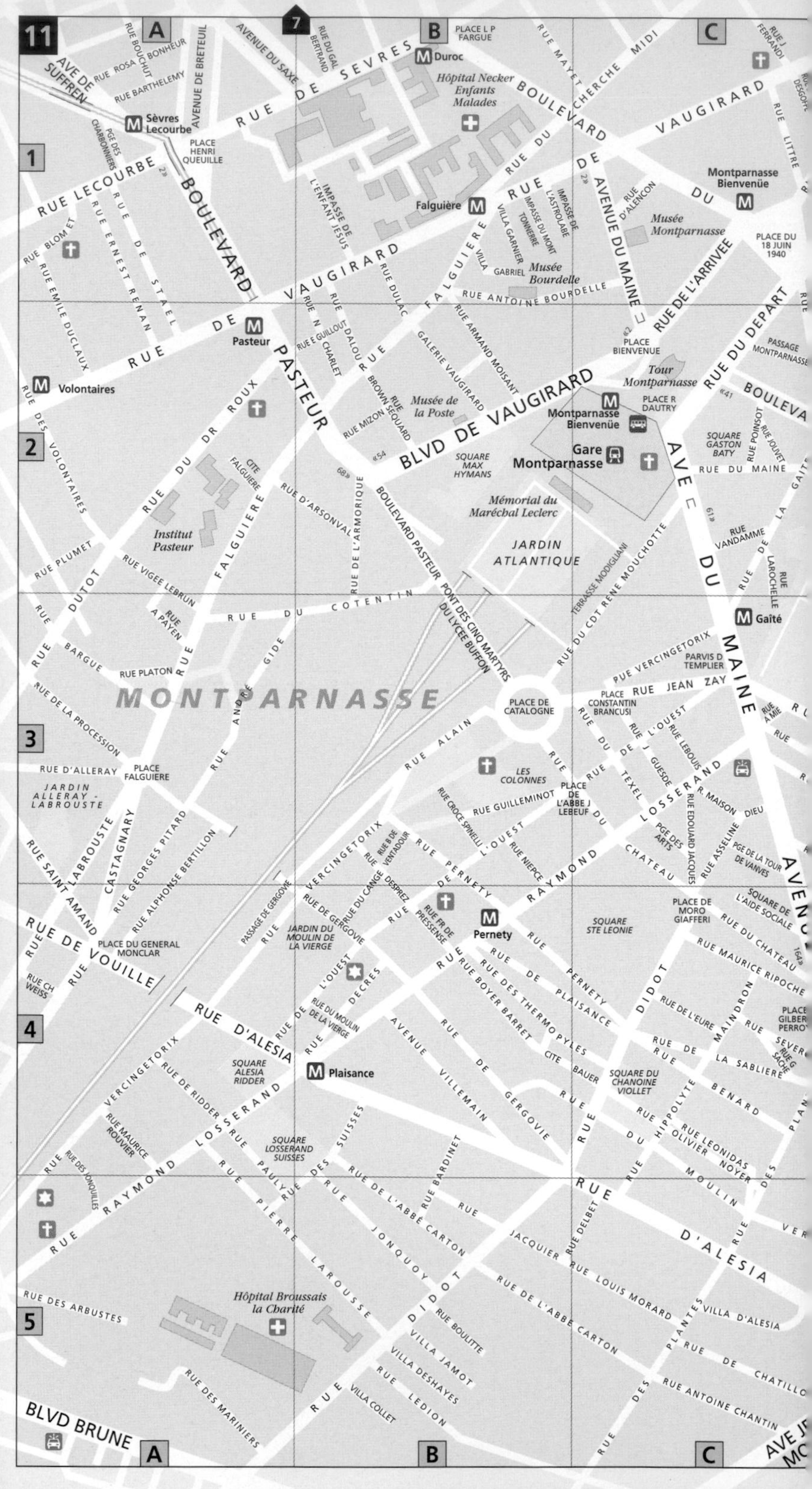

11
7
A
B
C
1
2
3
4
5
AVE DE SUFFREN
RUE ROSA BONHEUR
RUE BOUCHUT
RUE BARTHELEMY
AVENUE DE BRETEUIL
AVENUE DU SAXE
RUE DU GAL BERTRAND
RUE DE SEVRES
PLACE L P FARGUE
Duroc
Hôpital Necker Enfants Malades
RUE MAYET
RUE DU CHERCHE MIDI
BOULEVARD DU MONTPARNASSE
RUE DE VAUGIRARD
RUE J FERRANDI
RUE DESGOFFE
RUE LITTRE
Sèvres Lecourbe
PGE DES CHARBONNIERS
PLACE HENRI QUEUILLE
RUE LECOURBE
BOULEVARD PASTEUR
IMPASSE DE L'ENFANT JESUS
Falguière
IMPASSE DU MONT TONNERRE
IMPASSE DE L'ASTROLABE
VILLA GARNIER
AVENUE DU MAINE
RUE D'ALENCON
Montparnasse Bienvenüe
Musée Montparnasse
PLACE DU 18 JUIN 1940
RUE BLOMET
RUE ERNEST RENAN
RUE DE STAEL
RUE EMILE DUCLAUX
RUE DULAC
RUE FALGUIERE
VILLA GABRIEL
Musée Bourdelle
RUE ANTOINE BOURDELLE
RUE DE L'ARRIVEE
RUE DU DEPART
Pasteur
RUE N CHARLET
RUE E GUILLOUT
RUE DALOU
GALERIE VAUGIRARD
RUE ARMAND MOISANT
PLACE BIENVENUE
PASSAGE MONTPARNASSE
Tour Montparnasse
Volontaires
RUE DES VOLONTAIRES
RUE DU DR ROUX
RUE BROWN SEQUARD
RUE MIZON
Musée de la Poste
BLVD DE VAUGIRARD
PLACE R DAUTRY
Gare Montparnasse
BOULEVARD EDGAR QUINET
SQUARE GASTON BATY
RUE POINSOT
RUE JOLIVET
RUE DU MAINE
RUE DE LA GAITE
CITE FALGUIERE
RUE D'ARSONVAL
SQUARE MAX HYMANS
Mémorial du Maréchal Leclerc
AVENUE DU MAINE
Institut Pasteur
RUE DE L'ARMORIQUE
JARDIN ATLANTIQUE
TERRASSE MODIGLIANI
RUE DU CDT RENE MOUCHOTTE
RUE VANDAMME
RUE DE LAROCHELLE
RUE PLUMET
RUE DUTOT
RUE VIGEE LEBRUN
RUE DU COTENTIN
PONT DES CINQ MARTYRS DU LYCEE BUFFON
Gaîté
RUE A PAYEN
RUE BARGUE
RUE PLATON
RUE ANDRE GIDE
RUE VERCINGETORIX
PARVIS D TEMPLIER
MONTPARNASSE
PLACE DE CATALOGNE
PLACE CONSTANTIN BRANCUSI
RUE JEAN ZAY
RUE DE LA PROCESSION
RUE ALAIN
RUE DE L'OUEST
RUE DU TEXEL
RUE J GUESDE
RUE LEBOUIS
RUE D'ALLERAY
PLACE FALGUIERE
LES COLONNES
PLACE DE L'ABBE J LEBEUF
RUE LOSSERAND
RUE MAISON DIEU
JARDIN ALLERAY - LABROUSTE
RUE CROCE SPINELLI
RUE GUILLEMINOT
PGE DES ARTS
RUE EDOUARD JACQUES
RUE ASSELINE
PGE DE LA TOUR DE VANVES
RUE SAINT AMAND
RUE LABROUSTE
RUE CASTAGNARY
RUE GEORGES PITARD
RUE ALPHONSE BERTILLON
RUE B DE VENTADOUR
RUE NIEPCE
RUE DU CHATEAU
RUE RAYMOND LOSSERAND
RUE DESPREZ
RUE PERNETY
PLACE DE MORO GIAFFERI
SQUARE DE L'AIDE SOCIALE
PASSAGE DE GERGOVIE
RUE DE GERGOVIE
RUE DU CANGE
RUE FR DE PRESSENSE
Pernety
SQUARE STE LEONIE
RUE DE VOUILLE
PLACE DU GENERAL MONCLAR
JARDIN DU MOULIN DE LA VIERGE
RUE MAURICE RIPOCHE
RUE CH WEISS
RUE DECRES
RUE BOYER BARRET
RUE DES THERMOPYLES
RUE DE PLAISANCE
RUE DIDOT
PLACE GILBERT PERROY
RUE DU MOULIN DE LA VIERGE
RUE DE L'EURE
RUE MAINDRON
RUE SEVERO
RUE G SACHE
RUE D'ALESIA
AVENUE VILLEMAIN
CITE BAUER
RUE DE LA SABLIERE
SQUARE ALESIA RIDDER
Plaisance
SQUARE DU CHANOINE VIOLLET
RUE BENARD
RUE VERCINGETORIX
RUE DE RIDDER
RUE DE GERGOVIE
RUE HIPPOLYTE
RUE LEONIDAS
RUE OLIVIER NOYER
RUE MAURICE ROUVIER
SQUARE LOSSERAND SUISSES
RUE DES SUISSES
RUE BARDINET
RUE DU MOULIN VERT
RUE DES DES PLANTES
RUE DES JONQUILLES
RUE PAULY
RUE PIERRE LAROUSSE
RUE DE L'ABBE CARTON
RUE DELBET
RUE D'ALESIA
RUE JACQUIER
RUE JONQUOY
RUE LOUIS MORARD
RUE DES ARBUSTES
Hôpital Broussais la Charité
RUE DIDOT
RUE BOULITTE
VILLA D'ALESIA
RUE DE CHATILLON
VILLA JAMOT
VILLA DESHAYES
RUE ANTOINE CHANTIN
RUE DES MARINIERS
RUE VILLA COLLET
RUE LEDION
BLVD BRUNE
AVE JEAN MOULIN

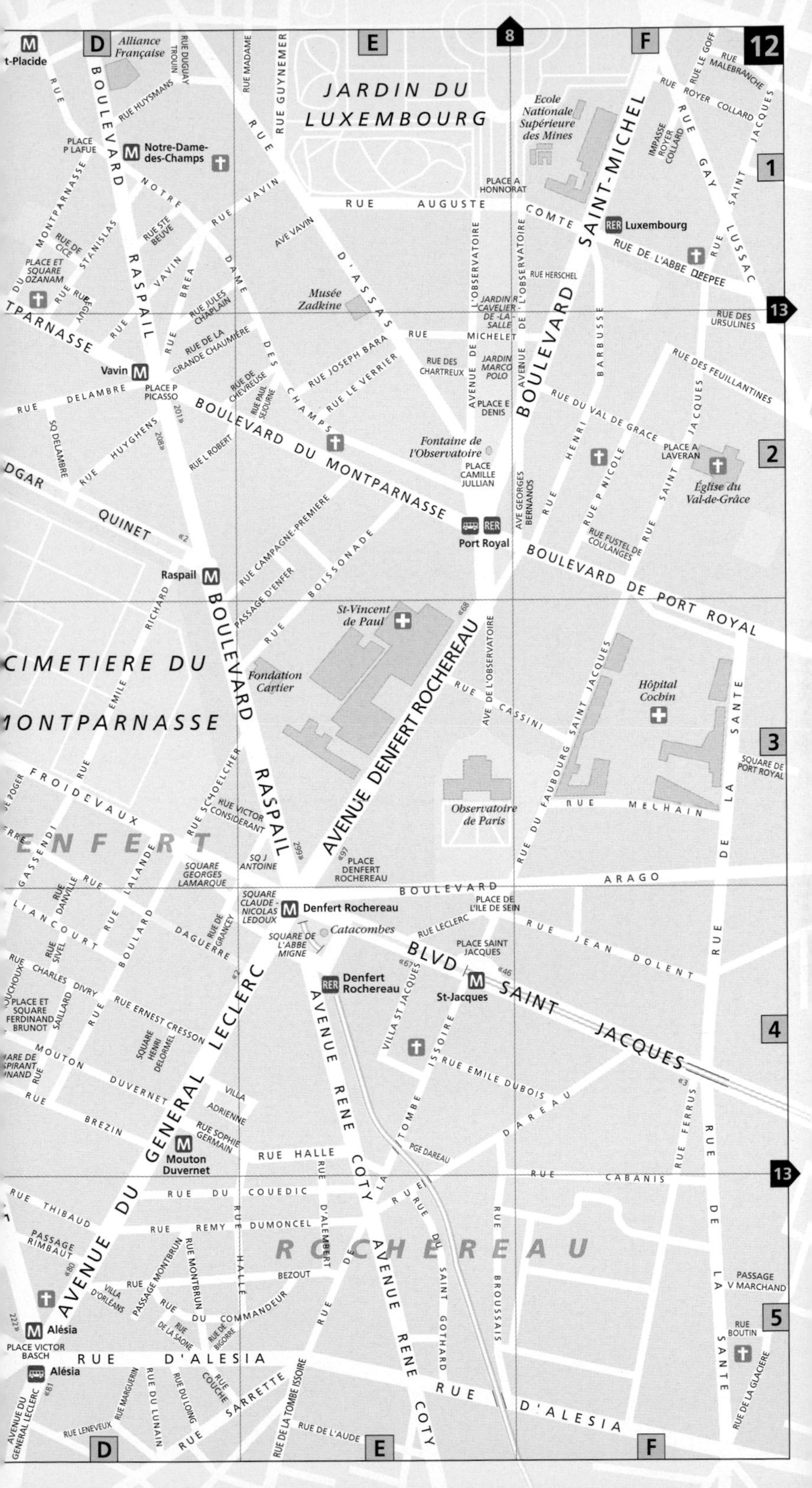

12
JARDIN DU LUXEMBOURG
Alliance Française
Ecole Nationale Supérieure des Mines
Notre-Dame-des-Champs
Luxembourg
Musée Zadkine
Vavin
BOULEVARD RASPAIL
BOULEVARD SAINT-MICHEL
BOULEVARD DU MONTPARNASSE
Fontaine de l'Observatoire
Port Royal
Église du Val-de-Grâce
BOULEVARD DE PORT ROYAL
Raspail
St-Vincent de Paul
Fondation Cartier
CIMETIERE DU MONTPARNASSE
AVENUE DENFERT ROCHEREAU
Hôpital Cochin
Observatoire de Paris
DENFERT
Denfert Rochereau
Catacombes
BLVD SAINT JACQUES
St-Jacques
AVENUE DU GENERAL LECLERC
AVENUE RENE COTY
Mouton Duvernet
ROCHEREAU
Alésia
RUE D'ALESIA
D
E
F
8
13
1
2
3
4
5

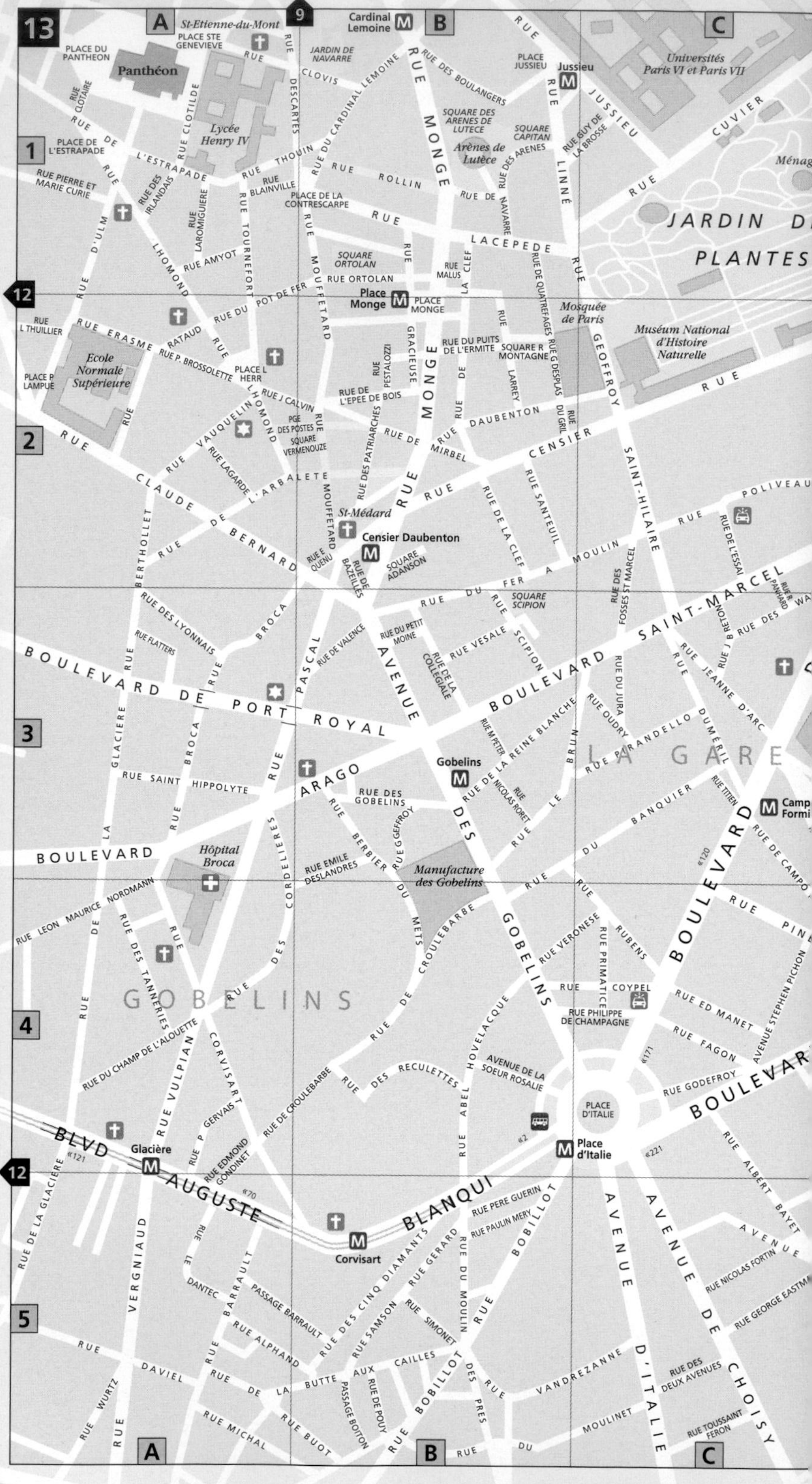

St-Etienne-du-Mont
Panthéon
Lycée Henry IV
Jardin de Navarre
Cardinal Lemoine
Jussieu
Universités Paris VI et Paris VII
Arènes de Lutèce
Square des Arenes de Lutece
Square Capitan
Jardin des Plantes
Place de la Contrescarpe
Square Ortolan
Place Monge
Mosquée de Paris
Muséum National d'Histoire Naturelle
Ecole Normale Supérieure
St-Médard
Censier Daubenton
Square Adanson
Square Scipion
Boulevard de Port Royal
Boulevard Saint-Marcel
Avenue des Gobelins
Boulevard Arago
Gobelins
La Gare
Hôpital Broca
Manufacture des Gobelins
Gobelins
Place d'Italie
Glacière
Blvd Auguste Blanqui
Corvisart
Avenue d'Italie
Avenue de Choisy
Rue Mouffetard
Rue Monge
Rue Claude Bernard
Rue Lacepede
Rue Censier
Rue Geoffroy Saint-Hilaire
Rue de la Glacière
Rue Vergniaud
Rue Bobillot

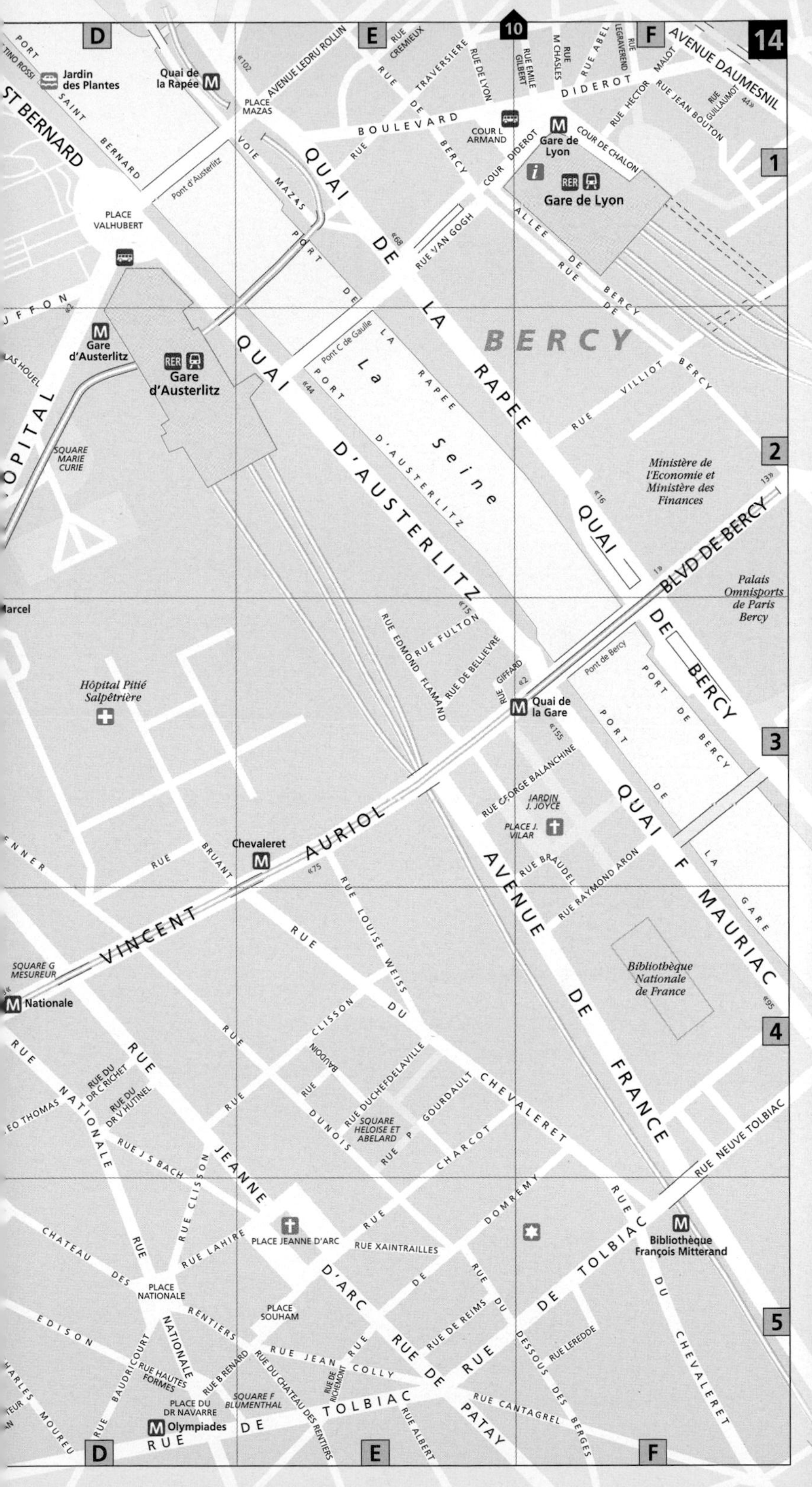

14
D
E
F
10
1
2
3
4
5
Jardin des Plantes
Quai de la Rapée
Place Mazas
Place Valhubert
Gare d'Austerlitz
Gare de Lyon
Cour Diderot
Bercy
La Seine
Quai de la Rapée
Quai d'Austerlitz
Quai de Bercy
Quai F Mauriac
Boulevard Diderot
Avenue Daumesnil
Avenue Ledru Rollin
Boulevard Saint Bernard
Quai St Bernard
Blvd de Bercy
Blvd Vincent Auriol
Avenue de France
Ministère de l'Economie et Ministère des Finances
Palais Omnisports de Paris Bercy
Hôpital Pitié Salpêtrière
Square Marie Curie
Quai de la Gare
Chevaleret
Jardin J. Joyce
Place J. Vilar
Bibliothèque Nationale de France
Nationale
Square G Mesureur
Bibliothèque François Mitterand
Place Jeanne d'Arc
Place Nationale
Place Souham
Square Heloise et Abelard
Square F Blumenthal
Place du Dr Navarre
Olympiades
Rue de Tolbiac
Rue Jeanne d'Arc
Rue du Chevaleret
Rue Clisson
Rue Louise Weiss
Rue Nationale
Rue Neuve Tolbiac
Rue de Patay
Rue du Dessous des Berges
Rue Edmond Flamand
Rue Fulton
Rue de Bellievre
Rue Giffard
Rue George Balanchine
Rue Raymond Aron
Rue Braudel
Rue Bruant
Rue Dunois
Rue Baudoin
Rue Duchefdelaville
Rue Gourdault
Rue Charcot
Rue Domremy
Rue Xaintrailles
Rue Lahire
Rue de Reims
Rue Leredde
Rue Cantagrel
Rue Albert
Rue Jean Colly
Rue de Richemont
Rue du Chateau des Rentiers
Rue B Renard
Rue Hautes Formes
Rue Baudricourt
Rue Edison
Rue Charles Moureu
Rue du Chateau
Rue des Rentiers
Rue J S Bach
Rue du Dr V Hutinel
Rue du Dr C Richet
Rue Van Gogh
Rue de Bercy
Rue Villiot
Allée de Bercy
Cour de Chalon
Rue Jean Bouton
Rue Hector Malot
Rue Guillaumot
Rue Crémieux
Rue Traversière
Rue de Lyon
Rue Emile Gilbert
Rue M Chasles
Rue Abel
Rue Legraverend
Voie Mazas
Port de la Rapée
Port d'Austerlitz
Port de Bercy
Port de la Gare
Pont d'Austerlitz
Pont C de Gaulle
Pont de Bercy
Cour L Armand

ILE-DE-FRANCE

Set at the heart of France, with Paris as its hub, the Ile-de-France extends well beyond the densely populated suburbs of the city. Its rich countryside incorporates a historic royal region of monumental splendour central to *"la gloire de la France"*.

The region became a favourite with French royalty after François I transformed Fontainebleau into a Renaissance palace in 1528. Louis XIV kept the Ile-de-France as the political axis of the country when he started building Versailles in 1661. This Neo-Classical château, created by the combined genius of Le Nôtre, Le Vau, Le Brun and Jules Hardouin-Mansart, is France's most visited sight. It stands as a monument to the power of the Sun King and is still used for state occasions. Rambouillet, closely linked with Louis XVI, is now the summer residence of the French president, while Malmaison was the favourite home of Empress Josephine. To the north, the Musée National de la Renaissance in the Château d'Ecouen offers a showcase of Renaissance life and to the south Vaux-le-Vicomte boasts some of the loveliest formal gardens in France.

Nourished by the Seine and Marne rivers, the Ile-de-France is a patchwork of chalky plains, wheatfields and forests. The serene, poplar-lined avenues and rustic charm of the region have been an inspiration to painters such as Corot, Rousseau, Pissarro and Cézanne.

Sights at a Glance

Châteaux and Museums

- 2 Musée National de la Renaissance
- 5 Château de Malmaison
- 6 *Château de Versailles pp178–81*
- 7 Château de Sceaux
- 8 Sèvres: Cité de la Céramique
- 9 Château de Rambouillet
- 11 Château de Vaux-le-Vicomte
- 13 *Château de Fontainebleau pp184–5*

Towns

- 4 St-Germain-en-Laye
- 12 Provins

Abbeys and Churches

- 1 Abbaye de Royaumont
- 3 Basilique St-Denis

Theme Parks

- 10 Disneyland® Resort Paris

Key

- Greater Paris
- Central Paris
- Motorway
- Major road
- Minor road

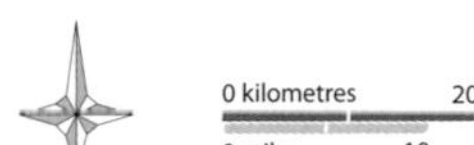

Ile-de-France

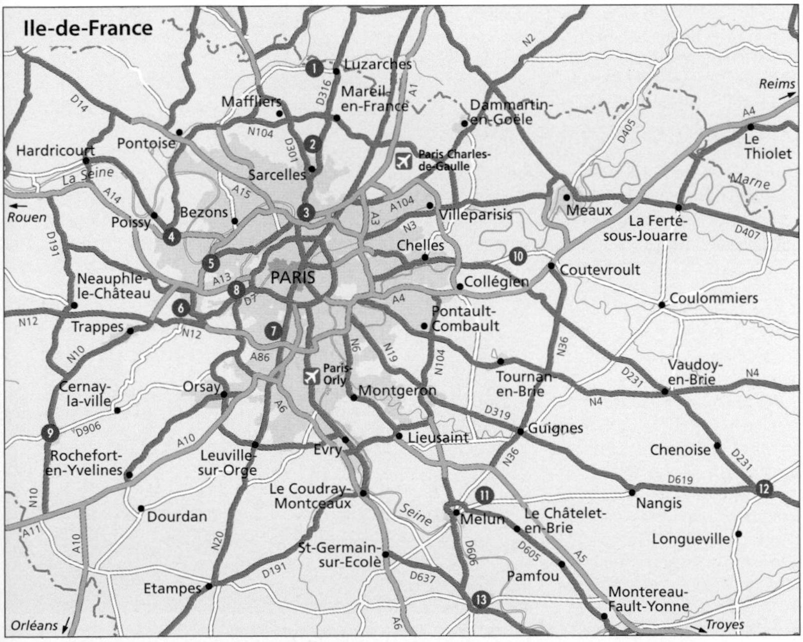

◀ Stunning formal gardens at the Château de Fontainebleau

The vaulted Gothic refectory of the Abbaye de Royaumont

❶ Abbaye de Royaumont

Fondation Royaumont, Asnières-sur-Oise, Val-d'Oise. **Tel** 01 30 35 59 00. **Open** 10am–6pm daily (Nov–Feb: to 5:30pm). Concerts. **royaumont.com**

Set among woods 35 km (22 miles) north of Paris, Royaumont is the finest Cistercian abbey in the Ile-de-France. Chosen for its remoteness, the abbey has stark stonework and a simplicity of line that reflect the austere teachings of St Bernard. However, unlike his Burgundian abbeys, Royaumont was founded in 1228 by Louis IX and his mother, Blanche de Castille. "St Louis" showered the abbey with riches and chose it as a royal burial site.

The abbey retained its royal links until the Revolution, when much of it was destroyed. It was then a textiles mill and orphanage, until its revival as a cultural centre. The original pillars still remain, along with a gravity-defying corner tower and the largest Cistercian cloisters in France, which enclose a charming Classical garden. The monastic quarters border one side of the cloisters.

The Château de Royaumont, erected as the abbot's palace on the eve of the Revolution, is set apart and resembles an Italianate villa. In the grounds are monks' workshops, woods, ponds and Cistercian canals.

In summer, concerts are held in the abbey on weekends *(01 34 68 05 50 for details; www.3emeacte.com for tickets).*

❷ Musée National de la Renaissance

Rue Jean Bulant, Château d'Ecouen, Val-d'Oise. **Tel** 01 34 38 38 52. **Open** 9:30am–12:45pm, 2–5:15pm Wed–Mon (mid-Apr–Sep: to 5:45pm). **Closed** 1 Jan, 1 May, 25 Dec. Park: no animals. museum only. **musee-renaissance.fr**

The imposing, moated Château d'Ecouen, now a Renaissance museum, provides an authentic setting for an impressive collection of paintings, stained glass, jewellery, tapestries, coffers, carved doors and staircases salvaged from this and other 16th-century châteaux.

Ecouen was built in 1538 for Anne de Montmorency, adviser to François I and Commander-in-Chief of his armies. As the second most powerful person in the kingdom, he employed Ecole de Fontainebleau artists and craftsmen to adorn his palace. Their influence is apparent in the painted fireplaces, depicting biblical and Classical themes in mysterious landscapes. The most striking room is the chapel, containing a gallery and vaulted ceilings painted with the Montmorency coat of arms.

Upstairs is one of the finest series of 16th-century tapestries in France. Equally compelling are the princely apartments, the library of illuminated manuscripts, vivid ceramics from Lyon, Nevers, Venice, Faenza, and Iznik, and a display of early mathematical instruments. There are also 16th- and 17th-century engravings from France, Italy and Germany. The castle is set within lovely formal gardens.

❸ Basilique St-Denis

1 rue de la Légion d'Honneur, St-Denis, Seine-St-Denis. **Tel** 01 48 09 83 54. Line 13 Basilique de St-Denis. **Open** 10am–6:15pm Mon–Sat, noon–6:15pm Sun (Oct–Mar: 10am–5pm Mon–Sat, noon–5:15pm Sun). **Closed** 1 Jan, 1 May, 25 Dec. 8:30am & 10am Sun. **saint-denis.monuments-nationaux.fr**

Statue of Louis XVI at St-Denis

According to legend, St-Denis struggled here clutching his decapitated head, and an abbey was erected to commemorate him. Following the burial of Dagobert I in the basilica in 638, a royal link with St-Denis began, that was to span 12 centuries. Most French kings were entombed in St-Denis, and all the queens of France were crowned here.

The elegant, early Gothic basilica rests on Carolingian and Romanesque crypts. Of the medieval effigies, the most impressive are of Charles V (1364) and a 12th-century

The west wing of Musée National de la Renaissance

The Renaissance tomb of Louis XII and Anne de Bretagne in St-Denis

likeness in enamelled copper of Blanche de France with her dog. The mask-like serenity of these effigies contrasts with the graphically realistic Renaissance portrayal of agony present in the grotesque mausoleum of Louis XII and Anne de Bretagne. Both are represented as naked figures, their faces eerily captured at the moment of death. Above the mausoleum, effigies of the finely dressed royal couple contemplate their own nakedness.

❹ St-Germain-en-Laye

Yvelines. 41,000. Maison Claude Debussy, 38 rue au Pain. **Tel** 01 30 87 20 63. **Open** Oct–Apr: Tue–Sat; May–Sep: daily. Tue, Wed, Fri–Sun.
ot-saintgermainenlaye.fr

Dominating place Général de Gaulle in this chic suburb is the legendary Château de St-Germain, birthplace of Louis XIV. Louis VI built the original stronghold in 1122, but only the keep and St-Louis chapel remain. Under François I and Henri II, the medieval upper tiers were demolished, leaving a moated pentagon. Henri IV built the pavilion and terraces that run down to the Seine, and Louis XIV had Le Nôtre landscape the gardens before leaving for Versailles in 1682.

Today the château houses the **Musée d'Archéologie Nationale**, with archaeological finds from prehistory to the Middle Ages. Created by Napoleon III, the collection includes a 22,000-year-old carved female, a megalithic tomb, a bronze helmet from the 3rd century BC and Celtic jewellery. The finest treasure is the Gallo-Roman mosaic pavement.

Musée d'Archéologie Nationale
Château de St-Germain-en-Laye, pl Charles de Gaulle. **Tel** 01 39 10 13 00.
Open 10am–5pm Wed–Mon.
Closed 1 Jan, 25 Dec.
musee-archeologienationale.fr

❺ Château de Malmaison

Rueil-Malmaison, Hauts-de-Seine, av du Château de Malmaison. **Tel** 01 41 29 05 55. **Open** 10am–12:30pm, 1:30–5:15pm daily (to 5:45pm Apr–Sep and weekends year-round).
Closed 1 Jan, 25 Dec.
chateau-malmaison.fr

Situated 15 km (9 miles) west of Paris, this 17th-century estate is best known for its Napoleonic associations. Bought by Josephine as a retreat from the formality of the Emperor's residences at the Tuileries and Fontainebleau, it has charming rural grounds. While Josephine loved this country manor, Napoleon scorned its entrance as fit only for servants, and so he had a curious drawbridge built at the back of the château.

The finest rooms are the frescoed and vaulted library, the canopied campaign room and the sunny Salon de Musique. Napoleon's restrained, yellow canopied bedroom contrasts with the bedchamber in which Josephine died, a magnificent indulgence bedecked in red. Many of the rooms overlook the romantic "English" gardens and the rose garden the Josephine cultivated after her divorce.

Memorabilia abounds, from imperial eagles to David's moody portrait of Napoleon, or Gérard's painting of the languid Josephine reclining on a chaise-longue.

The nearby Château Bois Préau, set in the wooded grounds, houses a museum dedicated to Napoleon's exile and death.

Empress Josephine's bed at the Château de Malmaison

❻ Château de Versailles

The present palace, started by Louis XIV in 1668, grew around Louis XIII's original hunting lodge. Architect Louis Le Vau built the first section, which expanded into an enlarged courtyard. From 1678, Jules Hardouin-Mansart added north and south wings and the Hall of Mirrors. He also designed the chapel, completed in 1710. The Opera House (L'Opéra) was added by Louis XV in 1770. André Le Nôtre enlarged the gardens and broke the monotony of the symmetrical layout with expanses of water and creative use of uneven ground. Opposite the château is the Académie du Spectacle Equestre, where you can watch dressage shows.

★ Formal Gardens
Geometric paths and shrubberies are features of the gardens.

★ Château
Under Louis XIV, Versailles became the centre of political power in France.

Fountain of Latona
Four marble basins rise to Balthazar Marsy's statue of the goddess Latona.

KEY

① **Fountain of Neptune** sculptures spray spectacular jets of water in Le Nôtre's 17th-century garden.

② **Ornamental Pools (Parterre d'Eau)**

③ **The Orangery** was built beneath the Parterre du Midi to house exotic plants in winter.

④ **The king's garden** features a mirror pool in the 19th-century garden created by Louis XVIII.

⑤ **Colonnade** is a series of marble arches designed by Mansart in 1685.

Dragon Fountain
The fountain's centrepiece is a winged monster.

The Grand Canal was the setting for Louis XIV's boating parties.

VISITORS' CHECKLIST

Practical Information
Pl d'Armes, Versailles, Yvelines. **Tel** 01 30 83 78 00. Château: **Open** 9am–6:30pm (5:30pm Nov–Mar) Tue–Sun. **Closed** some public hols; phone to check. Grand Trianon, Petit Trianon: **Open** noon–6:30pm (5:30pm Nov–Mar) Tue–Sun. Gardens: **Open** 8am–8:30pm daily. Park: **Open** 7am–8:30pm daily (7pm for cars; 6pm Nov–Mar). **Closed** 1 Jan, 1 May, 25 Dec. Les Fêtes de Nuit (Aug–Sep); Les Grandes Eaux Nocturnes (Apr–Sep: Sat). **chateauversailles.fr**

Transport
171 from Paris. RER Versailles Rive Gauche. Versailles Chantiers, Versailles Rive Droite.

Petit Trianon
Built in 1762 as a retreat for Louis XV, this small château became a favourite with Marie Antoinette.

Interior of the chapel at Versailles

★ Grand Trianon
Louis XIV built this small palace of stone and pink marble in 1687 to escape the rigours of court life, and to enjoy the company of Madame de Maintenon.

Inside the Château de Versailles

The sumptuous main apartments are on the first floor of this vast château complex. Around the Marble Courtyard are the private apartments of the king and queen. The apartments of the *dauphin* (the heir) and the *mesdames* (the daughters of Louis XV), on the ground floor, are also open to visitors. On the garden side are the state apartments, where official court life took place. These were richly decorated by Charles Le Brun with marble, stone and woodcarvings, murals, velvet, silver and gilded furniture. Beginning with the Salon d'Hercule, each state room is dedicated to an Olympian deity. The climax is the Hall of Mirrors, where 17 vast mirrors face tall arched windows. Not all rooms are open at the same time, so check on arrival.

★ Queen's Bedroom
In this room the queens of France gave birth to the royal children in public view.

The Salle du Sacre is adorned with huge paintings of Napoleon by Jacques-Louis David, including his vast, celebrated *The Coronation of Napoleon (Le Sacre du Napoléon)*, of 1807.

The Marble Courtyard is overlooked by a gilded balcony.

Stairs to ground-floor reception area

★ Chapelle Royale
The chapel's first floor was reserved for the royal family and the ground floor for the court. The beautiful interior is lavishly decorated with Corinthian columns and white marble, gilding and Baroque murals.

Key to Floorplan

- South wing
- Coronation room
- Madame de Maintenon's apartments
- Queen's apartments and private suite
- State apartments
- King's apartments and private suite
- North wing

For hotels and restaurants in this region see pp555–6 and p579

★ Hall of Mirrors
Great state occasions were held in this room stretching 70 m (233 ft) along the west façade. Here, in 1919, the Treaty of Versailles was ratified, ending World War I.

Salon de Oeil-de-Boeuf

The King's Bedroom is where Louis XIV died in 1715.

The Cabinet du Conseil was used by the king to receive his ministers and family.

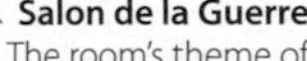

Salon de la Guerre
The room's theme of war is reinforced by Antoine Coysevox's stuccoed relief of Louis XIV riding to victory.

Louis XVI's library features Neo-Classical panelling and the king's terrestrial globe.

★ Salon de Vénus
A statue of Louis XIV stands amid the rich marble decor of this room.

Salon d'Apollon
Designed by Le Brun and dedicated to the god Apollo, this was Louis XIV's throne room. A copy of Hyacinthe Rigaud's famous portrait of the king (1701) hangs here.

Salon d'Hercule

1667 Grand Canal begun

1668 Construction of new château by Le Vau

Louis XV

1722 12-year-old Louis XV occupies Versailles

1793 Louis XVI and Marie Antoinette executed

1837 Inauguration of the museum of the Château de Versailles

1650 | 1700 | 1750 | 1800 | 1850 | 1900

1671 Interior decoration by Le Brun begun

1661 Louis XIV enlarges château

1715 Death of Louis XIV. Versailles abandoned by court

1682 Louis XIV and Marie-Thérèse move to Versailles

1789 King and Queen forced to leave Versailles for Paris

1774 Louis XVI and Marie Antoinette live at Versailles

1919 Treaty of Versailles signed on 28 June

❼ Château de Sceaux

Domaine de Sceaux, Hauts-de-Seine. **Tel** 01 41 87 29 50. **Open** Apr–Oct: 10am–6pm Wed–Mon (to 6:30pm Sun); Nov–Mar: 10am–5pm Wed–Mon. **Closed** public hols & lunchtimes. **W domaine-de-sceaux.hauts-de-seine.net**

The Parc de Sceaux, bounded by elegant villas, is an appealing mixture of formal gardens, woods and water. The gardens, designed by Le Nôtre, use water to great effect, with tiered waterfalls and fountains presenting a moving staircase that cascades into an octagonal basin. This feeds into the Grand Canal and offers a poplar-lined view to the Pavillon de Hanovre. This elegant pavilion is one of several that adorn the park, which also contains Mansart's Classical Orangerie. Today it hosts exhibitions and music concerts.

Built for Colbert in 1670, the original château was demolished and rebuilt in Louis XIII style in 1856. The stylish reconstruction contains the Musée de l'Ile-de-France, which celebrates the landscapes and châteaux of the region with paintings, furniture and sculpture.

❽ Sèvres: Cité de la Céramique

Place de la Manufacture, 92310 Sèvres. **Tel** 01 46 29 22 00. **Open** 10am–5pm daily. **Closed** Tue. **W sevresciteceramique.fr**

With over 50,000 objects on display, this fascinating museum traces the history of porcelain around the world from antiquity onward. The building was erected in 1756 as a royal factory under Louis XV and has remained under state ownership ever since. In 1824 it became home to the world's first ceramics museum. The collections include the latest pieces by 21st-century designers. Visitors can explore objects from America, Japan and all across Europe as they discover how techniques for making and decorating porcelain and ceramics have changed over the centuries.

Château de Rambouillet

❾ Château de Rambouillet

Rambouillet, Yvelines. **Tel** 01 34 83 00 25. **Open** 9:50am–6pm Wed–Mon (Oct–Mar: to 5pm). **W chateau-rambouillet.fr**

Bordering the deep Forêt de Rambouillet, once the favourite royal hunting ground, this ivy-covered red-brick château, flanked by five stone towers, is beautiful. Adopted as a feudal castle, country estate, royal palace and Imperial residence, it reflects a composite of French royal history. Since 1897, it has been the president's official summer residence.

Inside, oak-panelled rooms are adorned with Empire-style furnishings and Aubusson tapestries. The main façade overlooks Classical parterres. Nearby is the Queen's Dairy, given by Louis XVI to Marie Antoinette, so that she could play milkmaid.

Environs

About 27 km (17 miles) north on the D11, the **Château de Thoiry** has a safari park and an innovative play area for children.

❿ Disneyland® Resort Paris

Marne-la-Vallée, Seine-et-Marne. **Tel** 08 25 30 05 00. **Open** hours vary according to season – check website. RER Marne-la-Vallée-Chessy. TGV from Lille or Lyon. from both airports. **W disneylandparis.com**

Disneyland® Resort Paris has two theme parks, seven hotels, facilities for shopping and dining and convention centres. Most interesting are the Parks – the first with its five themed Lands, offering magic dominated by Sleeping Beauty Castle, and Walt Disney Studios®.

Minnie Mouse

⓫ Château de Vaux-le-Vicomte

Maincy, Seine-et-Marne. **Tel** 01 64 14 41 90. shuttle from Melun railway station (runs Apr–mid-Nov: weekends & hols). late Mar–early Nov: 10am–7pm (6 May–7 Oct: till midnight Sat); late Nov–early Jan: 11am–7pm. **Closed** 2 wks in Nov. **W vaux-le-vicomte.com**

Set north of Melun, not far from Fontainebleau, the château enjoys a peaceful rural location.

Sèvres Porcelain

In 1756 Madame de Pompadour and Louis XV opened a porcelain factory near Versailles at Sèvres to supply the royal residences with tableware and objets d'art. Thus began the production of exquisite dinner services, statuettes, Etruscan-style vases, romantic cameos and porcelain paintings, depicting grand châteaux or mythological scenes. Sèvres porcelain is typified by its translucence, durability and narrow palette of colours.

Le Pugilat (1832), one of a pair of vases from Sèvres

For hotels and restaurants in this region see pp555–6 and p579

André Le Nôtre

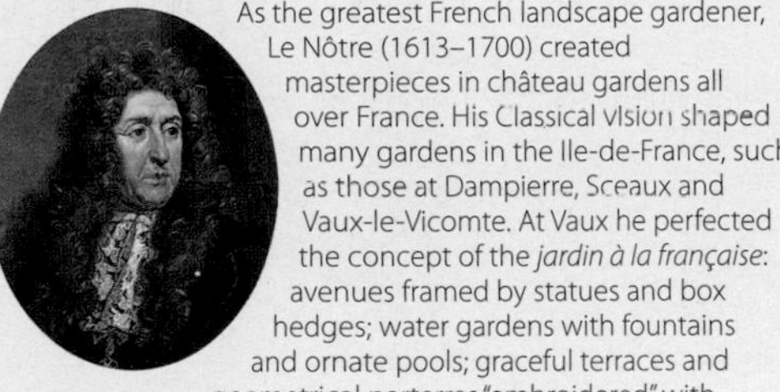

As the greatest French landscape gardener, Le Nôtre (1613–1700) created masterpieces in château gardens all over France. His Classical vision shaped many gardens in the Ile-de-France, such as those at Dampierre, Sceaux and Vaux-le-Vicomte. At Vaux he perfected the concept of the *jardin à la française*: avenues framed by statues and box hedges; water gardens with fountains and ornate pools; graceful terraces and geometrical parterres "embroidered" with motifs. His genius lay in architectural orchestration and a sense of symmetry, typified by the sweeping vistas of Versailles, his greatest triumph.

Nicolas Fouquet, a powerful court financier to Louis XIV, challenged the architect Le Vau and the decorator Le Brun to create the most sumptuous palace of the day. The result is one of the greatest 17th-century French châteaux. However, it also led to his downfall. Louis and his ministers were so enraged – because its luxury cast the royal palaces into the shade – that they arrested Fouquet.

The interior is a gilded banquet of frescoes, stucco, caryatids and giant busts. The Salon des Muses boasts Le Brun's magnificent frescoed ceiling of dancing nymphs and poetic sphinxes. La Grande Chambre Carrée is decorated in Louis XIII style with panelled walls and an impressive triumphal frieze, evoking Rome. However, its many rooms feel intimate and the scale is not overwhelming.

Yet Vaux-le-Vicomte's continuing fame is due to André Le Nôtre's stunning gardens. The landscape designer's early training as a painter is evident in the magnificent succession of terraces, ornamental lakes and fountains, which descend to a formal canal. On Saturday evenings from May to October, the castle is lit with over 2,000 candles, and classical music is played in the lounge bar in the gardens.

⓬ Provins

Seine-et-Marne. 12,500. Chemin de Villecran 77482 (01 64 60 26 26). Sat. **provins.net**

As a Roman outpost, Provins commanded the border of Ile-de-France and Champagne. Today, it offers a coherent vision of the medieval world. Ville Haute, the upper town, is clustered within 12th-century ramparts, complete with crenellations and defensive ditches. The ramparts to the west are the best preserved. Here, between the fortified gateways of Porte de Jouy and Porte St-Jean, the fortifications are dotted with square, round and rectangular towers.

The town is dominated by Tour César, a keep with four corner turrets and a pyramid shaped roof. The moat and fortifications were added by the English during the Hundred Years' War. A guardroom leads to a gallery and views over place du Chatel, a busy square of medieval gabled houses, and over the wheatfields beyond.

Provins is proud of its crimson roses. In addition to a daily medieval show, a floral celebration is held in the riverside rose garden every June, an event marked by a medieval festival with falconry and jousting.

Aerial view of the splendid Château de Vaux-le-Vicomte, with its gardens designed by Le Nôtre

⓭ Château de Fontainebleau

Fontainebleau is not the product of a single vision but is a bewildering cluster of styles from different periods. Louis VII built an abbey here, which was consecrated by Thomas Becket in 1169. A medieval tower survives, but the present château harks back to François I. Originally drawn by the local hunting, the Renaissance king created a decorative château modelled on Florentine and Roman styles.

Fontainebleau's abiding charm comes from its relative informality and spectacular forest setting. The *grands appartements* provide a sumptuous introduction to this royal palace.

Jardin de Diane
Now more romantic than Classical, the garden features a bronze fountain of Diana as huntress.

★ Escalier du Fer-à-Cheval
This imposing horseshoe-shaped staircase, built in 1634, by Jean Androuet du Cerceau, lies at the end of Cour du Cheval Blanc. Its ingenious design allowed carriages to pass beneath the two arches.

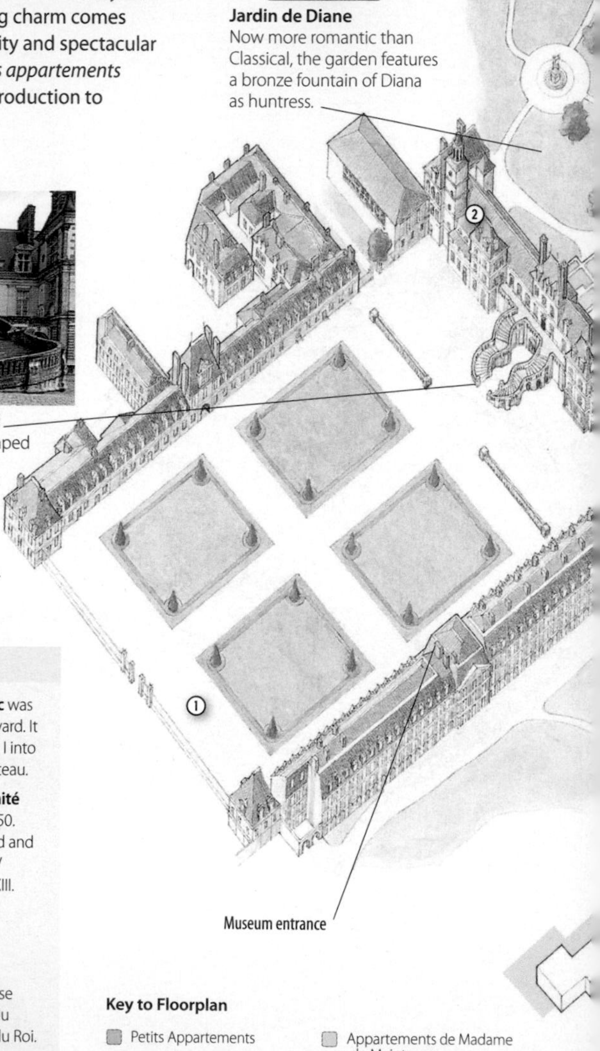

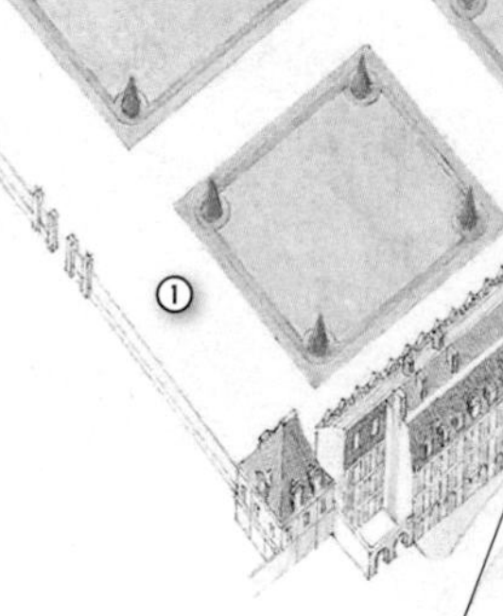

KEY

① **The Cour du Cheval Blanc** was once a simple enclosed courtyard. It was transformed by Napoleon I into the main approach to the château.

② **Chapelle de la Sainte Trinité** was designed by Henri II in 1550. The chapel acquired its vaulted and frescoed ceiling under Henri IV and was completed by Louis XIII.

③ **Cour Oval**

④ **Cour de la Fontaine**

⑤ **The Appartements de Napoléon I** house his grandiose throne in the Emperor's Salle du Trône, formerly the Chambre du Roi.

⑥ **The Jardin Anglais** is a romantic "English" garden, planted with cypress and plantain trees. It was redesigned in the 19th century by Maximilien-Joseph Hurtault.

Key to Floorplan

- Petits Appartements
- Galerie des Cerfs
- Musée Chinois
- Musée Napoléon
- Grands Appartements
- Salle Renaissance
- Appartements de Madame de Maintenon
- Grands Appartements des Souverains
- Escalier de la Reine/ Appartements des Chasses

For hotels and restaurants in this region see pp555–6 and p579

Porte Dorée
Originally a feudal gatehouse, this was transformed into the entrance pavilion to the forest by Gilles Le Breton for François I.

VISITORS' CHECKLIST

Practical Information
Seine-et-Marne. **Tel** 01 60 71 50 70. **Open** 9:30am–5pm Wed–Mon (6pm Apr–Sep). Gardens: **Open** 9am–5pm daily (6pm Mar–Apr & Oct, 7pm May–Sep). **Closed** 1 Jan, 1 May, 25 Dec. **musee-chateau-fontainebleau.fr**

First floor

3

5

4

★ Salle de Bal
The Renaissance ballroom, designed by Primaticcio (1552), was finished under Henri II. His emblems adorn the walnut coffered ceiling, forming a pattern reflected in the parquet floor.

★ Galerie François I
This gilded gallery is a tribute to the Italian artists in the Ecole de Fontainebleau. Rosso Fiorentino's allegorical frescoes pay homage to the king's wish to create "a second Rome".

The Barbizon School

Artists have been drawn to the glades of Fontainebleau since the 1840s, when a group of landscape painters, determined to paint only from nature, formed around Théodore Rousseau and Millet. They settled in the nearby hamlet of Barbizon, where the Auberge Ganne, a museum dedicated to the Ecole de Barbizon, is located.

Spring at Barbizon, painted by Jean-François Millet (1814–75)

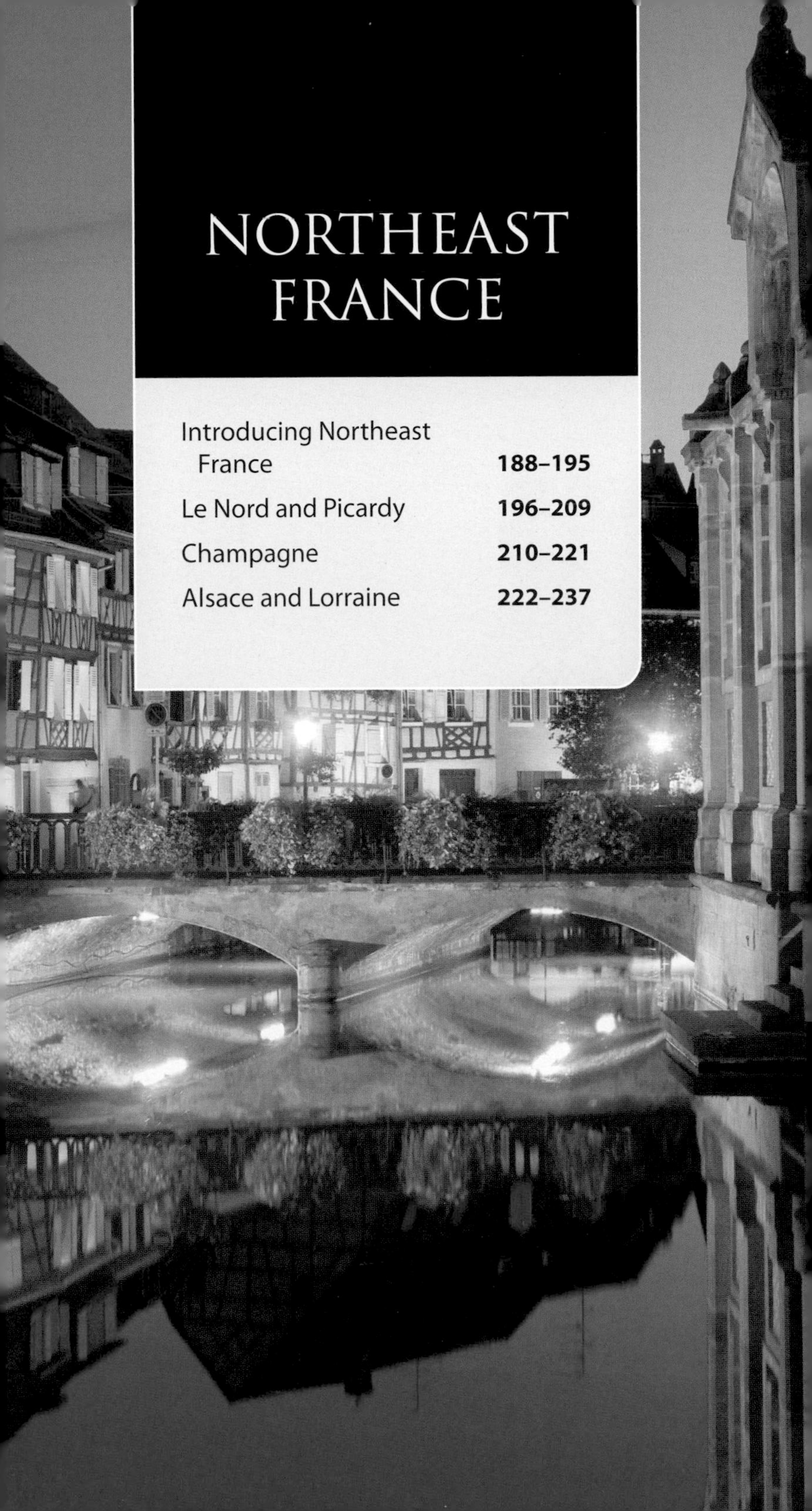

NORTHEAST FRANCE

Introducing Northeast France

The rolling plains of Northern France run from the English Channel to the wooded Ardennes hills and the Vosges mountains of Alsace. Apart from sombre battle memorials, the area has France's finest Gothic cathedrals – and a long tradition of brewing good-quality beers. There is fine wine, too, in Champagne and Alsace. The old heavy industry has gone, while Lille's growth as a transport hub has brought new prosperity. This map shows some of the most notable sights.

Amiens Cathedral is renowned for its fine woodcarvings and its nave, the highest in France *(see pp206–7)*.

Compiègne *(see p205)*

Reims Cathedral *(see pp216–17)*

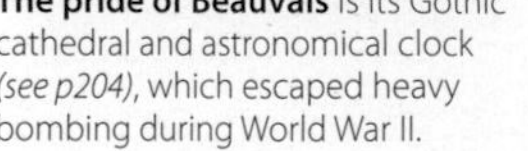

The pride of Beauvais is its Gothic cathedral and astronomical clock *(see p204)*, which escaped heavy bombing during World War II.

Half-timbered houses and Renaissance mansions line the streets and alleys of Troyes' Old Town *(see p220)*, rebuilt after the great fire in 1524. Its cathedral has remarkable stained-glass windows.

◀ River Lauch by night, Colmar

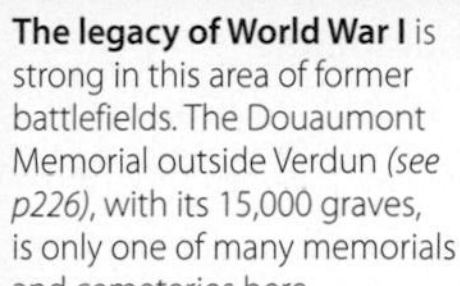

The legacy of World War I is strong in this area of former battlefields. The Douaumont Memorial outside Verdun *(see p226)*, with its 15,000 graves, is only one of many memorials and cemeteries here.

Haut-Koenigsbourg, a castle painstakingly rebuilt by Kaiser Wilhelm II when Alsace-Lorraine was under German rule, is one of Alsace's most popular attractions *(see p232)*.

Strasbourg, seat of the Council of Europe, has a fine Gothic cathedral *(see pp234–5)*, built using the red-pink sandstone from the Vosges.

Porte Chaussée, Verdun *(see p226)*

Place Stanislas, Nancy *(see p228)*

Rocrol
Charleville-Mézières
Sedan
Longwy
Thionville
Verdun
Metz
Sarreguemines
lons-en-mpagne
ALSACE AND LORRAINE
(See pp222–37)
Haguenau
Saverne
Toul
Nancy
-le-çois
St-Dizier
Lunéville
Strasbourg
Joinville
Sélestat
Neufchâteau
St-Dié
CHAMPAGNE
(See pp210–21)
Epinal
Colmar
Chaumont
Langres
Mulhouse

0 kilometres 50
0 miles 50

The Flavours of Northeast France

The cuisine of northeast France is robust and warming, with rich beef stews, suckling pig, sausages and hams, dumplings and sauerkraut dishes, many of them closely related to German or Flemish staples. There is good fish from the Atlantic and from freshwater lakes and rivers. Vegetables and fruit are produced in abundance, and often served in a variety of savoury and sweet tarts, of which *quiche lorraine*, with bacon, eggs and cream, is the best known. Rich cakes are popular, especially *kougelhopf*, a ring-shaped cake of raisins and almonds soaked in kirsch, and madeleine sponge cakes.

Leeks from a local market

Golden mirabelle plums alongside the more usual variety

Le Nord and Picardy

The northern coast offers a wide variety of fish and shellfish dishes, the most popular being steamed mussels served with chips (fries). Herrings are pickled, soused, grilled or smoked and North Sea shrimps fried and eaten whole. Chicken may be cooked in beer, duck is made into pies and terrines, and eel is served smoked as a starter. The market gardens *(hortillons)* of Picardy are famous for their vegetables, often made into delicious soups. Leeks or chicory, braised or in gratins, accompany many dishes. Strong, washed-rind cheeses, such as Maroilles, are typical of the region.

Beer is often drunk with meals in the northeast, where traditional methods and small breweries thrive.

Champagne

Champagne encompasses arable plains and wooded uplands as well as vineyards, and produces game, *charcuterie* and delicious freshwater fish. Nothing, however, can compete with its main claim to fame, Champagne itself, which is often used as a luxury cooking ingredient as well as, of course, being enjoyed in its own right.

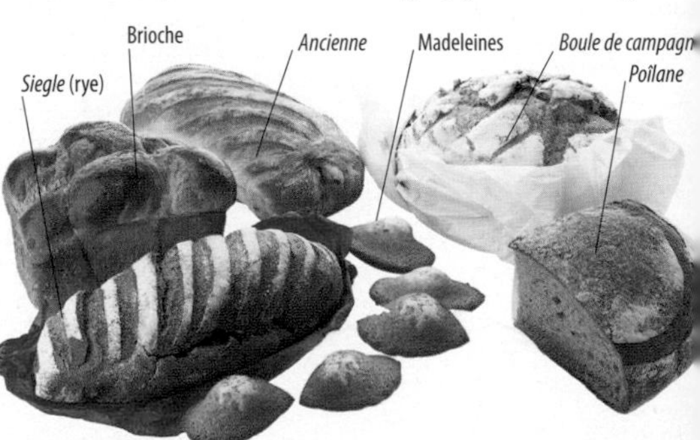

Selection of typical regional breads and patisserie

Regional Dishes and Specialities

Beetroot

The classic dish of the region is *choucroute garni*, a platter of pickled cabbage, flavoured with juniper berries, and cooked with white wine, ham hock and smoked pork belly. Smoked Montbeliard and Strasbourg sausages are added towards the end of cooking. Sausages come in many variations, from *saucisses de Strasbourg* to *bratwurst*, made from veal and pork, *lewerzurscht* (liver sausage), *andouillettes* (spicy chitterling sausages), *boudin noir* (black pudding of pork and pig's blood) and *boudin blanc* (white meat without blood). There are also smoked hams, cooked hams and many different terrines, such as *presskopf* (pig's brawn in jelly) and the jellied white meat terrine, *potjevleesch*. *Langue lucullus* is smoked ox tongue studded with *foie gras*, a speciality of Valenciennes.

Ficelle picardie Pancakes are filled with mushrooms and ham in a crème fraîche sauce, and baked with grated cheese.

Display of traditional northern French *charcuterie*

Wild boar, deer, rabbit, hare, quail, partridge and woodcock are all found in the Ardennes, made into game pâtés and terrines as well as roasts and stews. The Ardennes is also noted for its fine-quality smoked ham, while *jambon de Reims* is cooked ham with mustard, Champagne and Reims vinegar. Troyes is famous for its *andouillettes*, usually served with onions or baked in a creamy mustard sauce. Fish come from the small lakes east of Troyes and trout are abundant in the clear streams of the Ardennes. The two best cheeses of Champagne are Chaource and Langres.

Alsace and Lorraine

Rolling pastures, orchards, pine forests and rivers produce the ingredients of Alsatian cooking. Meat is important, particularly pork, roasted or made into hams and sausages. In winter, game stews abound. There is a strong tradition of raising geese; after all, *foie gras* production originated in Strasbourg. The rivers are a good source of pike, trout, crayfish and carp, often cooked in beer and served on festive occasions. Locally grown vegetables include cabbage, potatoes and turnips, and fruit includes bilberries, quince, redcurrants and the golden mirabelle plums of Lorraine, the latter prized for both jam and *eau de vie* (fruit brandy). The best-known cheese is Münster, a soft cow's milk cheese.

Shopping at the fish market in the port of Boulogne

The white wines of Alsace range from steely, bone-dry Riesling (the region's finest variety) to aromatic Muscat and Gerwurztraminer. For more on the wines of Alsace, *see pp236–7*.

ON THE MENU

Anguille au vert Eel baked with green herbs and potatoes.

Cassolette de petits gris Snails in Champagne sauce.

Flamiche aux poireaux Leek tart.

Flammekueche Pizza-style tart topped with bacon, crème fraîche and onions.

Marcassin à l'Ardennaise Wild boar with celeriac.

Potée champenoise Pork, ham, sausage, beans and vegetable stew.

Potée Lorraine Casserole of salt pork with vegetables.

Zewelwai A rich onion tart.

Truite à l'Ardennaise Trout is stuffed with breadcrumbs and finely chopped Ardennes ham, then baked.

Carbonnade de boeuf Steak and caramelized onions are covered with beer and cooked for 3 hours.

Babas au rhum These are dry yeast cakes of raisins, eggs and butter, doused in rum and served with cream.

France's Wine Regions: Champagne

Since its fabled "invention" by the monk Dom Pérignon in the 17th century, no other wine has rivalled Champagne as the symbol of luxury and celebration. Only wines made in this region by the *Méthode Champenoise* can be called Champagne *(see p214)*. Most Champagne is non-vintage: the skill of the blenders, using reserves of older wines, creates consistency and excellence year on year. The "big names" (*grandes marques*) command the prestige and prices, but many small growers and cooperatives also produce excellent-value wines well worth seeking out.

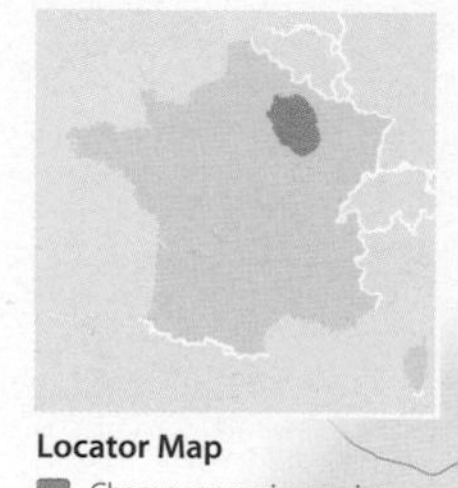

Locator Map

Champagne wine region

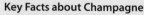

Grapes going for pressing, Montagne de Reims

Wine Regions

Champagne is a compact wine region, largely in the French département *of the Marne. Certain areas within it are particularly identified with certain styles of wine. The Aube produces 25 per cent of all Champagne as well as the exclusive Rosé des Riceys.*

Key Facts about Champagne

Location and Climate
The cool, marginal climate creates the finesse that other sparkling wines strive for, but seldom achieve. Chalky soils and east- and north-facing aspects help produce the relatively high acidity that Champagne needs.

Grape Varieties

Three varieties are grown, red ***Pinot Noir*** and ***Pinot Meunier***, and white ***Chardonnay***. Most Champagne is a blend of all three, though Blanc de Blancs is 100 per cent Chardonnay and Blanc de Noirs, although white, is made only from red grapes.

Good Producers
Grandes Marques: Bollinger, Gosset, Krug, Möet et Chandon, Joseph Perrier, Louis Roederer, Pol Roger, Billecart-Salmon, Veuve Clicquot, Taittinger, Ruinart, Laurent Perrier, Mumm, Lanson and Pommery.
Négociants, cooperatives and growers: Boizel, M Arnould, Cattier, Bricout, Drappier, Ployez-Jacquemart, H Blin, Gimmonet, André Jacquart, Chartogne-Taillet, Vilmart, Alfred Gratien, Emile Hamm, B Paillard, P Gerbais.

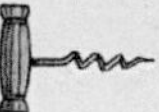

Good Vintages
2015, 2012, 2009, 2008, 2005, 2003.

From a name famous even to non-wine lovers, this is in the classic *brut* (dry) style; only *brut non dosage* or *brut sauvage* is drier.

Key

- Vallée de la Marne district
- Montagne de Reims district
- Côte de Sézanne district
- Côte des Blancs district
- Aube district

0 kilometres 15
0 miles 15

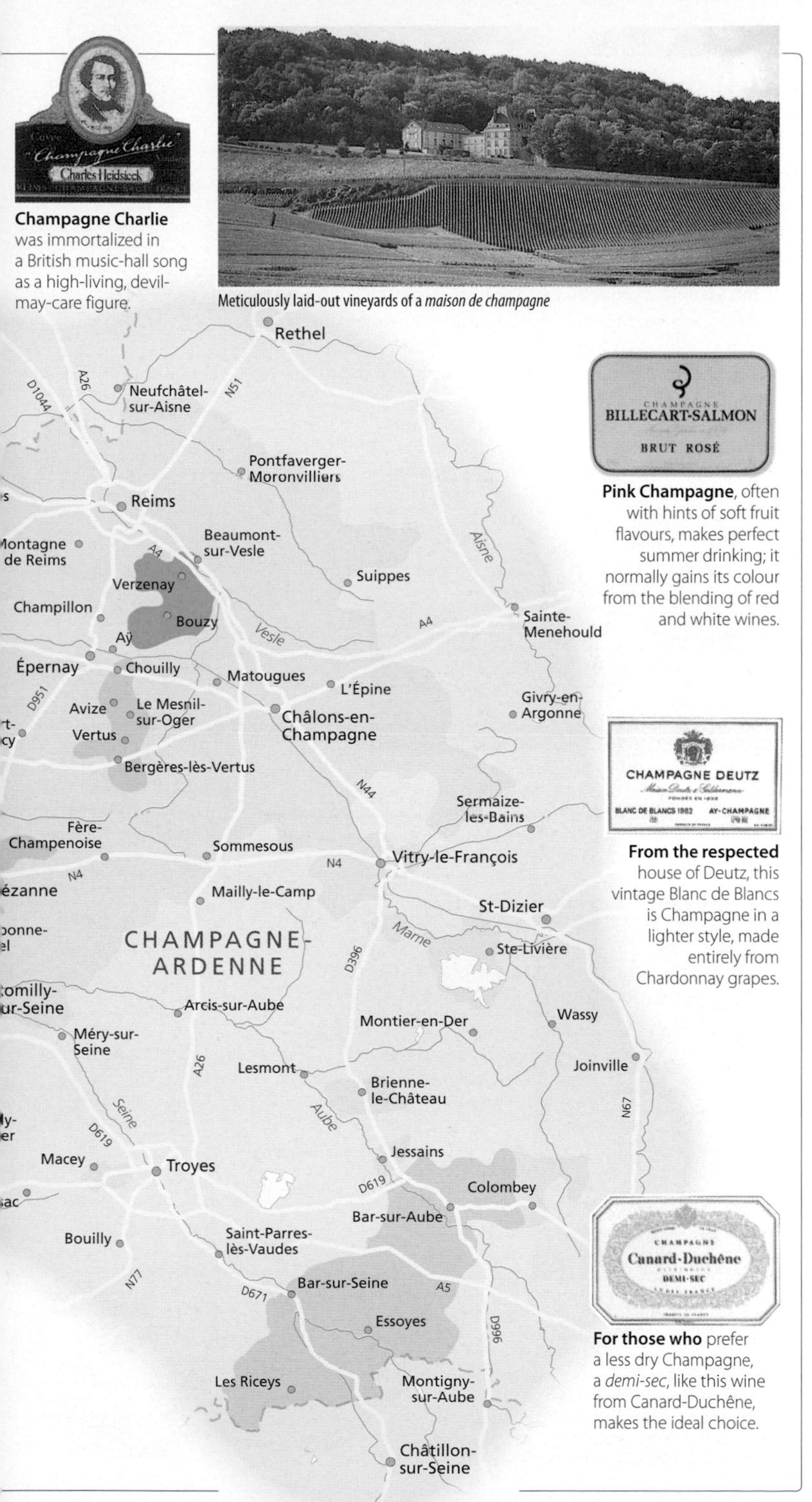

Champagne Charlie was immortalized in a British music-hall song as a high-living, devil-may-care figure.

Meticulously laid-out vineyards of a *maison de champagne*

Pink Champagne, often with hints of soft fruit flavours, makes perfect summer drinking; it normally gains its colour from the blending of red and white wines.

From the respected house of Deutz, this vintage Blanc de Blancs is Champagne in a lighter style, made entirely from Chardonnay grapes.

For those who prefer a less dry Champagne, a *demi-sec*, like this wine from Canard-Duchêne, makes the ideal choice.

The Battle of the Somme

The many cemeteries that cover the Somme region serve as a poignant reminder of the mass slaughter that took place on the Western Front in World War I (which ended with the Armistice on 11 November 1918). Between 1 July and 21 November 1916, the Allied forces lost more than 600,000 men and the Germans at least 465,000. The Battle of the Somme, a series of campaigns conducted by British and French armies against fortified positions held by the Germans, relieved the hard-pressed French at Verdun; but hopes of a breakthrough never materialized, and the Allies only managed to advance 16 km (10 miles).

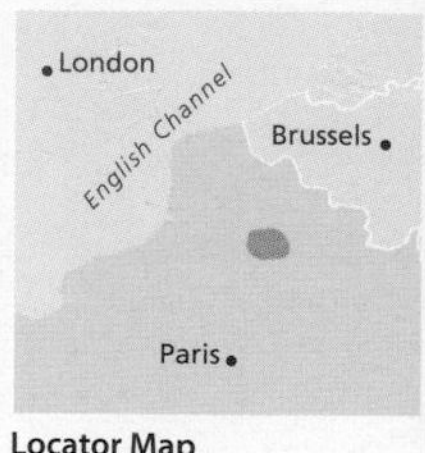

Locator Map

Somme battlefield

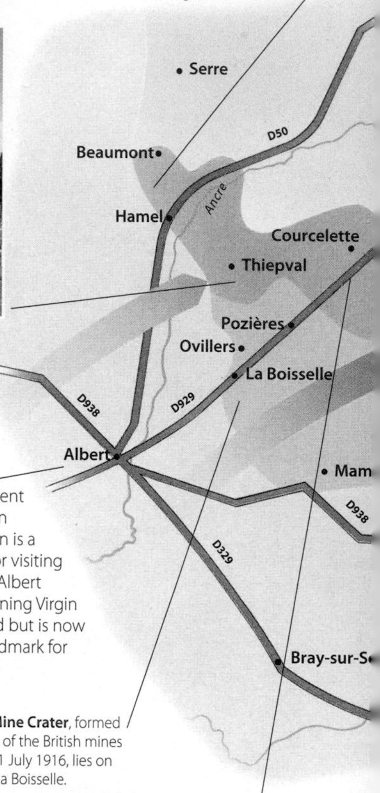

Beaumont Hamel Memorial Park, a tribute to the Royal Newfoundland Regiment, has a huge bronze caribou.

Thiepval Memorial was designed by Sir Edwin Lutyens. It dominates the landscape of Thiepval, one of the most hard-fought areas of the battle, appropriately chosen as a memorial to the 73,367 British soldiers with no known graves.

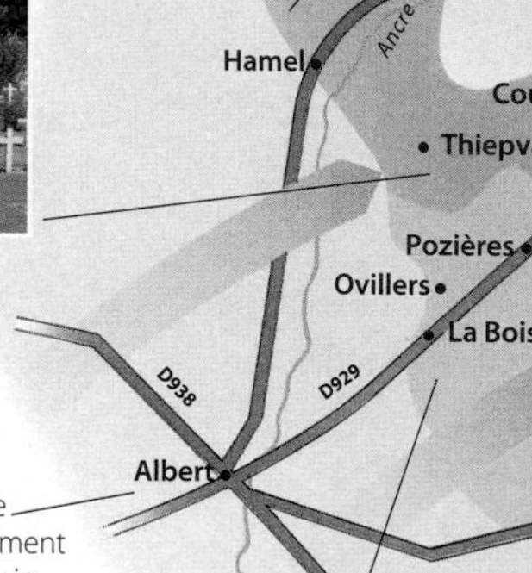

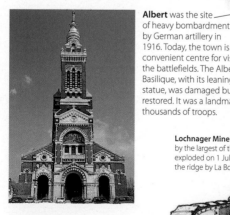

Albert was the site of heavy bombardment by German artillery in 1916. Today, the town is a convenient centre for visiting the battlefields. The Albert Basilique, with its leaning Virgin statue, was damaged but is now restored. It was a landmark for thousands of troops.

Lochnager Mine Crater, formed by the largest of the British mines exploded on 1 July 1916, lies on the ridge by La Boisselle.

The British Tank Memorial, on the main road from Albert to Bapaume, commemorates the first use of tanks in warfare on 15 September 1916. The attack was a limited success; the tanks of World War I were too few before 1918 to transform warfare dominated by artillery, machine guns and barbed wire.

Propaganda in World War I was employed by both sides to maintain support at home. This French postcard has a popular image for civilian consumption. It shows a dying soldier kissing the flag, under the tender gaze of a ministering nurse, affirming his faith in the cause with his last breath.

VISITORS' CHECKLIST

Practical Information
D929, D938 from Albert.
30 pl de la République, 80800 Corbie. **Tel** 03 22 96 95 76.
somme-tourisme.com
Albert Basilique, Beaumont Hamel Memorial Park, La Boisselle, Thiepval & Pozières memorials: **Open** daily. Ulster Tower: **Tel** 03 22 74 81 11. **Open** Feb–Mar: Tue–Sun; Apr–Nov: daily. South African Memorial, Delville Wood, Longueval. **Tel** 03 22 85 02 17. **Open** Feb–Nov: Tue–Sun. **Closed** hols. Historial de Péronne: **Tel** 03 22 83 14 18. **Open** Apr–Sep: daily; Oct–Mar: Tue–Sun. **Closed** mid-Dec–mid-Jan.
historial.org

Delville Wood South African Memorial and Museum show the importance of Commonwealth forces in the Somme.

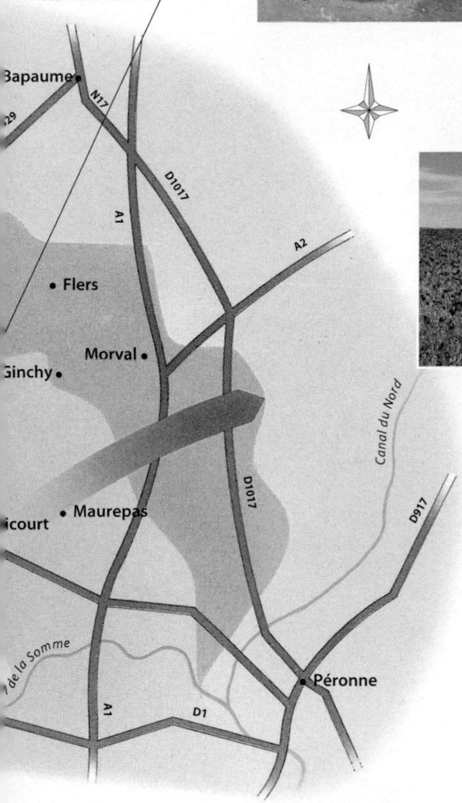

Bapaume
N17
D1017
A1
A2
Flers
Morval
Ginchy
Canal du Nord
Maurepas
D1017
D917
de la Somme
Péronne
A1
D1

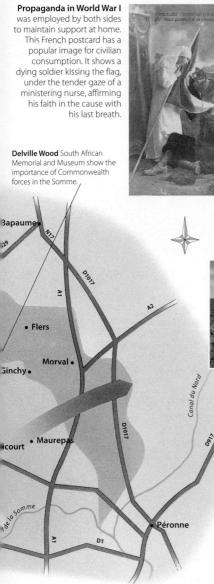

Poppies were one of the few plants to grow on the battlefield. Genghis Khan brought the first white poppy from China and, according to legend, it turned red after battle. Today poppies are a symbol of remembrance.

0 kilometres 5
0 miles 5

Key

- Allied forces
- German forces
- Front Line before 1 July 1916
- Front Line progress July–September 1916
- Front Line progress September–November 1916

The Front Line trenches stretched from the North Sea to the Swiss frontier; only by keeping underground could men survive the terrible conditions. Trenches remain in a few areas, including the Beaumont Hamel Memorial Park.

LE NORD AND PICARDY

Pas de Calais · Nord · Somme · Oise · Aisne

Beneath the modern skin of France's northernmost region, the sights and monuments bear witness to the triumphs and turbulence of its past: soaring Gothic cathedrals, stately châteaux, and the battlefields and memorials of World War I.

The Channel ports of Dunkerque, Calais and Boulogne, and the refined resort of Le Touquet, are the focal points along a busy coastline that stretches from the Somme estuary to the Belgian frontier. Boulogne has a genuine maritime flavour, and the white cliffs running from here to Calais provide the most dramatic scenery along the Côte d'Opale.

Flemish culture holds sway along the border with Belgium: an unfamiliar France of windmills and canals, where the local taste is for beer, hotpots and festivals with gallivanting giants. Lille is the dominant city here, a sprawling modern metropolis with a lively historic heart and an excellent art museum. To the southwest, the grace of Flemish architecture is handsomely displayed in the central squares of Arras, the capital of Artois. From here to the Somme Valley, the legacy of World War I, with its memorial cemeteries and poppy-strewn battlefields, makes compelling viewing.

Cathedrals are the main appeal of Picardy. In Amiens, its capital, Cathédrale Notre-Dame is a pinnacle of the Gothic style – its magnificence echoed by the dizzying achievements at Beauvais further south. Splendid cathedrals at Noyon, Senlis and the delightful hilltop town of Laon chart the evolution of the Gothic. Closer to Paris, two châteaux command attention. Chantilly, the epicentre of French equestrianism, boasts gardens by Le Nôtre and a 19th-century château housing copious art treasures. Compiègne, bordered by a large and inviting forest, plays host to a lavish royal palace favoured by French rulers from Louis XV to Napoleon III.

Memorial cemetery in the Vallée de la Somme, an area still haunted by the memory of World War I

◀ Château de Pierrefonds, overlooking the Forêt de Compiègne

Exploring Le Nord and Picardy

As the gateway to England and Belgium, this northern corner of France is buzzing with business and industries, with the large, Euro-oriented city of Lille offering great culture as well as a new high-tech district. Yet peace and quiet are never far away. The coast between the historic port of Boulogne-sur-Mer and the Vallée de la Somme has a rich birdlife and is perfect for a relaxing seaside visit. Inland, the many Gothic cathedrals such as Amiens and Beauvais make an impressive tour, and the World War I battlefields and memorials provide an important insight into 20th-century history. Further south, the grand châteaux at Compiègne and Chantilly – which has the fascinating Musée Condé – are easily visited en route to or from Paris.

DUNKERQ
4
Gravelines
A16
3 CALAIS
Channel Tunnel
Cap Blanc-Nez
Cap Griz Nez
Canal de la Basse Colme
Bergue
6
A16
D940
Guînes
FLANDRE MARITI
Cassel
Wimereux
ST-OMER 5
Arques
BOULOGNE-SUR-MER 2
N42
La Coupole
Hazeb
Desvres
D341
A26
N43
Samer
Aire-sur
Fauquembergues
D901
Béthu
D928
LE TOUQUET 1
Étaples
Bruay-la-Buissière
Montreuil-sur-Mer
Canche
D941
D939
Berck-sur-Mer
Hesdin
Saint-Pol-sur-Ternoise
Tinc
Fort-Mahon-Plage
Authie
Vron
D940
Crécy-en-Ponthieu
D1001
Frévent
Le Crotoy
NORD
Nouvion
Saint-Valéry-sur-Somme
A16
Doullens
La Pom
Abbeville
Bernaville
Ault
VALLÉE DE LA SOMME
N25
D925
Fressenneville
Somme
A28
Dieppe
Gamaches
Flixecourt
9
Alb
Airaines
Samara
Rouen
Picquigny
D901
AMIENS 10
Co
Hornoy
A29
Saint-Sauflieu
Aumale
D1029
Poix-de-Picardie
D935
Essertaux
Bo
Grandvilliers
D1001
A16
Breteuil
Marseille-en-Beauvaisis
Mont
Crèvecoeur-le-Grand
Songeons
D901
Wavignies
Gournay-en-Bray
Saint-Just-en-Chaussée
N31
D916
BEAUVAIS 11
N31
Bresles
D981
Clerm
Noailles
Mouy
Gisors
D1001
Creil
A16
Méru
CHANTILLY 16
PARC ASTÉRI
Paris
0 kilometres 25
0 miles 25

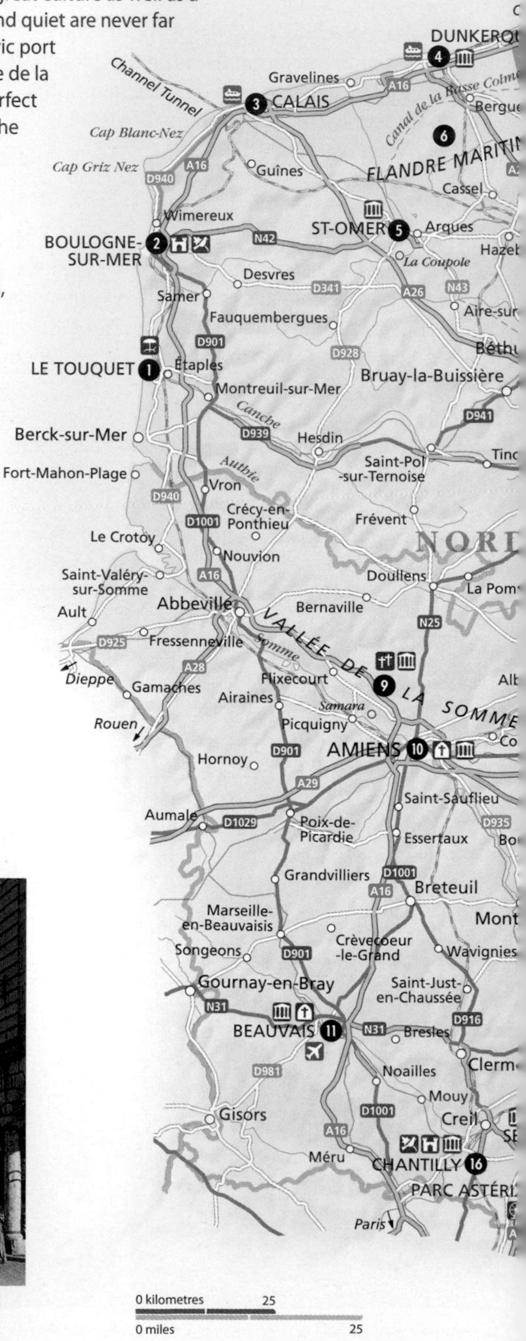

Key

- Motorway
- Major road
- Secondary road
- Minor road
- Scenic route
- Main railway
- Minor railway
- International border
- Regional border

STELLA ARTOIS

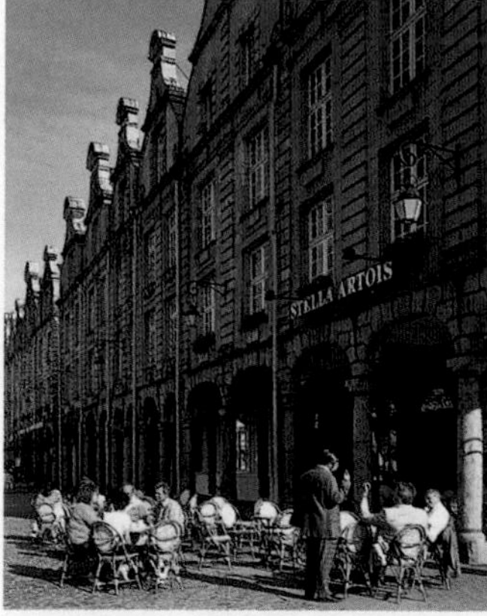

Lively outdoor café in the historic Grand'Place in the heart of Arras

For keys to symbols *see back flap*

Sights at a Glance

1. Le Touquet
2. Boulogne-sur-Mer
3. Calais
4. Dunkerque
5. St-Omer
6. Flandre Maritime
7. Lille
8. Arras
9. Vallée de la Somme
10. Amiens
11. Beauvais
12. Noyon
13. Compiègne
14. Château de Pierrefonds
15. Senlis
16. Chantilly
17. Parc Astérix
18. Laon

The meandering waters in the Vallée de la Somme

Getting Around

The main entry point into the region is Calais (and the Channel Tunnel terminal 3 km/ 2 miles south). From here, *autoroutes* A16 and A26/A1, several major N and D roads, and main-line rail services run directly to Paris. In addition, TGVs serve Calais-Frethun, Lille and Paris. There is a dense road network throughout the region.
With their many local bus and train connections, Lille and Amiens make good bases. The A26 (or *Autoroute des Anglais*) crosses the whole region from Calais to Troyes, via Arras and Laon, giving easy access to eastern Picardy. It's also a useful route if you're heading south and want to avoid Paris. Finally, the airport at Beauvais is a convenient entry point.

Poppies, the symbol of World War I battlefields, in the Vallée de la Somme

Le Touquet beach at low tide

❶ Le Touquet

Pas de Calais. 5,500. Palais du Congrès, pl de l'Hermitage (03 21 06 72 00). Thu & Sat (Jun–mid-Sep: also Mon). **letouquet.com**

Properly known as Le Touquet Paris-Plage, this resort was created in the 19th century and became fashionable with the rich and famous between the two world wars. A vast pine forest, planted in 1855, spreads around the town sheltering stately villas. To the west, a grid of smart hotels, holiday residences and sophisticated shops and restaurants borders a long, sandy beach. A racecourse and two casinos are complemented by seaside amusements and sports facilities, including two excellent golf courses, horse riding and land yachting.

Further inland, the hilltop town of **Montreuil** has lime washed 17th-century houses, abundant restaurants and a tree-shaded rampart walk.

❷ Boulogne-sur-Mer

Pas de Calais. 45,000. Parvis de Nausicaa (03 21 10 88 10). Wed & Sat *(pl Dalton)*, Sun *(pl Vignon & pl Gambetta)*. **tourisme-boulognesurmer.com**

An important fishing port and busy marina, Boulogne rewards its visitors well. Its attractions come neatly boxed in a walled Haute Ville, with the Porte des Dunes opening on to a 17th- to 19th-century ensemble of Palais de Justice, Bibliothèque and Hôtel de Ville in **place de la Résistance**.

The 19th-century **Basilique Notre-Dame** is capped by a dome visible for miles. Inside, a bejewelled wooden statue represents Boulogne's patroness, Notre-Dame de Boulogne. She is wearing a *soleil*, a headdress also worn by women during the *Grande Procession* held annually in her honour. Nearby, the powerful moated 13th-century **Château**, built for the Counts of Boulogne, is now a well-organized historical museum.

In the centre of town, shops, hotels and fish restaurants line quai Gambetta on the east bank of the River Liane. To the north lie Boulogne's beach and **Nausicaa**, a vast, spectacular and innovative aquarium and Sea Centre.

North of the town, the **Colonne de la Grande Armée** was erected in 1841 as a monument to Napoleon I's planned invasion of England in 1803–5. From the top there is a panoramic view along the coast towards Calais. This is the most scenic stretch of the Côte d'Opale (Opal Coast), with the windblown headlands of **Cap Gris-Nez** and **Cap Blanc-Nez** offering breathtakingly extensive views across the Channel.

Château
Rue de Bernet. **Tel** 03 21 10 02 20. **Open** Wed–Mon. **Closed** 1 May, 25 Dec, 1st wk Jan.

Aquarium Nausicaa
Bd Sainte-Beuve. **Tel** 03 21 30 98 98. **Open** daily. **Closed** 3 wks Jan, 25 Dec. **nausicaa.fr**

❸ Calais

Pas de Calais. 76,000. 12 bd Clémenceau (03 21 96 62 40). Wed, Thu & Sat. **calais-cotedopale.com**

Calais is a busy cross-Channel port with a sandy beach to the west. Clumsily rebuilt after World War II, it seems to have little to offer at first sight. Many visitors never get closer than the huge Cité Europe shopping mall by the Eurotunnel exit.

The **Musée des Beaux Arts**, however, has works by the Dutch and Flemish Schools. Also on show are studies for Auguste Rodin's famous statue *The Burghers of Calais* (1895). The statue stands outside the Hôtel de Ville and celebrates an event during Edward III's

The windswept Cap Blanc-Nez on the Côte d'Opale

The Burghers of Calais by Auguste Rodin (1895)

siege of Calais in 1347, when six burghers offered their lives to save the rest of the town.

The **Cité de la Dentelle et de la Mode** recalls the town's lace-making industry. **Musée Mémoire 1939–1945**, housed in a battle-scarred German blockhouse, offers a detailed account of local events during World War II.

Musée des Beaux-Arts
25 rue Richelieu. **Tel** 03 21 46 48 40.
Open Tue–Sun pms.

Cité de la Dentelle et de la Mode
Quai du Commerce. **Tel** 03 21 00 42 30. **Open** Wed–Mon. **Closed** first 2 weeks of Jan, 1 May, 25 Dec.
cite-dentelle.fr

Musée Mémoire 1939–1945
Parc St Pierre. **Tel** 03 21 34 21 57.
Open Mon & Wed–Sat; May–Sep: daily. **Closed** Jan & Dec.

4 Dunkerque

Nord. 375,000. Le Beffroi, rue Amiral Ronarc'h (03 28 66 79 21). Wed, Sat. **ot-dunkerque.fr**

Though a major industrial port, Dunkerque has much Flemish character. Start a tour from place du Minck, with its fresh fish stalls. Nearby **Musée Portuaire** celebrates the town's maritime history. In the old centre, a statue commemorates local hero Jean Bart, a 17th-century corsair, who lies in **Eglise St-Eloi**. Its belfry (1440) offers fine views.

Le Mémorial du Souvenir has an exhibition of the dramatic evacuation of 350,000 British and French troops in 1940. The **Lieu d'Art et d'Action Contemporaine (LAAC)** features ceramics and glassware.

Musée Portuaire
9 quai de la Citadelle. **Tel** 03 28 63 33 39. **Open** Wed–Mon (Jul & Aug: daily). **Closed** 1 Jan, 1 May, 25 Dec.

The port at Dunkerque

Le Memorial du Souvenir
Rue des Chantiers de France. **Tel** 03 28 66 79 21. **Open** Apr–Sep: daily.
ground floor only.

Lieu d'Art et d'Action Contemporaine
Jardin des Sculptures. **Tel** 03 28 29 56 00. **Open** Tue–Sun. **Closed** public hols.

5 St-Omer

Pas de Calais. 15,000. 7, pl Victor Hugo (03 21 98 08 51). Sat. **tourisme-saintomer.com**

With its cobbled streets and 17th- and 18th-century buildings, St-Omer appears untouched. The **Hôtel Sandelin** houses a fine and decorative arts museum, while the cathedral boasts 13th-century tiles and a huge organ. The **Bibliothèque d'Agglomération** contains rare manuscripts from the Abbaye St-Bertin, a ruined 15th-century abbey nearby. Five km (3 miles) from St-Omer, **La Coupole** is a World War II museum inside a converted bunker.

Hôtel Sandelin
14 rue Carnot. **Tel** 03 21 38 00 94.
Open Wed–Sun. ground floor.

Bibliothèque d'Agglomération
40 rue Gambetta. **Tel** 03 21 38 35 08.
Open Tue, Wed, Fri & Sat. **Closed** public hols.

La Coupole
Rue Clabaux, 62570 Helfaut. **Tel** 03 21 12 27 27. **Open** daily. **Closed** 2 wks in Jan, 24 & 25 Dec.

Channel Crossings

Calais is only 35 km (22 miles) southeast of the English coast, and crossing the waters of the Channel – which the French know as *la Manche* (the Sleeve) – has inspired many intrepid exploits. The first crossing by balloon was in 1785 by Jean-Pierre Blanchard; Captain M Webb made the first swim in 1875; and Louis Blériot's pioneering flight followed in 1909. Plans for an undersea tunnel, first laid as early as 1751, were finally achieved in 1994 with the opening of a railway link between Fréthun and Folkestone.

Children watching Louis Blériot taking off, 1909

6 Flandre Maritime

Nord. 5,000. Lille. Bergues. Dunkerque. Bergues, Le Beffroi, pl Henri Billiaert (03 28 68 71 06). **bergues-tourisme.fr**

South of Dunkerque lies a flat, agricultural plain with narrow waterways and expansive skies – an archetypal Flemish landscape with canals, cyclists and ancient windmills. The **Noordmeulen**, built just north of Hondschoote in 1127, is thought to be the oldest windmill in Europe.

From Hondschoote the D3 follows the Canal de la Basse Colme west to Bergues, a fortified wool town with fine 16th- to 17th-century Flemish works in its **Musée Municipal**. Further south, the hilltop town of **Cassel** has a cobbled Grande Place with 16th- to 18th-century buildings, and views across Flanders and Belgium from its Jardin Public.

Musée Municipal
1 rue du Mont de Piété, Bergues. **Tel** 03 28 68 13 30. **Open** Thu–Mon pms. **Closed** Nov–Apr.

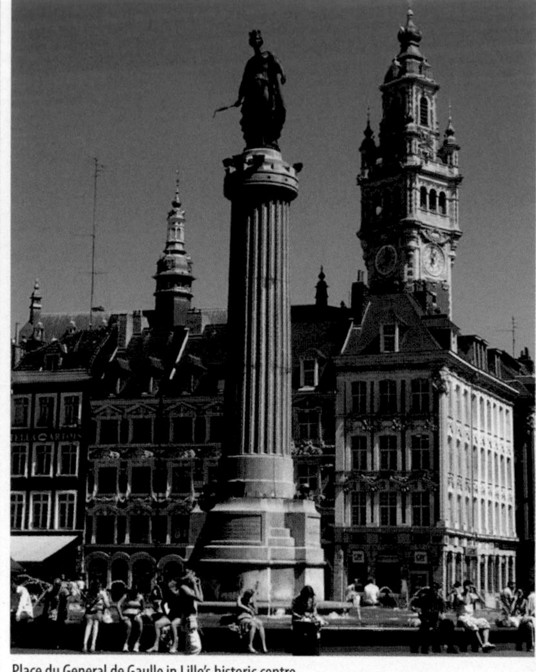
Place du General de Gaulle in Lille's historic centre

7 Lille

Nord. 230,000. 1 rue du Palais Rihour (08 91 56 20 04). Tue–Sun. **lilletourism.com**

Lille has excellent shops and markets and a powerful sense of its historic Flemish identity – the Flemish name, Rijssel, is still used and some of the area's one million residents speak a Franco-Flemish patois. With heavy industry declining, the city has turned to high tech. A modern commercial quarter, including the ultramodern Euralille shopping complex, adjoins Lille Europe station, the TGV/Eurostar/Thalys rail interchange. The city's "Métro", VAL, is a driverless automatic train.

Flower stalls in the arcades of the Vieille Bourse in Lille

However, the city's charm lies in its historic centre, Vieux Lille – a mass of cobbled squares and narrow streets that are packed with stylish shops, cafés and restaurants. Place du Général de Gaulle forms its hub, with façades including the 17th-century **Vieille Bourse** (Old Exchange). Adjacent stand the **Nouvelle Bourse** and the **Opéra**, both built in the early 20th century. The moated five-point brick Citadel by Vauban is also worth a look.

Musée de l'Hospice Comtesse
32 rue de la Monnaie. **Tel** 03 28 36 84 00. **Open** Wed–Sun, Mon pm.

A hospital was founded here in 1237. Now its 15th- and 17th- century buildings house exhibitions. The Sick Room has a barrel-vaulted ceiling; the Community Wing has a Delft kitchen. There is also a collection of ancient instruments.

Palais des Beaux-Arts
Pl de la République. **Tel** 03 20 06 78 00. **Open** Wed–Sun, Mon pm. **Closed** 1 Jan, 1 May, 14 Jul, 1 Nov, 25 Dec.

One of the best art collections outside Paris, the museum is strong on Flemish works, including Rubens and Van Dyck. Other highlights are *Paradise and Hell* by Dirk Bouts, van Goyen's *The Skaters*, Goya's *The Letter*, Delacroix's *Médée*, as well as works by Courbet and Impressionist paintings.

Musée d'Art Moderne, d'Art Contemporain et d'Art Brut (LaM)
1 Allée du Musée, 59650 Villeneuve-d'Ascq. **Tel** 03 20 19 68 68. **Open** Tue–Sun. **Closed** 1 Jan, 1 May, 25 Dec

Lille's contemporary art museum and sculpture park focuses on 20th- and 21st-century art. The collection showcases works by Picasso, Modigliani, Miró, Braque and Léger. It also boasts the largest permanent collection of outsider (brut) art in France.

For hotels and restaurants in this region see pp556–7 and pp579–80

8 Arras

Pas de Calais. 45,000. Hôtel de Ville, pl des Héros (03 21 51 26 95). Wed, Thu, Sat, Sun. **explorearras.com**

The centre of Arras, capital of the Artois region, is graced by two picturesque cobbled squares enclosed by 155 houses with 17th-century Flemish-style façades. A triumph of postwar reconstruction, each residence in the **Grand'Place** and the smaller place des Héros has a slightly varying design, with some original shop signs still visible.

A monumental **Hôtel de Ville** rebuilt in the Flamboyant Gothic style stands at the west end of place des Héros – in the foyer are four giants, Colas, Dédé, Ami Bidasse and Jacqueline, who swagger round the town during local festivals. From the basement you can take a lift up to the belfry for superb views, or take a guided tour into the labyrinth of underground passages below Arras. These were cut in the limestone in the 10th century. They have often served as shelter, during World War I notably, as a subterranean army camp.

The huge Abbaye St-Vaast includes an 18th- to 19th-century Neo-Classical cathedral and the **Musée des Beaux-Arts**. The museum contains some fine examples of medieval sculpture, including a pair of beautiful 13th-century angels. Among other exhibits are a local *arras* (hanging tapestry) and 19th-century works by the School of Arras, a group of Realist landscape painters.

Hôtel de Ville
Pl des Héros. **Tel** 03 21 51 26 95. **Open** Jul–Aug: Sun pm, Mon–Fri. Tunnels: **Open** Feb–Dec: daily. Belfry: **Open** daily. **Closed** 25 Dec, 1 Jan. obligatory for tunnels.

Musée des Beaux-Arts
22 rue Paul Doumer. **Tel** 03 21 71 26 43. **Open** Wed–Mon. **Closed** pub hols.

9 Vallée de la Somme

Somme. Amiens. 16 pl André Audinot, Péronne (03 22 84 42 38). **somme-tourisme.com**

The name of the Somme is synonymous with the slaughter and horror of trench warfare during World War I *(see pp194–5)*. Yet the Somme Valley also means pretty countryside, a vast estuary wetland and abundant wildlife. Lakes and woods alongside provide enjoyable camping, walking and fishing. Battlefields lie along the river and its tributaries north and northeast of Amiens, and extend north to Arras. Neat World War I Commonwealth cemeteries cover the area. The **Historial de la Grande Guerre** at Péronne gives a thoughtful introduction. Parc Mémorial Beaumont-Hamel, near Albert, is a real battlefield being allowed to disappear in its own time. Travel to Vimy Ridge Canadian Memorial, near Arras, to see a bloodbath battle site preserved as it was, and to Notre-Dame de Lorette, the landmark French National Cemetery.

Roadside shrine, Somme Valley

Boating on the River Somme

West of Amiens, **Samara** – Amiens' Gallo-Roman name – is France's largest archaeological park, with reconstructions of prehistoric dwellings, and exhibitions explaining early crafts such as flint-cutting and corn-grinding. Further downstream, Eglise St-Vulfran at Abbeville is noted for its Flamboyant Gothic west front with beautifully carved 16th-century door panels.

St-Valéry-sur-Somme is a charming harbour resort with a historic upper town and a tree-lined promenade looking across the estuary. William departed for England from here in 1066. Birdwatchers should visit the Maison de la Baie de Somme et de l'Oiseau nearby at Lanchéres, or the Parc Ornithologique de Marquenterre on the far shore near delightful Le Crotoy. In summer, a little train links the two sides, passing through dunes and marshes.

The 16th-century carvings on Eglise St-Vulfran in Abbeville, Somme Valley

Historial de la Grande Guerre
Château de Péronne. **Tel** 03 22 83 14 18. **Open** Apr–Sep: daily; Oct–Mar: Thu–Tue. **Closed** mid-Dec–mid-Jan. **historial.org**

Samara
La Chaussée-Tirancourt. **Tel** 03 22 51 82 83. **Open** Apr–Oct: daily. **samara.fr**

⑩ Amiens

Somme. 130,000. 23 pl Notre Dame (03 22 71 60 50). Wed & Sat. **amiens-tourisme.com**

There is more to Amiens, the capital of Picardy, than its **Cathédrale Notre-Dame** *(see pp206–7)*. The picturesque St-Leu quarter is a pedestrianized area of low houses and flower-lined canals with waterside restaurants and artisans' shops. Further east are the colourful **Les Hortillonnages**, a patchwork of marshland market gardens, once tended by farmers using punts that now ferry visitors around the protected natural site.

The **Musée de Picardie** has many fine medieval and 19th-century sculptures and 16th- to 20th-century paintings, including a set of 16th-century group portraits, commissioned as offerings to the cathedral. To the south is the Cirque d'Hiver, which Jules Verne (1828–1905) inaugurated in 1889. **Maison de Jules Verne** has over 700 objects spread over four floors relating to the famous author, who lived here from 1882 until 1900.

Musée de Picardie
48 rue de la République. **Tel** 03 22 97 14 00. **Closed** for renovation until 2019.

Maison de Jules Verne
2 rue Charles Dubois. **Tel** 03 22 45 45 75. **Open** Wed–Mon & Tue pm (mid-Oct–Easter: Mon & Wed–Fri; Sat & Sun pms).

The clock depicts Christ surrounded by the 12 apostles.
Mechanical figures perform scenes from the Last Judgment.
Solstice indicator
Clock showing the age of the world

Astronomical clock in Beauvais Cathedral

⑪ Beauvais

Oise. 61,000.
1 rue Beauregard (03 44 15 30 30).
Mon, Wed, Thurs, Sat.
visitbeauvais.fr

Heavily bombed in World War II, Beauvais is now a modern town with one outstanding jewel. Though never completed, **Cathédrale St-Pierre** is a poignant, neck-cricking finale to the vaulting ambition that created the great Gothic cathedrals. In 1227, work began on a building designed to soar above all predecessors, but the roof of the chancel caved in twice from lack of support before its completion in the early 14th century. Delayed by wars and inadequate funds, the transept was not completed until 1550. In 1573 its crossing collapsed after a tower and spire were added.

What remains today is nevertheless a masterpiece, rising 48 m (157 ft) high. In the transept much of the original 16th-century stained glass survives, while near the north door is a 90,000-part astronomical clock assembled in the 1860s. Displays take place daily at 30 minutes past the hour (€5). What would have been the nave is still occupied by the remnants of a 10th-century church known as the Basse-Oeuvre.

The former Bishop's Palace is now home to **Le MUDO – Musée de l'Oise**. The collection includes archaeological finds, medieval sculpture, tapestries and local ceramics. Beauvais has a long tradition of tapestry

Viollet-le-Duc

The renowned architectural theorist Viollet-le-Duc (1814–79) was the first to fully appreciate Gothic architecture. His 1854 dictionary of architecture celebrated medieval building techniques, showing that the arches and tracery of Gothic cathedrals were solutions to architectural problems, not mere decoration. His restoration work included Château de Pierrefonds, Notre-Dame in Paris *(see pp90–91)* and Carcassonne *(see pp492–3)*.

Medieval architects, as drawn by Viollet-le-Duc

production. The tourist office organizes visits to the local **Manufacture Nationale de la Tapisserie** factory at Beauvais.

Le MUDO – Musée de l'Oise
Ancien Palais Episcopal, 1 rue du Musée. **Tel** 03 44 10 40 50. **Open** Wed–Mon. **Closed** 1 Jan, Easter, 1 May, 9 Jun, 1 Nov, 25 Dec.

Manufacture Nationale de la Tapisserie
24 rue Henri-Brispot. Contact tourist office for reservations. Jul & Aug: Wed pm.

The rib-vaulted nave of Cathédrale de Notre-Dame, Noyon

⓬ Noyon

Oise. 15,000. pl Bertrand Labarre (03 44 44 21 88). Wed & Sat, first Tue of each month. **noyon-tourisme.com**

Noyon has long been a religious centre. The **Cathédrale de Notre-Dame**, dating from 1150, is the fifth to be built on this site and was completed by 1290. It provides a harmonious example of the transition from Romanesque to Gothic style.

A local history museum, the **Musée du Noyonnais**, occupies part of the former Bishop's Palace, and at the cathedral's east end is a rare half-timbered chapter library built in 1506.

Jean Calvin, the Protestant theologian and one of the leaders of the Reformation, was born here in 1509 and is commemorated in the small **Musée Jean Calvin.**

Musée du Noyonnais
Ancien Palais Episcopal, 7 rue de l'Evêché. **Tel** 03 44 09 43 41. **Open** Tue-Sun. **Closed** 1 Jan, 11 Nov, 24 Dec–2 Jan.

⓭ Compiègne

Oise. 70,000. pl de l'Hôtel de Ville (03 44 40 01 00). Tue–Sat. **compiegne-tourisme.fr**

Compiègne is where Joan of Arc was captured by the Burgundians in 1430. A 16th-century Hôtel de Ville with a towering belfry rules over the centre, but the town is most famous for its royal **Château**.

Designed as a summer residence for Louis XV, the château was completed by Louis XVI, restored by Napoleon and later became a residence of Napoleon III and Empress Eugénie. Tours of the Imperial Apartments take in private chambers, such as the sumptuous bedrooms of Napoleon I and Marie-Louise.

Within the Château, the Musée du Second Empire and Musée de l'Impératrice display furniture, memorabilia and portraits, while the Musée de la Voiture is an assembly of historic carriages, bicycles and early motor cars.

South and east of the town, the old hunting grounds of the **Forêt de Compiègne** spread as far as Pierrefonds, with ample space for walks and picnics beneath its oaks and beeches. East of the D130, Les Beaux Monts provide majestic views back to the château.

The Clairière de l'Armistice, north of the N31, marks the spot where the armistice of World War I was signed on 11 November 1918. The small **Musée Wagon de l'Armistice** has a replica of the railway carriage where the ceremony took place, which was used again in World War II by Hitler as a humiliating venue for the signing of the French surrender on 22 June 1940.

Château de Compiègne
Pl du Général de Gaulle. **Tel** 03 44 38 47 00. **Open** Wed–Mon. **Closed** 1 Jan, 1 May, 25 Dec. **palais-decompiegne.fr**

Musée Wagon de l'Armistice
Clairière de l'Armistice. **Tel** 03 44 85 14 18. **Open** Wed–Mon (Apr–mid-Sep: daily). **Closed** 1 Jan, 25 Dec.

⓮ Château de Pierrefonds

Oise. **Tel** 03 44 42 72 72. **Open** daily. **Closed** 1 Jan, 1 May, 25 Dec. Concerts. **chateau-pierrefonds.fr**

The immense Château de Pierrefonds dominates the small village below. A mighty castle was constructed here by Louis d'Orléans in the 14th century, but by 1813 it had become a picturesque ruin, which Napoleon I purchased for less than 3,000 francs.

In 1857, Napoleon III commissioned the architect Viollet-le-Duc to restore it, and in 1884 Pierrefonds was reborn as a museum of fortification. The exterior, with its moat, drawbridge, towers and double sentry walks, is a diligent reconstruction of medieval military architecture. The interior, by contrast, is enlivened by romantic fancies. There are guided tours and a historical exhibition.

Path through the Forêt de Compiègne

Amiens Cathedral

Work on France's largest cathedral started around 1220. It was built to house the head of St John the Baptist, brought back from the Crusades in 1206 and is still displayed here. Within 50 years, Notre-Dame was complete, a masterpiece of engineering – Gothic architecture carried to a bold extreme. Restored in the 1850s by Viollet-le-Duc *(see p204)*, and having miraculously survived two world wars, the cathedral is famous for its statues and reliefs, which inspired John Ruskin's *The Bible of Amiens* in 1884. The La Cathédrale en Couleurs sound-and-light show re-creates the original colours of the statuary around the west door.

★ West Front
The King's Gallery, a row of 22 colossal statues representing the kings of France, spans the west front. The statues are also thought to symbolize the Kings of Judah.

Weeping Angel
Sculpted by Nicolas Blasset in 1628, this sentimental statue in the ambulatory became a popular image during World War I.

KEY

① **The Calendar** shows signs from the zodiac, with the corresponding monthly labours below. It depicts everyday life in the 13th century.

② **St Firmin Portal** is decorated with figures and scenes from the life of St Firmin, the martyr who brought Christianity to Picardy and became the first bishop of Amiens.

③ **The Flamboyant tracery** of the rose window was created in the 16th century.

④ **A double row** comprising 22 elegant flying buttresses supports the construction.

⑤ **The flooring** was laid down in 1288 and reassembled in the late 19th century. The faithful followed its labyrinthine shape on their knees.

Central Portal
Scenes from the Last Judgment adorn the tympanum, with the *Beau Dieu*, a statue of Christ, between the doors.

For hotels and restaurants in this region see pp556–7 and pp579–80

Towers
Two towers of unequal height frame the west front. The south tower was completed in 1366; the north in 1402. The spire was replaced twice, in 1627 and 1887.

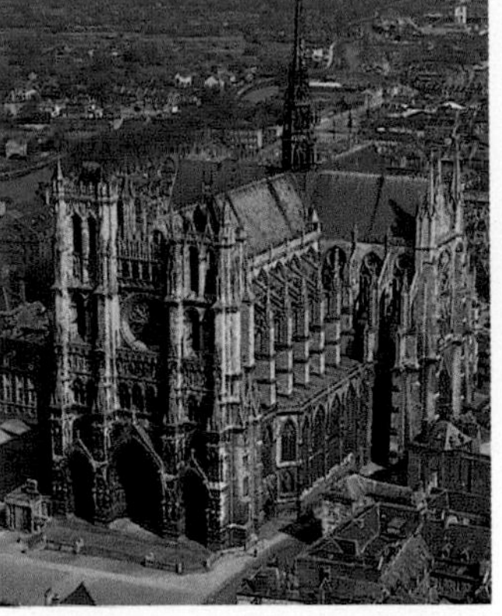

VISITORS' CHECKLIST

Practical Information
Pl Notre-Dame. **Tel** 03 22 80 03 41. **Open** 8:30am–6:15pm (Oct–Mar: to 5.15pm). La Cathédrale en Couleurs light show: Jun–Sep & Christmas hols (nightly). Towers: **Open** Mon, Wed–Sat & Sun pm. **Closed** 1 Jan, last Sun Sep. 9am daily; 9am, 10:30am Sun.
amiens-cathedrale.fr

★ Nave
Soaring 42 m (138 ft) high, with support from 126 slender pillars, the brightly illuminated interior of Notre-Dame is a hymn to the vertical.

★ Choir Stalls
The 110 oak choir stalls (1508–19) are delicately carved with over 4,000 biblical, mythical and real-life figures.

★ Choir Screens
Vivid scenes from the lives of St Firmin and St John, carved in the 15th- to the 16th centuries, adorn the ambulatory.

⓯ Senlis

Oise. 17,000. pl du Parvis Notre-Dame (03 44 53 06 40). Tue & Fri. senlis-tourisme.fr

Senlis, 10 km (6 miles) east of Chantilly, is worth visiting for its Gothic cathedral and the well-preserved historic streets that surround it. **Cathédrale Notre-Dame** was constructed during the 12th century, and the sculpted central doorway of its west front, depicting the Assumption of the Virgin, influenced later cathedrals such as Amiens *(see pp206–7)*. The south tower's spire dates from the 13th century, while the Flamboyant south transept, built in the mid-16th century, makes an ornate contrast with the austerity of earlier years. Opposite the west front, a gateway leads to the ruins of the Château Royal and its gardens. Here the **Musée de la Vénerie**, housed in a former priory, celebrates hunting through paintings, old weapons and trophies.

The **Musée d'Art** recalls the town's Gallo-Roman past, and also has an excellent collection of early Gothic sculpture.

Musée de la Vénerie
Château Royal, pl du Parvis Notre-Dame. **Tel** 03 44 29 49 93. **Open** Wed–Sun. **Closed** 1 Jan, 1 May, 25 Dec. obligatory for upper floor rooms, pms only.

Musée d'Art et d'Archéologie
Ancien Evêché, 2 pl Notre-Dame. **Tel** 03 44 24 86 72. **Open** Wed–Sun.

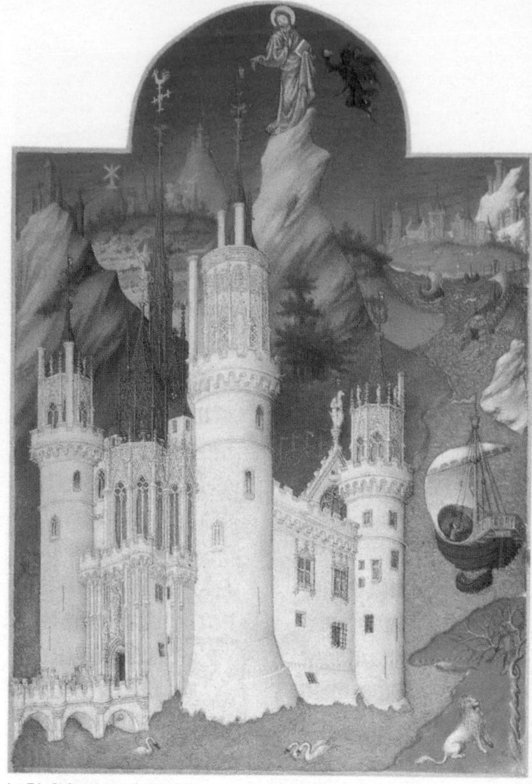

Les Très Riches Heures du Duc de Berry, on show in Chantilly

⓰ Chantilly

Oise. 11,000. 73 rue du Connétable (03 44 67 37 37). Wed & Sat. chantilly-tourisme.com

The horse-racing capital of France, Chantilly offers a classy combination of château, park and forest that has long made it a popular excursion. With origins in Gallo-Roman times, the château of today started to take shape in 1528, when Anne de Montmorency, Constable of France, had the old fortress replaced and added the Petit Château. During the time of the Great Prince of Condé (1621–86), renovation work continued and André Le Nôtre created a park and fountains that made even Louis XIV jealous. Destroyed in the Revolution, the Grand Château was again

Chantilly Horse Racing

Chantilly is the capital of thoroughbred racing in France, a shrine to the long-standing love affair between the French upper classes and the world of horses. It was the firm belief of Prince Louis-Henri de Bourbon, creator of Chantilly's monumental Grandes Ecuries, that he would one day be reincarnated as a horse. Horse racing was introduced from England around 1830 and soon became very popular. The first official race meeting was held here in 1834 and today around 3,000 horses are trained in the surrounding forests and countryside. Every June, Chantilly becomes the focus of the social and flat racing season when top riders and their thoroughbreds compete for its two historic trophies, the Prix du Jockey-Club and Prix de Diane-Hermès.

Prix de Diane-Hermès, one of many prestigious races at Chantilly

rebuilt and its receptions and hunting parties became crowded by the fashionable high society of the 1820s and 1830s. It was finally replaced by a Renaissance-style château in the late 19th century.

Today the Grand Château and the Petit Château form the **Musée Condé**, displaying art treasures collected by its last private owner, the Duke of Aumale. These include work by Raphael, Botticelli, Poussin and Ingres, and an entertaining gallery of 16th-century portraits by the Clouet brothers. Among the most precious items is the famous 15th-century illuminated manuscript *Les Très Riches Heures du Duc de Berry*, reproductions of which are on view. You can also tour the stately apartments, with decorative conceits ranging from frolicking monkeys to triumphant battles.

Asterix with friends, Parc Astérix

Both châteaux are somewhat upstaged by the magnificent stables (Grandes Ecuries), an equestrian palace designed by Jean Aubert in 1719 to accommodate 240 horses and 500 dogs. It is occupied by the **Musée du Cheval**, presenting various breeds of horses and ponies, and riding displays.

Musée Condé
Château de Chantilly. **Tel** 03 44 62 62 62. **Open** daily (Dec–Mar: Wed–Mon).

Musée du Cheval
Grandes Ecuries du Prince de Condé, Chantilly. **Tel** 03 44 27 31 80. **Open** daily (Dec–Mar: Wed–Mon).
domainedechantilly.com

⓱ Parc Astérix

Plailly. **Tel** 08 26 46 26 26. **Open** Apr–early Nov (times vary, check website).
parcasterix.fr

Near Charles de Gaulle airport a small fortified Gaulish village has its own customs controls, currency and radio station (Menhir FM). One of the most popular theme parks in France, it is dedicated to Asterix the Gaul and all the other characters in Goscinny and Uderzo's famous cartoon strip: Getafix, Obelix, Cacofonix et al. The Romans are driven crazy as they try to subdue these larger-than-life Gauls, who dodge patrolling Roman centurions. Hilarious battles take place.

The Parc is as much about French history as about the cartoons. Via Antiqua and the Roman City are lighthearted but still genuinely educational. Rue de Paris shows Paris through the centuries, including the construction of Notre-Dame cathedral. There are non-historical attractions too, such as a dolphinarium and Zeus' Thunder high-speed roller coaster. Check out the latest rides – there's usually something new every year.

⓲ Laon

Aisne. 27,000. Hôtel-Dieu, pl du Parvis Gauthier de Montagne (03 23 20 28 62). Tue–Sat.
tourisme-paysdelaon.com

The capital of the Aisne *département*, Laon occupies a dramatic site on top of a long, narrow ridge surrounded by wide plains. The old town, on top of the mount, is best approached by Poma, an automated cable car that swings up from the railway station to the place du Général Leclerc.

The pedestrianized rue Châtelaine, a main shopping street in Laon

Rose window in the 13th-century Cathédrale de Notre-Dame, Laon

The pedestrianized rue Châtelaine leads to Laon's splendid **Cathédrale de Notre-Dame**. Completed in 1235, the cathedral lost two of its original seven towers in the Revolution but remains an impressive monument to the early Gothic style.

Details include the deep porches of the west façade, the four-storey nave and the carved Renaissance screens enclosing its side chapels. The immense 13th-century rose window in the apse represents the Glorification of the Church. Protruding from the cathedral's western towers are statues paying tribute to the oxen that were used to haul up stone for its construction.

The rest of medieval Laon rewards casual strolling: a promenade rings the 16th-century **Citadelle** further east, while to the south you can follow the ramparts past the Porte d'Ardon and Porte des Chenizelles to **Eglise St-Martin**, with views of the cathedral from rue Thibesard.

South of Laon is Chemin des Dames, named after Louis XV's daughters, who used to take this route, but more often remembered as a World War I battlefield and lined with cemeteries and memorials.

CHAMPAGNE

Marne · Ardennes · Aube · Haute-Marne

Champagne is a name of great resonance, conjuring up images of celebration and the world-famous cathedral at Reims. Yet beyond the glamour lies an unspoiled rural idyll of two strikingly contrasting landscapes: the rolling plains of Champagne, giving way to lakes and water meadows to the south and the dense forests and hills of the Ardennes in the north.

The so-called "sacred triangle of Champagne", linking Epernay, Reims and Châlons-en-Champagne, is like a magnet for wine lovers. Here, the experience of drinking fine Champagne is enhanced by gourmet meals of stuffed trout, Ardennes ham and the famous tripe sausages called *andouillettes*.

The sign posted *route touristique du champagne* wends its way through vineyards towards endless cereal plains stretching southward to the "lake district", an area of oak forests, water meadows and streams.

On the border between France and Belgium lies the Ardennes, named after the Celtic word for "deep forest". This wild border land of dramatic valleys, deciduous forests and hills is cut by the meanderings of the River Meuse. Border fortifications include the vast citadel of Sedan and the star-shaped town and fortress of Rocroi, as well as the Maginot Line outposts built before World War II. The Ardennes may offer appealing countryside, but Champagne is culturally superior, with impressive towns that have painstakingly restored historic centres. It has some striking churches, from the Gothic majesty of Reims Cathedral to the rustic charm of its typical half-timbered *champenoises* churches. These feature vivid stained-glass windows by the famous School of Troyes, whose subtle craftsmanship seems to typify the appeal of this quiet region.

Timber-framed *champenoise* church at Lac du Der-Chantecoq

◀ Interior of Cathédrale Notre-Dame, Reims

Exploring Champagne

Champagne's fizz draws wine lovers to the sacred triangle between Reims, Epernay and Châlons-en-Champagne, but the region also attracts culture lovers to its great churches, notably Reims Cathedral. Reims abounds in gastronomic restaurants, but Troyes, the former capital of Champagne, makes the most delightful base. Much of Champagne is flat or gently undulating, and the wild and wooded Ardennes to the north attracts walkers and nature lovers. North of Reims, the Ardennes canal can be explored by barge or pleasure boat from Rethel; to the south, water sports are popular on the lakes to the east of Troyes.

Fishing by a canal in Montier-en-Der near Lac du Der-Chantecoq

Getting Around

The region's main *autoroute* is the A26, which gives access to Reims in under 3 hours from Calais, and also provides easy connection to most of the region all the way down to Troyes and Langres (via the A5). The A4 motorway also links Reims to Paris and Alsace. Paris–Reims by the TGV high-speed train takes 45 minutes. Rail transport within the region is reasonably good, and so are the roads. To explore the wine-growing region, follow the signposted roads marked "Route de Champagne".

Windmill at Verzenay, Parc Naturel de la Montagne de Reims

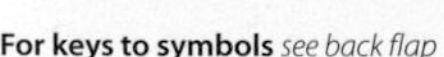

For keys to symbols *see back flap*

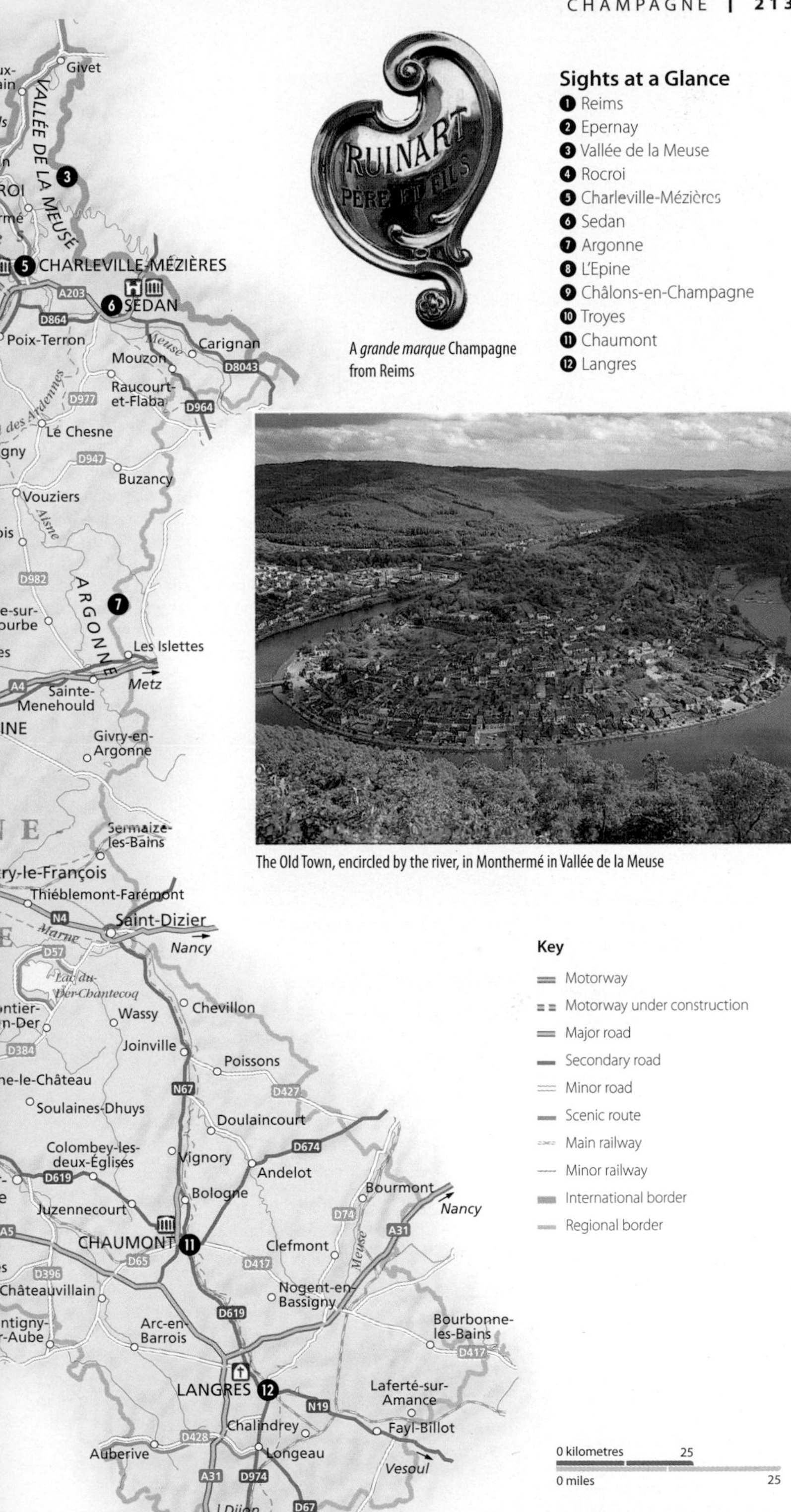

A *grande marque* Champagne from Reims

The Old Town, encircled by the river, in Monthermé in Vallée de la Meuse

Sights at a Glance

1. Reims
2. Epernay
3. Vallée de la Meuse
4. Rocroi
5. Charleville-Mézières
6. Sedan
7. Argonne
8. L'Epine
9. Châlons-en-Champagne
10. Troyes
11. Chaumont
12. Langres

Interior of Basilique St-Remi, Reims

❶ Reims

Marne. 185,000.
6 rue Rockefeller (03 26 77 45 00).
daily. **reims-tourisme.com**

Reims is home to some of the best-known *grandes marques* in Champagne, and several are grouped around the Basilique St-Remi. But the city has another, much earlier, claim to fame: since the 11th century, all the kings of France have come here to be crowned in the city's remarkable Gothic **Cathédrale Notre-Dame** *(see pp216–17)*.

Although World War II bombing destroyed much of Reims's architectural coherence, there are some remarkable monuments here. The **Cryptoportique**, part of the forum, and Porte Mars, a triumphal Augustan arch, recall the Roman past. The **Musée des Beaux-Arts** (open Wed–Thu) houses a fine collection of 15th- and 16th-century canvases depicting biblical scenes, portraits by the Cranachs, *The Death of Marat* by David and landscapes by Corot. Also here are the Barbizons, Impressionists and modern masters.

In 1996 Reims celebrated the 1,500-year anniversary of the baptism of Clovis, first king of the Franks, in its cathedral.

Musée de la Reddition

12 rue F Roosevelt. **Tel** 03 26 47 84 19. **Open** Wed–Mon. **Closed** 1 Jan, 1 May, 14 Jul, 1 & 11 Nov, 24, 25 & 31 Dec. (free 1st Sun of month).

In 1945, the German surrender was signed here, Eisenhower's French HQ during World War II.

Musée Hôtel le Vergeur

36 pl du Forum. **Tel** 03 26 47 20 75. **Open** 2–6pm Tue–Sun.
museelevergeur.com

This early Renaissance town house was bought by traveller and photographer Hugues Krafft in 1910. He dedicated his time and fortune to restoring the mansion after it was badly damaged in World War I. An avid collector, he filled the rooms with Renaissance and Neo-Gothic furniture, 16th–20th-century works of art and photographs and objects from his travels in Asia. Many of the artifacts and works of art illustrate the history of Reims. The highlight of the collection is a set of original prints of *Apocalypse* and the *Large Passion* by Albrecht Dürer (1471–1528).

Basilique St-Remi

Pl St-Rémi. **Open** daily.

This Benedictine abbey church, the oldest church in Reims, began as a Carolingian basilica dedicated to St Remi (440–533). Inside, an Early Gothic choir and radiating chapels can be seen, as well as sculpted Romanesque capitals in the north transept.

Porte Mars, a reminder of Reims in Roman times

Méthode Champenoise

To produce its characteristic bubbles, Champagne has to undergo a process of double fermentation. **First fermentation:** The base wine, made from rather acidic grapes, is fermented at 20–22°C in either stainless-steel tanks or, occasionally, in oak barrels. It is then siphoned off from the sediment and kept at colder temperatures to clear completely, before being drawn off and blended with wines from other areas and years (except in the case of vintage Champagne). The wine is bottled and the *liqueur de tirage* (sugar, wine and yeast) is added. **Second fermentation:** The bottles are stored for a year or more in cool, chalky cellars. The yeast converts the sugar to alcohol and carbon dioxide, which produces the sparkle, and the yeast cells die leaving a deposit. To remove this, the inverted bottles are turned and tapped daily *(remuage)* to shift the deposits into the neck of the bottle. Finally, the deposits are expelled by the process known as *dégorgement*, and a bit of sugar syrup *(liqueur d'expédition)* is added to adjust the sweetness before the final cork is inserted.

Champagne Mumm of Reims

Musée St-Remi

53 rue Simon. **Tel** 03 26 35 36 90. **Open** daily pm only. **Closed** 1 Jan, 1 May, 14 Jul, 1 & 11 Nov, 25 Dec.

Set in the former abbey, the adjoining museum encloses the original Gothic chapterhouse within its cloistered 17th-century shell. On display are archaeological artifacts, 15th-century tapestries depicting the life of St Remi, and a collection of weapons dating from the 16th–19th centuries.

Fort de la Pompelle

8 km (5 miles) southeast of Reims. **Tel** 03 26 49 11 85. **Open** Tue–Sun. **Closed** 1 May, 14 Jul, 1 Nov, mid-Dec–mid-Jan.

Built to protect Reims after the Franco-Prussian War, this fort houses a museum of German Imperial military headgear.

2 Epernay

Marne. 25,000. 7 av de Champagne (03 26 53 33 00). Wed, Thu, Sat & Sun. **ot-epernay.fr**

The main reason for visiting Epernay is to burrow into the chalky *caves* and taste the Champagne. The town lives off the fruits of its profitable Champagne industry. As proof, the avenue de Champagne

Statue of Dom Perignon at Moët

quarter abounds in mock-Renaissance mansions. **Moët & Chandon**, dating back to 1743, is the largest and slickest *maison*, the star of the Moët-Hennessy stable. Its cellars stretch some 28 km (18 miles) underground.

The group also owns other Champagne houses, such as Mercier, Krug, Veuve Clicquot and Ruinart.There is little to choose between a visit to the cellars of Moët & Chandon or **Mercier** – both are in avenue de Champagne. Mercier has the distinction of displaying a giant tun (cask) created for the 1889 Paris Exhibition, and takes you through the *caves* in an electric train.

De Castellane offers a more personalized tour, accompanied by a heady *dégustation*.

Moët & Chandon

20 av de Champagne. **Tel** 03 26 51 20 20. **Open** by appt only. Apr–mid-Nov: daily; mid-Nov–Dec & Feb–Mar: Mon–Fri. only. **moet.com**

Mercier

70 av de Champagne. **Tel** 03 26 51 22 22. **Open** Apr–mid-Nov: daily; mid-Nov–mid-Dec & mid-Feb–Mar: Thu–Mon. obligatory. **champagnemercier.fr**

De Castellane

57 rue de Verdun. **Tel** 03 26 51 19 19. **Open** mid-Mar–Dec: daily. restr. oblig. **castellane.com**

Dégorgement is the final removal of the yeast deposits from the bottle. The neck of the bottle is plunged in freezing brine and the frozen block of sediment is then removed.

Seductive marketing of champagne since the 19th century has ensured its continuing success.

The bubbles in champagne are produced during the second fermentation. Champagnes, especially vintage ones, improve with ageing.

Reims Cathedral

The magnificent Gothic Cathédrale Notre-Dame at Reims is noted for its monumentality. A cathedral has stood on this site since 401, but the present building was begun in 1211. Reims has been the backdrop for coronations from medieval times till 1825, when Charles X was crowned. The coronation of Charles VII here in 1429 was attended by Joan of Arc.

During the Revolution, the rood screen and windows were destroyed, but the stonework survived. World War I damage was fully restored in 1996, to coincide with the 1,500th anniversary of the baptism of Clovis, King of the Franks, at Reims – considered the first coronation of a French king.

The Nave
Compared with the nave at Chartres *(see pp312–15)*, Reims is taller. Its elegant capitals are decorated with naturalistic floral motifs such as ivy and berries.

★ Great Rose Window
Best seen at sunset, the 13th-century window shows the Virgin surrounded by the apostles and angel musicians. It is set within a larger window, a feature common in 13th-century architecture.

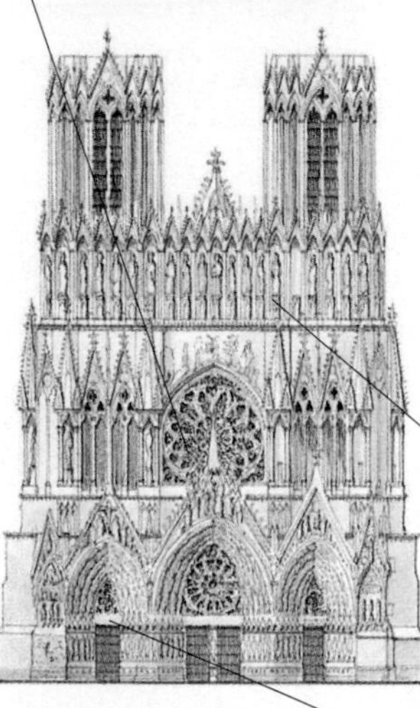

WEST FACADE

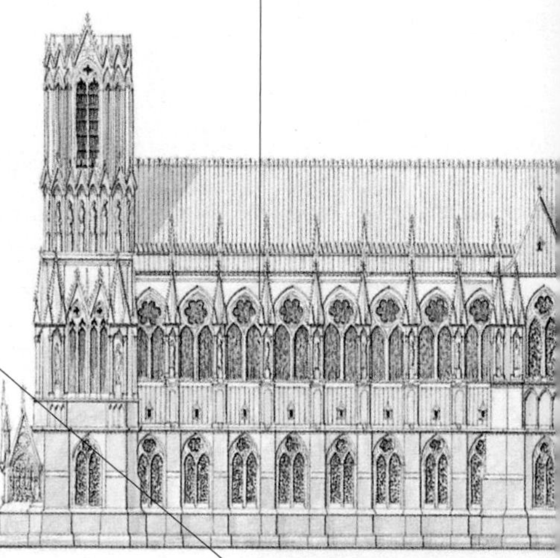

SOUTH FACADE

KEY

① **South transept**

② **The clerestory windows** pioneered Gothic tracery by dividing the lights with slender bars of stone, creating a decorative, intersecting pattern.

③ **The radiating chapels** of the apse are supported by flying buttresses and adorned with octagonal pinnacles.

④ **Pinnacles** on the flying buttresses shelter guardian angels, symbolic protectors of the cathedral.

★ Smiling Angel
Rich in statuary, Reims is often called "the cathedral of angels." Situated above the left (north) portal, this enigmatic angel with unfurled wings is the most celebrated of the many that grace the building.

★ Gallery of the Kings
The harmonious west façade, decorated with over 2,300 statues, is the most notable feature at Reims. Fifty-six stone effigies of French kings form the Gallery of the Kings.

Palais du Tau

The archbishop's palace adjoining the cathedral is named after its T-shaped design, based on early episcopal crosses. (*Tau* is Greek for "T".) The palace, built in 1690 by Mansart and Robert de Cotte, encloses a Gothic Chapel and the 15th-century Salle du Tau, rooms associated with French coronations. On the eve of a coronation, the future king would spend the night in the palace. After being crowned in the cathedral, he held a magnificent banquet in the palace. The Salle du Tau, or banqueting hall, is the finest room in the palace, with a magnificent barrel-vaulted ceiling and walls hung with 15th-century Arras tapestries. The palace now houses a museum of statuary and tapestries from the cathedral, including a 15th-century tapestry of the baptism of Clovis, the first French Christian king.

Salle du Tau – the banqueting hall

VISITORS' CHECKLIST

Practical Information
Cathédrale Notre-Dame, pl du Cardinal Luçon.
Tel 03 26 47 81 79.
Open 7:30am–7:30pm daily. Towers: **Open** mid-Mar–Apr, Sep & Oct: 2, 3 & 4pm Sat & Sun (also 10 & 11am Sat); May–Aug: 10 & 11am, 2, 3, 4 & 5pm Tue–Sun (pm only on Sun).
8am & 7pm Mon, Wed, Fri, 8am Tue, Thu, Sat, 9:30am & 11am Sun. by appt only.
cathedrale-reims.fr
Palais du Tau: **Tel** 03 26 47 81 79.
Open Tue–Sun. **Closed** 1 Jan, 1 May, 1 & 11 Nov, 25 Dec.
palais-du-tau.fr

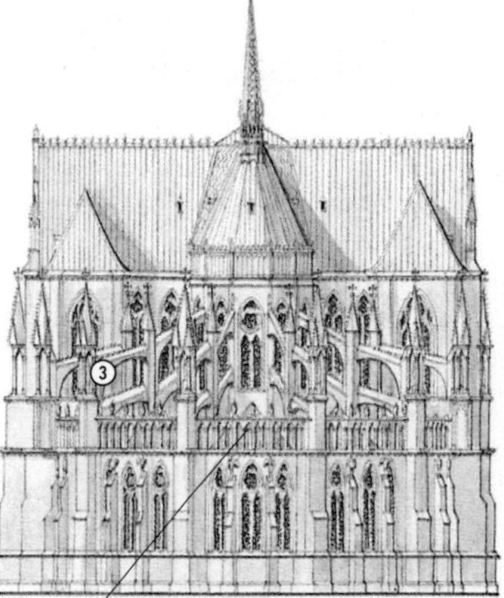

APSE

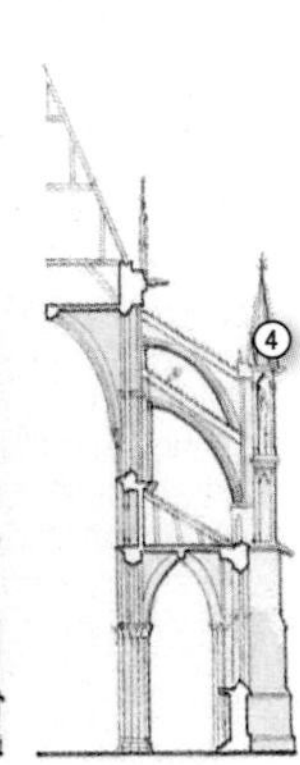

SIDE SECTION

Apse Gallery
The restored *claire-voie* (open work) gallery on the apse is crowned by statues of mythological beasts.

Chagall Window
The windows in the axial chapel were designed by the 20th-century artist Marc Chagall and made by local craftsmen. This one depicts the Crucifixion and the Sacrifice of Isaac.

The *sentier touristique*, a walk along the ramparts of Rocroi

❸ Vallée de la Meuse

Ardennes. 9,000. Monthermé. Rue Jean Baptiste Clément, Monthermé (03 24 54 46 73). **tourisme-meuse.com**

The Meuse meanders through the Ardennes among spectacular scenery of wild gorges, woods and warped rock formations of granite or schist.

Dramatically set on a double meander of the Meuse, **Revin** is a rather unremarkable town in an exceptional site, its Vieille Ville enfolded in the north bend. From the quay, you can see wooded **Mont Malgré Tout** and a route dotted with observation points and steep trails. Just south is **Dames de la Meuse**, a rocky outcrop over the river gorge.

Monthermé lies on two banks, with the Vieille Ville clustered on the charming left bank. The rocky gorges around **Roche à Sept Heures** on the far bank entice climbers and ramblers. The jagged crest of **Rocher des Quatre Fils d'Aymon** suggests the silhouette of four legendary local horsemen.

❹ Rocroi

Ardennes. 2,400. Monthermé. 1ter rue du Pavillon (03 24 54 20 06). Tue & first Mon of month. **otrocroi.com**

Set on the Ardennes plateau, the star-shaped citadel of Rocroi was originally built under Henri II in 1555, and later made impregnable by Vauban in 1675 *(see p226)*. The main attraction is the walk along the ramparts from the southern gateway. The nature reserve at Rièzes is home to orchids and carnivorous plants.

❺ Charleville-Mézières

Ardennes. 58,000. 4 pl Ducale (03 24 55 69 90). Tue, Thu & Sat. **charleville-tourisme.com**

This riverside ford was originally two towns. The medieval citadel of Mézières only merged with the neat Classical town of Charleville in 1966. Mézières has irregular slate-covered houses curving around a bend in the Meuse. Battered fortifications and gateways are visible from avenue de St-Julien. Tucked into the ramparts is the much remodelled Gothic **Notre-Dame de l'Espérance**.

The centrepiece of Charleville is **place Ducale**, a model of Louis XIII urban planning, echoing place des Vosges in Paris *(see p93)*. The poet Arthur Rimbaud was born nearby in 1854. His modest birthplace at No. 12 rue Bérégovoy is still there, along with his childhood home on the Meuse at what is now 7 quai Arthur Rimbaud.

Just along the quayside is the Vieux Moulin, the town house whose view inspired "Le Bateau Ivre", Rimbaud's greatest poem. Inside is the **Musée Rimbaud**, with manuscripts and photographs by the poet.

Musée Rimbaud
Quai A Rimbaud. **Tel** 03 24 32 44 65. **Open** Tue–Sun. **Closed** 1 Jan, 1 May, 25 Dec. (free 1st Sun of month).

❻ Sedan

Ardennes. 20,000. 32 rue du Menil (03 24 27 73 73). Wed & Sat. **tourisme-sedan.fr**

Just to the east of Charleville is the **Château de Sedan**, the largest fortified castle in Europe. There has been a bastion on these slopes since the 11th century, but each Ardennes conflict has spelled a new tier of defences for Sedan.

In 1870, during the Franco-Prussian War, with 700 Prussian cannons turned on Sedan, Napoleon III surrendered and 83,000 French prisoners were deported to Prussia. In May 1940, after capturing Sedan, German forces reached the French coast a week later.

The seven-storey bastion contains sections dating from medieval times to the 1550s.

The poet Rimbaud, whose birthplace was Charleville, painted by Jef Rosman (1873)

Highlights include the ramparts, the 16th-century fortifications and the magnificent 15th-century eaves in one tower. The **Musée du Château** has a fine collection of armour, brought here by Napoleon Bonaparte. There are also tableaux of wax figures illustrating medieval life.

The bastion is surrounded by 17th-century slate-roofed houses, which hug the banks of the Meuse. These reflect the city's earlier prosperity as a Huguenot stronghold.

Musée du Château
1 pl du Château. **Tel** 03 24 29 98 80. **Open** daily.

Environs
Further south is **Fort de Villy-la-Ferté**, one of the few forts on the Maginot Line to have been captured in devastating combat with the enemy in 1940.

Courtyard inside the heavily fortified Château de Sedan

Gargoyle on the Basilique de Notre-Dame de L'Epine

7 Argonne

Ardennes & Meuse. Châlons. Ste-Menehould. 5 pl du Général Leclerc, Ste-Menehould (03 26 60 85 83). **argonne.fr**

East of Reims, the Argonne is a compact region of picturesque valleys and forests, dotted with priories, trenches and war cemeteries.

As a wooded border between the rival bishoprics of Champagne and Lorraine, the Argonne was home to abbeys and priories. Now ruined, the Benedictine abbey of **Beaulieu-en-Argonne** boasts a 13th-century wine press and has forest views. Just north is **Les Islettes**, known for its faïence pottery and tiles. The hilly terrain here was a battleground during the Franco-Prussian War and World War I. The disputed territory of **Butte de Vauquois**, north of Les Islettes, bears a war memorial.

8 L'Epine

Marne. 650. Châlons. 3 quai des Arts, Châlons en Champagne (03 26 65 17 89).

L'Epine is worth visiting if only for a glimpse of the **Basilique de Notre-Dame de l'Epine**, surrounded by wheatfields. Designed on the scale of a cathedral, this 15th-century Flamboyant Gothic church has been a pilgrimage site since medieval times. Even French kings have come here to venerate a "miraculous" statue of the Virgin.

On the façade, three gabled portals are offset by floating tracery, a gauzy effect reminiscent of Reims Cathedral. All around are gruesome gargoyles, symbolizing evil spirits and deadly sins, chased out by the holy presence within. Unfortunately, the most risqué sculptures were destroyed, judged obscene by 19th-century puritans. The subdued Gothic interior contains a 15th-century rood screen and the venerated statue of the Virgin.

Champagne Timber Churches

Skirting Lac du Der-Chantecoq lies a region of woodland and water meadows, containing 12 Romanesque and Renaissance half-timbered churches with curious pointed gables and *caquetoirs*, rickety wooden porches. They have intimate and often beautifully carved interiors with stained-glass windows designed in the vivid colours of the School of Troyes. Rural roads link churches at Bailly-le-Franc, Châtillon-sur-Broué, Lentilles, Vignory, Outines, Chavanges and Montier-en-Der.

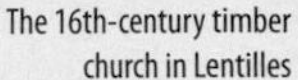

The 16th-century timber church in Lentilles

⑨ Châlons-en-Champagne

Marne. 48,000. 3 quai des Arts (03 26 65 17 89). Wed, Fri am, Sat, Sun am. **chalons-tourisme.com**

Encircled by the River Marne and minor canals, Châlons has a sleepy bourgeois charm thanks to its half-timbered houses and gardens mirrored in canals. Nearby are vineyards producing Blanc de Blancs.

From quai de Notre-Dame there are views of old bridges and the Romanesque towers of **Notre-Dame-en-Vaux**, a masterpiece of Romanesque Gothic. Behind the church is a well-restored medieval quarter and the **Musée du Cloître**, containing the original Romanesque cloisters.

Cathédrale St-Etienne, by the canal, is a cool Gothic affair with a Baroque portal, Romanesque crypt and vivid medieval windows. Beyond is **Le Petit Jard**, riverside gardens overlooking the Château du Marché, and a turreted tollgate built by Henri IV. Excellent river tours of the city are available from the tourist office.

Musée du Cloître de Notre-Dame-en-Vaux

Rue Nicolas Durand. **Tel** 03 26 69 38 53. **Open** Wed–Mon. **Closed** 1 Jan, 1 May, 1 & 11 Nov, 25 Dec.

⑩ Troyes

Aube. 63,000. 16 rue Aristide Briand (08 92 22 46 09). daily. **tourisme-troyes.com**

Troyes is a delight, a city of magnificent Gothic churches and charming 16th-century half-timbered houses, in a historical centre shaped like a champagne cork. The city is famous for its heritage of stained glass and sausages *(andouillettes)*, and its hosiery industry and factory shops.

The battered Flamboyant Gothic west front of the **Cathédrale St-Pierre-et- St-Paul** opens on to a splendid vaulted interior. The nave is bathed in mauvish-red rays from the 16th-century rose window, complemented by the discreet turquoise of the Tree of Jesse window and the intense blue of the medieval windows of the apse.

Statuary in the Cathédrale St-Pierre-et-St-Paul, Troyes

Nearby, **Eglise St-Nizier** glitters in the faded quarter behind the cathedral with its shimmering tiled Burgundian roof. Inside, it is lit by windows in a range of warm mauves and soothing blues.

The Gothic **Basilique St-Urbain** boasts grand flying buttresses and fine 13th-century windows. **Eglise Ste-Madeleine** is noted for its elaborate 16th-century rood screen resembling lacy foliage, grapes and figs. Beyond is a wall of windows in browns, reds and blues. The quaint ruelle des Chats, a covered passageway, connects rue Charbonnet and rue Champeaux.

Set in one of the best-preserved quarters is the **Eglise St-Pantaléon**. Its Gothic and Renaissance interior houses an imposing collection of 16th-century statuary and severe *grisaille* windows. The 17th-century **Hôtel de Vauluisant** contains the Musée d'Art Champenois (Regional Art Museum) and the Musée de la Bonneterie, dedicated to hosiery.

Rue Larivey, a typical street with half-timbered houses, in Troyes

Musée d'Art Moderne

14 pl St-Pierre. **Tel** 03 25 76 26 80. **Open** Tue–Sun. **Closed** public hols.

Beside the cathedral, the former episcopal palace is now a museum of modern art, with a sculpture by Rodin and an especially fine collection of Fauvist paintings, as well as other modern art.

Cité du Vitrail

1 rue Roger-Salengro. **Tel** 03 25 42 52 87. **Open** Tue–Sun. **Closed** 1 Jan, 1 May, 11 Nov, 25 & 26 Dec.

A short walk from the cathedral, this museum in the 18th-century Hôtel-Dieu presents a collection of stained glass from the middle ages to the present day.

Hôtel du Petit Louvre

Rue de la Montée St-Pierre. Courtyard only **Open** daily.

Set off quai Dampierre, this well-restored *hôtel particulier* boasts a fish-scale roof, medieval tower, Renaissance courtyard, staircase and well. The highlight is a façade adorned with quizzical multicoloured faces.

For hotels and restaurants in this region see pp557–8 and pp580–82

Environs
The city's green playground, **Lac et Forêt d'Orient**, is 24 km (15 miles) east of Troyes. The forest is dotted with marshes, nature reserves and smaller lakes. Lac d'Orient, the largest artificial lake in Europe, is popular for sailing, with water-skiing on Lac Amance and fishing at Lac du Temple.

⓫ Chaumont

Haute-Marne. 26,000. 7 av du Général de Gaulle (03 25 03 80 80). Wed & Sat. **tourisme-chaumont-champagne.com**

As the former residence of the Counts of Champagne, this feudal town enjoyed great prestige in the 13th century. On the far side of a ravine, the old town is on a rocky spur, with the Palais de Justice and the medieval castle keep dominating.

The keep is a reminder that this quiet administrative centre had a formidable past. This impression is confirmed by the Renaissance town houses, which are bulging with *tourelles d'escaliers*, turreted staircases.

Basilique St-Jean-Baptiste, a grey-stone Champenois church, is the most remarkable monument in Chaumont. The interior is enlivened by a spider's web of vaulting, a striking turreted staircase and Renaissance galleries. Near the entrance is a tiny chapel containing an unsettling *Mise au Tombeau* (1471), an intense multicoloured stone group of ten mourners gathered around Christ laid out on a shroud in his tomb. In the left transept is a bizarre but beguiling *Tree of Jesse*. On this ill-lit Renaissance stone relief, a family tree sprouts from the sleeping Jesus.

Environs
Twenty-three kilometres (14 miles) northwest of Chaumont, **Colombey-les-Deux-Eglises** will forever be associated with General Charles de Gaulle (1890–1970). The de Gaulles bought their home, **La Boisserie,** in 1933, but had to

Cathédrale St-Mammès in Langres

abandon it during the war, when it was badly damaged. After its restoration, de Gaulle would return to La Boisserie from Paris at weekends to write his memoirs. He died here on 9 November 1970. The house is now a museum.

In the village churchyard, the General lies in a simple tomb, but a giant granite cross of Lorraine, erected in 1972, dominates the skyline. At its foot is the **Mémorial**, a museum dedicated to de Gaulle's life.

La Boisserie
Colombey-les-Deux-Eglises. **Tel** 03 25 01 52 52. **Open** daily (Oct–Mar: Wed–Mon). **Closed** mid-Dec–Jan.

Mémorial Charles de Gaulle
Tel 03 25 30 90 80. **Open** Oct–Apr: Wed–Mon. **Closed** Jan, 24, 25 & 31 Dec. **memorial-charlesdegaulle.fr**

⓬ Langres

Haute-Marne. 9,000. square Olivier Lahalle (03 25 87 67 67). Fri. **tourisme-langres.com**

Set on a rocky spur, Langres lies beyond Chaumont, in the backwaters of southern Champagne. This ancient bishopric was one of the gateways to Burgundy and the birthplace of the encyclopedist Denis Diderot (1713–84). Langres promotes itself as a land of springs, claiming that its proximity to the sources of the Seine and Marne grant it mystical powers.

Virtually the whole town is enclosed by medieval ramparts, Langres's undoubted attraction. A succession of towers and parapets provide glimpses of romantic town gates and sculpted Renaissance mansions, with panoramic views of the Marne Valley, the Langres plateau, the Vosges and, on a clear day, even Mont Blanc.

Near Porte Henri IV is the much-remodelled **Cathédrale St-Mammès**. The gloomy vaulted interior, in Burgundian Romanesque style, is redeemed by the sculpted capitals in the apse, reputedly taken from a temple of Jupiter. The town's Musée d'Art et d'Histoire has some interesting collections.

Langres's lively summer season includes historical re-enactments, theatre and fireworks.

Memorial to General de Gaulle at Colombey-les-Deux-Eglises

ALSACE AND LORRAINE

Meuse · Meurthe-et-Moselle · Moselle · Vosges · Haut-Rhin · Bas-Rhin

As border regions, Alsace and Lorraine have been fought over for centuries by France, Austria and Germany, their beleaguered past recalled by many a military stronghold and cemetery. Today, the region presents only a peaceful aspect with pastel-painted villages, fortified towns and sleepy vineyards.

At the northeast frontier of France, bordered by the Rhine, Alsace forms a fertile watershed between the mountains of the Vosges and the Black Forest in Germany. Lorraine, with its rolling landscape on the other side of the mountains, is the poorer cousin but is more overtly French in character.

Embattled Territory

Caught in the wars between France and Germany, Alsace and part of Lorraine have changed nationality four times since 1871. Centuries of strife have made border citadels of Metz, Toul and Verdun in Lorraine, while Alsace abounds with castles, from the faithfully reconstructed Haut-Koenigsbourg to Saverne's ruined fortress, built to guard a strategic pass in the Vosges. However, the area has a strong identity of its own, taking pride in local costumes, traditions and dialects. In Alsace, Route des Vins vineyards nudge pretty villages in the Vosges foothills. Strasbourg, the capital, is a cosmopolitan city with a 16th-century centre, while Nancy, Lorraine's historical capital, represents elegant 18th-century architecture.

Much of the attraction of this region lies in its cuisine. Lorraine offers beer and quiche lorraine. In Alsace, cosy *winstubs*, or wine cellars, serve sauerkraut and flowery white wines, such as Riesling and Gewurztraminer. There are also fine restaurants here.

Villagers enjoying the view from their window in Hunspach, north of Strasbourg in the northern Vosges

◀ Half-timbered houses lining the canals of Petite Venise, Colmar

Exploring Alsace and Lorraine

Visitors seeking art and architecture will be amply rewarded by the charming medieval towns and excellent city museums of the region. Undiscovered Lorraine is the place to clamber over military citadels, walk in unspoiled countryside and unwind at relaxing spas. By contrast, Alsace offers magnificent forests, rugged mountain drives in the Vosges, quaint villages and rich wines. The Route des Vins *(see pp236–7)* is one of the region's many scenic routes. It is particularly popular during the wine harvest festivities but is worth visiting in any season.

Sights at a Glance

1. Verdun
2. Toul
3. Metz
4. Nancy
5. Gérardmer
6. Mulhouse
7. Guebwiller
8. Neuf-Brisach
9. Eguisheim
10. Colmar
11. Riquewihr
12. Ribeauvillé
13. Château du Haut-Koenigsbourg
14. Sélestat
15. Obernai
16. Strasbourg
17. Saverne
18. Betschdorf

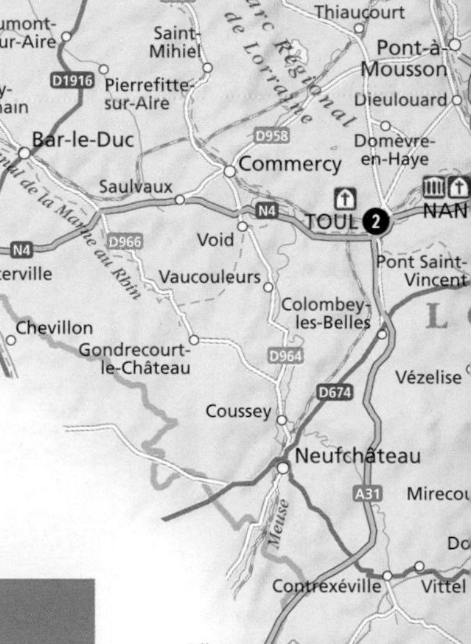

Field of sunflowers just outside the village of Turckheim

For keys to symbols *see back flap*

The picturesque village of Riquewihr on the Route des Vins

Getting Around

There are good roads and rail links between Strasbourg, Colmar, Metz and Nancy, and on to Switzerland and Germany. The main roads to and through the regions are the N4, A31, A35, A4 to Paris and N59, and the tunnel under the Vosges. The spectacular journey over the Vosges and along the Route des Vins is best made by car or on organized trips from Colmar or Strasbourg. The TGV link to the region from Paris takes 2 hours 20 minutes.

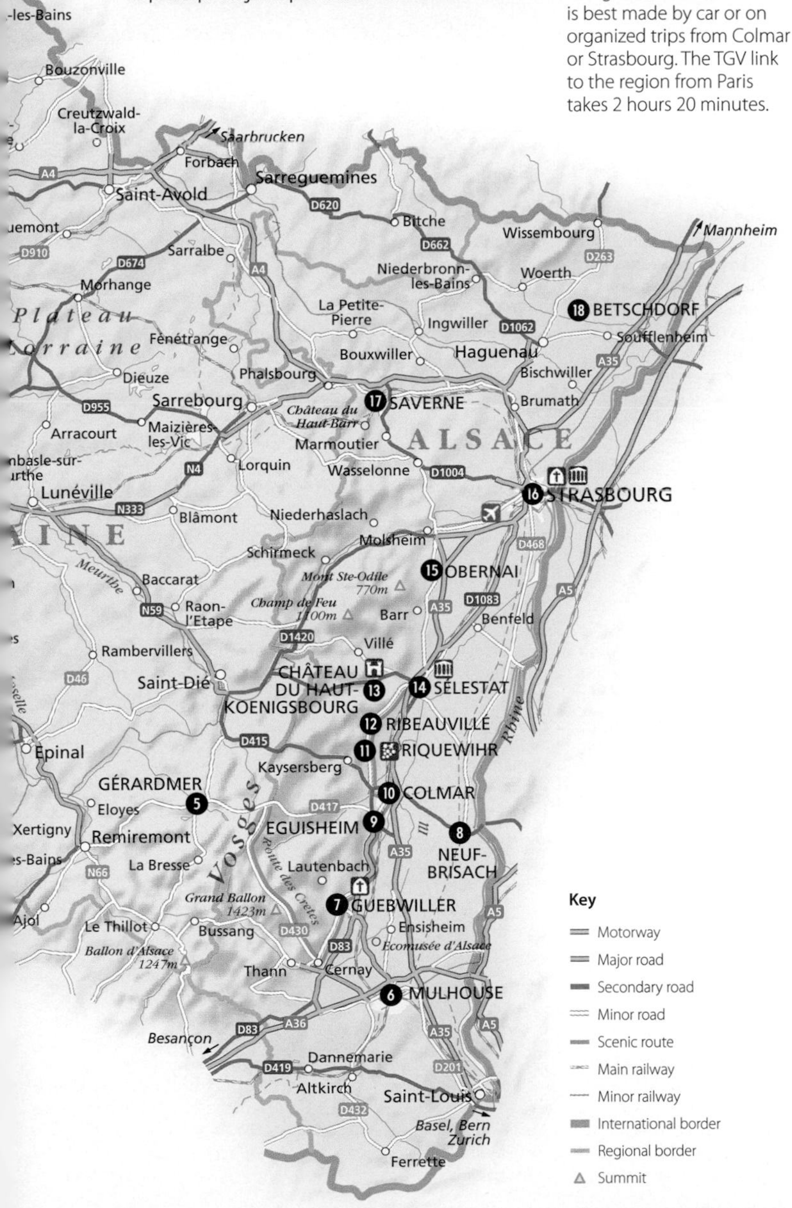

Key

- Motorway
- Major road
- Secondary road
- Minor road
- Scenic route
- Main railway
- Minor railway
- International border
- Regional border
- △ Summit

The Ossuaire de Douaumont, a sentinel for the regiments of crosses on the battlefields of Verdun

❶ Verdun

Meuse. 21,000. pl de la Nation (03 29 86 14 18). Fri.
verdun-tourisme.com

Verdun will be forever remembered for the horrors of the 1916 Battle of Verdun, when about a million men died in almost a whole year of continuous bloodshed that is considered the worst single battle of the Great War. The Germans intended to strike a blow at French morale by destroying the forts of Douaumont and Vaux (which had been built to prevent a repeat of the humiliating French defeat of the Franco-Prussian War of 1870) and capture Verdun, France's northeastern stronghold. The French fought simply to prevent the town being taken. The stalemate and the killing continued here right up to the end of the war, and not until 1918 did the Germans draw back from their positions just 5 km (3 miles) from the town.

Several poignant museums, memorials, battle sites and cemeteries can be visited in the hills just outside Verdun on the north side. In this devastated region, nine villages were obliterated without trace. The **Musée-Memorial de Fleury** tells their story. Nearby, the **Ossuaire de Douaumont** contains the unidentified bones of over 130,000 French and German dead. One of the most striking monuments to the Battle of Verdun is Rodin's memorial in Verdun itself. It depicts the winged figure of Victory unable to soar triumphant because she has become caught in the remains of a dead soldier.

The town of Verdun was heavily fortified over the centuries. The crenellated **Porte Chaussée**, a medieval river gateway, still guards the eastern entrance to the town and is the most impressive of the remaining fortifications.

Although battered by war damage, the **Citadelle de Verdun** retains its 12th-century tower, the only relic from the original abbey that Vauban incorporated into his new military design. Now a war museum, the **Citadelle Souterraine**, it re-creates Verdun's role in World War I. The citadel casemates come to life as grim trenches, and the presentation ends by showing how the "Unknown Soldier" was chosen for the symbolic tomb under the Arc de Triomphe in Paris *(see p111)*.

The town centre is dominated by the cathedral, where Romanesque elements were rediscovered after the 1916 bombardments.

The 16th-century cloisters of Eglise St-Gengoult in Toul

Citadelle Souterraine
Ave du Soldat Inconnu. **Tel** 03 29 84 84 42. **Open** daily. **Closed** 24 Dec–late Jan.

❷ Toul

Meurthe-et-Moselle. 17,000. 1 pl Charles de Gaulle (03 83 64 90 60). Wed, Fri & Sat.
lepredenancy.fr

Lying within dark forests west of Nancy, the octagonal fortress city of Toul is encircled by the Moselle and the Canal de la Marne. Along with Verdun and Metz, Toul was one of the 4th-century bishoprics. In the early 18th century, Vauban built the citadel, from which the ring of defensive waterways, the octagonal city ramparts and the **Porte de Metz** remain.

The **Cathédrale St-Etienne**, begun in the 13th century, took over 300 years to build. It suffered damage in World War II but the purity of the Champenois style has survived, notably in the arched, high-galleried interior. The imposing Flamboyant Gothic façade is flanked by octagonal towers. Rue du Général-Gengoult, behind the Gothic **Eglise St-Gengoult**, contains a clutch of sculpted Renaissance houses. North of the city the local "grey" Côtes de Toul wines are produced.

Environs

South of Toul, near the town of Neufchâteau, is the birthplace of Joan of Arc at Domrémy-La-Pucelle. Next door to the house where she was born is an exhibition about her remarkable life.

The vast **Parc Régional de Lorraine** takes in red-tiled cottages, vineyards, forests, cropland, *chaumes* (high pasture-land), marshes and lakes. Inns in the area are especially noted for their quiche lorraine and *potée lorraine*, a bacon casserole.

Jupiter Slaying a Monster on the Column of Merten in La Cour d'Or

❸ Metz

Moselle. 125,000. pl d'Armes (03 87 39 00 00). Tue, Thu & Sat. **tourisme.metz.fr**

An austere yet appealing city, Metz sits at the confluence of the Moselle and the Seille. Twenty bridges crisscross the rivers and canals, and there are pleasant walks along the banks. This Gallo-Roman city, now the capital of Lorraine, has always been a pawn in the game of border chess – annexed by Germany in 1871, regained by France in 1918.

Set on a hill above the Moselle, the **Cathédrale St-Etienne** overlooks the historic centre. Inside, there are stained-glass windows, including some by Marc Chagall.

To the northwest of the cathedral, a narrow wooden bridge leads across to the island of Petit Saulcy, site of the oldest French theatre still in use. Located on the other side of the cathedral, the **Porte des Allemands**, spanning a river, resembles a medieval castle because of its bridge, defensive towers and 13th-century gate with pepper-pot towers.

In the Vieille Ville, the delightful place St-Louis is bordered by arcaded 14th-century mansions. **Eglise St-Pierre-aux-Nonnains** claims to be one of France's oldest churches. The external walls and façade date from Roman times, while much of the rest belongs to the 7th century. Nearby is the 13th-century **Chapelle des Templiers**, built by the Knights Templar; it can be visited by guided tour.

Centre Pompidou Metz

1 parvis des Droits de l'Homme. **Tel** 03 87 15 39 39. **Open** Wed–Mon. **Closed** 1 May.

This museum is an annexe to the Centre Pompidou in Paris *(see pp96–7)*. Modern European art is displayed inside an unusual hexagonal building.

Musée de la Cour d'Or

2 rue du Haut-Poirier. **Tel** 03 87 20 13 20. **Open** Wed–Mon. **Closed** pub hols.

Also known as the Musée d'Art et d'Histoire, this is set in the Petits-Carmes, a deconsecrated 17th-century monastery incorporating Gallo-Roman baths and a medieval barn. On display are Merovingian stone carvings; Gothic painted ceilings and a variety of German, Flemish and French paintings.

White Storks

The white stork, traditionally a symbol of good fortune in Alsace, used to be a frequent sight in northeast France. White storks spend the winter in Africa but migrate north to breed. However, the gradual draining of marshy ground, pesticides and electric cables have threatened their survival here. A programme to reintroduce them to the area has set up breeding centres, as at Molsheim and Turckheim, which means that these striking birds can once again be seen in Alsace-Lorraine.

The 13th-century Chapelle des Templiers, with restored frescoes, in Metz

Place Stanislas in Nancy, with statue of Stanislas Leczinski, Duke of Lorraine and father-in-law of Louis XV

❹ Nancy

Meurthe-et-Moselle. 105,000. 14 pl Stanislas (03 83 35 22 41). Tue–Sat. **nancy-tourisme.fr**

Lorraine's historic capital backs on to the Canal du Marne and the River Meurthe. In the 18th century, Stanislas Leczinski, Duke of Lorraine *(see p306)*, transformed the city, making it a model of 18th-century town planning.

Nancy's second golden age was the turn of the 20th century, when glassmaker Emile Gallé founded the Ecole de Nancy, a forerunner of the Art Nouveau Movement in France.

Nancy's principal and most renowned landmark is **place Stanislas**. Laid out in the 1750s, this elegantly proportioned square is enclosed by highly ornate gilded wrought-iron gates and railings, which have been beautifully restored. Lining the square are fine *hôtels particuliers* (town houses) and chic restaurants.

An Arc de Triomphe leads to Place de la Carrière, a gracious, tree-lined square. At the far end, flanked by semicircular arcades, is the Gothic **Palais du Gouvernement**. Next door in the Parc de la Pépinière is Rodin's statue of Claude Lorrain, the landscape painter, born near Nancy.

Grande Rue provides a glimpse of medieval Nancy. Of the original fortifications the only remaining one is the Porte de la Craffe, which was used as a prison after the Revolution.

Eglise et Couvent des Cordeliers et Musée Régional des Arts et Traditions Populaires

64 & 66 Grande Rue. **Tel** 03 83 32 18 74. **Open** Tue–Sun. **Closed** 1 Jan, Easter Sun, 1 May, 14 Jul, 1 Nov, 25 Dec.

The dukes of Lorraine are buried in the crypt, and the adjoining converted monastery contains the Musée Régional des Arts et Traditions Populaires, covering folklore, furniture, costumes and crafts.

Musée des Beaux-Arts

3 pl Stanislas. **Tel** 03 83 85 30 72. **Open** Wed–Mon. **Closed** some public hols.

A renovation and modern extension have enabled 40 per cent more of the museum's remarkable collection of 14th- to 20th-century European art to be seen, including works by Delacroix, Manet, Monet, Utrillo and Modigliani. The Daum glassware is stunning.

Musée Historique Lorraine

Palais Ducal, 64 Grande Rue. **Tel** 03 83 32 18 74. **Closed** for renovation until 2020.

The Museum of the History of Lorraine has a rich collection of archaeological finds, sculptures and paintings, including two by Georges de la Tour.

Musée de l'Ecole de Nancy

36–38 rue de Sergent Blandan. **Tel** 03 83 40 14 86. **Open** Wed–Sun. **Closed** 1 Jan, 1 May, 14 July, 1 Nov, 25 Dec.

Exhibits in reconstructed Art Nouveau settings include furniture, fabrics and jewellery, as well as the fanciful glassware of Emile Gallé, founder of the Ecole de Nancy.

Arc de Triomphe in place Stanislas, leading to place de la Carrière

Vosges landscape seen from the Route des Crêtes

The Route des Crêtes

This strategic mountain road, 83 km (52 miles) long, connects the Vosges valleys from Col du Bonhomme to Cernay, east of Thann, often through woodland. Hugging the western side of the Vosges, the Route des Crêtes was created during World War I to prevent the Germans from observing French troop movements. When not shrouded in mist, there are breathtaking views over Lorraine from its many "ridges" *(crêtes)*.

5 Gérardmer

Vosges. 10,000. 4 pl des Déportés (03 29 27 27 27). Thu & Sat. **gerardmer.net**

Nestling on the Lorraine side of the Vosges, on the shore of a magnificent lake stretching out before it, Gérardmer is a setting rather than a city. In November 1944, just before its liberation, Gérardmer was razed by the Nazi scorched-earth policy, but has since been reconstructed. Sawmills and woodcarving remain local trades, though tourism is fast replacing the textile industry.

Gérardmer is now a popular holiday resort. In winter, the steep slopes of the Vosges Cristallines around the town turn it into a ski resort, while the lake is used for water sports in summer. The town's attractions also include lake-side walks and boat trips, as well as Géromée cheese, similar to the more famous Munster, from just over the Alsatian border. Gérardmer also boasts the oldest tourist information office in the country, dating from 1875.

The scenic drives and mountain hikes in the Vosges attract adventurous visitors. Most leave the lakeside bowl to head for the Alsatian border and the magnificent **Route des Crêtes**, which can be joined at the mountain pass of Col de la Schlucht.

Re-creating village crafts in the Ecomusée d'Alsace in Ungersheim

6 Mulhouse

Haut-Rhin. 115,000. 1 av Robert Schuman (03 89 35 48 48). Tue, Thu & Sat. **tourisme-mulhouse.com**

Close to the Swiss border, Mulhouse is an industrial city, which was badly damaged in World War II. However, there are technical museums and shopping galleries, as well as Alsatian taverns and Swiss wine bars. Most visitors use the city as a base for exploring the rolling hills of the Sundgau on the Swiss border.

Of the museums, **Musée de l'Impression sur Etoffes**, at 14 rue Jean-Jacques Henner, is devoted to textiles and fabric painting, while the **Musée Français du Chemin de Fer**, at 2 rue Alfred Glehn, has a collection of steam and electric locomotives. A revamped **Cité de l'Automobile**, at 15 rue de l'Epée, boasts over 100 Bugattis, a clutch of Mercedes and Ferraris, and Charlie Chaplin's Rolls-Royce. In the Renaissance former town hall, on place de la République, is the **Musée Historique**.

Alsatian black pig in the Ecomusée d'Alsace in Ungersheim

The lake at Gérardmer, offering sporting and leisure activities

Environs

At Ungersheim, north of Mulhouse, the **Ecomusée d'Alsace** displays and preserves the region's rural heritage. The 12th-century fortified house from Mulhouse is a dramatic building, complete with Gothic garden. Farms are run along traditional lines, with livestock such as the Alsatian black pig. Rural crafts can be seen in their original settings.

Ecomusée d'Alsace
Chemin du Grosswald. **Tel** 03 89 74 44 74. **Open** Tue–Sun (Jun–Aug: daily). **Closed** Jan–Mar, Nov. **ecomusee.alsace**

7 Guebwiller

Haut-Rhin. 12,000. 71 rue de la République (03 89 76 10 63). Tue & Fri. **tourisme-guebwiller.fr**

Surrounded by vineyards and flower-filled valleys, Guebwiller is known as "the gateway to the valley of flowers". However, as an industrial town producing textiles and machine tools, it feels cut off from this rural setting. The *caves* and churches make it worth a visit.

Set on a pretty square, **Eglise Notre-Dame** combines Baroque theatricality with Neo-Classical elegance, while **Eglise des Dominicains** boasts Gothic frescoes and a fine rood screen. **Eglise St-Léger**, the richly decorated Romanesque church, is the most rewarding, especially the façade, triple porch and portal.

Eglise St-Léger in Guebwiller

Environs

The scenic Lauch valley, north-west of Guebwiller, is known as "Le Florival" because of its floral aspect. **Lautenbach** is used as a starting point for hikes through this recognized *zone de tranquillité*. The village has a pink Romanesque church, with a portal depicting human passion and the battle between Good and Evil. The square leads to the river, a small weir, *lavoir* (public washing place) and houses overhanging the water.

8 Neuf-Brisach

Haut-Rhin. 2,100. Palais du Gouverneur, 6 pl d'Armes (03 89 72 56 66). Sat. **tourisme-paysrhinbrisach.com**

Situated near the German border, this octagonal citadel is the military strategist Vauban's masterpiece. Built between 1698 and 1707, the citadel forms a typical star-shaped pattern, with symmetrical towers enclosing 48 equal squares. In the centre, from where straight streets radiate for ease of defence, is

The Citadel of Neuf-Brisach

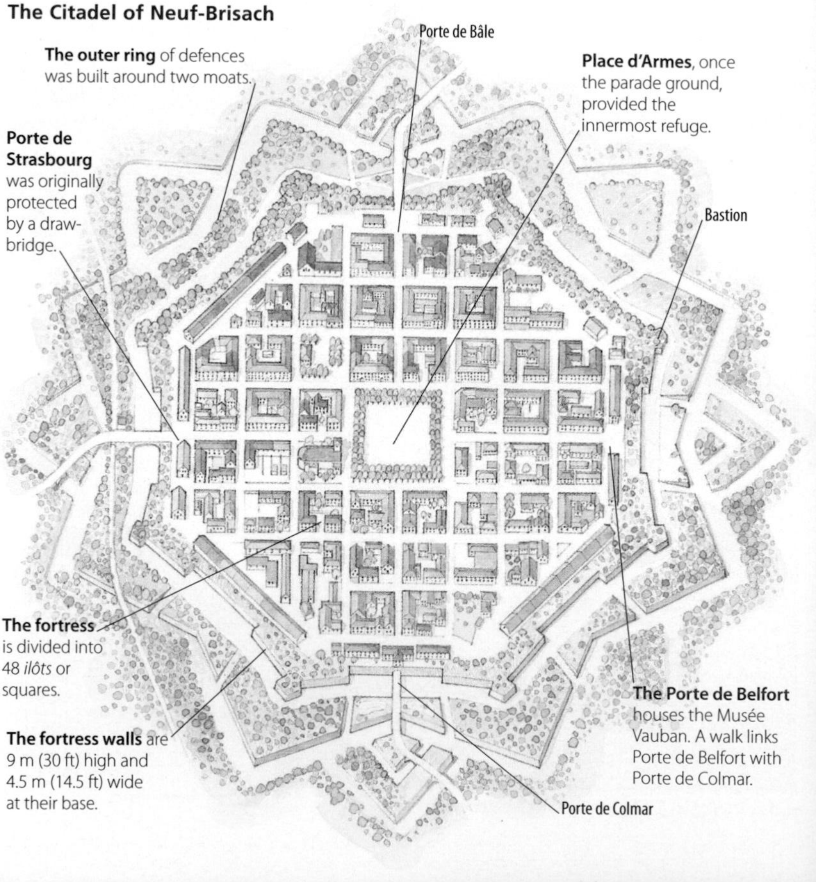

The outer ring of defences was built around two moats.

Porte de Bâle

Place d'Armes, once the parade ground, provided the innermost refuge.

Porte de Strasbourg was originally protected by a draw-bridge.

Bastion

The fortress is divided into 48 *îlôts* or squares.

The fortress walls are 9 m (30 ft) high and 4.5 m (14.5 ft) wide at their base.

The Porte de Belfort houses the Musée Vauban. A walk links Porte de Belfort with Porte de Colmar.

Porte de Colmar

The celebrated Issenheim altarpiece by Matthias Grünewald in Colmar

place d'Armes and the Eglise St-Louis, which was added in 1731–6. This was the usual homage to Louis XV, implying that the church was dedicated to the king, rather than the saint.

The Porte de Belfort houses the **Musée Vauban**, which includes a model of the town, showing the outlying defences, now concealed by woodland. They represent Vauban's barrier to the fortress and it is to his credit that the citadel was never taken.

Musée Vauban
Pl Porte de Belfort. **Tel** 03 89 72 03 93.
Open May–Sep: Wed–Mon; Oct–Apr: groups only, by appt.

❾ Eguisheim

Haut-Rhin. 1,600. 22a Grand'Rue (03 89 23 40 33).
ot-eguisheim.fr

Eguisheim is an exquisite small town, laid out within three concentric rings of 13th-century ramparts. The ensemble of austere fortifications and elegance within makes for a surprisingly harmonious whole.

In the centre of town is the octagonal feudal **castle** of the Counts of Eguisheim. A Renaissance fountain in front has the statue of Bruno Eguisheim, born here in 1002. He became Pope Léon IX and was later canonized.

The Grand'Rue is lined with half-timbered houses. Close to the castle is the **Marbacherhof**, a monastic tithe barn and corn hall. On a neighbouring square, the modern parish church retains the original Romanesque sculpted tympanum.

The rest of the town has its share of Hansel-and-Gretel atmosphere, while inviting courtyards offer tastings of *grands crus*. From rue de Hautvilliers, outside the ramparts, a marked path leads through scenic vineyards.

❿ Colmar

Haut-Rhin. 68,000.
Rue Unterlinden (03 89 20 68 92).
Mon, Wed, Thu & Sat.
tourisme-colmar.com

Colmar is the best-preserved city in Alsace. As a trading post and river port, it had its heyday in the 16th century, when wine merchants shipped their wine along the waterways running through the picturesque canal quarter, now known as **Petite Venise**. "Little Venice" is best seen on a leisurely boat trip that takes you from the tanners' quarter to rue des Tanneurs. The adjoining place de l'Alsacienne Douane is dominated by the **Koifhüs**, a galleried customs house with a Burgundian tiled roof, overlooking half-timbered pastel houses sporting sculpted pillars.

Nearby, place de la Cathédrale quarter is full of 16th-century houses. **Eglise St-Martin**, essentially Gothic, has a noted south portal. To the west, the place des Dominicains, busy with cafés, is dwarfed by the Gothic **Eglise Dominicaine**. Inside is *La Vierge au Buisson de Roses* (1473), the red-and-gold "Virgin of the Rosebush" by Martin Schongauer, a renowned painter and native son of Colmar.

The adjoining square, Place d'Unterlinden, has the **Musée d'Unterlinden**. Set in a Dominican monastery, it displays early Rhenish paintings. The highlight is the Issenheim altarpiece. A masterpiece of emotional intensity, it is part of an early 16th-century Alsatian panel painting by Matthias Grünewald. A three-storey wing houses modern and contemporary art.

In the historic centre, the quaint rue des Têtes has the former wine exchange, a Renaissance town house known as the Maison des Têtes because of the grimacing heads on the gabled façade. And in rue Mercière, **Maison Pfister**, with its slender stair turret and galleried flower-decked façade, has come to typify the city.

The **Musée Bartholdi**, on rue des Marchands, is devoted to Colmar-born Frédéric-Auguste Bartholdi, designer of the Statue of Liberty.

Along quai de la Poissonnerie in the Petite Venise area of Colmar

For hotels and restaurants in this region see p558 and pp582–3

⓫ Riquewihr

Haut-Rhin. 1,300. 2 rue de la 1ère Armée (03 89 73 23 23). Fri. **ribeauville-riquewihr.com**

Vineyards run right up to the ramparts of Riquewihr, the prettiest village on the Route des Vins *(see pp236–7)*. Deeply pragmatic, Riquewihr winemakers plant roses at the end of each row of vines – both for their pretty effect and as early detectors of parasites. The village belonged to the counts of Wurttemberg until the Revolution and has grown rich on wine, from Tokay and Pinot Gris to Gewurztraminer and Riesling. Virtually an open-air museum, Riquewihr abounds in cobbled alleys, geranium-clad balconies, galleried courtyards, romantic double ramparts and watchtowers.

From the Hôtel de Ville, **rue du Général de Gaulle** climbs gently past medieval and Renaissance houses, half-timbered, stone-clad, or corbelled. Oriel windows vie with sculpted portals and medieval sign boards. On the right lies the idyllic **place des Trois Eglises**. A passageway leads through the ramparts to the vineyards on the hill. Further up lies the **Dolder**, a 13th-century belfry, followed by the **Tour des Voleurs** (both are museums, the latter with a medieval torture chamber), marking the second tier of ramparts. Beyond the gateway is the **Cour des Bergers**, gardens laid out around the 16th-century ramparts. Visitors outnumber the locals in summer or during the superb Christmas market.

The pretty – and popular – village of Riquewihr, set among vineyards

⓬ Ribeauvillé

Haut-Rhin. 5,000. 1 Grand'Rue (03 89 73 23 23). Fri & Sat. **ribeauville-riquewihr.com**

Overlooked by three ruined castles, Ribeauvillé is stiflingly prettified, as may be expected from a favoured town on the Route des Vins. This status is partly due to healthy sales of the celebrated *grands crus* of Alsace, especially Riesling. There are ample opportunities for tastings, particularly near the park, in the lower part of town *(see p236)*.

On Grand'Rue (No. 14) is the **Pfifferhüs**, the minstrels' house. As locals declare, Ribeauvillé is the capital of the *kougelhopf*, the almond-flavoured Alsatian cake.

Tortuous alleys wind past steep-roofed artisans' and *vignerons'* houses in the upper part of the town. Beyond are Renaissance fountains, painted façades and **St-Grégoire-le-Grand**, the Gothic parish church. A marked path, which begins in this part of town, leads into the vineyards.

⓭ Château du Haut-Koenigsbourg

Orschwiller, Bas-Rhin. **Tel** 03 69 33 25 00. **Open** daily. **Closed** 1 Jan, 1 May, 25 Dec. **haut-koenigsbourg.fr**

Looming above the pretty village of St-Hippolyte, this castle is the most popular attraction in Alsace. In 1114, the Swabian Emperor, Frederick of Hohenstaufen, built the first Teutonic castle here, which was destroyed in 1462. Rebuilt and added to under the Habsburgs, it burned down in 1633. At the end of the 19th century, Kaiser Wilhelm II commissioned Berlin architect Bodo Ebhardt to restore the castle. The result of his painstaking work was a precise reconstruction of the original building.

With a drawbridge, fierce keep and rings of fortifications, this warm sandstone hybrid is a sophisticated feudal château. The Cour d'Honneur is a breathtaking re-creation, with a pointed corner turret and creaky arcaded galleries. Inside are gloomy "Gothic" chambers and "Renaissance" rooms. La Grande Salle is the most far-fetched, with a Neo-Gothic gallery and ornate panelling. From the battlements, almost 760 m (2,500 ft) above the Alsace plain, stretches a Rhineland panorama, bordered by the Black Forest and the Alps. On the other side are views from the high Vosges to villages and vineyards below.

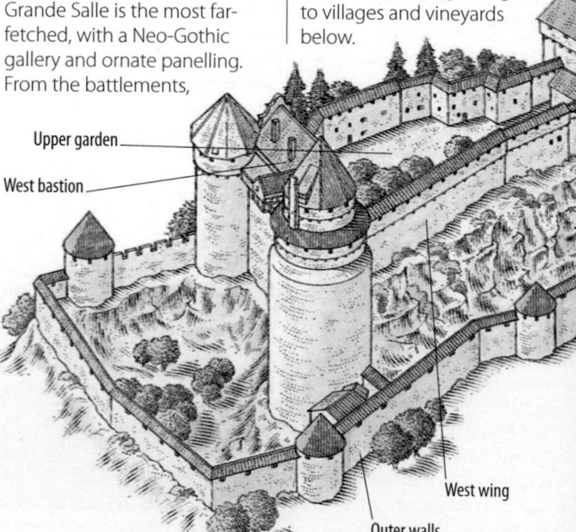

Chapelle St-Sébastien outside Dambach-la-Ville, along the Route des Vins

⓮ Sélestat

Bas-Rhin. 17,000. Commanderie Saint Jean, bd du Général Leclerc (03 88 58 87 20). Tue, Sat.
selestat-haut-koenigsbourg.com

During the Renaissance, Sélestat was the intellectual centre of Alsace, with a tradition of humanism fostered by Beatus Rhenanus, a friend of Erasmus. The **Bibliothèque Humaniste** has a collection of editions of some of the earliest printed books, including the first book to name America, in 1507. Nearby are the Cour des Prélats, a turreted ivy-covered mansion, and the Tour de l'Horloge, a clocktower. **Eglise Ste-Foy** is 12th century, with an octagonal bell tower. Opposite is **Eglise St-Georges**, glittering with green and red "Burgundian tiles".

Bibliothèque Humaniste
1 rue de la Bibliothèque.
Tel 03 88 58 07 20.
Closed until mid-2018 due to major reconstruction.
bibliotheque-humaniste.eu

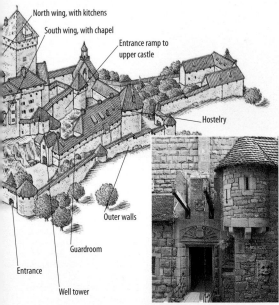

North wing, with kitchens
South wing, with chapel
Entrance ramp to upper castle
Hostelry
Outer walls
Guardroom
Entrance
Well tower

Drawbridge within the walls of Château du Haut-Koenigsbourg

Environs

Medieval **Dambach-la-Ville**, another pretty town, is linked to Andlau and red-tiled Itterswiller by a delightful rural road through vineyards.

Ebersmunster, a picturesque hamlet, has an onion-domed abbey church, with a Baroque interior that is a sumptuous display of gilded stucco.

⓯ Obernai

Bas-Rhin. 11,000. pl du Beffroi (03 88 95 64 13). Thu.
tourisme-obernai.fr

Young *Alsaciens* in traditional costume

At the north end of the Route des Vins, Obernai retains a flavour of authentic Alsace: residents speak Alsatian, at festivities women wear traditional costume, and church services are well attended in the cavernous Neo-Gothic **Eglise St-Pierre-et-St-Paul**.

Place du Marché is well preserved, and features the gabled **Halle aux Blés**, a 16th-century corn hall (now a restaurant) above a former butcher's shop, with a façade adorned with cows' and dragons' heads. Place de la Chapelle, the adjoining square, has a Renaissance fountain and the 16th-century **Hôtel de Ville** and the **Kapellturm**, the galleried Gothic belfry. Side streets have Renaissance and medieval timber-framed houses. A stroll past the cafés on rue du Marché ends in a pleasant park by the ramparts.

Environs

Odile, Alsace's 7th-century patron saint, was born in Obernai, but she is venerated on **Mont Sainte-Odile**, to the west.

Molsheim, a former bishopric and fortified market town 10 km (6 miles) north, is noted for its Metzig, a Renaissance-style butchers' guildhall.

Le Mémorial de l'Alsace-Moselle at Schirmeck commemorates the 10,000 who died at the Struthof concentration camp across the valley.

⑯ Strasbourg

Halfway between Paris and Prague, Strasbourg is not surprisingly often known as "the crossroads of Europe". The city wears its European cosmopolitanism with ease – after all, its famous cathedral has catered to both Catholic and Protestant congregations – and as one of the capitals of the European Union has sensibly located the futuristic European Parliament building some way from the historic centre. One of the ways to see this, along with the more traditional city sights, is to take a boat trip along the waterways encircling the Old Town. On the way you will take in the Ponts-Couverts, covered bridges linked by medieval watchtowers that provide an observation point for the four Ill canals, and the scenic Petite France, once the tanners' district, dotted with mills and crisscrossed by bridges.

Pont-Couvert, linked by medieval watchtowers

The central portal of the west façade of the cathedral

Cathédrale Notre-Dame

A masterpiece of stone lacework, the sandstone cathedral "rises like a most sublime, wide-arching tree of God", as Goethe marvelled. Though construction began in the late 11th century (the choir is Romanesque, the nave is Gothic), it ended only in 1439, with the completion of the west façade, begun in 1277. The three portals are ornamented with statues. But the crowning glory is the rose window. The south portal leads to the Gothic Pillar of Angels (c.1230), set beside the Astronomical Clock: mechanical figures appear accompanied by chimes at 12:31pm. There are wonderful views over the city from the viewing platform, and on some summer evenings there are organ concerts.

In place de la Cathédrale, **Maison Kammerzell**, now a popular restaurant, was once a rich merchant's mansion, its highly elaborate, carved façade, dating from the mid-15th to late-16th centuries.

Palais Rohan

2 pl du Château. **Tel** 03 68 98 51 60. **Open** Wed–Mon. **Closed** 1 Jan, Good Fri, 1 May, 1 & 11 Nov, 25 Dec. **musees.strasbourg.eu**

Designed by the king's architect, Robert de Cotte, in 1730, this grand Classical palace was intended for the prince-bishops of Strasbourg. It houses three museums: the Musée des Beaux-Arts; the Musée Archéologique; and the Musée des Arts Décoratifs, which contains the sumptuous State Apartments and one of the finest collections of ceramics in France.

For hotels and restaurants in this region see p558 and pp582–3

The Musée d'Art Moderne et Contemporain on Strasbourg's waterfront

Strasbourg City Centre

① Cathédrale Notre-Dame
② Maison Kammerzell
③ Palais Rohan
④ Musée Historique
⑤ Musée Alsacien
⑥ Musée de l'Oeuvre Notre-Dame
⑦ Musée d'Art Moderne et Contemporain

0 metres 250
0 yards 250

Musée Historique

2 rue du Vieux-Marché-aux-Poissons. **Tel** 03 68 98 51 60. **Open** Tue–Sun. **Closed** 1 Jan, Good Fri, 1 May, 1 & 11 Nov, 25 Dec.

The museum occupies the 16th-century city abattoir and focuses on Strasbourg's political and military history.

Musée Alsacien

23 quai St-Nicolas. **Tel** 03 68 98 51 52. **Open** Wed–Mon. **Closed** 1 Jan, Good Fri, 1 May, 1 Nov, 25 Dec.

Housed in a series of interconnecting Renaissance buildings, the museum has fascinating exhibits on local traditions and popular arts and crafts.

VISITORS' CHECKLIST

Practical Information

Bas-Rhin. 500,000.
17 pl de la Cathédrale (03 88 52 28 28). Wed, Fri & Sat.
Festival Musica (Sep & Oct).
otstrasbourg.fr

Transport

12 km (7.5 miles) SW Strasbourg. pl de la Gare (08 92 35 35 35). pl des Halles (03 88 23 43 23).

Musée de l'Oeuvre Notre-Dame

3 pl du Château. **Tel** 03 68 98 51 60. **Open** Tue–Sun. **Closed** 1 Jan, Good Fri, 1 May, 1 Nov, 25 Dec. ground fl.

The cathedral's impressive museum contains much of its original sculpture, as well as magnificent 11th-century stained glass. This sombre gabled house also displays a collection of Medieval and Renaissance Alsatian art.

Musée d'Art Moderne et Contemporain

1 pl Hans-Jean Arp. **Tel** 03 68 98 51 55. **Open** Tue–Sun. **Closed** 1 Jan, Good Fri, 1 May, 1 & 11 Nov, 25 Dec.

Adrien Fainsilber's cultural flagship for the 21st century is a marvel of glass and light (particularly at night, when it appears to float on the river). Its superb collections run from 1860 to 1950 (modern) and from 1950 onwards (contemporary). The Art Café is welcome respite for art-weary feet.

MM Park Museum

4 rue Gutenberg, La Wantzenau 67610. **Tel** 03 88 59 25 43. **Open** daily. **Closed** 25 Dec & 1 Jan.

The largest private collection of World War II artifacts in Europe is housed in this museum 12 km (7.5 miles) north of Strasbourg. The collection includes around 120 vehicles, about 400 male and female uniforms and numerous weapons. A highlight are the objects and documents from the 1944 Sussex Plan to spy on Nazi troops before and after the D-Day landings.

For keys to symbols *see back flap*

The Alsace Route des Vins

Meandering over 180 km (110 miles) from Marlenheim to Thann, the picturesque wine route takes in historic towns with cobbled streets, medieval timber-framed houses and Renaissance fountains. Romantically appointed *winstubs,* or cellars, offer traditional *choucroute garnie* and flowery white Alsatian wines. Dedicated wine lovers could spend two or three days covering the route at leisure, or may want to make shorter trips in either direction to or from Colmar. For a refreshing contrast from the unremitting charm of the towns and villages, escape occasionally into *sentiers viticoles* – lovely paths through the vineyards themselves.

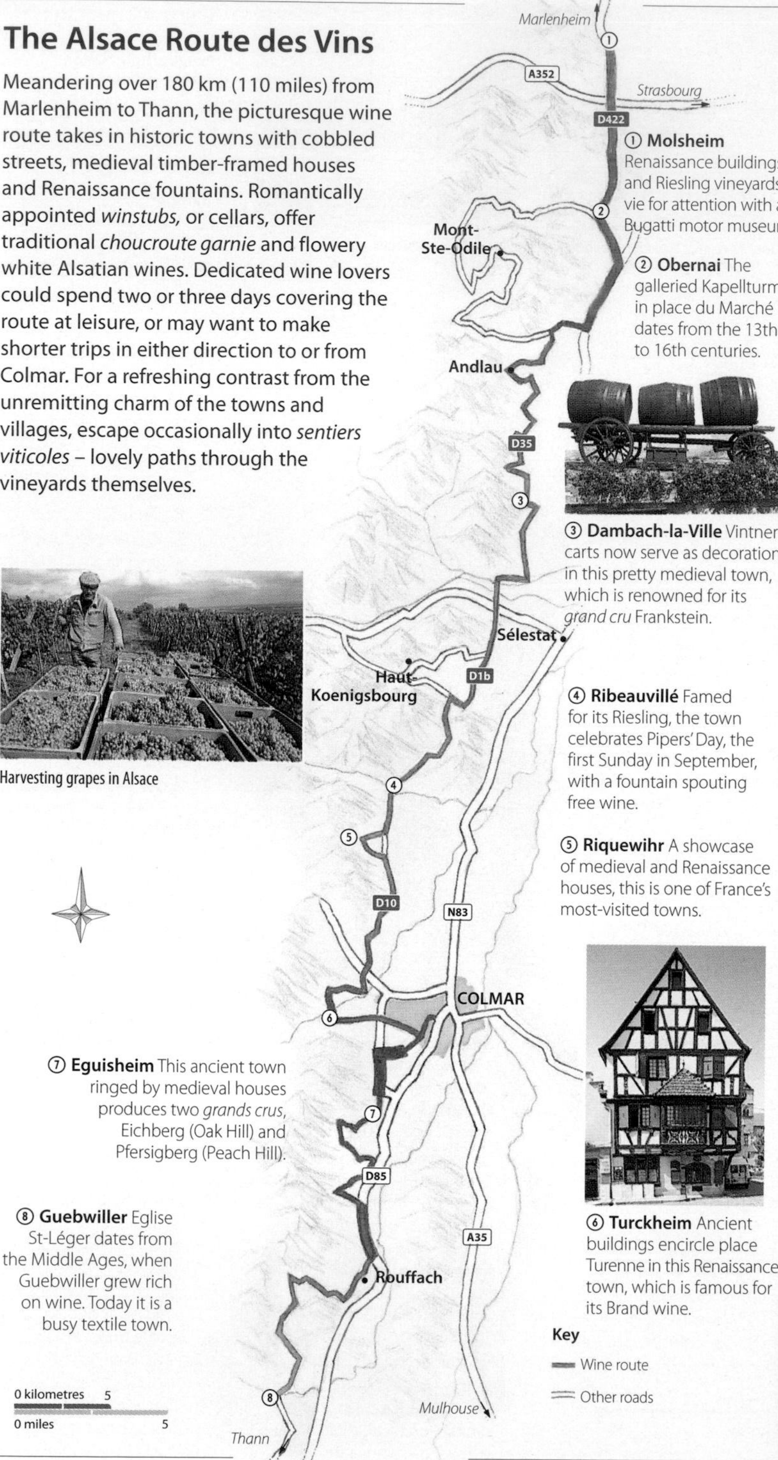

Harvesting grapes in Alsace

① **Molsheim** Renaissance buildings and Riesling vineyards vie for attention with a Bugatti motor museum.

② **Obernai** The galleried Kapellturm in place du Marché dates from the 13th to 16th centuries.

③ **Dambach-la-Ville** Vintner's carts now serve as decoration in this pretty medieval town, which is renowned for its *grand cru* Frankstein.

④ **Ribeauvillé** Famed for its Riesling, the town celebrates Pipers' Day, the first Sunday in September, with a fountain spouting free wine.

⑤ **Riquewihr** A showcase of medieval and Renaissance houses, this is one of France's most-visited towns.

⑥ **Turckheim** Ancient buildings encircle place Turenne in this Renaissance town, which is famous for its Brand wine.

⑦ **Eguisheim** This ancient town ringed by medieval houses produces two *grands crus,* Eichberg (Oak Hill) and Pfersigberg (Peach Hill).

⑧ **Guebwiller** Eglise St-Léger dates from the Middle Ages, when Guebwiller grew rich on wine. Today it is a busy textile town.

Key

Wine route

Other roads

lsace Wine

sace wines are usually aromatic, y and full-bodied. All are white cept Pinot Noir, used for light reds.

ate-harvested Alsatian classic

Key Facts

Location and climate
Protected by the Vosges, Alsace has a warm climate and France's owest annual rainfall.

Grape varieties
Alsace wines are known simply by their grape variety. ***Gewurztraminer***, with its exotic rose-petal character, is most typically Alsatian, although the ***Riesling*** is arguably the finest. ***Muscat*** s another aromatic variety. Spicy out less assertive than Gewurztraminer, ***Pinot Gris*** and the crisper, dry ***Pinot Blanc*** go well with food. ***Pinot Noir*** s the only red variety.
Lusciously rich, sweet, late-harvested wines are an Alsace speciality.

Best producers
Albert Boxler, Marcel Deiss, Rolly Gassmann, Beyer, Meyer-Fonne, Kuentz-Bas, Domaine Weinbach, Dopff & Irion, Olivier Zind-Humbrecht, Charles Schléret, Domaines Schlumberger, Domaine Ostertag, Domaine Trimbach, Hugel & Fils, Cave de Turckheim.

Good vintages
2015, 2012, 2010, 2008, 2004, 2001, 1998, 1996.

The 12th-century chapel of the Château du Haut-Barr, near Saverne

⓱ Saverne

Bas-Rhin. 12,000. 37 Grand'Rue (03 88 91 80 47). Tue & Thu. **tourisme-saverne.fr**

Framed by hills, and situated on the River Zorn and the Marne–Rhine canal, Saverne is a pretty sight. The town was a fief of the prince-bishops of Strasbourg and its sandstone Château des Rohan was a favourite summer residence. Today, it houses the **Musée du Château de Rohan-Pontivy**, with a collection tracing Saverne's past. On the far side of the château, the Grand'Rue is studded with restaurants and timber-framed Renaissance houses.

Musée du Château de Rohan-Pontivy
Château des Rohan. **Tel** 03 88 71 63 95. **Open** Jan–mid-Jun & mid-Sep–Dec: Mon–Fri pm, 10am–6pm Sat & Sun; mid-Jun–mid-Sep: 10am–noon, 2–6pm daily. **Closed** Tue. restricted.

Environs
To the southwest, perched on a rocky spur, the ruined **Château du Haut-Barr** – the "Eye of Alsace" – once commanded the pass of Col de Saverne. In **Marmoutier**, 6 km (4 miles) south, is an abbey church with a Romanesque-Lombard façade and octagonal towers.

⓲ Betschdorf

Bas-Rhin. 4,000. 1 rue des Francs, La Mairie (03 88 54 48 00). **betschdorf.com**

The vibrant village of Betschdorf borders the Forêt de Haguenau, 45 km (28 miles) north of Strasbourg. Many residents occupy timber-framed houses dating from the 18th century, when pottery made the village prosperous. Generations of potters have passed down the knowledge of the characteristic blue-grey glaze to their sons, while the women have been entrusted with decorating it in cobalt blue. A pottery museum, with a workshop attached, displays rural ceramics. Betschdorf is a good place to try *tartes flambées* – hot, crispy bases topped with cheese or fruit.

Betschdorf pottery

Environs
Another pottery village, **Soufflenheim**, lies 10 km (6 miles) southeast. Its earth-coloured pottery is usually painted with bold flowers. To the north, close to the German border, the picturesque town of **Wissembourg** has many half-timbered houses and the second-largest church in Alsace after Strasbourg Cathedral, Eglise St-Pierre et St-Paul.

WESTERN FRANCE

Introducing Western France

The western regions of France have played very different historical roles, from the royal heartland of the Loire Valley to separatist Celtic Brittany. These are mainly rich farming regions, with fishing important along the coasts. Heavy industry and oil refineries are concentrated around Rouen and Le Havre. Visitors come for the wonderful beaches, quiet rural byways and the sumptuous Loire châteaux. This map shows some of the region's most celebrated sights.

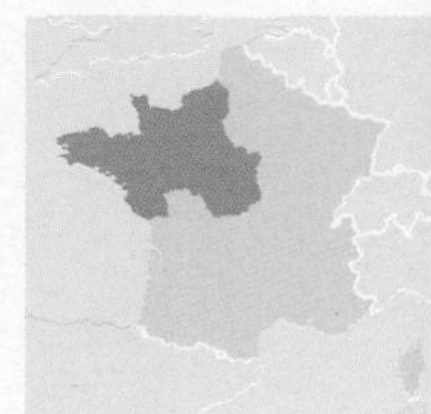

The evocative profile of Mont-St-Michel has welcomed pilgrims since the 11th century. Today nearly one million visitors a year walk across the footbridge to the island abbey *(see pp260–65).*

Guimiliau Parish Close *(see pp280–81)*

The megaliths of Carnac are evidence of early settlers in Brittany. These ancient granite blocks, arranged in intriguing patterns, date back to 4000 BC and are thought to have had a religious or astronomical purpose *(see p283).*

◀ Château de Chambord, reflected in the River Cossan

The Bayeux Tapestry *(see pp256–7)* shows William the Conqueror's invasion of England from the French point of view. Among its 58 scenes, key events such as the Battle of Hastings in 1066 are depicted with great vigour and finesse. Here, two of William's messengers are shown hurrying to meet him.

Château de Chambord is the largest and most extravagant of the Loire châteaux *(see pp306–7)*. François I transformed the original hunting lodge into a luxurious moated castle in 1519. Its splendour was completed by Louis XIV in 1685. Inside the 440 rooms are François's salamander emblem and 365 fireplaces, one for every day of the year.

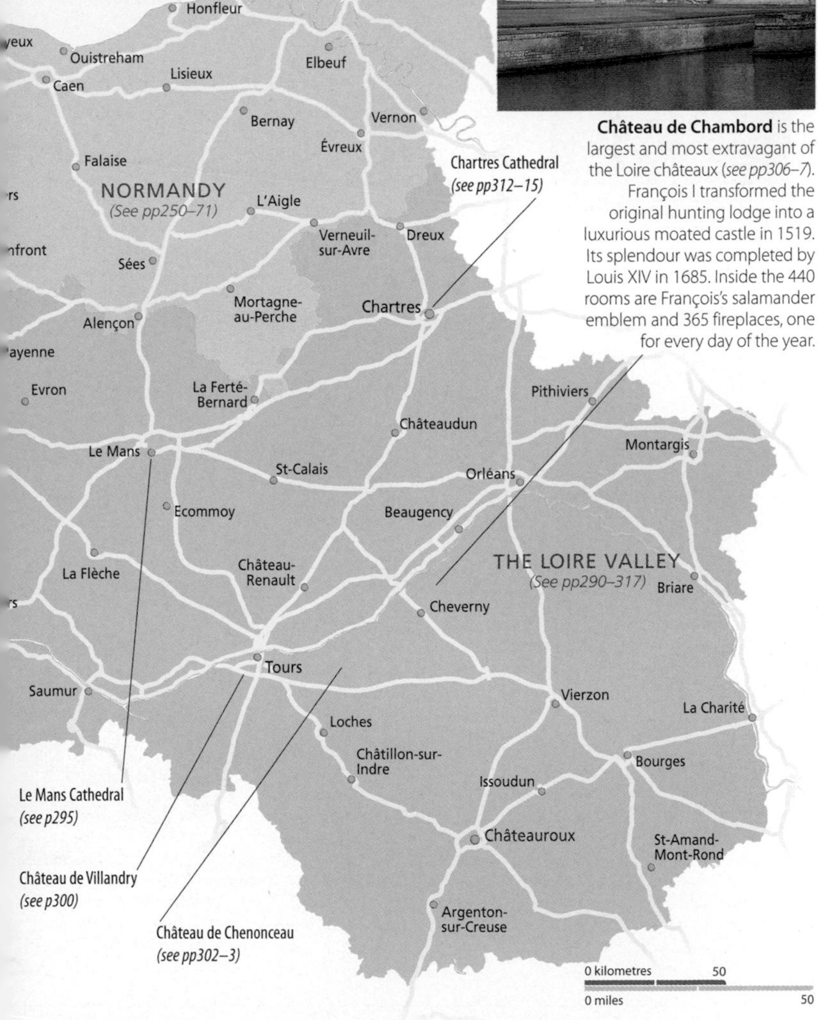

Rouen Cathedral *(see pp268–9)*

Chartres Cathedral *(see pp312–15)*

NORMANDY *(See pp250–71)*

THE LOIRE VALLEY *(See pp290–317)*

Le Mans Cathedral *(see p295)*

Château de Villandry *(see p300)*

Château de Chenonceau *(see pp302–3)*

Le Tréport
Dieppe
St-Valery-en-Caux
Tôtes
Etretat
Yvetot
Harfleur
Rouen
Honfleur
Elbeuf
Ouistreham
Caen
Lisieux
Bernay
Vernon
Évreux
Falaise
L'Aigle
Verneuil-sur-Avre
Dreux
Sées
Mortagne-au-Perche
Chartres
Alençon
Evron
La Ferté-Bernard
Pithiviers
Châteaudun
Montargis
Le Mans
St-Calais
Orléans
Ecommoy
Beaugency
La Flèche
Château-Renault
Briare
Cheverny
Tours
Saumur
Vierzon
La Charité
Loches
Châtillon-sur-Indre
Bourges
Issoudun
Châteauroux
St-Amand-Mont-Rond
Argenton-sur-Creuse

0 kilometres 50
0 miles 50

The Flavours of Western France

The Atlantic coast, the rich agricultural hinterland of dairy farms, orchards and vegetable fields, and the rivers of the Loire Valley combine to produce some of France's best-loved food. Vegetables are grown in abundance in Brittany and the alluvial soils of the Loire, and the orchards of Normandy are bountiful. Fish from the wind-swept coast of Brittany or the channel ports of Normandy play a key role in the cuisine. Hearty meat dishes range from the celebrated Rouen duck to rabbit and game of the Sologne in the Loire. Fine cheeses are made here, and butter is the favoured cooking medium.

Normandy apples

Norman cheese producer displaying his wares

Normandy

Normandy's lush green pastures, dotted with brown-and-white cows, and orchards heavy with apples, make it a great source of veal, milk, cheese, cream, butter, apples and pears. Duck is a speciality, as is *pre-salé* lamb from the salt-rich marshes around Mont-St-Michel. Many vegetables are grown and wild mushrooms thrive in the damp meadows and woodlands in autumn. Fish is important, with catches of sole, plaice and mackerel, skate and herrings, and 80 per cent of France's scallops, plus a great variety of shellfish.

Camembert is Normandy's most famous cheese; others include Pont l'Evêque, the pungent-smelling Livarot, rich Brillat-Savarin and Petit-Suisse, a small, fresh white cheese eaten with sugar. Apples symbolize Normandy above all, and cider is traditionally drunk with food, while Calvados, the fiery apple brandy, is served with meals as *le trou normand*.

Brittany

Thousands of kilometres of coastline yield an abundance of fish and shellfish. Oysters are highly prized, as are mussels,

Some of the favourite vegetables of western France

Regional Dishes and Specialities

Fish dominates the menus here, most spectacularly in the *plateau de fruits de mer*, featuring oysters, crabs, langoustines, prawns, shrimps, cockles and clams, piled on a bed of ice. Oysters are served simply with lemon or shallot vinegar, but can also come stuffed, gratinéed or wrapped in pastry. Fresh fish may be grilled, baked in sea salt (*sel de Guérande* is the best), braised in cider or served with *beurre blanc* ("white butter" sauce with shallots, wine vinegar and cream). Lobster is often served *à l'Armoricaine*. *Cotriade*, the Breton fish stew, combines a selection of the catch of the day with onions and potatoes. *Moules marinières* (mussels steamed in white wine with shallots and butter) is the popular classic. As a change from fish, look for *gigot de sept heures* – lamb slowly pot-roasted for seven hours.

Pears

Homard à l'armoricaine
Lobster, served in a herby tomato-and-onion sauce, enriched with brandy.

Superb Breton oysters for sale at a regional fish market

harvested both wild and cultivated. Other fish caught include monkfish, tuna, sardines, scallops and lobster. Pig-rearing is important, so expect roast pork, smoked sausages, hams and *boudin noir* (black/blood pudding), delicious served with apples. A great delicacy is the *pre-salé* lamb from Ile de Ouessant, served with haricot beans. Artichokes are the symbol of Brittany, an indication of the importance of vegetables, especially winter produce such as cauliflower, onions and potatoes.

Crêpes (pancakes), both sweet and savoury, are a key element of the Breton diet. They come as buckwheat *galettes* with savoury fillings such as ham, cheese, spinach or mushrooms, or as lacy, light dessert versions with sweet fillings and known as *crêpes dentelles* (*dentelle* meaning "lace").

The Loire Valley

This huge region takes pride in a truly diverse range of specialities. Grass-fed cattle are raised in Anjou, and sheep are breed in the Berry region. Excellent free-range chickens, *poulet fermier*

Cheese and charcuterie at Loches market in the Loire Valley

Loué, are raised in Touraine and the Orléanais. The forests and lakes of the Sologne yield deer, wild boar, pheasant, partridge, hare and duck. *Charcuterie* includes *rillettes* (shredded and potted pork) and ham from the Vendée. The Atlantic coast produces a variety of fish and the Loire itself is a source of pike, shad, tench, salmon, eels and lampreys. Mushrooms are cultivated in the limestone caves around Saumur, but of the many vegetables grown, the best of all is Sologne asparagus. Superb goat's cheeses include Sainte-Maure de Touraine, ash-coated Valençay and the little Crottins de Chavignol.

ON THE MENU

Alose à l'oseille Shad in a sorrel sauce.

Côte de veau vallée d'Auge Veal in mushrooms, cream and cider or Calvados.

Far aux pruneaux Egg batter pudding baked with prunes.

Kig ha farz Meat-and-vegetable hotpot with buckwheat dumpling.

Marmite Dieppoise Assorted fish stewed in cider or white wine with cream.

Tergeule Creamy baked rice pudding with cinnamon.

Tripes à la Mode de Caen Tripe with calves' feet, onions or leeks, herbs and cider.

Sole Normande Baked sole in sauce of egg and cream, garnished with mussels, oysters, mushrooms and prawns.

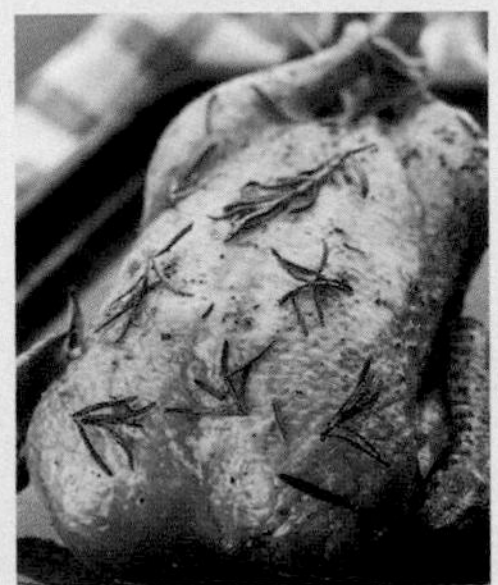
Canard á la rouennaise Duclair duck, part-roasted then finished in a rich sauce of duck liver and shallots.

Tarte Tatin Caramelized upside-down apple tart, originally made at the Hotel Tatin in the Loire Valley.

France's Wine Regions: the Loire

With a few exceptions, the Loire is a region of good rather than great wines. The fertile agricultural soils of the meandering flatlands of the "Garden of France" are fine for fruit and vegetables, less so for the production of great wines. The cool, northern, Atlantic-influenced climate nonetheless produces refreshing reds and summer rosés, both dry and lusciously sweet white wines and attractively bracing sparkling wines. Very much in the majority here, and usually intended for early consumption, are the dry white wines, so vintages in the Loire tend to matter less than in the classic red wine regions.

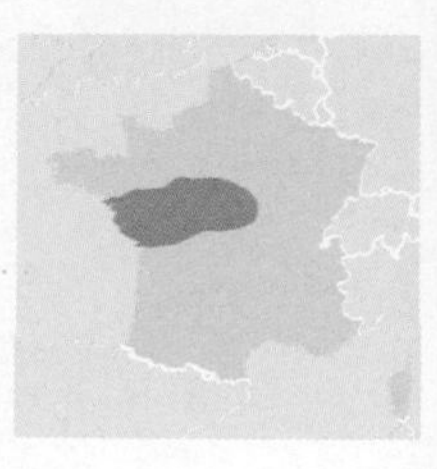

The sweet wine of Quarts de Chaume , within the Coteaux du Layon *appellation*, is little-known outside France.

Muscadet with the words *sur lie* on the label has been aged on its "lees" *(see p31)*, giving the wine a greater amount of flavour and interest.

Wine Regions

The Loire, flowing for some 1,000 km (620 miles), links the major wine areas of the Loire Valley. From its source in the Ardèche, it flows north through the centre of France to the Sancerre and Pouilly-Fumé vineyards, then west through Touraine and Anjou, finally reaching the coastal flats of the Pays Nantais, home of Muscadet.

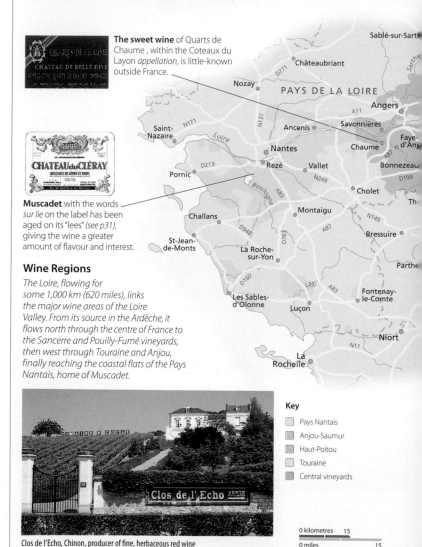

Clos de l'Echo, Chinon, producer of fine, herbaceous red wine

Key

- Pays Nantais
- Anjou-Saumur
- Haut-Poitou
- Touraine
- Central vineyards

0 kilometres 15

0 miles 15

This red wine has been made using grapes from *vieilles vignes* – the oldest and the best vines on the grower's property.

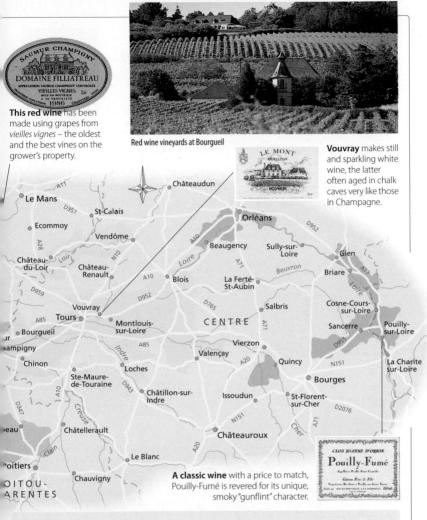

Red wine vineyards at Bourgueil

Vouvray makes still and sparkling white wine, the latter often aged in chalk caves very like those in Champagne.

A classic wine with a price to match, Pouilly-Fumé is revered for its unique, smoky "gunflint" character.

Key Facts About Loire Wines

Location and Climate

Fertile agricultural soils support fruit, vegetables and cereals; the poorer soils support grapes. The climate is cool, influenced by the Atlantic, giving the wines a refreshing acidity.

Grape Varieties

The ***Melon de Bourgogne*** makes simple, dry white wines. The ***Sauvignon*** makes gooseberryish, flinty dry whites, finest in Sancerre and Pouilly Fumé but also good in Touraine. The ***Chenin Blanc*** makes dry and medium Anjou, Savennières, Vouvray, Montlouis and Saumur, sparkling Vouvray and Saumur, and the famous sweet whites,

Bonnezeaux, Vouvray and Quarts de Chaume. Summery reds are made from the ***Gamay*** and the fruity, herbaceous ***Cabernet Franc***.

Good Producers

Muscadet: Sauvion, Guy Bossard, Michel Brégeon. *Anjou, Savennières, Vouvray*: Richou, Ogereau, Nicolas Joly, Huet, Domaine des Aubuissières, Bourillon Dorléans, Jacky Blot, François Pinon. *Touraine* (white): Pibaleau. *Saumur-Champigny* (red): Filliatreau, Château du Hureau. *Chinon, Bourgueil*: Couly-Dutheil, Frédéric Mabileau. *Sancerre, Pouilly-Fumé, Ménétou-Salon*: François Cotat, Vacheron, Mellot, Vincent Pinard.

From Defence to Decoration

The great châteaux of the Loire Valley gradually evolved from purely defensive structures to decorative palaces. With the introduction of firearms, castles lost their defensive function and comfort and taste predominated. Defensive elements such as towers, battlements, moats and gatehouses were retained largely as symbols of rank and ancestry. Renaissance additions, from galleries to dormer windows, added elegance.

Salamander emblem of François I

Angers *(see p295)*, a fortress built from 1230 to 1240 by Louis IX, stands on a rocky hill in the town centre. In 1585, Henri III removed the pepper-pot-shaped towers from 17 fortifications which were formerly 30 m (98 ft) high.

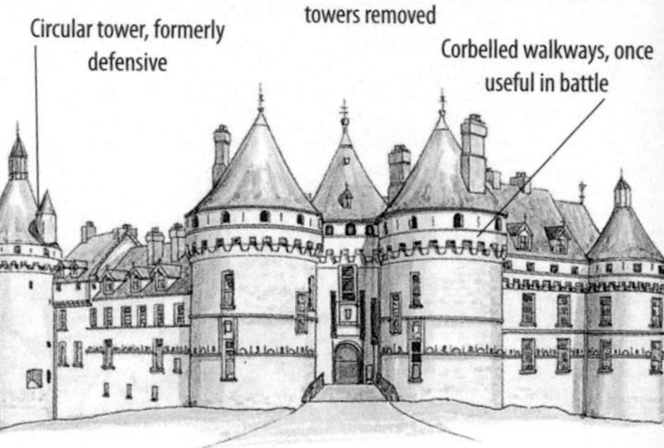

Chaumont *(see p310)* was rebuilt in 1445–1510 in Renaissance style by the Amboise family. Although it has a defensive appearance, with circular towers, corbelled walkways and a gatehouse, these features are mainly decorative. It was restored after c.1833.

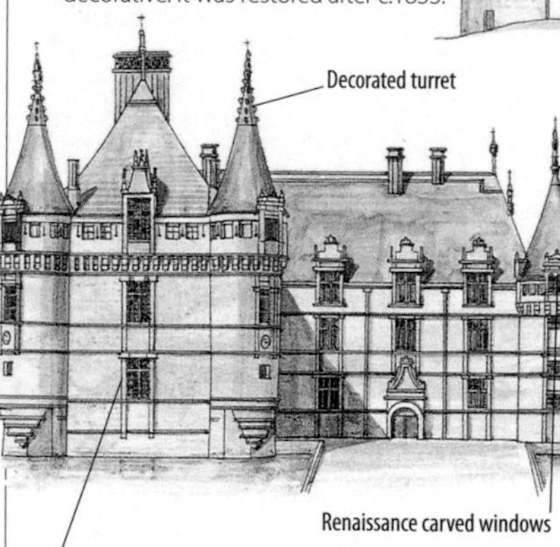

Azay-le-Rideau *(see p300)*, regarded as one of the most elegant and well-designed Renaissance châteaux, was built from 1518 to 1527 by finance minister Gilles Berthelot and his wife Philippa Lesbahy. It is a mixture of traditional turrets with Renaissance pilasters and pinnacles. Most dramatic is the interior staircase with its three storeys of twin bays and an intricately decorated pediment.

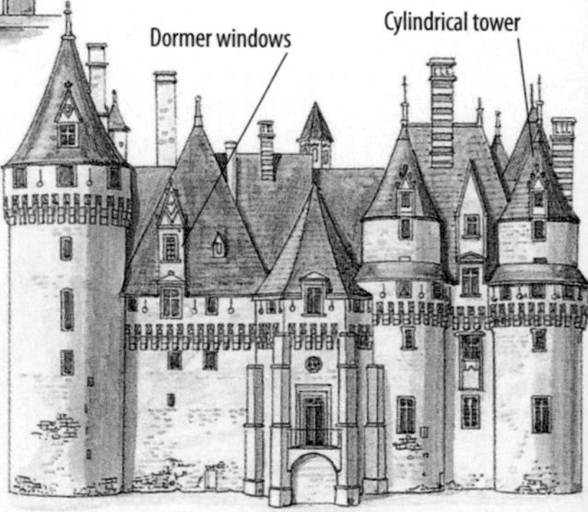

Ussé *(see p299)* was built in 1462 by Jean de Bueil as a fortress with parapets containing openings for missiles, battlements and gunloops. The Espinay family, chamberlains to both Louis XI and Charles VIII, bought the château and changed the walls overlooking the main courtyard to Renaissance style with dormer windows and pilasters. In the 17th century the north wing was demolished to create palatial terraces.

Breton Traditions

Brittany was christened Breiz Izel (Little Britain) by the Welsh and Cornish migrants who fled here in the 5th and 6th centuries AD and imposed their customs, language and religion on the local Gauls. Brittany resisted Charlemagne, the Vikings, the Normans, English alliances and even French rule until 1532. Today, Breton is taught in some schools, and a busy calendar keeps Brittany in touch with its past and with other Celtic regions.

Bigouden lace headdresses

Breton music has strong Celtic links. Instruments including the *biniou*, similar to the bagpipes, and the oboe-like *bombarde*, are often heard at local festivals.

A *pardon* is an annual religious festival honouring a local saint. The name derives from the granting of indulgences to pardon the sins of the past year. Some *pardons*, such as those at Ste-Anne d'Auray and Ste-Anne-la-Palud, still attract thousands of pilgrims, who carry banners and holy relics through the streets. Most *pardons* take place between April and September.

Breton costumes, still seen at *pardons* and weddings, varied, as each area had distinctive headdresses or *coiffes*. Artists such as Gauguin often painted the costumes. There are good museum collections in Quimper *(see p278)* and Pont l'Abbé in Pays Bigouden *(see p277)*.

Brittany's Coastal Wildlife

With its granite cliffs, sweeping bays, rias and deep estuaries, the Brittany coastline contains a wealth of varied wildlife habitats. Parts of the coast have a tidal range of more than 50 m (150 ft), the highest in France, and this great variation in sea level divides marine life into several distinct zones. Most of the region's famous shellfish, including mussels, clams and oysters, live on the lower shore, either on rocks or in muddy sand, where they are submerged for most of the day. Higher zones are the preserve of limpets and barnacles and several kinds of seaweed, which can survive out of the water for long periods. Above the sea, towering cliffs offer a nursery for seabirds and a foothold for many kinds of wild flowers.

Cliffs at the Pointe du Raz, Brittany

The Ile de Bréhat at low tide

Features of the Coast

This scene shows some of the wildlife habitats found on the Brittany coastline. When exploring the shore, make a note of the tide times, particularly if you plan to walk along the foot of the cliffs.

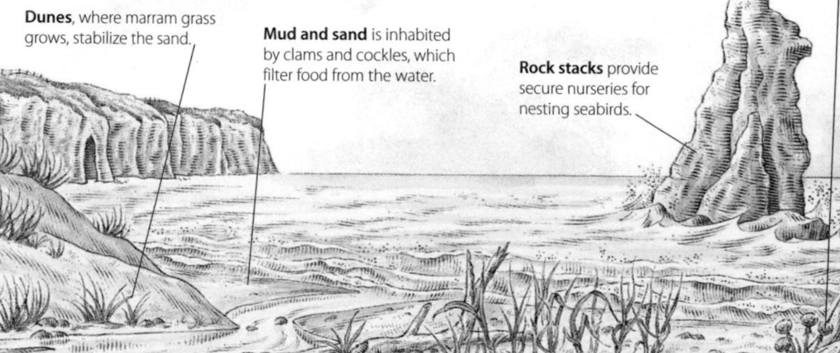

Salt-marsh flowers are at their best in late summer.
Dunes, where marram grass grows, stabilize the sand.
Mud and sand is inhabited by clams and cockles, which filter food from the water.
Rock stacks provide secure nurseries for nesting seabirds.

Oyster Beds

Like most marine molluscs, oysters begin their lives as tiny floating larvae. The first step in *ostréiculture*, or oyster cultivation, consists of providing the larvae with somewhere to settle, which is usually a stack of submerged tiles. The developing oysters are later transferred to beds and left to mature before being collected for the market.

Oyster beds at Cancale

Clifftop turf often contains a narrow band of wild flowers sandwiched between fields and the sea.
Rock pools are flooded twice daily by the tide. They are inhabited by fish, molluscs, sea anemones and sponges.

Coastal Wildlife

The structure of this shore determines the wildlife that lives on it. In a world beset by wind and waves, rocks provide solid anchorage for plants and a secure habitat for many small animals. Muddy sand is rich in nutrients, and has a greater abundance of life – although most of this is concealed beneath the surface.

Cliffs

The rock dove is a cliff-dwelling ancestor of the well-known city pigeon.

Thrift is a common spring flower, found on exposed ledges near the sea.

Rocks and Rock Pools

Seaweed of many different varieties is exposed each day by the falling tide.

The limpet, a slow-moving creature, scrapes tiny plants from the rock surface.

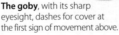

The goby, with its sharp eyesight, dashes for cover at the first sign of movement above.

Crabs live at many different water depths. Some species are extremely good swimmers.

Mud and Sand

Cockles live in large numbers just beneath the surface of muddy sand.

The curlew has a forceps-like curved beak for extracting shell-fish from mud and sand.

catamarans.com
LE CLIPPER

NORMANDY

Manche · Calvados · Orne · Seine-Maritime · Eure

The quintessential image of Normandy is of a lush, pastoral region of apple orchards, contented cows, cider and pungent cheeses – but the region also spans the windswept beaches of the Cotentin and the wooded banks of the Seine Valley. Highlights include the great abbey churches of Caen, the mighty island of Mont-St-Michel and Monet's garden at Giverny.

Normandy gets its name from the Viking Norsemen who sailed up the River Seine in the 9th century. Pillagers-turned-settlers, they made their capital at Rouen – today a cultured cathedral city that commands the east of the region. Here the Seine meanders seaward past ancient abbeys at Jumièges and St-Wandrille to a coast that became an open-air studio for Impressionist painters during the mid- and late 19th century.

North of Rouen are the chalky cliffs of the Côte d'Albâtre. The mood softens at the port of Honfleur and the elegant resorts of the Côte Fleurie to the west. Inland lies the Pays d'Auge, with its half-timbered manor houses and patch-eyed cows. The western half of Normandy is predominantly rural, a *bocage* countryside of small, high-hedged fields with windbreaks composed of beech trees.

The modern city of Caen is worth visiting for its two great 11th-century abbey churches built by William the Conqueror and his queen, Matilda. Close by, in Bayeux, the story of William's invasion of England is told in detail by the town's famous tapestry. Memories of another invasion, the D-Day landings of 1944, still linger along the Côte de Nacre and the Cotentin Peninsula. Thousands of Allied troops poured ashore on to these magnificent beaches in the closing stages of World War II. The Cotentin Peninsula is capped by the port of Cherbourg, still a strategic naval base. At its western foot stands one of France's greatest attractions: the monastery island of Mont-St-Michel.

Half-timbered manor house in the village of Beuvron-en-Auge, near Lisieux

◀ The harbour at Honfleur, Calvados

Exploring Normandy

Normandy's rich historical sights and diverse landscape make it ideal for touring by car or bicycle. Rewarding coastal drives and good beaches can be found along the windswept Côte d'Albâtre and the Cotentin Peninsula. Further south is one of France's most celebrated sights, Mont-St-Michel. Inland, follow the meanders of the Seine Valley, passing cider orchards and half-timbered houses along the way, to visit historic Rouen and Monet's garden at Giverny.

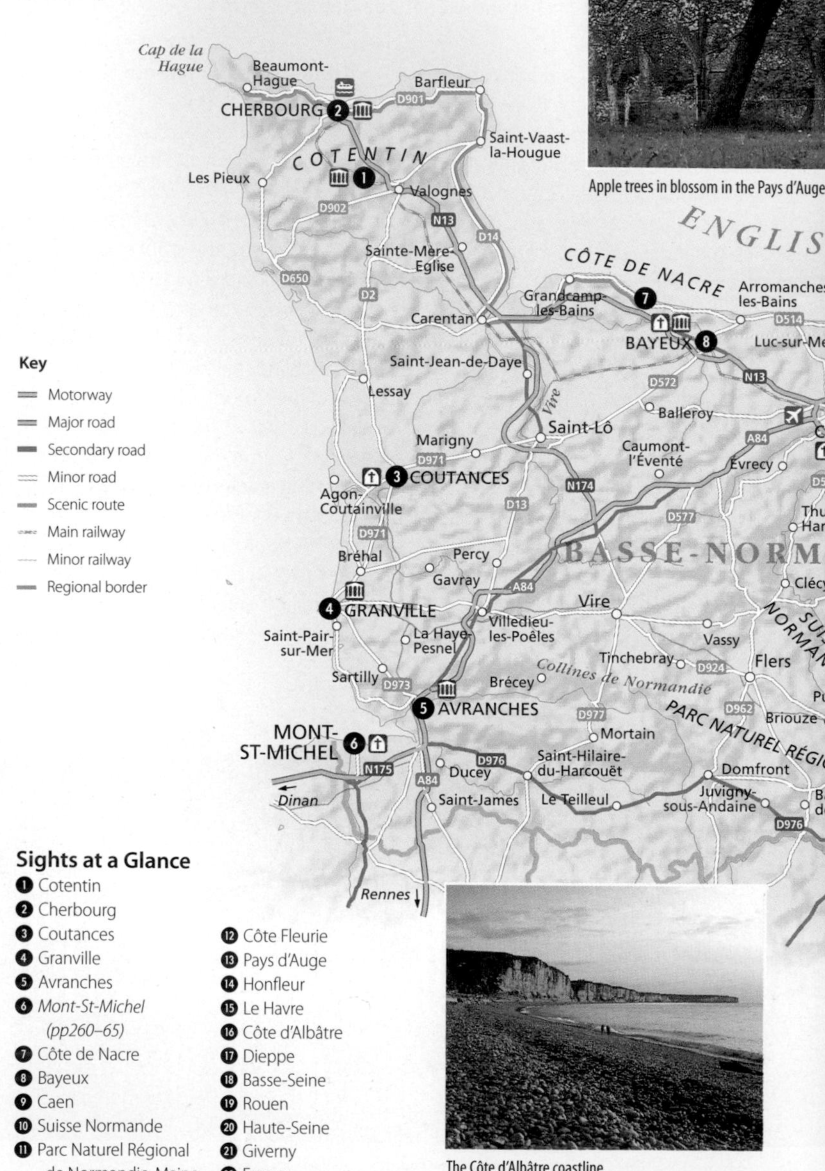

Apple trees in blossom in the Pays d'Auge

The Côte d'Albâtre coastline

Key

- Motorway
- Major road
- Secondary road
- Minor road
- Scenic route
- Main railway
- Minor railway
- Regional border

Sights at a Glance

1. Cotentin
2. Cherbourg
3. Coutances
4. Granville
5. Avranches
6. *Mont-St-Michel (pp260–65)*
7. Côte de Nacre
8. Bayeux
9. Caen
10. Suisse Normande
11. Parc Naturel Régional de Normandie-Maine
12. Côte Fleurie
13. Pays d'Auge
14. Honfleur
15. Le Havre
16. Côte d'Albâtre
17. Dieppe
18. Basse-Seine
19. Rouen
20. Haute-Seine
21. Giverny
22. Evreux

For keys to symbols *see back flap*

Getting Around

Access to and through the region from Calais is quick and direct on the A16, which links up with the A28–A29 and A13 motorways to Paris, and runs west to Caen, and beyond on the A84. There are also main road and rail links to the cross-Channel ports of Dieppe, Le Havre, Caen (Ouistreham) and Cherbourg. Travel by public transport beyond these arteries is limited. The region is threaded with minor roads, particularly delightful in the Pays d'Auge and Cotentin Peninsula. The main airports are at Rouen, Le Havre and Caen.

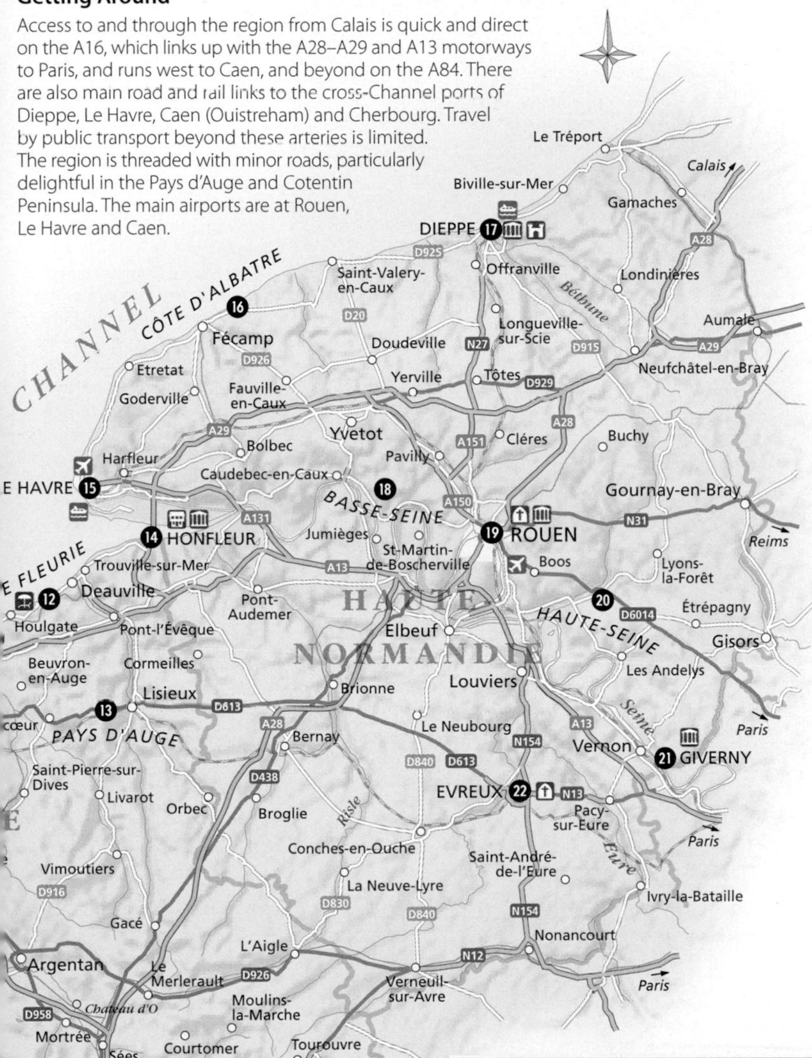

The town of Les Andelys shrouded in mist

Rugged cliffs on the Cotentin Peninsula

❶ Cotentin

Manche. Cherbourg. 2 quai Alexandre III, Cherbourg (02 33 93 52 02).
manchetourisme.com

Thrusting into the English Channel, the Cotentin Peninsula has a landscape similar to Brittany's. Its long sandy beaches have wild and windblown headlands around Cap de la Hague and Nez de Jobourg. The latter is popular among birdwatchers – gannets and shearwaters fly by in large numbers. Along the east coast stretches Utah Beach, where American troops landed as part of the Allied invasion on 6 June 1944. Inland, Ste-Mère-Eglise commemorates these events with its **Musée Airborne** (Airborne Troops Museum). Just outside Ste-Mère-Eglise, the **Ferme-Musée du Cotentin** has farm animals and activities, which give an insight into rural life in the early 1900s, while further north, in the market town of Valognes, the **Musée Régional du Cidre et du Calvados** celebrates the thriving local talent for making cider and Calvados.

Two fishing ports command the Peninsula's northeast corner: Barfleur and St-Vaast-la-Hougue, the latter famous for oysters and a base for boat trips to the Ile de Tatihou. The Val de Saire is ideal for a scenic drive, with a view point at La Pernelle, the best place to survey the coast. On the west side of the Peninsula, warmed by the Gulf Stream, the resort of Barneville-Carteret offers sandy beaches and summer boat trips to the Channel Islands. The low-lying, marshy landscape east of Carentan forms the heart of the Parc Régional des Marais du Potentin et du Bessin.

Musée Airborne
14 rue Eisenhower, Ste-Mère-Eglise. **Tel** 02 33 41 41 35. **Open** Feb–Nov: daily. **Closed** Jan & Dec.
airborne-museum.org

Ferme-Musée du Cotentin
Rte de Beauvais, Ste-Mère-Eglise. **Tel** 02 33 95 40 20. **Open** Jul–Aug: daily; Apr–Jun, Easter & Nov school hols: Sun–Fri pms only. **Closed** 1 May.

Musée Régional du Cidre et du Calvados
Rue du Petit-Versailles, Valognes. **Tel** 02 33 40 11 55 (Office du Tourisme). **Open** Apr–Sep: Wed–Sun pms only (Jun–Aug: Mon–Sat & Sun pm).

❷ Cherbourg

Manche. 44,000. 2 quai Alexandre III (02 33 93 52 02). Tue, Thu & Sat. **cherbourg tourisme.com**

Cherbourg has been a strategic port and naval base since the mid-19th century. The French Navy still uses its harbours, as do transatlantic ships and cross-Channel ferries from England and Ireland. For a good view of the port, drive to the hilltop **Fort du Roule**, which houses the **Musée de la Libération**, recalling the D-Day invasion and the subsequent liberation of Cherbourg. Most activity is centred on the flower-filled market square, place Général de Gaulle, and along shopping streets such as rue Tour-Carrée and rue de la Paix. The fine art in the **Musée Thomas-Henry** includes 17th-century Flemish works, and portraits by Jean François Millet, born in Gréville-Hague. **Parc Emmanuel Liais** has small botanical gardens and a densely packed **Musée d'Histoire Naturelle**.

The **Cité de la Mer**, a bilingual centre, has a deep-sea aquarium, the world's largest visitable submarine and other wonders.

Cherbourg town centre

Musée de la Libération
Fort du Roule. **Tel** 02 33 20 14 12. **Open** Tue–Fri, Sat & Sun pms. **Closed** public hols.

Musée Thomas-Henry
Esplanade de la Laïcité. **Tel** 02 33 23 39 30. **Open** Tue–Fri & Sat & Sun pms.

La Cité de la Mer
Gare Maritime Transatlantique. **Open** Feb, Apr–Oct: daily; Mar, Nov & Dec: Tue–Sun. **Closed** Jan, 25 Dec. **Tel** 02 33 20 26 69.
citedelamer.com

❸ Coutances

Manche. 12,000. pl Georges Leclerc (02 33 19 08 10). Thu. **tourisme-coutances.fr**

From Roman times until the Revolution, the hill top town of Coutances was the capital of the Cotentin. The slender **Cathédrale Notre-Dame**, a fine example of Norman Gothic architecture, has a soaring 66-m (217-ft) lantern tower. Founded in the 1040s by Bishop Geoffroi de Montbray, it was financed by the local de Hauteville family using money gained in Sicily, where they had founded a kingdom a few years earlier. The town was badly damaged during World

War II, but the cathedral, the churches of St Nicholas and St Peter, and the beautiful public gardens with their rare plants, all survived.

The back of Coutances Cathedral with its squat lantern tower

❹ Granville

Manche. 14,000.
4 cours Jonville (02 33 91 30 03).
Sat. ville-granville.fr

Ramparts enclose the upper town of Granville, which sits on a spur overlooking the Baie du Mont-St-Michel. The walled town was developed from fortifications built by the English in 1439.

The chapel walls of the **Eglise de Notre-Dame** are lined with tributes from local fishermen to their patroness, Notre-Dame du Cap Lihou. The lower town is an old-fashioned seaside resort with a casino, promenades and public gardens. From the port there are boat trips to the Iles Chausey, a scattering of low-lying granite islands.

The **Musée d'Art Moderne Richard Anacréon** houses a collection of early 20th-century art. Surrounded by a beautiful cliff garden, the **Musée Christian Dior** is housed in Villa Les Rhumbs, the fashion designer's fine childhood home.

Musée d'Art Moderne Richard Anacréon
pl de l'Isthme, La Haute-Ville.
Tel 02 33 51 02 94. **Open** Feb–May, Oct & Nov: Fri–Sun pms; Jun–Sep: Tue–Sun.

Musée Christian Dior
Villa Les Rhumbs. **Tel** 02 33 61 48 21.
Open Apr–Sep: daily; Oct–Apr: Wed–Sun pms. Gardens: open all year.

D-Day Landings

In the early hours of 6 June 1944, Allied forces began landing on the shores of Normandy, the first step in a long-planned invasion of German-occupied France, known as Operation Overlord. Parachutists were dropped near Ste-Mère-Eglise and Pegasus Bridge, and sea-borne assaults were made along a string of code-named beaches. US troops landed on Utah and Omaha in the west, while British and Canadian troops, which included a contingent of Free French commandos, landed at Gold, Juno and Sword. The beaches are still referred to by their code names. Pegasus Bridge, where the first French house was liberated, is a natural starting point for a tour around the sights and memorials. Further west, evocative ruins of the artificial harbour towed across from England survive at Arromanches-les-Bains.

American troops coming ashore during the Allied invasion of France

There are British, German and American war cemeteries at La Cambe, Ranville and St-Laurent-sur-Mer. War museums at Bayeux, Caen, St-Mère-Eglise and Cherbourg provide background on D-Day and the ensuing Battle of Normandy.

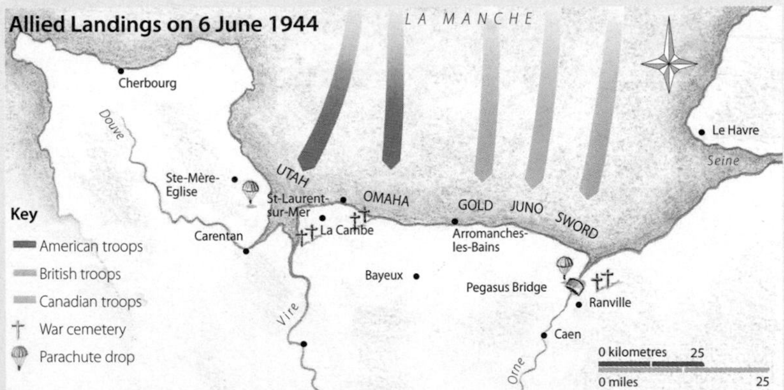

By the end of D-Day, over 135,000 men had been brought ashore, with losses totalling around 10,000

5 Avranches

Manche. 9,500. 2 rue Général-de-Gaulle (02 33 58 00 22). Sat. **cc-avranchesmont saintmichel.fr**

Avranches has been a religious centre since the 6th century and is the final staging post for visitors to the abbey on Mont-St-Michel. The origins of the famous abbey lie in a vision experienced by Aubert, the bishop of Avranches. One night in 708 the Archangel Michael instructed him to build a church on the nearby island. Aubert's skull, with the fingerhole made in it by the angel, can be seen in the treasury of **St-Gervais** in Avranches. The best views of Mont-St-Michel are from the **Jardin des Plantes**. After the Revolution, 203 illuminated manuscripts were rescued from Mont-St-Michel's abbey. These and many others are held in the **Musée des Manuscrits du Mont-St-Michel**. Multimedia displays show how monks copied and illuminated the texts. The **Musée d'Art et d'Histoire** highlights life in the Cotentin during World War II.

Musée des Manuscrits du Mont-St-Michel
Pl d'Estouteville. **Tel** 02 33 79 57 00. **Open** Tue–Sat pms (Apr–Sep: Tue–Sun). **Closed** Jan, 1 May, 1 Nov, 25 Dec.

Musée d'Art et d'Histoire
Pl Jean de Saint-Avit. **Tel** 02 33 79 57 00. **Open** Wed–Sun.

Remains of the Mulberry Harbour from World War II off the Côte de Nacre

6 Mont-St-Michel

See pp260–65.

7 Côte de Nacre

Calvados. Caen. Caen, Bayeux. Caen-Ouistreham. pl St-Pierre, Caen (02 31 27 14 14). Fri, Sun. **caen-tourisme.fr**

The stretch of coast between the mouths of the rivers Orne and Vire was dubbed the Côte de Nacre (Mother-of-Pearl Coast) in the 19th century. More recently it has become known as the site of the D-Day landings, when Allied troops poured ashore at the start of Operation Overlord *(see p255)*. The associated cemeteries, memorials and museums, and the remnants of the Mulberry Harbour at Arromanches-les-Bains, provide focal points for a visit. However, the coastline is equally popular as a summer holiday destination, offering long, sandy beaches backed by seaside resorts such as Courseulles-sur-Mer and Luc-sur-Mer, which are more relaxed than the resorts of the Côte Fleurie further east.

8 Bayeux

Calvados. 16,000. Pont-St-Jean (02 31 51 28 28). Sat, Wed. **bayeux-bessin-tourisme.com**

Bayeux was the first town to be liberated by the Allies in 1944 and fortunate to escape war damage. Today, an attractive nucleus of 15th- to 19th-century buildings remains around its central high streets, rue St-Martin and rue St-Jean. The latter is lined with shops and cafés.

Bayeux Tapestry

A lively comic strip justifying William the Conqueror's invasion of England, this 70-m- (230-ft-) long embroidered hanging was commissioned by Bishop Odo of Bayeux. Offering insights into 11th-century life, and an action-packed account of the defeat of Harold, King of England, at the Battle of Hastings, the tapestry is valued as a work of art, a historical document, an early example of spin and an entertaining read.

Harold's retinue sets off for France to inform William that he will succeed to the English throne.

Trees with interlacing branches are sometimes used to divide the tapestry's 58 scenes.

Above the town rise the spires and domed lantern tower of the Gothic **Cathédrale Notre-Dame**. Beneath its interior is an 11th-century crypt decorated with restored 15th-century frescoes of angels playing musical instruments. The original Romanesque church that stood here was consecrated in 1077, and it is likely that Bayeux's famous tapestry was commissioned for this occasion by one of its key characters, Bishop Odo.

The tapestry is displayed in a renovated seminary, **Centre Guillaume-le-Conquérant-Tapisserie de Bayeux**, which gives a detailed audio-visual explanation of events leading up to the Norman conquest. On the southwest side of the town, the restored **Musée Mémorial de la Bataille de Normandie** traces the events of the Battle of Normandy in World War II, with an excellent film compilation made from contemporary newsreels.

Centre Guillaume-le-Conquérant-Tapisserie de Bayeux
Rue de Nesmond. **Tel** 02 31 51 25 50. **Open** daily. **Closed** 3 wks early Jan, 25–26 Dec. **tapisserie-bayeux.fr**

Musée Mémorial de la Bataille de Normandie
Bd Fabian-Ware. **Tel** 02 31 51 46 90. **Open** mid-Feb–Dec: daily. **Closed** 1 Jan, 25 Dec.

The Abbaye aux Hommes in Caen

9 Caen

Calvados. 115,000. pl St-Pierre (02 31 27 14 14). Fri & Sun. **caen-tourisme.fr**

In the mid-11th century Caen became the favoured residence of William the Conqueror and Queen Matilda, and despite the destruction of three-quarters of the city during World War II much remains of their creation. The monarchs built two great abbeys and a castle on the north bank of the River Orne, bequeathing Caen a core of historic interest that justifies penetrating its industrial estates and postwar housing. Much-loved by the citizens of Caen, the **Eglise St-Pierre** was built on the south side of the castle in the 13th and 14th centuries, with an impressively ornate Renaissance east end added in the early 16th century. The frequently copied 14th-century bell tower was destroyed in 1944, but has now been restored. To the east, rue du Vaugeux is the central street in Caen's small Vieux Quartier (Old Quarter). Now pedestrianized, the street still has some lovely half-timbered buildings. A walk west, along rue St-Pierre or boulevard du Maréchal Leclerc, leads to the city's main shopping district.

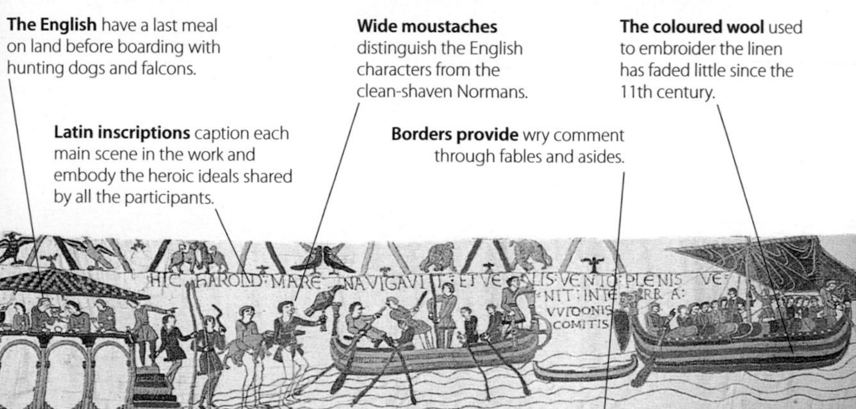

The English have a last meal on land before boarding with hunting dogs and falcons.
Wide moustaches distinguish the English characters from the clean-shaven Normans.
The coloured wool used to embroider the linen has faded little since the 11th century.
Latin inscriptions caption each main scene in the work and embody the heroic ideals shared by all the participants.
Borders provide wry comment through fables and asides.
HIC HAROLD MARE NAVIGAVIT ET VELIS VENTO PLENIS VE
NIT IN TERRA
VVIDONIS
COMITIS

Caen City Centre

① Abbaye aux Hommes
② Eglise St-Etienne
③ Château Ducal
④ Eglise St-Pierre
⑤ La Trinité
⑥ Abbaye aux Dames

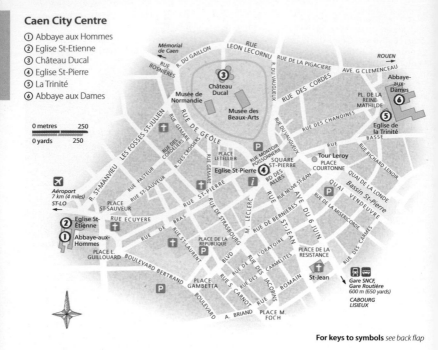

For keys to symbols *see back flap*

Abbaye-aux-Hommes

Esplanade Jean-Marie Louvel. **Tel** 02 31 30 42 81. **Open** for visits daily except during services. **Closed** 1 Jan, 1 May, 25 Dec. guided tour. (no tours Oct–Mar). restr.

Work began on William's Abbey for Men in 1063 and was almost complete by his death 20 years later. The abbey church, **Eglise St-Etienne**, is a masterpiece of Norman Romanesque, with a severe west front crowned with 13th-century spires. The sparingly decorated nave was roofed in the early 1100s with stone vaulting that anticipates the Gothic style.

Abbaye-aux-Dames

Pl de la Reine Mathilde. **Tel** 02 31 06 98 98. **Open** daily pms only. **Closed** 1 Jan, 1 May, 25 Dec. obligatory.

Like the Abbaye-aux-Hommes, Matilda's Abbey for Women also has a Norman Romanesque church, **La Trinité**, flanked by 18th-century buildings. Begun in 1060, it was consecrated six years later. Queen Matilda lies buried in the choir under a slab of black marble, and her restored abbey, with its creamy Caen stone, makes a serene, dignified mausoleum.

Château Ducal

Esplanade du Château. Musée des Beaux-Arts: **Tel** 02 31 30 47 70. **Open** daily (Nov–May: Wed–Mon). Musée de Normandie: **Tel** 02 31 30 47 60. **Open** Jun–Oct: daily: Nov–May: Wed–Mon. **Closed** 1 Jan, Easter, 1 May, Ascension, 1 Nov, 25 Dec (both museums).

The ruins of Caen's castle, one of the largest fortified enclosures in Europe, offer spacious lawns, museums and rampart views. A fine art collection, strong on 17th-century French and Italian painting, is exhibited in the **Musée des Beaux-Arts**. The **Musée de Normandie** recalls traditional life in the region with utensils and displays on farming and lace.

Mémorial de Caen

Esplanade Dwight-Eisenhower. **Tel** 02 31 06 06 45. **Open** mid-Feb–Oct: daily; Nov–mid-Feb: Tue–Sun. **Closed** 3 weeks in Jan, 25 Dec.
memorial-caen.fr

Northwest of Caen, close to the N13 ring road (exit 7), this museum is dedicated to peace, placing D-Day into the context of World War II using a host of interactive and audiovisual techniques, including stunning compilations of archive and fictional film.

A modern extension gives a wider perspective on cultural, religious, border and ecological conflicts in the second half of the 20th century.

Lush Orne Valley in the Suisse Normande

For hotels and restaurants in this region see pp559–60 and pp583–5

⑩ Suisse Normande

Calvados & Orne. Caen. Caen, Argentan. 2 pl St-Sauveur, Thury-Harcourt (02 31 79 70 45). **suisse-normande-tourisme.com**

Though hardly the mountains of Switzerland, the cliffs and valleys carved out by the River Orne as it winds north to Caen have become popular for walking, climbing, camping and river sports. The area is also ideal for a rural drive. Its highest and most impressive point is the Oëtre Rock, off the D329, where you can look down over the dramatic gorges created by the River Rouvre.

⑪ Parc Naturel Régional de Normandie-Maine

Orne & Manche. Alençon. Argentan. Carrouges (02 33 81 75 75). **parc-naturel-normandie-maine.fr**

The southern fringes of central Normandy have been incorporated into France's largest regional park. Among the farmland and forests of oak and beech are several small towns. **Domfront** rests on a spur overlooking the River Varenne. The spa town **Bagnoles-de-l'Orne** offers a casino and sports facilities, while **Sées** has a Gothic cathedral. The **Maison du Parc** at Carrouges has information on walks, cycling and canoeing.

Poster of Deauville, about 1930

Maison du Parc
Carrouges. **Tel** 02 33 81 13 33. **Open** Apr–mid-Oct & 6–21 Dec: daily. **Closed** 1 May.

Environs
Just north of the park is the **Château d'O**, a Renaissance château with fine 17th-century frescoes. The **Haras du Pin** is France's national stud, called "a horses' Versailles" for its 17th-century architecture. Horse shows, dressage events and various tours take place throughout the year.

⑫ Côte Fleurie

Calvados. Deauville. 112 rue Victor Hugo, Deauville (02 31 14 40 00). **deauville.org**

The Côte Fleurie (Flowery Coast) between Villerville and Cabourg has been planted with chic resorts, which burst into bloom every summer. **Trouville** was once a humble fishing village, but in the mid-19th century caught the attention of writers Gustave Flaubert and Alexandre Dumas. By the 1870s Trouville had acquired grand hotels, a railway station and pseudo-Swiss villas along the beachfront. It has, however, long been outclassed by its neighbour, **Deauville**, created by the Duc de Morny in the 1860s. This resort boasts a casino, racecourses, marinas and the famous beachside catwalk, Les Planches.

For something quieter, head west to smaller resorts such as Villers-sur-Mer or Houlgate. **Cabourg** further west is dominated by the turn-of-the-century Grand Hôtel, where novelist Marcel Proust spent many summers. Proust used the resort as a model for the fictional Balbec in his novel *Remembrance of Things Past*.

⑬ Pays d'Auge

Calvados. Deauville. Lisieux. 11 rue d'Alençon, Lisieux (02 31 48 18 10). **lisieux-tourisme.com**

Inland from the Côte Fleurie, the Pays d'Auge is classic Normandy countryside, lushly woven with fields, wooded valleys, cider orchards, dairy farms and manor houses. Its capital is **Lisieux**, a cathedral town devoted to Ste Thérèse of Lisieux, who was canonized in 1925 and still attracts hundreds of thousands of pilgrims each year. Lisieux is an obvious base for exploring the region, but nearby market towns, such as St-Pierre-sur-Dives and Orbec, are smaller and more attractive.

The best way to enjoy the Pays d'Auge is to potter around its minor roads. There is a tourist route devoted to cider, and picturesque manor houses, farmhouses and châteaux testify to the wealth of this fertile land. **St-Germain-de-Livet** can be visited, as can **Crèvecoeur-en-Auge**, and the half-timbered village of **Beuvron-en-Auge** is charming.

Apples and Cider

Apple orchards are a familiar feature of the Normandy countryside, and their fruit a fundamental ingredient in the region's gastronomic repertoire. No self-respecting patisserie would be without its *tarte normande* (apple tart), and every country lane seems to sport an *Ici Vente Cidre* (Cider Sold Here) sign. Much of the harvest forms the raw material for cider and Calvados, an apple brandy aged in oak barrels for at least two years. A local brew is also made from pears, and known as *poiré* (perry).

A crop ranging from sour cider apples to sweet eating varieties

6 Mont-St-Michel

Shrouded by mist, encircled by sea, soaring proudly above glistening sands – the silhouette of Mont-St-Michel is one of the most enchanting sights in France. Now linked to the mainland by a causeway, the island of Mont-Tombe (Tomb on the Hill) stands at the mouth of the River Couesnon, crowned by a fortified abbey that almost doubles its height. Lying strategically on the frontier between Normandy and Brittany, Mont-St-Michel grew from a humble 8th-century oratory to become a Benedictine monastery that had its greatest influence in the 12th and 13th centuries. Pilgrims known as *miquelots* journeyed from afar to honour the cult of St Michael, and the monastery was a renowned centre of medieval learning. Major engineering works to reverse the silting up of the sea around the island have been completed.

St Aubert's Chapel
A small 15th-century chapel built on an outcrop of rock is dedicated to Aubert, the founder of Mont-St-Michel.

★ Gabriel Tower
Three floors of cannons point in all directions from this imposing 16th-century tower.

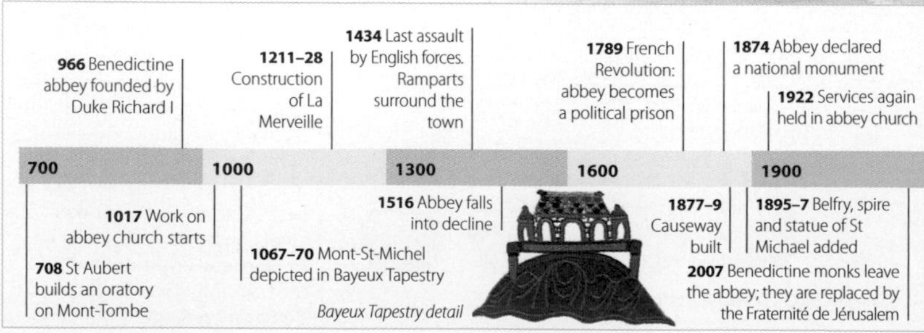

966 Benedictine abbey founded by Duke Richard I
1211–28 Construction of La Merveille
1434 Last assault by English forces. Ramparts surround the town
1789 French Revolution: abbey becomes a political prison
1874 Abbey declared a national monument
1922 Services again held in abbey church
700
1000
1300
1600
1900
708 St Aubert builds an oratory on Mont-Tombe
1017 Work on abbey church starts
1067–70 Mont-St-Michel depicted in Bayeux Tapestry
1516 Abbey falls into decline
1877–9 Causeway built
1895–7 Belfry, spire and statue of St Michael added
2007 Benedictine monks leave the abbey; they are replaced by the Fraternité de Jérusalem

Bayeux Tapestry detail

Tides of Mont-St-Michel
Extremely strong tides in the Baie du Mont-St-Michel act as a natural defence. They rise and fall with the lunar calendar and can reach speeds of 10 km/h (6 mph).

VISITORS' CHECKLIST

Practical Information
bd de l'Avancée (02 33 60 14 30). **ot-montsaintmichel.com** Abbey: **Tel** 02 33 89 80 00. **Open** May–Aug: 9am–7pm; Sep–Apr: 9:30am–6pm. **Closed** 1 Jan, 1 May, 25 Dec. 12:15pm Tue–Sat, 11:30am Sun. **abbaye-mont-saint-michel.fr**

Transport
to Pontorson, then bus.

★ Abbey
Protected by high walls, the abbey and its church occupy an impregnable position on the island.

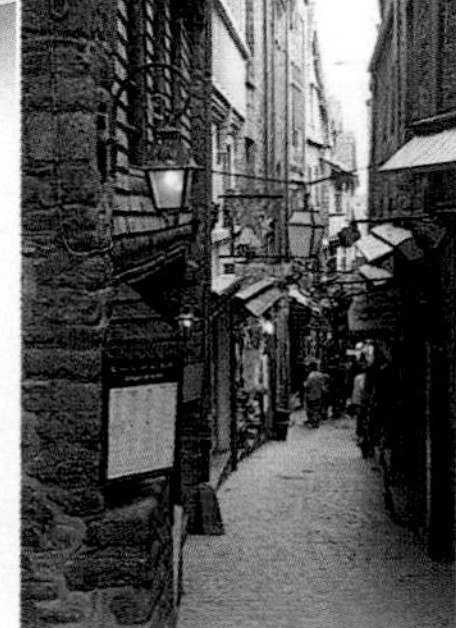

★ Grande Rue
Now crowded with restaurants, the pilgrims' route, followed since the 12th century, climbs up past Eglise St-Pierre to the abbey gates.

KEY

① **Gautier's Leap**, the terrace at the top of the Inner Staircase, is named after a prisoner who leaped to his death.

② **Eglise St-Pierre**

③ **Liberty Tower**

④ **The Arcade Tower** provided lodgings for the abbot's soldiers.

⑤ **King's Tower**

The Abbey of Mont-St-Michel

The present buildings bear witness to the time when the abbey served both as a Benedictine monastery and, for 73 years after the Revolution, as a political prison. In 1017 work began on a Romanesque church at the island's highest point, building over its 10th-century predecessor, now the Chapel of Our Lady Underground. A monastery built on three levels, La Merveille (The Miracle) was added to the church's north side in the early 13th century.

★ Church
Four bays of the Romanesque nave survive. Three were pulled down in 1776, creating the West Terrace.

Refectory
The monks took their meals in this long, narrow room, which is flooded with light through tall windows.

★ La Merveille
The Miracle is a Gothic masterpiece – a three-storey monastic complex built in only 16 years.

Knights' Room
The rib vaults and finely decorated capitals are typically Gothic.

Crypt of the Thirty Candles is one of two 11th-century crypts built to support the transepts of the main church.

★ Cloisters
The cloisters with their elegant columns in staggered rows are a beautiful example of early 13th-century Anglo-Norman style.

For hotels and restaurants in this region see pp559–60 and pp583–5

Visiting the Abbey

The three levels of the abbey reflect the monastic hierarchy. The monks lived at the highest level, in an enclosed world of church, cloister and refectory. The abbot entertained his noble guests on the middle level. Soldiers and pilgrims further down on the social scale were received at the lowest level. Guided tours begin at the West Terrace at the church level and end in the almonry, where alms were dispensed to the poor. The almonry is now a bookshop and souvenir hall.

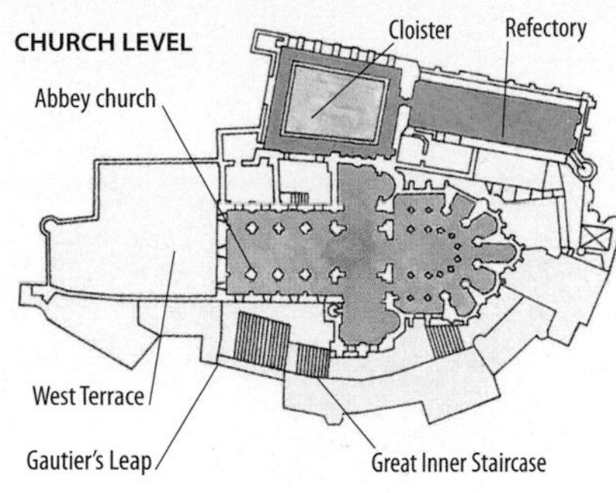

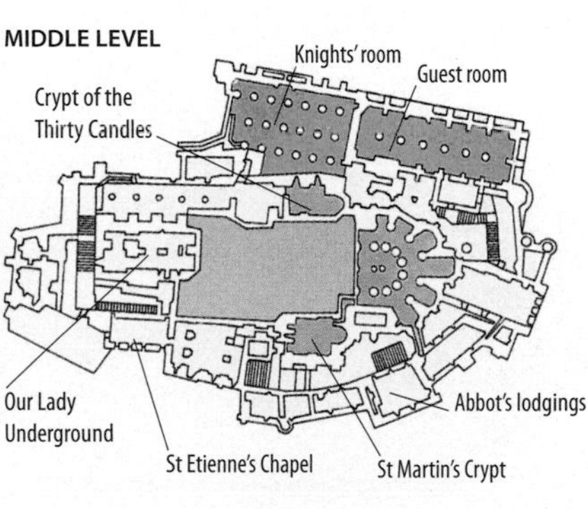

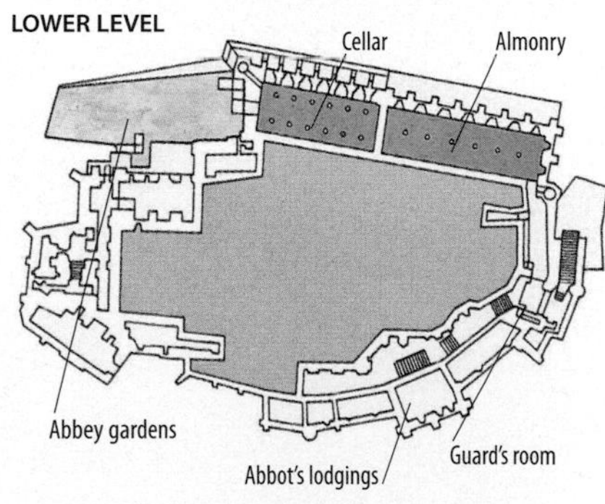

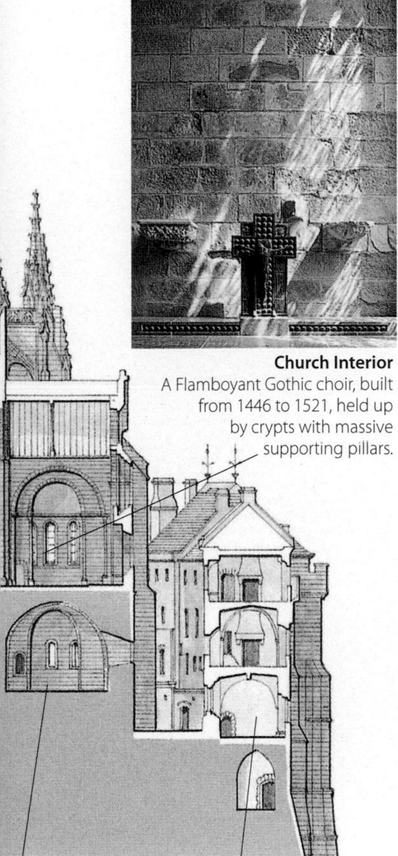

Church Interior
A Flamboyant Gothic choir, built from 1446 to 1521, held up by crypts with massive supporting pillars.

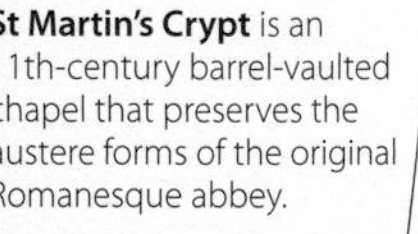

St Martin's Crypt is an 11th-century barrel-vaulted chapel that preserves the austere forms of the original Romanesque abbey.

The abbot's lodgings were close to the abbey entrance, and he received prestigious visitors in the guest room. Poorer pilgrims were received in the almonry.

West Terrace
Guided tours start here, at the West Terrace. The Fraternité de Jérusalem, a small monastic community, lives in the abbey and welcomes visitors.

Mont-St-Michel by night ▶

⓮ Honfleur

Calvados. 8,500. Deauville. quai Lepaulmier (02 31 89 23 30). Wed, Sat; Thu, Sun: fish market at harbour. **ot-honfleur.fr**

A major defensive port in the 15th century, Honfleur has become one of Normandy's most appealing harbours. At its heart is the 17th-century **Vieux Bassin** (Old Dock), with its pretty, tall houses (6–7 storeys).

Honfleur became a centre of artistic activity in the 19th century. Eugène Boudin, the painter, was born here in 1824, as was the composer Erik Satie in 1866. Courbet, Sisley, Renoir, Pissarro and Cézanne all visited Honfleur, often meeting at the Ferme St-Siméon, now a luxury hotel. Painters still work from Honfleur's quayside, and exhibit in the **Greniers à Sel**, two salt warehouses built in 1670. These lie to the east of the Vieux Bassin in an area known as l'Enclos, which made up the fortified heart of the town in the 13th century.

The **Musée d'Ethnographie et d'Art Populaire Normand** displays mementos of Honfleur's nautical past, with a warren of Norman interiors next door in the former prison. Place Ste-Catherine has an unusual 15th-century church built by ship's carpenters. The **Musée Eugène-Boudin** documents the artistic appeal of Honfleur and the Seine estuary, with works from Boudin to Raoul Dufy. **Les Maisons Satie** use extracts from Satie's music to guide you round reconstructions of the rooms.

Greniers à Sel
Rue de la Ville. 02 31 89 23 30. **Open** for guided tours & exhibitions. obligatory, except during summer exhibs (contact the tourist office for details).

Musée d'Ethnographie et d'Art Populaire Normand
Quai St-Etienne. **Tel** 02 31 89 14 12. **Open** mid-Feb–Mar, Oct–Nov: Tue–Fri (pms only), Sat, Sun; Apr–Sep: Tue–Sun. **Closed** 1 May, 14 Jul.

Musée Eugène-Boudin
Pl Erik Satie, rue de l'Homme de Bois. **Tel** 02 31 89 54 00. **Open** mid-Mar–Sep: Wed–Mon; mid-Feb–mid-Mar & Oct–Dec: Tue–Fri pms, Sat & Sun.

Les Maisons Satie
67 bd Charles V. **Tel** 02 31 89 11 11. **Open** mid-Feb–Dec: Wed–Mon. **Closed** public hols.

Quai St-Etienne in Honfleur

⓯ Le Havre

Seine-Maritime. 195,000. 186 bd Clemenceau (02 32 74 04 04). daily. **lehavretourisme.com**

Strategically positioned on the Seine estuary, Le Havre (The Harbour) was created in 1517 by François I after the nearby port of Harfleur silted up. During World War II it was virtually obliterated by Allied bombing, but despite a vast industrial zone, which stands beside the port it still has appeal. It is an important yachting centre, and its beach has two blue flags (very clean).

Much of the city centre was rebuilt in the 1950s–60s by Auguste Perret, whose towering **Eglise St-Joseph** (a UNESCO World Heritage Site) pierces the skyline. On the seafront, the **Musée Malraux** has works by, amongst others, local artist Raoul Dufy. France's biggest skateboard park is also on the seafront.

Musée Malraux
2 bd Clemenceau. **Tel** 02 35 19 62 62. **Open** Tue–Sun. **Closed** public hols. **muma-lehavre.fr**

⓰ Côte d'Albâtre

Seine-Maritime. Pont Jehan Ango, Dieppe (02 32 14 40 60). **dieppetourisme.com**

The Alabaster Coast gets its name from the chalky cliffs and milky waters that characterize the Normandy coastline between Le Havre and Le Tréport. It is best known for the **Falaise d'Aval**, west of **Etretat**, eroded into an arch. The author Guy de Maupassant, born near Dieppe in 1850, compared these cliffs to an elephant dipping its trunk into the sea. From Etretat, a chain of coastal roads runs east across a switchback of breezy headlands and wooded valleys to Dieppe.

Fécamp is the only major town along this route. Its Benedictine abbey was once an important pilgrimage centre after a tree trunk said to contain drops of Christ's blood was washed ashore here in the 7th century. This is enshrined in a reliquary at the entrance to the Lady Chapel of the abbey church, La Trinité.

The vast **Palais Bénédictine** is a Neo-Gothic and Renaissance homage to the ego of Alexander Le Grand, a local wine and spirits merchant who rediscovered the monks' recipe for Bénédictine, the famous herbal liqueur. Built in 1882, it incorporates a distillery and an

Woman with Parasol (1880) by Boudin in the Musée Eugène-Boudin

For hotels and restaurants in this region see pp559–60 and pp583–5

The cliffs at Falaise d'Aval, famously likened to an elephant dipping its trunk into the sea

eccentric museum packed with curios. The adjacent halls provide an aromatic account and tastings of the 27 herbs and spices that make up the elixir.

Palais Bénédictine
110 rue Alexandre Le Grand, Fécamp. **Tel** 02 35 10 26 10. **Open** daily. **Closed** Jan–mid-Feb, 1 May, 25 Dec.

View of Dieppe from the château and museum above the town

17 Dieppe

Seine-Maritime. 36,000. Pont Jean Ango (02 32 14 40 60). Tue, Thu & esp. Sat.
dieppetourisme.com

Dieppe exploits a break in the chalky cliffs bordering the Pays de Caux, and has won historical prestige as a Channel fort, port and resort. Prosperity came during the 16th and 17th centuries, when local privateer Jehan Ango raided the Portuguese and English fleets, and a trading post called Petit Dieppe was founded on the West African coast. At that time, Dieppe's population was already 30,000, and included a 300-strong community of craftsmen carving imported ivory. This maritime past is celebrated in **Le Château-Musée**, the 15th-century castle crowning the headland to the west of the seafront. Here you can see historical maps and model ships, a collection of Dieppe ivories, and paintings that evoke the town's development as a fashionable seaside resort during the 19th century. Dieppe had the nearest beach to Paris and quickly responded to the developing passion for promenading, seawater cures and bathing.

Today Dieppe's broad seafront is given over to lawns, seaside amusements and car parks, and its liveliest streets surround the battle-scarred **Eglise St-Jacques** to the south. If the weather is poor, visit **L'Estran-La Cité de la Mer**, an exhibition centre with models on maritime themes, and an aquarium.

Le Château-Musée
Tel 02 35 06 61 99. **Open** Wed–Mon. **Closed** 1 Jan,1 May, 1 Nov, 25 Dec.

L'Estran-La Cité de la Mer
37 rue de l'Asile Thomas. **Tel** 02 35 06 93 20. **Open** daily. **Closed** 1 Jan, 25 Dec.

18 Basse-Seine

Seine-Maritime & Eure. Le Havre, Rouen. Yvetot. Le Havre. Yvetot (02 32 70 99 96).

Meandering seaward from Rouen to Le Havre, the River Seine is crossed by three spectacular road bridges: the Pont de Brotonne, the Pont de Tancarville and the Pont de Normandie (linking Le Havre and Honfleur). The grace and daring of these modern bridges echo the soaring aspirations of the abbeys founded on the river's banks in the 7th and 8th centuries. The abbeys now provide good stepping stones for a tour of the Lower Seine valley.

West of Rouen is the harmonious Eglise de St-Georges at **St-Martin-de-Boscherville**, which until the Revolution was the church of a small walled abbey. Its 12th-century chapter-house has remarkable biblical statues and carved capitals. From here the D67 runs south to the riverside village of La Bouille.

As you head northwest, an hourly car ferry at Mesnil-sous-Jumièges takes you over to the colossal ruins of the **Abbaye de Jumièges**. The abbey was founded in 654 and once housed 900 monks and 1,500 servants. The main abbey church dates from the 11th century; its consecration in 1067 was a major event, with William the Conqueror in attendance.

The D913 strikes through oak and beech woods in the Parc Régional de Brotonne to the Benedictine **Abbaye de St-Wandrille**, founded in the 7th century. The Musée de la Marine de Seine at **Caudebec-en-Caux** gives an engrossing account of many aspects of life on this great river since the late 19th century.

Monk from Abbaye de St-Wandrille

⑲ Rouen

Founded at the lowest point where the Seine could be bridged, Rouen has prospered through maritime trade and industrialization to become a rich and cultured city. Despite the severe damage of World War II, the city boasts a wealth of historic sights on its right bank, all within walking distance of the central Cathédrale Notre-Dame, frequently painted by Monet.

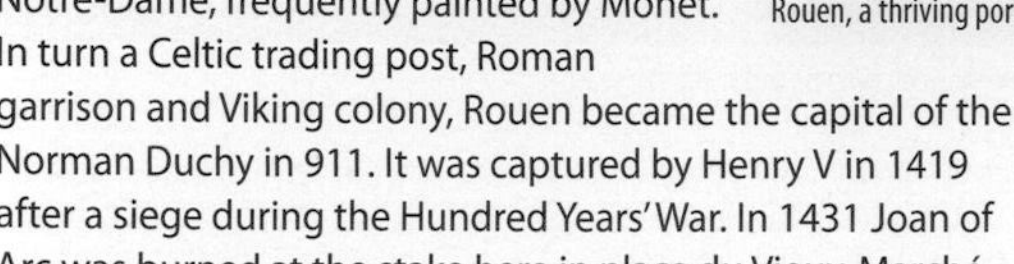

In turn a Celtic trading post, Roman garrison and Viking colony, Rouen became the capital of the Norman Duchy in 911. It was captured by Henry V in 1419 after a siege during the Hundred Years' War. In 1431 Joan of Arc was burned at the stake here in place du Vieux-Marché.

Rouen, a thriving port on the River Seine

Exploring Rouen

From **place du Vieux Marché** and the 1979 **Eglise Ste-Jeanne-d'Arc,** rue du **Gros Horloge** runs east under the city's Great Clock. Rue aux Juifs leads past the 15th-century Gothic **Palais de Justice**, once Normandy's parliament, to the smart shops and cafés around rue des Carmes. Further east, between the St-Maclou and St-Ouen churches, are half-timbered houses in rue Damiette and rue Eau de Robec.

Cathédrale Notre-Dame

Jun–Sep: Sound and light show.

This Gothic masterpiece is dominated by the famous west façade *(see p271)*, painted by Monet, and framed by two unequal towers – the northern Tour St-Romain, and the later Tour du Beurre, supposedly paid for by a tax on butter consumption in Lent. Above the central lantern tower rises a Neo-Gothic cast iron spire, erected in 1876. Both the 14th-century northern Portail des Libraires and southern Portail de la Calende stand out for their precise sculpting and delicate tracery. Many of the cathedral's riches are accessible by guided tour only, including the tomb of Richard the Lionheart, whose heart was buried here, and the rare 11th-century semi-circular hall crypt, rediscovered in 1934.

Cathédrale Notre-Dame, Rouen

Historial Jeanne d'Arc

7 rue Saint Romain. **Tel** 02 35 52 48 00. **Open** Tue–Sun. **Closed** public hols. **historial-jeannedarc.fr**

Mulitmedia displays trace the story of Joan of Arc at this museum in the former archbishop's palace where she was sentenced.

Sights at a Glance

① Place du Vieux Marché
② Gros Horloge
③ Palais de Justice
④ Cathédrale Notre-Dame
⑤ Historial Jeanne d'Arc
⑥ Eglise St-Maclou
⑦ Aître St-Maclou
⑧ Eglise St-Ouen
⑨ Hôtel de Ville
⑩ Musée le Secq des Tournelles
⑪ Musée des Beaux-Arts
⑫ Musée de la Céramique
⑬ Musée d'Histoire Naturelle

Eglise St-Maclou

This Flamboyant Gothic church has an intensively decorated west façade with a five-bay porch and carved wooden doors depicting biblical scenes. Behind the church, the **Aitre St-Maclou**, or ossuary, is a rare surviving example of a medieval cemetery for the burial of plague victims. The timbers of its buildings, set around the quadrangle, are carved with a macabre array of grinning skulls, crossed bones, coffins and gravediggers' implements.

Eglise St-Ouen

Once part of a formadable Benedictine abbey, St-Ouen is a solid Gothic church with a lofty, unadorned interior made all the more beautiful by its restored 14th- century stained glass. Next to the church is the 18th-century **Hôtel de Ville**.

Musée Le Secq des Tournelles

Rue Jacques-Villon. **Tel** 02 35 88 42 92. **Open** Wed–Mon pms. **Closed** public hols. ground floor only.

Located in a 15th-century church, this wrought-ironwork museum exhibits antique iron-mongery ranging from keys to corkscrews and Gallo-Roman spoons to mighty tavern signs.

Musée des Beaux-Arts

Square Verdrel. **Tel** 02 35 71 28 40. **Open** Wed–Mon. **Closed** some public hols.

The city's collection includes major art works: masterpieces by Caravaggio and Velázquez, and paintings by Normandy-born artists Théodore Géricault, Eugène Boudin and Raoul Dufy. Also on display is Monet's *Rouen Cathedral, The Portal, Grey Weather*.

VISITORS' CHECKLIST

Practical Information
Seine Maritime. 110,000. 25 pl de la Cathédrale (02 32 08 32 40). Tue–Sun. Feast of Joan of Arc (late May).
rouentourisme.com

Transport
11 km (7 miles) SE of Rouen. gare Rive Droite, pl Bernard Tissot (08 92 35 35 35). 25 rue des Charrettes. **Tel** 02 35 52 52 52.

Musée de la Céramique

Hôtel d'Hocqueville,1 rue Faucon. **Tel** 02 35 07 31 74. **Open** Wed–Mon pms. **Closed** public hols.

Exhibits of 1,000 pieces of Rouen faïence – colourful glazed earthenware – together with other pieces of French and foreign china are displayed in a 17th-century town house. The works trace the history of Rouen faïence to its zenith in the 18th century.

Musée d'Histoire Naturelle

198 rue Beauvoisine. **Tel** 02 35 71 41 50. **Open** Tue–Sun pms. **Closed** public hols.

The second-largest museum of its kind in France, this museum holds more than 800,000 objects.

Musée Flaubert

51 rue de Lecat. **Tel** 02 35 15 59 95. **Open** Tue & Wed–Sat pm. **Closed** public hols.

Flaubert's father was a surgeon at Rouen Hospital, and his family home combines memorabilia with an awesome – and occasionally gruesome – display of 17th- to 19th-century medical equipment.

Gustave Flaubert

The novelist Gustave Flaubert (1821–80) was born and raised in Rouen, and the city provides the backdrop for some memorable scenes in his masterpiece, *Madame Bovary*. Published in 1856–7, this realistic study of a country doctor's wife driven to despair by her love affairs provoked a scandal that made Flaubert's name. His famous stuffed green parrot, which can be seen in the Musée Flaubert, was always perched on his writing desk.

Flaubert's stuffed parrot

For keys to symbols *see back flap*

Château Gaillard and the village of Les Andelys, in a loop of the River Seine

⑳ Haute-Seine

Eure. Rouen. Vernon, Val de Reuil. Gisors, Les Andelys. Les Andelys (02 32 54 41 93). **lesandelys-tourisme.fr**

Southeast of Rouen, the river Seine follows a convoluted course, with most points of interest on its north bank. At the centre of the Forêt de Lyons, once the hunting ground for the dukes of Normandy, is the country town of **Lyons-la-Forêt**, with half-timbered houses and an 18th-century covered market.

To the south the D313 follows the gracefully curving Seine to the town of **Les Andelys**. Above it tower the ruins of Château Gaillard, which Richard the Lionheart, as King of England and Duke of Normandy, built in 1197 to defend Rouen from the French. They eventually took the castle in 1204.

㉑ Giverny

Eure. 600. 80 rue Claude Monet, Giverny 27620 (02 32 64 45 01). **normandie-giverny.fr**

In 1883 the Impressionist painter Claude Monet rented a house in the small village of Giverny, and worked here until his death. The house, known as the **Fondation Claude Monet**, and its garden are open to the public. The house is decorated in the colour schemes that Monet admired; the glorious gardens are famous as the subject of some of the artist's studies. Only copies are on show, but there are outstanding original 19th- and 20th-century artworks in the **Musée des Impressionnismes** nearby.

Fondation Claude Monet
Giverny, Gasny. **Tel** 02 32 51 28 21. **Open** Apr–Oct: daily.
fondation-monet.com

Musée des Impressionnismes
99 rue Claude Monet, Giverny. **Tel** 02 32 51 94 65. **Open** daily.

㉒ Evreux

Eure. 55,000. 1ter pl du Général de Gaulle (02 32 24 04 43). Wed & Sat. **grandevreuxtourisme.fr**

Though considerably damaged in the war, Evreux is a pleasant cathedral town set in wide, agricultural plains. At its heart, the **Cathédrale Notre-Dame** is renowned for its 14th- to 15th-century stained glass. The building is predominantly Gothic, though Romanesque arches survive in the nave, and Renaissance screens adorn its chapels. Next door, the former Bishop's Palace houses the **Musée de l'Ancien Evêché**, with Roman bronze statues of Jupiter and Apollo and fine 18th-century furniture and decorative art.

Monet's garden at Giverny, restored to its original profuse glory

For hotels and restaurants in this region see pp559–60 and pp583–5

Monet's Cathedral Series

In the 1890s Claude Monet made almost 30 paintings of Rouen's cathedral, several of which are now in the Musée d'Orsay in Paris *(see pp124–5)*. He studied the effects of changing light on its façades, and described both the surface detail and huge bulk, putting colour before contour. The archetypal Impressionist, Monet said he conceived this series when he watched the effects of light on a country church, "as the sun's rays slowly dissolved the mists… that wrapped the golden stone in an ideally vaporous envelope".

Harmony in Blue and Gold (1894)

Monet selected a close vantage point for the series and was keen on this southwest view. The sun would cast afternoon shadows across the carved west front, accentuating the cavernous portals and the large rose window.

Monet's sketch, one of many of Rouen, parallels the shimmering effect of the paintings.

Harmony in Brown (1894) is the only finished version of a frontal view of the west façade. Analysis has shown that it was begun as a southwest view like the others.

Harmony in Blue (1894), compared with Harmony in Blue and Gold, shows the stone of the west façade further softened by the diffuse light of a misty morning.

The Portal, Grey Weather (1894) was one of several canvases in the grey colour group, which showed the cathedral façade in the soft light of an overcast day.

BRITTANY

Finistère · Côtes-d'Armor · Morbihan · Ille-et-Vilaine

Jutting defiantly into the Atlantic, France's northwest corner has long been culturally and geographically distinct from the main bulk of the country. It was known to the Celts as Armorica, the land of the sea, and Brittany's past swirls with the legends of drowned cities and Arthurian forests. Prehistoric megaliths arise mysteriously from land and sea, and the medieval is never far from the modern.

A long, jagged coastline is the region's great attraction. Magnificent beaches line its northern shore, swept clean by huge tides and interspersed with well-established seaside resorts, seasoned fishing ports and abundant oysterbeds. The south coast is gentler, with wooded river valleys and a milder climate, while the west, being exposed to the Atlantic winds, has a drama that justifies the name Finistère – the End of the Earth.

Inland lies the Argoat – once the Land of the Forest, now a patchwork of undulating fields, woods and rolling moorland. The Parc Naturel Régional d'Armorique occupies much of central Finistère, and it is in western Brittany that Breton culture remains most evident. In Quimper, and in the Pays Bigouden, crêpes and cider, traditional costumes, and Celtic music are still a genuine part of the Breton lifestyle. Eastern Brittany has a more conventional appeal. Vannes, Dinan and Rennes, the Breton capital, have well-preserved medieval quarters, where half-timbered buildings shelter inviting markets, shops, *crêperies* and restaurants. The walled port of St-Malo on the Côte d'Emeraude recalls the region's maritime prowess, while the remarkably intact castles at Fougères and Vitré are reminders of the mighty border-fortresses that protected Brittany's eastern frontier before its final union with France in 1532.

Fort la Latte, a medieval castle, offers spectacular views of the Côte d'Emeraude

◀ The sun sets over the dramatic coastline at the Pointe du Raz

Exploring Brittany

Ideal for a seaside holiday, Brittany offers enjoyable drives along the headlands and beaches of the northern Côte d'Emeraude and Côte de Granit Rose, while the south coast boasts wooded valleys and the prehistoric sites of Carnac and the Golfe du Morbihan. The parish closes *(see pp280–81)* provide intriguing insight into Breton culture, as does the cathedral town of Quimper. Be sure to visit the regional capital, Rennes, and the great castle at Fougères, and in summer take a boat trip to one of Brittany's islands.

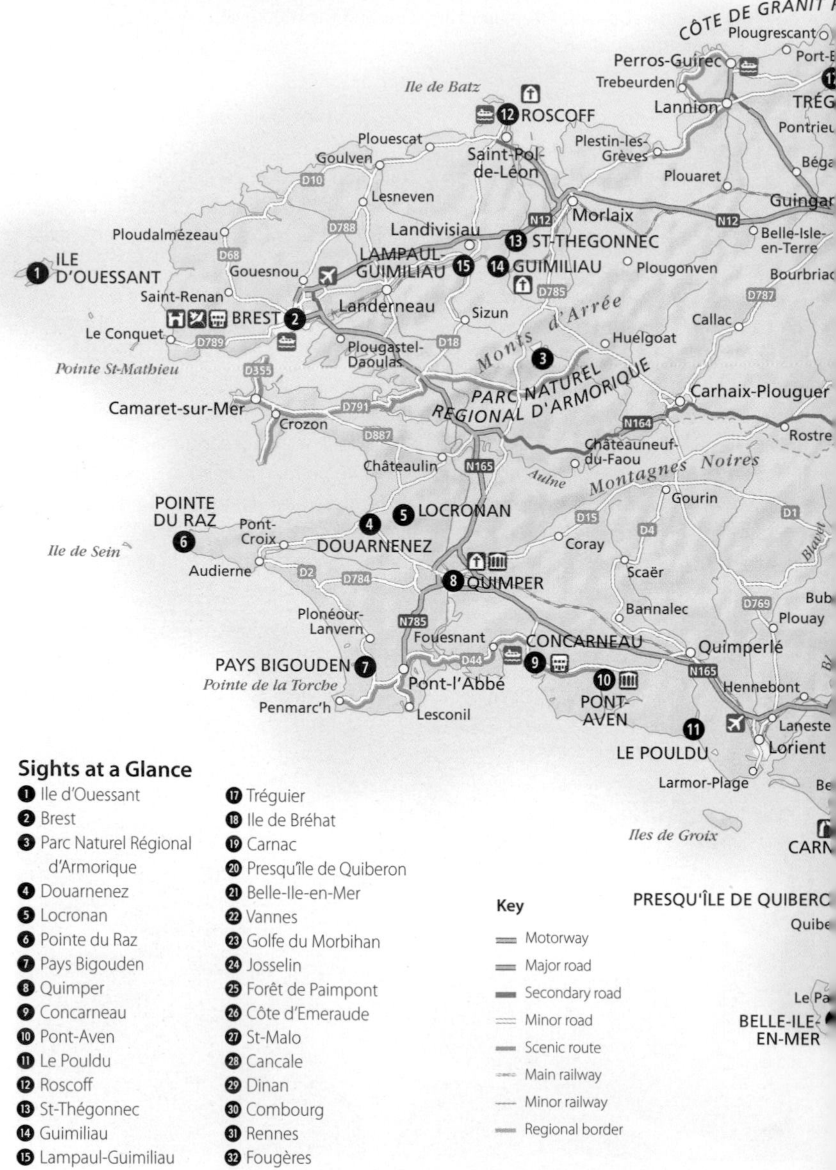

Sights at a Glance

1 Ile d'Ouessant
2 Brest
3 Parc Naturel Régional d'Armorique
4 Douarnenez
5 Locronan
6 Pointe du Raz
7 Pays Bigouden
8 Quimper
9 Concarneau
10 Pont-Aven
11 Le Pouldu
12 Roscoff
13 St-Thégonnec
14 Guimiliau
15 Lampaul-Guimiliau
16 Côte de Granit Rose
17 Tréguier
18 Ile de Bréhat
19 Carnac
20 Presqu'île de Quiberon
21 Belle-Ile-en-Mer
22 Vannes
23 Golfe du Morbihan
24 Josselin
25 Forêt de Paimpont
26 Côte d'Emeraude
27 St-Malo
28 Cancale
29 Dinan
30 Combourg
31 Rennes
32 Fougères
33 Vitré

For keys to symbols *see back flap*

Lighthouse on the Île de Bréhat, Côte de Granit Rose

Getting Around

Expressways N12/N165 encircle Brittany, giving easy access to coastal areas, while the N12 and N24 give direct access to Rennes, Brittany's capital. Brittany can be reached by air to Brest, Nantes, Rennes and Dinard airports, by Channel ferries to St-Malo and Roscoff, by *autoroutes* from Normandy, the Loire and the A11 from Paris, or by TGV direct from Paris and Lille.

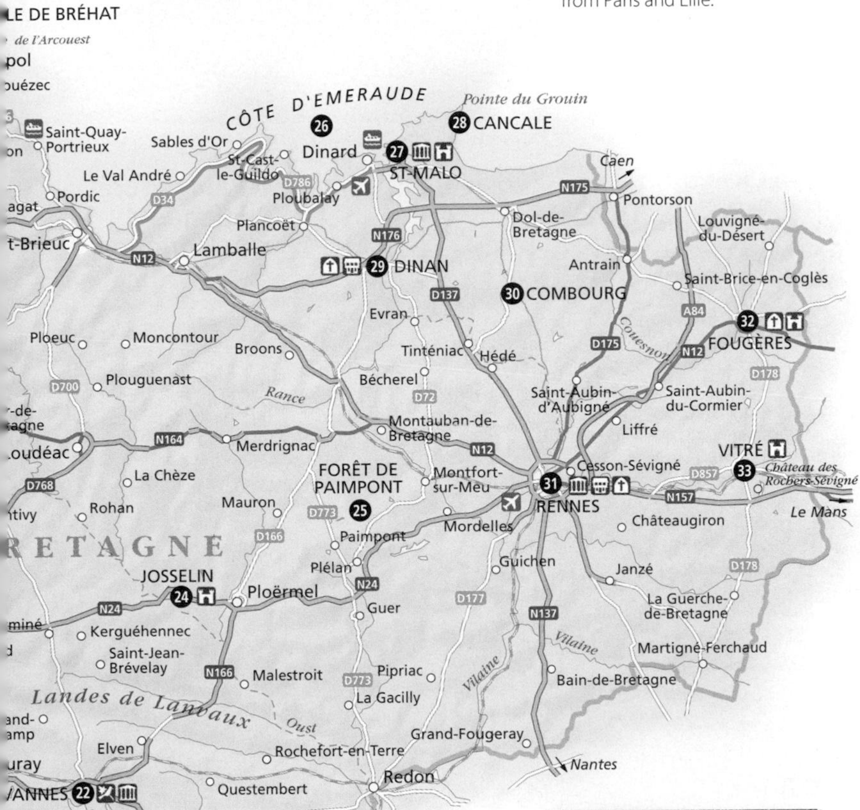

Half-timbered houses in the medieval part of Rennes

❶ Ile d'Ouessant

Finistère. 900. Ouessant (via Brest). Brest, then boat. Le Conquet, then boat. pl de l'Eglise, Lampaul (02 98 48 85 83). **ot-ouessant.fr**

A well-known Breton proverb declares "He who sees Ouessant sees his own blood". Also known as Ushant, the island is notorious among sailors for its fierce storms and strong currents. However, this westerly point of France has a pleasant climate in summer and, though often bleak and stormy, can be surprisingly mild in winter. Part of the Parc Naturel Régional d'Armorique, the windswept island supports migrating birds and a small seal population, which may be observed from the Pern and Pen-ar-Roc'h headlands.

Two museums shed light on the island's defiant history, dogged by shipwreck and tragedy. At Niou Uhella, the **Ecomusée du Niou** has furniture made from driftwood and wrecks, often painted blue and white in honour of the Virgin Mary. Nearby at Phare du Créac'h, the **Musée des Phares et Balises** explains the history of Brittany's many lighthouses and their keepers.

Ecomusée du Niou
Maison du Niou. **Tel** 02 98 48 86 37. **Open** Apr–Sep: daily; Oct–Mar: Tue–Sun pms.

Musée des Phares et Balises
Pointe de Créac'h. **Tel** 02 98 48 80 70. **Open** Apr–Sep: daily; Oct–Mar: Tue–Sun pms.

❷ Brest

Finistère. 155,000. to islands only. 8 av Georges Clemenceau (02 98 44 24 96). daily. **brest-metropole-tourisme.fr**

A natural harbour, protected by the Presqu'île de Crozon, Brest is France's premier Atlantic naval port, with a rich maritime history. Heavily bombed during World War II, it is now a modern commercial city, where cargo vessels, yachts and fishing boats ply the waters. The Cours Dajot promenade has good views of the Rade de Brest (Bay of Brest).

Windswept moorlands near Ménez-Meur, Parc Naturel Régional d'Armorique

The **Château** houses a naval museum with historic maps, maritime paintings, model ships, carved wooden figureheads and nautical instruments.

Across the Penfeld river – reached by Europe's largest lifting bridge, Pont de Revouvrance – is the 14th- century **Tour de la Motte Tanguy**. By the Port de Plaisance, **Océanopolis** "sea centre" has three vast pavilions simulating temperate, tropical and polar ecosystems.

Château de Brest
Tel 02 98 22 12 39. **Open** Feb–Mar & Oct–Dec: Wed–Mon pms only; Apr–Sep: daily. **Closed** 1 May, 25 Dec.

Tour de la Motte Tanguy
Sq Pierre Peron. **Tel** 02 98 00 87 93. **Open** Jun–Sep: daily; Oct–May: Mon, Wed–Thu pm, Sat–Sun pms. **Closed** 1 Jan, 1 May, 25 Dec.

Océanopolis
Port de Plaisance du Moulin Blanc. **Tel** 02 98 34 40 40. **Open** Apr–mid-Sep: daily; mid-Sep–Mar: Tue–Sun. **Closed** 3 wks Jan, 25 Dec. **oceanopolis.com**

The 14th-century Tour de la Motte Tanguy, housing a museum on the history of Brest

❸ Parc Naturel Régional d'Armorique

Finistère. Brest. Chateaulin, Landernau. Le Faou, Huelgoat, Carhaix. Le Faou (02 98 81 90 08). **pnr-armorique.fr**

The Armorican Regional Nature Park stretches west from the moorlands of the Monts d'Arrée to the Presqu'île de Crozon and Ile d'Ouessant. Within this protected area lies a mixture of farmland, heaths, remains of ancient oak forest and wild, open spaces. The park and its scenic coastline is ideal for walking, riding and touring by bicycle or car.

Huelgoat is a good starting point for inland walks, while **Ménez-Hom** (330 m/1,082 ft), at the start of the Crozon Peninsula, has excellent views. The main park information centre is at **Le Faou**. Nearby at **Ménez-Meur** is a wooded estate with wild and farm animals, and a Breton horse museum. Scattered around the park are 16 small specialist museums, some paying tribute to country traditions such as hunting, fishing and tanning. The **Musée de l'Ecole Rurale** (open Feb–Oct) at Trégarvan re-creates an early 20th-century rural school. Other museums cover subjects such as medieval monastic life, rag-and-bone men and the lifestyle of a Breton country priest. The **Ferme d'Antéa** in Brasparts displays contemporary crafts and art.

For hotels and restaurants in this region see pp560–61 and pp585–6

❹ Douarnenez

Finistère. 17,000. 2 rue du Docteur Mével (02 98 92 13 35). Mon–Sat. **douarnenez-tourisme.com**

At the start of the 20th century Douarnenez used to be France's leading sardine port; today it is still devoted to fishing, but is also a tourist resort with beaches on both sides of the Pouldavid estuary.

Nearby lies the tiny **Ile Tristan**, linked with the tragic love story of Tristan and Iseult. In the 16th century it was the stronghold of a notorious brigand, La Fontenelle.

The picturesque **Port du Rosmeur** offers cafés, fish restaurants and boat trips around the bay, with a lively early morning *criée* (fish auction) held in the nearby Nouveau Port. The Port-Rhu has been turned into a floating museum, **Le Port Musée**, with over 100 boats and several shipyards. Some of the larger vessels can be visited.

Le Port Musée
Pl de l'Enfer. **Tel** 02 98 92 65 20. **Open** Jul–Aug: daily; Feb–Jun & Sep–Oct: Tue–Sun. **port-musee.org**

Locronan's 15th-century Eglise St-Ronan, seen from the churchyard

❺ Locronan

Finistère. 1,000. pl de la Mairie (02 98 91 70 14). **locronan-tourisme.com**

During the 15th–17th centuries Locronan grew wealthy from the manufacture of sailcloth. After Louis XIV ended the Breton monopoly on this trade, the town declined – leaving an elegant ensemble of Renaissance buildings that attract many visitors. In the town's central cobbled square stands a late 15th-century church dedicated to the Irish missionary St-Ronan. Down Rue Moal is the delightful **Chapelle Notre-Dame-de-Bonne-Nouvelle**, with a calvary and a fountain. Every July Locronan is the scene of a *Troménie,* a hilltop pilgrimage held in honour of St Ronan. The more elaborate *Grande Troménie* takes place every six years.

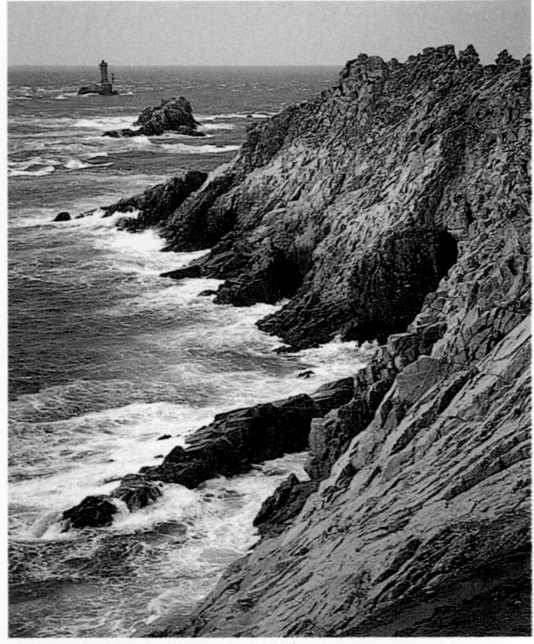

The awe-inspiring cliffs of Pointe du Raz

❻ Pointe du Raz

Finistère. Quimper. Quimper, then bus. Audierne (02 98 70 12 20); Maison du Site (02 98 70 67 18). **pointeduraz.com**

The dramatic Pointe du Raz, almost 80 m (262 ft) high, is a headland jutting into the Atlantic at the tip of Cap Sizun. The views of jagged rocks and pounding seas are breathtaking. Further west is the flat Ile de Sein and beyond that the lighthouse of Ar Men. Despite being only 1.5 m (5 ft) above sea level, Ile de Sein is nevertheless home to 260 inhabitants, and can be reached by boat from Audierne in an hour.

❼ Pays Bigouden

Finistère. Pont l'Abbé. Pont l'Abbé (02 98 82 37 99). **ot-pontlabbe29.fr**

Brittany's southwest tip is known as the Pays Bigouden, a windy peninsula with proud and ancient traditions. The region is famous for the women's tall *coiffes* still worn at festivals and *pardons* *(see p247)*, which can also be seen at the **Musée Bigouden**.

Along the Baie d'Audierne is a brooding landscape of hamlets and isolated chapels – the 15th-century calvary at **Notre-Dame-de-Tronoën** is the oldest in Brittany. There are invigorating sea views from **Pointe de la Torche** (a good surfing spot) and from the **Eckmühl lighthouse**.

Musée Bigouden
Le Château, Pont l'Abbé. **Tel** 02 98 66 09 03. **Open** Apr–Jun & Sep & Oct: Tue–Sun pm only; Jul & Aug: daily. **Closed** 1 May.

❽ Quimper

Finistère. 70,000. pl de la Résistance (02 98 53 04 05). Wed, Sat. **quimper-tourisme.com**

The ancient capital of Cornouaille, Quimper has a distinctly Breton character. Here you can find Breton language books and music on sale, buy a traditional costume and tuck into some of the best *crêpes* and cider in Brittany. Quimper gets its name from *kemper*, a Breton word meaning "the confluence of two rivers", and the Steir and Odet still flow through this relaxed cathedral city.

West of the cathedral lies a pedestrianized area known as **Vieux Quimper**, full of shops, *crêperies* and half-timbered houses. Rue Kéréon is the main thoroughfare, with place au Beurre and the picturesque *hôtels particuliers* (mansions) of rue des Gentilshommes to the north.

Quimper has been producing faïence, elegant hand-painted pottery, since 1690. The design often features decorative flowers and animals framed by blue and yellow borders. Now mainly decorative, faïence is today exported to collectors all over the world. In the southwest of the city lies the oldest factory, **Faïenceries HB-Henriot**, which is open to visitors all year round.

Typical faïence plate from Quimper

Cathédrale St-Corentin

Quimper's cathedral is dedicated to the city's founder-bishop St Corentin. Begun in 1240 – its colourfully painted interior now restored – it is the earliest Gothic building in Lower Brittany, and was bizarrely constructed with its choir at a slight angle to the nave, perhaps to fit in with some since-disappeared buildings. The two spires of the west façade were added in 1856. Between them rides a statue of King Gradlon, the mythical founder of the drowned city of Ys. After this deluge he chose Quimper as his new capital and St Corentin as his spiritual guide.

View of the Harbour of Quimper (1857) by Eugène Boudin at the Museé des Beaux-Arts, Quimper

Musée des Beaux-Arts

40 pl St-Corentin. **Tel** 02 98 95 45 20. **Open** Jul–Aug: daily; Sep–Jun: Wed–Mon. **Closed** most public hols; Nov–Mar: Sun am. **mbaq.fr**

Quimper's art museum is one of the best in the region. The collection is strong on late 19th- and early 20th-century artists, and their work – such as Jean-Eugène Buland's *Visite à Ste-Marie de Bénodet*, offering a valuable insight into the way visiting painters perpetuated a romantic view of Brittany. Also on show are works by members of the Pont-Aven School and local artists such as J-J Lemordant and Max Jacob.

Musée Départemental Breton

1 rue de Roi-Gradlon. **Tel** 02 98 95 21 60. **Open** mid-Jun–mid-Sep: daily; mid-Sep–mid-Jun: Tue–Sat; Sun pm.

The 16th-century Bishop's Palace has collections of Breton costumes, furniture and faïence, including Cornouaille *coiffes*, ornately carved box-beds and wardrobes, and turn-of-the-20th-century tourist posters for Brittany.

❾ Concarneau

Finistère. 20,000. only for islands. quai d'Aiguillon (02 98 97 01 44). Mon & Fri. **tourismeconcarneau.fr**

An important fishing port, Concarneau's principal attraction is its 14th-century **Ville Close** (walled town), built on an island in the harbour and encircled by massive lichen-covered granite ramparts. Access is by bridge from place Jean Jaurès. Parts of the ramparts can be toured, and the narrow streets are full of shops and restaurants. The **Musée de la Pêche**, housed in the port's ancient barracks, explains the local techniques and history of sea-fishing.

Musée de la Pêche

3 rue Vauban. **Tel** 02 98 97 10 20. **Open** Feb, Mar, Nov & Dec: Tue–Sun pm; Apr–Jun & Sep–Oct: Tue–Sun; Jul & Aug: daily. **Closed** Jan, public hols.

Fishing boats in Concarneau's busy harbour

For hotels and restaurants in this region see pp560–61 and pp585–6

⑩ Pont-Aven

Finistère. 3,000. 5 Pl Julia (02 98 06 04 70). Tue, Sat. **pontaven.com**

Port-Avon was once a market town of "14 mills and 15 houses", but its picturesque location in the wooded Aven estuary made it attractive to many late 19th-century artists.

In 1888 Paul Gauguin, along with like-minded painters Emile Bernard and Paul Sérusier, developed a crude, colourful style of painting known as Synthetism. Drawing inspiration from the Breton landscape and its people, the Ecole de Pont-Aven (Pont-Aven School) worked here and in nearby Le Pouldu until 1896.

The town is devoted to art and has 50 private galleries, along with the informative **Musée de Pont-Aven**, which documents the achievements of the Pont-Aven School. The surrounding woods proved inspirational to many artists, and offer pleasant walks – one leads through the Bois d'Amour to the **Chapelle de Trémalo**, where the wooden Christ in Gauguin's *Le Christ Jaune* still hangs.

Musée de Pont-Aven
Place Julia. **Tel** 02 98 06 14 43. **Open** Feb, Mar, Nov & Dec: Tue–Sun pms; Apr–Jun, Sep & Oct: Tue–Sun; Jul & Aug: daily. **Closed** 1 Jan, 25 Dec.

Notre-Dame-de-Kroaz-Baz, Roscoff

⑪ Le Pouldu

Finistère. 4,000. Pl Ocean Le Pouldu, Clohars (02 98 39 93 42). **quimperle-terreoceane.com**

A quiet port at the mouth of the River Laïta, Le Pouldu has a small beach and good walks. Its main attraction is **Maison Musée du Pouldu**, a reconstruction of the inn where Paul Gauguin and other artists stayed between 1889 and 1893. They covered every inch of the dining room, including the window-panes, with self-portraits, caricatures and still-lifes. These were discovered in 1924 beneath layers of wallpaper.

Maison Musée du Pouldu
10 rue des Grands Sables. **Tel** 02 98 39 98 51. **Open** Apr–mid-Jun & mid-Sep–Nov: Sat & Sun pm; mid-Jun–mid-Sep: Tue–Sun.

⑫ Roscoff

Finistère. 3,700. Quai d'Auxerre (02 98 61 12 13). Wed. **roscoff-tourisme.com**

Roscoff is a thriving Channel port and beach resort. Signs of its wealthy sea-faring past can be found along rue Amiral Réveillère and in place Lacaze-Duthiers. The granite facades of the 16th- and 17th- century shipowners' mansions, and the weatherbeaten caravels and cannon on the **Eglise Notre-Dame-de-Kroaz-Baz**, testify to the days when Roscoff privateers were as notorious as those of St.-Malo *(see p286)*.

The famous French onion sellers (Johnnies) first crossed the Channel in 1828, selling plaited onions door to door. The **Maison des Johnnies** tells their history.

To find out more about the manufacture and taste of products made with seaweed, visit **Algoplus**. From the harbour you can take a boat trip to the peaceful **Ile de Batz**. Near Pointe de Bloscon are tropical gardens.

Maison des Johnnies
48 rue Brizeux. **Tel** 02 98 61 25 48. **Open** mid-Apr–end Apr: Thu–Sat pm; May–mid-Jun & mid-Sep–Oct: Tue–Sat pm; mid-Jun–mid-Sep: Tue, Thu–Sat & Wed pm. **Closed** Nov–mid-Apr. obligatory.

Algoplus
Zone de Bloscon. **Tel** 02 98 61 14 14. call ahead.

Paul Gauguin in Brittany

Carving, Chapelle de Trémalo

Paul Gauguin's (1848–1903) story reads like a romantic novel. At the age of 35 he left his career as a stockbroker to become a full-time painter. From 1886 to 1894 he lived and worked in Brittany, at Pont-Aven and Le Pouldu, where he painted the landscape and its people. He chose to concentrate on the intense, almost "primitive" quality of the Breton Catholic faith, attempting to convey it in his work. This is evident in *Le Christ Jaune* (The Yellow Christ), inspired by a woodcarving in the Trémalo chapel. In Gauguin's painting, the Crucifixion is a reality in the midst of the contemporary Breton landscape, rather than a remote or symbolic event. This theme recurs in many of his paintings from the period, including *Jacob Wrestling with the Angel* (1888).

Le Christ Jaune (1889) by Paul Gauguin

⓭ St-Thégonnec

Finistère. **Open** daily.

This is one of the most complete parish closes in Brittany. As you pass through its triumphal archway, the ossuary is to the left. The calvary, directly ahead, was built in 1610 and perfectly illustrates the extraordinary skills Breton sculptors developed as they worked with the local granite. Among the many animated figures surrounding the central cross, a small niche contains a statue of St Thégonnec with a cart pulled by wolves.

⓮ Guimiliau

Finistére. **Open** daily.

Almost 200 figures adorn Guimiliau's intensely decorated calvary (1581–8), many wearing 16th-century dress. Among them you can contemplate the legendary torment of Katell Gollet, a servant girl tortured by demons for stealing a consecrated wafer to please her lover.

The church is dedicated to St Miliau and has a richly decorated south porch. The baptistry's elaborate carved oak canopy dates from 1675.

Font canopy from 1675, Guimiliau

⓯ Lampaul-Guimiliau

Finistère. **Open** daily.

Entering through the monumental gate, the chapel and ossuary lie to the left, while the calvary is to the right. Here, however, it is the church that demands most attention. The interior is zealously painted and carved, including some naive scenes from the Passion depicted along the 16th-century rood-beam dividing the nave and choir.

Parish Closes

Reflecting the religious fervour of the Bretons, the Enclos Paroissiaux (parish closes) were built during the 15th–18th centuries. At that time Brittany had few urban centres but many wealthy rural settlements that profited from maritime trading and the manufacture of cloth. Grand religious monuments, some taking over 200 years to complete, were built by small villages inspired by spiritual zeal and the more earthly desire to rival their neighbours. Some of the finest parish closes lie in the Elorn Valley, linked by a well-signposted Circuit des Enclos Paroissiaux.

The enclosure, surrounded by a stone wall, is the hallowed area. By following the wall, visitors are drawn towards the triumphal arch, shown here in Pleyben.

The small cemetery reflects the size of the community that built these great churches.

Guimiliau Parish Close

The three essential features of a parish close are a triumphal gateway marking the entry into the hallowed enclosure, a calvary depicting scenes from the Passion and Crucifixion, and an ossuary beside the church porch.

The calvary is unique to Brittany, and may have been inspired by the crosses set on top of menhirs *(see p283)* by the early Christians. They provide a walk-around Bible lesson, often with the characters in 17th-century costumes as in this example from St-Thégonnec.

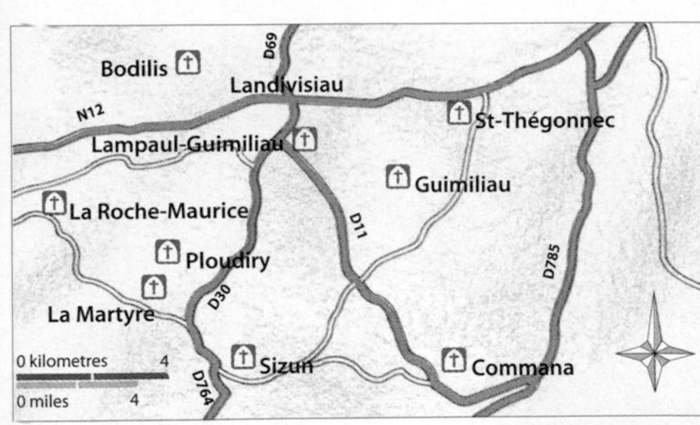

Brittany's parish closes are mostly in the Elorn Valley. As well as St-Thégonnec, Lampaul-Guimiliau and Guimiliau, other parish closes to visit include Bodilis, La Martyre, La Roche-Maurice, Ploudiry, Sizun and Commana. Further afield lie Plougastel-Daoulas and Pleyben, while Guéhenno is in the Morbihan region. i rue de Kerven, Landivisiau (02 98 68 33 33).

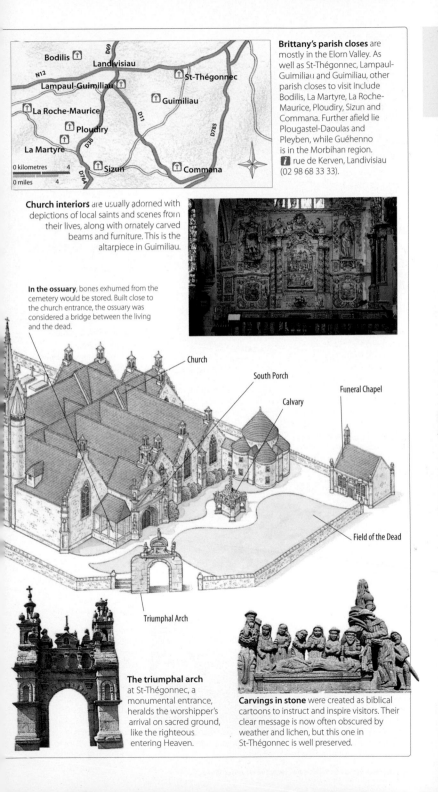

Church interiors are usually adorned with depictions of local saints and scenes from their lives, along with ornately carved beams and furniture. This is the altarpiece in Guimiliau.

In the ossuary, bones exhumed from the cemetery would be stored. Built close to the church entrance, the ossuary was considered a bridge between the living and the dead.

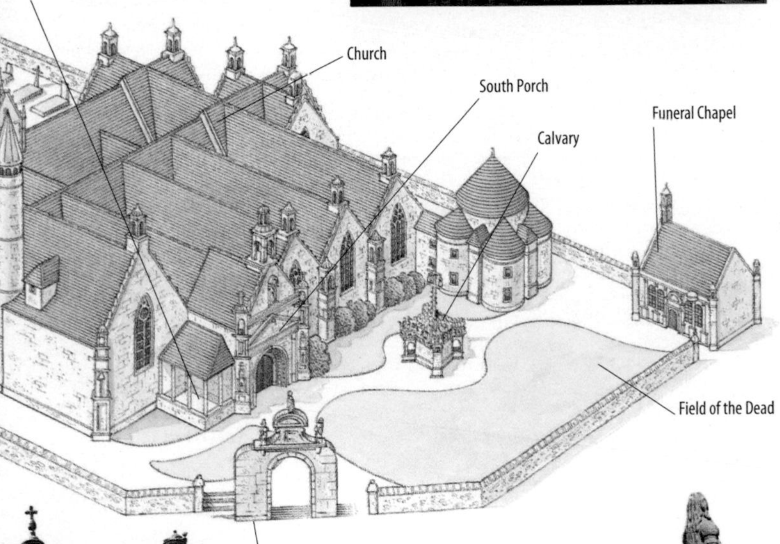

The triumphal arch at St-Thégonnec, a monumental entrance, heralds the worshipper's arrival on sacred ground, like the righteous entering Heaven.

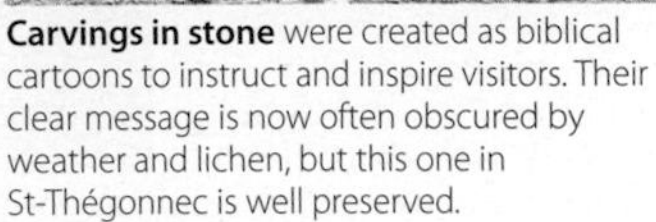

Carvings in stone were created as biblical cartoons to instruct and inspire visitors. Their clear message is now often obscured by weather and lichen, but this one in St-Thégonnec is well preserved.

The chapel of Notre-Dame, perched on the cliffs above the beach of Port-Blanc, Côte de Granit Rose

⓰ Côte de Granit Rose

Côtes d'Armor. Lannion. Lannion (02 96 05 60 70). Thu. **bretagne-cotedegranitrose.com**

The coast between Paimpol and Trébeurden is known as the Côte de Granit Rose due to its pink cliffs. These are best between Trégastel and Trébeurden; their granite is also used in neighbouring towns. The coast between Trébeurden and Perros-Guirec is one of Brittany's most popular family holiday areas.

Further east there are quieter beaches and coves, as at **Trévou-Tréguignec** and **Port-Blanc**. Beyond Tréguier, **Paimpol** is a working fishing port that once sent huge cod and whaling fleets to fish off Iceland and Newfoundland.

⓱ Tréguier

Côtes d'Armor. 3,000. Port de Plaisance (02 96 92 22 33). Wed. **tregor-cotedajoncs-tourisme.com**

Overlooking the estuary of the Jaundy and Guindy rivers, Tréguier stands apart from the resorts of the Côte de Granit Rose. It is a typically Breton market town, with one main attraction, the 14th- to 15th-century **Cathédrale St-Tugdual**. It has three towers: one Gothic, one Romanesque and one 18th century. The last, financed by Louis XVI with winnings from the Paris Lottery, has holes in the shapes of playing-card suits.

Environs

Chapelle St-Gonery in Plougrescant has a leaning lead spire and a 15th-century painted wooden ceiling.

⓲ Ile de Bréhat

Côtes d'Armor. 420. Paimpol, then bus to Pointe de l'Arcouest (Mon–Sat winter; daily summer), then boat. Office de tourisme de l'île de Bréhat (02 96 20 04 15). **brehat-infos.fr**

A 15-minute crossing from the Pointe de l'Arcouest, the Île de Bréhat is actually two islands, joined by a bridge, which together are only 3.5 km (2 miles) long. With motorized traffic banned, and a climate mild enough for mimosa and a variety of fruit trees to flourish, it has a relaxing atmosphere. Bicycle hire and boat tours are available in the main town, **Port-Clos**, and you can walk to the island's highest point, the **Chapelle St-Michel**.

Chapelle St-Michel, a landmark on Île de Bréhat

⓳ Carnac

Morbihan. 4,600. 74 avenue des Druides (02 97 52 13 52). **ot-carnac.fr**

Carnac, a popular seaside resort, is also one of the world's great prehistoric sites, with almost 3,000 menhirs in parallel rows, and an excellent **Musée de Préhistoire**.

The 17th-century **Eglise St-Cornély** is dedicated to St Cornelius, patron saint of horned animals. His life is depicted on its ceiling.

Maison des Megaliths
Tel 02 97 52 29 81. **Open** daily. **Closed** 1 Jan, 1 May, 25 Dec.

Musée de Préhistoire
10 pl de la Chapelle. **Tel** 02 97 52 22 04. **Open** Apr–Oct: Wed–Mon(Jul & Aug: daily); Mar & Nov: Wed–Mon pms only. **Closed** Jan, 1 May, Dec.

⓴ Presqu'île de Quiberon

Morbihan. 5,000. Quiberon (via Lorient). Jul–Aug. Quiberon. Quiberon (02 97 50 07 84). Sat, Wed (summer). **quiberon.com**

Once an Island, the slender Quiberon peninsula has a bleak west coast with sea-punished cliffs, known as the Côte Sauvage. The east is more benign. At the peninsula's southern tip is the fishing port and resort of **Quiberon**, with a car ferry to Belle-Ile. In 1795, 10,000 Royalist troops were massacred here in an ill-fated attempt to reverse the French Revolution.

For hotels and restaurants in this region see pp560–61 and pp585–6

Brittany's Prehistoric Monuments

At Carnac, thousands of ancient granite rocks were arranged in mysterious lines and patterns by Megalithic tribes as early as 4000 BC. Their original purpose remains obscure: the significance was probably religious, but the precise patterns also suggest an early astronomical calendar. Celts, Romans and Christians have since adapted them to their own beliefs.

The Gavrinis Tumulus, Golfe du Morbihan

Megaliths

There are many different formations of megaliths, all with a particular purpose. Words from the Breton language, such as men *(stone),* dole *(table) and* hir *(long), are still used to describe them.*

Menhirs, the most common megaliths, are upright stones, standing alone or arranged in lines. Those in circles are known as cromlechs.

Dolmen, two upright stones roofed by a third, were used as a burial chamber, such as the Merchant's Table at Locmariaquer.

Allée couverte, upright stones placed in a row and roofed to form a covered alley, can be seen at Carnac.

A tumulus is a dolmen covered with stones and soil to form a burial mound.

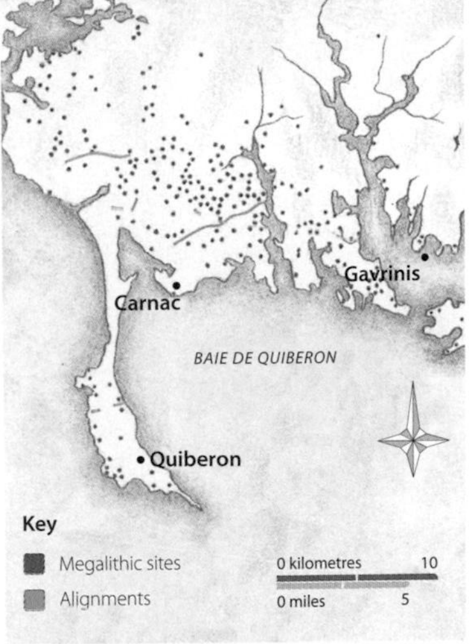

Brittany's major megalithic sites

Alignment at Carnac

Menhirs of all shapes in a field near Carnac

21 Belle-Ile-en-Mer

Morbihan. 5,000. Quiberon (via Lorient). from Quiberon. quai Bonnelle, Le Palais (02 97 31 81 93). daily. **belle-ile.com**

Brittany's largest island lies 14 km (9 miles) south of Quiberon and can be reached in 45 minutes by car ferry from Quiberon. The coast has cliffs and good beaches; inland lie exposed highlands intersected by sheltered valleys. In the main town, Le Palais, stands the **Citadelle Vauban**, a 16th-century star-shaped fortress, and there are fine walks and views along the southern Côte Sauvage.

22 Vannes

Morbihan. 58,000. 1 quai Tabarly (02 97 47 24 34). Wed & Sat. **tourisme-vannes.com**

Standing at the head of the Golfe du Morbihan, Vannes was the capital of the Veneti, a seafaring Armorican tribe defeated by Caesar in 56 BC. In the 9th century Nominoë, the first Duke of Brittany, made it his power base. The city remained influential up until the signing of the union with France in 1532, when Rennes became the Breton capital. Today it is a busy commercial city with a well-preserved medieval quarter, and a good base for exploring the Golfe du Morbihan.

The impressive eastern walls of old Vannes can be viewed from promenade de la Garenne. Two of the city's old gates survive at either end: Porte-Prison in the north, and the southern Porte-Poterne with a row of 17th-century washhouses close by.

Walking up from Porte St-Vincent, you find the city's old market squares, still in use today. **Place des Lices** was once the scene of medieval tournaments and the streets around rue de la Monnaie are full of well-preserved 16th-century houses.

Begun in the 13th century, **Cathédrale St-Pierre** has since been drastically remodelled and restored. The Chapel of the Holy Sacrament houses the

Cloisters of St-Pierre in Vannes

revered tomb of Vincent Ferrier, a Spanish saint who died in Vannes in 1419.

Opposite the west front of the cathedral, the old covered market **La Cohue** (meaning "throng" or "hubbub") was once the city's central meeting place. Parts of the building date from the 13th century. A museum inside features works by contemporary artists such as Tal-Coat, Soulages and Genevieve, plus a small collection related to seafaring.

Housed in the 15th-century Château Gaillard, the **Musée d'Histoire** is a rich assembly of finds from Morbihan's many prehistoric sites, including jewellery, pottery and weapons. There is also a gallery of medieval and Renaissance objets d'art.

Musée d'Histoire
Château Gaillard, 2 rue Noé. **Tel** 02 97 01 63 00. **Open** Jun–Sep: pm only. **Closed** public hols.

Environs

To the south of the city the **Parc du Golfe** is a beautiful leisure park with waterfront attractions, including a butterfly garden, a conservatory set in a tropical forest and an aquarium that boasts over 400 species of fish. Northeast of Vannes, off the N166, lie the romantic ruins of the imposing 15th-century castle, **Tours d'Elven**. Very near Parc du Golfe is **Le Ker**, an educational theme park, which includes a museum and cinema. It recounts the history of Brittany from prehistoric times to the arrival of the Romans through interactive exhibits and 4D films.

Le Ker
1 rue Gilles Gahinet, Parc du Golfe, 56000 Vannes. **Tel** 02 97 47 60 22. **Open** 12:30–6pm Mon–Fri, 10am–6pm Sat & Sun.

23 Golfe du Morbihan

Morbihan. Lorient. Vannes. Vannes (02 97 47 24 34). **tourisme-vannes.com**

Morbihan means "little sea" in Breton, an apt description for this landlocked expanse of tidal water. Only connected to the Atlantic by a small channel between the Locmariaquer and Rhuys peninsulas, the gulf is dotted with islands. Around 40 are inhabited, with the **Ile d'Arz** and the **Ile-aux-Moines** the largest. These are served by regular ferries from Conleau and Port-Blanc respectively.

Around the gulf several small harbours earn a living from fishing, oyster cultivation and tourism. There is a wealth of

The picturesque fishing port of Le Bono in Golfe du Morbihan

For hotels and restaurants in this region see pp560–61 and pp585–6

The seaside resort of Dinard, on the Côte d'Emeraude

megalithic sites, notably the island of **Gavrinis**, where stone carvings have been excavated *(see p283)*. There are boat trips to Gavrinis from Larmor-Baden and around the gulf from Locmariaquer, Auray, Vannes and Port-Navalo.

The medieval Château de Josselin on the banks of the River Oust

㉔ Josselin

Morbihan. 2,500. 21 rue Olivier de Clisson (02 97 22 36 43). Sat. **josselin-tourisme.fr**

Overlooking the River Oust, Josselin is dominated by a medieval **Château** owned by the de Rohan family since the end of the 15th century. Only four of its nine towers survive. The elaborate inner granite façade incorporates the letter "A" – a tribute to the much-loved Duchess Anne of Brittany (1477–1514), who presided over Brittany's "Golden Age". Tours are given of the 19th-century interior, and in the former stables there is a Musée des Poupées with 600 dolls. In the town, **Basilique Notre-Dame-du-Roncier** contains the mausoleum of the castle's most famous owner and constable of France, Olivier de Clisson (1336–1407). West of Josselin at Kerguéhennec, the grounds of an 18th-century château have become a modern sculpture park.

Château de Josselin
Tel 02 97 22 36 45. **Open** Apr–Aug: daily (Apr–mid-Jul & Sep: pms only); Oct: Sat & Sun pms.
chateaujosselin.com

㉕ Forêt de Paimpont

Ille-et-Vilaine. Rennes. Monfort-sur-Meu. Rennes. Pl du Roi St-Judicael, Paimpont (02 99 07 84 23). **tourisme-broceliande.bzh**

Also known as the Forêt de Brocéliande, this is a remnant of the dense primeval woods that once covered much of Armorica. It has long been associated with the legends of King Arthur, and visitors still search for the magical spring where the sorcerer Merlin first met the Lady of the Lake. The small village of **Paimpont** is a good base for exploring both the forest and its myths.

Legendary sorcerer Merlin and Viviane, the Lady of the Lake

㉖ Côte d'Emeraude

Ille-et-Vilaine & Côtes d'Armor. Dinard–St-Malo. Dinard (08 21 23 55 00). **ot-dinard.com**

Between Le Val-André and the Pointe du Grouin, near Cancale, sandy beaches, rocky headlands and classic seaside resorts stretch along Brittany's northern shore. Known as the Emerald Coast, its self-proclaimed Queen is the aristocratic resort of **Dinard**, "discovered" in the 1850s and still playing host to the international rich.

To its west are resorts including St-Jacut-de-la-Mer, St-Cast-le-Guildo, Sables d'Or-les-Pins and Erquy, all with tempting beaches. In the Baie de la Frênaye, the medieval **Fort La Latte** provides good views from high in its ancient watchtower, while the lighthouse that dominates **Cap Fréhel** nearby offers even more extensive panoramas.

East of Dinard, the D186 runs across the **Barrage de la Rance** to St-Malo. Built in 1966 it was the world's first dam to generate electricity by using tidal power. Beyond St-Malo, coves and beaches surround La Guimorais, while around the Pointe du Grouin the seas are often truly emerald.

Seafarers of St-Malo

St-Malo owes its wealth and reputation to the exploits of its mariners. In 1534 Jacques Cartier, born in nearby Rothéneuf, discovered the mouth of the St Lawrence river in Canada and claimed the territory for France. It was Breton sailors who voyaged to South America in 1698 to colonize the Iles Malouines, known today as Las Malvinas or the Falklands. By the 17th century St-Malo was the largest port in France and famous for its corsairs – privateers licensed by the king to prey on foreign ships. The most illustrious were the swashbuckling René Duguay-Trouin (1673–1736), who captured Rio de Janeiro from the Portuguese in 1711, and the intrepid Robert Surcouf (1773–1827), whose ships hounded vessels of the British East India Company. The riches won by trade and piracy enabled St-Malo's shipowners to build great mansions known as *malouinières*.

Explorer Jacques Cartier (1491–1557)

㉗ St-Malo

Ille-et-Vilaine. 53,000. Esplanade St-Vincent (08 25 13 52 00). Tue & Fri. **saint-malo-tourisme.com**

Once a fortified island, St-Malo stands in a commanding position at the mouth of the River Rance.

The city is named after Maclou, a Welsh monk who came here in the 6th century to spread the Christian message. During the 16th–19th centuries the port won prosperity and power through the exploits of its seafarers. St-Malo was heavily bombed in 1944 but has since been scrupulously restored and is now a major port and ferry terminal as well as a resort.

The old city is encircled by ramparts that provide fine views of St-Malo and its islands. Take the steps up by the **Porte St-Vincent** and walk clockwise, passing the 15th-century **Grande Porte**.

Within the city is a web of cobbled streets with tall 18th-century buildings housing shops, fish restaurants and crêperies. Rue Porcon-de-la-Barbinais leads to **Cathédrale St-Vincent**, with its sombre 12th-century nave contrasting with the stained glass of the chancel. On cour La Houssaye, the 15th-century Maison de la Duchesse Anne has been carefully restored.

St-Malo seen at low tide through the gate of Fort National

Château de St-Malo

Pl Châteaubriand, near the Marina. **Tel** 02 99 40 71 57. **Open** Apr–Sep: daily; Oct–Mar: Tue–Sun. **Closed** 1 Jan, 1 May, 1 & 11 Nov, 25 Dec.

St-Malo's castle dates from the 14th–15th centuries. The great keep contains a museum of the city's history, including the adventures of its state-sponsored corsairs. From its watchtowers there is an impressive view. Nearby, in place Vauban, a tropical aquarium has been built into the ramparts, while on the edge of town the Grand Aquarium has a shark tank and simulated submarine rides.

Fort National

Open Jun–Sep: daily at low tide.

Constructed in 1689 by Louis XIV's famous military architect, Vauban, this fort can be reached on foot at low tide and offers good views of St-Malo and its ramparts. At low tide you can also walk out to **Petit Bé Fort** (open Easter–mid-Nov) and **Grand Bé**, where St-Malo-born writer François-René de Chateaubriand lies buried. From the top there are great views along the whole of Côte d'Emeraude *(see p285)*.

Tour Solidor

St-Servan. **Tel** 02 99 40 71 58. **Open** Apr–Sep: daily; Oct–Mar: Tue–Sun. **Closed** 1 Jan, 1 May, 1 & 11 Nov, 25 Dec.

To the west of St-Malo in St-Servan, the three-towered Tour Solidor was built in 1382. Formerly a toll house, it was also a prison under the Revolution, and now houses an intriguing museum devoted to the ships and sailors that rounded Cape Horn, with ship models, logs and various nautical instruments.

Environs

When the tide is out, good beaches are revealed around St-Malo and in the nearby suburbs of St-Servan and Paramé. A passenger ferry runs to Dinard in summer *(see p285)* and the Channel Islands and there are boat trips up the Rance to Dinan, and out to the Iles Chausey, Ile de Cézembre and Cap Fréhel.

At Rothéneuf you can visit the **Manoir Limoëlou**, home of the navigator Jacques Cartier. Nearby, on the coast, Les Rochers Sculptés is a beguiling array of

A stone sculpture at Les Rochers Sculptés created by the abbé Fouré near St-Malo

granite faces and figures carved into the cliffs by a local priest, Abbé Fouré, at the end of the 19th century.

Manoir Limoëlou
Rue D Macdonald-Stuart, Limoëlou-Rothéneuf. **Tel** 02 99 40 97 73. **Open** Jun–Sep: daily; Oct–May: Mon–Sat. **Closed** public hols. oblig.

㉘ Cancale

Ille-et-Vilaine. 5,500. 44 rue du Port (02 99 89 63 72). Sun.
cancale-tourisme.fr

A small port with views across the Baie du Mont-St-Michel, Cancale is entirely devoted to the cultivation and consumption of oysters. Prized by the Romans, the acclaimed flavour of Cancale's oysters is said to derive from the strong tides that wash over them daily. You can survey the beds from a *sentier des douaniers* (coastguards' footpath, the GR34) running along the cliffs.

There are plenty of opportunities for sampling the local speciality provided by a multitude of bars and restaurants along the busy quays of the Port de la Houle, where the fishing boats arrive at high tide. Devotees should pay a visit to the **Musée de l'Huître, du Coquillage et de la Mer.**

Musée de l'Huître, du Coquillage et de la Mer – La Ferme Marine
Aurore. **Tel** 02 99 89 69 99. **Open** mid-Feb–Jun & mid-Sep–Oct: Mon–Fri pms; Jul–mid-Sep: daily.

㉙ Dinan

Côtes d'Armor. 10,000. 9 rue du Château (02 96 87 69 76). Thu. **dinan-tourisme.com**

Set on a hill overlooking the wooded Rance Valley, Dinan is a modern market town with a medieval heart. Surrounded by ramparts, the half-timbered houses and cobbled streets of its Vieille Ville have an impressive, unforced unity best appreciated by climbing to the top of its 15th-century **Tour d'Horloge**, in rue de l'Horloge. Nearby, **Basilique St-Sauveur** contains the heart of Dinan's most famous son, the 14th-century warrior Bertrand du Guesclin.

Behind the church, Les Jardins Anglais offer good views of the River Rance and the viaduct spanning it. A couple of streets further north, the steep, geranium-decorated rue du Jerzual winds down through the 14th-century town gate to the port. Once a busy harbour from which cloth was shipped, it is now a quiet backwater, where you can take a pleasure cruise, or walk along a towpath to the restored 17th-century **Abbaye St-Magloire** at Léhon.

The **Château de Dinan** is flanked by the 14th-century Duc de Bretagne Jean IV keep and the 15th-century Tour de Coëtquen. In contrast to the military-style exterior, the inside comprises a kitchen, chapel and residential rooms with monumental fireplaces.

View over Dinan and the Gothic bridge crossing the River Rance

Château de Dinan
rue du Château. **Tel** 02 96 87 58 72. **Open** Jun–Sep: daily; Easter–May & Oct–mid-Nov: daily pms only. **Closed** mid-Nov–Easter, public hols.

Author and diplomat François-René de Chateaubriand (1768–1848)

㉚ Combourg

Ille-et-Vilaine. 5,000. 9 rue Notre Dame (02 99 73 13 93). Mon.
tourisme.bretagneromantique.fr

A small, sleepy town beside a lake, Combourg is completely overshadowed by the great, haunting **Château de Combourg**. The buildings seen today date from the 14th and 15th centuries. In 1761 the château was bought by the Comte de Chateaubriand, and the melancholic childhood spent there by his son, the author and diplomat François-René de Chateaubriand (1768–1848), is candidly described in his entertaining chronicle *Mémoires d'Outre-Tombe*.

Empty after the Revolution, the château was restored in the 19th century and is open for tours. One room has the belongings of François-René de Chateaubriand.

Château de Combourg
23 rue des Princes. **Tel** 02 99 73 22 95. **Open** Apr–Jun, Sep & Oct: Mon–Fri & Sun pm; Jul & Aug: daily.
chateau-combourg.com

Rennes City Centre

① Portes Mordelaises
② Cathédrale St-Pierre
③ Eglise St-Sauveur
④ Hôtel de Ville
⑤ Opéra de Rennes
⑥ Eglise St-Germain
⑦ Parc du Thabor
⑧ Palais du Parlement de Bretagne
⑨ Musée des Beaux-Arts

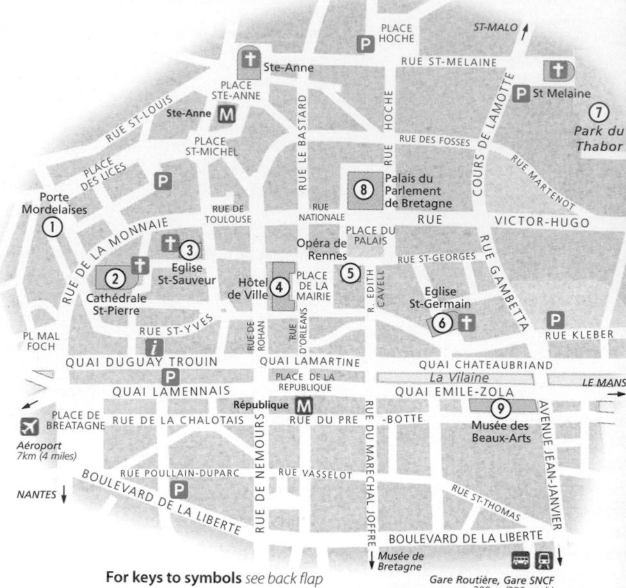

0 metres 250
0 yards 250

For keys to symbols *see back flap*

㉛ Rennes

Ille-et-Vilaine. 215,000. 11 rue St-Yves (02 99 67 11 11). Tue–Sat. **tourisme-rennes.com**

Founded by the Gauls and colonized by the Romans, Rennes is strategically located where the Vilaine and Ille rivers meet. After Brittany's union with France in 1532, the town became regional capital. In 1720 a fire lasting for six days devastated the city. Today a small part of the medieval city survives, together with the neat grid of 18th-century buildings that arose from the ashes.

The imposing Neo-Classical façade of Cathédrale St-Pierre

Around this historic core are the tower blocks and high-tech factories of modern Rennes – a confident provincial capital with two universities and a thriving cultural life.

Wandering through the streets that radiate from place des Lices and place Ste-Anne, it is easy to imagine what Rennes was like before the Great Fire. Now mostly pedestrianized, this area has become the city's youthful heart with plenty of bars, *crêperies* and designer shops. At the western end of rue de la Monnaie stands the 15th-century **Portes Mordelaises**, once part of the city's ramparts.

Close by, **Cathédrale St-Pierre** was completed in 1844, the third on this site. Note the carved 16th-century Flemish altarpiece. Nearby is the 18th-century **Eglise St-Sauveur**. In the place de la Mairie stands the early 18th-century **Hôtel de Ville** and the Neo-Classical **Opéra de Rennes**. Just south of the attractive rue St-George, **Eglise St-Germain** has a typically Breton belfry and wooden vaulting. The **Parc du Thabor**, once part of a Benedictine monastery, is ideal for walks and picnics.

Half-timbered houses lining the narrow streets of old Rennes

Palais du Parlement de Bretagne

Pl du Parlement. **Open** Tourist Office for guided tours (02 99 67 11 66). **tourisme-rennes.com**

Rennes' Law Courts, built in 1618–55, formed the seat of the region's governing body until the Revolution. Severely damaged by fire during riots over fish prices in 1994, the major restoration work is all but complete, including the unique coffered ceiling and gilded woodwork of the Grande Chambre. Today, the Salle des Pas Perdus, with its vaulted ceilings, can again be admired by the public.

Musée des Beaux-Arts

20 quai Zola. **Tel** 02 23 62 17 45. **Open** Tue–Sun. **Closed** public hols. **W** **mbar.org**.

The Musée des Beaux-Arts has a wide-ranging collection of art from the 14th century to the present, including a room of art on Breton themes. There are paintings by Gauguin, Bernard and other members of the Pont-Aven School *(see p279)*, and three works by Picasso, including the lively *Baigneuse* painted at Dinard in 1928.

Musée de Bretagne

10 cours des Alliés. **Tel** 02 23 40 66 00. **Open** Tue–Sun pm only. **Closed** public hols. **W** **musee-bretagne.fr**

Housed in the Rennes cultural centre along with the Science Museum and Planetarium, the Musée de Bretagne includes examples of traditional Breton furniture and costume, and displays on Brittany's prehistoric megaliths, the growth of Rennes, rural crafts and the fishing industry.

Environs

Just south of Rennes, the **Ecomusée du Pays de Rennes** traces the history of a local farm since the 17th century.

Some 16 km (10 miles) to the southeast of Rennes is **Châteaugiron**, a charming medieval village, with an imposing castle and houses preserving their wooden eaves.

Ecomusée du Pays de Rennes

Ferme de la Bintinais, rte de Châtillon-sur-Seiche. **Tel** 02 99 51 38 15. **Open** Tue–Fri (Sat, Sun pm only). **Closed** public hols. **W** **ecomusee-rennes-metropole.fr**

Château de Châteaugiron

Open Jul & Aug: Mon–Sat & Sun pm; call 02 99 37 89 02.

32 Fougères

Ille-et-Vilaine. 23,000. 2 rue Nationale (02 99 94 12 20). Sat. **W** **ot-fougeres.fr**

A fortress town close to the Breton border, Fougères rests on a hill overlooking the Nançon river. In the valley below, and still linked to the Haute Ville by a curtain of ancient ramparts, stands

The mighty fortifications of Château de Fougères

the mighty 11th- to 15th-century **Château de Fougères**. To get a good overview of the château, go to the gardens of place aux Arbres behind the 16th-century **Eglise St-Léonard**. From here you can descend to the river and the medieval houses around place du Marchix. The Flamboyant Gothic **Eglise St-Sulpice**, with its 18th-century wood-panelled interior and granite retables, is well worth visiting.

A walk around the castle's massive outer fortifications reveals the ambitious scale of its construction, with 13 towers and walls over 3 m (10 ft) thick. You can still climb the castle's ramparts to get a feel of what it was like to live within its staggered defences. Much of the action in Balzac's novel *Les Chouans* (1829) takes place in and around Fougères and its castle.

Château de Fougères

Pl Pierre-Simon. **Tel** 02 99 99 79 59. **Open** Jun–Sep: daily; Oct–May: Tue–Sun. **Closed** Jan, 25 Dec. **W** **chateau-fougeres.com**

Overhanging timber-frame houses on rue Beaudrairie, Vitré

33 Vitré

Ille-et-Vilaine. 16,000. pl Général de Gaulle (02 99 75 04 46). Mon & Sat. **W** **bretagne-vitre.com**

The fortified town of Vitré is set high on a hill overlooking the Vilaine Valley. Its medieval **Château** is complete with pencil-point turrets and picturesque 15th- to 16th-century buildings in attendance. The castle was rebuilt in the 14th–15th centuries and follows a triangular plan, with some of its ramparts walkable. There is a museum in the Tour St-Laurent.

To the east, rue Beaudrairie and rue d'Embas have overhanging timber-frame houses with remarkable patterning.

The 15th- to 16th-century **Cathédrale Notre-Dame**, built in Flamboyant Gothic style, has a south façade with an exterior stone pulpit. Further along rue Notre-Dame, the promenade du Val skirts around the town's ramparts.

To the southeast of Vitré on the D88, the **Château des Rochers-Sévigné** was once the home of Mme de Sévigné (1626–96), famous letter-writer and chronicler of life at the court of Louis XIV. The park, chapel and some of her rooms are open to the public.

Château de Vitré

Tel 02 99 75 04 54. **Open** Apr–Sep: daily; Mar & Oct: Wed–Mon; Nov–Feb: Mon, Wed–Fri & Sun pm. **Closed** 1 Jan, Easter, 1 Nov, 25 Dec.

Château des Rochers-Sévigné

Tel 02 99 96 76 51. **Open** Mar & Oct: Wed–Mon; Apr–Sep: daily. **Closed** Nov–Feb. obligatory. restricted.

THE LOIRE VALLEY

Loire-Atlantique · Vendée · Maine-et-Loire · Sarthe · Indre-et-Loire Loir-et-Cher · Loiret · Eure-et-Loir · Cher

Renowned for its sumptuous châteaux, the glorious valley of the Loire, now classified a UNESCO World Heritage Site, is rich both in history and architecture. Like the River Loire, this vast region runs through the heart of French life. Its sophisticated cities, luxuriant landscape and magnificent food and wine add up to a bourgeois paradise.

The lush Loire Valley is supremely regal. Orléans was France's intellectual capital in the 13th century, attracting artists, poets and troubadours to the royal court. But the medieval court never stayed in one place for long, which led to the building of magnificent châteaux all along the Loire. Chambord and Chenonceau, the two greatest Renaissance châteaux, remain prestigious symbols of royal rule, resplendent amid vast hunting forests and waterways.

Due to its central location, culture and fine cuisine, Tours is the visitors' capital. Angers is a close second, but more authentic are the historic towns of Saumur, Amboise, Blois and Beaugency, strung out like jewels along the river. This is the classic Loire Valley, a château trail that embraces the Renaissance gardens of Villandry and the fairy-tale turrets of Ussé. Venture northwards and the cathedral cities of Le Mans and Chartres reign supreme, their medieval centres bordered by Gallo-Roman walls. Nantes in the west is a breezy, forward-looking port and gateway to the Atlantic.

Southwards, the windswept Vendée is edged by a wild, sandy coastline that is perfect for windsurfers and nature lovers alike. Inland, the Loire's more peaceful tributaries and the watery Sologne beg to be explored. Also ripe for discovery are troglodyte caves, sleepy hamlets and small Romanesque churches decorated with frescoes. Inviting inns offer game, fish and abundant fresh vegetables to be lingered over with a light white Vouvray wine or a fruity Bourgeuil. Overindulgence is no sin in this rich region.

The River Loire at Montsoreau, southeast of Saumur

◀ Formal gardens at the Château de Villandry

Exploring the Loire Valley

The lush valley landscape, studded with France's greatest châteaux, is the main attraction. Numerous river cruises are available, while the sandy Atlantic coast offers beach holidays. Peaceful country holidays can be had in the Vendée, and in the Loir and Indre valleys. Wine tours focus on Bourgueil, Chinon, Muscadet, Saumur and Vouvray vintages. The most charming bases are Amboise, Beaugency, Blois and Saumur, but culture lovers are well provided for throughout the region.

Countryside around Vouvray

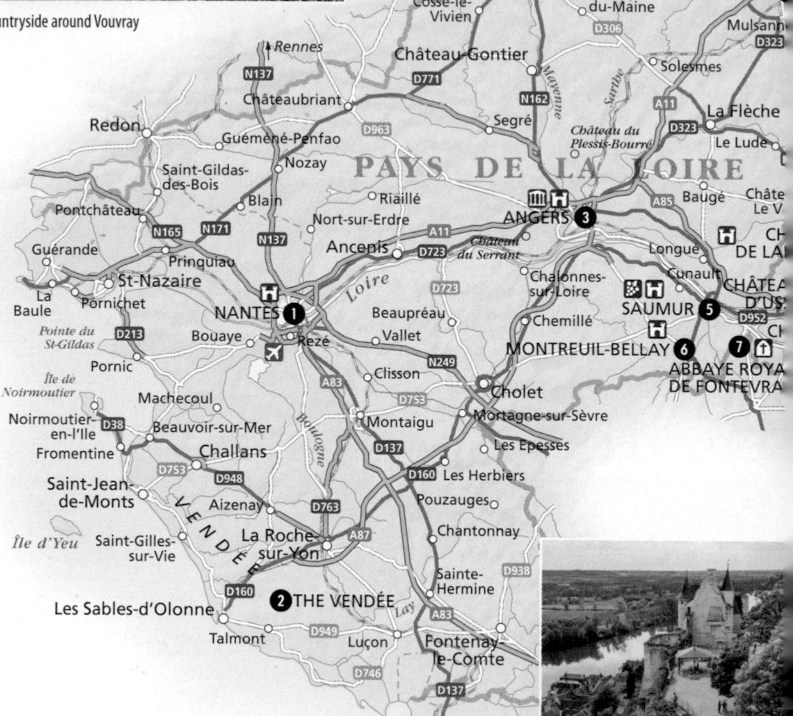

Getting Around

The region is well-served by transport links. Nantes and Tours airports have international flights; Tours airport also serves Marseille and Figari (Corsica). Chartres, Le Mans, Angers and Nantes are reached from Paris by the A11, and the A10 links Orléans, Blois and Tours. The TGV train travels from Paris to Le Mans (1 hr); Tours (1 hr); Angers (90 mins); and Nantes (2 hrs). There is also TGV access from Lille (Eurostar interchange). The smaller châteaux can be difficult to reach by public transport, but there are tours from major tourist centres.

The Château de Chinon, on a rocky outcrop above the Vienne river

For keys to symbols *see back flap*

Sights at a Glance

1. Nantes
2. The Vendée
3. Angers
4. Le Mans
5. Saumur
6. Montreuil-Bellay
7. Abbaye Royale de Fontevraud
8. Chinon
9. Château d'Ussé
10. Château de Langeais
11. Château d'Azay-le-Rideau
12. Château de Villandry
13. Tours
14. Vouvray
15. Loches
16. Montrésor
17. *Château de Chenonceau pp302–3*
18. Amboise
19. *Château de Chambord pp306–7*
20. Blois
21. Beaugency
22. Vendôme
23. The Loir
24. *Chartres pp311–15*
25. Orléans
26. St-Benoît-sur-Loire
27. Bourges

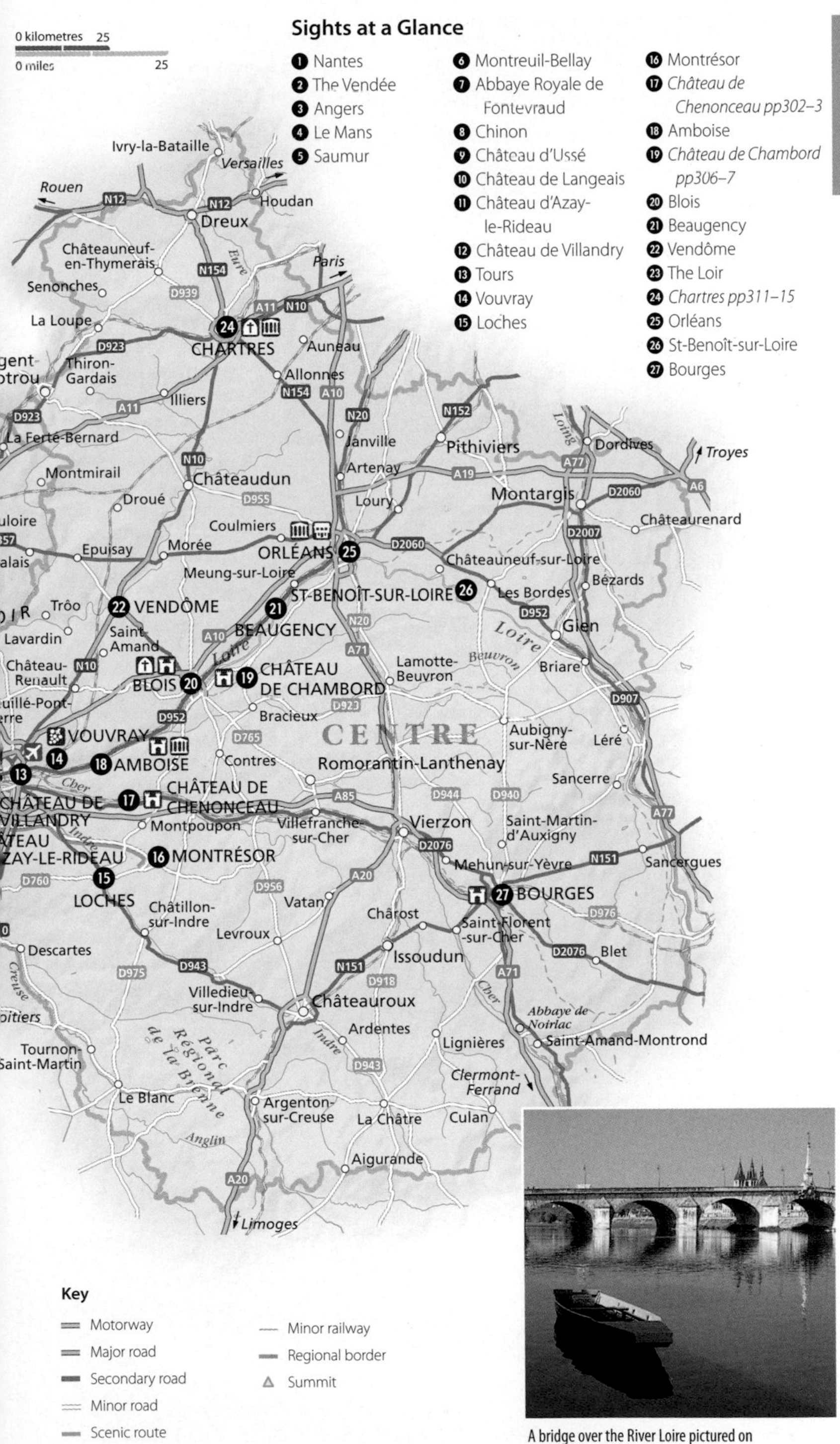

A bridge over the River Loire pictured on a clear day

Tomb of François II and his wife, Marguerite de Foix, in Cathédrale St-Pierre, Nantes

❶ Nantes

Loire-Atlantique. 270,000. Nantes. 9 rue des Etats (08 92 46 40 44). Tue–Sun. **nantes-tourisme.com**

For centuries, Nantes disputed with Rennes the title of capital of Brittany. Yet links with the Plantagenets and Henri IV also bound it to the "royal" River Loire. Since the 1790s it has officially ceased to be part of Brittany, and, though still Breton at heart, it is today capital of the Pays de la Loire.

Visually, Nantes is a city of variety, with high-tech towers overlooking the port, canals and Art Nouveau squares. Chic bars and restaurants cram the medieval nucleus, bounded by place St-Croix and the château.

The **Cathédrale St-Pierre et St-Paul**, completed in 1893, is notable both for its sculpted Gothic portals and Renaissance tomb of François II, the last duke of Brittany.

More impressive is the **Château des Ducs de Bretagne**, where Anne of Brittany was born in 1477 and where the Edict of Nantes was signed by Henri IV in 1598, granting Protestants religious freedom. Following major restoration work the château now houses the lively, interactive **Musée d'Histoire**. It charts the history of Nantes through 32 rooms of exhibits, including Turner's painting of the Loire embankments in Nantes and a virtual visit of the city in 1757.

Château des Ducs de Bretagne
Pl Marc Elder. **Tel** 08 11 46 46 44. **Open** Jul & Aug: daily; Sep–Jun: Tue–Sun. **Closed** 1 Jan, 1 May, 1 Nov, 25 Dec.

Environs

From Nantes, boats cruise the Erdre and Sèvre Nantaise rivers, passing châteaux and vineyards. Some 32 km (20 miles) southeast of Nantes is **Clisson**, a town razed to the ground during the Vendée Uprising of 1793, and later rebuilt by sculptor François-Frédéric Lemot along Italian lines, with Neo-Classical villas and red-tiled roofs. On a spur overlooking the Sèvre Nantaise river is the ruined 13th-century **Château de Clisson**.

Château de Clisson
Tel 02 40 54 02 22. **Open** Feb–Apr & Oct–Dec: Wed–Mon pms; May–Jun & Sep: Wed–Mon; Jul & Aug: daily. **Closed** Jan, 1 May, Christmas hols.

❷ The Vendée

Vendée and Maine-et-Loire. Nantes. La Roche-sur-Yon. La Roche-sur-Yon (02 51 36 00 85). **vendee-tourisme.com**

The counter-revolutionary movement that swept western France between 1793 and 1799 began as a series of uprisings in the Vendée, still an evocative name to the French. As a bastion of the ancien régime, the region rebelled against urban Republican values. But a violent massacre in 1793 left 80,000 royalists dead in one day, as they tried to cross the Loire at St-Florent-le-Vieil. The Vendée farmers were staunch royalists, and, although they ultimately lost, the region remains coloured by conservatism and religious fervour to this day.

This local history is dramatically retraced at **Le Puy du Fou** in Les Epesses, south of Cholet, with its spectacular summer evening live show, *Cinéscénie*. More sober accounts are given at Logis de La Chabotterie, near St-Sulpice-de-Verdon, and the Musée du Textile in Cholet, whose flax and hemp textiles provided the royalist heroes with their kerchiefs: originally white, then blood red.

The tranquil Vendée offers green tourism inland, in the *bocage vendéen*, a wooded backwater with paths and nature trails. The Atlantic coast between the Loire and La Rochelle has beaches, yet the only sizable resort here is **Les Sables d'Olonne**, with boat trips to the salt-marshes, out to sea or to the nearby **Ile d'Yeu**. To the north,

The harbour at Ile de Noirmoutier in the Vendée

For hotels and restaurants in this region see pp561–2 and pp586–9

the marshy **Ile de Noirmoutier** is connected to the mainland at low tide via the Gois causeway.

Inland lies the remote **Marais Poitevin** *(see pp412–13)*, its marshes home to bird sanctuaries and fine churches (Maillezais, Vix, Maillé) in hamlets bordered by canals. It is France's largest complex of man-made waterways, largely reclaimed for farming in the west, while further east is a nature lover's paradise. Coulon is the main centre for hiring punts.

The Apocalypse tapestry in Angers

❸ Angers

Maine-et-Loire. 155,000. 7 pl Kennedy (02 41 23 50 00). Tue–Sun. **angersloiretourisme.com**

Angers is the historic capital of Anjou, home of the Plantagenets and gateway to the Loire Valley. The town has a formidable 13th-century **Château** *(see p246)*. Inside is the longest (103 m/ 338 ft) and one of the finest medieval tapestries in the world. It tells the story of the Apocalypse, with battles between hydras and angels.

A short walk from the castle is the **Cathédrale St-Maurice**, noted for its façade and 13th-century stained-glass windows. Close by is Maison d'Adam, with carvings showing the tree of life. The nearby **Galerie David d'Angers**, housed in the glass-covered ruins of a 13th-century church, celebrates the sculptor born in Angers. Across the River Maine, the Hôpital St-Jean, a hospital for the poor from 1174 to 1854, houses the **Musée Jean Lurçat**. Its prize exhibit is the exquisite *Chant du Monde* tapestry, which was created by Lurçat in 1957. In the same building is **Le Musée de la Tapisserie Contemporaine**, with displays of ceramics and paintings.

Château d'Angers
Tel 02 41 86 48 77. **Open** daily. **Closed** 1 Jan, 1 May, 1 & 11 Nov, 25 Dec.

Galerie David d'Angers
33bis rue Toussaint. **Tel** 02 41 05 38 90. **Open** Tue–Sun. **Closed** most pub hols.

Musée Jean Lurçat/Le Musée de la Tapisserie Contemporaine
4 bd Arago. **Tel** 02 41 24 18 45. **Open** Tue–Sun. **Closed** most public hols.

Environs

Within a 21-km (13-mile) radius of Angers lie the Renaissance **Château de Serrant** and the moated **Château du Plessis-Bourré**, a decorative pleasure dome encased in a feudal shell. Follow the Loire east along the sandbanks and dykes, enjoying the fish restaurants en route.

Château de Serrant
St-Georges-sur-Loire. **Tel** 02 41 39 13 01. **Open** mid-Feb–mid-Jul & Sep–Oct: Wed–Sun; mid-Jul–Aug: daily. **Closed** Nov–mid-Feb obligatory.
chateau-serrant.net

Château du Plessis-Bourré
Ecuillé. **Tel** 02 41 32 06 72. **Open** mid-Feb–Mar & Oct: Tue–Sun pms; Apr–Jun & Sep: Tue–Sun; Jul–Aug: daily; Nov: daily pms. obligatory.
plessis-bourre.com

❹ Le Mans

Sarthe. 150,000. 16 rue de l'Etoile (02 43 28 17 22). Tue–Sun. **lemans-tourisme.com**

Ever since Monsieur Bollée became the first designer to place an engine under a car bonnet, Le Mans has been synonymous with the motor trade. Bollée's son created an embryonic Grand Prix, and the event *(see p41)* and the associated **Musée des 24 Heures du Mans** have remained star attractions ever since. Cité Plantagenet, the ancient fortified centre, is surrounded by the greatest Roman walls in France, best seen from the quai Louis Blanc. Once abandoned, the area has been restored, and is now used for filming epics such as *Cyrano de Bergerac*, set amongst Renaissance mansions, half-timbered houses, arcaded alleys and tiny courtyards. The crown is the Gothic **Cathédrale St-Julien**, borne aloft by flying buttresses, with its Romanesque portal rivalling that of Chartres. Inside, the Angevin nave opens into a Gothic choir, complemented by sculpted capitals and a 12th-century Ascension window.

Stained-glass Ascension window in the Cathédrale St-Julien, Le Mans

Musée des 24 Heures du Mans
9 pl Luigi Chinetti. **Tel** 02 43 72 72 24. **Open** daily.

Le Mans racetrack: a 1933 print from the French magazine *Illustration*

5 Saumur

Maine-et-Loire. 32,000.
8bis quai Carnot (02 41 40 20 60).
Thu, Sat. **ot-saumur.fr**

The Château de Saumur and spire of St-Pierre seen from the Loire

Saumur is celebrated for its fairy-tale château, cavalry school, mushrooms and sparkling wines. Its stone mansions recall the city's 17th-century heyday, when it was a bastion of Protestantism and vied with Angers as the intellectual capital of Anjou.

High above both town and river is the turreted **Château de Saumur**. The present structure was started in the 14th century by Louis I of Anjou and remodelled later by his grandson, King René. Collections include medieval sculpture, and equestrian exhibits.

King René's coat of arms

The Military Cavalry School, established in Saumur in 1814, led to the creation of the **Musée des Blindés**, which exhibits 150 different armoured vehicles, and of the prestigious Cadre Noir horse-riding formation.

Morning training sessions and stable visits, along with occasional evening performances, can be seen at the **Ecole Nationale d'Equitation**. The nearby subterranean **Parc Pierre et Lumière** (sculptures in the tufa cave walls of prominent local tourist sites), is well worth a visit; as is Europe's largest dolmen, with its collection of prehistoric implements, in Bagneux.

Before you leave the area, be sure to sample the local *méthode champenoise* sparkling wine – the best in France outside Champagne – in one of the many wine cellars or at the Maison des Vins in town.

Château de Saumur
Tel 02 41 40 24 40. **Open** Apr–Oct: Tue–Sun (mid-Jun–mid-Sep: daily).

Ecole Nationale d'Equitation
St-Hilaire-St-Florent. **Tel** 02 41 53 50 60. **Open** Feb–mid-Nov for guided tours; Apr–Oct: call for performance times. **Closed** public hols. oblig.
cadrenoir.fr

Environs

Eglise Notre-Dame at Cunault, an 11th-century Romanesque priory church, has a fine west door and carved capitals, while a subterranean fort and myriad caves and tunnels can be seen at **Château de Brézé**.

Troglodyte Dwellings

Some of the best troglodyte settlements in France have been carved out of the soft limestone (tufa) of the Loire Valley, especially around Saumur, Vouvray and along the River Loir. The caves, cut out of cliff-faces or dug underground, have been a source of cheap, secure accommodation for centuries. Today they are popular as *résidences secondaires*, or used for wine storage and mushroom growing. Some are now restaurants or hotels, and old quarries at Doué-la-Fontaine accommodate a zoo and a 15th-century amphitheatre. At Rochemenier, near Saumur, is a well-preserved troglodyte village museum. A central pit is surrounded by a warren of caves, barns, wine cellars, dwellings and even a simple underground chapel.

Heralded by chimneypots, the underground hamlet of La Fosse was inhabited until the late 20th century by three families, and is now a museum of family life underground.

A typical troglodyte dwelling

6 Montreuil-Bellay

Maine-et-Loire. 4,500.
pl du Concorde (02 41 52 32 39).
Tue (mid-Jun–mid-Sep: also Sun).
ville-montreuil-bellay.com

Set on the River Thouet 17 km (11 miles) south of Saumur, Montreuil-Bellay is one of the region's most gracious small towns and is an ideal base for touring Anjou. The towering roofline of the Gothic collegiate church overlooks walled mansions and surrounding vineyards (wine tasting recommended). The **Chapelle St-Jean** was an ancient hospice and pilgrimage centre.

The imposing **Château de Montreuil-Bellay**, established in 1025, is a veritable fortress with its 13 interlocking towers, barbican and ramparts.

A 15th-century house lies beyond the fortified gateway, complete with vaulted medieval kitchen and an oratory decorated with 15th-century frescoes.

Château de Montreuil-Bellay
Tel 02 41 52 33 06. **Open** Apr–early Nov: Wed–Mon (Jul–Aug: daily).

For hotels and restaurants in this region see pp561–2 and pp586–9

Court Life in the Renaissance

François I's reign, from 1515 to 1547, witnessed the apogee of the French Renaissance, characterized by an intense period of château-building and an interest in humanism and the arts. The itinerant court travelled between the pleasure palaces of Amboise, Blois and Chambord in the Loire. Days were devoted to hunting, falconry, *fêtes champêtres* (country festivals) or *jeu de paume*, a forerunner of tennis. Nights were given over to feasting, balls, poetry and romantic assignations.

Lute and mandolin music were much in vogue, as were Italian recitals and masquerades. Musicians played at the twice-weekly balls, where the pavane and galliard were danced.

The antics of François I's fools, Triboulet and Caillette, amused the court. Yet they were often mistreated: courtiers regularly nailed Caillette's ears to a post for fun, daring him to remain silent.

Renaissance Feasts

Dinner usually took place before 7pm to the accompaniment of Italian music. Humanist texts were read aloud and the king's fools amused the courtiers.

Courtiers used their own knives at dinner. Forks were still rare, although their use was spreading from Italy.

A typical royal dinner comprised smoked eel, salted ham, veal *pâté*, egg and saffron soups, roast game and boiled meats, as well as fish dishes in lemon or gooseberry sauce.

The cost of lavish damask, satin and silk costumes often sent courtiers into debt.

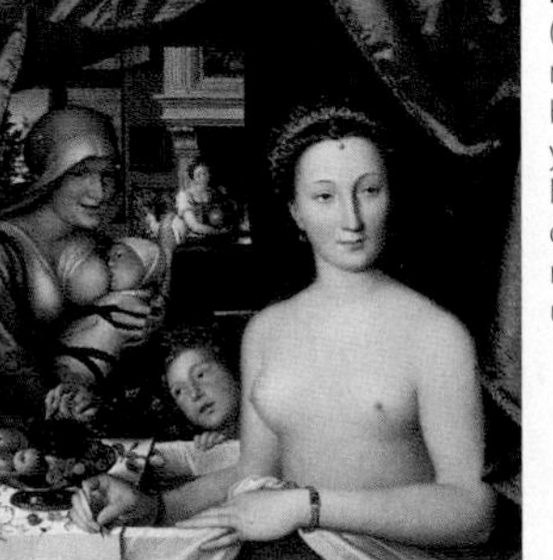

Diane de Poitiers (1499–1566) became the mistress of the future Henri II when he was 12 years old. Two years later he married Catherine de'Medici, but Diane remained his favourite until his death.

Artists symbolized love in different ways during the Renaissance. Winged hearts charmingly perform the function here.

The Grand Moûtier cloisters

The Plantagenets

The legendary counts of Anjou were named after the *genêt*, the sprig of broom Geoffrey Plantagenet wore in his cap. He married Matilda, daughter of England's Henry I. In 1154, when their son Henry – who married Eleanor of Aquitaine *(see p55)* – acceded to the English throne, the Plantagenet dynasty of English kings was founded, fusing French and English destinies for 300 years.

Effigies of Henry II, Plantagenet King of England, and Eleanor of Aquitaine

❼ Abbaye Royale de Fontevraud

Maine-et-Loire. 🚌 from Saumur.
Tel 02 41 51 73 52. **Open** daily.
Closed Jan, 25 Dec.

The Abbaye Royale de Fontevraud is the largest and most remarkably intact medieval abbey in Europe. It was founded in the early 12th century by Robert d'Arbrissel, a visionary itinerant preacher, who set up a Benedictine community of monks, nuns, nobles, lepers and vagabonds. The radical founder entrusted the running of the abbey to an abbess, usually from a noble family, and the abbey became a favourite sanctuary for the female aristocracy, including Eleanor of Aquitaine.

From 1804 to 1963 the abbey was used as a prison, since when the buildings have been undergoing painstaking restoration by the French State. Wandering around the abbey buildings and gardens gives a fascinating insight into monastic life.

Tour Evraud

Pepper-pot chimneys top the towers of the kitchen, restored in the 20th century.

Fireplace alcoves that look like side chapels housed the ovens.

The focal point was the Romanesque abbey church, consecrated in 1119. It boasts beautifully carved capitals and an immense nave with four domes, one of the finest examples of a cupola nave in France. Inside are the painted effigies of the Plantagenets, dating from the early 13th century: Henry II of England, his redoubtable wife Queen Eleanor of Aquitaine, their crusading son Richard the Lionheart and Isabelle d'Angoulême, widow of his infamous brother, King John of England.

The abbey's nuns lived around the Renaissance **Grand Moûtier cloisters**, forming one of the largest nunneries in France. The leper colony was once housed in the **St-Lazare priory**, now a hotel and restaurant. The monastic quarters of **St-Jean de l'Habit** no longer exist. Most impressive is the octagonal kitchen with its fireplaces and chimneys in the **Tour Evraud**, a rare example of secular Romanesque architecture.

The abbey, now an important arts centre, regularly hosts concerts and exhibitions.

❽ Chinon

Indre-et-Loire. 9,000.
i 1 rue Rabelais (02 47 93 17 85).
Thu. **W** **chinon-valdeloire.com**

The Château de Chinon is an important shrine in Joan of Arc country and, as such, wheedles money from all passing pilgrims. It was here in 1429 that the saint first recognized the disguised dauphin (later Charles VII), and persuaded him to give her an army to drive the English out of France. Before that, Chinon was the Plantagenet kings' favourite castle. Although the **château** is now mostly in ruins, the ramparts are an impressive sight from the opposite bank of the Vienne river. The town's bijou centre is like a medieval film set. **Rue Voltaire**, lined with 15th- and 16th-century houses and once enclosed by the castle walls, represents a cross-section of Chinonais history. At No. 12 is the **Musée Animé du Vin**, where animated figures tell the story of wine making. Nearby, at 44 rue Haute St-Maurice, is the Musée d'Art et d'Histoire, a stone

Stallholder at Chinon's 1900s market

Vineyard in the Chinon wine region

mansion, where, in 1199, Richard the Lionheart is said to have died. The grandest mansion is the **Palais du Gouverneur**, with its double staircase and loggia. More charming is the **Maison Rouge** in the Grand Carroi, studded with a red-brick herringbone pattern.

The neighbouring 15th-century **Château de Marçay**, built on an earlier 11th-century fortress *(see p561)* now offers luxurious rooms for a stay in the Loire Valley.

The 1900s market, with stall-holders in period costume, folk dancing and music, is a must (third Saturday of August).

Musée Animé du Vin
12 rue Voltaire. **Tel** 02 47 93 25 63. **Open** mid-Mar–mid-Oct: daily.

Environs
5 km (3 miles) southwest of Chinon is **La Devinière,** birthplace of François Rabelais, the 16th-century writer, priest, doctor and humanist scholar.

La Devinière
Seuilly. **Tel** 02 47 95 91 18. **Open** Apr–Sep: daily; Oct–Mar: Wed–Mon. **Closed** 1 Jan, 25 Dec.

9 Château d'Ussé

Indre-et-Loire. Chinon, then taxi. **Tel** 02 47 95 54 05. **Open** mid-Feb–mid-Nov: daily. W **chateaudusse.fr**

The fairy-tale Château d'Ussé enjoys a bucolic setting by the River Indre. Its romantic turrets, pointed towers and chimneys inspired the writer Charles Perrault's *Sleeping Beauty*.

Constructed in the 15th century, the castle was gradually transformed into an aristocratic château, which is still privately owned *(see p246)*. However, the sunless and musty interior is rather disappointing and the *Sleeping Beauty* tableaux are clumsily presented.

The château's delightful Renaissance chapel, framed by the oak forest of Chinon, has lost its Aubusson tapestries, but retains a lovely della Robbia terracotta *Virgin*.

10 Château de Langeais

Indre-et-Loire. Langeais. **Tel** 02 47 96 72 60. **Open** daily. **Closed** 1 Jan, 25 Dec. W **chateau-de-langeais.com**

Compared with neighbouring towns, Langeais is distinctly untouristy and has a welcoming, unpretentious feel. Its château is fiercely feudal, built strictly for defence with a drawbridge, portcullis and no concessions to the Renaissance. It was constructed by Louis XI in just four years, from 1465 to 1469, with hardly an alteration since then. The ruins of an impressive keep, built by Foulques Nerra in AD 994, stand in the small château courtyard.

A *son-et-lumière* display in the Salle de Mariage represents the marriage of Charles VIII and Anne of Brittany in 1491. Many of the rooms have intricate designs on the tiled floors, and all are hung with fine 15th- and 16th-century Flemish and Aubusson tapestries.

François Rabelais

Rabelais, born in 1494, was a priest, doctor, diplomat and humanist scholar noted for his wisdom and tolerance. He is best remembered for his many ribald satires (written as "medicine" for his patients), such as *Pantagruel* and *Gargantua*, set around his native Chinon.

Infant Pantagruel, depicted by Doré in 1854, was fed on the milk of 17,913 cows

⓫ Château d'Azay-le-Rideau

Indre-et-Loire. 🚉 🚌 Azay-le-Rideau. **Tel** 02 47 45 42 04. **Open** daily; call ahead for opening times. **Closed** 1 Jan, 1 May, 25 Dec. **azay-le-rideau.fr**

Balzac called Azay-le-Rideau "a multifaceted diamond set in the Indre". It is the most beguiling and feminine of Loire châteaux, created in the early 16th century by Philippa Lesbahy, wife of François I's corrupt finance minister. Although Azay is superficially Gothic *(see pp60–61, 246)*, it clearly shows the transition to the Renaissance: the turrets are purely decorative and the moats are picturesque pools. Azay was a pleasure palace, lived in during fine weather and deserted in winter.

The interior is equally delightful, an airy, creaking mansion smelling faintly of cedarwood and full of lovingly re-created domestic detail. The first floor is furnished in the Renaissance style, with a fine example of a portable Spanish cabinet and exquisite tapestries. The ground floor has 19th-century furniture, dating from the period of the château's restoration. The four-storey grand staircase is unusual for its time, being straight as opposed to spiral. In July and August, from 9pm until midnight, a sound and light show takes place.

Wine-tasting opportunities in the village are a welcome reminder that vineyards are all around.

The Château de Villandry's *jardin d'ornement*

⓬ Château de Villandry

Indre-et-Loire. 🚉 Tours, then taxi. **Tel** 02 47 50 02 09. **Open** Château: mid-Feb–mid-Nov & mid-Dec–early Jan: daily. Gardens: daily. Mar–Oct. **chateauvillandry.fr**

Villandry was the last great Renaissance château built in the Loire Valley, a perfect example of 16th-century architecture. Its gardens were restored to their original splendour early in the last century by Dr Joachim Carvallo, whose grandson continues his work.

The result is a patchwork of sculpted shrubs and flowers on three levels: the kitchen garden *(jardin potager)*, the ornamental garden *(jardin d'ornement)* and, on the highest level, the water garden *(jardin d'eau)*. There are signs to explain the history and meaning behind each plant: the marrow, for instance, symbolized fertility; the cabbage, sexual and spiritual corruption. Plants were also prized for their medicinal properties: cabbage was thought to help cure hangovers, while pimento aided digestion.

The delicate roots of the 51 km (32 miles) of box hedge that outline and highlight each section mean that the whole 40,000 sq m (430,000 sq ft) of gardens must be hand-weeded.

A *chocolatier* in Tours

⓭ Tours

Indre-et-Loire. 140,000. ✈ 🚉 🚌 ℹ 78 rue Bernard Palissy (02 47 70 37 37). Tue–Sun. **tours-tourisme.fr**

Tours is the most appealing of the major Loire cities, thanks to bourgeois prosperity, an intelligent restoration programme and its university population. It is built on the site of a Roman town, and was a centre of Christianity in the 4th century under St Martin, bishop of Tours. In 1461 Louis XI made the city the French capital. However, during Henri IV's reign the city lost favour with the monarchy and the capital left Tours for Paris.

Bombarded by the Prussians in 1870, and bombed in World War II, Tours suffered extensive damage. By 1960, the middle classes had abandoned the historic centre and it became a slum, full of crumbling medieval masonry.

Château d'Azay-le-Rideau reflected in the River Indre

Regeneration of the city has succeeded due to the popular policies of Jean Royer, mayor of Tours from 1958 to 1996.

The pedestrianized **place Plumereau** is Tours's most atmospheric quarter, set in the medieval heart of the city and full of cafés, boutiques and galleries. Streets such as rue Briçonnet reveal half-timbered façades, hidden courtyards and crooked towers. A gateway leads to place St-Pierre-le-Puellier, a square with sunken Gallo-Roman remains and a Romanesque church converted into a café. A few streets away in place de Châteauneuf lies the Romanesque **Tour Charlemagne**, all that remains of St Martin's first church. West of here is the highly upmarket artisans' quarter, centred on rue du Petit St-Martin.

On rue du Commerce lies the **Hôtel Goüin**, with its stunning façade. Just behind it is a contemporary art museum, **Centre de Création Contemporain Olivier Debré**, named after the 20th-century artist inspired by the Touraine region. It displays several of Olivier Debré's large-scale works and also hosts regular

Cathédrale St-Gatien in Tours

temporary exhibitions of contemporary art throughout the year. A little further west is the **Eglise St-Julien**, whose Gothic monastic cells and chapterhouse contain a small wine museum. Next door, the **Musée du Compagnonnage** displays hundreds of finely crafted works by master craftsmen of the guilds.

The **Cathédrale St-Gatien**, in the eastern sector of the city, was begun in the early 13th century and completed in the 16th. Its Flamboyant Gothic façade is blackened and crumbling but still truly impressive, as are the medieval stained-glass windows.

The **Musée des Beaux-Arts**, set in the former archbishop's palace nearby, overlooks Classical gardens and a giant cedar of Lebanon. Its star exhibits are *Christ in the Garden of Olives* and *The Resurrection* by Mantegna.

Centre de Création Contemporain Olivier Debré
Jardin François 1er, Tours.
Tel 02 47 66 50 00. **Open** Winter: Wed–Sun; Summer: Tue–Sun.

Musée des Beaux-Arts
18 pl François Sicard. **Tel** 02 47 05 68 73. **Open** Wed–Mon. **Closed** 1 Jan, 1 May, 14 Jul, 1 & 11 Nov, 25 Dec.

Musée du Compagnonnage
8 rue Nationale. **Tel** 02 47 21 62 20. **Open** mid-Jun–mid-Sep: daily; mid-Sep–mid-Jun: Wed–Mon. **Closed** 1 Jan, 1 May, 14 Jul, 1 & 11 Nov, 25 Dec.

Environs

Just outside Céré la Ronde, on the D764 from Montrichard to Loches, lies the 15th-century **Château de Montpoupon** and its excellent Musée du Veneur, which looks at the important role of horses in hunting.

Tours Town Centre

① Place Plumereau
② Tour Charlemagne
③ Hôtel Goüin
④ Centre de Création Contemporain Olivier Debré
⑤ Eglise St-Julien
⑥ Cathédrale St-Gatien
⑦ Musée des Beaux-Arts

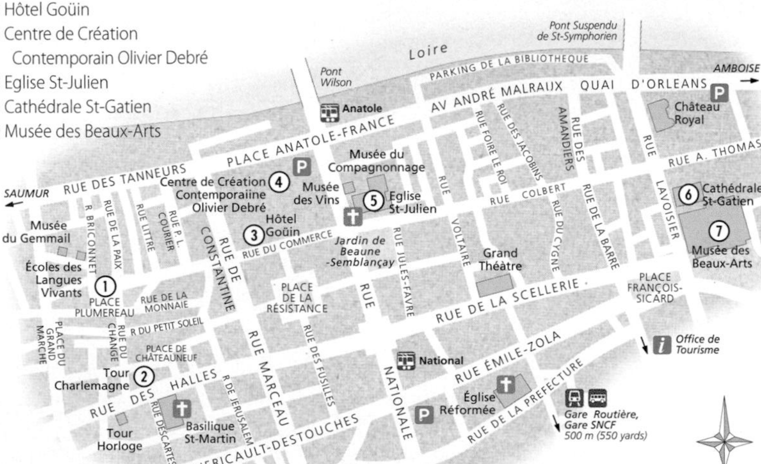

For keys to symbols *see back flap*

⓮ Château de Chenonceau

A romantic pleasure palace, Chenonceau was created from the Renaissance onwards by a series of aristocratic women. A magnificent avenue bordered by plane trees leads to symmetrical gardens and the serene vision that Flaubert praised as "floating on air and water". The château stretches across the River Cher with a 60-m (197-ft) gallery built over a series of arches, its elegant beauty reflected in the languid waters. The grandeur continues inside with splendidly furnished rooms, airy bedchambers and fine paintings and tapestries.

Turreted Pavilion
This was built between 1513 and 1521 by Catherine Briçonnet and her husband, Thomas Bohier, over the foundations of an old watermill.

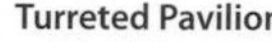

Chapelle
The chapel has a vaulted ceiling and pilasters sculpted with acanthus leaves and cockleshells. The stained glass, destroyed by a bomb in 1944, was replaced in 1953.

Catherine de' Medici's Garden
Lavish court receptions and transvestite balls were held under Catherine's auspices.

1533 Marriage of Catherine de' Medici (1519–89) to Henri II (1519–59). Chenonceau becomes a Loire royal palace

1547 Henri II offers Chenonceau to Diane de Poitiers, his lifelong mistress

Catherine de' Medici

1789 Chenonceau is spared in the French Revolution, thanks to Madame Dupin

1500 | **1600** | **1700** | **1800**

1513 Thomas Bohier acquires medieval Chenonceau. His wife, Catherine Briçonnet, rebuilds it in Renaissance style

1575 Louise de Lorraine (1554–1601) marries Henri III, Catherine's third and favourite son

1559 On Henri's death, Catherine forces the disgraced Diane to accept the Château de Chaumont in exchange for Chenonceau

1863 Madame Pelouze restores château to its original s

1730–99 Madame Dupin, a "farmer-general's" wife, makes Chenonceau a salon for writers and philosophers

VISITORS' CHECKLIST

Practical Information
Tel 08 20 20 90 90. **Open** daily. gr. fl. only.
Promenades Nocturnes: Jul–Aug (walks in the illuminated grounds to the sound of classical music). **chenonceau.com**

Transport
Chenonceaux. from Tours.

Grande Galerie
The elegant gallery crowning the bridge is Florentine in style. It was created by Catherine de'Medici from 1570 to 1576.

1913 The château is bought by the Menier family, the chocolatiers who still own it today

1900

1941 Chenonceau chapel is damaged in a bombing raid

Diane de Poitiers

The Creation of Chenonceau

The women responsible for Chenonceau each left their mark. Catherine Briçonnet, wife of the first owner, built the turreted pavilion and one of the first straight staircases in France; Henri II's mistress, Diane de Poitiers, added the formal gardens and arched bridge over the river; Catherine de' Medici transformed the bridge into an Italian-style gallery (having evicted Diane following her husband's death in 1559); Louise de Lorraine, bereaved wife of Henri III, inherited the château in 1590 and painted the ceiling of her bedchamber black and white (the colour of royal mourning); Madame Dupin, a cultured 18th-century chatelaine, saved the château from destruction in the Revolution; and Madame Pelouze undertook a complete restoration in 1863.

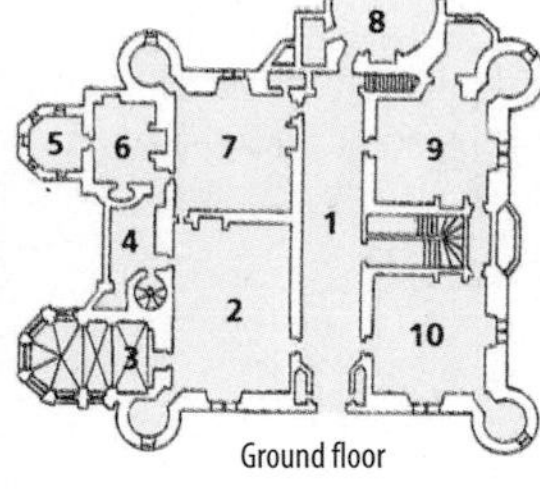

Ground floor

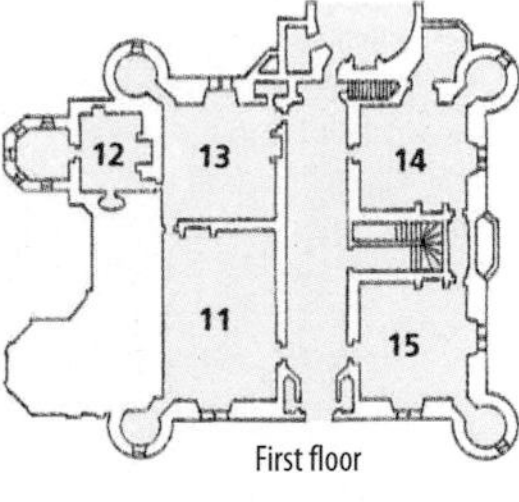

First floor

Château Guide

The main living area was in the square-shaped turreted pavilion in the middle of the River Cher. Four principal rooms open off the Vestibule on the ground floor: the Salle des Gardes and the Chambre de Diane de Poitiers, both hung with 16th-century Flemish tapestries; the Chambre de François I, with a Van Loo painting; and the Salon Louis XIV. On the first floor, reached via the Italianate staircase, are other sumptuous apartments, including the Chambre de Catherine de' Médici and the Chambre de César de Vendôme.

1 Vestibule
2 Salle des Gardes
3 Chapelle
4 Terrasse
5 Librairie de Catherine de' Médicis
6 Cabinet Vert
7 Chambre de Diane de Poitiers
8 Grande Galerie
9 Chambre de François I
10 Salon Louis XIV
11 Chambre des Cinq Reines
12 Cabinet des Estampes
13 Chambre de Catherine de' Médici
14 Chambre de César de Vendôme
15 Chambre de Gabrielle d'Estrées

Chambre de Catherine de' Médici

15 Vouvray

Indre-et-Loire. 3,500. 12 rue Rabelais (02 47 52 68 73). Tue & Fri. **tourismevouvray-valdeloire.com**

Just east of Tours is the village of Vouvray, home of the delicious white wine that Renaissance author Rabelais likened to taffeta.

The star vineyard is **Huet**, where, since 1990, grapes have been grown according to biodynamic methods: manual weeding and natural fertilizers. In the preface to his novel *Quentin Durward,* Sir Walter Scott sang the praises of its dry white wines, which are still matured in chestnut barrels. Gaston Huet also hit the headlines in 1990 with his protests against the building of tracks for the TGV train over Vouvray vineyards. A compromise was reached and tunnels were built under the hilly vineyards.

The **Château de Montcontour**, where monks first planted vines in the 4th century, has its own winemaking museum in the 10th-century cellars hewn out of the tufa rock.

Huet
11–13 rue de la Croix-Buisée. **Tel** 02 47 52 78 87. **Open** Tue–Sat; wine tastings and cellar visits by reservation only. **Closed** public hols. for groups.

The medieval town of Loches

Château de Moncontour
Route de Rochecorbon. **Tel** 02 47 52 60 77. **Open** Apr–Sep: daily; Oct–Mar: Mon–Fri & Sat am. Visits can be followed by wine tastings. **moncontour.com**

16 Loches

Indre-et-Loire. 7,000. pl de la Marne (02 47 91 82 82). Wed & Sat. **loches-tourainecotesud.com**

This picturesque, unspoiled medieval town is removed from the château trail in the Indre Valley. It is a backwater of late Gothic gateways and sculpted façades. Its keep boasts the deepest dungeons in the Loire. The **Logis Royal de Loches** is associated with Charles VII and his mistress Agnès Sorel. It is also where Joan of Arc pleaded with Charles to go to Reims and be crowned. Anne of Brittany's chapel is decorated with ermines, and contains an effigy of Agnès Sorel.

Logis Royal de Loches
Tel 02 47 59 01 32. **Open** daily. **Closed** 1 Jan, 25 Dec.

The Heroine of France

Joan of Arc is the quintessential French national heroine, a virginal warrior, a woman martyr, a French figurehead. Her divinely led campaign to "drive the English out of France" during the Hundred Years' War has inspired plays, poetry and films from Voltaire to Cecil B de Mille. Responding to heavenly voices, she appeared on the scene as champion of the dauphin, the uncrowned Charles VII. He faced an Anglo-Burgundian alliance, which held most of northern France, and had escaped to the royal châteaux on the Loire. Joan convinced him of her mission, mustered the French troops and in May 1429 led them to victory over the English at Orléans. She then urged the dithering Charles to go to Reims to be crowned. However, in 1430 she was captured and handed over to the English. Accused of witchcraft, she was burned at the stake in Rouen in 1431 at the age of 19. Her legendary bravery and tragic martyrdom led to her canonization in 1920.

Earliest known drawing of Joan of Arc (1429)

Portrait of Joan of Arc in the Archives Nationales in Paris. She saved the city from the English on 8 May 1429, a date the Orléanais still celebrate annually *(see p316).*

⓱ Montrésor

Indre-et-Loire. 400. 43 grande rue (02 47 92 70 71). **tourisme-valdindrois-montresor.com**

Classed as one of "the most beautiful villages in France", Montrésor does not disappoint. Set on the River Indrois, it became a Polish enclave in the 1840s. In 1849 a Polish nobleman, Count Branicki, bought the 15th-century **Château**, built on the site of one of Foulques Nerra's 11th-century fortifications. One of the most charming castles in the Loire Valley, Château de Montrésor has remained in the family ever since, its interior unchanged since the mid-19th century.

Farm building and poppy fields near the village of Montrésor

Château de Montrésor
Tel 02 47 92 60 04. **Open** daily (mid-Nov–mid-Apr: Sat & Sun).

⓲ Amboise

Indre-et-Loire. 12,000. quai du Général de Gaulle (02 47 57 09 28). Fri & Sun am. **amboise-valdeloire.com**

Few buildings are more historically important than the **Château d'Amboise**. Louis XI lived here; Charles VIII was born and died here; François I was brought up here, as were Catherine de'Medici's ten children. The château was also the setting for the 1560 Amboise Conspiracy, an ill-fated Huguenot plot against François II. Visitors are shown the metal lacework balcony that served as a gibbet for 12 of the 1,200 conspirators who were put to death. The **Tour des Minimes**, the château's original entrance, is famous for its huge spiral ramp, up which horsemen could ride to deliver provisions.

Amboise seen from the Loire

On the ramparts is the beautifully restored Gothic **Chapelle St-Hubert**, Leonardo da Vinci's burial place. Under the patronage of François I, the artist lived in the nearby manor house of **Clos-Lucé** between 1516 and 1519. The Clos-Lucé contains a museum exhibiting models of Leonardo's inventions constructed from his sketches.

Château d'Amboise
Tel 02 47 57 00 98. **Open** daily. **Closed** 1 Jan, 25 Dec.
chateau-amboise.com

Clos-Lucé
2 rue de Clos-Lucé. **Tel** 02 47 57 00 73. **Open** daily. **Closed** 1 Jan, 25 Dec. restricted.
vinci-closluce.com

A romantic heroine, Joan of Arc was a popular subject for artists. This painting of her is by François-Léon Benouville (1821–59).

Burned at the stake – a scene from *St Joan*, Otto Preminger's 1957 epic film, which starred Jean Seberg.

⑲ Château de Chambord

Henry James once said, "Chambord is truly royal – royal in its great scale, its grand air, and its indifference to common considerations." The Loire's largest residence, brainchild of the extravagant François I, began as a hunting lodge in the Forêt de Boulogne. In 1519 this was razed and the creation of present-day Chambord began, to a design probably initiated by Leonardo da Vinci. By 1537 the towers, keep and terraces had been completed by 1,800 men and three master masons. At one point, François suggested diverting the Loire to flow in front of his château, but he settled for redirecting the nearby Cosson instead. His son Henry II continued his work, and Louis XIV completed the 440-roomed edifice in 1685.

The Château de Chambord with the River Cosson, a tributary of the Loire, in the foreground

★ Roof Terraces
This skyline of delicate cupolas has been likened to a miniature Oriental town. The roof terraces include a forest of elongated chimney-pots, miniature spires, shell-shaped domes and richly sculpted gables.

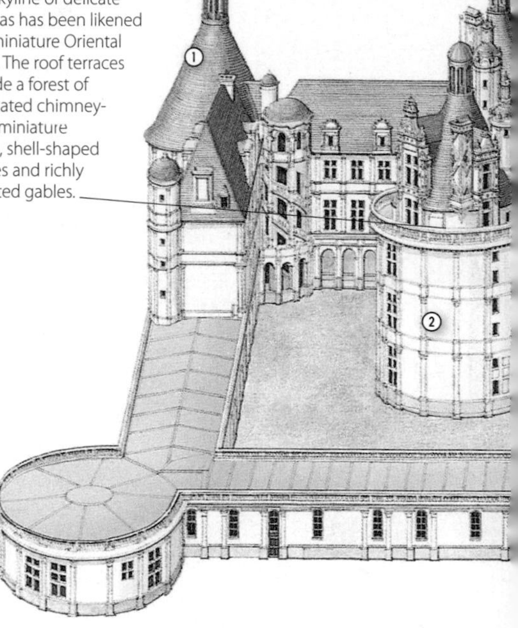

KEY

① **The chapel** was begun by François I shortly before his death in 1547. Henri II added the second storey and Louis XIV the roof.

② **The central keep** (donjon), with its four circular towers, forms the nucleus of the château.

③ **The lantern tower** is 32 m (105 ft) high. Surmounting the terrace, it is supported by arched buttresses and crowned by a fleur-de-lys.

④ **François I's Bedchamber** is where the king, hurt by a failed romance, scratched a message on a pane of glass: "Souvent femme varie, bien fol est qui s'y fie." (Every woman is fickle, he who trusts one is a fool.)

1519–47 The Count of Blois's hunting lodge demolished by François I and the château created

1547 Death of François I

1547–59 Henri II adds the west wing and second storey of the chapel

1669–85 Louis XIV completes the building, then abandons it

1670 Molière's *Le Bourgeois Gentilhomme* staged at Chambord

1725–33 Inhabited by Stanislas Leczinski, exiled king of Poland who was made duke of Lorraine

1748 The Maréchal de Saxe acquires Chambord. On his death, two years later, the château yet again falls into decline

1840 Chambord declared a *Monument Historique*

1970s Chambord is restored and refurnished and the moats re-dug

1500 | 1600 | 1700 | 1800 | 1900

Molière

★ Vaulted Guardrooms
Arranged in the form of a Greek cross around the Grand Staircase, the vaulted guardrooms were once the setting for royal balls and plays. Their ceilings are decorated with François I's initials and salamander motif.

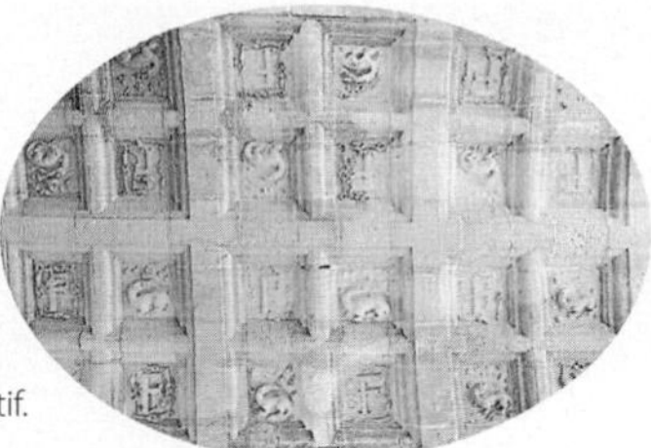

VISITORS' CHECKLIST

Practical Information
Tel 02 54 50 40 00. **Open** Nov–Mar. 9am–5pm daily; Apr–Oct: 9am–6pm daily. **Closed** 1 Jan, 1 May, 25 Dec. Apr–Sep: events include carriage rides, boat trips and equestrian shows. **chambord.org**

Transport
Blois, then taxi, bus (2, 4) or shuttle to Chambord (Apr–early Sep only). 02 54 90 41 41.

The Salamander
François I chose the salamander as his enigmatic emblem. It appears over 800 times throughout the château.

Cabinet de François I
The king's barrel-vaulted study *(cabinet)* in the outer north tower was turned into an oratory in the 18th century by Queen Catherine Opalinska, wife of Stanislas Leczinski (Louis XV's father-in-law).

★ Grand Staircase
This innovative double-helix staircase was supposedly designed by Leonardo da Vinci. It ensures that the person going up and the person going down cannot meet.

Louis XIV's Bedchamber
Within the Sun King's apartments, the grandest quarters in the château, is Louis XIV's bedchamber.

Blois's Cathédrale St-Louis and Hôtel de Ville seen from across the Loire

⑳ Blois

Loir-et-Cher. 60,000.
23 pl du château (02 54 90 41 41).
Wed, Sat. **bloischambord.com**

Once a fief of the counts of Blois, the town rose to prominence as a royal domain in the 15th century, retaining its historic façades and refined atmosphere to this day. Architectural interest abounds in Vieux Blois, the hilly, partially pedestrianized quarter enclosed by the château, cathedral and river. Four well-signposted walking tours act as a gentle introduction to the noble mansions and romantic courtyards that grace the Loire's most beguiling town.

Set back from the north bank of the river, the **Château Royal de Blois** was the principal royal residence until Henri IV moved the court to Paris in 1598 – Louis XIV's creation of Versailles *(see pp178–81)* was to mark the final eclipse of Blois. The château's four contrasting wings make a harmonious whole. The Salle des Etats Généraux, the only part of the building surviving from the 13th century, housed the council and court, and is the largest and best-preserved Gothic hall in France. The adjoining late 15th-century Louis XII wing, which houses the **Musée des Beaux-Arts**, infuses Gothic design with Renaissance spirit, sealed with the king's porcupine symbol.

The 16th-century François I wing is a masterpiece of the French Renaissance, containing a monumental spiral staircase in an octagonal tower. By contrast, the 17th-century Gaston d'Orléans wing is a model of Classical sobriety.

Blois is authentically furnished and hung with paintings interpreting its troubled past. These include a portrayal of the murder of the Duc de Guise in 1588. Suspected of heading a Catholic plot against Henri III, he was stabbed to death by guards in the king's chamber.

King Louis XII's porcupine symbol

The most intriguing room is Catherine de' Medici's study where, of the 237 carved wooden wall panels, four are secret cabinets said to have stored her poisons. Dominating the eastern

François I Staircase
Built between 1515 and 1524, this octagonal staircase is a masterpiece of the early French Renaissance.

The gallery provided an ideal setting for viewing jousts and receptions held in the inner courtyard.

François I's salamander motif adorns the openwork balustrades.

The staircase within the tower slopes appreciably more steeply than the balustrades.

Louis XII wing of the Château Royal de Blois

For hotels and restaurants in this region see pp561–2 and pp586–9

sector of the city, the **Cathédrale St-Louis** is a 17th-century reconstruction of a Gothic church that was almost completely destroyed by a hurricane in 1678. Behind the cathedral the former bishop's palace, built in 1700, is the **Hôtel de Ville** (town hall). The surrounding terraced gardens have lovely views over the city and river. Opposite the cathedral is the **Maison des Acrobates**, carved with characters from medieval farces including acrobats and jugglers.

Place Louis XII, the marketplace, is overlooked by splendid 17th-century façades. Rue Pierre de Blois, a quaint alley straddled by a Gothic passageway, winds downhill to the medieval Jewish ghetto. Rue des Juifs boasts several distinguished *hôtels particuliers* (mansions), including the galleried **Hôtel de Condé**, with its Renaissance archway and courtyard, and the **Hôtel Jassaud**, with magnificent 16th-century bas-reliefs above the main doorway. On rue du Puits-Châtel, which is also rich in Renaissance mansions, is the galleried **Hôtel Sardini**.

Place Vauvert is the most charming square in Vieux Blois, with a fine example of a half-timbered house.

Château Royal de Blois
Tel 02 54 90 33 33. **Open** Jan–Mar & Nov–Dec: 10am–5pm daily; Apr–Jun & Sep–Oct: 9am– 6:30pm daily; Jul–Aug: 9am–7pm daily. **Closed** 1 Jan, 25 Dec. *Son-et-lumière* show: Apr–Sep nightly (with audioguides in English).

Covered Gothic passageway in rue Pierre de Blois

The nave of the abbey church of Notre-Dame in Beaugency

㉑ Beaugency

Loiret. 7,500. 3 pl de Docteur-Hyvernaud (02 38 44 54 42). Sat. **tourisme-beaugency.fr**

The eastern gateway to the Loire, the compact medieval town of Beaugency makes a peaceful base for exploring the Orléanais region. Exceptionally for the Loire, it is possible to walk along the riverbanks and stone levees. At quai de l'Abbaye there is a good view of the 11th-century bridge, which, until modern times, was the only crossing point between Blois and Orléans. An obvious target for enemy attack, it was captured four times by the English during the Hundred Years' War, before being retaken by Joan of Arc in 1429.

The town centre is dominated by a ruined 11th-century watchtower. It stands on **place St-Firmin**, along with a 16th-century bell tower (the church was destroyed in the Revolution) and a statue of Joan of Arc. Period houses line the square.

Further down is the **Château de Beaugency**, built on the site of the feudal castle by one of Joan of Arc's *compagnons d'armes*, Jean de Dunois. Highlights include the 16th-century seigneural lodgings and the kitchen. Facing the Château de Beaugency is **Notre-Dame**, a Romanesque abbey church that witnessed the annulment of the marriage between Eleanor of Aquitaine and Louis VII in 1152, leaving Eleanor free to marry the future Henry II of England.

Nearby is the medieval clock tower in rue du Change and the Renaissance **Hôtel de Ville**, its façade adorned with the town's arms. Equally lovely is the nearby ancient mill district around rue du Pont and rue du Ru, with its streams and riot of flowers.

Château de Beaugency
3 pl Dunois. **Tel** 02 38 44 36 47. **Open** mid-Feb–late-Feb: Tue–Sun pms; Mar: Sat & Sun pms; Apr–Jun & Sep–Oct: Tue–Sun; Jul–Aug: daily. **Closed** Nov–mid-Feb.

Châteaux Tour of the Sologne

The mysterious Sologne is a secretive landscape of woods and marshes edged by vineyards. Wine lovers can indulge in tastings of Loire Valley wines accompanied, in season, by a dinner of succulent wild game from the region's forests, popular hunting grounds for centuries. The Sologne is a hunter's paradise, and devotees of the sport can see today's hounds, as well as hunting trophies of the past.

This ambling rural route takes in some of the Loire's most varied châteaux. The five on this tour – for which a couple of days is required – represent a delightful encapsulation of regional architecture. All styles are here, from feudal might to Renaissance grace and Classical elegance. Several are inhabited but can still be visited.

② Château de Beauregard
Beauregard was built around 1520 as a hunting lodge for François I. It contains a gallery with 327 portraits of royalty.

D751
D952
①
← Amboise

① Château de Chaumont
Chaumont is a feudal castle with Renaissance embellishments and lofty views over the River Loire (*see p246*).

Pontlevoy

0 kilometres 5
0 miles 5

Key

Tour route

Other roads

㉒ Vendôme

Loir-et-Cher. 19,000. 47 rue Poterie (02 54 77 05 07). Fri & Sun. **vendome-tourisme.fr**

Once an important stop for pilgrims en route to Compostela in Spain, Vendôme is still popular with modern pilgrims, thanks to the TGV rail service. Though a desirable address with Parisian commuters, the town still manages to retain its provincial charm. Vendôme's old stone buildings are encircled by the River Loir. Its lush gardens invite a relaxed exploration, especially Parc Ronsard. Reached by a footbridge across the Loir, this park boasts a plane tree planted in 1759 and a medieval *lavoir*.

The town's greatest monument is the abbey church of **La Trinité**, founded in 1034. Its Romanesque bell tower (all that remains of the original structure) is overshadowed by the church portal, a masterpiece of Flamboyant Gothic tracery. The interior is embellished with Romanesque capitals and 15th-century choir stalls. Commanding a rocky spur high above the Loir is the ruined **château**, built by the counts of Vendôme in the 13th–14th centuries. The garden around the château is remarkable for its collection of hydrangeas.

Vendôme's native son Rochambeau, hero of the American Revolution

㉓ The Loir

Loir-et-Cher. Tours. Vendôme. Montoire-sur-le-Loir. 16 pl Clémenceau, Montoire-sur-le-Loir (02 54 85 23 30). **otsi-montoire.fr**

Compared with the royal River Loire, the tranquil Loir to the north has a more rural charm. The stretch between Vendôme and Trôo is the most rewarding, offering troglodyte caves (*see p296*), walking trails, wine tasting, fishing and boat trips.

Les Roches-l'Evêque is a fortified village with cave dwellings visible in the cliff face. Just downstream is **Lavardin**, with its Romanesque church, half-timbered houses, Gothic bridge and ruined château ringed by ramparts. In **Montoire-sur-le-Loir**, the Chapelle St-Gilles, a former leper colony, has Romanesque frescoes. **Trôo**, the next major village, is known for its Romanesque Eglise de St-Martin and a

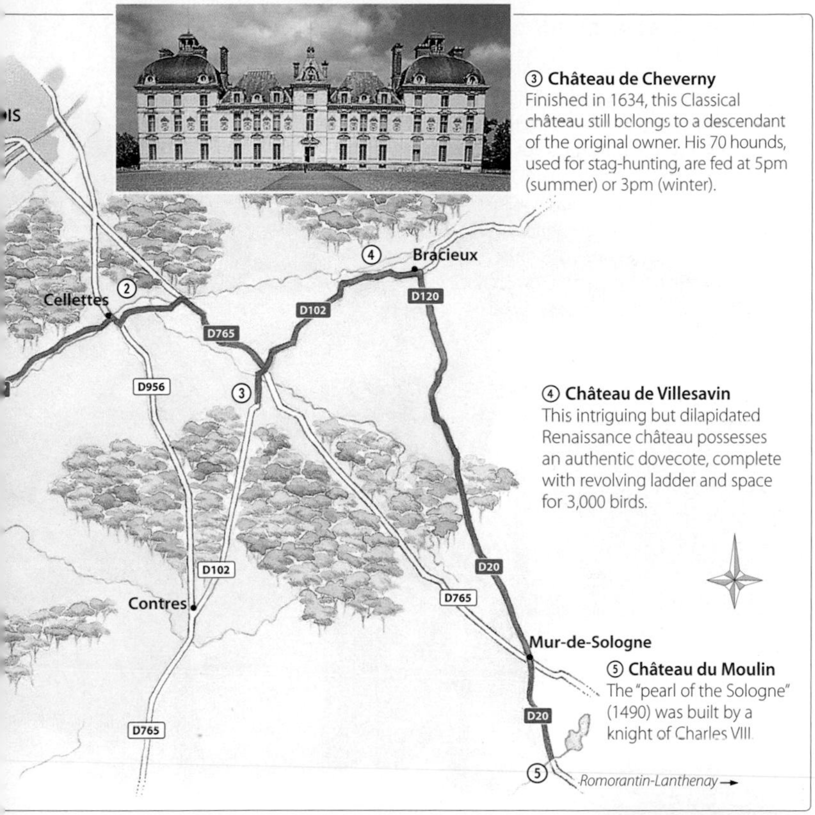

③ Château de Cheverny
Finished in 1634, this Classical château still belongs to a descendant of the original owner. His 70 hounds, used for stag-hunting, are fed at 5pm (summer) or 3pm (winter).

④ Château de Villesavin
This intriguing but dilapidated Renaissance château possesses an authentic dovecote, complete with revolving ladder and space for 3,000 birds.

⑤ Château du Moulin
The "pearl of the Sologne" (1490) was built by a knight of Charles VIII.

labyrinth of troglodyte dwellings. **St-Jacques-des-Guérets**, facing the village of Trôo, has a frescoed Romanesque chapel, as does **Poncé-sur-le-Loir**, farther downstream. On the slopes are vineyards producing Jasnières and Côteaux du Vendômois. Wine tastings enliven sleepy **Poncé** and **La Chartre-sur-le-Loir**. The cliffs on the opposite bank are studded with caves, commonly used as wine cellars.

Northward, the **Forêt de Bercé** abounds with paths and streams, while to the west the small town of **Le Lude** sits on the south bank of the Loir, dominated by its romantic 15th-century château.

Some 20 km (12 miles) west of Le Lude lies the town of **La Flèche**, where the main attraction is the Prytanée Nationale Militaire, originally a Jesuit college founded by Henri IV in 1603. Philosopher René Descartes was one of the college's earliest and most illustrious pupils.

㉔ Chartres

Eure-et-Loir. 42,000.
8–10 rue de la Poissonnerie (02 37 18 26 26). Tue, Thu, Sat.
chartres-tourisme.com

Chartres has the greatest Gothic cathedral in Europe *(see pp312–15)*, and its churches should not be ignored. The Benedictine abbey church of **St-Pierre** has lovely medieval stained-glass windows, while **St-Aignan** abuts 9th- century ramparts. By the river is the Romanesque **Eglise de St-André**, a deconsecrated church used for art exhibitions and concerts.

Chartres is also one of the first urban conservation sites in France. Half-timbered houses abound along such cobbled streets as rue des Ecuyers. Steep staircases known as *tertres* lead down to the River Eure, providing views of mills, humpback stone bridges, washhouses and the cathedral.

One of the many washhouses along the Eure river

In the Grenier de Loens, next to the cathedral, is the **Centre International du Vitrail** (stained-glass centre). The building's 13th-century vaulted storerooms house a museum for temporary exhibitions of contemporary stained glass and the techniques of making it. There is a permanent exhibition of Renaissance stained-glass panels. The centre provides courses for beginners and experienced artists.

Centre International du Vitrail
5 rue du Cardinal Pie. **Tel** 02 37 21 65 72. **Open** Mon–Sat & Sun pm.

Chartres Cathedral

According to art historian Emile Mâle, "Chartres is the mind of the Middle Ages manifest." Begun in 1020, the Romanesque cathedral was destroyed by fire in 1194. Only the north and south towers, south steeple, west portal and crypt remained; the sacred *Veil of the Virgin* relic was the sole treasure to survive. Peasant and lord alike helped to rebuild the church in just 25 years. Few alterations were made after 1250, and fortunately, Chartres was unscathed by the Wars of Religion and the French Revolution. The result is a Gothic cathedral with a true "Bible in stone" reputation.

Elongated Statues
These statues on the Royal Portal represent Old Testament figures.

Gothic Nave
As wide as the Romanesque crypt below it, the nave reaches a lofty height of 37 m (121 ft).

★ Royal Portal
The central tympanum of the Royal Portal (1145–55) shows *Christ in Majesty*.

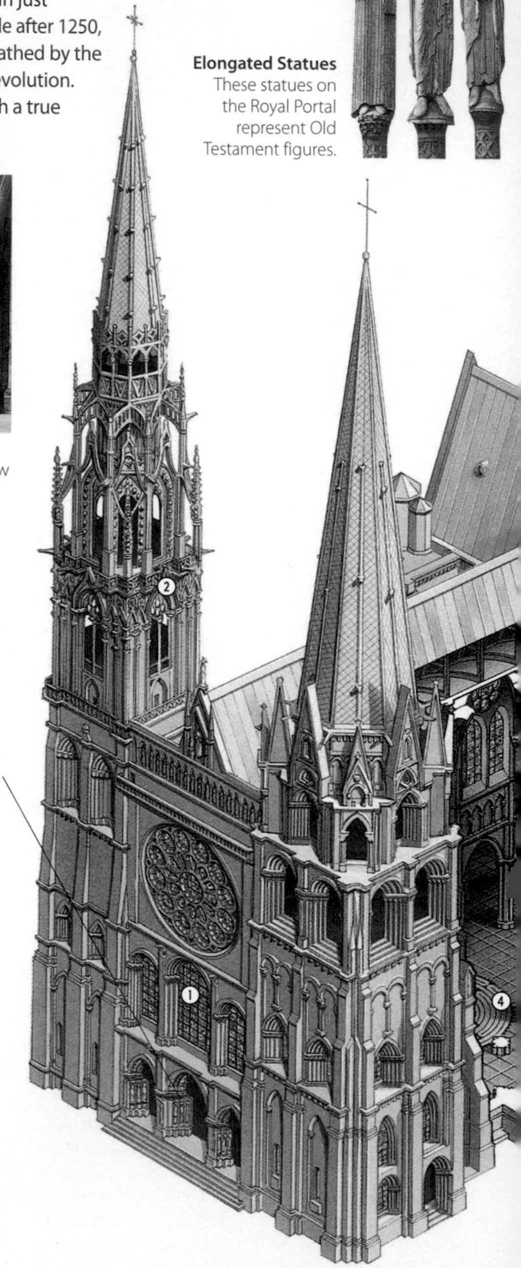

KEY

① **The lower half** of the west front is a survivor of the original Romanesque church, with the portal and the three windows dating from the mid-12th century.

② **The taller** of the two spires dates from the start of the 16th century. Flamboyant Gothic in style, it contrasts sharply with the solemnity of its Romanesque counterpart.

③ **The vaulted ceiling** is supported by a network of ribs.

④ **Labyrinth**

The Labyrinth

The 13th-century labyrinth, inlaid in the nave floor, was a feature of most medieval cathedrals. Pilgrims followed the tortuous route on their knees, echoing the way to Jerusalem and the complexity of life, in order to reach Christ. The journey – 259 m (851 ft) of broken concentric circles – took at least an hour.

VISITORS' CHECKLIST

Practical Information
Pl de la Cathédrale. **Tel** 02 37 21 59 08. **Open** 8:30am–7:30pm daily. 9am Tue & Fri, 11:45am & 6:15pm Mon–Sat (6pm Sat), 9:15am (in Latin) & 11am Sun. for crypt and tower.
cathedrale-chartres.org

Our Lady of the Pillar
Carved from dark pear wood, this 16th-century replica of a 13th-century statue is a striking shrine, which is often surrounded by candles.

★ Stained-Glass Windows
The windows cover a surface area of over 2,600 sq m (28,000 sq ft).

★ South Porch
Sculpture on the South Porch (1197–1209) reflects New Testament teaching.

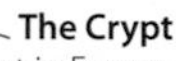

The Crypt
This is the largest crypt in France, most of it dating from the early 11th century. It houses the *Veil of the Virgin* relic and comprises two galleries, a series of chapels and the 9th-century St Lubin's vault.

The Stained Glass of Chartres

Donated by royalty, aristocracy, priests and the merchant brotherhoods between 1210 and 1240, this glorious collection of stained glass is world renowned. Around 176 windows illustrate biblical stories and daily life in the 13th century. During both world wars the windows were dismantled piece by piece and removed for safety. There is an on-going programme, begun in the 1970s, to restore the windows in the cathedral.

Stained glass above the apse

Redemption Window
Six scenes illustrate *Christ's Passion* and death on the Cross (c.1210).

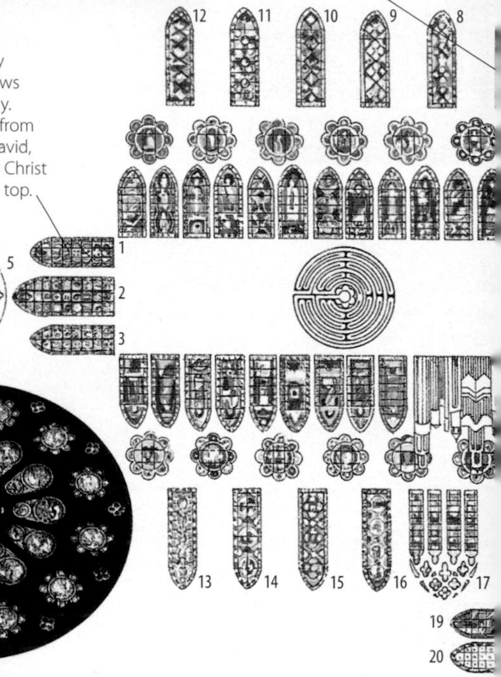

★ Tree of Jesse
This 12th-century stained glass shows Christ's genealogy. The tree rises up from Jesse, father of David, at the bottom, to Christ enthroned at the top.

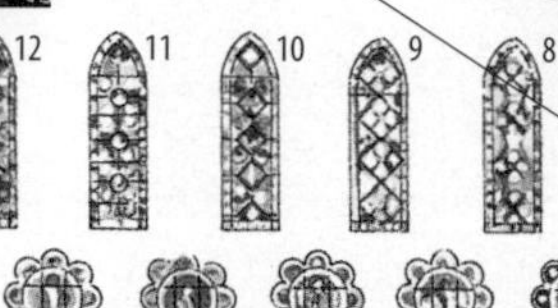

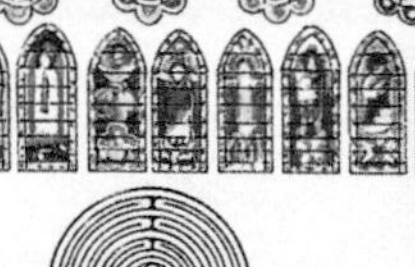

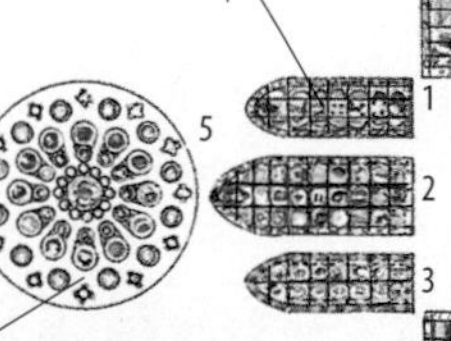

★ West Rose Window
This window (1215), with Christ seated in the centre, shows the *Last Judgment*.

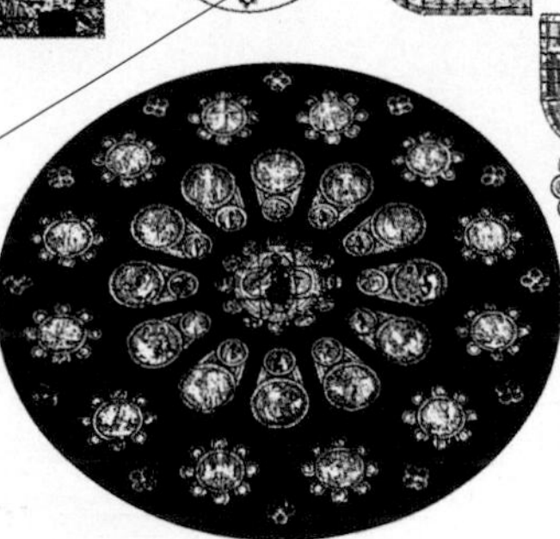

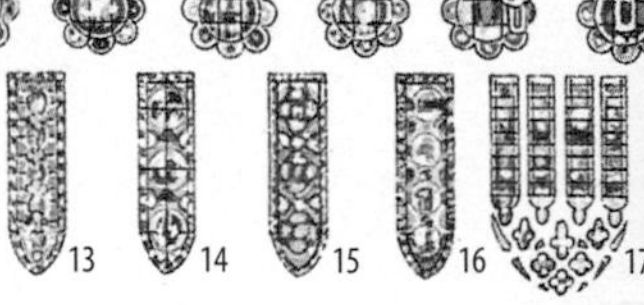

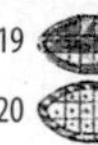

Key

1 Tree of Jesse
2 Incarnation
3 Passion and Resurrection
4 North Rose Window
5 West Rose Window
6 South Rose Window
7 Redemption Window
8 St Nicholas
9 Joseph
10 St Eustache
11 St Lubin
12 Noah
13 St John the Evangelist
14 Mary Magdalene
15 Good Samaritan and Adam and Eve
16 Assumption
17 Vendôme Chapel Windows
18 Miracles of Mary
19 St Apollinaris
20 Modern Window
21 St Fulbert
22 St Anthony and St Paul
23 Blue Virgin
24 Life of the Virgin
25 Zodiac Window
26 St Martin
27 St Thomas Becket
28 St Margaret and St Catherine
29 St Nicholas
30 St Remy
31 St James the Greater
32 Charlemagne
33 St Theodore and St Vincent
34 St Stephen
35 St Cheron
36 St Thomas
37 Peace Window
38 Modern Window
39 Prodigal Son
40 Ezekiel and David
41 Aaron
42 Annunciation-Visitation
43 Isaiah and Moses
44 Daniel and Jeremiah

North Rose Window
This depicts the *Glorification of the Virgin*, surrounded by the kings of Judah and the prophets (c.1230).

Guide to Reading the Windows

Each window is divided into panels, usually read from left to right, bottom to top (Earth to Heaven). The number of figures or abstract shapes used is thought to be symbolic: three stands for divinity, while the number four symbolizes the material world or the four elements.

Upper panels of the Incarnation Window

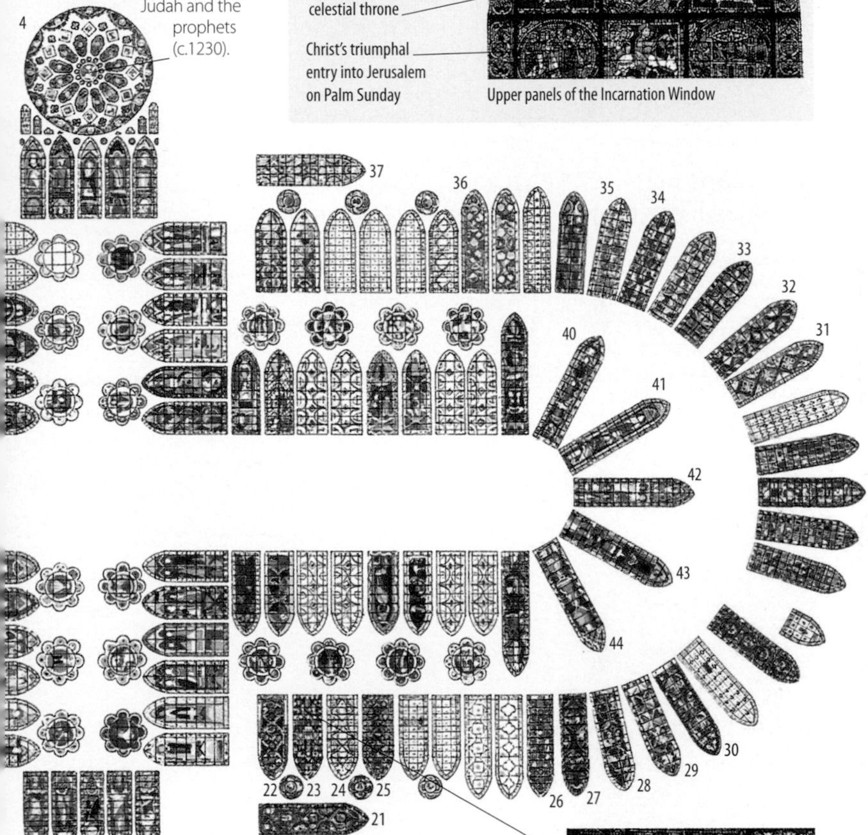

4

37

36

35

34

33

32

31

40

41

42

43

44

30

29

28

27

26

22 23 24 25

21

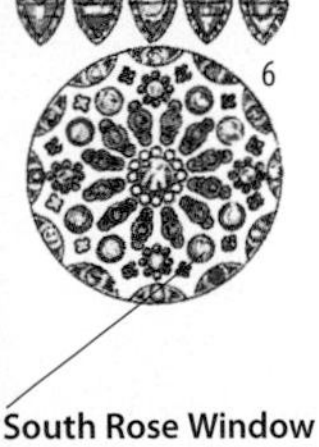

6

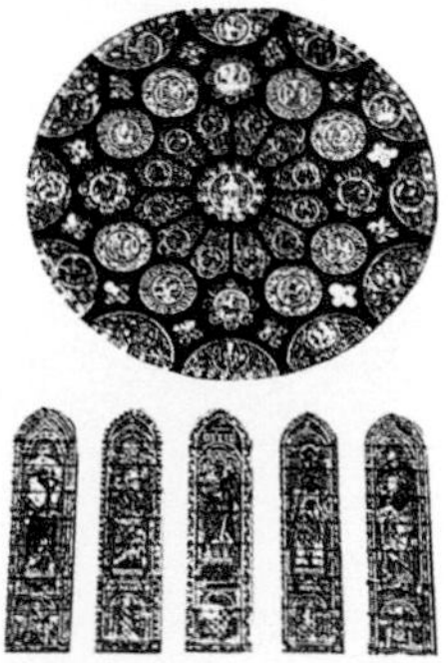

South Rose Window
This illustrates the *Apocalypse*, with *Christ in Majesty* (c.1225).

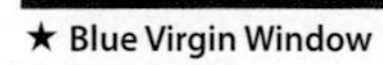

★ Blue Virgin Window
The window's bottom panel depicts the conversion of water into wine by Christ at *The Wedding at Cana*.

Orléans's Cathédrale Sainte-Croix

㉕ Orléans

Loiret. 110,000. 2 pl Etape (02 38 24 05 05). Tue–Sun.
tourisme-orleans.com

Orléans's dazzling contemporary bridge symbolizes the city's increasing importance at the geographic heart of both France and Europe. As a tourist, however, one is struck by the city's continued attachment to its past, most particularly to Joan of Arc. It was from here that the Maid of Orléans saved France from the English in 1429 *(see pp304–5)*. Since her martyrdom at Rouen in 1431, Joan remains a presence in Orléans. Every 29 April and 1 and 7–8 May her liberation of the city is re-enacted in a pageant and a blessing in the cathedral.

Orléans's historic centre was badly damaged in World War II, but much has been reconstructed, and a faded grandeur lingers in Vieil Orléans, the quarter bounded by the cathedral, the River Loire and **place du Martroi**. The latter, a Classical but rather windswept square, has an equestrian statue of the city's heroine. Nearby the half-timbered **Maison de Jeanne d'Arc**, rebuilt from period dwellings in 1961 on the site where Joan had lodgings in 1429, has multimedia displays telling her story.

From place du Martroi, rue d'Escures leads past Renaissance mansions to the cathedral. **Hôtel Groslot** is the grandest, a 16th-century red-brick mansion, where kings Charles IX, Henri III and Henri IV all stayed. The 17-year-old François II died here in 1560 after attending a meeting of the Etats Généraux with his child bride, Mary, later Queen of Scots. The building served as Orléans's town hall from 1790 to 1982, and the sumptuously decorated interior, with its Joan memorabilia, is still used for marriages and official ceremonies.

Virtually opposite the Hôtel Groslot and alongside the new town hall is the **Musée des Beaux-Arts**, displaying European works of art from the 16th to the 20th centuries.

The **Cathédrale Sainte-Croix** nearby is an imposing edifice begun in the late 13th century, destroyed by the Huguenots (Protestants) in 1568, and then rebuilt in supposedly Gothic style between the 17th and 19th centuries.

Maison de Jeanne d'Arc
3 pl du Général de Gaulle. **Tel** 02 38 68 32 63. **Open** Tue–Sun (Oct–Mar: pms only).

Hôtel Groslot
Pl de l'Etape. **Tel** 02 38 79 22 30. **Open** Sun–Fri, Sat am. **Closed** sporadically.

Musée des Beaux-Arts
Pl Ste-Croix. **Tel** 02 38 79 21 55. **Open** Tue–Sun. **Closed** 1 Jan, 1 & 8 May, 14 Jul, 1 & 11 Nov, 25 Dec. free 1st Sun of month.

Orléans City Centre

① Maison de Jeanne d'Arc
② Hôtel Groslot
③ Musée des Beaux-Arts
④ Cathédrale Sainte-Croix

0 metres 250
0 yards 250

For keys to symbols *see back flap*

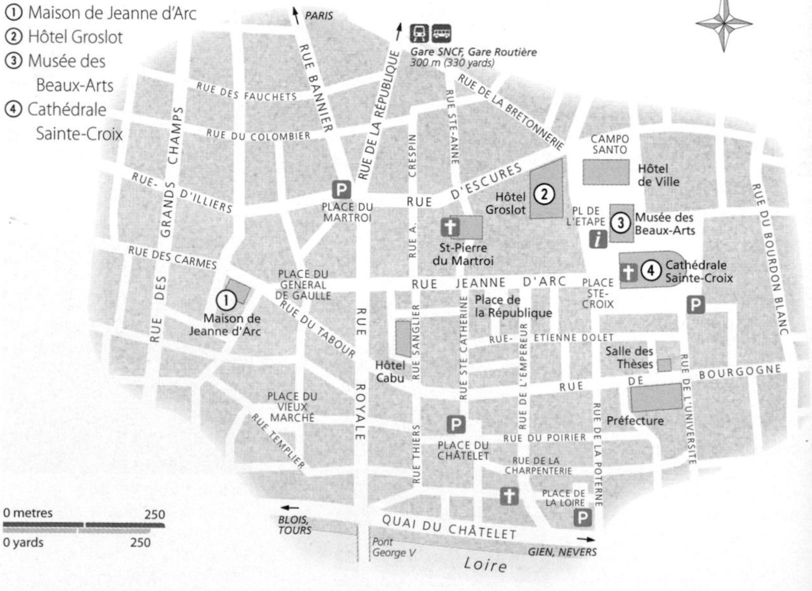

Joan of Arc stained-glass window in Orléans' Cathédrale Sainte-Croix

26 St-Benoît-sur-Loire

Loiret. 2,000. 44 rue Orléanaise (02 38 35 79 00).
W **tourisme-loire-foret.com**

Situated along the River Loire between Orléans and Gien, St-Benoît-sur-Loire boasts one of the finest Romanesque abbey churches (1067–1108) in France. It is all that survives of an important monastery founded in AD 650 and named after St Benedict, patron saint of Europe. His relics were brought from Italy at the end of the 7th century.

The church's belfry porch is graced with carved capitals depicting biblical scenes. The nave is tall and light, and the choir floor is an amazing patchwork of Italian marble. Daily services with Gregorian chant are open to the public.

27 Bourges

Cher. 80,000. 21 rue Victor Hugo (02 48 23 02 60). Tue–Sun. W **bourges-tourisme.com**

This Gallo-Roman city retains its original walls but is best known as the city of Jacques Coeur, financier and foreign minister to Charles VII. The greatest merchant of the Middle Ages and a self-made man *par excellence*, it was in his capacity as an arms dealer that he established a tradition maintained for four centuries, as Napoleon III had cannons manufactured here in 1862.

Built over part of the walls, the **Palais Jacques Coeur** is a Gothic gem and a lasting memorial to its first master. It was finished in 1453, and incorporates Coeur's two emblems, scallop shells and hearts, as well as his motto: *"A vaillan coeur, rien impossible"* – to the valiant heart, nothing is impossible. The guided tour reveals a barrel-vaulted gallery, a painted chapel and a chamber that had Turkish baths.

Bourges also flourishes as a university town and cultural mecca, renowned for its spring festival of music.

Rue Bourbonnoux leads to **St-Etienne**, a cathedral very similar to Paris's Notre-Dame. The grand west façade, the widest among France's Gothic cathedrals, has five sculpted portals, the central one depicting an enthralling Last Judgment. In the choir are vivid 13th-century stained-glass windows presented by the guilds. The crypt holds the marble tomb of the 14th-century Duc de Berry, best known for commissioning the illuminated manuscript the *Très Riches Heures* (see *pp208–9*). From the top of the north tower stretch views of the beautifully restored medieval quarter and the marshes beyond. Beside the cathedral is a tithe barn and the remains of the Gallo-Roman ramparts. The **Jardin des Prés Fichaux**, set along the River Yèvre, contains pools and an open-air theatre. To the north lie the **Marais de Bourges**, where gardeners transport their produce by boat.

Statue of Jacques Coeur

Palais Jacques Coeur

Rue Jacques Coeur. **Tel** 02 48 24 79 42. **Open** daily. **Closed** 1 Jan, 1 May, 1 & 11 Nov, 25 Dec.

Environs

About 35 km (22 miles) south of Bourges in the Berry region is the **Abbaye de Noirlac**. Founded in 1136, it is one of the best-preserved Cistercian abbeys in France.

Statue in the Jardin des Prés Fichaux

For hotels and restaurants in this region see pp561–2 and pp586–9

CENTRAL FRANCE AND THE ALPS

Introducing Central France and the Alps

The geological contrasts of this region reflect its enormous variety, from the industrial and gastronomic metropolis of Lyon to the largely agricultural landscape of Burgundy. The mountains of the Massif Central and the Alps attract visitors for winter sports, superb walking and other outdoor activities. The major sights of this richly rewarding area, both natural and architectural, are shown here.

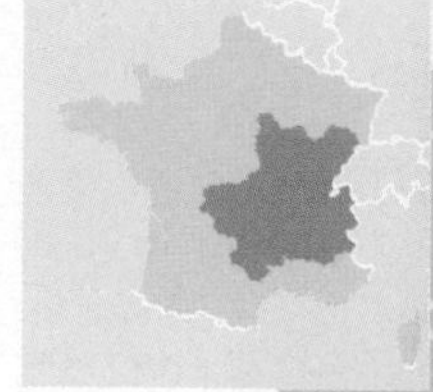

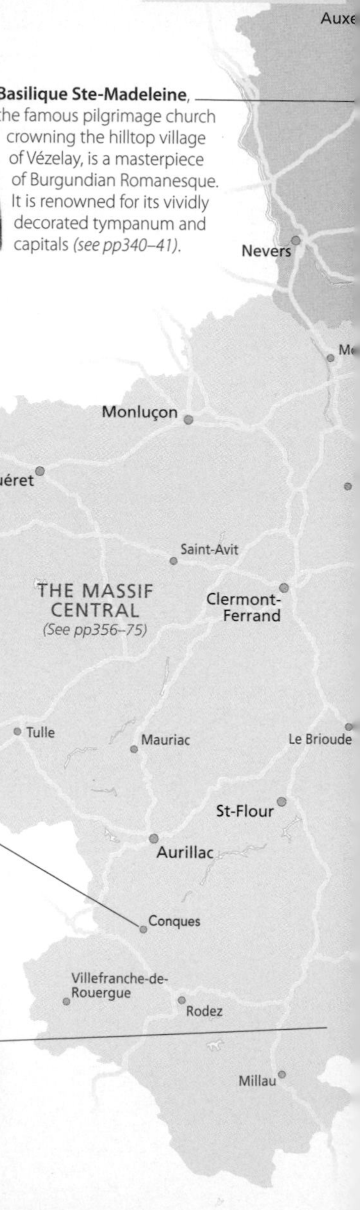

Basilique Ste-Madeleine, the famous pilgrimage church crowning the hilltop village of Vézelay, is a masterpiece of Burgundian Romanesque. It is renowned for its vividly decorated tympanum and capitals *(see pp340–41)*.

The Abbaye de Ste-Foy in the village of Conques *(see pp372–3)* is one of the great pilgrimage churches of France, with a fabulous treasury of medieval and Renaissance gold reliquaries.

The Gorges du Tarn have some of France's most spectacular natural scenery. The road which follows the plunging course of the River Tarn gives dramatic viewpoints along the canyon and across the limestone Causses *(see pp374–5)*.

◀ The magnificent peak of Puy de Dôme, the tallest extinct volcano in the Monts Dôme range

The Abbaye de Fontenay, founded by St Bernard in the early 12th century, is the oldest Cistercian monastery in France (see pp336–7). This well-preserved Romanesque abbey is a perfect testimony to the severe ideal of the Cistercian life.

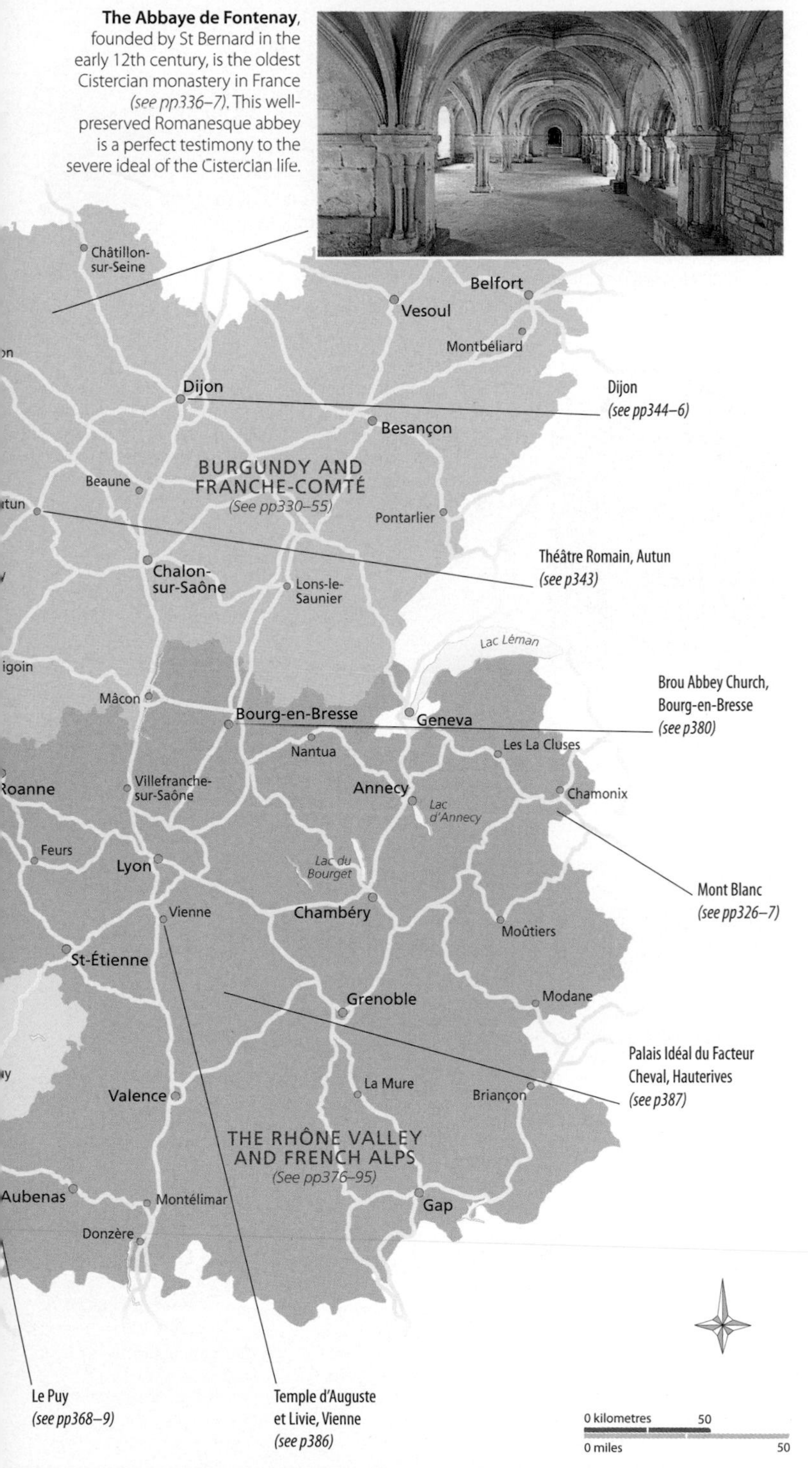

Dijon (see pp344–6)

Théâtre Romain, Autun (see p343)

Brou Abbey Church, Bourg-en-Bresse (see p380)

Mont Blanc (see pp326–7)

Palais Idéal du Facteur Cheval, Hauterives (see p387)

Le Puy (see pp368–9)

Temple d'Auguste et Livie, Vienne (see p386)

The Flavours of Central France

The renowned gastronomic tradition of Lyon and the rich wine and food of Burgundy combine to make central France a gourmet paradise. The great chefs of the region have a wide choice of excellent local produce: fine Bresse chicken, Charolais beef and Morvan ham; wildfowl and frogs from the marshes of the Dombe; fish from the Saône and the Rhône; and fat snails called "escargots de Bourgogne". Franche-Comté and the Jura contribute smoked sausages, farmhouse cheeses, walnut oil and fish from glacier-fed lakes. In the Massif Central, sturdy regional fare features salted hams, pork, Cantal cheese, the celebrated green lentils of Le Puy and wild mushrooms.

Chanterelle mushrooms

A mountain farmer shows off his fine salt-cured ham

Burgundy and Franche-Comté

Burgundy is one of France's top wine regions, so, not surprisingly, wine plays a major role in the cuisine, such as in the signature dish, *boeuf bourguignon*, made from Charolais beef marinated and then stewed in good red wine, with baby onions, bacon and mushrooms added. Other specialities include *coq au vin* and *oeufs en meurette*. Dijon's famous mustard appears most classically with steak and in *moutarde au lapin*, rabbit in a creamy mustard sauce. Burgundy and Franche-Comté produce some of the most celebrated French cheeses: Epoisses, a cow's-milk cheese washed with *marc de Bourgogne*; Cîteaux, made by monks; and the magnificent Vacherin-Mont d'Or, a winter treat to be scooped straight from its wooden box. Blackcurrants are widely grown and contribute to many desserts as well as the famous Kir: white wine with cassis (blackcurrant liqueur).

The Massif Central

The peasant cuisine of the Auvergne is well-known in France due to the many cafés run by

Mouthwatering array of classic French cheeses

Regional Dishes and Specialities

String of onions

The cuisine of central France is rich with sauces using wine, butter and cream, which enhance almost every dish: snails in butter and garlic; potatoes cooked with cheese and cream; and beef, lamb and chicken stewed slowly in reduced wine sauces, often with cream or butter added at the end of cooking. Mushrooms are served in cream sauces, and fish is often baked in a creamy *gratin*. Most indulgent of all is the Alpine fondue, where cheeses are melted, together with Kirsch and wine, in a special earthenware fondue pot. This is placed on a burner on the table, and cubes of bread are speared onto special long forks and dipped into the cheese. Traditionally, anyone who loses their bread in the pot must kiss everyone else at the table.

Oeufs en meurette This Burgundian dish is eggs poached in red wine with onions, mushrooms and bacon.

Traditional *charcuterie* on sale in a Lyon market

Auvergnats in Paris, where they serve local dishes such as pork stuffed with cabbage, or *aligot*. Le Puy lentils, grown in the fertile volcanic soils of the Puy-en-Velay basin, combine well with sausages or *petit salé*, or are served cold as a salad. Good beef comes from the Salers cattle of the Auvergne or from the Limousin, where there is also plentiful game. Wild mushrooms are eagerly sought in season. Cheeses include Cantal, one of the country's oldest, and similar in flavour to Cheddar, and the famous blue Roquefort, ripened in the limestone caves of the Lozère.

The Rhône Valley and French Alps

Lyon is famous for its traditional bistros, *bouchons*, where the cooks are often women, known as *mères*, who dish up substantial fare such as onion soup, *lyonnais* sausages and *charcuterie*. The markets of Lyon are equally famous, stocked with the region's wide range of fruit, particularly apricots, peaches and juicy berries. Vegetables include onions, chard and cardoons,

Redcurrants and blackberries for sale by the punnet

and the most northerly outpost of the olive is at Nyons. The Bresse region is famous for its high-quality chickens.

The Dombes lakes and the Alps are good sources of fish, such as perch, trout and lake salmon. Bony perch is most delicious eaten as *quenelles de brochet*, filleted fish blended, made into dumplings and baked in a creamy sauce. From the Alps comes a wide range of cheeses. As well as being delicious to eat fresh, they will often be found melted in *raclettes* or fondues, or layered with sliced potato to make an unctuous *gratin dauphinois*.

ON THE MENU

Chou farci Cabbage stuffed with pork and herbs.

Gigot Brayaude Leg of lamb baked over sliced potatoes and *lardons* of bacon.

Gougère Cheesy *choux* pastry baked in a ring shape.

Jambon persillé Ham and parsley in aspic jelly.

Pochouse Freshwater fish (carp, pike, eel and trout) stewed in white wine.

Potée savoyarde Hotpot made with vegetables, chicken, ham and sausage.

Salade auvergnate Cubes of Auvergne ham, Cantal cheese and walnuts.

Petit salé A speciality of the Auvergne region, salt pork is cooked in wine with tiny green Puy lentils.

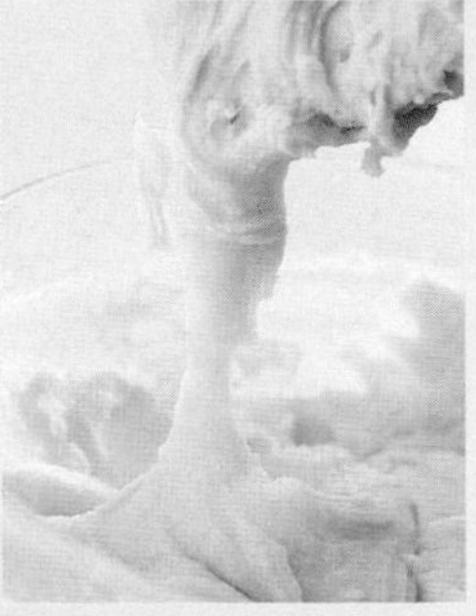

Aligot Slivers of Cantal cheese are beaten into buttery, garlicky mashed potato until the mixture forms long strands.

Clafoutis This is usually made with black cherries, baked in batter and laced with Kirsch, a cherry liqueur.

France's Wine Regions: Burgundy

Burgundy and its fine wines have inspired awe for centuries. The fame of the region's wines spread throughout Europe in the 14th century, under the Valois Dukes of Burgundy. The system of dividing wine areas into designated *appellations*, of which there are a bewildering number, came into effect in 1935. Even today, the classification system remains dauntingly complex. But, despite its impenetrable image, this is unmissable territory for the "serious" wine lover, with its rich vinous history and tradition and dazzling *grands crus*.

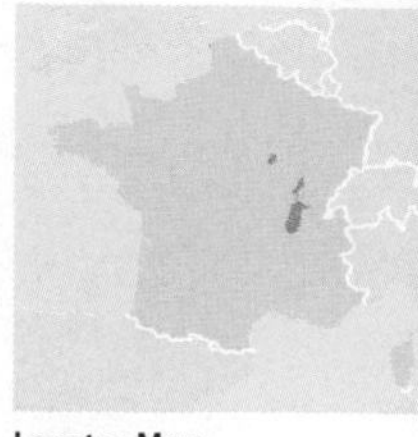

Locator Map

Burgundy wine region

Clos de Vougeot on the Côte de Nuits

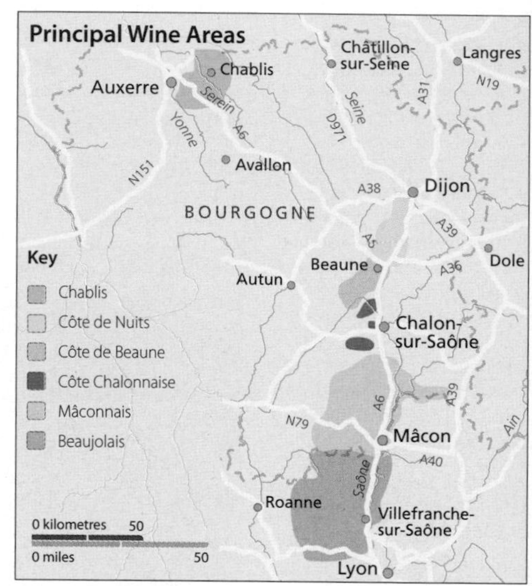

Wine Regions

Between Chablis in the north and the Côte Chalonnaise and Mâconnais in the south is the Côte d'Or, incorporating Côte de Nuits and Côte de Beaune. The Beaujolais region (see p381) *lies below Mâcon.*

Key Facts About Burgundy

Location and Climate

The continental climate (bleak winters and hot summers) can be very variable, making vintages a crucial quality factor. The best vineyards have chalky soil and face south or east.

Grape Varieties

Burgundy is at least relatively simple in its grape varieties. Red Burgundy is made from ***Pinot Noir***, with its sweet flavours of raspberries, cherries and strawberries, while the ***Gamay*** makes red Mâcon and Beaujolais. ***Chardonnay*** is the principal white variety for Chablis and white Burgundy, though small amounts of ***Aligoté*** and ***Pinot Blanc*** are grown and the ***Sauvignon*** is a speciality of St-Bris.

Good Producers

White Burgundy: Jean-Marie Raveneau, René Dauvissat, La Chablisienne, Comtes Lafon, Guy Roulot, Etienne Sauzet, Pierre Morey, Louis Carillon, Jean-Marc Boillot, André Ramonet, Hubert Lamy, Jean-Marie Guffens-Heynen, Olivier Merlin, Louis Latour, Louis Jadot, Olivier Leflaive.
Red Burgundy: Denis Bachelet, Daniel Rion, Domaine Dujac, Armand Rousseau, Joseph Roty, De Montille, Domaine de la Pousse d'Or, Domaine de l'Arlot, Jean-Jacques Confuron, Robert Chevillon, Georges Roumier, Leroy, Drouhin.

Good Vintages

(Reds) 2015, 2012, 2010, 2009, 2005.
(Whites) 2014, 2012, 2010, 2008, 2005.

So elaborate are Burgundy's *appellations* that individual vineyards, such as Clos la Roche, may have their own designation.

Grand cru vineyards are at the top of the quality pyramid; they also tend to occupy the upper slopes of the Côte d'Or.

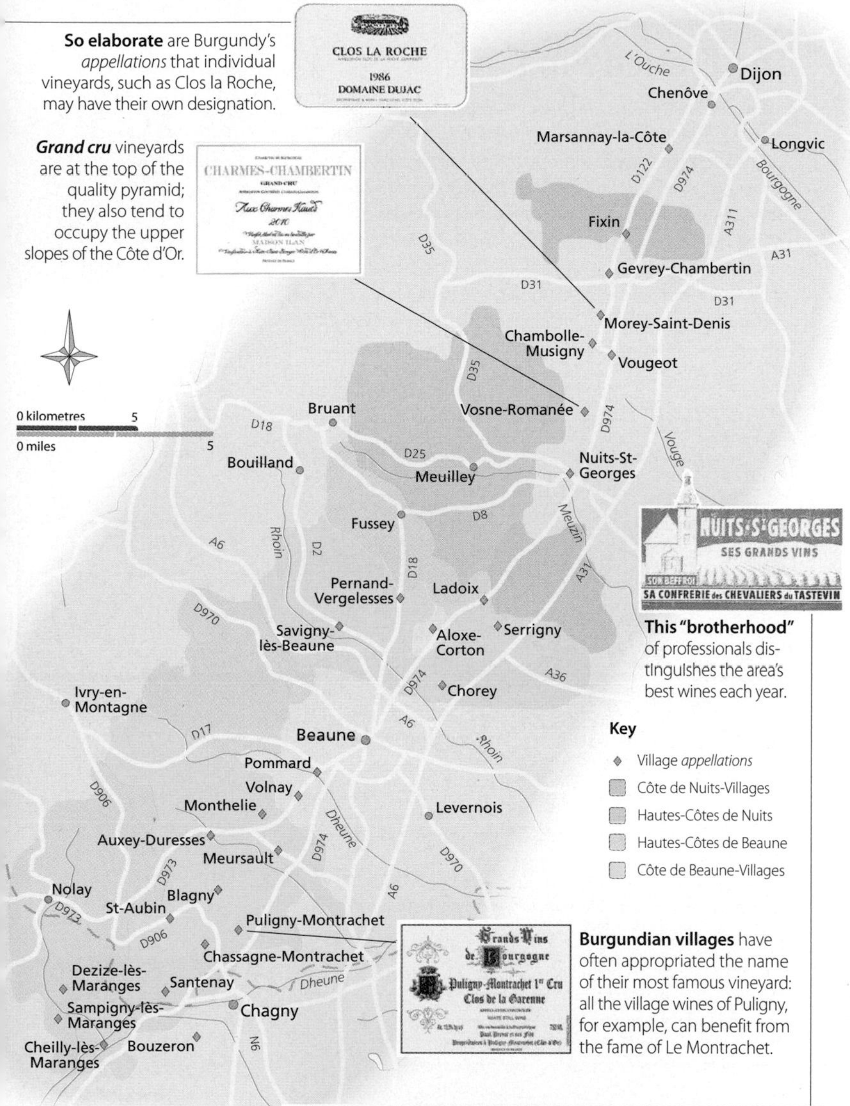

This "brotherhood" of professionals distinguishes the area's best wines each year.

Key

- Village *appellations*
- Côte de Nuits-Villages
- Hautes-Côtes de Nuits
- Hautes-Côtes de Beaune
- Côte de Beaune-Villages

Burgundian villages have often appropriated the name of their most famous vineyard: all the village wines of Puligny, for example, can benefit from the fame of Le Montrachet.

The Côte d'Or

The Côte de Nuits and Côte de Beaune, together forming the "golden" Côte d'Or (see p348), *meet at the historic town of Beaune, which hosts the most famous annual wine auction in the world* (see p350). "Hautes-Côtes" *and* "Villages" *wines, from a different* terroir, *are less sought after than wines from the starry individual* appellations.

Teams of grape-pickers at the vineyards of Nuits-St-Georges

The French Alps

In any season, the Alps are one of the most spectacular regions of France – a majestic mountain range stretching south from Lake Geneva almost to the Mediterranean, and climaxing in Europe's loftiest peak, the 4,800-m (15,770-ft) Mont Blanc. The area encompasses the old regions of Dauphiné and Savoie, once remote and independent (Savoie only became part of France in 1860). They have prospered since Alpine holidays and skiing became popular over the last century, but are still very conscious of their distinct identity.

Children in traditional Savoie costumes

The Alpine landscape in winter: chalets and skiers on the slopes at Courchevel

Winter

The ski season usually starts just before Christmas, and finishes at the end of April. Most resorts offer both cross-country and downhill skiing, with many pistes linking two or more ski stations. The less energetic can still enjoy the landscape from some of the highest cable cars *(téléphériques)* in the world.

A cable car at Courchevel, part of Les Trois Vallées complex

Of the 100 or more French Alpine resorts, the most popular include **Chamonix-Mont Blanc**, the historic capital of Alpine skiing and site of the first Winter Olympics in 1924; **Megève**, which boasts one of the best ski schools in Europe; **Morzine**, a year-round resort on the Swiss border, overlooked by the modern, car-free resort of **Avoriaz**; modern **Albertville**, site of the 1992 Winter Olympics; **Les Trois Vallées**, which include glamorous **Courchevel** and **Méribel**, and the lesser-known **Val Thorens/Les Ménuires**; **Tignes**, a year-round resort; **Les Arcs** and **La Plagne**, both purpose-built; and **Val d'Isère**, a favourite among the rich and famous.

A downhill skier at Val d'Isère

Alpine Flowers

In spring and early summer the pastures of the French Alps are ablaze with flowers. These include blue-and-yellow gentians, bellflowers, lilies, saxifrages and a variety of orchids. Steep mountain meadows cannot be farmed intensively, and the absence of fertilizers and weed killers enables wild flowers to flourish.

Spring gentian *(Gentiana verna)*

Martagon lily *(Lilium martagon)*

The French Alps in summer: flower-filled meadows overlooked by brilliant white peaks

Spring and Summer

The Alpine summer season starts in late June, extending to early September – most resorts close in October and November between the hiking and skiing seasons. After the spring thaw, flower-filled pastures, snow-fed mountain lakes and a huge number of marked trails make this area a hiker's paradise. In the Chamonix area alone there are over 310 km (195 miles) of hiking trails. The best-known long-distance route is the **Tour du Mont Blanc**, a ten-day hike via France, Italy and Switzerland. The **GR5** traverses the entire Alps, passing through the **Parc National de la Vanoise** and **Parc Régional du Queyras** *(see p391)* to the south. *Téléphériques* give access to the higher trails, where the views are even more awesome. Be sure to bring plenty of warm, waterproof clothing, as the weather can change very quickly.

Bell-ringing dairy cows in an Alpine pasture

Many resorts are now concentrating on broadening their summer appeal – golf, tennis, mountain biking, horse riding, paragliding, canoeing, white-water rafting, glacier skiing and mountain climbing are all widely available.

Mountain climbers scaling the heights around Mont Blanc

Geology of the Massif Central

The Massif Central covers almost one-fifth of France and is over 250 million years old. Most of its peaks have been eroded to form a vast plateau split into deep valleys. The heart of the Massif consists of hard, igneous rocks such as granite, with softer rocks such as limestone at its margins. Different rock types are reflected in the landscape and buildings; in the eroded Gorges du Tarn, the houses are built of russet-coloured limestone. Massive granite farmhouses are a feature of Limousin and Le Puy-en-Velay is distinguished by its giant basalt pillars.

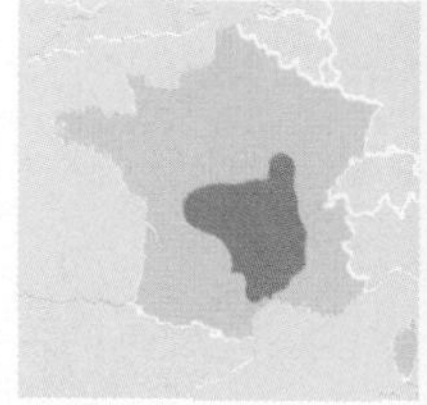

Locator Map

Extent of the Massif Central

This granite portal is found in the Romanesque church at Moutier d'Ahun *(see pp360–61)*. Granite underlies much of the Massif Central.

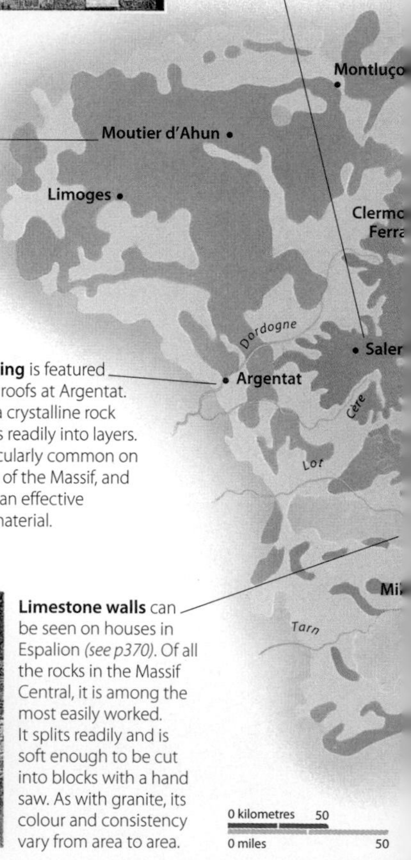

Basalt is a dark, fine-grained rock formed by volcanic lava. A common building stone in the Auvergne, it is often cut into blocks and bonded with lighter-coloured mortar. In the medieval town of Salers *(see p367)*, basalt was used for most of the buildings, including this one in the Grande Place.

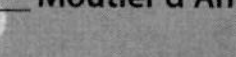

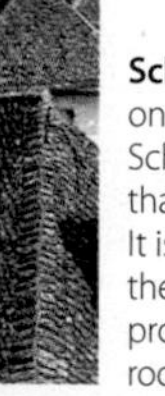

Schist tiling is featured on these roofs at Argentat. Schist is a crystalline rock that splits readily into layers. It is particularly common on the edge of the Massif, and provides an effective roofing material.

Limestone walls can be seen on houses in Espalion *(see p370)*. Of all the rocks in the Massif Central, it is among the most easily worked. It splits readily and is soft enough to be cut into blocks with a hand saw. As with granite, its colour and consistency vary from area to area.

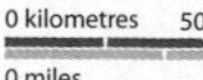

Crystallized lava, for example this dramatic curtain of columns at Prades, formed when liquid basalt seeped through the surrounding rock and solidified to form giant crystals.

Key

- Sedimentary rock
- Surface volcanic rock
- Granite
- Metamorphic rock

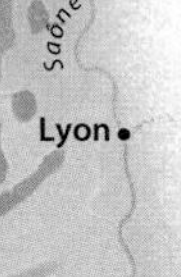

Limestone plateaux *(causses)* are typical of this region. Gorges, where rivers have cut through layers of this slightly soluble rock, run deep into the Massif Central.

This mature landscape at Mont Aigoual is the highest point in the Cévennes *(see p375)*, dividing rivers flowing into the Atlantic and the Mediterranean. Its granite and schist rocks show erosion.

Recognizing Rocks

Geologists divide rocks into three groups. Igneous rocks, such as granite, are formed by volcanic activity and either extruded on to the surface or intrude into other rocks below ground. Sedimentary rocks are produced by sediment build-up. Metamorphic rocks have been transformed by heat or pressure.

Sedimentary Rock

Oolitic limestone often contains fossils and small amounts of quartz.

Surface Volcanic Rock

Basalt, which can form very thick sheets, is the most common lava rock.

Granite

Pink granite, a coarse-grained rock, is formed deep in the earth's crust.

Metamorphic Rock

Muscovite schist is a medium-grained mud- or clay-based rock.

BURGUNDY AND FRANCHE-COMTE

Yonne · Niévre · Côte d'Or
Saône-et-Loire · Jura · Doubs · Haute-Saône

Burgundy considers itself the heart of France, a prosperous region with world-renowned wine, earthy but excellent cuisine and magnificent architecture. Franche-Comté, to the east, combines gentle farmland with lofty Alpine forests.

Under the dukes of Valois, Burgundy was France's most powerful rival, with territory extending well beyond its present boundaries. By the 16th century, however, the duchy was ruled by governors appointed by the French king, but it still retained its privileges and traditions. Once a part of Burgundy, Franche-Comté – the Free County – struggled to remain independent of the French crown, and was a province of the Holy Roman Empire until annexed by Louis XIV in 1674.

Burgundy, now as in the past, is a rich region, a centre of medieval religious faith, which produced renowned Romanesque masterpieces at Vézelay, Fontenay and Cluny. Dijon is a splendid city, filled with the great palaces of the old Burgundian nobility and a collection of great paintings and sculptures in the Musée des Beaux-Arts. The vineyards of the Côte d'Or, the Côte de Beaune and Chablis yield some of the world's most venerated wines. Other varied landscapes – from the wild forests of the Morvan to the lush farmland of the Brionnais – produce snails, Bresse chickens and Charolais beef.

Franche-Comté has none of this opulence, though its capital, Besançon, is a fine 17th-century city with a tradition of clockmaking. Topographically the Franche-Comté is divided into two, with gently rolling farmland in the Saône Valley and high Alpine scenery to the east. This forest country of Alpine torrents filled with trout is also the home of great cheeses, notably Vacherin and Comté, and of the characteristic yellow wine of Arbois.

The prehistoric site of the Roche de Solutré near Mâcon

◀ A view of Semur-en-Auxois, Burgundy, from the banks of the River Armançon

Exploring Burgundy and Franche-Comté

Burgundy is arguably France's richest province – historically, culturally, gastronomically and economically. This lush kernel of a once-great power possesses a concentration of unique Romanesque architecture in Fontenay and Vézelay, along with some of the world's most venerated wines. Dijon is a must for lovers of art, architecture, and food. Franche-Comté is better suited for outdoor holidays, such as trekking and canoeing in wild scenery and crystal-clear rivers.

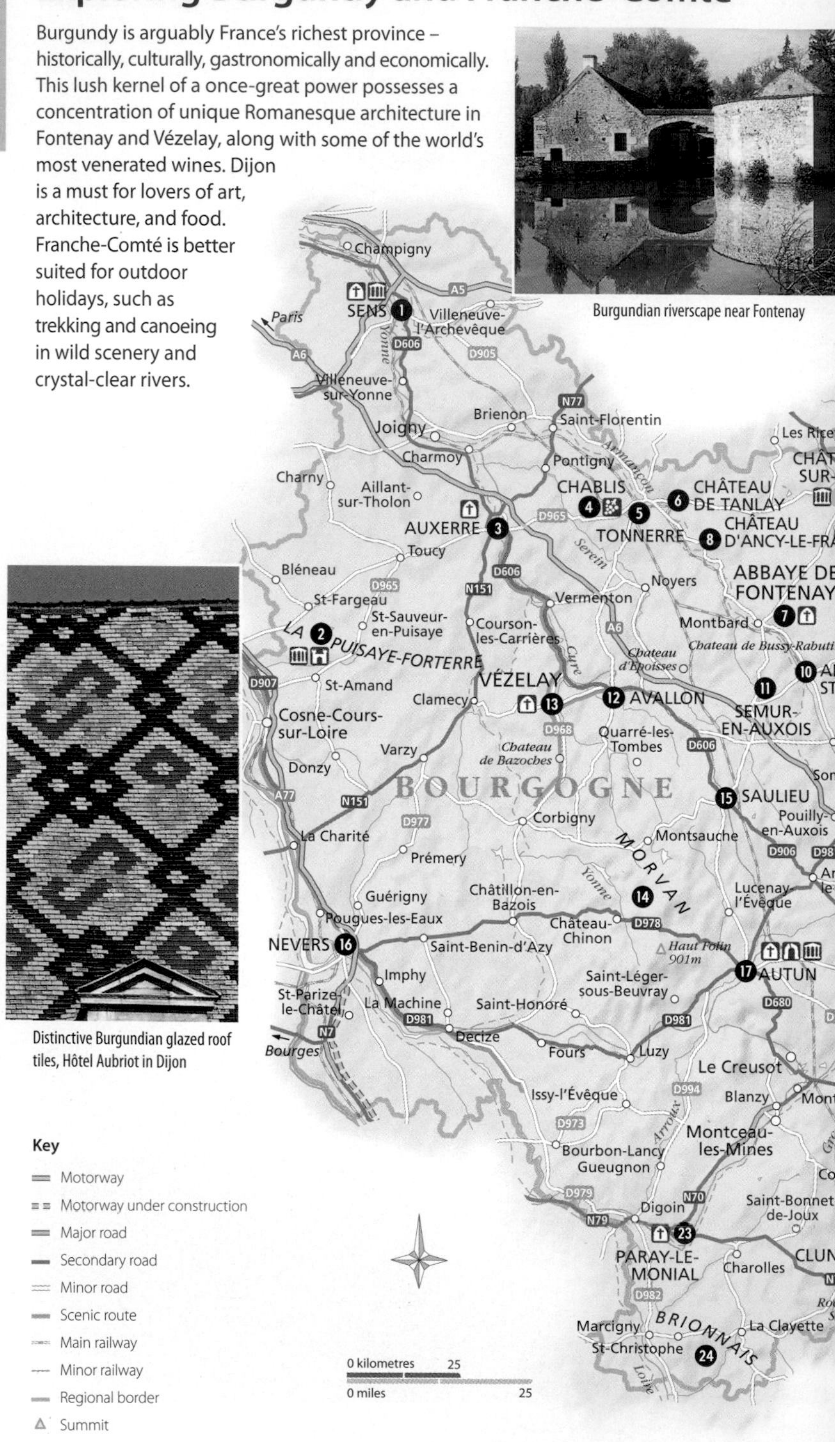

Burgundian riverscape near Fontenay

Distinctive Burgundian glazed roof tiles, Hôtel Aubriot in Dijon

Key

- Motorway
- Motorway under construction
- Major road
- Secondary road
- Minor road
- Scenic route
- Main railway
- Minor railway
- Regional border
- Summit

For keys to symbols *see back flap*

Sights at a Glance

1. Sens
2. La Puisaye-Forterre
3. Auxerre
4. Chablis
5. Tonnerre
6. Château de Tanlay
7. *Abbaye de Fontenay pp336–7*
8. Château d'Ancy-le-Franc
9. Châtillon-sur-Seine
10. Alise-Ste-Reine
11. Semur-en-Auxois
12. Avallon
13. *Vézelay pp340–41*
14. Morvan
15. Saulieu
16. Nevers
17. Autun
18. *Dijon pp344–6*
19. Côte d'Or
20. Beaune
21. Tournus
22. Cluny
23. Paray-le-Monial
24. Brionnais
25. Mâcon
26. Cascades du Hérisson
27. Arbois
28. Dole
29. Arc-et-Senans
30. Champlitte
31. Besançon
32. Ornans
33. Belfort
34. Ronchamp

Wine harvest in Nuits-St-Georges, Côte d'Or

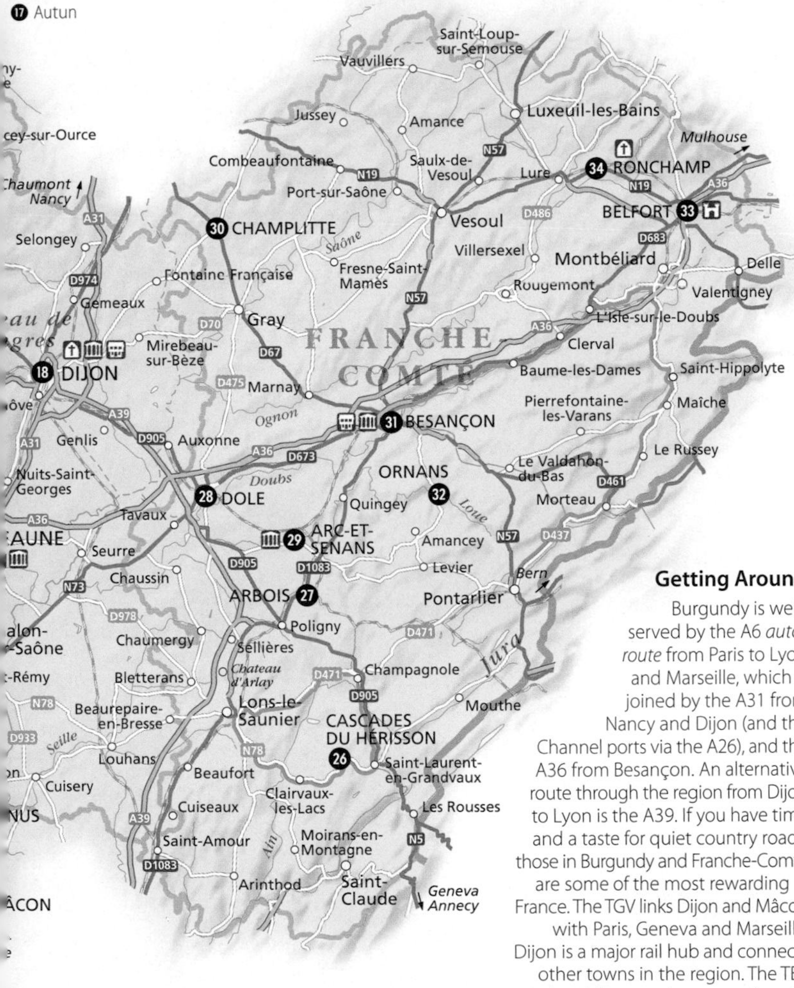

Getting Around

Burgundy is well-served by the A6 *autoroute* from Paris to Lyon and Marseille, which is joined by the A31 from Nancy and Dijon (and the Channel ports via the A26), and the A36 from Besançon. An alternative route through the region from Dijon to Lyon is the A39. If you have time and a taste for quiet country roads, those in Burgundy and Franche-Comté are some of the most rewarding in France. The TGV links Dijon and Mâcon with Paris, Geneva and Marseille. Dijon is a major rail hub and connects other towns in the region. The TER network has regular connections to Dijon, Sens, Beaune and Auxerre.

La Sainte Châsse, 11th-century reliquary in the Treasury in Sens

❶ Sens

Yonne. 30,000. pl Jean-Jaurès (03 86 65 19 49). Mon, Wed, Fri, Sat & Sun. **tourisme-sens.com**

The little town of Sens, at the confluence of the rivers Yonne and Vanne, was important before Caesar came to Gaul. It was the Senones whose attempt to sack the Roman Capitol in 390 BC was thwarted by a flock of geese.

The **Cathédrale St-Etienne** is Sens's outstanding glory. Begun before 1140, it is the oldest of the great Gothic cathedrals and its noble simplicity influenced many other churches. Louis IX *(see pp56–7)* did the town the honour of getting married here in 1234.

The exquisite stained-glass windows from the 12th to 16th centuries show biblical scenes, including the Tree of Jesse, and a tribute to Thomas Becket, who was exiled here. His liturgical robes are in the Treasury (part of the **Musées de Sens**), which has one of the finest collections in France, including a beautiful Byzantine reliquary.

Les Musées de Sens
Pl de la Cathédrale. **Tel** 03 86 64 46 22. **Open** Jun–Sep: Wed–Mon; Oct–May: Wed, Sat, Sun (Mon, Thu, Fri pm only). **Closed** 1 Jan, 1 May, 14 Jul, 1 Nov & 25 Dec.

❷ La Puisaye-Forterre

Yonne, Nièvre. Auxerre, Clamecy, Bonny-sur-Loire, Cosne-Cours-sur-Loire. St-Fargeau, St-Sauveur-en-Puisaye. Charny (03 86 63 65 51).

The secret forest country of La Puisaye-Forterre was immortalized by Colette (1873–1954), who was born at **St-Sauveur** in "a house that smiled only on its garden side". This 17th-century château now houses the **Musée Colette**.

The best way to explore the region is on foot or by bike around its watery woodlands, orchards and meadows. Alternatively, take a ride on the *Transpoyaudin*, a 27-km (17-mile) train ride from St-Sauveur to Villiers St-Benoît.

A hands-on visit can be made to **Château de Guédelon**, a 25-year project begun in 1997 to re-create a medieval castle, using only original building methods and materials found locally. Nearby is the genuine 13th-century **Château de Ratilly**, where art exhibitions, concerts and music workshops take place in summer. More of this can be seen in **St-Amand**, the centre of Puisaye stoneware production, much of which was traditionally fired in the 18th-century horizontal kiln at Moutiers. Both the pottery and local frescoes

Château de St-Fargeau in the Puisaye-Forterre region

Colette in the 1880s at St-Sauveur

(see the churches at **Moutiers** and **La Ferté-Loupière**) made use of locally mined ochre, a major export in the 19th century. The pink brick **Château de St-Fargeau** housed the exiled Grande Mademoiselle *(p61)*.

Musée Colette
Château St-Sauveur-en-Puisaye. **Tel** 03 86 45 61 95. **Open** Apr–Oct: Wed–Mon.

❸ Auxerre

Yonne. 40,000. 1–2 quai de la République (03 86 52 06 19). Tue & Wed. **ot-auxerre.fr**

Beautifully sited overlooking the Yonne river, Auxerre justly prides itself on a fine collection of churches along with a charming pedestrianized main square, place Charles-Surugue.

The Gothic **Cathédrale St-Etienne** took over three centuries to build and was completed in about 1560. It is famous for its intricate 13th-century stained glass. The choir with its slender columns and *colonnettes* is the epitome of Gothic elegance, while the western portals are decorated with beautiful flamboyant sculpture that has been sadly mutilated by war and weather. The Romanesque crypt is adorned by 11th- to 13th-century frescoes, including one depicting Christ on a white horse. The badly pillaged treasury is less impressive, but has an interesting collection of illuminated manuscripts. St Germanus, mentor of St Patrick and bishop of Auxerre in the 5th century, was buried at the former abbey church of **St-Germain**. The abbey was founded by Queen Clothilde, wife of Clovis *(see pp54–5)*, the first Christian king of France, and is an important shrine. The crypt is partly Carolingian, with tombs and 11th- to 13th-century frescoes. The former abbey houses the **Musée St-Germain** with local Gallo-Roman finds.

Musée St-Germain
2 pl St-Germain. **Tel** 03 86 18 05 50. **Open** Wed–Sun. **Closed** 1 & 8 May, 1 & 11 Nov, last week Dec. crypt only.

Medieval fresco in Cathédrale St-Etienne at Auxerre

❹ Chablis

Yonne. 2,700. 1 rue du Maréchal de Lattre de Tassigny (03 86 42 80 80). Sun. **tourisme-chablis.fr**

There can be no question that Chablis tastes best in Chablis. Although this is one of the most famous wine villages on earth, its narrow stone streets still have an air of sleepy prosperity. February processions in nearby Fyé, attended by the wine brotherhood of Piliers Chablisiens, honour St Vincent, patron saint of wine growers.

The intriguing spring of Fosse Dionne in Tonnerre

❺ Tonnerre

Yonne. 6,000. pl Marguerite de Bourgogne (03 86 55 14 48). Sat & Wed. **tourisme-tonnerre.fr**

The mystical cloudy-green spring of **Fosse Dionne** is a good reason to visit the small town of Tonnerre. An astonishing volume of water bursts up from the ground into an 18th-century washing place. Due to its depth and strong currents, it has never been thoroughly explored and local legend has it that a serpent lives on undisturbed.

The **Hôtel-Dieu** is 150 years older than the more famous one in Beaune *(see pp350–51)*. It was founded by Margaret of Burgundy in 1293 to care for the poor. In the Revolution it lost its tiling, but the barrel-vaulted oak ceiling survived.

Hôtel-Dieu & Musée
Rue du Prieuré. **Tel** 03 86 55 14 48. **Open** daily (mid-Oct–mid-Apr: closed Mon, Wed & Sun). **Closed** some public hols.

❻ Château de Tanlay

Yonne. **Tel** 03 86 75 70 61. **Open** Apr–early Nov: Wed–Mon. obligatory.

Built in the mid-16th century, the moated Château de Tanlay is a beautiful example of French Renaissance architecture. There is a trompe l'oeil in the Grande Galerie and, in the corner tower, an intriguing School of Fontainebleau painted ceiling. Its antique divinities represent famous Protestants and Catholics in the 16th century, such as Diane de Poitiers as Venus.

The Renaissance façade and *cour d'honneur* of Château de Tanlay

❼ Abbaye de Fontenay

The tranquil Abbey of Fontenay is the oldest surviving Cistercian foundation in France and offers a rare insight into the Cistercian way of life. It represents the spirit of the order in the sublime gravity of its Romanesque church and its plain but elegant chapterhouse, in early Gothic style. The abbey was founded in 1118 by St Bernard. Situated deep in the forest, it offered the peace and seclusion the Cistercians sought. Supported by the local aristocracy, the abbey began to thrive and remained in use until the Revolution, when it was sold and converted into a paper mill. In 1906 the abbey came under new ownership and was restored to its original appearance.

Dovecote
A magnificent circular dovecote, built in the 13th century, is situated next to the kennel where the precious hunting dogs of the dukes of Burgundy were guarded by servants.

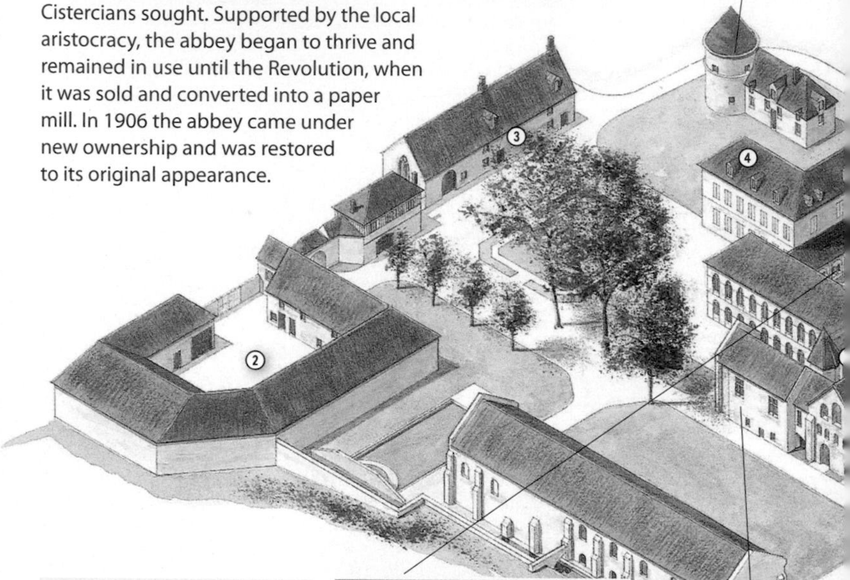

KEY

① **In the forge** monks produced their own tools and hardware.

② **The visitors' hostel** is where weary wanderers and pilgrims were offered board and lodging.

③ **The bakehouse** is no longer intact, but the 13th-century oven and chimney have survived.

④ **The 17th-century** abbot's lodgings were built when the abbots were appointed by royal favour.

⑤ **Warming Room**

⑥ **The scriptorium** is where manuscripts were copied. The adjacent Warming Room was used to warm chilled hands.

⑦ **The herb garden** was skilfully cultivated by the monks in order to grow healing herbs for medicines and potions.

⑧ **Infirmary**

★ Cloisters
For a 12th-century monk, a walk through the cloisters was an opportunity for meditation, as well as providing shelter from the weather.

Fontenay "Prison"
It may be that this 15th-century building was actually used to lock up not local miscreants but important abbey archives, in order to protect them against damage by rats.

For hotels and restaurants in this region see pp562–3 and pp589–91

★ Abbey Church
Rich decoration has no place in this church from the 1140s. But the severe architectural forms, the warm colour of the stone and the diffused light convey a grandeur of their own.

VISITORS' CHECKLIST

Practical Information
Côte-d'Or. **Tel** 03 80 92 15 00.
Open 10am–6pm daily (mid-Nov–Mar: 10am–noon, 2–5pm).
(Apr–mid-Nov only).
abbayedefontenay.com

Transport
Montbard.

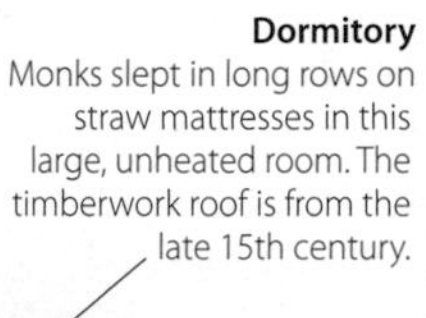

Dormitory
Monks slept in long rows on straw mattresses in this large, unheated room. The timberwork roof is from the late 15th century.

Chapterhouse
Once a day, monks and abbot assembled in this room to discuss matters concerning the community. It derives much of its charm from the elegant 12th-century piers and the rib vaults.

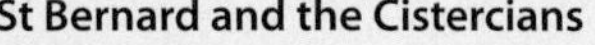

St Bernard and the Cistercians

In 1112 Bernard, a young Burgundian nobleman, joined the Cistercians. At the time the order was still obscure, founded 14 years earlier by a group of monks who wanted to turn their back on the elaborate lifestyle of Cluny *(see pp54–5)*, renounce the world, and espouse poverty and simplicity of life. During Bernard's lifetime the Cistercians became one of the largest and most famous orders of its time. Part of this success was clearly due to Bernard's powerful personality and his skills as a writer, theologian and statesman. He reinforced the poverty rule, rejecting all forms of embellishment. In 1174, only 21 years after his death, he was canonized.

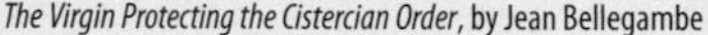

The Virgin Protecting the Cistercian Order, by Jean Bellegambe

8 Château d'Ancy-le-Franc

Yonne. **Tel** 03 86 75 14 63. **Open** Apr–mid-Nov: Tue–Sun; Jul–Aug: Mon pm. **chateau-ancy.com**

The Renaissance façade of the Château d'Ancy-le-Franc gives an austere impression. Its inner courtyard, however, has rich ornamentation. The château was constructed during the 1540s by the Italian Sebastiano Serlio, for the Duke of Clermont-Tonnerre. Most of the interior decorations were carried out by Primaticcio and other members of the Fontainebleau School *(see pp184–5)*. Diane de Poitiers, the duke's sister-in-law and mistress of Henry II, is portrayed in the *Chambre de Judith et Holophernes*. Diane's apartments, including her bedroom, decorated with murals, can also be visited.

The staid façade of the Château d'Ancy-le-Franc

Vase of Vix in the Musée du Payes du Châtillonnais, Châtillon-sur-Seine

9 Châtillon-sur-Seine

Côte d'Or. 6,000. rue du Bourg (03 80 91 13 19). Sat. **chatillonnais-tourisme.fr**

World War II left Châtillon a ruin, hence the town's largely modern aspect. But the past is still present in the **Musée du Pays du Châtillonnais**, where the Vix treasure is displayed. In 1953, the tomb of a Gaulish princess, from the 6th century BC, was discovered near Vix at Mont Lassois. The trove of jewellery and artifacts of Greek origin includes a stunning bronze vase, an impressive 164 cm (66 in) high and weighing 208 kg (459 lb). Also of interest in the town is the Romanesque **Eglise St-Vorles**, containing an *Entombment* with Christ and mourners splendidly sculpted (1527).

Nearby are the sources of the River Seine, between St-Seine-l'Abbaye and Chanceau, and its tributory, the River Douix, each marked by a beautiful grotto.

Musée du Pays du Châtillonnais
Rue de la Libération. **Tel** 03 80 91 24 67. **Open** Jul–Aug: daily; Sep–Jun: Wed–Mon. **Closed** 1 Jan, 1 May, 24–25 & 31 Dec.
musee-vix.fr

10 Alise-Ste-Reine

Côte d'Or. 3,300. 1 av de la Gare, Venarey-Les Laumes 21150 (03 80 96 89 13). **alesia-tourisme.net**

Mont Auxois, above the village of Alise-Ste-Reine, was the site of Caesar's final victory over the heroic Gaulish chieftain Vercingétorix in 52 BC after a six-week siege *(see p52)*. The first excavations here were undertaken in the mid-19th century, and they uncovered the vestiges of a thriving Gallo-Roman town, with theatre, forum and well-laid-out street plan. The **Alésia MuséoParc** includes a historical discovery centre with interactive media displays and life-size reconstructions of siege engines.

Alise is dominated by Aimé Millet's gigantic moustachioed statue of Vercingétorix, which was placed here in 1865 to commemorate the first excavations. Cynics feel that it bears a more than passing resemblance to Napoleon III, who sponsored the dig.

Alésia MuséoParc
Rue de l'Hôpital. **Tel** 03 80 96 96 23. **Open** Feb–Nov: daily.
alesia.com

Environs

In the vicinity lies **Château de Bussy-Rabutin**. The spiteful 17th-century soldier and wit

Excavations at the Roman site near Alise-Ste-Reine

Roger de Bussy-Rabutin created its highly individualistic decor, while exiled from Louis XIV's court. One room is dedicated to portraits of his many mistresses, as well as a couple of imaginary ones.

Château de Bussy-Rabutin
Bussy-le-Grand. **Tel** 03 80 96 00 03. **Open** daily. **Closed** 1 Jan, 1 May, 1 & 11 Nov, 25 Dec.

⓫ Semur-en-Auxois

Côte d'Or. 5,000. 2 pl Gaveau (03 80 97 05 96). Sun.
tourisme-semur.fr

Approached from the west, Semur-en-Auxois comes as a surprise on an otherwise uneventful road. Its massive round bastions built in the 14th century (one of them with an unnerving gash in it) suddenly appear, towering over the Pont Joly and the peaceful River Armançon.

The **Eglise Notre-Dame** dates from the 13th and 14th centuries, and was modelled on the cathedral of Auxerre. The fragile high walls had to be restored in the 15th and 19th centuries. The church houses significant artworks, from the tympanum showing the legend of Doubting Thomas on the north doorway, to the 15th-century *Entombment* by Antoine le Moiturier. The stained glass presents the legend of St Barbara, and the work of different guilds such as butchers and drapers.

Environs
The village of Epoisses is the site of the moated **Château d'Epoisses**, its 11th- to 18th-century construction blending medieval towers with fine Renaissance details, and a huge 15th-century dovecote. Epoisses is also the home of one of Burgundy's most revered cheeses, to be sampled at the local café or *fromagerie*.

Stained-glass window in Eglise Notre-Dame at Semur-en-Auxois

Semur-en-Auxois by the River Armançon

Château d'Epoisses
Epoisses. **Tel** 01 42 27 73 11. **Open** Jul–Aug: Wed–Mon (grounds: all year). ground floor only.

⓬ Avallon

Yonne. 9,000. 6 rue Bocquillot (03 86 34 14 19). Sat & Thu. **avallon-morvan.com**

A fine old fortified town, Avallon is situated on a granite spur between two ravines by the River Cousin. It suffered in the wars of Saracens, Normans, English and French, which accounts for its defensive aspect. The town is quiet and full of charming details. The main monument is the 12th-century Romanesque **Eglise St-Lazare**, with two carved doorways. The larger illustrates the signs of the zodiac, the labours of the month, and the horsemen of the Apocalypse. The nave is decorated with sophisticated acanthus capitals and polychrome statuary.

The **Musée de l'Avallonnais** features an intricate Venus mosaic from the 2nd century AD, and Georges Rouault's (1871–1958) series of Expressionist etchings, the *Miserere*.

Musée de l'Avallonnais
5 rue du College. **Tel** 03 86 34 03 19. **Open** Apr–Sep: Wed–Mon pms; Oct–mid-Nov & mid-Feb–Mar: Sat–Sun pms. **Closed** mid-Nov–mid-Feb.

Environs
To the southwest of Avallon is the 12th-century **Château de Bazoches**, which was given to Maréchal de Vauban by Louis XIV in 1675, and transformed by him into a military garrison.

Miserere by Georges Rouault in the Musée d'Avallonnais, Avallon

13 Vézelay

The golden glow of the Basilique Ste-Madeleine crowning Vézelay's hill is visible from afar. Tourists follow in the footsteps of medieval pilgrims, ascending the narrow street up to the former abbey church. In the 12th century, at the height of its glory, the abbey claimed to house relics of Mary Magdalene and was also an important meeting point for pilgrims en route to Santiago de Compostela in Spain *(see pp404–5)*. Today its attraction lies in the Romanesque church with its magnificent sculpture and Gothic choir.

View of Vézelay
The abbey dominates Vézelay's surroundings, as it once dominated the religious and worldly affairs of the area.

Nave of Ste-Madeleine
The nave was rebuilt between 1120 and 1135, using alternate dark and light stone in the transverse arches.

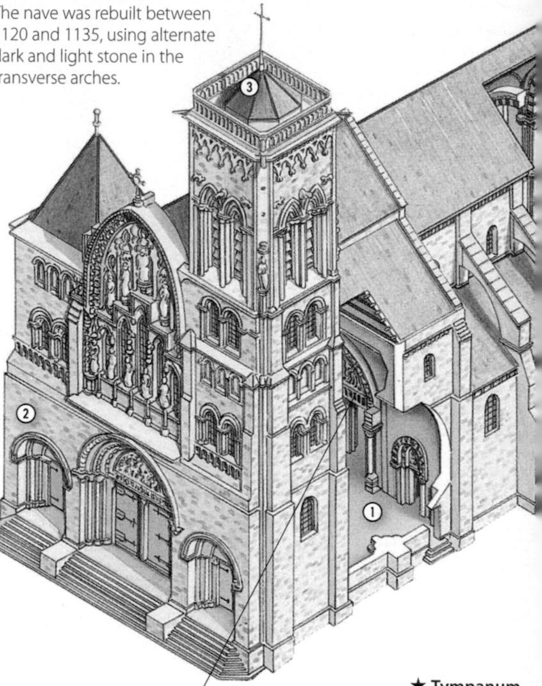

★ Tympanum
This masterpiece of sculpture (1120–35) shows Christ on his throne, stretching out his hands from which rays of light descend on to the apostles.

KEY

① **The narthex** used to be a gathering point for medieval processions.

② **The façade** dates from 1150 and has a large 13th-century window. It was about to collapse, when in 1840 Viollet-le-Duc was commissioned to restore it, according to old plans.

③ **Tour St-Michel** was built from 1150 to 1250. It derives its name from the statue of the archangel in the tower's southwest corner.

④ **Nave of Ste-Madeleine**

⑤ **Tour St-Antoine** was built at the same time as the choir, in the late 12th century. Its counterpart on the north side was never finished.

⑥ **The chapterhouse** and cloister are the only parts remaining from the 12th-century monastic buildings. Viollet-le-Duc rebuilt part of the cloister and restored the rib-vaulted chapterhouse, once a graceful background for the monks' daily assemblies.

VISITORS' CHECKLIST

Practical Information
Basilique Ste-Madeleine, Vézelay. **Tel** 03 86 33 39 50 or 03 86 33 23 69 (tourist office). **Open** 7am–8pm daily (7am–dusk winter). 6:30pm Mon–Fri; 12:30pm, 6pm (winter), 7pm (summer) Sat; 11am Sun.
basiliquedevezelay.org

Transport
Sermizelles.

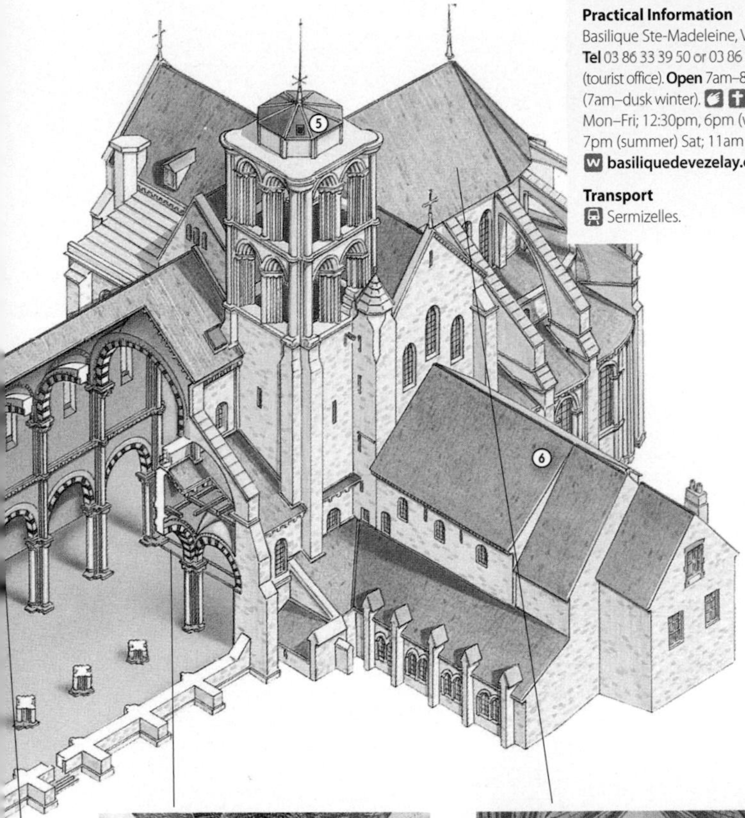

Crypt of Ste-Madeleine
The Romanesque crypt houses relics once thought to be Mary Magdalene's. The vault was rebuilt in 1165.

★ Capitals
The capitals in the nave and narthex are exquisitely carved, and give a vivid rendering of the stories of classical antiquity and the Bible. The master who created them remains unknown.

Choir of Ste-Madeleine
The choir was rebuilt in the last quarter of the 12th century in the then-modern Gothic style of the Ile-de-France.

Morvan, a region of rivers and forests, well suited to fishing and other outdoor pursuits

⓮ Morvan

Yonne, Côte d'Or, Nièvre, Saône-et-Loire. Dijon. Autun, Mombard. Château-Chinon, Saulieu, Avallon. 6 bd République, Château-Chinon (03 86 85 06 58); Maison du Parc, St-Brisson (03 86 78 79 57). **tourisme.parcdumorvan.org**

Morvan is a Celtic word meaning "Black Mountain", which is a good description of this area seen from afar. The immense, sparsely inhabited plateau of granite and woodland appears suddenly in the centre of the rich Burgundy hills and farmland. Stretching roughly north to south, it gains altitude as it proceeds southwards, reaching a culminating point of 901 m (2,956 ft) at **Haut-Folin**.

The Morvan's two sources of natural wealth are abundant water and dense forests of oak, beech and conifer. In the old days lumber used to be floated out of the area to Paris via a network of lakes and rivers. Today it travels by truck, and the Yonne, Cousin and Cure rivers are instead used for recreation and the production of electricity.

The Morvan has always been a poor, remote area. Each of its largest towns, Château-Chinon in the centre and Saulieu on the outskirts, has barely 3,000 inhabitants.

During World War II, the Morvan was a bastion of the French Resistance. Today a Regional Nature Park, its attraction is its wildness. Information on a wide variety of outdoor activities, including cycling, canoeing, skiing and horse trekking, is available at the **Maison du Parc** at St-Brisson, where there is also the very moving **Musée de la Resistance**. There are plenty of short walking trails, and two well-signed long-distance paths: the GR13 (Vézelay to Autun) and the Tour du Morvan par les Grands Lacs.

Musée de la Résistance
Maison du Parc, St-Brisson. **Tel** 03 86 78 72 99. **Open** Easter–mid-Nov: Sat pm–Mon, Wed–Fri (Jul & Aug: daily). **Closed** Sat am.

⓯ Saulieu

Côte d'Or. 3,000. 24 rue d'Argentine (03 80 64 00 21). Sat. **saulieu.fr**

On the edge of the Morvan, Saulieu has been a shrine of Burgundian cooking since the 17th century. The town was then a staging post on the Paris to Lyon coach road.

The stylized animal sculptures of François Pompon can be admired at the **Musée Pompon**, which also houses a collection of Gallo-Roman stelae on the ground floor.

The Romanesque **Basilique St-Andoche**, built in the early 12th century, has decorated capitals with representations of the Flight into Egypt and a comical version of the story of Balaam and his donkey waylaid by the Angel.

Nevers faïence vase

⓰ Nevers

Nièvre. 41,000. Palais Ducal, rue Sabatier (03 86 68 46 00). Sat. **nevers-tourisme.com**

Like all Burgundian towns fronting the Loire, Nevers should be approached from the west side of the river for a full appreciation of its noble site. Though lacking historical importance, the town has much to show. Considered to be the earliest of the Loire châteaux, the **Palais Ducal** has a long Renaissance façade framed by polygonal towers and a broad esplanade. The Romanesque 11th-century **Eglise St-Etienne** has graceful monolithic columns and a wreath of radiating chapels. In the crypt of the Gothic **Cathédrale St-Cyr** is a 16th-century sculpted *Entombment*, and the foundations of a 6th-century baptistry, discovered in 1944, after heavy bombing.

The contemporary stained-glass windows are also noteworthy. The overlordship of Nevers passed to the Gonzaga family in the 16th century. They brought with them an Italian school of artists skilled in faïence-making and glass-blowing.

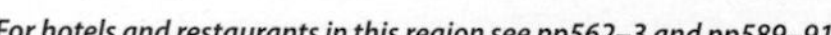
For hotels and restaurants in this region see pp562–3 and pp589–91

The industry has remained and the modern pottery is still traditionally decorated in blue, white, yellow and green, with its curious trademark, the little green arabesque knot, or *noeud vert*. The best place to view it is at the **Musée Municipal**. There are also several pottery workshops in the town centre.

Musée Municipal Frédéric Blandin
16 rue Saint-Genest. **Tel** 03 86 68 44 60. **Open** Tue–Sun (Oct–Apr: Tue–Fri pms only; Sat & Sun all day).

Environs

Just south of Nevers, the majestic 19th-century **Pont du Guetin** carries the Loire Canal across the Allier river. The church at **St-Parize-le-Châtel** has a jolly Burgundian menagerie sculpted on the capitals of the crypt.

The *Temptation of Eve* in Autun

17 Autun

Saône-et-Loire. 18,000. 13 rue Général Demetz (03 85 86 80 38). Wed & Fri, Journées Romaines d'Autun: 1st weekend of Aug.
autun-tourisme.com

Augustodunum, the town of Augustus, was founded in the late 1st century BC. It was a great centre of learning, with a population four times what it is today. Its theatre, built in the 1st century AD, could seat 20,000 people.

Today Autun is still a delight, deserving gastronomic as well as cultural investigation.The magical **Cathédrale St-Lazare** was built in the 12th century. It is notable for its sculptures, most of them by the mysterious 12th-century artist Gislebertus. He sculpted both the capitals inside and the glorious Last Judgment tympanum over the main portal. This masterpiece, called a "Romanesque Cézanne" by André Malraux, escaped notice and was saved from destruction during the Revolution because it had been plastered over in the 18th century. Inside, some of the capitals can be seen close-up in the Salle Capitulaire. Look also for the sculpture of Pierre Jeannin and his wife.

Autun's imposing Porte St-André, once part of the Roman wall

Jeannin was the president of the Dijon parliament that prevented the Massacre of St Bartholomew *(see pp60–61)* spreading, with the perceptive remark, "the commands of very angry monarchs should be obeyed very slowly".

The collection of medieval art at the **Musée Rolin** includes the bas-relief *Temptation of Eve* by Gislebertus, the 15th-century painted stone Virgin of Autun and the *Nativity of Cardinal Rolin* by the Master of Moulins, from about 1480.

The **Porte St-André** and **Porte d'Arroux**, and the ruins of the **Théâtre Romain** and the **Temple de Janus**, are reminders of Autun's glorious Roman past.

Musée Rolin
3 rue des Bancs. **Tel** 03 85 52 09 76. **Open** mid-Feb–Mar & mid-Oct–Nov: Wed–Sat, Sun pm; Apr–mid-Oct: Wed–Mon. **Closed** Dec–mid-Feb, public hols.

Remains of Autun's Roman theatre, dating from the 1st century AD

⑱ Street-by-Street: Dijon

The centre of Dijon is noted for its architectural splendour – a legacy from the dukes of Burgundy *(see p347)*. Wealthy parliament members also had elegant *hôtels particuliers* built in the 17th–18th centuries. The capital of Burgundy, Dijon today has a rich cultural life and a renowned university. The city's great art treasures are housed in the Palais des Ducs. Dijon is also famous for its mustard *(see p322)* and *pain d'épices* (gingerbread), a reminder of the town's position on the spice route. It became a major rail hub during the 19th century and now has a TGV link to Paris.

Hôtel de Vogüé
This elegant 17th-century mansion is decorated with Burgundian cabbages and fruit garlands by Hugues Sambin.

★ Notre-Dame
This magnificent 13th-century Gothic church has a façade with gargoyles, columns and the popular Jacquemart clock. The *chouette* (owl) is reputed to bring good luck when touched.

Musée des Beaux-Arts
The collection of Flemish masters here includes this 14th-century triptych by Jacques de Baerze and Melchior Broederlam.

Place de la Libération was created by Mansart in the 17th century.

★ Palais des Ducs
The dukes of Burgundy held court here, but the building seen today was mainly built in the 17th century for the parliament. It now houses the Musée des Beaux-Arts.

Rue Verrerie
This cobbled street in the old merchants' quarter is lined with medieval half-timbered houses. Some have fine woodcarvings, such as Nos. 8, 10 and 12.

VISITORS' CHECKLIST

Practical Information
Côte d'Or. 155,000.
15 cour de la Gare & 11 rue des Forges (08 92 70 05 58). Tue, Fri, Sat. Florissimo (2020); Fêtes de la Vigne (2018); Festival International de Musique Mécanique (2018). Hôtel de Vogüé: inner courtyard open. Musée Magnin: (03 80 67 11 10). **Open** Tue–Sun. **Closed** 1 Jan, 25 Dec.
destinationdijon.com

Transport
cour de la Gare.

★ St-Michel
Begun in the 15th century and completed in the 17th century, St-Michel's façade combines Flamboyant Gothic with Renaissance details. On the richly carved porch, angels and biblical motifs mingle with mythological themes.

Musée Magnin
A collection of French and foreign 16th- to 19th-century paintings are displayed among period furniture in this 17th-century mansion.

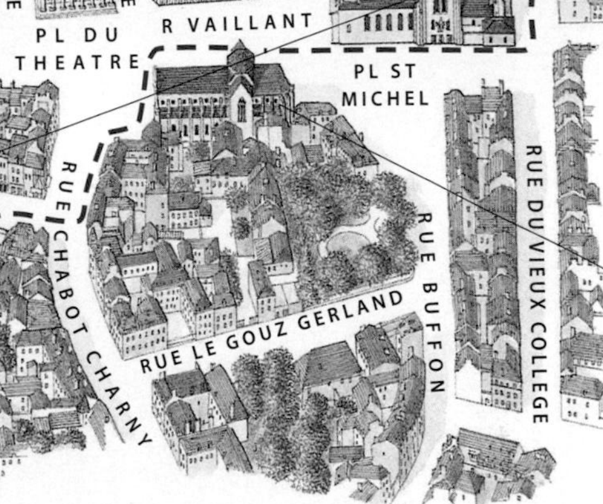

Eglise St-Etienne dates back to the 11th century but has been rebuilt many times. Its characteristic lantern was added in 1686.

Key
Suggested route

0 metres 100
0 yards 100

Well of Moses by Claus Sluter, in the Chartreuse de Champmol

Exploring Dijon

The centre of Dijon is a warren of little streets that reward exploration. Rue des Forges, behind the Palais de Ducs, was the main street until the 18th century and is named after the jewellers and goldsmiths who had workshops there. At No. 34 Hôtel Chambellan is Flamboyant Gothic with a stone spiral staircase and wooden galleries. At No. 38 the Maison Maillard, built in 1560, has a stone façade decorated by Hugues Sambin.

Rue Chaudronnerie has a number of houses of note, especially the Maison des Cariatides at No. 28, with ten fine stone carved caryatids framing the windows. Place Darcy is lined with hotels and restaurants; the Jardin Darcy, with its polar bear sculpture *(L'Ours Blanc)* by François Pompon, is delightful.

Musée des Beaux-Arts

Palais des Etats de Bourgogne, Cour de Bar. **Tel** 03 80 74 52 70. **Open** Wed–Mon. **Closed** 1 Jan, 1 & 8 May, 14 Jul, 1 & 11 Nov, 25 Dec. limited.

Dijon's prestigious art collection is housed in the former Palais des Ducs *(see p344)*. The Salle des Gardes on the first floor is dominated by the giant mausoleums of the dukes, with tombs sculpted by Claus Sluter (c.1345–1405). Other exhibits include two gilded Flemish retables and a portrait of Philip the Good by Rogier van der Weyden.

The collection has Dutch and Flemish masters and sculpture by Sluter and Rude, as well as Swiss and German primitives, 16th- to 18th-century French paintings, the Donation Granville of 19th- and 20th-century French art and sculptures by François Pompon. Note the ducal kitchens with six fireplaces, and the Tour Philippe le Bon, 46 m (150 ft) tall with a fine view of Burgundian tiled roof tops.

Cathédrale St-Bénigne

Pl St-Bénigne. **Tel** 03 80 30 39 33. **Open** daily. for crypt.

Little remains of the 11th-century Benedictine abbey first founded in honour of St Bénigne. Beneath the church is a Romanesque crypt with a fine rotunda ringed by three circles of columns.

Musée Archéologique

5 rue du Docteur Maret. **Tel** 03 80 48 83 70. **Open** Apr–Oct: Wed–Mon; Nov–Mar: Wed, Sat & Sun. **Closed** most public hols.

The museum is housed in the old dormitory of the Benedictine Abbey of St Bénigne. The 11th-century chapterhouse, its stocky columns supporting a barrel-vaulted roof, houses a fine collection of Gallo-Roman sculpture. The ground floor, with its lovely fan vaulting, houses the famous head of Christ by Claus Sluter, originally from the *Well of Moses*.

Chartreuse de Champmol

1 bd Chanoine Kir. **Open** daily (08 92 70 05 58).

This was originally the site of a family necropolis built by Philip the Bold, but destroyed during the Revolution. All that remains is a chapel doorway and the famous *Well of Moses* by Claus Sluter. It is now in the grounds of a psychiatric hospital east of Dijon railway station – it is not very easy to find but worth the effort. The statue, representing Moses and five other prophets, is set on a hexagonal base above a basin. Sluter is renowned for his deeply cut carving and his work here is exquisitely lifelike.

The tomb of Philip the Bold by Claus Sluter, now in the Grande Salle of the Musée des Beaux-Arts

The Golden Age of Burgundy

While the French Capetian dynasty fought in the Hundred Years' War *(see pp58–9)*, the dukes of Burgundy built up one of Europe's most powerful states, which included Flanders and parts of Holland. From the time of Philip the Bold (1342–1404), the ducal court became a cultural force, supporting many of Europe's finest artists, such as painters Rogier van der Weyden and the van Eyck brothers and the sculptor Claus Sluter. The duchy's dominions were, however, broken up after the death of Duke Charles the Bold in 1477.

The tomb of Philip the Bold in Dijon was made by the Flemish sculptor Claus Sluter, who was among the most brilliant artists of the Burgundian Golden Age. The dramatic realism of the mourners is one of the most striking features of this spectacular tomb, begun while the duke was still alive.

Burgundy In 1477

Extent of the duchy at its peak

The Marriage of Philip the Good

Philip the Good, duke from 1419 to 1467, married Isabella of Portugal in 1430. This 17th-century copy of a painting by van Eyck shows the sumptuous wedding feast, when Philip also inaugurated the chivalric Order of the Golden Fleece.

The dukes surrounded themselves with luxury, including fine gold and silverware.

Isabella of Portugal

The Duchess of Bedford, Philip's sister

Greyhounds were popular hunting animals at the Burgundian court.

Philip the Good is dressed in white ceremonial finery.

Burgundian art, such as this Franco-Flemish Book of Hours, reflected the Flemish origins of many of the dukes' favourite artists.

Dijon's Palais des Ducs was rebuilt in 1450 by Philip the Good to reflect the glory of the Burgundian court, a centre of art, chivalry and glorious feasts. Empty after Charles the Bold's death, it was reconstructed in the 17th century.

Wine harvest in the vineyards of Nuits-St-Georges, part of the Côte d'Or district

⑲ Côte d'Or

Côte d'Or. ✈ Dijon. 🚉 🚌 Dijon, Nuits-St-Georges, Beaune, Santenay. ℹ Dijon (08 92 70 05 58). **W cotedor-tourisme.com**

In winemaking terms, the Côte d'Or includes the Côte de Beaune and the Côte de Nuits in a nearly unbroken line of vines from Dijon to Santenay. Squeezed in between the flat plain of the Saône to the south-east and a plateau of woodland to the northwest, this narrow escarpment is about 50 km (30 miles) long. The grapes of the great Burgundy vineyards grow in the golden reddish soil of the slope (hence the area's name).

The classification of the characteristics of the land is fabulously technical and elaborate, but for the layman a rough rule of thumb might be that 95 per cent of the best vines are on the uphill side of the D974 thoroughfare *(see pp324–5)*. The names on the signposts haunt the dreams of wine lovers the world over: Gevrey-Chambertin, Vougeot, Chambolle-Musigny, Vosne-Romanée, Nuits-St-Georges, Aloxe-Corton, Meursault and Chassagne Montrachet.

Narrow street in Beaune's historic centre

Typical grape basket in the Musée du Vin de Bourgogne at Beaune

⑳ Beaune

Côte d'Or. 👥 23,000. 🚉 🚌 ℹ 6 bd Perpeuil (03 80 26 21 30). Sat, Wed. Baroque Music (Jul). **W beaune-tourisme.fr**

The old centre of Beaune, snug within its ramparts and encircling boulevards, is easy to explore on foot. Its indisputable treasure is the **Hôtel-Dieu** *(see pp350–51)*. The Hôtel des Ducs de Bourgogne, built in the 14th–16th centuries, houses the **Musée du Vin de Bourgogne**. The building, with its flamboyant façade, is as interesting as its display of traditional winemaking equipment.

Farther to the north lies the **Collégiale Notre-Dame**, begun in the early 12th century. Inside this mainly Romanesque church hang five very fine 15th-century woollen and silk tapestries. With hints of early Renaissance style, they delicately illustrate the life of the Virgin Mary in 19 scenes.

Musée du Vin de Bourgogne
Rue d'Enfer. **Tel** 03 80 22 08 19. **Open** Wed–Sun (Apr–Sep: Wed–Mon). **Closed** Dec–mid-Mar.

㉑ Tournus

Saône-et-Loire. 👥 6,500. 🚉 🚌 ℹ pl de l'Abbaye (03 85 27 00 20). Sat. **W tournugeois.fr**

The Abbaye de St-Philibert is one of Burgundy's oldest and greatest Romanesque buildings. It was founded by a group of monks from Noirmoutier, who had been driven from their island by invading Normans in the 9th century, and brought with them relics of their patron saint, Philibert (still in the choir). Rebuilt in the 10th–12th centuries, the well-fortified abbey church is made from lovely

Dovecote in Cormatin château gardens, Mâconnais

Nave of St-Philibert in Tournus

pale pink stone, with black-and-white vaulting inside.

The 17th-century Hôtel-Dieu has its original rooms intact with the furniture, equipment and pharmacy on display. It also houses the **Musée Greuze** (open Apr–Oct) dedicated to Tournus's most famous son, the artist Jean-Baptiste Greuze (1725–1805).

Environs

Southwest of Tournus lies the Mâconnais landscape of hills, vineyards, orchards, red-tiled farmhouses and Romanesque churches. **Brancion** is a pretty hill village, **Chapaize** has an 11th-century church and there is a sumptuous Renaissance château at **Cormatin**. The village of **Taizé** is the centre of a world-famous ecumenical community. To the north, **Chalon-sur-Saône** features the Musée Niépce, dedicated to the inventor of photography.

22 Cluny

Saône-et-Loire. 4,800. 6 rue Mercière (03 85 59 05 34). Sat. **cluny-tourisme.com**

The little town of Cluny is overshadowed by the ruins of its great abbey. The **Ancienne Abbaye de Cluny** was once the most powerful monastic foundation in Europe *(see pp54–5)*. The abbey was founded by William the Pious, Duke of Aquitaine in 910. Within 200 years, Cluny had become the head of a major reforming order with monasteries all over Europe. Its abbots were considered to be as powerful as monarchs or popes, and four of them are venerated as saints. By the 14th century, however, the system was in decline. The abbey was closed in 1790 and the church was later dismantled.

The guided tour presents the abbey remains, notably the Clocher de l'Eau Bénite (Holy Water Bell Tower); the remains of figured capitals, displayed in the 13th-century flour store; and the **Musée d'Art & Archéologie**, in the former abbot's palace. In the town, don't miss the 12th-century **Eglise St-Marcel**.

Southwest of the town, the chapel in **Berzé-la-Ville** is decorated with superb 12th-century frescoes, similar to those once seen at Cluny.

Ancienne Abbaye de Cluny
Tel 03 85 59 15 93. **Open** daily. **Closed** 1 Jan, 1 May, 1 & 11 Nov, 25 Dec.

Musée d'Art & Archéologie
Palais Jean de Bourbon. **Tel** 03 85 59 89 99. **Open** daily. **Closed** 1 Jan, 1 May, 1 & 11 Nov, 25 Dec.

23 Paray-le-Monial

Saône-et-Loire. 10,000. 25 av Jean-Paul II (03 85 81 10 92). Fri. **tourisme-paraylemonial.fr**

Dedicated to the cult of the Sacred Heart of Jesus, the **Basilique du Sacré-Coeur** has made Paray-le-Monial one of the most important sites of pilgrimage in modern France. Marguerite-Marie Alacoque, who was born here in 1647, had rather gory visions, from which the cult later developed, sweeping across France in the 19th century. The church is a small version of the now-lost abbey church of Cluny, with particularly harmonious and pure Romanesque architecture.

A visit to the **Musée du Hiéron** (open mid-Mar–Dec) provides an insight into industrial artistic tile production in the 19th and 20th centuries.

Situated on place Guignaud is the ornate **Maison Jayet**, dating from the 16th century, which houses the town hall.

Basilique du Sacré-Coeur at Paray-le-Monial

Hôtel-Dieu

After the Hundred Years' War, many of Beaune's inhabitants suffered the effects of poverty and famine. To remedy this, the chancellor, Nicolas Rolin, and his wife founded a hospice here in 1443, inspired by the architecture of northern French hospitals. The Rolins provided an annual grant and saltworks for income. Today the hospice is considered a medieval jewel, with its superb geometric, multi-coloured Burgundian roof tiles. It houses two religious masterpieces: the *Christ-de-Pitié* statue, carved from oak, and Rogier van der Weyden's *Last Judgment* polyptych.

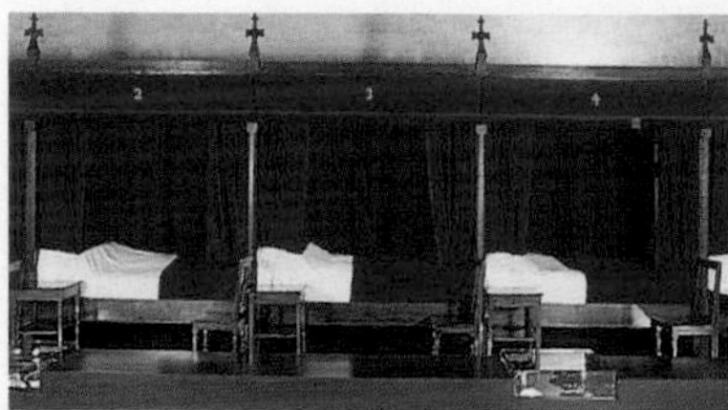

★ Great Hall of the Poor
The hall, with its carved, painted roof, has 28 four-poster beds, each often used by two patients at a time. Meals were served at central tables.

Tribute to Rolin's Wife
A recurring motif features the entwined letters N and G, birds and stars, and the word *Seulle*, referring to Rolin's wife Guigone, his "one and only".

KEY

① **St Anne's Room** has a tableau of nuns working in what was once the linen room, and a colourful feast-day tapestry.

② **St Hugues's Room** contains a painting of the saint curing two children. Frescoes by Isaac Moillon show the miracles of Christ.

③ **Glazed roof tiles**, in a colourful geometric pattern, are the most dramatic feature of the Hôtel-Dieu.

④ **St Louis's Room**

Annual Charity Wine Auction

On the third Sunday in November, an annual charity auction in Beaune is the centrepiece of three days of festivities known as *Les Trois Glorieuses*. Saturday sees the banquet of the Confrérie des Chevaliers du Tastevin at the Château Clos de Vougeot. On Sunday the auction of wine from vineyards owned by nearby hospitals takes place. Its prices are the benchmark for the entire vintage. On Monday, at La Paulée de Meursault, there is a party, where growers bring along bottles of their best vintages to enjoy.

Wine sold at the famous auction

Kitchen
The centrepiece of the kitchen is a Gothic fireplace with a dual hearth and a mechanical spit, made in 1698 and is turned by a wooden "robot".

VISITORS' CHECKLIST

Practical Information
Rue de l'Hôtel Dieu, Beaune.
Tel 03 80 24 45 00. **Open** Apr–mid Nov: 9–6:30pm daily; mid-Nov–Mar: 9–11:30am, 2–5:30pm daily.
Wine Auction: 3rd Sun Nov: Les Halles de Beaune (03 80 24 45 00).
hospices-de-beaune.com

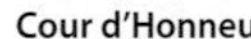

Cour d'Honneur
The buildings of Hôtel-Dieu are arranged around a splendid central courtyard. This is flanked by a wooden gallery, above which rise high dormer windows topped by weather vanes. The courtyard well is a fine example of Gothic wrought-iron work.

Pharmacy
Unusual potions with names such as woodlouse powder, shrimps' eyes and vomit nut powder are stored in these earthenware pots. Nearby is a bronze mortar used to prepare the remedies.

★ Last Judgment Polyptych
The naked figures shown in Rogier van der Weyden's 15th-century polyptych were briefly given clothing in the 19th century. At the same time, the altarpiece was cut in half so that the outer and inner panels could be seen together.

Château de Pierreclos in the Mâconnais region

24 Brionnais

Saône-et-Loire. Mâcon. Paray-le-Monial, Roanne. Paray-le-Monial. Marcigny (03 85 25 39 06).

The Brionnais is a small and peaceful rural district, squeezed between the River Loire and the Beaujolais foot-hills in the far south of Burgundy.

Its agricultural staple is the white Charolais cow, which can be seen grazing everywhere. For a closer look at this regional symbol, visit the lively cattle-market in **St-Christophe** on Wednesdays.

The area has an abundance of Romanesque churches, most of which are built of the local ochre-coloured stone. The 11th-century church of **Anzy-le-Duc** has a majestic three-tiered polygonal tower and exquisitely carved capitals. **Semur-en-Brionnais** was the birthplace of Cluny's famous abbot St Hugues. Its church is inspired by his great monastery. The church at **St-Julien-de-Jonzy** has a very finely carved tympanum.

Capital in St-Julien-de-Jonzy

A small town by the River Genette, **La Clayette** is graced by a château set in a lake (not open to the public). In nearby Curbigny, it is possible to visit the 18th-century **Château de Drée**, with its Louis XV and Louis XVI salons and its chapel.

Southeast of La Clayette the lonely **Montagne de Dun** rises just over 700 m (2,300 ft) and offers a panorama over the gentle, green Brionnais hills. This is some of the best picnic country in Burgundy, full of sleepy corners and quiet byways.

25 Mâcon

Saône-et-Loire. 36,000. 1 pl Saint Pierre (03 85 21 07 07). Sat. **macon-tourism.com**

At the frontier between Burgundy and the south, Mâcon is an industrial town and wine centre on the Saône.

The lack of churches is due to fervent anti-clericalism during the Revolution, when 14 were destroyed. A 17th-century convent has been turned into the **Musée des Ursulines**. Its collections include French and Flemish painting and an exhibition on the prehistoric site of Solutré. On the charming place aux Herbes, where the market is held, the **Maison de Bois** is a 15th-century wooden house covered with bizarre carvings.

Musée des Ursulines
Allée de Matisco. **Tel** 03 85 39 90 38. **Open** Tue–Sat & Sun pm. **Closed** 1 Jan, 1 May, 14 Jul, 1 Nov, 25 Dec.

Environs

The great **Roche de Solutré** rises dramatically above the Pouilly-Fuissé vineyards in the Mâconnais district *(see p349)*. Below the rock, finds from the Stone Age have established it as a major archaeological site.

Mâconnais is also the land of the Romantic poet Lamartine (1790–1869). Born in Mâcon, he spent his childhood at Milly Lamartine and later lived at Château de St-Point. **Château de Pierreclos** is associated with his epic poem *Jocelyn*.

Charolais cattle grazing on the gentle hills of the Brionnais

Franche-Comté

A region of woods and water, the Franche-Comté offers exceptional natural beauty combined with opportunities for canoeing, trekking and skiing. Apart from towns well worth visiting, this is a region to explore in the wild. Glorious scenery with grottoes and cascading waterfalls can be found all along the Vallée du Doubs. Further south are the spectacular sources of the rivers Lison and Loue. The Reculées is an area of extraordinary formations of ridges and waterfalls such as Baume-les-Messieurs. In Région des Lacs, the silent, peaceful lakes are surrounded by mountain peaks and virgin forests.

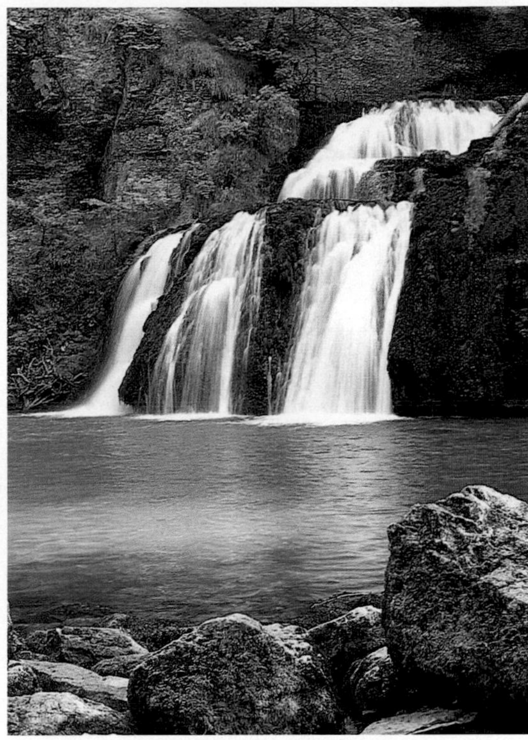

Nature at its purest at Source du Lison in the Franche-Comté

26 Cascades du Hérisson

Jura. Clairvaux-les-Lacs (03 84 25 27 47). Wed.

The village of Doucier, at the foot of the Pic de l'Aigle, is the starting point for the valley of the River Hérisson, one of the finest natural settings in the Jura. Leave the car at the park by the Moulin Jacquand and walk up the trail through the woods to a spectacular waterfall, the 65-m (213-ft) Cascade de L'Eventail, and beyond to the equally impressive Cascade du Grand Saut. The walk, which takes about 2 hours there and back, is steep at times and can be slippery, so proper shoes are essential.

27 Arbois

Jura. 3,600. 17 rue de l'Hôtel de Ville (03 84 66 55 50). Fri.
tourisme.arbois.com

The jolly wine town of Arbois lies on the vine-covered banks of the River Cuisance. It is famous for the sherry-like *vin jaune* (yellow wine) of the district. On the north side of the town is **Maison de Pasteur**, the preserved house and laboratory of the great scientist Louis Pasteur (1822–95), the first to test vaccines on humans.

Environs
Southeast of Dole is the 18th-century **Château d'Arlay**, with immaculately kept gardens.

28 Dole

Jura. 28,000. 6 pl Grévy (03 84 72 11 22). Tue & Fri.
tourisme-paysdedole.fr

The busy town of Dole lies where the Doubs meets the Rhine-Rhône canal. The former capital of the Comté was always a symbol of the region's resistance to the French. The region had become used to relative independence, first under the counts of Burgundy and then as part of the Holy Roman Empire. Though always French-speaking, its people did not appreciate the idea of the French absolute monarchy and in 1636 endured a very long siege. The town finally submitted to Louis XIV, first in 1668 and again in 1674.

There is a charming historic quarter in the centre of town, full of winding alleys, houses dating back to the 15th century, and quiet inner courtyards. Place aux Fleurs offers an excellent view of this part of town and the mossy-roofed, 16th-century **Eglise Notre-Dame**.

Virgin and Child on the north portal of Eglise Notre-Dame, Dole

The Saline Royale at Arc-et-Senans

㉙ Arc-et-Senans

Doubs. 1,400. 3A rue de la Saline (03 81 57 43 21). **destinationlouelison.com**

Designated a World Heritage Site since 1982, the **Saline Royale** (Royal Saltworks) at Arc-et-Senans were designed by the great French architect Claude-Nicolas Ledoux (1736–1806). He envisaged a development built in concentric circles around the main buildings. However, the only ones to be completed (in 1775) were the buildings used for salt production. Nevertheless, these show the staggering scale of Ledoux's idea: salt water was to be piped from Salins-les-Bains nearby, and fuel to reduce it was to come from the Chaux forest. The enterprise, which was never a success, was closed down in 1895, but the salt production buildings can be visited. The **Musée Ledoux Lieu du Sel** displays intriguing models of the grand projects imagined by the visionary architect.

Musée Ledoux Lieu du Sel
Saline Royale. **Tel** 03 81 54 45 45.
Open daily. **Closed** 1 Jan, 25 Dec.
gr. floor.

㉚ Champlitte

Haute-Saône. 1,900. 2 allée du Sainfoin (03 84 67 67 19).
ot-champlitte.fr

In the small town of Champlitte, the **Musée des Arts et Traditions Populaires** was created by a local shepherd, who collected artifacts connected with disappearing local customs. One of the poignant displays housed in this Renaissance château recalls the emigration of 400 citizens to Mexico in the mid-19th century.

Musée des Arts et Traditions Populaires
Pl de l'Eglise. **Tel** 03 84 67 82 00.
Open Jul & Aug: daily (Sat & Sun pms only); Mar–Jun & Sep–Nov: Wed–Mon (Sat & Sun pm only). **Closed** Dec–Feb.

㉛ Besançon

Doubs. 120,000. 2 pl de la Première Armée Française (03 81 80 92 55). Tue–Sat & Sun am.
besancon-tourisme.com

Besançon supplanted Dole as the capital of the Franche-Comté in the 17th century. It began as an ecclesiastical centre and is now an industrial one, specializing in precision engineering. The stately architecture of the old town, with its elegant wrought-iron work, is a 17th-century legacy.

Behind the Renaissance façade of the Palais Granvelle, in the Grande Rue, is the **Musée du Temps**, a fine collection of time-pieces of all ages – a tribute to Besançon's renown as a clock- and watchmaking centre. An interactive exhibition on the third floor invites reflection on the relativity of the notion of time.

Further along the same street are the birthplaces of novelist Victor Hugo (1802–85) at No. 140 and the Lumière brothers *(see p67)* at place Victor Hugo. Behind **Porte Noire**, a Roman arch, is the 12th-century Cathédrale St-Jean. In its bell tower is the **Horloge Astronomique** with its automatons that pop out on the hour.

The stunning **Musée des Beaux-Arts et d'Archéologie**, in the old corn market, houses works by Fragonard, Cranach, Rubens, Ingres, Goya, Matisse and Picasso.

Vauban's citadel, overlooking the River Doubs, has great views, plus three museums, including the **Musée Comtois**, with a collection of local artifacts, and a natural history museum with an insectarium and an aquarium.

Musée du Temps
Palais Granvelle, 96 Grande Rue. **Tel** 03 81 87 81 50. **Open** Tue–Sun. **Closed** 1 Jan, 1 May, 1 Nov, 25 Dec.

Horloge Astronomique
Rue de la Convention. **Tel** 03 81 81 12 76. **Open** Apr–Sep: Wed–Mon (winter: Thu–Mon). **Closed** Jan, 1 May, 1 & 11 Nov, 25 Dec.

Musée des Beaux-Arts et d'Archéologie
1 pl de la Révolution. **Tel** 03 81 87 80 67. **Closed** for renovation until late 2018.
free Sun.

Musée Comtois
La Citadelle, rue des Fusillés de la Résistance. **Tel** 03 81 87 83 33.
Open daily. **Closed** 3 wks Jan, 25 Dec.

Besançon's astronomical clock, made in 1857–60

㉜ Ornans

Doubs. 4,300. 7 rue Pierre Vernier (03 81 62 21 50). 3rd Tue of month. **destinationlouelison.com**

The great Realist painter Gustave Courbet was born at Ornans in 1819. He painted the town in every possible light. His *Enterrement à Ornans* proved to be one of the most influential

The striking Chapelle Notre-Dame-du-Haut by Le Corbusier at Ronchamp

paintings of the 19th century. Courbet's work is displayed in three historic buildings, including his childhood home, which make up the **Musée Courbet.**

Musée Courbet

Pl Robert Fernier. **Tel** 03 81 86 22 88. **Open** Wed–Mon. Closed 1 Jan, 1 May, 1 Nov, 25 Dec.
doubs.fr

Environs

A canoeist's paradise, the **Vallée de la Loue** is the loveliest in the Jura. The D67 follows the river from Ornans eastwards to Ouhans, from where it is only a 15-minute walk to its magnificent source. Various belvederes offer splendid views over the area.

Southwest of Ornans, the spectacular **Source du Lison** *(see p353)* is a 20-minute walk from Nans-sous-Ste-Anne.

33 Belfort

Territoire de Belfort. 52,000. 2 bis rue Clemenceau (03 84 55 90 90). Wed–Sun. **belfort-tourisme.com**

The symbol of Belfort is an enormous pink sandstone lion. It was built (rather than carved) by Frédéric-Auguste Bartholdi (1834–1904), whose other major undertaking was the Statue of Liberty.

Belfort's immensely strong **citadel**, designed by Vauban under Louis XIV, withstood three sieges, in 1814, 1815 and 1870. Today this remarkable array of fortifications provides an interesting walk and extensive views of the surroundings. The **Musée d'Histoire** is housed in the citadel and displays models of the original fortifications as well as regional art and artifacts (closed Tue).

34 Ronchamp

Haute-Saône. 3,000. 25 rue Le Corbusier (03 84 63 50 82). Sat. **ot-ronchamp.fr**

Le Corbusier's **Chapelle Notre-Dame-du-Haut** dominates this former miners' town. A sculpture rather than a building, its swelling concrete form was finalized in 1955. Inside, light, shape and space form a unity.

There is also a **Musée de la Mine** evoking the industry and the life of local miners.

Le Miroir d'Ornans in the Musée Courbet, Ornans

THE MASSIF CENTRAL

Haute-Vienne · Creuse · Allier · Puy de Dôme · Corrèze · Cantal Haute-Loire · Aveyron · Lozère·

The Massif Central is a region of strange, wild beauty – one of France's best-kept secrets. It is surprisingly little known beyond its sprinkling of spas and the major cities of Clermont-Ferrand, Vichy and Limoges. However, the new *autoroutes* through the heart of its uplands have started to open up this previously remote region.

The huge central plateau of ancient granite and crystalline rock that makes up the Massif Central embraces the dramatic landscapes of the Auvergne, Limousin, Aveyron and Lozère. Once a testing crossroads for pilgrims, and strung with giant volcanoes, it is a region of unsuspected richness, from the spectacular town of Le Puy-en-Velay, to the unique treasures at Conques.

With its crater lakes and hot springs, the Auvergne is the Massif Central's lush volcanic core, an outdoor paradise offering activities from hiking in summer to skiing in winter. It also has some of France's most beautiful Romanesque churches, medieval castles and Renaissance palaces. To the east are the mountain ranges of Forez, Livardois and Velay; to the west are the giant chains of extinct volcanoes, the Monts Dômes, Monts Dore and the Monts du Cantal. The Limousin, on the northwestern edge of the Massif Central, is gentler country with green pastures and blissfully empty roads.

The Aveyron spreads into the south-west from the Aubrac mountains, carrying with it the rivers Lot, Aveyron and Tarn through gorges and valleys with their cliff-hanging villages. To the east in the Lozère are the Grands Causses, the vast, isolated uplands of the Cévennes. These barren plateaux give farmers a poor living, but have been a favourite route with adventurous travellers across the centuries.

La Bourboule, a spa town in the Monts Dore

◀ The spectacular Gorges du Tarn

Exploring the Massif Central

Nature is at its most magnificent in the volcanic mountain ranges and wild river gorges of the Massif Central. This is a vast and unspoiled territory, which offers spectacular sightseeing and every imaginable outdoor activity, with rafting, paragliding, canoeing and hiking among the many choices. There are hundreds of churches, châteaux and museums to nourish lovers of history, architecture and art; and good, hearty regional cooking and interesting local wines for lovers of good living.

0 kilometres 25

0 miles 25

Key

- Motorway
- Motorway under construction
- Major road
- Secondary road
- Minor road
- Scenic route
- Main railway
- Minor railway
- Regional border
- △ Summit

Limestone cliffs of the Gorges du Tarn

Getting Around

There are good air and rail services connecting Paris with the major towns of Limoges and Clermont-Ferrand. Many of the most interesting towns and sights are easily accessible only by car, and AutoTrain from Paris to Brive is an effortless way of getting to the region with a car. Most minor roads are well-kept, but slow going in the mountains. A few roads are vertiginous, especially the road to the summit of Puy Mary, which is utterly breath-taking. The A71/A75 (toll-free) through the Auvergne is a magnificent road.

For keys to symbols *see back flap*

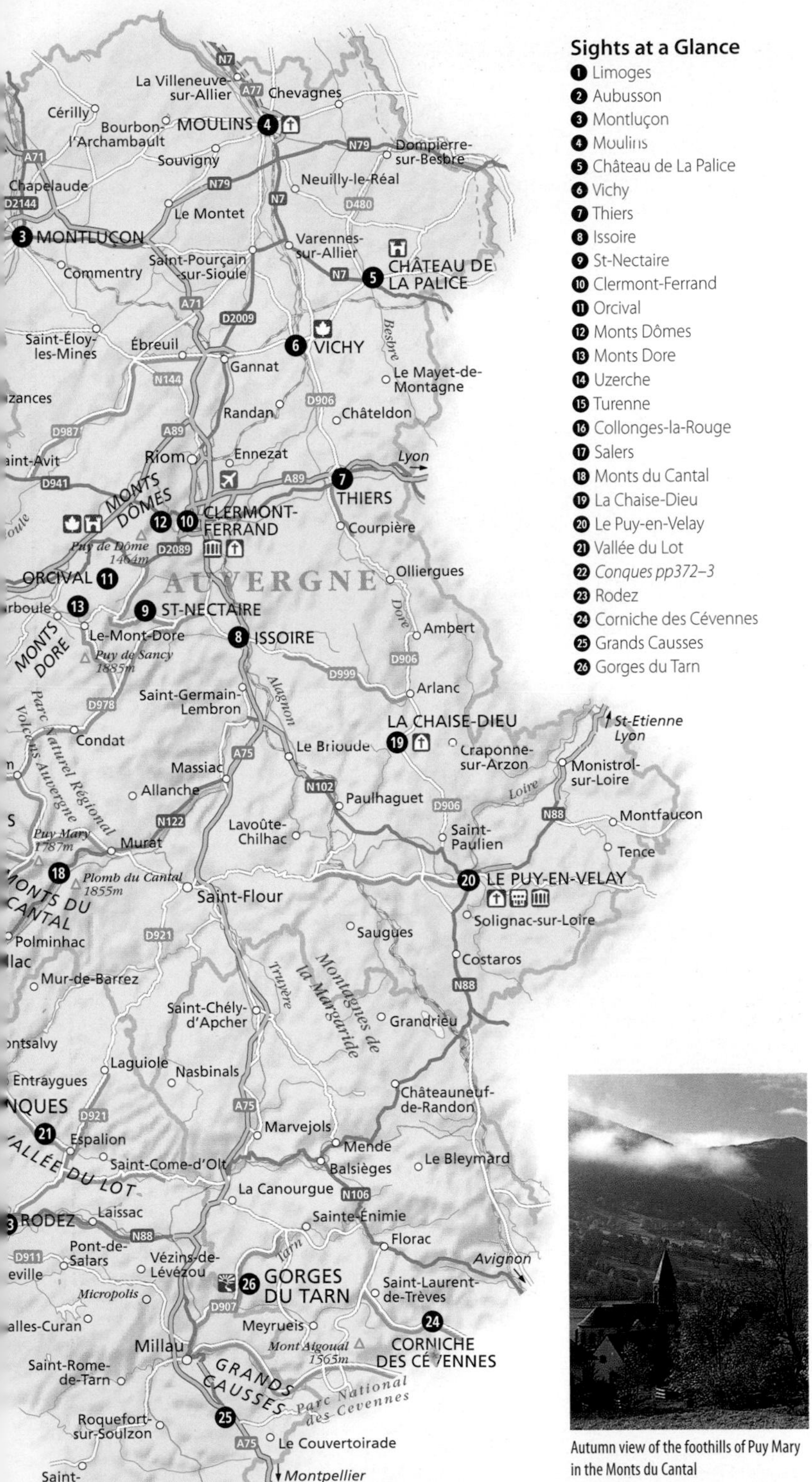

Sights at a Glance

1 Limoges
2 Aubusson
3 Montluçon
4 Moulins
5 Château de La Palice
6 Vichy
7 Thiers
8 Issoire
9 St-Nectaire
10 Clermont-Ferrand
11 Orcival
12 Monts Dômes
13 Monts Dore
14 Uzerche
15 Turenne
16 Collonges-la-Rouge
17 Salers
18 Monts du Cantal
19 La Chaise-Dieu
20 Le Puy-en-Velay
21 Vallée du Lot
22 *Conques pp372–3*
23 Rodez
24 Corniche des Cévennes
25 Grands Causses
26 Gorges du Tarn

Autumn view of the foothills of Puy Mary in the Monts du Cantal

A Limoges enamel plaque, *The Bad Shepherd*

❶ Limoges

Haute-Vienne. 200,000. 12 bd de Fleurus (05 55 34 46 87). daily. **limoges-tourisme.com**

The capital of the Limousin has two hearts: the old Cité and the rival château, now the commercial centre of the modern city. The Cité was ravaged by the Black Prince during the Hundred Years' War and today it is a quiet place of half-timbered houses and narrow streets.

It was not until the 1770s that Limoges became synonymous with porcelain. The legendary local ware is on display at the superb **Musée National Adrien-Dubouché**. More than 10,000 exhibits trace the history of ceramics. The **Musée des Beaux-Arts de Limoges** houses an Egyptian collection, archaeological artifacts tracing the history of Limoges, over 600 Limousin enamels and Impressionist paintings. This area was a centre of Resistance operations in World War II; the **Musée de la Résistance et de la Déportation** has a collection of exhibits relating to Resistance activities.

Musée National Adrien-Dubouché
Pl Winston Churchill. **Tel** 05 55 33 08 50. **Open** Wed–Mon. **Closed** 1 Jan, 25 Dec. **musee-adriendebouche.fr**

Musée des Beaux-Arts de Limoges
1 pl de l'Evêché. **Tel** 05 55 45 98 10. **Open** Wed–Mon. **Closed** Oct–Mar: Sun am, 1 Jan, 1 May, 1 & 11 Nov, 25 Dec. **museebal.fr**

Musée de la Résistance et de la Déportation
Rue Neuve Saint-Etienne. **Tel** 05 55 45 84 44. **Open** mid-Sep–mid-Jun: Wed–Sat, Sun pm & Mon; mid-Jun–mid-Sep: Wed–Mon. **Closed** 1 Jan, 1 May, 25 Dec.

Environs

Resistance activity led to severe reprisals in Limousin. On 10 June 1944, SS troups shot the entire population of the village of **Oradour-sur-Glane**, 25 km (16 miles) northwest of Limoges. The ruins have been kept as a shrine, and a new village was built nearby.

Close by, **St-Junien**, a glove-making town since the Middle Ages, still supplies designers today with luxury leather items.

❷ Aubusson

Creuse. 5,000. rue Vieille (05 55 66 32 12). Sat. **tourisme-aubusson.com**

Aubusson owes its renown to the exceptionally pure waters of the Creuse, perfect for making the delicately coloured dyes used for tapestries and rugs. Tapestry production was at its zenith in the 16th and 17th centuries, but by the end of the 18th century the Revolution and patterned wallpaper had swept away the clientele.

In the 1940s, Aubusson was revived, largely due to the artist Jean Lurçat, who persuaded other modern artists to design for tapestry. The **Cité Internationale de la Tapisserie** houses a museum with a permanent collection of these modern works. All 30 workshops welcome visitors – at the **Manufacture St-Jean** you can watch tapestries and custom-made carpets being made by hand and restored.

Cité Internationale de la Tapisserie
rue Williams-Dumazet. **Tel** 05 55 66 66 66. **Open** Wed–Mon. **Closed** Jan. **cite-tapisserie.fr**

Manufacture St-Jean
3 rue St-Jean. **Tel** 05 55 66 10 08. **Open** Mon–Fri.

Environs

A single street of 15th-century houses and a Roman bridge comprise **Moûtier-d'Ahun**, tucked into the lush Creuse

Tapestry restoration at the Manufacture St-Jean in Aubusson

For hotels and restaurants in this region see pp563–4 and pp591–3

Church at Moûtier-d'Ahun, near Aubusson

Valley. Vestiges of a Benedictine abbey can still be detected in the half-Romanesque, half-Gothic church with its elaborate stone portal. The choir has wooden stalls, and it is worth paying a visit to the church just to see them. They are masterpieces of late 17th-century carving with fantastical and intricately worked motifs of flora and fauna representing the many different facets of Good and Evil in figurative form. Today, there is a garden where the nave once was.

❸ Montluçon

Allier. 45,000. 67ter bd de Courtais (04 70 05 11 44). Tue, Thu–Sun. **montlucontourisme.com**

Montluçon is the economic centre of the region, a small town with a medieval core. At its heart there is a Bourbon château, which now houses temporary exhibitions. **Jardin Wilson**, a pleasant *jardin à la française* in the medieval quarter, sits on the original ramparts of the town. Mostly destroyed in the 18th century, little remains of the ramparts now. The restored rose garden and spectacular flowerbeds are worth a visit. The 12th-century **Eglise de St-Pierre** is a surprise, with giant stone columns and a huge barrel-vaulted ceiling.

❹ Moulins

Allier. 23,000. rue François Péron (04 70 44 14 14). Fri, Sun. **moulins-tourisme.com**

Capital of the Bourbonnais and seat of the Bourbon Dukes since the 10th century, Moulins flourished during the early Renaissance. Its most celebrated sight is the Flamboyant Gothic **Cathédrale Notre-Dame**, where members of the Bourbon court appear amid the saints in the 15th- and 16th-century stained-glass windows. The treasury contains a luminous 15th-century Virgin and Child triptych by the "Master of Moulins". Benefactors Pierre II, Duke of Bourbon, and his wife Anne de Beaujeu, bedecked in embroidery and jewels, are shown being introduced to a less richly dressed Madonna.

The tower keep and the single remaining wing of the Bourbon **Vieux Château** house a superb collection of sculpture, painting and decorative art from the 12th to the 16th centuries. Housed in the former cavalry barracks is a magnificent collection of 10,000 theatrical costumes.

Cathédrale Notre-Dame
Pl des Vosges. **Tel** 04 70 20 57 77.
Treasury: **Open** Tue–Sat & Sun pm.
Closed 25 Dec.

Stained-glass windows at the Cathédrale Notre-Dame in Moulins

❺ Château de La Palice

Allier. **Tel** 04 70 99 37 58. **Open** Apr–Oct: Wed–Mon.

In the early 16th century, the Marshal of France, Jacques II de Chabannes, hired Florentine architects to reconstruct the feudal château-fort at Lapalisse, creating a refined Renaissance castle, which has been inhabited ever since by his descendants. The *salon doré* (gilded room) has a beamed ceiling panelled in gold, and two huge 15th-century Flemish tapestries showing the Crusader Knight Godefroy de Bouillon and Greek hero Hector, two of the nine classic braves of chivalric legend.

Environs

From Lapalisse, the D480 leads up through the beautiful Besbre Valley past a handful of other small, well-preserved châteaux, including **Château de Thoury** and **Château Beauvoir**. Though neither is open to the public, they can be admired from the outside.

Gilded ceiling, Château de La Palice

❻ Vichy

Allier. 27,000. 19 rue du Parc (08 25 77 10 10). Wed.
vichy-destinations.fr

This small city on the River Allier has long been known for its hot and cold springs, and reputed cures for rheumatism, arthritis and digestive complaints. The letter-writer Madame de Sévigné and the daughters of Louis XV visited in the late 17th and 18th centuries – the former compared the showers to "a rehearsal for Purgatory". The visits of Napoleon III in the 1860s put Vichy on the map and made taking the waters fashionable. The small town was spruced up and became a favourite among the French nobility and the world's wealthy middle classes. These days, the grand old **Thermal Establishment**, built in 1900 lies abandoned, but it is possible to walk in and admire the architecture. The modern baths are state-of-the-art and strictly for medical purposes. A doctor's prescription and a reservation 30 days in advance are required for all treatments.

Interior of the original Thermal Establishment building in Vichy

An Art Nouveau travel poster from 1895 promoting Vichy

Vichy's fortunes changed for the better once again in the 1960s with the damming of the Allier, creating a huge lake in the middle of town, which rapidly became a thriving centre for water sports and international events. For a small fee, you can have a taste of sports from aikido to waterskiing or learn canoeing on the 3-km- (2-mile-) long artificial river.

The focal point of life in Vichy is the **Parc des Sources** in the centre of town, with its turn-of-the-20th-century bandstand (afternoon concerts in season), *belle époque* glass-roofed shopping galleries, and the Grand Casino and Opera House. Here there is gambling every afternoon and musical performances in the evenings, and an atmosphere of gaiety pervades. Also open to the public are the beautiful bronze taps of the **Source Célestin**, in a riverside park containing vestiges of a convent bearing the same name. Only by making an effort to imagine the city in grainy black-and-white newsreel style is there the slightest reminder of the wartime Vichy government, which was based in the town from 1940 to 1944 *(see p69)*.

Source Célestin
Bd du Président Kennedy. **Open** daily. **Closed** Dec–Jan.

❼ Thiers

Puy de Dôme. 13,500.
pl de Pirou (04 73 80 65 65).
Thu & Sat. **thiers-tourisme.fr**

According to the writer La Bruyère, Thiers "seems painted on the slope of the hill", hanging dramatically as it does on a ravine over a sharp bend in the River Durolle. The city has been renowned for cutlery since the Middle Ages, when legend has it that Crusaders brought back techniques of metalwork from the Middle East. With grindstones powered by dozens of waterfalls on the opposite bank of the river, Thiers produced everything from table knives to guillotine blades, and cutlery remains its major industry today, much of it on display in the Cutlery Museum, the **Musée de la Coutellerie**.

The Old Town is filled with mysterious quarters including "the Corner of Chance" and "Hell's Hollow", honeycombed with tortuous streets and well-restored 14th- to 17th-century houses. Many have elaborately carved wooden façades, notably the Maison du Pirou in place Pirou. The view to the west from the rampart terrace, towards Monts Dômes and Monts Dore, is particularly splendid at sunset.

Musée de la Coutellerie
58 rue de la Coutellerie. **Tel** 04 73 80 58 86.
Open Jun–Sep: daily; mid-Feb–May & Oct: Tue–Sun; Nov–Christmas hols Tue–Sun pm. **Closed** Jan–mid-Feb.

❽ Issoire

Puy de Dôme. 15,000.
9 pl St-Paul (04 73 89 15 90).
Sat. **issoire-tourisme.com**

Most of old Issoire was destroyed in the 16th-century Wars of Religion. The present-day town has been an important industrial centre since the end of World War II. Not only does Issoire have a thriving aeronautical tradition, it is also a mecca for glider pilots, who come from miles around to take advantage of the strong local air currents.

Issoire's colourful 12th-century abbey church of **St-Austremoine** is one of the great Romanesque churches of the region. The capitals depict scenes from the *Life of Christ* (one of the Apostles at the Last Supper has fallen asleep at table), and imaginary demons and beasts. The 15th-century fresco of the *Last Judgment* shows Bosch-like figures of sinners being cast into the mouth of a dragon or carted off to hell. The nearby Tour de l'Horloge has scenes of Renaissance history.

Pilgrimages and Ostensions

Parishes in the Auvergne and the Limousin are renowned for honouring their saints in outdoor processions. Ascension Day sees the Virgin of Orcival carried above the village by night, accompanied by gypsies and their children for baptism. Every seven years a score of villages in the Limousin hold *Ostensions*, when the saints' relics are paraded through the streets into the surrounding woods. The *Ostension* season begins the Sunday after Easter and runs until June. The next event in the seven-year cycle will be held in 2023.

The Saint-Martial reliquary parade during the Ostensions in Limoges

Viewed here from the south, thiers spread over the slopes above the River Durolle

9 St-Nectaire

Puy de Dôme. 750. Les Grands Thermes (04 73 88 50 86). Jul–Aug: Sun am. **sancy.com**

The Auvergne is noted for Romanesque churches. The **Eglise St-Nectaire** in the upper village of St-Nectaire-le Haut, with its soaring, elegant proportions, is one of the most beautiful. The 103 stone capitals, 22 of them polychrome, are vividly carved, and the treasury includes a gold bust of St Baudime and a wooden Notre-Dame-du-Mont-Cornadore, both marvels of 12th-century workmanship. The lower village, St-Nectaire-le-Bas, has more than 40 hot and cold springs.

Environs

The 12th-century citadel of **Château de Murol**, partially in ruins, offers costumed guides demonstrating medieval life and knightly pursuits. It is wonderful for children.

Château de Murol
Murol. **Tel** 04 73 88 82 50. **Open** Apr–Sep: daily; Oct–Mar: Sat & Sun. **Closed** 1 Jan, 14 Jul, 25 Dec.
murolchateau.com

Fontaine d'Amboise (1515) in Clermont-Ferrand

10 Clermont-Ferrand

Puy de Dôme. 140,000. pl de la Victoire (04 73 98 65 00). Mon–Sat. **clermont-fd.com**

Clermont-Ferrand began as two distinct cities, united only in 1630. Clermont is a lively commercial centre and student town, with thriving cafés and restaurants. It was a Celtic settlement before the Roman era, had a cathedral as early as the 5th century, and by 1095 was significant enough for the pope to announce the First Crusade there. The counts of Auvergne, challenging the episcopal power of Clermont, made their base in what is now old Montferrand, a short drive from Clermont city centre. Built on a bastide pattern, it is a time warp of quiet streets and Renaissance houses.

Clermont's more ancient origins are well illustrated at the **Musée Bargoin** with its remarkable collections of locally found Roman domestic artifacts (closed Mondays and Sunday mornings).

Place St-Pierre is Clermont's principal marketplace, with a daily food market – especially good on Saturdays. Nearby, the pedestrianized rue du Port leads steeply downhill from the **Fontaine d'Amboise** (1515) to the **Basilique Notre-Dame-du-Port**. This is one of the most important Romanesque churches in the region and has benefited from extensive renovations. The stone interior is beautifully proportioned, with a magnificent raised choir and vivid carved capitals showing Charity battling Avarice, in the form of two knights.

The contrast with the black lava **Cathédrale Notre-Dame-de-l'Assomption** is startling, from austere 12th-century

Raised choir in the Basilique Notre-Dame-du-Port

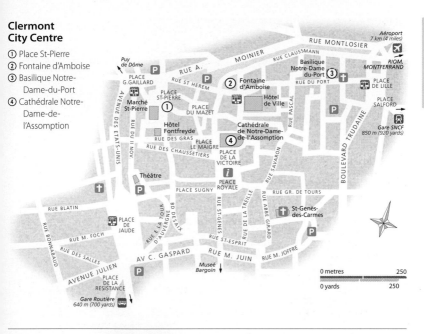

Clermont City Centre

① Place St-Pierre
② Fontaine d'Amboise
③ Basilique Notre-Dame-du-Port
④ Cathédrale Notre-Dame-de-l'Assomption

0 metres 250
0 yards 250

Romanesque to high-flying 13th-century Gothic. The graceful lines of the interior are due to the strong local stone used for construction, allowing pillars to be thinner and the whole structure to be lighter. The dark volcanic rock provides a foil for the jewel-like 12th- to 15th-century stained-glass windows, which are believed to be from the same workshop as Sainte-Chapelle's in Paris *(see p88)*.

The old section of Montferrand thrived from the 13th to the 17th centuries, and many fine houses – known as *hôtels particuliers* – built by prosperous merchants – have survived. Some of the best of these, with Italianate loggias, mullioned windows and intriguing courtyards, line the ancient **rue Kléber**. Between Clermont and old Montferrand lies a third mini-city, the headquarters and factories of the Michelin rubber-and-tyre company. Founded here in 1830 it dominates the town.

Michelin man, c.1910

Choir inside the Cathédrale Notre-Dame-de-l'Assomption, Clermont-Ferrand

Environs

Once the rival of Clermont-Ferrand for supremacy in Auvergne, **Riom** is a sombre provincial town of black stone houses and lava fountains. The 14th-century château of Duke Jean de Berry was razed in the 19th century to build the Palais de Justice; all that remains is the Sainte-Chapelle with its lovely 15th-century stained-glass windows.

Riom's greatest treasure is a graceful Madonna holding an infant with a small bird in his hand. The statue is housed in the Eglise de Notre-Dame-du-Marthuret, originally built in the 14th century, but greatly altered since then.

⓫ Orcival

Puy de Dôme. 300.
Le Bourg (04 73 65 89 77).
tourisme-sancy-artense.com

Crowded in summer, Orcival is nevertheless well worth visiting for its Romanesque church, the **Basilique d'Orcival**, which many would say is the best in the region. Completed at the beginning of the 12th century, and typically Auvergne Romanesque in style, the apse is multi-tiered, and the side walls are supported by powerful buttresses and strong arches. Inside, the ornate silver and vermilion *Virgin and Child* (in the forward-facing position known as "in majesty") is enigmatic, with an unusual, rigid, square chair. With an interior lit by 14 windows and a spacious crypt, the proportions of the building itself are the most graceful aspect.

Virgin and Child in the Basilique d'Orcival

Aerial view of Puy de Dôme in the Monts Dômes range

⓬ Monts Dômes

Puy de Dôme. Clermont-Ferrand. Aydat (04 73 65 64 26). **parcdesvolcans.fr**

The youngest range of the Auvergne volcanoes at 4,000 years old, the Monts Dômes, or Chaîne des Puys, encompass 112 extinct volcanoes aligned over a 30-km (19-mile) stretch just west of Clermont-Ferrand. At the centre, the **Puy de Dôme** towers above a high plateau. A mountain railway spirals up the peak at a steady 12 per cent gradient, taking 15 minutes to reach the top, while the steeper Roman path is still used by hikers. (No cars or buses ascend the Puy de Dôme; phone 08 26 39 96 15 for train information).

At the summit are the vestiges of the Roman temple of Mercury and a meteorological/telecommunications tower. On a rare clear day, the view across the volcano will take away whatever breath you have left.

The volcanic Roche Tuilière below Col de Guéry in the Monts Dore

The controversial **Parc Européen du Volcanisme, Vulcania** uses the latest technology to simulate volcanic activity in its underground circuit.

In the southwest corner of the Monts Dômes region is the **Château de Cordès**, a small, privately owned 15th-century manor house with formal gardens designed by Le Nôtre *(see p183)*.

Vulcania
D941B, Saint-Ours-les-Roches. **Tel** 04 73 19 70 00. **Open** mid-Mar–mid-Nov; see website for times. Documentation centre. **vulcania.com**

Château de Cordès
Orcival. **Tel** 04 73 21 15 89. **Open** Jul & Aug: daily; Jun: Sun pm (gardens only).

⓭ Monts Dore

Puy de Dôme. Clermont-Ferrand. Le Mont-Dore. Montlosier, Aydat (04 73 65 64 26).

Three giant volcanoes – the Puy de Sancy, the Banne d'Ordanche and the Puy de l'Aiguiller – and their secondary cones make up the Monts Dore: dark green, heavily wooded mountains laced with rivers and lakes and dotted with summer and winter resorts for skiing, hiking, paragliding, canoeing and sailing.

The 1,885-m (6,185-ft) **Puy de Sancy** is the highest point in central France. It can be reached by taking a shuttle from the town of Le Mont-Dore to the cable car, which goes up to the peak, followed by a long hike across open terrain. From Le Mont-Dore there is a scenic drive on the D36, which leads to the **Couze-Chambon Valley**, a beautiful stretch of high moorland threaded with waterfalls.

The area has two popular spa towns, **La Bourboule**, for children's ailments, with its casino, and Le Mont-Dore, with its grandiose turn-of-the-20th-century **Etablissement Thermal**.

Below the Col de Guéry on the D983, the eroded volcanic **Roche Sanadoire** and **Roche Tuilière** stand up like two gigantic gateposts. From their peaks are far-reaching views over the wooded Cirque de Chausse and beyond.

Church at La Bourboule in the Monts Dore

⓮ Uzerche

Corrèze. 3,000. pl de la Libération (05 55 73 15 71). Sat. **uzerche-tourisme.com**

Uzerche is an impressive sight: grey slate roofs, turrets and bell towers rising from a hill above the Vézère river. This prosperous town never capitulated during the conflicts of the Middle Ages, and earlier withstood a seven-year siege by Moorish forces in 732: the townspeople sent a feast out to their enemy – in fact, the last of their supplies. The Moors, thinking such lavish offerings meant the city had stores to spare, gave up.

The Romanesque **Eglise St-Pierre** crests the hill above the town. Beyond Uzerche, the Vézère cuts through the green gorges of the Saillant.

Cantal Cheese

Transhumance is still practised in the Auvergne, with the local Salers cattle kept in barns in the valleys during winter and led up to mountain pastures for the summer. The robust grasses and flowers – gentian, myrtle, anemone – on which the cows graze produce a flavoursome milk that is the basis for the region's excellent cheese, Cantal. Curds were once turned and pressed through cheesecloth by hand, but now modern methods prevail. Cantal is the key ingredient in *aligot* – the potato-and-cheese purée flavoured with garlic that is one of the region's most famous dishes.

Salers cattle enjoying rich pastures

⓯ Turenne

Corrèze. 750. Brive-la-Gaillarde (05 55 24 08 80).

Turenne is one of the most appealing medieval towns in the Corrèze. Crescent-shaped and clustered on the cliff-side, the town was the last independent feudal fiefdom in France, under the absolute rule of the La Tour d'Auvergne family until 1738. Henri de la Tour d'Auvergne, their most illustrious member, was a marshal of France under Louis XIV, and one of the greatest soldiers of modern times.

Now the sole remains of the **Château de Turenne** are the 13th-century Clock Tower and 11th-century Tower of Caesar, from which there is a quite stunning 360-degree view of the Cantal mountains across to the Dordogne Valley. Not far away is the 16th-century collegiate church and the **Chapelle des Capucins** dating from the 18th century.

Château de Turenne
Tel 05 55 85 90 66. **Open** Apr–Oct: daily; Nov–Mar: Sun pm.
chateau-turenne.com

⓰ Collonges-la-Rouge

Corrèze. 400. Brive, then bus to Collonges. 13 rue de la République, Bellegarde-sur-Valserine (01200 (04 50 48 48 68). **valle-dordogne.com**

There's something a little unsettling about Collonges' carmine sandstone architecture, quite beautiful in individual houses, though the overall effect is both austere and fairy-tale-like.

Founded in the 8th century, Collonges came under the rule of Turenne, whose burghers built the sturdy turreted houses in the surrounding vineyards. Look out for the communal bread oven in the marketplace, and the 11th-century church, later fortified with a tower keep. The church's unusual carved white limestone tympanum shows a man driving a bear, and other lively figures.

Medieval Château de Val at Bort-les-Orgues near Salers

⓱ Salers

Cantal. 400. summer only. pl Tyssandier d'Escous (04 71 40 58 08). Wed. **salers-tourisme.fr**

A handsome town of grey lava houses and 15th-century ramparts, Salers sits atop a steep escarpment at the edge of the Cantal mountains. It is one of few virtually intact Renaissance villages in the region. The church has an admirable polychrome *mise au tombeau* (entombment), dated 1495, and five 17th-century Aubusson tapestries.

From the fountain, streets lead up to the cliff edge, and allow views of the surrounding valleys, with the ever-present sound of cowbells in the distance. The town is very crowded in summer, but it makes a good starting point for excursions to the Puy Mary *(see p368)*, the huge barrage at Bort-les-Orgues, the nearby Château de Val and the Cère Valley to the south.

Puy Mary peak in the volcanic Monts du Cantal

⑱ Monts du Cantal

Cantal. Aurillac. Lioran. Aurillac (04 71 48 46 58). **iaurillac.com**

The Cantal mountains were originally one enormous volcano – the oldest and the largest in Europe, dating from the Tertiary period. The highest peaks, the **Plomb du Cantal** at 1,855 m (6,086 ft) and the **Puy Mary** at 1,787 m (5,863 ft), are surrounded by crests and deep river valleys. Driving the narrow roads is a thrill, compounded by the views at every hairpin turn. Between peaks and gorges, rich mountain pastures provide summer grazing for red-gold Salers cows *(see p367)*. From the **Pas de Peyrol**, the highest road pass in the country at 1,582 m (5,191 ft), it's about a 25-minute journey on foot to the summit of the Puy Mary.

Environs

One of the finest of the Auvergne châteaux, **Château d'Anjony** was built by Louis II d'Anjony, a supporter of Joan of Arc *(see p304)*. Highlights are the 16th-century frescoes: in the chapel, scenes from the Life and Passion of Christ, and, upstairs, in the *Salle des Preux* (Knights' Room), a dazzling series of the nine heroes of chivalry. To the south lies the small town of **Aurillac**, a good base for exploring the Cantal region.

Château d'Anjony

Tournemire. **Tel** 04 71 47 61 67. **Open** mid-Feb–Jun & Sep–mid-Nov: daily pms; Jul–Aug: daily (closed Sun am). obligatory.

⑲ La Chaise-Dieu

Haute-Loire. 700. rue Saint-Esprit (04 71 00 01 16). Thu. **la-chaise-dieu.info**

Sombre and massive, midway between Romanesque and Gothic, the 14th-century abbey church of St-Robert is the prime reason to visit the small village of La Chaise-Dieu. The building is an amalgam of styles; the choir, however, is sensational: 144 oak stalls carved with figures of Vice and Virtue. Above them, entirely covering the walls, are some of the loveliest tapestries in France. Made in Brussels and Arras in the early 16th century and depicting scenes from the Old and New Testaments, they are rich in colour and detail.

Statue of Notre-Dame-de-France at Le Puy

On the outer walls of the choir the 15th-century wall painting of the *Danse Macabre* shows Death in the form of skeletons leading rich and poor alike to their inevitable end. Beyond the cloister is the Echo room, in which two people whispering in opposite corners can hear one another perfectly. A Baroque Music Festival from mid-August to September makes the abbey crowded.

Detail of *Danse Macabre* at St-Robert, in La Chaise-Dieu

⑳ Le Puy-en-Velay

Haute-Loire. 21,000. 2 pl de Clauzel (04 71 09 38 41). Sat. Sep. **ot-lepuyenvelay.fr**

Located in the bowl of a volcanic cone, the town of Le Puy, a UNESCO World Heritage site, teeters on a series of rock outcrops and giant basalt pillars. The town has three peaks, each topped with a landmark church or statue. Seen from afar, this is one of the most impressive sights in France.

The town is now a commercial and tourist-oriented place, but its star attraction is its medieval **Holy City**. This became a pilgrimage centre after the Bishop of Le Puy, Gotescalk, made one of the first pilgrimages to Santiago de Compostela in 962, and built the **Chapelle St-Michel**

The Auvergne's Black Madonnas

The cult of the Virgin Mary has always been strong in the Auvergne and this is reflected in the concentration of her statues in the region. Carved in dark walnut or cedar, now blackened with age, the Madonnas are believed to originate from the Byzantine influence of the Crusaders. Perhaps the most famous Madonna is the one in Le-Puy-en-Velay, a 17th-century copy of one that belonged to Louis IX in the Middle Ages.

Louis IX's Black Virgin

d'Aiguilhe on his return. Pilgrims from eastern France and Germany assembled at the **Cathédrale de Notre-Dame** with its famous Black Madonna and "fever stone" – a Druid ceremonial stone believed to have healing powers embedded in one of its walls – before setting off for Compostela.

Built on an early pagan site, the Cathédrale de Notre-Dame is a huge Romanesque structure. Multiform arches, carved palm and leaf designs and a chequerboard façade show the influences of Moorish Spain, and indicate the considerable cultural exchange that took place with southern France in the 11th and 12th centuries. In the transept are Romanesque frescoes, notably an 11th- to 12th-century St Michael; in the sacristy, the treasury includes the Bible of Theodolphus, a handwritten document from the era of Charlemagne. The cathedral is the centre of the Holy City complex that dominates the upper town, encompassing a baptistry, cloister, Prior's house and Penitents' chapel.

The colossal red statue of **Notre-Dame-de-France**, on the pinnacle of the Rocher Corneille, was erected in 1860, cast from 213 cannons captured at Sebastopol during the Crimean War. The statue is reached by a steep pathway, and can be climbed by an iron ladder on the inside.

The **Chapelle St-Michel d'Aiguilhe**, like the cathedral, shows Moorish influences in the trefoil decoration and coloured mosaics on the rounded arch over the main entrance. It seems to grow out of a giant finger of lava rock and is reached by a steep climb. The church is thought to be located on the site of a Roman temple to Mercury, and its centre dates from the 10th century, although most of the building was constructed a century later. The floor has been constructed to follow the contours of the rock in places, and the interior is ornamented with faded 10th-century murals and 20th-century stained glass.

In the lower city, narrow streets of 15th- and 16th-century houses lead to the Vinay Garden and the **Musée Crozatier**, which has a collection of handmade lace from the 16th century to the present. The museum also has a good collection of archaeological artifacts, medieval objets d'art, 15th-century paintings and natural sciences exhibits.

In mid-September, Le Puy transforms itself entirely for a masked and costumed Renaissance carnival for The Bird King Festival, an ancient tradition celebrating the skill of the city's best archers *(see p42)*.

Notre-Dame-de-France
Rocher Corneille. **Tel** 04 71 04 11 33.
Open daily. **Closed** mid-Nov–Jan (except Christmas hols).

Chapelle St-Michel d'Aiguilhe
Aiguilhe. **Tel** 04 71 09 50 03.
Open mid-Feb–mid-Dec: daily.

Musée Crozatier
Jardin Henri Vinay. **Tel** 04 71 06 62 40. **Open** call for up-to-date information.

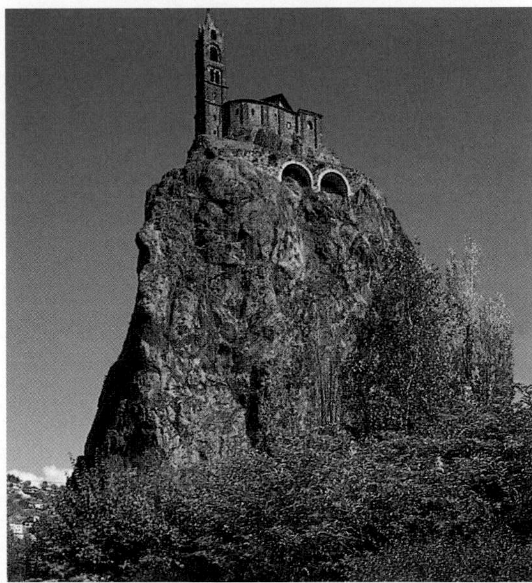

Chapelle St-Michel d'Aiguilhe, standing on a finger of lava rock

Ruins of the Castle of Calmont d'Olt at Espalion in the Lot Valley

㉑ Vallée du Lot

Aveyron. Aurillac, Rodez. Rodez, Séverac-le-Château. Espalion, Rodez. Espalion (05 65 44 10 63). **valleedulot.com**

From Mende and the old river port of La Canourgue all the way to Conques, the River Lot (or Olt in old usage) courses through its fertile valley past orchards, vineyards and pine forests. **St Côme d'Olt**, near the Aubrac mountains, is an unspoiled, fortified village with a 15th-century church surrounded by Medieval and Renaissance houses. At **Espalion**, the pastel stone houses and a turreted 16th-century castle are reflected in the river, which runs beneath a 13th-century arched stone bridge. The town has one of the best markets in the region on Friday mornings. Just outside town is the 11th-century Perse Church, with carved capitals portraying battling knights and imaginary birds sipping from a chalice.

Estaing was once the fiefdom of one of the greatest families of the Rouergue, dating back to the 13th century. The village nestles beneath its massive château (open May–mid-Oct) on the riverbank. The road passes through the Lot Gorge on the way to **Entraygues** ("between waters"), where the old quarter and 13th-century Gothic bridge are worth a visit. Beyond Entraygues, the river widens to join the Garonne.

㉒ Conques

See pp372–3.

㉓ Rodez

Aveyron. 26,000. place de la Cité (05 65 75 76 77). Wed, Sat. **tourisme.grand-rodez.com**

Like many medieval French cities, Rodez was politically divided: the shop-lined **place du Bourg** on one side of town and **place de la Cité**, near the cathedral, on the other, reflect conflicting secular and ecclesiastical interests. Rodez's commercial centre is the region's largest. The 13th-century huge pink stone **Cathédrale Notre-Dame** is worth a look, with its fortress-like west façade and its magnificent bell tower. The 15th-century choir stalls show a panoply of creatures, including a winged lion and one naughty fellow exposing his derrière.

The striking steel **Musée Soulages** houses over 500 paintings and other works by the artist Pierre Soulages, who was born in Rodez in 1919. It also hosts temporary exhibitions of modern and contemporary art.

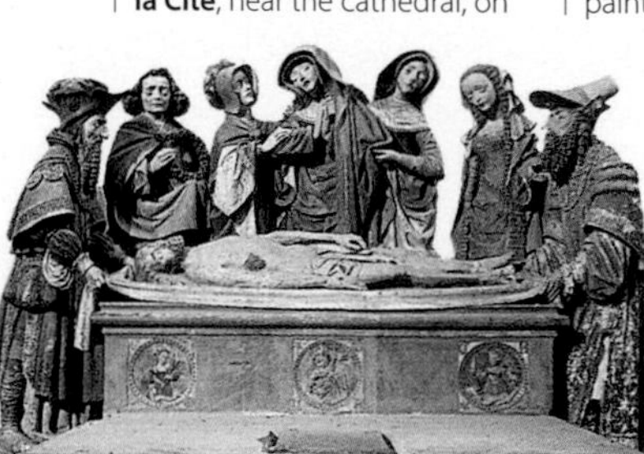
Entombment in Rodez Cathedral

Environs

Southeast (45km/28 miles) lies Saint Léons, birthplace of Jean-Henri Fabre, the entymologist. Here is **Micropolis**, part

Robert Louis Stevenson

Robert Louis Stevenson (1850–94), best known for his novels *Treasure Island, Kidnapped* and *Strange Case of Dr Jekyll and Mr Hyde,* was also an accomplished travel writer. In 1878, he set off across the remote Cévennes mountain range with only a small donkey, Modestine, for company. His classic account of this eventful journey, *Travels with a Donkey in the Cévennes*, was published in the following year.

Robert Louis Stevenson

interactive museum, part theme park, dedicated to the glory of insects (closed Nov–mid-Feb). Watch the breathtaking film of the same name, if nothing else.

Musée Soulages
Jardin du Foirail, av Victor Hugo.
Tel 05 65 73 82 60. **Open** Tue–Sun (Jul–Aug: Mon pm).

㉔ Corniche des Cévennes

Lozère, Gard. Nîmes. Alès. St-Jean-du-Gard. Parc National de Cévennes, 6bis pl du Palais, Florac 48400 (04 66 49 53 00).
cevennes-parcnational.fr

The dramatic Corniche road from Florac on the Tarn to St-Jean-du-Gard was cut in the early 18th century by the army of Louis XIV in pursuit of the Camisards, Protestant rebels who had no uniforms but fought in their ordinary shirts (*camiso* in the *langue d'oc*). The route of the D983 makes a spectacular drive. Fascination with the history of the Camisards was one of the reasons that Robert Louis Stevenson undertook his fabled trek in the Cévennes with Modestine, recounted in his *Travels with a Donkey in the Cévennes*.

At St-Laurent-de-Trèves, where fossil remains suggest dinosaurs once roamed, there is a view of the Grands Causses and the peaks of Lozère and Aigoual. The Corniche ends in St-Jean-du-Gard.

Dramatic scenery in Corniche des Cévennes national park

㉕ Grands Causses

Aveyron. Rodez-Marcillac. Millau. Millau (05 65 60 02 42). Wed & Fri. **millau-viaduc-tourisme.fr**

The Causses are vast, arid limestone plateaux, alternating with green, fertile canyon valleys. The only sign of life at times is a bird of prey wheeling in the sky, or an isolated stone farm or shepherd's hut. The whole area makes for some desolate hiking for those who like solitude.

The four Grands Causses – Sauveterre, Méjean, Noir and Larzac – stretch out east of the city of Millau, which boasts the tallest vehicular bridge in the world. They extend from Mende in the north to the valley of the Vis river in the south.

Among the sights in the Causses are the *chaos* – bizarre rock formations reputed to resemble ruined cities, and named accordingly: there's the *chaos* of **Montpellier-le-Vieux**, **Nîmes-le-Vieux** and **Roquesaltes**. **Aven Armand** and the **Dargilan Grotto** are vast and deep natural underground grottoes.

A good place to head for in the Larzac Causse is the strange, rough-hewn stone village of **La Couvertoirade**, a fully enclosed citadel of the Knights Templar in the 12th century. The unpaved streets and medieval houses are an austere reminder of the dark side of the Middle Ages. Entry to the village is free, with a fee for the tour of the ramparts.

The Causse du Larzac's best-known village is probably **Roquefort-sur-Soulzon**, a small grey town terraced on the side of a crumbled lime-stone outcrop. It has one main street and one major product, Roquefort cheese. This is made from unpasteurized sheep's milk, seeded with a distinctive blue mould grown on loaves of bread, and aged in the warren of damp caves above the town.

View over Méjean, one of the four plateaux of the Grands Causses

22 Conques

The village of Conques clusters around the splendid Abbaye de Ste-Foy, hemmed into a rugged site against the hillside. St Foy was a young girl who became an early Christian martyr; her relics were first kept at a rival monastery in Agen. In the 9th century a monk from Conques stole the relics, thereby attracting pilgrims to this remote spot and firmly establishing Conques as a halt on the route to Santiago de Compostela *(see pp404–5)*. The treasury holds the most important collection of medieval and Renaissance gold work in Western Europe. Some of it was made in the abbey's own workshops as early as the 9th century. The Romanesque abbey church has beautiful stained-glass windows by Pierre Soulages (1994), and its tympanum is a triumph of medieval sculpture.

View of the church from the village

Nave Interior
Pure and elegantly austere, the Romanesque interior dates from 1050–1135. The short nave soars to a height of 22 m (72 ft), with three tiers of arches topped by 250 decorative carved capitals.

Tympanum
This sculpture from the early 12th century depicts the *Last Judgment*, with the Devil in Hell (shown) in the lower part of the sculpture and Christ in Heaven in the tympanum's central position.

KEY

① **The broad transepts** were able to accommodate crowds of pilgrims.

② **The Cloister** consists of a reconstructed square: only two sections of the original early 12th-century arcades remain. However, 30 of the original carved capitals are displayed in the refectory and in the Musée Fau.

Conques' Treasures

The treasures date from the 9th to the 19th century, and are prized for both their beauty and their rarity. The gold-plated wood and silver reliquary of Ste-Foy is studded with gems, rock crystal and even an *intaglio* of the Roman Emperor Caracalla. The body is 9th century, but the face may be older, possibly 5th century. Other magnificent pieces include an "A"-shaped reliquary, said to be a gift from Charlemagne; the small but exquisite Pépin's shrine from AD 1000; and a late 16th-century processional cross.

The precious reliquary of Ste-Foy

VISITORS' CHECKLIST

Practical Information
Aveyron. 1,600. Pl de l'Eglise (05 65 72 85 00). Treasury/museum: **Open** daily: Apr–Sep: 9:30am–12:30pm, 2–6:30pm; Oct–Mar: 10am–noon, 2–6pm. 8am Mon–Sat, 11am Sun. restr. **tourisme-conques.fr**

Transport
to St-Christophe, then a bus. from Rodez.

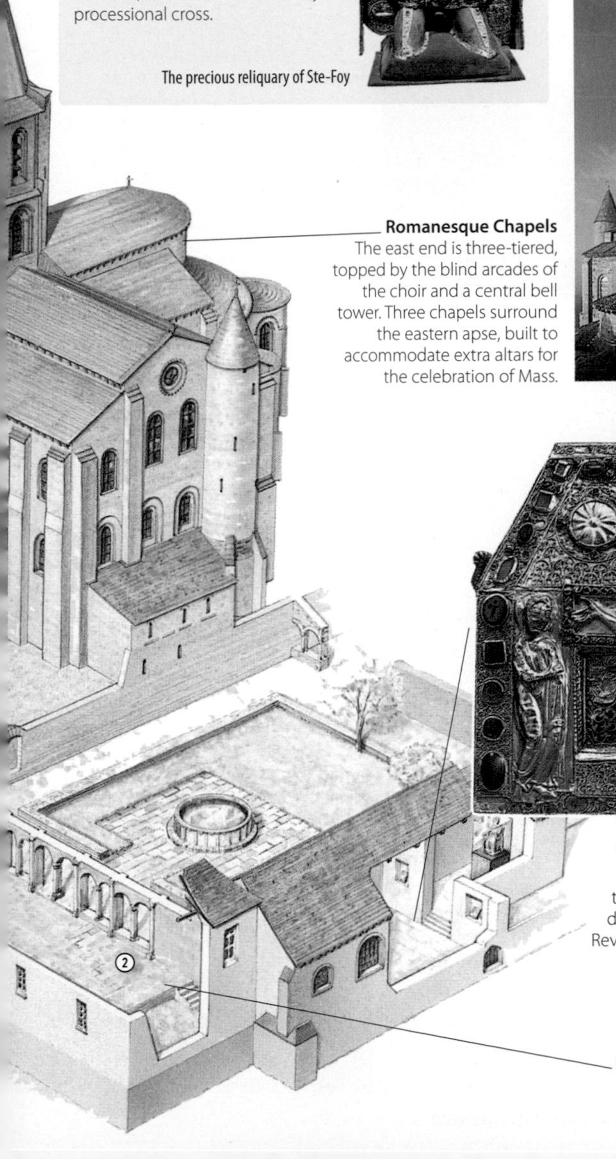

Romanesque Chapels
The east end is three-tiered, topped by the blind arcades of the choir and a central bell tower. Three chapels surround the eastern apse, built to accommodate extra altars for the celebration of Mass.

Treasury
The precious contents of the Treasury were hidden by the townspeople to prevent their destruction during the French Revolution. Perhaps surprisingly, all were returned.

②

Entrance to the Treasury

㉖ Gorges du Tarn

Near the beginning of its journey to meet the River Garonne, the Tarn flows through some of Europe's most spectacular gorges. For millions of years, the Tarn and its tributary the Jonte have eaten their way down through the limestone plateaux of the Cévennes, creating a sinuous forked canyon some 24 km (15 miles) long and nearly 400 m (1,300 ft) deep. The UNESCO-listed gorges are flanked by rocky bluffs and scaled by roads with dizzying bends and panoramic views, which are very popular in the high season. The surrounding plateaux, or *causses*, are eerily different, forming an open, austere landscape, dry in summer and snow-clad in winter, where wandering sheep and isolated farms are sometimes the only signs of life.

Point Sublime
From 800 m (2,600 ft) up, there are stunning views of a major bend in the Tarn gorge, with the Causse Méjean visible in the distance.

Outdoor Activities
The Tarn and Jonte gorges are popular for canoeing and river-rafting. Although the rivers are relatively placid in summer, melting snow can make them hazardous in spring.

Pas de Souci
Just upriver from Les Vignes, Pas de Souci flanks a narrow point in the gorge as the Tarn makes its way northwards.

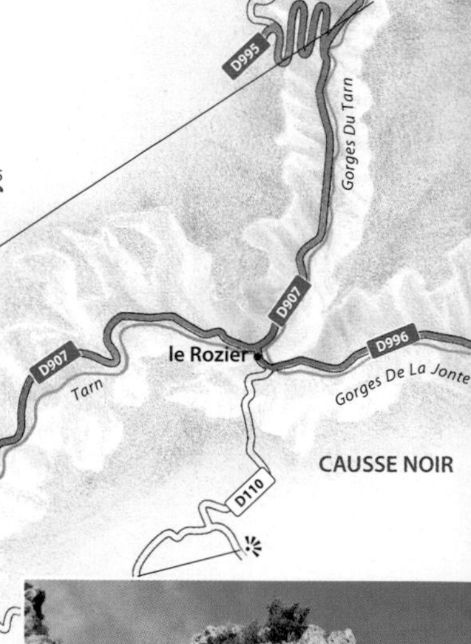

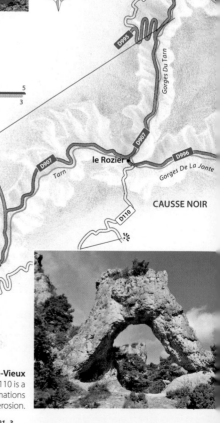

Chaos de Montpellier-le-Vieux
Situated on the flank of the Causse Noir off the D110 is a remarkable geological site – bizarre rock formations created by limestone erosion.

For hotels and restaurants in this region see pp563–4 and pp591–3

La Malène
An old crossing-point between the Causse de Sauveterre and the Causse Méjean, this village, with its 16th-century fortified manor, is a good starting point for boat trips.

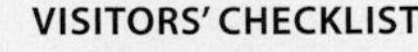

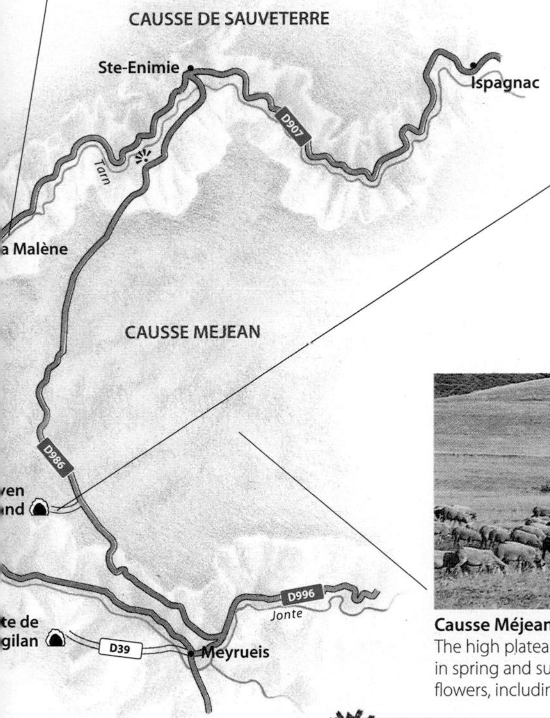

VISITORS' CHECKLIST

Practical Information
Lozère. Le Rozier (05 65 62 60 89), St-Enimie (04 66 48 53 44).
gorgesdutarn.net

Transport
Rodez-Marcillac. Mende, Banassac, Séverac-le-Château. Milau.

CAUSSE DE SAUVETERRE
Ste-Enimie
Ispagnac
D907
Tarn
a Malène
CAUSSE MEJEAN
D986
ven
nd
D996
Jonte
te de
gilan
D39
Meyrueis

Aven Armand Caves
On the Causse Méjean, many stalactites in the caves are tinted by minerals that are deposited by the slowly trickling water.

Causse Méjean
The high plateaux or *causses* are a botanist's paradise in spring and summer, with over 900 species of wild flowers, including orchids.

The Wild Cévennes

One of the least populated parts of France, this area is well-known for its wild flowers and birds of prey, and griffon vultures were once common here. These giant but harmless scavengers nearly died out in the 20th century through being hunted, but now a reintroduction programme has led to growing numbers breeding in the Gorges de la Jonte.

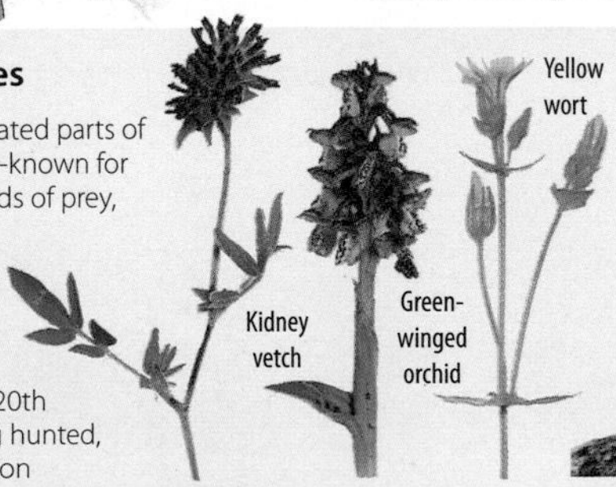

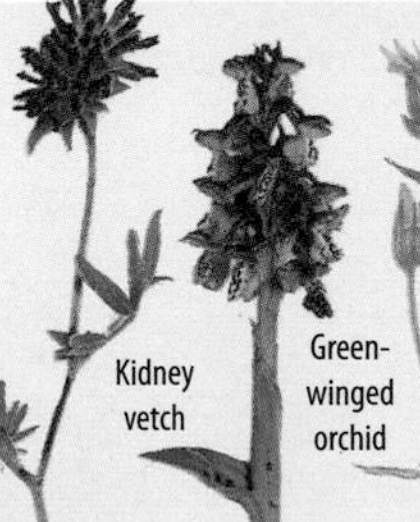

Wild flowers found in this thinly populated area include unusual Alpine plants.

The griffon vulture, which now breeds in the region, has a wingspan of over 2.5 m (8 ft).

THE RHONE VALLEY AND FRENCH ALPS

Ain · Rhône · Isère · Loire · Drôme · Ardèche
Hautes-Alpes · Savoie · Haute-Savoie

Its two most important geographical features, the Alps and the River Rhône, give this region both its name and its dramatic character. The east is dominated by majestic snowcapped peaks, while the Rhône provides a vital conduit between north and south.

The Romans recognized this strategic route when they founded Lyon over 2,000 years ago. Today Lyon, with its great museums and fine Renaissance buildings, is the second city of France. It is one of the country's most vital commercial and cultural centres, as well as the undisputed capital of French gastronomy. To the north lie the flat marshlands of the Dombes and the rich agricultural Bresse plain. Here, too, are the famous Beaujolais vineyards, which, along with the Rhône ones, make the region such an important wine producer.

The French Alps are among the most popular year-round resort areas in the world, with internationally renowned ski stations such as Chamonix, Mégève and Courchevel, and historic cities including Chambéry, capital of Savoy before it joined France. Elegant spa towns line the shores of Lac Léman (Lake Geneva). Grenoble, a bustling university city and high-tech centre, is flanked by two of the most spectacular nature reserves in France, the Chartreuse and the Vercors.

To the south, orchards and fields of sunflowers give way to brilliant rows of lavender interspersed with vineyards and olive groves. Châteaux and ancient towns dot the landscape. Mountains and pretty, old-fashioned spa towns characterize the rugged Ardèche, and the deeply scoured gorges along the River Ardèche offer some of the wildest scenery in France.

The restored Ferme de la Forêt at St-Trivier-de-Courtes, north of Bourg-en-Bresse

◀ Chapelle Sainte-Marie-Madeleine set against the dramatic scenery of the Vallée de la Clarée, close to Briançon

Exploring the Rhône Valley and French Alps

Lyon is the region's largest city, famed for its historic buildings and gastronomic tradition. Wine lovers can choose between the vineyards of the Beaujolais, Rhône Valley and Drôme region to the south. To the west, the Ardèche offers rugged wilderness, canoeing and climbing. Spa devotees from around the world flock to Evian-les-Bains and Aix-les-Bains, while the Alps are a favourite destination for sports enthusiasts *(see pp326–7)*.

Sights at a Glance

1. Bourg-en-Bresse
2. The Dombes
3. Pérouges
4. *Lyon pp382–5*
5. Vienne
6. St-Romain-en-Gal
7. St-Etienne
8. Palais Idéal du Facteur Cheval
9. Tournon-sur-Rhône
10. Valence
11. The Ardèche
12. Vals-les-Bains
13. Montélimar
14. Grignan
15. Nyons
16. Briançon
17. Le Bourg d'Oisans
18. Grenoble
19. The Vercors
20. The Chartreuse
21. Chambéry
22. Aix-les-Bains
23. Annecy
24. Lac Léman

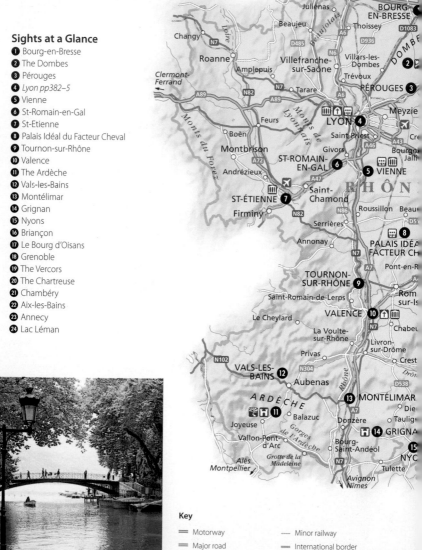

The Pont des Amours in Annecy

Key

- Motorway
- Major road
- Secondary road
- Minor road
- Scenic route
- Main railway
- Minor railway
- International border
- Regional border
- △ Summit

For keys to map symbols *see back flap*

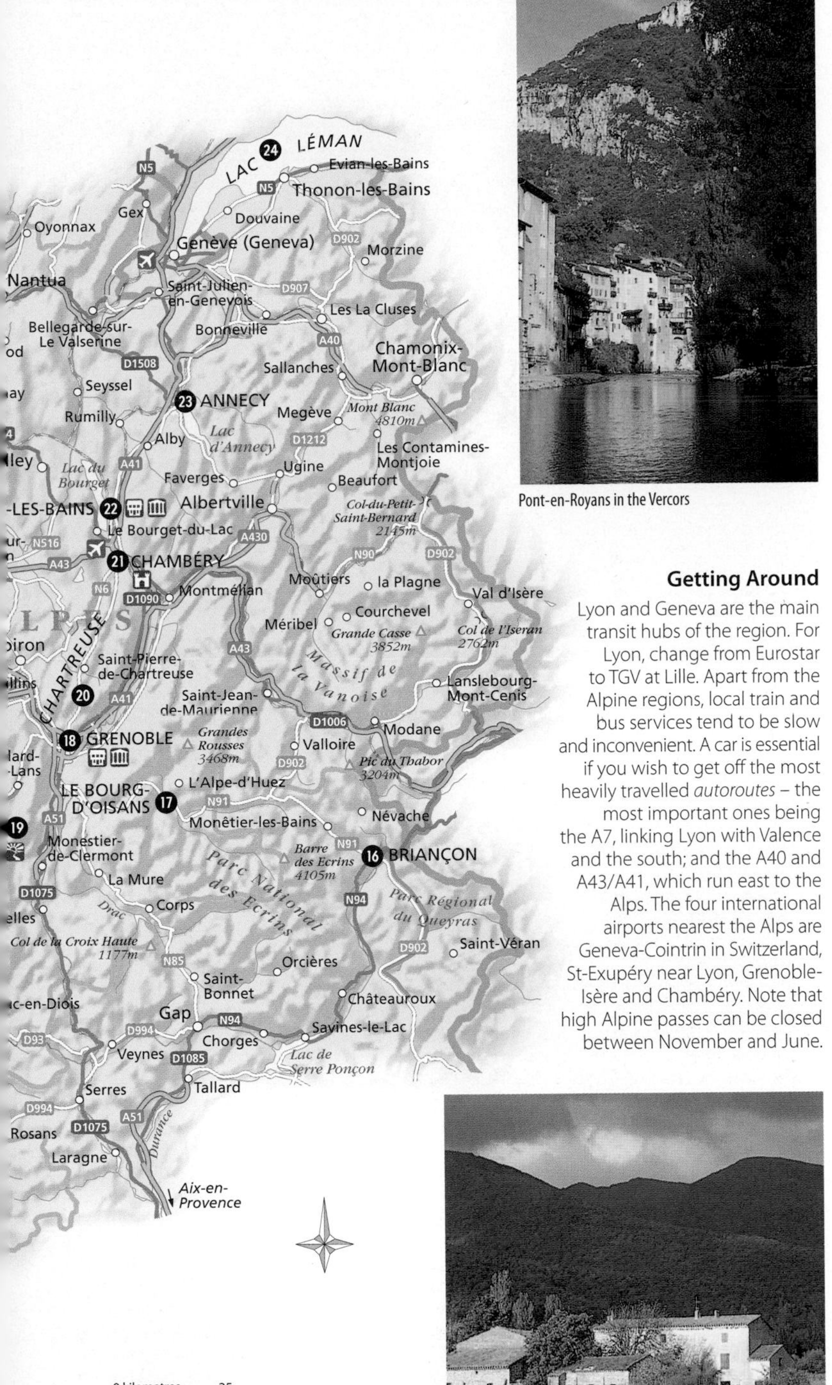

Pont-en-Royans in the Vercors

Getting Around

Lyon and Geneva are the main transit hubs of the region. For Lyon, change from Eurostar to TGV at Lille. Apart from the Alpine regions, local train and bus services tend to be slow and inconvenient. A car is essential if you wish to get off the most heavily travelled *autoroutes* – the most important ones being the A7, linking Lyon with Valence and the south; and the A40 and A43/A41, which run east to the Alps. The four international airports nearest the Alps are Geneva-Cointrin in Switzerland, St-Exupéry near Lyon, Grenoble-Isère and Chambéry. Note that high Alpine passes can be closed between November and June.

Farms around Le Poët Laval, near Montélimar

1 Bourg-en-Bresse

Ain. 43,000. Centre Culturel Albert Camus, 6 av Alsace-Lorraine (04 74 22 49 40). Wed & Sat. **bourgenbressetourisme.fr**

Bourg-en-Bresse is a busy market town, with some beautifully restored half-timbered buildings. It is best known for its tasty *poulet de Bresse* (chickens raised in the flat agricultural region of Bresse and designated *appellation d'origine protégée, or AOP*); and its abbey church of **Brou** on the southeast edge of town.

The latter, no longer a place of worship, has become one of the most visited sites in France. Flamboyant Gothic in style, it was built between 1505 and 1536 by Margaret of Austria after the death of her husband Philibert, Duke of Savoy, in 1504.

The couple's finely sculpted Carrara marble tombs can be seen in the choir, along with the tomb of Margaret of Bourbon, Philibert's mother, who died in 1483. Notice also the beautifully carved choir stalls, stained-glass windows, and rood screen with its elegant basket-handle arching.

The adjacent cloisters house a small museum with a good collection of 16th- and 17th-century Dutch and Flemish masters, as well as contemporary works by local artists.

Environs

About 24 km (15 miles) north of Bourg-en-Bresse at St-Trivier-de-Courtes, the restored **Ferme-Musée de la Forêt** offers a look at farm life in the region during the 17th century. The ancient house has what is known locally as a Saracen chimney, with a brick hood in the centre of the room, similar to constructions in Sicily and Portugal, and a collection of antique farm implements.

Bresse chickens

Ferme-Musée de la Forêt
Tel 04 74 30 71 89. **Open** Apr–Oct: Sat & Sun (mid-Jun–Sep: Tue–Sun).

Tomb of Margaret of Austria in the abbey church of Brou at Bourg-en-Bresse

2 The Dombes

Ain. Lyon. Lyon, Villars les Dombes, Bourg-en-Bresse. Villars-les-Dombes (from Bourg-en-Bresse). 3 pl de Hôtel de Ville, Villars-les-Dombes (04 74 98 06 29).

This flat, glacier-gouged plateau south of Bourg-en-Bresse is dotted with small hills, ponds and marshes, making it popular with anglers and bird-watchers. In the middle of the area at **Villars-les-Dombes** is an ornithological park, the **Parc des Oiseaux**. Over 400 species of native and exotic birds live here, including tufted herons, vultures, pink flamingoes, emus and ostriches.

Parc des Oiseaux
Route Nationale 83, Villars-les-Dombes.
Tel 04 74 98 05 54. **Open** daily. **Closed** mid-Nov–Mar.

3 Pérouges

Ain. 900. Meximieux-Pérouges. 09 67 12 70 84. **perouges.org**

Originally the home of immigrants from Perugia, Pérouges is a fortified hilltop village of medieval houses and cobblestone streets. In the 13th century it was a centre of linen-weaving, but with the mechanization of the industry in the 19th century, the local population fell from 1,500 to 90.

Restoration of its historic buildings and a new influx of craftsmen have breathed new life into Pérouges. Not surprisingly, the village has often been used as the setting for historical dramas such as *The Three Musketeers* and *Monsieur Vincent*. The village's main square, place de la Halle, is shaded by a huge lime tree planted in 1792 to honour the Revolution.

For hotels and restaurants in this region see pp564–5 and pp593–4

A Tour of Beaujolais

Beaujolais is an ideal area for wine tasting, offering delicious, affordable wine and glorious countryside. The south of the region produces most of the Beaujolais Nouveau, released fresh from the cellars on the third Thursday of November each year. In the north are the ten superior quality *cru* wines – St-Amour, Juliénas, Moulin-à-Vent, Chénas, Fleurie, Chiroubles, Morgon, Brouilly, Côte de Brouilly and Regnié – most of which can be visited in a day's drive. The distinctive *maisons du pays* have living quarters built over the wine cellar. Almost every village has its *cave* (wine cellar), offering tastings and a glimpse of the wine culture that dominates local life.

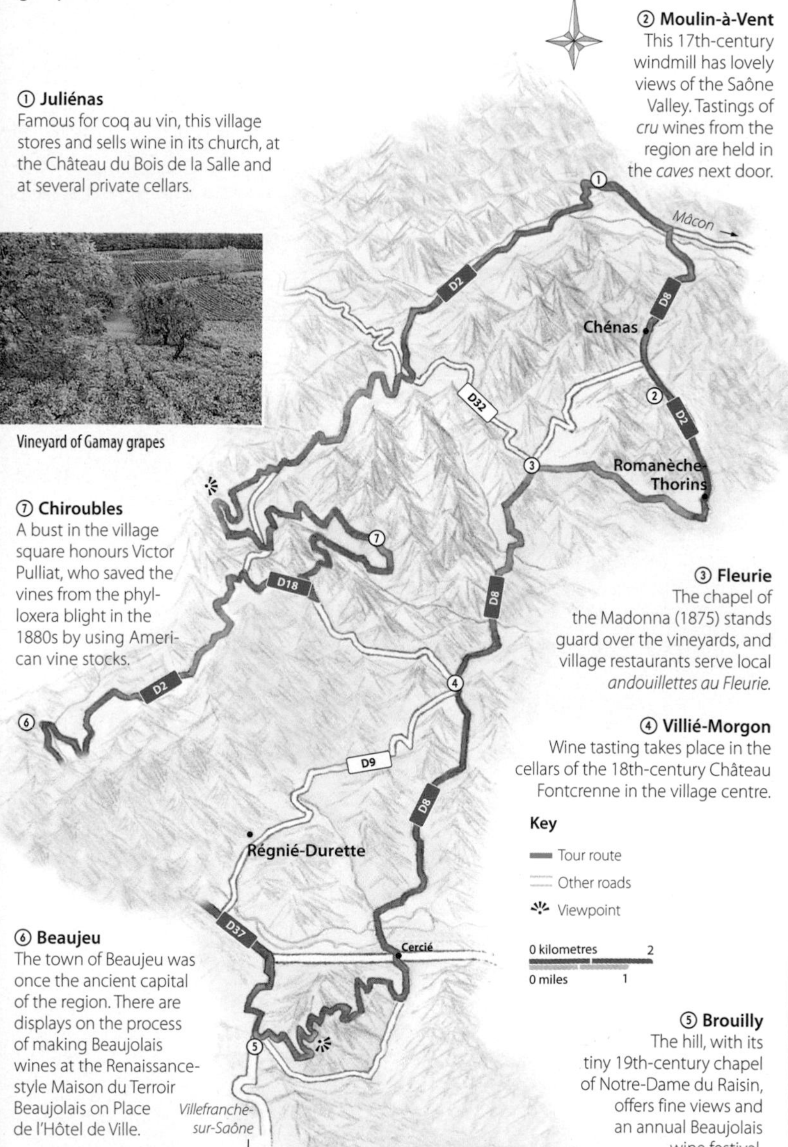

Vineyard of Gamay grapes

① Juliénas
Famous for coq au vin, this village stores and sells wine in its church, at the Château du Bois de la Salle and at several private cellars.

② Moulin-à-Vent
This 17th-century windmill has lovely views of the Saône Valley. Tastings of *cru* wines from the region are held in the *caves* next door.

③ Fleurie
The chapel of the Madonna (1875) stands guard over the vineyards, and village restaurants serve local *andouillettes au Fleurie.*

④ Villié-Morgon
Wine tasting takes place in the cellars of the 18th-century Château Fontcrenne in the village centre.

⑤ Brouilly
The hill, with its tiny 19th-century chapel of Notre-Dame du Raisin, offers fine views and an annual Beaujolais wine festival.

⑥ Beaujeu
The town of Beaujeu was once the ancient capital of the region. There are displays on the process of making Beaujolais wines at the Renaissance-style Maison du Terroir Beaujolais on Place de l'Hôtel de Ville.

⑦ Chiroubles
A bust in the village square honours Victor Pulliat, who saved the vines from the phylloxera blight in the 1880s by using American vine stocks.

❹ Street-by-Street: Lyon

On the west bank of the River Saône, the restored old quarter of Vieux Lyon is an atmospheric warren of cobbled streets, *traboules* (covered passageways), Renaissance palaces, first-class restaurants, lively *bouchons* (bistros) and bohemian shops. It is also the site of the Roman city of Lugdunum, the commercial and military capital of Gaul founded by Julius Caesar in 44 BC. Vestiges of this prosperous city can be seen in the superb Gallo-Roman museum at the top of Fourvière hill. Two excavated Roman theatres still stage performances, from opera to rock concerts. At the foot of the hill is the finest collection of Renaissance mansions in France. The Musée des Confluences sits in a spectacular structure of stainless steel and glass.

★ Théâtres Romains
There are two Roman amphitheatres here: the Grand Théâtre, the oldest theatre in France, built in 15 BC to seat 30,000 spectators and still used for modern performances; and the smaller Odéon, with its geometric tiled flooring.

★ Musée de la Civilisation Gallo-Romaine
This underground museum contains a rich collection of statues, mosaics, coins and inscriptions evoking Lyon's Roman past.

Entrance to funicular

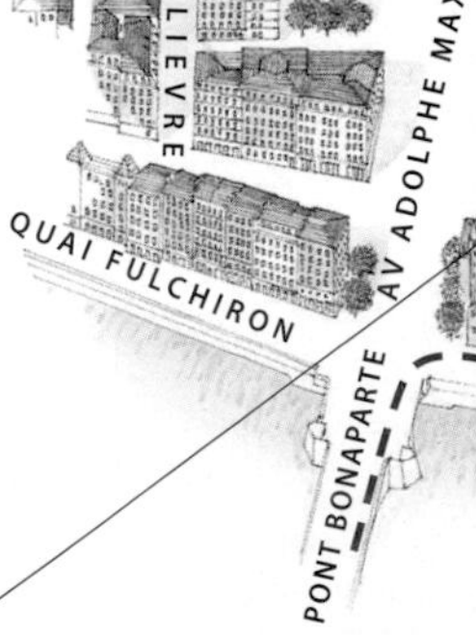

Cathédrale St-Jean
Begun in the late 12th century, the cathedral has a 14th-century astronomical clock that shows religious feast days till the year 2019.

For hotels and restaurants in this region see pp564–5 and pp593–4

★ Basilique Notre-Dame de Fourvière
This gaudy mock-Byzantine creation – a riot of turrets and crenellations, marble and mosaic – was built in the late 19th century and has become one of the symbols of Lyon.

The Chemin du Rosaire is a beautiful path leading down from Notre-Dame de Fourvière, with spectacular views of the sprawling metropolis below.

The Tour Métallique was erected in 1893 and is now used as a television transmitter.

Rue Juiverie boasts a number of splendid Renaissance mansions – look out for the Hôtel Paterin at No. 4 and the Hôtel Bullioud at No. 8.

Rue St-Jean and rue du Boeuf are lined with Renaissance mansions, the former homes of bankers and silk merchants.

The 15th-century Hôtel Gadagne houses two museums: the **Musée Historique de Lyon** and the **Musée des Marionnettes du Monde**, which exhibits the famous Lyonnais puppets.

Key

– Suggested route

VISITORS' CHECKLIST

Practical Information
Rhône. 455,000. pl Bellecour (04 72 77 69 69). daily. Biennale Internationale d'Art Contemporain (Sep–Jan), Biennale Internationale de la Danse (Sep).
lyon-france.com
Musée de la Civilisation Gallo-Romaine: **Tel** 04 72 38 49 30. **Open** Tue–Sun.
museegalloromain. grandlyon.com
Hôtel Gadagne: **Tel** 04 78 42 03 61. **Open** Wed–Sun.

Transport
25 km (16 miles) E Lyon. Perrache, Part-Dieu (SNCF **Tel** 3635). Perrache.

Exploring Lyon

France's second city, dramatically sited on the banks of the Rhône and Saône rivers, has been a vital gateway between the north and south since ancient times. On arriving you immediately feel a *brin du sud*, or touch of the south. The crowds are not as quick-stepping as they are in Paris, and the sun is often shining here when it's rainy and cold in the north. Despite its importance as a banking, textile and pharmaceutical centre, most of the French immediately associate Lyon with their palates. The city is packed with restaurants, ranging from simple *bouchons* (bistros) to some of the most opulent tables in France.

Lyon's ornate 17th-century Hôtel de Ville

The Presqu'île

The heart of Lyon is the Presqu'île, a narrow peninsula of land just north of the confluence of the Saône and Rhône rivers. Rue de la République, a pedestrianized shopping street, links the twin poles of civic life: the vast place Bellecour, with its equestrian statue of Louis XIV in the middle, and **place des Terreaux**. The latter is overlooked by Lyon's ornate 17th-century **Hôtel de Ville** (town hall) and the Palais St-Pierre, a former Benedictine convent and now the home of the **Musée des Beaux-Arts**. In the middle of the square is a monumental 19th-century fountain by Bartholdi, sculptor of the Statue of Liberty.

Behind the town hall, architect Jean Nouvel's futuristic **Opéra de Lyon** – a black barrel vault of steel and glass encased in a Neo-Classical shell – was remodelled to a controversial design in 1993.

A few blocks to the south, the **Musée de l'Imprimerie** illustrates Lyon's contribution to the early days of printing in the late 15th century. Three other museums worth visiting are the **Musée des Tissus**, which houses a collection of silks and tapestries dating from early Christian times to the present day; the **Musée des Arts Décoratifs**, which displays a range of tapestries, furniture, porcelain and objets d'art; and the **Musée des Confluences**, a history and anthropology museum in a glass-and-steel structure.

Nearby, the **Abbaye St-Martin d'Ainay** is a restored Carolingian church dating from 1107.

Lyon City Centre

① Hôtel de Ville
② Musée des Beaux-Arts
③ Opéra de Lyon
④ Musée de l'Imprimerie
⑤ Musée des Tissus
⑥ Musée des Arts Décoratifs
⑦ Abbaye St-Martin d'Ainay
⑧ Eglise St-Polycarpe
⑨ Amphithéâtre des Trois Gaules

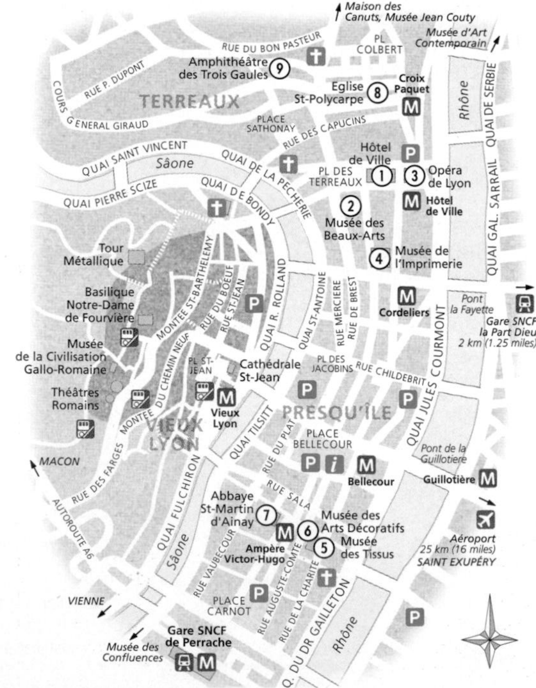

For keys to symbols *see back flap*

La Croix-Rousse
This area north of Presqu'île became the centre of the city's silk-weaving industry in the 15th century. It is traced with covered passages known as *traboules*, used by weavers to transport their finished fabrics. To get a sense of them, enter at No. 6 place des Terreaux and continue along till you reach the **Eglise St-Polycarpe**. From here, it is a short walk to the ruins of the **Amphi-théâtre des Trois Gaules**, built in AD 19, and the **Maison des Canuts**, with its traditional silk loom. A little north of here is **Musée Jean Couty**, which houses works by the Lyonnais 20th-century artist and modern and contemporary art exhibitions. Northeast is the **Musée d'Art Contemporain**.

La Part-Dieu
This modern business area on the east bank of the Rhône has a huge shopping complex and the **Auditorium Maurice-Ravel** for cultural events.

Musée de l'Imprimerie
13 rue de la Poulaillerie. **Tel** 04 78 37 65 98. **Open** Wed–Sun. **Closed** public hols.

Musée des Tissus
34 rue de la Charité. **Tel** 04 78 38 42 00. **Open** Tue–Sun. **Closed** public hols.

Musée des Arts Décoratifs
30 rue de la Charité. **Tel** 04 78 38 42 00. **Open** Tue–Sun. **Closed** pub hols.

Musée des Confluences
86 quai de Perrache. **Tel** 04 28 38 12 12. **Open** Tue–Sun. **Closed** 1 Jan, 1 May, 1 Nov, 25 Dec.

Maison des Canuts
10–12 rue d'Ivry. **Tel** 04 78 28 62 04. **Open** Mon–Sat. **Closed** public hols.

Musée Jean Couty
1 pl Henri Barbusse. **Tel** 04 72 42 20 00. **Open** 11am–6pm Wed–Sun.

Musée d'Art Contemporain
81 quai Charles de Gaulle. **Tel** 04 37 61 09. **Open** 11am–6pm Wed–Sun.

Environs
Bourgoin-Jallieu, southeast of Lyon, still prints silk for fashion houses, and has a fine textile collection in its museum.

Musée des Beaux-Arts

Lyon's Musée des Beaux-Arts showcases the country's largest and probably most important collection of art after the Louvre. The museum is housed in the 17th-century Palais St-Pierre, a former Benedictine convent for the daughters of the nobility. The Musée d'Art Contemporain, formerly located in the Palais St-Pierre, is now at 81 quai Charles de Gaulle, north of the Parc Tête d'Or. Housed in a building designed by Renzo Piano, it specializes in works dating from after the mid-20th century.

Antiquities

Included in this wide-ranging collection on the first floor are Egyptian archaeological finds, Etruscan statuettes and 4,000-year-old Cypriot ceramics. Temporary exhibits, with a separate entrance on 16 rue Edouard Herriott, are also on the ground and first floors.

Sculpture and Objets d'Art

Occupying the old chapel on the ground floor, the sculpture department includes works from the French Romanesque period and Italian Renaissance, as well as late 19th- and early 20th-century pieces. Represented are Rodin and Bourdelle (whose statues also appear in the courtyard), Maillol, Despiau and Pompon, among others. The huge objets d'art collection, on the first floor, comprises medieval ivories, bronzes and ceramics, coins, medals, weapons, jewellery, furniture and tapestries.

Odalisque (1841) by James Pradier

Paintings and Drawings

The museum's superb collection of paintings occupies the second floor. It covers all periods and includes works by Spanish and Dutch masters, the French schools of the 17th, 18th and 19th centuries, Impressionist and modern paintings, as well as works

Fleurs des Champs (1845) by Louis Janmot of the Lyon School

by the Lyon School, whose exquisite flower paintings were used as sources of inspiration by the designers of silk fabrics through the ages. On the first floor, the Cabinet d'Arts Graphiques has over 4,000 drawings and etchings by such artists as Delacroix, Poussin, Géricault, Degas and Rodin (by appointment only).

Musée des Beaux-Arts
Palais St-Pierre, 20 pl des Terreaux. **Tel** 04 72 10 17 40. **Open** Wed–Mon. **Closed** public hols.

La Méduse (1923) by Alexeï von Jawlensky

Châtiment de Lycurgue in the Musée Archéologique, St-Romain-en-Gal

5 Vienne

Isère. 30,000. cours Brillier (04 74 53 70 10). Tue–Sat. International Jazz Festival (end Jun–mid-Jul). **vienne-tourisme.com**

No other city in the Rhône Valley offers such a concentration of architectural history as Vienne. Located in a natural basin of land between the river and the hills, this site was recognized for both its strategic and aesthetic advantages by the Romans, who vastly expanded an existing village when they invaded the area in the 1st century BC.

The centre of the Roman town was the **Temple d'Auguste et Livie** (10 BC) on place du Palais, a handsome structure supported by Corinthian columns. Not far away off place de Miremont are the remains of the **Jardin Archéologique de Cybèle**, a temple dedicated to the goddess Cybele.

Vienne's Temple d'Auguste et Livie (1st century BC)

The **Théâtre Romain**, at the foot of Mont Pipet off rue du Cirque, was one of the largest amphitheatres in Roman France, capable of seating over 13,000 spectators. It was restored in 1938, and is now used for a variety of events, including an international jazz festival. From the very top seats the view of the town and river is spectacular.

Other interesting Roman vestiges include a fragment of Roman road in the public gardens and, on the southern edge of town, the **Pyramide du Cirque**, a curious structure about 20 m (65 ft) high that was once the centrepiece of the chariot racetrack. The **Musée des Beaux-Arts et d'Archéologie** also has a good collection of Gallo-Roman artifacts, as well as 18th-century French faïence.

The **Cathédrale de St-Maurice** is the city's most important medieval monument. It was built between the 12th and 16th century and represents an unusual hybrid of Romanesque and Gothic styles. Two of Vienne's earliest Christian churches are the 12th-century **Eglise St-André-le-Bas**, with richly carved capitals in its nave and cloister, and the **Eglise St-Pierre**, parts of which date from the 5th and 6th centuries. The latter houses the **Musée Lapidaire**, a museum of stone-carving, with bas-reliefs and statues from Gallo-Roman buildings.

Musée des Beaux-Arts et d'Archéologie
Pl de Miremont. **Tel** 04 74 78 71 04. **Open** Apr–Oct: Tue–Sun; Nov–Mar: Tue–Fri & Sat–Sun pm. **Closed** 1 Jan, 1 May, 1 & 11 Nov, 25 Dec.

Musée Lapidaire
Pl St-Pierre. **Tel** 04 74 85 20 35. **Open** Apr–Oct: Tue–Sun; Nov–Mar: Tue–Fri & Sat–Sun pm. **Closed** 1 Jan, 1 May, 1 & 11 Nov, 25 Dec.

Ornate doorway of Cathédrale de St-Maurice

6 St-Romain-en-Gal

Rhône. 1,300. Vienne. Vienne (04 74 53 70 10).

In 1967, building work in this commercial town directly across the Rhône from Vienne revealed extensive remains of a significant Roman community dating from 100 BC to AD 300. It comprises the remnants of villas, public baths, shops and warehouses. Of particular interest is the House of the Ocean Gods, with a magnificent mosaic floor depicting the bearded Neptune and other ocean images.

Much of what has been unearthed so far is housed in the **Musée Archéologique** near the ruins. The impressive collection includes household objects, murals and mosaics. The star exhibit is the *Châtiment de Lycurgue*, a mosaic discovered in 1907.

Musée Archéologique
Tel 04 74 53 74 01. **Open** Tue–Sun. **Closed** some pub hols. restricted. **musee-site.rhone.fr**

7 St-Etienne

Loire. 180,000. 16 av de la Libération (04 77 49 39 00). daily. International Design Biennial (mid-Mar–mid-Apr, in odd-numbered years). **saint-etiennetourisme.com**

The dour renown brought to this city by coal-mining and armaments is slowly being shaken off, with urban redevelopment well under way and an efficient tramway network. The downtown area around place du Peuple is lively. Nearby, Jean-Michel Wilmotte has overhauled the **Musée d'Art et d'Industrie**, which covers St-Étienne's industrial history, including the development of the revolutionary Jacquard loom, and world-class collections of cycles and ribbon-making machines.

To the north of the city, the **Musée d'Art Moderne** has a collection of 20th-century art, including works by Andy Warhol and Frank Stella.

Detail of the bizarre Palais Idéal du Facteur Cheval at Hauterives

Musée d'Art et d'Industrie
2 pl Louis Comte. **Tel** 04 77 49 73 00. **Open** Wed–Mon. **Closed** some public hols.

Musée d'Art Moderne
Saint Priest en Jarez. **Tel** 04 77 79 52 52. **Open** Wed–Mon. **Closed** some public hols & when exhibitions change. **mam-st-etienne.fr**

The Bridges of the Rhône

The Rhône has played a crucial role in French history, transporting armies and commercial traffic between the north and south. It has always been dangerous, a challenge to boatmen and builders for centuries. In 1825 the brilliant engineer Marc Seguin built the first suspension bridge using steel-wire cables. This was followed by another 20 along the length of the Rhône, forever transforming communications between east and west.

Suspension bridge over the Rhône at Tournon-sur-Rhône *(see p388)*

8 Palais Idéal du Facteur Cheval

Hauterives, Drôme. Romans-sur-Isère. **Tel** 04 75 68 81 19. **Open** daily. **Closed** 1, 15–31 Jan, 25 Dec. restricted. **facteurcheval.com**

At Hauterives, 24 km (15 miles) north of Romans-sur-Isère on the D538, is one of the greatest follies of France, an eccentric "palace" made of stones and evoking Egyptian, Roman, Aztec and Siamese styles of architecture. It was built by a local postman, Ferdinand Cheval, who collected the stones during his daily rounds. His neighbours thought him mad, but the project attracted the admiring attention of Picasso, the Surrealist André Breton and others.

The interior of the palace is inscribed with Cheval's numerous mottoes and exhortations, the most poignant of which refers to his assiduous efforts to realize his lifelong fantasy: "1879–1912: 10,000 days, 93,000 hours, 33 years of toil". Concerts are held here on summer evenings.

Parc Jouvet in Valence

9 Tournon-sur-Rhône

Ardèche. 10,000. Hôtel de la Tourette (04 75 08 10 23). Wed & Sat. Festival de Shakespeare (Jul). **hermitage-tournonais-tourisme.com**

Situated at the foot of impressive granite hills, Tournon is a lovely town with gracious tree-lined promenades and an imposing 11th- to 16th-century **château**. The latter houses a museum of local history, and has fine views of the town and river from its terraces.

The adjacent **Collégiale St-Julien**, with its square bell tower and elaborate façade, is an interesting example of the Italian influence on architecture in the region during the 14th century. Inside is a powerful *Résurrection*, painted in 1576 by Capassin, a pupil of Raphael.

On quai Charles de Gaulle, the **Lycée Gabriel-Fauré** is the oldest secondary school in France, dating from 1536. Directly across the Rhône from Tournon, the village of **Tain l'Hermitage** is famous for its steep-climbing vineyards, which produce both red and white Hermitage, the finest of all Rhône wines.

Environs

From Tournon's main square, place Jean Jaurès, a twisting road signposted **Route Panoramique** leads via the villages of Plats and St-Romain-de-Lerps to St-Péray. This route offers breathtaking views at every turn, and at St-Romain you are rewarded with a superb panorama extending over 13 *départements*.

10 Valence

Drôme. 67,000. 11 bd Bancel (04 75 44 90 40). Thu & Sat. Summer Music (Jul). **valence-romans-tourisme.com**

Valence is a large, thriving market town set on the east bank of the Rhône and looking across to the cliffs of the Ardèche. Its principal sight is the Romanesque **Cathédrale St-Apollinaire** on place des Clercs, founded in 1095 and rebuilt in the 17th century.

Alongside the cathedral in the former bishop's palace, the small **Musée de Valence** contains a collection of late 18th-century chalk drawings of Rome by Hubert Robert.

A short walk from here are two Renaissance mansions. The **Maison des Têtes** at No. 57 Grande Rue was built in 1532 and is embellished with the sculpted heads of ancient Greeks including Hippocrates, Aristotle and Homer. On rue Pérollerie, the **Maison Dupré-Latour** has a finely sculptured porch and staircase.

The **Parc Jouvet**, south of avenue Gambetta, offers lovely pools and gardens, with fine views across the river to the ruined **Château de Crussol**.

Musée de Valence
4 pl des Ormeaux. **Tel** 04 75 79 20 80. **Open** Tue pm & Wed–Sun. **Closed** some pub hols.

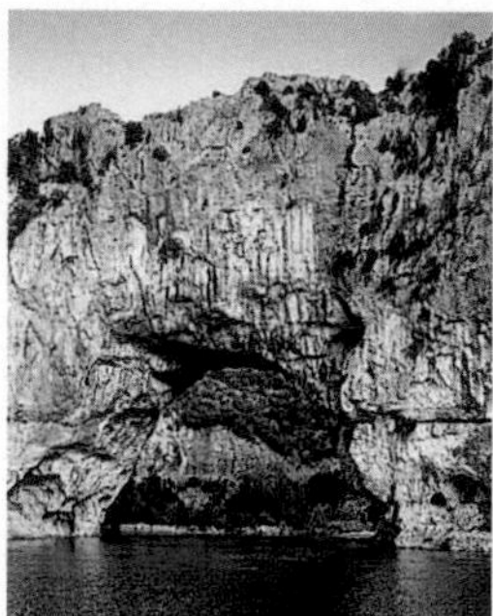

The limestone Pont d'Arc

11 The Ardèche

Ardèche. Avignon. Montélimar. Montélimar, Vallon Pont d'Arc. Vallon Pont d'Arc (04 28 91 24 10). **vallon-pont-darc.com**

Over the course of thousands of years, wind and water have endowed this south-central region of France with such a

Côtes du Rhône

Rising in the Swiss Alps and flowing south to the Mediterranean, the mighty Rhône is the common thread that links the many vineyards of the Rhône Valley. A hierarchy of *appellations* divides into three levels of quality: at the base, the regional Côtes du Rhône provides the bulk of the Rhône's wines; next, Côtes du Rhône-Villages comprises a plethora of picturesque villages; and, at the top, there are 13 individual *appellations*. The most famous are the steep slopes of Hermitage and Côte Rôtie in the northern Rhône, and historic Châteauneuf-du-Pape *(see pp506–7)* in the south. The lion's share of production is of red wine, which, based on the Syrah grape, is often spicy, full-bodied and robust.

Harvest in a Côtes du Rhône vineyard

rugged landscape that it is more reminiscent of the American southwest than the verdure commonly associated with the French countryside. This visible drama is repeated underground as well, since the Ardèche is honeycombed with enormous stalagmite- and stalactite-ornamented caves. The most impressive are the **Grotte de la Madeleine**, reached via a signposted path from the D290, and the cave and museum **La Cité de la Préhistoire** (open Feb–mid-Nov) to the south of Vallon-Pont-d'Arc.

For those who prefer to stay above ground, the most arresting natural scenery in the region is the **Gorges de l'Ardèche**, best seen from the D290, a two-lane road that parallels the recessed river for 32 km (20 miles). Close to the head of the gorge, heading west, is the **Pont d'Arc**, a natural limestone "bridge" spanning the river and created by erosion and the elements. Nearby is **Grotte Chauvet**, a replica of the oldest known decorated cave in the world, now closed to the public, and a UNESCO World Heritage site. Painted up to 36,000 years ago, the cave contains hundreds of animal paintings demonstrating astonishing technical ability.

Canoeing and white-water rafting are the two most popular sports here. All the equipment necessary can be rented locally; operators at Vallon-Pont-d'Arc (among many other places) rent out two-person canoes and organize return transport

The Gorges de l'Ardèche, between Vallon-Pont-d'Arc and Pont St-Esprit

The village of Vogüé on the banks of the River Ardèche

from St-Martin d'Ardèche, 32 km (20 miles) downstream.

The softer side of the region is found in its ancient and picturesque villages, gracious spa towns, vineyards and plantations of Spanish chestnuts (from which the delectable *marron glacé* is produced).

Some 13 km (8 miles) south of Aubenas, the 12th-century village of **Balazuc** is typical of the region, its stone houses built on a clifftop overlooking a secluded gorge of the Ardèche. There are fine views as you approach on the D294.

Neighbouring **Vogüé** is nestled between the River Ardèche and a limestone cliff. A tiny but atmospheric village, its most commanding sight is the 12th-century **Château de Vogüé**, once the seat of the barons of Languedoc. Rebuilt in the 17th century, the building houses a museum featuring exhibitions about the region.

Château de Vogüé
Tel 04 75 37 01 95. **Open** Apr–Oct: Wed–Sun (Jul–Sep: daily). **Closed** 1 wk Jun. **chateaudevogue.net**

⓱ Vals-les-Bains

Ardèche. 3,700. Montélimar. rue Jean Jaurès (04 75 89 02 03). Thu & Sun (& Tue in summer). **aubenas-vals.com**

This small spa town retains a hint of its past elegance. It is situated in the valley of the Volane, where there are at least 150 springs, of which all but two are cold. The water, which contains bicarbonate of soda and other minerals, is said to help with digestive problems, rheumatism and diabetes.

Discovered around 1600, Vals-les-Bains is one of the few spas in southern France to have been overlooked by the Romans. The town reached the height of its popularity in the late 19th century, and most of its parks and architecture retain something of the *belle époque*. Vals is a convenient first stop for an exploration of the Ardèche, with plenty of hotels and restaurants.

Environs

About 8 km (5 miles) east of Vals is the superb Romanesque church of **St-Julien du Serre**.

A farm near Le Poët Laval, east of Montélimar

⓭ Montélimar

Drôme. 33,000. Montée St-Martin, allées Provençales (04 75 01 00 20). Wed–Sat. **montelimar-tourisme.com**

Whether you choose to make a detour to Montélimar will largely depend on how sweet a tooth you might have. The main curiosity of this market town is its medieval centre, chock-full of shops selling almond-studded nougat. This splendid confection has been made here since the start of the 17th century, when the almond tree was first introduced into France from Asia.

The **Château des Adhémar**, a mélange of 12th-, 14th- and 16th- century architecture, surveys the town from a tall hill to the east.

Château des Adhémar
Tel 04 75 91 83 50. **Open** May–Oct: daily. **Closed** 1 Jan, 11 Nov, 25 Dec.

Environs

The countryside east of Montélimar is full of picturesque medieval villages and scenic routes. **La Bégude-de-Mazenc** is a thriving little holiday centre, with its fortified Old Town perched on a hilltop. Further east is **Le Poët Laval**, a tiny medieval village set in the Alpine foothills. **Dieulefit**, the capital of this beautiful region, has several small hotels and restaurants, as well as facilities for tennis, swimming and fishing. To the south, the fortified village of **Taulignan** is known for its truffles.

⓮ Grignan

Drôme. 1,500. pl du Jeu de Ballon (04 75 46 56 75). Tue. **tourisme-paysdegrignan.com**

Attractively situated on a rocky hill surrounded by fields of lavender, this charming little village owes its fame to Madame de Sévigné *(see p95)*, who wrote many of her celebrated letters while staying at the **Château de Grignan**.

Built during the 15th and 16th centuries, the château is one of the finest Renaissance structures in this part of France. Its interior contains a good collection of Louis XII furniture and Aubusson tapestries.

From the château's terrace, a panoramic view extends as far as the Vivarais mountains in the Ardèche. Directly below the terrace, the **Eglise de St-Saveur** was built in the 1530s, and contains the tomb of Madame de Sévigné, who died here in 1696 at the age of 70.

Château de Grignan
Tel 04 75 91 83 55. **Open** Apr–Oct: daily; Nov–Mar: Wed–Mon. **Closed** 1 Jan, 11 Nov, 25 Dec.

⓯ Nyons

Drôme. 7,000. pl de la Libération (04 75 26 10 35). Thu. **paysdenyons.com**

As a major centre of olive production, Nyons is synonymous with olives in France. All manner of olive products are on sale at the Thursday-morning market, from soap to *tapenade*, the olive paste so popular in the south.

The **Quartier des Forts** is Nyons' oldest quarter, a warren of narrow streets and stepped alleyways, the most rewarding of which is the covered rue des Grands Forts. Spanning the River Aygues is a graceful 13th-century bridge; on its town side are several old mills turned into shops, where you can see the enormous presses once used to extract olive oil. The **Espace Vignolis – Musée de l'Olivier** further explains the cultivation of the olive tree and the myriad local uses found for its fruit.

There is a fine view from the belvedere overlooking the town. Sheltered by mountains, Nyons enjoys an almost exotic climate, with all the trees and plants of the Riviera to be found here.

Espace Vignolis – Musée de l'Olivier
Pl Olivier de Serres. **Tel** 04 75 26 95 00. **Open** Mon–Fri.

Environs

From Nyons, the D94 leads west to **Suze-la-Rousse**, a pleasant wine-producing village, which, during the Middle Ages, was the most important town in the area. Today, it is best known for its "university of wine", one of the most respected centres of oenology in the world. It is

The hilltop town of Grignan and its Renaissance château

Olive groves just outside Nyons

housed in the 14th-century **Château de Suze-la-Rousse**, the hunting lodge of the princes of Orange. The interior courtyard is a masterpiece of Renaissance architecture, and some rooms preserve original paint and stuccowork.

Château de Suze-la-Rousse
Tel 04 75 04 81 44. **Open** Apr–Oct: daily; Nov–Mar: Wed–Mon. **Closed** 1 Jan, 11 Nov, 25 Dec.

Playing *boules* in Nyons

16 Briançon

Hautes-Alpes. 12,000. 1 pl du Temple (04 92 24 98 98). Wed. Altitude Jazz Festival (early Feb). **serre-chevalier.com**

Briançon – the highest town in Europe at 1,320 m (4,330 ft) – has been an important stronghold since pre-Roman times, guarding as it does the road to the Col de Montgenèvre, one of the oldest and most important passes into Italy. At the beginning of the 18th century, the town was fortified with ramparts and gates – still splendidly intact – by Louis XIV's military architect, Vauban. If driving, park at the Champs de Mars, and enter the pedestrianized Old Town via the **Porte de Pignerol**.

This leads to the **grande rue**, a steep, narrow street with a stream running down the middle and bordered by lovely period houses. The nearby **Eglise de Notre-Dame** dates from 1718, and was also built by Vauban with an eye to defence. To visit Vauban's **citadel**, stop by the tourist office, which organizes guided tours.

Briançon is a major sports centre, with skiing in winter, and rafting, cycling and paragliding in summer *(see pp614–15)*.

Environs
Just west of Briançon, the **Parc National des Ecrins** is the largest of the French national parks, offering lofty peaks and glaciers, and a magnificent variety of Alpine flowers.

The **Parc Régional du Queyras** is reached from Briançon over the rugged Col de l'Izoard. A wall of 3,000-m (9,850-ft) peaks separates this wild and beautiful national park from neighbouring Italy.

17 Le Bourg d'Oisans

Isère. 3,000. to Grenoble. to Le Bourg d'Oisans. quai Docteur Girard (04 76 80 03 25). Sat. **bourgdoisans.com**

Le Bourg d'Oisans is an ideal base from which to explore the Romanche Valley, providing opportunities for cycling, rock-climbing and skiing in the nearby resort of **L'Alpe d'Huez**.

Silver and other minerals have been mined here since the Middle Ages, and the town still has a reputation as a centre for geology and mineralogy. Its **Musée des Minéraux et de la Faune des Alpes** is renowned for its collection of crystals and precious stones.

Musée des Minéraux et de la Faune des Alpes
Pl de l'Eglise. **Tel** 04 76 80 27 54. **Open** pm (days vary – check website). **Closed** 1 Jan, mid-Nov–mid-Dec, 25 Dec. **bourgdoisans.com**

Life on High

The Alpine ibex is one of the rarest inhabitants of the French Alps, living high above the tree line for all but the coldest part of the year. Until the creation of the Parc National de la Vanoise *(see p327)*, this sure-footed climber had become almost extinct in France, but after rigorous conservation there are now over 500. Both males and females have horns; in the oldest males they can be almost 1 m (3 ft) long.

An ibex in the Parc National de la Vanoise

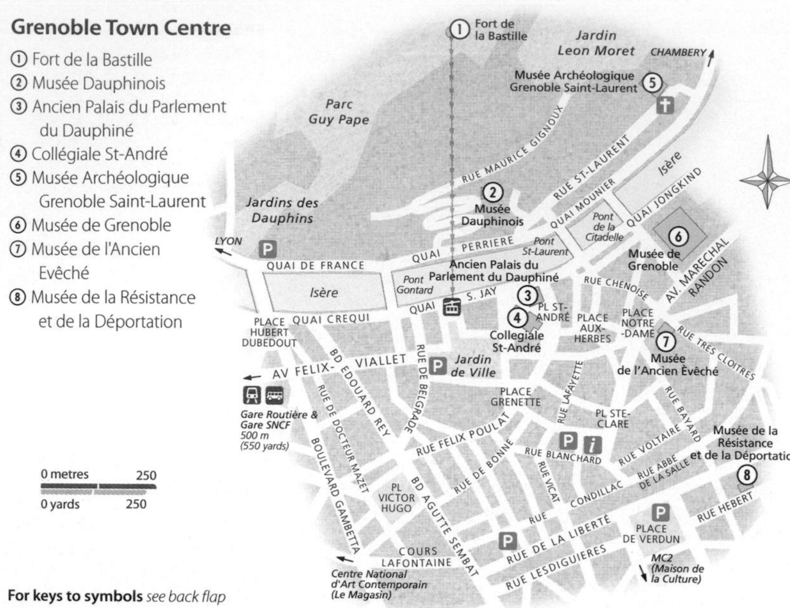

For keys to symbols *see back flap*

Fort de la Bastille on the Chartreuse mountain range, with views of Grenoble

⓲ Grenoble

Isère. 165,000.

14 rue de la République (04 76 42 41 41). Tue–Sun.

grenoble-tourisme.com

Ancient capital of the Dauphiné region and site of the 1968 Winter Olympics, Grenoble is a thriving city at the confluence of the Drac and Isère rivers, with the Vercors and Chartreuse massifs rising to the west and north. It is home to the science-oriented University of Grenoble, and is a centre of chemical and electronics industries and nuclear research.

A cable car starting at quai Stéphane-Jay whisks you up to the 19th-century **Fort de la Bastille**, which has superb views of the city and surrounding mountains. Paths lead down through Parc Guy Pape and Jardin des Dauphins to the **Musée Dauphinois**, a regional museum in a 17th-century convent devoted to local history, arts and crafts. Nearby, **Musée Archéologique Grenoble Saint-Laurent**, located in a former church with a 6th-century crypt, exhibits medieval artifacts and decorative and religious art.

On the left bank of the Isère, the focus of life is the pedestrian area around place Grenette. Nearby, place St-André is the heart of the medieval city, overlooked by Grenoble's oldest buildings, including the 13th-century **Collégiale St-André** and the 16th-century **Ancien Palais du Parlement du Dauphiné**.

The **Musée de Grenoble** exhibits works by Chagall, Picasso and Matisse. The **Musée de l'Ancien Evêché** recounts the history of Isère, and includes the 4th-century baptistry. On rue Hébert, the **Musée de la Résistance et de la Déportation** has documents relating to the French Resistance. Displays of contemporary art can be seen at **Le Magasin** (Centre National d'Art Contemporain) in a renovated warehouse. In the Quartier Malherbe, **MC2** (Maison de la Culture) hosts concerts, dance and theatre.

Musée Dauphinois
30 rue Maurice Gignoux. **Tel** 04 57 58 89 01. **Open** Wed–Mon. **Closed** 1 Jan, 1 May, 25 Dec.

Musée Archéologique Grenoble Saint-Laurent
Pl St-Laurent. **Tel** 04 76 44 78 68. **Open** Wed–Mon. **musee-archeologique-grenoble.fr**

Musée de Grenoble
5 pl de Lavalette. **Tel** 04 76 63 44 44. **Open** Wed–Mon. **Closed** 1 Jan, 1 May, 25 Dec.

Grenoble's gondola cable car

Musée de l'Ancien Evêché
2 rue Très Cloîtres. **Tel** 04 76 03 15 25. **Open** Thu–Tue. **Closed** 1 Jan, 1 & 8 May, 25 Dec.

Musée de la Résistance et de la Déportation
14 rue Hébert. **Tel** 04 76 42 38 53. **Open** daily. **Closed** Tue am, 1 Jan, 1 May, 25 Dec.

Le Magasin (CNAC)
8 esplanade Andry Farcy. **Tel** 04 76 21 95 84. **Open** times vary – phone for details. **magasin-cnac.org**

MC2
4 rue Paul Claudel. **Tel** 04 76 00 79 00. **Open** times vary – phone for details. **mc2grenoble.fr**

⑲ The Vercors

Isère & Drôme. Grenoble. Romans-sur-Isère, St-Marcellin, Grenoble. Pont-en-Royans, Romans-sur-Isère. Pont-en-Royans (04 76 36 09 10). Maison du Parc: 255 chemin des Fusillés, Lans-en-Vercors 38250 (04 76 94 38 26) **parc-du-vercors.fr**

To the south and west of Grenoble, the Vercors is one of France's most magnificent regional parks – a wilderness of pine forests, mountains, waterfalls, caves and deep, narrow gorges.

The D531 out of Grenoble passes through **Villard-de-Lans** – a good base for excursions – and continues west to the dark **Gorges de la Bournes**. About 8 km (5 miles) further west, the hamlet of **Pont-en-Royans** is sited on a limestone gorge, its stone houses built into the rocks overlooking the River Bourne.

South of Pont-en-Royans along the D76, the **Route de Combe-Laval** snakes along a sheer cliff above the roaring river. The **Grands Goulets**, 7 km (4 miles) to the east, is a spectacularly deep, narrow gorge overlooked by sheer cliffs that virtually shut out the sky above. The best-known mountain in the park is the **Mont Aiguille**, a soaring outcrop of 2,086 m (6,844 ft).

The Vercors was a key base for the French Resistance during World War II. In July 1944 the Germans launched an aerial attack on the region, flattening several of its villages. There are Resistance museums at Vassieux and Grenoble.

Cows grazing in the Chartreuse

⑳ The Chartreuse

Isère & Savoie. Grenoble, Chambéry. Grenoble, Voiron. St-Pierre-de-Chartreuse. St-Pierre-de-Chartreuse (04 76 88 62 08). **st-pierre-chartreuse.com**

From Grenoble, the D512 leads north towards Chambéry into the Chartreuse, a majestic region of mountains and forests, where hydroelectricity was invented in the late 1800s. The **Monastère de la Grande Chartreuse**, just west of St-Pierre-de-Chartreuse off the D520-B, is the main local sight.

Founded by St Bruno in 1084, the monastery owes its fame to the sticky green and yellow Chartreuse liqueurs first produced by the monks in 1605. The recipe, based on a secret herbal elixir of 130 ingredients, is now produced in the nearby town of Voiron.

The monastery itself is inhabited by about 40 monks, who live in silence and seclusion. It is not open to visitors, but there is a museum at the entrance, the **Musée de la Correrie**, which faithfully depicts the daily routine of the Carthusian monks.

Musée de la Correrie
St-Pierre-de-Chartreuse. **Tel** 04 76 88 60 45. **Open** Apr: daily pms; May–Sep: daily; Oct–mid-Nov: Mon–Fri pm only, Sat & Sun.

A farm in the pine-clad mountains of the Chartreuse

㉑ Chambéry

Savoie. 61,000. 5bis pl Palais de Justice (04 79 33 42 47). Tue, Sat. **chambery-tourisme.com**

Once the capital of Savoy, this dignified city has aristocratic airs and a distinctly Italianate feel. Its best-loved monument is the extravagant **Fontaine des Eléphants** on rue de Boigne, erected in 1838 to honour the Comte de Boigne, who left to his home town some of the fortune he amassed in India.

The 14th-century **Château des Ducs de Savoie**, at the opposite end of rue de Boigne, is now occupied by the Préfecture. Only parts of the building, such as the late Gothic Ste-Chapelle, can be visited, via guided tours arranged with the tourist office.

On the southeast edge of town is the 17th-century country house **Les Charmettes**, where the philosopher Rousseau lived with his mistress Madame de Warens. It is worth a visit for its gardens and museum of memorabilia.

Les Charmettes
892 chemin des Charmettes. **Tel** 04 79 33 39 44. **Open** Wed–Mon (Dec–late Mar: Sat & Sun). **Closed** public hols. with fee.

The Lac du Bourget at Aix-les-Bains

㉒ Aix-les-Bains

Savoie. 26,000. pl Maurice Mollard (04 79 88 68 00). Wed & Sat am. Festival Musilac (Jul). **aixlesbains.com**

The Romantic poet Lamartine rhapsodized over the beauty of Lac du Bourget, site of the gracious spa town of Aix-les-Bains. The heart of the town is the 19th-century **Thermes Nationaux**, thermal baths, first enjoyed by the Romans over 2,000 years ago – in the basement are the remains of the original Roman baths. The ruins can be visited on a guided tour. Opposite the baths, the 2nd-century AD **Temple of Diana** contains Gallo-Roman artifacts. The tourist office runs guided tours (Feb–Nov). The nearby **Musée Faure** has some stunning Impressionist paintings by Degas and Sisley, Rodin sculptures and Lamartine memorabilia.

Roman statue in the Temple of Diana

Thermes Nationaux
Pl Maurice Mollard. call 04 79 88 68 00 for guided tours.

Musée Faure
Villa des Chimères, 10 bd des Côtes. **Tel** 04 79 61 06 57. **Open** Wed–Mon. **Closed** Mon & Tue Nov–Mar, 20 Dec–5 Jan, public hols.

Environs

Boats leave from Aix's Grand Port and sail across Lac du Bourget to the **Abbaye d'Hautecombe**, a Benedictine abbey containing the mausoleum of the Savoyard dynasty.

The small town of **Le Revard**, just east of Aix on the D913, has spectacular views of the lake and Mont Blanc.

㉓ Annecy

Haute-Savoie. 51,000. 1 rue Jean Jaurès (04 50 45 00 33). Tue, Fri–Sun. Fête du Lac (firework display; 1st Sat Aug). **lac-annecy.com**

Annecy is one of the most charming towns in the Alps, set at the northern tip of Lac

Annecy's 12th-century Palais de l'Isle in the middle of Thiou canal

For hotels and restaurants in this region see pp564–5 and pp593–4

Cycling along the shores of Lac Léman (Lake Geneva)

d'Annecy and surrounded by snowcapped mountains. Its small medieval quarter is laced with canals, flower-covered bridges and arcaded streets. Strolling around is the main attraction here, though there are a couple of specific sights worth having a look at more closely: the formidable **Palais de l'Isle**, a 12th-century prison in the middle of the Thiou canal; and the turreted **Château d'Annecy**, set high on a hill above the town with impressive views of Vieil Annecy and the crystal-clear lake beyond.

The best spot for swimming and water sports is at the eastern end of the avenue d'Albigny near the Imperial Palace hotel, while boat trips leave from quai Napoléon III.

Environs

One of the best ways to enjoy the area's spectacular scenery is to take a boat from Annecy to **Talloires**, a tiny lakeside village celebrated for its hotels and restaurants. Facing Talloires across the lake is the 15th-century **Château de Duingt** (not open to visitors).

On the west bank of the lake, the Semnoz mountain and its summit, the **Crêt de Châtillon**, offer superb views of Mont Blanc and the Alps *(see pp326–7)*.

㉔ Lac Léman

Haute-Savoie & Switzerland.
✈ Geneva. 🚉 🚌 Geneva, Thonon-les-Bains, Évian-les-Bains.
ℹ Thonon-les-Bains (04 50 71 55 55).
W **thononlesbains.com**

The stirring scenery and gentle climate of the French shore of Lake Geneva (Lac Léman to the French) has made it a popular and fashionable resort area since the first spa buildings were erected at Évian-les-Bains in 1839.

Yvoire is a fine place to begin a visit to the area. This medieval port is guarded by a 14th-century castle, and its houses are bedecked with colourful flower boxes.

Further east along Lake Geneva is **Thonon-les-Bains**, a prosperous, well-manicured little spa town perched on a cliff overlooking the lake. A funicular takes you down to Rives, the small harbour at the foot of the cliffs, where sailboats can be rented and excursion boats to the Swiss cities of Geneva and Lausanne call in. Just outside the town is the 15th-century **Château de Ripaille**, made famous by its one-time resident Duke Amadeus VIII, who later became antipope (Felix V).

Though it has been modernized and acquired an international reputation for its eponymous spring water, **Evian-les-Bains** still exudes a polite *vie en rose* charm. The tree-lined lakefront promenade teems with leisurely strollers, while more energetic types can avail themselves of all kinds of sporting facilities including tennis, golf, riding, sailing and skiing in the winter. State-of-the-art spa treatments are available, and the exotic domed casino is busy at night, offering blackjack, roulette and baccarat among other games.

From Evian there are daily ferries across Lake Geneva to Lausanne in Switzerland, as well as coach excursions into the surrounding mountains.

The 14th-century castle at Yvoire, overlooking Lake Geneva (Lac Léman)

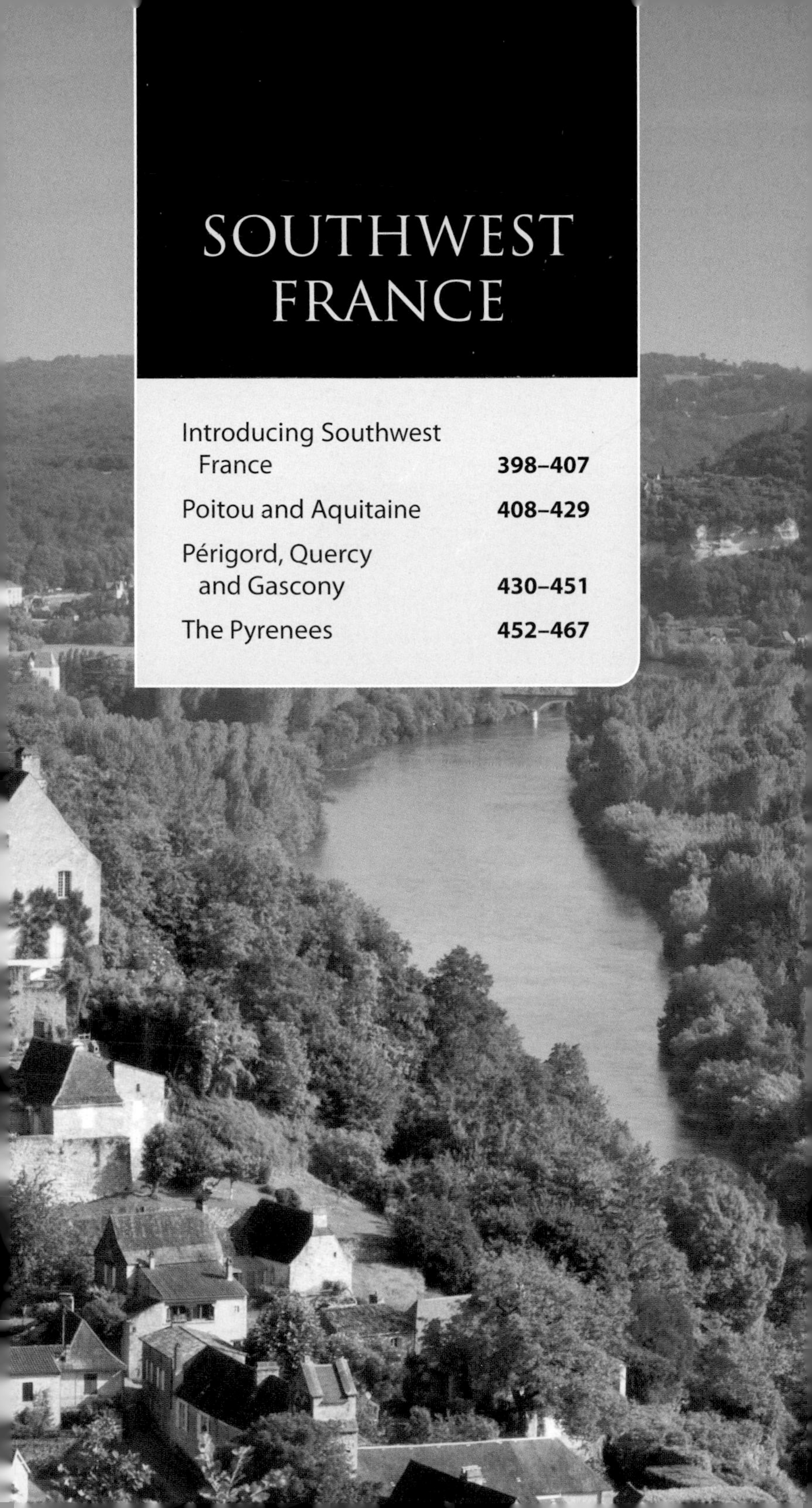

SOUTHWEST
FRANCE

Introducing Southwest France

The southwest is farming France, a green and peaceful land nurturing produce from sunflowers to *foie gras*. Other key country products include Landes forest timber, Bordeaux wines and Cognac. Major modern industries, including aerospace, are focused on the two chief cities, Bordeaux and Toulouse. Visitors are mainly drawn to the wide Atlantic beaches, the ski slopes of the Pyrenees and the rural calm of the Dordogne. The major sights of this favoured region are shown here and include some of France's most celebrated Romanesque buildings.

Thouar
Bressu
Parthena
Niort
La Rochelle
St-Jean-d'Angély
Rochefort

Roman Ruins, Saintes
(see p422)

Saintes
La Palmyre
Pons
Soulac-sur-Mer
Barbezieu
Mirambea
Pauillac
Lac d'Hourtin-Carcans
Coutra
Bordeaux
Libou
Arès
Arcachon
Gujan-Mestras
Langon
Biscarrosse
Bazas
Mimizan

POITOU AND AQUITAINE
(See pp408–29)

Mont-de-Marsan
Léon
Dax
Aire-sur-l'Adour
Bayonne
Biarritz
Orthez
Saint Jean de Luz
Pau
Oloron-Ste-Marie
St-Jean-Pied-de-Port
Lourde
Cauterets

0 kilometres 50
0 miles 50

Cirque de Gavarnie
(see p463)

La Rochelle's harbour is today a haven for pleasure yachts as well as an important commercial port *(see p420)*. Tour de la Chaîne and Tour St-Nicolas protect the entrance of the old port. The town's historic centre is filled with cobbled streets lined by merchants' houses.

Bordeaux is a town of grand 18th- and 19th-century buildings and monuments, including its theatre and the Monument aux Girondins. A 21st-century addition is the Cité du Vin museum, which celebrates the region's wine production *(see pp424–6)*.

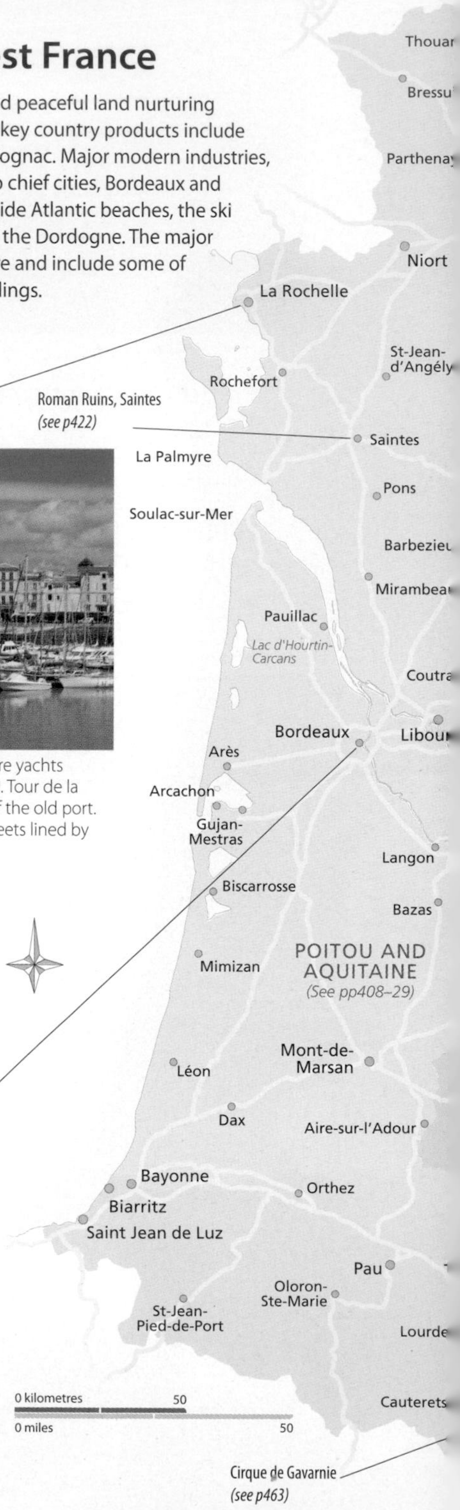

◀ Château de Castelnaud, overlooking the River Dordogne

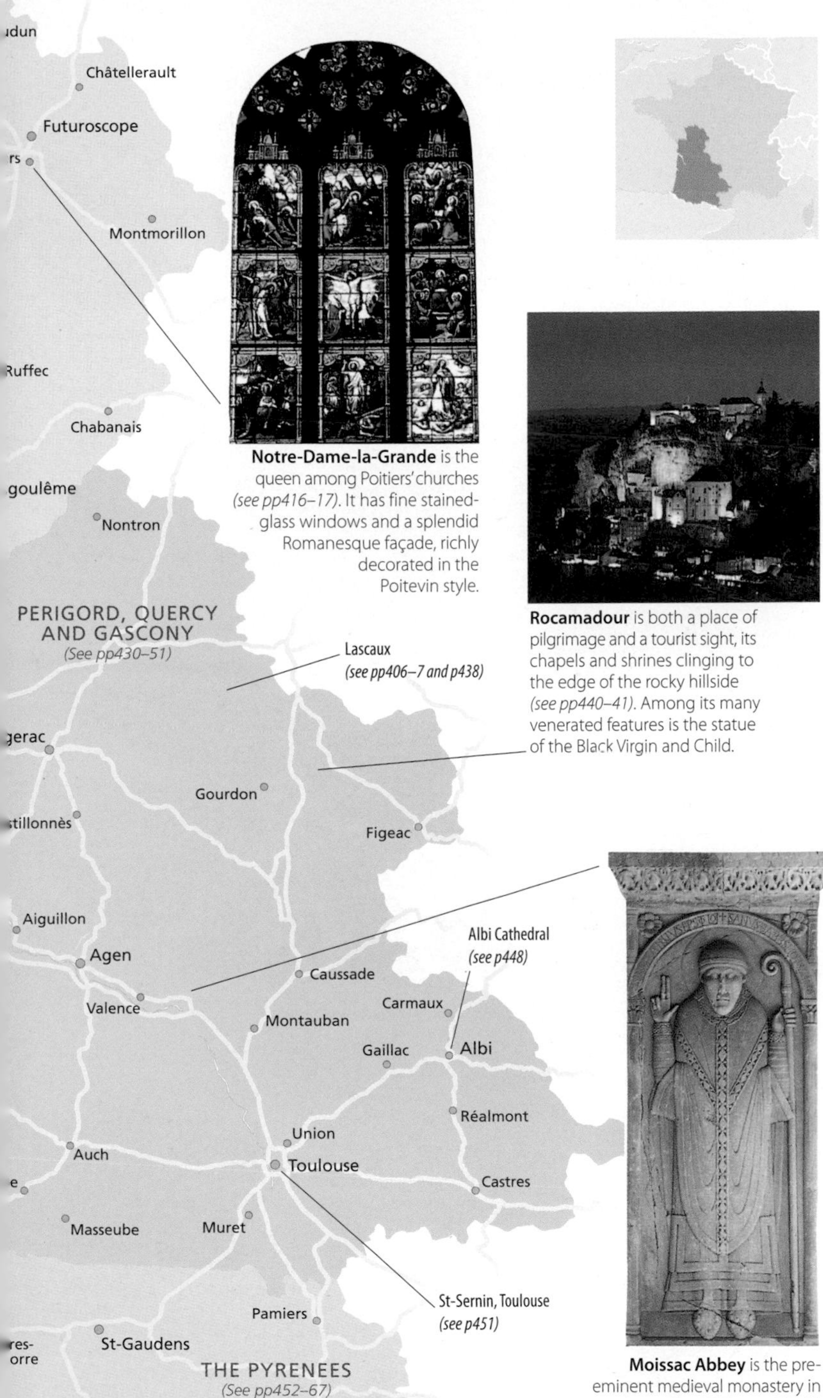

Notre-Dame-la-Grande is the queen among Poitiers' churches *(see pp416–17)*. It has fine stained-glass windows and a splendid Romanesque façade, richly decorated in the Poitevin style.

Rocamadour is both a place of pilgrimage and a tourist sight, its chapels and shrines clinging to the edge of the rocky hillside *(see pp440–41)*. Among its many venerated features is the statue of the Black Virgin and Child.

Moissac Abbey is the pre-eminent medieval monastery in southwest France *(see pp446–7)*. Its tympanum, representing the Apocalypse, and the cloister capitals are outstanding examples of Romanesque sculpture.

The Flavours of Southwest France

"Great cooking and great wines make a paradise on earth", said Henri IV of his own region, Gascony. The southwest does indeed fulfil the requirements of the most demanding gourmet. The Atlantic coast supplies fine seafood; Bordeaux produces some of France's best wines to complement its rich cooking; geese and ducks provide the fat that is key to local cuisine; and regional produce includes delicacies such as *foie gras*, truffles and wild mushrooms. The Pyrenees offer beef and lamb grazed on mountain pastures, cheese and *charcuterie*, and the Basque country adds the spicy notes of red peppers and fine chocolate.

Espelette peppers

Walnuts, one of the southwest's most famous products

Poitou and Aquitaine

The coast is famous for its seafood, and is the most important oyster-producing region of France – the oysters of Marennes-Oleron are of especially high quality. The species of blue algae on which they feed gives them a distinctive green colouring. Oysters are usually served simply with lemon or shallot vinegar, but in Bordeaux they like to eat them with little sausages. Mussels are also raised here, and the sea yields a variety of fish. Eels, lamprey and sturgeon are caught in the Gironde estuary.

Poitou-Charentes is one of France's main goat-rearing areas, producing cheeses such as *chabichou de Poitou*, a small, soft, cylindrical cheese of distinct flavour.

Périgord, Quercy and Gascony

High-quality ducks, geese and poultry form the basis of the cuisine of this region, and their fat is a key ingredient of many dishes from simple *pommes sarladaises* (potatoes cooked in goose fat) to *confit*, where entire duck legs are preserved in their own fat. The ultimate

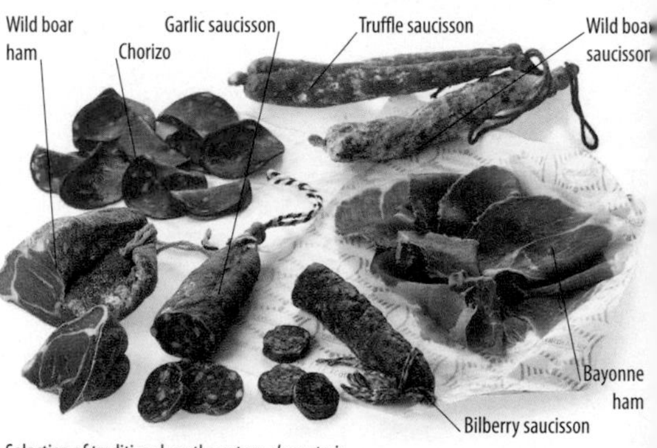

Selection of traditional southwestern *charcuterie*

Regional Dishes and Specialities

Pink garlic

Duck is one of the essential ingredients of southwestern cooking, and is served in a variety of ways. The *magret* is the breast – the best of all coming from a duck that has been bred for *foie gras*. Usually served pink *(rose)*, it may come with a variety of sauces but is most perfectly complemented by the smoky flavour of local *cèpe* mushrooms in season. Duck *confit* is usually made with the legs, but gizzards are also preserved in this way. *Foie gras* is the most expensive (and controversial) product, resulting from the process of *gavage*, when the duck or goose is force-fed maize to enlarge and enrich its liver. *Foie gras* can be eaten freshly cooked, served with sauce or fruit, or preserved and served with toast or brioche, ideally accompanied by a sweet white wine such as Sauternes.

Omelette aux truffes For this luxurious omelette the filling is local black truffles, with more sliced over the top.

Fattened Toulouse geese, the source of *foie gras*

southwestern dish has to be *cassoulet*, a stew of duck or goose, sausages, pork and white beans topped with a crust of breadcrumbs; it arouses fierce competition among the dedicated chefs of the region.

Luxury ingredients enhance these basics: walnut oil is added to salads, and slivers of expensive truffles perfume sauces or omelettes. Wild mushrooms are eagerly sought in season, and are most delicious cooked simply with garlic, shallots and parsley. The region is one of the main producers of garlic, which appears studded into meat or served as whole baked heads. The finest fruits include *reines-claudes* (greengages) and the celebrated plums of Agen, which are dried as prunes or added to dishes of rabbit or hare.

The Pyrenees

From the mountain pastures come beef and lamb of high quality, including Barèges mutton, as well as river trout and an array of excellent *charcuterie*. Strong cheeses of goat's or ewe's milk are sometimes served with jam made from the black cherries

Fishermen opening oysters at a local maritime festival

of Itxassou. One of the most popular dishes is *garbure*, a hearty stew of cabbage, bacon and confit of duck or goose.

Basque cuisine has its own distinct identity, with the red Espelette pepper adding a touch of spice to chorizo, *piperade* or *chipirones* (baby squid cooked in their own ink). Succulent Bayonne ham is made from pigs that forage for acorns and chestnuts. Bayonne was also home to the first chocolatiers in France – 17th-century Jewish refugees from the Inquisition – and the town still makes top-quality dark, bitter chocolate.

ON THE MENU

Cagouilles à la charentaise Snails with sausage meat, herbs and wine.

Entrecôte à la bordelaise Steak in sauce of red wine, shallots and bone marrow.

Farçi poitevin Cabbage stuffed with bacon, pork and sorrel.

Gasconnade Leg of lamb with garlic and anchovy.

Mouclade Mussels in curry sauce, from the spice port of La Rochelle.

Salade landaise Salad of foie gras, gizzards and *confit*.

Ttoro Basque mixed fish and shellfish stew with potatoes, tomatoes and onions.

Cassoulet This is a stew of white beans cooked with a variety of sausages and cuts of meat, such as pork or duck.

Piperade Eggs are added to a stew of peppers, onions, tomatoes and garlic, with Bayonne ham laid on top.

Croustade Thin pastry is layered with melted butter and apples, perfumed with Armagnac and vanilla.

France's Wine Regions: Bordeaux

Bordeaux is the world's largest fine wine region, and, for red wines, certainly the most familiar outside France. Following Henry II's marriage to Eleanor of Aquitaine, three centuries of courtly commerce with England ensured that claret was served at the finest foreign tables. In the 19th century, canny merchants capitalized on this fame and brought fantastic financial prosperity to the region and, with it, the famous 1855 Classification of the Médoc, a league table of châteaux that is still very much in force today.

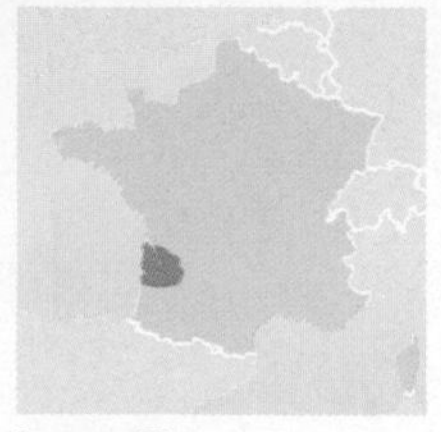

Locator Map

Bordeaux wine region

Picking red Merlot grapes at Château Palmer

Wine Regions

The great wine-producing areas of Bordeaux straddle two great rivers; the land between the rivers ("Entre-Deux-Mers") produces lesser, mainly white wines. The rivers, and the river port of Bordeaux itself, have been crucial to the trade in Bordeaux wines; some of the prettiest châteaux line the river banks, enabling easy transportation.

0 kilometres 15

0 miles 15

Key

- Médoc
- Blaye
- Bourg
- Entre-Deux-Mers
- Graves
- Pessac-Léognan
- Cérons
- Barsac
- Sauternes
- Libournais District
- Pomerol
- Saint-Emilion

Key Facts About Bordeaux Wines

Location and Climate
Climatic conditions may vary not only from one year to another, but also within the region itself. The soils tend to be gravelly in the Médoc and Graves, and clayey on the right bank.

Grape Varieties

The five main red grape varieties are ***Cabernet Franc***, ***Cabernet Sauvignon***, ***Merlot, Petit Verdot*** and ***Malbec***. Cabernet Sauvignon is the dominant grape on the west side of the Gironde, Merlot to the east. Most Bordeaux reds are, however, a blend of grapes. ***Sauvignon Blanc*** and ***Sémillon*** are grown and often blended for both dry and sweet whites.

Good Producers
(Reds) Latour, Margaux, Haut-Brion, Cos d'Estournel, Léoville Las Cases, Léoville Barton, Lascombes, Pichon Longueville, Pichon Lalande, Lynch-Bages, Palmer, Rausan-Ségla, Duhart Milon, d'Angludet, Léoville Poyferré, Branaire Ducru, Ducru Beau-caillou, Malescot St-Exupéry, Cantemerle, Phélan-Ségur, Chasse-Spleen, Poujeaux, Domaine de Chevalier, Pape Clément, Cheval Blanc, Canon, Pavie, l'Angelus, Troplong Mondot, La Conseillante, Lafleur, Trotanoy.

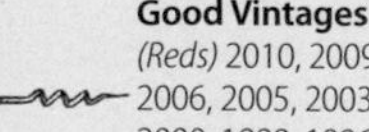

Good Vintages
(Reds) 2010, 2009, 2006, 2005, 2003, 2000, 1998, 1996.

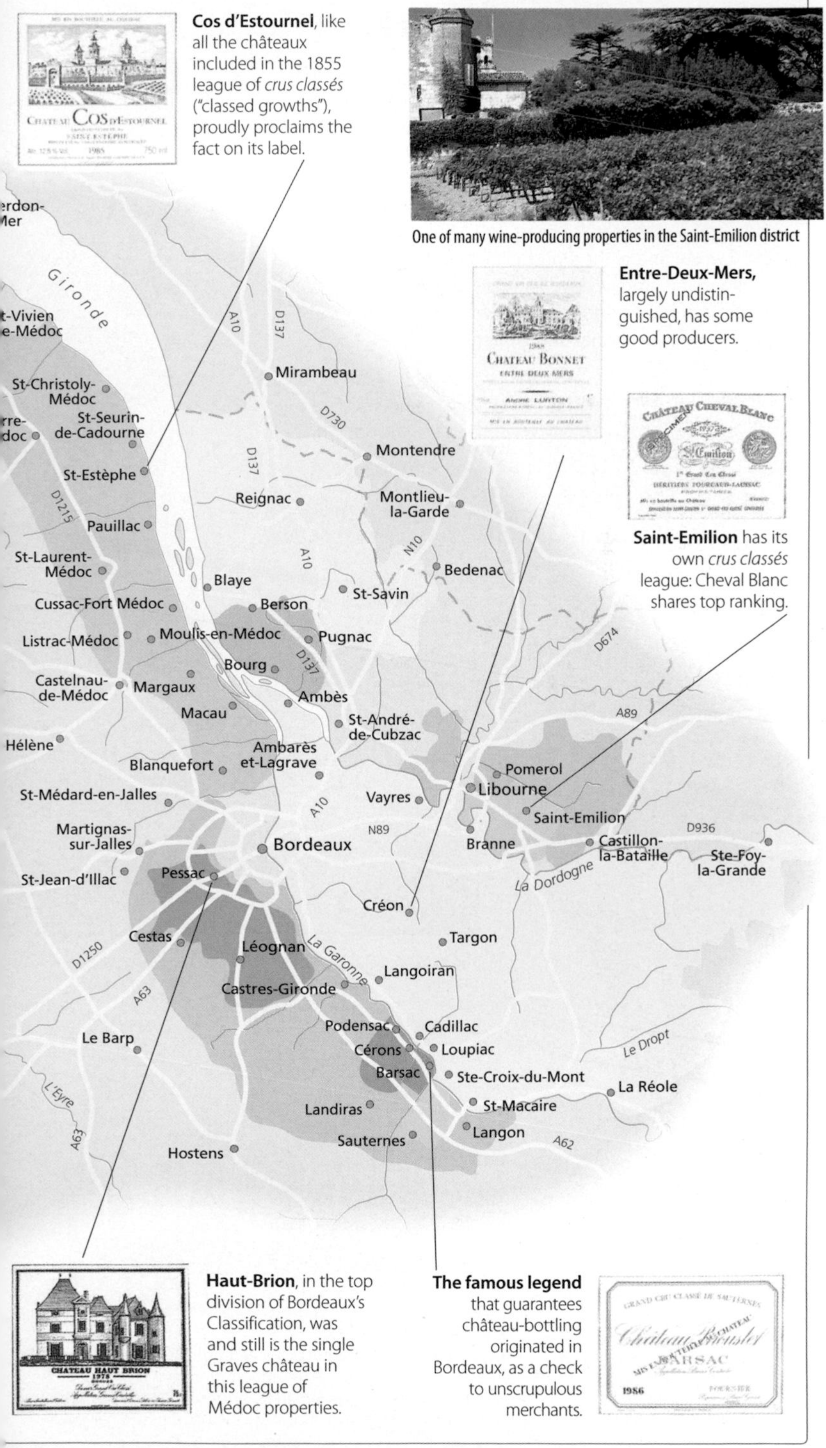

Cos d'Estournel, like all the châteaux included in the 1855 league of *crus classés* ("classed growths"), proudly proclaims the fact on its label.

One of many wine-producing properties in the Saint-Emilion district

Entre-Deux-Mers, largely undistinguished, has some good producers.

Saint-Emilion has its own *crus classés* league: Cheval Blanc shares top ranking.

Haut-Brion, in the top division of Bordeaux's Classification, was and still is the single Graves château in this league of Médoc properties.

The famous legend that guarantees château-bottling originated in Bordeaux, as a check to unscrupulous merchants.

The Road to Compostela

Throughout the Middle Ages millions of Christians visited Santiago de Compostela in Spain to pay homage at the shrine of St James (Santiago). They travelled across France staying in monasteries or simple shelters and would return with a scallop shell, the symbol of St James, as a souvenir. Most pilgrims went in hope of redemption and were often on the road for years. In 1140, a monk called Picaud wrote one of the world's first travel guides about the pilgrimage. Today, travellers can follow the same routes, passing through ancient towns and villages with their magnificent shrines and churches.

The original cathedral of Santiago de Compostela was built in 813 by Alfonso II over the tomb of St James. In 1075, construction started on the grandiose Romanesque church seen today, which has, among other later additions, a resplendent 17th- to18th-century Baroque façade.

Foreign pilgrims joined at ports such as St-Malo.

The routes converged on Santiago de Compostela.

Most pilgrims crossed the Pyrenees at Roncesvalles.

James the Greater, an apostle, came to Spain to spread the Gospel, according to legend. On his return to Judaea, he was martyred by Herod. His remains were taken to Spain by boat and lay hidden for 800 years.

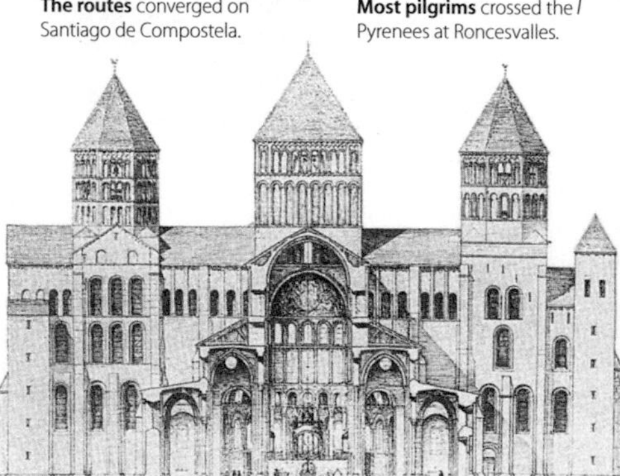

The powerful Cluny monastery in Burgundy *(see pp54–5)*, and its affiliated monasteries, played an important role in promoting the pilgrimage. They built shelters and set up churches and shrines housing precious relics, to encourage the pilgrims on their way.

The Pilgrims' Way

Paris, Vézelay (see pp340–41), *Le Puy* (see pp368–9) *and Arles* (see pp512–13) *are the rallying points for the four "official" routes across France. They cross the Pyrenees at Roncesvalles and Somport, and merge at Puente la Reina to form one route, culminating at the shrine on the Galician coast*

Conques purloined relics to boost its prestige.

Le Puy was a main rallying point for pilgrims.

The reliquary of Ste-Foy, at Conques, is in one of many elaborate shrines that drew crowds of pilgrims on the way to Santiago de Compostela. A saint's relics were thought to have miraculous powers.

What to See Today

Huge Romanesque churches, including Ste-Madeleine at Vézelay *(see p340)*, Ste-Foy at Conques *(pp372–3)* and St-Sernin at Toulouse *(p451)*, along with many small chapels, were built to accommodate large numbers of pilgrims.

Basilique Ste-Madeleine, Vézelay

The first recorded pilgrim was the bishop of Le Puy in 951. But pilgrims have probably been coming to Santiago since 814, soon after the saint's tomb was found.

The name Santiago de Compostela is believed to originate from the Latin *Campus stellae* (field of stars). Legend has it that strange stars were seen hovering over a field in 814 and on 25 July, now the feast of Santiago, the saint's remains were found. Subsequent evidence showed that St James's remains were never in Compostela after all.

Caves of the Southwest

Southwest France is well-known for its spectacular rock formations, created by the slow accumulation of dissolved mineral deposits. Caves and rock shelters exist throughout limestone country in France. But in the foothills of the Pyrenees and the Dordogne they also have something else to offer the visitor: a collection of extraordinary rock paintings, some dating back to the last Ice Age. These art forms were created when prehistoric peoples evolved and began engraving, painting and carving. This unique artistic tradition lasted for more than 25,000 years, reaching its zenith around 17,000 years ago. Some very fine examples of cave painting are still visible today.

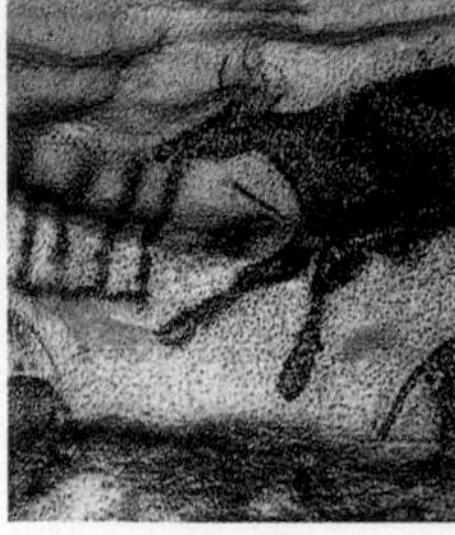

Ancient cave paintings at Lascaux

Caves of the Dordogne

There are many different cave systems to visit in or near the Dordogne Valley. The entire Périgord region contains one of the densest concentrations of prehistoric sites anywhere in the world. In an uncertain climate, its rivers flanked by caves and rock shelters proved very attractive to prehistoric man.

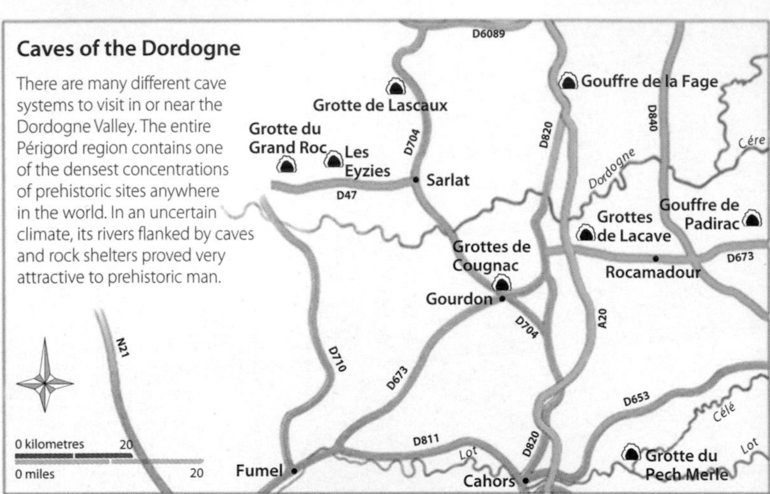

Cave Formation

Limestone is laid down in layers containing fissures that allow water to penetrate beneath the surface. Over thousands of years, the water slowly dissolves the rock, first forming potholes and then larger caverns. Stalactites develop where water drips from the cave roof; stalagmites grow upwards from the floor.

Grotte du Grand Roc in the Vézère Valley, Périgord

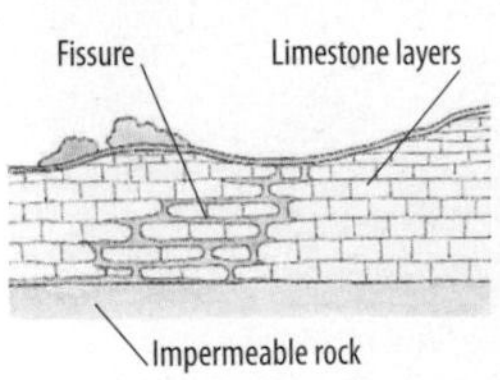

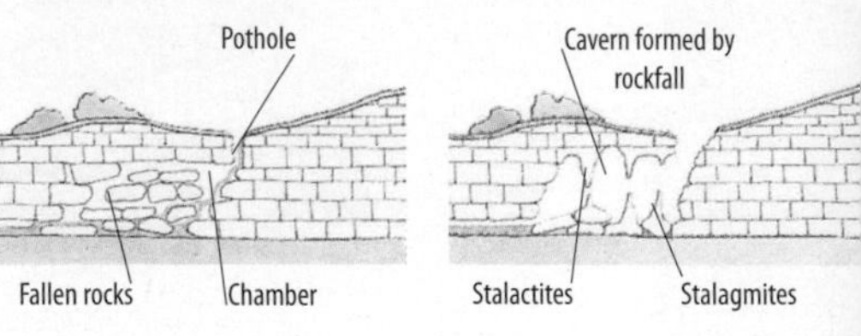

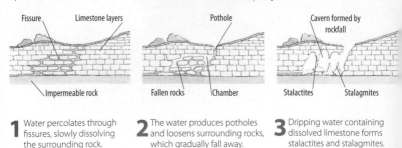

1 Water percolates through fissures, slowly dissolving the surrounding rock.

2 The water produces potholes and loosens surrounding rocks, which gradually fall away.

3 Dripping water containing dissolved limestone forms stalactites and stalagmites.

Gouffre de Padirac

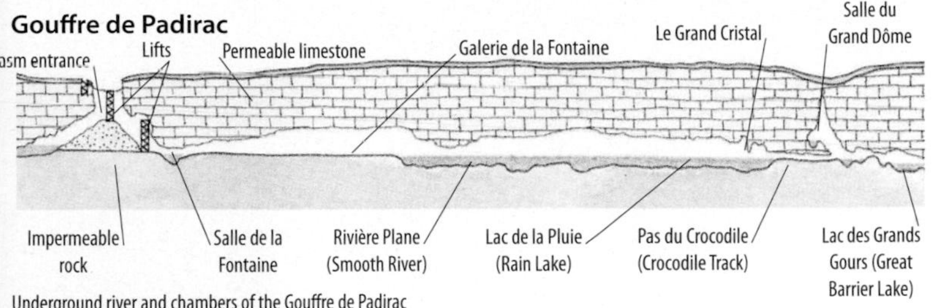

Underground river and chambers of the Gouffre de Padirac

Prehistoric caves at Les Eyzies

Visiting the Caves

Cougnac contains chasms (*gouffres*) and galleries and its prehistoric paintings include human figures. Around **Les Eyzies** *(see pp438–9)* are the caves of **Les Combarelles**, and **Font de Gaume**, which have beautiful prehistoric paintings, drawings and engravings, as does **Rouffignac** in its network of caves. **Grand Roc** has chambers containing a profusion of stalactites and stalagmites. Northeast of Les Eyzies is the rock shelter of **L'Abri du Cap Blanc**, with its rare frieze of horses and bison dating from around 14,000 years ago.

On the south bank of the Dordogne, an underground river and lake with extraordinary rock formations can be seen at **Lacave**. The gigantic chasm and caverns at **Gouffre de Padirac** *(p442)* are even more spectacular. The caves at **Lascaux** with the finest prehistoric paintings have been closed but the exceptional replica at **Lascaux IV** *(p438)* is well worth seeing. Further south, **Pech-Merle's** caverns *(pp442–3)* have impressive rock formations. **Niaux**, in the foothills of the Pyrenees, can also be visited.

The Story of Cave Art

The first prehistoric cave paintings in Europe were discovered in northwest Spain in 1879. Since then, over 200 decorated caves and rock shelters have been found in Spain and France, mainly in the Dordogne region. A wide range of clues, from stone lamps to miraculously preserved footprints, has helped prehistorians to work out the techniques the cave artists used. But their motives are still not clear. Nearly all the paintings are of animals, with few humans, and many of them are in inaccessible underground chambers. The paintings undoubtedly had a symbolic or magical significance; a new theory suggests they were the work of shamans.

The techniques used by Ice Age artists, who worked by lamplight, included cutting outlines into soft rock, using natural contours as part of the design. Black lines and shading were produced by charcoal, while colour washes were applied with mineral pigments such as kaolin and haematite. Hand silhouettes were made by sucking up diluted pigment and blowing it through a plant stem to form a fine spray. When the hand was removed from the rock, its eerie shape was left behind.

Decorated stone lamp discovered in Lascaux cave

Kaolin

Charcoal

Haematite

The Great Bull from the Hall of Bulls frieze at Lascaux

POITOU AND AQUITAINE

Deux-Sèvres · Charente-Maritime · Vendée · Vienne · Charente
Gironde · Landes

This vast area of southwest France spans a quarter of the country's windswept Atlantic coastline, a great expanse of fine sandy beaches. The region stretches from the marshes of the Marais Poitevin to the great pine forests of the Landes. Central to it is the celebrated wine region of Bordeaux and its great châteaux.

The turbulent history of Poitou and Aquitaine, fought over for centuries, has left a rich architectural and cultural heritage. The great arch and amphitheatre at Saintes bear witness to Roman influence in the area. In the Middle Ages, the pilgrimage route to Santiago de Compostela *(see pp404–5)* created an impressive legacy of Romanesque churches, such as those at Poitiers and Parthenay, as well as tiny chapels and glowing frescoes. The Hundred Years' War *(see pp58–9)* caused great upheaval but also resulted in the construction of mighty defence keeps by the English Plantagenet kings. As a result of the Wars of Religion *(see pp60–61)*, many towns, churches and châteaux were destroyed and had to be rebuilt.

Present-day Poitiers is a big, thriving commercial centre. To the west are the historic ports of La Rochelle and Rochefort. Further south, the wine-producing district of Bordeaux combines with Cognac, famous for its brandy, to supply an important part of the region's income. The city of Bordeaux is as prosperous today as in Roman times, combining a lively cultural scene with elegant 18th-century architecture. Its wines complement the region's cuisine: lampreys, mussels and oysters from the coast; and salty lamb and goat's cheeses from the inland pastures.

Shuttered houses in St-Martin-de-Ré, on Ile de Ré, off the coast of La Rochelle

◀ Aerial view of Pointe de la Fumée, famous for its seafood restaurants, near Fouras, south of La Rochelle

Exploring Poitou and Aquitaine

Blessed with a seemingly endless Atlantic coastline, abundant navigable waterways, excellent ports and the finest wine and brandy in the world, the region is ideal for a relaxing holiday. Today most summer visitors head straight for the beaches with their thundering waves, but there is also a lush countryside inland with a lot to offer. Fine medieval architecture can be seen along the pilgrim's route to Santiago de Compostela *(see pp404–5)*, and châteaux of all shapes and sizes characterize the wine districts around Bordeaux. The only modern city of major importance in the region, Bordeaux is worth a visit for its elegant 18th-century architecture as well as for its rich cultural life. The vast man-made forest of Les Landes also adds to this greatly undervalued corner of France.

Beach life in Bassin d'Arcachon on the Côte d'Argent

Getting Around

The region's main motorway is the A10 connecting Paris and Poitiers with Bordeaux and points east, such as Toulouse, west to Rochefort and south to Bayonne and Spain. This road carries most of the area's heavy traffic, relieving the excellent smaller roads. Bordeaux can be reached by TGV direct from Lille (Eurostar interchange) and from Paris via the superfast TGV L'Océane, with a journey time of only 2 hours. Bordeaux, Poitiers and La Rochelle have international airports (direct flights to UK), and Bordeaux also has coach services to most European capitals. Poitiers has buses to nearby towns.

For keys to symbols *see back flap*

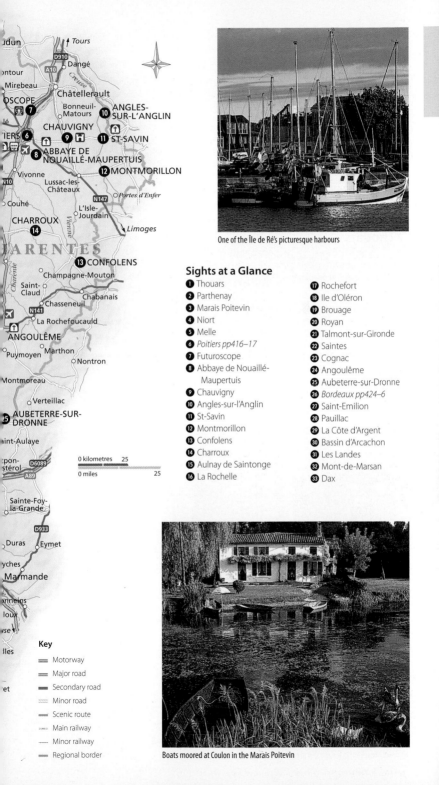

One of the Île de Ré's picturesque harbours

Sights at a Glance

1. Thouars
2. Parthenay
3. Marais Poitevin
4. Niort
5. Melle
6. *Poitiers pp416–17*
7. Futuroscope
8. Abbaye de Nouaillé-Maupertuis
9. Chauvigny
10. Angles-sur-l'Anglin
11. St-Savin
12. Montmorillon
13. Confolens
14. Charroux
15. Aulnay de Saintonge
16. La Rochelle
17. Rochefort
18. Ile d'Oléron
19. Brouage
20. Royan
21. Talmont-sur-Gironde
22. Saintes
23. Cognac
24. Angoulême
25. Aubeterre-sur-Dronne
26. *Bordeaux pp424–6*
27. Saint-Emilion
28. Pauillac
29. La Côte d'Argent
30. Bassin d'Arcachon
31. Les Landes
32. Mont-de-Marsan
33. Dax

Key

- Motorway
- Major road
- Secondary road
- Minor road
- Scenic route
- Main railway
- Minor railway
- Regional border

Boats moored at Coulon in the Marais Poitevin

Rose window of St-Médard, Thouars

❶ Thouars

Deux-Sèvres. 10,000. 32 pl St-Médard (05 49 66 17 65). Tue & Fri. **tourisme-pays-thouarsais.fr**

Thouars, on a rocky outcrop surrounded by the River Thouet, is on the border between Anjou and Poitou. There are as many roofs of northern slate as of southern red tiles.

In the centre stands **Eglise St-Médard**. Its Romanesque façade is a perfect example of the Poitevin style that is typical of the region *(see p416)*, although a splendid Gothic rose window has been added. Lined with half- timbered medieval houses, rue du Château leads up to the 17th- century château which now houses a school and is open to the public from April to September.

East of Thouars lies the moated **Château d'Oiron**, which now hosts contemporary art exhibitions. A masterpiece of Renaissance architecture, it was largely built from 1518 to 1549.

Château d'Oiron
10 rue du Château, 79100 Oiron.
Tel 05 49 96 51 25. **Open** daily.
Closed some public hols.
ground floor. **oiron.fr**

❷ Parthenay

Deux-Sèvres. 11,000. 8 rue de la Vau-St-Jacques (05 49 64 24 24). Wed. **tourisme-gatine.com**

Parthenay is a sleepy provincial town, except on Wednesday mornings, when France's second-biggest livestock market is held here. In the Middle Ages, the town was an important halt on the route to Santiago de Compostela *(see pp404–5)* and it is easy to imagine the processions of pilgrims in the medieval quarter. Steep and cobbled, rue de la Vau-St-Jacques winds up to the 13th-century ramparts, leading on from the fortified Porte St-Jacques, which guards a 13th-century bridge over the River Thouet.

West of Parthenay, the 12th-century church of **St-Pierre de Parthenay-le-Vieux** has a splendid Poitevin façade, featuring Samson and the Lion and a cavalier with a falcon.

Medieval houses lining the cobbled rue de la Vau-St-Jacques in Parthenay

❸ Marais Poitevin

Charente-Maritime, Deux-Sèvres, Vendée. La Rochelle. Niort, La Rochelle. Coulon, Arçais, Marans. 2 rue Brisson, Niort (05 49 24 18 79). **niortmarais poitevin.com**

The Poitevin marshes, which have been slowly drained with canals, dykes and sluices for a thousand years, cover about 800 sq km (309 sq miles) between Niort and the sea. The area is now a regional park, divided into two parts. To the north and south of the Sèvre estuary is the Marais Désséché (dry marsh), where cereal and other crops are grown. The huge swathe of the Marais Mouillé (wet marsh) is upstream towards Niort.

The wet marshes, known as the Venise Verte (Green Venice), are the most interesting. They are crisscrossed by a labyrinth of weed-choked canals, adorned by waterlilies, and irises, shaded by poplars and beeches, and support a rich variety of birds and other wildlife. The *maraîchins* who live here stoutly maintain that much of the huge, water-logged forest is unexplored. The picturesque whitewashed villages hereabouts are all built on higher ground, and the customary means of transport is a flat-bottomed boat, known as a *platte*.

Coulon, St-Hilaire-la-Palud, La Garette and Arçais, as well as Damvix and Maillezais in the Vendée, are all convenient

Flat-bottomed boats moored at Coulon in the Marais Poitevin

starting points for boat trips around the marshes. Boats can be rented with or without a guide. Make sure you bring plenty of insect repellent.

Coulon is the largest and best-equipped village, and a popular base for visiting the area. **La Maison du Marais Poitevin** presents an account of life in the marshes in times gone by, along with details of the wetlands' flora and fauna.

The Plantagenet donjon in Niort, now housing a local museum

❹ Niort

Deux-Sèvres. 60,000. 2 rue Brisson (05 49 24 18 79). Thu & Sat. **niortmaraispoitevin.com**

Once a medieval port by the green waters of the Sèvre, Niort is now a prosperous industrial town specializing in machine tools, electronics, chemicals and insurance.

Its closeness to the marshes is evident in local specialities – eels, snails and angelica. The last, a herb, has been cultivated in the wetlands for centuries and is used for anything from liqueur to ice cream.

The town's immediate attraction is the huge 12th-century donjon overlooking the Vieux Pont. Built by Henry II and Richard the Lion-Heart, it played an important role during the Hundred Years' War and was later used as a prison. One prisoner was the father of Madame de Maintenon *(see p62)*, who spent her childhood in Niort. The donjon is now a museum of local arts and crafts, and archaeology. The **Musée d'Agesci** in avenue de Limoges exhibits ceramics, sculpture and paintings from the 16th to 20th centuries.

Environs

Halfway to Poitiers is the small town of **St-Maixent-L'Ecole**. A marvel of light and space, its abbey church is a Flamboyant Gothic reconstruction by François Le Duc (1670) of a building destroyed during the Wars of Religion. Further west, the **Tumulus de Bougon** consists of five tumuli (burial mounds), the oldest dating from 4500 BC.

❺ Melle

Deux-Sèvres. 4,000. 3 rue E Traver (05 49 29 15 10). Fri.
decouvertes.paysmellois.org

A Roman silver mine was the origin of Melle, which in the 9th century had the only mint in Aquitaine. Later its fame derived from the *baudet du Poitou*, an especially sturdy mule bred in the area. Now Melle is better known for its churches, of which the finest is **St-Hilaire**. It has a 12th-century Poitevin façade with an equestrian statue of the Emperor Constantine above the north door.

Environs

To the northwest, the abbey in **Celles-sur-Belle** has a great Moorish doorway which contrasts strongly with the rest of the church, a 17th-century restoration in Gothic style.

Equestrian statue of Constantine on the façade of St-Hilaire, Melle

A canal in the Marais Poitevin ▶

6 Poitiers

Three of the greatest battles in French history were fought around Poitiers, the most famous in 732, when Charles Martel halted the Arab invasion. After two periods of English rule the town thrived during the reign of Jean de Berry (1369–1416), the great sponsor of the arts. Its university, founded in 1431, made Poitiers a major intellectual centre and saw Rabelais among its students. The Wars of Religion left Poitiers in chaos and not until the late 19th century did any major development take place. Today, however, the town is a modern and dynamic regional capital with a rich architectural heritage in its historic centre.

Fresco in Eglise St-Hilaire-le-Grand

Notre-Dame-la-Grande

Despite its name, Notre-Dame-la-Grande is not a large church. One of Poitiers' great pilgrim churches, it is most celebrated as a masterpiece of lively 12th-century Poitevin sculpture, notably its richly detailed façade. In the choir is a Romanesque fresco of Christ and the Virgin. Most of the chapels were added in the Renaissance.

Palais de Justice

Pl Alphonse Lepetit. **Tel** 05 49 50 22 00. **Open** 8:30am–noon & 1:30–5pm Mon–Fri.

Behind the bland Renaissance façade is the 12th-century great hall of the palace of the Angevin kings, Henry II and Richard the Lionheart. This is thought to be the scene of Joan of Arc's examination by a council of theologians in 1429.

Cathédrale St-Pierre

The 13th-century carved choir stalls in St-Pierre are by far the oldest in France. Note the huge

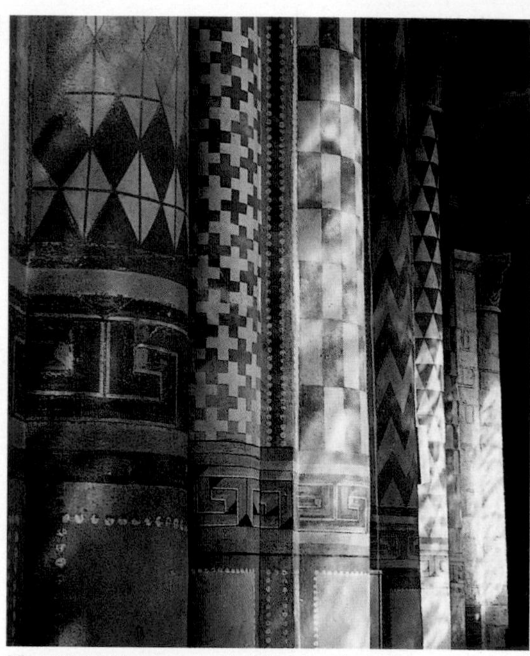

Pillars with colourful geometrical patterns in Notre-Dame-la-Grande

Notre-Dame-la-Grande

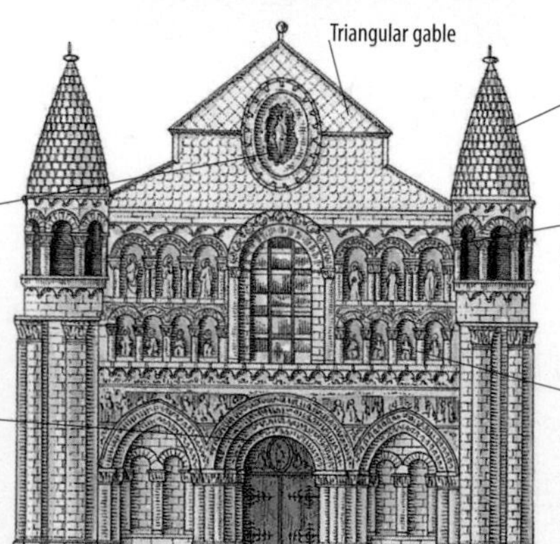
Triangular gable
Cone-shaped pinnacles
Christ in Majesty is shown in the centre of the gable, surrounded by symbols of the evangelists.
Blind arcading is a distinctive feature of the Poitevin façade.
The portals on the Poitevin façade are deep and richly sculpted, often showing a pronounced Moorish influence.
The 12 apostles are represented by statues in the arcatures, together with the first bishop St Hilaire and his disciple St Martin.

For hotels and restaurants in this region see pp565–6 and pp594–6

12th-century east window showing the Crucifixion. The tiny figures of the cathedral's patrons (Henry II and Eleanor of Aquitaine) are crouched at the foot of the window. Its organ (1787–91), made by François-Henri Cliquot, is one of the finest in Europe.

Espace Mendès France

1 pl de la Cathédrale. **Tel** 05 49 50 33 08. **Open** 9am–6:30pm Tue–Fri, 2–6:30pm Sat & Sun. **Closed** 1 Jan; Sun in Jul–Aug.

This museum contains a state-of-the-art planetarium, with laser shows to explain the mysteries of the universe, plus exhibitions.

Baptistère St-Jean

Rue Jean Jaurès. **Open** Tue–Sun; mid-Jun–Sep: daily.

The polygonal 4th-century Baptistère St-Jean is one of the oldest Christian buildings in France. It is now a museum, with Romanesque frescoes of Christ and Emperor Constantine, and some Merovingian sarcophagi.

Musée Sainte-Croix

3bis rue Jean Jaurès. **Tel** 05 49 41 07 53. **Open** Tue–Sun. **Closed** some public hols.

Musée Sainte-Croix exhibits prehistoric, Gallo-Roman and medieval archaeology, and a wide range of paintings and 19th-century sculpture. Seven bronzes by Camille Claudel are on show, including *La Valse*. There is also a collection of contemporary art.

VISITORS' CHECKLIST

Practical Information
Vienne. 91,000. 45 pl Charles de Gaulle (05 49 41 21 24). Sat, Tue & Thu. Les Expressifs (Oct). **ot-poitiers.fr**

Transport
5 km (3 miles) W Poitiers.

Eglise St-Hilaire-le-Grand

Fires and reconstructions have made St-Hilaire a mosaic of different styles. With its origins in the 6th century, the church still displays an 11th-century bell tower and a 12th-century nave.

Médiathèque François Mitterrand

4 rue de l'Université. **Tel** 05 49 52 31 51. **Open** Tue–Sat. **Closed** public hols.

This modern building, located in the historic quarter, is home to the **Maison du Moyen Age**, which displays a collection of medieval manuscripts, maps and engravings.

One of Futuroscope's most popular attractions: the large-screen cinema

❼ Futuroscope

Av René Monory, Chasseneuil-du-Poitou, Jaunay-Clan. **Tel** 05 49 49 11 12. **Open** daily. **Closed** Jan–early Feb. **futuroscope.com**

Futuroscope is a fantastic theme park 7 km (4 miles) north of Poitiers, exploring visual technology in a futuristic environment. Attractions evolve yearly and include simulators, 3-D and 360-degree screens and the "magic carpet" cinema, with one of its screens on the floor, creating the sensation of flying. The cinema has the biggest screen in Europe.

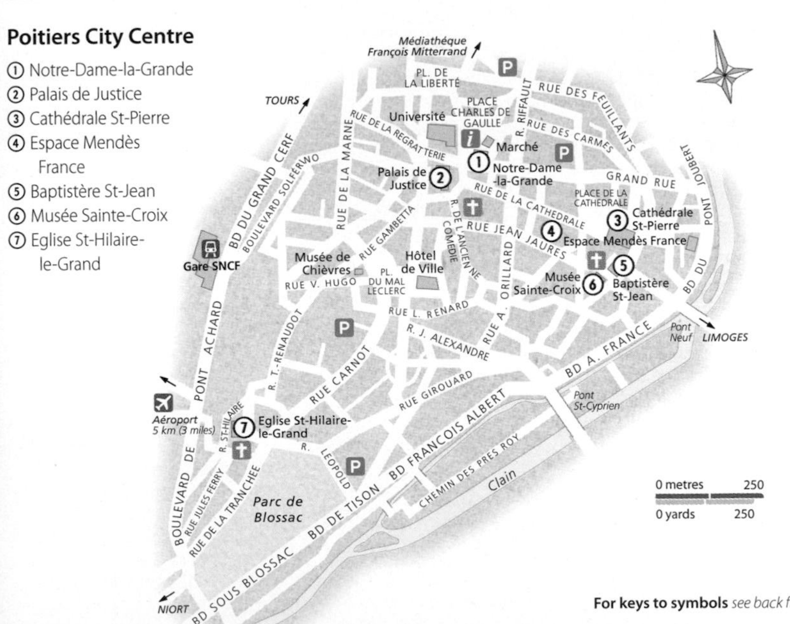

For keys to symbols *see back flap*

The castle ruins of Angles-sur-l'Anglin with the old watermill in the foreground

❽ Abbaye de Nouaillé-Maupertuis

Vienne. **Tel** 05 49 55 35 69. Church: **Open** 9am–6pm (7pm in summer). summer only.

On the banks of the River Miosson lies the Abbaye de Nouaillé-Maupertuis. First mentioned at the end of the 7th century, the abbey became independent in the late 700s and followed the Benedictine rule. The church was built at the start of the 12th century and reconstructed several times. Behind the altar is the 11th-century sarcophagus of St-Junien, with three great eagles painted on the front.

More interesting is the nearby battlefield, scene of the great English victory at Poitiers Nouaillé by the Black Prince in 1356. The view has altered little since the 14th century. Drive down the small road to La Cardinerie (to the right off the D142), which leads to the river crossing at Gué de l'Omme, the epicentre of the battle. There is a monument commemorating the battle halfway up the hill, where the heaviest fighting took place and where the French king Jean le Bon was captured. He had put up a heroic resistance with only his battle-axe and his small son Philippe to tell him where the next English knight was coming from.

❾ Chauvigny

Vienne. 7,000. 5 rue St-Pierre (05 49 46 39 01). Tue, Thu, Sat. **tourisme-chauvigny.com**

Chauvigny, on its steep promontory overlooking the broad River Vienne, displays the ruins of no fewer than four fortified medieval castles. Stone from the local quarry was so plentiful that nobody ever bothered to demolish earlier castles for building material.

Nevertheless, the best thing in this town is the 11th- to12th-century **Eglise St-Pierre**, whose decorated capitals are a real treasure – particularly those in the choir stalls. The carvings represent biblical scenes along with monsters, sphinxes and sirens. Look for the one that says *Gofridus me fecit* (Gofridus made me), with wonderfully natural scenes of the Epiphany.

Monster capitals in the Eglise St-Pierre in Chauvigny

Environs

Nearby is the lovely **Château de Touffou**, a Renaissance dream on the banks of the Vienne, with terraces and hanging gardens.

Château de Touffou

Bonnes. **Tel** 05 49 56 40 08. **Open** only by guided tour. Apr–Sep: 10am–noon, 2–6pm Sat & Sun: . **touffou.com**

❿ Angles-sur-l'Anglin

Vienne. 380. 2 rue du Four Banal (05 49 48 86 87). Roc-aux-Sorciers: 2 Les Certaux, 05 49 83 37 27. **anglessuranglin.com**

The village of Angles lies in a stunning riverside setting, dominated by its castle ruins. Adding to the charm is an old watermill by the slow-running River Anglin, graced by waterlilies and swaying reeds.

Angles is famous for its tradition of fine needlework, the *jours d'Angles*, which is determinedly maintained by the local women today.

Located just outside the village is the Roc-aux-Sorciers, a sculpted rock shelter which dates back 15,000 years and is one of the world's most important Paleolithic cave art sites.

⓫ St-Savin

Vienne. 900. 20 pl de la Libération (05 49 84 30 00). Fri. saintsavin.com

The glory of St-Savin is its 11th-century abbey church with its slender Gothic spire and huge nave.

The abbey had enormous influence until the Hundred Years' War, when it was burned down. It was later pillaged several times during the Wars of Religion. Despite restoration work by monks in the 17th century and again in the 19th century, the church appears quite untouched.

Its interior contains the most magnificent series of 12th-century Romanesque frescoes in Europe. These wallpaintings were among the very first in France to be classified as a *monument historique* in 1836. Some of the frescoes were restored in 1967–74 and have been protected by UNESCO since 1983. A full-scale replica of the St-Savin murals can be seen at the Palais de Chaillot in Paris *(see pp114–15)*. The abbey-museum explains the historical context and techniques of these murals.

The gothic spire of St-Savin

⓬ Montmorillon

Vienne. 6,500. 2 pl du Maréchal Leclerc (05 49 91 11 96). Wed; la Foire des Hérolles: 29th of each month (28th in Feb). tourisme-montmorillon.fr

Montmorillon, built on the River Gartempe, has its origins in the 11th century. Like most towns in the region, it had a difficult time during the Hundred Years' War and the Wars of Religion. Some buildings survived, such as **Eglise Notre-Dame**, which has beautiful frescoes in its 12th-century crypt (contact the tourist office for key). These include scenes from the life of St Catherine of Alexandria.

Environs

A short walk from the Pont de Chez Ragon, south of Montmorillon, is the **Portes d'Enfer**, a dramatically shaped rock above the rapids of the Gartempe. In nearby Coulonges, the animal market **la Foire des Hérolles** draws people from across France.

St-Savin Wall Paintings

The frescoes of St-Savin represent Old Testament history from the Creation to the Ten Commandments. The sequence starts to the left of the entrance with the Creation of the stars and of Eve. It continues with scenes from Noah's Ark to the Tower of Babel, the story of Joseph and the parting of the Red Sea. It is believed that all the frescoes were created by the same group of artists, due to the similarity in style. Their harmonious colours – red, ochre, green, black and white – have been softened by time.

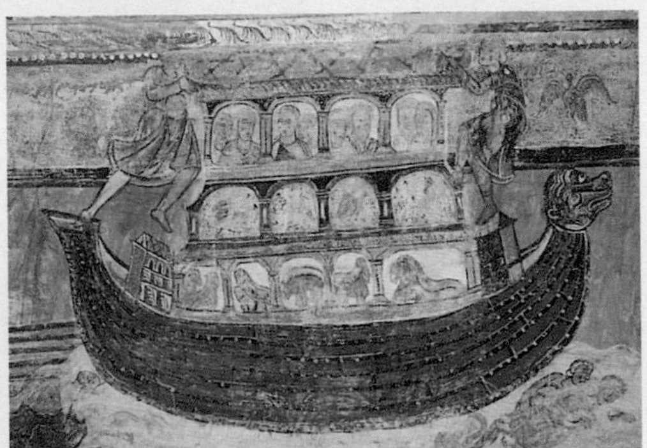

Noah's Ark, from a 12th-century wall painting in St-Savin

⓭ Confolens

Charente. 2,900. 8 rue Fontaine des Jardins (05 45 84 14 08). Wed & Sat. mairie-confolens.fr

On the border with Limousin, Confolens was once an important frontier town but now suffers from rural exodus. Efforts to prevent the town's isolation include the annual international folklore festival. Every August the town is transformed by a mix of music, costumes and crafts from all over the world.

Of historical interest is the medieval bridge that runs across the Vienne and was heavily restored in the early 18th century.

⓮ Charroux

Vienne. 1,200. 2 rte de Chatain (05 49 87 60 12). Thu. civraisiencharlois.com

The 8th-century **Abbaye St-Sauveur** in Charroux was once one of the richest abbeys in the region. Today it is a ruin open to the sky (phone the tourist office to arrange a visit).

Its chief contribution to history was made in the 10th century, when the Council of Charroux declared the "Truce of God", the earliest-known attempt to regulate war in the manner of the Geneva convention. Rules included: "Christian soldiers may not plunder churches, strike priests or steal peasants' livestock while campaigning."

A huge tower marks what was once the centre of the church, and some superb sculpture from the original abbey portal can be seen in the small museum.

⓯ Aulnay de Saintonge

Charente-Maritime. 1,500. 290 av de l'Eglise (05 46 32 60 71). Thu & Sun. **saintongedoree-tourisme.com**

Perhaps the most unusual fact about the lovely 12th-century **Eglise St-Pierre** at Aulnay is that it was all built at once; there is no ill-fitting apse or transept added to an original nave. Surrounded by nothing but cypresses, it has remained the same since the time of the great pilgrimages.

The church is covered in glorious sculpture, particularly the outside of the south transept. It is a rare example of a complete Romanesque façade, with rank on rank of raucous monsters and graceful human figures. Look for the donkey with a harp. Inside the church there is a pillar decorated with elephants.

Façade of Eglise St-Pierre at Aulnay

⓰ La Rochelle

Charente-Maritime. 78,000. 2 quai Georges Simenon, Le Gabut (05 46 41 14 68). daily. **larochelle-tourisme.com**

La Rochelle, a commercial centre and busy port since the 11th century, has suffered much from a distressing tendency to back the wrong side – the English and the Calvinists, for example. This led to the ruthless siege of the city by Cardinal Richelieu in 1628, during which 23,000 people starved to death. The walls were destroyed and the city's privileges withdrawn.

Tour St-Nicolas in La Rochelle

The glory of La Rochelle is the old harbour surrounded by stately buildings. The harbour is now the biggest yachting centre on France's Atlantic coast. On either side of its entrance are **Tour de la Chaîne** and **Tour St-Nicolas**. A huge chain used to be strung between them to ward off attack from the sea.

La Rochelle is easy to explore on foot, though its cobbled streets and arcades can be congested in high summer. To get an overview, climb the 15th-century **Tour de la Lanterne**. Its inner walls were covered in graffiti by prisoners, mostly mariners, in the 17th–19th centuries. Ships are the most common motif.

The study of the 18th-century scientist Clément Lafaille is preserved in the renovated **Muséum d'Histoire Naturelle**, complete with shell collection and display cabinets. There are also stuffed animals and African masks. The town's relation to the New World is treated in the **Musée du Nouveau Monde**. Emigration, commerce and the slave trade are explained through old maps, paintings and artifacts.

The **Bunker of Rochelle** is well worth a visit. Constructed in secret for World War II submarine commanders, it has remained in its original condition for more than 70 years.

Next to the Vieux Port is the huge **Aquarium**. Transparent tunnels lead through tanks with different marine biotopes, including sharks and turtles.

Tours de la Rochelle
Rue des Murs, Le Port. **Tel** 05 46 41 74 13. **Open** daily. **Closed** 1 Jan, 1 May, 25 Dec. **tours-la-rochelle.fr**

Muséum d'Histoire Naturelle
28 rue Albert Premier. **Tel** 05 46 41 18 25. **Open** Tue–Sun. **Closed** 1 Jan, 1 May, 14 Jul, 1 & 11 Nov, 25 Dec. **museum-larochelle.fr**

Musée du Nouveau Monde
10 rue Fleuriau. **Tel** 05 46 41 46 50. **Open** Wed–Mon. **Closed** Sat am (Oct–Mar), Sun am, 1 Jan, 1 May, 14 Jul, 1 & 11 Nov, 25 Dec.

Bunker de la Rochelle
8 rue des Dames. **Tel** 05 46 42 52 89. **Open** daily. **Closed** 30 Dec–mid-Feb.

Aquarium
Bassin des Grands Yachts, quai Louis Prunier. **Tel** 05 46 34 00 00. **Open** daily. **aquarium-larochelle.com**

Environs

Ile de Ré is a long stretch of chalky cliffs and dunes, with a rich birdlife. It is linked to the mainland by a 3-km (2-mile) bridge. Its main town, **St-Martin-de-Ré**, has many seafood restaurants serving local oysters.

A tank with an array of marine animals at La Rochelle Aquarium

⓱ Rochefort

Charente-Maritime. 25,000. av Sadi-Carnot (05 46 99 08 60). Tue, Thu & Sat; flea market: 2nd Thu at Cour Roy Bry. **rochefort-ocean.com**

The historic rival of La Rochelle, Rochefort was purpose-built by Colbert *(see pp62–3)* in the

Phare des Baleines on the eastern point of the Ile de Ré, opposite La Rochelle

17th century to be the greatest shipyard in France, producing over 300 sailing vessels per year.

This maritime heritage can be traced in the beautifully restored **Corderie Royale** from 1670. The building houses an exhibition on ropemaking. The **Musée National de la Marine** displays models of the ships built in the arsenal.

Rochefort is also the birthplace of the writer Pierre Loti (1850–1923). His extravagant **Maison de Pierre Loti** is filled with lush souvenirs in an Oriental decor.

Outside the town is **Pont Transbordeur**, France's last transporter bridge, built in 1897 to connect Rochefort with southern points.

La Corderie Royale
Centre International de la Mer, rue Audebert. **Tel** 05 46 87 01 90. **Open** daily. **Closed** 1, 7–25 Jan, 25 Dec. **W** **corderie-royale.com**

Musée National de la Marine
Pl de la Gallissonnière. **Tel** 05 46 99 86 57. **Open** daily (Oct–Mar: Wed–Mon). **Closed** Jan, 1 May, 25 Dec. **W** **musee-marine.fr**

Maison de Pierre Loti
141 rue Pierre Loti. **Tel** 05 46 82 91 94. **Closed** for renovation; call for information. only. **W** **maisondepierreloti.fr**

Pont Transbordeur
3 av Maurice Chupin, Parc des Fourriers. **Tel** 05 46 83 30 86. **Open** Apr–mid-Nov: daily; call for opening times. **W** **pont-transbordeur.fr**

Environs

Île d'Aix is served by a ferry from Fouras on the mainland. Napoleon was briefly kept here before being exiled to St-Helena. There are Napoleonic mementos in the **Musée Napoléonien**.The camel he rode in the Egyptian campaign is in the **Musée Africain**.

Musée Napoléonien
30 rue Napoléon. **Tel** 05 46 84 66 40. **Open** Wed–Mon (Apr–Sep: daily). **Closed** 1 May.

Musée Africain
Rue Napoléon. **Tel** 05 46 84 66 40. **Open** Wed–Mon (Apr–Sep: daily). **Closed** 1 May.

Napoleon, who was detained at Île d'Aix in 1814

⑱ Île d'Oléron

Charente-Maritime. 22,000. La Rochelle. Rochefort, La Rochelle, Saintes then bus. from La Rochelle (in summer). 22 rue Dubois Meynardie, Marennes (05 46 85 65 23). **W** **oleron-island.com**

Accessible from the mainland by bridge, Oléron is the second-largest French island after Corsica, and a very popular holiday resort. Its south coast, the **Côte Sauvage**, is all dunes and pine forest, with excellent beaches at Vert Bois and Grande Plage, near La Cotinière, and a series of colourful ports. The north is used for farming, fishing and winegrowing.

The train from **St-Trojan** makes a fine excursion through dunes and woodlands to the Pointe de Maumusson (Easter–October).

⑲ Brouage

Charente-Maritime. 600. 2 rue de l'Hospital (05 46 85 19 16). **W** **hiers-brouage-tourisme.fr**

Cardinal Richelieu's fortress at Brouage, his base during the Siege of La Rochelle (1627–8), once overlooked a thriving harbour, but its wealth and population declined in the 18th century, as the ocean receded. In 1659, Marie Mancini was sent into exile here by her uncle, Cardinal Mazarin, who did not approve of her liaison with Louis XIV. The king never forgot the beautiful Marie. Even on his way back from his wedding, he stayed alone at Brouage in the room once occupied by his first great love. Today the **ramparts** are a peaceful place to stroll and admire the view.

Environs

There are two reasons to go to Marennes, southwest of Brouage: the famous green-tinged oysters and the view from the steeple of Eglise St-Pierre-de-Sales. Nearby is the 18th-century **Château de la Gataudière** with an exhibition of horse-drawn vehicles.

Saintes' Roman amphitheatre, with the Eglise St-Eutrope in the background

⓴ Royan

Charente-Maritime. 19,000. to Verdon only. 1 bd de la Grandière (05 46 23 00 00). Tue–Sun; daily in summer. **royan-tourisme.com**

Badly damaged by Allied bombing in World War II, Royan is now thoroughly modern and different in tone from the rest of the towns on this weather-beaten coast. With five beaches of fine sand, here called *conches*, it becomes a heavily populated resort in the summer months.

Built between 1955 and 1958, **Eglise Notre-Dame** is a remarkable early example of reinforced concrete architecture. Its interior is flooded with colour and light by the stained-glass windows.

The outstanding Renaissance **Phare de Cordouan**, visible in the distance from the coast, offers a change from all the modern architecture. Various lighthouses have been erected on the site since the 11th century. The present one was finished in 1611, with a chapel inside. The construction was later reinforced and heightened. Since 1789, nothing has changed but the lighting method. Boat trips in summer ferry visitors to Phare de Cordouan from Royan harbour.

㉑ Talmont-sur-Gironde

Charente-Maritime. 100. rue de l'Église (05 46 90 16 25). **talmont-sur-gironde.fr**

The tiny Romanesque **Eglise Ste-Radegonde** is perched on a spit of land overlooking the Gironde. Built in 1094, the church's apse was designed to resemble the prow of a ship – which is apt, since the nave has already fallen into the estuary. A 15th-century façade closes off what's left. Inside are richly decorated capitals, including a tableau of St George and the Dragon.

Talmont is a jewel of a village, packed full of little white houses and colourful hollyhocks in summer.

㉒ Saintes

Charente-Maritime. 27,000. Place Bassompierre (05 46 74 23 82). Tue–Sun. **saintes-tourisme.fr**

Capital of the Saintonge region, Saintes has an extraordinarily rich architectural heritage. For centuries it boasted the only bridge over the lower Charente, well used by pilgrims on their way to Santiago de Compostela. The Roman bridge no longer exists, but you can still admire the magnificent **Arc de Germanicus** (AD 19), which used to mark its entrance.

On the same side of the river is the beautiful **Abbaye aux Dames**. Consecrated in 1047, it was modernized in the 12th century. During the 17th and 18th centuries noble ladies were educated here. Look for the decorated portal and the vigorous 12th-century head of Christ in the apse.

On the left bank is the 1st-century Roman **amphitheatre**. Further away lies the rather unknown gem, **Eglise St-Eutrope**. In the 15th century, this church had the misfortune to effect a miraculous cure of the dropsy on Louis XI. In a paroxysm of gratitude, he did his best to wreck it with ill-considered Gothic additions. Luckily, its rare Romanesque capitals have survived.

Arc de Germanicus in Saintes

㉓ Cognac

Charente. 19,000. 16 rue du 14 Juillet (05 45 82 10 71). Tue–Sun. **tourism-cognac.com**

Wherever you spot the black lichen stains from alcohol evaporation on the exterior of the buildings in this river port,

Necropolis in the monolithic Eglise St-Jean in Aubeterre-sur-Dronne

you may be sure that you are looking at a storehouse of cognac.

All the great cognac houses do tours – a good one is at **Cognac Otard** in the 15th- to 16th-century château where François I was born. The distillery was established in 1795 by a Scot named Otard, who demolished an old chapel in the process. Luckily, much of the Renaissance architecture was saved and can be seen during the tour, which includes a cognac tasting.

Cognac in traditional snifter

The basic material for cognac is local white wine low in alcohol, which is then distilled. The resultant pale spirit is aged in oak barrels for 4–40 years before being bottled. The skill lies in the blending – therefore the only guide to quality is the name and the duration of ageing.

Cognac Otard
Château de Cognac, 127 bd Denfert-Rochereau. **Tel** 05 45 36 88 86. **Open** daily. **Closed** Jan, 1 May & public hols in winter. obligatory. **baronotard.com**

㉔ Angoulême

Charente. 45,000. 7 bis rue du Chat (05 45 95 16 84). daily. **angouleme-tourisme.com**

The celebrated 12th-century **Cathédrale St-Pierre**, which dominates this industrial centre, is the fourth to be built on the site. One of its most interesting features is the Romanesque frieze on the façade. The cathedral's liturgical treasures are on show in a stunning display designed by contemporary artist Jean-Michel Othoniel. Some restoration work to the cathedral was carried out by the 19th-century architect Abadie. In his eagerness to wipe out all details added after the 12th century, he destroyed a 6th-century crypt.

Unforturnately, he was also let loose on the old château, transforming it into a Neo-Gothic **Hôtel de Ville** (town hall). However, the 15th-century tower, where Marguerite d'Angoulême, sister of François I, was born in 1492, still stands. A statue of her can be seen in the garden. She spoke six languages, had a major role in foreign policy and wrote a popular work, *Heptaméron*. The ramparts offer a bracing walk with views over the Charente Valley.

Angoulême has become the capital of comic book *(bande dessinée)* art, hosting the prestigious Festival de la Bande Dessinée (Jan/Feb). The **Cité Internationale de la Bande-Dessinée et de l'Image** has a reference collection of French print and film cartoons dating back to 1946. From here, a footbridge leads to the Musée de la Bande Dessinée, where the history, techniques and aesthetics of the art form are explained.

Cité Internationale de la Bande-Dessinée et de l'Image
121 rue de Bordeaux. **Tel** 05 45 38 65 65. **Open** Tue–Sun (w/e pms only). **Closed** public hols. Cinema: **citebd.org**

㉕ Aubeterre-sur-Dronne

Charente. 420. 8 pl du Champ de Foine (05 45 98 57 18). Sun. **sudcharentetourisme.fr**

The chief ornament of this pretty white village is the staggering monolithic **Eglise St-Jean**. Dug out of the white chalky cliff that gave the village its name (Alba Terra – White Earth), some parts of it date back to the 6th century. Between the Revolution and 1860, it served as the village's cemetery. It contains an early Christian baptismal font and an octagonal reliquary.

The Romanesque Eglise St-Jacques is also of note for its fine sculpted façade.

Detail from the Romanesque façade of Cathédrale St-Pierre in Angoulême

㉖ Street-by-Street: Bordeaux

Built on a curve of the River Garonne, Bordeaux has been a major port since pre-Roman times and for centuries a crossroads of European trade. Today Bordeaux shows little visible evidence of the Romans, Franks, English or the Wars of Religion that have marked its past. This forward-looking town, the seventh largest in France and a UNESCO World Heritage site, is an industrial and maritime sprawl surrounding a noble 18th-century centre.

Along the waterfront of this wealthy wine metropolis is a long sweep of elegant Classical façades, first built to mask the medieval slums behind. Adding to the magnificence are the Esplanade des Quinconces, the Grand Théâtre and the place de la Bourse.

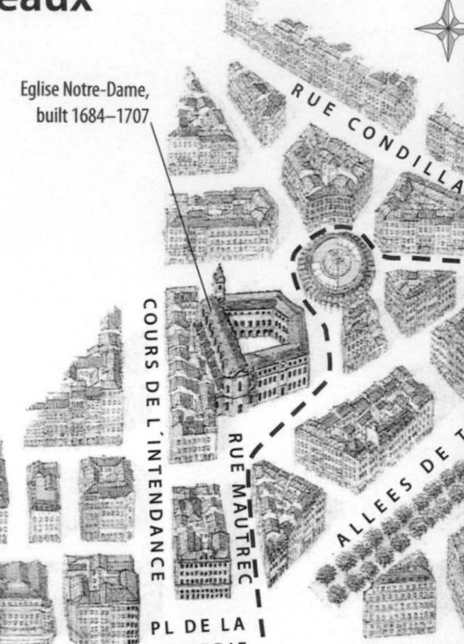

Eglise Notre-Dame, built 1684–1707

★ Grand Théâtre
Built in 1773–80, the theatre is a masterpiece of the Classical style, crowned by nine statues of the muses.

Key

▬ Suggested route

0 metres 100
0 yards 100

The *quais*, lined with graceful façades, make a beautiful walk along the Garonne.

★ Place de la Bourse
This elegant and harmonious square is flanked by two majestic 18th-century buildings, Palais de la Bourse and Hôtel des Douanes. In front of them, next to the river, is the Miroir d'Eau water feature.

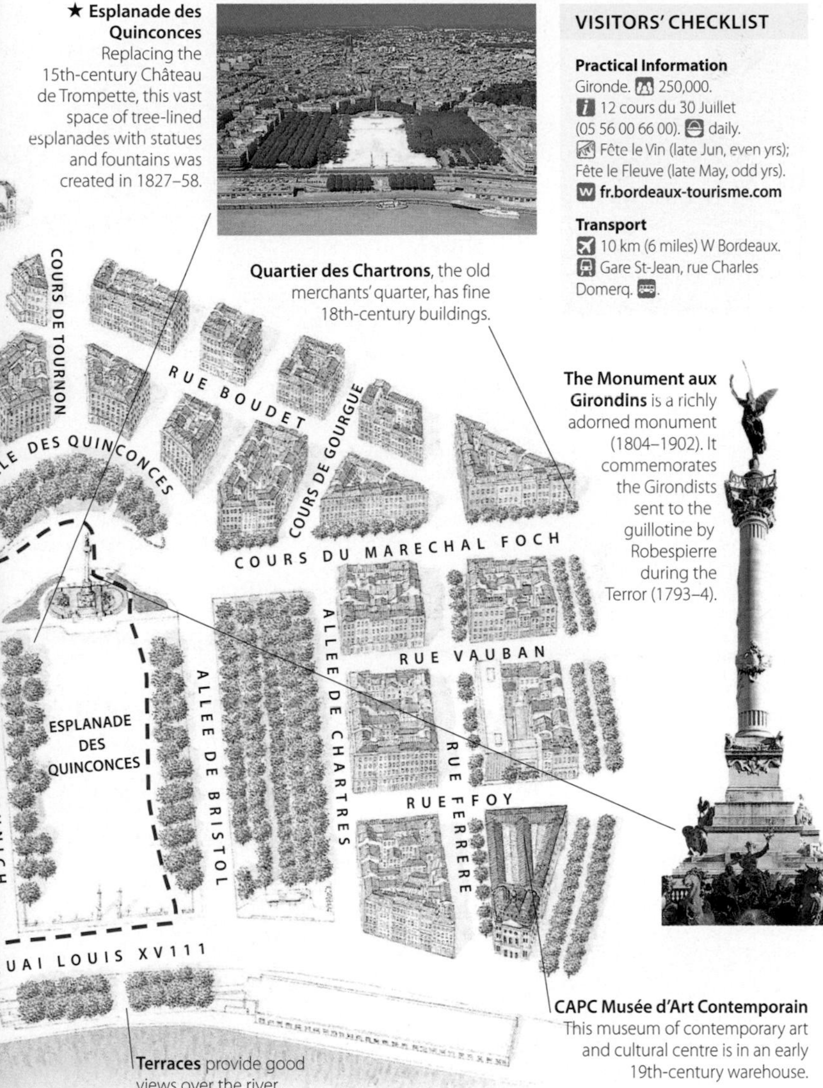

★ Esplanade des Quinconces
Replacing the 15th-century Château de Trompette, this vast space of tree-lined esplanades with statues and fountains was created in 1827–58.
Quartier des Chartrons, the old merchants' quarter, has fine 18th-century buildings.
The Monument aux Girondins is a richly adorned monument (1804–1902). It commemorates the Girondists sent to the guillotine by Robespierre during the Terror (1793–4).
CAPC Musée d'Art Contemporain
This museum of contemporary art and cultural centre is in an early 19th-century warehouse.
Terraces provide good views over the river.
COURS DE TOURNON
RUE BOUDET
COURS DE GOURGUE
CLE DES QUINCONCES
COURS DU MARECHAL FOCH
ALLEE DE CHARTRES
RUE VAUBAN
ESPLANADE DES QUINCONCES
ALLEE DE BRISTOL
RUE FERRERE
RUE FOY
QUAI LOUIS XV111

VISITORS' CHECKLIST

Practical Information
Gironde. 250,000.
12 cours du 30 Juillet (05 56 00 66 00). daily.
Fête le Vin (late Jun, even yrs); Fête le Fleuve (late May, odd yrs).
fr.bordeaux-tourisme.com

Transport
10 km (6 miles) W Bordeaux.
Gare St-Jean, rue Charles Domerq.

Transporting wine barrels in 19th-century Aquitaine

The Bordeaux Wine Trade

After Marseille, Bordeaux is the oldest trading port in France. From Roman times the export of wine was the basis for a modest prosperity, but under English rule (1154–1453, *see pp56–9*), the merchants began making immense fortunes from their monopoly of wine sales to England. After the discovery of the New World, Bordeaux took advantage of its Atlantic position to diversify and extend its wine market. Today the Bordeaux region produces over 60 million cases of wine per year.

Grand Theâtre de Bordeaux

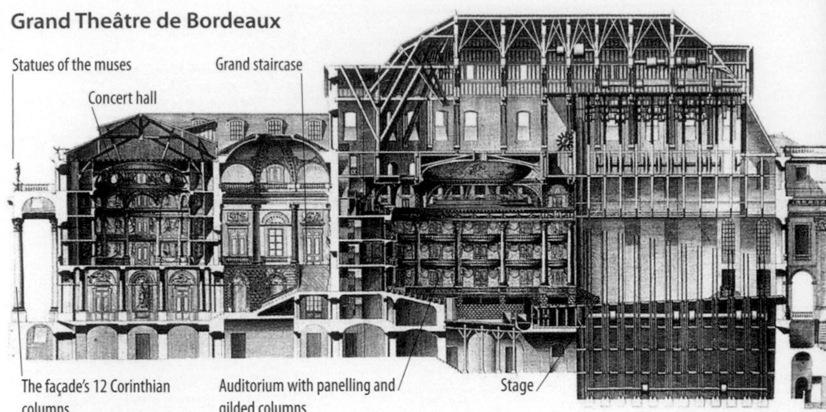

Exploring Bordeaux

Much of central Bordeaux is grand streets and 18th-century mansions. A triangle made by cours Clemenceau, cours de l'Intendance and allées de Tourny has chic boutiques and cafés. Cathédrale St-André is another focal point, with good museums nearby. Both the *quais* and the Chartrons district around the Jardin Public are worth exploring.

Grand Théâtre

Pl de la Comédie. **Tel** 05 56 00 85 95. **Open** by appointment only.

Built by architect Victor Louis, the 18th-century Grand Théâtre is one of the finest Classical edifices of its type in France. The auditorium is renowned for its acoustics. The grand main staircase was later imitated by Garnier for the Paris Opéra *(see p101)*.

Cité du Vin

quai de Bacalan. **Tel** 05 56 16 20 20. **Open** daily. **Closed** Mon in winter, 1 Jan & 25 Dec. **W laciteduvin.com**

The City of Wine Museum offers the opportunity to discover the world of wine-making from its origins to the present day, and includes a tasting.

Basilique St-Michel

Pl Canteloup et Meynard. **Open** daily.

It took 200 years to build the Basilique St-Michel, begun in 1350. This triple-naved edifice has a remarkable statue of St Ursula. Its freestanding belfry, built in 1472–92, is the tallest in southern France (114 m/374 ft).

Musée des Beaux-Arts

20 cours d'Albret. **Tel** 05 56 10 20 56. **Open** Wed–Mon. **Closed** public hols. **W musba-bordeaux.fr**

Housed in two wings of the Hôtel de Ville, the excellent collection of paintings here ranges from the Renaissance to the present. Masterpieces include works by Titian, Veronese, Rubens, Delacroix, Corot, Renoir, Matisse and Boudin.

Musée des Arts Décoratifs

39 rue Bouffard. **Tel** 05 56 10 14 00. **Open** Wed–Mon. **Closed** public hols.

If you're interested in elegant furnishings and fine porcelain, stop off at this exceptional collection, housed in the suitably refined 18th-century Hôtel de Lalande.

Musée d'Aquitaine

20 cours Pasteur. **Tel** 05 56 01 51 00. **Open** Tue–Sun. **Closed** public hols. **W musee-aquitaine-bordeaux.fr**

This important museum traces life in the region from prehistoric times to the present, through artifacts, furniture and viticulture tools. Among its exhibits are the Tayac treasure from the 2nd century BC, and the Garonne treasure, a hoard of Roman coins.

The 15th-century Porte Cailhou, once the main gate to the city of Bordeaux

Cathédrale St-André

Pl Pey Berland. **Tel** 05 56 52 68 10.

The nave of this gigantic church was begun in the 11th century and modified 200 years later. The Gothic choir and transepts were added in the 14th and 15th centuries. The excellent medieval sculptures on the Porte Royale include scenes from the Last Judgement.

CAPC Musée d'Art Contemporain

Entrepôt Lainé, 7 rue Ferrère. **Tel** 05 56 00 81 50. **Open** Tue–Sun. **Closed** pub hols. **W capc-bordeaux.fr**

This converted 19th-century warehouse merits a visit, whatever you make of its temporary exhibitions and permanent collection of contemporary art.

27 Saint-Emilion

Gironde. 2,000. pl des Créneaux (05 57 55 28 28). Sun. **W saint-emilion-tourisme.com**

This charming village in the middle of the red wine district to which it gives its name, dates back to an 8th-century hermit, Emilion, who dug out a cave for himself in the rock. A monastery followed, and by the Middle Ages Saint-Emilion had become a small town. Medieval houses still line the narrow streets, and parts of the 12th-century

For hotels and restaurants in this region see pp565–6 and pp594–6

ramparts remain. The interior of the church dug out of the chalky cliff by followers of St Emilion after his death is somewhat ruined by concrete columns put up to prevent its collapse.

Famous châteaux in the district include the elegant **Figeac**, **Cheval Blanc** and **Ausone**, all of them Saint-Emilion premiers grands crus classés.

Vineyard close to Margaux in the Médoc region west of Bordeaux

28 Pauillac

Gironde. 5,000.
La Verrerie (05 56 59 03 08).
Sat. **pauillac-medoc.com**

One of the most famous areas in the Médoc wine region *(see pp402–3)* is the commune of Pauillac. Three of its châteaux are Médoc premiers grands crus classés. The **Château Mouton Rothschild** uses leading artists to create its wine labels and has a small museum of paintings on wine themes from all over the world. The **Château Lafite Rothschild** is of medieval origin and the **Château Latour** is recognizable by its distinctive stone turret. They can be visited by appointment (contact the tourist office well in advance of your visit).

The town of Pauillac is situated on the west bank of the Gironde. In the 19th century it was the bustling arrival point for transatlantic steamships, but now the sleepy port is mostly used by pleasure boats. There are picturesque river views from the *quais* and plenty of cafés serving the local wine.

Bordeaux Wine Châteaux

The château is at the heart of the quality system in Bordeaux, the world's largest fine wine region. A château includes a vineyard and a building which can range from the most basic to the grandest, most historic as well as modern. But the château is also the symbol of a tradition and the philosophy that a wine's quality and character spring from the soil. Some châteaux welcome visitors for wine tasting as well as buying. Every major wine town has a Maison du Vin, which can provide information on visits to a château.

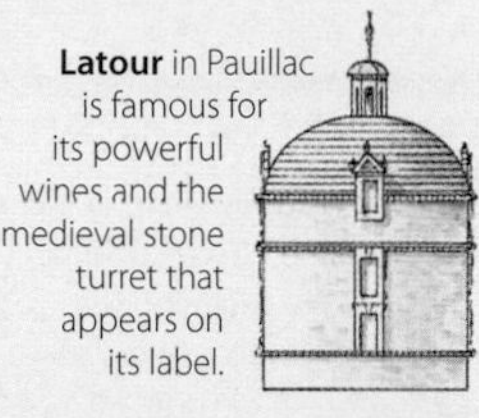

Latour in Pauillac is famous for its powerful wines and the medieval stone turret that appears on its label.

Cheval Blanc, a great château in the St-Emilion area, boasts a rich, spicy premier grand cru.

Margaux, built in 1802, produces a classic Margaux premier cru of the same elegant proportions as its Palladian façade.

Palmer, dating from 1856, is Neo-Renaissance in style and produces a very fine Margaux troisième cru.

Gruaud-Larose is a cream-coloured château with a Classical façade, distinguished by its full-bodied St-Julien deuxième cru classé.

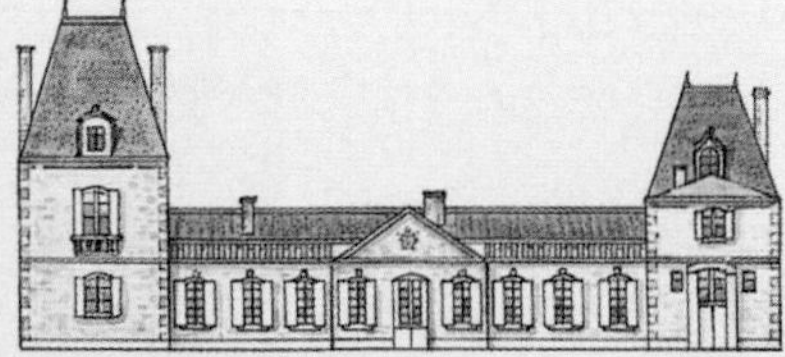

Vieux Château Certan is Belgian-owned and one of the great historic properties of Pomerol. Its wines are consistently in the first rank in the district, challenged only by Pétrus.

The immense Dune du Pilat, stretching almost 3 km (2 miles) south of the inlet to Bassin d'Arcachon

29 La Côte d'Argent

Gironde, Landes. ✈ Bordeaux, Biarritz. 🚉 Soulac-sur-Mer, Arcachon, Labenne, Dax. 🚌 Lacanau, Arcachon, Mimizan. ℹ Lacanau (05 56 03 21 01), Mimizan-Plage (05 58 09 11 20), Capbreton (05 58 72 12 11).

The long stretch of coast between Pointe de Grave on the Gironde estuary and Bayonne *(see p456)* is called La Côte d'Argent – the Silver Coast. It is virtually one vast beach of shifting sand dunes. Tree-planting has now slowed down their progress.

The coast is dotted with seaside resorts renowned for surfing, such as **Soulac-sur-Mer** in the north, followed by the big **Lacanau-Océan** and **Mimizan-Plage**. Down in the south is **Hossegor** with its salty lake, and **Capbreton**. Modern holiday resorts have been integrated with the old.

Inland are lakes popular for fishing and boating. They are connected to each other and the ocean by lively water currents, such as the **Courant d'Huchet** from Etang de Léon. Boat trips are available.

30 Bassin d'Arcachon

Gironde. 👥 12,000. ⛴ to Cap Ferret. 🚉 🚌 ℹ espl Georges Pompidou (05 57 52 97 97). 🛒 daily. **W arcachon.com**

In the middle of the Côte d'Argent the straight coastline suddenly forms a lagoon. Famous for its natural beauty, fine beaches and oysters, the Bassin d'Arcachon is a protected area, perfect for holidaymakers, sailing enthusiasts and oyster-eaters.

The basin is dotted with smaller amorphous resorts, beaches and fishing/oyster villages, all worth exploring.

Cap Ferret, the northern headland that protects the basin from stiff Atlantic winds, is a preserve of the wealthy, whose luxurious villas stand among the pines. Look for the small road under the trees from Lège, which leads to the wild, magnificent beach of Grand-Crohot.

Between Cap Ferret and Arcachon, near Gujan-Mestras, the **Parc Ornithologique du Teich** provides care and shelter for damaged birds and endangered species. For the birdwatcher, there are two fascinating walks, each carefully marked: an introductory one, and another of greater length. Both provide concealed observation points from which people can watch the wildfowl without disturbing them.

Arcachon was created as a seaside resort in 1845. Its popularity grew and in the late 19th and early 20th centuries the elegant villas in Ville d'Hiver were built. The livelier Ville d'Eté, facing the lagoon, has a casino and sports facilities.

The immense **Dune du Pilat** is the largest sand dune in Europe. It is nearly 3 km (2 miles) long, 104 m (340 ft) high and 500 m (1,625 ft) wide. Aside from the view, the dune is a great vantage point in autumn for viewing flocks of migratory birds, as they pass overhead on their way to the sanctuary at Le Teich.

Parc Ornithologique du Teich
Le Teich, rue du Port. **Tel** 05 56 22 80 93. **Open** daily.
W reserve-ornithologique-du-teich.com

Parc Ornithologique du Teich, a bird sanctuary in Bassin d'Arcachon

Landes Forest

The vast, totally artificial 19th-century forest of Les Landes was an ambitious project to make use of an area of sand and marshes. Pines and grasses were planted to anchor the coastal dunes, and inland dunes were stabilized with a mixture of pines, reeds and broom. In 1855 the land was drained – it is now covered with pine groves and undergrowth, preserving a delicate ecological balance.

Pine trees in the Landes forest

㉛ Les Landes

Gironde, Landes. Bordeaux, Biarritz. Morcenx, Dax, Mont-de-Marsan. Mont-de-Marsan. Mont-de-Marsan (05 58 05 87 37).

Almost entirely covered by an immense pine forest, the Landes area extends over the two *départements* of Gironde and Landes. The soil here is uniformly sandy. Until the mid-19th century the whole region became a swamp in winter, because of a layer of tufa (porous rock) just under the surface which retained water from the brackish lakes. Any settlement or agriculture close to the sea was impossible due to the constantly shifting dunes. Furthermore, the mouth of the Adour river kept moving from Capbreton to Vieux-Boucau and back, a distance of 32 km (20 miles).

The Adour was fixed near Bayonne by a canal in the 16th century. This was the start of the slow conquest of the Landes. The planting of pine trees ultimately wiped out the migrant shepherds and their flocks. Today the inner Landes is still very underpopulated, but wealthy from its pinewood and pine derivatives. The coastal strip also has a large influx of holidaymakers.

In 1970, part of the forest was made into a nature park. At **Marquèze**, in the **Ecomusée Marquèze**, a typical 19th-century *airial* (clearing) has been restored. It commemorates the vanished world of Les Landes before the draining of the marshes, when shepherds still used stilts to get about. There are traditional *auberges landaises* (wooden houses with sloping roofs), as well as henhouses built on stilts because of foxes.

Ecomusée Marquèze
Route de la Gare, 40630 Sabres.
Tel 05 58 08 31 31. **Open** Apr–Oct daily. **marqueze.fr**

㉜ Mont-de-Marsan

Landes. 33,000.
1 pl Charles de Gaulle (05 58 05 87 37). Tue & Sat.
visitmontdemarsan.fr

A bullfighting mecca, Mont-de-Marsan attracts all the great bullfighters of France and Spain in summer. A less-bloodthirsty local variant of the sport is the *course landaise*, in which the object is to vault over the horns and back of a charging bull.

The administrative capital of the Landes is also known for its hippodrome, poultry farming and *foie gras* production.

Sculpture from the first half of the 20th century can be seen at **Musée Despiau-Wlérick**.

㉝ Dax

Landes. 22,000. 11 cours Foch (05 58 56 86 86). Tue–Sun am.
dax-tourisme.com

The thermal spa of Dax is second only to Aix-les-Bains *(see p394)* in importance. Its hot springs, with a constant temperature of 64° C (147° F) and tonic mud from the Adour, have been soothing aches and pains since the time of Emperor Augustus.

Apart from the 13th-century doorway of the otherwise 17th-century **Cathédrale Notre-Dame**, there isn't much of architectural interest in this peaceful town. But the promenade along the River Adour is charming and the bullring is world renowned.

La Force (1937) by Raoul Lamourdedieu, in the bullfighting capital of Mont-de-Marsan

PERIGORD, QUERCY AND GASCONY

Dordogne · Lot · Haute-Garonne · Lot-et-Garonne
Gers · Tarn-et-Garonne · Tarn

Southwest France is an archaeologist's heaven, for the region has been continuously inhabited by mankind for tens of thousands of years, longer than any other area in Europe. The landscape of these historic regions seems to have an ancient familiarity, derived from centuries of people living in harmony with the land.

The great cave sites around Les Eyzies and Lascaux harbour the earliest evidence we possess of primitive art. The castles, bastides *(see p449)* and churches that grace the countryside from Périgueux to the Pyrenees, from the Bay of Biscay to Toulouse and beyond to the Mediterranean, belong to a far more recent past. From the coming of Christianity until the late 18th century, this fine region was the battlefield for a string of conflicts. The English fought and lost the Hundred Years' War *(see pp58–9)* for Aquitaine (1345–1453); this was followed by intermittent Wars of Religion, in which Catholics fought Huguenots (French Protestants) in a series of massacres and guerrilla wars.

Today, nothing is left of these old struggles but crumbling ramparts, keeps and bastides, which are part of the region's cultural and artistic heritage, attracting thousands of visitors every year. Yet it is as well to remember that all the great sights here, from the abbey church at Moissac, whose 12th-century portal is a masterpiece of Romanesque art, to the awesome clifftop site of Rocamadour, have suffered at one time or another from the attacks of marauding soldiers.

Since the mid-20th century, the rural southwest has gone through a radical demographic shift. There has been a continual decline in the old peasant way of life with fewer and fewer people cultivating the land. A steady migration by the young to the cities has been matched by an influx of downsizers and commuters looking for a more relaxed way of life.

Périgord geese, reared for the area's celebrated *foie gras*

◀ Limestone cliffs tower over the beautiful countryside of the Gorges de l'Aveyron

Exploring Périgord, Quercy and Gascony

The towns of Périgueux, Cahors and Albi make good bases for exploring the region, and are quieter alternatives to Toulouse – the only major urban centre. Elsewhere, the green hills and sleepy villages of Gascony and Périgord (also known as the Dordogne) are mainly for those who appreciate the slow pace of life in the countryside. But if you want more than peace and good food, this region offers some of France's finest medieval architecture, and Europe's most important prehistoric caves, notably Lascaux.

A narrow street in the medieval hilltop town of Cordes sur Ciel

Key

- Motorway
- Major road
- Secondary road
- Minor road
- Scenic route
- Main railway
- Minor railway
- Regional border

Getting Around

The west–southeast Autoroute des Deux Mers (A62–A61) is the main road through the region, linking Bordeaux, the Atlantic coast and the Mediterranean. The A20 from Montauban to Limoges provides access to the Dordogne and Quercy. Buses and mainline railways, including a Bordeaux–Marseille TGV, pass along the same two axes. They meet at Toulouse, where an international airport has daily flights to and from most European destinations.

For keys to symbols *see back flap*

Sights at a Glance

1. St-Jean-de-Côle
2. Hautefort
3. Brantôme
4. Bourdeilles
5. Périgueux
6. St-Amand-de-Coly
7. Lascaux IV
8. Bergerac
9. Les Eyzies
10. Dordogne Valley
11. *Sarlat pp436–7*
12. Domme
13. *Rocamadour pp440–41*
14. Gouffre de Padirac
15. Autoire
16. Cahors
17. Agen
18. Larressingle
19. Condom
20. Auch
21. Auvillar
22. *Moissac pp446–7*
23. Montauban
24. Gorges de l'Aveyron
25. Cordes-sur-Ciel
26. Albi
27. Castres
28. *Toulouse pp450–51*

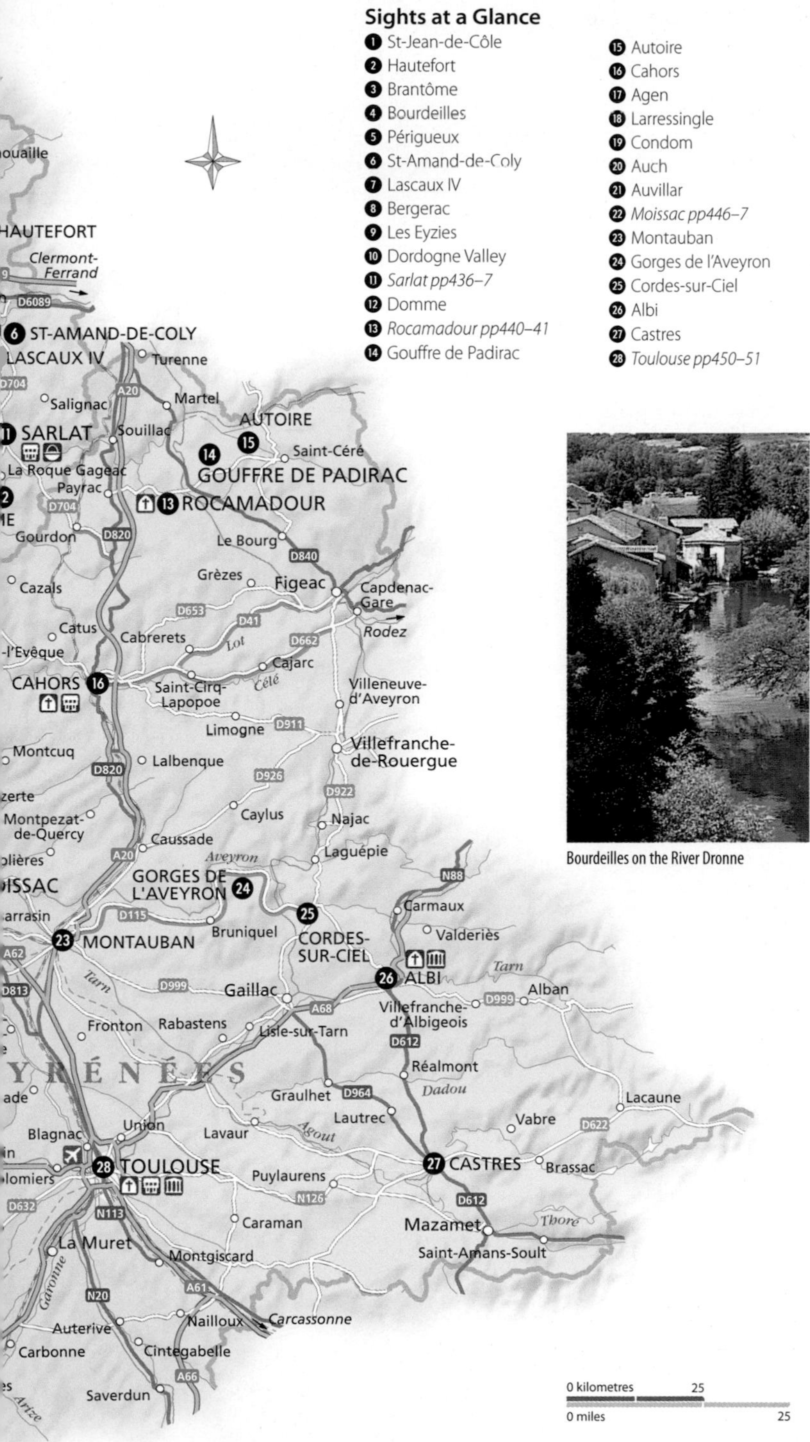

Bourdeilles on the River Dronne

❶ St-Jean-de-Côle

Dordogne. 360. 19 rue du Château (05 53 62 14 15). Floralies (Apr–May). **perigordgourmand.com**

St-Jean-de-Côle's medieval, humpbacked bridge gives the best view of this lovely Dordogne village set in hilly countryside. Stone and half-timbered houses, roofed with the distinctive red-brown tiles of the region, cram the narrow streets around the main square. Here stand a covered marketplace, château and 12th-century church.

The cupola of the church used to be the largest in the region – too large, it seems, for it fell down twice in the 18th and 19th centuries. The second time it happened, the builders gave up, and there has been a plank ceiling ever since.

Main square in the lovely village of St-Jean-de-Côle

❷ Hautefort

Dordogne. **Tel** 05 53 50 51 23. Le Bourg: **Open** Apr–Sep: daily (Mar & early Nov: Sat, Sun & hols, pm only; Oct: daily, pm only). **Closed** mid-Nov–Feb. obligatory. limited. **chateau-hautefort.com**

Hautefort clings to the sides of a steep hill topped by a massive 17th-century château, one of the finest in southwest France. Partially fortified and built as a pleasure palace in honour of King Louis XIII's secret love, the Marquis de Hautefort's sister Marie, the castle sits among French gardens on terraces with superb views of the rolling countryside of northeast Périgord. In the village, the hospice, of a similar date, has a museum of early medical implements.

Brantôme Abbey

❸ Brantôme

Dordogne. 2,200. Notre Dame church (05 53 05 80 63). Fri. **perigord-dronne-belle.fr**

Surrounded by the River Dronne, Brantôme is often called the Venice of the Périgord Vert. Its medieval abbey and 11th-century belfry (reputedly the oldest in France), together with the verdant rockface behind, provide a dramatic backdrop for this picturesque town.

The poet Pierre de Bourdeille (1540–1614) was appointed abbot here in his youth. His lovers allegedly included Mary, Queen of Scots. After a crippling fall, Bourdeille retired here in 1569 to write his racy memoirs. It is possible to wander the stone staircases and cloisters, and through the main courtyard to the troglodyte dwellings in the cliff behind. In one are two scenes (the Last Judgment and the Crucifixion) that were cut into the stone between the 16th and 17th centuries.

Just 12 km (7 miles) northeast lies the Renaissance **Château de Puyguilhem** and **Grotte de Villars**. As well as spectacular rock formations, these caves house some marvellous 19,000-year-old cave paintings.

Château de Puyguilhem
Villars. **Tel** 05 53 54 82 18. **Open** Apr–Sep: daily; Oct–Mar: Wed–Sun. **Closed** 1 Jan, 1 May, 1 &11 Nov, 25 Dec. **chateau-puyguilhem.fr**

Grotte de Villars
Villars. **Tel** 05 53 54 82 36. **Open** Apr–mid-Nov: daily. obligatory. **grotte-villars.com**

❹ Bourdeilles

Dordogne. 800. 63 place Tilleuls (05 53 05 62 43). **perigord-dronne-belle.fr**

This town may be small, but it has much to offer – a Gothic bridge with cutwater piers, a mill and a medieval **château**. The 16th-century additions to the castle were designed in a hurry by the châtelaine Jacquette de Montbron, when expecting a visit from Queen Catherine de' Medici. After the royal visit was called off, so were the building works. The highlight is the gilded salon, decorated in the 1560s by Ambroise le Noble, of the Fontainebleau School.

Château de Bourdeilles
Tel 05 53 03 73 36. **Open** Feb–Mar & Nov–mid-Dec: Tue–Sun; Apr–Oct: daily. **Closed** Jan. **semitour.com**

The impressive Château de Bourdeilles towering above the town

Périgueux's Cathédrale St-Front, restored in the 19th century

❺ Périgueux

Dordogne. 32,000.
26 pl Francheville (05 53 53 10 63).
daily. tourisme-perigueux.fr

The ancient and truly gastronomic city of Périgueux, like its neighbours Bergerac and Riberac, should be visited on market day, when stalls in the lively squares in the medieval part of town offer the pick of local specialities, including truffles (Nov–Mar), *charcuterie* and the succulent pies called *pâtés de Périgueux*.

Périgueux, now the busy regional capital, has long been the crossroads of Périgord. The earliest part remaining today is the quarter known as **La Cité**, once the important Gallo-Roman settlement of Vesunna. From Roman times to the Middle Ages, this was the focus of Périgueux. Most of the fabric of Vesunna was pulled down in the 3rd century, but some vestiges of a temple, a huge arena and a sumptuous villa remain. The **Eglise St-Etienne** nearby dates to the 12th century. La Domus de Vesonne, a Gallo-Roman museum, is also in La Cité.

Walking up the hill to the city's dazzling white cathedral you pass through bustling streets and squares, each with its market activity. This is the medieval quarter of **Le Puy St-Front**, which began to flourish as pilgrims on their way to Santiago de Compostela *(see pp404–5)* visited the cathedral. As they brought prestige and wealth to the quarter, it gradually eclipsed La Cité.

At the top stands the imposing **Cathédrale St-Front**, the largest in southwestern France. The Romanesque construction was heavily restored in the 19th century, when architect Paul Abadie added the fancy domes and cones.

Elaborate 19th-century stained glass in Cathédrale St-Front

He later used St-Front as inspiration for the Sacré-Coeur in Paris *(see p138)*.

Other gems of medieval and Renaissance architecture include **Maison Estignard**, at No. 3 rue Limogeanne, with its unusual corkscrew staircase, and houses along rue Aubergerie and rue de la Constitution.

Also in the cathedral quarter is the **Musée d'Art et d'Archéologie du Périgord**, one of the most comprehensive prehistory museums in France, with remnants of burials dating back 70,000 years. Beautiful Roman glass, mosaics, earthenware and other artifacts from Vesunna are in the Gallo-Roman museum.

Musée d'Art et d'Archéologie du Périgord
22 cours Tourny. **Tel** 05 53 06 40 70.
Open Wed–Mon. **Closed** public hols.
perigueux-maap.fr

❻ St-Amand-de-Coly

Dordogne. **Tel** Maison du Patrimoine (09 64 01 46 39, summer only); La Mairie (05 53 51 47 85). **Open** daily.
Mon, Wed, Fri (call 05 53 50 74 32).
saint-amand-de-coly.org

This abbey church is an outstanding example of fortress architecture, built in the 12th to 13th centuries by Augustinian monks to protect their monastery. There are two lines of defence: a high stone rampart and, behind it, the arched tower of the church itself. The tower looks more like a castle keep, and was once pierced by arrow slits.

Inside, the church is beautifully simple, with pure lines, a flat ribbed vault, 12th-century cupola, a soaring nave and a stone floor sloping up to the altar. Yet even this interior was arranged for defence, with a gallery from which enemies within the building could be attacked.

St-Amand was damaged during the Hundred Years' War. In 1575, it survived a siege by Huguenot cavalry and a six-day bombardment by cannon. Religious life here ended after the Revolution.

⓫ Sarlat

Sarlat-la-Canéda possesses the highest concentration of medieval, Renaissance and 17th-century façades of any town in France. Its prosperity was a reflection of the privileged status it was granted in return for loyalty to the French crown during the Hundred Years' War. Behind the nondescript rue de la République are narrow lanes and archways, and ancient, ochre-coloured stone town houses rich in ornamental detail. Protected by law since 1962, Sarlat's buildings now form an open-air museum. The town is also famous for having one of the best markets in France.

Place de la Liberté
The Renaissance heart of Sarlat is now lined with luxury shops and cafés.

Rue des Consuls contains 15th-, 16th- and 17th-century mansions, built for the town's middle-class merchants, magistrates and church officials.

Rue Jean-Jacques Rousseau was the main street until rue de la République (known as "La Traverse") was built in the 19th century.

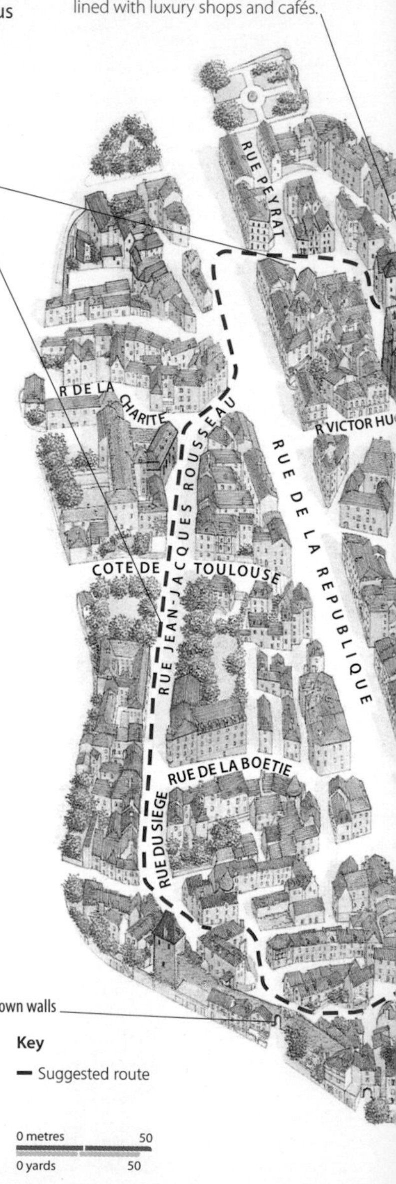

Town walls

Key

— Suggested route

0 metres 50
0 yards 50

Walnuts, a key Périgord crop

Sarlat Market

Every Wednesday, the great Sarlat food market is held in place de la Liberté; every Thursday organic markets meet at 5pm, and every Saturday there is a full-scale fair that attracts locals from all around. There is a daily indoor market at Eglise Sainte-Marie. Sarlat lies at the heart of the nation's *foie gras* and walnut trades. These typical Périgord products absorb much of the town's attention and supply a good proportion of its revenue, as they did during Sarlat's heyday in the 14th and 15th centuries. Other local specialities are black truffles, dug up in the woods in January, and wild mushrooms. Seek out the cheeses of every shape, age and hue, and the huge range of pork delicacies: potted, fresh, smoked, dried, salted, fried, baked or boiled.

Bulbs of pink garlic

VISITORS' CHECKLIST

Practical Information
Dordogne. 10,000. 3 rue Tourny (05 53 31 45 45). Wed & Sat. Theatre (Jul–Aug); Film (Nov). **sarlat-tourisme.com**

Transport
av de la Gare.

Rue de la Salamandre
This lane was named after the salamander emblem of François I. It is seen on many of the town's 16th-century houses.

Eglise Sainte-Marie, built in1365, now houses an indoor market offering local products. A panoramic lift has been built up to the top of the church's steeple, providing a great view of Sarlat from above.

Lanterne des Morts
(Lantern of the Dead) The conical tower in the cemetery was built to commemorate the sermons of St Bernard in Sarlat in August 1147.

Cathédrale St-Sacerdos
Built largely in the 16th and 17th centuries, the cathedral is remarkable for its magnificent 18th-century organ.

The Chapelle des Pénitents Bleus, built in pure Romanesque style, is the last vestige of the 12th-century abbey.

The former Bishop's Palace, with remains of a 16th-century loggia and a Renaissance interior, is now a tourist office, which puts on excellent summer exhibitions.

Cour des Fontaines
A pure spring here attracted the monks who founded Sarlat's first abbey in the 9th century.

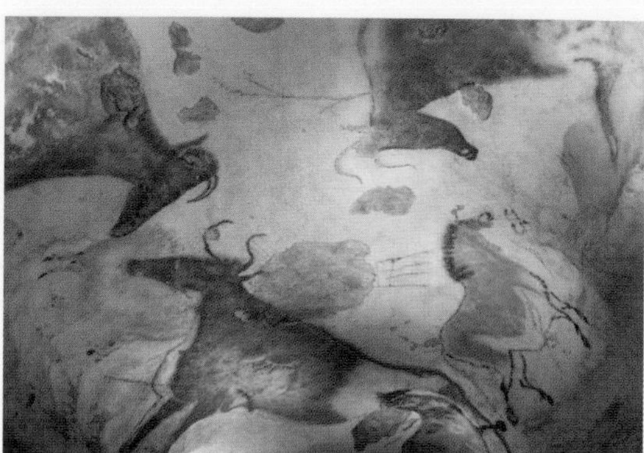
Replica of bulls and horses cave paintings at the Lascaux Centre International de l'Art Pariétal

7 Lascaux IV

Lascaux Centre International de l'Art Pariétal, Dordogne. **Tel** 05 53 50 99 10. **Open** 9am–7pm daily. **Closed** 1 Jan, 25 Dec.
W **lascaux.fr**

Lascaux is the most famous of the prehistoric sites located on the River Vézère *(see pp406–7)*. Four boys came across the caves and their astonishing Palaeolithic paintings in 1940, and the importance of their discovery was swiftly recognized.

Lascaux has been closed to the public since 1963 because of deterioration, but the Centre International de l'Art Pariétal provides state-of the art replicas of the vivid cave paintings of bulls, high-antlered elk, bison and horses. It includes an interactive exhibition using digital touchscreens that retraces the history of the discovery of Lascaux and a virtual reality tour of the caves. The on-site café serves excellent regional food.

8 Bergerac

Dordogne. 29,000. **i** 97 rue Neuve d'Argenson (05 53 57 03 11). Wed & Sat; organic market: Tue. **W** **bergerac-tourisme.com**

This small port, a tobacco farming and commercial centre, spreads itself over both sides of the Dordogne. Chief attractions are its extraordinary **Musée du Tabac** (tobacco museum), and its food and wine, which are invariably excellent. Bergerac's most celebrated wine is Monbazillac, a sweet white wine, often drunk on ceremonial occasions. On show in the small, lively museum are some Native American pipes.

Musée du Tabac
Maison Peyrarède, pl du Feu.
Tel 05 53 63 04 13. **Open** Tue–Sun. **Closed** Sun ams (Oct–Mar: Sun all day), public hols.

9 Les Eyzies

Dordogne. 850. **i** 19 av de la Préhistoire (05 53 06 97 05). Mon (Apr–Oct). **W** **lascaux-dordogne.com**

Four major prehistoric sites and a group of smaller caves cluster around the unassuming village of Les Eyzies. Head first for the **Musée National de Préhistoire**, in a modern building at the foot of a 16th-century castle overlooking the village. The timelines and other exhibits are useful for putting the vast warren of prehistoric painting and sculpture into context.

The **Grotte de Font de Gaume** is the logical first stop after the museum. This cave, discovered in 1901, contains probably the finest prehistoric paintings still on public view in France.

Close by is the **Grotte des Combarelles**, with engravings of bison, reindeer, magic symbols and human figures. Further on, you reach the rock shelter of **Abri du Cap Blanc**, discovered in 1909,

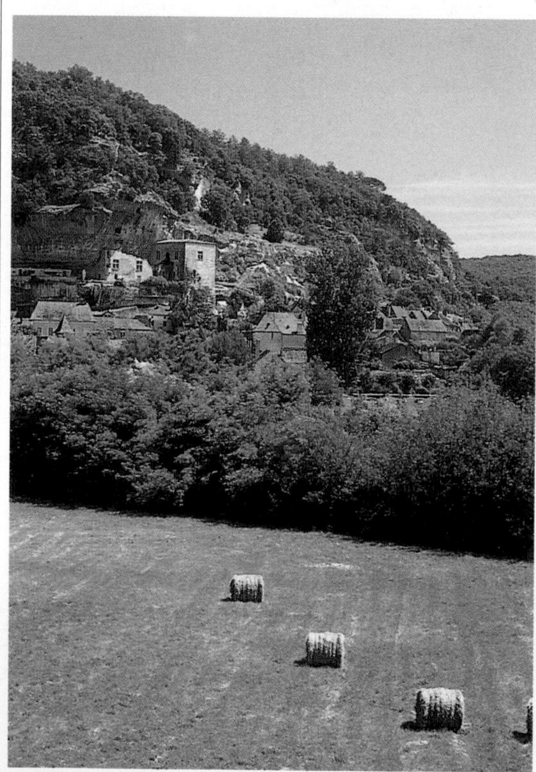
Les Eyzies, a centre for the area's concentration of prehistoric caves

For hotels and restaurants in this region see pp566–8 and pp596–8

with a rare, life-size frieze of horses and bison sculpted in the rock.

On the other side of Les Eyzies is the cave system at **Rouffignac**, a favourite place for excursions since the 15th century. There are 8 km (5 miles) of caves here, 2.5 km (1.5 miles) of which are served by electric train. The paintings include drawings of mammoths, and a frieze of two bison challenging each other to combat.

Tickets for the caves sell out fast, especially in summer, so arrive early or book ahead. Note that tickets for Combarelles must be purchased at the Grotte de Font de Gaume.

Musée National de Préhistoire

Musée National de Préhistoire
Tel 05 53 06 45 65. **Open** Jul & Aug: daily; Sep–Jun: Wed–Mon. **Closed** 1 Jan, 25 Dec.

Grotte de Font de Gaume
Tel 05 53 06 86 00. **Open** Sun–Fri by appt; book ahead. **Closed** some public hols.

Grotte des Combarelles
Tel 05 53 06 86 00. **Open** Sun–Fri (book ahead). **Closed** some public hols.

Abri du Cap Blanc
Marquay, Les Eyzies. **Tel** 05 53 06 86 00. **Open** Sun–Fri.

Grotte de Rouffignac
Tel 05 53 05 41 71. **Open** Apr–Oct: daily (tickets at 9am and 2pm).
grottederouffignac.fr

⑩ Dordogne Valley

Dordogne. Bergerac. Bergerac, Le Buisson de Cadouin. Beynac. Le Buisson de Cadouin (05 53 22 06 09).

Probably no river in France crosses so varied a landscape and such different geological formations as the Dordogne. Starting in deep granite gorges in the Massif Central, it continues through fertile lowlands, then enters the limestone Causse country around Souillac. By the time the Dordogne has wound down to the Garonne, it is almost 3 km (2 miles) wide.

Don't be put off by the valley's touristy image. It is a beautiful area for wandering. Several villages make good stopping-off points, such as Limeuil, Beynac and La Roque-Gageac, from where *gabarres* (river boats) ferry visitors (Easter–Oct).

Perched high above the river, southwest of Sarlat, is the 17th-century **Château de Marqueyssac**. Its topiary park offers panoramic views from Domme to Beynac, and of the Château de Castelnaud on the opposite riverbank.

View of Domme from the medieval gateway of Porte de la Combe

⑪ Sarlat

See pp436–7.

⑫ Domme

Dordogne. 1,000. pl de la Halle (05 53 31 71 00). Thu. **perigord-noir-valleedordogne.com**

Henry Miller wrote: "Just to glimpse the black, mysterious river at Domme from the beautiful bluff…is something to be grateful for all one's life." Domme itself is a neat bastide *(see p449)* of golden stone, with medieval gateways still standing. People come here to admire the view, which takes in the Dordogne Valley from Beynac in the west to Montfort in the east, and to wander the maze of old streets inside the walls. There is also a large cavern under the 17th-century covered market, where the inhabitants hid at perilous moments during the Hundred Years' War and the 16th-century Wars of Religion. Despite a seemingly impregnable position, 30 intrepid Huguenots managed to capture Domme by scaling the cliffs under cover of night and opening the gates.

A *cingle* (loop) of the River Dordogne, seen from the town of Domme

⓭ Rocamadour

Rocamadour became one of the most famous centres of pilgrimage following a spate of miracles heralded, it is claimed, by the bell above the Black Virgin and Child in the Chapel of Notre-Dame. This was followed by the discovery in 1166 of an ancient grave and sepulchre containing an undecayed body, said to be that of the early Christian hermit St Amadour. Although the town suffered with the decline of pilgrimages in the 17th and 18th centuries, it was heavily restored in the 19th century. Still a holy shrine, as well as a popular tourist destination, Rocamadour enjoys a phenomenal site on a rocky plateau above the Alzou Valley. The best views are to be had from the ramparts of the château, reached from the hamlet of L'Hospitalet.

General View
Rocamadour is at its most breathtaking in the sunlight of early morning: the cluster of medieval houses, towers and battlements seems to sprout from the base of the cliff.

KEY

① **The Tomb of St Amadour** once held the body of the hermit called *roc amator* (lover of rock), from whom the town took its name.

② **St Michael's Chapel** contains well-preserved 12th-century frescoes.

③ **The château** stands on the site of a fort that protected the sanctuary from the west.

④ **Ramparts**

⑤ **Cross of Jerusalem**

⑥ **The Basilica of St-Sauveur**, a late 12th-century sanctuary, backs on to the bare rock face.

⑦ **The Chapel of St John the Baptist** faces the fine Gothic portal of the Basilica of St-Sauveur.

⑧ **St Anne's Chapel** dates from the 13th century, and contains a 17th-century gilded altar screen.

⑨ **Chapel of St Blaise** (13th century)

Grand Stairway
Pilgrims would climb this broad flight of steps on their knees as they said their rosaries. The stairway leads to a square on the next level, around which the main pilgrim chapels are grouped.

VISITORS' CHECKLIST

Practical Information
Lot. 650. L'Hospitalet, Cour du Prieuré (05 65 33 22 00). Chapel of Notre-Dame: **Open** 9am–6:30pm daily (to 9pm Jun–Sep).
vallee-dordogne.com

Transport
5 km (3 miles) SW Rocamadour.

Stations of the Cross
Pilgrims encounter the Cross of Jerusalem and 14 stations marking Jesus's journey to the Cross on their way up the hillside to the château.

Rocamadour Town
Now a pedestrian precinct, the main street is lined with souvenir shops to tempt the throngs of pilgrims.

Chapel of Notre-Dame (Miracles)
St Amadour's body was found in the cliff, near the Black Virgin Chapel. A statue of the Black Virgin, the supreme object of veneration, stands on the altar.

⓮ Gouffre de Padirac

Lot. **Tel** 05 65 33 64 56. **Open** Apr–mid-Nov: daily.
gouffre-de-padirac.com

Formed by the collapse of a cave, this huge crater measures 115 ft (35 m) wide and 337 ft (103 m) deep. The underground river and stunning succession of galleries *(see pp406–7)* were discovered in 1889. The immense Salle du Grand Dôme chamber dwarfs the tallest of cathedrals. Take a jacket; the cave is 13° C (55° F).

⓯ Autoire

Lot. 360. Saint Céré (05 65 10 01 10). **vallee-dordogne.com**

This is one of the loveliest places in Quercy, the fertile area east of Périgord. There are no grand monuments or dramatic history, just an unspoiled site at the mouth of the Autoire gorge. The **Château de Limarque** on the main square, and the **Château de Busqueille** overlooking it, are both built in characteristic Quercy style, with turrets and towers. Elsewhere, elaborate dovecotes stand in fields or are attached to houses.

Outside Autoire, past a 100-ft (30-m) waterfall, a path climbs to a rock amphitheater giving panoramic views of the region.

The picturesque village of Autoire, seen from across the gorge

⓰ Cahors

Lot. 21,000. pl François Mitterrand (05 65 53 20 65). Wed & Sat am. **tourisme-cahors.fr**

The capital of the Lot *département*, Cahors is renowned for its dark, heady wine, which was produced as far back as Roman times. It is also famous for being the birthplace of the statesman Léon Gambetta (1838–82), who led France to recovery after the war with Prussia in 1870. The main street of Cahors – like many towns in France – is named after him.

Cathédrale de St-Etienne, entrenched behind the narrow streets of Cahors' Old Town, dates back to 1119. It has some fine medieval details: don't miss the lively figures of the Romanesque north door and tympanum, which depict the Ascension, or the huge cupola above the nave (said to be the

A Tour of Two Rivers

Flanked by spectacular limestone cliffs, the beautiful Lot and Célé valleys feature ancient medieval villages and castles, narrow gorges and rushing waterfalls along lazy stretches of river. An unhurried tour of both valleys, around 100 miles (160 km), is best spread over two days, to savor the gastronomic delights as well as the superb views.

From Cahors, the route follows the Lot, then meanders slowly up the peaceful and picturesque Célé Valley to reach Figeac, a handsome town full of charming shops, cafés and restaurants. The return route is via the busier Lot Valley, which has more sights, including the spectacular village of St-Cirq-Lapopie (allow time to park above or below the village and enter on foot).

① **Grotte de Pech-Merle**
This 29,000-year-old prehistoric site outside Cabrerets has huge chambers painted with mammoths, horses, bison and human figures.

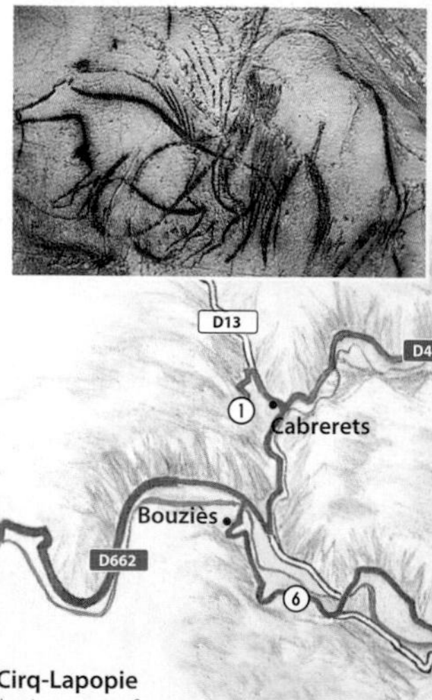

⑥ **St-Cirq-Lapopie**
Perched high above the Lot, one of France's prettiest villages has a 15th-century church and timber-framed houses built into the cliffs.

largest in France). They are covered in 14th-century frescoes depicting the stoning of St. Stephen (St-Etienne). The Renaissance cloisters are decorated with some intricate, though damaged, carvings.

Also worth seeking out in the cathedral quarter is the ornate 16th-century **Maison de Roaldès**, its north facade decorated with tree, sun, and rose of Quercy motifs. It was here that Henri of Navarre (who later became Henri IV) stayed for one night in 1580 after besieging and capturing Cahors.

The town's landmark monument is the **Pont Valentré**, a fortified bridge that spans the river. With seven pointed arches and three towers, it was built between 1308 and 1360, and has withstood many attacks since then. It is claimed that the bridge is one of the most photographed monuments in France. An alternative way to enjoy the scenery is to take a leisurely 90-minute boat trip through the lock from a wharf near the bridge (Apr–Oct).

The fortified Pont Valentré, spanning the River Lot at Cahors

Environs

Cahors makes a good base from which to explore the sights of the Lot. Visit the historic towns of Figeac – birthplace of Jean-François Champollion, who first deciphered Egyptian hieroglyphics – and the **Grotte de Pech-Merle** with its extraordinary painted walls.

Grotte de Pech-Merle
Cabrerets. **Tel** 05 65 31 27 05.
Open Apr–Oct daily.
pechmerle.com

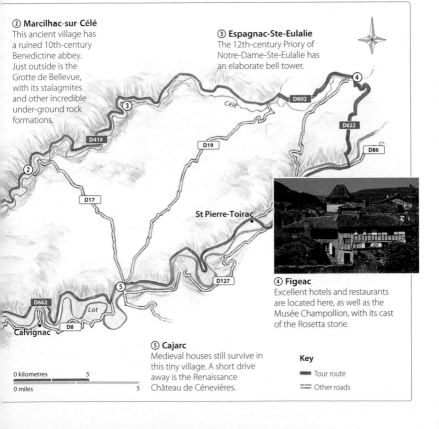

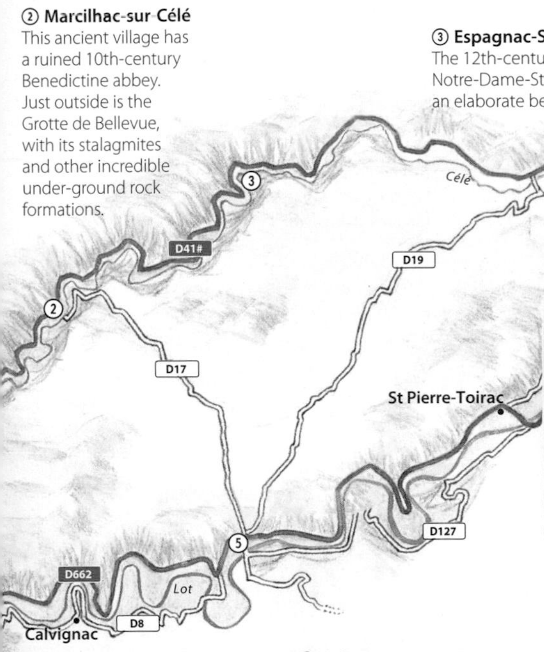

② Marcilhac-sur-Célé
This ancient village has a ruined 10th-century Benedictine abbey. Just outside is the Grotte de Bellevue, with its stalagmites and other incredible under-ground rock formations.

③ Espagnac-Ste-Eulalie
The 12th-century Priory of Notre-Dame-Ste-Eulalie has an elaborate bell tower.

④ Figeac
Excellent hotels and restaurants are located here, as well as the Musée Champollion, with its cast of the Rosetta stone.

⑤ Cajarc
Medieval houses still survive in this tiny village. A short drive away is the Renaissance Château de Cénevières.

Key
Tour route
Other roads

0 kilometres 5
0 miles 5

Orchards and vineyards outside Agen

17 Agen

Lot-et-Garonne. 35,000. 38 rue Garonne (05 53 47 36 09. Wed, Sat & Sun. **destination-agen.fr**

Vast orchards of regimented plum trees – producing the celebrated *pruneaux d'Agen* – characterize the landscape around this small provincial city. Crusaders returning from the Middle East brought the fruit to France in the 11th century, and monks in the Lot Valley nearby were the first to dry plums for prunes in commercial quantities.

Agen's **Musée Municipal des Beaux-Arts** contains paintings by Goya, including a self-portrait, Sisley's *September Morning*, Corot's landscape *L'Etang de Ville d'Avray* and works by Picabia. Undisputed jewel of the collection is the *Vénus du Mas*, a beautifully proportioned marble statue dating from the 1st century BC, discovered nearby in 1876.

Musée Municipal des Beaux-Arts
Pl du Docteur Esquirol. **Tel** 05 53 47 77 88. **Open** Wed–Mon. **Closed** 1 Jan, Easter Mon, 1 & 8 May, Ascension Thu, 1 & 11 Nov, 25 Dec.

Environs
The fortified village of Moirax, 8 km (5 miles) south of Agen, has a beautiful 12th-century Romanesque church. Two of the sculpted capitals depict biblical accounts of Daniel in the lions' den, and Original Sin.

The bastide town (see p449) of Villeneuve-sur-Lot, 34 km (21 miles) south of Agen stands astride the River Lot. It has a tall 14th-century tower that once formed a defensive gateway. The red-brick Romano-Byzantine church of Ste-Catherine was built in 1909 but contains restored 15th-century stained-glass windows. Just to the east of Villeneuve is the pretty medieval hilltop village of Penne D'Agenais.

18 Larressingle

Gers. 220. to Condom. Larressingle (05 62 68 22 49). **tourisme-condom.com**

With its ramparts, ruined donjon (defence tower) and fortress gate, Larressingle is a tiny fortified village in the middle of the Gascon countryside. It dates from the 13th century, and is one of the last remaining Gascon villages with its walls still intact. The state of preservation is unique, and gives an idea of what life must have been like for the small, embattled local communities who had to live for decades under conditions of perpetual warfare.

19 Condom

Gers. 7,000. 5 pl St-Pierre (05 62 28 00 80). Wed, Sat am & Sun am. **tourisme-condom.com**

Long a centre for the Armagnac trade, Condom is a market town built around the late-Gothic **Cathédrale St-Pierre**. In 1569 during the Wars of Religion, the Huguenot (French Protestant) army threatened to demolish the cathedral, but Condom's citizens averted this by paying a huge ransom.

The river Baïse skirts the town centre. Notable among Condom's fine 17th- to 18th-century mansions is the **Hôtel de Cugnac** on rue Jean-Jaurès, with its ancient *chai* (wine and spirit storehouse) and distillery. On the other side of the town centre, the **Musée de l'Armagnac** is the place to find out, finally, what the difference between the brandy of Armagnac and Cognac really is.

Musée de l'Armagnac
2 rue Jules Ferry. **Tel** 05 62 28 47 17. **Open** Apr–Oct: Wed–Mon; Nov–Mar: Wed–Sun pms. **Closed** Jan, public hols.

Armagnac

Armagnac is one of the world's most expensive brandies. It is also one of the leading products of southwest France: approximately 6.5 million bottles are produced annually, 45 per cent of which are exported to 132 countries. The vineyards of Armagnac roughly straddle the border between the Gers and the Lot-et-Garonne regions and the Landes. Similar in style to Cognac, its more famous neighbour, Armagnac's single distillation leaves more individual flavours in the spirit. The majority of small, independent producers offer direct sale to the public: look out for the battered, often half-hidden farm signs advertising *Vente Directe*.

A Tenarèze Armagnac

D'Artagnan

Gascons call their domain the "Pays d'Artagnan", after Alexandre Dumas' rollicking hero from *The Three Musketeers* (1844). The character of d'Artagnan was based on Charles de Batz, a typical Gascon, whose chivalry, passion and impetuousness made him ideal as a musketeer, or royal bodyguard. De Batz's life was as fast and furious as that of the fictional hero, and he performed a feat of courtliness by arresting Louis XIV's most formidable minister without causing the slightest offence. The French have other opinions on the Gascon nature, too: a *promesse de Gascon*, for example, means an empty promise.

Statue of Dumas' musketeer d'Artagnan in Auch

20 Auch

Gers. 23,000. 1 rue Dessoles (05 62 05 22 89). Tue am, Thu & Sat. W **auch-tourisme.com**

The ancient capital of the Gers department, Auch (pronounced "Ohsh") has long been a sleepy place, which comes alive on market days. The new town by the station is not a place that encourages you to linger. Head instead for the Old Town on the outcrop overlooking the River Gers. If you climb the 234 stone steps from the river, you arrive directly in front of the restored late Gothic **Cathédrale Ste-Marie**, begun in 1489. The furnishings of the cathedral are remarkable: highlights are the carved wooden choir stalls depicting more than 1,500 biblical, historical and mythological characters, and the equally magnificent 15th-century stained glass, attributed to Arnaud de Moles. The windows show a mix of prophets, patriarchs and apostles, with 360 individually characterized figures and exceptional colours. Three depict the key biblical events of Creation, the Crucifixion and the Resurrection.

Medallion from Cathédrale Ste-Marie

Auch went through an urbanization programme in the 18th century, when the allées d'Etigny, flanked by the grand Hôtel de Ville and Palais de Justice, were built. Some fine houses from this period line the pedestrianized rue Dessoles. Auch's restaurants are known for their hearty dishes, including *foie gras de canard* (fattened duck liver).

21 Auvillar

Tarn-et-Garonne. 1,000. pl de la Halle (05 63 39 89 82).

A perfect complement to the high emotion of Moissac *(see pp446–7)*, Auvillar is one of the loveliest hilltop villages in France. It has a triangular marketplace lined with half-timbered arcades at its centre, and extensive views from the promenade overlooking the River Garonne. There are picnic spots along this panoramic path plus an orientation map. This includes all but the chimneys visible in the distance, belonging to the nuclear plant at Golfech.

Sunflowers, a popular crop in southwest France grown for their seeds and oil

㉒ Moissac

At the core of this otherwise unremarkable riverside town is the abbey of St-Pierre, one of the undisputed masterpieces of French Romanesque art. Founded in the 9th century by a Benedictine monk, the abbey was subsequently ransacked by Arabs, Normans and Hungarians. In 1047, Moissac abbey was united with the rich foundation at Cluny and prospered under the direction of Abbot Durand de Bredon. By the 12th century it had become the pre-eminent monastery in southwest France. The superb south portal was created during this period.

Abbey of St-Pierre
The church's exterior belongs to two periods: one part, in stone, is Romanesque; the other, in brick, is Gothic.

Christ in Majesty
The figure of Christ sits in judgment at the centre of the scene. He holds the Book of Life in his left hand and raises his right in benediction.

Tympanum
The lower register of the balanced, compact tympanum shows the expressive "24 Elders with crowns of gold" from St John's vision.

★ South Portal
The carved south portal (1100–1130) is a masterful translation into stone of St John's dramatic vision of the Apocalypse (Book of Revelation, Chapters 4 and 5). The Evangelists Matthew, Mark, Luke and John appear as "four beasts full of eyes". Moorish details on the door jambs reflect the contemporary cultural exchange between France and Spain.

VISITORS' CHECKLIST

Practical Information
Tarn-et-Garonne. 13,000. 6 pl Durand de Bredon (05 63 04 01 85). Sat, Sun ams. Abbey: **Open** daily. Cloisters: **Open** daily. 6:30pm Mon–Fri, 9am Sat, 11am Sun. **tourisme.moissac.fr**

Transport

★ Cloister
The late 11th-century cloister is lined with alternate double and single columns in white, pink, green and grey marble. In all, there are 76 richly decorated arches.

Floorplan: Church and Cloister

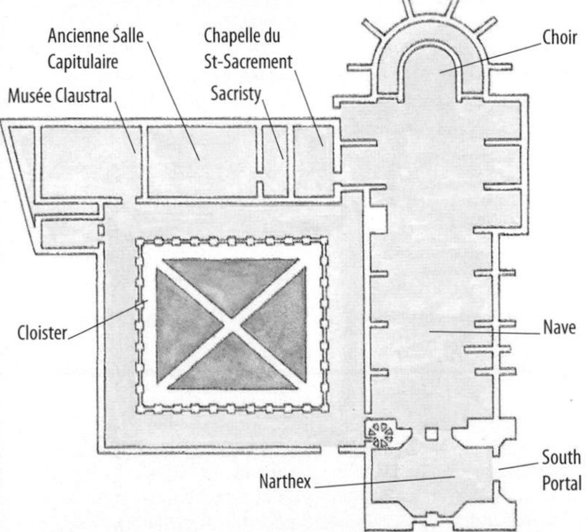

Cloister Capitals
Flowers, beasts and scenes from both the Old and New testaments are featured in these superbly sculptured 11th-century Romanesque capitals.

㉓ Montauban

Tarn-et-Garonne. 60,000. 4 rue du Collège (05 63 63 60 60). Wed & Sat; organic market: Thu pm. **montauban-tourisme.com**

Toulouse's little pink-brick sister and the capital of the 17th-century "Protestant Republic" of southern France, Montauban was the birthplace of the painter Jean-Auguste-Dominique Ingres (1780–1867). The town's great treasure is the **Musée Ingres**, a 17th-century palace with an exceptional bequest of paintings and 4,000 drawings, plus works by Van Dyck, Tintoretto, Courbet and the sculptor Emile Bourdelle, who was also born here.

Above all, Montauban has a pleasant shopping area, with a double-arcaded main square (place Nationale) built in the 17th and 18th centuries. A few streets away lies the stark white **Cathédrale Notre-Dame**, built on the orders of Louis XIV in 1692 in the backlash against Protestant heresy. It houses *The Vow of Louis XIII* by Ingres (1824).

Musée Ingres
Palais Episcopal, 19 rue de l'Hôtel de Ville. **Tel** 05 63 22 12 91. **Closed** for renovation until end 2019.

㉔ Gorges de l'Aveyron

Tarn-et-Garonne. Toulouse. Montauban, Lexos. Montauban. 10 rue de la Pélisserie (05 63 30 63 47). **tourisme-saint-antonin-noble-val.com**

At the Gorges de l'Aveyron, the sweltering plains of Montauban change abruptly to cool, chestnut-wooded hills. Here the villages are of a different stamp from those of Périgord and Quercy, displaying an obsession with defence.

The château at Bruniquel, founded in the 6th century, is built over the lip of a precipice. Further along the D115, the village of Penne's position on the tip of a giant rock fang is even more extreme. The gorge narrows and darkens; from St-Antonin-Noble-Val, beside the river, the valley turns towards Cordes.

25 Cordes-sur-Ciel

Tarn. 1,000. Maison Gaugiran, 38–42 rue Grand Raimond (05 63 56 00 52). Sat.
cordessurciel.fr

Cordes-sur-Ciel is a fitting description as the town seems suspended against the skyline. During the 13th-century Cathar wars the entire town was excommunicated. Devastating epidemics of plague later sent it into decline, and the town was in an advanced state of decay at the beginning of the 20th century.

Restoration work began in the 1940s and the ramparts and many of the gates built in 1222 have been well preserved. Also intact are Gothic houses such as the 14th-century **Maison du Grand Fauconnier**.

Today, Cordes still exudes a sense of loss. The town of which Albert Camus wrote "Everything is beautiful there, even regret", is now dependent on tourism. "Medieval" crafts aimed at visitors abound and a collection at the **Musée d'Art Moderne et Contemporain** evokes Cordes' former embroidery industry. The museum also houses works of modern art by such artists as Picasso and Mirô. The **Jardin des Paradis** offers a corner of beauty and hope in which to reflect .

Musée d'Art Moderne et Contemporain
Maison du Grand Fauconnier.
Tel 05 63 56 14 79. **Open** mid-Mar–mid-Nov: Wed–Mon.

Cathédrale Ste-Cécile perched above the town of Albi

26 Albi

Tarn. 52,000. Palais de la Berbie, pl Ste-Cécile (05 63 36 36 00). Tue–Sun. **albi-tourisme.fr**

Like many large towns in this region, Albi is not only red, but also can become red hot, and not ideal for afternoon visits in summer. You need to get up in the cool early morning to walk the streets around the market and the cathedral.

Try to make for the **Musée Toulouse-Lautrec** in the Palais de la Berbie ahead of the crowds. The museum contains the most complete permanent collection of the artist's work in existence, including paintings, drawings and his famous posters for the Moulin Rouge. There are also canvases by Matisse, Dufy and Yves Brayer. After a stroll around the beautiful terraced gardens, step next door to the vast red-brick **Cathédrale Ste-Cécile**, built in the aftermath of the Albigensian crusade in 1265. It was intended as a reminder to potential heretics that the Church meant business. From a distance, its semicircular towers and narrow windows give it the appearance more of a fortress than a place of worship. Every feature, from the huge bell tower to the apocalyptic fresco of the *Last Judgment*, is on a giant scale, built deliberately to dwarf the average person. The effect is breathtaking.

Musée Toulouse-Lautrec
Palais de la Berbie. **Tel** 05 63 49 48 70. **Open** Apr–Sep: daily; Oct–Mar: Wed–Mon. **Closed** 1 Jan, 1 May, 1 Nov, 25 Dec.
museetoulouselautrec.net

Toulouse-Lautrec

Comte Henri de Toulouse–Lautrec was born in Albi in 1864. Crippled at 15 as a result of two falls, he moved to Paris in 1882, recording the life of the city's cabarets, brothels, racecourses and circuses. He was a dedicated craftsman and his bold, vivid posters did much to establish lithography as a major art form. Alcoholism and syphilis led to his early death at the age of 36.

Lautrec's *La Modiste* (1900)

27 Castres

Tarn. 43,000. 2 pl de la République (05 63 62 63 62). Tue–Sun. **tourisme-castres.fr**

A centre for the cloth industry since the 14th century, today Castres is also the headquarters of one of France's biggest pharmaceutical companies. In the large collection of Spanish art in the **Musée Goya – Musée d'Art Hispanique**, the artist himself is well represented by a large, misty council scene and by a series of powerful prints, *Los Caprichos*. Outside, the formal gardens between the town hall and the River Agout were designed in the 17th century by André Le Nôtre *(see p183)*, the landscape architect of Vaux-le-Vicomte and Versailles.

Musée Goya – Musée d'Art Hispanique
Hôtel de Ville. **Tel** 05 63 71 59 30 or 05 63 71 59 27. **Open** Jul–Aug: daily; Sep–Jun: Tue–Sun. **Closed** 1 Jan, 1 May, 14 Jul, 1 Nov, 25 Dec.

Bastide Towns

Bastide towns were hurriedly built in the 13th century by both the English and the French to encourage settlement of empty areas before the Hundred Years' War. They are the medieval equivalent of "new towns", with planned grids of streets and fortified perimeters. Over 300 bastide towns and villages still survive between Périgord and the Pyrenees.

A broad arcaded marketplace is the central feature of most bastides. Montauban's arcades still shelter a variety of shops.

Lauzerte, founded in 1241 by the Count of Toulouse, is a typical bastide town of grey-stone houses. The town, long an English outpost, is perched for security on the brow of a hill.

The church could be used as a keep when the bastide's outer fortifications had been breached.

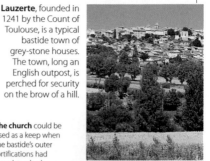

The central square is surrounded by a grid of interconnecting streets and alleys. This differs markedly from the usual jumble of medieval houses and lanes.

Stone houses protected the perimeter.

Monflanquin

This military bastide town was built by the French in 1256 on a strategic north–south route. It changed hands several times during the Hundred Years' War.

Today, the bastides form a convenient network of market towns, known as the *route des bastides*. Enquire at the local tourist office about market days, the busiest but best time to visit.

Porte de la Jane in Cordes-sur-Ciel is a typical bastide feature. These narrow gateways were easily barred by portcullises.

㉘ Toulouse

Toulouse, the most important town in southwest France, is the country's fourth largest metropolis, and a major industrial and university city. The area is also famous for being the centre of Europe's aerospace industry (both Concorde and Airbus originated here), as shown by the Cité de l'Espace, just outside the city.

Best seen on foot, Toulouse has fine cuisine, one of France's most striking churches, Basilique St-Sernin, lively street life and a rose-brick Old Town, which is described as "pink at dawn, red at noon and mauve at dusk".

The River Garonne, crossed by the Pont Neuf

Houseboats at their moorings on the Canal du Midi

Exploring Toulouse

This warm southern city has steadily expanded, crescent-like, from its original Roman site on the Garonne. First it was a flourishing Visigoth city, then a Renaissance town of towered brick palaces built with the wealth generated by the *pastel* (blue pigment) and grain trades. The grandest of these palaces still survive in the Old Town, centred around place du Capitole and the huge 18th-century **Hôtel de Ville**. Here, and in place St-Georges and rue Alsace-Lorraine, is the main concentration of shops, bars and cafés. The city's large student population keeps prices down in the numerous cafés, tapas bars and bookstores, and in the flea market on Sundays in place St-Aubin and allées Jules Guesde et Paul Fuegaplace.

A ring of 18th- and 19th-century boulevards encircles the city, surrounded in turn by a tangle of *autoroutes*. The left bank of the Garonne is under development (St-Cyprien) and is linked by Toulouse's driverless metro. The former abattoir has been superbly converted into a centre for modern and contemporary art, **Les Abattoirs** (Wed–Sun), the highlight of which is Picasso's theatre backdrop *Minotaur Disguised as Harlequin*.

Les Jacobins

Rue Lakanal. **Tel.** 05 61 22 23 82. **Open** Tue–Sun. **jacobins.toulouse.fr**

This church was begun in 1229 and completed over the next two centuries. It was the first Dominican convent, founded to combat dissent. The Jacobins' convent became the founding institution of Toulouse University. Its church, a Gothic masterpiece, features a soaring, 22-branched palm tree vault in the apse. The delicate Gothic Chapelle St-Antonin (1337) contains frescoes of the Apocalypse dating from 1341.

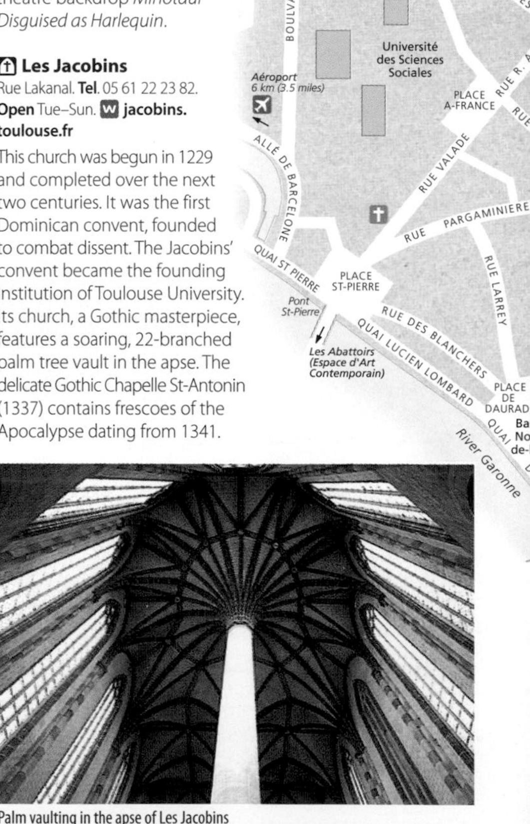

Palm vaulting in the apse of Les Jacobins

Fondation Bemberg

Hôtel d'Assézat, 7 pl d'Assézat. **Tel** 05 61 12 06 89. **Open** Tue–Sun. **Closed** 1 Jan, 25 Dec. **fondation-bemberg.fr**

This 16th-century palace houses the collection of local art lover Georges Bemberg, and covers Renaissance paintings, 19th- to 20th-century French paintings and drawings, including Impressionist, Post-Impressionist and Fauvist works, objets d'art and bronzes.

Musée des Augustins

21 rue de Metz. **Tel** 05 61 22 21 82. **Open** Wed–Mon. **Closed** 1 Jan, 1 May, 25 Dec. **augustins.org**

Toulouse became a centre of Romanesque art due to its position on the route to Santiago de Compostela *(see pp404–5)*. The museum has sculpture from the period and cloisters from a 14th-century Augustinian priory. There are also 16th- to 19th-century French, Italian and Flemish paintings, including work by Ingres, Delacroix, Constant and Laurens.

Sights at a Glance

① Les Jacobins
② Fondation Bemberg
③ Musée des Augustins
④ Basilique St-Sernin

VISITORS' CHECKLIST

Practical Information

Haute-Garonne. 474,000. Donjon du Capitole (08 92 180 180). daily. Piano aux Jacobins (Sep). **toulouse-tourisme.com**

Transport

6 km (4 miles) NW Toulouse. bd Pierre Semard (trains: Gare Matabiau). Guided minibus tours: **citytour-toulouse.com**

Basilique St-Sernin

Pl St-Sernin. **Tel** 05 61 21 80 45. **Open** daily. **basilique-saint-sernin.fr**

This is the largest Romanesque basilica in Europe, built in the 11th–12th centuries to accommodate pilgrims. Highlights are the octagonal brick belfry, with rows of decorative brick arches topped by an enormously tall spire. Beautiful 11th-century marble bas-reliefs of Christ and the symbols of the Evangelists by Bernard Gilduin are in the ambulatory.

Cité de l'Espace

Av Jean Gonord. **Tel** 05 67 22 23 24. **Open** Tue–Sun (daily Apr–Sep). **Closed** Jan. **cite-espace.com**

Southeast of the city centre, this vast "space park" includes two planetariums, interactive exhibits related to space exploration, an IMAX cinema and a lifesize replica of the Ariane 5 rocket, where visitors can learn how, in theory at least, to launch rockets and satellites.

The tiered, 12th-century tower of Basilique St-Sernin

For keys to symbols *see back flap*

THE PYRENEES

Pyrénées-Atlantiques · Hautes-Pyrénées · Haute-Garonne · Ariège

The mountains of the Pyrenees form a conspicuous frontier across southwestern France. Over centuries this remote terrain has fostered tenacious people, many descended from Spanish emigrants and refugees. Today it is the last remaining wilderness in southern Europe and a habitat for rare animal species.

Heading east from the Atlantic coast, the hills are wonderfully lush after the plains of Aquitaine. The deeper the Pyrenees are penetrated, the steeper the valley sides and the more gigantic the snow-clad peaks become. This is magnificent, empty, dangerous country, to be approached with caution and respect. In summer the region offers over 1,600 km (1,000 miles) of walking trails, as well as camping, fishing and climbing. In winter there is both cross-country and downhill skiing at the busy resorts along the border, much livelier than their Spanish counterparts.

Historically, the Pyrenees are known as the birthplace of Henri IV, who put an end to the Wars of Religion in 1593 and united France, though the region has been characterized more often by independent fiefdoms. The region's oldest inhabitants, the Basque people *(see p459)*, have maintained their own language and culture, and their resorts of Bayonne, Biarritz and St-Jean-de-Luz reflect this, looking to the sea and to summer visitors for their livelihood.

Inland, Pau, Tarbes and Foix rely on tourism and medium-scale industry, while Lourdes receives five million pilgrims every year. For the rest, life has been regulated by agriculture, though economic constraints today are causing an exodus from the land.

Countryside around St-Lizier, in the heart of the Pyrenean countryside

◀ The Ariège river in Foix

Exploring the Pyrenees

The towering Pyrenees cut across southwest France from the Mediterranean to the Atlantic coast, encompassing the craggy citadel of Montségur; the pilgrimage centre of Lourdes; Pau, capital of the hilly Béarn country; and the Basque port of Bayonne. This formidable range, an unspoiled paradise for walkers, fishermen and skiers, is as lush on its French side as it is arid in Spain, and contains the wild and beautiful Parc National des Pyrénées. Throughout the region, visitors can expect cool temperatures and grandiose scenery. Lovers of history and architecture will be richly rewarded by St-Bertrand-de-Comminges and St-Jean-de-Luz, among the region's important sights.

Marzipan sweets, a speciality of southwest France

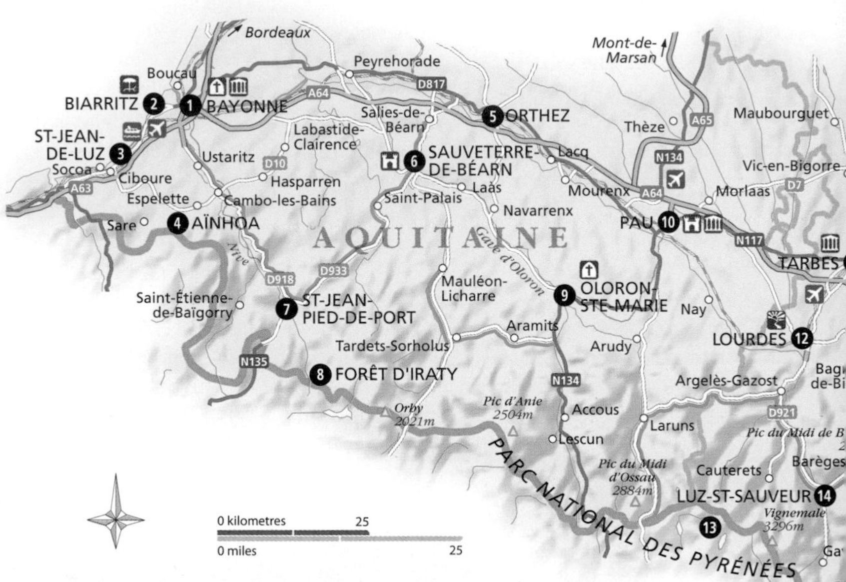

Getting Around

Access to the Basque coast in the western Pyrenees is via the A63/N10 from Bordeaux. The length of the Pyrenees, including the mountain valleys, is served by the A64, which runs from Bayonne to Toulouse, via Orthez, Pau, Tarbes and St-Gaudens. Once you are high up, expect narrow, twisting roads and slow driving. The scenic but demanding D918/D618 road crosses 18 high passes between the Atlantic and the Mediterranean.

There are airports at Biarritz, Pau and Lourdes. Both Pau and Lourdes, together with Orthez and Tarbes, are on the rail route that loops south between Bordeaux and Toulouse.

The galleried church in the Basque village of Espelette

For keys to symbols *see back flap*

Sights at a Glance

1. Bayonne
2. Biarritz
3. St-Jean-de-Luz
4. Aïnhoa
5. Orthez
6. Sauveterre-de-Béarn
7. St-Jean-Pied-de-Port
8. Forêt d'Iraty
9. Oloron-Ste-Marie
10. Pau
11. Tarbes
12. Lourdes
13. *Parc National des Pyrénées pp464–5*
14. Luz-St-Sauveur
15. Arreau
16. St-Bertrand-de-Comminges
17. St-Lizier
18. Foix
19. Montségur
20. Mirepoix

Wild *pottock* ponies on moorland in the Forêt d'Iraty

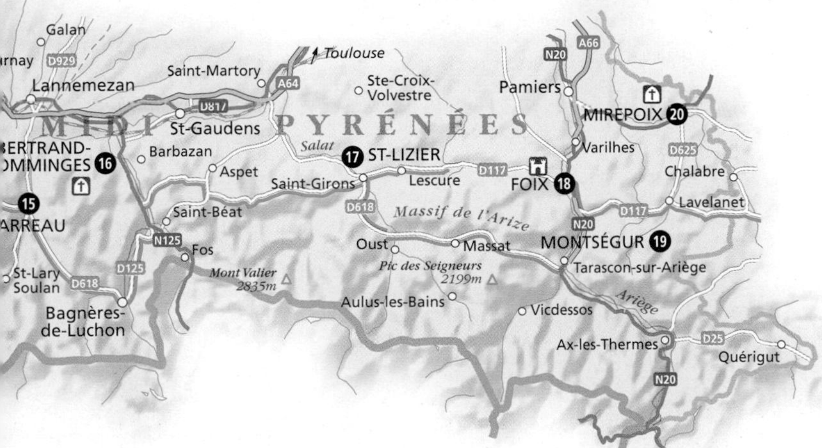

St-Jean-de-Luz seen from Ciboure, across the Nivelle estuary

Key

- Motorway
- Major road
- Secondary road
- Minor road
- Scenic route
- Main railway
- Minor railway
- International border
- Regional border
- △ Summit

❶ Bayonne

Pyrénées-Atlantiques. 49,500. pl des Basques (05 59 46 09 00). daily. **bayonne-tourisme.com**

Bayonne, capital of the French Basque country, lies between two rivers – the turbulent Nive, which arrives straight from the mountains, and the wide, languid Adour. An important town since Roman times because of its command of one of the few easily passable roads to Spain, Bayonne prospered as a free port under English rule from 1154 to 1451. Since then it has successfully withstood 14 sieges, including a particularly bloody one directed by Wellington in 1813.

Grand Bayonne, the district around the cathedral, can be easily explored on foot. The 13th-century **Cathédrale Ste-Marie** was begun under English rule and is northern Gothic in style. Look for the handsome cloister and the 15th-century knocker on the north door – if a fugitive could put a hand to this, he was entitled to sanctuary. The pedestrianized streets around form a lively shopping area, especially the arcaded rue Port Neuf, with cafés serving hot chocolate, a Bayonne speciality. (Fine-quality chocolate-making was introduced by the Jews who fled Spain at the end of the 15th century, and it has remained a speciality of the town.) Bayonne is also famous for its ham.

Grand Bayonne, clustered around the twin-spired cathedral

Lighthouse at Biarritz

Petit Bayonne lies on the opposite side of the quay-lined River Nive. The **Musée Basque** gives an excellent introduction to the customs and traditions of the Basque nation, with reconstructed house interiors and exhibits on seafaring. Nearby, the **Musée Bonnat-Helleu** has a superb art gallery. The first floor here is a must for art lovers, with sketches by Leonardo, Van Dyck, Rubens and Rembrandt and paintings by Goya, Corot, Ingres and Constable.

Musée Basque
37 quai des Corsaires. **Tel** 05 59 59 08 98. **Open** Tue–Sun (Jul–Aug: daily). **Closed** public hols.
musee-basque.com

Musée Bonnat-Helleu
5 rue Jacques Lafitte. **Tel** 05 59 46 63 60. **Closed** for renovation.
musee-bonnat.com

❷ Biarritz

Pyrénées-Atlantiques. 26,000. Javalquinto, square d'Ixelles (05 59 22 37 00). daily. **tourisme.biarritz.fr**

Biarritz, west of Bayonne, has a grandiose centre, but has been developed along the coast by residential suburbs. The resort began as a whaling port but was transformed into a playground for the European rich in the 19th century. Its popularity was assured when Empress Eugénie discovered its mild winter climate during the reign of her husband, Napoleon III. The town has three good beaches, with some of the best surfing in Europe, two casinos, and one of the last great luxury hotels in Europe, the Palais, formerly the residence of Eugénie.

In the port des Pêcheurs, the **Aquarium de Biarritz** is home to specimens of some of the marine life found in the Bay of Biscay. Below it, a narrow cause-way leads across to the Rocher de la Vierge, offering far-reaching views along the whole of the Basque coast. The Planète Musée du Chocolat is fine compensation for a rainy day.

Aquarium de Biarritz
Esplanade du Rocher-de-la-Vierge, 14 plateau de l'Atalaye. **Tel** 05 59 22 75 40. **Open** daily. **Closed** 1 Jan, 2nd–3rd wk Jan, 25 Dec.
aquariumbiarritz.com

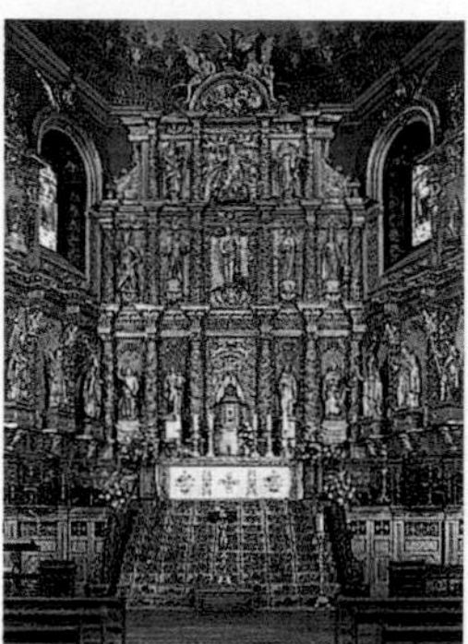

Altar in Eglise St-Jean-Baptiste

❸ St-Jean-de-Luz

Pyrénées-Atlantiques. 14,000. Biarritz. 20 bd Victor Hugo (05 59 26 03 16). daily. **saint-jean-de-luz.com**

St-Jean is a quiet fishing town out of season and a scorching tourist resort in August, with shops to rival the chic rue du Faubourg St-Honoré in Paris. In the 11th century whale carcasses were towed here to feed the whole village. The natural harbour protects the shoreline, making it one of the few beaches safe for swimming along this stretch of coast.

An important historical event took place in St-Jean: the wedding of Louis XIV and the Infanta Maria Teresa of Spain in 1660, a union that had the

For hotels and restaurants in this region see pp568–9 and pp598–9

St-Jean-de-Luz, a fishing village that explodes into life in summer

effect of sealing the long-awaited alliance between France and Spain, only to embroil the two countries ultimately in the War of the Spanish Succession. This wedding took place at the **Eglise St-Jean-Baptiste**, still the biggest and best of the great Basque churches, a triple-galleried marvel with a glittering 17th-century altar-piece and an atmosphere of gaiety and fervour. The gate through which the Sun King led his bride was immediately walled up by masons: a plaque now marks the spot. The **Maison Louis XIV**, with its contemporary furnishings, is where the king stayed in 1660, and is worth a look.

The port is busy in summer, while the restaurants behind the covered markets serve sizzling bowls full of *chipirons* – squid cooked in their own ink – a local speciality. Place Louis XIV is a lovely place to sit and watch the world go by.

Maison Louis XIV
Place Louis XIV. **Tel** 05 59 26 27 58.
Open Apr–Oct: Wed–Mon.
maison-louis-xiv.fr

Environs
On the other side of the River Nivelle, Ciboure was the birth-place of composer Maurice Ravel. It is characterized by 18th-century merchants' houses, steep narrow streets and seafood restaurants. A coastal walk of 1 hour leads to the neighbouring village of **Socoa**, where the lighthouse on the clifftop offers a fine view of the coast all the way to Biarritz.

Basque men in traditional berets

❹ Aïnhoa

Pyrénées-Atlantiques. 700.
Maison du Patrimoine (05 59 29 93 99). **ainhoa-tourisme.com**

A tiny township on the road to the Spanish border, Aïnhoa was founded in the 12th century as a waystation on the road to Santiago de Compostela *(see pp404–5)*. The main street of 17th-century whitewashed Basque houses and a galleried church from the same period survive.

Environs
There is a similar church in the village of Espelette nearby. Typically Basque in style, the galleries boosted the seating capacity and separated the men from the women and children. Espelette is the trading centre for *pottocks*, an ancient local breed of pony, auctioned here at the end of January. It is also the shrine of the local crop, the red pimento pepper, especially in October when a pepper festival is held here.

At the foot of the St-Ignace pass lies the mountain village of **Sare**. From the pass you can reach the summit of La Rhune by cog railway. This provides the best vantage point in the entire Pays Basque. The descent on foot is worthwhile.

The 11th-century château, Espelette

Sauveterre-de-Béarn and the remains of the fortified bridge over the Gave d'Oloron, the Pont de la Légende

5 Orthez

Pyrénées-Atlantiques. 12,000. 58 rue du Commerce, Monein (05 59 12 30 40). Tue; Nov–Mar: *foie gras* market Sat. **coeurdebearn.com**

Orthez is an important Béarn market town, its 13th- to 14th-century fortified bridge a vital river-crossing point over the Gave de Pau in the Middle Ages. It has a spectacular Saturday-morning market held from November to February, selling *foie gras*, smoked and air-cured Bayonne hams, and all kinds of fresh produce. Fine buildings line rue Bourg Vieux, especially the house of Jeanne d'Albret, the mother of Henry IV, on the corner of rue Roarie. Jeanne's enthusiasm for the Protestant faith alienated both her own subjects and Charles X, and ultimately caused the Béarn region to be drawn into the Wars of Religion (1562–98).

6 Sauveterre-de-Béarn

Pyrénées-Atlantiques. 1,500. pl Royale (05 59 38 32 86). Sat. **tourisme-bearn-gaves.com**

An attractive market town, Sauveterre is well worth a night's stay. It has stunning views southward over the Gave d'Oloron, the graceful single arch of the river's fortified bridge, and the 16th-century **Château de Nays**. Fishermen gather here for the annual salmon-fishing championships, in the fast-flowing Oloron (April to July).

Be sure to visit the **Château de Laàs**, 9 km (6 miles) along the D27 from Sauveterre, which has an excellent collection of 18th-century decorative art and furniture – notably the bed Napoleon slept in on the night after his defeat at Waterloo. There is also a pretty park with romantic Italian gardens.

Château de Laàs
Tel 05 59 38 91 53. **Open** Apr–Oct: 2–6pm Tue–Fri, 10am–6pm Sat & Sun (Jul–Aug: daily).

The Château de Nays at Sauveterre in the Béarn region

7 St-Jean-Pied-de-Port

Pyrénées-Atlantiques. 1,800. 14 pl du Général de Gaulle (05 59 37 03 57). Mon. **saintjeanpied deport-paysbasque-tourisme.com**

The old capital of Basse-Navarre, St-Jean-Pied-de-Port lies at the foot of the Roncesvalles Pass. Here the Basques crushed the rear-guard of Charlemagne's army in 778 and killed its commander, Roland, later glorified in the *Chanson de Roland*.

Throughout the Middle Ages this red sandstone fortress town was famous as the last rallying point before entering Spain on the pilgrim road to Santiago de Compostela *(see pp404–5)*. Tall booths were erected next to the gates for additional security.

Visitors and pilgrims in all seasons still provide St-Jean with its income. They enter the narrow streets of the upper town on foot from the Porte d'Espagne, and pass cafés, hotels and restaurants on the way up. The ramparts are worth the steep climb, as is the citadel with panoramic views.

On Mondays the town hosts a craft market, Basque *pelota* matches and, in summer, shows with bulls.

8 Forêt d'Iraty

Pyrénées-Atlantiques. St-Jean-Pied-de-Port. St-Jean-Pied-de-Port (05 59 37 03 57), Larrau (05 59 28 62 80).

A plateau of beech woods and moorland, the Forêt d'Iraty is famous for its cross-country skiing and walking. Here the ancient breed of Basque ponies, the *pottocks*, run half-wild. These creatures have not changed since the prehistoric inhabitants of the region traced their silhouettes on the walls of local caves.

The tourist office at St-Jean-Pied-de-Port publishes maps of local walks. The best begins at the Chalet Pedro car park, south of the lake on the Iraty plateau, and takes you along the GR10 to 3,000-year-old standing stones on the western side of the Sommet d'Occabé.

9 Oloron-Ste-Marie

Pyrénées-Atlantiques. 12,000. allées du Comte de Tréville (05 59 39 98 00). Fri & Sun.
tourisme-oloron.com

Oloron, a small town at the junction of the Aspe and the Ossau valleys, has grown from a Celtiberian settlement. There are huge agricultural fairs here in May and September, and the town is famed for producing the famous classic French berets.

Basque Culture

Most of Basque country is in Spain, but around 10 per cent lies within France. The Basque people have their own complex language, isolated from other European tongues, and their music, games and folklore are equally distinct. French Basques are less fiercely separatist than their Spanish counterparts, but both are still deeply attached to their unique way of life.

Pelota, the traditional Basque game

Cathédrale Ste-Marie, Oloron

The town's great glory is the doorway of the Romanesque **Cathédrale Ste-Marie**, with its biblical and Pyrenean scenes. Spain lies just on the other side of the Somport pass at the head of the mountainous Aspe Valley, and the influence of Spanish stonemasons is evident in Oloron's **Eglise Sainte-Croix** with its Moorish-style vaulting.

Environs

Head up the Aspe Valley to try one of the area's famous ewe's cheeses, or mixed cow and goat's cheeses. A side road leads to Lescun, huddled around its church, beyond which is a spectacular range of saw-toothed peaks topped by the **Pic d'Anie** at 2,504 m (8,215 ft), one of the most beautiful sights in the Pyrenees. This is also one of the last refuges of the Pyrenean brown bear, whose numbers have been drastically diminished by human activity, particularly hunting and the building of roads and houses.

High moorland above the Forêt d'Iraty, long denuded of timber for use by the French and Spanish navies

Gobelin tapestry in the Château de Pau

⑩ Pau

Pyrénées-Atlantiques. 79,000. pl Royale (05 59 27 27 08). Mon–Sat. **pau-pyrenees.com**

A lively university town, with elegant *belle époque* architecture and shady parks, Pau is the capital of the Béarn region, and the most interesting big town in the central Pyrenees. The weather in autumn and winter is mild, so this has been a favourite resort of affluent foreigners, especially the English, since the early 19th century.

Pau is chiefly famous as the birthplace of Henry IV. His mother, Jeanne d'Albret, travelled for 19 days from Picardy, in the eighth month of her pregnancy, just to have her baby here. She sang during her labour, convinced that if she did so, Henry would grow up as tough as she was. As soon as the infant was born, his lips were smeared with garlic and local Jurançon wine, in keeping with the traditional custom.

The town's principal sight is the **Château de Pau**, first remodelled in the 14th century for the ruler of Béarn, Gaston Phoebus *(see p467)*. It was heavily restored 400 years later. Marguerite d'Angoulême, sister of the King of France, resided here in the late 16th century, and transformed the town into a centre for the arts and free thinking. The château's 16th-century Gobelin tapestries, made by Flemish weavers working in Paris, are fabulous. (The Maison Carrée in Nay – 18 km/ 11 miles towards Lourdes – exhibits the former Musée Béarnais' collection of artifacts retracing the history, traditions and culture of the Béarn.)

Outside, the boulevard des Pyrénées affords glorious views of some of the highest Pyrenean peaks, often snow-capped year round. Continue from here to the eclectic **Musée des Beaux-Arts**, where there is a splendid Degas, the *Cotton Exchange, New Orleans*, as well as two works by Rubens.

Château de Pau
Rue du Château. **Tel** 05 59 82 38 02. **Open** daily. **Closed** 1 Jan, 1 May, 25 Dec. restricted.
chateau-pau.fr

Musée des Beaux-Arts
Rue Mathieu Lalanne. **Tel** 05 59 27 33 02. **Open** Wed–Mon. **Closed** some public hols. restricted.
museedesbeauxartsdepau.com

⑪ Tarbes

Hautes-Pyrénées. 42,500. 3 cours Gambetta (05 62 51 30 31). Thu. **tarbes-tourisme.fr**

Tarbes is the capital of the Bigorre region and hosts a major agricultural fair. The **Jardin Massey** in the middle of town was designed at the turn of the 19th century and is one of the loveliest parks in the southwest, with many rare plants, including the North American sassafras, and a 14th-century cloister with finely carved capitals.

In the gardens is the **Musée Massey**, housing a unique collection on the history of French and international hussars and a fine arts collection.

Musée Massey
Jardin Massey. **Tel** 05 62 44 36 95. **Open** Wed–Mon. **Closed** 1 Jan, 1 May, 25 Dec.
musee-massey.com

⑫ Lourdes

Hautes-Pyrénées. 15,000. pl Peyramale (05 62 42 77 40). daily. **lourdes-infotourisme.com**

Lourdes, one of the great shrines of Europe, owes its celebrity to visions of the Virgin experienced by 14-year-old Bernadette Soubirous in 1858. Five million people annually

Château de Pau, birthplace of Henry IV in 1553

◀ The lush Forêt d'Iraty and surrounding moorland

visit **Grotte Massabielle**, where the visions occurred, and rue des Petits-Fossés where Bernadette lived, in search of a miracle cure. The **Musée du Petit Lourdes** gives information about Bernadette and the shrine.

Visit the **Grottes de Bétharram** for underground rides by boat and train, or the **Musée Pyrénéen**, about the pioneers who opened up these ranges.

Musée du Petit Lourdes
68 ave Peyramale. **Tel** 05 62 94 24 36. **Open** Apr–Oct: daily.
musee-lourdes.fr

Grottes de Bétharram
St-Pé-de-Bigorre. **Tel** 05 62 41 80 04. **Open** Feb–late Mar: Mon–Fri pms; late Mar–Oct: daily.
betharram.com

Spectacular limestone formations at the Grottes de Bétharram

Pilgrims participating in open-air Mass at Lourdes

Musée Pyrénéen
rue du Fort. **Tel** 05 62 42 37 37. **Open** daily. **Closed** 1 Jan, 1 & 11 Nov, 25 Dec. restricted. **lourdes-visite.fr**

⓭ Parc National des Pyrénées

See pp464–5.

⓮ Luz-St-Sauveur

Hautes-Pyrénées. 1,000. to Lourdes. pl du 8 mai 1945 (05 62 92 30 30). Mon am. **luz.org**

Luz-St-Sauveur is an attractive spa town, with an unusual church built in the 14th century by the Hospitaliers de Saint Jean de Jérusalem (later the Knights of Malta), an order established to protect pilgrims. The church is fortified with gun slits that provided protection for pilgrims on the way to Santiago de Compostela *(see pp404–5)*.

Environs
The elegant spa town of **Cauterets** makes a good base for climbing, skiing and walking in the rugged mountains of the Bigorre region.

Gavarnie is a former way-station on the Santiago de Compostela pilgrim route. A good track, accessible on foot or by donkey, leads from the village to the spectacular natural rock amphitheatre known as the **Cirque de Gavarnie**. Here the longest waterfall in Europe, at 420 m (1,378 ft), cascades off the mountain into space, encircled by eleven 3,000-m (9,800-ft) peaks.

Tourists can now share much of the **Observatoire Pic du Midi de Bigorre** with scientists. It is even possible to spend the night here. Access is by cable car from La Mongie. Alternatively there are a number of walks up to the Pic (4 hours minimum).

The French are justly proud of the Observatory, which has supplied some of the clearest images of Venus and other planets so far obtained from Earth. The 1-m (3.2-ft) telescope mapped out the moon for NASA's Apollo missions.

Observatoire Pic du Midi de Bigorre
Tel 08 25 00 28 77. **Open** daily. **Closed** 18 Apr, May, 6 Nov & Dec.
picdumidi.com

The Miracle of Lourdes

In 1858 a young girl named Bernadette Soubirous experienced 18 visions of the Virgin at the Grotte Massabielle near the town. Despite being told to keep away from the cave by her mother – and the local magistrate – she was guided to a spring with miraculous healing powers. The church endorsed the miracles in the 1860s, and since then many people claim to have been cured by the holy water. A religious city of shrines, churches and hospices has since grown up around the spring, with a dynamic tourist industry to match.

Bernadette's vision

⓭ Parc National des Pyrénées

The Pyrenees National Park, designated in 1967, extends 100 km (62 miles) along the French and Spanish frontier. It boasts some of the most spectacular scenery in Europe, ranging from meadows glimmering with butterflies to high peaks, snowcapped even in summer. Variations in altitude and climate make the park rich in flora and fauna. One of the most enjoyable ways to see it is on foot: within the park are 350 km (217 miles) of well-marked footpaths.

Vallée d'Aspe
Jagged peaks tower above the Vallée d'Aspe and the Cirque de Lescun. An access road to Somport Tunnel has been built here.

Pic d'Anie
The limestone-flanked 2,504-m (8,215-ft) Pic d'Anie overlooks rich upland pastures watered by melting snow. In spring, the ground is ablaze with Pyrenean varieties of gentian and columbine, found nowhere else.

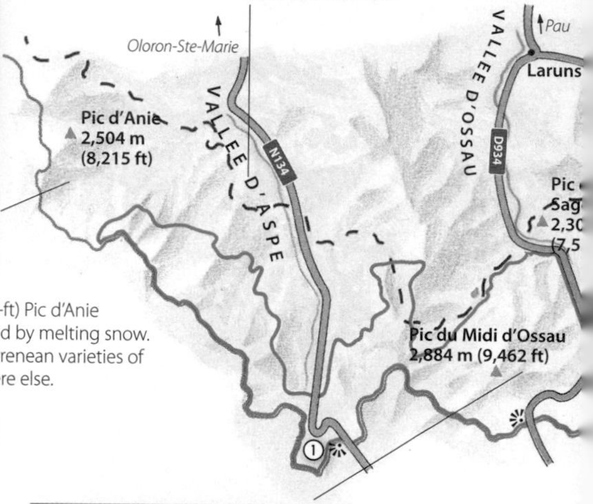

Oloron-Ste-Marie
Pau
Laruns
Pic d'Anie 2,504 m (8,215 ft)
VALLEE D'ASPE
N134
VALLEE D'OSSAU
D934
Pic du Midi d'Ossau 2,884 m (9,462 ft)
①

KEY

① **Col du Somport**, the Somport pass (1,632 m/5,354 ft), is a rugged route into Spain that is now bypassed by a tunnel.

② **The GR10 long-distance trail** is one of the great walks of France, linking the Atlantic with the Mediterranean.

③ **Brèche de Roland**

Pic du Midi d'Ossau
A tough trail leads from the Bious-Artigues lake at the base of the Pic du Midi d'Ossau and encircles the formidable, tooth-shaped summit (2,884 m/9,462 ft).

Pyrenean Wildlife

The Pyrenees are home to a rich variety of wild creatures, many of them unique to the range. The ibex, a member of the antelope family, is still numerous in the valleys of Ossau and Cauterets. Birds of prey include the Egyptian, griffon and bearded vultures. Ground predators range from the pine marten to the stoat. The desman, a tiny aquatic mammal related to the mole, is found in many of the mountain streams.

Pyrenean fritillary flowers through late spring and early summer in mountain pastures.

The Turk's Cap Lily comes into flower June–August on rocky slopes at up to 2,200 m (7,218 ft).

Brèche de Roland
The famous breach in the sheer crest of the Cirque de Gavarnie forms a gateway for climbers between France and Spain.

Tips for Walkers

The park is crossed by a network of numbered trails. Each is well signposted and shows the length of time needed. Mountain huts offer a meal and a bed for the night. For maps and information, visit the Park Office at Cauterets (tel: 05 62 92 52 56) or at Luz-St-Sauveur (tel: 05 62 92 38 38), both open year round, or visit www.parc-pyrenees.com.

Walking the trail in high summer

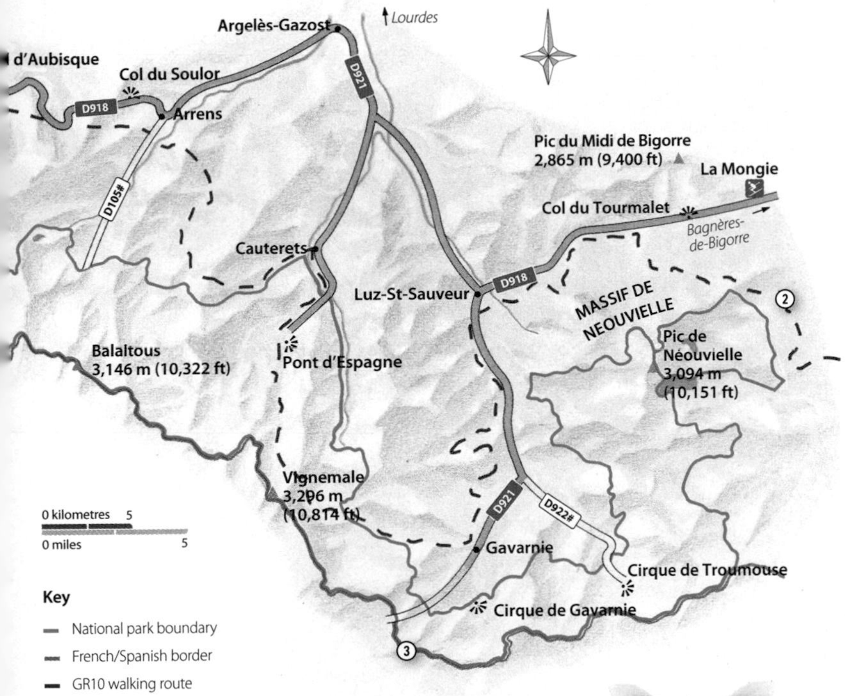

Lourdes
Argelès-Gazost
d'Aubisque
Col du Soulor
D918
Arrens
D921
D105#
Pic du Midi de Bigorre
2,865 m (9,400 ft)
La Mongie
Col du Tourmalet
Bagnères-de-Bigorre
Cauterets
D918
Luz-St-Sauveur
MASSIF DE NEOUVIELLE
Pic de Néouvielle
3,094 m
(10,151 ft)
Balaïtous
3,146 m (10,322 ft)
Pont d'Espagne
Vignemale
3,296 m
(10,814 ft)
D921
D922#
Gavarnie
Cirque de Troumouse
Cirque de Gavarnie
0 kilometres 5
0 miles 5

Key

- National park boundary
- French/Spanish border
- GR10 walking route

The Egyptian vulture is seen all over the Pyrenees, especially on rocky cliff faces.

Pyrenean bears are close to extinction, but a few still live in this park, especially in the west.

These butterflies are among several colourful species found at high altitudes.

15 Arreau

Hautes-Pyrénées. 850. Château des Nestes (05 62 98 63 15). Thu. **vallee-aure.com**

Arreau stands at the junction of the rivers Aure and Louron. A small, bustling half-timbered town with good shops and restaurants, this is the place to buy the basics for hiking or fishing in the mountains. The town surrounds a handsome town hall with a covered marketplace beneath it. Next door is a 16th-century house, the Maison de Lys, which has a façade ornamented with the fleur-de-lys motifs.

Environs

St-Lary Soulan is a nearby ski resort and a good base for exploring the entire Massif du Néouvielle. Head for the village of Fabian and the smattering of lakes above it, where the GR10 *(see pp464–5)* and other well-marked trails crisscross the peaks. Here you may see golden eagles or an enormous lammergeier.

Cloisters in the Cathédrale Ste-Marie, St-Bertrand-de-Comminges

16 St-Bertrand-de-Comminges

Haute-Garonne. 250. Montrejeau, then taxi. Les Olivetains, parvis de la Cathédrale (05 61 95 44 44). music festival (mid-Jul–end Aug). **tourisme-stgaudens.com**

The pretty hilltop town of St-Bertrand is the most remarkable artistic and historic site in the Central Pyrenees and the venue for an acclaimed music festival in summer *(see p41)*. Some of the best sculpture in the region adorns the portal of the **Cathédrale Ste-Marie**. The adjoining Romanesque and Gothic cloisters contain sarcophagi, carved capitals and statues of the four Evangelists.

St-Bertrand's origins lie on the plain below, in the city founded by the great Roman statesman Pompey in 72 BC. At that time it consisted of two thermal baths, a theatre, a temple, a market and a Christian basilica. All were destroyed by Gontran, the grandson of Clovis *(see p54)* in 585, and six centuries were to pass before the Bishop of Comminges, Bertrand de l'Isle, saw the site as a potential location for a new cathedral and monastery. The town, which was relatively unimportant in political terms, became a major religious centre.

Inside the cathedral, look out for the 66 magnificent carved choirstalls and the 16th-century organ case. The tomb of Bertrand de l'Isle is situated at the far end of the choir, with an altar beside it; the beautiful marble tomb in the Virgin's chapel just off the nave is that of Hugues de Châtillon, a bishop who provided funds for the completion of the cathedral in the 14th century.

Cathédrale Ste-Marie
Tel 05 61 95 44 44. **Open** daily. **Closed** Sun am.

The imposing 12th-century Cathédrale Ste-Marie in St-Bertrand

Fresco in the Cathédrale St-Lizier

17 St-Lizier

Ariège. 1,500. pl de l'Eglise (05 61 96 77 77). **tourisme-stgirons-stlizier.fr**

St-Lizier is located in the Ariège, a region famous for its steep-sided valleys and wild mountain scenery. The village dates back to Roman times, and by the Middle Ages was an important religious centre. St-Lizier has two cathedrals; the finer is the 12th- to 14th-century **Cathédrale St-Lizier** in the lower town. The **Cathédrale de la Sède** in the upper town has the best view. Nearby is the **Bishop's Palace**, which houses a museum of local history.

St-Lizier, with snowcapped mountains in the distance

⑱ Foix

Ariège. 10,000. rue Bayle (05 61 65 12 12). Fri & 1st, 3rd & 5th Mon of each month, also Tue, Wed all day in Jul–Aug. **foix-tourisme.com**

With its battlements and towers, Foix stands foursquare at the junction of the rivers Arget and Ariège. In the Middle Ages, Foix's dynasty of counts ruled the whole of the Béarn area. Count Gaston Phoebus (1331–91) was the most flamboyant, a poet who wrote a famous treatise on hunting. He was a ruthless politician, who had his brother and his son put to death.

Some of the pleasures of the medieval court are re-created in the local summer fair, the largest in the southwest. At any time, the 15th-century keep of the **Château de Foix** is worth climbing just for the view. The restored 14th-century **Eglise de St-Volusien** is delightful in its simplicity and grace.

Château de Foix
Tel 05 61 05 10 10. **Open** daily. **Closed** 1 Jan, 25 Dec. **sites-touristiques-ariege.fr**

Environs
The **Grotte de Niaux**, 15 km (9 miles) south of Foix, features some prehistoric cave paintings.

Grotte de Niaux
Tel 05 61 05 10 10. **Open** daily. **sites-touristiques-ariege.fr**

⑲ Montségur

Ariège. 130. 05 61 03 03 03. **Open** Feb–Dec: daily. **Closed** 25 Dec. (May–Sep). **montsegur.fr**

Montségur is famous as the last stronghold of the Cathars *(see p495)*. From the car park at the foot of the mount, a path leads up to the small castle above, which was occupied in the 13th century by *faidits* (dispossessed aristocrats) and a Cathar community. The Cathars themselves lived outside the fortress, in houses clinging to the rock. Opposed to Catholic authority, Cathar troops marched on Avignonnet in 1243 and massacred members of the Inquisitional tribunal. In retaliation, an army of 10,000 laid siege to Montségur for ten months. When captured, 205 Cathars refused to convert and were burned alive.

⑳ Mirepoix

Ariège. 3,300. pl du Maréchal Leclerc (05 61 68 83 76). Mon & Thu. **tourisme-mirepoix.com**

Mirepoix is a solid country bastide town *(see p449)* with a huge main square – one of the loveliest in the southwest – surrounded by beamed 13th- to 15th-century arcades and half-timbered houses.

The **cathedral**, begun in 1317 with the last additions made in 1867, boasts the widest Gothic nave (22 m/72 ft) in France.

The best times to visit the town are on market days, when stalls in the square sell a mass of local produce.

The arcaded main square at Mirepoix

THE SOUTH OF FRANCE

Introducing the South of France

The South is France's most popular holiday region, drawing millions of visitors each year to the Riviera resorts, and modern beach cities to the west. Agriculture is a mainstay of the economy, producing early fruits and an abundance of affordable wine. The new high-tech industries of Nice and Montpellier reflect the region's key role in the developing south coast sunbelt, while Corsica still preserves much of its natural beauty. The map shows the major sights of this sun-blessed region.

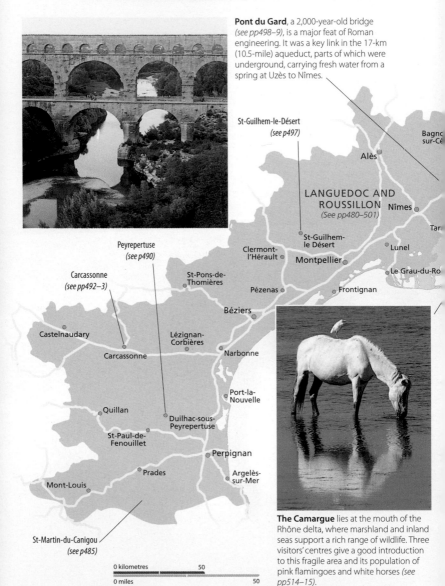

Pont du Gard, a 2,000-year-old bridge *(see pp498–9)*, is a major feat of Roman engineering. It was a key link in the 17-km (10.5-mile) aqueduct, parts of which were underground, carrying fresh water from a spring at Uzès to Nîmes.

St-Guilhem-le-Désert *(see p497)*

Peyrepertuse *(see p490)*

Carcassonne *(see pp492–3)*

LANGUEDOC AND ROUSSILLON *(See pp480–501)*

Alès
Nîmes
St-Guilhem-le Désert
Lunel
Clermont-l'Hérault
Montpellier
St-Pons-de-Thomières
Pézenas
Frontignan
Béziers
Castelnaudary
Lézignan-Corbières
Carcassonne
Narbonne
Port-la-Nouvelle
Quillan
Duilhac-sous-Peyrepertuse
St-Paul-de-Fenouillet
Perpignan
Prades
Argelès-sur-Mer
Mont-Louis

St-Martin-du-Canigou *(see p485)*

0 kilometres 50
0 miles 50

The Camargue lies at the mouth of the Rhône delta, where marshland and inland seas support a rich range of wildlife. Three visitors' centres give a good introduction to this fragile area and its population of pink flamingoes and white horses *(see pp514–15)*.

◄ A field of sunflowers in Languedoc

Avignon, enclosed by massive ramparts, became papal territory when popes decamped from Rome *(see pp507–9)* in the 14th century, taking up residence in the Palais des Papes, which towers over the town. In the summer the town is the scene of the popular Avignon Festival.

Giacometti Statue, St-Paul de Vence *(see pp528–9)*

Musée Matisse, Nice *(see pp530–31)*

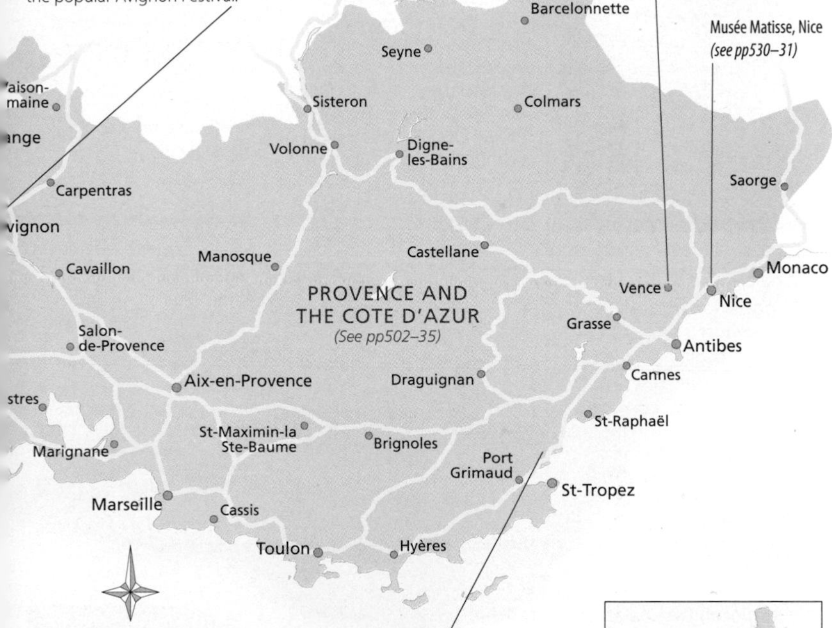

Barcelonnette
Seyne
'aison-maine
Sisteron
Colmars
ange
Volonne
Digne-les-Bains
Carpentras
Saorge
vignon
Castellane
Manosque
Cavaillon
Monaco
PROVENCE AND THE COTE D'AZUR
(See pp502–35)
Vence
Nice
Grasse
Salon-de-Provence
Antibes
Aix-en-Provence
Draguignan
Cannes
stres
St-Raphaël
St-Maximin-la Ste-Baume
Brignoles
Marignane
Port Grimaud
St-Tropez
Marseille
Cassis
Toulon
Hyères

Bastia
Calvi
Statue of Napoleon, Ajaccio *(see p546)*
CORSICA
(See pp536–47)
Ajaccio
Bonifacio

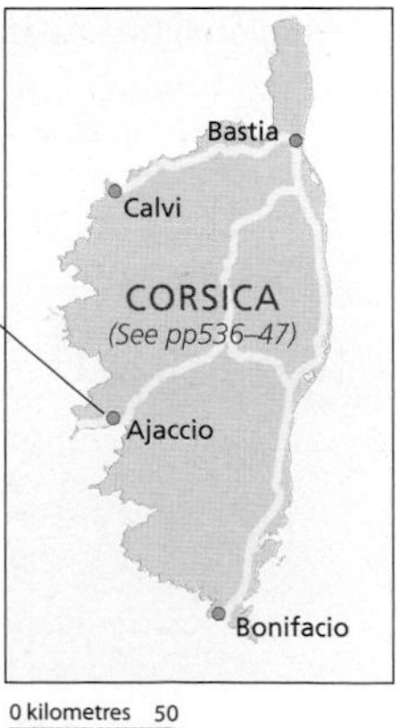

0 kilometres 50
0 miles 50

The Côte d'Azur has attracted sun-worshippers and celebrities since the 1920s *(see pp478–9)*. The coast also offers some prize collections of 20th-century art *(pp476–7)* and yearly events such as the Cannes Film Festival and Jazz à Juan.

For keys to symbols *see back flap*

The Flavours of the South of France

Mediterranean France has a fresh, sunny cuisine, with ripe and flavourful fruit and vegetables, fresh fish and seafood, and lean meat from mountain pastures. Good dishes are enhanced by key ingredients: olive oil, garlic and aromatic herbs. Markets are a colourful feast of seasonal produce all year round. Whether you opt for a picnic choice of local hams, sausage, bread and cheese to eat on the beach, share a simple lunch of tomato salad and grilled fish or lamb in a village bistro, or indulge in the sophisticated cuisine of one of France's top chefs, you can be sure of food that is not only authentic and delicious, but healthy too.

Local olives and olive oil

Preserving anchovies in seasoned olive oil in Languedoc and Roussillon

Languedoc and Roussillon

There is a robust Catalan flavour to the food in this area bordering Spain. Spices and almonds add an exotic touch to the fruit and vegetables produced in abundance on the Roussillon plain, and the grass-fed beef and lamb of the Mediterranean Pyrenees. Fish is plentiful: Sète is the largest fishing port on the French Mediterranean, huge oyster and mussel beds thrive in the saltwater lagoons of the coast and the little fishing port of Collioure is famous for its anchovies. Local dishes include *brandade de morue*, a speciality of Nîmes, squid stuffed with anchovies and snails with garlic and ham. Roussillon is famous for its peaches and apricots, and the cherries of Ceret are always the first to be harvested in France. Goat's milk is the main source of cheese, with round, orange-rinded Pélardon the most common.

Provence and the Côte d'Azur

This is the land of the olive and of rich green olive oil. These are

Selection of Mediterranean seafood available in the south of France

Regional Dishes and Specialities

The *cuisine du soleil* ("cuisine of the sun") has produced several classic dishes, of which *bouillabaisse* is the most famous. The ingredients of this fish stew vary from place to place, though Marseille claims the original recipe. A variety of local seafood (always including *rascasse*, or scorpion fish) is cooked in stock with tomatoes and saffron. The fish liquor is traditionally served first, with croûtons spread with *rouille*, a spicy mayonnaise, and the fish served afterwards. Once a fisherman's supper, it is now a luxury item you may need to order 24 hours in advance. A simpler version is *bourride*, a garlicky fish soup. Rich red wine stews, known as *daubes*, are another speciality, usually made with beef, but sometimes with tuna or calamari. Other classics include *ratatouille* and *salade niçoise*.

Fresh figs

Artichauts à la barigoule Small violet artichokes are stuffed with bacon and vegetables, cooked in wine.

Dried spices and herbs on sale at the market in Nice

evident in a wide range of dishes, such as *aioli*, a rich mayonnaise of olive oil and garlic, served with vegetables or fish; *tapenade*, a purée of olives, anchovies and capers; and *pissaladière*, a type of pizza made with onions, olives and anchovies, with a distinct Italian accent. Vegetables play a leading role: courgettes (zucchini) or tomatoes stuffed in the *niçois* style with meat, rice and herbs; baby artichokes sautéed with bacon; or aromatic *pistou*, a bean and vegetable soup laced with a sauce of basil and garlic. Mediterranean fish is highly prized, and is often best appreciated simply grilled. Meat includes game and rabbit; Sisteron lamb, grazed on high mountain pastures; and the bull's meat stew of the Camargue, served with nutty local red rice. There is also ripe fruit aplenty, from juicy figs to fragrant Cavaillon melons to the vivid lemons of Menton.

Corsica

The cuisine of Corsica is a robust version of the Mediterranean diet. Chestnuts were once the staple food of the island, and the flour is still widely used. There is a huge variety of *charcuterie*, including flavoursome hams and sausages, smoked, cured or air-dried in the traditional way. Wild boar is a delicacy, stewed with chestnuts in red wine. Roast goat *(cabri rôti)* is served as a festive meal, spiked with garlic and rosemary. Game, from rabbit to pigeon and partridge, is also very popular. On the coast there is locally caught fish and seafood, including monkfish, squid, sea urchins and sardines, the latter most delicious stuffed with herbs and Brocciu, a ricotta-style soft cheese. Local honey is redolent of mountain herbs, and jams are made from a huge variety of ingredients.

Ripe chestnuts on the tree in a Corsican forest

ON THE MENU

Beignets des fleurs de courgette Courgette (zucchini) flower fritters.

Estoficada Salt cod stewed with tomatoes, potatoes, garlic and olives.

Fougasse Flat olive oil bread often studded with olives.

Ratatouille Stew of aubergine (eggplant), tomatoes, courgettes (zucchini) and peppers.

Salade niçoise Lettuce with hard-boiled egg, olives, green beans, tomatoes and anchovies.

Socca Chickpea (garbanzo) pancakes, a speciality of Nice.

Tourte des blettes Pie of chard, raisins and pine kernels.

Brandade de morue Dried salted cod is cooked in water, then beaten with olive oil and milk to make a purée.

Daube de boeuf Beef is marinated in red wine, onions and garlic, then stewed with orange peel and tomato.

Crème catalane Originating in Spain, this dessert is an eggy custard topped with a flambéed sugar crust.

France's Wine Regions: the South

A massive arc stretching from Banyuls, in the extreme southern corner of France, to Nice, close to the Italian border, encompasses the Mediterranean vineyards of Languedoc and Roussillon and Provence. This was for a century an area of mass-produced wine, and much is still of *vin de France* quality. Today, however, the more dynamic producers are applying new technology to traditional and classic grape varieties to revive southern France's nobler heritage of generous, warm, aromatic wines, redolent of sun-baked stone, the scent of wild herbs, and the shimmering waters of the Mediterranean.

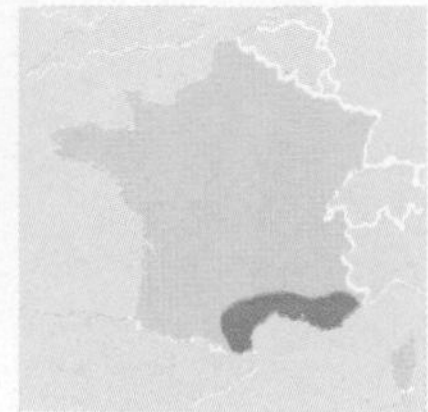

Locator Map

Languedoc and Roussillon & Provence

Coteaux du Languedoc (since 2012, just "Languedoc") is a large and varied *appellation* stretching from Narbonne towards Nîmes.

The quality wines produced by Mass de Daumas Gassac have earned this vineyard its reputation as the *grand cru* of Languedoc.

Stop here to try the wines of Côtes du Roussillon – idiosyncratic yet characterful, dry white wines, dry rosés and medium reds.

0 kilometres 25

0 miles 25

Key

- Collioure & Banyuls
- Côtes de Roussillon
- Côtes de Roussillon Villages
- Fitou
- Corbières
- Minervois
- Coteaux du Languedoc/Languedoc
- Costières du Gard
- Coteaux d'Aix en Provence
- Côtes de Provence
- Bandol & Côtes de Provence
- Coteaux Varois
- Bellet

Rugged valley slopes in Corbières

Hand-picking grapes for Côtes de Provence red wine

Wine Regions

Both in the Provence wine region, east of Aix and Marseille, and in the larger Languedoc and Roussillon area to the west, new quality wine appellations, *such as Cabardès (north of Carcassonne), are joining the more familiar names.*

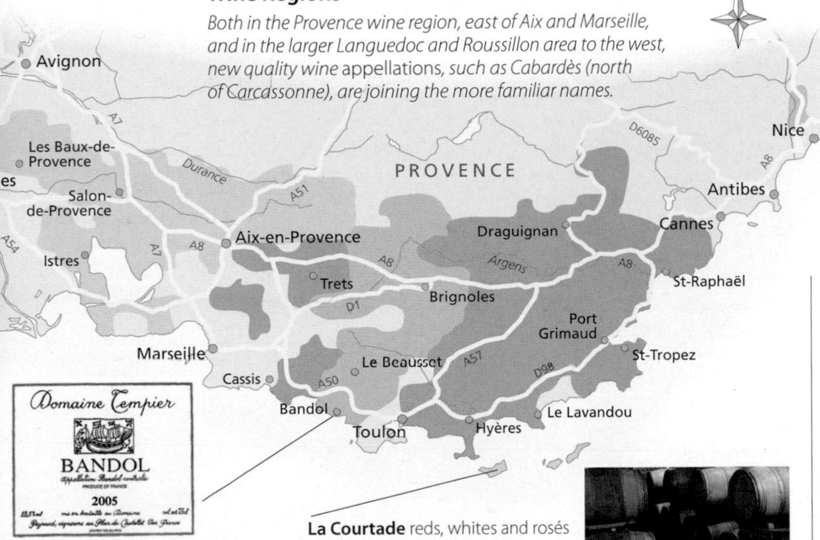

Bandol is a small *appellation* that uses a traditional southern French red grape, the *Mourvèdre*, to produce its quality reds.

La Courtade reds, whites and rosés are produced by the Domaine de la Courtade, one of three vineyards located on the Ile de Porquerolles off the coast of Provence.

Key Facts About Wines of the South

Location and Climate

A warm and sunny climate helps to create generously alcoholic wines. The flat coastal plains support acres of vines, but generally the best sites are on the schist and limestone hillsides.

Grape Varieties

Mass-production grapes such as ***Aramon*** are giving way to quality varieties such as ***Syrah***, ***Mourvèdre*** and ***Grenache***. ***Cabernet Sauvignon***, ***Merlot*** and ***Syrah***, and the whites ***Chardonnay***, ***Sauvignon Blanc*** and ***Viognier***, are increasingly used for *IGPs* *(see p30)*. Rich, sweet whites are made from the aromatic, honeyed ***Muscat*** grape.

Good Producers

Corbières & Minervois: La Voulte Gasparets, Saint Auriol, Lastours, Villerambert-Julien. *Faugères*: Château des Estanilles, Château de la Liquiere. *St Chinian*: Château Cazal-Viel, Domaine Navarre, Cave de Roquebrun. *Coteaux du Languedoc/Languedoc* and *IGPs*: Mas Jullien, Château de Capitoul, Domaine de la Garance, Mas de Daumas Gassac, Pech-Celeyran. *Roussillon*: Domaine Gauby, Domaine Sarda Malet. *Provence:* Domaine Tempier, Château Pibarnon, Domaine de Trévallon, Mas de la Dame, Domaine Richeaume, La Courtade, Château Simone, Château Pradeaux, Château de Bellet.

Artists and Writers in the South of France

Artists and writers have helped to create our image of the South of France – the poet Stephen Liégeard even gave the Côte d'Azur its name in 1887. Many writers, French and foreign, found a haven in the warmth of the south. From Cézanne to van Gogh, Monet to Picasso, artists have been inspired by the special light and brilliant colours of this seductive region. Today, it is rich in art museums, some devoted to single artists including Matisse, Picasso and Chagall, others with varied collections such as those in Céret *(see p486)*, Nîmes *(see pp500–1)*, Montpellier *(see pp498–9)*, St-Tropez *(see p520)*, St-Paul de Vence *(see pp528–9)* and Nice *(see pp530–31)*.

Picasso and Françoise Gilot on the Golfe Juan, 1948

Paul Cézanne's studio in Aix-en-Provence *(see p515)*

Festive Light

The Impressionists were fascinated by the effects of light, and Monet was entranced by "the glaring festive light" of the south, which made colours so intense he said no one would believe they were real if painted accurately. In 1883 Renoir came with him to the south, returning often to paint his voluptuous nudes in the filtered golden light. Bonnard too settled here, painting endless views of the red-tiled roofs and palm trees.

Post-Impressionists van Gogh and Gauguin arrived in 1888, attracted by the region's rich colours. Cézanne, who was born in Aix in 1839, analysed and painted the structure of nature, above all the landscape of Provence and his beloved Mont-Ste-Victoire. Pointillist Paul Signac came to St-Tropez to paint sea and sky in a rainbow palette of dots.

The Wild Beasts

The Fauves, dubbed "Wild Beasts" for their unnaturally bright and wild colours, led one of the first 20th-century avant-garde movements, founded by Matisse in Collioure in 1905 *(see p487)*. Other Fauves included Derain, Vlaminck, Marquet, Van Dongen and Dufy. Matisse visited Corsica in 1898, and then St-Tropez, and was inspired by the sensuality of Provence to paint the celebrated *Luxe, Calme et Volupté*. Eventually he settled in Nice, where he painted his great series of Odalisques. He wrote, "What made me stay are the great coloured reflections of January, the luminosity of daylight." The exquisite blue-and-white chapel he designed in Vence is one of the most moving of his later works *(see p527)*.

Vincent van Gogh's *Sunflowers* (1888)

Picasso Country

The South of France is, without question, Picasso country. His nymphs and sea urchins, his monumental women running on the beach, his shapes and colours, ceramics and sculpture are all derived from the hard shadows and bright colours of the south.

Pablo Picasso was born in Málaga in Spain in 1881, but he spent much of his life on the French Mediterranean, developing Cubism with Braque in Céret in 1911, and arriving in Juan-les-Pins in 1920. He was in Antibes, when war broke out in 1939, where he painted *Night Fishing at Antibes*, a luminous nocturnal seascape. He returned in 1946 and was given the Grimaldi Palace to use as a studio. It is now a Picasso Museum *(see p525)*. He also worked in Vallauris, producing ceramics and sculptures *(see p526)*.

Deux Femmes Courant sur la Plage (1922) by Pablo Picasso

Lost Caviar Days

Just as F Scott Fitzgerald wrote the Jazz Age into existence, he created the glittering image of life on the Riviera with *Tender is the Night*. He and Zelda arrived in 1924, attracted, like many expatriate writers, by the warm climate and the cheap, easy living. "One could get away with more on the summer Riviera, and whatever happened seemed to have something to do with art," he wrote. They passed their villa on to another American, Ernest Hemingway. Many other writers flocked there including Katherine Mansfield, D H Lawrence, Aldous Huxley, Friedrich Nietzsche, Lawrence Durrell and Graham Greene. Some, including Somerset Maugham, led glamorous lifestyles surrounded by exotic guests. Colette was an early visitor to St-Tropez, and in 1954, Françoise Sagan captured the youthful hedonism of the time in her novel *Bonjour Tristesse*.

Scott and Zelda Fitzgerald with daughter Scottie

New Realism

In the 1950s Nice produced its own school of artists, the Nouveaux Réalistes, including Yves Klein, Arman, Martial Raysse, Tinguely, César, Niki de Saint Phalle and Daniel Spoerri *(see pp530–31)*. They explored the possibilities of everyday objects – Arman sliced violins, packaged and displayed trash; Tinguely exploded TV sets and cars. They had a light-hearted approach: "We live in a land of vacations, which gives us the spirit of nonsense," said Klein. He painted solid blue canvases of his personal colour, International Klein Blue, taking the inspiration of the Mediterranean to its limit.

Provençal Writers

The regions of Provence and Languedoc have always had a distinct literary identity, ever since the troubadours in the 12th–13th centuries composed their love poetry in the *langue d'oc* Provençal, a Latin-based language. In the 20th century, many regional writers have been inspired by the landscape and local traditions. They were influenced by the 19th-century Felibrige Movement to revive the language, led by Nobel Prize-winning poet Frédéric Mistral. Some, including Daudet and film-maker-turned-writer Marcel Pagnol, celebrate the Provençal character; others, such as Jean Giono, explore the connection between nature and humanity.

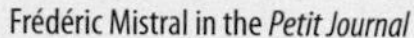

Frédéric Mistral in the *Petit Journal*

Beaches in the South of France

The glamorous Mediterranean coast is France's foremost holiday playground. To the east lie the Riviera's big, traditional resorts such as Menton, Nice, Cannes and Monte-Carlo. To the west are smaller resorts in coves and bays including St-Tropez and Cassis. Further on is the Camargue Regional Nature Park at the mouth of the Rhône. West of the Rhône, making a majestic curve reaching almost to the Spanish border, is the long, sandy shore of Languedoc and Roussillon, where a string of purpose-built resorts range from modernistic beach cities to replicas of fishing villages.

The beaches are sandy west of Antibes; eastwards, they are naturally shingly, so any sand is imported. Anti-pollution drives mean that most beaches are now clean, except in a few spots west of Marseille and around Nice. Private beaches are plentiful and pricey but are usually well equipped.

A rail poster by David Dellepiane advertising the Côte d'Azur

LANGUEDOC AND ROUSSILLON
Montpellier
Le Grande-Motte
Camargue
Rhône
Stes-Maries-de-la-Mer
Martigues
Carro
Sète
Golfe du Lion
Beziers
Agde
Narbonne
Gruissan
Port Leucate
Le Barcarès
Canet-Plage
Argelès-Plage
Collioure

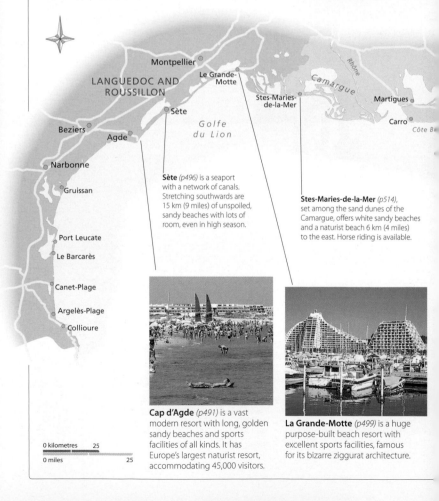

Sète *(p496)* is a seaport with a network of canals. Stretching southwards are 15 km (9 miles) of unspoiled, sandy beaches with lots of room, even in high season.

Stes-Maries-de-la-Mer *(p514)*, set among the sand dunes of the Camargue, offers white sandy beaches and a naturist beach 6 km (4 miles) to the east. Horse riding is available.

0 kilometres 25
0 miles 25

Cap d'Agde *(p491)* is a vast modern resort with long, golden sandy beaches and sports facilities of all kinds. It has Europe's largest naturist resort, accommodating 45,000 visitors.

La Grande-Motte *(p499)* is a huge purpose-built beach resort with excellent sports facilities, famous for its bizarre ziggurat architecture.

In Victorian times the Côte d'Azur, or Riviera, was the fashionable holiday venue of Europe's royalty and rich. They came to gamble and escape northern winters. Summer bathing did not come into vogue until the 1920s. Today the Riviera is busy all year round, with the glamorous beaches and nightlife still a major attraction.

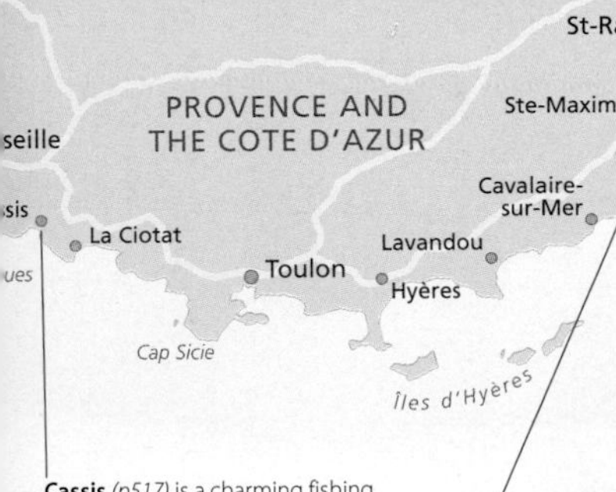

Menton *(p533)* has a warm climate in winter, giving beach weather all year. Its sheltered, shingly beaches are backed by beautiful villas.

Cannes *(pp524–5)* takes great pride in its golden beaches, keeping them scrupulously clean: most are private with entrance fees.

Cassis *(p517)* is a charming fishing village with a popular casino, white cliffs and some lovely hidden creeks nearby.

St-Tropez *(p520)* is flanked by golden beaches, mostly occupied by stylish "clubs" offering amenities at a price.

Nice *(pp530–31)* has a visually dramatic waterfront with a wide, handsome promenade, but the beach itself is stony and has a busy highway alongside.

Cap Ferrat *(p532)* is a wooded peninsula with a 10-km (6-mile) craggy cliff walk, offering glimpses of grand villas and private beaches.

LANGUEDOC AND ROUSSILLON

Pyrénées-Orientales · Aude · Gard · Hérault

The southern area of Languedoc and Roussillon stretches from the foothills of the Pyrenees to the mouth of the Rhône. The flat beaches and lagoons of the coast form a popular sunbelt. In between is a dry, scorched land producing half of France's table wine and the season's first peaches and cherries.

Beyond such sensuous pleasures are many layers of history, not least the amalgamation of Languedoc and Roussillon within the new region of Occitanie, created in 2016. Languedoc is where Occitan, the tongue of the troubadours, was once spoken and the area still cherishes its linguistic and cultural identity. Roussillon was a Spanish possession until the treaty of the Pyrenees in 1659. Catalan heritage is displayed everywhere from the road signs to the Sardana dance, and the flavour of Spain is evident in the popularity of paella and gaudily painted façades.

This stretch of coastline was the first place in Gaul to be settled by the Romans, their enduring legacy evident in the great amphitheatre at Nîmes and the magnificent engineering of the Pont du Gard. The abbeys of St-Martin-du-Canigou, St-Michel-de-Cuxa and St-Guilhem-le-Désert are superb examples of early Romanesque architecture, unaffected by Northern Gothic. The great craggy Cathar castles and the perfectly restored medieval city of Carcassonne bear witness to the bloody battles of the Middle Ages.

In parts, the area remains wild and untamed: from the high plateaux of the Cerdagne, to the wild hills of the Corbières, or the remote uplands of Haut Languedoc. But it also has the most youthful and progressive cities in France: Montpellier, the ancient university city and capital of the region, and Nîmes with its exuberant *feria*. The whole area is typified by an insouciant mixture of ancient and modern, from Roman temples and Postmodern architecture in its cities to solar power and ancient abbeys in the mountains.

The coastline at La Vieux Cap, Cap d'Agde

◀ The citadel of Carcassonne

Exploring Languedoc and Roussillon

Languedoc and Roussillon combine miles of gentle coastline with a rugged hinterland. The clean, sandy beaches are perfect for family holidays, with resorts ranging from traditional fishing villages to new purpose-built resorts. Inland is quieter, with acres of vineyards in the Corbières and Minervois and mountain walks in the Haut Languedoc and Cerdagne. A rich architectural heritage ranges from Roman to Romanesque, contrasting with the modern, vibrant atmosphere of the main cities.

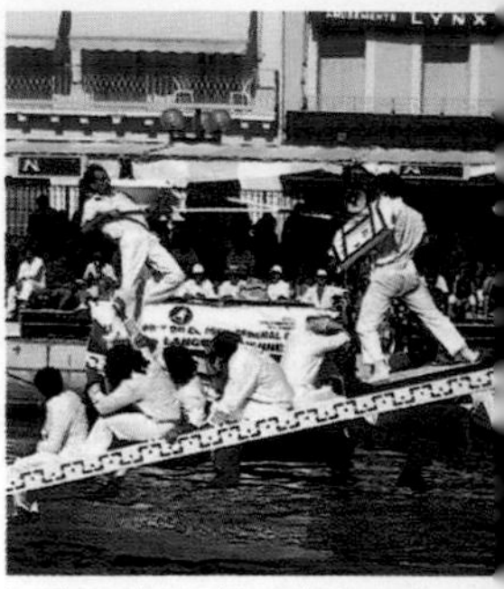

Jousting on the canal, a regular summer event in Sète

Sights at a Glance

1. Cerdagne
2. Villefranche-de-Conflent
3. St-Michel-de-Cuxa
4. St-Martin-du-Canigou
5. Prieuré de Serrabone
6. Céret
7. Côte Vermeille
8. Collioure
9. Elne
10. Perpignan
11. Forteresse de Salses
12. Corbières
13. Narbonne
14. Golfe du Lion
15. *Carcassonne (pp492–3)*
16. Minerve
17. Béziers
18. Sète
19. Pézenas
20. Parc Naturel Régional du Haut Languedoc
21. St-Guilhem-le-Désert
22. Montpellier
23. La Grande-Motte
24. Aigues-Mortes
25. *Nîmes (pp500–1)*
26. Pont du Gard

For keys to symbols *see back flap*

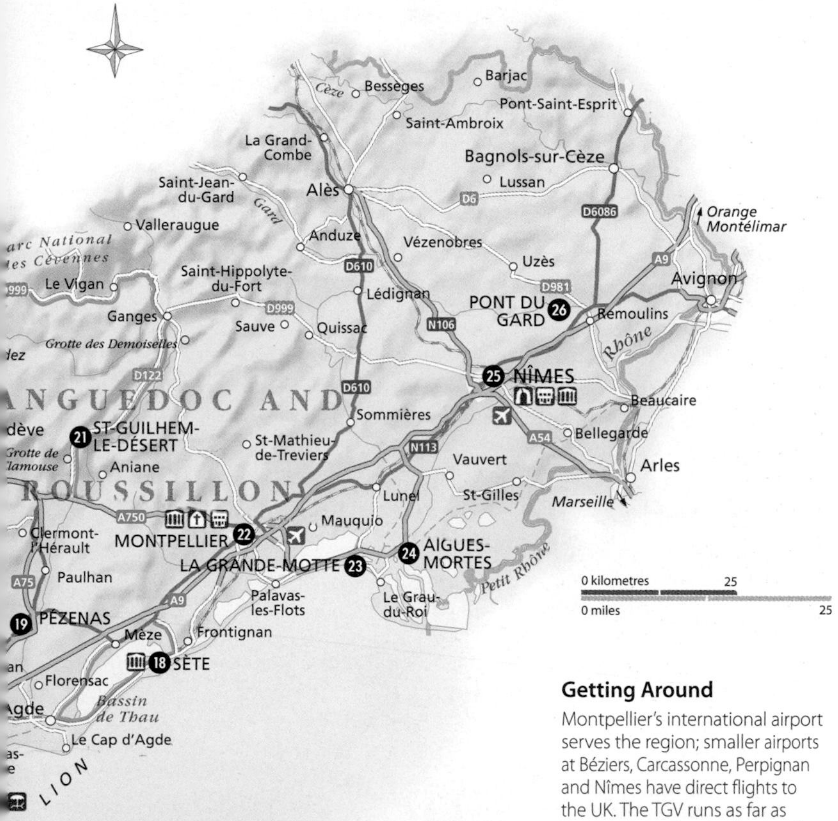

Getting Around

Montpellier's international airport serves the region; smaller airports at Béziers, Carcassonne, Perpignan and Nîmes have direct flights to the UK. The TGV runs as far as Perpignan, and a good rail and bus network connects the region's main towns. The A61 motorway provides access from the west and the A9 follows the coast. The A75 now enters from the north. Smaller roads, even in the mountains, are well maintained. Barges along the Canal du Midi are a leisurely alternative.

The ruined Barbarossa tower at Gruissan on the Golfe du Lion

Key

- Motorway
- Major road
- Secondary road
- Minor road
- Scenic route
- Main railway
- Minor railway
- International border
- Regional border
- △ Summit

❶ Cerdagne

Pyrénées-Orientales. Perpignan. Mont Louis, Bourg Madame, Latour de Carol Enveitg. 1 pl de Roser, Saillagouse (04 68 04 15 47); Mont Louis (04 68 04 21 97).
pyrenees-cerdagne.com
mont-louis.net

The remote Cerdagne, an independent state in the Middle Ages, is today divided between Spain and France. Its high plateaux offer skiing and walking among clear mountain lakes and pine and chestnut forests. The Little Yellow Train (08 00 88 60 91, www.ter-sncf.com) is an excellent way to sample it in a day. Stops include **Mont Louis**, a town fortified by Vauban, Louis XIV's military architect, and which still accommodates French troops; the huge ski resort of **Font-Romeu**; **Latour-de-Carol** and the tiny village of **Yravals** below it. Nearby **Odeillo** is the site of a solar furnace, 45 m (150 ft) tall and 50 m (165 ft) wide, and its giant curved mirrors create a remarkable sight in the valley.

❷ Villefranche-de-Conflent

Pyrénées-Orientales. 230. 33 rue Saint Jacques (04 68 96 22 96). **villefranchedeconflent.fr**

In medieval times Villefranche's position at the narrowest point of the Têt Valley made it an eminently defensible fortress against Moorish invasion. Fragments of 11th-century walls remain, along with massive ramparts, gates and Fort Liberia high above the gorge, and all built by Vauban in the 17th century. The 12th-century **Eglise de St-Jacques** has fine carved capitals from the workshops of St-Michel-de-Cuxa, and Catalan painted wooden statues, including a 14th-century Virgin and Child. The 13th-century oak door is embellished with intricate local wrought ironwork, a craft that still features on many of the shop signs in town. From the streets of locally quarried pink marble you can make the climb up to the **Grottes des Canalettes**, a superb underground setting for concerts. The Little Yellow Train will take you to the magnificent mountain plain of the Cerdagne.

Abbey cloisters of St-Michel-de-Cuxa

Statue in St-Jacques, Villefranche

The Little Yellow Train

Arrive early for the best seats in the carriages of *Le Petit Train Jaune*, which winds its way on narrow-gauge tracks through gorges and across towering viaducts up into the Cerdagne, stopping at small mountain stations along the way. Built in 1910 to improve access to the mountains, it now operates mainly for tourists, beginning at Villefranche-de-Conflent and terminating at Latour-de-Carol.

The Little Yellow Train, with open carriages for summer visitors

❸ St-Michel-de-Cuxa

Abbey of St-Michel-de-Cuxa: Rte de Tourinya Codalet, Prades, Pyrénées-Orientales. **Tel** 04 68 96 15 35.
Open May–Sep: 9:30–11:50am & 2–6pm; Oct–Apr: 2–5pm.
Closed 1 Jan, Easter Sunday, 25 Dec.
abbaye- cuxa.com
10 pl de la République, Prades (04 68 05 41 02). **prades-tourisme.fr**

Prades, a small, pink marble town in the Têt Valley, is typical of the local style. The **Eglise St-Pierre** has a southern Gothic wrought iron belfry and a Baroque Catalan interior. But the town is distinguished by the pre-Romanesque **abbey of St-Michel-de-Cuxa**, which lies 3 km (2 miles) further up the valley, and by the legacy of the Spanish cellist Pablo Casals, who spent many years here in exile from Franco's Spain; the Prades music festival is held every year in the abbey in his memory.

St-Michel-de-Cuxa abbey was founded by Benedictine monks in 878 and rapidly became renowned throughout France and Spain. Distinctive, Moorish-influenced keyhole arches pierce the massive walls of the abbey church, which was consecrated in 974. The mottled pink marble cloisters, with their superbly carved capitals, were added in the 12th century.

After the Revolution the building was abandoned, and its famous carvings looted. From 1913, George Grey Bernard, a visiting American artist, began to discover some of the capitals incorporated in local buildings. In 1925 he sold the carvings to the Metropolitan Museum of Art in New York, where they formed the basis of the Cloisters Museum – a faithful re-creation of a Romanesque abbey in the unlikely setting of Manhattan.

❹ St-Martin-du-Canigou

Casteil. **Tel** 04 68 05 50 03. **Open** (guided tours only: tours last an hour; times vary with seasons) Jun–Sep: daily; Oct–May: Tue–Sun. **Closed** Jan, Good Friday. **stmartinducanigou.org**

St-Martin-du-Canigou is situated in a spectacularly remote site a third of the way up Pic du Canigou, on a jagged spur of rock approached only by a 40-minute climb on foot from Casteil, a special shuttle (Jul–Aug: daily) or hired transport. Built at the beginning of the 11th century, the abbey was financed by Guifred, Count of Cerdagne, who entered the monastery in 1035. He was buried there 14 years later in a tomb he carved from the rock himself, and which can still be seen. The early Romanesque church is based on a simple basilican plan. Two churches built quite literally one on top of the other make the lower church the crypt for the upper building.

The abbey complex is best viewed from above, by continuing up the path. From there, its irregular design clinging to the rock is framed by the dramatic mountain setting – the ensemble a tribute to the ingenuity and vitality of its early builders.

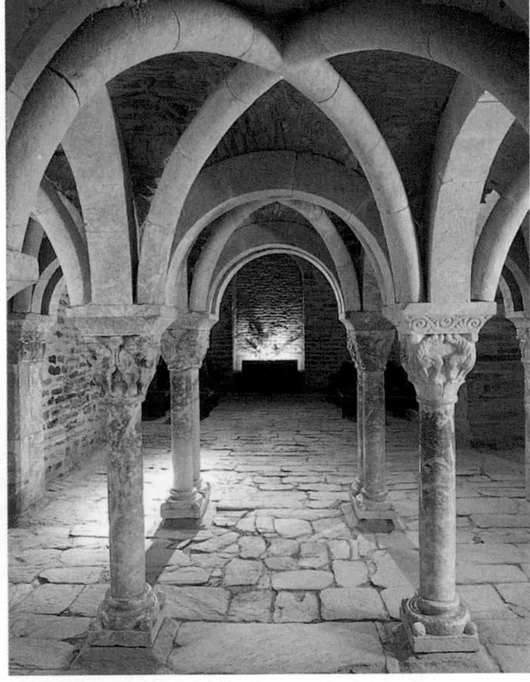

Serrabone priory's chapel tribune, with columns of local marble

The 11th-century cloister of St-Martin-du-Canigou

❺ Prieuré de Serrabone

Boule d'Amont. **Tel** 04 68 84 09 30 (tourist office). **Open** 10am–6pm daily. **Closed** 1 Jan, 1 May, 1 Nov, 25 Dec.

Perched high up on the northern flanks of Pic du Canigou, the sacred mountain of the Catalans, is the priory of Serrabone. A final lap of hairpin bends on the approach road (the D618) reveals the simple square tower and round apse of this remote Romanesque abbey, surrounded by a botanical garden of local herbs and woodland plants clinging to the mountain side.

Inside the cool, austere 12th-century building is a surprisingly elaborate chapel tribune, its columns and arches glowing from the local red-veined marble, carved by the anonymous Master of Cuixà, whose work appears throughout the region. Note the strange beasts and verdant flora featured in the capital carvings, especially the rose of Roussillon.

6 Céret

Pyrénées-Orientales. 8,000. 1 av Clémenceau (04 68 87 00 53). Sat, Tue eve Jul–Aug. Fête des Cerises (May/Jun). ot-ceret.fr

Surrounded by a cloud of pink blossom in the early spring, Céret produces the very first cherries of the year. The annual cherry festival is held in early June. The tiled and painted façades and loggias of the buildings have a Spanish feel. The town was popular with Picasso, Braque and Matisse, and today the sophisticated **Musée d'Art Moderne** houses a remarkable collection, which includes Catalan artists Tapiès and Capdeville; 50 works donated by Picasso, including a series of bowls painted with bullfighting scenes; and works by Matisse, Chagall, Juan Gris and Salvador Dalí.

The town's Catalan heritage is evident in regular bullfights held in the arena, and in its Sardana dance festivals in July.

Musée d'Art Moderne
8 bd Maréchal Joffre. **Tel** 04 68 87 27 76. **Open** 10am–5:30pm Tue–Sun (Jul–Sep: to 7pm daily) . **Closed** Tue (Oct–Jun), 1 Jan, 1 May, 1 Nov & 25 Dec. **musee-ceret.com**

Environs
From Céret the D115 follows the Tech Valley to the spa town of **Amélie-les-Bains**, where fragments of Roman baths have been discovered. Beyond, in **Arles-sur-Tech**, the Eglise de Ste-Marie contains 12th-century frescoes, and, beside the church door, a sarcophagus, which, according to local legend, produces drops of unaccountably pure water every year.

Statue by Aristide Maillol, Banyuls

7 Côte Vermeille

Pyrénées-Orientales. Perpignan. Collioure, Cerbère. Collioure, Banyuls-sur-Mer. Collioure (04 68 82 15 47). **collioure.com**

Here the Pyrenees meet the Mediterranean, the coast road twisting and turning around secluded pebbly coves and rocky outcrops. The *vermeille* (vermilion-tinted) rock of the headlands gives this stretch of coast, the loveliest in the region, its name.

The Côte Vermeille extends all the way to the Costa Brava in northern Spain. With its Catalan character, it is as redolent of Spain as of France. **Argelès-Plage** has three sandy beaches and a palm-fringed promenade, and is the largest camping centre in Europe. The small resort of **Cerbère** is the last French town before the border, flying the red-and-gold Catalan flag to signal its true allegiance. All along the coast, terraced vineyards cling to the rocky hillsides, producing strong, sweet wines such as Banyuls and Muscat. The difficult terrain makes harvesting a laborious process. Vines were first cultivated here by Greek settlers in the 7th century BC, and Banyuls itself has wine cellars dating back to the Middle Ages.

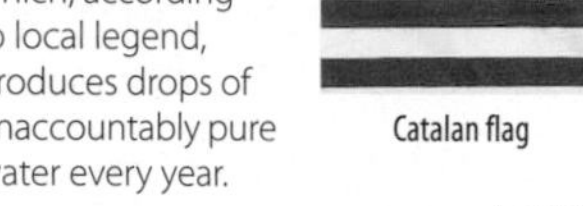
Catalan flag

Banyuls is also famous as the birthplace of Aristide Maillol, the 19th-century sculptor, whose work can be seen all over the region. **Port Vendres**, with fortifications built by the indefatigable Vauban (architect to Louis XIV), is a fishing port, renowned for its anchovies and sardines.

The spectacular Côte Vermeille, seen from the coast road south of Banyuls

For hotels and restaurants in this region see p569 and pp599–601

Collioure harbour, with one of its beaches and the Eglise Notre-Dame-des-Anges

8 Collioure

Pyrénées-Orientales. 3,000. pl du 18 juin (04 68 82 15 47). Wed & Sun. **collioure.com**

The colours of Collioure first attracted Matisse here in 1905: brightly stuccoed houses sheltered by cypresses and gaily painted fishing boats, all bathed in the famous luminous light, and washed by a gentle sea. Other artists including André Derain worked here under Matisse's influence and were dubbed *fauves* (wild beasts) for their wild experiments with colour. Art galleries and souvenir shops now fill the cobbled streets, but this small fishing port has changed little since then, with anchovies still its main business. Two salting houses, which can be visited, are evidence of this tradition.

Three sheltered beaches, both pebble and sand, nestle round the harbour, dominated by the bulk of the **Château Royal**, which forms part of the harbour wall. It was first built by the Knights Templar in the 13th century, and Collioure became the main port of entry for Perpignan, remaining under the rule of Spanish Aragon until France took over in 1659. The outer fortifications were reinforced ten years later by Vauban, who demolished much of the original town in the process. Today the château can be toured, or visited for its exhibitions of modern art.

The **Eglise Notre-Dame-des-Anges** on Collioure's quayside was rebuilt in the 17th century to replace the church that was destroyed by Vauban. A former lighthouse was incorporated as a bell tower. Inside the church are no fewer than five Baroque altarpieces by Joseph Sunyer and other Catalan masters of the genre.

Be warned that Collioure is extremely popular in July and August, with visitors cramming the tiny streets. Long queues of traffic are possible, too, though the building of another route, the D86, has helped to ease congestion.

Château Royal
Tel 04 68 82 06 43. **Open** daily. **Closed** 1 Jan, 1 May, 15 & 16 Aug, 25 Dec.

9 Elne

Pyrénées-Orientales. 8,500. 14 bd Voltaire (04 68 22 05 07). Mon, Wed, Fri. **elne-tourisme.com**

This ancient town accommodated Hannibal and his elephants in 218 BC on his epic journey to Rome, and was one of the most important towns in Roussillon until the 16th century. Today it is famed for the 11th-century **Cathédrale de Ste-Eulalie et Ste-Julie**, with its superb marble cloister. Its sculpted capitals are embellished with flowers, figures and arabesques. The side nearest the cathedral dates from the 1100s; the remaining three from the 13th and 14th centuries.

Cathédrale de Ste-Eulalie et Ste-Julie
Tel 04 68 22 70 90/05 07. **Open** Oct–Apr: Tue–Sun; May–Sep: daily. **Closed** 1 Jan, 1 May & 25 Dec.

Carved capital at Elne, showing "The Dream of the Magi"

Entrance to the Palais des Rois de Majorque, Perpignan

⑩ Perpignan

Pyrénées-Orientales. 122,000. Place Arago (04 68 66 30 30). daily.
perpignantourisme.com

Catalan Perpignan has a distinctly southern feel, with palm trees lining place Arago, house and shop façades painted vibrant turquoise and pink, and the streets of the Arab quarter selling aromatic spices, couscous and paella.

Today, Perpignan is the vibrant capital of Roussillon, and has an important position on the developing Mediterranean sunbelt. But it reached its zenith in the 13th and 14th centuries under the kings of Majorca and the kings of Aragón, who controlled great swathes of northern Spain and southern France. Their vast **Palais des Rois de Majorque** still straddles a substantial area in the southern part of the city.

Perpignan's strong Catalan identity is evident during the weekly summer celebrations when the Sardana – a key Catalan symbol – is danced. Arms raised, concentric circles of dancers keep step to the accompaniment of a Catalan woodwind band.

One of Perpignan's finest buildings, the **Loge de Mer**, lies at the head of the square. It was built in 1397 to house the Maritime Exchange, but only the eastern section retains the original Gothic design. The rest of the building was rebuilt in Renaissance style in 1540 with sumptuous carved wooden ceilings and sculpted window frames. The Loge de Mer has avoided becoming a hushed museum piece. Instead, it remains the centre of Perpignan life – elegant cafés cluster round it, producing a constant buzz of activity.

Next door is the **Hôtel de Ville** with its pebble stone façade and wrought-iron gates. Inside, parts of the arcaded courtyard date back to 1315; at the centre is Aristide Maillol's allegorical sculpture, *The Mediterranean* (1950).

To the east is the labyrinthine cathedral quarter of St-Jean, made up of small streets and squares containing some fine 14th- and 15th-century buildings.

Devout Christ in St-Jean

Cathédrale St-Jean

Pl de Gambetta. **Tel** 04 68 51 33 72. **Open** 8am–6pm Mon–Sat (7pm summer months); 2–6pm Sun.
cathedraleperpignan.fr

Topped by a wrought-iron belfry, this cathedral was begun in 1324 and was finally ready for use in 1509. It is constructed almost entirely from river pebbles layered with red brick, a style common throughout the region due to the scarcity of other building materials.

Inside the gloomy interior the nave is flanked by gilded altarpieces and painted wooden statues, with a massive pre-Romanesque marble font. A cloistered cemetery adjoins the church and the Chapel of the Devout Christ with its precious, poignantly realistic medieval wooden Crucifixion. The cathedral replaced the

The Annual Procession de la Sanch

There is a very Catalan atmosphere in Perpignan during the annual Good Friday procession of the Confraternity of La Sanch (Brotherhood of the Holy Blood). Originally dedicated to the comfort of condemned prisoners in the 15th century, members of the brotherhood still wear macabre red or black robes as they carry sacred relics and the crucifix from the Chapel of the Devout Christ to the cathedral.

11th-century church of St-Jean-le-Vieux, whose superb Romanesque doorway can be glimpsed to the left of the main entrance. Some areas may be restricted due to ongoing restoration work.

Palais des Rois de Majorque

2 rue des Archers. **Tel** 04 68 34 96 26. **Open** Oct–May: 9am–5pm; Jun–Sep: 10am–6pm. **Closed** 1 Jan, 1 May, 1 Nov & 25 Dec.

Access to the vast 13th-century fortified palace of the Kings of Majorca is as circuitous today as it was intended to be for invading soldiers. Flights of steps zigzag within the sheer red-brick ramparts, begun in the 15th century and added to successively over the next two centuries. Eventually, the elegant gardens and substantial castle within are revealed, entered by way of the Tour de l'Hommage, from the top of which is a panoramic view of city, mountains and sea.

The palace itself is built around a central arcaded courtyard, flanked on one side by the Salle de Majorque, a great hall with a triple fireplace and giant Gothic arched windows. Adjacent, two royal chapels built one above the other show southern Gothic style at its best: pointed arches, patterned frescoes and elaborate tilework demonstrating a distinct Moorish influence. The fine rose marble doorway of the upper King's Chapel is typical of the Roussillon Romanesque style, although the sculpted capitals are Gothic. Today the great courtyard is sometimes used for concerts.

Palais des Rois de Majorque

Musée des Arts et Traditions Populaires Catalans

pl de Verdun, Le Castillet. **Tel** 04 68 35 42 05. **Open** times vary with season. **Closed** bank holidays.

The red-brick tower and pink belfry of the Castillet, built as the town gate in 1368, was at one time a prison and is all that remains of the town walls. It now houses a traditional Catalan kitchen with furniture, looms and terracotta pots for storing water and oil.

Musée d'Art Hyacinthe Rigaud

21 rue Mailly. **Tel** 04 68 66 19 83. **Open** Oct–May: 11am–5:30pm Tue–Sun; Jun–Sep: 10:30am–7pm daily (Jul & Aug: till 9pm). **Closed** public hols. **musee-rigaud.fr**

Two magnificient mansions dating from the 17th and 18th centuries house an eclectic permanent collection dominated by the work of Hyacinthe Rigaud (1659–1743), who was born in Perpignan and was the court painter to Louis XIV and Louis XV. This is complemented by a display of the city's medieval art, whose *chef d'oeuvre* is the 15th-century *Retable de la Trinité* by the Master of the Loge de Mer. There is also a room dedicated to Aristide Maillol, whose work is on show alongside his contemporaries such as Alphonse Mucha and Picasso; the latter had several prolonged stays in the building and his studio on the second floor is open to the public.

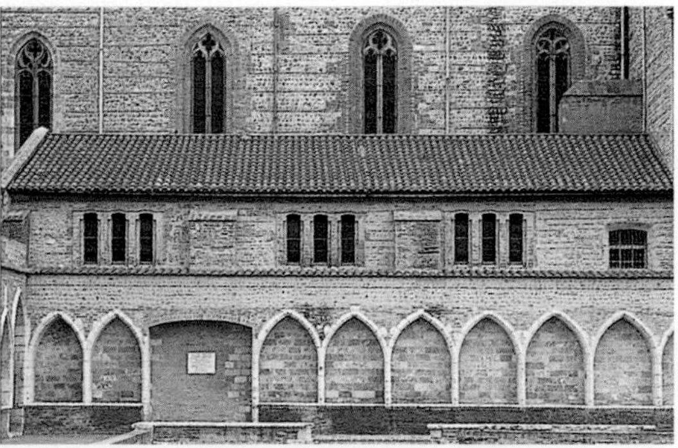

The pebble and red-brick Cathédrale St-Jean in Perpignan

Fortress tower and ramparts, Salses

⓫ Forteresse de Salses

Pyrénées-Orientales. 3,000. Salses-le-Château 66600 (04 68 38 60 13). **Open** 10am–5:15pm daily. **Closed** 1 Jan, 1 May, 1 & 11 Nov, 25 Dec. Wed. **forteresse-salses.fr**

Looking like a giant sandcastle against the ochre earth of the Corbières vineyards, the **Forteresse de Salses** stands at the old frontier of Spain and France. It guards the narrow defile between the Mediterranean lagoons and the mountains, and was built by King Ferdinand of Aragon between 1497 and 1506 to defend Spain's possession of Roussillon. Its massive walls and rounded towers are typical of Spanish military architecture, designed to deflect the new threat posed by gunpowder.

Inside were underground stables for 300 horses and a subterranean passageway.

Vineyards covering the hilly terrain of the Corbières

⓬ Corbières

Aude. Perpignan. Narbonne, Carcassonne, Lézignan-Corbières. Narbonne, Carcassonne, Lézignan-Corbières. 9 cours de la République, Lézignan-Corbières (04 68 27 05 42). **tourisme-corbieres-minervois.com**

Still one of the wildest parts of France with few roads, let alone villages, the Corbières is best known for its wine and the great craggy hulks of the Cathar castles *(see p495)*. Much of the land is untamed *garrigue* (scrubland), fragrant with honeysuckle and broom; south-facing slopes have been cleared and planted with vines.

To the south are the spectacular medieval castles of **Peyrepertuse** and **Quéribus**, the latter one of the last Cathar strongholds. The guided visits around the remarkable Cathar château at **Villerouge-Termenes** reveal some of its turbulent past. To the west is the barren, uninhabited Razès area in the upper Aude Valley. Its best-kept secret is the village of **Alet-les-Bains**, with beautifully preserved half-timbered houses and the remains of a Benedictine abbey, battle-scarred from the Wars of Religion.

⓭ Narbonne

Aude. 54,000. 31 rue Jean Jaurès (04 68 65 15 60). Thu & Sun. **narbonne-tourisme.com**

Narbonne is a medium-sized, cheerful town profiting from the booming wine region that surrounds it. The town is bisected by the tree-shaded Canal de la Robine; to the north is the restored medieval quarter with many good shops and restaurants. Located here is one of Narbonne's most intriguing tourist attractions, the Roman **Horreum**. This underground warehouse dates back to the 1st century BC, when Narbonne was a major port and capital of the largest Roman province in Gaul.

The town prospered through the Middle Ages until the 15th century, when the harbour silted up and the course of the river Aude altered, taking Narbonne's fortunes with it. By then, an important bishopric had been established and an ambitious cathedral project, modelled on the great Gothic cathedrals of the north, was under way. However, the full grandiose design was abandoned, and just the chancel, begun in 1272, became the **Cathédrale St-Just et St-Pasteur** we see today.

It is still enormous, enhanced by 14th-century sculptures, fine stained-glass windows and an 18th-century carved organ. Aubusson and Gobelin tapestries adorn the walls, and above the Chapel of the Anonciade it is possible to visit a treasury of manuscripts, jewelled reliquaries and tapestries.

The unfinished transept now forms a courtyard, and between the cathedral and the **Palais des Archevêques** (Archbishops' Palace) lies a cloister with four galleries of 14th-century vaulting.

This huge palace and cathedral complex dominates the centre of Narbonne. Between the Palais des Archevêques' massive 14th-century towers is the town hall, with a 19th-century Neo-Gothic façade by Viollet-le-Duc *(see p204)*, the architect who so determinedly restored medieval France. The palace itself is divided into

The vaulted chancel of Cathédrale St-Just et St-Pasteur in Narbonne

Canal du Midi

From Sète to Toulouse the 240-km (149-mile) Canal du Midi flows between plane trees, vineyards and villages. The complex system of locks, aqueducts and bridges is a remarkable feat of engineering, built by the Béziers salt-tax baron Paul Riquet. Completed in 1681, it encouraged Languedoc trade and created a vital link, via the Garonne river, between the Atlantic and the Mediterranean. Today it is plied by holiday barges.

Tranquil waterway of the Canal du Midi

The Cistercian Abbaye de Fontfroide (1093), nestled amongst trees southwest of Narbonne

the Palais Vieux (Old Palace) and the Palais Neuf (New Palace). Narbonne's most important museums are in the Palais Neuf, on the left as you enter through the low medieval arches of the passage de l'Ancre. The **Musée d'Archéologie** collection includes fragments of Narbonne's Roman heritage, from remarkable Roman frescoes, milestones and parts of the original walls to an assemblage of domestic objects, coins, tools and glassware. Those with a head for heights shouldn't miss climbing to the top of the 42-m (138-ft) dungeon, Donjon Gilles Aycelin.

In the archbishops' former apartments is the **Musée d'Art et d'Histoire**, which is as interesting for its luxurious furnishings and richly decorated ceilings as for its art collection. This includes some fine paintings by Canaletto, Brueghel, Boucher and Veronese as well as a large selection of local earthenware. In addition, the museum houses an outstanding collection of Orientalist paintings.

South of the Canal de la Robine are a number of fine mansions, including the Renaissance **Maison des Trois Nourrices** on the corner of rue des Trois-Nourrices and rue Edgard Quinet. Nearby is the **Musée Lapidaire**, with architectural fragments from Gallo-Roman Narbonne, and the 13th-century Gothic **Basilique St-Paul-Serge**. The collection will transfer to the new **Musée de la Romanité** when it opens in 2019.

Horreum
Rue Rouget-de-l'Isle. **Tel** 04 68 90 30 65. **Open** Jun–Sep: daily; Oct–May: Wed–Mon. **Closed** 1 Jan, 1 May, 1 & 11 Nov, 25 Dec.

Musée d'Archéologie/Musée d'Art et d'Histoire
Palais des Archevêques. **Tel** 04 68 90 30 65. **Open** Jun–Sep: daily; Oct–May: Wed–Mon. **Closed** 1 Jan, 1 May, 1 & 11 Nov, 25 Dec.

Musee Lapidaire
Eglise Notre-Dame de Lamourguier. **Tel** 04 68 90 30 65. **Open** Jun–Sep: daily; Oct–May: Wed–Mon. **Closed** 1 Jan, 1 May, 1 & 11 Nov, 25 Dec.

Environs
Southwest (13 km/8 miles), the Cistercian **Abbaye de Fontfroide** has an elegant cloister. The abbey is tucked away in a quiet valley, surrounded by cypress trees.

⓮ Golfe du Lion

Aude, Hérault. Montpellier. Sète. 55 rue du Port, La Grande-Motte (04 67 56 42 00).
lagrandemotte.com

Languedoc and Roussillon's shoreline forms an almost unbroken sweep of sandy beach. Only at its southern limits does it break into the rocky inlets of the Côte Vermeille. Purpose-built resorts created since the 1960s emphasize eco-friendly, low-rise family accommodation, some in local styles, others with imaginative architecture.

La Grande-Motte marina has distinctive ziggurat-style buildings *(see p499)*. **Cap d'Agde** has Europe's largest naturist quarter. Inland **Agde**, founded by ancient Greek traders, is built of black basalt and has a fortified cathedral. **Port Leucate** and **Port Bacarès** are ideal for water sports. An older town is **Sète** *(see p496)*. A feature of the flat Languedoc coast is its *étangs* – large shallow lagoons. Those nearest the Camargue are the haunt of thousands of wading birds.

A wide, sandy beach on the Cap d'Agde

⑮ Carcassonne

The citadel of Carcassonne is a perfectly restored medieval town, and protected by UNESCO. It crowns a steep bank above the River Aude, a fairy-tale sight of turrets and ramparts overlooking the Basse Ville below. The strategic position of the citadel between the Atlantic and the Mediterranean and on the corridor between the Iberian peninsula and the rest of Europe led to its original settlement, consolidated by the Romans in the 2nd century BC. It became a key element in medieval military conflicts. At its zenith in the 12th century, it was ruled by the Trencavels, who built the château and cathedral. Military advances and the Treaty of the Pyrenees in 1659, which relocated the French–Spanish border, hastened its decline. The attentions of architectural historian Viollet-le-Duc *(see p204)* led to its restoration in the 19th century.

The Restored Citadel
Restoration of La Cité has always been controversial. Critics complain that it looks too new, favouring a more romantic ruin.

★ Basilique St-Nazaire
Within the Romanesque and Gothic cathedral is the famous Siege Stone, said to depict the 1209 Siege of Carcassonne by crusaders.

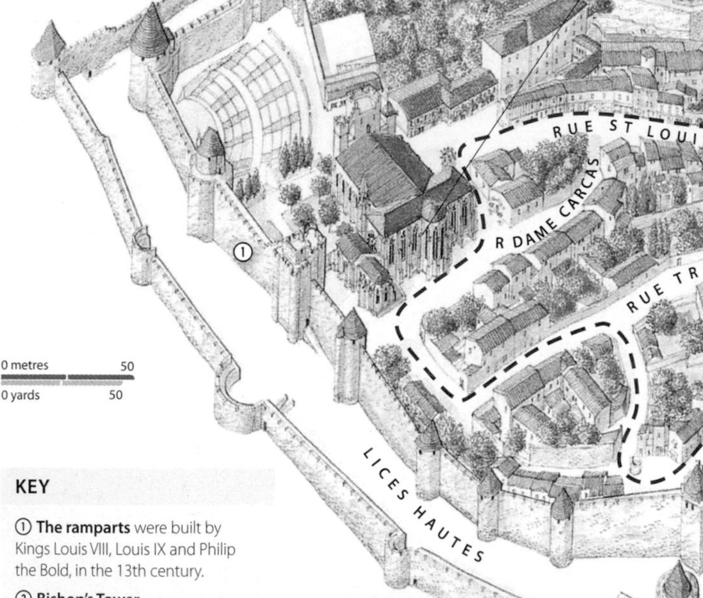

KEY

① **The ramparts** were built by Kings Louis VIII, Louis IX and Philip the Bold, in the 13th century.

② **Bishop's Tower**

③ **Porte d'Aude**

④ **Gallo-Roman walls**

⑤ **The Great Well**

⑥ **The *lices***, the easily defended spaces between the inner and outer ramparts, were also used for jousting, for crossbow practice and for storage of timber and other materials.

★ Le Château
A fortress within a fortress, the château has a moat, five towers and defensive wooden galleries on the walls.

Religious Persecution

Carcassonne's strategic position meant it was often at the centre of religious conflict. The Cathars *(see p495)* were given sanctuary here in 1209 by Raymond-Roger Trencavel when besieged by Simon de Montfort in his crusade against heresy. In the 14th century the Inquisition continued to root out the Cathars. This painting depicts intended victims in the Inquisition Tower.

Les Emmurés de Carcassonne, J P Laurens

VISITORS' CHECKLIST

Practical Information

Aude. 47,000. 28 rue de Verdun (04 68 10 24 30). Tue, Thu & Sat. Festival de Carcassonne (Jul–Aug); l'Embrasement de la Cité (14 Jul). Le Château: **Open** 9:30am–5pm daily (Apr–Sep: to 6.30pm). **Closed** 1 Jan, 1 May, 14 July, 1 & 11 Nov, 25 Dec. **tourisme-carcassonne.fr**

Transport

4 km (2 miles) W Carcassonne.
Port du Canal du Midi.
30 rue Georges Brassens.

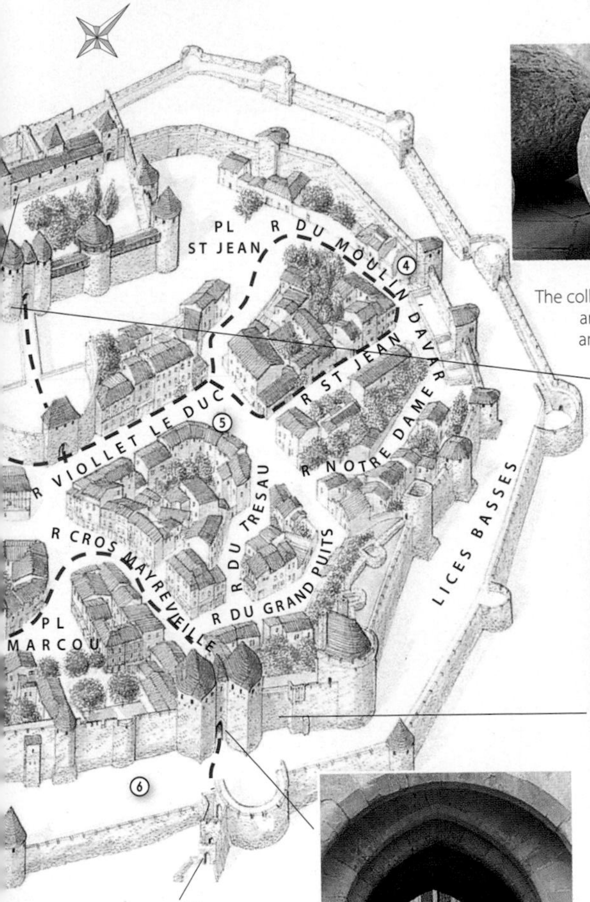

Musée Lapidaire
The collection includes Roman amphorae and terracotta, Romanesque murals and fragments from the cathedral, a set of Gothic windows and these medieval stone missiles.

Porte Narbonnaise
Flanked by two sandstone towers, built in 1280, the defences included two portcullises, two iron doors, a moat and a drawbridge.

Main entrance to La Cité

Old City Entrance
Entering La Cité is still a step back in time, although it is one of France's top tourist destinations, filled with souvenir shops.

Key

— Suggested route

Béziers with its medieval cathedral, seen from Pont Vieux in the southwest

⓰ Minerve

Hérault. 130. 9 rue des Martyrs (04 68 91 81 43). **minervois-tourisme.fr**

In the parched, arid hills of the Minervois, surrounded by vines and not much else, Minerve appears defiant on its rocky outcrop at the confluence of the rivers Cesse and Briant. It is defended by what the Minervois call the "Candela" (Candle), an octagonal tower that is all that remains of the medieval château. In 1210, the small town resisted the vengeful Simon de Montfort, scourge of the Cathars, in a siege lasting seven weeks. This culminated in the execution of 140 Cathars, who were burned at the stake.

Today visitors enter Minerve by a high bridge spanning the gorge. Turn right and follow the route of the Cathars past the Romanesque arch of the Porte des Templiers to the 12th-century **Eglise St-Etienne**. Outside the church is a crudely carved dove, symbol of the Cathars, and within is a 5th-century white marble altar table, one of the oldest artifacts in the region.

A rocky path follows the riverbed below the town, where the water has cut out caves and two bridges – the Grand Pont and the Petit Pont – from the soft limestone.

⓱ Béziers

Hérault. 77,000. Pl du Forum (04 99 41 36 36). Fri. **beziers-mediteranee.com**

Famous for its bullfights and rugby, and the wine of the surrounding region, Béziers has several other points of interest. The town seems turned in on itself, its roads leading up to the massive 14th-century **Cathédrale St-Nazaire**, with its fine sculpture, stained glass and frescoes. In 1209, several thousand citizens were massacred in the crusade against the Cathars. The papal legate's troops were ordered not to discriminate between Catholics and Cathars, but to "Kill them all. God will recognize his own!" The **Musée du Biterrois** holds exhibitions (in French only) on local history, wine and the Canal du Midi, engineered in the late 17th century by Paul Riquet, Béziers' most famous son *(see p490)*. His statue presides over the Allées Paul Riquet, which is lined by rows of plane trees and large canopied restaurants, a civilized focus to this otherwise businesslike town.

Statue of the engineer Paul Riquet in the allées Paul Riquet, Béziers

Musée du Biterrois
Ramp du 96ème, Caserne St-Jacques. **Tel** 04 67 36 81 60. **Open** 10am–6pm Tue–Sun (Oct–May: to 5pm Tue–Fri). **Closed** 1 Jan, Easter, 1 May, 25 Dec.

Environs

Overlooking the Béziers plain and the mountains to the north is Oppidum d'Ensérune, a superb Roman site. The **Musée de l'Oppidum d'Ensérune** has a good archaeological collection, from Celtic, Greek and Roman vases to jewellery and weapons.

The **Château de Raissac** (between Béziers and Lignan) houses an unusual 19th-century faïence museum in its stables.

Musée de l'Oppidum d'Ensérune
Nissan-lez-Ensérune. **Tel** 04 67 37 01 23. **Open** daily (Sep–Apr: Tue–Sun). **Closed** public hols. limited. **enserune.fr**

Château de Raissac
Rte de Lignan sur Orr. **Tel** 04 67 49 17 60. **Open** by appt. **raissac.com**

For hotels and restaurants in this region see p569 and pp599–601

The Cathars

The Cathars (from Greek *katharos*, meaning "pure") were a 12th- to 14th-century Christian sect critical of corruption in the established Catholic Church. Cathar dissent flourished in independent Languedoc as an expression of separatism, but the rebellion was rapidly exploited for political purposes. Peter II of Aragon was keen to annex Languedoc, and Philippe II of France joined forces with the pope to crush the Cathar heretics in a crusade led by Simon de Montfort in 1209. This began over two centuries of ruthless killing and torture.

Cathar Castles
The Cathars took refuge in the defensive castles of the Corbières and Ariège. Peyrepertuse is one of the most remote and difficult to get to even today: a long, narrow stone citadel hacked from a high, craggy peak over 609 m (2,000 ft) high.

Cathars (also known as Albigensians) believed in the duality of good and evil. They considered the material world entirely evil. To be truly pure they had to renounce the world, and be non-violent, vegetarian and sexually abstinent.

The crusade against the Cathars was vicious. Heretics' land was promised to the crusaders by the pope, who assured forgiveness in advance of their crimes. In 1209, 20,000 citizens were massacred in Béziers, and, in 1210 some 140 were burned to death in Minerve. In 1244, another 225 Cathars died defending one of their last fortresses at Montségur.

Cathar Country
Castles and towns with a Cathar association, some of them spectacular sites, are concentrated in Languedoc, the centre of Catharism in the Middle Ages.

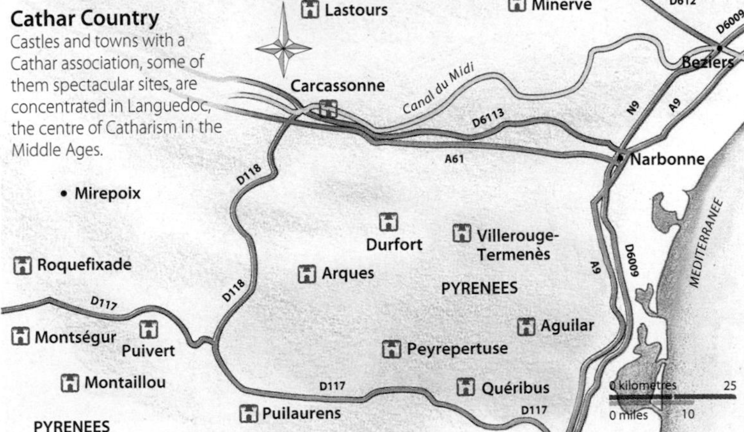

The impressive Grand Hôtel *(see p569)* with the Canal Royal in the foreground

⓲ Sète

Hérault. 45,000. 60 grand' rue Mario Roustan (04 99 04 71 71). daily. **tourisme-sete.com**

Sète is a major fishing and industrial port. It has a gutsier, more raffish air than much of the leisure-oriented Mediterranean, with its shops selling ships' lamps and propellers, and its quayside restaurants full of hungry sailors demolishing vast platters of mussels, oysters and sea snails straight off the boat. Most of Sète's restaurants can be found in a stroll along the Grand Canal, with its Italianate houses painted in pastel colours and with wrought-iron balconies overlooking Sète's network of canals and bridges. Boisterous water jousting tournaments on Canal Royal, dating back to 1666, form part of the patron saint's festival in August *(see p42)*.

To the west of the town, next to the open-air Théâtre de la Mer, is the **Musée de la Mer**, which explores Sète's maritime and water jousting history from the 18th century to the present day.

Nearby is the **Cimetière Marin**, where Sète's most famous son, poet Paul Valéry (1871–1945), is buried. There is a small art museum and breathtaking views of the coast and the mountains from the lookout on Mont St-Clair.

Cimetière Marin in Sète, burial place of the poet Paul Valéry

Musée de la Mer
1 rue Jean Vilar. **Tel** 04 99 04 71 55. **Open** Tue–Sun. **Closed** 1 Jan, 1 May, 25 Dec.

⓳ Pézenas

Hérault. 8,500. Pl des Etats de Languedoc (04 67 98 36 40). Sat. **pezenas-tourisme.fr**

Pézenas is a charming little town, easily appreciated in a gentle stroll of its main sights, and abounding in revealing details, fragmentary evidence of its past brilliance as the seat of local government in the 16th–17th centuries. Then the town also played host to many troupes of musicians and actors, including Molière.

The narrow streets in the old town are beautifully preserved. Best of all are the glimpses of fine houses through courtyard doorways, such as the **Hôtel des Barons de Lacoste**, at 8 rue François-Oustrin, with its beautiful stone staircase, and the **Maison des Pauvres** at 12 rue Alfred Sabatier, with its three galleries and staircase.

Look out for the medieval shop window on rue Triperie-Vieille, and just within the 14th-century **Porte Faugères**, the streets of the Jewish quarter (rue Juiverie and rue des Litanies), with their chilling feeling of enclosure. Shops selling antiques, second-hand goods and books abound. All around the town, vines stretch as far as the eye can see.

The stone foyer of the Hôtel des Barons de Lacoste in Pézenas

⑳ Parc Naturel Régional du Haut Languedoc

Hérault, Tarn. ✈ Béziers. 🚂 Béziers, Bédarieux. 🚌 St-Pons-de-Thomières. ℹ St-Pons-de-Thomières (04 67 97 38 22). **W** **parc-haut-languedoc.fr**

The high limestone plateaux and wooded slopes of upper Languedoc are a world away from the coast. From the Montagne Noire, a mountainous region between Béziers and Castres, up into the Cévennes is a landscape of remote sheep farms, eroded rock formations and deep river gorges. Much of this area has been designated the Parc Naturel Régional du Haut Languedoc, one of the largest of the French regional parks.

You can enter the park at **St-Pons-de-Thomières**, with access to forest and mountain trails for walking and riding, plus a wildlife research centre, where one can glimpse the mouflons (wild mountain sheep), eagles and wild boar, which were once a common sight in the region. You can also enter the park at Revel, Castres, St-Chinian and Lodéve.

If you take the D908 from St-Pons through the park, you pass the village of **Olargues** with its 12th-century bridge over the River Jaur. **Lamalou-les-Bains**, on the park's eastern edge, is a small spa town with a restored *belle époque* spa building and theatre, and a soporifically slow pace.

Outside the park boundaries to the northeast there are spectacular natural phenomena. At the **Cirque de Navacelles**, the River Vis has joined up with itself cutting out an entire island. On it sits the peaceful village of Navacelles, visible from the road higher up. The **Grotte des Demoiselles** is one of the most magnificent in an area full of caves, where you walk through a calcified world. A funicular train takes visitors from the foot of the mountain to the top.

The **Grotte de Clamouse** is also an extraordinary experience, the reflections from underground rivers and pools flickering on the cavern roofs. The Spéléopark offers caving activities.

The picturesque village of St-Guilhem-le-Désert

Grotte des Demoiselles
St-Bauzille-de-Putois, Ganges. **Tel** 04 67 73 70 02. **Open** daily. **Closed** Jan, 25 Dec. **W** **demoiselles.com**

Grotte de Clamouse
Rte de St-Guilhem-le-Désert, St-Jean-de-Fos. **Tel** 04 67 57 71 05. **Open** daily. **W** **clamouse.com**

Grotte des Demoiselles

㉑ St-Guilhem-le-Désert

Hérault. 270. 🚌 ℹ 2 pl de la Liberté (04 67 56 41 97). **W** **saintguilhem-valleeherault.fr**

Tucked away in the Celette mountains, St-Guilhem-le-Désert is no longer as remote as when Guillaume of Aquitaine retired here as a hermit in the 9th century. After a lifetime as a soldier, Guillaume received a fragment of the True Cross from Emperor Charlemagne and established a monastery in this ravine above the River Hérault.

Vestiges of the first 10th-century church have been discovered, but most of the building is a superb example of 11th- to 12th-century Romanesque architecture. Its lovely apsidal chapels dominate the heights of the village, behind which the carved doorway opens on to a central square.

Within the church is a sombre barrel-vaulted central aisle leading to the sunlit central apse. Only two galleries of the cloisters remain: the rest are in New York, along with carvings from St-Michel-de-Cuxa *(see p484–5)*.

Montpellier City Centre

① Place de la Comédie
② CORUM
③ Tour de la Babote
④ Tours des Pins
⑤ Cathédrale St-Pierre
⑥ Notre-Dame des Tables
⑦ Hôtel de Manse
⑧ Hôtel de Mirman
⑨ Hôtel des Trésoriers de la Bourse
⑩ Musée Fabre
⑪ Promenade de Peyrou
⑫ Château d'Eau
⑬ Jardin des Plantes

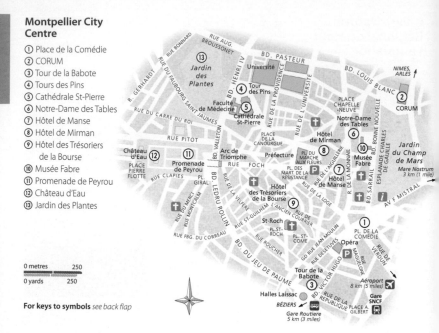

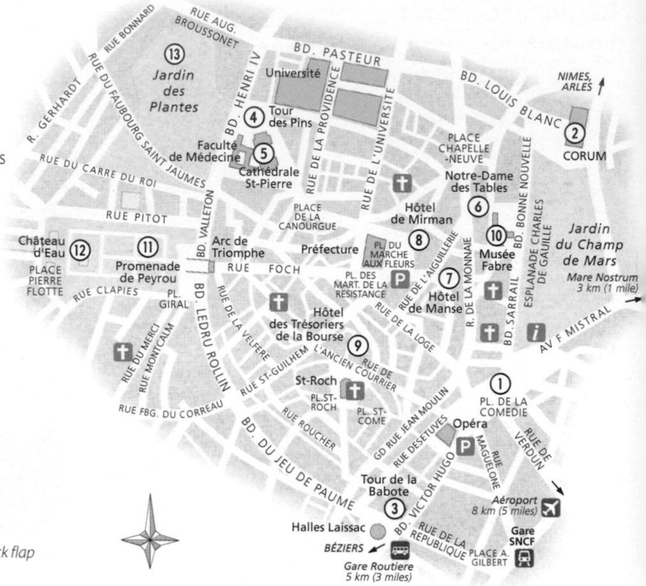

0 metres 250
0 yards 250

For keys to symbols *see back flap*

Open-air café in place de la Comédie, in the heart of Montpellier

㉒ Montpellier

Hérault. 279,000. 30 allée Jean de Lattré de Tassigny (04 67 60 60 60). daily. Festival International Montpellier Danse (Jun–Jul). **montpellier-france.com**

Montpellier is one of the liveliest and most forward-looking cities in the south, with a quarter of its population under 25. Sometimes on an evening in university term time it resembles a rock festival more than the second-largest city in Occitanie. Centre of the action is the egg-shaped **place de la Comédie**, known as "l'Oeuf" ("the egg"), with its 19th-century opera house fronted by the Fontaine des Trois Graces and surrounded by buzzing cafés. An esplanade of plane trees and fountains leads to the **CORUM**, an opera and conference centre typical of the city's brave new architectural projects. The best of these is Ricardo Bofill's Postmodern housing complex, known as Antigone, and modelled on St Peter's in Rome, Jean Nouvel and François Fortes's city hall, and La Nuage, a Philippe-Starck-designed sports and wellness centre.

Montpellier was founded relatively late, developing in the 10th century as a result of the spice trade with the Middle East. The city's medical school was founded in 1220, partly as a result of this cross-fertilization of knowledge between the two cultures, and remains one of the most respected in France.

Most of Montpellier was ravaged by the Wars of Religion in the 16th century. Only the **Tour de la Babote** and the **Tours des Pins** remain of the 12th-century fortifications. There are few fine churches, the exceptions being the **Cathédrale St-Pierre** and the 18th-century **Notre-Dame des Tables**.

The 1600s saw the building of mansions with elegant courtyards, stone staircases and balconies. Examples open to the public include **Hôtel de Manse** on rue Embouque-d'Or, **Hôtel de Mirman** near place des Martyrs de la Resistance and **Hôtel des Trésoriers de la Bourse**.

Another 17th-century building houses the **Musée Fabre**, with its collection of mainly French art. Highlights include Courbet's *Bonjour M. Courbet*, Berthe Morisot's *L'Eté*, and some evocative paintings of the region by Raoul Dufy. Look out

Pont du Gard

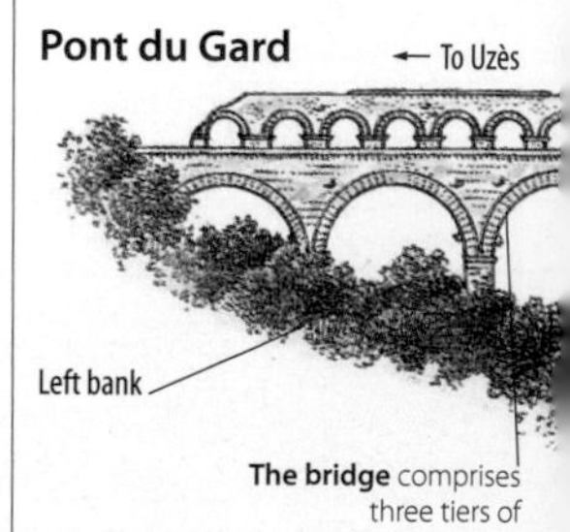

The bridge comprises three tiers of continuous arches.

for paintings by a local Impressionist artist, Frédéric Bazille, who died tragically young at the age of 29.

To view the city's position between mountains and sea, go to the **Promenade de Peyrou**, a grand 18th-century square dominated by the **Château d'Eau** and the aqueduct that used to serve the city. North of here is the **Jardin des Plantes**, France's oldest botanical gardens (1593). Not to be missed is **Mare Nostrum**, the aquarium in the Odysseum leisure zone, which has over 300 marine species.

Musée Fabre
39 bd Bonne Nouvelle. **Tel** 04 67 14 83 00. **Open** Tue–Sun.
W museefabre.montpellier3m.fr

Mare Nostrum
Allée Ulysse, Odysseum. **Tel** 04 67 13 05 50. **Open** daily. **Closed** 1 Jan, 25 Dec.
W aquariummarenostrum.fr

Château d'Eau, Montpellier

23 La Grande-Motte

Hérault. 8,700. 55 rue du Port (04 67 56 42 00). Sun (& Thu: mid-Jun–mid-Sep).
W lagrandemotte.fr

The bizarre white ziggurats of this modern marina exemplify the development of France's

La Grande-Motte

southwest coast. One of several on the lagoons south of Montpellier, there are marinas and facilities for every kind of sport from tennis and golf to water sports, all flanked by golden beaches and pine forests. To the east are Le Grau-du-Roi, once a tiny fishing village, and Port-Camargue, with its big marina.

24 Aigues-Mortes

Gard. 8,500. pl St Louis (04 66 53 73 00). Wed & Sun.
W ot-aiguesmortes.fr

The best approach to this perfectly preserved walled town is across the salt marshes of the Camargue Gardoise. Now marooned 5 km (3 miles) from the sea, the imposing defences of this once-important port have become a tourist experience, worth visiting more for the effect of the ensemble than the touristy shops within. Aigues-Mortes ("Place of Dead Waters") was established by Louis XI in the 13th century to consolidate his power on the Mediterranean, and built according to a strict grid pattern. By climbing up the **Tour de Constance** you can walk out onto the rectangular walls, which afford a superb view over the Camargue.

Environs

To the northeast is **St-Gilles-du-Gard**, also once an important medieval port. Today it is worth a detour to see the superbly sculpted 12th-century façade of its abbey church. This was originally established by the monks of Cluny abbey as a shrine to St Gilles, and a resting place on the famous pilgrimage route to Santiago de Compostela *(see pp404–5)*.

25 Nîmes

See pp500–1.

26 Pont du Gard

400 rte du Pont du Gard-La Bégud, Gard. from Nîmes. 04 66 37 50 99. Open daily.
W pontdugard.fr

No amount of fame can diminish the first sight of the 2,000-year-old Pont du Gard, a UNESCO World Heritage site. The Romans considered it the best testimony to the greatness of their empire, and at 49 m (160 ft) it was the highest bridge they ever built.

It is made from blocks of stone, hauled into place by slaves using an ingenious system of pulleys. The huge build-up of calcium in the water channels suggests the aqueduct was in continuous use for 400 to 500 years, carrying water to Nîmes along a 50-km (31-mile) route from the springs at **Uzès**. This charming town has an arcaded marketplace and several fine medieval towers.

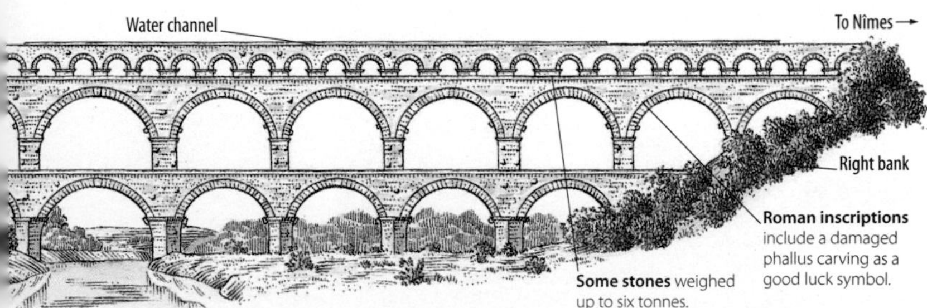
Water channel
To Nîmes →
Right bank
Roman inscriptions include a damaged phallus carving as a good luck symbol.
Some stones weighed up to six tonnes.

25 Nîmes

One of the most popular sites in Nîmes is the bus stop designed by Philippe Starck, who is also credited with reworking the city's pedestrian zone. Such innovations are part of the city's design renaissance. Architectural projects range from imaginative housing to a glittering arts complex, under the guidance of a dynamic mayor. An important crossroads in the ancient world, Nîmes is equally well known for its Roman antiquities such as the amphitheatre, the best preserved of its kind. The city is also famous for its festivals and bullfights (*ferias*). These are good times to see the rest of Nîmes with its museums, archaeological collections and Old Town of narrow streets and intimate squares.

Arches of the Roman amphitheatre

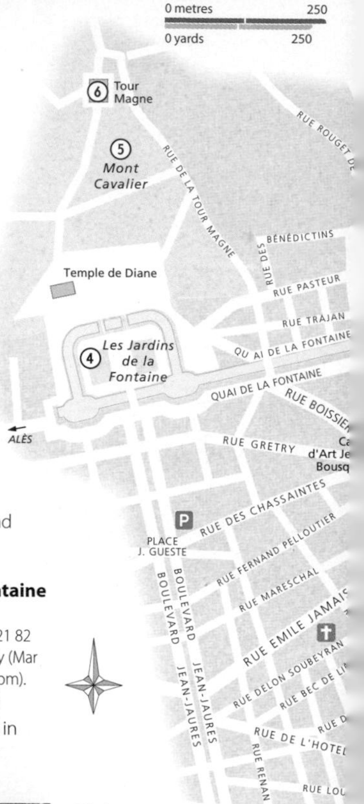

Historic Nîmes

Nîmes has had a turbulent history, suffering particularly during the 16th-century Wars of Religion, when the Romanesque **Cathédrale Notre-Dame et St-Castor** was badly damaged. During the 17th and 18th centuries the town prospered from textile manufacturing, one of the most enduring products being denim, or "de Nîmes". Many of the fine houses of this period have been restored – elegant examples can be seen on rue de l'Aspic, rue des Marchands and rue du Chapitre in the Old Town. Just outside the town centre is a futuristic apartment building, **Nemausus I**.

The Roman gate, the **Porte Auguste** was once part of one of the longest city walls in Gaul. Of the original arches still standing, two (large ones) were for chariots and carts, and two (smaller ones) for pedestrians. The other major Roman remnant is the **Castellum**. Water used to arrive here from the Pont du Gard *(see pp498–9)* to be distributed around the city.

Jug from Musée Archéologique

Les Jardins de la Fontaine (Tour Magne)

Quai de la Fontaine. **Tel** 04 66 21 82 56. **Open** 7:30am–6:30pm daily (Mar & Sep: to 8pm; Apr–Aug: to 10pm). reserve at tourist office.

When the Romans arrived in Nîmes, they found a town established by the Gauls,

Sights at a Glance

1. Cathédrale Notre-Dame et St-Castor
2. Porte Auguste
3. Castellum
4. Les Jardins de la Fontaine
5. Mont Cavalier
6. Tour Magne
7. Les Arènes
8. Maison Carrée
9. Musée des Beaux-Arts
10. Carré d'Art Jean Bousquet/ Musée d'Art Contemporain

Les Jardins de la Fontaine, with a view over the city

For hotels and restaurants in this region see p569 and pp599–601

centred on the source of a spring. They named the town Nemausus, after their river god. In the 18th century, formal gardens were constructed, and a network of limpid pools and cool stone terraces remains. High above the garden on **Mont Cavalier** is the octagonal **Tour Magne**, once a key part of the Roman walls, offering a great view of the city.

Castellum
RUE GRAVEROL
RUE RANGUEIL
RUE BAUDIN
RUE BACHALAS
RUE CLERISSEAU
PLACE ST CHARLES
BOULEVARD GAMBETTA
AVIGNON
RUE NATIONALE
R DU MERIER D'ESPAGNE
RUE DES ORANGERS
RUE DES LOMBARDS
Porte Auguste
PL DU CHÂTEAU
Grand Temple
RUE ROUSSY
AVE DU GENERAL PERRIER
RUE GUIZOT
PL AUX HERBES
Cathédrale Notre-Dame et St-Castor
Musée du VieuxNîmes
RUE DE L'HORLOGE
RUE DE LA MADELEINE
RUE FRESQUE
RUE DE L'ASPIC
RUE DOREE
RUE DES GREFFES
BD AMIRAL COURBET
PLACE DE LA MADELAINE
RUE DE L'ETOILE
BD VICTOR-HUGO
Hôtel de Ville
PLACE DU MARCHÉ
RUE RÉGALE
SQ DE LA COURONNE
Palais de Justice
BD DES ARÈNES
BD DE LA LIBERATION
Esplanade Charles de Gaulle
BD DE PRAGUE
Les Arènes
PLACE DES ARÈNES
RUE JEAN-REBOUL
PORTE DE FRANCE
RUE DE LA REPUBLIQUE
RUE DE LA CITE
RUE BRICONNET
Gare SNCF, Gare Routière 200 m (420 yards)
ARLES, MONTPELLIER Nemausus I
RUE BOURDALOUE
Musée des Beaux-Arts
Aeroport 12 km (7.5 miles)

Les Arènes (L'Amphithéâtre)

10 bd des Arènes. **Tel** 04 66 21 82 56. **Open** daily. **Closed** Feria des Vendanges, Feria de Pentecôte, performance days. **arenes.nimes.fr**

All roads lead to the amphitheatre, Les Arènes. Built at the end of the 1st century AD, the design of the oval arena and tiers of stone seats accommodated huge crowds of up to 20,000 spectators. Today it is a perfect venue for concerts, sporting events and bullfights.

Les Grands Jeux Romains, a three-day reenactment of traditional Roman games at the end of April, are a sight to behold. Facing Les Arènes, the Musée de la Romanité houses ancient Roman statues, ceramics, coins, glass and mosaics.

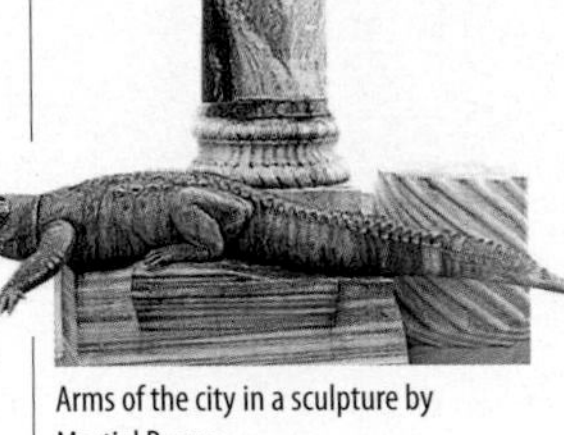

Arms of the city in a sculpture by Martial Raysse

Maison Carrée

Pl de la Maison Carrée. **Tel** 04 66 21 82 56. **Open** daily.

This elegant Roman temple built around AD 2 is one of the best preserved in the world. Inside, a multimedia experience, "Nemausus", illustrates the birth of the city.

Musée des Beaux-Arts

Rue Cité Foulc. **Tel** 04 66 28 18 32. **Open** 10am–6pm Tue–Sun. **Closed** 1 Jan, 1 May, 1 Nov, 25 Dec.

This fine arts museum houses an eclectic collection of 16th–19th-century Dutch, French, Italian and Flemish works, notably Jacopo Bassano's *Susanna and the Elders* and the *Mystic Marriage of St Catherine* by Michele Giambono. The Gallo-Roman mosaic of *The Marriage of Admetus*, discovered in 1882, is on the main floor.

VISITORS' CHECKLIST

Practical Information
Gard. 154,000. 6 rue Auguste (04 66 58 38 00). daily. Ferias: Pentecôte (Pentecost), Vendanges (Sep). **ot-nimes.fr**

Transport
12 km (7 miles) SE Nîmes-Arles-Camargues. bd Talabot (SNCF: 36 35). Rue St Félicité (09 70 81 86 38).

The Maison Carrée

Carré d'Art Jean Bousquet/Musée d'Art Contemporain

Pl de la Maison Carrée. **Tel** 04 66 76 35 70 (Mon–Fri), 04 66 76 35 35 (Sat & Sun). **Open** 10am–6pm Tue–Sun. **Closed** 1 Jan, 1 May, 1 Nov, 25 Dec. **carreartmusee.com**

Nîmes' glass-and-steel arts complex, designed by the British architect Sir Norman Foster, was built in tribute to the Maison Carrée opposite. Five of its floors lie underground. The complex has a library, a roof-terrace restaurant around a huge glass atrium, and the Musée d'Art Contemporain. The collection covers the main European art movements from the 1960s on, and includes works by French artists Raysse, Boltanski and Lavier.

Virgil, Horace and Varius in Mecene's home (1846) by Charles Jalabert at the Musée des Beaux-Arts

For keys to symbols *see back flap*

NICE
STEPHAN

PROVENCE AND THE COTE D'AZUR

Vaucluse · Bouches-du-Rhône · Var
Alpes-de-Haute-Provence · Alpes-Maritimes

No other region of France fires the imagination as strongly as Provence, with its herb-scented hills to its yacht-filled harbours. The vivid landscape and luminous light have inspired artists and writers from van Gogh to Picasso, and F Scott Fitzgerald to Pagnol.

The borders of Provence are defined by nature: to the west, the Rhône; south, the Mediterranean; and north, where the olive trees end. To the east are the Alps and a border that has shifted over the centuries between France and Italy. Within is a contrasting terrain of plummeting gorges, Camargue salt flats, lavender fields and sun-drenched beaches.

Past visitors have left their mark. In Orange and Arles, the buildings of Roman Provincia are still in use. Fortified villages such as Eze were built to withstand the Saracen pirates who plagued the coast in the 6th century. In the 19th century, rich Europeans sought winter warmth on the Riviera; by the 1920s, high society was in residence all year round, and their elegant villas remain. The warm sunlight nurtures intense flavours and colours. Peppers, garlic and olives transform a netful of Mediterranean fish into that vibrant epitome of Provençal cuisine, *bouillabaisse*.

The image of Provence bathed in sunshine is marred only when the bitter Mistral wind scours the land. It has shaped a people as hardy as the olive tree, yet quick to embrace life to the full the moment the sun returns.

Cap Martin, seen from the village of Roquebrune

◀ Boats moored in the harbour at Nice

Exploring Provence

This sun-drenched southeastern region is France's most popular holiday destination. Sun-worshippers cram the beaches in the summer months, and entertainment includes opera, dance and jazz festivals, bullfights, casinos and *boules* games. Inland is a paradise for walkers and nature lovers, with remote mountain plateaux, perched villages and dramatic river gorges.

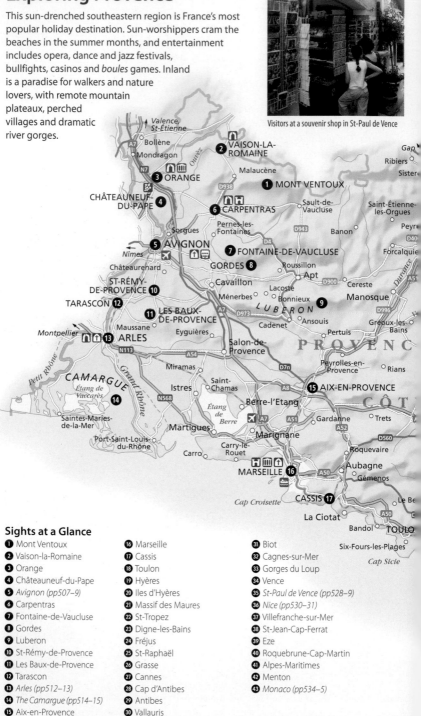

Visitors at a souvenir shop in St-Paul de Vence

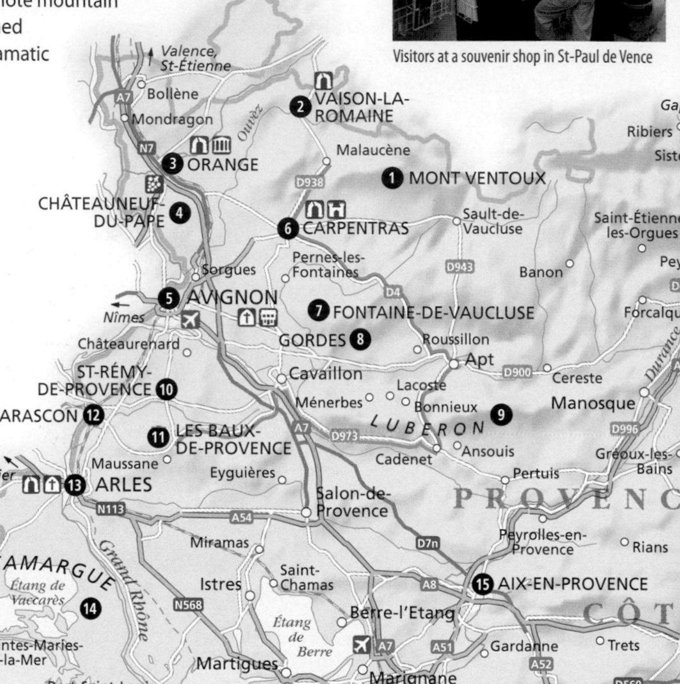

Sights at a Glance

1 Mont Ventoux
2 Vaison-la-Romaine
3 Orange
4 Châteauneuf-du-Pape
5 *Avignon (pp507–9)*
6 Carpentras
7 Fontaine-de-Vaucluse
8 Gordes
9 Luberon
10 St-Rémy-de-Provence
11 Les Baux-de-Provence
12 Tarascon
13 *Arles (pp512–13)*
14 *The Camargue (pp514–15)*
15 Aix-en-Provence
16 Marseille
17 Cassis
18 Toulon
19 Hyères
20 Iles d'Hyères
21 Massif des Maures
22 St-Tropez
23 Digne-les-Bains
24 Fréjus
25 St-Raphaël
26 Grasse
27 Cannes
28 Cap d'Antibes
29 Antibes
30 Vallauris
31 Biot
32 Cagnes-sur-Mer
33 Gorges du Loup
34 Vence
35 *St-Paul de Vence (pp528–9)*
36 *Nice (pp530–31)*
37 Villefranche-sur-Mer
38 St-Jean-Cap-Ferrat
39 Eze
40 Roquebrune-Cap-Martin
41 Alpes-Maritimes
42 Menton
43 *Monaco (pp534–5)*

For keys to symbols *see back flap*

Getting Around

The largest airport in the region, and second busiest in France, is Nice. Fly-drive packages are popular, although mainly recommended for touring inland. Traffic jams on coastal roads in high season can usually be avoided by using the *autoroutes*. Main coastal towns have good bus and rail links, and bikes can be hired at most rail stations. The Chemin de Fer de Provence railway line runs from Nice to Digne-les-Bains through spectacular mountain scenery. Mountain roads, though tortuous, are good.

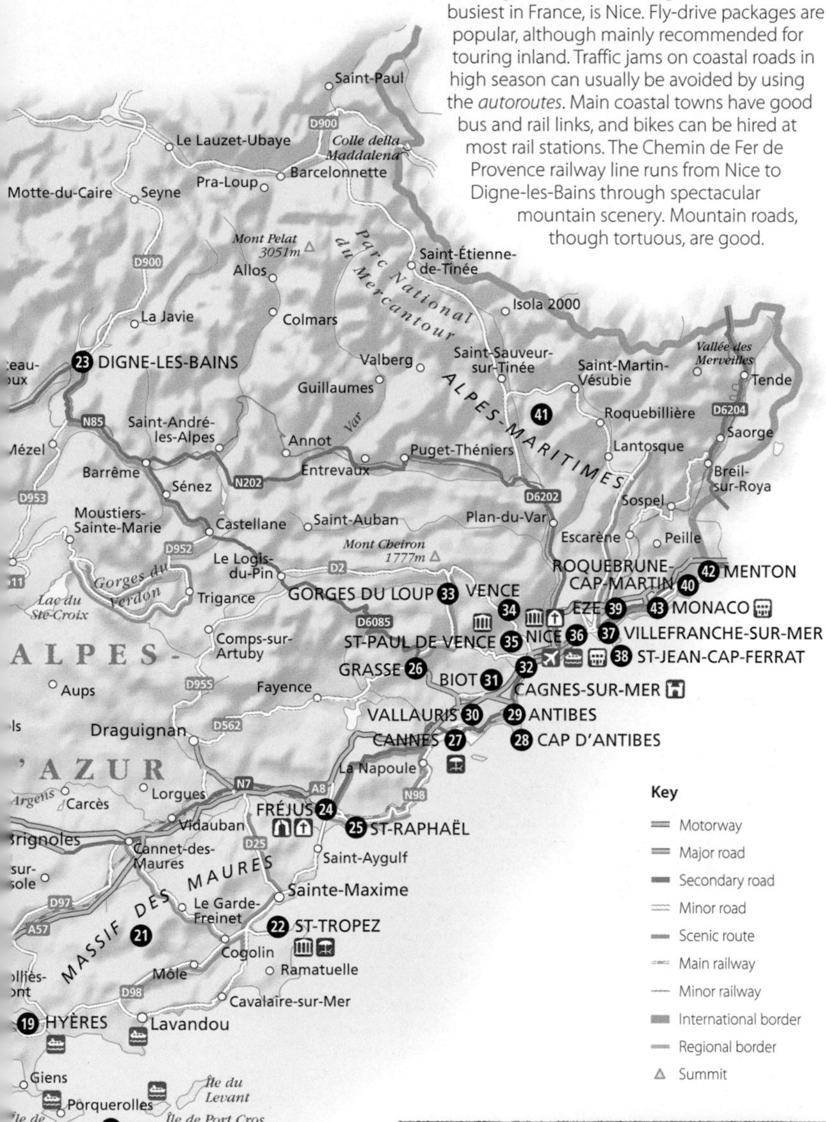

Key

- Motorway
- Major road
- Secondary road
- Minor road
- Scenic route
- Main railway
- Minor railway
- International border
- Regional border
- Summit

0 kilometres 25

0 miles 25

Spectacular scenery near the quiet market town of Forcalquier

❶ Mont Ventoux

Vaucluse. Avignon. Avignon. Carpentras. av de la Promenade, Sault-en-Provence (04 90 64 01 21). **ventoux-en-provence.com**

The name means "Windy Mountain" in Provençal. A variety of flora and fauna may be found on the lower slopes but only moss survives at the peak, where the temperature can drop to –27°C (–17° F). The bare white scree at the summit makes it look snow-capped even during summer.

The legendary British cyclist Tommy Simpson died during 1967's Tour de France on Mont Ventoux. Today, a road leads up to the radio beacon pinnacle, but the trip should not be attempted in bad weather. At other times, spectacular views from the top make the effort worthwhile.

Roman mosaic from the Villa du Paon in Vaison-la-Romaine

❷ Vaison-la-Romaine

Vaucluse. 6,200. pl du Chanoine Sautel (04 90 36 02 11). Tue. **vaison-ventoux-tourisme.com**

This site has been settled since the Bronze Age, but its name stems from five centuries as a Roman town. Although the upper town, dominated by the ruins of a 12th-century castle, has some charming narrow streets, stone houses and fountains, Vaison's main attractions lie on the opposite side of the river.

The **Roman City** is split into two districts: Puymin and La Villasse. At Puymin, an opulent mansion, the Villa du Paon, and a Roman theatre have been uncovered.

In 1992, the River Ouvèze burst its banks, taking many lives in Vaison and the nearby area. Damage to some ruins, such as the Roman bridge, has since been repaired. Also at Vaison is the fine Romanesque **Cathédrale Notre-Dame-de-Nazareth**, with medieval cloisters.

Roman City

Fouilles de Puymin & Musée Théo Desplans, pl du Chanoine Sautel. **Tel** 04 90 36 50 48. **Open** daily. **Closed** Jan–mid-Feb, 25 Dec.

❸ Orange

Vaucluse. 30,000. 5 cours Aristide Briand (04 90 34 70 88). Thu. **orange-tourisme.fr**

Orange is a thriving regional centre in the Rhône Valley, an important marketplace for produce such as grapes, olives, honey and truffles. Visitors should explore the area around the 17th-century Hôtel de Ville, where attractive streets open on to quiet, shady squares. Orange also has two of the greatest Roman monuments in Europe: the **Théâtre Antique** and the **Arc de Triomphe**.

Roman Theatre (Théâtre Antique)

1 rue Madeleine-Roch. **Tel** 04 90 51 17 60. **Open** daily. also valid for Musée d'Orange. **theatre-antique.com**

Dating from the 1st-century-AD reign of Augustus, the well-preserved theatre, a UNESCO World Heritage Site, has perfect acoustics. It is still used for theatre performances and concerts. The back wall rises to a height of 37 m (120 ft) and is 103 m (338 ft) wide. In 2006 an immense glass roof, built high above the theatre so as not to affect the acoustics, replaced the original roof, which was destroyed in a fire.

Statue of Augustus Caesar in the Roman Theatre at Orange

Arc de Triomphe

Av de l'Arc de Triomphe.

The triple-arched monument, built about AD 20, is decorated with battle scenes, trophies and inscriptions to the honour of Tiberius and the conquest of Rome after the Battle of Actium.

Musée d'Art et d'Histoire d'Orange

1 rue Madeleine-Roch. **Tel** 04 90 51 17 60. **Open** daily.

Relics here reflect the Roman presence in Orange, including 400 marble fragments, some of which date to Emperor Vespasian's reign in the 1st century BC.

❹ Châteauneuf-du-Pape

Vaucluse. 2,200. Sorgues, then taxi. from Avignon or Orange. 3 rue de la République (04 90 83 71 08). Fri. **chateauneuf-du-pape-tourisme.fr**

Here, in the 14th century, the popes of Avignon chose to build a new castle *(château neuf)* and

View across the vineyards of Châteauneuf-du-Pape

For hotels and restaurants in this region see pp569–71 and pp601–3

plant the vineyards from which one of the finest wines of the Côtes du Rhône is produced. Now almost every doorway in this attractive little town seems to open into a *vigneron*'s cellar.

After the Wars of Religion *(see pp60–61)*, all that remained of the papal fortress were a few fragments of walls and tower, but the ruins look spectacular and offer magnificent views across to Avignon and the Vaucluse uplands beyond.

Wine festivals punctuate the year, including the Fête de la Véraison in August *(see p42)*, when the grapes start to ripen, and the Châteauneuf-du-Pape Spring Wine Fair, hosted by local growers.

5 Avignon

Vaucluse. 94,000. 41 cours Jean Jaurès (04 32 74 32 74). Tue–Sun. Festival d'Avignon (3 wks Jul). **avignon-tourisme.com**

Massive ramparts enclose one of the most fascinating towns in southern France. The **Palais des Papes** *(see pp508–9)* dominates, but there are also other riches, including the nearby Carré du Palais, a showcase for Rhône valley wines and comprising a wine school, bar and restaurant. North of the Palais is the 13th-century **Musée du Petit Palais**, once the Archbishop of Avignon's residence. Now a museum, it displays Romanesque and Gothic sculpture and medieval paintings, with works by Botticelli and Carpaccio.

Rue Joseph-Vernet and rue du Roi-René are lined with 17th- and 18th-century houses. There are also fine churches, such as the **Cathédrale de Notre-Dame-des-Doms** and the 14th-century **Eglise St-Didier**. The **Musée Lapidaire** contains statues, mosaics and carvings from pre-Roman Provence. The **Musée Calvet** features a superb array of exhibits, including wrought-iron works and Roman finds. It also gives an overview of French art during the past 500 years, with works by Rodin, Utrillo and Dufy.

Two major modern and contemporary art collections, the **Musée Angladon** and the **Collection Lambert**, have been added to the city's cultural repertoire. The former has works by Degas, van Gogh, Cézanne, Picasso and Modigliani, while the latter features minimalist and conceptual art.

Place de l'Horloge is the social centre of Avignon, with pavement cafés and a 1900 merry-go-round. One of the prettiest streets is rue des Teinturiers.

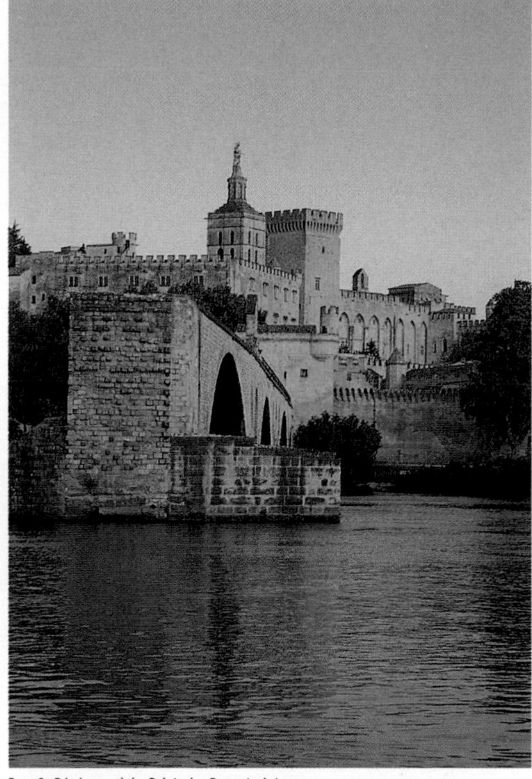

Pont St-Bénézet and the Palais des Papes in Avignon

Actors in historical costume at the Avignon Theatre Festival

Avignon's renowned 12th-century bridge, the **Pont St-Bénézet**, was largely destroyed by floods in 1668. People danced on an island below the bridge but over the years, as the famous song testifies, *sous* has become *sur*.

Avignon hosts France's largest festival, which includes ballet, drama and classical concerts. The "Off" festival features 600 companies from all areas of show business.

Musée du Petit Palais
Pl du Palais. **Tel** 04 90 86 44 58. **Open** Wed–Mon. **Closed** 1 Jan, 1 May, 25 Dec. **petit-palais.org**

Musée Lapidaire
27 rue de la République. **Tel** 04 90 85 75 38. **Open** Tue–Sun. **Closed** 1 Jan, 1 May, 25 Dec. restricted. **musee-lapidaire.org**

Musée Calvet
65 rue Joseph Vernet. **Tel** 04 90 86 33 84. **Open** Wed–Mon. **Closed** 1 Jan, 1 May, 25 Dec. **musee-calvet-avignon.org**

Palais des Papes

Confronted with factional strife in Rome and encouraged by the scheming of Philippe IV of France, Pope Clement V moved the papal court to Avignon in 1309. Here it remained until 1377, during which time his successors transformed the modest episcopal building into the present magnificent palace. Its heavy fortification was vital to defend against rogue bands of mercenaries. Today, it is empty of the luxurious trappings of 14th-century court life, as virtually all the furnishings and works of art were destroyed or looted in the course of the centuries.

★ Consistory Hall
Simone Martini's frescoes (1340) were taken from the cathedral to replace works destroyed by fire in the papal reception hall in 1413.

Military Architecture
The palace and its ten towers were designed as an impregnable fortress. It eventually covered an area of 15,000 sq m (161,500 sq ft).

KEY

① **Champeaux gate**

② **Corner tower**

③ **Bell tower**

④ **Trouillas tower**

⑤ **Benedict XII's cloister** incorporates the guest and staff wings, and the Benedictine chapel.

⑥ **La Gache tower**

⑦ **Angels' tower**

⑧ **Pope's chamber**

⑨ **Great courtyard**

⑩ **The Great Chapel** is 20 m (66 ft) high and covers an area of 780 sq m (8,400 sq ft).

⑪ **The Great Audience Hall** is divided into two naves by five columns with bestiary sculpture on their capitals.

The Avignon Popes

Seven "official" popes reigned in Avignon until 1376. They were followed by two "anti-popes", the last of whom, Benedict XIII, fled in 1403. Popes or anti-popes, few were known for their sanctity. Clement V died eating powdered emeralds, prescribed as an indigestion cure; Clement VI (1342–52) thought that the best way to honour God was through luxury. Petrarch was shocked by "the filth of the universe" at court. In 1367, Urban V tried to return the Curia (papal court) to Rome, a move that became permanent in 1377.

Benedict XII (1334–42)

For hotels and restaurants in this region see pp569–71 and pp601–3

Papal Power
More like a warlord's citadel than a papal palace, the building's heavy fortification reflects the insecure climate of 14th-century religious life.

VISITORS' CHECKLIST

Practical Information
Pl du Palais, Avignon. **Tel** 04 90 27 50 00. **Open** Apr–Jun: 9am–7pm; Jul: 9am–8pm; Aug: 9am–8:30pm; Sep–Oct: 9am–7pm; Nov–Mar: 9:30am–6:30pm (Mar: from 9am). Last adm: 1 hr before closing. in 11 languages.
palais-des-papes.com

★ Stag Room
Fourteenth-century hunting frescoes and ceramic tiles adorn Clement VI's study, making it the palace's most lovely room.

Building the Palace

The palace comprises Pope Benedict XII's simple Palais Vieux (1334–42) and Clement VI's flamboyant Palais Neuf (1342–52). Ten towers, some of which are more than 50 m (164 ft) high, are set in the walls to protect its four wings.

Key

- By Benedict XII (1334–42)
- By Clement VI (1342–52)

❻ Carpentras

Vaucluse. 30,000. Maison de Pays, 97 pl du 25 Août 1944 (04 90 63 00 78). Fri. **carpentras-ventoux.com**

In 1320, Carpentras became capital of the papal county of Venaissin, and remained so until 1791. Modern boulevards trace the former ramparts, with one original gate, the Porte d'Orange, surviving.

In the Middle Ages the town was home to a large Jewish community. The 1367 **Synagogue** is the oldest in France. The Sanctuary has been restored.

While not openly persecuted under papal rule, many Jews changed faith, entering **Cathédrale St-Siffrein** by the Porte Juive (Jews' Door).

The Law Courts were built in 1640 as the episcopal palace. The Criminal Court has 17th-century carved tablets of the local towns. In the pharmacy of the Hôtel-Dieu, the 18th-century cupboards are painted with quaint figures of monkey "doctors". More regional art and history is on show at the **Musée Sobirats**.

Synagogue
15 pl Maurice Charretier. **Tel** 04 90 63 39 97. **Open** Mon–Fri. **Closed** Jewish feast days. **synagoguecarpentras.fr**

Musée Sobirats
112 rue du Collège. **Tel** 04 90 63 04 92. **Open** Wed–Mon. **Closed** Oct–Mar & public hols.

Riverfront and watermill at Fontaine-de-Vaucluse

❼ Fontaine-de-Vaucluse

Vaucluse. 650. Avignon. Av Robert Garcin, Residence Jean Garcin (04 90 20 32 22). **oti-delasorgue.fr**

The main attraction here is the source of the River Sorgue. It is the most powerful spring in France, gushing at up to 90,000 litres (19,800 gallons) per second from an underground river at the foot of a cliff. It powers the Moulin à Papier Vallis Clausa (papermill), which produces handmade paper using the same methods as in the 15th century, and now sells maps, prints and lampshades. There are also several museums. One is devoted to the poet Petrarch, who lived and wrote here, and another to the French Resistance of World War II.

Perched village of Gordes

❽ Gordes

Vaucluse. 2,000. pl du Château (04 90 72 02 75). Tue. **gordes-village.com**

Dominated by a 16th-century **château**, the perched village of Gordes forms such a harmonious whole that it might have been designed by an architect. The arcaded medieval lanes add to the attractive hilltop position.

Just south lies the **Village des Bories**, a primitive habitat of tiny beehive-shaped huts built of overlapping dry stones. The construction techniques are thought to date back to Neolithic times. This group was inhabited from the 16th to the early 20th century.

The **Abbaye de Sénanque**, to the north, is a fine Romanesque Cistercian monastery.

Château de Gordes
Pl du Château. **Tel** 04 90 72 98 64. **Open** Apr–Sep: Tue–Sun. **Closed** 1 Jan, 25 Dec.

Village des Bories
Rte de Gorde. **Tel** 04 90 72 03 48. **Open** daily. **Closed** 1 Jan, 25 & 31 Dec. **levillagedesbories.com**

❾ Luberon

Vaucluse. Avignon. Cavaillon, Avignon. Apt. pl François Tourel, Cavaillon (04 90 71 32 01). **luberoncoeurdeprovence.com**

A huge limestone range, the Montagne du Luberon is one of the most appealing areas of Provence. Rising to 1,125 m (3,690 ft), it combines wild areas

For hotels and restaurants in this region see pp569–71 and pp601–3

with picturesque villages. Almost the entire area is designated a regional nature park. Within it are more than 1,000 plant species and cedar and oak forests. The wildlife is varied, with eagles, vultures, snakes, beavers, wild boar and the largest lizards in Europe.The park headquarters are in **Apt**, the capital of the Luberon.

Once notorious as the haunt of highwaymen, the Luberon hills now hide sumptuous holiday homes. The major village is **Bonnieux**, with its 12th-century church and 13th-century walls. Also popular are **Roussillon**, with red ochre buildings, **Lacoste**, the site of the ruins of the Marquis de Sade's castle, and **Ansouis**, with its 14th-century Eglise St-Martin and 17th-century castle. **Ménerbes** drew to it the writer Peter Mayle, whose tales of life here brought this quiet region a worldwide audience.

Herb stall at St-Rémy-de-Provence

⑩ St-Rémy-de-Provence

Bouches-du-Rhône. 10,000. Avignon. pl Jean Jaurès (04 90 92 05 22). Wed. saintremy-de-provence.com

For centuries St-Rémy, with its boulevards, fountains and narrow streets, had two claims to fame. One was that Vincent van Gogh spent a year here, in 1889–90, at the St-Paul-de-Mausole hospital. *Wheat Field with Cypress* and *Ravine* are among the 150 works he produced here. St-Rémy-de-Provence was also, in 1503, the birthplace of Nostradamus, known for his prophecies. But, in 1921, it found new fame when archaeologists unearthed the Roman ruins at the **Site Archéologique de Glanum**. Little remains of the ancient city, sacked in AD 480 by the Goths, but the site impresses. Around the ruins of a Roman arch is a mausoleum, decorated with scenes such as the death of Adonis.

Site Archéologique de Glanum
Tel 04 90 92 23 79. **Open** Apr–Aug: daily; Sep–Mar: Tue–Sun. **Closed** 1 Jan, 1 May, 1 & 11 Nov, 25 Dec. **site-glanum.fr**

⑪ Les Baux-de-Provence

Bouches-du-Rhône. 470. Arles. La Maison du Roy (04 90 54 34 39). **lesbauxdeprovence.com**

One of the strangest places in Provence, the deserted citadel of Les Baux stands like a natural extension of a huge rocky plateau. The ruined castle and old houses overlook the Val d'Enfer (Infernal Valley), with its weird rocks.

In the Middle Ages Les Baux was home to powerful feudal lords, who claimed descent from the Magus Balthazar. It was the most famous of the Provençal Cours d'Amour, at which troubadours sang the praises of high-born ladies. The ideal of ever-lasting but unrequited courtly love contrasts with the warlike nature of the citadel's lords.

The glory of Les Baux ended in 1632. It had become a Protestant stronghold and Louis XIII ordered its destruction. The ruins of **Château de Baux de Provence** are a reminder of a turbulent past and offer spectacular views. The living village below has a pleasant little square, the 12th-century **Eglise St-Vincent** and the **Chapelle des Pénitents Blancs**, decorated by local artist Yves Brayer, whose work can be seen in the **Musée Yves Brayer**.

Deserted medieval citadel of Les Baux-de-Provence

In 1821 bauxite, a deep-red mineral, was discovered here and named after the town. Deposits were intensely exploited until they ran out at the end of the 20th century.

To the southwest are the ruins of the **Abbaye de Montmajour** with its fine 12th-century Romanesque church.

Parading the Tarasque, 1850

⑫ Tarascon

Bouches-du-Rhône. 14,000. Les Panaromiques, av de la République (04 90 91 03 52). Tue & Fri. **tarascon.org**

According to legend, the town takes its name from the Tarasque, a monster, half-animal and half-fish, which terrorized the countryside. It was tamed by Ste Marthe, who is buried in the church here. An effigy of the Tarasque is still paraded through the streets each June *(see p41)*.

The striking 15th-century **Château Royal de Provence** on the banks of the Rhône is one of the finest examples of Gothic military architecture in Provence. Its sombre exterior gives no hint of the beauties within: the Flemish-Gothic courtyard; and the spiral staircase; the painted ceilings of the banqueting hall.

Opposite is Beaucaire, a ruined castle and gardens.

Château Royal de Provence (Tarascon)
Bd du Roi René. **Tel** 04 90 91 01 93. **Open** daily. **Closed** some public hols. **chateau.tarascon.fr**

⑬ Arles

Few other towns in Provence combine all the region's charms as well as Arles. Its position on the Rhône makes it a natural, historic gateway to the Camargue *(see pp514–15)*. Its Roman remains, such as the arena and Constantine's baths, are complemented by the ochre walls and Roman-tiled roofs of later buildings. A bastion of Provençal tradition and culture, it has museums that are among the best in the region. Van Gogh spent time here in 1888–9, but Arles is no longer the industrial town he painted. Visitors are now its main business, and entertainment ranges from the Arles Festival to bullfights.

Palais Constantine was once a grand imperial palace. Now only its vast Roman baths remain, dating from the 4th century AD. They are remarkably well preserved and give an idea of the luxury that bathers enjoyed.

Musée Réattu
This museum, in the old Commandery of the Knights of Malta, houses witty Picasso sketches, paintings by the local artist Jacques Réattu (1760–1833) and sculptures by Ossip Zadkine, including *La Grande Odalisque* (1932), above.

Hôtel de Ville and entrance to Cryptoportiques

Museon Arlaten
In 1904 the poet Frédéric Mistral used his Nobel Prize money to establish this museum devoted to his beloved native Provence. Parts of the collection are arranged in room settings, and even the museum attendants wear traditional Arles costume. (Note that the museum is closed for renovation until 2019.)

Espace Van Gogh, in a former hospital where the artist was treated in 1889, is a cultural centre devoted to his life and work.

★ Eglise St-Trophime
This church combines a noble 12th-century Romanesque exterior with superb Romanesque and Gothic cloisters. The ornate main portal is carved with saints and apostles.

Tourist information

Les Alyscamps by Paul Gauguin

Les Alyscamps

A tree-lined avenue of broken medieval tombs is the focal point of these "Elysian Fields" to the southeast of Arles. It became Christian in the 4th century and was a prestigious burial ground until the 12th century. Some sarcophagi were sold to museums; others have been neglected. Mentioned in Dante's *Inferno*, painted by van Gogh and Gauguin, it is a place for thought and inspiration.

VISITORS' CHECKLIST

Practical Information

Bouches-du-Rhône. 53,000.
arlestourisme.com
bd des Lices (04 90 18 41 20).
Wed, Sat. Arles Festival (Jul); Prémice du Riz (Sep). Musée Réattu: **Open** Tue–Sun. **Closed** 1 Jan, 1 May, 1 Nov, 25 Dec. Museon Arlaten: **Closed** until 2019. **museonarlaten.fr**

Transport

25 km (16 miles) NW Arles.
 av Paulin Talabot.

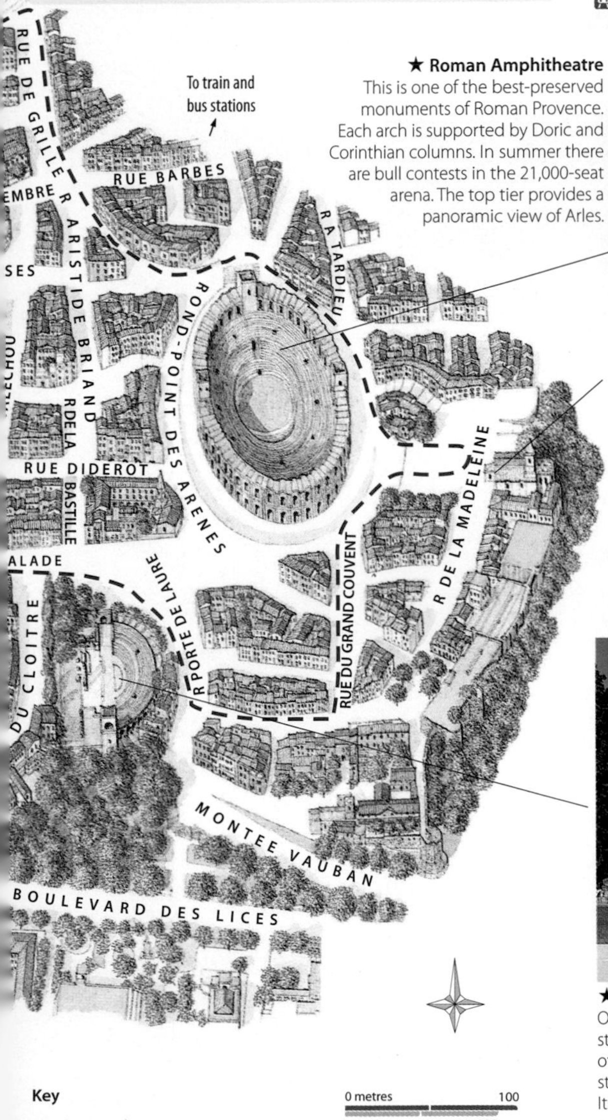

To train and bus stations

RUE DE GRILLE
RUE BARBES
EMBRE
R ARISTIDE BRIAND
SES
RA TARDIEU
ROND-POINT DES ARENES
RDELA BASTILLE
RUE DIDEROT
ALADE
R DE LA MADELEINE
RUE DU GRAND COUVENT
R PORTE DE LAURE
DU CLOITRE
MONTEE VAUBAN
BOULEVARD DES LICES

★ Roman Amphitheatre

This is one of the best-preserved monuments of Roman Provence. Each arch is supported by Doric and Corinthian columns. In summer there are bull contests in the 21,000-seat arena. The top tier provides a panoramic view of Arles.

Eglise Notre-Dame-de-la-Major is the church in which the *gardians* (cowboys) of the Camargue celebrate the feast day of their patron saint, St George. Although the building dates from the 12th to 17th centuries, a Roman temple existed on this spot hundreds of years earlier.

★ Roman Theatre

Once a fortress, the theatre's stones were later used for other buildings. Today, it stages the Arles Festival. Its remaining columns are called the "two widows".

Key

— Suggested route

0 metres 100
0 yards 100

⓮ The Camargue

The Rhône delta was responsible for the formation of more than 1,120 sq km (432 sq miles) of wetlands, pastures, dunes and salt flats that make up the Camargue, but human efforts are needed to preserve it. The region now maintains a fragile ecological balance, in which a unique collection of flora flourishes, including tamarisk and narcissi, and fauna such as egrets and ibises. The pastures provide grazing for sheep, cattle and small white Arab-type horses, ridden by the *gardians* or cowboys, a hardy community who traditionally lived in thatched huts *(cabanes)* and still play their part in keeping Camargue traditions alive.

Sunset over the Camargue

Black Bulls
In a Provençal bull contest (known as a *course*), the animals are not killed. Instead, red rosettes are plucked from between their horns with a small hook.

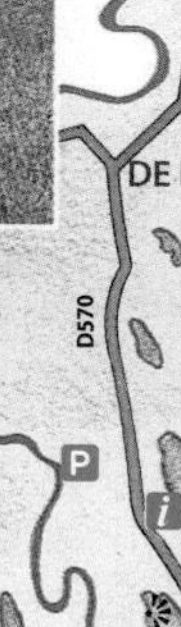

Les Saintes-Maries-de-la-Mer
The May gypsy pilgrimage to this fortified church marks the legendary arrival by boat in AD 18 of Mary Magdalene, St Martha and the sister of the Virgin Mary. Statues in the church depict the event.

Flamingoes
These striking birds are always associated with the Camargue, but the region supports many other breeds, including herons, kingfishers, owls and birds of prey. The area around Ginès is the best place to see them.

VISITORS' CHECKLIST

Practical Information
Bouches-du-Rhône. Mas du Pont de Rousty. **Tel** 04 90 97 10 40. Les Pèlerinages (end May, end Oct), Festival du Cheval (14 Jul). Musée de la Camargue, Pont de Rousty: **Tel** 04 90 97 10 82. **Open** daily. **Closed** 1 Jan, 1 May, 25 Dec. **saintes maries.com**; **parc-camargue.fr**

Transport
Montpellier-Méditerranée, 90 km (56 miles) east. av Paulin Talabot, Arles.

Key

- Nature reserve boundary
- Walking routes
- Walking and cycling routes

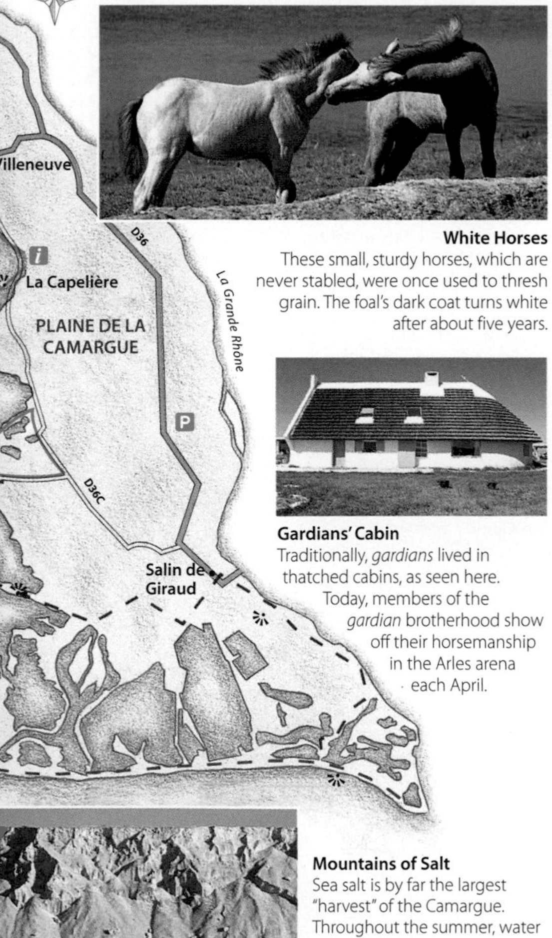

White Horses
These small, sturdy horses, which are never stabled, were once used to thresh grain. The foal's dark coat turns white after about five years.

Gardians' Cabin
Traditionally, *gardians* lived in thatched cabins, as seen here. Today, members of the *gardian* brotherhood show off their horsemanship in the Arles arena each April.

Mountains of Salt
Sea salt is by far the largest "harvest" of the Camargue. Throughout the summer, water collected in vast brine pans evaporate and the crystals are heaped into shimmering *camelles* up to 8 m (26 ft) high.

⓯ Aix-en-Provence

Bouches-du-Rhône. 145,000. Les allées provençales, 300 ave Giuseppe Verdi (04 42 16 11 61). daily. **aixenprovencetourism.com**

Founded by the Romans in 103 BC, Aix was frequently attacked, first by the Visigoths in AD 477, later by Lombards, Franks and Saracens. Despite this, the city prospered. By the end of the 12th century it was capital of Provence. A centre of art and learning, it reached its peak in the 15th century during the reign of "Good King" René. He is shown in Nicolas Froment's *Triptych of the Burning Bush* in the 13th- century Gothic **Cathédrale St-Sauveur**, also noted for its 16th-century walnut doors, Merovingian baptistry and Romanesque cloisters.

Aix is still a centre of art and learning, and its many museums include the **Musée Granet** of fine arts and archaeology in the Palais de l'Archevêché.

Aix has been called "the city of a thousand fountains". Three of the best are on cours Mirabeau. On one side are 17th- and 18th-buildings with wrought-iron balconies; on the other are cafés. The Old Town centres on place de l'Hôtel de Ville, with its colourful flower market. The **Caumont Centre d'Art**, located in one of the city's most stunning mansions, is an art gallery and cultural centre.

Aix's most famous son is Paul Cézanne (1839–1906). The **Atelier de Cézanne** is kept as it was when he died. Montagne Ste-Victoire, inspiration for many of his paintings, is 15 km (9 miles) east of Aix.

Musée Granet
pl St-Jean de Malte. **Tel** 04 42 52 88 32. **Open** Tue–Sun. **Closed** 1 Jan, 1 May, 25 Dec. **museegranet-aixenprovence.fr**

Caumont Centre d'Art
3 rue Joseph Cabassol. **Tel** 04 42 20 70 01. **Open** daily.

Atelier de Cézanne
9 av Paul Cézanne. **Tel** 04 42 21 06 53. **Open** daily. **Closed** Dec–Feb: S... 1–10 Jan, 1 May, 25 Dec. **atelier-cezanne.con**

For keys to symbols *see*

Old harbour of Marseille, looking towards the quai de Rive Neuve

⑯ Marseille

Bouches-du-Rhône. 866,000. 11 La Canebière (0826 500 500). Mon–Sat. **marseille-tourisme.com**

A Greek settlement, founded in the 7th century BC, then called Massilia, Marseille was seized by the Romans in 49 BC. It became the "Gateway to the West" for most Oriental trade. France's largest port and lively second-largest city has close links with the Middle East and North Africa. Designated a European Capital of Culture in 2013, Marseille has renovated its old harbour and port terminal.

Narrow stepped streets, quiet squares and fine 18th-century façades contrast with the bustle of boulevard Canebière and the Cité Radieuse, Le Corbusier's post-war radical housing complex.

The old harbour now only handles small boats, but its daily fish market is renowned.

Marseille has many excellent museums. Those in the old harbour area include the **Musée des Docks Romains**, the **Musée d'Histoire de Marseille** and the upbeat **Musée de Savon**.

The **Musée Cantini**, to the south, houses the 20th-century art collection of sculptor Jules Cantini. It includes Surrealist, Cubist and Fauve paintings. On the other side of the city is the **Château Borély**, home to the Musée des Arts Décoratifs and the Musée de la Mode. Marseille has an extensive tramway system and has introduced a bike-rental scheme that allows people to rent a bike in one part of town and deposit it in another.

Musée des Beaux-Arts

Palais Longchamp, pl Aile Gauche (left wing). **Tel** 04 91 14 59 30. **Open** Tue–Sun. **Closed** 1 Jan, 1 May, 1 Nov, 25, 26 Dec.

This museum is housed in the handsome 19th-century Palais Longchamp. Works include Michel Serre's graphic views of Marseille's plague of 1721, Pierre Puget's town plans for the city and murals depicting it in Greek and Roman times.

Château d'If

Vieux Port. **Tel** 06 03 06 25 26. **Open** Apr–Sep: daily; Oct–Mar: Tue–Sun. **chateau-if.fr**

The Château d'If (Castle of Yew) stands on a tiny island 2 km (1 mile) southwest of the port. A formidable fortress, it was built in 1529 to house artillery, but never put to military use and later became a prison. Alexandre Dumas' fictional Count of Monte Cristo was supposed to have been imprisoned here, and visitors can see a special cell, complete with escape hole. Most real-life inmates were either common criminals or political prisoners.

Basilique de Notre-Dame-de-la-Garde

Built between 1853 and 1864, this Neo-Byzantine basilica dominates the city. Its belfry, 46 m (151 ft) high, is capped by a huge gilded statue of the Virgin. The lavishly decorated interior has coloured marble and mosaic facings.

Abbaye de St-Victor

Similar to a fortress in appearance, the abbey was rebuilt in the 11th century after destruction by the Saracens. In the French Revolution, the rebels used it as a barracks and prison. There is an intriguing crypt in the abbey's church, with an original catacomb chapel and a number of pagan and Christian sarcophagi.

On 2 February each year, St-Victor becomes a place of pilgrimage. Boat-shaped cakes are sold to commemorate the legendary arrival of St Mary Magdalene, Lazarus and St Martha nearly 2,000 years ago.

Cathédrale de la Major

Built in Neo-Byzantine style, this is the largest 19th-century church in France, 141 m (463 ft) long and 70 m (230 ft) high. In the crypt are the tombs of the bishops of Marseille. The small and beautiful Ancienne Cathédrale de la Major is close by.

La Vieille Charité

2 rue de la Charité. **Tel** 04 91 14 58 11. **Open** Tue–Sun. **Closed** public hols. **vieille-charite-marseille.com**

In 1640, construction of a shelter "for the poor and beggars" of Marseille was begun by royal decree. A hundred years later, Pierre Puget's hospital and church opened. The restored building houses the Musée d'Archéologie Méditerranéenne; the Musée des Arts Africains, Océaniens et Amérindiens (MAAOA) is on the second floor.

Fish seller at the fish market in Marseille

Musée des Civilisations de l'Europe et de la Méditerranée (MuCEM)
1 esplanade de J4, 201 quai du Port (VJ4 and Fort Saint-Jean). **Tel** 04 84 35 13 00. **Open** Wed–Mon. **mucem.org**

Linking Marseille's harbour, a former port terminal and the 17th-century Fort St-Jean, this cultural centre facing the Mediterranean Sea focuses on the history of civilization in the European and Mediterranean region. Its ethnographical collection includes over 500,000 items, some dating back to 1884, plus drawings, paintings, photographs and books.

17 Cassis

Bouches-du-Rhône. 8,000. quai des Moulins, Le Port (08 92 39 01 03). Wed & Fri. **ot-cassis.com**

Many villages along this coast have been built up and have all but lost their original charm, but Cassis is still much the same little fishing port that attracted artists such as Dufy, Signac and Derain. This is a place in which to relax at a waterside café, watching the fishermen or street performers, while enjoying the seafood and a bottle of the local dry white wine for which Cassis is noted.

From Marseille to Cassis the coastline forms narrow inlets, the **Calanques**, their jagged white cliffs (some as high as 400 m/1,312 ft) reflected in dazzling turquoise water. Wildlife abounds here, with countless seabirds, foxes, stone martens, bats, large snakes and lizards. The flora is no less impressive, with more than 900 plant species, of which 50 are classified as rare. The En-Vau and Sormiou Calanques are especially lovely. The Massif de Calanque and Cap Canaille are designated national parks.

18 Toulon

Var. 167,000. 12 pl Louis-Blanc (04 94 18 53 00). Tue–Sun. **toulontourisme.com**

In 1793 this naval base was captured by an Anglo-Spanish fleet, but was retaken by the young Napoleon Bonaparte. The impressive collection of the **Musée National de la Marine** explores maritime history. The **Musée d'Art de Toulon**, housed in an Italian Renaissance building, has a collection representing Fauvism, Minimalism and Realism. The war-damaged Old Town has a few original buildings, and the fish market is worth a visit. For lovely views, the boat trip around the bay and the cable car ride up to Mont Faron are highly recommended.

Musée National de la Marine
Pl Monsenergue. **Tel** 04 22 42 02 01. **Open** daily. **Closed** Tue (Sep–Jun), 1 May, 25 Dec. restr. **musee-marine.fr**

Musée d'Art de Toulon
113 bd Mar Leclerc. **Tel** 04 94 36 81 01. **Open** Tue–Sun pms only. **Closed** public hols.

Paul Signac's *Cap Canaille*, painted at Cassis in 1889

Tour of the Gorges du Verdon

The Verdon Gorges constitute one of the most dramatic natural sights in Europe. The dark green River Verdon flows through a deeply cut valley with twisted rocks and cone-shaped peaks. In places, the Gorges reach depths of 700 m (2,297 ft), passing through largely uninhabited country between the vast natural amphitheatre of Moustiers-Ste-Marie and the narrow streets of Castellane. Dramatic viewpoints include the Balcons de la Mescla, beyond the Pont de l'Artuby, and the Point Sublime. A detour southwest of Moutiers to Quinson's Musée de Préhistoire is worthwhile.

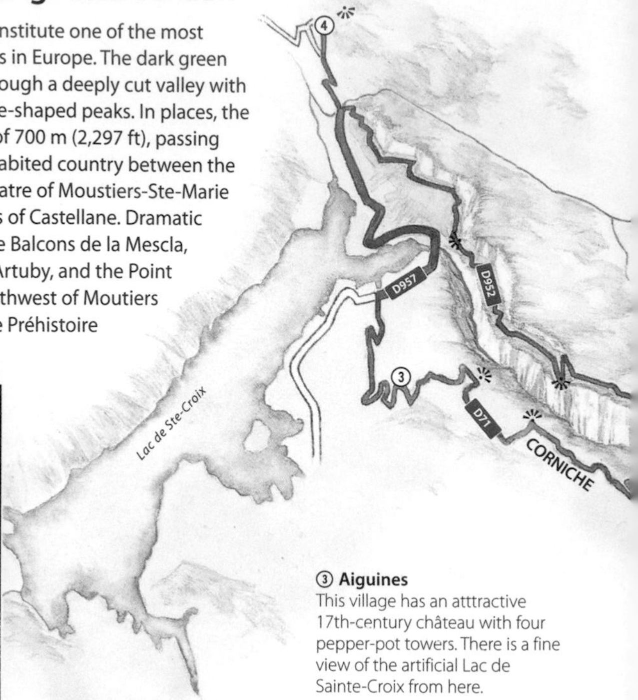

Verdon Gorges from the Castellane road

③ Aiguines
This village has an atttractive 17th-century château with four pepper-pot towers. There is a fine view of the artificial Lac de Sainte-Croix from here.

⓳ Hyères

Var. 57,000. Rotonde du Park Hotel, av de Belgique (04 94 01 84 50). Tue, Thu & Sat. **hyeres-tourisme.com**

Towards the end of the 18th century, Hyères became one of the first health resorts of the Côte d'Azur. Among its subsequent visitors were Queen Victoria and writers Robert Louis Stevenson (1850–94) and Edith Wharton (1862–1937).

The main sights are found in the Vieille Ville's medieval streets, which lead past the spacious, flagstoned place Massillon to a ruined castle and views over the coast.

Modern Hyères is imbued with a lingering *belle époque* charm, which has become popular with experimental film-makers. It continues to attract a health-conscious crowd and is a major centre for aquatic sports.

Porquerolles island marina

hotels and restaurants in this region see pp569–71 and pp601–3

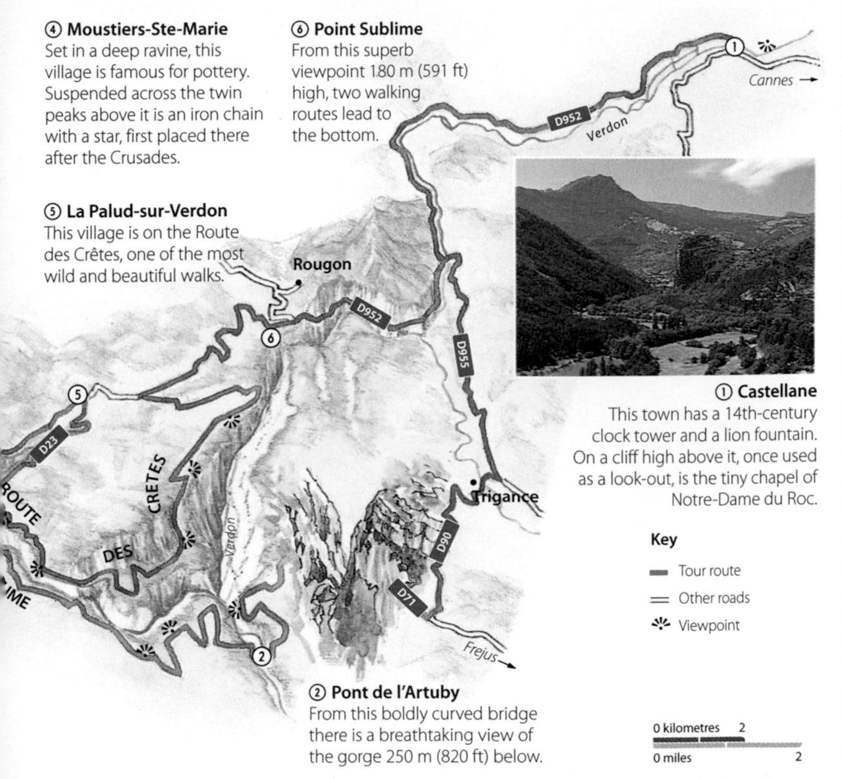

④ Moustiers-Ste-Marie
Set in a deep ravine, this village is famous for pottery. Suspended across the twin peaks above it is an iron chain with a star, first placed there after the Crusades.
⑥ Point Sublime
From this superb viewpoint 180 m (591 ft) high, two walking routes lead to the bottom.
Cannes
D952
Verdon
⑤ La Palud-sur-Verdon
This village is on the Route des Crêtes, one of the most wild and beautiful walks.
Rougon
D952
D955
D23
ROUTE
DES
CRETES
Verdon
Trigance
D90
D71
Frejus
① Castellane
This town has a 14th-century clock tower and a lion fountain. On a cliff high above it, once used as a look-out, is the tiny chapel of Notre-Dame du Roc.
Key
Tour route
Other roads
Viewpoint
② Pont de l'Artuby
From this boldly curved bridge there is a breathtaking view of the gorge 250 m (820 ft) below.
0 kilometres 2
0 miles 2

⑳ Iles d'Hyères

Var. Toulon-Hyères. Hyères. Hyères (Porquerolles office: 04 94 58 33 76). **hyeres-tourisme.com** **porquerolles.com**

Locally known as the Iles d'Or ("Golden Islands"), after the gold colour of their cliffs, this lovely trio of islands can be reached by boat from Hyères, Tour Fondue, Le Lavandou, La Croix Valmer, Cavalaire and St Tropez.

Porquerolles, the largest of the three, measures 7 km (4 miles) by 2.5 km (1.5 miles). It is covered in rich vegetation, much of which, for instance the Mexican bellombra tree, was introduced from a variety of exotic foreign climes.

The island's main town, also known as Porquerolles, looks more like a North African colonial settlement than a Provençal village. It was established in 1820 as a retirement town for Napoleon's most honoured troops. All the island's beaches lie along the northern coastline. The best, the long, sandy Plage Notre-Dame, one of the finest beaches in Provence, sits in a sheltered bay about an hour's walk from Porquerolles village.

A stroll around lush **Port-Cros**, covering 2.5 sq km (1 sq mile), takes the best part of a day. It rises to 195 m (640 ft), the highest point on any of the islands.

Both Porquerolles and Port-Cros are national parks. Unique reserves of flora and fauna, their waters are also protected. There is even a 300-m (984-ft) scenic swimming route. You can buy a waterproof guide to the underwater wildlife.

The wild, virtually treeless **Ile du Levant** is reached by boat from Port-Cros. Its main draw is the oldest naturist resort in France, Héliopolis, founded in 1931. The eastern half of the island, controlled by the French navy, is permanently closed to the public.

㉑ Massif des Maures

Var. Toulon-Hyères. Hyères, Toulon or Fréjus. Bormes-les-Mimosas. Toulon. 1 pl Gambetta, Bormes-les-Mimosas (04 94 01 38 38). **bormeslesmimosas.com**

The dense wilderness of pine, oak and chestnut covering the Maures mountains probably gave rise to its name, meaning "dark" or "gloomy". It extends nearly 65 km (40 miles) between Hyères and Fréjus. The D558 north of Cogolin leads to the heart of the Maures. Along the way is La Garde-Freinet, well-known for its bottle-cork industry.

Northwest of Cannet-des-Maures lies the Abbaye de Thoronet. With the abbeys at Sénanque, in Vaucluse, and Silvacane, in the Bouches-du-Rhône, it is known as one of the "Three Sisters" of Provence.

Harbourside at St-Tropez

22 St-Tropez

Var. 4,500. quai Jean Jaurès (08 92 68 48 28 or, from abroad, 04 94 97 45 21). Tue & Sat.
sainttropeztourisme.com

The geography of St-Tropez kept it untouched by the earliest development of the Côte d'Azur. Tucked away at the tip of a peninsula, it is the only north-facing town on the coast and so did not appeal to those seeking a warm and sheltered winter resort. In 1892 the painter Paul Signac was among the first outsiders to respond to its unspoiled charm, encouraging friends, such as the painters Matisse and Bonnard, to join him. In the 1920s the Parisian writer Colette also made her home here. St-Tropez also began to attract star-spotters, hoping for a glimpse of celebrities such as the Prince of Wales.

During World War II the beaches around St-Tropez were the scene of Allied landings, and part of the town was heavily bombed. Then, in the 1950s, young Parisians began to arrive, and the Bardot-Vadim film helped to create the reputation of modern St-Tropez as a playground for gilded youth. The wild public behaviour and turbulent love affairs of Roger Vadim, Brigitte Bardot, Sacha Distel and others left fiction far behind. Mass tourism followed, with visitors once again more interested in spotting a celebrity than in visiting the **Musée de l'Annonciade** with its outstanding collection of works by Signac, Derain, Rouault, Bonnard and others.

Today, there are far more luxury yachts than fishing boats moored in St-Tropez harbour. Its cafés make ideal bases for people- and yacht-watching. Another centre of the action is place des Lices, both for the Harley-Davidson set and the morning market. The **Musée de l'Histoire Maritime**, located in the tower of the citadel from where there are great views, recounts the village's impressive seafaring past.

The best beaches are found outside the town, including the golden curve of Pampelonne, with its beach clubs and restaurants. This is the beach on which to see and be seen. St-Tropez has no train station, so driving and parking can be a nightmare in summer – it is best to get the boat from St Raphaël or St Maxime.

It is said that St-Tropez takes its name from a Roman soldier martyred as a Christian by the Emperor Nero. Each May a *bravade* in his honour takes place, whereby an effigy of the saint is carried through the town to the accompaniment of musket fire.

Nearby are two small towns of differing character but equal charm. **Port-Grimaud** was only built in 1966, but the sensitive use of traditional architecture makes it seem older. Most of its "streets" are canals. Up in the hills, the winding streets of **Ramatuelle** have been restored to perfection by the largely celebrity population.

Musée de l'Annonciade
2 rue l'Annociade, pl Grammont. **Tel** 04 94 17 84 10. **Open** Wed–Mon. **Closed** 1 Jan, Ascension, 1 & 17 May, 1 Nov, 25 Dec.

Musée de l'Histoire Maritime
Citadelle de Saint Tropez. **Tel** 04 94 97 59 43. **Open** daily. **Closed** 1 Jan, 1 & 17 May, 11 Nov, 25 Dec.

Scooters, a stylish solution to the traffic problems in St-Tropez

Brigitte Bardot

In 1956, Brigitte Bardot's film *And God Created Woman* was shot in St-Tropez by her new husband, Roger Vadim. By settling in St-Tropez, "BB" the sex goddess (b.1934) changed the fortunes of the sleepy little fishing village and ultimately the Côte d'Azur, making it the centre of her then-hedonistic lifestyle. In 1974, on her 40th birthday, she celebrated her retirement from films at Club 55 on Pampelonne Beach. She now devotes her time to her animal sanctuary.

Brigitte Bardot in 1956

For hotels and restaurants in this region see pp569–71 and pp601–3

23 Digne-les-Bains

Alpes-de-Haute-Provence. 17,000. Le Rond Point (04 92 36 62 62). Wed, Sat.
ot-dignelesbains.fr

This charming spa town in the foothills of the Alps features in Victor Hugo's *Les Misérables*. A trip on the Train des Pignes from Nice offers superb views. Apart from the spa, Digne-les-Bains also offers a lavender festival *(see p42)* and **Le Jardin des Papillons**, France's only butterfly garden.

Le Jardin des Papillons
St Benoît. **Tel** 04 92 36 70 70. **Open** Apr–Sep. in summer.

24 Fréjus

Var. 54,000. 249 rue Jean Jaurès (04 94 51 83 83). Wed, Fri–Sun. **frejus.fr**

The modern town of Fréjus is dwarfed in importance by two impressive historic sites. The remains of the Roman **Amphithéâtre** (founded by Julius Caesar in 49 BC) may not be as complete as those at Orange or Arles but they are of exceptional variety. A great amphitheatre, fragments of an aqueduct, a theatre and part of a rampart gateway remain. The sea has receded over the centuries and there are few traces of the original harbour.

The cathedral on rue de Fleury marks the entrance to the **Groupe Episcopal**. The fortified enclave includes the 5th-century baptistry, one of the oldest in France, and the cathedral cloister, its coffered medieval roof decorated with a spectacular bestiary.

In 1959 Fréjus was hit by a wall of water, as the Malpasset Barrage burst. To the north, the ruined dam can still be seen.

Amphithéâtre
Rue Henri Vadon. **Tel** 04 94 51 34 31. **Open** Tue–Sun (Oct–Mar: Tue–Sat). **Closed** 1 Jan, 1 May, 25 Dec.

Groupe Episcopal
48–58 rue de Fleury. **Tel** 04 94 51 26 30. **Open** Tue–Sun (Jun–Sep: daily). **Closed** 1 Jan, 1 May, 1 & 11 Nov, 25 Dec. cloisters. **cloitre-frejus.fr**

The Creation of a Perfume

The best perfumes begin as a formula of essential oils extracted from natural sources. The blend of aromas is created by a perfumer called a "nose" because of his or her exceptional sense of smell. A perfume may use as many as 300 essences, all painstakingly extracted from plants by various methods: steam distillation, extraction by volatile solvents and *enfleurage à froid* (for costly or potent essences). With this process, pungent blossoms are placed onto layers of fats for several days until the fats are saturated. The oils are then "washed" out with alcohol, and, when this evaporates, it leaves the "pure" perfume essence behind.

Lavender water

Grasse flowers

25 St-Raphaël

Var. 35,000. 99 quai Albert 1er (04 94 19 52 52).
saint-raphael.com

Delightfully situated, St-Raphaël is a charming, old-style Côte d'Azur resort with *belle époque* architecture and a palm-fronded promenade. Aside from its beaches, it offers a marina, a casino, a Neo-Byzantine basilica, a 12th-century church and an archaeology museum with treasures from prehistorical underwater wrecks.

It was here that Napoleon Bonaparte landed in 1799 on his return from Egypt.

26 Grasse

Alpes-Maritimes. 52,000. pl de la Buanderie (04 93 36 66 66).
grassetourisme.fr

Cradled by hills, with views out to sea, Grasse is surrounded by fields of lavender, mimosa, jasmine and roses. Grasse has been the centre of the world's perfume industry since the 16th century, when Catherine de' Medici set the fashion for scented leather gloves. At that time, Grasse was also known as the centre for leather tanning. The tanneries have gone, but the perfume houses founded in the 18th and 19th centuries are still in business, although today Grasse perfumes are made from imported flowers or chemicals. Fragonard and Molinard have museums, but the best place to learn the history of perfume is at the **Musée Internationale de la Parfumerie**, which has a garden of fragrant plants.

Grasse was the birthplace of the artist Jean-Honoré Fragonard (1732–1806). The late 17th-century **Villa-Musée Fragonard** is decorated with murals by his son. Fragonard's only religious work is in the **Cathédrale de Notre-Dame-du-Puy** in the Old Town, which also has three paintings by Rubens. Place aux Aires and place du Cours typify Grasse's charm, surrounded by streets with Renaissance staircases and balconies.

Musée International de la Parfumerie
2 bd de Jeu du Ballon. **Tel** 04 97 05 58 00. **Open** daily. **Closed** 1 Jan, 1 May, 25 Dec. **museesdegrasse.com**

Villa-Musée Fragonard
23 bd Fragonard. **Tel** 04 93 36 52 98. **Open** Jul–Sep daily.

Statue honouring Jean-Honoré Fragonard in Grasse

Menton at dusk ▶

High summer on the beach at Cannes, overlooked by the Carlton Hotel

㉗ Cannes

Alpes-Maritimes. 75,000. Palais des Festivals, 1 bd de la Croisette (04 92 99 84 22). Tue–Sun. **cannes-destination.com**

Just as Grasse is synonymous with the perfume industry, the first thing that most people associate with Cannes is its many festivals, especially the Film Festival. There is much more to the city than these glittering events. It was Lord Brougham, the British Lord Chancellor, who put Cannes on the map, although Prosper Mérimée, Inspector of Historic Monuments, allegedly visited Cannes two months before him. Lord Brougham stopped here in 1834, unable to reach Nice due to a cholera outbreak there. Struck by the beauty and mild climate of what was then just a small fishing port, he built a villa here. Other foreigners followed and Cannes became established as a top Mediterranean resort.

The Old Town that Lord Brougham knew is centred in the district of Le Suquet, on the slopes of Mont Chevalier. Part of the old city wall can still be seen on place de la Castre, which is dominated by the **Notre-Dame de l'Espérance**, built in the 16th and 17th centuries in the Provençal Gothic style. An 11th-century watchtower is another attractive feature of the quarter, and the castle keep houses the **Musée de la Castre**, the eclectic finds of a 19th-century Dutch explorer, Baron Lycklama.

The famed **boulevard de la Croisette** is lined with gardens and palm trees. One side is occupied by luxury boutiques and hotels such as the Carlton, built in *belle époque* style, with twin cupolas modelled on the breasts of La Belle Otero, a famous member of the 19th-century *demi-monde*. Opposite are some of the finest sandy beaches on this coast. The glamour of the Croisette, once one of the world's grandest thoroughfares, seems faded in the noise and fumes of summer.

Iles de Lérins

depart from: le Quai des Iles. Horizon (04 92 98 71 36 for Ile Ste-Marguerite), Planaria (04 92 98 71 38 for Ile St-Honorat).

Just off the coast from Cannes are the Iles de Lérins. The fort on **Ile Sainte-Marguerite** is where the mysterious Man in the Iron Mask was imprisoned in the late 17th century. A popular theory

Cannes Film Festival

The first Cannes Film Festival took place in 1946 and, for almost 20 years, it remained a small and exclusive affair, attended by the artists and celebrities who lived or were staying on the coast. The arrival of the "starlet", especially Brigitte Bardot, in the mid-1950s marked the change from artistic event to media circus, but Cannes remains the international marketplace for film-makers and distributors, with the *Palme d'Or* award conferring high status on its winner. The annual film festival is held in May in the huge Palais des Festivals et des Congrés, opened in 1982. It has 13 auditoriums, two exhibition halls, conference rooms, a casino and a nightclub.

The red carpet at the Cannes Film Festival

is that his face had to be hidden because he resembled someone very important indeed – possibly even Louis XIV. Visitors can see the tiny cell that held him for over ten years.

Ile Saint-Honorat has an 11th-century tower in which the resident monks took refuge during raids by the Saracens. There are also five ancient chapels. Both islands offer peaceful woodland walks, fine views and quiet coves for swimming.

Beside the boulevard de la Croisette

28 Cap d'Antibes

Alpes-Maritimes. Nice. Antibes. Nice. 42 av Robert Soleau, Antibes (04 22 10 60 10).
antibesjuanlespins.com

With its sumptuous villas, this rocky peninsula, also known as "the Cap", has been a symbol of luxury life on the Riviera since it was frequented by F Scott Fitzgerald and the rich American set in the 1920s. The magnate Frank Jay Gould invested in the resort of Juan-les-Pins, and it became the focus of high life on the Cap. Today, memories of the Jazz Age live on at the Jazz Festival held here and in Antibes, when international stars perform *(see p41)*.

At the highest point of the peninsula, the sailors' chapel of **La Garoupe** has a collection of votive offerings and a 14th-century Russian icon. Nearby is the **Jardin Botanique de la Villa Thuret**, created in 1856 to acclimatize tropical plants. Much of the exotic flora of the region began its naturalization here.

Jardin Botanique de la Villa Thuret
90 chemin Raymond, Antibes Juan-les-Pins. **Tel** 04 97 21 25 00. **Open** Mon–Fri. **Closed** public hols.

29 Antibes

Alpes-Maritimes. 77,000. 42 av Robert Soleau (04 22 10 60 10). Tue–Sun (Jul–Aug: daily).
antibesjuanlespins.com

The lively town of Antibes was founded by the Greeks as Antipolis and settled by the Romans. In the 14th century, Savoy's possession of the town was contended by France until it fell to them in 1481, after which **Fort Carré** was built and the port, now the base of many luxury superyachts, was remodelled by Vauban.

The Château Grimaldi, formerly a residence of Monaco's ruling family, was built in the 12th century. It now houses the **Musée Picasso**. In 1946 the artist used part of the castle as a studio and, in gratitude, donated 23 paintings and 44 drawings, including *The Goat*. Most are inspired by his love of the Mediterranean, including *La Joie de Vivre*.

The Goat (1946) by Pablo Picasso

Over the years, the collection has grown to include more than 150 works.

The pottery in the **Musée d'Archéologie** includes objects salvaged from shipwrecks from the Middle Ages to the 18th century.

Musée Picasso
Château Grimaldi. **Tel** 04 92 90 54 20/26. **Open** Tue–Sun. **Closed** 1 Jan, 1 May, 1 Nov, 25 Dec.

Musée d'Archéologie
Bastion St-André. **Tel** 04 93 95 85 98. **Open** Tue–Sun. **Closed** public hols.

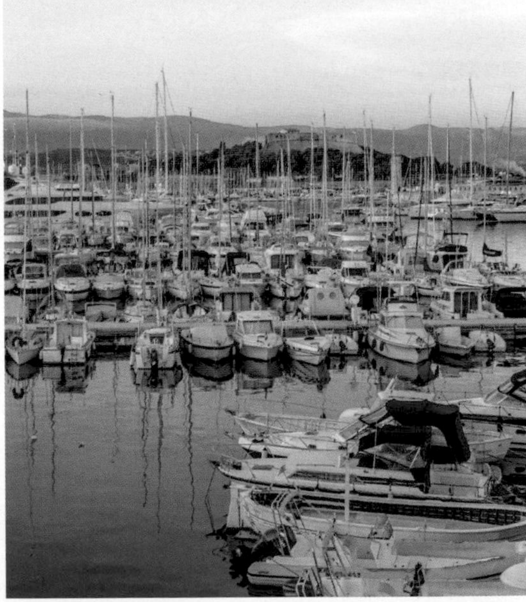

Yachts in the harbour at Antibes

㉚ Vallauris

Alpes-Maritimes. 26,000. 4 av Georges Clémenceau (04 93 63 18 38); Golfe Juan Vieux Port (04 93 63 73 12). Tue–Sun. **vallauris-golfe-juan.fr**

Vallauris owes its fame to Pablo Picasso, who rescued the town's pottery industry. In 1951, the village authorities commissioned Picasso to paint a mural in the deconsecrated chapel next to the castle, and his *War and Peace* (1952) is the chief exhibit of the **Musée National Picasso**. In the main square is a bronze statue, *Man with a Sheep* (1943), donated by Picasso.

Musée National Picasso
Place de la Libération. **Tel** 04 93 64 71 83. **Open** Wed–Mon (Jul & Aug: daily). **Closed** 1 Jan, 1 May, 1 & 11 Nov, 25 Dec. **musees-nationaux-alpesmaritimes.fr**

㉛ Biot

Alpes-Maritimes. 11,000. 4 Chemin Neuf (04 93 65 78 00). Tue. **biot-tourisme.com**

A typical hill village, charming Biot has always attracted artists and artisans. The best known is Fernand Léger, who made his first ceramics here in 1949. Some of these and other works by him are in the **Musée National Fernand Léger** outside town.

The town is also famous for its bubble-flecked glassware. The craft of the glassblowers can be seen (and purchased) at the **Verrerie de Biot**.

Musée National Fernand Léger
316 chemin du Val-de-Pome. **Tel** 04 92 91 50 30. **Open** Wed–Mon. **Closed** 1 Jan, 1 May, 25 Dec. **musee-fernandleger.fr**

La Verrerie de Biot
5 chemin des Combes. **Tel** 04 93 65 03 00. **Open** daily. **Closed** 1 & 15–27 Jan. **verreriebiot.com**

Renoir's studio at the Musée Renoir, Chemin des Collettes, in Cagnes-sur-Mer

㉜ Cagnes-sur-Mer

Alpes-Maritimes. 48,000. 6 bd Maréchal Juin (04 93 20 61 64). Tue–Sun. **cagnes-tourisme.com**

Cagnes-sur-Mer is divided into three districts. The oldest and most interesting is Haut-de-Cagnes, with its steep streets, covered passageways and ancient buildings, including a number of Renaissance arcaded houses. The other districts are Cagnes-Ville, the modern town where hotels and shops are concentrated, and Cros-de-Cagnes, a seaside fishing resort and yachting harbour.

The **Château Grimaldi** in Haut-de-Cagnes was built in the 14th century and reworked in the 17th by Henri Grimaldi. Behind the fortress walls is a shady courtyard. The surrounding marble columns conceal a museum devoted to the olive tree and a small collection of modern Mediterranean art. There is also a group of paintings bequeathed by *chanteuse* Suzy Solidor. The 40 works, all portraits of her, are by artists such as Lolita Lempicka and Kees van Dongen. On the ceiling of the banqueting hall is a vast illusionistic fresco of the *Fall of Phaeton*, attributed to Carlone in the 1620s.

The last 12 years of Pierre-Auguste Renoir's life were spent in Cagnes, at the **Musée Renoir**. The house has been kept almost exactly as it was when he died in 1919 and contains 14 of his paintings as well as 17 plaster

Exterior of the Musée National Fernand Léger in Biot, with a mural by the artist

For hotels and restaurants in this region see pp569–71 and pp601–3

sculptures. The views from the garden across the countryside down to the sea are simply stunning.

Château Grimaldi
pl du Château. **Tel** 04 92 02 47 30. **Open** mid-Dec–mid-Nov: Wed–Mon. **Closed** 1 Jan, 25 Dec.

Musée Renoir
Tel 04 93 20 61 07. **Open** Wed–Mon (call to confirm opening hours). **Closed** 1 May, 1 Jan, 25 Dec.

㉝ Gorges du Loup

Alpes-Maritimes. Nice. Cagnes-sur-Mer. Grasse. Nice. 2 pl de la Libération, Tourrettes-sur-Loup (04 93 24 18 93). **tourrettessurloup.com**

The River Loup rises in the Pre-Alps behind Grasse and cuts a deep path down to the sea. Along its route are dramatic cascades and spectacular views. The superb countryside is crowned by the perched villages for which the region is famous.

Gourdon owes much of its appeal to its ancient houses, grouped round a 12th-century **château** built on the site of a Saracen stronghold and perched high on the cliffside. Its terraced gardens were laid out by André Le Nôtre *(see p183)*.

Tourrettes-sur-Loup is a fortified village, in which the ramparts are formed by the outer houses. It is famous for its fields of violets, grown for use in perfume and candied sweets. The **Bastide aux Violettes** museum explores the role of the flower in the village's history and economy.

La Bastide aux Violettes
quartier de La Ferrage. **Tel** 04 93 59 06 97. **Open** Tue–Sat (Jul & Aug: daily). **tourettessurloup.com**

㉞ Vence

Alpes-Maritimes. 19,000. pl du Grand Jardin (04 93 58 06 38). Tue & Fri. **vence-tourisme.fr**

Vence's gentle climate has always been its main attraction; today it is surrounded by holiday villas. It was an important religious centre in the Middle Ages. The **Cathédrale** was restored by Vence's most famous bishop, Antoine Godeau. A 5th-century Roman sarcophagus serves as its altar and there are Carolingian wall carvings. Note, too, the 15th-century carved choir stalls and Godeau's tomb.

Within the ramparts of the Old Town, which retains its 13th- to 14th-century town gates, is place du Peyra, once a Roman forum. Its fountain, built in 1822, still provides fresh water. Found on the edge of town, the **Chapelle du Rosaire**, built in 1947 to 1951, was decorated by Henri Matisse, in gratitude to the nuns who nursed him during an illness. On its white walls, biblical scenes are reduced to simple black lines tinted by splashes of light from the blue and yellow stained-glass windows.

Domed roof in Vence

Chapelle du Rosaire
466 av Henri Matisse. **Tel** 04 93 58 03 26. **Open** Tue, Thu & Fri am and pm, Wed & Sat pm. **Closed** public hols.
Sun 10am.

Chapelle du Rosaire in Vence, whose architecture and interior were designed and decorated by Matisse

35 Street-by-Street: St-Paul de Vence

One of the most famous and frequently visited hill villages of the Nice hinterland, St-Paul de Vence was once a French frontier post facing Savoy. Its 16th-century ramparts offer views over a landscape of cypress trees and red-roofed villas with palm trees and swimming pools. The village has been heavily restored, but its winding streets and medieval buildings are authentic. It has proved a magnet for artists, both established and aspiring, throughout the 20th century. Today galleries and studios dominate the village.

View of St-Paul de Vence
The local landscape is a favourite subject for artists. Neo-Impressionist Paul Signac (1863–1935) painted this view of St-Paul.

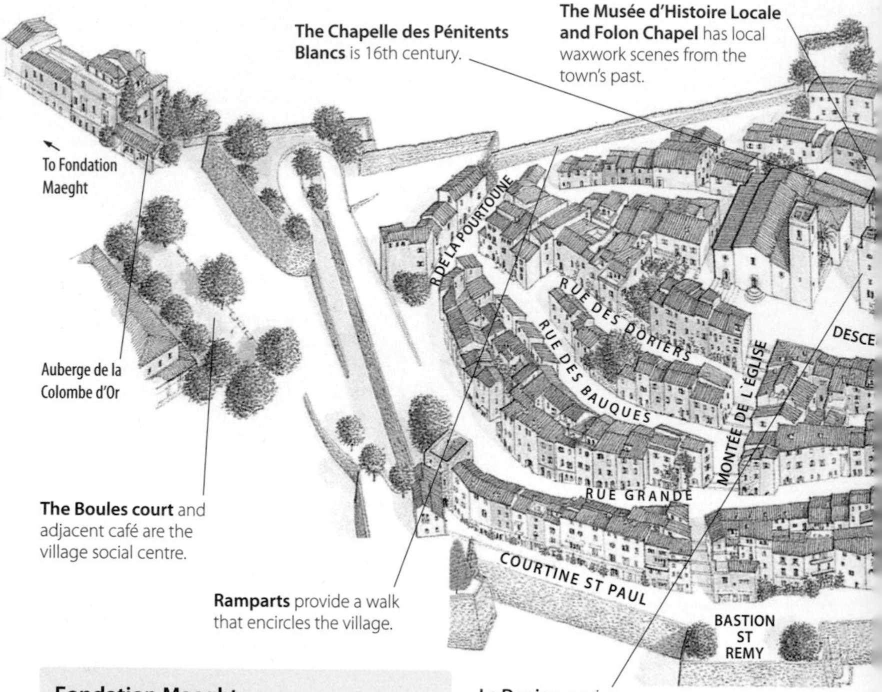

The Chapelle des Pénitents Blancs is 16th century.

The Musée d'Histoire Locale and Folon Chapel has local waxwork scenes from the town's past.

To Fondation Maeght

R DE LA POURTOUNE

RUE DES DORIERS

RUE DES BAUQUES

MONTÉE DE L'ÉGLISE

DESCE

RUE GRANDE

COURTINE ST PAUL

BASTION ST REMY

Auberge de la Colombe d'Or

The Boules court and adjacent café are the village social centre.

Ramparts provide a walk that encircles the village.

Le Donjon, a grim medieval building, was used as a prison until the 19th century.

Fondation Maeght

Built in 1964 by Paris art dealers Aimé and Marguerite Maeght, this is one of Europe's finest museums of modern art. The striking pink and white building, set outside St-Paul, was designed by Catalan architect José-Luis Sert, who worked on it directly with artists such as Miró and Chagall. Inside are paintings by Bonnard, Braque, Kandinsky, Chagall and others. There are also summer concerts, exhibitions, a library and lectures. In the terraced gardens, sculptures, mobiles and mosaics by Arp, Calder, Miró, Giacometti and Hepworth are set amid the pine trees.

L'Homme qui Marche by Giacometti

The Colombe d'Or
This famous auberge includes a Léger mural (above) on the terrace; a Braque dove by the pool; and a Picasso and a Matisse in the dining room.

For hotels and restaurants in this region see pp569–71 and pp601–3

Eglise Collégiale
Begun in the 12th century, the church has treasures including a painting of St Catherine, attributed to Claudio Coello.

VISITORS' CHECKLIST

Practical Information
Alpes-Maritimes. 3,500.
2 rue Grande (04 93 32 86 95).
saint-pauldevence.com
Fondation Maeght: 623 chemin Gardettes (04 93 32 81 63). **Open** 10am–6pm (Jul–Sep: to 7pm).

Transport
840 av Emile Hugues, Vence (04 93 58 37 60).

Grand Fountain
This charming cobble-stoned *place* has a pretty urn-shaped fountain.

Rue Grande
The doors of the 16th- and 17th-century houses bear coats of arms.

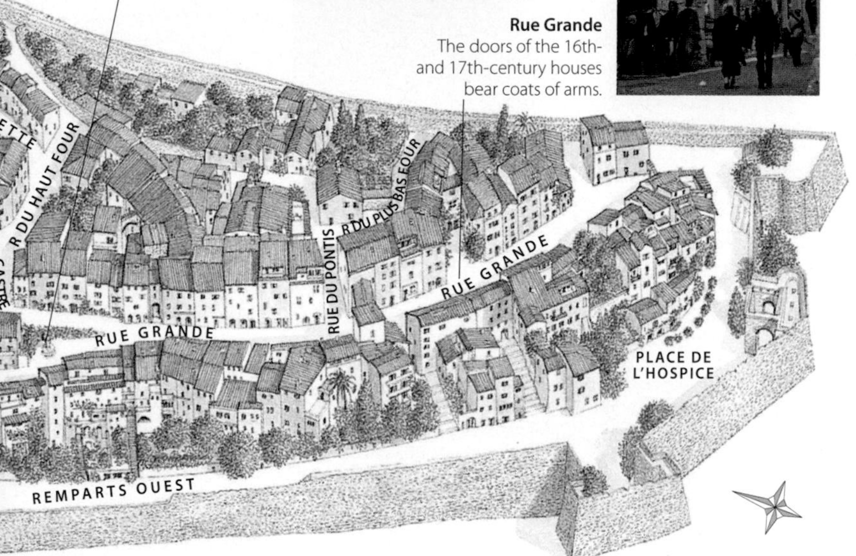

Celebrity Village

The Colombe d'Or (Golden Dove) auberge *(see p602)* was popular with many of the artists and writers who flocked to the Riviera in the 1920s. Early patrons included Picasso, Soutine, Modigliani, Signac, Colette and Cocteau. Thanks to a friendship with the owners, these artists often paid for their rooms and meals with paintings, resulting in the priceless collection that can be seen by diners today. The rich and famous have continued to come to St-Paul de Vence: Zelda and F Scott Fitzgerald had a dramatic fight over Isadora Duncan at dinner here one night, and Yves Montand married Simone Signoret on the terrace. Modern-day fans include Elton John, Michael Caine, Roger Moore and Hugh Grant.

Artist Marc Chagall (1887–1985), who moved to St-Paul de Vence in 1950

36 Nice

The largest resort on the Mediterranean coast and the fifth biggest city in France, with its second busiest airport, Nice was founded by the Greeks and colonized by the Romans. Its temperate winter climate and verdant subtropical vegetation have long attracted visitors. Until World War II it was favoured by aristocrats, including Tsar Nicholas I's widow, who visited in 1856 and Queen Victoria, who stayed in 1895. This glittering past has contributed to Nice becoming capital of the Côte d'Azur, and today it is also a centre for business conferences and package holidays. Nice has worthy museums, good beaches and an atmospheric street life. Best of all is Carnival: 18 days of celebrations finishing on Shrove Tuesday in a fireworks display and the Battle of the Flowers *(see p43)*.

Nice's Old Quarter

Yachts at anchor in Nice harbour

Exploring Nice

The promenade des Anglais, along the seafront, was built in the 1830s with funds raised by the English colony. Today it is an eight-lane, 8-km (5-mile) highway, with galleries, shops and grand hotels such as the 1913 **Negresco**, reflecting Nice's prosperity.

Nice was Italian until 1860, and the pastel façades and balconies of the Old Town have a distinctly Italianate feel. It lies at the foot of a hill still known as the Château for the castle that once stood there. The district's tall, narrow buildings house artists and galleries, boutiques and restaurants. The daily flower market in cours Saleya should not be missed. The **Cimiez** district, on the hills overlooking the town, is the fashionable quarter of Nice. The old monastery of Notre-Dame-de-Cimiez is well worth a visit. Lower down the hillside are Les Arènes, remains of a Roman settlement with vestiges of the great baths and an amphitheatre. Excavated artifacts are on show at the archaeological museum, next to the Musée Matisse. At the foot of the Cimiez hill is the **Musée National Marc Chagall**. The promenade du Paillon, a strip of park with a central waterway, runs from the Old Town through the centre to the promenade des Anglais.

As well as guided tours on foot or by bike, it is possible to explore the foodie side of the city on a culinary tour.

Musée National Marc Chagall

36 av du Docteur Ménard. **Tel** 04 93 53 87 20. **Open** Nov–Apr: 10am–5pm Wed–Mon (May–Oct: to 6pm). **Closed** 1 Jan, 1 May, 25 Dec. **w musee-chagall.fr**

The largest collection of works by Marc Chagall, includes paintings, drawings, sculpture and 17 canvases of the artist's *Biblical Message*.

Villa Masséna

65 rue de France. **Tel** 04 93 91 19 10. **Open** Wed–Mon.

Housed in a 19th-century Italianate mansion, the Villa Masséna exhibits trace the history of Nice.

Cathédrale Ste-Réparate

3 pl Rossetti. **Tel** 08 92 70 74 07 or 04 93 92 01 35 for guided tours. **Open** daily.

This 17th-century Baroque building has a handsome tiled dome and is lavishly decorated with marble and original panelling.

Palais Lascaris

15 rue Droite. **Tel** 04 93 62 72 40. **Open** Wed–Mon. **Closed** 1 Jan, Easter, 1 May, 25 Dec.

Ornate woodwork, Flemish tapestries and illusionistic

An azure view – relaxing on the promenade des Anglais

ceilings thought to be by Carlone adorn this stuccoed 17th-century palace. Its small but delightful collection includes a reconstruction of an 18th-century apothecary's shop.

Musée d'Art Moderne et d'Art Contemporain (MAMAC)

pl Yves Klein. **Tel** 04 97 13 42 01. **Open** Tue–Sun. **Closed** 1 Jan, Easter, 1 May, 25 Dec.
mamac-nice.org

The museum occupies a strikingly original complex of four marble-faced towers linked by glass passageways. The collection is particularly strong in Neo-Realism and Pop Art, with works by Andy Warhol, Jean Tinguely and Niki de Saint Phalle. Also well-represented are such Ecole de Nice artists as César, Arman and Yves Klein.

Musée Matisse

164 av des Arènes de Cimiez. **Tel** 04 93 81 08 08. **Open** Wed–Mon. **Closed** some public hols.
musee-matisse-nice.org

Inspired by the Mediterranean light, Matisse spent many years in Nice. The museum, housed in and below the 17th-century Arena Villa, displays drawings, paintings, bronzes, fabrics and artifacts. Highlights include *Still Life With Pomegranates* and Matisse's last completed work, *Flowers and Fruits*.

Blue Nude IV (1952) by Henri Matisse

Musée National du Sport

Stade Allianz Riviera, bd des Jardiniers. **Tel** 04 89 22 44 00. **Open** Tue–Sun.
museedusport.fr

With its superb collection of memorabilia and photographs, this museum gives an interactive view of France's sporting history.

VISITORS' CHECKLIST

Practical Information
Alpes-Maritimes. 350,000. 5 prom des Anglais (04 92 14 46 14). Tue–Sun. Carnival.
nicetourism.com

Transport
7 km (4 miles) SW. av Thiers (36 35). 4 bd Jean Jaurès (08 10 06 10 06). quai du Commerce (04 93 21 72 17).

Musée des Beaux-Arts

33 av des Baumettes. **Tel** 04 92 15 28 28. **Open** Tue–Sun. **Closed** 1 Jan, Easter, 1 May, 25 Dec. restr.
musee-beaux-arts-nice.org

The 19th-century home of a Ukrainian princess displays works sent to Nice by Napoleon III after Italy ceded the city to France.

Musée des Arts Asiatiques

405 prom des Anglais. **Tel** 04 92 29 37 00. **Open** May–mid-Oct: 10am–6pm Wed–Mon (mid-Oct–Apr: to 5pm). **Closed** 1 Jan, 1 May, 25 Dec.
arts-asiatiques.com

Ancient and contemporary Asian art is displayed in Kenzo Tange's white marble and glass setting.

Nice

① Musée National Marc Chagall
② Villa Masséna
③ Cathédrale Ste-Réparate
④ Palais Lascaris
⑤ Musée d'Art Moderne et d'Art Contemporain

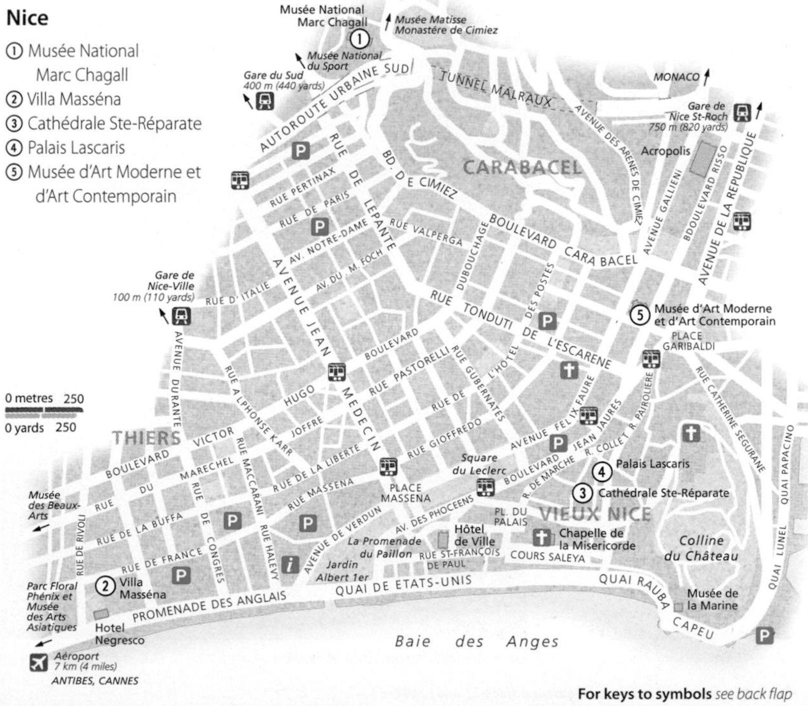

For keys to symbols *see back flap*

Chapelle de St-Pierre, Villefranche

㊲ Villefranche-sur-Mer

Alpes-Maritimes. 5,000. Jardin François Binon (04 93 01 73 68). Wed, Sat, Sun. **tourisme-villefranche-sur-mer.com**

One of the most perfectly situated towns on the coast, Villefranche lies at the foot of hills forming a sheltered amphitheatre. The town overlooks a beautiful natural harbour, which is deep enough to be a naval port of call.

The bright and animated waterfront is lined by Italianate façades, with cafés and bars from which to watch the fishermen. Here, too, is the **Chapelle de St-Pierre**, which, after years of service storing fishing nets, was restored in 1957 and decorated by Jean Cocteau. His frescoes depict non-religious images and the life of St Peter.

Also worth a visit is the 16th-century **Citadelle St-Elme**, incorporating three museums, an exhibition room, a congress room and a garden.

Behind the harbour, the streets are narrow, winding and often stepped. Walking through them, you get the odd glimpse of the harbour. The vaulted 14th-century rue Obscure has always provided shelter from bombardment, right up to World War II.

Chapelle de St-Pierre
Quai Amiral Courbet. **Tel** 04 93 76 90 70. **Open** Wed–Mon. **Closed** mid-Nov–mid-Dec, 25 Dec.

㊳ St-Jean-Cap-Ferrat

Alpes-Maritimes. 1,600. Nice. Nice. Beaulieu-sur-Mer. 5/59 av Denis Semeria (04 93 76 08 90). **saintjeancapferrat-tourisme.fr**

This peninsula boasts some of the most sumptuous villas on the Riviera. From 1926 until the author's death, the best-known was Somerset Maugham's Villa Mauresque, where he received celebrities from Noël Coward to Winston Churchill.

High walls shield most of the exclusive villas, but possibly the best one is open to the public. The **Villa Ephrussi de Rothschild** is a terracotta and marble mansion set in themed gardens on the crest of the cape. It belonged to the Baroness Ephrussi de Rothschild, who bequeathed it to the Institut de France in 1934. It is furnished as she left it, with her collections of priceless porcelain, items that belonged to Marie Antoinette and a unique collection of drawings by Fragonard.

The town of **Beaulieu-sur-Mer** lies where the cape joins the mainland. A pleasant marina with an exceptionally mild climate and very fine hotels, it is the site of another unique house, the extraordinary **Villa Grecque Kérylos**. Built between 1902 and 1908 for archaeologist Theodore Reinach in imitation of an ancient Greek residence, it contains lovingly reproduced mosaics, frescoes and furniture.

Villa Ephrussi de Rothschild
1 av Ephrussi de Rothschild, Cap Ferrat. **Tel** 04 93 01 45 90. **Open** Mar–Oct: 10am–6pm daily (Jul & Aug: to 7pm); Nov–Feb: pms daily (10am–6pm w/e & school hols). restricted. **villa-ephrussi.com**

Villa Grecque Kérylos
Imp Gustave Eiffel, Beaulieu. **Tel** 04 93 01 01 44. **Open** as above. **villakerylos.fr**

Greek-style Villa Grecque Kérylos at Beaulieu-sur-Mer

For hotels and restaurants in this region see pp569–71 and pp601–3

Louis XV salon at the Villa Ephrussi de Rothschild, St-Jean-Cap-Ferrat

❸❾ Eze

Alpes-Maritimes. 2,500. pl Général de Gaulle (04 93 41 26 00). **eze-tourisme.com**

For many, Eze is the ultimate perched village, balancing on a rocky pinnacle high above the Mediterranean. Every summer, thousands of visitors stream through the 14th-century fortified gate. The flower-decked buildings are almost all shops, galleries and craft workshops. At the top of the village, the château is surrounded by the lush tropical plants of the **Jardin Exotique**. The view from here is superb.

Further along the Upper Corniche is the Roman Alpine **Trophée d'Auguste à La Turbie** *(see pp52–3)*. This vast 6 BC structure dominates the surrounding village, with fine views towards Monaco and Italy.

Jardin Exotique
Rue du Château. **Tel** 04 93 41 10 30. **Open** daily. **Closed** Christmas wk.

Trophée d'Auguste à La Turbie
Open Tue–Sun. **Closed** public hols. **trophee-auguste.fr**

❹⓿ Roquebrune-Cap-Martin

Alpes-Maritimes. 13,000. Nice. 218 av Aristide Briand (04 93 35 62 87). Wed. **rcm-tourisme.com**

The medieval village of Roquebrune overlooks the wooded cape where the villas of the rich and famous still stand. Residents have included Coco Chanel and Empress Eugenie. The cape has not always been kind – poet W B Yeats died here in 1939 and architect Le Corbusier was drowned off the coast in 1965.

In 1467 Roquebrune believed that by performing scenes from the Passion it escaped the plague, and every August it continues this tradition.

❹❶ Alpes-Maritimes

Alpes-Maritimes. Nice. Nice. Peille. Nice. 15 rue Centrale, Peille (04 93 82 14 40). **peille.fr**

In the hinterland of the Côte d'Azur, it is still possible to find quiet, unspoiled villages off the tourist track. The tiny twin villages of **Peille** and **Peillon** are typical. Both have changed little since the Middle Ages, perched on outcrops over the Paillon river, their streets a mass of steps and arches. Peille, the more remote, even has its own dialect. The Alpes-Maritimes countryside is also unspoiled, its craggy gorges, tumbling rivers and windswept plateaux just a few hours from the coast. Of note are the ancient rock carvings of the **Vallée des Merveilles** and rare wildlife in the **Parc National du Mercantour**.

❹❷ Menton

Alpes-Maritimes. 30,000. Palais de l'Europe, 8 av Boyer (04 92 41 76 76). Tue–Sun. **tourisme-menton.fr**

Menton's beaches, with the Alps and the golden buildings and *belle époque* villas of the Old Town as a backdrop, would be enough to lure most visitors. Tropical gardens and citrus fruits thrive in the town's glorious climate, mild even in February for the lemon festival *(see p43)*.

The **Basilica St-Michel** is a superb example of Baroque architecture. The square before it is paved with a mosaic of the Grimaldi coat of arms. The **Salle des Mariages** in the Hôtel de Ville was decorated in 1957 by Jean Cocteau. Drawings, paintings, ceramics and stage designs by the renowned artist are displayed in the **Musée Jean Cocteau Collection Séverin Wunderman**, housed in a striking modern building. Inside the Palais Carnolès, the **Musée des Beaux-Arts** features works from the Middle Ages to the 20th century.

Salle des Mariages
Hôtel de Ville, pl Ardoino. **Tel** 04 92 10 50 00. **Open** Mon–Fri. **Closed** public hols.

Musée Jean Cocteau Collection Séverin Wunderman
2 quai de Monléon. **Tel** 04 89 81 52 50. **Open** Wed–Mon. **Closed** pub hols. **museecocteaumenton.fr**

Musée des Beaux-Arts
Palais Carnolès, 3 av de la Madone. **Tel** 04 93 35 49 71. **Open** Wed–Mon. **Closed** public hols.

The façade of the Musée Jean Cocteau Collection Séverin Wunderman

43 Monaco

Travellers to Monaco by car would do well to take the Moyenne Corniche, one of the most beautiful highways in the world, with incomparable views of the Mediterranean coastline. Arriving among the skyscrapers of Monaco today, it is hard to envisage the turbulence of its history. At first a Greek settlement, later taken by the Romans, it was bought from the Genoese in 1297 by the Grimaldis, who, in spite of bitter family feuds and at least one political assassination, are still the world's oldest ruling dynasty. Monaco covers 1.9 sq km (0.74 sq miles) and, although its size has increased by one-third in the form of landfills, it still occupies an area smaller than that of New York's Central Park.

Skyscrapers and apartment blocks of modern Monte Carlo

Casino de Monte Carlo

Exploring Monaco

Monaco owes its renown principally to its casino. Source of countless legends, it was instituted in 1878 by Charles III to save himself from bankruptcy. The first casino was opened in 1865 on a barren promontory (later named Monte Carlo in his honour) across the harbour from ancient Monaco-Ville. So successful was Charles's money-making venture that, by 1870, he was able to abolish taxation for his people. Today, Monaco is a tax haven for thousands, and its residents have the highest per capita income in the world.

Visitors come from all over the world for the Grand Prix de Monaco in May *(see p40)* and the Monte Carlo Rally in January *(see p43)*. Many of the greatest singers perform in the opera season. There is a fireworks festival (July–August), and an international circus festival at the end of January as well as world-class ballet and concerts. Facilities exist for every sort of leisure activity, and there is much else to enjoy without breaking the bank, including **Fort Antoine** and the Neo-Romanesque **Cathédrale**.

Casino de Monte Carlo

Place du Casino. **Tel** 00 377 98 06 21 21. **Open** daily, from 2pm (for players). **casinomontecarlo.com**

Renovated in 1878 by Charles Garnier, architect of the Paris Opéra *(see p101)*, and set in formal gardens, the Casino de Monte Carlo gives a splendid view over Monaco. The lavish interior is still decorated in *belle époque* style, recalling an era when this was the rendezvous of Russian Grand Dukes. Anyone can play the odds on the one-armed bandits of the Salon Blanc or the roulette wheels of the Salons Européens. Tours run daily from 9am to noon. Check the website for rules, regulations and dress code.

Palais Princier

Place du Palais. **Tel** 00 377 93 25 18 31. **Open** Apr–Oct: daily. **palais.mc**

Monaco-Ville, the seat of government, is the site of the 13th-century Palais Princier. The interior, with its priceless furniture and carpets and its magnificent frescoes of

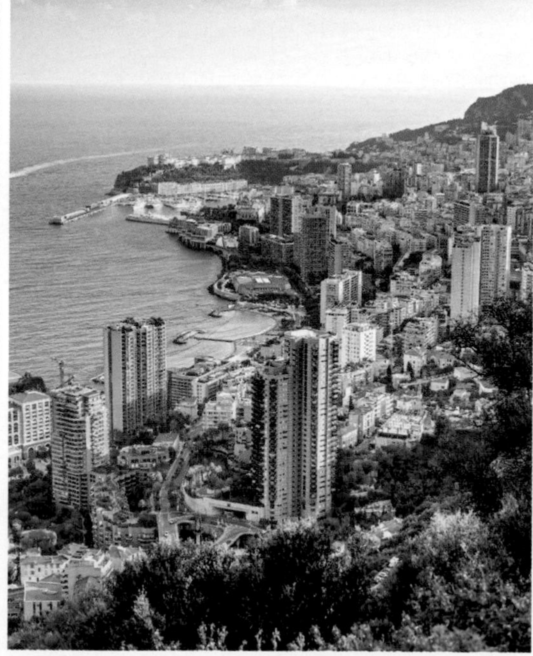

Aerial view of Monaco

Monaco's Royal Family

Prince Albert II assumed the Monaco throne in July 2005, three months after his father Prince Rainier III died, aged 81, ending a reign of over 55 years. Rainier was descended from a Grimaldi who entered the Monaco fortress in 1297. His wife, former film star Grace Kelly, died tragically in 1982. In 2011 Prince Albert married the South African Charlene Wittstuck; they welcomed their twin children in December 2014.

The wedding of Prince Albert and Princess Charlene

mythological figures, is only open to the public in the summer. The Changing of the Guard takes place at 11:55am.

Musée du Vieux Monaco

2 rue Emile de Loth. **Tel** 00 377 93 50 57 28. **Open** Jun–Sep: Wed & Fri. **traditions-monaco.com**

This museum aims to preserve and promote Monaco's historic national identity through a collection of paintings, ceramics, furniture, traditional costumes and reconstructed interiors typical of the area.

Guard outside the Palais Princier

Musée Océanographique

Av Saint-Martin. **Tel** 00 377 93 15 36 00. **Open** daily. **Closed** 1 Jan, Grand Prix, 25 Dec. **oceano.mc**

This museum was founded in 1910 by Prince Albert I. Its aquarium, fed with seawater, holds rare species of marine plants and animals. The museum houses an important scientific collection, diving equipment and model ships. Marine explorer Jacques Cousteau established his research centre here.

VISITORS' CHECKLIST

Practical Information

Monaco. 38,000. 2a bd des Moulins (00 377 92 16 61 16). daily. Festival du Cirque (Jan); International Fireworks Festival (Jul–Aug); Fête Nationale Monégasque (19 Nov).
visitmonaco.com

Transport

15 km (9 miles) SW Nice. pl Ste-Dévote (00 377 93 10 60 05).

Jardin Exotique

62 bd du Jardin Exotique. **Tel** 00 377 93 15 29 80. **Open** daily. **Closed** 19 Nov, 25 Dec. **jardin-exotique.mc**

These gardens are considered to be the finest in Europe, with a huge range of tropical and sub-tropical plants. A museum of anthropology offers evidence that mammoths once lived on the coast here.

Nouveau Musée National de Monaco

Villa Sauber, 17 av Princesse Grace. **Tel** 00 377 98 98 91 26. **Open** daily. **Closed** Grand Prix and public hols.

Villa Sauber and Villa Paloma are the two magnificent *belle époque* villas that make up this museum, which hosts temporary exhibitions on themes of art and performance.

Monaco

① Jardin Exotique
② Musée du Vieux Monaco
③ Palais Princier
④ Cathédrale
⑤ Musée Océanographique
⑥ Casino de Monte Carlo

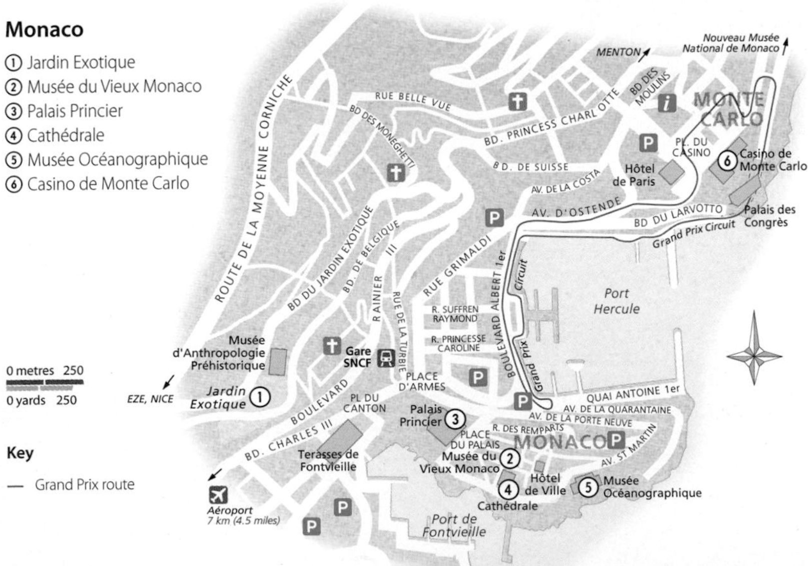

Key

— Grand Prix route

For keys to symbols *see back flap*

CORSICA

Haute-Corse · Corse-du-Sud

Corsica, where the people speak their own language, has all the attributes of a mini-continent. There are tropical palm trees, vineyards, olive and orange groves, forests of chestnut and indigenous pine, alpine lakes and cool mountain torrents filled with trout. Most distinctive of all is the parched maquis (scrub), heavy with the scent of myrtle, which Napoleon swore he could smell from Elba.

The fourth-largest island in the Mediterranean after Sicily, Sardinia and Cyprus, Corsica has been a problem and a bafflement to mainland France ever since 1769, when it was "sold" to Louis XV by the Genoese for 40 million francs. Before that, following years of struggle, the Corsican people had enjoyed 14 years of independence under the revered leadership of Pasquale Paoli. They understandably felt cheated by the deal with the French, and have resented them ever since. To holiday-makers visiting the island – in July and August tourists outnumber the inhabitants six to one – the Corsican–French relationship may be a matter of indifference. However, there is a strong (and sometimes quite violent) separatist movement, which does deter some tourists. As a result, Corsica's wild beauty has been preserved to an extent not seen in the rest of the Mediterranean.

For 200 years, from the 11th to the 13th century, Corsica was a colony of the old Tuscan republic of Pisa, whose builders founded beautifully proportioned Romanesque churches. These edifices are, along with the megalithic stone warriors in Filitosa, the noblest monuments to be seen here. For the rest, the birthplace of Napoleon is a place of wild seacoasts and mountain peaks, one of the last unspoiled corners of the Mediterranean: poor, depopulated, beautiful, old-fashioned and doggedly aloof.

The village of Oletta in the Nebbio region around St-Florent

◀ Dramatic limestone cliffs at Bonifacio

Exploring Corsica

Corsica's main appeal is its scenery: a wildly beautiful landscape of mountains, forests, myrtle-scented maquis and countless miles of sandy beaches. Late spring (when the wild flowers are in bloom) and early autumn are the best times to visit – the temperature is moderate and there aren't too many visitors. The island is renowned for its superb hiking trails, some of which become cross-country skiing trails during the winter. Downhill skiing is also possible in February and March.

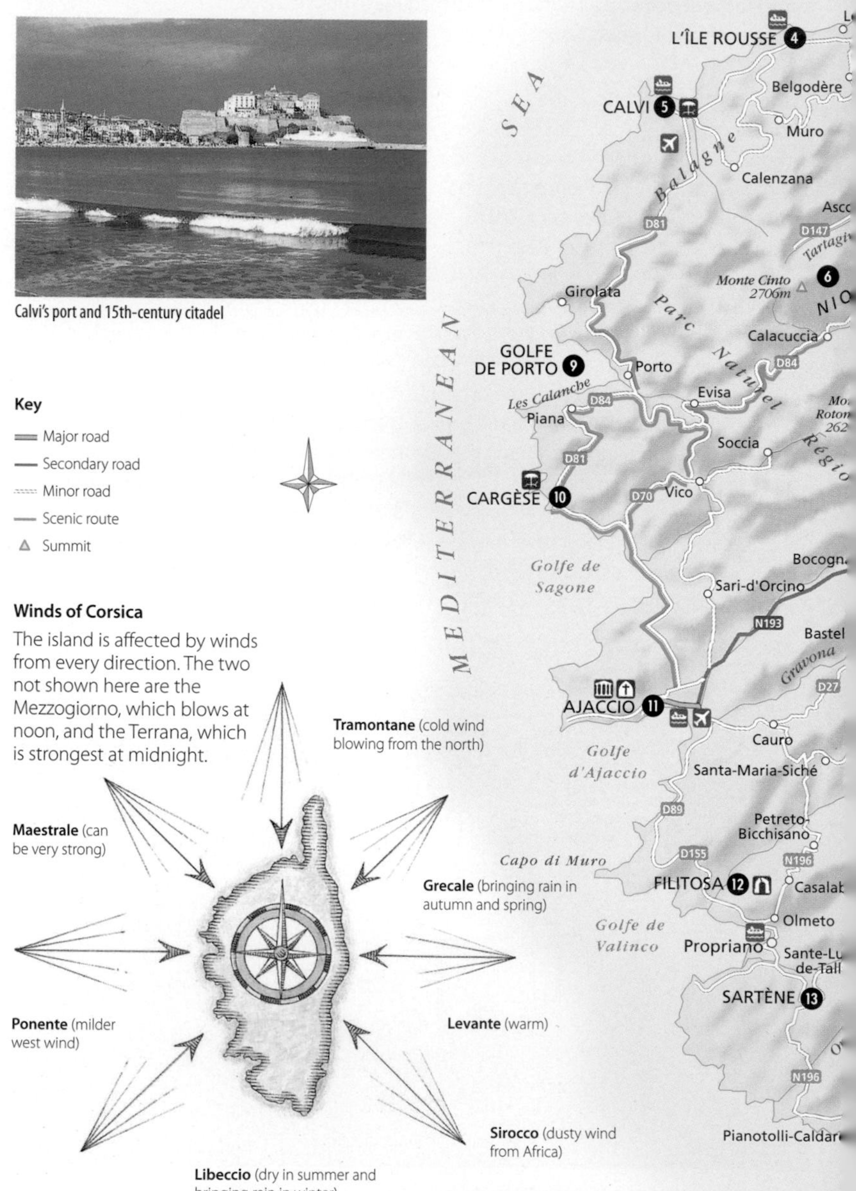

Calvi's port and 15th-century citadel

For keys to symbols see back flap

CAP CORSE 1
Centuri-Port
Rogliano
Macinaggio
Pino
Luri
D80
Canari
Golfe de St-Florent
D80
Monte Stello
1307m
Nonza
Erbalunga
Lavasina
Désert des Agriates
Patrimonio
ST-FLORENT 3
2 BASTIA
D81
Oletta
D82
Casatorra
Santo-Pietro-di-Tenda
Murato
Borgo
Casamozza
Golo
Ponte-Nuovo
Vescovato
Ponte-Leccia
N198
Morosaglia
N193
Figareto
Francardo
CASTAGNICCIA
8
Moriani-Plage
Piedicroce
Cervione
D71
7 CORTE
Prunete
Phare-d'Alistro
Venaco
Bravone
N200
Vezzani
Tavignano
Vivario
Vizzavona
Aléria
D344
CÔTE ORIENTALE
Ghisonaccia
15
Mignataja
D69
Travo
Zicavo
Solenzara
Monte Incudine
2136m
D268
N198
Zonza
Conca
Lecci
D368
Porto-Vecchio
D859
Figari
N198
14 BONIFACIO

Sights at a Glance

1. Cap Corse
2. Bastia
3. St-Florent
4. L'Ile Rousse
5. Calvi
6. The Niolo
7. Corte
8. The Castagniccia
9. Golfe de Porto
10. Cargèse
11. Ajaccio
12. Filitosa
13. Sartène
14. Bonifacio
15. Côte Orientale

The Calanche cliffs in the Golfe de Porto

Getting Around

Car ferries (which should be booked well in advance) depart from Marseille, Nice and Toulon, arriving at Bastia, L'Ile Rousse, Calvi, Ajaccio, Propriano and Porto-Vecchio. There are also ferries from Sardinia to Bonifacio and Propriano, and from several Italian ports. There are small airports at Ajaccio, Bastia, Calvi and Figari. Corsica's roads are narrow, twisting and often tortuously slow, though breathtaking views reward the effort. A car is a must for exploring the island, as public transport is limited. Carry spare petrol – filling stations are few and far between.

0 kilometres 20
0 miles 10

Corte's Old Town, with its citadel high up on a rocky outcrop

❶ Cap Corse

Haute-Corse. Bastia. Bastia. Bastia. Port de Plaisance, Macinaggio (04 95 35 40 34); Port Toga, Pietrabugna (04 95 31 02 32). **macinaggiorogliano-capcorse.fr**

Cap Corse is the northern tip of Corsica, 40 km (25 miles) in length but seldom more than 12 km (7 miles) wide, pointing like an accusatory finger towards Genoa.

There are two roads out of Bastia to the cape: the D81 leading west across the mountains and joining up with the D80 after the wine village of Patrimonio; and the D80 travelling north along the eastern shore to **Erbalunga** and **Macinaggio**. The road is narrow and twisting, a taste of what awaits you in Corsica.

From the coastal village of **Lavasina**, the D54 leads left off the D80 to Pozzo; from here it is a 5-hour round trip on foot to the 1,307-m (4,288-ft) summit of **Monte Stello**, the highest peak on the cape. The 360-degree view from the top takes in St-Florent to the west, the massif of central Corsica to the south and the Italian island of Elba to the east.

Further up the coast, the restored **Tour de Losse** is one of many 16th-century Genoese towers along the coast – part of an elaborate system that enabled all Corsican towns to be warned within 2 hours of impending barbarian raids.

The charming 18th-century fishing port of **Centuri**, near the tip of the peninsula on the west coast, is an ideal spot for a delicious seafood feast. **Pino**, a pretty little village straggling down the green mountainside further to the south, has no hotel, only a lovely little church dedicated to the Virgin, full of model ships placed there by mariners grateful for her protection.

On the way south along the vertiginous lower corniche, be sure to turn left up the hill to **Canari**. One of the larger villages in this area, Canari has a jewel of a 12th-century Pisan church, Santa Maria Assunta, a magnificent view across the sea and a thoroughly convivial hotel-restaurant. All the byroads in this thickly wooded area seem to lead somewhere interesting. There are dozens of picturesque hamlets in the vicinity, and it should be borne in mind that from this point onwards the landscape becomes steadily less attractive, as the road winds on past the old asbestos workings and beaches of black sand below the village of **Nonza**.

The village of Erbalunga on the east coast of Cap Corse

❷ Bastia

Haute-Corse. 44,000. north end of pl St-Nicolas (04 95 54 20 40). Tue–Sun. **bastia-tourisme.com**

A thriving port and the administrative capital of Upper Corsica, Bastia is utterly different in style from its sedate west coast rival, Ajaccio. The Genoese citadel and colourful 19th-century Italianate buildings around the old port are for many people their first taste of the authentic Mediterranean – as it was half a century ago, and as it stubbornly remains in our imagination.

The centre of Bastia's life is **place St-Nicolas**, facing the wharf where ferries from the mainland and Italy arrive. Heading south along the waterfront, you come to **place de l'Hôtel de Ville**, site of a daily food market. Bordering the square are the early 17th century **Chapelle de l'Immaculée Conception**, with its ornate 18th-century interior, and the mid-17th-century **Eglise de St-Jean-Baptiste**, whose façade dominates the Vieux Port.

From here it is a short walk up to the 16th-century **citadel** housing the **Musée de Bastia**, which recounts the town's history from its medieval origins in an impressive setting.

Musée de Bastia
Pl du Dujon. **Tel** 04 95 31 09 12.
Open Oct–Apr: Tue–Sat; May, Jun & Sep: Tue–Sun; Jul–Aug: daily.
musee-bastia.com

Bastia's Vieux Port seen from the Jetée du Dragon

For hotels and restaurants in this region see p571 and p603

❸ St-Florent

Haute-Corse. 1,700.
Bâtiment Administratif, BP 53 (04 95 37 06 04). first Wed of month.
corsica-saintflorent.com

St-Florent is almost a Corsican St-Tropez – chic, affluent and packed with yachts. Its citadel, which showcases photography exhibitions, dates from 1439, and is a fine example of Genoese military architecture. The town itself is pleasant to wander around; its main attraction, the 12th-century Pisan **Cathédrale de Santa Maria Assunta**, lies just inland on the road to Poggio-d'Oletta.

Environs

A leisurely 4-hour circuit by car of the **Nebbio** region, which extends in an amphitheatre shape around St-Florent, might take in the following: **Santo-Pietro-di-Tenda**; **Murato**, famous for its magnificent **Eglise de San Michele de Murato**, a 12th-century Pisan Romanesque construction built of white and green stone; the **San Stefano** pass, with the sea on either side; **Oletta**, which produces a special blue cheese made from ewe's milk; the **Teghime** pass; and finally the wine village of **Patrimonio**, where there is a strange, big-eared menhir dating from 900–800 BC.

Along the coast to the west of St-Florent lies the barren, uninhabited **Désert des Agriates**. If you can face the 10-km (6-mile) haul to the sea – on foot, by bike or by motorbike – the Saleccia beach is the most beautiful on the island.

San Michele de Murato

❹ L'Ile Rousse

Haute-Corse. 3,400.
av Calizi (04 95 60 04 35).
summer: daily; winter: Tue & Fri.
ot-ile-rousse.fr

Founded in 1758 by Pasquale Paoli, leader of independent Corsica, L'Ile Rousse is today a major holiday resort and ferry terminal. The centre of town is dominated by a marble statue of Corsica's national hero, Paoli. On the north side of the square is the covered market, with the Old Town located just beyond.

In summer, L'Ile Rousse becomes overcrowded, its beaches a mass of bodies. It is worth travelling 10 km (6 miles) up the coast to **Lozari**, which offers a magnificent, virtually unspoiled stretch of sand.

Environs

One very pleasant way to discover the **Balagne** region is to take the tram-train from L'Ile Rousse to Calvi and back. This odd little service runs all year (more frequent in summer), roughly keeping to the coastline and stopping at Algajola, Lumio and various villages along the way.

❺ Calvi

Haute-Corse. 5,500.
97 Port de Plaisance, chemin de la Plage (04 95 65 16 67). daily.
balagne-corsica.com;
calvi-tourisme.com

Calvi, where Nelson lost his eye in an "explosion of stones" in 1794, is today half military town, half cheap holiday resort. Its 15th-century Genoese citadel sitting high above Calvi port, from where it towers over the sea, is one of the most beautiful sights on the island.

The town makes a half-hearted case for being the birthplace of Christopher Columbus, but there is no evidence to support this. A much better claim to fame is the food, which is very good and reasonably priced. There is also a respectable jazz festival towards the end of June.

Outside town, the 19th-century **Chapelle de Notre-Dame de la Serra** is gloriously sited on a hilltop commanding extensive views in all directions.

French foreign legionnaire

The Chapelle de Notre-Dame de la Serra, 6 km (3 miles) southwest of Calvi

Corte's 15th-century citadel perched on a rocky outcrop above the town

6 The Niolo (Niolu)

Haute-Corse. Corte. rte de Cuccia, Calacuccia (04 95 48 05 22). **office-tourisme-niolu.com**

The Niolo, west of Corte, extends westward to the Vergio pass and the upper Golo basin, and to the east as far as the Scala di Santa Regina. It includes Corsica's highest mountain, the 2,706-m (8,878-ft) **Monte Cinto**, and its biggest river, the **Golo**, which meets the sea south of Bastia.

Of the various regions of Corsica, the Niolo is the only one to persist in the cultivation of livestock for its economic mainstay.

The main town, **Calacuccia**, is suitable for excursions to Monte Cinto. The nearby ski resort of **Haut Asco** is best reached by the D147 from **Asco**, but enthusiasts can walk from Calacuccia (8–9 hours). To the south is the huge forest of **Valdu Niello**.

7 Corte

Haute-Corse. 7,500. La Citadelle (04 95 46 26 70). Fri. **corte-tourisme.com**

In the geographical centre of Corsica, Corte was the chosen capital of the independence leader Pasquale Paoli from 1755 to 1769, and today is the seat of the island's university. In the Old Town is the 15th-century citadel, housing the **Musée de la Corse**. Its exhibits relate to traditional Corsican life and anthropology.

Corte is the best base for exploring nearby mountain areas, especially as it stands exactly halfway along the GR20, the legendary 220-km (137-mile) trail from Calenzana to Conca.

Musée de la Corse
La Citadelle. **Tel** 04 95 45 25 45. **Open** Tue–Sun (mid-Jun–mid-Sep: daily; Nov–Mar: Tue–Sat). **Closed** public hols. **musee-corse.com**

Environs
Don't miss the beautiful **Gorges de la Restonica**, about 12 km (7 miles) out of town via the D623. Above these gorges adventurous walkers may wish to make the well-marked climb to the snow-fed **Lac de Melo** (allow 60–90 minutes); or the **Lac de Capitello**, 30 minutes further on, where the snow stays as late as early June. The path – in winter a cross-country ski trail – follows the river.

South of Corte, the **Forêt de Vizzavona** features beech and pine woodland crisscrossed by trout-filled streams and walking trails (notably the GR20). It is a fine refuge from the summer heat and is also an excuse to take the small-gauge train up from Ajaccio or Bastia, stopping at Vizzavona.

8 The Castagniccia

Haute-Corse. Bastia. Corte, Ponte Leccia. Piedicroce, La Porta, Valle-d'Alesani. Maison des Enterprises, Folelli, Piedicroce (04 95 35 82 54 or 04 95 33 38 21). **castagniccia.fr**

East of Corte is the hilly, chestnut-covered region of Castagniccia (literally "small chestnut grove"), which most Corsicans agree is the very heart and kernel of the island. It was here that independence leader Pasquale Paoli was born in 1725, and where the revolts against Genoa and later France began in earnest in 1729. Alas, many of the villages in this beautiful, remote area are nearly empty, their inhabitants having joined the 800,000 or so Corsicans (almost three times the present population) who live and work in mainland France or Italy. It seems hard to believe that in the 17th century, when the great chestnut forests introduced here by the Genoese were at the height of their production, this was the most prosperous and populated region in Corsica.

The D71 from Ponte Leccia (north of Corte) to the east coast winds through the centre of the Castagniccia region, and to see it at a leisurely pace will take the best part of a week. Stock up on groceries before you start, as there is little to be had in the way of supplies en route.

◀ One of the Genoese towers on the beautiful Iles Sanguinaires

9 Golfe de Porto

Corse-du-Sud. Ajaccio. Porto. Quartier la Marine (04 95 26 10 55). **porto-tourisme.com**

Porto is sited at the head of the Golfe de Porto, one of the most beautiful bays in the Mediterranean, which for the sake of its fauna and flora has been included among UNESCO's World's Heritage sites. The town has a magnificent Genoese watchtower – the perfect spot for admiring the sunset – and regular boat excursions (Apr–Oct) to the Calanche, Scandola and Girolata.

The **Calanche** begin 8 km (5 miles) out of Porto, on the road to Piana. These 300-m (1,000-ft) red-granite cliffs plunge sheer to the sea, and are quite simply breathtaking. They are accessible by boat or on foot: well-defined trails start from the Tête du Chien and the Pont de Mezanu, while boat tickets are available at Porto's Hôtel Le Cyrnée and a few other places in the marina.

East of Porto are the Gorges de la Spelunca, accessed by a mule route punctuated by Genoese bridges.

Just south of Porto, along a spectacular corniche drive passing under granite archways, lies the pretty village of **Piana**, a good base for visiting this whole area, with information on recommended walks. One worthwhile destination is the cove at **Ficajola** just below Piana – a truly delightful beach.

Genoese watchtower at Golfe de Porto

Environs

The road over the mountains from Porto to Calvi offers no more than a taste of this grandiose corner of Corsica – you have to take to the sea to view it properly (ferries from Porto and Galéria). **Girolata**, a tiny hamlet north of Porto, can be reached only by sea or via a mule track (4 hours round trip on foot) from a clearly marked point 23 km (14 miles) north of Porto on the D81.

At the mouth of the Golfe de Girolata, the **Réserve Naturelle de Scandola**, instituted in 1975, is the first land and sea reserve in France, covering over 10 sq km (4 sq miles) of sea, and a similar area of cliffs, caves and maquis. Marine life is abundant in these clear, protected waters; the birds include ospreys, puffins and falcons.

The town of Piana with the Calanche in the background

Corsican Flowers

For lovers of wild flowers, Corsica is a Mediterranean jewel. Much of the island is covered with maquis, a tangle of aromatic shrubs and low trees that flowers from late winter onwards. Among its dense variety are showy rockroses, which shower the ground with short-lived pink or white petals, and brilliant yellow broom. Grassy and rocky slopes are good places to spot the widespread tassel hyacinth and the Illyrian sea lily, which grows only in Corsica and Sardinia.

Rock-rose

For hotels and restaurants in this region see p571 and p603

Cargèse's Greek rite church

⑩ Cargèse

Corse-du-Sud. 1,300. *i* rue du Docteur Dragacci (04 95 26 41 31). **cargese.net**; **ouestcorsica.com**

Cargèse overlooks the sea from a promontory between the bays of Sagone and Pero. It is a small town with an odd history: many of the people who live here are the descendants of 17th-century Greek refugees from Turkish rule, and given asylum in Corsica.

A few Cargésiens still speak Greek, and their icon-filled Eastern (Greek) rite church faces its Catholic counterpart in an attitude that must once have seemed confrontational. Nowadays the old rivalries have vanished, and the Orthodox priest and Catholic *curé* often stand in for one another.

There are many splendid beaches in the vicinity, notably at **Pero** and **Chiuni** just to the north, and at **Ménasina** and **Stagnoli** to the south.

⑪ Ajaccio

Corse-du-Sud. 69,000. *i* 3 bd du Roi Jérôme (04 95 51 53 03). Tue–Sun. **ajaccio-tourisme.com**

Ajaccio, a noisy, busy town by Corsican standards, was the birthplace of Napoleon Bonaparte in 1769. Napoleon never returned to Corsica after crowning himself emperor of the French in 1804, but the town – modern capital of nationalist Corsica – celebrates his birthday every 15 August.

The 16th-century **Cathédrale Notre-Dame de la Miséricorde**, where Napoleon was baptized in 1771, houses Delacroix's painting *Vierge du Sacré-Coeur*.

A few streets away, the **Musée National de la Maison Bonaparte**, where Napoleon was born and spent his childhood, contains family portraits, period furniture and assorted memorabilia.

Much more extraordinary is the art collection assembled by Napoleon's unscrupulous uncle, Cardinal Fesch, who merrily looted churches, palaces and museums during the Italian campaign and brought the swag home to Ajaccio. Housed in the 19th-century **Palais Fesch**, the **Musée des Beaux-Arts** contains the finest collection of Italian primitive art in France after the Louvre. Among its masterpieces are works by Bellini, Botticelli, Titian, Veronese, Bernini and Poussin. Next to the Palais Fesch stands the **Chapelle Impériale**, built in 1855 by Napoleon III to accommodate the tombs of the Bonapartes. From here, walk back along the quay to the Jetée de la Citadelle, which offers superb views of the town, the marina and the Golfe d'Ajaccio. The adjacent 16th-century **citadel** is occupied by the army.

Statue of Napoleon by Laboureur in place Maréchal Foch, Ajaccio

Musée National de la Maison Bonaparte
Rue St-Charles. **Tel** 04 95 21 43 89. **Open** Tue–Sun.
musee-maisonbonaparte.fr

Palais Fesch, Musée des Beaux-Arts
50–52 rue Cardinal Fesch. **Tel** 04 95 26 26 26. **Open** Wed–Mon.
musee-fesch.com

Environs

From the Quai de la Citadelle there are daily excursions to the **Îles Sanguinaires** at the mouth of the Golfe d'Ajaccio.

At Vero, 21 km (13 miles) northeast on the N193, is an unusual park, **A Cupulatta**, with over 170 species of tortoises and turtles (Apr–Oct).

A statue-menhir at Filitosa

⑫ Filitosa

Station Préhistorique de Filitosa, Sollacaro, Corse-du-Sud.
Tel 04 95 74 00 91. **Open** Apr–Oct: daily. **filitosa.fr**

The 4,000-year-old, life-size stone warriors of Filitosa are the most spectacular relics of megalithic man in Corsica. Discovered in 1946, these phallus-like granite menhirs represent an interesting progression from mere silhouettes to detailed sculpture etched with human features.

The five most recent and most sophisticated figures (about 1500 BC) stand around

For hotels and restaurants in this region see p571 and p603

The fortified Old Town of Bonifacio, with the harbour in the foreground

a 1,000-year-old olive tree, in the field below a tumulus. Other finds, which include a heavily armed warrior with shield, helmet and sword, can be seen in the site's archaeological museum.

⓭ Sartène

Corse-du-Sud. 3,500.
14 cours Soeur Amélie (04 95 77 15 40). summer: daily; winter: Sat.
lacoursedesorigines.com

Sartène is a medieval fortified town of narrow cobbled streets and grey granite houses rising above the Rizzanese Valley. Founded by the Genoese in the early 16th century, it has survived attacks by Barbary pirates and centuries of bloody feuding among the town's leading families.

Despite all this, Sartène has a reputation for deep piety, reinforced each year by the oldest and most intense Christian ceremony in Corsica, the Good Friday Catenacciu (literally, the "chained one"). A red-hooded penitent, bare-foot and in chains, drags a wooden cross through the Old Town in a re-enactment of Christ's ascent to Golgotha.

Environs

In the town centre, the **Musée Départemental de la Préhistoire et d'Archéologie** has a collection of Neolithic, Bronze and Iron Age artifacts.

Musée Départemental de la Préhistoire et d'Archéologie
Bd Jacques Nicolaï. **Tel** 04 95 77 01 09.
Open Jun–Sep: daily; Oct–May: Mon–Fri. **prehistoire-corse.org**

⓮ Bonifacio

Corse-du-Sud. 3,000.
2 rue Fred Scamaroni (04 95 73 11 88). Wed. **bonifacio.fr**

Bonifacio is the southernmost town in Corsica, dramatically sited on a limestone and granite cliff peninsula with stunning views *(see p536)*. Its handsome harbour at the foot of the cliffs is the focus of life: cafés, restaurants and boutiques abound and boats depart regularly for neighbouring Sardinia and the uninhabited island of Lavezzi.

From the harbour, steps lead up to Bonifacio's fortified Old Town. The citadel, which was built by the conquering Genoese at the end of the 12th century, has long been the town's main defensive post, and from 1963 to 1983 was the headquarters of the French foreign legion. From here, wander down to the tip of the promontory to see the three old windmills and the ruins of a Franciscan monastery.

⓯ Côte Orientale

Haute-Corse & Corse-du-Sud. Bastia. 80 av St-Alexandra, Aléria (04 95 57 01 51); rue Maréchal Leclerc, BP 92, Porto-Vecchio (04 95 70 09 58). Bastia, Porto-Vecchio. **oriente-corsica.com**; **ot-portovecchio.com**.

The flat, rather dreary alluvial plain stretching from Bastia to Solenzara has been rich farmland since 1945, the year it was finally drained and rid of malaria. More recently, seaside resorts and even high-rise hotels have mushroomed along the coast, cashing in on its long, sandy beaches.

The best sight in **Mariana**, which is otherwise uncomfortably close to the Bastia-Poretta airport, is the early 12th-century cathedral of Mariana known as **La Canonica**. A short distance away is the slightly older **Eglise de San Perteo**, surrounded by meadows.

About halfway down the coast, the port of **Aléria**, originally a Greek colony and the base for Rome's conquest of Corsica in 259 BC, is interesting for its rich archaeological heritage. Just outside town, a museum housed in the 15th-century Fort de Matra chronicles daily life in Roman Aléria.

Towards the southern tip of the island, the fortified town of **Porto-Vecchio**, built by Corsica's Genoese conquerors, is now an extremely popular resort. The setting is perfect for the conventional seaside holiday, with umbrella pines, cork oak forests and glorious white sandy beaches within easy reach of the town, especially at **Palombaggia** and **Pinarello**.

The Golfe de Porto-Vecchio

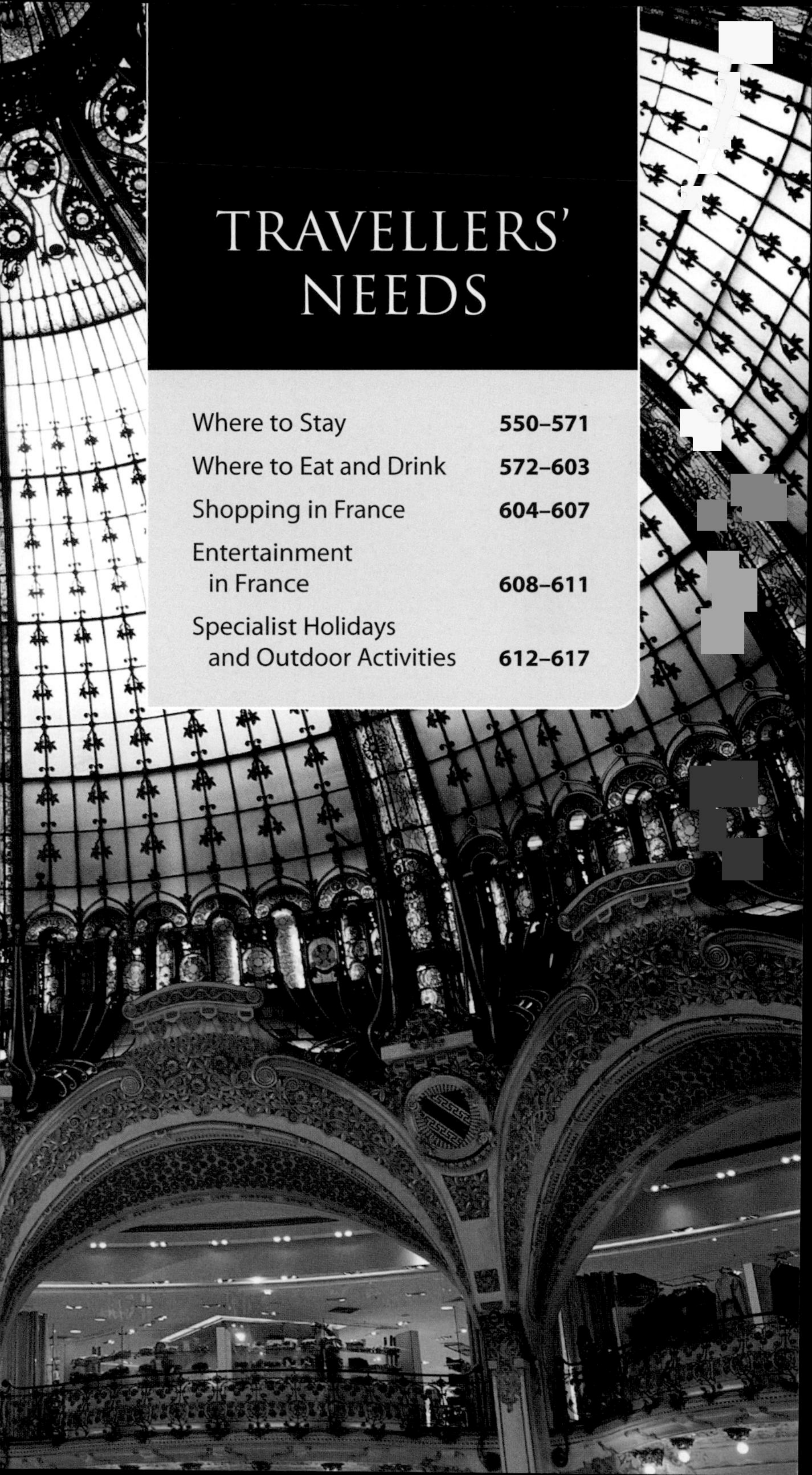

TRAVELLERS' NEEDS

WHERE TO STAY

France has thousands of registered hotels that range from some of the most glamorous establishments in the world to charming and idiosyncratic little inns tucked away in the countryside. On these four pages, the types of hotels on offer are summarized with tips on what to expect. The hotel listings pages *(see pp554–71)* describe some of the best hotels around the country in every price category and style. Alternatively, you can choose from the increasingly popular *chambres d'hôtes* (bed and breakfasts), which range from simple farms to grandiose châteaux. As France is one of the most popular countries in the world for self-catering holidays, there is also information on renting a rural home or *gîte*, and how to get the most out of a camping holiday.

Entrance to the Hôtel-Restaurant Euzkadi at Espelette in the Pyrenees *(see p568)*

Gradings

French hotels are graded from one star to five stars, based on the range of facilities they offer. Hotels with two or more stars must have a lift, where appropriate. Three-star hotels must have 80 per cent rooms en suite. Four- and five-star hotels must have room service, air conditioning and all of their rooms en suite. The very best five-star hotels are known as palace hotels.

Meals and Facilities

In high season, many resort hotels insist on half board or *demi-pension* (a rate per person for the room, dinner and breakfast). There is also full board or *pension*, which covers lunch too. While it is cheaper to opt for inclusive rates, set or limited-choice menus often omit the more interesting dishes. And if you do not have *pension* or *demi-pension* accommodation, breakfast is often charged as an extra. Go instead to the local café, as it tends to be cheaper and more filling.

Many hotels do not provide meals on Sunday evenings and often stop serving dinner as early as 9pm on other days.

Rooms usually have double beds; twin or single beds must be requested when booking. All mid-range hotels, with a few historic exceptions mostly in Paris, are en suite. Elsewhere, there are still a handful of budget options with separate bathrooms down the corridor, but the majority now offer en-suite facilities. A bathroom with a *bain* (bath) is usually more expensive than one with a *douche* (shower).

Prices

Rates, inclusive of tax and service, are quoted per room (apart from *pension* and *demi-pension* arrangements). There is usually a small surcharge for a third person in a room for two, and little reduction for single travellers.

As a rule, the higher the star rating, the more you pay. Rates for a double room start from about €50 in a cheap chain hotel on the outskirts of town, €70–€80 per night for a one-star city-centre hotel, and upwards of €160 for a four-star hotel. The best palace hotels charge as much as €1,000 per night. Costs also vary geographically, with remote rural areas like Brittany being the cheapest. For equivalent accommodation in fashionable areas such as Dordogne and Provence, expect to pay 20 per cent more, plus another 20 per cent for Paris and the Côte d'Azur. Prices vary seasonally too, with coastal and Alpine areas increasing their tariffs by up to 50 per cent during peak periods.

Booking

Advance booking is always wise, especially for Paris and hotels in popular tourist areas over the holiday months of July and August. Places where you

Imposing white exteriors of Le Negresco in Nice, Côte d'Azur *(see p570)*

◀ Interior of the Galeries Lafayette department store in Paris

The comfortable lounge area in the lobby at the Jeu du Paume, Paris *(see p554)*

think hotels should be easy to find can suddenly fill up, thanks to a sporting event or concert. Even the chain hotels by the motorways tend to be full out of season. Choice can also be limited, because many hotels are seasonal: many seaside resorts shut down from October to March, and ski resort hotels often close in April.

These days most people book their accommodation in France online, either through a hotel booking site or directly via the hotel's own website, paying for at least one night's stay to hold the reservation – although there may be web discounts for paying all in advance. It is advisable to read the small print carefully about cancellations and refunds. Those who want to book on arrival can do so from tourist offices in all main cities and towns – they offer reservations up to eight days in advance.

Hotel Chains

France's hotel chains vary from cheap and cheerful pit stops, situated on the outskirts of towns by motorways or main roads, to sleek and upmarket four-star business hotels and self-catering suites in city centres. Almost all of them offer the usual conveniences and free Wi-Fi access.

Among the cheapest are the one-star, no-frills **Formule 1** motels, offering bedrooms with twins or a double and single bed but no en-suite facilities. **Hotels Première Classe** fall under the two-star category – they offer en-suite rooms and charge the same low rates for up to three people sharing. Other options in this category include **Ibis**, which also offers reasonably good deals, and **Campanile**. Three-star chains include **Novotel** and **Mercure** – both offer en-suite accommodation and usually allow one child with no charge, provided the whole family sleeps in one room. Novotel allows two under-16s. **Adagio** offers apartments in city centres, sleeping up to six for a minimum of four nights. The top spots in the hotel chain accommodation list undoubtedly belong to the boutique-style **MGallery** hotels and the international luxury chain **Sofitel**. Most of these chains are now part of the vast **Accor** hotel empire.

Stone steps leading to the charmingly rustic Hôtel de l'Abbaye in Longpont *(see p556)*

Self-Catering

A *gîte* is a rural holiday home, often a converted farmhouse or its outbuildings. *Gîte* holidays are a popular and relatively cheap way to see France, particularly out of season, but you should book many months in advance in order to secure the best self-catering properties in summer or for skiing holidays in winter.

Gîtes de France registers some 60,000 *gîtes*, all inspected and graded to indicate the level of facilities. Book directly on their website by region or by theme – country, charm, children, hiking, extreme sports, wellbeing and many others. They also list city-break rentals, B&Bs, camp sites and cottages.

Clévacances, another reliable national organization, also lists good-quality *gîtes* throughout France.

France has numerous other kinds of self-catering options such as stately south-coast villas, stunning ski-resort chalets, and modern city and coastal apartments. **Allo Vacances** provides a booking service for holiday lets throughout the different regions.

Lovely dining area at the Hôtel de la Cité, Carcassonne *(see p569)*

Camping

There are 11,000 official camp sites spread around France's diverse countryside. The **Fédération Française de Camping et de Caravaning (FFCC)** publishes a comprehensive list, which is updated every year. There is a wide range of camp sites listed on the Gîtes de France website too. **Bienvenue à la Ferme** offers a number of sites as well as *gîtes* and B&Bs, on farms.

Camp sites are graded from one to four stars. Three- and four-star sites are usually impressively spacious with plenty of amenities and electricity connections for a percentage of tents and caravans. One- and two-star sites always have toilets, a public phone and running water, although some one-star sites may have only cold water. However, what they lack in facilities, they often make up for with peaceful surroundings and rural charm. Glamping (glamorous camping) is also popular. Luxury camp sites offer a range of unusual accommodation: **Belrepayre Trailer Park** has a range of 1950s trailers; **La Cabane en l'Air** offers tree cabins; and **Carre d'Etoiles** has wood cabins with glass roofs for star-gazing.

Camping Card International (CCI), available through various national camping clubs, offers campers, especially in France, numerous discounts and third party liability insurance.

Hostels

Hostels are a money-saving option for single travellers, though cheap hostels don't remain as inexpensive for those travelling with a partner.

The IYHF's hostelling guide details the 220 hostels around France offered by the **Fédération Unie des Auberges de Jeunesse (FUAJ)**, open to all ages and providing decent dormitory accommodation. Those who are not members of the **Youth Hostel Association (YHA)** in their home country will have to pay a small surcharge each time they stay in a French youth hostel. **Ethic Etapes** has 50 centres with a cultural bent scattered all over France. All have a restaurant and single, shared and dormitory accommodation for groups, individuals and families. *Gîtes d'étape* are usually large farm-houses with dormitories close to walking, cycling and horse-riding routes.

Disabled Travellers

A number of associations publish information on accommodation throughout France with wheelchair access, notably the **Association des Paralysés de France (APF)** and the Gîtes de France's guide *Accessibles*. **Les Compagnons du Voyage** can organize escorted door-to-door transport on all public transport networks throughout France. **Guide Accessible** (in French) is a useful website that lists, region by region, trans-portation companies and lodgings adapted for wheelchair users.

Further Information

The French tourism development agency, **Atout France**, offers a wide range of informative brochures on France, and most of them can be downloaded for easy reference. The first port of call for all non-hotel accommodation in the French countryside, however, should be **Gîtes de France**.

Recommended Hotels

The accommodation options featured in this guide – listed by area and then by price – have been selected across a wide price range for their excellent facilities and unique appeal. They cover categories such as family, value for money, romantic, luxury, boutique, rooms with views and B&Bs.

Family hotels are especially suited for visitors travelling with children, offering either rooms with multiple beds or inter-connected rooms. Both independent and chain hotels have rooms and facilities geared to handle guests travelling with their families.

Holiday-makers enjoying the pool at a camp site in high season

Value for money hotels offer great rates for their facilities, location or service. Select from a range of independent establishments of character offering excellent deals in cities and the countryside. A large proportion of these hotels are part of the **Logis de France** organization.

Romantic hotels are aimed at couples. Hotels that feature in this category may either have special decor, or four-poster beds, or perhaps a romantic spa.

Many of France's châteaux and historic mansions have been converted into hotels – from Renaissance piles with sweeping lawns to medieval castles with battlements. Lots of these **historic** hotels belong to the **Relais et Châteaux** group, which guarantees beautifully designed rooms and top-notch fine dining. From glamorous hotels in Paris to swanky seaside resorts, the **luxury** category features all the plush places to splurge on.

Chic **boutique** hotels are springing up in many French cities – these are generally small but full of character with smart designs and all the modern conveniences. They tend to be pricey, but the experience is usually worth it.

A deluxe room at the Mandarin Oriental Hotel Paris *(see p554)*

Rooms with views are hotels set in scenic locations – high in the mountains, on the coast or in some of France's most beautiful landscapes.

Bed and breakfasts (B&Bs), or *chambres d'hôtes,* have increased by a huge margin all over the country, primarily due to strict EU regulations that have led to the closing of lots of the old family-run hotels, with many B&Bs springing up in their place. Most of these establishments are full of character and range from tiny cottages to elaborate châteaux full of family portraits and antiques, to boutique suites for couples in historic town houses. B&Bs located on farms are called *fermes-auberges* (farm inns). Besides breakfast, many B&Bs offer dinner on request. Over 10,000 B&Bs are inspected and registered by Gîtes de France. Many others are not registered, but information on these is available from local tourist offices or online.

For choosing the very best in hospitality and lodging, look out for hotels marked **DK Choice** – highlighted in recognition of a superlative feature. It may have beautiful surroundings, be a historically important building, have a noteworthy sustainable outlook or just be incredibly charming. Whatever the reason, it is a guarantee of an especially memorable stay.

DIRECTORY

Hotels

Accor (Formule 1, Ibis, MGallery, Mercure, Novotel, Adagio, Sofitel)
Tel 0871 663 0624 (UK).
Tel 0825 012 011 (France).
W accorhotels.com

Campanile
Tel 020 7519 5045 (UK); 08 92 23 48 12 (France).
W campanile.com

Hotels Première Classe
Tel 08 92 23 48 14 (France).
W premiereclasse.com

Logis de France
Tel 01 45 84 83 84 (France).
W logishotels.com

Relais et Châteaux
Tel 01 76 49 39 39 (France).
W relaischateaux.com

B&B & Self-Catering

Allo Vacances
W allovacances.com

Clévacances
Tel 05 32 10 82 30.
W clevacances.com

Gîtes de France
W gites-de-france.com

Camping

Belrepayre Trailer Park
W airstreameurope.com

Bienvenue à la Ferme
Tel 01 53 57 11 50.
W bienvenue-a-la-ferme.com

La Cabane en l'Air
W lacabaneenlair.com

Camping Card International (CCI)
W campingcard international.com

Carre d'Etoiles
W carre-detoiles.com

Fédération Française de Camping et de Caravaning (FFCC)
78 rue de Rivoli, 75004 Paris.
Tel 01 42 72 84 08.
W ffcc.fr

Hostels

Ethic Etapes
27 rue de Turbigo, 75002 Paris. **Tel** 01 40 26 57 64.
W ethic-etapes.fr

FUAJ (Fédération Unie des Auberges de Jeunesse)
27 rue Pajol, 75018 Paris.
Tel 01 44 89 87 27.
W fuaj.org

YHA (Youth Hostel Association)
Trevelyan House, Matlock, Derbyshire DE4 3YH.
Tel 01629 592 600.
W yha.org.uk

Disabled Travellers

Association des Paralysés de France (APF)
13 pl de Rungis, 75013 Paris.
Tel 01 53 80 92 97.
W apf.asso.fr

Les Compagnons du Voyage
34 rue Championnet, LAC CG25, 75018 Paris.
Tel 01 58 76 08 33.
W compagnons.com

Guide Accessible
W guide-accessible.com

Further Information

Atout France
Lincoln House, 300 High Holborn, London W1V 7JH.
Tel 020 7061 6600 (within UK only).
W uk.france.fr

Where to Stay

Paris

Ile de la Cité, Marais and Beaubourg

Britannique €€
B&B **Map** 9 A3
20 av Victoria, 75001
Tel *01 42 33 74 59*
W hotel-britannique.fr
British seascapes and other details adorn this hotel on a tree-lined street. Personalized romantic weekend packages are available.

Caron de Beaumarchais €€
Boutique **Map** 9 C3
12 rue Vieille-du-Temple, 75004
Tel *01 42 72 34 12*
W carondebeaumarchais.com
This elegant hotel is gracefully decorated with colours, fabrics and upholstered furniture from the 18th century.

Hospitel €€
B&B **Map** 9 A4
1 pl du Parvis Notre-Dame, 75004
Tel *01 44 32 01 00*
W hotel-hospitel.fr
Bright, comfortable accommodation can be found at this central hotel above a hospital. Welcoming staff and free Wi-Fi.

Hôtel de la Bretonnerie €€
Historic **Map** 9 C3
22 rue Ste-Croix de la Bretonnerie, 75004
Tel *01 48 87 77 63*
W hotelbretonnerie.com
Exposed beams, stone vaulting, canopy beds and rich fabrics give this hotel a medieval ambience.

St-Louis en l'Isle €€
Romantic **Map** 9 C4
75 rue St-Louis en l'Ile, 75004
Tel *01 46 34 04 80*
W saintlouisenlisle.com
Enjoy great service in this stylish hotel with peaceful rooms in neutral shades. Excellent location.

DK Choice

Jeu du Paume €€€
Historic **Map** 9 C4
54 rue St-Louis en l'Ile, 75004
Tel *01 43 26 14 18*
W jeudepaumehotel.com
What were the Royal Tennis Courts under Louis XIII now house a rustic-chic hotel with exposed wooden beams, grand ceilings and well-appointed rooms. Equipped with all modern comforts.

Le Pavillon de la Reine €€€
Luxury **Map** 10 D3
28 pl des Vosges, 75003
Tel *01 40 29 19 19*
W pavillon-de-la-reine.com
Overlooking the city's most beautiful square, this hotel has an unrivalled setting. The 17th-century mansion has been refurbished in elegant country-house style, and it offers romantic bedrooms and a lovely spa.

DK Choice

Le Petit Moulin €€€
Boutique **Map** 10 D2
29–31 rue de Poitou, 75003
Tel *01 42 74 10 10*
W paris-hotel-petitmoulin.com
The oldest *boulangerie* (bakery) in Paris now houses this petite, quirky hotel. All the individually decorated rooms reflect Christian Lacroix's love for colour and opulence, and they are wildly romantic, with audacious murals. There is wheelchair access, free Wi-Fi and private parking for guests.

Tuileries & Opéra

Citadines Prestige Opéra Vendôme €€
Family **Map** 4 D5
2 rue Edouard VII, 75009
Tel *01 40 15 14 00*
W citadines.com
The self-catered and well-equipped apartments on offer here are a practical option and perfect for families. Friendly and accommodating staff.

Entrance to the gorgeous Caron de Beaumarchais hotel

Price Guide
Prices are based on one night's stay in high season for a standard double room, inclusive of service charges and taxes.

€	up to €100
€€	€100 to €250
€€€	over €250

Brighton €€€
Luxury **Map** 8 D1
218 rue de Rivoli, 75001
Tel *01 47 03 61 61*
W paris-hotel-brighton.com
Enjoy breathtaking views of the Tuileries amid antique furnishings, glittering chandeliers and faux-marble columns. Family-friendly.

Mandarin Oriental €€€
Luxury **Map** 8 D1
251 rue St-Honoré, 75001
Tel *01 70 98 78 88*
W mandarinoriental.com
Oriental charm meets Parisian style at this luxurious world-class establishment. Spacious rooms have Art Deco details.

Le Meurice €€€
Luxury **Map** 8 D1
228 rue de Rivoli, 75001
Tel *01 44 58 10 10*
W lemeurice.com
This celebrated plush palace offers glittering rooms, glorious views and great service. There is also a luxurious spa.

Champs-Elysées and Invalides

Mayet €€
Boutique **Map** 11 B1
3 rue Mayet, 75006
Tel *01 47 83 21 35*
W mayet.com
Bright, jazzy murals decorate this well-run, small hotel with chic urban design.

Le Bristol €€€
Luxury **Map** 3 A4
112 rue de Faubourg-St-Honoré, 75008
Tel *01 53 43 43 00*
W lebristolparis.com
Admire the antiques, chandeliers and tapestries at this elegant hotel. A children's club and pool will keep the little ones happy.

Four Seasons George V €€€
Luxury **Map** 2 E5
31 av George V, 75008
Tel *01 49 52 70 00*
W fourseasons.com/paris
Guests at this iconic establishment enjoy modern comforts in a luxurious setting. A Parisian symbol of opulence.

Hôtel Daniel €€€
Romantic **Map** 2 F4
8 rue Frédéric Bastiat, 75008
Tel *01 42 56 17 00*
W hoteldanielparis.com
Located near the Champs-Elysées, this flamboyant hotel has Oriental fabrics, wallpaper and carpets.

Hôtel de la Tour Maubourg €€€
Romantic **Map** 7 B3
150 rue de Grenelle, 75007
Tel *01 47 05 16 16*
W hoteltourmaubourgparis.com
Boasting a great location, this charming boutique hotel has eclectic and delightful decor.

The Peninsula Paris €€€
Historic
19 av Kléber, 75016
Tel *01 58 12 28 88*
W paris.peninsula.com
This opulent hotel set in a 1908 building has 200 elegant rooms and suites. The rooftop restaurant has great skyline views.

Shangri La €€€
Romantic **Map** 6 D1
10 av d'Iéna, 75116
Tel *01 53 67 19 98*
W shangri-la.com/paris/shangrila
Housed in a *belle époque* palace, the Shangri La has parquet floors, chandeliers and two luxe eateries.

The Left Bank

Les Degrés de Notre Dame €€
B&B **Map** 9 B4
10 rue des Grands Degrés, 75005
Tel *01 55 42 88 88*
This vintage charmer offers attractive beamed bedrooms leading off a frescoed stairway.

Hôtel des Grandes Ecoles €€
Family **Map** 9 B5
75 rue Cardinal Lemoine, 75005
Tel *01 43 26 79 23*
W hotel-grandes-ecoles.com
The charming breakfast room and flowery bedrooms at this hotel are reminiscent of a Provençal villa.

Hôtel des Grands Hommes €€
Romantic **Map** 13 A1
17 pl du Panthéon, 75005
Tel *01 46 34 19 60*
W hoteldesgrandshommes.com
Enjoy views of the Panthéon from this Empire-style hotel. The deluxe rooms have quaint terraces.

Hôtel de Buci €€€
Romantic **Map** 8 E4
22 rue de Buci, 75006
Tel *01 55 42 74 74*
W buci-hotel.com
Antiques, rich colours, four-poster beds and plush fabrics lend this hotel a distinctly 18th-century feel.

Relais Christine €€€
Historic **Map** 8 F4
3 rue Christine, 75006
Tel *01 40 51 60 80*
W relais-christine.com
Built on the remains of a 13th-century abbey, this is a luxurious and impressive haven of calm.

Relais St-Germain €€€
Romantic **Map** 8 F4
9 Carrefour de l'Odéon, 75006
Tel *01 44 27 07 97*
W hotel-paris-relais-saint-germain.com
This 17th-century conversion is irresistibly Parisian and has plush, soundproofed bedrooms.

Résidence Le Prince Regent €€€
Boutique **Map** 8 F5
28 rue Monsieur le Prince, 75006
Tel *01 56 24 19 21*
W leprinceregent.com
These modern apartments offer great services, from babysitting to spa relaxation and housekeeping.

Further Afield

Loft Paris €
B&B
7 cité Véron, 75018
Tel *06 14 48 47 48*
W loft-paris.fr
Four neat apartments have quirky decor and lots of character. The one on the fourth floor has a view of the Moulin Rouge windmill.

DK Choice

Arvor St-Georges €€
B&B
8 rue Laferrière, 75009
Tel *01 48 78 60 92*
W hotelarvor.com
This family-friendly B&B with charming rooms and suites has been furbished in smart retro-contemporary style. The open-plan reception, which includes a bar and breakfast area, is decorated with conceptual artist Daniel Buren's striped posters.

L'Ermitage €€
B&B
24 rue Lamarck, 75018
Tel *01 42 64 79 22*
Light, floral-themed bedrooms offer hilltop views over the city. There is also a lovely garden.

Mama Shelter €€
Boutique
109 rue de Bagnolet, 75020
Tel *01 43 48 48 48*
W mamashelter.com/en/paris
Super-trendy, Philippe Starck-designed rooms have iMacs, microwaves and mood lighting.

The classic exterior of the Terrass hotel, located in the Montmartre district, Paris

Le Relais Montmartre €€
Romantic
6 rue Constance, 75018
Tel *01 70 64 25 25*
W hotel-relais-montmartre.com
Rooms here have pretty fabrics, exposed beams and dainty period furniture. Attactive courtyard, too.

DK Choice

Terrass €€
Romantic
12–14 rue Joseph de Maistre, 75018
Tel *01 46 06 72 85*
W terrass-hotel.com
This relaxed four-star hotel with elegant rooms is perfect in any season. In winter, guests enjoy the piano bar, with its open fire and comfy armchairs. In summer, sofas dot the roof, allowing visitors to take in the views.

La Villa Paris €€
B&B
33 rue de la Fontaine à Mulard, 75013
Tel *01 43 47 15 66*
W la-villa-paris.com
Enjoy all the comforts of home at this lovely 1920s B&B with parquet floors and refined decor.

Ile-de-France

CERNAY LA VILLE: Abbaye des Vaux de Cernay €€
Rooms with views
Domaine des Vaux de Cernay, 78720
Tel *01 34 85 23 00*
W abbayedecernay.com
Beautifully restored, this 12th-century abbey has large vaulted rooms and stunning grounds.

ST-GERMAIN-EN-LAYE: Pavillon Henri IV €€
Historic
19–21 rue Thiers, 78100
Tel *01 39 10 15 15*
W pavillonhenri4.fr
The birthplace of Louis XIV, this beautiful château near a pleasant park has fine views of Paris.

For more information on types of hotels *see pp552–3*

VERSAILLES: Hôtel des Roys €€
Value for money
14 av de Paris, 78000
Tel *01 39 50 56 00*
W hotel-roys-versailles.com
In a great location, this elegant town house provides its guests with simple and neat rooms.

DK Choice

VILLIERS LE MAHIEU: Château de Villiers le Mahieu €€
Luxury
rue du Centre, 78770
Tel *01 34 87 44 25*
W chateauvilliers.com
Set within a moated fortress, this 17th-century château strikes a balance between conservation and comfort. Superb courtyard and grounds.

Le Nord and Picardy

AMIENS: Victor Hugo €
Value for money
2 rue de l'Oratoire, 80000
Tel *03 22 91 57 91*
W hotel-a-amiens.com
Stay in basic but pleasant rooms at this cheerful family-run hotel next to the cathedral.

AMIENS: Hôtel Marotte €€
Boutique
3 rue Marotte, 80000
Tel *03 60 12 50 00*
W hotel-marotte.com
Housed in a beautifully restored building, this family-run hotel has gracefully decorated rooms.

DK Choice

BUSNES: Château de Beaulieu €€
Luxury
1098 rue de Lillers, 62350
Tel *03 21 68 88 88*
W lechateaudebeaulieu.fr
Seamlessly converted into a contemporary hotel, this 18th-century château is surrounded by sprawling elegant gardens. Herbs from the grounds are used in the luxury Michelin-starred restaurant.

CALAIS: Les Dunes €
Family
48 rte Nationale, Blériot Plage, 62231
Tel *03 21 34 54 30*
W les-dunes.com
Rooms have no frills at this small hotel with a beach location, just a 5-minute drive from the city centre. Good restaurant on site.

Elegant, well-appointed rooms at the Hôtel Marotte in Amiens

FERE EN TARDENOIS: Château de Fère €€€
Historic
Rte de Fismes, 02130
Tel *03 23 82 21 13*
W chateaudefere.com
There are stylish rooms and a well-stocked wine cellar at this stunning 16th-century château hotel just 1 hour from Paris.

GOSNAY: La Chartreuse du Val St-Esprit €€
Luxury
1 rue de Fouquières, 62199
Tel *03 21 62 80 00*
W lachartreuse.com
This 18th-century château built on medieval ruins offers large delightful rooms, a lovely park and three restaurants.

GOUVIEUX: Château de la Tour €€
Luxury
Chemin de la Chaussée, 60270
Tel *03 44 62 38 38*
W lechateaudelatour.fr
The pretty rooms at this hotel not far from Chantilly have views over the expansive garden or the forest. Guests also enjoy a restaurant, tennis courts, and an outdoor heated pool, plus impeccable service.

LAON: La Maison des Trois Rois €€
Value for money
17 rue Saint-Martin, 02000
Tel *03 23 20 74 24*
W lamaisondes3rois.com
Friendly and very comfortable, this B&B is set in a beautiful 14th-century mansion with five excellently restored rooms.

LE TOUQUET: Le Castel – Victoria €
Value for money
11 rue de Paris, 62520
Tel *03 21 90 01 00*
W castelvictoria.com
Close to the beach and town centre, this sleek hotel has tasteful rooms and a great roof terrace.

LILLE: Alliance Couvent des Minimes €€
City centre
17 quai du Wault, 59000
Tel *03 20 30 62 62*
W alliance-lille.com
This converted monastery has stylish rooms, lovely cloisters and a spectacular atrium with a trendy bar and restaurant.

LILLE: Hermitage Gantois €€
Luxury
224 rue de Paris, 59000
Tel *03 20 85 30 30*
W hotelhermitagegantois.com
The rooms at this 14th-century hospice are set around an indoor patio. Some have authentic fireplaces; others boast Louis XV-style wood panelling.

LONGPONT: Hôtel de l'Abbaye €
Value for money
8 rue des Tourelles, 02600
Tel *03 23 96 02 44*
W hotel-abbaye-longpont.fr
Stay in old-fashioned and comfortable rooms at this hotel opposite a 12th-century abbey.

LUMBRES: Moulin de Mombreux €
Family
70 rue Mombreux, 62380
Tel *03 21 98 68 72*
W moulindemombreux.com
The rooms at this attractive 18th-century mill on the banks of the River Bléquin are in an annexe building, some with pleasant river views.

MONTREUIL SUR MER: Château de Montreuil €€€
Luxury
4 chaussée des Capucins, 62170
Tel *03 21 81 53 04*
W chateaudemontreuil.com
There is a restaurant, plus lovely gardens, at this stylish manor house within the ramparts of the town.

REUILLY-SAUVIGNY: L'Auberge le Relais €€
Value for money
2 rue de Paris, 02850
Tel *03 23 70 35 36*
W relaisreuilly.com
In a scenic location, with views of Champagne's vine-covered hills, this hotel has cosy rooms, a good restaurant and fine service.

Key to Price Guide *see p554*

SAINTE-PREUVE: Château de Barive €€
Rooms with views
Domaine du Château de Barive, 02350
Tel *03 23 22 15 15*
W domainedebarive.com
Guests here stay in large rooms in beautifully converted 18th-century stables. There is also a gourmet restaurant.

ST-QUENTIN: Hôtel des Cannoniers €
Value for money
15 rue des Cannoniers, 02100
Tel *03 23 62 87 87*
W hotel-cannoniers.com
The rooms at this period town house with a courtyard for summer breakfasts have vibrant colour schemes and floral fabrics. Opt for a suite, at little extra cost.

WIMEREUX: Hôtel St-Jean €
Family
1 rue Georges Romain, 62930
Tel *03 21 83 57 40*
W hotel-saint-jean.fr
Located very close to the beach, this hotel offers brightly coloured but stylishly decorated rooms. Spa facilities are also available.

Champagne

AUBERIVE: Auberge du Palais Abbatial €€
Historic
Pl de l'Abbaye, 52160
Tel *03 25 84 33 66*
W auberge-abbatiale.com
The stately rooms at this medieval auberge feature stone floors and fireplaces, canopy beds and timbered ceilings. There is also a pleasant garden, plus a restaurant with exposed-brick walls decorated with tapestries.

AY: Le Castel Jeanson €€
Family
24 rue Jeanson, 51560
Tel *03 26 54 21 75*
W casteljeanson.fr
Guests at this neat 18th-century converted château can relax in the Art Deco veranda by the indoor pool or with a book from the hotel library.

CHALONS-EN-CHAMPAGNE: Hôtel d'Angleterre €€
City centre
19 pl Monseigneur Tissier, 51000
Tel *03 26 68 21 51*
W hotel-dangleterre.fr
The spacious, individually decorated guest rooms at the Hôtel d'Angleterre boast sleek marble bathrooms.

DK Choice

CHARLEVILLE MEZIERES: Le Dormeur du Val €€
Boutique
32 bis rue de la Gravière, 08000
Tel *03 24 42 04 30*
W hotel-dormeur-du-val.com
This remarkable hotel has zany modern interiors and vibrant, well-appointed rooms. Enjoy a drink at the lively bar or sit down with a book in the well-stocked hotel library. Le Dormeur du Val also has a gym, plus saunas and Turkish baths.

COLOMBEY-LES-DEUX-EGLISES: La Grange du Relais €
Family
26 rte Nationale 19, 52330
Tel *03 25 02 03 89*
W lagrangedurelais.fr
The rooms at this simple hotel with an excellent restaurant open out on to a flower-filled terrace.

COURCELLES-SUR-VESLE: Château de Courcelles €€€
Luxury
8 rue du Château, 02220
Tel *03 23 74 13 53*
W chateau-de-courcelles.fr
Sumptuous bedrooms and a stately reading room await at this magnificent château.

EPERNAY: Hôtel de la Cloche €
Value for money
3 pl Mendès-France, 51200
Tel *03 26 55 15 15*
W hotel-la-cloche.com
A practical base from which to explore neighbouring areas, this cheerful establishment offers simple but immaculate rooms.

ETOGES: Château d'Etoges €€
Luxury
4 rue Richebourg, 51270
Tel *03 26 59 30 08*
W etoges.com
This fairy-tale castle offers period rooms, large grounds, a moat and an excellent restaurant.

Rustic setting of the grand Château de Barive, Sainte-Preuve

MESNIL-SAINT-PERE : Auberge du Lac €
Value for money
5–7 rue du 28 Août 1944, 10140
Tel *03 25 41 27 16*
W auberge-du-lac.fr
Located in the Lac et Forêt d'Orient Natural Park, this family hotel has nicely restored half-timbered buildings.

MOUSSEY: Domaine de la Creuse €€
Family
Domaine de la Creuse, 10800
Tel *03 25 41 74 01*
W domainedelacreuse.fr
The five ground-floor rooms at this charming B&B in an old farm with a courtyard are decorated in soothing natural tones, apart from the bright-pink Peony Room.

PEIGNEY: Auberge des Voiliers €
Value for money
1 chemin du bord de Lac de la Liez, 52200
Tel *03 25 87 05 74*
W hotel-voiliers.com
The rooms at this hotel-restaurant alongside the Lac de la Liez are basic, but some have lakeside views.

REIMS: Hôtel de la Paix €€
City centre
9 rue de Buirette, 51100
Tel *03 26 40 04 08*
W bestwestern-lapaix-reims.com
Guest rooms here are housed within contemporary buildings with an elegant central courtyard.

REIMS: Château Les Crayères €€€
Luxury
64 bd Henry Vasnier, 51100
Tel *03 26 24 90 00*
W lescrayeres.com
There is an excellent restaurant at this splendid château in lovely grounds with a wooded park.

SEDAN: Le Château Fort €
Value for money
Port des Princes, 08200
Tel *03 24 26 11 00*
W chateaufort-sedan.fr
Some rooms have wheelchair access at this exceptional hotel in Europe's largest fortress.

TROYES: Champs des Oiseaux €€
City centre
20 rue Linard Gonthier, 10000
Tel *03 25 80 58 50*
W champdesoiseaux.com
The stunningly restored 15th- and 16th-century half-timbered buildings housing this hotel also offer delightful courtyards.

For more information on types of hotels *see pp552–3*

VIENNE-LE-CHATEAU: Le Tulipier €€
Family
Rue Saint-Jacques, 51800
Tel *03 26 60 69 90*
W letulipier.com
Deep in the forests of the Argonne, this modern hotel has a heated indoor pool and a well-stocked bar. Free bicycles.

VILLIERS SUR MARNE: La Source Bleue €
Value for money
La Papeterie, 52320 Gudmont
Tel *03 25 94 70 35*
W hotelsourcebleue.com
Smartly designed rooms and suites, some with balconies, can be found at this old mill in the country.

VINAY: Hostellerie La Briqueterie €€
Luxury
4 rte de Sézanne, 51530
Tel *03 26 59 99 99*
W labriqueterie.fr
Guests at this hotel situated among the vineyards of Champagne enjoy spacious rooms and an excellent gourmet restaurant. There is also a spa offering treatments and a pool.

Alsace and Lorraine

AMNEVILLE: Diane €
Family
rue de la Source, 57360
Tel *03 87 70 16 33*
W acceuil-amneville.com
Located at the edge of the forest, close to the Amneville's famous leisure park, this hotel offers affordable, sleek and elegant rooms decorated in brown and beige tones.

COLMAR: Hostellerie Le Marechal €€
City centre
4–6 pl des Six Montagnes Noires, Petite Venise, 68000
Tel *03 89 41 60 32*
W hotel-le-marechal.com
Rooms at this romantic riverside hotel in the heart of the Petite Venise area are extravagantly decorated.

DIEVE: Hostellerie du Château des Monthairons €€
Family
26 rte de Verdun, Les Monthairons, 55320
Tel *03 29 87 78 55*
W chateaudesmonthairons.com
This palatial château has two chapels, extensive grounds and a private beach on the Meuse.

DRACHENBRONN: Auberge du Moulin des 7 Fontaines €
Family
1 Sept Fontaines, 67160
Tel *03 88 94 50 90*
W 7fontaines.fr
Set in a working farm, this 18th-century house offers simple rooms and an on-site restaurant serving great food.

KAYSERSBERG: Hôtel Constantin €
Value for money
10 rue Père Kohlman, 68240
Tel *03 89 47 19 90*
W hotel-constantin.com
An old winemaker's house, this is now a pleasant, quiet hotel with unpretentious rooms and a warm Alsatian welcome.

LAPOUTROIE: Les Alisiers €
Rooms with views
5 rue du Faudé, 68650
Tel *03 89 47 52 82*
W alisiers.com
This farmhouse hotel offers no-frills chalet-style rooms and a terrace with scenic views of the Vosges mountains.

METZ: La Cathédrale €€
Historic
25 pl de Chambre, 57000
Tel *03 87 75 00 02*
W hotelcathedrale-metz.fr
Located in the historic centre, facing the cathedral of St-Etienne, this hotel is made up of two elegant 17th-century buildings. It is worth paying a little extra to stay in a room with a view of the cathedral.

MULHOUSE: Hôtel du Parc €€
City centre
26 rue de la Sinne, 68100
Tel *03 89 66 12 22*
W hotelduparc-mulhouse.com
The comfortable, Art Deco-style rooms at this hotel feature white marble bathrooms.

NANCY: Grand Hôtel de la Reine €€
Luxury
2 pl Stanislas, 54000
Tel *03 83 35 03 01*
W hoteldelareine.com
Stay in a refurbished Neo-Classical building in one of Europe's finest 18th-century squares.

OBERNAI: Hôtel du Parc €€
Family
169 rte de Otrott, 67210
Tel *03 88 95 50 08*
W hotel-du-parc.com
A historic Alsatian exterior contrasts with modern interiors at this hotel. Excellent facilities.

Elegant bedroom at Le Bouclier d'Or in Strasbourg

RIQUEWIHR: L'Oriel €
Value for money
3 rue Ecuries Seigneuriales, 68340
Tel *03 89 86 03 13*
W hotel-oriel.com
In a picturesque village, this hotel has a half-timbered façade and vibrant interiors. Lovely courtyard.

SELESTAT: Hôtel Illwald €€
Value for money
Le Schnellenbuhl, 67600
Tel *03 90 56 11 40*
W illwald.fr
On the edge of the Illwald forest, this auberge has a pleasant mix of traditional and contemporary styles, plus a good restaurant.

STRASBOURG: Le Bouclier d'Or €€
Luxury
1 rue du Bouclier, 67000
Tel *03 88 13 73 55*
W lebouclierdor.com
Comprising three restored Renaissance buildings, this hotel is furnished with Alsatian antiques. It also has a fully equipped spa.

STRASBOURG: Le Chut €€
Value for money
4 rue du Bain aux Plantes, 67000
Tel *03 88 32 05 06*
Situated in the centre of old Strasbourg, this hotel has sleek, modern rooms. Great restaurant.

DK Choice

STRASBOURG: Les Haras €€
Luxury
23 rue des Glacières, 67000
Tel *03 90 20 50 00*
W les-haras-hotel.com
A former Louis XV stud farm is now a chic, minimalist hotel featuring elegantly furnished rooms. Materials such as wood and saddle leather hint to the equestrian history. An upscale brasserie is in the ex-stables.

Key to Price Guide *see p554*

Normandy

AGNEAUX: Château d'Agneaux €€
Value for money
Av Ste-Marie, 50180
Tel *02 33 56 19 21*
W chateau-agneaux.com
This 13th-century hotel features period furniture, parquet floors and wood panelling.

DK Choice

BAGNOLES DE L'ORME: Le Manoir de Lys €€
Family
Rte de Juvigny, 61140
Tel *02 33 37 80 69*
W manoir-du-lys.fr
Surrounded by a lush deer-filled forest, this charming family hotel offers cozy, up-to-date rooms. Seven family suites, called "The Wood Pavilions", are dotted along the forest's edge – ideal for those seeking solitude. Lots of fun activities on offer for guests.

BAYEUX: Hôtel Bellefontaine €€
Family
49 rue de Bellefontaine, 14400
Tel *02 31 22 00 10*
W hotel-bellefontaine.com
The best rooms at this 18th-century château have Louis XV-style furniture and views of either the cathedral or the park.

CAEN: Best Western Le Dauphin €€
City centre
29 rue Gémare, 14000
Tel *02 31 86 22 26*
W bestwestern.fr
Top-notch facilities at this tastefully renovated 15th-century priory with comfortable rooms include a spa with *hammam* and sauna. On-site restaurant, too.

CHERBOURG: Le Louvre €
City centre
2 rue Henri Dunant, 50100
Tel *02 33 53 02 28*
W hotel-le-louvre-cherbourg.com
Stay in neat, bright and modern rooms at this no-frills hotel. Good breakfast buffet.

CREPON: La Ferme de la Rançonnière €€
Value for money
Rte d'Arromanches, 14480
Tel *02 31 22 21 73*
W ranconniere.fr
This 13th-century farmhouse offers large rooms with exposed beams, stone walls and Louis XV-style furnishings.

DEAUVILLE: Hôtel Normandy Barrière €€€
Luxury
38 rue Jean Mermoz, 14800
Tel *02 31 98 66 22*
W lucienbarriere.com
This Anglo-Normandy manor house has lavishly decorated rooms with 1920s charm.

DIEPPE: Hôtel La Présidence €€
Rooms with views
1 bd de Verdun, 76200
Tel *02 35 84 31 31*
W mercure.com
Behind the drab exterior, this hotel has smart, modern rooms, some with sea views.

ETRETAT: Domaine St-Clair €€€
Rooms with views
Chemin de St-Clair, 76790
Tel *02 35 27 08 23*
W hoteletretat.com
This 19th-century Anglo-Norman château has panoramic views of the village and the cliffs of Etretat.

FECAMP: Le Grand Pavois €€
Rooms with views
15 quai Vicomté, 76400
Tel *02 35 10 01 01*
W hotel-grand-pavois.com
Some of the bright rooms at this quayside hotel, with an attractive marine-themed decor, have balconies overlooking the port.

GRANVILLE: Brit Hotel Essential de Granville €
Family
57 av des Matignon, 50400
Tel *02 33 50 05 05*
W brithotel.fr
This modern chain hotel has good-value, functional rooms, including some for groups of three or four. Buffet breakfast and cheerful staff.

Open courtyard leading up to the stately Hôtel Normandy Barrière in Deauville

HONFLEUR: La Ferme Saint Siméon €€€
Luxury
rue Adolphe Marais, 14600
Tel *02 31 81 78 00*
W fermesaintsimeon.fr
Rooms are sumptuous at this 19th-century farmhouse mansion, once the haunt of Impressionist artists.

MACE: Hôtel l'Ile de Sées €
Value for money
Le Tour de Vandel, 61500
Tel *02 33 27 98 65*
W ile-sees.fr
Stay in pleasant, comfy rooms in an ivy-clad converted dairy. Good restaurant and fine service.

MESNIL-VAL: Hostellerie de la Vieille Ferme €€
Value for money
23 rue de la Mer, 76910
Tel *02 35 86 72 18*
W vieille-ferme.net
This hotel, close to the beach, is made up of Anglo-Norman-style buildings dating from the 18th to 20th centuries. Pretty garden terrace.

MONT-ST-MICHEL: Terrasses Poulard €€
Rooms with views
BP 18, 50170
Tel *02 33 89 02 02*
W terrasses-poulard.fr
Located in the heart of Mont-St-Michel, this hotel has stunning views of the bay and the abbey.

PONT DE L'ARCHE: Hôtel de la Tour €
Value for money
41 quai Foch, 27340
Tel *02 35 23 00 99*
W hoteldelatour.org
Next to the town's 13th-century ramparts, this place has stunning 18th-century Norman architecture. Rooms are spacious, with cosy, if a little time-worn, furnishings.

PONT AUDEMER: Belle Ile sur Risle €€
Luxury
112 rte de Rouen, 27500
Tel *02 32 56 96 22*
W bellile.com
Superb cuisine is served in the 19th-century rotunda at this elegant hotel on its own island. Classic-style rooms.

ROUEN: Inter Hôtel Notre Dame €
City centre
4 rue de la Savonnerie, 76000
Tel *02 35 71 87 73*
W hotelnotredame.com
This centrally located hotel offers guest rooms decorated in a chic contemporary style.

For more information on types of hotels *see pp552–3*

ROUEN: Hôtel de Bourgtheroulde €€
Luxury
15 pl de la Pucelle d'Orléans, 76000
Tel *02 35 14 50 50*
W hotelsparouen.com
The ornate Renaissance façade belies all the modern comforts of this boutique hotel. Great spa.

ST-PATERNE: Château de St-Paterne €€€
Historic
Le Château, 72610
Tel *02 33 27 54 71*
W chateau-saintpaterne.com
Henry IV's 15th-century love nest offers magnificent, stately rooms and dinner by candlelight.

ST-VAAST: Hôtel de France et Fuchsias €
Value for money
20 rue de Maréchal Foch, 50550
Tel *02 33 54 40 41*
W france-fuchsias.com
This country-house hotel has warm, snug rooms, most of them overlooking the garden.

Brittany

BENODET: Domaine de Kereven €
Value for money
Bénodet, 29950
Tel *02 98 57 02 46*
W kereven.fr
Beautifully decorated rooms overlook the expansive grounds of an 18th-century farm.

BREST: Hôtel de la Corniche €
Family
1 rue Amiral-Nicol, 29200
Tel *02 98 45 12 42*
W hotel-la-corniche.com
Set in a peaceful neighbourhood near the scenic coastline, this hotel offers pretty pastel-hued rooms.

CARNAC: Hôtel Tumulus €€
Rooms with views
Rte du Tumulus, 56340
Tel *02 97 52 08 21*
W hotel-tumulus.com
Enjoy fine views of Quiberon Bay from this 1920s villa with elegant, large rooms, some with private terraces. Lovely spa and pool.

COURNON: La Grée des Landes €€
Rooms with views
La Gacilly, 56200
Tel *02 99 08 50 50*
W lagreedeslandes.com
This eco-friendly hotel features minimalist rooms with terraces overlooking the lush countryside. It has an organic restaurant.

DINAN: L'Avaugour €€
Family
1 pl du Champ Clos, 22100
Tel *02 96 39 07 49*
W avaugourhotel.com
The best rooms overlook the garden at this family-run hotel in a traditional granite building near the ramparts. They are simply furnished, but spacious.

DINARD: Villa Reine Hortense €€
Rooms with views
19 rue Malouine, 35800
Tel *02 99 46 54 31*
W villa-reine-hortense.com
Relive the splendour of the *belle époque* at this romantic hotel in a clifftop setting. Rooms have garden or sea views, and three have private balconies.

DOL DE BRETAGNE: Domaine des Ormes €€
Family
35120
Tel *02 99 73 53 00*
W lesormes.com
These charming guest rooms are part of a resort with great facilities including a golf course, riding school and aquapark.

FOUESNANT: Hôtel l'Orée du Bois €
Value for money
4 rue Kergoadig, 29170
Tel *02 98 56 00 06*
W hotel-oreedubois.com
Some of the simply furnished guest rooms here have sea views. Lovely outdoor terrace.

LANDEDA: Hôtel La Baie des Anges €€
Family
350 rte des Anges, 29870
Tel *02 98 04 90 04*
W baie-des-anges.com
Stay in smartly decorated rooms at this family-friendly hotel with a pool, *hammam* and sauna.

LOCQUIREC: Le Grand Hôtel des Bains €€
Luxury
15 rue de l'Eglise, 29241
Tel *02 98 67 41 02*
W grand-hotel-des-bains.com
There are stylish rooms, most of them with balconies, at this *belle époque* hotel with direct access to the beach.

MORLAIX: Hôtel de l'Europe €€
City centre
1 rue d'Aiguillon, 29600
Tel *02 98 62 11 99*
W hoteleurope-morlaix.com
Boasting a great location and a good-value brasserie, this Second Empire hotel has an elegant, richly decorated interior.

Neat, well-kept room at the Manoir du Vaumadeuc, Pleven

PLEVEN: Manoir du Vaumadeuc €
Historic
Le Vaumadeuc, 22130
Tel *02 96 84 46 17*
W vaumadeuc.com
This authentic 15th-century granite manor house has a pretty Renaissance garden and a lake.

PLOUBAZLANEC: Les Agapanthes €€
Rooms with views
1 rue Adrien Rebours, 22620
Tel *02 96 55 89 06*
W hotel-les-agapanthes.com
Most of the beautiful rooms in this stone house on the village square have views of Paimpol Bay.

QUIBERON: Ker Noyal €
Value for money
43 chemin des Dunes, 56170
Tel *02 97 50 33 31*
W ker-noyal.com
Stay in spacious, modern rooms in a typical seaside hotel on a quiet street near the casino.

QUIMPER: Hôtel Gradlon €€
City centre
30 rue de Brest, 29000
Tel *02 98 95 04 39*
W hotel-gradlon.com
Rooms here are charming and quiet. Some overlook the hotel's flower garden and fountain.

RENNES: The Magic Hall Hotel €€
City centre
17 rue de la Quintaine, 35000
Tel *02 99 66 21 83*
W lemagichall.com
Choose from cinema-, theatre-, dance- and music-themed rooms at this quirky, theatrical-style hotel.

ROSCOFF: La Résidence €
Family
14 rue des Johnnies, 29680
Tel *02 98 69 74 85*
W hotelroscoff-laresidence.fr
Situated close to the port, this hotel is smartly decorated and has a great family room.

ST-MALO: La Maison des Armateurs €€
City centre
6 Grand Rue, 35400
Tel *02 99 40 87 70*
W maisondesarmateurs.com
This former shipowner's house in the old town is now a chic hotel with bright and modern rooms.

DK Choice

TREBOUL: Ty Mad €€
Boutique
Plage St-Jean, 29100
Tel *02 98 74 00 53*
W hoteltymad.com
Frequented in the 1920s by local artists such as Max Jacob, the eco-friendly Ty Mad has 15 individually decorated rooms with garden or sea views. Closed mid-Nov–Mar.

VANNES: Villa Kerasy €€
City centre
20 av Favrel et Lincy, 56000
Tel *02 97 68 36 83*
W villakerasy.com
Near the medieval town centre, this hotel features exotic decor inspired by the Spice Route.

The Loire Valley

AMBOISE: Le Choiseul €€
Rooms with views
36 quai Charles-Guinot, 37400
Tel *02 47 30 45 45*
W choiseul-hotelrestaurant.com
This 18th-century ivy-clad manor house is set in flower-filled grounds with views of the Loire.

ANGERS: Hôtel Mail €€
City centre
8 rue des Ursules, 49100
Tel *02 41 25 05 25*
W hoteldumail.fr
Charming and family-run, this hotel in a 17th-century building was once part of a convent.

AZAY-LE-RIDEAU: Manoir de la Rémonière €€
Value for money
La Chapelle Ste-Blaise, 37190
Tel *02 47 45 24 88*
W manoirdelaremoniere.com
The stately rooms at this hotel built on the site of a Roman villa have an old-world feel.

BOURGES: Le Bourbon €€
City centre
Bd République, 18000
Tel *02 48 70 70 00*
W hoteldebourbon.fr
Guests stay in elegant, spacious rooms in this renovated 17th-century abbey. Great restaurant.

CHAMPIGNE: Château des Briottières €€
Luxury
Rte Marigné, 49330
Tel *02 41 42 00 02*
W briottieres.com
This family-run 18th-century château has stately rooms with luxurious furnishings.

CHARTRES: Le Grand Monarque €€
Family
22 pl des Epars, 28005
Tel *02 37 18 15 15*
W bw-grand-monarque.com
A converted 16th-century staging post with modern rooms, this place has a bistro and a fine-dining restaurant.

CHENONCEAUX: Hôtel du Bon Laboureur €€
Luxury
6 rue de Dr Bretonneau, 37150
Tel *02 47 23 90 02*
W bonlaboureur.com
Situated very close to the Château de Chenonceau, this picturesque 18th-century inn has lovely gardens.

CHINON: Hôtel Diderot €
Value for money
4 rue Buffon, 37500
Tel *02 47 93 18 87*
W hoteldiderot.com
Located on a quiet street near the city centre, this tuffeau stone building dating from the 1600s has elegant rooms.

CHINON: Château de Marçay €€
Historic
Le Château, 37500
Tel *02 47 93 03 47*
W chateaudemarcay.com
Rooms in this restored 15th-century fortified château have a refined, aristocratic atmosphere. Views over the park and vineyards.

LA CHARTRE SUR LE LOIR: Hôtel de France €€
Value for money
20 pl de la République, 72340
Tel *02 43 44 40 16*
W lhoteldefrance.fr
Fully renovated, this ivy-clad hotel has smartly furnished, comfortable rooms that mix old and modern styles. Pretty terrace.

LE CROISIC: Fort de l'Océan €€
Rooms with views
Pointe du Croisic, 44490
Tel *02 40 15 77 77*
W hotelfortocean.com
This Vauban fortress facing the sea now houses a delightful hotel. Rooms are stylish and comfortable, and no traces remain of harsh military life.

LE MANS: Le Charleston €
City centre
18 rue Gastelier, 72000
Tel *02 43 24 87 46*
W lecharlestonhotel.com
Rooms at this pleasant and friendly hotel are attractive, and there is a small patio for breakfast in good weather.

LOCHES: Hôtel de France €
Value for money
6 rue Picois, 37600
Tel *02 47 59 00 32*
W hoteldefrance-loches.com
Modest but comfortable rooms are offered at this former staging post with a restaurant serving good regional food.

LOUE: Hôtel Ricordeau €
Family
13 rue de la Libération, 72540
Tel *02 43 88 40 03*
W hotel-ricordeau.fr
Some of the individually decorated rooms at this former coaching inn overlook the garden.

MONTLOUIS SUR LOIRE: Château de la Bourdaisière €€
Luxury
25 rue de la Bourdaisière, 37270
Tel *02 47 45 16 31*
W labourdaisiere.com
This luxury hotel is set within a magnificent château. Some of the guest rooms are furnished with antiques.

MUIDES SUR LOIRE: Château de Colliers €€
Rooms with views
Rte Départementale 951, 41500
Tel *02 54 87 50 75*
W chateau-colliers.com
Back in the 18th century, this château belonged to the governor of Louisiana. It is a rustic but grand building, with a number of delightfully romantic rooms.

Exquisitely decorated room at the Château des Briottières, Champigné

NANTES: Amiral €
City centre
26 bis rue Scribe, 44000
Tel *02 40 69 20 21*
W amiralhotelnantes.com
In addition to a central location, this hotel boasts comfortable, modern and soundproofed rooms.

NANTES: Hôtel La Pérouse €€
Boutique
3 allée Duquesne, 44000
Tel *02 40 89 75 00*
W hotel-laperouse.fr
Named after a French navigator, this chic hotel has rooms with designer furniture. Fine service.

NOIRMOITIER EN L'ILE: Hôtel Fleur de Sel €€
Family
Rue des Saulniers, 85330
Tel *02 51 39 09 07*
W fleurdesel.fr
Some guest rooms have a private terrace at this comfortable hotel with a vast garden and a pool.

DK Choice

ONZAIN: Domaine des Hauts de Loire €€€
Luxury
Rte d'Herbault, 41150
Tel *02 54 20 72 57*
W domainehautsloire.com
This turreted, ivy-clad hunting lodge with large grounds boasts lavishly furnished interiors. Rooms in the old coach house are the most opulent. The chef prepares cutting-edge food, served with superb local wines.

ORLEANS: Hôtel de l'Abeille €€
City centre
64 rue Alsace Lorraine, 45000
Tel *02 38 53 54 87*
W hoteldelabeille.com
This grand Neo-Classical building offers well-decorated, old-style rooms. Rooftop terrace.

ROMORANTIN-LANTHENAY: Grand Hôtel du Lion d'Or €€
Luxury
69 rue Georges Clémenceau, 41200
Tel *02 54 94 15 15*
W hotel-liondor-romorantin.fr
Stay in well-furnished rooms at this Renaissance mansion with authentic Empire-style decor.

ST-MARC-SUR-MER: Hôtel de la Plage €
Rooms with views
Plage de M. Hulot, 44600
Tel *02 40 91 99 01*
W hotel-delaplage.fr
This lovely seaside hotel featured in the film *Les Vacances de Monsieur Hulot*. Modern rooms.

SAUMUR: Hôtel Anne d'Anjou €
Rooms with views
32–34 quai Mayaud, 49400
Tel *02 41 67 30 30*
W hotel-anneanjou.com
Some of the rooms at this elegant building on the banks of the Loire are decorated in Empire style. There is also a grand staircase.

SILLE-LE-GUILLAUME: Relais des Etangs de Guibert €
Value for money
Neufchâtel-en-Saosnois, 72600
Tel *02 43 97 15 38*
W lesetangsdeguibert.com
Overlooking a lake, this rustic farmhouse is in a romantic setting deep in the forest.

TOURS: Hôtel l'Adresse €
City centre
12 rue de la Rôtisserie, 37000
Tel *02 47 20 85 76*
W hotel-ladresse.com
In the historic Plumereau district, this modern hotel is set within an elegant 18th-century town house.

Burgundy and Franche-Comté

ARC-ET-SENANS: La Saline Royale €€
Historic
Arc-et-Senans, 25610
Tel *03 81 54 45 32*
W salineroyale.com
A World Heritage Site, this hotel features sleek, contemporary rooms. Good service.

AUXERRE: Le Parc des Maréchaux €€
City centre
6 av Foch, 89000
Tel *03 86 51 43 77*
W leparcdesmarechaux.com
The Empire-style rooms here are named after French marshals. The best ones overlook the park.

Extensive gardens and inviting pool at Hôtel Fleur de Sel, Noirmoitier en L'Ile

BEAUNE: Hôtel Grillon €
Value for money
21 rte de Seurre, 21200
Tel *03 80 22 44 25*
W hotel-grillon.fr
This charming hotel is set within a walled garden. Rooms in the extension are more spacious.

BEAUNE: Hôtel Le Cep €€
Romantic
27 rue Maufoux, 21200
Tel *03 80 22 35 48*
W hotel-cep-beaune.com
In the old town, this hotel has rooms named after local wines and furnished with antiques.

BESANCON: Hôtel Le Sauvage €€
City centre
6 rue du Chapitre, 25000
Tel *03 81 82 00 21*
W hotel-lesauvage.com
Some of the stylish rooms in this former monastery have a view of the citadel.

CHABLIS: Hostellerie des Clos €€
Value for money
Rue Jules-Rathier, 89800
Tel *03 86 42 10 63*
W hostellerie-des-clos.fr
Enjoy delightful rooms and top-notch dining in this restored medieval convent.

DK Choice

CHAGNY: Lameloise €€
Luxury
36 pl d'Armes, 71150
Tel *03 85 87 65 65*
W lameloise.fr
Lameloise is a beautifully restored old house with classic decor that includes oak-beamed ceilings and period furniture. Large rooms and impeccable bathrooms. It is also home to one of Burgundy's best restaurants.

DIJON: Le Jacquemart €
Value for money
32 rue Verrerie, 21000
Tel *03 80 60 09 60*
W hotel-lejacquemart.fr
This rambling 17th-century building in the historic centre has rooms with rustic furniture.

DIJON: Hostellerie du Chapeau Rouge €€
Romantic
5 rue Michelet, 21000
Tel *03 80 50 88 88*
W chapeau-rouge.fr
In the heart of the city, this smart 16th-century hotel offers slick, contemporary rooms and an impressive dining space.

Key to Price Guide *see p554*

The vibrant exterior of Le Relais Bernard Loiseau, Saulieu

DOLE: La Chaumière €€
Family
346 av du Maréchal-Juin, 39100
Tel *03 84 70 72 40*
W lachaumiere-dole.fr
Run by one of the region's top chefs, this ancient farmhouse has a chic ambience. Rooms are floral, Zen or colour-themed.

JOIGNY: La Côte St-Jacques €€€
Luxury
14 faubourg de Paris, 89300
Tel *03 86 62 09 70*
W cotesaintjacques.com
This classy hotel overlooking the Yonne river has a pretty garden leading to the water's edge.

LEVERNOIS: Hostellerie de Levernois €€€
Romantic
Rue du Golf, 21200
Tel *03 80 24 73 58*
W levernois.com
Near Beaune, in the Burgundian countryside, this 17th-century manor-house hotel features a large park and gardens.

MALBUISSON: Le Bon Accueil €
Value for money
Rue de la Source, 25160
Tel *03 81 69 30 58*
W le-bon-accueil.fr
Rooms have simple pine furniture and patterned fabrics at this friendly hotel. Good restaurant.

MARTAILLY-LES-BRANCION: La Montagne de Brancion €€
Rooms with views
Col de Brancion, 71700
Tel *03 85 51 12 40*
W lamontagnedebrancion.com
This modern hotel on a hillside overlooks vineyards and lush countryside. Impressive cuisine.

NEVERS: Clos Ste-Marie €
Value for money
25 rue du Petit-Mouësse, 58000
Tel *03 86 71 94 50*
W clos-sainte-marie.fr
Some of the rooms at this serene hotel have antique furniture and quaint decor, others are modern.

NITRY: Auberge de la Beursaudière €
Value for money
5 & 7 rue Hyacinthe-Gautherin, 89310
Tel *03 86 33 69 70*
W beursaudiere.com
The attractive rooms in this 12th-century former priory have been named after ancient trades. Breakfast is served in a wine cellar.

RULLY: Le Vendangerot €
Value for money
6 pl Sainte-Marie, 71150
Tel *03 85 87 20 09*
W vendangerot.fr
This welcoming hotel has neat and unpretentious rooms, and a popular restaurant serving local delicacies.

SAULIEU: Le Relais Bernard Loiseau €€€
Luxury
2 rue d'Argentine, 21210
Tel *03 80 90 53 53*
W bernard-loiseau.com
Enjoy refined rooms and Michelin-starred dining at this upmarket hotel with impeccable service and authentic Burgundy charm.

VALLEE DE COUSIN: Hostellerie du Moulin des Ruats €€
Romantic
9 rue des Isles Labaumes, 89200
Tel *03 86 34 97 00*
W moulindesruats.com
A former flour mill has been turned into a hotel-restaurant with beautifully furnished rooms.

VONNAS: Georges Blanc €€€
Luxury
Pl Marché, 01540
Tel *04 74 50 90 90*
W georgesblanc.com
Plush hotel-restaurant with a glitzy spa and sauna, and one of the region's top restaurants.

The Massif Central

BEAULIEU-SUR-DORDOGNE: Manoir de Beaulieu €
Family
4 pl Champ de Mars, 19120
Tel *05 55 91 01 34*
W hotelbeaulieudordogne.com
This traditional hotel offers nicely renovated rooms – some rustic, some modern.

BELCASTEL: Du Vieux Pont €€
Family
Le Bourg, 12390
Tel *05 65 64 52 29*
W hotelbelcastel.com
All the rooms at this modest hotel by the Aveyron river have wonderful views. The owners run a superb restaurant just across the bridge.

CANTAL: Instants d'Absolu Ecolodge & Spa €€
Rooms with view
Le Lac du Pêcher, Fons Nostre 15300
Tel *04 71 20 83 09*
W ecolodge-france.com
This 17th-century lava-stone farm-house has been converted into an eco-friendly hotel. Complete the detox experience with a spa and hot basalt stone massage.

DK Choice

CHAMALIERES: Hôtel Radio €€
Rooms with views
43 av Pierre et Marie Curie, 63400
Tel *04 73 30 87 83*
W hotel-radio.fr
Fans of Art Deco will love this 1930s gem situated on a hill overlooking Clermont Ferrand. Original floor mosaics, mirrors and wrought-iron decor sit side-by-side with radio memorabilia. The spacious rooms have period furnishings. Opt for a room with a balcony.

CONQUES: Hôtel Ste-Foy €€
Romantic
Le Bourg, 12320
Tel *05 65 69 84 03*
W hotelsaintefoy.com
This 17th-century Aveyron inn features stone walls, low-beamed ceilings and modern amenities.

LE BOURG: Auberge des Montagnes €
Value for money
Pailherols, 15800
Tel *04 71 47 57 01*
W auberge-des-montagnes.com
On the flanks of the Monts du Cantal, this auberge has snug chalet-style rooms and a good restaurant serving regional fare.

LIMOGES: Hôtel Jeanne d'Arc €
City centre
17 av du Général-de-Gaulle, 87000
Tel *05 55 77 67 77*
W hoteljeannedarc.fr
Behind the façade of a 19th-century coaching inn is a tastefully renovated hotel with stylish, well-equipped rooms.

MENDE: Hôtel de France €€
Family
9 bd Lucien-Arnault, 48000
Tel *04 66 65 00 04*
W hoteldefrance-mende.com
A renovated 1856 staging post, this hotel has comfortable, chic rooms and a fabulous terrace.

For more information on types of hotels *see pp552–3*

Pleasant, simply furnished room at Château d'Ygrande, Ygrande

MILLAU: Château de Creissels €€
Romantic
Rte de St-Afrique, 12100
Tel *05 65 60 16 59*
W chateau-de-creissels.com
This atmospheric 12th-century château has fine views of the Tarn Valley and the Millau viaduct. Rooms in the 1970s extension are comfortable and quiet.

ORCIVAL: Hôtel Notre Dame €
Value for money
Pl de la Basilique, 63210
Tel *04 73 65 82 02*
W hotelnotredame-orcival.com
Opposite the basilica, this cosy, family-run hotel has cheerful rooms. It serves hearty breakfasts.

PEYRELEAU: Grand Hôtel de la Muse et du Rozier €€
Rooms with views
Rue des Gorges du Tarn, 12720
Tel *05 65 62 60 01*
W hotel-delamuse.fr
In an idyllic setting overlooking the Tarn river, this historic country inn has a quaint exterior that contrasts with its contemporary features inside.

RODEZ: La Ferme de Bourran €€
Rooms with views
Quartier de Bourran, 12000
Tel *05 65 73 62 62*
W fermedebourran.com
On a secluded hillock, this renovated farmhouse has bright, contemporary rooms in soothing tones of white, grey and ivory.

SALERS: Le Bailliage €
Value for money
Rue Notre-Dame, 15410
Tel *04 71 40 71 95*
W salers-hotel-bailliage.com
Rooms at this grand old house with a delightful garden are simple and well kept. Some have mountain views.

SALERS: Hôtel Saluces €
Family
Rue de la Martille, 15140
Tel *04 71 40 70 82*
W hotel-salers.fr
Relax in stylish rooms with wooden flooring in this gorgeous family-run 16th-century mansion.

ST-ALBAN-SUR-LIMAGNOLE: Relais St-Roch €€
Luxury
Château de la Chastre, chemin du Carreirou, 48120
Tel *04 66 31 55 48*
W relais-saint-roch.fr
There is a well-stocked lounge bar with over 300 whiskies at this 18th-century mansion with elegant rooms and classy decor.

ST-BONNET-LE-FROID: Le Clos des Cimes €€€
Luxury
Le Bourg, 43290
Tel *04 71 59 93 72*
W regismarcon.fr
Luxurious rooms, original works of art and wonderful valley views can all be found at this fabulous country auberge for gourmands.

ST-GERVAIS D'AUVERGNE: Castel-Hôtel 1904 €
Value for money
rue de Castel, 63390
Tel *04 73 85 70 42*
W castel-hotel-1904.com
This turreted château features oak beams, classy wooden floors and period furniture.

ST-MARTIN-VALMEROUX: Hostellerie de la Maronne €€
Romantic
Le Theil, 15140
Tel *04 71 69 20 33*
W maronne.com
Tastefully renovated, this 19th-century manor house offers beautifully decorated rooms and a great restaurant.

VICHY: Aletti Palace Hôtel €€
City centre
3 pl Joseph-Aletti, 03200
Tel *04 70 30 20 20*
W hotel-aletti.fr
This hotel oozes *belle époque* grandeur, from its stately reception hall to the crystal chandeliers. Fine restaurant and a terraced pool. Good service.

YGRANDE: Château d'Ygrande €€
Luxury
Le Mont, 03160
Tel *04 70 66 33 11*
W chateauygrande.fr
Meticulously renovated, this 19th-century château situated in vast grounds offers a number of bright and elegant rooms.

The Rhône Valley and French Alps

ANNECY: Hôtel Palais de l'Isle €€
City centre
13 rue Perrière, 74000
Tel *04 50 45 86 87*
W palaisannecy.com
On the Thouin canal, this renovated 18th-century house has comfortable rooms and modern decor.

BRIANCON: Hôtel Cristol €
Value for money
6 rte d'Italie, 05100
Tel *04 92 20 20 11*
W hotel-cristol-briancon.fr
Ideal for families, this unpretentious hotel has bright, airy, contemporary rooms.

CHAMBERY: Hôtel des Princes €€
City centre
4 rue de Boigne, 73000
Tel *04 79 33 45 36*
W hoteldesprinces.com
Quiet and comfortable rooms can be found at this lovely hotel near the Fontaine des Eléphants.

CHAMONIX-MONT BLANC: Le Hameau Albert 1er €€€
Luxury
119 impasse du Montenvers, 74402
Tel *04 50 53 05 09*
W hameaualbert.fr
This chic hotel complex has various accommodation options and stunning views of Mont Blanc.

CHANTEMERLE-LES-GRIGNAN: Le Parfum Bleu €€
Value for money
615b rte de Valaurie, 26230
Tel *04 75 98 54 21*
W parfum-bleu.com
Take in the sound of cicadas and the smell of lavender at this stylish, restored farmhouse.

CLIOUSCLAT: La Treille Muscate €
Value for money
Le Village, 26270
Tel *04 75 63 13 10*
W hotelrestaurant-latreillemuscate.com
A pleasant inn with tasteful, individually decorated rooms, La Treille Muscate also has a vaulted dining room serving local cuisine.

GRENOBLE: Splendid Hôtel €
Value for money
22 rue Thiers, 38000
Tel *04 76 46 33 12*
W splendid-hotel.com
Centrally located in an oasis of tranquillity, the Splendid has a walled garden and brightly decorated rooms.

Key to Price Guide *see p554*

GRENOBLE: Le Grand Hôtel €€
City centre
5 rue de la République, 38000
Tel *04 76 51 22 59*
W grand-hotel-grenoble.com
This high-end hotel is in a central location, but the triple glazing ensures a peaceful night's sleep. Rooms are decorated in black, white and grey tones.

LE POET-LAVAL: Les Hospitaliers €
Romantic
Vieux Village, 26160
Tel *04 75 46 22 32*
W hotel-les-hospitaliers.com
Situated in a dreamy hilltop medieval hamlet, this classy hotel offers spacious rooms and a top-notch restaurant.

LYON: Hôtel des Artistes €€
City centre
8 rue Gaspard-André, 69002
Tel *04 78 42 04 88*
W hotel-des-artistes.fr
This cosy hotel featuring bright rooms is a popular haunt for the actors performing at the famous theatre opposite.

LYON: Cour des Loges €€€
Luxury
6 rue du Boeuf, 69005
Tel *04 72 77 44 44*
W courdesloges.com
The elegant rooms at this hotel blend Renaissance-period features and contemporary decor.

MANIGOD: Hôtel-Chalets de la Croix-Fry €€€
Luxury
Rte du Col de la Croix-Fry, 74230
Tel *04 50 44 90 16*
W hotelchaletcroixfry.com
Alpine rustic chic meets self-indulgent comfort at this classy chalet-style hotel with great log-cabin-style rooms.

MEGEVE: Les Fermes de Marie €€€
Luxury
163 chemin de Riante Colline, 74120
Tel *04 50 93 03 10*
W fermesdemarie.com
The chic Savoyard country-style chalets here have an air of relaxed sophistication. Guests can pamper themselves at the on-site spa, featuring a sauna, *hammam*, Jacuzzi and hairdresser.

MONTELIMAR: Le Sphinx €
Value for money
19 bd Desmarais, 26200
Tel *04 75 01 86 64*
W sphinx-hotel.fr
Old-school charm greets visitors to this 17th-century town-house mansion with a delightful terrace.

DK Choice

PEROUGES: Hostellerie du Vieux Pérouges €€
Historic
Pl du Tilleuil, 01800
Tel *04 74 61 00 88*
W hostelleriedeperouges.com
Set in a medieval hilltop village, this historic inn has rooms in four 13th-century timbered houses clustered around the cobbled square – the decor is different in each house. The on-site restaurant serves authentic traditional dishes with flair. A truly unique place.

ROMANS-SUR-ISERE: Hôtel l'Orée du Parc €€
Family
6 av Gambetta, 26100
Tel *04 75 70 26 12*
W hotel-oreeparc.com
An elegant bolthole, this hotel is perfect for exploring the Drôme region. Impeccably maintained rooms.

ST-CYR-AU-MONT-D'OR: L'Ermitage Hôtel €€
Rooms with views
Chemin de l'Ermitage Mont Cindre, 69450
Tel *04 72 19 69 69*
W ermitage-college-hotel.com
Rooms are bright, with quirky accessories and views of Fourvière, at this sleek, ultra-modern hotel.

TALLOIRES: Hôtel l'Abbaye €€€
Luxury
Chemin des Moines, 74290
Tel *04 50 60 77 33*
W abbaye-talloires.com
Relax in the wonderful rooms in this 17th-century Benedictine abbey on the shores of Lake Annecy. Cézanne was a fan.

VAL D'ISERE: Christiania €€€
Rooms with views
Chef Lieu, 73152
Tel *04 79 06 08 25*
W hotel-christiania.com
Deluxe Alpine-style rooms come with balconies and magnificent views at this modern chalet hotel.

VALLON-PONT D'ARC: Le Clos des Bruyères €€
Family
Rte des Gorges, 07150
Tel *04 75 37 18 85*
W closdesbruyeres.fr
At this modern Provençal-style hotel, rooms open onto the pool area via a balcony or terrace. The breakfast buffet has plenty of variety and the restaurant is excellent. Enjoy a treatment at the pleasant on-site spa.

Poitou and Aquitaine

ARCACHON: Hôtel Le Dauphin €€
Family
7 av Gounod, 33120
Tel *05 56 83 02 89*
W dauphin-arcachon.com
Leo Tolstoy spent a year at this attractive hotel that is just a short walk from Arcachon's beaches. Bright rooms and a nice pool.

BORDEAUX: La Maison du Lierre €€
B&B
57 rue Huguerie, 33000
Tel *05 56 51 92 71*
W hotel-maisondulierre-bordeaux.com
This charming hotel in central Bordeaux is set in a historic house with a pretty garden. Breakfast is served in a lovely inner courtyard.

BORDEAUX: Grand Hôtel de Bordeaux €€€
Luxury
2–5 pl de la Comédie, 33000
Tel *05 57 30 44 44*
W ghbordeaux.com
An outstanding spa and two restaurants run by Gordon Ramsay are on offer at this magnificent hotel in a great location. Guests can sign up for wine tours.

CAP-FERRET: La Maison du Bassin €€
Romantic
5 rue des Pionniers, 33950
Tel *05 56 60 60 63*
W lamaisondubassin.com
With the charm of a family home, this chic hotel has colonial decor in the rooms, a bar and restaurant.

COGNAC: Les Pigeons Blancs €
Historic
110 rue Jules Brisson, 16100
Tel *05 45 82 16 36*
W pigeons-blancs.com
Welcoming guests since the time of François I, this old coaching inn near the vineyards has lovely gardens and a famous restaurant.

Outdoor seating area at L'Ermitage Hôtel, St-Cyr-au-Mont-d'Or

COULON: Hôtel Le Central €
Boutique
4 rue d'Autremont, 79510
Tel *05 49 35 90 20*
W hotel-lecentral-coulon.com
This hotel combines romantic boutique style with comfort. Good location, along the "Venice Vert", and great food.

EUGENIE-LES-BAINS: Les Prés d'Eugénie €€€
Luxury
Pl de l'Impératrice, 40320
Tel *05 58 05 06 07*
W michelguerard.com
Run by chef Michel Guérard, this colonial-style hotel has a fabulous spa and gorgeous gardens.

HOSSEGOR: Les Hortensias du Lac €€
Romantic
1578 av du Tour du Lac, 40150
Tel *05 58 43 99 00*
W hortensias-du-lac.com
Located near France's best surfing beaches, this sprawling villa overlooks gardens and a lake. Delightful rooms.

ILE DE RE: Hôtel Le Sénéchal €€
Boutique
6 rue Gambetta, 17590 Ars-en-Ré
Tel *05 46 29 40 42*
W hotel-le-senechal.com
Rooms are distinctive at this laid-back village hotel on a pretty island, with exposed brick, wood beams and rural-chic decor.

LA ROCHELLE: Hôtel Les Brises €€
Rooms with views
Chemin de la Digue Richelieu, 17000
Tel *05 46 43 89 37*
W hotellesbrises.eu
Offering stunning views of the harbour, this popular hotel is close to several beaches. Ideal location, a short walk to town.

MAGESQ: Relais de la Poste €€€
Boutique
24 av de Maremne, 40140
Tel *05 58 47 70 25*
W relaisposte.com
This peaceful, family-owned hotel is set in beautiful gardens with a large pool. There is also a spa and a Michelin-starred restaurant.

PAUILLAC: Château Cordeillan-Bages €€
Historic
Rte des Châteaux, 33250
Tel *05 56 59 24 24*
W cordeillanbages.com
Set amid the Médoc vineyards, this magnificent 17th century, château offers splendid gardens, Michelin-starred dining and elegant rooms. Closed Dec–Feb.

POITIERS: Château du Clos de la Ribaudière €€
Romantic
10 rue du Champ de Foire, 86360 Chasseneuil du Poitou
Tel *05 49 52 86 66*
W ribaudiere.com
This delightful hotel offers elegantly modernized rooms and excellent service. The grounds comprise large gardens, a pool and a relaxing spa.

POITIERS: Les Cours du Clain €€
Family
117 chemin de la Grotte à Calvin, 86000
Tel *06 10 16 09 55*
W lescoursduclain-poitiers.com
Set in a historic 1830 house with gardens, this is a beautiful, quiet B&B near central Poitiers. A generous breakfast is served on a terrace overlooking the swimming pool. Closed Nov–Mar.

ROYAN: Domaine de Saint-Palais €€
Value for money
50 rue du Logis, 17420 Saint-Palais-sur-Mer
Tel *05 46 39 85 26*
W domainedesaintpalais.eu
Close to both woods and beaches, this charming former hunting lodge dating to the 17th century offers bright, elegant rooms. There is also a Cognac-tasting facility.

SAINT-EMILION: Au Logis des Remparts €€
Rooms with views
18 rue Guadet, 33330
Tel *05 57 24 70 43*
W logisdesremparts.com
This boutique hotel is ideal for wine touring and exploring the medieval town. Some rooms have views of the gardens and swimming pool.

Communal area looking out to the gardens at Les Prés d'Eugénie, Eugénie-les-Bains

DK Choice

ST-LOUP-SUR-THOUET: Château de Saint-Loup €€
Historic
79600 St-Loup-sur-Thouet
Tel *05 49 64 81 73*
W chateaudesaint-loup.com
A magical experience is guaranteed at this moated medieval château in the countryside north of Poitiers. Choose from several exquisite rooms in the 17th-century main house – the most fascinating ones are in a medieval keep and round tower.

SEIGNOSSE: Villa de l'Etang Blanc €€
Romantic
2265 route de l'Etang Blanc, 40510
Tel *05 58 72 80 15*
W villaetangblanc.fr
Stay in beautifully stylish rooms at this calm country house by a lake. An excellent restaurant and cooking classes are also available.

Périgord, Quercy and Gascony

AGEN: Hôtel Château des Jacobins €€
Historic
2 rue Jacob, 47000
Tel *05 53 47 03 31*
W chateau-des-jacobins.com
Housed in a 19th-century mansion near the old town, this hotel is opposite a 13th-century church.

ALBI: L'Autre Rives €
B&B
60 rue Cantepau, 81000
Tel *06 75 47 01 51*
W lautrerives.com
In a 1930s house, this stylish B&B has five large rooms furnished with designer accessories.

BERGERAC: Le Clos d'Argenson €€
B&B
99 rue Neuve d'Argenson, 24100
Tel *06 12 90 59 58*
W leclosdargenson.com
This beautiful B&B offers four ultra-comfortable suites, plus a pool in the garden.

BOURDEILLES: Hostellerie Les Griffons €€
Rooms with views
24310 Bourdeilles
Tel *05 53 45 45 35*
W griffons.fr
Most of the characterful rooms at this lovely 16th-century house in a gorgeous village have river views. Closed Nov–Apr.

Key to Price Guide *see p554*

BRANTOME: Le Chatenet €€
B&B
24310 Brantôme
Tel *05 53 05 81 08*
W lechatenet.com
Housed in a Périgord stone manor house, this B&B offers a pool and gardens. Closed mid-Oct–Mar.

BRANTOME: Le Moulin de l'Abbaye €€
Family
1 rte de Bourdeilles, 24310
Tel *05 53 05 80 22*
W moulinabbaye.com
Stay in sumptuous rooms at this beautiful riverside mill with delightful garden terraces. The Michelin-starred restaurant uses locally sourced produce.

CHANCELADE: Château des Reynats €€
Romantic
15 av des Reynats, 24650
Tel *05 53 03 53 59*
W chateau-hotel-perigord.com
Rooms are divided between the main house and the orangerie at this grand Périgord château-hotel with a pool and tennis courts.

CORDES-SUR-CIEL: Hostellerie du Vieux Cordes €
Historic
Haut de la Cité, 21 rue St-Michel, 81170
Tel *05 63 53 79 20*
W hostelleriehvc.com
In a superb hill-town, this medieval mansion offers great views and charming rooms. The restaurant has a good regional menu. Ask for a table on the terrace.

CORDES-SUR-CIEL: Le Secret du Chat €€
B&B
Haut de la Cité, Le Planol, 81170
Tel *06 95 48 18 10*
W chambres-cordes-tarn-charme-lesecretduchat.com
This gorgeous B&B and *gîte* set in an old town house affords amazing views. Closed Nov–Mar.

DK Choice

CUQ-TOULZA: Hôtel Cuq en Terrasses €€
Rooms with views
Cuq le Château, 81470
Tel *05 63 82 54 00*
W cuqenterrasses.com
Rising up on a hilltop east of Toulouse, this renovated 18th-century manor house feels a part of the Languedoc landscape. The pool is set in lush, picturesque gardens, and the views from the terrace restaurant are glorious. Closed mid-Oct–mid-Apr.

Bright, well-furnished room at the Le Pont de l'Ouysse, Lacave

DOMME: L'Esplanade €
Rooms with views
2 rue Pontcarral, 24250
Tel *05 53 28 31 41*
W esplanade-perigord.com
Enjoy the warm welcome from the mother-and-daughter team running this clifftop hotel. Superb views from most rooms and an excellent restaurant. Closed Nov–Feb.

LACAVE: Le Pont de l'Ouysse €€
Luxury
Lacave, 46200
Tel *05 65 37 87 04*
W lepontdelouysse.com
Rooms are bright and sunny, with hardwood floors, at this indulgent retreat with a spa, a terrace pool and a Michelin-starred restaurant.

LASCABANES: Le Domaine de Saint-Géry €€
Historic
Le Bourg, 46800
Tel *05 65 31 82 51*
W saint-gery.com
Tall ceilings and parquet floors add to the luxurious ambience at this palatial B&B set in a historic manor. Magnificent grounds.

LECTOURE: Hôtel de Bastard €€
Value for money
Rue Lagrange, 32700
Tel *05 62 68 82 44*
W hotel-de-bastard.com
A beautiful wooden staircase leads to the sleeping quarters at this comfortable small-town hotel with a garden pool and a good restaurant.

LES EYZIES-DE-TAYAC: Les Glycines €€
Boutique
4 av de Laugerie, 24620
Tel *05 53 06 97 07*
W les-glycines-dordogne.com
This small and mellow hotel combines a country location with boutique style. Especially lovely restaurant, pool and garden on site.

MAUROUX: Hostellerie Le Vert €€
Historic
Lieu dit "Le Vert", 46700 Mauroux
Tel *05 65 36 51 36*
W hotellevert.com
Rooms have heaps of character at this family-friendly, 17th-century house in the Cahors wine country. Closed Nov–Mar.

ROCAMADOUR: Domaine de la Rhue €
Boutique
La Rue, 46500
Tel *05 65 33 71 50*
W domainedelarhue.com
This hotel is an ideal base for exploring the countryside and has spacious rooms and a pool. Closed mid-Oct–Mar.

ST-EUTROPE-DE-BORN: Le Moulin de Labique €€
Romantic
47210 St-Eutrope-de-Born
Tel *05 53 01 63 90*
W moulin-de-labique.net
Rooms at this good-value B&B in a 13th-century manor house are decorated with antiques.

SARLAT: Le Moulin Pointu €
Value for money
Ste-Nathalène, 24200
Tel *05 53 28 15 54*
W moulinpointu.com
Start the day with an organic breakfast at this B&B with charming rooms, large gardens and a pool.

SARLAT: La Villa des Consuls €€
Family
3 rue Jean-Jacques Rousseau, 24200
Tel *05 53 31 90 05*
W villaconsuls.fr
These modern, self-catering rooms and apartments are set in different historic buildings in the old town.

TOULOUSE: Hotel Saint-Sernin €
Value for money
2 rue St-Bernard, 31000
Tel *05 61 21 73 08*
W hotelstsernin.com
There are 17 bright, stylish rooms in this 19th-century town house near the Saint-Sernin basilica.

For more information on types of hotels *see pp552–3*

TOULOUSE: La Cour des Consuls €€
Luxury
46 rue des Couteliers, 31000
Tel *05 67 16 19 99*
W sofitel.com
Housed in two former lords' mansions, this stunning five-star hotel features contemporary design, a gourmet restaurant and an elegant spa.

TOULOUSE: Hôtel des Beaux Arts €€
City centre
1 pl du Pont-Neuf, 31000
Tel *05 34 45 42 42*
W hoteldesbeauxarts.com
Smartly modernized rooms, some with great views of the Garonne river, can be found in this *belle époque* building. Friendly, helpful staff.

The Pyrenees

AINHOA: Hôtel Ithurria €€
Family
Place de Fronton, 64250
Tel *05 59 29 92 11*
W ithurria.com
Housed in a giant Basque-style chalet at the foot of the Pyrenees, this charming hotel features an excellent pool and a *hammam*. The restaurant serves generous portions and makes use of the eggs laid daily by the resident hens. Closed Nov–Mar.

ANGLET: Château de Brindos €€
Luxury
1 allée du Château, 64600
Tel *05 59 23 89 80*
W chateaudebrindos.com
Exquisite attention to detail rules at this spacious country-house hotel situated by the Etang de Brindos lake near Biarritz. Visit the sauna or the steam room, then grab a cocktail at their lakeside pub.

ARREAU: Hôtel d'Angleterre €
Family
Rte de Luchon, 65240
Tel *05 62 98 63 30*
W hotel-angleterre-saint-lary.com
Stay in an 18th-century coaching inn in a stunning mountain location. Pretty garden and a pool.

BIARRITZ: Villa le Goëland €€
Historic
12 rue Grande Atalaye, 64200
Tel *05 59 24 25 76*
W villagoeland-biarritz.com
There are views of the ocean from the high-ceilinged rooms at this 19th-century villa on the cliffs.

BIARRITZ: Hôtel du Palais €€€
Luxury
1 av de l'Impératrice, 64200
Tel *05 59 41 64 00*
W hotel-du-palais.com
Enjoy the opulent spa, pool and other facilities at this hotel in a superb location. The building's history adds to the romantic vibe.

CAMON: L'Abbaye-Château de Camon €€
B&B
3 place Philippe de Lévis, 09500
Tel *05 61 60 31 23*
W chateaudecamon.com
A restored 10th-century monastery, this hotel is located in a historic village. Gracefully decorated rooms. Closed Nov–Mar.

DK Choice

ESPELETTE: Hôtel-Restaurant Euzkadi €
Rooms with views
285 Karrika Nagusia, 64250
Tel *05 59 93 91 88*
W hotel-restaurant-euzkadi.com
The family-run Euzkadi offers well-appointed rooms, lovely terrace views and a large swimming pool. An ideal place for sampling Basque-influenced dishes. Impeccable service. Closed mid-Feb–mid-Mar.

Elegant, gracefully decorated room at the Hôtel du Palais, Biarritz

FOIX: Hôtel-Restaurant Lons €
Value for money
6 pl Georges Dutilh, 09000
Tel *05 34 09 28 00*
W hotel-lons-foix.com
Close to the historic Château de Foix, this traditional hotel has old-fashioned but comfortable rooms. The courtyard overlooks the town square.

LOURDES: Grand Hôtel Belfry €€
B&B
66 rue de la Grotte, 65100
Tel *05 62 94 58 87*
W belfry.fr
Large, black-and-white hued rooms combine modern features with traditional style.

MIREPOIX: Maison des Consuls €€
Historic
6 pl du Maréchal Leclerc, 09500
Tel *05 61 68 81 81*
W maisondesconsuls.com
Enjoy pleasant views across the cathedral square from the rooms at this hotel housed in a 13th-century building.

ORTHEZ: Hôtel Reine Jeanne €
Romantic
44 rue Bourg Vieux, 64300
Tel *05 59 67 00 76*
W reinejeanne.com
This 18th-century building has chic, modern rooms set around a courtyard, plus a fine restaurant.

PAU: Hôtel Bristol €
Family
3 rue Gambetta, 64000
Tel *05 59 27 72 98*
W hotelbristol-pau.com
Some rooms at this pleasant hotel in the centre of Pau have balconies with great views of the Pyrenees.

ST-ETIENNE-DE-BAIGORRY: Hôtel-Restaurant Arcé €€
Romantic
St-Etienne-de-Baïgorry, 64430
Tel *05 59 37 40 14*
W hotel-arce.com
This hotel blends boutique style and Basque architecture. Pool and gardens, plus a restaurant. Closed mid-Nov–mid-Apr.

ST-JEAN-DE-LUZ: Hôtel La Devinière €€
Romantic
5 rue Louis-Fortuné Loquin, 64500
Tel *05 59 26 05 51*
W hotel-la-deviniere.com
The former home of the author Rabelais, this hotel has antique furnishings and modern comforts. Terraces of the rooms overlook the Eglise St-Jean-Baptiste.

Key to Price Guide *see p554*

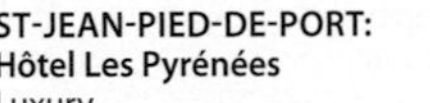

ST-JEAN-PIED-DE-PORT: Hôtel Les Pyrénées €€
Luxury
19 pl Charles de Gaulle, 64220
Tel *05 59 37 01 01*
W hotel-les-pyrenees.com
Enjoy breakfast around the pool at this prestigious hotel with elegant rooms and gardens.

ST-LIZIER: Villa Belisama €€
Rooms with views
3 rue Notre Dame, 09190
Tel *05 61 65 65 65*
W lecarredelange.com
Take in the views of the Salat river valley from this charming B&B in a historic hilltop village. Half-board accommodation only.

SARE: Ttakoinenborda €
Value for money
Rte de Lizarrieta, 64310
Tel *05 59 47 51 42*
W chambredhotebasque.fr
Built in 1680, this B&B in a Basque farmhouse amid rolling fields is excellent for exploring the area.

Languedoc and Roussillon

BEZIERS: Hôtel des Poètes €
B&B
80 allées Paul Riquet, 34500
Tel *04 67 76 38 66*
W hoteldespoetes.net
Free bikes for exploring the Canal du Midi are available at this hotel overlooking the Parc des Poètes.

CARCASSONNE: Hôtel du Pont Vieux €
Value for money
32 rue Trivalle, 11000
Tel *04 68 25 24 99*
W hotelpontvieux.com
This attractively furnished hotel has 19 rooms, an inner courtyard and views of the citadel.

CARCASSONNE: Hôtel de la Cité €€€
Luxury
Pl August-Pierre Pont, 11000
Tel *04 68 71 98 71*
W hoteldelacite.com
Expect impeccable service and period rooms at this hotel with gardens, a pool and a restaurant.

CERET: Le Mas Trilles €€
Historic
Av du Vallespir, Le Pont de Reynes, 66400
Tel *04 68 87 38 37*
W le-mas-trilles.com
This stone-built 14th-century farmhouse has charming rooms and a pleasant rooftop terrace. Closed mid-Oct–mid-Apr.

Comfortable room at Le Mas Trilles in a 14th-century farmhouse in Ceret

COLLIOURE: Relais des Trois Mas €€
Boutique
Rte de Port-Vendres, 66190
Tel *04 68 82 05 07*
W relaisdestroismas.com
A calm retreat in pine-shaded gardens, this hotel boasts great bay views. Michelin-starred restaurant.

DK Choice

MOLITG-LES-BAINS: Château de Riell €€
Rooms with views
66500
Tel *04 68 05 04 40*
W chateauderiell.com
This Baroque-style château offers fabulous views over forests and Mount Canigou. The interiors are decorated with antiques and exotic furniture.

MONTPELLIER: Hôtel du Palais €
City centre
3 rue Palais des Guilhem, 34000
Tel *04 67 60 47 38*
W hoteldupalais-montpellier.fr
Located in the old town, just steps away from the Peyrou Gardens, this historic building has cosy, classic rooms and a relaxed atmosphere.

NARBONNE: Hotel La Résidence €€
City centre
6 rue du 1er Mai, 11100
Tel *04 68 32 19 41*
W hotel-laresidence-narbonne.fr
Rooms are spacious, with high ceilings, and there is a good wine bar at this hotel with friendly, knowledgeable hosts.

NIMES: Hotel de l'Amphithéâtre €
Boutique
4 rue des Arènes, 30000
Tel *04 66 67 28 51*
W hoteldelamphitheatre.com
This small hotel located near the historic amphitheatre features rooms decorated in Provençal style. Delicious breakfast.

PERPIGNAN: Hôtel de la Loge €
Value for money
1 rue des Fabriques d'en Nabot, 66000
Tel *04 68 34 41 02*
W hoteldelaloge.fr
In the city centre, but close to the beaches and mountains, this 16th-century Catalan mansion has lots of character, including a wrought-iron staircase.

PERPIGNAN: Villa Duflot €€
Boutique
7 Rond Point Albert Donnezan, 66000
Tel *04 68 56 67 67*
W villa-duflot.com
This Italian-style villa features stylish decor and striking modern sculptures. Guests enjoy fine dining next to the exquisite gardens and pool.

PEZENAS: Aire de Vacances €
Historic
1 rue Calquières Basses, 34120
Tel *09 50 58 99 11*
W air-de-vacances.com
Tuck into a breakfast made with local organic products at this delightful 19th-century house near the town centre.

SETE: Grand Hôtel €€
Rooms with views
17 Quai de Tassigny, 34200
Tel *04 67 74 71 77*
W legrandhotelsete.com
Overlooking Sète's grand canal, this traditional 19th-century hotel has an excellent conservatory-restaurant.

UZES: Hostellerie Provençale €€
City centre
1–3 rue de la Grande Bourgade, 30700
Tel *04 66 22 11 06*
W hostellerieprovencale.com
This small, friendly hotel in an 18th-century building features terracotta tiled floors, rustic furniture and up-to-date amenities. Plentiful breakfast.

Provence and the Côte d'Azur

AIX-EN-PROVENCE: Hôtel Cézanne €€
Boutique
40 av Victor Hugo, 13100
Tel *04 42 91 11 11*
W hotelaix.com
The decor at this hotel is arty and chic. The individually decorated rooms ensure a comfortable stay. Breakfast is served until noon on the terrace, and there is an attractive outdoor bar.

For more information on types of hotels *see pp552–3*

ANTIBES: Mas Djoliba €€
B&B
29 av Provence, 06600
Tel *04 93 34 02 48*
W hotel-djoliba.com
Some rooms have views of the gardens at this farmhouse with palm trees around its pool.

DK Choice

ARLES: L'Hôtel Particulier à Arles €€€
Historic
4 rue de la Monnaie, 13200
Tel *04 90 52 51 40*
W hotel-particulier.com
Step into a world of rich elegance and opulent living at this historic hotel. A walled garden, a pool and an ultra-sophisticated spa and *hammam* all make for a dreamy stay.

AVIGNON: Hôtel Bristol €€
Family
44 cours Jean Jaurès, 84000
Tel *04 90 16 48 48*
W bristol-avignon.com
Classy and conveniently located, this pet-friendly hotel has several family rooms and refined decor.

AVIGNON: La Mirande €€€
Luxury
4 pl de la Mirande, 84000
Tel *04 90 14 20 20*
W la-mirande.fr
Renovated in 18th-century style, this hotel is in a splendid cardinal's mansion by the Palais des Papes.

BORMES-LES-MIMOSAS: Domaine du Mirage €€
Family
38 rue de la Vue des Iles, 83230
Tel *04 94 05 32 60*
W domainedumirage.com
The service is impeccable at this Victorian-style hotel with family rooms, sea views and a pool.

CANNES: Hotel de Provence €€
City centre
9 rue Molière, 06400
Tel *04 93 38 44 35*
W hotel-de-provence.com
This lovely three-star hotel in the shopping district features contemporary rooms and studios and a lovely garden.

CASTELLANE: Nouvel Hôtel du Commerce €€
Value for money
Pl Marcel Sauvaire, 04120
Tel *04 92 83 61 00*
W hotel-du-commerce-verdon.com
An excellent stopover option, this place has clean, simple rooms, a fine garden restaurant and a pool. Closed Nov–mid-Mar.

Lush trees shading the charming La Bastide de Voulonne in Gordes

DK Choice

CHATEAU-ARNOUX: La Bonne Etape €€
Romantic
Chemin du Lac, 04160
Tel *04 92 64 00 09*
W bonneetape.com
At this 18th-century posthouse inherited by current owner and master chef Jany Gleize, rooms are stunningly done up with antiques. Excellent heated pool amid the olive groves.

EZE: La Chèvre d'Or €€€
Luxury
Rue du Barri, 06360
Tel *04 92 10 66 66*
W chevredor.com
Romantic, individually decorated rooms and suites have Jacuzzis and private gardens. The pool and terrace have views of the Mediterranean Sea.

FAYENCE: Moulin de la Camandoule €
Historic
159 chemin de Notre-Dame des Cyprès, 83440
Tel *04 94 76 00 84*
W camandoule.com
Rooms are decorated in rustic Provençal style at this hotel in a converted 15th-century olive mill with beautiful grounds and a pool.

DK Choice

GORDES: La Bastide de Voulonne €€
Family
Cabrières d'Avignon, 84220
Tel *04 90 76 77 55*
W bastide-voulonne.com
This guesthouse in a Provençal farmhouse is an idyllic spot for a family break – the heated pool and terrace have spectacular views over the Luberon. Family suites and lush gardens.

ILE DE PORT-CROS: Le Manoir €€€
Romantic
Port-Cros, 83400
Tel *04 94 05 90 52*
W hotel-lemanoirportcros.com
Surrounded by palm trees, this historic mansion has balconies overlooking the sea.

JUAN-LES-PINS: Hôtel des Mimosas €€
Value for money
Rue Pauline, 06160
Tel *04 93 61 04 16*
W hotelmimosas.com
This elegant hotel is surrounded by a park full of exotic flowers. Simple rooms decorated with splashes of colour.

MARSEILLE: Hotel La Résidence du Vieux Port €€
Family
18 quai du Port, 13002
Tel *04 91 91 91 22*
W hotel-residence-marseille.com
Most rooms overlook the Old Port and the Basilica at this hotel with colourful 1950s-style decor.

MONACO: Columbus Monte-Carlo €€
Boutique
23 av des Papalins, 98000
Tel *00 377 92 05 92 22*
W columbushotels.com
The sleek rooms at this hotel are decorated in dark stone and polished metal. Good restaurant and cigar bar with sea views.

MOUSTIERS-STE-MARIE: La Bastide de Moustiers €€€
Boutique
Chemin de Quinson, 04360
Tel *04 92 70 47 47*
W bastide-moustiers.com
Created by Alain Ducasse in a 17th-century building, La Bastide has a superb restaurant, gorgeous gardens and mountain views. Closed Nov–Mar.

NICE: Hôtel Windsor €€
Romantic
11 rue Dalpozzo, 06000
Tel *04 93 88 59 35*
W hotelwindsornice.com
Art-filled rooms and a pool inside an exotic garden await here. Dine alfresco in summer or next to the fireplace in winter.

NICE: Le Negresco €€€
Luxury
37 promenade des Anglais, 06000
Tel *04 93 16 64 00*
W hotel-negresco-nice.com
Designed by Henri Négresco, this vintage hotel has superb works of art and top-notch facilities. Private beach on La Promenade.

Key to Price Guide *see p554*

ST-PAUL DE VENCE: Hostellerie des Remparts €
Value for money
72 rue Grande, 06570
Tel *04 93 24 10 47*
W hostellerielesremparts.com
Modern comforts, antique-filled rooms and marvellous views of the Mediterranean can all be found at this medieval building. Gracious, warm hosts.

ST-REMY DE PROVENCE: Hôtel du Soleil €
Boutique
35 av Pasteur, 13210
Tel *04 90 92 00 63*
W hotelsoleil.com
Featuring contemporary rooms with minimalist decor, this stylish three-star hotel and spa is located in an old farmhouse on the edge of the town. It has a heated pool.

ST-TROPEZ: Lou Cagnard €
B&B
18 av Paul Roussel, 83990
Tel *04 94 97 04 24*
W hotel-lou-cagnard.com
Conveniently situated a few minutes walk from the port and town centre, this elegant Provençal town house has airy rooms and a lush garden. Closed Oct–Feb.

DK Choice

ST-TROPEZ: Pastis Hôtel St-Tropez €€€
Boutique
6 av du Général Leclerc, 83990
Tel *04 98 12 56 50*
W pastis-st-tropez.com
This intimate hideaway, filled with 20th-century art, has stylish rooms that are all beautifully furnished and have lovely garden or sea views. The pool, surrounded by palm trees, is the perfect spot for breakfast. The hotel is a 10 minute walk from the port and main attractions. Attentive and welcoming staff.

SAINTES-MARIES-DE-LA-MER: Mas de la Fouque €€€
Boutique
rte du Petit Rhône, 13460
Tel *04 90 97 81 02*
W masdelafouque.com
Overlooking a lagoon and boasting views of the Camargue Nature Park, this chic hotel and spa features a fine restaurant, plus pool, tennis and riding facilities.

SEILLANS VAR: Hôtel des Deux Rocs €
Historic
1 pl Font d'Amont, 83440
Tel *04 94 76 87 32*
W hoteldeuxrocs.com
An 18th-century mansion with graceful decor, this is great for families. Closed mid-Nov–mid-Mar.

VAISON LA ROMAINE: Les Tilleuls d'Elisée €
B&B
1 av J. Mazen, chemin Bon Ange, 84110
Tel *04 90 35 63 04*
W vaisonchambres.info
In an idyllic rural setting, this charming B&B is set in a 19th-century Provençal farmhouse.

VILLEFRANCHE-SUR-MER: Hôtel Welcome €€
Boutique
1 quai Amiral Courbet, 06230
Tel *04 93 76 27 62*
W welcomehotel.com
Artist Jean Cocteau's favourite hotel is full of arty, period charm. A sailboat is available to rent.

Corsica

AJACCIO: Les Mouettes €€
Boutique
9 cours Lucien Bonaparte, 20000
Tel *04 95 50 40 40*
W hotellesmouettes.fr
Enjoy airy Riviera-style rooms in a 19th-century seaside mansion with stunning views of the bay. Closed Nov–Mar.

Colourful decor in the lobby at Château Hôtel La Signoria in Calvi

BASTIA: Hôtel Pietracap €
Boutique
20 rte San Martino, San Martino di Lota, 20200
Tel *04 95 31 64 63*
W pietracap.com
In a beautiful seaside park, this hotel offers views of the island of Elba. Closed Nov–Mar.

BONIFACIO: Hôtel des Etrangers €
Value for money
Av Sylvère Bohn, 20169
Tel *04 95 73 01 09*
W hoteldesetrangers.fr
Stay in beautifully furnished, bright en-suite rooms at this family-owned hotel. Closed Nov–Mar.

CALVI: Château Hôtel La Signoria €€€
Luxury
Rte de la Forêt de Bonifato, 20260
Tel *04 95 65 93 00*
W hotel-la-signoria.com
There are chic rooms and villas, a *hammam* and a private beach, at this hotel. Closed Nov–Mar.

CORTE: Hôtel Dominique Colonna €€
B&B
Vallée de la Restonica, BP 83, 20250
Tel *04 95 45 25 65*
W dominique-colonna.com
In the middle of a nature reserve, this smart hotel has stylish decor and a lovely pool. Closed Nov–Mar.

DK Choice

ERBALUNGA: Hôtel Demeure Castel Brando €€
Historic
Erbalunga, Brando, 20222
Tel *04 95 30 10 30*
W castelbrando.com
Built in 1853, Castel Brando is set in a park of ancient olive trees and exotic palms. Rooms are spacious and elegant. There are two pools, a breakfast patio and top-notch staff. Closed Nov–Mar.

PIANA: Les Roches Rouges €€
Romantic
Rte de Porto, 20115
Tel *04 95 27 81 81*
W lesrochesrouges.com
Dating from 1912, this hotel boasts a magical location, with a view of the gulf. Closed Nov–Mar.

PORTO-VECCHIO: E Casette Private Hotel €€
Boutique
Rte de Palombaggia, 20137
Tel *04 95 70 13 66*
W private-hotel-corsica.com
This romantic hotel has views across the gulf. All rooms have a private Jacuzzi. Closed Oct–Apr.

For more information on types of hotels *see pp552–3*

WHERE TO EAT AND DRINK

The French consider eating well an essential part of their national birthright. Restaurant reviews, as well as cooking and food shows on television, are avidly followed, and the general quality of both fresh food and restaurant offerings is excellent. This introduction to the restaurant listings, which are arranged by region and town *(see pp576–603)*, looks at the different types of restaurants in France. Find practical tips on eating out, reading menus, ordering and service – everything you need to know to enjoy your meal. At the front of the book is a guide to a typical menu and an introduction to French wine *(see pp28–31)*. The main food and wine features are at the beginning of each of the five regional sections.

French Eating Habits

The traditional main meal at midday survives mainly in rural regions. In cities, French families get together for Sunday lunches that can last 3 hours or more. However, a weekday city lunch is increasingly likely to consist of a sandwich, salad or steak in a café, while dinner is the main meal of the day. Usually, lunch is from noon to 2pm and dinner from 8 to 10pm, with last orders taken 30 minutes before closing time.

Some family-owned places and restaurants in city centres, catering mainly to workers, close on the weekends.
A large proportion of French restaurants, even the ones in hotels, close on Sunday night, so be sure to check in advance – though there is likely to be a pizzeria open somewhere. Off the beaten track and in resort towns, restaurants and hotels are often closed out of season or open only on Friday and Saturday nights. It is always advisable to call ahead.

Over the past few decades, French eating habits have changed dramatically, becoming much more international in outlook. The growing popularity of foods from former French colonies and beyond means that North African and Vietnamese establishments are easy to find, as are Chinese and Italian restaurants. Burger and Tex-Mex joints are also popular with young people.

Brasseries

The brasserie has its origins in the region of Alsace and they were originally attached to breweries; the name *brasserie* actually means "brewery".

The *belle époque* interior of La Cigale, a brasserie in Nantes *(see p588)*

Customers tuck into Lyonnais specialities at the Benoît restaurant, Paris *(see p576)*

Usually found in larger cities and towns, they are big, bustling places, many with fresh shellfish stands outside. They serve beer on tap as well as a *vin de la maison* (house wine) and a variety of regional wines. Menus usually include simple fish and grilled meat dishes along with Alsatian specialty such as *choucroute garnie* (sauerkraut with sausage and pork). Prices are very much on par with those charged at bistros. Like cafés, brasseries usually serve food from morning until night.

Ferme-Auberges

In the country, a simple "farm inn", or *ferme-auberge*, serves good, inexpensive meals prepared with fresh farm produce. *Ferme-auberges* can be dining rooms attached to a working farm, offering in many cases – as in parts of Corsica – an accurate reflection of authentic regional cuisine. Other *ferme-auberges* may be part of a farm's lodgings, where meals are taken with the host's family as part of the room and board.

Cafés

The soul of France, cafés serve drinks, coffee, tea, simple meals and snacks such as salads, omelettes and sandwiches throughout the day, and usually provide a cheaper breakfast than most hotels. In addition to serving refreshments, cafés are a good source of information and provide the traveller with endless opportunities to people-watch at leisure.

In villages, almost the entire population may drift in and out of a single café during the course of the day, while large cities have cafés that cater to a specific clientele such as workers or students. Paris's most famous cafés were traditional meeting places for intellectuals and artists to exchange ideas *(see p156)*.

Bistro Annexes, Salons du Thé and Wine Bars

Since the 1990s, bistro annexes have appeared in many cities. They are lower-priced sister eateries of famous – and much more expensive – restaurants run by well-known chefs. Many of them offer *formule* or *prix-fixe* (fixed-price) menus and the chance to sample the cooking of a celebrated chef.

Salons du thé (tearooms) are also good-value options for light meals, generally offering a choice of salads, savoury tarts and sandwiches. Wine bars offer light suppers in the evenings, with a choice of Spanish-style tapas, *charcuterie* (cured meats), breads and cheeses on the menu.

Reservations

In cities, larger towns and major resorts, it is always best to make a reservation, especially from May to September, and for evening meals or a Sunday lunch. But this rarely applies to cafés or in the country, where one can walk into most places. However, when travelling in remote rural and resort areas off season, it is advisable to check whether the restaurant is open all year.

The bar at La Ferme aux Grives in Eugénie-les-Bains *(see p595)*

If you have a reservation and your plans change, then call and cancel – smaller restaurants, in particular, must fill all their tables to make a profit.

Reading the Menu and Ordering

When the menu is presented, it is common practice for guests to be asked their choice of apéritif, which could be Kir (white wine mixed with a dash of black-currant liqueur), vermouth, light port – drunk in France as a cocktail – or, seeing as many French people do not drink spirits before a meal, a soft drink.

The menu opens with *les entrées* (starters) and is followed by *les plats* (main courses); most restaurants will also offer a *plat du jour*, or daily special, for lunch. A selection of dishes from a classic French menu is given on pages 28–9.

Cheese is served as a separate course between the main course and dessert. Coffee is always black, unless one specifies "*crème*", and served after dessert. Alternatively, one can ask for a *tisane* (herbal tea).

Many restaurants offer a choice of fixed-price menus for lunch or dinner. These usually comprise several *entrées*, *plats* and desserts to choose from in each price category – which generally works out to be cheaper than ordering à la carte. Many chefs in upmarket restaurants also offer a *menu dégustation* (tasting menu) that has numerous courses of small portions, allowing diners to try a variety of the chef's dishes. Because tasting menus are complex for both the chef and wait staff, the whole table is often required to order the same menu.

Wine

As restaurants put a large mark-up on wine, it is more affordable to further your connoisseurship with bottles purchased in shops. Local or house wine, however, is often served in carafes, and is generally quite acceptable. If in doubt, ordering a small carafe is a cheaper way to test it out; ask for a *demi* (50 cl) or *quart* (25 cl).

French law divides the country's wines into three classes, in ascending order of quality: *Vin de France*, *Indication Géographique Protégée* (IGP) and *Appellation d'Origine Protégée* (AOP). The Vin de France wines are rarely found in restaurants. For help in choosing a regional wine (IGP upwards), refer to the wine features in the regional sections of this book. For an introduction to French wine, see pages 30–31.

Classic wood interiors at Auberge du XIIème Siècle, Saché *(see p588)*

The well-kept grounds and attractive façade of Les Ursulines, Autun *(see p589)*

Water

A carafe of *eau du robinet* (tap water) is supplied on request free of charge and is perfectly safe to drink. The French also pride themselves on their wide range of mineral waters. Favourite mealtime brands include Evian and the slightly fizzy Badoit.

Prices

Prices for restaurants of the same rating are more or less consistent throughout France, except in large cities and the more fashionable resort areas, where they can be significantly more expensive. The quality of food and service is the most decisive price factor, and one can easily spend over €150 per head to eat at one of the top establishments – much more if you choose a prestigious wine.

How to Pay

Visa/Carte Bleue (V) is the most widely accepted credit card in France. MasterCard (MC) is also commonly accepted, while American Express (AE) and Diners Club (DC) tend to be accepted only in upmarket establishments. However, it is best to always carry plenty of cash, especially when touring the countryside, as small family-run restaurants and *ferme-auberges* may not take any credit cards. If in doubt, ask when making the reservation.

Service and Tipping

French meals are generally enjoyed at a leisurely pace. People think nothing of spending 4 hours at the table, so, if pressed for time, it is better to go to a café, bistro or brasserie.

A service charge of 12.5 to 15 per cent is almost always included in the price of the meal, but most French people leave a few euro cents behind in a café, and an additional 5 per cent or so of the total bill in other restaurants. In the grander restaurants, which pride themselves on their service, an additional tip of 5 to 10 per cent is expected. Around €0.50 to €0.70 is appropriate for cloakroom assistants, and €0.30 is sufficient for toilet attendants.

Dress Code

Even when dressed casually, the French are generally well turned out; visitors should aim for the same level of presentable comfort. Running shoes, shorts, beach clothes or active sportswear are unacceptable everywhere except in cafés or beachside places.

Children

French children are introduced from an early age to restaurants and as a rule are very well behaved. Some restaurants provide equipment such as highchairs or baby seats. There is often not much room for pushchairs.

A plate of delicious oysters, a popular dish on the menu of many seafood restaurants

Pets

Dogs are usually accepted at all but the most elegant restaurants. The French are great dog lovers, so do not be surprised to see your neighbour's lapdog sitting on the next-door *banquette*.

Smoking

The French now adhere to government regulations that prohibit smoking inside restaurants and cafés. However, smoking is generally permitted at outdoor tables.

Wheelchair Access

Though newer restaurants usually provide wheelchair access, it is often restricted elsewhere. A word when booking should ensure that you are given a conveniently located table and assistance, if needed, upon arrival.

Vegetarian Food

France remains difficult for vegetarians, although some progress has been made in recent years. In most restaurants

Bright, spacious sitting area at La Tour d'Argent, Paris *(see p578)*

the main courses are firmly orientated towards meat and fish. However, you can often fare well by ordering from the *entrées* and should not shy away from asking for a dish to be served without its meat content. Provided you make the request in advance, most smart restaurants will prepare a special vegetarian dish.

Only larger cities and university towns are likely to have fully fledged vegetarian restaurants. Otherwise cafés, pizzerias, creperies and Oriental restaurants are good places to find vegetarian meals.

Picnics

Picnicking is the best way to enjoy France's wonderful fresh produce while taking in the delights of the French countryside. Select local bread, cheeses and *charcuterie* from markets and enticing shops.

Picnic areas along major roads are well marked and furnished with tables and chairs, but country lanes are better still.

Recommended Restaurants

The restaurants in this guide have been carefully selected to reflect the wide range that France offers when it comes to eating out – suitable for every budget. The listings are organized by area, then by price.

At the top of the list are the country's **fine dining** restaurants, including some of the torch-bearers for the nation's world-renowned culinary art. Some of them, however, still serve classic, sauce-based haute cuisine.

Most top chefs take great pride in their individual styles and recipes, adapting haute cuisine techniques to modern tastes. Their restaurants are invariably expensive, but often make for an unforgettable dining experience. Many of these establishments are located inside elegant hotels, but are open to non-guests as well.

Traditional French restaurants concentrate on the country's classic dishes such as *escargots* (snails), pâté, *foie gras*, *steak au poivre* (pepper steak), *sole meunière* (sole pan-fried with brown butter sauce and lemon), *crème brûlée* (rich creamy custard topped with hard caramel) and chocolate mousse. Then there are **modern French** restaurants, generally with a casual-chic atmosphere – the heirs of the nouvelle cuisine movement that began in the 1960s, emphasizing fresh, top-quality ingredients and inventive food pairings that are beautifully presented and consider modern dietary needs. Contemporary chefs also tend to be more open to inspiration from across a wide spectrum of culinary styles, notably Mediterranean, Asian, North African and North American.

For a foodie, the best aspect of travelling across France has to be the country's many restaurants that specialize in authentic **regional** cuisine – eateries that lay genuine emphasis on local ingredients and traditional recipes. Many such dishes have now attained popularity around the world, such as the cheese fondues of the Alps, the rich seafood *bouillabaisse* of Marseille in Provence, the *cassoulet* – duck and bean stew – of southwest France, and the crêpes and cider of Brittany.

Although Paris may have the country's most famous restaurants, Lyon as a whole is acknowledged as France's gastronomic capital, known for its fabulous array of hearty meat dishes, such as sausages, duck pâté and roast pork.

Bistros, varying widely in size and services offered, are often informal and affordable, and stay open later than the average restaurant. Generally they offer a good, moderately priced meal from a traditional menu of an *entrée* or *hors d'oeuvre* (starter), *plats mijotés* (simmered dishes) and *grillades* (grilled fish and meats), followed by cheese and dessert. They may also have a reasonably priced three- or four-course meal, usually featuring comfort dishes such as onion soup and *boeuf bourguignon* (beef stewed in red wine).

The establishments labelled **DK Choice** are places that have been highlighted in recognition of a special feature – a celebrity chef, exquisite food, an inviting ambience or simply great value for money. Most of these eateries are popular among locals and visitors, so be sure to inquire regarding reservations well in advance to avoid waiting in long queues. Entries with the DK Choice label provide not only a delicious meal, but also a superb dining experience.

A beautifully presented plate of food at Le Jardin Gourmand, Auxerre *(see p589)*

Wine is served by the glass at Le Baron Rouge, Paris *(see p578)*

Where to Eat and Drink

Paris
Ile de la Cité, Marais and Beaubourg

DK Choice

L'As du Fallafel €
Israeli **Map** 9 C3
34 rue des Rosiers, 75004
Tel *01 48 87 63 60* **Closed** *Sat*
The falafels here are arguably the best in town, perhaps even in France, so expect to find very long queues for the famous sandwiches snaking down the street at lunchtime. The hummus is a velvety delight.

Chez H'Anna €
Israeli **Map** 9 C3
54 rue des Rosiers, 75004
Tel *01 42 74 74 99* **Closed** *Mon*
Sample creamy home-made hummus and exquisite falafels at this delightful Israeli eatery.

L'Ambassade d'Auvergne €€
Auvergnat **Map** 9 B2
22 rue du Grenier St-Lazare, 75003
Tel *01 42 72 31 22* **Closed** *Sat*
Typical Auvergne dishes such as *aligot* (mashed potatoes with cheese and garlic) are served at this rustic, dark-beamed inn.

Frenchie €€
Bistro **Map** 9 A1
5–6 rue du Nil, 75002
Tel *01 40 39 96 19* **Closed** *Sat & Sun*
Book months ahead for a chance to dine at one of Paris's hottest bistros. Try the exquisite dishes on the fixed-price menus.

Le Garde Robe €€
Tapas **Map** 8 F2
41 rue de l'Arbre Sec, 75001
Tel *01 49 26 90 60* **Closed** *Sun*
Charcuterie, cheese and oysters are served as tasty accompaniments to an outstanding wine menu.

Le Hangar €€
Traditional French **Map** 9 B2
12 impasse Berthaud, 75003
Tel *01 42 74 55 44* **Closed** *Sun & Mon*
Cheerful staff serve delicious food in this modest setting. Savour pan-fried *foie gras* on pureéd potatoes.

Les Philosophes €€
Traditional French **Map** 9 C3
28 rue Vieille du Temple, 75004
Tel *01 48 87 49 64*
Visit this delightful all-day café for first-rate onion soup, *steak frites* and the house speciality, tomato *tarte Tatin*. There is a good fixed-price menu.

Benoît €€€
Bistro **Map** 9 B3
20 rue St-Martin, 75004
Tel *01 58 00 22 05*
Enjoy hearty food in this Michelin-starred Alain Ducasse bistro. Don't miss the veal sweetbreads and *cassoulet*.

Spring €€€
Modern French **Map** 8 F2
6 rue Bailleul, 75001
Tel *01 45 96 05 72* **Closed** *Sun & Mon*
Creative versions of French classics are paired with outstanding wines at Spring. Excellent fixed-price tasting menu.

Yam'Tcha €€€
Asian **Map** 8 F2
121 rue St-Honoré, 75001
Tel *01 40 26 06 06* **Closed** *Sun–Tue*
The name means "drink tea". Try different brews to complement the mouthwatering Chinese-influenced dishes. A tea boutique is nearby, at 4 rue Sauval.

Tuileries and Opéra

Bouillon Chartier €
Brasserie **Map** 4 F4
7 rue du Faubourg Montmartre, 75009
Tel *01 47 70 86 29*
Enjoy great food in glorious *belle époque* surroundings. Try the house pâté, snails or the tender meat stew.

Bistrot Victoires €€
Traditional French **Map** 8 F1
6 rue la Vrillière, 75001
Tel *01 42 61 43 78*
Confit, *steak frites* and other tasty dishes are served in impeccable surroundings. Great value.

Le Grand Véfour, which has retained much of its original 18th-century decoration

Price Guide
Price categories are for a three-course meal for one, including tax and all service charges.

€	under €30
€€	€30 to €65
€€€	over €65

Chez Georges €€
Traditional French **Map** 8 F1
1 rue du Mail, 75002
Tel *01 42 60 07 11* **Closed** *Sat & Sun*
Try the exceptional *steak au poivre* at this vintage treasure, beloved of cookery writer Julia Child.

Pascade €€
Auvergnat **Map** 4 D5
14 rue Daunou, 75002
Tel *01 42 60 11 00* **Closed** *Sun & Mon*
Come here for *pascade* – a crispy, thick savoury or sweet *crêpe* filled with gourmet ingredients.

DK Choice

Racines €€
Wine bar **Map** 4 F5
8 passage des Panoramas, 75002
Tel *01 40 13 06 41* **Closed** *Sat & Sun*
Racines has a short menu that combines French and Italian dishes. Choose from a selection of very good wines, and try the excellent *charcuterie*, *ratatouille*, lamb and pork. Save room for the seriously seductive desserts.

Caviar Kaspia €€€
Russian **Map** 3 C5
17 pl de la Madeleine, 75008
Tel *01 42 65 33 32* **Closed** *Sun*
Sample caviar, smoked salmon and chilled vodka in the plush surroundings of an early 20th-century Russian aristocrat's salon.

Le Grand Véfour €€€
Fine dining **Map** 8 F1
17 rue de Beaujolais, 75001
Tel *01 42 96 56 27* **Closed** *Sat & Sun*
The decor in this 18th-century room has barely altered since Napoleon brought Josephine here to dine. Innovative cuisine.

Champs-Elysées and Invalides

Korean Barbecue Champs-Elysées €
Korean **Map** 3 A5
7 rue de Ponthieu, 75008
Tel *01 42 25 35 41* **Closed** *Sun*
Tuck into unbelievably tender, paper-thin beef teamed with crisp greens. Great gyoza and sushi.

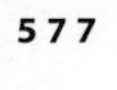

Gorgeous dining space with a retractable roof at Lasserre

Bistrot de Paris €€
Bistro **Map** 8 D3
33 rue de Lille, 75007
Tel *01 42 61 16 83* **Closed** *Sun & Mon*
This delighful Art Nouveau gem rustles up tasty bistro classics for a busy crowd of loyal customers.

Café Constant €€
Bistro **Map** 6 E3
139 rue St-Dominique, 75007
Tel *01 47 53 73 34*
Arrive early to get a seat at this popular bistro where comfort food takes centre stage. Try the veal *cordon bleu*.

Le Florimond €€
Traditional French **Map** 6 F3
19 av de la Motte-Picquet, 75007
Tel *01 45 55 40 38* **Closed** *Sun & first Sat of every month*
Hearty food such as tasty lobster ravioli is served in a bright locale. End with the vanilla *millefeuille*.

La Fontaine de Mars €€
Southwest French **Map** 6 E3
129 rue St-Dominique, 75007
Tel *01 47 05 46 44*
Duck *cassoulet* is the flagship dish at this family-friendly bistro with beautiful interiors. Great service.

Huîtrier €€
Seafood **Map** 2 D2
16 rue Saussier-Leroy, 75017
Tel *01 40 54 83 44*
The oysters steal the show at this modern, minimalist restaurant that also serves classic French fare.

Minipalais €€
Fine dining **Map** 7 A1
Grand Palais, 3 av Winston Churchill, 75008
Tel *01 42 56 42 42*
Diners are in for a gastronomic treat in a trendy setting with floor-to-ceiling windows, a fabulous terrace and a grand cocktail bar.

DK Choice

Relais de l'Entrecôte €€
Steakhouse **Map** 2 F5
15 rue Marbeuf, 75008
Tel *01 49 52 07 17*
This place is a true carnivore's paradise. The high-quality beef is cut thin, the *frites* are cooked to perfection and the secret-recipe sauce is really something to write home about.

DK Choice

Antoine €€€
Seafood **Map** 6 E1
10 av de New York, 75116
Tel *01 40 70 19 28* **Closed** *Sun & Mon*
Enjoy sensational seafood and spectacular views across the Seine to the Eiffel Tower. Try the signature sea bass for two, grilled on fennel wood and served with steamed vegetables.

L'Arpège €€€
Fine dining **Map** 7 B3
84 rue de Varenne, 75007
Tel *01 47 05 09 06* **Closed** *Sat & Sun*
Home-grown organic vegetables take pride of place in this establishment run by Michelin-starred chef Alain Passard.

L'Astrance €€€
Modern French **Map** 5 C3
4 rue Beethoven, 75016
Tel *01 40 50 84 40* **Closed** *Sat–Mon*
Book months in advance to secure a table at this intimate, globally celebrated restaurant. Sample the inspired tasting menu.

Hiramatsu €€€
Modern French **Map** 5 C1
52 rue de Longchamp, 75116
Tel *01 56 81 08 80* **Closed** *Sat & Sun*
Diners are treated to a flawless blend of French cuisine with Japanese influences in elegant surroundings. Great service.

Le Jules Verne €€€
Fine dining **Map** 6 D3
5 av Gustave Eiffel, 75007
Tel *01 45 55 61 44*
Alain Ducasse's restaurant on the Eiffel Tower's second platform offers stylish dining to complement the 360-degree view over Paris.

Lasserre €€€
Fine dining **Map** 7 A1
17 av Franklin Delano Roosevelt, 75008
Tel *01 43 59 02 13* **Closed** *Sun & Mon*
Linger over deliciously refined cooking in an elegantly decorated dining room. The retractable roof opens to the stars, and the service is impeccable.

Prunier €€€
Seafood **Map** 2 D4
16 av Victor-Hugo, 75116
Tel *01 44 17 35 85* **Closed** *Sun*
Enjoy a seasonal menu of inventive fish dishes, plus an impressive variety of caviars, at this beautiful Art Deco gem.

Left Bank

Breakfast in America €
American **Map** 9 A5
17 rue des Ecoles, 75005
Tel *01 43 54 50 28*
All-day breakfasts and other US staples – bacon, pancakes, burgers and more – are served at this classic diner. There is another branch on the Right Bank.

Le Loubnane €
Lebanese **Map** 9 A4
29 rue Gallande, 75005
Tel *01 43 26 70 60* **Closed** *Mon*
Delicious meze is dished up at this family-run establishment. Don't miss the exceptional pistachio-stuffed *crêpes*.

L'Agrume €€
Bistro **Map** 13 C3
15 rue des Fossés St-Marcel, 75005
Tel *01 43 31 86 48* **Closed** *Sun & Mon*
Foodies line up to sample Franck Marchesi-Grandi's delicious five-course tasting menu.

DK Choice

Brasserie Balzar €€
Brasserie **Map** 9 A5
49 rue des Ecoles, 75005
Tel *01 43 54 13 67*
Skilled waiters in long aprons serve typical brasserie fare, such as onion soup, at this venerable institution, the former haunt of many great artists and literary figures. There is a separate café and bar section.

L'Epigramme €€
Bistro **Map** 8 F4
9 rue de l'Eperon, 75006
Tel *01 44 41 00 09* **Closed** *Sun & Mon*
Enjoy bistro classics such as Basque pork with turnip *choucroute* and traditional *escargots*.

Kitchen Galerie Bis €€
Modern French **Map** 8 F4
25 rue des Grands Augustins, 75006
Tel *01 46 33 00 85* **Closed** *Sun & Mon*
This place, the younger sibling to the celebrated original, offers contemporary French cuisine with an Asian twist. Fabulous starters.

For more information on types of restaurants *see p575*

Mavrommatis €€
Greek **Map** 13 B2
42 rue Daubenton, 75005
Tel *01 43 31 17 17* **Closed** *Mon*
Beautifully presented dishes and stylish decor are teamed with friendly service at Mavrommatis. Be sure to try the *moussaka*.

Les Papilles €€
Bistro **Map** 12 F1
30 rue Gay Lussac, 75005
Tel *01 43 25 20 79* **Closed** *Sun & Mon*
There are daily changing menus at this deli, coffee bar, wine shop and bistro all rolled into one.

Le Procope €€
Traditional French **Map** 8 F4
13 rue de l'Ancienne Comédie, 75006
Tel *01 40 46 79 00*
Opened in 1686, the city's oldest restaurant is delightfully nostalgic. Great selection of desserts.

Shu €€
Japanese **Map** 8 F4
8 rue Suger, 75006
Tel *01 46 34 25 88* **Closed** *Sun*
There's no menu in this *omakase*-style restaurant. The traditional dishes look and taste stunning.

Terroir Parisien €€
Traditional French **Map** 9 B5
20 rue St-Victor, 75005
Tel *01 44 31 54 54*
This beautifully designed space serves delicious, locally sourced food cooked by an award-winning chef.

Le Timbre €€
Bistro **Map** 12 D1
3 rue Ste-Beuve, 75006
Tel *01 45 49 10 40* **Closed** *Sun & Mon*
All the dishes here are prepared using only the finest, freshest ingredients. Delicious *millefeuille*.

Le Comptoir du Relais €€€
Bistro **Map** 8 F4
9 carrefour de l'Odéon, 75006
Tel *01 44 27 07 97*
Try the lobster bisque at this much celebrated temple to French bistro cuisine. No bookings, so get there early.

DK Choice

La Tour d'Argent €€€
Fine dining **Map** 9 B5
15 quai de la Tournelle, 75005
Tel *01 43 54 23 31* **Closed** *Sun & Mon*
This family-run Paris institution, with its romantic sixth-floor dining room and panoramic views, is world-famous. The ground-floor bar doubles as a gastronomic museum.

Lovely *belle époque* interior of popular Bofinger brasserie

Further Afield

Amici Miei €
Italian
44 rue St-Sabin, 75011
Tel *01 42 71 82 62* **Closed** *Sun & Mon*
This popular, unpretentious *trattoria* rolls out some of the best thin-crust pizzas in Paris. Try the authentic Sardinian specialties, too. Arrive early to avoid the queue.

Arbre de Sel €
Korean
138 rue de Vaugirard, 75015
Tel *01 47 83 29 52* **Closed** *Sun*
The beautifully presented dishes here range from spicy to very spicy. Vegetarian options are also available. Friendly and efficient service.

DK Choice

Le Baron Rouge €
Wine bar
1 rue Théophile Roussel, 75012
Tel *01 43 43 14 32*
Fresh, succulent oysters brought directly from the Atlantic coast can be eaten inside the tiny bustling bar or on the pavement, standing around large barrels. They also have a great selection of cheese, *charcuterie* and wine by the glass. Great, fun vibe.

Chez Gladines €
Basque
30 rue des Cinq Diamants, 75013
Tel *01 45 80 70 10*
Huge salads, smothered with sautéed potatoes, are served in earthenware bowls at this no-frills eatery.

Chez Toinette €
Traditional French
20 rue Germain Pilon, 75018
Tel *01 42 54 44 36* **Closed** *Sun & Mon*
Enjoy delectable duck *foie gras*, snails, lamb shank and sea bass at this unassuming restaurant with a cosy interior.

Rose Bakery €
Vegetarian
46 rue des Martyrs, 75009
Tel *01 42 82 12 80*
This is the haunt of British expatriates homesick for scones. The home-made carrot cake is legendary. Fabulous coffee and Neal's Yard cheeses, plus a selection of healthy brunches.

La Balançoire €€
Traditional French
6 rue Aristide Bruant, 75018
Tel *01 42 23 70 83* **Closed** *Sun & Mon*
Filled with jars of sweets, this child-friendly restaurant has a menu that features lots of classics. The steak and *foie gras* are particularly noteworthy. Helpful and friendly staff.

Le Bistrot Paul Bert €€
Bistro
18 rue Paul Bert, 75011
Tel *01 43 72 24 01* **Closed** *Sun & Mon*
Generous portions of top-notch food, a serious wine list and lovely prewar decor await at this ever-popular bistro. The fixed-priced lunch menu is great value. Booking ahead is recommended.

Bofinger €€
Brasserie
5–7 rue de la Bastille, 75004
Tel *01 42 72 87 82*
The city's most beautiful brasserie has a perfectly preserved *belle époque* interior. On the menu are classic Alsatian dishes, plus beer on tap.

La Cantine du Troquet €€
Basque
101 rue de l'Ouest, 75014
Tel *01 45 40 04 98* **Closed** *Sun & Mon*
This is a popular restaurant where mouthwatering regional food is served up with a unique touch at canteen-style tables. The desserts are excellent, too.

La Coupole €€
Brasserie
102 bd du Montparnasse, 75014
Tel *01 43 20 14 20*
Seafood platters draw the crowds at this historic 600-seat brasserie with authentic Art Deco interiors. A veritable Parisian landmark.

Marty €€
Brasserie
20 av des Gobelins, 75005
Tel *01 43 31 39 51*
Robust cooking is served in original 1913 interiors. Sample the roast duck or the seafood platters. For a truly unique experience, book a seat at the chef's table.

Le Miroir €€
Bistro
94 rue des Martyrs, 75018
Tel *01 46 06 50 73* **Closed** *Mon*
Comfort food and lovely desserts (try the lemon pie) are cooked by haute cuisine-trained chefs.

La Villa Corse €€
Corsican
164 bd de Grenelle, 75015
Tel *01 53 86 70 81* **Closed** *Sun*
An inventive Corsican menu is delivered in a hospitable setting, with a cosy bar and a library.

DK Choice

La Closerie des Lilas €€€
Traditional French
171 bd du Montparnasse, 75006
Tel *01 40 51 34 50*
Splash out on classic dishes, such as *boeuf bourguignon*, in the restaurant proper, or head for the brasserie and bar, where a pianist plays every evening. Hemingway was a regular at this historic establishment.

Ile-de-France

BRAY SUR SEINE: Au Bon Laboureur €
Seafood
2 rue Grande, 77480
Tel *01 60 67 10 81* **Closed** *Wed & Sun eve*
An unassuming exterior belies the award-winning fare on offer at this great-value hotel restaurant.

DAMPIERRE: Auberge Saint-Pierre €
Traditional French
1 rue de Chevreuse, 78720
Tel *01 30 52 53 53* **Closed** *Sun eve, Mon & Tue*
This 17th-century half-timbered house offers a welcoming dining room and very good food.

FONTAINEBLEAU: L'Axel €€
Modern French
43 rue de France, 77300
Tel *01 64 22 01 57* **Closed** *Mon & Tue, Wed lunch*
Rising star Kunihisa Goto and his team run this Michelin-starred kitchen with Japanese creativity. Try the chef's tasting menu.

LE PERREUX SUR MARNE: Les Magnolias €€
Fine dining
48 av de Bry, 94170
Tel *01 48 72 47 43* **Closed** *Sat lunch, Sun & Mon*
For an avant-garde take on classic dishes, try the lobster ravioli or one of the delicious desserts.

NEUILLY-SUR-SEINE: Le Zinc Zinc €
Bistro
209 ter av du Général-de-Gaulle, 92200
Tel *01 40 88 36 06*
Offering great food and wines from all over France, this lively bistro is also open for breakfast.

PROVINS: Aux Vieux Remparts €€
Bistro
3 rue Couverte, 77160
Tel *01 64 08 94 00*
In a half-timbered building, this eatery offers dishes such as mascarpone, white radish with shiso, and smoked salmon. Alfresco dining in the summer.

RAMBOUILLET: Le Cheval Rouge €€
Traditional French
78 rue du Général de Gaulle, 78120
Tel *01 30 88 80 61* **Closed** *Tue & Wed*
This is the place for top-notch French cuisine. Try *foie gras* and *morilles* mushrooms, and roast lamb with thyme.

ST-GERMAIN-EN-LAYE: Le Saint Exupéry €€
Traditional French
11 av des Loges, 78100
Tel *01 39 21 50 90* **Closed** *Sat & Sun*
Diners choose this pleasant restaurant for specialities such as shellfish and grilled meat.

DK Choice

VERSAILLES: Ramsay Trianon Palace €€€
Fine dining
1 bd de la Reine, 78000
Tel *01 30 84 50 18* **Closed** *Sun*
Gordon Ramsay's restaurant is the jewel in the crown of this superb royal château hotel. Expect a culinary extravaganza in majestic surroundings, but be prepared to feel considerably lighter in the pockets after the meal. Dinner only.

The façade of L'Axel, a Michelin-starred restaurant in Fontainebleau

Le Nord and Picardy

AIRE-SUR-LA-LYS: Hostellerie des Trois Mousquetaires €€
Traditional French
Château de la Redoute, rte de Béthune, 62120
Tel *03 21 39 01 11* **Closed** *Sun eve*
Good old-fashioned cooking such as turbot with Saint Omer cauliflower and Rossini steak can be sampled here.

AMIENS: L'Aubergade €€€
Regional
78 rte Nationale
Tel *03 22 89 51 41* **Closed** *Sun & Mon*
Located just outside Amiens, this prestigious restaurant has lovely decor and excellent regional fare.

ARRAS: La Faisanderie €€
Traditional French
45 Grand Place, 62000
Tel *03 21 48 20 76* **Closed** *Sun eve, Mon, Thu lunch*
This superb restaurant with a Baroque brick-vaulted dining room offers a traditional menu.

BEAUVAIS: Le Palais d'Antan €€
Traditional French
75 rue St-Pierre, 60000
Tel *03 44 45 06 52* **Closed** *Tue*
Enjoy inventive cuisine with a great view of the impressive cathedral. Try grilled monkfish with vegetables, potatoes and Camembert sauce.

BELLE-EGLISE: La Grange de la Belle Eglise €€€
Traditional French
28 bd René-Aimé-la-Gabrielle, 60540
Tel *03 44 08 49 00* **Closed** *Sun eve, Mon & Tue lunch*
Specialities at this luxury restaurant include lobster and scallops with Sauternes sauce.

BOULOGNE-SUR-MER: La Plage €€
Seafood
124 bd Sainte-Beuve, 62200
Tel *03 21 99 90 90* **Closed** *Wed eve*
Located on the waterfront, La Plage is the place for modern takes on classic seafood dishes. Try the tartare of beef with fresh oysters and wasabi, or roast monkfish with parsnip purée and grilled hazelnuts.

CALAIS: Histoire Ancienne €€
Traditional French
20 rue Royale, 62100
Tel *03 21 34 11 20* **Closed** *Sun & Mon eves; Jul–Aug: Mon & Sun*
Come to the Histoire Ancienne for old-world bistro-style cooking: marrowbones, snails in garlic butter and pepper steak.

The rustic interior decor of Estaminet T'Kasteel Hof, in Cassel

CALAIS: La Sole Meunière €€
Seafood
1 bd de la Résistance 62100
Tel *03 21 34 43 01* **Closed** *Sun eve, Mon*
The fish served here comes straight from the harbour. Do not miss the seafood platter.

CAMBRAI: L'Escargot €€
Bistro
10 rue du Général de Gaulle, 59400
Tel *03 27 81 24 54* **Closed** *Wed & Fri eve*
Savour simple dishes such as lamb chops, veal kidneys, trout and bream at this cosy, rustic eatery.

CASSEL: Estaminet T'Kasteel Hof €€
Traditional French
Rue St-Nicolas, 59670
Tel *03 28 40 59 29* **Closed** *Mon–Wed*
This no-frills Flanders café has fantastic views and a shop selling local produce. Booking advised.

COMPIEGNE: Bistrot de Flandre €€
Traditional French
2 rue d'Amiens, 60200
Tel *03 44 83 26 35* **Closed** *Sun eve*
Try the roast fillet steak with peppers at this classic bistro with hearty meals and a good wine list.

DOUAI: La Terrasse €€
Seafood
36 Terrasse St-Pierre, 59500
Tel *03 27 88 70 04*
Hidden in a side street, this restaurant dishes up fantastic fresh fish and delectable *fois gras*.

DUNKERQUE: L'Auberge de Jules €€
Seafood
9 rue de la Poudrière, 59140
Tel *03 28 63 68 80* **Closed** *Sat & Sun; 2 weeks in Aug*
Fresh fish and shellfish dishes are prepared at this popular bistro near the port. Cheery atmosphere.

FAVIERES: La Clé des Champs €€
Traditional French
13 pl Frères Caudron, 80120
Tel *03 22 27 88 00* **Closed** *Mon & Tue*
Specialities at this great-value eatery include Saint Vaast oysters and pigeon with cabbage and chicory-flavoured sauce.

LAON: Zorn-La Petite Auberge €€
Modern French
45 bd Brossolette, 02000
Tel *03 23 23 02 38* **Closed** *Sat lunch, Sun, Mon eve*
Enjoy creative cooking with an emphasis on fish. Stylish decor and an excellent wine list.

LENS: L'Atelier de Marc Meurin €€
Regional
Parc du Musée du Louvre-Lens, 97 rue Paul Bert, 62300
Tel *03 21 18 24 90* **Closed** *Tue & Sun eves*
Just steps from the Louvre-Lens museum, Marc Meurin creates great dishes from local produce.

LILLE: Au Vieux de la Vieille €€
Regional
2–4 rue des Vieux-Murs, 59800
Tel *03 20 13 81 64*
This café specializes in Flemish cuisine. Try the chicken in *Maroilles* cheese.

LILLE: Le Compostelle €€
Traditional French
4 rue Saint-Etienne, 59800
Tel *03 28 38 08 30* **Closed** *Sun eve*
Great food and delicious desserts are served in a fine 16th-century Renaissance interior.

LILLE: N'Autre Monde €€
Bistro
1 bis rue du Cure Saint-Etienne, 59000
Tel *03 20 15 01 31* **Closed** *Mon*
The menu changes seasonally at this bijou bistro, and it includes innovative dishes with an exotic touch such as bream served with potato and coconut cream.

DK Choice

MONTREUIL SUR MER: Auberge de la Grenouillère €€€
Traditional French
19 rue de la Grenouillère, La Madelaine sous Montreuil, 62170
Tel *03 21 06 07 22* **Closed** *Mon lunch, Tue & Wed*
Diners come to enjoy the creative 11-course tasting menu at this riverside farm restaurant with traditional interiors. Located in a tranquil setting by a stream.

POIX-DE-PICARDIE: L'Auberge de la Forge €€
Traditional French
14 rue du 49ème Régiment BCA Caulières, 80290
Tel *03 22 38 00 91* **Closed** *Sun eve*
There are great-value meals to be had at this half-timbered Picardy coaching inn, plus a brasserie for those who just want to grab a quick bite to eat.

ROYE: La Flamiche €€
Traditional French
20 pl de l'Hôtel de Ville, 80700
Tel *03 22 87 00 56* **Closed** *Sun eve, Mon & Tue*
Seasonal dishes are prepared with great originality at this top-notch restaurant. Try the scallops and oysters wrapped in spinach and served with a Japanese seaweed sauce.

STEENVOORDE: Auberge du Noord Meulen €
Traditional French
rte du Whormhout, 59112
Tel *03 28 48 11 18*
Delicious food is served in wonderfully quaint surroundings. Try the *ficelle picarde* (baked pancake with ham, mushrooms and cream).

Champagne

CHALONS-EN-CHAMPAGNE: Au Carillon Gourmand €€
Traditional French
15 pl Monseigneur Tissier, 51000
Tel *03 26 64 45 07* **Closed** *Sun eve, Mon & Wed eve*
This welcoming restaurant offers a traditional menu that features dishes such as saddle of rabbit served with mustard sauce and beef fillet in bread crust with chorizo.

CHALONS-EN-CHAMPAGNE: Le Petit Pasteur €€
Bistro
42 rue Pasteur, 51000
Tel *03 26 68 24 78* **Closed** *Sun & Wed eves, Mon*
Diners can choose from bistro, regional and traditional menus at this unpretentious restaurant with simple decor. There is terrace seating on sunny days.

CHARLEVILLE-MEZIERES: Au Cochon Qui Louche €€
Traditional French
31 rue Victoire Cousin 08000
Tel *03 24 35 49 05* **Closed** *Sun & Mon*
Enjoy a bistro menu and home-style cooking at this fun eatery. The desserts are delicious –don't miss the chocolate mousse.

Key to Price Guide *see p576*

COLOMBEY-LES-DEUX-EGLISES: Hostellerie La Montagne €€
Traditional French
10 rue Pisseloup, 52330
Tel *03 25 01 51 69* **Closed** *Mon & Tue*
Don't miss the Ile d'Yeu sole with parsnip gnocchi at this elegant restaurant with friendly service.

CUMIERES: Le Caveau €€
Traditional French
44 rue de la Coopérative, 51480
Tel *03 26 54 83 23* **Closed** *Sun & Tue eves, Mon*
Dine on excellent *foie gras* salad and duck breast in red wine inside a rustic old vaulted cellar.

EPERNAY: La Cave à Champagne €€
Traditional French
16 rue Gambetta, 51200
Tel *03 26 55 50 70* **Closed** *Tue & Wed*
Try the steak with Pinot Noir sauce or the cod in Chardonnay at this cosy restaurant that reinvents classic French dishes using local wines.

EPERNAY: Les Berceaux €€€
Regional
13 rue des Berceaux, 51200
Tel *03 26 55 28 84* **Closed** *Mon & Tue*
This centrally located hotel houses both an upscale restaurant and an informal bistro. They both serve classic local cuisine, which includes game dishes in season.

GIFFAUMONT-CHAMPAUBERT: La Grange aux Abeilles €
Creperie
4 rue du Grand Der, 51290
Tel *03 26 72 61 97* **Closed** *Mon & Tue, Wed eve*
An ancient beekeepers' barn has been converted into a restaurant and creperie. It is possible to buy pots of honey, too. Good service.

LANGRES: Restaurant Diderot €€
Traditional French
4 rue de l'Estres, 52200
Tel *03 25 87 07 00* **Closed** *Wed lunch*
This elegant, beamed restaurant specializes in putting creative twists on classic French dishes. Try the loin of lamb with fig juice, or haddock in a bacon crust with red wine. Hearty portions.

MAGNANT: Le Val Moret €€
Modern French
Rue du Maréchal Leclerc, 10110
Tel *03 25 29 85 12*
Chef Julien Lasserre offers original takes on classic dishes. Meat is sourced from the adjacent farm owned by the restaurant. The creative menu changes seasonally.

MAISONS LES CHAOURCE: Aux Maisons €€
Regional
11 rue Anciens Combattants d'AFN, 10210
Tel *03 25 70 07 19* **Closed** *Sun eve*
Authentic local fare with creative variations is served in a converted barn. The guinea fowl breast with Marc de Champagne sauce is a menu highlight.

NOGENT-SUR-SEINE: Le Beau Rivage €€
Traditional French
20 rue Villiers-aux-Choux, 10400
Tel *03 25 39 84 22* **Closed** *Sun eve & Mon*
Expect delicious food, old-school service, and fabulous views of the Seine at this restaurant. The desserts are superb.

PONT-SAINTE-MARIE: Bistrot DuPont €€
Traditional French
5 pl Charles de Gaulle, 10150
Tel *03 25 80 90 99* **Closed** *Mon, Thu & Sun eves*
Staple bistro choices are on the menu at this lively eatery. House specials include home-made *foie gras*, *coq au vin*, grilled steak and *andouillette de Troyes* (pork sausages).

REIMS: Brasserie du Boulingrin €€
Traditional French
48 rue de Mars, 51100
Tel *03 26 40 96 22* **Closed** *Sun*
A very popular meeting place for locals, this eatery serves excellent oysters and steak tartare.

DK Choice

REIMS: Café du Palais €€
Traditional French
14 pl Myron Herrick, 51100
Tel *03 26 47 52 54* **Closed** *Sun, Mon; Tue–Fri dinner*
Enter an Aladdin's cave of theatrical memorabilia under a heritage-listed stained-glass roof. A much-loved family-run brasserie, the Café du Palais offers excellent main dishes, great desserts and a fine selection of Champagne.

SERMIERS: Lys du Roy €
Traditional French
1 rte de Damery, 51500
Tel *03 26 97 66 11* **Closed** *Mon & Tue eves, Wed*
Quaint old-world exteriors and a menu of classic choices with a refined twist await here. The specialities include home-made *foie gras* and the entrecote steak with Chaource cheese sauce.

SEZANNE: Le Relais Champenois €€
Traditional French
157 rue Notre Dame, 51120
Tel *03 26 80 58 03* **Closed** *Sun & Fri eves*
Eat among rustic beams and copper saucepans. The chef showcases local products in dishes such as red mullet fillets with Ratafia sauce, and duck breast with Griotte cherries.

TINQUEUX: Assiette Champenoise €€€
Traditional French
40 av Paul Vaillant-Couturier, 51430
Tel *03 26 84 64 64* **Closed** *Tue & Wed*
Enjoy exquisitely prepared dishes of lobster, scallops, turbot and venison at this delightful restaurant with stylish modern interiors. There is a choice of menus – the lunchtime taster menu is particularly recommended.

TROYES: Aux Crieurs de Vin €€
Bistro
4 pl Jean Jaurès, 10000
Tel *03 25 40 01 01* **Closed** *Sun & Mon*
The home-made cooking at this lively wine shop and bistro with an informal atmosphere and wooden tables and chairs attracts both families and local businesspeople. Try the local speciality – *andouillette* sausage – and wash it down with their good choice of natural wines.

TROYES: Le Valentino €€
Regional
35 rue Paillot de Montabert, 10000
Tel *03 25 73 14 14* **Closed** *Sun & Mon*
The innovative menu at this picturesque half-timbered house with a courtyard for outdoor dining features dishes such as turbot with morel mushroom sauce.

Exquisite fare laid out at the brasserie Café du Palais, Reims

Gracefully laid table at the refined L'Arnsbourg in Baerenthal

VILLIERS-SUR-SUIZE: Auberge de la Fontaine €€
Traditional French
2 pl de la Fontaine, 52210
Tel *03 25 31 22 22* **Closed** *Sat lunch & Sun eve*
The menu offers lots of choice, the food is good and prices are fairly low. Great rustic setting.

VINAY: La Briqueterie €€€
Modern French
4 rte de Sézanne, 51530
Tel *03 26 59 99 99* **Closed** *Sat lunch*
Sitting pretty amid Champagne vineyards, this plush restaurant prepares creative dishes. The wine list showcases local champagnes.

Alsace and Lorraine

BAERENTHAL: L'Arnsbourg €€€
Traditional French
18 Untermuhlthal, 57230
Tel *03 87 06 50 85* **Closed** *Mon & Tue*
Enjoy an outstanding dining experience at one of France's finest restaurants, tucked away in the countryside.

BITCHE: Le Strasbourg €€
Traditional French
24 rue Col. Teyssier, 57230
Tel *03 87 96 00 44* **Closed** *Sun eve, Mon, Tue lunch*
Try a wide range of fish dishes – Guilvinec sole, lobster, pike-perch – at this first-class restaurant with a big dining room. The home-made *foie gras* is also delicious.

COLMAR: Wistub Brenner €€
Regional
1 rue de Turenne, 68000
Tel *03 89 41 42 33*
Wistub Brenner is famous for its Alsatian dishes and cheery, unpretentious atmosphere. The salad with potent Munster cheese is especially popular.

COLMAR: JY's €€€
Modern French
17 rue de la Poissonerie 68000
Tel *03 89 21 53 60* **Closed** *Sun & Mon*
Contemporary dining based on an audacious fusion of flavours can be sampled in this 17th-century building. Excellent wine list. Reasonable prices.

ILLHAEUSERN: L'Auberge de l'Ill €€€
Regional
2 rue de Collonges, 68970
Tel *03 89 71 89 00* **Closed** *Mon & Tue*
This Michelin-starred establishment offers a varied selection of Alsatian dishes. Try the truffle wrapped in *fois gras*.

KAYSERSBERG: Restaurant Saint Alexis €
Traditional French
Lieu-dit Saint Alexis, 68240
Tel *03 89 73 90 38* **Closed** *Fri*
This eatery in the mountains offers excellent traditional cooking, including delicious soups and omelettes, plus game dishes and sauerkraut.

LEMBACH: Gimbelhof €€
Traditional French
Rte Forestière, 67510
Tel *03 88 94 43 58* **Closed** *Mon & Tue*
Surrounded by a forest and ruined medieval castles, Gimbelhof is a successful family-run hotel-restaurant.

LES THONS: Le Couvent des Cordeliers €
Regional
Les Thons, 88410
Tel *03 29 07 90 84* **Closed** *Mon & Tue–Fri eves*
The owner roasts slices of gammon on an open fire at this popular, friendly eatery. The steak with fried mushrooms is also recommended.

MARLENHEIM: Le Cerf €€€
Traditional French
30 rue Général de Gaulle, 67520
Tel *03 88 87 73 73* **Closed** *Tue & Wed*
At this half-timbered coaching inn with a cobbled courtyard, guests can dine on delicious dishes such as fillet of beef cooked in Licorne Black Beer served with seasonal vegetables.

METZ: Le Bistro des Sommeliers €€
Bistro
10 rue Pasteur, 57000
Tel *03 87 63 40 20* **Closed** *Sat lunch, Sun*
Sample excellent food and a wide range of wines in a brasserie setting. The fixed-price menu is great value.

METZ: Le Magasin aux Vivres €€
Traditional French
5 av Ney, 57000
Tel *03 87 17 17 17* **Closed** *Sat lunch, Sun eve & Mon*
This is a great place to enjoy good food in elegant historic surroundings. The dessert menu is outstanding. Cookery lessons are also offered.

NANCY: Au Grand Serieux €
Brasserie
27 rue Raugraff, 54000
Tel *03 83 36 68 87* **Closed** *Sun & Mon, Tue–Sat lunch, Fri eve*
A popular institution since 1870, this eatery serves a daily changing menu based on fresh market produce. Good local wine list. Friendly service.

NANCY: La Poule'Ange €€
Modern French
74 rue Saint-Julien, 54000
Tel *03 83 34 19 62* **Closed** *Sun eve, Mon*
Rustic-chic decor with comfortable chairs sets the scene at this landmark restaurant just five minutes' walk from Place Stanislas. The menu offers beautifully presented dishes such as seared prawns with carrot mousse and *langoustine bisque*.

NIEDERSTEINBACH: Au Wasigenstein €€
Regional
32 rue Principale Wengelsbach, 67510
Tel *03 88 09 50 54* **Closed** *Mon & Tue; Nov–Feb: Sun–Thu*
This excellent village auberge in a stunning location boasts a lovely terrace for outdoor dining. On the menu is superb wild game.

OBERNAI: La Fourchette des Ducs €€€
Traditional French
6 rue de la Gare, 67210
Tel *03 88 48 33 38* **Closed** *Sun eve, Mon, Tue–Sat lunch*
A sophisticated dining experience based on authentic local flavours is guaranteed at this luxury restaurant, founded in the 1920s by local motoring genius Ettore Bugatti.

RIBEAUVILLE: Zum Pfifferhüs €€
Regional
14 Grand'Rue, 68150
Tel *03 89 73 62 28* **Closed** *Wed & Thu*
An authentic *winstub* on the main street, this charming wine bar and restaurant serves dishes such as ham hock, *choucroute* and Mirabelle plum tart. There's a good selection of wine by the glass.

Key to Price Guide *see p576*

RIQUEWIHR: Le Sarment d'Or €€
Traditional French
4 rue du Cerf, 68340
Tel *03 89 86 02 86* **Closed** *Sun eve, Mon, Tue lunch*
Fabulous food is served in this 17th-century house in a quiet corner of this pretty village. The elegantly decorated beamed dining room adds to the charm. Great attention to detail.

SAVERNE: Taverne Katz €€
Regional
80 Grand Rue, 67700
Tel *03 88 71 16 56* **Closed** *Mon & Thu eves*
The braised hock in beer is the highlight of the menu at this restaurant with stunning exterior and beautifully panelled interiors.

STRASBOURG: Winstub Zuem Strissel €
Regional
5 pl de la Grande Boucherie, 67000
Tel *03 88 32 14 73*
Good-value brasserie-style food is served at this restaurant dating from the 1300s. Try the *bibelekäse* (cream cheese and chips).

DK Choice

STRASBOURG: Buerehiesel €€€
Traditional French
4 Parc de Orangerie, 67000
Tel *038 84 56 65* **Closed** *Sun & Mon*
Buerehiesel is a unique Michelin-starred restaurant that gave up its three Rosettes to give clients a better deal. Now it serves great food without all the bells and whistles that go with such star-rated establishments.

WISSEMBOURG: Daniel Rebert €
Bistro
7 pl du Marché aux Choux, 67100
Tel *03 88 94 01 66* **Closed** *Mon*
This lovely patisserie has a discreet tearoom at the back serving light lunches and coffee, plus exquisite cakes.

Normandy

ACQUIGNY: Hostellerie d'Acquigny €€
Traditional French
1 rue Evreux, 27400
Tel *02 32 50 20 05* **Closed** *Sun eve, Mon & Tue*
This former coaching inn houses a smart restaurant with good-value set menus, which include vegetarian options, great service and an eclectic wine list.

ALENCON: Le Bistro €€
Bistro
21 rue de Sarthe, 61000
Tel *02 33 26 51 69* **Closed** *Sun & Mon*
Featuring a well-stocked wine list, this classic French bistro also has a distinctive green-painted façade, red-chequered tablecloths and old film posters.

AUMALE: La Villa des Houx €€
Regional
6 av Général de Gaulle, 76390
Tel *02 35 93 93 30* **Closed** *Oct–Mar: Sun eve*
Housed in a former police station, this restaurant offers a taste of real Normandy cuisine. Try the apricot *foie gras* starter.

BARNEVILLE-CARTERET: Marine €€
Traditional French
11 rue de Paris, 50270
Tel *02 33 53 83 31* **Closed** *Nov–mid-Mar*
The wine list matches the exquisite food at this modern, stylish dining room with a panoramic view of the port. Excellent service.

BAYEUX: Le Lion d'Or €€
Traditional French
71 rue St-Jean, 14400
Tel *02 31 92 06 90* **Closed** *Tue & Sat lunch; mid-Nov–mid-Mar: Mon eve*
Le Lion d'Or serves a range of well-prepared, traditional Normandy dishes in a converted 18th-century post office. The desserts are a highlight. Advance booking recommended.

BEUVRON-EN-AUGE: Le Pavé Auge €€
Regional
Les Halles, 14430
Tel *02 31 79 26 71* **Closed** *Mon & Tue*
Once a village market hall, this restaurant uses locally sourced produce. The focus is on fish.

Beautiful glass-covered dining area at Buerehiesel in Strasbourg

BLAINVILLE-SUR-MER: Le Mascaret €€
Modern French
1 rue de Bas, 50560
Tel *02 33 45 86 09* **Closed** *Sep–mid-Jul: Sun & Mon*
Experience top experimental cuisine, made with fresh, home-grown produce. The five-course tasting menu is great value.

BRICQUEVILLE-SUR-MER: Couleurs Saveurs €€
Modern French
2 rte de Bretonnière, 50290
Tel *02 33 61 65 62* **Closed** *Wed; Mon & Sun eves*
The modern dining room of this coastal restaurant sets the stage for a menu where regional produce meets Oriental spices.

CAEN: Le Pressoir – Ivan Vautier €€€
Fine dining
3 av Henry-Chéron, 14000
Tel *02 31 73 32 71* **Closed** *Mon & Sun eve*
Award-winning chef Ivan Vautier creates delectable dishes for discerning guests, with emphasis on using the best local produce.

CHERBOURG: Le Faitout €€
Bistro
25 rue Tour-Carrée, 50100
Tel *02 33 04 25 04* **Closed** *Sun; Mon–Wed lunch*
A bastion of culinary tradition, Le Faitout is an animated bistro-style restaurant serving wholesome dishes.

DEAUVILLE: Le Spinnaker €€
Seafood
52 rue Mirabeau, 14800
Tel *02 31 88 24 40* **Closed** *Mon & Tue*
One of Normandy's finest fish restaurants, Le Spinnaker has an attractive modern dining room. It also offers grilled meat dishes.

DIEPPE: Bistrot du Pollet €€
Bistro
23 rue Tête de Boeuf, 76200
Tel *02 35 84 68 57* **Closed** *Sun & Mon*
Reservations are strongly recommended at this small, friendly eatery with a simple but wholesome menu. Try the haddock salad or grilled sardines.

FALAISE: L'Attache €€
Traditional French
Rte de Caen, 14700
Tel *02 31 90 05 38* **Closed** *Tue & Wed*
The chef uses unusual plants and aromatic herbs to flavour his cooking at this beautifully renovated former staging post.

For more information on types of restaurants *see p575*

FECAMP: La Marée €€
Seafood
77 quai Bérigny, 76400
Tel *02 35 29 39 15* **Closed** *Mon, Thu & Sun eves*
This very popular and lively first-floor restaurant offers huge seafood platters and views of the fishing port.

GISORS: Le Cappeville €€
Regional
17 rue Cappeville, 27410
Tel *02 32 55 11 08* **Closed** *Wed & Thu*
Sample the refined dishes at this elegantly furbished converted town house. Impressive cheeseboard on offer.

GRANVILLE: La Citadelle €€
Seafood
34 rue du Port, 50406
Tel *02 33 50 34 10* **Closed** *Wed; Oct–Mar: Tue*
Overlooking the bay of St-Michel, this charming restaurant is said to serve the biggest portions of sole in town. There are various fixed menus to choose from.

HONFLEUR: La Ferme St-Siméon €€€
Fine dining
Rue A. Marais, 14600
Tel *02 31 81 78 00*
There is an excellent wine list to go with the delectable fish on offer at this luxurious spa-hotel restaurant.

JUVIGNY-SOUS-ANDAINE: Au Bon Accueil €€
Traditional French
23 pl St-Michel, 61140
Tel *02 33 38 10 04* **Closed** *Sun eve, Mon*
Good menus are prepared from fresh local produce at this stylish restaurant offering creative French cuisine.

LA CROIX ST-LEUFROY: Le Cheval Blanc €€
Traditional French
27 rue de Louviers, 27490
Tel *02 32 34 82 86* **Closed** *Sun & Tue eves, Wed*
Drive out to a quiet village in the Eure Valley for a taste of top-notch cuisine. Excellent cheese selection and good-value fixed-price menu.

LA FERRIERE AUX ETANGS: Auberge de la Mine €€
Regional
Le Gué-Plat, 61450
Tel *02 33 66 91 10* **Closed** *Sun eve, Mon & Tue*
Authentic Norman dishes are prepared with refreshing originality at this auberge. The desserts are to die for.

Entrance to the ever-popular brasserie La Mère Poulard, Mont-St-Michel

LE BREUIL-EN-AUGE: Le Dauphin €€
Traditional French
2 rue de l'Eglise, 14130
Tel *02 31 65 08 11* **Closed** *Sun eve, Mon*
The chef at this restaurant in a half-timbered Normandy house reinvents classic dishes using the best local produce.

LE HAVRE: Jean-Luc Tartarin €€€
Fine dining
73 av Foch, 76600
Tel *02 35 45 46 20* **Closed** *Sun & Mon*
Diners come to this restaurant for the imaginative dishes based on produce sourced from local farms and fishing harbours, accompanied by fine service.

LES ANDELYS: La Chaine d'Or €€
Traditional French
27 rue Grande, 27700
Tel *02 32 54 00 31* **Closed** *Sun eve, Tue*
Exquisite culinary classics, perfectly prepared, can be enjoyed in a romantic setting on the banks of the Seine.

LYONS-LA-FORET: Le Grand Cerf €€
Bistro
20 pl Isaac Benserade, 27480
Tel *02 32 49 50 50* **Closed** *Mon & Tue*
Hearty home-made fare is complemented by the rustic setting at Le Grand Cerf. Oak beams and bare red-brick walls add to the charm.

MONT-ST-MICHEL: La Mère Poulard €€€
Brasserie
Grande Rue, 50170
Tel *02 33 89 68 68*
Visitors from across the world stop at this historic restaurant for omelettes cooked in a long-handled pan over a fire.

PONT L'EVEQUE: Auberge des Deux Tonneaux €€
Bistro
Pierrefitte en Auge, 14130
Tel *02 31 64 09 31* **Closed** *Mon eve, Tue*
Robust dishes and local ciders are served at this thatched cottage. The shady terrace has valley views.

PONT SAINT-PIERRE: Auberge de l'Andelle €€
Traditional French
27 Grande Rue, 27360
Tel *02 32 49 70 18* **Closed** *Oct–mid-Mar: Tue eve*
Pick a live lobster from the tank and have it cooked to perfection at this rustic dining room.

ROUEN: Le 37 €€
Bistro
37 rue St-Etienne-des-Tonneliers, 76000
Tel *02 35 70 56 65* **Closed** *Sun & Mon*
This attractive city-centre bistro serves modern cuisine. Find the daily specials on the chalkboard.

DK Choice

ROUEN: Restaurant Gill €€€
Fine dining
8–9 quai de la Bourse, 76000
Tel *02 35 71 16 14* **Closed** *Sun & Mon*
This highly recommended restaurant is located on the banks of the Seine and has an elegant dining room. Try the roast turbot. There is also a tasting menu available.

STE-CECILE: Le Manoir de l'Archerie €€
Traditional French
37 rue Michel de l'Epinay, 50800
Tel *02 33 51 13 87* **Closed** *Mon; Oct–Mar: Sun eve*
Fresh Normandy produce is served in a beautiful manor house. Also on the menu is a good selection of local cheeses.

TROUVILLE-SUR-MER: La Régence €€
Seafood
132 bd Fernand Moureaux, 14360
Tel *02 31 88 10 71* **Closed** *Winter: Wed & Thu*
The shellfish is a house speciality at La Régence, a beautiful restaurant featuring mirrors and 19th-century wood panelling.

VEULES LES ROSES: Les Galets €€
Seafood
3 rue Victor Hugo, 76980
Tel *02 35 97 61 33* **Closed** *Wed (except Aug) & Tue*
Close to the pebbly beach, this traditional restaurant has a comfortable dining area.

Key to Price Guide *see p576*

VILLERS BOCAGE:
Les Trois Rois €€
Traditional French
2 pl Jeanne d'Arc, 14310
Tel *02 31 77 00 32* **Closed** *Winter: Sun eve & Mon lunch*
Situated on a vast square surrounded by gardens, this restaurant serves generous portions of classic local dishes.

Brittany

ARRADON:
Les Logoden €
Creperie
24 rue Albert-Danet, 56610
Tel *02 97 46 79 03* **Closed** *Sun lunch, Mon & Tue*
The authentic and delicious *crêpes* prepared here feature a different filling each week. The produce is sourced from neighbouring farms.

AUDIERNE: Le Goyen €€
Seafood
Pl Jean-Simon, 29770
Tel *02 98 70 08 88* **Closed** *Jan–Mar*
Sample fresh oysters and excellent seafood platters at this hotel-restaurant by the sea. Try the scrumptious pan-fried scallops.

BELLE ILE EN MER:
La Désirade €€
Seafood
Le Petit Cosquet, 56360
Tel *02 97 31 70 70* **Closed** *Mon–Fri lunch*
This farmhouse restaurant offers a great breakfast menu in addition to fantastic seafood.

BREST: Le M €€€
Fine dining
22 rue du Commandant Drogou, 29200
Tel *02 98 47 90 00*
A typical granite-built manor house with a contemporary dining room, Le M serves a range of inventive dishes. Pretty garden terrace with outdoor tables for alfresco dining in good weather.

CARANTEC:
Restaurant Patrick Jeoffroy €€€
Fine dining
20 rue Kélénn, 29660
Tel *02 98 67 00 47* **Closed** *Sun eve, Mon & Tue*
Classic food with a modern twist is served in this sleek restaurant with views over Kélénn beach. Try the line-caught sea bass.

CARNAC: Le Calypso €€
Seafood
158 rte du Pô, 56340
Tel *02 97 52 06 14* **Closed** *Sun eve, Mon*
This popular seafood restaurant overlooks the oyster beds of Anse du Pô. Great service.

CONCARNEAU:
Le Petit Chaperon Rouge €
Creperie
7 pl Duguesclin, 29900
Tel *02 98 60 53 32* **Closed** *Sun eve, Mon*
Near the harbour, this lovely creperie has decor inspired by "Little Red Riding Hood".

DINAN: Ma Mère Pourcel €€
Traditional French
3 pl des Merciers, 22100
Tel *02 96 39 03 80* **Closed** *Sun & Tue eves, Wed*
Enjoy locally reared lamb and a variety of innovative fish dishes at this restaurant inside a medieval half-timbered building.

DOUARNENEZ: Insolite €€
Modern French
4 rue Jean Jaurès, 29100
Tel *02 98 92 00 02* **Closed** *Sun eve, Mon*
Original dishes blended with regional produce and Eastern spices at this stylish restaurant.

FOUESNANT CAP COZ: Restaurant de la Pointe du Cap Coz €€
Traditional French
153 av de la Pointe, 29170
Tel *02 98 56 01 63* **Closed** *Mon & Wed; Sep–Jun: Sun & Tue eves*
Top-notch cuisine is served in a dining room decorated to complement the coastal setting.

Spacious dining area at Restaurant Patrick Jeoffroy, Carantec

FOUGERES: Haute Sève €€
Regional
37 bd Jean Jaurès, 35300
Tel *02 99 94 23 39* **Closed** *Sun eve, Mon*
The timbered façade belies the vibrant modern interior that acts as a backdrop for a range of regional classics with a twist.

GUIMILIAU: Ar Chupen €
Creperie
43 rue de Calvaire, 29400
Tel *02 98 68 73 63* **Closed** *Winter: Fri eve & Sat lunch*
Traditional galettes and *crêpes* made to order ensure that this renovated Breton farmhouse is a budget winner.

GUINGAMP:
Le Clos de la Fontaine €€
Traditional French
9 rue du Général de Gaulle, 22200
Tel *02 96 21 33 63* **Closed** *Sun eve, Mon; Sep–Jun: Tue eve*
Wonderful fish dishes are served with delicate sauces at this eatery. The chef uses only the best local produce.

HEDE: L'Hostellerie du Vieux Moulin €€
Traditional French
Ancienne rte de St-Malo, 35630
Tel *02 99 45 45 70* **Closed** *Mon, Sun & Thu lunch*
There are good-value lunchtime menus to be had at this place overlooking Hédé Castle. The menu changes seasonally.

ILE DE NOIRMOUTIER:
Le Grand Four €€
Seafood
1 rue de la Cure, 85330
Tel *02 51 39 61 97* **Closed** *Jan & Dec; Winter: Sun eve, Thu lunch; Jul–Aug: Mon*
Dine in a 17th-century house with pink shutters and cloaked in green ivy. Also on offer is a decent selection of Loire wines.

LORIENT: Le Neptune €€
Seafood
15 av de la Perrière, 56100
Tel *02 97 37 04 56* **Closed** *Sun*
The haul at the nearby Keroman fishing port determines the dish of the day at Le Neptune. Trendy modern decor.

LORIENT: L'Amphitryon €€€
Fine dining
127 rue du Colonel Jean Müller, 56100
Tel *02 97 83 34 04* **Closed** *Sun & Mon*
Inspirational cuisine is prepared with simplicity in the stylish surroundings of L'Amphitryon. There is a good choice of wines by the glass.

For more information on types of restaurants *see p575*

PAIMPOL: L'Islandais €
Creperie
19 quai Morand, 22500
Tel *02 96 20 93 80*
A quayside restaurant with an aquatic theme, L'Islandais serves a wide range of tasty sweet and savoury galettes.

DK Choice

PLOMODIERN: Auberge des Glazicks €€€
Fine dining
7 rue de la Plage, 29550
Tel *02 98 81 52 32* **Closed** *Mon & Tue*
Headed by Olivier Bellin, this award-winning restaurant has stunning views over the Bay of Douarnenez. The celebrated chef uses Breton produce to create sublime and original food.

PLOUBALAY: La Gare €€
Regional
4 rue des Ormelets, 22650
Tel *02 96 27 25 16* **Closed** *Jul & Aug: Mon & Tue; Sep–Jun: Mon & Tue eves, Wed*
Market-driven dishes are given a modern twist in this restaurant with two dining rooms, one of which opens out on to a terrace.

QUIMPER: L'Ambroisie €€
Modern French
49 rue Elie Fréron, 29000
Tel *02 98 95 00 02* **Closed** *Sun eve, Mon*
Located close to the cathedral, this atmospheric restaurant offers both modern and classical fare.

RENNES: Essential €€
Modern French
11 rue Armand Rébillon, 35000
Tel *02 99 14 25 14* **Closed** *Sat lunch & Sun*
Dine on contemporary bistro-style cuisine in a distinctive glass cube-shaped restaurant.

RENNES: La Fontaine aux Perles €€€
Fine dining
96 rue de la Poterie, 35000
Tel *02 99 53 90 90* **Closed** *Sun eve, Mon; Aug: Sun–Tue*
This manor house provides the perfect setting for delights such as John Dory flavoured with sweet spices and pineapple.

ROSCOFF: L'Ecume des Jours €€
Traditional French
Quai d'Auxerre, 29680
Tel *02 98 61 22 83* **Closed** *Sep–Jul: Tue & Wed*
An authentic 16th-century ship-owner's house offers a wide range of local coastal produce.

ST-BRIEUC: Air du Temps €€
Bistro
4 rue du Gouët, 22000
Tel *02 96 68 58 40* **Closed** *Sun & Mon*
Try the pork casserole at this pleasant eatery, where the modern decor offsets the historic stone walls.

ST-MALO: Le Chalut €€
Seafood
8 rue de la Corne de Cerf, 35400
Tel *02 99 56 71 58* **Closed** *Mon & Tue*
Fishing nets, buoys and an aquarium provide the perfect ambience to this seafood eatery.

TREGUIER: Aigue Marine €€€
Seafood
5 rue Marcelin Berthelot, 22220
Tel *02 96 92 97 00* **Closed** *Sun eve, Mon, Sat lunch; Jan & Feb*
This fine restaurant in a harbour-front hotel serves sublime fish. Fixed-price menus available.

VANNES: Dan Ewen €
Creperie
3 pl Général de Gaulle, 56000
Tel *02 97 42 44 34* **Closed** *Sun*
The decor may be a little worn and rustic, but this creperie serves the best buckwheat pancakes in town.

VANNES: L'Eden €€
Modern French
3 rue Pasteur, 56000
Tel *02 97 46 42 62* **Closed** *Sun & Mon*
A local favourite, this restaurant prepares contemporary dishes with originality.

The Loire Valley

AMBOISE: Le 36 €€€
Fine dining
36 quai C. Guinot, 37400
Tel *02 47 30 63 36* **Closed** *Nov–Mar: Tue & Wed*
Serving seasonal food, Le 36 also offers a pretty garden and Loire views from the dining room.

Exquisitely decorated dining space at Le 36, Amboise

ANCENIS: Les Terrasses de Bel Air €€
Traditional French
Rte d'Angers, 44150
Tel *02 40 83 02 87* **Closed** *Sun eve, Mon*
Classic cuisine is prepared creatively in this 18th-century manor house with a garden.

ANGERS: Ma Campagne €€
Traditional French
14 promenade de la Reculée, 49000
Tel *02 41 48 38 06* **Closed** *Sun eve, Mon*
Select one of the chef's famous chocolate creations for dessert at this country-style auberge very close to the town centre.

BEAUGENCY: Le Petit Bateau €€
Modern French
54 rue du Pont, 45190
Tel *02 38 44 56 38* **Closed** *Mon & Tue*
This appealing restaurant reinvents classic dishes. Specialities include fresh fish and wild mushrooms.

BLOIS: Côté Loire €€
Traditional French
2 pl de la Grève, 41000
Tel *02 54 78 07 86* **Closed** *Sun & Mon*
Enjoy the simple but delicious menu at this old-fashioned hotel-restaurant overlooking the River Loire.

BLOIS: Orangerie du Château €€€
Fine dining
1 av Jean Laigret, 41000
Tel *02 54 78 05 36* **Closed** *Sun & Mon*
Excellent regional food and wines are served in the beautiful winter gardens of this château.

BOURGES: Le Cercle €€
Modern French
44 bd Lahitolle, 18000
Tel *02 48 70 33 27* **Closed** *Sun & Mon*
In a lovely manor house, this contemporary restaurant offers modern, inventive cuisine.

BOURGES: Le Louis XI €€
Bistro
11 rue Porte Jaune, 11000
Tel *02 48 70 92 14* **Closed** *Sep–Jun: Sun & Mon*
Enjoy large portions of classic, no-frills bistro fare and a convivial ambience. Good service.

BOURGUEIL: Le Moulin Bleu €€
Traditional French
7 rue du Moulin Bleu, 37140
Tel *02 47 97 73 13* **Closed** *Wed & Sun–Tue eves; off-season: Sun–Thu, Fri lunch & Sat lunch*
Traditional dishes are served in two vaulted dining rooms at Le Moulin Bleu. Great location and friendly service.

Key to Price Guide *see p576*

BRACIEUX: Le Rendez-vous des Gourmets €€
Regional
20 rue Roger Brun, 41250
Tel *02 54 46 03 87* **Closed** *Wed, Sat lunch; mid-Aug & mid-Jul: Sun eve, Mon lunch*
Make sure you book in advance at this very popular auberge serving traditional regional food.

CHARTRES: Le Grand Monarque – Le Georges €€€
Fine dining
22 pl des Epars, 28000
Tel *02 37 18 15 15* **Closed** *Sun & Mon*
Grands crus wines accompany the very best of classic French cuisine at this gourmet restaurant.

Entrance to Le Georges, the restaurant of Le Grand Monarque, Chartres

CHINON: Les Années 30 €€
Modern French
78 rue Haute St-Maurice, 37500
Tel *02 47 93 37 18* **Closed** *Wed; Sep–Jun: Tue*
Interesting dishes such as fillet of veal with a tajine of dried fruit and sweet potato gnocchi feature on the menu at this elegant eatery.

CLISSON: La Bonne Auberge €€
Traditional French
1 rue Olivier de Clisson, 44190
Tel *02 40 54 01 90* **Closed** *Sun eve, Mon, Tue lunch, Wed eve*
This auberge has three dining rooms. Specialities include seafood, fish and game (in season).

CONTRES: La Botte d'Asperges €
Traditional French
52 rue Pierre-Henri Mauger, 41700
Tel *02 54 79 50 49* **Closed** *Sun eve, Mon*
Locally grown asparagus features prominently on the menu, when in season. Delicious food served in a contemporary setting.

DOUE LA FONTAINE: Auberge Bienvenue €€
Traditional French
104 rte de Cholet, 49700
Tel *02 41 59 22 44* **Closed** *Sun eve, Mon*
Hearty meals made with local produce, often doused in regional wines, are on the menu at this pretty inn. Opt for the roast turbot with a creamy Savennieres sauce.

FONTEVRAUD ABBAYE: La Licorne €€
Traditional French
allée Sainte-Catherine, 49590
Tel *02 41 51 72 49* **Closed** *Mon, Sun & Wed eves; Oct–Easter*
Next to the splendid abbey, this popular restaurant has a lovely courtyard terrace and an elegant dining room. It serves delicately flavoured dishes. Book ahead.

GENNES: Auberge du Moulin de Sarré €
Traditional French
Rte de Louerre, 49350
Tel *02 41 51 81 32* **Closed** *Mon–Fri (but will open for parties of at least 12 people)*
Sample robust cuisine in a 16th-century watermill. Ask for the local speciality, *fouées* (warm bread puffs cooked in a wood-burning oven).

GENNES: L'Aubergade €€€
Fine dining
7 av des Cadets de Saumur, 49350
Tel *02 41 51 81 07* **Closed** *Tue & Wed*
Two elegantly laid-out dining rooms serve up a variety of dishes with exotic flavours.

ILE D'YEU: Les Bafouettes €€
Seafood
8 rue Gabriel-Guist'Hau, 84350
Tel *02 51 59 38 38* **Closed** *Mon; Sep–Mar: Sun*
Traditional fish dishes and *foie gras* feature prominently on the menu of this unpretentious restaurant. The small dining room fills up quickly, so book ahead.

LA FERTE IMBAULT: La Tête de Lard €€
Traditional French
13 pl des Tilleuls, 41300
Tel *02 54 96 22 32* **Closed** *Sun eve, Mon, Tue lunch*
Housed in a refurbished country hotel, La Tête de Lard has a great menu that offers seasonal choices. It features a lovely summer terrace.

LAMOTTE BEUVRON: Hôtel Tatin €€
Traditional French
5 av de Vierzon, 41600
Tel *02 54 88 00 03* **Closed** *Sun eve, Mon, Tue lunch*
Serving fresh local produce, *foie gras* and home-made *pâté*, this hotel-restaurant is also a great place to try a typical *tarte Tatin*.

LANGEAIS: Au Coin des Halles €€
Bistro
9 rue Gambetta, 37120
Tel *02 47 96 37 25* **Closed** *Wed & Thu*
Combining chic interiors with excellent cuisine, Au Coin des Halles is a top-notch bistro. In summer, ask for a table in the garden. Reservations essential.

LE MANS: Auberge des 7 Plats €€
Traditional French
79 Grande Rue
Tel *02 43 24 57 77* **Closed** *Sun & Mon*
Select from the seven starters, seven mains and 14 desserts on the menu at this unique eatery located in the old town.

LE MANS: Le Beaulieu €€
Fine dining
34 bis place de la République, 72000
Tel *02 43 87 78 37* **Closed** *Sat & Sun*
This sophisticated city-centre restaurant offers superb seasonal menus accompanied by fine service.

MALICORNE-SUR-SARTHE: La Petite Auberge €€
Traditional French
5 pl du Guesclin, 72270
Tel *02 43 94 80 52* **Closed** *Sun–Thu eves; Mon*
Gourmet food can be enjoyed in a charming setting at La Petite Auberge. In summer, it is possible to dine on the lovely terrace; in winter, diners take refuge around the huge fireplace.

MONTBAZON: La Chancelière €€
Modern French
1 pl des Marronniers, 37250
Tel *02 47 26 00 67* **Closed** *Sun & Mon*
Modern, sophisticated cuisine is prepared with great precision and attention to detail at this chic and elegant restaurant.

For more information on types of restaurants *see p575*

MONTSOREAU: Diane de Méridor €€
Fine dining
12 quai Philippe de Commines, 49730
Tel *02 41 51 71 76* **Closed** *Tue & Wed*
Carved out of tuffeau rock, this restaurant has exposed beams and an open fireplace. Specializes in freshwater fish dishes.

NANTES: La Cigale €€
Brasserie
4 pl Graslin, 44000
Tel *02 51 84 94 94*
This ornate *belle époque* brasserie dates from 1895. The quality of food perfectly matches the exceptional interiors.

NANTES: L'Océanide €€
Seafood
2 rue Paul Bellamy, 44000
Tel *02 40 20 32 28* **Closed** *Sun, Mon lunch*
A first-class seafood restaurant, this place was designed during World War II to resemble the interior of an ocean liner.

DK Choice

NANTES: L'U.Ni €€
Modern French
36 rue Fouré
Tel *02 40 75 53 05* **Closed** *Mon & Tue*
Serving creative food in a modern setting, L'U.Ni has made a name for itself in gourmet circles. Good-value lunch menus include dishes such as monkfish with yellow carrot purée flavoured with citrus fruit, followed by hazelnut dacquoise.

ONZAIN: Domaine des Hauts de Loire €€€
Fine dining
Rte de Herbault, 41150
Tel *02 54 20 72 57* **Closed** *Wed–Fri lunch; Oct–Apr: Mon & Tue*
Award-winning cuisine is served in a former hunting lodge set within its own park.

ORLEANS: La Dariole €€
Traditional French
25 rue Etienne Dolet, 45000
Tel *02 38 77 26 67* **Closed** *Sat & Sun; Mon, Wed & Thu eves*
A 15th-century half-timbered building houses this little restaurant and tearoom. Great cakes.

ORLEANS: Le Lièvre Gourmand €€
Modern French
28 quai de Chatelet, 45000
Tel *02 38 53 66 14* **Closed** *Tue*
The all-white decor belies the exciting menu at this restaurant. Original dishes include mullet with seaweed and coriander.

ROCHECORBON: Les Hautes Roches €€€
Fine dining
86 quai Loire, 37210
Tel *02 47 52 88 88* **Closed** *Sun eve, Mon*
This château dining room with an elegant and contemporary interior serves meticulously prepared classic cuisine.

SACHE: Auberge du XIIème Siècle €€
Traditional French
1 rue du Château, 37190
Tel *02 47 26 88 77* **Closed** *Sun eve, Mon, Tue lunch*
A good choice of fixed-price menus built around classic dishes is served in historic surrounds.

ST-OUEN LES VIGNES: L'Aubinière €€
Traditional French
29 rue Jules Gautier, 37530
Tel *02 47 30 15 29* **Closed** *Mon; Oct–May: Tue lunch*
L'Aubinière is a small but lovely restaurant that produces outstanding dishes. It features a pretty garden leading down to the river.

SANCERRE: Auberge La Pomme d'Or €€
Traditional French
Pl de la Mairie, 18300
Tel *02 48 54 13 30* **Closed** *Tue & Wed; Oct–Mar: Sun eve*
Enjoy Chavignol goat's cheese and other flavoursome dishes based on seasonal, regional produce with a glass of Sancerre wine.

SANCERRE: La Tour €€
Modern French
31 Nouvelle Place, 18300
Tel *02 48 54 00 81* **Closed** *Sun eve, Mon*
With views over the Sancerre vineyards, this elegant restaurant serves contemporary cuisine using the best local produce. Fine selection of red and white wines from Sancerre.

The exterior of Domaine des Hauts de Loire, a popular restaurant in Onzain

SAUMUR: L'Escargot €€
Traditional French
30 rue du Maréchal Leclerc, 49400
Tel *02 41 51 20 88* **Closed** *Tue, Wed, Sat lunch*
Unpretentious eatery serving good, simple dishes, including turbot and slow-braised lamb.

TOURS: L'Atelier Gourmand €€
Traditional French
37 rue Etienne Marcel, 37000
Tel *02 47 38 59 87* **Closed** *Sat lunch–Mon*
This charming restaurant in the old part of Tours offers an interesting menu at competitive prices. The dishes are beautifully presented. Good wine list.

TOURS: L'Odéon €€
Brasserie
10 pl du Général Leclerc, 37000
Tel *02 47 20 12 65* **Closed** *Mon & Sat lunch; Sun*
A quality Art Deco-style restaurant, L'Odéon creatively reinvents traditional French regional dishes.

TOURS: Les Saveurs €€
Bistro
1 pl Gaston Paillhou, 37000
Tel *02 47 37 03 13* **Closed** *Sun & Mon*
The tasty dishes at this chic, modern city-centre bistro are based around seasonal produce sourced from the daily market.

TOURS: La Roche Le Roy €€€
Fine dining
55 rte de St-Avertin, 37000
Tel *02 47 27 22 00* **Closed** *Sun & Mon*
Fine Loire and Bordeaux wines accompany the classic top-notch French cuisine at this Michelin-starred restaurant.

VALAIRE: L'Herbe Rouge €
Bistro
Le Bourg, 41120
Tel *02 54 44 98 14* **Closed** *Mon & Tue; winter*
At this excellent country bistro nestled in tiny Valaire, the focus is firmly on organic vegetables, farm-reared meat and natural wines.

VENDOME: La Vallée €€
Traditional French
34 rue Barré-de-St-Venant, 41100
Tel *02 54 77 29 93* **Closed** *Sun eve, Mon & Tue*
Diners flock here to enjoy well-prepared traditional dishes in a rustic dining room. Good choice of regional wines.

Key to Price Guide *see p576*

The elegant, minimalist lines of Le Jardin Gourmand, Auxerre

VIGNOUX-SUR-BARANGEON: Le Prieuré €€
Traditional French
2 rte de St-Laurent, 18500
Tel *02 48 51 58 80* **Closed** *Oct–May: Tue & Wed*
Meals for the discerning diner are served in the elegant dining room or on the covered terrace.

VOUVRAY: Les Geules Noires €€
Traditional French
66 vallée Coquette, 37210
Tel *02 47 52 62 18* **Closed** *Sun eve, Mon; Sep–May: Tue*
Carved into a cave, this place is ideal for wine lovers. Be sure to try sweet Vouvray with your dessert. Daily changing menu.

Burgundy and Franche-Comté

ARBOIS: Jean-Paul Jeunet €€€
Fine dining
9 rue de l'Hôtel de Ville, 39600
Tel *03 84 66 05 67* **Closed** *Jul–Aug: lunch; Sep–Jun*
The famous chef creates dishes such as Bresse chicken gently poached in Jura wine, or guinea fowl cooked with Danané pepper and served with Trousseau jelly. In a lovely location, the restaurant has a pretty terrace and attentive staff.

ARNAY LE DUC: Chez Camille €€
Traditional French
1 pl Edouard Herriot, 21230
Tel *03 80 90 01 38*
Come to Chez Camille's stone-walled dining room to savour hearty dishes such as rabbit *pâté* and game.

AUTUN: Les Ursulines €€
Fine dining
14 rue de Rivault, 71400
Tel *03 85 86 58 58* **Closed** *Mon–Fri lunch*
The turbot and duck fillet are superb at this elegant restaurant serving gourmet fare.

AUXERRE: Le Jardin Gourmand €€
Modern French
56 bd Vauban, 89000
Tel *03 86 51 53 52* **Closed** *Mon & Tue; Sep–Jun: Sun eve*
Inventive dishes and a legendary veal are served in an attractive room. The chef grows his own herbs and vegetables.

AVALLON: Relais des Gourmets €€
Traditional French
45–47 rue de Paris, 89200
Tel *03 86 34 18 90* **Closed** *Sun eve, Mon*
Choose from unpretentious fixed-priced menus at this traditional auberge with two dining rooms.

BEAUNE: Le Bistro de L'Hôtel €€
Bistro
3 rue Samuel Legay, 21200
Tel *03 80 25 94 10* **Closed** *Sun & lunch*
This chic bistro uses high-quality ingredients sourced from local suppliers. It also has an excellent selection of wines.

BEAUNE: La Ciboulette €€
Bistro
69 rue Lorraine, 21200
Tel *03 80 24 70 72* **Closed** *Mon & Tue*
The simple decor belies the high culinary standards here. Expect Burgundian classics, such as Charolais steak with Epoisses cheese sauce and pear poached in red wine.

BEAUNE: L'Ecusson €€
Modern French
Pl Malmedy, 21200
Tel *03 80 24 03 82* **Closed** *Wed & Sun*
Daring, inventive cuisine can be enjoyed in L'Ecusson's pleasant interior of wooden floors and oak beams.

BELFORT: Le Pot au Feu €€
Traditional French
27 bis Grand'Rue, 90000
Tel *03 84 28 57 84* **Closed** *Sat & Mon lunch, Sun*
A 17th-century vaulted cellar is the setting for homely dishes, such as the *pot au feu* (braised beef-and-vegetable stew). An extensive selection of wines.

BONLIEU: La Poutre €€
Regional
25 Grande Rue, 39130
Tel *03 84 25 57 77* **Closed** *Nov–Apr; May–Oct: Mon lunch*
Enjoy hearty home-cooked food in an 18th-century farmhouse with stone walls and oak beams. Try the tasting menu.

CHABLIS: La Cuisine au Vin €€
Regional
16 rue Auxerroise, 89800
Tel *03 86 18 98 52* **Closed** *Mon & Tue; Sun–Thu eves*
Diners can expect innovative takes on classics such as Burgundy snails and *boeuf bourguignon* at this place atmospherically located in an old wine cellar. Friendly staff.

CHAGNY: Lameloise €€€
Fine dining
36 pl Armes, 71150
Tel *03 85 87 65 65* **Closed** *Jul–Sep: Tue–Thu lunch; Oct–Jun: Tue & Wed*
This is the place for fine Burgundian cooking prepared with only the best ingredients Everything is cooked to perfection.

CHAINTRE: La Table de Chaintré €€
Regional
Le Bourg, 71570
Tel *03 85 32 90 95* **Closed** *Sun eve–Tue*
La Table de Chaintré is a well-established restaurant with a menu that changes weekly.

CHALON-SUR-SAONE: Le Bistrot €€
Bistro
31 rue de Strasbourg
Tel *03 85 93 22 01* **Closed** *Sat & Sun*
Try the seafood risotto or the Bresse chicken at this friendly bistro-style restaurant.

CHAROLLES: Restaurant Frédéric Doucet €€€
Modern French
2 av de la Libération, 71120
Tel *03 85 24 11 32* **Closed** *Sun eve, Mon, Tue lunch*
For a modern spin on traditional dishes, try this chic restaurant serving sizzling Charolais steak.

DIJON: La Dame d'Aquitaine €€
Traditional French
23 pl Bossuet, 21000
Tel *03 80 30 45 65* **Closed** *Mon–Wed lunch, Sun*
This eatery in an 18th-century stone-walled crypt offers regional specialities using local produce.

For more information on types of restaurants *see p575*

DIJON: DZ'Envies €€
Modern French
12 rue Odebert, 21000
Tel *03 80 50 09 26* **Closed** *Sun*
Facing the marketplace, this eatery has a minimalist decor that provides the ideal backdrop to its simple gourmet dishes.

DIJON: Hostellerie du Chapeau Rouge €€€
Modern French
5 rue Michelet, 21000
Tel *03 80 50 88 88* **Closed** *Sun & Mon*
Try scallops and *foie gras* ravioli with truffle and creamy soy sauce and other creative dishes in a sleek setting.

DOLE: La Chaumière €€€
Modern French
346 av du Maréchal Juin, 39100
Tel *03 84 70 72 40* **Closed** *Sat & Mon lunch, Sun*
Come to this delightful eatery for dishes such as chicken with mushrooms cooked in *vin jaune*, and carrots flavoured with ginger.

FONTANGY: Ferme-Auberge de la Morvandelle €
Traditional French
Précy-sous-Thil, 21390
Tel *06 78 80 88 68* **Open** *Apr–mid-Nov: Sat eve & Sun lunch; groups of minimum 10 people on weekdays*
Many ingredients used in the dishes are grown at this farm with a dining area in a converted barn.

GEVREY-CHAMBERTIN: Chez Guy €€
Regional
3 pl de la Mairie, 21220
Tel *03 80 58 51 51* **Closed** *Nov–Mar: Sun*
At this chic restaurant with exposed beams and a terrace, you can try simple cuisine such as *coq au vin* and rabbit *fricassée*.

IGUERANDE: La Colline du Colombier €€
Modern French
Colombier, 71340
Tel *03 85 84 07 24* **Closed** *Tue & Wed (Jul & Aug: Wed only)*
At this ancient farmhouse renovated by legendary chefs Michel and Marie-Pierre Troigros, the cuisine focuses on local meat and organic produce.

LONS-LE-SAUNIER: La Comédie €€
Modern French
65 pl de la Comédie, 39000
Tel *03 84 24 20 66* **Closed** *Sun & Mon*
The fixed-price menus change daily at this contemporary restaurant, while the desserts and the à la carte choices are seasonal.

MAGNY-COURS: Absolue Renaissance €€
Modern French
2 rue de Paris, 58470
Tel *03 86 58 10 40* **Closed** *Sun, Mon eve*
Set in a vast garden with its own vegetable patch, this restaurant puts a new spin on classic dishes.

MALBUISSON: Le Bon Acceuil €€
Modern French
Rue de la Source, 25160
Tel *03 81 69 30 58* **Closed** *Sun eve, Mon, Tue lunch*
Sample Lake Geneva *féra* trout with a watercress sauce and other creative seasonal dishes in a converted farmhouse.

MONTFAUCON: La Cheminée €€
Regional
3 rue de la Vue des Alpes, 25660
Tel *03 81 81 17 48* **Closed** *Sun & Wed eves, Mon*
Enjoy spectacular Alpine scenery from this rustic eatery serving dishes based on local produce.

NEVERS: Jean-Michel Couron €€
Modern French
21 rue St-Etienne, 58000
Tel *03 86 61 19 28* **Closed** *Sun eve–Tue*
The chef at this intimate restaurant selects top produce to create perfectly balanced flavours.

NITRY: Auberge de la Beursaudière €€
Traditional French
Chemin de Ronde, 89310
Tel *03 86 33 69 69*
Hearty local dishes such as braised steak are served up by staff in regional dress.

NUITS-ST-GEORGES: L'Alambic €€
Regional
Rue de Général de Gaulle, 21700
Tel *03 80 61 35 00* **Closed** *Mon, Tue lunch; Nov–Mar: Sun eve*
There is a vast selection of wines to go with the classic dishes on offer in this Cistercian dining room.

PORT LESNEY: Le Bistro Pontarlier €€
Bistro
Port Lesney, 39600
Tel *03 84 37 83 27* **Closed** *Mon & Tue eves, Wed & Thu (except Jul & Aug)*
This much-loved bistro is in the old schoolhouse of a pretty wine-producing village near Arbois.

PULIGNY-MONTRACHET: La Table d'Olivier Leflaive €€€
Regional
Pl du Monument, 21190
Tel *03 80 21 95 27* **Closed** *Sun*
Try the speciality wine-tasting lunches at this rustic spot with a background in wine production. The seasonal menu uses locally grown produce.

QUARRE LES TOMBES: Auberge de Atre €€
Traditional French
Les Lavaults, 89630
Tel *03 86 32 20 79* **Closed** *Tue & Wed*
Classic dishes such as roast duck with pepper sauce are served in a cosy dining room.

DK Choice

ST-AMOUR BELLEVUE: L'Auberge du Paradis €€€
Modern French
Le Plâtre Durand, 71570
Tel *03 85 37 10 26* **Closed** *Mon, Tue, Wed–Sat lunch*
The monthly changing menu at this exciting restaurant may include Iberian black pig served with a mousse of Brie de Meaux, flavoured with grainy mustard. The dining room is modern and quirky, with forks hanging from lampshades.

ST-ROMAIN: Les Roches €€
Regional
Pl de la Mairie, 21190
Tel *03 80 21 21 63* **Closed** *Tue & Wed*
Simple, no-frills cooking is served at this small hotel-restaurant. Try the four-course set menu.

Smart, modern dining space at La Table d'Olivier Leflaive, Puligny-Montrachet

Key to Price Guide *see p576*

SAULIEU:
Le Relais Bernard Loiseau €€€
Fine dining
2 rue d'Argentine, 21210
Tel *03 80 90 53 53* **Closed** *Tue & Wed; Feb*
Renowned across France, this restaurant creates masterful interpretations of traditional dishes.

SENS: La Madeleine €€€
Fine dining
1 rue Alsace-Lorraine, 89100
Tel *03 86 65 09 31* **Closed** *Sun, Mon, Tue lunch*
The seasonal menus at this smart establishment offer dishes such as scallop *carpaccio*.

TOURNUS:
Le Restaurant Greuze €€€
Traditional French
1 rue A. Thibaudet, 71700
Tel *03 85 51 13 52* **Closed** *Wed; Nov–Mar*
Enjoy classic cuisine in simple but charming surroundings. Try the Bresse chicken and pair with a good Mâcon or Beaujolais wine.

VENOY: Le Moulin de la Coudre €€
Traditional French
2 rue des Gravottes, La Coudre, 89290
Tel *03 86 40 23 79* **Closed** *Sun eve, Mon lunch*
The menu changes weekly here, according to the seasonal produce available. Creatively prepared classic cuisine.

VERDUN-SUR-LE-DOUBS:
L'Hostellerie Bourguignonne – Didier Denis €€
Traditional French
2 av Pdt-Borgeot, 71350
Tel *03 85 91 51 45* **Closed** *Tue & Wed lunch; winter: Sun eve*
This rustic venue specializes in honest, straightforward cooking made with local ingredients. Enjoy the superb Charolais beef fillet and the excellent wines.

VEZELAY: Le Bougainville €€
Regional
28 rue Saint-Étienne, 89450
Tel *03 86 33 27 57* **Closed** *Tue & Wed; mid-Nov–mid-Mar*
Expect Burgandy favourites such as home-made terrine, *jambon persillé*, hare stew and snails.

VILLENEUVE SUR YONNE:
Auberge La Lucarne aux Chouettes €€
Regional
7 quai Bretoche, 89500
Tel *03 86 87 18 26* **Closed** *Sun eve, Mon*
The menu at this 17th-century inn by the River Yonne features dishes such as eggs poached in red wine, snails and more.

Rustic exteriors of the Georges Blanc restaurant in Vonnas

VILLERS-LE-LAC: Le France €€
Modern French
8 pl Cupillard, 25130
Tel *03 81 68 00 06* **Closed** *Sun eve, Mon*
The delicious dishes served at this hotel-restaurant are infused with herbs from the hotel garden. Try the Bresse chicken with morel mushrooms. Great service.

VINCELOTTES:
Auberge des Tilleuils €€
Traditional French
12 quai de l'Yonne, 82290
Tel *03 86 42 22 13* **Closed** *Tue & Wed*
Enjoy mouthwatering cuisine in this attractive riverside auberge. Fish specialities include oyster soup, scallops and langoustines.

VONNAS: Georges Blanc €€€
Fine dining
Pl Marché, 01540
Tel *04 74 50 90 90* **Closed** *Mon & Tue, Wed & Thu lunch*
A gourmet shrine, Georges Blanc offers such inventive cuisine as lobster cooked in *vin jaune* and served with morel mushroom ravioli. Excellent wines.

The Massif Central

DK Choice

ALLEYRAS: Le Haut Allier €€
Modern French
Pont d'Alleyras, 43580
Tel *04 71 57 57 63* **Closed** *Mon & Tue; mid-Nov–Mar*
Nestled in the Allier gorge, this hotel-restaurant believes in local produce. Enjoy traditional dishes such as saddle of Saugues lamb, or more imaginative ones such as pigeon breast in a cep mushroom crumble with corn flour gnocchi. The set menus are great value.

BELCASTEL: Vieux Pont €€€
Modern French
Le Bourg, 12390
Tel *05 65 64 52 29* **Closed** *Jan–mid-Mar; Sun & Mon (except Jul & Aug)*
Straddling a medieval bridge, this place produces creative dishes with flair. Try Ségela veal cooked with kaffir lime, and mashed potatoes with almond, lemon and ginger oil.

BOUDES: La Vigne €€
Modern French
Pl de la Mairie, 63340
Tel *04 73 96 55 66* **Closed** *Sun eve, Mon & Tue*
The chef constantly seeks out new ideas for his changing menu at this creative restaurant on the main square of this wine village. Great set menus.

BRIVE-LA-GAILLARDE:
Chez Francis €€
Bistro
61 av de Paris, 19100
Tel *05 55 74 41 72* **Closed** *Sun & Mon*
This Paris-style bistro serves well-prepared reworkings of regional favourites. Good selection of southern French wines.

CLERMONT-FERRAND:
Amphitryon Capucine €€
Traditional French
50 rue Fontgiève, 63000
Tel *04 73 31 38 39* **Closed** *Sun & Mon*
Try the roast turbot basted with cep mushroom sauce at this stately dining room complete with a fireplace and oak beams. Excellent wine list.

CLERMONT-FERRAND:
Le Caveau €€
Regional
1 rue Tour de la Monnaie, 63000
Tel *04 73 14 07 03* **Closed** *Sun*
Rustic and traditional, Le Caveau is a meat eater's paradise serving huge chunks of Salers or Aubrac beef and *coq au vin*.

For more information on types of restaurants *see p575*

CLERMONT-FERRAND: Goûts et Couleurs €€
Modern French
6 pl Champgil, 63000
Tel *04 73 19 37 82* **Closed** *Sat lunch, Sun & Mon lunch*
The geometric decor is softened by an ancient vaulted ceiling in this former mirror workshop serving modern, inventive cuisine.

LAGUIOLE: Michel Bras €€€
Fine dining
rte de l'Aubrac, 12210
Tel *05 65 51 18 20* **Closed** *Mon & Tue, Wed lunch*
A wall of glass overlooks the beautiful Aubrac countryside from this hilltop restaurant renowned for its cutting-edge cuisine.

LE PUY-EN-VELAY: Tournayre €€
Regional
12 rue Chênebouterie, 43000
Tel *04 71 09 58 94* **Closed** *Sun & Wed eves, Mon*
Vaulted ceilings and stone walls distinguish this 12th-century town house. Try typical Auvergnat dishes such as lentils or Velay veal.

LE ROUGET: Hôtel des Voyageurs €
Traditional French
20 av de 15 Septembre 1945, 15290
Tel *04 71 46 10 14* **Closed** *Sep–May: Sun lunch*
This stone-built Cantal hotel-restaurant serves well-prepared traditional dishes. Go for the *menu du terroir*. The fish with chorizo is especially good.

LES ESTABLES: Auberge des Fermiers du Mézenc €€
Regional
Le Bourg, 43150
Tel *04 71 08 34 30*
A restored 18th-century stone farmhouse, this place serves local produce, such as Mézenc beef, *crique* (fried potato galette) and regional cheeses.

LIMOGES: Chez Alphonse €€
Bistro
5 pl de la Motte, 87000
Tel *05 55 34 34 14* **Closed** *Sun*
There are good *prix-fixe* menus at this lively bistro serving regional cuisine. The chef sources all the ingredients from the local market.

LIMOGES: L'Amphitryon €€€
Modern French
26 rue de la Boucherie, 87000
Tel *05 55 33 36 39* **Closed** *Sun & Mon*
The food is sophisticated and the flavours are delicate at this contemporary dining space. The Limousin beef is a perennial favourite.

Striking, contemporary interiors of the refined Michel Bras restaurant, Laguiole

MILLAU: La Braconne €€
Traditional French
7 pl Maréchal Foch, 12100
Tel *05 65 60 30 93* **Closed** *Sun eve, Mon*
Specialities at this 13th-century vaulted restaurant on an arcaded square include flambéed leg of lamb. Classic cuisine.

MONTLUCON: Le Grenier à Sel €€
Traditional French
10 rue Ste-Anne, 03100
Tel *04 70 05 53 79* **Closed** *Sun eve, Mon*
Dine in an elegant pastel-hued room set in an impressive ivy-clad 18th-century mansion with massive fireplaces.

MONTSALVY: L'Auberge Fleurie €€
Traditional French
Pl du Barry, 15120
Tel *04 71 49 20 02* **Closed** *Sun eve; Sep–Jun: Mon; mid-Nov–mid-Mar*
This charming auberge has oak beams, an open fireplace and a rustic feel. The roast hen with chestnut charlotte is a must.

MOULINS: Le Trait d'Union €€
Bistro
16 rue Gambetta, 3000
Tel *04 70 34 24 61* **Closed** *Sun & Mon*
Sizzling dishes such as Monts du Forez veal and steak Rossini can be found on the menu at this upmarket bistro.

MURAT: Le Jarrousset €€
Modern French
Rte de Clermont-Ferrand, 15300
Tel *04 71 20 10 69* **Closed** *Sun, Tue & Wed eves; Sep–Jun: Mon*
The emphasis here is on using top-quality seasonal ingredients, most of them sourced locally.

RODEZ: Goûts en Couleurs €€
Modern French
38 rue Bonald, 12000
Tel *05 65 42 75 10* **Closed** *Sun & Mon*
At this charming eatery with a garden terrace in the old town, the chef prepares imaginative fare such as line-caught whiting served with a mussel and vervain tart.

ST-BONNET-LE-FROID: Auberge des Cimes €€€
Fine dining
Le Bourg, 43290
Tel *04 71 59 93 72* **Closed** *Tue & Wed*
The delicious, seasonally determined dishes on the menu at the rustically decorated Auberge des Cimes include roast quail with caramelized pear, and monkfish served with assorted pumpkins.

ST-JULIEN-CHAPTEUIL: Vidal €€
Traditional French
Pl du Marché, 43260
Tel *04 71 08 70 50* **Closed** *Sun & Mon*
Opt for the juicy stuffed fillet of beef or the Velay lamb at this family-run restaurant serving authentic cuisine in a quaint village. There's an excellent dessert menu, too.

UZERCHE: Restaurant Jean Teyssier €€
Mediterranean
Rue du Pont-Turgot, 19140
Tel *05 55 73 10 05* **Closed** *Sep–Jun: Tue & Wed*
The chef at Jean Teyssier serves Mediterranean dishes such as grilled red mullet fillets on parmesan shortbread and *tapenade (see p473)* in an elegant dining room with a chandelier and great views of the Vezère.

VICHY: Brasserie du Casino €€
Brasserie
4 rue du Casino, 03200
Tel *04 70 98 23 06* **Closed** *Tue & Wed*
Housed in a stylish Art Deco salon decked out with wood and mirrors, the Brasserie du Casino is a veritable institution on the Vichy restaurant scene. The excellent menu features classic upmarket brasserie fare. Impeccable service.

Key to Price Guide *see p576*

VICHY: Jacques Decoret €€€
Modern French
15 rue du Parc, 3200
Tel *04 70 97 65 06* **Closed** *Tue & Wed*
The finest regional produce is used in refined dishes that are prepared with great skill. The setting is also lovely – in a huge conservatory.

The Rhône Valley and French Alps

ANNECY: Le Belvédère €€€
Modern French
7 chemin Belvédère, 74000
Tel *04 50 45 04 90* **Closed** *Sun eve, Wed; Oct–May: Tue eve*
Enjoy lake views and appetizing contemporary food – *foie gras* perfumed with vanilla, and desserts such as the chocolate cigar filled with coffee mousse.

ARGENTIERE: Le Chêne Vert €€
Regional
Rocher, 7110 Tel
Tel *04 75 88 34 02*
This traditional Ardèchois hotel and restaurant offers a number of regional classics. Try the *foie gras* served with a fig *confit*.

CHAMBERY: Château de Candie – Orangerie €€
Modern French
Rue de Bois de Candie, Chambéry le Vieux, 73000
Tel *04 79 96 63 00*
At this elegant restaurant you can choose such experimental dishes as fera fish fillet served with olives and chorizo, accompanied by carrot, orange and fennel sauce.

DK Choice

CHAMONIX: La Calèche €€
Traditional French
Rue Dr. Paccard, 74400
Tel *04 50 55 94 68*
This mountain restaurant serves typical Savoyard cuisine, including *tartiflette* (a gratin made with *lardons*, cheese, potatoes and onions), fondue, and grilled meats. The dining room is crammed with Swiss clocks, copper pans and a bobsleigh from the 1924 Winter Olympics.

CHAMONIX: Les Jardins du Mont Blanc €€€
Modern French
62 allée du Majestic, 74400
Tel *04 50 53 05 64*
Housed in a charming mountain hotel, this smart restaurant offers modern Alpine cuisine prepared with the best regional produce.

COLLONGES MONT D'OR: Paul Bocuse €€€
Fine dining
40 quai de la Plage, 69660
Tel *04 72 42 90 90*
National treasure Paul Bocuse makes dishes such as black truffle soup topped with pastry, or his legendary gratin of crayfish. The restaurant is decorated with chandeliers and gilded mirrors.

COURCHEVEL: Le Chabichou €€€
Modern French
Quartier des Chenus, 73120
Tel *04 79 08 00 55* **Closed** *Summer: Tue*
Experience creative cuisine while enjoying breathtaking mountain views. Old-school favourites on offer include pork from the Cantal region.

COURCHEVEL: Le Genépi €€€
Traditional French
Courchevel 1850, 73120
Tel *04 79 08 08 63* **Closed** *Sep–Nov: Sat & Sun*
Savour traditional mountain fare at this excellent dining establishment, located within a luxury ski resort. Good wine and cocktail list.

GRENOBLE: A Ma Table €€
Traditional French
92 cours Jean-Jaurès, 38000
Tel *04 76 96 77 04* **Closed** *Sat–Mon, Tue, Wed & Fri eves*
This beautiful restaurant serves tasty dishes such as breast of farm-reared guinea fowl cooked in cider, duck *foie gras* with cocoa, and roast squid with truffle cream.

GRENOBLE: Badine €€
Modern French
168 cours Berriat, 38000
Tel *04 76 21 95 33* **Closed** *Sat & Sun*
The dishes at Badine reflect the creativity of the young chef. The seasonal menu uses local produce. In summer, tables are set up outside, under the ancient wisteria.

LE BOURGET-LAC: Beaurivage €€
Regional
Bd du Lac, 73370
Tel *04 79 25 00 38* **Closed** *Sun eve, Wed (except Jul & Aug) & Thu*
Diners flock here to sample classic Savoyard cuisine. This lakeside auberge features a lovely terrace overhung with plantain trees.

LE CLUSAZ: La Scierie €€
Modern French
321–331 rte du Col des Aravis, 74220
Tel *04 50 63 34 68*
Dishes at this restaurant in a former sawmill range from local mountain *charcuterie* to John Dory fillet with Mondeuse wine sauce and creamy risotto, served in a friendly ambience.

LYON: 33 Cité €€
Brasserie
33 quai Charles de Gaulle, 69006
Tel *04 37 45 45 45* **Closed** *Sun*
A modern brasserie located in the city centre, 33 Cité offers carefully prepared classic and contemporary cuisine in a stylish dining room. The extensive wine list is excellent.

LYON: Brasserie Georges €€
Bistro
30 cours Verdun, 69002
Tel *04 72 56 54 54*
Dating to 1836, Brasserie Georges is a huge, bustling city-centre bistro with Art Deco interiors. The menu covers Lyonnais specialities, seafood dishes and sauerkraut.

LYON: La Gargotte €€
Modern French
15 rue Royale, 69001
Tel *04 78 28 79 20* **Closed** *Sat, Sun, Mon lunch & Tue*
Classic dishes are reworked with originality at this friendly restaurant in an old pastry shop with retro decor and mirrored walls.

LYON: L'Alexandrin €€€
Regional
83 rue Moncey, 69003
Tel *04 72 61 15 69* **Closed** *Sun & Mon*
L'Alexandrin specializes in exquisite gourmet reinventions of typical Lyonnais dishes, including roast turbot on a *carpaccio* of mango, and lobster ravioli with celery tagliatelle, served in a warm and elegant interior or on the outside terrace.

Brightly lit, vibrant dining room at Le Chabichou in Courchevel

For more information on types of restaurants *see p575*

The charming dining room at La Taverne du Mont d'Arbois in Megeve

MEGEVE: La Petite Ravine €€
Traditional French
743 chemin de la Ravine, Demi Quartier Combloux, 74120
Tel *04 50 21 38 67*
The limited selection of dishes at this alpine chalet restaurant with a warm ambience includes cheese-based regional classics.

MEGEVE: La Taverne du Mont d'Arbois €€
Modern French
3001 rte Edmond de Rothschild, 74120
Tel *04 50 21 03 53*
This authentic chalet attracts a chic Megève crowd with its modern reworkings of traditional recipes. Old favourites such as *raclette* and fondue also on offer.

MORZINE: La Chamade €€
Traditional French
La Crusaz, 90 rte de la Plagne, 74110
Tel *04 50 79 13 91*
Choose from a wide-ranging menu that features wood-oven pizzas and regional fare such as *charcuterie*. Alternatively, try the warm Reblochon salad.

OUCHES: Troisgros €€€
Fine dining
728 rte de Villerest, 42155
Tel *04 77 71 66 97* **Closed** *Mon lunch; Tue & Wed*
One of the country's top restaurants, Troisgros features striking contemporary decor, pure lines and a Zen atmosphere, plus an exceptionally high calibre of cooking.

ST-AGREVE: Domaine de Rilhac €€
Modern French
Rilhac, 07320
Tel *04 75 30 20 20* **Closed** *Tue eve, Wed & Thu lunch; mid-Dec–mid-Mar*
Chef Ludovic Sinz reinvents classic fare in this smartly renovated farmhouse. Try the pumpkin soup with snails or the pan-fried chicory.

ST-ETIENNE: Le Bistrot de Paris €€
Bistro
7 pl Jean Jaurès, 42000
Tel *04 77 21 56 74* **Closed** *Sun eve*
This jovial bistro has a simple menu that changes in accordance with what is in season.

ST-MARTIN-DE-BELLEVILLE: La Bouitte €€€
Modern French
St-Marcel, 73440
Tel *04 79 08 96 77*
Order the farm-reared chicken with truffles at this Alpine chalet restaurant. Inventive dishes.

TAIN L'HERMITAGE: Lycée Hotelier de l'Hermitage €
Traditional French
Rue Jean Monnet, 26600
Tel *04 75 07 57 14* **Closed** *Sat, Sun, Mon–Wed eve & Fri eve*
Students training to become chefs run two restaurants serving classic gourmet dishes. Only open during the school term.

TALLOIRES: La Villa des Fleurs €€
Regional
Rte du Port, 74290
Tel *04 50 60 71 14* **Closed** *Sun eve, Mon*
Fish caught in Lake Annecy features prominently on the seasonal menu at this lovely waterside villa.

TOURNON: Le Tournesol €€
Modern French
44 av Maréchal Foch, 07300
Tel *04 75 07 08 26* **Closed** *Sun eve, Tue & Wed*
Sample the home-made duck and pistachio terrine at this smart restaurant with views of the Hermitage vineyards.

URIAGE-LES-BAINS: Les Terrasses d'Uriage €€€
Modern French
Pl de la Déesse-Hygie, 38410
Tel *04 76 89 10 80* **Closed** *Sun eve, Mon, Tue–Thu lunch; late Dec–Jan*
Les Terrasses is an upscale restaurant in a Napoleon III building that opens out onto a lovely park. The place for creative, beautifully presented dishes.

VALENCE: Restaurant Pic €€€
Fine dining
285 av Victor Hugo, 26000
Tel *04 75 44 15 32* **Closed** *Sun eve & Mon*
A chic restaurant in a luxury hotel, Pic features a constantly evolving menu. Excellent Rhône wines.

DK Choice

VIENNE: La Pyramide €€€
Fine dining
14 bd Fernand Point, 38200
Tel *04 74 53 01 96* **Closed** *Tue & Wed*
Beautifully presented, the gastronomic creations at La Pyramide are based on regional produce – try the saddle of lamb cooked in a bread crust and served with a leek *tarte tatin*. Excellent wine list. A classic Michelin-starred establishment.

Poitou and Aquitaine

ANGOULEME: Le Terminus €
Bistro
3 pl de la Gare, 16000
Tel *05 45 95 27 13* **Closed** *Sun*
Stylish and modern, Le Terminus has a lovely summer terrace. On the menu is a great selection of seafood purchased from the local market.

ARCACHON: La Cabane de L'Aiguillon €
Seafood
Bd Pierre Loti, 33120
Tel *05 56 54 88 20* **Closed** *Oct–Easter*
Enjoy a platter of oysters on the terrace of this family-run eatery on the beach.

ARCACHON: Chez Yvette €€
Seafood
59 bd du Général Leclerc, 33120
Tel *05 56 83 05 11*
Set on the waterfront, this lively and atmospheric local institution has been serving plates of fish and oysters since 1962. There is a good wine list to complement the dishes.

ARCINS: Le Lion d'Or €€
Regional
11 rte de Pauillac, 33460
Tel *05 56 58 96 79* **Closed** *Sun & Mon*
An intimate restaurant in a Médoc wine village, Le Lion d'Or is renowned for great local cuisine and superb wines.

Key to Price Guide *see p576*

BORDEAUX: Tante Charlotte €
Traditional French
7 rue des Bahutiers, 33000
Tel *09 82 60 13 12* **Closed** *Sun & Mon*
Traditional cuisine made with seasonal, organic produce is on offer at this cosy, modern bistro.

BORDEAUX: Le Chapon Fin €€€
Fine dining
5 rue Montesquieu, 33000
Tel *05 56 79 10 10* **Closed** *Sun & Mon*
Exquisite creative fare is dished up at this historic restaurant with glorious *belle époque* decor. Impressive selection of wines.

COGNAC: Les Pigeons Blancs €€
Regional
110 rue Jules Brisson, 16100
Tel *05 45 82 16 36*
This traditional restaurant serves locally based cuisine. Highlights on the menu include the succulent beef and duck dishes.

COULON: Le Central €
Regional
4 rue d'Autremont, 79510
Tel *05 49 35 90 20* **Closed** *Mon*
For innovative regional cuisine and an excellent range of fruit desserts, head to Le Central. The dining room and terrace overlook the Poitevin marshes.

EUGENIE-LES-BAINS: La Ferme aux Grives €€
Fine dining
11 rue des Thermes, 40320
Tel *05 58 05 05 06* **Closed** *Tue & Wed*
Chef Michel Guérard's upscale restaurant serves sublime French fare with a modern twist. Try the suckling pig or chicken cooked on the spit in their fireplace.

ILE D'OLERON: Ecailler €
Seafood
65 rue du Port, 17310 St-Pierre-d'Oléron
Tel *05 46 47 10 31* **Closed** *mid-Dec–Feb*
Great local oysters, crab and other seafood specialities are served at this harbourside eatery that sources its ingredients from the market at the end of the pier.

ILE DE RE: La Baleine Bleue €€
Brasserie
Quai Launay Razilly, 17410 St-Martin-de-Ré
Tel *05 46 09 03 30* **Closed** *Mon eve, Tue (except Jul & Aug)*
In a great harbourside location, this stylish bar and brasserie sells fish, seafood and fine wines.

JARNAC: Restaurant du Château €€
Fine dining
15 pl du Château, 16200
Tel *05 45 81 07 17* **Closed** *Mon, Wed & Sun eves*
This elegant restaurant provides refined dishes such as roast pheasant in cognac sauce.

LA ROCHELLE: Le Boute en Train €
Bistro
7 rue des Bonnes Femmes, 17000
Tel *05 46 41 73 74* **Closed** *Sun & Mon*
Enjoy hearty classic fare made with market-fresh ingredients at this eatery. Great service, too.

LA ROCHELLE: Coquillages et Crustacés €
Seafood
Port du Plomb (côté l'Houmeau), 17000
Tel *05 46 45 32 52* **Closed** *Mon, Sun eve*
This waterside restaurant offers all types of seafood, including platters of shells, lobsters, crustaceans and fish. Some dishes have an Asian touch

LA ROCHELLE: L'Entracte €€
Brasserie
35 rue St-Jean-du-Pérot, 17000
Tel *05 46 52 26 69*
The friendly staff at L'Entracte plate up inventive takes on simple regional cuisine in a stylish interior with an open kitchen.

LANGON: Restaurant Claude Darroze €€
Fine dining
95 cours du Général Leclerc, 33210
Tel *05 56 63 00 48*
Enjoy excellent Southwestern French cooking and Bordeaux wines in this intimate restaurant with striking decor.

Guests dining alfresco at La Ferme aux Grives in Eugènie-les-Bains

Stone façade with red awnings of Restaurant du Château, Jarnac

MARGAUX: Le Pavillon de Margaux €
Traditional French
3 rue Georges Mandel, 33460
Tel *05 57 88 77 54* **Closed** *Jun–Sep: Tue; Oct–May: Tue & Wed*
Set in a villa hotel, this mellow dining room serves a great selection of light lunches.

MONTMORILLON: Le Lucullus €
Regional
4 bd de Strasbourg, 86500
Tel *05 49 84 09 09* **Closed** *Mon & Tue, Sun eve*
Refined regional cuisine and an excellent wine list await at this bar-bistro. Casual dining.

NIORT: Bloom Restaurant €€
Bistro
9 rue de l'Hotel de Ville, 79000
Tel *05 49 77 44 35* **Closed** *Sun*
Chic, airy modern bistro where local fish is the highlight of the varied menus.

PAUILLAC: Château Cordeillan-Bages €€
Fine dining
Rte des Châteaux, 33250
Tel *05 56 59 24 24* **Closed** *Mon & Tue; Dec–Mar*
Gourmet cuisine is dished up at this lavish Médoc château-hotel. Excellent Bordeaux wines.

POITIERS: Les Bons Enfants €
Regional
11bis rue Cloche Perse, 86000
Tel *05 49 41 49 82* **Closed** *Sun & Mon*
Snug and tightly packed, this eatery serves generous portions of duck and other local specialities.

POITIERS: Le Pince Oreille €€
Bistro
11 rue des Trois Rois, 86000
Tel *05 49 60 25 99* **Closed** *Sun & Mon*
At this laid-back bar-restaurant with live music there is a good selection of wholesome meals.

For more information on types of restaurants *see p575*

ROCHEFORT: La Belle Poule €€
Regional
102 av du 11 Novembre, 17300
Tel *05 46 99 71 87* **Closed** *Fri*
Sample regionally inspired cooking at this lovely restaurant with a terrace by the River Charente.

SABRES: Auberge des Pins €€
Fine dining
Rte de la Piscine, 40630
Tel *05 58 08 30 00* **Closed** *Sep–Jun: Mon*
Enjoy delicate cuisine in serene environs. The menu features pigeon, langoustines and ice-cream cannelloni. Convivial host.

SAINT-EMILION: L'Envers du Décor €€
Bistro
11 rue du Clocher, 33330
Tel *05 57 74 48 31*
This award-winning bistro and wine bar serves healthy salads and snacks as well as intricate dishes.

DK Choice

SAINT-EMILION: Restaurant Le Tertre €€
Fine dining
5 rue du Tertre de la Tente, 33330
Tel *05 57 74 46 33* **Closed** *Feb–Mar: Wed & Thu; Apr–Nov: Wed; mid-Nov–Jan*
Le Tertre has won many fans with its outstanding food, warm service and superb wines. Choose from classic local dishes such as duck, *foie gras* or line-caught *maigre* fish – all of which are prepared with great flair.

SAUTERNES: Le Saprien €
Regional
14 rue Principale, 33210
Tel *05 56 76 60 87* **Closed** *Sun eve & Mon*
In a converted farmhouse, this smart restaurant serves good-value, traditional French dishes.

Cooking wood pigeon over coals, Auberge des Pins, Sabres

TALMONT-SUR-GIRONDE: Hôtel-Restaurant L'Estuaire €
Seafood
1 av de l'Estuaire, 17120
Tel *05 46 90 43 85* **Closed** *Oct–Mar: Mon & Tue*
A selection of local fish and seafood can be enjoyed in a lovely, remote location beside the Gironde estuary.

Périgord, Quercy and Gascony

AGEN: Mariottat €€
Fine dining
25 rue Louis Vivent, 47000
Tel *05 53 77 99 77* **Closed** *Mon, Sat lunch & Sun eve; Nov–May: Wed lunch*
Refined food made with fresh produce is served in a beautiful 19th-century town mansion furnished with antiques.

ALBI: L'Épicurien €
Bistro
42 pl Jean Jaurès, 81000
Tel *05 63 53 10 70* **Closed** *Sun & Mon*
This smart, contemporary bistro offers creative takes on classic French dishes. Great local wines.

ALBI: Le Jardin des Quatre Saisons €
Regional
5 rue de la Pompe, 81000
Tel *05 63 60 77 76* **Closed** *Mon; Thu & Sun eves*
In the heart of historic Albi, this lovely eatery serves great local favourites. Truffle and mushroom dishes are highly recommended.

AUCH: Le Papillon €
Regional
rte d'Agen (RN 21), 32810 Montaut-les-Créneaux
Tel *05 62 65 51 29* **Closed** *Sun eve & Mon*
Gascon specialities such as *cassoulet* and lamb are served in a tranquil room beside a lovely garden. Perfect for big groups.

BERGERAC: La Flambée €€
Regional
49 av Marceau Feyry, 24100
Tel *05 53 57 52 33*
In addition to an excellent wine list, this place offers great local fare such as duck, *foie gras* and goat's cheese.

BRANTOME: Au Fil du Temps €
Bistro
1 chemin du Vert Galant, 24310
Tel *05 53 05 24 12* **Closed** *Sun eve*
This popular bistro with a lively atmosphere and nostalgic decor specializes in dishes prepared on a traditional *rôtissoire*.

BRANTOME: Les Frères Charbonnel €€
Regional
Rue Gambetta, 24310
Tel *05 53 05 70 15*
Duck and truffles are the house specialities at this renowned hotel-restaurant situated beside the River Dronne.

CAHORS: Auberge du Vieux Cahors €
Regional
144 rue St-Urcisse, 46000
Tel *05 65 35 06 05*
Hearty local dishes can be enjoyed at this atmospheric 15th-century inn with friendly service.

CAHORS: Le Balandre €€
Fine dining
Hôtel Terminus, 5 av Charles de Freycinet, 46000
Tel *05 65 53 32 00* **Closed** *Sun & Mon*
Cahors' most elegant restaurant presents an entire truffle-based tasting menu – and more. It also offers a range of cooking classes.

CASTRES: La Lanterne des Salvages €€
Bistro
1 av du Sidobre, Les Salvages, 81100 Burlats
Tel *05 63 35 08 21*
An eatery with a riverside terrace in a village north of Castres, La Lanterne provides fresh, seasonal menus and an inviting bar.

CHAMPAGNAC-DE-BELAIR: Le Moulin du Roc €€€
Fine dining
Av Eugene Leroy, 24530 Champagnac-de-Bélair
Tel *05 53 02 86 00* **Closed** *Tue; mid-Nov–mid-Mar*
The Michelin-starred Moulin du Roc offers beautifully presented Périgord cuisine in the romantic setting of a converted 1670s mill.

CONDOM: La Table des Cordeliers €
Traditional French
1 rue des Cordeliers, 32100
Tel *05 62 68 43 82* **Closed** *Sun & Mon*
Enjoy impeccable service and creative cuisine in this bistro housed in a 13th-century convent. Exceptional value for money.

CORDES-SUR-CIEL: Bistrot Tonin'ty €€
Regional
Hostellerie du Vieux Cordes, Haut de la Cité, 81170
Tel *05 63 53 79 20* **Closed** *Sun eve, Mon & Tue lunch*
Bistrot Tonin'ty is renowned for the irresistible desserts

Key to Price Guide *see p576*

created by Yves Thuries, master chocolatier and owner. Dine in the courtyard in good weather.

DOMME: L'Esplanade €€
Regional
2 rue Pontcarral, 24250
Tel *05 53 28 31 41* **Closed** *Mon; mid-Jan–mid-Feb; mid-Nov–mid-Dec*
There is a terrace overlooking the Dordogne Valley at this popular eatery with duck, *foie gras* and truffles as menu highlights.

FIGEAC: La Cuisine du Marché €€
Bistro
15 rue Clermont, 46100
Tel *05 65 50 18 55* **Closed** *Sun & Mon lunch*
The seasonal menus at this attractively converted stone wine cellar in medieval Figeac mix local favourites with Spanish dishes.

FRANCESCAS: Le Relais de la Hire €€
Regional
11 rue Porteneuve, 47600
Tel *05 53 65 41 59* **Closed** *Sun*
Fresh herbs from the chef's garden add bold flavours to the cuisine in this charming historic building.

ISSIGEAC: La Brucelière €€
Regional
Pl de la Capelle, 24560
Tel *05 53 73 89 61* **Closed** *May–Oct: Tue eve & Wed; Nov–Apr: Tue & Wed*
This rugged inn outside Bergerac serves lighter variations of local cuisine. Charming terrace.

LACAVE: Le Pont de l'Ouysse €€
Fine dining
Le Pont de l'Ouysse, 46200
Tel *05 65 37 87 04* **Closed** *Nov–Mar; weekly closing days vary*
This gorgeous restaurant has fabulous terrace views. Truffles are from the hotel's own grounds.

LES EYZIES-DE-TAYAC: Au Vieux Moulin €
Regional
2 rue du Moulin Bas, 24620
Tel *05 53 06 94 33* **Closed** *Tue, Wed & Sat lunch; Nov–Mar*
Classic local dishes are served in a very pretty old mill that overlooks a stream near the Lascaux caves.

MANCIET: La Bonne Auberge €
Regional
Pl du Pesquèrot, 32370
Tel *05 62 08 50 04* **Closed** *Mon*
Diners come to this family-run restaurant for the rich Gascon fare and the fine Armagnacs.

One of the many gastronomic creations at Le Pont de l'Ouysse, Lacave

MONBAZILLAC: La Tour des Vents €€
Traditional French
Moulin de Malfourat, 24240
Tel *05 53 58 30 10* **Closed** *Sun eve, Mon & Tue lunch*
There are stunning views of the Dordogne countryside from this Michelin-starred hilltop restaurant. Creative menus.

MONTAUBAN: Au Fil de l'Eau €
Bistro
14 quai du Dr Lafforgue, 82000
Tel *05 63 66 11 85* **Closed** *Sun & Mon*
A sizzling *cassoulet* heads the list of local specialities at this smart restaurant in the heart of old Montauban.

PERIGUEUX: Restaurant L'Essentiel €€
Regional
8 rue de la Clarté, 24000
Tel *05 53 35 15 15* **Closed** *Mon & Sun*
Sample subtle combinations of classic Périgord food and modern innovation at this local Michelin-starred favourite. The decor is warm and charming.

PUJAUDRAN: Le Puits Saint-Jacques €€€
Fine dining
Av Victor Capoul, 32600
Tel *05 62 07 41 11* **Closed** *Sun eve, Mon & Tue*
Exquisite cuisine and excellent wines are showcased at this prestigious restaurant in a historic farmhouse setting.

PUJOLS: La Toque Blanche €€
Regional
47300, Pujols
Tel *05 53 49 00 30* **Closed** *Sun & Mon*
Book in advance at this long-established restaurant with lovely views and an inventive chef.

ROCAMADOUR: Le Roc du Berger €
Regional
Bois de Belveyre, rte de Padirac, 46500
Tel *05 65 33 19 99* **Closed** *Oct: Mon–Fri; Nov–mid-Mar*
Local lamb and trout feature on the menu at this rustic eatery with tables inside wood cabins or under trees.

ST-MEDARD: Le Gindreau €€€
Fine dining
Le Bourg, 46150
Tel *05 65 36 22 27* **Closed** *Mon & Tue*
Savour gourmet meals in a converted village school. Delicious truffles and an exemplary wine cellar.

SARLAT: La Couleuvrine €
Regional
1 pl de la Bouquerie, 24200
Tel *05 53 59 27 80*
Enjoy hearty bistro-style food by the medieval fireplace in a tower in Sarlat's grand ramparts.

DK Choice

SORGES: Auberge de la Truffe €
Regional
Le Bourg, 24420
Tel *05 53 05 02 05*
Truffles figure prominently in Périgord cuisine, and Sorges proclaims itself the "world truffle capital". This inn is the ideal place to sample truffles in all their variety – *consommé*, omelettes, with scallops and in desserts.

TOULOUSE: Brasserie Flo – Les Beaux Arts €€
Brasserie
1 quai de la Daurade, 31000
Tel *05 61 21 12 12*
A local institution, Brasserie Flo has grand 1900s decor, a bustling atmosphere and a huge menu.

TOULOUSE: Le Louchebem €€
Traditional French
Marché Victor Hugo, 31000
Tel *05 67 00 51 75* **Closed** *Mon, dinner*
Carnivores will love this meat haven on the first floor of the Victor Hugo market. Try the Toulouse sausage or *cassoulet*.

TOULOUSE: Michel Sarran €€€
Fine dining
21 bd Armand Duportal, 31000
Tel *05 61 12 32 32* **Closed** *Wed lunch, Sat & Sun; Aug*
A real gourmet experience awaits at this elegant Michelin-starred restaurant. Try the creative and delicious chef's tasting menu.

For more information on types of restaurants *see p575*

TURSAC: La Source €
Regional
Le Bourg, 24620
Tel *05 53 06 98 00* **Closed** *Tue & Wed*
This friendly restaurant serves local dishes featuring herbs and mushrooms from the garden on site.

The Pyrenees

AINHOA: La Maison Oppoca €€
Regional
Le Bourg, 64250
Tel *05 59 29 90 72* **Closed** *Thu, Fri lunch, Sun eve*
Serving Basque cuisine, this stylish establishment specializes in crab dishes and inventive cooking.

ARGELES-GAZOST: Au Fond du Gosier €
Bistro
7 rue du Capitaine Digoy, 65400
Tel *05 62 90 13 40* **Closed** *Sat lunch, Sun & Mon*
Local dishes are prepared with fresh produce and culinary flair at this place. Original wine list.

ASCAIN: L'Atelier Gourmand Basque €
Regional
Pl du Fronton, 64310
Tel *05 59 54 46 82* **Closed** *Sun; Jul & Aug: Mon*
This lively bar-restaurant offers great local cuisine, plus a range of tapas dishes.

AX-LES-THERMES: Le Chalet €€
Regional
4 av Durandeau, 09110
Tel *05 61 64 24 31* **Closed** *Sun & Mon*
One of the best restaurants in the Ariège serves dishes such as local trout and deer in creative ways.

BAGNERES-DE-LUCHON: Les Caprices Etigny €
Regional
30 bis allées d'Etigny, 31110
Tel *05 61 94 31 05* **Closed** *Mon*
Try local lamb, organic trout or pork grilled over an open fire at this eatery with mountain views.

DK Choice

BAREGES: Auberge du Lienz Chez Louisette €
Regional
Rte de Lienz, 65120
Tel *05 62 92 67 17* **Closed** *mid-Apr–mid-May & Nov*
Few restaurants boast such a spectacular location, in the High Pyrenees. In winter, skiers warm up with *garbure* (thick soup); for summer hikers, there are dishes with wild flowers and fruits.

Chic, comfortable dining space at Le Sin restaurant, Biarritz

BAYONNE: Le Bayonnais €
Bistro
38 quai des Corsaires, 64100
Tel *05 59 25 61 19* **Closed** *Sun & Mon; 3 wks in Jun & 2 wks in Dec*
Enjoy Basque fare, including great squid, at this pleasant place with a terrace on a riverside quay.

BAYONNE: Auberge du Cheval Blanc €€
Fine dining
68 rue Bourgneuf, 64100
Tel *05 59 59 01 33* **Closed** *Mon, Sat lunch, Sun eve*
Family-run and Michelin-starred, this inn offers particularly good ham and Atlantic seafood.

BIARRITZ: Chez Albert €€
Seafood
51 bis allée Port des Pêcheurs, 64200
Tel *05 59 24 43 84* **Closed** *Feb–Jun & Sep–Nov: Wed; Dec–Jan*
Great sea views come as a bonus at this seafood brasserie located right on the port. The seafood platter is immense.

BIARRITZ: Le Sin €€
Fine dining
Cité de Océan, 1 av de la Plage, 64200
Tel *05 59 47 82 89* **Closed** *Sep–Jun: Mon, Sun eve*
Enjoy creative Basque cuisine based on local fish at this modern restaurant that comes with fabulous views.

ESPELETTE: Hôtel-Restaurant Euzkadi €
Regional
285 Karrika Nagusia, 64250
Tel *05 59 93 91 88***Closed** *Mon & Tue; mid-Feb–mid-Mar*
This charming eatery serves classic Basque fare, and the dishes often feature the village's famous fiery peppers.

FOIX: Le Phoebus €
Regional
3 cours Irénée Cros, 09000
Tel *05 61 65 10 42* **Closed** *Mon, Sat lunch, Sun eve; late July–mid-Aug*
Specialities here include duck, *foie gras* and chocolate fondant, but there are also vegetarian options. There are great views of the Ariège river and the château.

LARRAU: Etchemaïte €
Regional
Le Bourg, 64560
Tel *05 59 28 61 45* **Closed** *Jan–mid-Feb*
In the Pic d'Orhy, this family-run establishment boasts a gorgeous location. Lamb cooked in several ways is the star dish.

LOURDES: Le Magret €
Bistro
10 rue des 4 Frères Soulas, 65100
Tel *05 62 94 20 55* **Closed** *Wed*
Known for regional specialities from black pig, to *foie gras* and lamb, this small, relaxed bistro has good- value seasonal menus and wines.

MIREPOIX: Les Remparts €
Bistro
6 cours Louis Pons Tande, 09500
Tel *05 61 60 80 22*
Global touches are given to local produce and traditions at this historic inn. Great surf 'n' turf.

MONTSEGUR: La Patate Qui Fume €
Regional
118 rue du Village, 09300
Tel *05 61 02 65 07* **Closed** *Wed; Jul & Aug: Thu; Nov–Mar*
Set in a village house, this cosy restaurant serves hearty dishes made with local produce.

PAU: Restaurant Pierre €€
Bistro
14–16 rue Louis Barthou, 64000
Tel *05 59 27 76 86* **Closed** *Sat & Sun*
There are monthly menus at this snug spot with old-fashioned decor and an attached pub.

ST-GAUDENS: La Connivence €€
Fine dining
Chemin Ample, Valentine, 31800
Tel *05 61 95 29 31* **Closed** *Mon*
Sophisticated and family-owned, this restaurant offers excellent wines and regional specialities.

ST-JEAN-DE-LUZ: Chez Pablo €€
Regional
5 rue Mlle Etcheto, 64500
Tel *05 59 26 37 81* **Closed** *Wed*
Family-owned for three generations, this friendly eatery has a copious menu and specializes in Basque seafood.

Key to Price Guide *see p576*

ST-JEAN-DE-LUZ: Le Kaïku €€€
Fine Dining
17 rue de la République, 64500
Tel *05 59 26 13 20* **Closed** *Tue & Wed*
Enjoy inventive Basque cuisine and superb fish in a lovely old stone house. Good-value lunch menu.

ST-JEAN-PIED-DE-PORT: Relais de la Nive €
Brasserie
4 pl Charles de Gaulle, 64220
Tel *05 59 37 04 22*
This spacious brasserie with fine views over the River Nive makes great salads and light meals.

ST-LARY-SOULAN: Restaurant La Grange €
Regional
13 rte d'Autun, 65170
Tel *05 62 40 07 14* **Closed** *Sep–Jun: Tue & Wed; Nov*
Enjoy local bean stews and grilled meats at this large stone farmhouse in the High Pyrenees.

SAINT-GIRONS: L'Auberge d'Antan €€
Regional
Av de la Résistance, 09200
Tel *05 61 64 11 02* **Closed** *Mon, Sat lunch, Sun eve*
Savour spit-roast suckling pig – the house speciality – at this restaurant set in a renovated barn.

SARE: Baratxartea €
Regional
Ihalar, 64310
Tel *05 59 54 20 48* **Closed** *mid-Nov–mid-Mar*
The chef plates fine food made with vegetables from the hotel's garden at this large Basque chalet.

TARBES: L'Agora €
Fine dining
48 rue Abbé Torné, 65000
Tel *05 62 93 09 34* **Closed** *Mon*
Tarbes' top restaurant features fresh produce and fish. Excellent wines and a charming terrace.

Pretty shaded eating area at the popular La Marquière, Carcassonne

Languedoc and Roussillon

AIGUES-MORTES: Le Duendé €
Regional
13 rue Amiral Courbet, 30220
Tel *04 66 51 79 28*
This simple restaurant in an old townhouse is a good place to sample the local flavours of traditional Camargue cuisine in a warm ambience.

AIGUES-MORTES: Le Café des Bouzigues €€
Regional
7 rue Pasteur, 30220
Tel *04 66 53 93 95* **Closed** *most of Jan, late Nov–early Dec*
This cheerful restaurant with a terrace supplies a creative and hearty fixed-price menu.

ANDUZE: Auberge Les Trois Barbus €€
Fine dining
Rte de Mialet, Camaou et Roucan, Générargues, 30140
Tel *04 66 61 72 12* **Closed** *Mon & Tue; Nov–late Mar*
This elegant restaurant in a rustic setting has plenty of dishes featuring *foie gras* and wild mushrooms. Rich desserts, too.

ARGELLIERS: Auberge de Saugras €€
Traditional French
Domaine de Saugras, 34380
Tel *04 67 55 08 71* **Closed** *Tue & Wed*
There is an impressive cellar at this traditional farmhouse serving lots of duck and mountain trout.

BEZIERS: Octopus €€€
Fine dining
12 rue Boiledieu, 34500
Tel *04 67 49 90 00* **Closed** *Sun & Mon*
Béziers' best restaurant is a Michelin-starred affair with lots of truffles, a touch of Asia and a great wine selection.

BIZE MINERVOIS: La Bastide Cabezac €
Traditional French
18–20 Hameau de Cabezac, 11120,
Tel *04 68 46 66 10* **Closed** *Sun eve, Mon*
Come to this atttractive 18th-century staging post with refined creative fare such as Cathar chicken *fricassée*.

CAP D'AGDE: La Manade €
Regional
15 pl Saint-Clair, 34300
Tel *04 67 21 23 38* **Closed** *winter: Tue & Wed*
This is the place for affordable, tasty seafood and succulent steaks from the Camargue.

CARCASSONNE: L'Escargot €
Regional
7 rue Viollet le Duc, 11000
Tel *04 68 47 12 55* **Closed** *Wed*
A popular tapas and wine bar, L'Escargot offers a range of dishes with international influences made with local produce.

DK Choice

CARCASSONNE: La Marquière €€
Regional
13 rue St-Jean, 11000
Tel *04 68 71 52 00* **Closed** *Wed & Thu; Jan 10–Feb 10*
Located up in the Cité, La Marquière is a popular family-run local favourite. The food is authentic Southwestern – duck breasts and *confits*, *foie gras* and *cassoulet*. Oysters and other seafood are available as well.

CARCASSONNE: Le Parc Franck Putelat €€€
Fine dining
80 chemin des Anglais, 11000
Tel *04 68 71 80 80* **Closed** *Sun & Mon; 3 weeks in Jan*
Sample radically creative cuisine at this two-star restaurant with a good-value lunch menu.

CERET: Alcatalà €
Catalan
15 av Georges Clémenceau, 66400
Tel *04 68 87 07 91* **Closed** *Mon*
Creative cooking, exotic flavours and a dash of Catalan style can be enjoyed on a chic bamboo-shaded terrace.

CLARA: Les Loges du Jardin d'Aymeric €€
Traditional French
7 rue du Canigou, 66500
Tel *04 68 96 08 72* **Closed** *Sun eve & Mon; Jan*
Classic dishes with a contemporary twist are served in a tranquil garden setting.

COLLIOURE: Le 5e Péché €€
Regional
18 rue Fraternité, 66190
Tel *04 68 98 09 76* **Closed** *Sun & Mon*
A Japanese chef creates his own remarkable Languedoc-Asian fusion cuisine from a choice of fresh, local ingredients.

COLLIOURE: La Balette €€
Fine dining
114 rte de Port-Vendres, 66190
Tel *04 68 82 05 07* **Closed** *Mon (also Tue in low season); late Nov–early Feb*
Dine on elaborate creations in a beautiful setting with magical views of Collioure over the bay.

For more information on types of restaurants *see p575*

CUCUGNAN: Auberge du Vigneron €
Regional
2 rue Achille Mir, 11350
Tel *04 68 45 03 00* **Closed** *Mon; late Nov–early Mar*
The hearty Languedoc fare here uses produce from the kitchen garden. Good Corbières wines.

FONTJONCOUSE: Gilles Goujon €€€
Fine dining
5 av St-Victor, 11360
Tel *04 68 44 07 37* **Closed** *Mon; Dec–late Mar*
Culinary masterpieces are served at this Michelin-starred restaurant. Try the "truffle eggs".

LE BOULOU: Hostalet de Vivès €
Catalan
Le Village, Vivès, 66490
Tel *04 68 83 05 52* **Closed** *Mon & Tue; Jul & Aug: Mon*
Grilled snails, rabbit cooked on an open fire and all things Catalan are on offer at this rustic eatery.

MARAUSSAN: Le Parfum des Garrigues €€
Regional
37 rue de l'Ancienne Poste, 34370
Tel *09 70 35 53 34* **Closed** *Mon & Tue*
Fresh seafood, grilled meat and game dishes are delivered in a pretty courtyard.

MINERVE: Relais Chantovent €
Bistro
17 Grande Rue, 34210
Tel *04 68 91 14 18* **Closed** *Sun & Wed, Tue eve; mid-Dec–mid-Mar*
Terrace views over the Gorges du Brian accompany the creative cooking. Home-made ice cream.

MONTPELLIER: Au Bonheur des Tartes €
Bistro
4 rue des Trésoriers de la Bourse, 34000
Tel *04 67 02 77 38* **Closed** *Sun, Wed eve*
Enjoy perfect cooking and excellent *plats du jour* in this cosy eatery with a tearoom attached.

MONTPELLIER: La Diligence €€
Traditional French
2 pl Pétrarque, 34000
Tel *04 67 66 12 21* **Closed** *Sun, Mon & Sat lunch*
Set in a vaulted medieval hall, this city-centre restaurant serves grilled dishes, wines and desserts.

MONTPELLIER: Le Petit Jardin €€
Fine dining
20 rue Jean-Jacques Rousseau, 34000
Tel *04 67 60 78 78* **Closed** *winter: Sun & Mon*
Enjoy old-world elegance and refined cuisine at this eatery that boasts a lovely garden setting. The seasonally changing menu takes inspiration from cuisines across the world.

NARBONNE: Chez Bebelle €
Bistro
Halles de Narbonne, 1 bd Dr. Ferroul, 11100
Tel *06 85 40 09 01* **Closed** *Sun & Mon*
At this inexpensive, cheerful family-run steakhouse in the covered market, the meat is sourced daily from the neighbouring butcher.

NARBONNE: Le Table de St-Crescent €€
Fine dining
Rond pt de la Liberté, 68 av Général Leclerc, 11100
Tel *04 68 41 37 37* **Closed** *Mon & Tue (Jul–Sep: Mon only)*
An old medieval chapel provides the perfect setting for a special evening. A creative, seasonal menu is on offer.

NIMES: Aux Plaisirs des Halles €
Traditional French
4 rue Littré, 30000
Tel *04 66 36 01 02* **Closed** *Sun & Mon*
Classic dishes made from locally sourced ingredients, including lamb and olives, is served in a pleasant wood-panelled interior.

NIMES: Le Cheval Blanc €
Wine bar
1 pl des Arènes, 30000
Tel *04 66 76 19 59* **Closed** *Sun*
Facing the arena, this lively brasserie has a great cellar and Pyrenean *charcuterie* and cheeses.

PERPIGNAN: Le Grain de Folie €
Bistro
71 av Général Leclerc, 66000
Tel *04 68 51 00 50* **Closed** *Sun eve*
The dining room here may be austere, but the cooking is first rate. It provides good-value meals and great desserts.

The well-stocked Le Cheval Blanc wine bar in Nîmes

PERPIGNAN: La Galinette €€
Fine dining
23 rue Jean Payra, 66000
Tel *04 68 35 00 90* **Closed** *Sun & Mon*
Boasting a huge wine list, this is also the place for creative, critically acclaimed Catalan cuisine.

PEZENAS: L'Entre-Pots €€
Modern French
8 av Louis-Montagne, 34120
Tel *04 67 39 00 00* **Closed** *Jul & Aug: Mon; Sep–Jun: Sun & Mon*
In an old warehouse, this restaurant serves inventive food and boasts a large wine cellar.

PORT CAMARGUE: Le Spinaker €€
Traditional French
Pointe du Môle, Le Grau du Roi, 30240
Tel *04 66 53 36 37* **Closed** *Mon–Wed (out of season); Jan; Jul & Aug: Mon & Tue*
Seafood, grilled beef and duck are served on a terrace overlooking the marina. Decadent desserts.

PORT-VENDRES: La Cote Vermeille €€
Seafood
Quai Fanal, 66660
Tel *04 68 82 05 71* **Closed** *Mon*
Enjoying a quayside location, this famous seafood restaurant has delicious lobster and oysters.

SAILLAGOUSE: La Vieille Maison Cerdane €
Catalan
Pl de Cerdagne, 66800
Tel *04 68 04 72 08* **Closed** *Mon; mid-Nov–mid-Apr*
This old family-run coach inn specializes in venison and other game dishes.

SETE: Terre et Mer €€
Regional
Pl de Souras Bas, 34200
Tel *04 67 74 49 43* **Closed** *Tue & Wed*
Come here for fresh seafood, meat and *charcuterie* from the Aveyron. Great desserts, too.

SOURNIA: Auberge de Sournia €
Traditional French
4 rte de Prades, 66730
Tel *04 68 97 72 82* **Closed** *Wed & Sun eves; 2 weeks in Feb & Nov*
The hearty mountain cooking at this popular village inn includes steak, duck and a range of game dishes.

UZES: Au Petit Jardin €€
Bistro
4 bd Gambetta, 30700
Tel *04 66 81 56 88* **Closed** *Oct–Jun: Sun*
Enjoy good bistro food in a lovely garden setting. There is live jazz on Saturday evenings.

Key to Price Guide *see p576*

VILLEFRANCHE-DE-CONFLENT: Auberge St-Paul €€
Bistro
7 pl de Eglise, 66500
Tel *04 68 96 30 95* **Closed** *Mon*
Sample creative dishes with a Spanish touch, including a mushroom-themed "land and sea" menu.

Provence and the Côte d'Azur

AIX-EN-PROVENCE: Le Formal €€
Fine dining
32 rue Espariat, 13100
Tel *04 42 27 08 31* **Closed** *Sat lunch, Sun & Mon; late Aug–early Sep*
Choose from a range of truffle dishes at Le Formal. The lunch menus are good value.

ANTIBES: Aubergine €
Regional
7 rue Sade, 06600
Tel *04 93 34 55 93* **Closed** *Wed*
This popular restaurant is the place to visit for excellent Provençal dishes. Book ahead.

ARLES: La Grignotte €
Regional
6 rue Favorin, 13200
Tel *04 90 93 10 43* **Closed** *Sun & Mon*
Try the fish soup and beef stew with Camargue rice at this simple eatery. Good house wines.

ARLES: Lou Marques €€
Fine dining
9 bd Lices, 13200
Tel *04 90 52 52 52*
This elegant restaurant offers a garden terrace and beautifully presented classic Provençal dishes.

AVIGNON: La Fourchette €€
Regional
17 rue Racine, 84000
Tel *04 90 85 20 93* **Closed** *Sat & Sun*
Putting an innovative spin on Provençal classics, this quirky place offers tasty seafood and cheeses.

AVIGNON: Christian Etienne €€€
Fine dining
10 rue Mons, 84000
Tel *04 90 86 16 50* **Closed** *Wed & Thu*
This restaurant serves superb seasonal fare and an elaborate truffle menu in a stunning 14th-century dining room.

BIOT: Les Terraillers €€€
Fine dining
11 rte Chemin Neuf, 06410
Tel *04 93 65 01 59* **Closed** *Wed & Thu; mid-Oct–Nov*
Lobster, truffles and *foie gras* await here, along with an excellent list of Provençal wines.

Dining area at Les Terraillers in Biot, in a 16th-century stone house

BONNIEUX: Edouard Loubet €€€
Fine dining
Les Claparèdes, chemin des Cabanes, 84480
Tel *04 90 75 89 78* **Closed** *Wed; winter (except hols)*
Diners can enjoy ravishing dishes from one of France's top chefs at this gourmet restaurant in a great location with views of the Provençal countryside.

CAGNES-SUR-MER: Fleur de Sel €€
Traditional French
85 montée de la Bourgade, 06800
Tel *04 93 20 33 33* **Closed** *Wed & Thu*
The lofty Haut de Cagnes makes a lovely setting for some refined cooking. There are great-value set menus.

CANNES: Angolo Italiano €
Italian
18 rue du Commandant André, 06400
Tel *04 93 39 82 57* **Closed** *Mon*
This Neapolitan-run restaurant serves *charcuterie*, cheeses, grilled meat and seafood, as well as lots of pasta dishes.

CANNES: La Palme d'Or €€€
Fine dining
73 la Croisette, 06400
Tel *04 92 98 74 14* **Closed** *Sun–Tue; Jan & Feb*
Part of the famous Hôtel Martinez, this fashionable Michellin-starred restaurant has a terrace with stunning views of the Bay of Cannes. The exquisite food, wonderful atmosphere and great service make this a memorable experience.

CARPENTRAS: Chez Serge €
Bistro
90 rue Cottier, 84200
Tel *04 90 63 21 24*
Striking modern decor and imaginative food featuring fish and wild mushrooms can be found here. There is a huge wine list.

CASTELLANE: Auberge du Teillon €
Traditional French
Rte Napoléon le Garde, 04120
Tel *04 92 83 60 88* **Closed** *Mon; Nov–Mar*
This country inn is famed for fine dishes such as hand-smoked salmon and *foie gras millefeuille*.

CHATEAUNEUF-DU-PAPE: La Mère Germaine €€
Regional
3 rue Commandant Lemaitre, 84230
Tel *04 90 22 78 34* **Closed** *mid-Sep–mid-Mar: Wed*
The wide range of classic Provençal dishes is accompanied by an excellent list of wines.

EZE: Café La Gascogne €
Bistro
151 av de Verdun, 06360
Tel *04 93 41 18 50*
Enjoy no-frills wholesome fare in the Hotel du Golf – everything from *foie gras* to pizza. Fantastic selection of wines.

EZE: Château Eza €€€
Fine dining
Rue de la Pise, 06360
Tel *04 93 41 12 24* **Closed** *Mon & Tue; Jan–Mar*
Château Eza offers stunning terrace views and high-quality Michelin-star cooking.

DK Choice

FAYENCE: L'Escourtin €€
Bistro
159 chemin de Notre Dame des Cyprès, 83440
Tel *04 94 76 00 84* **Closed** *Wed*
Filled with antiques and flowers, L'Escourtin has an idyllic location inside an ancient olive mill with a delightful garden courtyard. The cuisine is authentic, with an emphasis on game dishes, *foie gras*, and fish in subtle sauces – all flavoured with the best garden produce and herbs.

For more information on types of restaurants *see p575*

ILE DE PORQUEROLLES: L'Olivier €€€
Seafood
Ile de Porquerolles Ouest, 83400
Tel *04 94 58 34 83* **Closed** *Mon & Tue (except Jul & Aug); Oct–Apr*
This isolated, semi-tropical island retreat offers a delightful culinary experience. Mostly seafood.

L'ISLE-SUR-LE SORGUE: Le Vivier €€
Regional
800 cours Fernande Peyre, 84800
Tel *04 90 38 52 80* **Closed** *Mon, Fri & Sat lunch*
Ask for the famous pigeon pie with porcini mushrooms and enjoy it on the magical riverside terrace.

LA TURBIE: Hostellerie Jérôme €€€
Fine dining
20 rue Comte de Cessole, 06320
Tel *04 92 41 51 51* **Closed** *Sep–Jun: Mon & Tue*
All dishes are prepared daily using market produce at this Michelin-starred establishment. Dinner only.

LES-BAUX-DE-PROVENCE: L'Oustau de Baumanière €€€
Fine dining
Rte Départementale 27, Le Val d'Enfer 13520
Tel *04 90 54 33 07* **Closed** *Jan & Feb*
Great for celebrity-spotting, this Michelin-starred gem has a great setting and inventive menus.

LES-SAINTES-MARIES-DE-LA-MER: El Campo €
Spanish
13 rue Victor Hugo, 13460
Tel *04 90 97 84 11* **Closed** *Sep–Jun: Wed*
Enjoy an evening with live flamenco and Gypsy-Kings-style guitar music. Paella is a speciality

MARSEILLE: Toinou €
Seafood
3 cours Saint-Louis, 13001
Tel *04 91 33 14 94*
Fresh oysters, mussels and prawns are served with crusty bread and white wine. Ideal seafood place.

DK Choice

MARSEILLE: L'Epuisette €€€
Seafood
158 rue du Vallon des Auffes, 13007
Tel *04 91 52 17 82* **Closed** *Sun & Mon; 1 week in Mar*
Heavenly *bouillabaisse*, lobster tajine and other seafood delicacies are accompanied by fine wines and followed by great desserts. Attentive staff ensure a memorable dining experience in a spectacular glass dining room overlooking the turquoise sea.

Refined and graceful dining room at the renowned Le Louis XV in Monaco

MENTON: Le Mirazur €€€
Fine dining
30 ave Aristide Briand, 06500
Tel *04 92 41 86 86* **Closed** *Mon & Tue; Nov–mid-Feb*
With magnificent views of the sea and the old town, the Michelin-starred Le Mirazur offers colourful dishes made with fresh seafood, local lamb and vegetables from the chef's own garden.

MONACO: Le Louis XV €€€
Fine dining
Hotel de Paris, pl du Casino, Monte Carlo, 98000
Tel *00 377 98 06 88 64* **Closed** *Tue & Wed*
Capital of Alain Ducasse's culinary empire since 1987, Le Louis XV is all about contemporary haute cuisine in a supremely elegant setting. It has a huge wine cellar. Dinner only.

DK Choice

MOUSTIERS-STE-MARIE: La Treille Muscate €
Regional
Pl de l'Eglise, 04360
Tel *04 92 74 64 31* **Closed** *Wed eve, Thu*
Near a waterfall, under the crags, this restaurant has a shady terrace under an ancient plane tree on which to savour Provençal and Mediterranean dishes such as *pieds et paquets* (sheeps' feet and stuffed sheep tripe) with baby vegetables.

NICE: Les Amoureux €
Italian
46 bd Stalingrad, 06300
Tel *04 93 07 59 73* **Closed** *Sun & Mon*
Visit Les Amoureux for some of the best Neapolitan pizzas on the Riviera, with the perfect crust, served in a convivial atmosphere.

NICE: Jan €€€
Fine dining
12 rue Lascaris, 06000
Tel *04 97 19 32 23* **Closed** *Sun & Mon*
Enjoy Michelin-starred cuisine from South African chef Jan Hendrik, who mixes French and South African flavours in his creative, contemporary dishes.

ROQUEBRUNE-CAP-MARTIN: Au Grand Inquisiteur €€
Traditional French
15–18 rue du Château, 06190
Tel *04 93 35 05 37* **Closed** *Mon*
This intimate, family-run restaurant rustles up authentic traditional dishes, including snails. Dinner only.

ST-JEAN-CAP-FERRAT: La Cabane de L'Écailler €€
Seafood **Map** F3
Nouveau Port, 06230
Tel *04 93 87 39 31* **Closed** *Nov–Mar*
Be sure to try the grilled fish, *bouillabaisse* and roast lobster at this delightful place on a picturesque port.

ST-PAUL DE VENCE: La Colombe d'Or €€
Regional
Pl du Général de Gaulle, 06570
Tel *04 93 32 80 02* **Closed** *Nov–mid-Dec*
A legendary artists' retreat, La Colombe d'Or offers simple but excellent Provençal cooking. Guests can eat al fresco on the garden terrace.

ST-REMY DE PROVENCE: La Cantina €
Italian
18 bd Victor Hugo, 13210
Tel *04 90 90 90 60* **Closed** *Mon*
There is an excellent selection of Italian wines at this informal restaurant specializing in thin-crust pizzas and pasta dishes.

Key to Price Guide *see p576*

ST-TROPEZ: Vague d'Or €€€
Fine dining
Plage de la Bouillabaisse, 83990
Tel *04 94 55 91 00* **Closed** *Early Oct–late Apr*
Sample a range of imaginative Mediterranean dishes using local ingredients in a romantic setting. Excellent service and fine wines. Dinner only.

STE-AGNES: Le Righi €
Regional
1 pl du Fort, 06500
Tel *04 92 10 90 88* **Closed** *Wed*
Enjoy food such as ravioli, gnocchi and lamb cooked in hay, while admiring the amazing views of the surrounding landscape.

VENCE: La Litote €€
Bistro
5 rue de l'Evêché, 06140
Tel *04 93 24 27 82* **Closed** *Sun eve, Mon*
On a little square, with tables under the trees, this laid-back restaurant offers inventive fare.

VILLEFRANCHE-SUR-MER: La Mère Germaine €€
Seafood
9 quai Courbet, 06230
Tel *04 93 01 71 39* **Closed** *mid-Nov–25 Dec*
A long-established favourite on the port since 1938, this place serves an excellent *bouillabaisse*.

VILLENEUVE-LES-AVIGNON: Guinguette du Vieux Moulin €€
Seafood
5 rue du Vieux Moulin, 30400
Tel *04 90 94 50 72*
This lively riverside restaurant specializes in grilled sardines and other fish. Live music.

Corsica

AJACCIO: A Nepita €
Bistro
4 rue St Lazaro, 20000
Tel *04 95 26 75 68* **Closed** *Sat lunch, Sun, Mon–Wed eves*
The chef here bases his daily-changing menu on produce fresh from the market.

DK Choice

AJACCIO: Le Week End €€
Regional
Rte des Sanguinaires, 20000
Tel *04 95 52 01 39* **Closed** *Winter*
This smart beach restaurant offers a mix of seafood and regional produce. Finish off with *limoncello* ice cream or a platter of Corsican cheeses.

Exterior of the popular restaurant La Mère Germaine in Villefranche-Sur-Mer

BASTIA: Chez Huguette €€
Seafood
Vieux Port, rue de la Marine, 20200
Tel *04 95 31 37 60* **Closed** *2 weeks at Christmas*
A favourite on the Vieux Port, Chez Huguette is ideal for oysters and grilled fish. Excellent wine cellar.

BONIFACIO: The Kissing Pigs €
Regional
15 quai Banda del Ferro, 20169
Tel *04 95 73 56 09*
This portside eatery and wine bar serves *charcuterie*, omelettes, grill, and a good range of wines.

BONIFACIO: Le Voilier €€
Fine dining
81 quai Jérôme Comparetti, 20169
Tel *04 95 73 07 06* **Closed** *Wed; mid-Jan–mid-Feb*
In summer this chic restaurant has a mozzarella bar that is perfect for a light lunch. Lovely tapas.

CALVI: A Casetta €
Regional
16 rue Clémenceau, 20280
Tel *04 95 65 32 15*
This deli stocking regional products has a "tasting terrace" that offers great views. Try a platter of local hams and cheeses.

CARGESE: Bel'Mare €
Mediterranean
Rte d'Ajaccio, 20130
Tel *04 95 26 40 13* **Closed** *Nov–Feb*
Enjoy the views from the terrace and choose from a range of pizzas, pasta dishes, steaks and salads. Evenings only.

CORTE: Osteria di l'Orta €€
Bistro
Casa Guelfucci, Pont de l'Orta, 20250
Tel *04 95 61 06 41* **Closed** *Sat & Sun; mid-Nov–Mar*
Meals here feature home-grown produce, plus meat raised and cured by the owners.

ERBALUNGA: Le Pirate €€€
Fine dining
Port, 20222
Tel *04 95 33 24 20* **Closed** *Jan–Feb; Sep–Jun: Mon & Tue*
Diners can sample organic lamb and veal, plus wonderful desserts, in a romantic, Michelin-starred spot on the water.

LEVIE: A Pignata €€
Regional
Rte du Pianu, 20170
Tel *04 95 78 41 90* **Closed** *Winter*
Book ahead to dine at A Pignata, a beautiful *ferme-auberge* that guarantees first-rate cooking.

PORTO-VECCHIO: Casa del Mare €€€
Fine dining
Rte de Palombaggia, 20137
Tel *04 95 72 34 34* **Closed** *Sun; mid-Nov–mid-Apr*
A modern seafront pavilion is the setting for sumptuous, Italian-influenced meals. Dinner only.

SAINT-FLORENT: Le Petit Caporal €€
Brasserie
Port de Plaisance, 20217
Tel *04 95 37 20 26* **Closed** *Wed & Thu*
As well as excellent pizzas, pasta, mussels and *frites*, the menu here includes steaks and seafood.

Sea views and a refined dining area at the waterside restaurant Le Pirate, Erbalunga

For more information on types of restaurants *see p575*

Shopping in France

Shopping in France is a delight. Whether you go to the hypermarkets and department stores, or seek out the small specialist stores and markets, you will be tempted by stylish French presentation and the quality of goods on offer. Renowned for its food and wine, France also offers world-famous fashion, perfume, pottery, porcelain and crystal. This section provides guidelines on opening hours and the range of goods stocked by the different types of stores. There are also details of quintessentially French products that are worth hunting down and a size conversion chart to aid clothes shopping.

Fresh nectarines and melons on sale at a market stall

Opening Hours

Food shops open anywhere between 7am and 8am and close around noon for lunch. In the north, the lunch break generally lasts for 2 hours; in the south, it is 3–4 hours (except in resorts, where it is shorter). After lunch, most food shops reopen until 7pm or later.

Bakeries open early and many stay open until early evening to catch the late baguette buyers. They also serve a range of lunchtime snacks.

Supermarkets, department stores and most hypermarkets remain open all day, with no lunchtime closure.

General opening hours for non-food shops are 9am–6pm Monday through Saturday, often with a break for lunch. Many of these shops are closed on Monday mornings, and the smaller shops may stay closed all day. In the tourist regions, however, shops usually open every day in high season.

Sunday is by far the quietest shopping day, although most food shops (and newsagents) open (usually for the morning), as do many shops in the main tourist areas of large cities.

Hypermarkets and Department Stores

Hypermarkets (*hypermarchés* or *grandes surfaces*) can be found on the outskirts of every sizable town: look for signs indicating *centre commercial*. Much bigger than supermarkets, they sell mainly groceries, but their other lines include clothing, home accessories and electronic equipment. They also sell discount petrol (gasoline). **Carrefour**, **Casino**, **Auchan**, **Leclerc** and **Intermarché** are the biggest.

Supermarkets and retail chains, such as **Monoprix** and **Franprix**, are usually found in town centres, as are the more upmarket department stores (*grands magasins*) **Printemps** and **Galeries Lafayette**.

A local bakery, which often sells pastries as well as bread

Specialist Shops

One of the pleasures of shopping in France is that specialist food shops continue to flourish, despite the influx of supermarkets and hypermarkets. The *boulangerie* (bakery) is frequently combined with a *pâtisserie* selling cakes and pastries. The *traiteur* sells prepared foods. *Fromagers* (cheese shops) and other shops specializing in dairy products *(produits laitiers)* may be combined, but the *boucherie* (butcher) and *charcuterie* (pork butcher-delicatessen) are often separate shops. For general groceries go to an *épicerie* or *alimentation*, but don't confuse this with an *épicerie fine* – a delicatessen.

Cleaning and household products are available from a *droguerie*, while hardware is bought from a *quincaillerie*. The term *papeterie* (stationer) covers both the expensive, specialist retailers and their hypermarket equivalents.

Markets

This guide lists the market day for most towns featured in the *Area by Area* section. To find out where the market is, ask a passerby for *le marché*. Markets are held in the morning and usually finish promptly at noon.

Look for local producers, including those with only one or two special items to sell, as their goods are often more reasonably priced and of better quality than stalls with multiple items. By law (but not always in practice) price tags include the origin of all produce: *pays* means "local". Chickens from Bresse are marketed featuring a red, white and blue badge with the name of the producer.

If you are visiting markets over several weeks, look for items just coming into season, such as fresh walnuts, the first wild asparagus, early artichokes or wild strawberries. At the market, you can also buy spices and herbs, some offbeat peculiarities (such as decorative cabbages), shoes and clothing.

The year is full of seasonal regional markets in France, specializing in such things as truffles, hams, garlic, *foie gras* and livestock. *Foires artisanales* may be held at the same time as the seasonal markets, selling local produce and crafts.

Sausages and cheeses, regional specialities on offer in a Lyon market

Regional Produce

French regional specialities are available outside their area of origin, but it is more interesting to buy them locally as their creation and flavour reflect the traditions, tastes and climate of the region.

Provence, in the south, prides itself on the quality of its olive oil, the best of which is made from the first cold pressing, lovingly decanted every day for a week. If you cannot get to a niche olive oil producer in Provence, head to **Oliviers et Co**, which has branches throughout the country, and sells an excellent selection of oils. Be sure to indulge in a tasting session to sample the flavours. In the temperate north, delicious Camembert cheese is the product of fresh Normandy milk that has been cured for at least 3 weeks.

Popular drinks are also associated with particular regions. Pastis, made from aniseed, is commonly drunk in the south. Calvados, made in Normandy from apples, is popular in the north. Fruit liqeur, the secret ingredient to many a good cocktail or dessert, comes in many flavours (from peach to wild strawberry) in addition to the well-known blackcurrant – **Crème de Cassis**. Visit local producers to buy good versions of this thick, alcoholic syrup.

Pastis 51, a popular *apéritif*

To a large extent, location determines the quality of regional produce. For example, the culinary tradition of Lyon *(see pp382–5)*, France's premier gastronomic city, stems from the proximity of Charolais cattle, Bresse chickens and pork, wild game from La Dombes, and the finest Rhône Valley wines.

Alongside sachets of dried herbs from Provence and plaited strings of garlic and onions, be sure to buy the seasoning loved by all self-respecting francophile cooks – salt from the Ile de Ré *(see p420)* or Guérande. If you happen to be visiting the area, check out the salt flats and pick up the crumbly coarse grains at a local market. The Fleur de Sel is a delicate, fine-grained variety and the Sel Marin is a grey, coarser type of salt.

Provençal dried herbs for culinary use and for making teas

Beauty Products

French women are renowned for their grooming, and there is a plethora of good beauty products in France. The major French labels, such as **Chanel** and **Guerlain**, are available overseas, but die-hard cosmetics fans should scour the local beauty counters to find special products that are only on sale in France.

While in Paris, beauty junkies must visit the Chanel store on rue Cambon and the Guerlain store on the Champs-Elysées to buy special scent that is only available in those particular shops.

Throughout the rest of the country, brands such as Evian, Eau Thermale d'Avène and Barbara Gould, available at many supermarkets, are popular. A visit to any branch of Monoprix, or especially to one of their Monop'Beauty outposts, will reveal a large selection of quality products, which can mostly only be found in department stores in other countries. The cosmetics chain Sephora has several hundred brands of skincare, fragrance and cosmetics. Likewise, pharmacies in every town also carry a range of high-end healthcare and beauty items not found in supermarkets. If you are looking for standard sun creams or hair products, don't expect to find too many low-end brands in pharmacies.

A more traditional approach to French grooming can be found by buying *savon de Marseille* – good-quality traditional soap made with plenty of olive oil.

True scent aficionados should head for Grasse *(see p521)*, the perfume capital of the world. Be sure to visit the three largest scent factories, **Fragonard**, **Molinard** and **Galimard**, all of which have scent available for purchase.

Accessories

French fashion is rightfully famous, but aside from the main couture labels and stores *(see pp146–8)*, the best way to get the French look is to accessorize *à la française*. In keeping with the French tradition of specialist local trades, there are certain regions that excel in producing accessories.

For a start, a handmade umbrella from Aurillac *(see p368)* is guaranteed to chase away rainy-day blues in style. The best-known umbrella manufacturers are **L'Ondée au Parapluie d'Aurillac**, **Piganiol** and **Delos**, who will customize one for you with a photograph of whomever you choose to protect you from the storms.

Beautiful hands are easily available courtesy of the glove trade in Millau. Visit **L'Atelier Gantier** (the Glove Workshop) to pick up a stunning pair of expertly hand-stitched leather gloves in one of a seemingly endless array of colours.

More casual chic can be found with brightly coloured wicker baskets from local markets and hardware stores. These quickly turn a casual ensemble into a boho-chic outfit. Beachside boutiques are great places for picking up stylish sarongs, beads and bracelets for any trip to *la plage* (the beach). **K Jacques** sandals from St-Tropez have long been must-have items among the fashion set.

When it is time to hit the slopes rather than the beach, French ski-wear labels such as Rossignol can be a good buy, but only at the end of the season. At the height of *piste* time, ski resort shops are expensive. Once the snow starts to melt, however, ex-rental gear including skis and boots can be picked up relatively cheaply, while ski jackets, hats and *après-ski*-wear tends to be gloriously cut-price.

Household Goods

If you are in the market for housewares, the best stores are **Conforama**, **Alinea** and **Habitat**. **Truffaut** sells garden furniture, and **Leroy Merlin** is the hypermarket of the DIY, home-improvement world.

It is surprisingly rare to see the whole range of kitchen goods in a specialist shop. Instead, try the kitchen section of department stores. General hardware shops stock cast-iron cooking equipment. White china is sold in specialist shops.

Travelling through Normandy provides the perfect excuse for sampling many wonderful products, not least the *crème Chantilly*, but for tableware fans or lingerie lovers the lace industry here is also guaranteed to please. While **Alençon** lace is extremely expensive and mainly finds its way onto couture sold in top Parisian stores, hitting the shops in Argentan, Chantilly *(see pp208–9)* and Bayeux *(see pp256–7)* is likely to yield exquisite yet affordable lace. For those who want to keep costs to a minimum, it is worth hunting around for small lace pieces that can be used to liven up an outfit, such as a delicate lace flower that can be added to a bag or blouse.

Lace curtains are easy to come by, as are lovely table-cloths. The best way to be sure to see or buy good lace is to take "the lace road" and visit the **Alençon Lace Museum** and the lace boutiques in Alençon, Argentan, Caen *(see pp257–8)*, Courseulles, Villedieu-les-Poêles and La Perrière.

With a beautiful tablecloth in place, you can proceed to pick up stunning crystal from which to sniff, swirl and sip great French wine. The most famous crystal maker in France, **Baccarat**, has a museum where you can take in some of their amazing creations and a store where you can buy a little Baccarat bauble to take home with you. A cheaper French crystal that is still elegant for every-day use is **Cristal d'Arques**. You can tour the small museum in the factory and buy stemware at discount prices in the factory store.

Pottery is available at reasonable prices, especially near centres of production, such as Quimper *(see p278)* in Brittany, Aubagne near Marseille and Vallauris *(see p526)* near Grasse.

Porcelain from Limoges *(see p360)* sets off any meal beautifully: a dinner set from the **Royal Limoges** factory store can be a great investment.

Similarly, stunning **Aubusson** tapestries are extremely expensive and unlikely to be an impulse holiday purchase. However, interior design fanatics could do worse than plan their tapestry or rug

Size Chart

Women's dresses, coats and skirts								
French	36	38	40	42	44	46	48	
British	8	10	12	14	16	18	20	
American	4	6	8	10	12	14	16	
Women's shoes								
French	36	37	38	39	40	41		
British	3	4	5	6	7	8		
American	5	6	7	8	9	10		
Men's suits								
French	44	46	48	50	52	54	56	58
British	34	36	38	40	42	44	46	48
American	34	36	38	40	42	44	46	48
Men's shirts								
French	36	38	39	41	42	43	44	45
British	14	15	15½	16	16½	17	17½	18
American	14	15	15½	16	16½	17	17½	18
Men's shoes								
French	39	40	41	42	43	44	45	46
British	6	7	7½	8	9	10	11	12
American	7	7½	8	8½	9½	10½	11	11½

purchase around a trip to the home of weaving in Aubusson *(see pp360–61)*.

Finishing touches are fun to shop for and can certainly be more frivolous. Be sure to visit the local markets for gingham cotton napkins, linen cleaning cloths and seafood accoutrements (such as lobster crackers and oyster forks). In Provence, stock up on inexpensive, brightly coloured cookware – tagines, terracotta bowls and painted plates can all be found in abundance.

Wine

To buy wine straight from the vineyards *(domaines)* and wine cooperatives, follow the tasting *(dégustation)* signs. You may be expected to buy at least one bottle, except where a small fee is charged for wine tasting. Wine cooperatives make and sell the wine of small producers. Here you can buy wine in 5- and 10-litre containers *(en tonneau)*, as well as in bottles. Wine sold *en tonneau*, once opened, needs to be consumed fairly quickly, as it will deteriorate within a few days. Wine sold in bottles travels better.

Nicolas is France's main off-licence, with many branches.

Factory Outlets

The French sales system is very rigid *(see p144)*, but true bargain hunters know that factory shops have some items on sale all year round. The biggest factory outlets in France can be found in and around Troyes in outlet malls called **Marques Avenue** (Brands Avenue), **Marques City** (Brands City) and **McArthurGlen**, a large American outlet. They sell everything from Yves Saint Laurent suits to Black and Decker drills, Cristofle silverware and Bonpoint babygros. As different an experience as you can get from browsing around French markets and local specialist stores, what factory outlets lack in charm they make up for in bargains. If a whole new wardrobe is in order, it is definitely worth a trip.

DIRECTORY

Hypermarkets and Department Stores

For details of addresses, visit the following websites.

Auchan
W auchan.fr

Carrefour
W carrefour.fr

Casino
W supercasino.fr

Franprix
W franprix.fr

Galeries Lafayette
W galerieslafayette.com

Intermarché
W intermarche.com

Leclerc
W e-leclerc.com

Monoprix
W monoprix.fr

Printemps
W printemps.com

Regional Produce

Crème de Cassis
Gabriel Boudier, 14 rue de Cluj, 21007 Dijon.
Tel 03 80 74 33 33.

Oliviers et Co
For details of addresses, visit W oliviers-co.com

Beauty Products

Chanel
31 rue Cambon, 75008 Paris. **Tel** 01 44 50 66 00.
W chanel.com

Fragonard
20 bd Fragonard, 06130 Grasse. **Tel** 04 93 36 44 65.
W fragonard.com

Galimard
73 route de Cannes, 06130 Grasse. **Tel** 04 93 09 20 00.
W galimard.com

Guerlain
68 av des Champs Elysées, 75008 Paris.
Tel 01 45 62 52 57.
W guerlain.com

Molinard
60 bd Victor Hugo, 06130 Grasse. **Tel** 04 93 36 01 62.
W molinard.com

Accessories

L'Atelier Gantier
21 rue Droite, 12100 Millau. **Tel** 05 65 60 81 50.
W atelierdugantier.fr

Delos
14 rue Rocher, 15000 Aurillac. **Tel** 04 71 48 86 85. W delos-france.com

K Jacques
32 rte Plages, 83990 St-Tropez. **Tel** 04 94 97 41 50. W kjacques.fr

L'Ondée au Parapluie d'Aurillac
27 rue Victor Hugo, 15000 Aurillac.
Tel 04 71 48 29 53.

Piganiol
9 rue Ampère 15000 Aurillac.
Tel 04 71 63 42 60.

Household Goods

Alençon Lace Museum
Cour carrée de la Dentelle, 61000 Alençon.
Tel 02 33 32 40 07.

Alinea
W alinea.fr

Aubusson
Manufacture Saint-Jean 3 rue Saint-Jean, 23200 Aubusson.
Tel 05 55 66 10 08
W manufacture-saint-jean.fr

Baccarat
20 rue des Cristalleries, 54120 Baccarat.
Tel 03 83 76 60 06.
W baccarat.com

Conforama
W conforama.fr

Cristal d'Arques
132 av Gén de Gaulle, 62510 Arques.
Tel 03 21 95 46 96.
W arcdecoration.com

Habitat
W habitat.net

Leroy Merlin
W leroymerlin.fr

Royal Limoges
28 rue Donzelot Accès par le quai du Port du Naveix, 87000 Limoges.
Tel 05 55 33 27 37.
W royal-limoges.fr

Truffaut
W truffaut.com

Wine

Nicolas
W nicolas.com

Factory Outlets

Marques Avenue
Av de la Maille, 10800 Saint-Julien-les-Villas.
Tel 03 25 82 80 80.
W marquesavenue.com

Marques City
21 rue Marc Verdier, 10150 Pont Sainte Marie.
Tel 09 71 27 02 66.
W marquescity.fr

McArthurGlen
McArthurGlen Troyes, Voie du Bois, 10150 Pont-Sainte-Marie.
Tel 03 25 70 47 10.
W mcarthurglen.com

Entertainment in France

Paris is one of the world's great entertainment cities, but France's reputation as a centre of excellence in the arts extends well beyond the capital. Whether you prefer to attend theatre or catch a film, listen to jazz or techno, or watch modern dance, the country has a wide array of choices. The regional chapters in this guide will give you an insight into local gems, while these pages provide an overview of entertainment trends and events. Major festivals, such as Avignon and Cannes, occupy an important place in French hearts, so book well ahead if you plan to attend. For small festivals and local happenings, tourist office websites have up-to-the-minute listings.

The spectacular setting of Avignon Theatre at night

Theatre

Going to the theatre in France can be as formal or intimate as you choose. A trip to a major theatre can involve dressing up, making special *souper* (late dinner) reservations at a nearby restaurant specializing in theatre-goers and quaffing Champagne during the interval. On the other hand, a trip to a small-scale theatre can be about casual dress, cheap tickets and an intimate experience.

Whatever the genre, the French love an evening *au théâtre*, be it a French farce or a festival of street theatre.

France's biggest theatre event is at **Avignon** *(see p507)*. It is held during three weeks in July and is mainly open-air. It also includes ballets, drama and classical concerts. Many outdoor theatres operate in summer and are often free – contact the town's tourist office for a programme. The **Off Festival** is also worth a look.

Circus is also popular with the French. In small towns, summertime is often heralded by the circus loudspeaker strapped to the top of a car cruising the streets and inviting adults and children alike to flock to the big top. For larger circus events, head to Monaco for the Festival International du Cirque de Monte-Carlo or visit the colourful Festival International du Cirque de Bayeux, or the Cirque d'Hiver Bouglione in Paris.

Large-scale *spectacles* or shows are another popular form of theatre, be they massive musicals or *son et lumière* performances. Marionettes are also given due respect in France, where puppet shows go beyond traditional Punch and Judy territory.

Film

Le Septième Art, as the French refer to film, reveals the respect with which the genre is held. From the Lumière brothers and their innovative technology to contemporary critical smashes, such as *The Chorus*, *Amélie*, *The Artist* and *The Intouchables*, France's influence on film is undeniable. The French are supportive of local, independent cinemas, and small towns are often fiercely protective of their screening centre. So, when visiting the cinema, don't be restricted to the behemoths of UGC and Gaumont and instead head to a tiny *salle de cinéma*. If your language skills won't stretch to seeing a French film while in France, be sure to catch the VO *(Version Originale)* of any other language films, which will be screened in the film's original language. VF *(Version Française)* denotes a dubbed screening in French. As any expatriate in France knows, hearing a strange French voice coming out of a Hollywood A-lister's mouth is likely to dull any enjoyment of a major blockbuster movie.

Another thing to bear in mind is the French attitude to snacking. Essentially it is only acceptable for children, and even then only at a designated time after school. While French cinemas do have concession stands selling popcorn and sweets, it is only the foreigners who can be heard munching throughout the tense parts of the film. On the other hand, some French cinemas have bars and restaurants attached, so that filmgoers can dissect the movie over a meal.

Many cinemas run mini directors' festivals with several films shown back to back, attracting serious film buffs and those curious to learn more.

As the fame of **Cannes** *(see pp524–5)* reflects, film festivals are taken seriously by the French. Cannes itself is a maelstrom of media hype, old-school glamour and shiny new cash. It is an amazing experience, if you can get tickets to any of the films or parties, but these are notoriously difficult to get, as they are by invitation only. An easier way to experience the fabulous side of film is to attend

Poster promoting La Rochelle international film festival

Red carpet and razzmatazz at the Cannes Film Festival

the lower-key American film festival in **Deauville** *(see p259)*. The former is seen as a major launch pad for US independent films looking for European release, and attracts big stars and cult directors alike. The competition section of the festival has ten films in the running each year. The chic town of Deauville is small and accessible and, while the chance of bumping into a huge star is slim, it feels possible.

The film festival in **La Rochelle** *(see p420)*, the second largest in France, does not attract big actors, but film fans will not be disappointed with the broad selection of movies.

A truly great way to catch a film in France is at an open-air festival. There are many such events throughout the country; check local listings, so as not to miss out. The Festival International du Film de la Rochelle and Toulouse's **Cinéma en Plein Air** both feature outdoor screenings in the summer, while **Cinéma en Plein Air à La Villette** in Paris attracts tourists and locals at the end of the summer to a series of themed films.

Dance

Dancing is a way of life in France. From formal lessons to spontaneous outbreaks of grooving in the village square, moving to music is central to all types of celebration. Most foreigners' first experience with French dancers occurs in a nightclub and, more often than not, is accompanied by an expression of surprise. In even the most upscale nightclub, it is not unusual to see trendy twentysomethings jiving away to *le rock*, a formal form of rock-and-roll dancing. French teens are taught *le rock* before being unleashed on the party scene, and a basic understanding of its signature twirls and twists is considered vital to being a good dancer.

The love affair with formal dance sessions starts young, but lasts until late in life: tea dances are a major fixture of most older people's social calendars. Community centres, sports halls, restaurants and chic nightclubs often host *thé dansants* (tea dances), normally in the late afternoon or early evening.

Another way to experience French dance culture is to head to a *guingette*, a moored party boat with a convivial, old-fashioned atmosphere. People here dance the *quadrille* or the *musette* to accordion music, spinning around on the banks of the river. While the *guingettes* were traditionally clustered around the Marne river, they have now spread throughout France and are definitely worth seeking out if your travels take you close to a major tributary.

In general, lots of dancing takes place near to water in France. Those looking to get into the groove in the south should take their dancing shoes to the quays in Bordeaux and Marseille.

Once a year, on 13 and 14 July, a most unusual impromptu dancing venue springs up around the country with the *Bals des Pompiers*. The "Firemen's Balls" are a national institution, when the French of all ages head down to their local fire station to celebrate Bastille day by dancing to everything from Edith Piaf to hip hop until the early hours of the morning.

If you would prefer to watch rather than participate, there are several major dance festivals that celebrate the dance traditions of different regions. The **Gannat festival** held in the Auvergne *(see p357)* is a fine example of a regional dance extravaganza, as is the **Festival Interceltique de Lorient** *(see p274)*, which celebrates Celtic music and dance. The main international dance festivals are held in **Montpellier** *(see pp498–9)* and **Lyon** *(see pp382–5)*. These provide a wonderful opportunity to enjoy major contemporary dance talent from around the world.

Wonderful costumes and choreography at the Montpellier dance festival

Music

The French music scene is about far more than Johnny Hallyday, although it must be said that the ageing rocker still manages to sell stacks of records, concert tickets and gossip magazines. It should also be pointed out that he is actually Belgian, but the French have taken him to their hearts anyway. Acts such as Bob Sinclar, Daft Punk, David Guetta and Christine and the Queens are big international names, catering to English-speaking audiences.

Chanson is ever popular, as the success of the movement's poster boy Benjamin Biolay reveals. The *nouvelle chanson* scene is dominated by Biolay, although other well-known artists in this genre include Vincent Delerm, Benabar, Olivia Ruiz and French-Canadian Coeur de Pirate.

"Le French Touch", a genre of house music originating in the 1990s, has been made popular by acts such as Daft Punk, Modjo and Cassius.

Well-known female singers include Lara Fabian and reality-TV pop star Chimène Badi.

France is the world's second-biggest market for hip-hop after the USA. The success of artists such as MC Solaar, IAM and Assassin have ensured international recognition for the country's thriving urban scene.

The event that best symbolizes this musical cornucopia is the **Fête de la Musique**. Every year, on 21 June, France resonates to the sound of this national music festival. Amateur and professional musicians alike set up their stages throughout villages and towns and perform. The best way to enjoy this is to walk around and try and take in as many different "concerts" as possible, but be aware that for some wannabe rock stars this is their only chance to shine, regardless of whether or not they can sing. Musical quality aside, what is most impressive about the Fête de la Musique is the sheer number of genres that one can hear in a few streets. Ranging from full orchestras to one-man rap artists, you can expect to hear everything from accordion music to panpipes, *chanson*, hip-hop and electro.

If you prefer your festivals a little more specialized, visit one of the events focusing on the very best of a particular genre from chamber music to jazz. The July **Festival of Francofolies** in La Rochelle *(see p420)* brings together French music enthusiasts from around the world, just as **Jazz in Antibes** draws top performers to this chic seaside town *(see p525)*. The **Chorégies d'Orange**, France's oldest opera festival, takes place throughout July and August in the well-preserved Roman amphitheatre, which retains perfect acoustics. The organ festival in **Aubusson** *(see pp360–61)* focuses around the glorious organ in the Sainte-Croix church and **La Roque d'Anthéron** continues to attract piano-loving crowds. The **Colmar International Festival** *(see p231)* is a major draw for classical music buffs, and the **Aix Festival** *(see p515)* is a must for any serious fan of classical music and opera, while the **Radio France Occitanie Montpellier Festival** has a wide-ranging appeal with symphony concerts, chamber music, jazz and world music.

Clubs

Cool clubs and artful partying most definitely exist outside the capital city, despite what Parisians may believe. There are, of course, bars and clubs throughout the country, and night owls looking to dance are unlikely to be disappointed by the range of options on offer. Small local venues can be great fun, and community events such as open-air parties and festivals are almost always worth a look-in.

In general, nightclubs open late and even in small towns, don't really get going till after midnight. The French are more likely to nurse a few drinks rather than dash around buying multiple rounds, and shots are almost unheard of over here. It is considered uncouth to drink wine outside of mealtimes, although Champagne is always a good thing! The prevailing custom is to club together with friends and buy a bottle of spirits between you. The nightclub will present you with plenty of mixers, and – the big benefit of going for this option – you will usually get a table all to yourselves. Tables are generally reserved for those in possession of a full bottle of spirits; a single gin and tonic does not warrant a seat. As extravagant as this may seem, it is generally cheaper than buying individual drinks for four or more people.

In terms of dress code, trainers are almost always forbidden in clubs, and the smarter the better could be seen as the rule. In house or hip-hop clubs strict dress codes tend to be relaxed. However, in more traditional *boîtes de nuit* (nightclubs) getting glammed up is the way to go. Clubs with difficult door policies can often be outfoxed by dining late. If you are worried about getting in, call ahead and make a dinner reservation. Alternatively flaunt designer labels at the doormen.

To experience one of France's most glamorous clubs head to **Les Planches** – an uber-chic spot outside Deauville *(see p259)*. Aside from its swimming pool, in which starlets frolic at 3am, Les Planches has a surprisingly inclusive, friendly and fun vibe. Vintage cars tear around town rounding up partygoers to keep the night going.

Up in the mountains **Le Privilege** in Chamonix *(see p326)* is a jumping Alpine party place.

The Côte d'Azur *(see pp502–35)* is, of course, renowned for its hedonistic nightlife. **Les Caves du Roy** in the Hotel Byblos and **Nikki Beach** in St-Tropez *(see p520)* are perfect for the jet set, while **Jimmy'z** in Monaco *(see pp534–5)* is the place to hang out with highrollers.

Spectator Sports

Sporting enthusiasts are spoiled for choice in France, with myriad opportunities to indulge in spectator sport throughout the country. If you don't want to wait to see the *grande finale* of the **Tour de France** in Paris, taking in the spectacle from a tiny village en route is a great experience (drivers beware: the Tour takes precedence and the traffic will be stopped for an extremely long time).

If football is more your thing, then head to the Olympic stadia to catch huge teams, such as **Lyon** and **Marseille**, in action.

Surfing fans should make for Biarritz *(see p456)*, Lacanau *(see p428)* and Hossegor *(see p428)* to watch the tournaments there, while ski aficionados might want to watch the European Cup in Les Trois Vallées *(see p326)*.

Golfers flock to the **PGA Open** held outside Paris and to the **LPGA in Evian,** which is the world's second most valuable tournament after the US Open.

Riders will be drawn to one of France's national studs at the **Haras National de Pompadour** for dressage, showjumping and other competitions throughout the year. Similarly, equine enthusiasts should not miss out on exciting horse racing at the renowned **Chantilly Racecourse**.

The **Le Mans** 24-hour car race is an institution, as is the famous **Grand Prix** in Monaco *(see pp534–5)*. The **French Grand Prix** at Magny Cours, south of Nevers *(see pp342–3)* is also well worth a visit.

No visitor to France in the summer should miss out on one of the greatest spectator sports of them all: head to the village square and take in a game of *pétanque* (also known as *boules*).

DIRECTORY

Theatre

Avignon Theatre Festival
Tel 04 90 27 66 50.
W festival-avignon.com

Off Festival
W avignonleoff.com

Film

Cannes Film Festival
W festival-cannes.fr

Cinéma en Plein Air Toulouse
W lacinemathequedetoulouse.com

Cinéma en Plein Air La Villette
W lavillette.com

Deauville Film Festival
W festival-deauville.com

La Rochelle Film Festival
W festival-larochelle.org

Dance

Festival Interceltique de Lorient
Tel 02 97 21 24 29.
W festival-interceltique.bzh

Gannat Festival
Tel 04 70 90 12 67.
W cultures-traditions.org

Lyon Festival
Tel 04 27 46 65 60. **W labiennaledelyon.com**

Montpellier Festival
W montpellierdanse.fr

Music

Aix Festival
Tel 04 42 17 34 00.
W festival-aix.com

Aubusson Festival
Tel 05 55 66 18 36.
W orgue-aubusson.org

Chorégies d'Orange
Tel 04 90 34 24 24.
W choregies.fr

Colmar International Festival
Tel 03 89 20 68 97.
W festival-colmar.com

Festival of Francofolies
Tel 05 46 50 55 77.
W francofolies.fr

Jazz in Antibes
W jazzajuan.com

Radio France Occitanie Montpellier Festival
Tel 04 67 02 02 01.
W festivalradiofrancemontpellier.com

La Roque d'Anthéron
Tel 04 42 50 51 15.
W festival-piano.com

Clubs

Les Caves du Roy
Av Paul Signac, 83990 St-Tropez.
Tel 04 94 56 68 00.

Jimmy'z
Le Sporting Club
Av Princesse Grace, Monte Carlo.
Tel 00 377 98 06 70 68.

Nikki Beach
Route de l'Epi, 83350 Ramatuelle.
Tel 04 94 79 82 04.
W nikkibeach.com

Les Planches
Les Longs Champs, 14910 Blonville sur Mer.
Tel 06 67 59 72 75.
W lesplanches.com

Le Privilege
52 rue des Moulins, 74400 Chamonix.
Tel 06 72 43 92 83.

Spectator Sports

Chantilly Racecourse
Rue Plaine des Aigles, Chantilly, Oise.
Tel 03 44 62 44 00.
W france-galop.com

French Grand Prix
58170 Magny Cours.
Tel 03 86 21 80 00.
W circuit magnycours.com

Grand Prix
Automobile Club de Monaco.
Tel 01 82 88 27 34.
W monaco-grand-prix.com

Haras National de Pompadour
Tel 08 11 90 21 31.
W ifce.fr/haras-nationaux/

LPGA in Evian
W lpga.com

Le Mans
Tel 02 43 40 24 00.
W lemans.org

Olympique Lyon
350 av Jean Jaurès, 69007 Lyon.
W olweb.fr

Olympique de Marseille
3 bd Michelet, 13008 Marseille.
W om.net

PGA Open
W pgafrance.net

Tour de France
W letour.fr

Specialist Holidays and Outdoor Activities

France offers an amazing variety of leisure and sport activities, making it a wonderful choice for a specialist holiday. The French take great pride in the *art de vivre*, which entails not only eating and drinking well, but also pursuing special interests and hobbies. For the best in entertainment and spectator sports, festivals and annual events, see *France Through the Year* on pages 40–43. Information on leisure and sporting activities in a particular region is available from the tourist offices listed for each town in this guide. The suggestions below cover the most popular, and also some more unusual, pursuits.

Students honing their culinary skills on a Hostellerie Bérard cookery course

Specialist Holidays

French government tourist offices *(see p623)* have a wide range of information on travel companies that offer special-interest holidays. The official website for tourism in France is www.rendezvousenfrance.com, and it is an excellent source of information.

If you want to improve your French, many language courses are available. These are very often combined with other activities, such as cooking or painting. For more information, request *cours de français pour étudiants étrangers* (French courses for foreign students) from the **French Institute** in London.

Young people can enjoy a French-speaking holiday by working part time on restoration of historic sites with **Union REMPART** *(Union pour la Réhabilitation et Entretien des Monuments et du Patrimoine Artistique)*.

A tantalizing array of gastronomic courses is on offer, to introduce you to classical French cuisine or the cooking of a particular region. For experienced cooks, advanced and specialist courses are available too. Wine-appreciation courses can also be found and are always very popular.

There are numerous art and crafts courses throughout the country, catering to everyone from the absolute beginner to the most accomplished artist.

Nature lovers can enjoy the national parks *(parcs nationaux)* and join organized birdwatching and botanical trips in many areas, including the Camargue, the Cévennes and Corsica.

Le Guide des Jardins en France, published by Actes Sud, is a useful reference guide when visiting France's many beautiful gardens.

Painting the picturesque French landscape

Golf

There are golf courses all over France, especially along the north and south coasts and in Aquitaine. Players have to reach a minimum standard and obtain a licence in order to play, so be sure to take your handicap certificate with you. Top courses offer weekend or longer tutored breaks geared to all levels of experience. The **Fédération Française de Golf** will provide a list of all the courses throughout France.

Specialist golf packages, including deluxe hotel accommodation, can be ideal for serious golfers and any non-golfing partners alike. The spectacular Evian Resort and its renowned **Evian Championship Golf Course** is a very exclusive, pampering option. The 18-hole course is guaranteed to appeal to fans. There is also a spa and five swimming pools, perfect for lazing. The climbing wall, squash and tennis courts will appeal to more active visitors.

In the south, the **American Golf Academy** offers a team of golf pros who are adept at coaching children, beginners and also experts through their eight different courses and private lessons. Their summer schools and master classes are highly sought after.

The **Hotel de Mougins**, with a lovely address on the "avenue du Golf", is situated near to ten prestigious golf courses, including the Golf Country Club Cannes, the Royal Mougins Golf Club and the Golf d'Opio-Valbonne. The hotel can arrange rounds at the different clubs, and offers packages that include extras, such as lunch in the clubhouse.

The **Golf Hotel Grenoble Charmeil** can organize green fees for three courses, including the Grenoble International course. In Brittany, the **St-Malo Golf and Country Club** has a 19th-century manor-house interior and an impressive 27-hole golf course, surrounded by the Mesnil forest.

Tennis

Tennis is a very popular sport in France, and courts for hourly hire can be found in almost every town. It is a good idea to bring your own equipment with you, as hire facilities may not be available.

Hiking

In France, more than 60,000 km (38,000 miles) of long-distance tracks, known as *Grandes Randonnées* (GR), are clearly marked. There are also 80,000 km (50,000 miles) of the shorter *Petites Randonnées* (PR).

The routes vary in difficulty and include long pilgrim routes, Alpine crossings and tracks through national parks. Some *Grandes* and *Petites Randonnées* are open for mountain biking as well as horse riding.

Topo Guides, published by **Féderation Française de la Randonnée Pédestre**, describe the tracks, providing details of transport, places for overnight stops and food shops. A useful book series geared specifically toward families is *Les 200 Plus Belles Balades en France en Famille*, which can be ordered online.

Cycling

For advice on cycling in France, contact the British **CTC** (Cyclists' Touring Club) or the **Fédération Française de Cyclisme**.

Serious cyclists could live their dreams by joining up for a Tour de France stage vacation with the **Velo Echappe** *Etape du Tour* team. The company organizes two types of adventure – a fully guided programme or a self-guided option. They handle all the registration forms and paperwork, and on the guided option they will put you up in a hotel a block away from the end of the stage. Applications to the tour company must be received by the end of March every year to have a chance to ride along with the Tour de France professionals.

Escaping into the forest at Fontainebleau *(see pp184–5)*

At the other end of the scale, people who enjoy a gentle bike ride could opt for a wine cycling tour through the vineyards of France. Freewheeling down the Route des Grands Crus in Burgundy may be more than enough holiday exercise for some.

Duvine Adventures organize tours that take in famed vineyards such as La Tache, Romanée-Conti and Nuit-St-Georges. The riding includes flat spells and hills, and there are excellent lunches.

Local tourist offices provide details about riding facilities in their areas. **Voies Vertes** offers information on "greenways", easy rides through some of France's loveliest countryside. *Gîtes de France (see p551)* offer dormitory accommodation in the vicinity of well-known tracks.

Mountain biking – a great way to explore

Horse Riding

There are many reputable companies that offer riding breaks, from one-hour treks to long weekends or holidays of a week or more. The best way to choose is to decide which type of countryside you would prefer to see from the saddle. If the Mont-St-Michel (*see pp260–63*) and the beaches of Brittany appeal, then **A La Carte Sportive** offer stables with horses trained in trekking for beginners and intermediates. For more experienced riders, riding a Camargue mount through the countryside of Provence (*see pp514–15*) is a wonderful treat. **Ride in France** organizes rides through beautiful scenery, vineyards and picturesque villages, allowing riders to experience the flora and fauna of the area. Horse lovers with a taste for the historical, or those hankering after a little luxury, could do worse than to sign up for a break with the **Cheval et Châteaux** company which organizes horse-riding tours around châteaux in the Loire. Not only do riders get to take in the majesty of the châteaux of the region, the overnight accommodation also comes courtesy of a castle. It makes an ideal way to play lord or lady of the manor, while indulging in a passion for trekking.

Hiking along the Gorges du Verdon in Provence *(see pp518–19)*

Mountain Sports

The French mountains, especially the Alps and the Pyrenees, provide a wide range of sporting opportunities. In addition to winter downhill skiing and *ski de fond* (cross-country skiing), the mountains are enjoyed in the summer by rock-climbers and mountaineers, and by those skiers who can't wait for winter and so indulge in some of Europe's best glacier skiing.

Mountain climbing is possible not just in summer, but all year round, although some high routes will be snowbound until quite late in the year and require special equipment such as ice axes. These should not be attempted without experience or a local guide. Climbers should contact the **Fédération Française de la Montagne et de l'Escalade** for more information on the best climbing locations and other useful tips.

Winter sports fans should join the serious skiers and snowboarders who head to the French hills in droves every season. The mountains here have terrain to satisfy all levels of expertise from toddlers in the kids' club through to death-defying off-piste athletes, adrenalin-junkie snowboarders, kitesurfers and middle-of-the-road snow fans who are happiest cruising blue runs and eating in slope-side restaurants.

Skiing

Undoubtedly, France has some of the best ski resorts anywhere in the world. The sheer scale of some of the larger areas can be quite daunting if you're on a week-long trip – especially to those who insist on covering all the trails on the map. The Trois Vallées ski area *(see p326)*, for example, is made up of three valleys, which include the resorts of Courchevel, Méribel, Val Thorens and Les Ménuires. Added together, they comprise a staggering 600 km (375 miles) worth of pistes.

The Trois Vallées is an excellent example of how French ski resorts differ wildly in style. Super-chic stations such as Courchevel and Méribel draw skiers from around the world, often dressed in cutting-edge ski fashion and using the latest high-tech equipment. In these resorts the hotels – especially those dubbed to be "in" – are expensive, and eating and drinking in the "see and be seen spots" here puts a significant dent in the most generous of holiday budgets. On the other hand, resorts that are considered less glamorous, such as Vals Thorens and Les Menuires, can be enjoyed without designer labels and huge credit card limits.

The main consideration when choosing a resort should be the percentage of terrain to suit your ability. For example, a beginner might be miserable in a resort aimed at experts and offering only a few green runs. Similarly, a more confident intermediate looking to improve will be frustrated by a ski area full of easy cruising slopes that are overrun with beginners.

It is also important to think about whether or not it matters to you if the village is picturesque. Die-hard ski fans can overlook ugly concrete architecture in towns such as Flaine, while those looking for the bigger picture would be best off heading to somewhere pretty, such as La Clusaz or Megève *(see p326)*.

The proximity of accommodation to piste is also very important; most people find it is worth paying a premium for accommodation near the slopes and lifts, rather than having to stagger back in heavy boots carrying your skis after a long day's schussing.

Aside from obvious concerns such as nightlife, children's créches and the efficiency of lift networks, it can also be useful to look at historic snow reports for the last few years for the time you are planning your trip. The weather can be unpredictable, though, so be sure to also check the resorts' snow-making capabilities.

Armed with these details, you should be in a good position to pick the right resort for you, but remember, while the Alps get most of the attention, the Pyrenees can offer some seriously good skiing, too.

Aeronautical Sports

Learning to fly in France can be relatively inexpensive. Information on the different flying schools is available from the **Fédération Nationale Aéronautique**. There are also plenty of opportunities to learn the exhilarating skills of gliding, paragliding and hang-gliding, popular in the Alps of Provence, in the Pyrenees and Corsica. For more information, contact the **Fédération Française de Vol Libre**.

If piloting a plane is a little too much, you can opt for ballooning instead. France has an illustrious ballooning history, being the birthplace of the Montgolfier brothers, who pioneered the art in 1783. **Ballon de Paris** provide a tethered taste of adventure in Paris with a trip into the air in the Parc André-Citroën, but floating unfettered over the countryside can be arranged by several companies around the country. **France Montgolfières** can organize trips over Fontainebleau *(see pp184–5)* outside Paris or over the Burgundian vineyards. Alternatively, they offer the opportunity to appreciate the spectacular châteaux of the Loire from a balloon. In Provence the same company can float you over the picturesque villages, cornfields and vines of the Luberon *(see pp510–11)*.

Water Sports

Whitewater rafting, kayaking and canoeing all take place on many French rivers, especially in the Massif Central and the Southwest. More information on these sports and the best places to take part can be obtained from the **Fédération Française de Canoë-Kayak**.

The Atlantic coast around Biarritz *(see p456)* offers some

of the best surfing and windsurfing in Europe. Excellent windsurfing can also be found in Brittany, with **Wissant** in particular being a big draw. A charming small fishing village, Wissant is considered a decent stop on any windsurf tour. The western Mediterranean is also popular with windsurfers. Surfers who prefer to do it without the sail head to **Hossegor** outside Biarritz *(see p456)* for spectacular waves. The surfing here is world-class and perhaps not ideal for beginners, but the after-surf scene is great fun for anyone who is more interested in lying on the beach or paddling at the shore than carving up the water.

Similarly the town of **Lacanau** *(see p428)* plays host to international surf competitions, drawing wave fans from all over the world.

Sailing and waterskiing are also very popular in France. Contact the **Fédération Française de Voile** for more details. Training schools and equipment hire are found at numerous places along the coast and on lakes. In particular, the seaside towns of Brittany have a good choice of sailing schools.

If cruising on a boat is your kind of thing, there are many outlets that can help. One of the swankier options is to take a **Sunsail** bareboat tour around the Côte d'Azur, although this option is only available to those who have reached a certain level of boatmanship. The company also offers a range of skippered tours around the beautiful coastline.

Swimming facilities throughout the country are generally good, although swimming on the Atlantic coast can be dangerous and may be forbidden outside patrolled areas. The beaches in the South of France can be very crowded in high season *(see pp478–9)*.

For diving enthusiasts, the Côte d'Azur, which has a number of World War II wrecks, offers good opportunities, as does Corsica. More information is available from **Fédération Française d'Études et de Sports Sous-Marins**.

Naturism

There are nearly 90 naturism centres in France. These are mostly located in the south and southwest of the country, as well as in Corsica. Information in English can be obtained from French Government Tourist Offices *(see p620)*, or from the **Fédération Française de Naturisme**.

Public Events

To join the French as they enjoy their spare time, look out for local football and rugby matches, cycling races or other sporting events suited to spectators.

Special seasonal markets and local *fêtes* often combine antiques fairs and *boules* tournaments with rock and pop concerts, making an enjoyable day out.

Spa Holidays

France is renowned for its seawater-based thalassotherapy spa techniques, with many centres, salons and hotels offering "thalasso" treatments. The seaside towns and resorts seem to be the most logical place to head for ocean-based treatments, and, not surprisingly, there are some excellent spots dotted around the coastline.

Chic seaside town Deauville *(see p259)* plays host to upscale spa seekers in the **Algotherm Thalassotherapy Spa**. Similarly the **Hôtel Thalasso Sofitel** in Quiberon *(see p282)* offers top-class water therapy. More water therapy can be found near the springs at Vichy *(see pp362–3)* at the **Les Celestins** spa and at **Evian-les-Bains** *(see p395)*.

Wine in France is considered to be almost as important as water, so it is not surprising that a spa specializing in "vinotherapy" or wine therapy has hordes of loyal fans. Head to **Les Sources de Caudalie** spa among the vines near Bordeaux and indulge in a vinosource grape facial and cabernet scrub.

If big-name treatments are your thing, you should head to **Le Mas Candille**, which hosts the first Shiseido spa in continental Europe. The products used are as exceptional as one would expect from such a swanky brand, and the techniques are Oriental-inspired.

Finally, if a thoroughly indulgent approach to a spa session is your idea of holiday heaven, then splurge at the **Terre Blanche Hôtel Spa Golf Resort** in Provence. The half-day retreat of total indulgence involves an aromatherapy massage, a Provençal body wrap, and relaxing in the sauna, spa, hammam or laconium. If you want to go à la carte, you can choose from a wide range of delights, such as an eye-lifting facial, a body-toning massage or an Oshadi clay wrap.

If you can't escape from the city, the Valmont spa at the **Hotel Meurice** and the **Four Seasons** spa at the George V can provide the ultimate escape and spa break right in the centre of Paris.

Yoga

The beautiful countryside in France provides the perfect backdrop for a restorative yoga retreat holiday. The **Manolaya Yoga Centre** offers relaxing and fun hatha yoga holidays throughout Provence and at its Avignon-based centre. For the more relaxing style of hatha yoga, try **Silvananda Ashram Yoga** retreats held near Orléans in the beautiful Loire.

Another excellent option is a break at the **Domaine de la Grausse** in the foothills of the Pyrenees, where walking and visiting local waterfalls, châteaux, medieval villages and even taking in some cave paintings are all on the agenda. Those with any energy left over can take advantage of options to go mountain biking, riding, playing golf and fishing.

Beginners and experienced yoga fans alike are welcome at **Les Passeroses**, near Angoulême, which specializes in hatha and vinyasa yoga. Boutique accommodation with en-suite bathrooms and a vegetarian menu are part of the package here.

Gourmet

For gourmets looking to learn how to re-create some of the stunning meals enjoyed in French restaurants, or wine buffs seeking to increase their knowledge and cellar at the same time, there are many excellent options. The sheer number of cookery classes available throughout the country may seem overwhelming, so the first step in choosing an activity holiday of this kind is to consider your initial skill level and what you wish to achieve from the break. From die-hard kitchen disasters to budding restaurateurs, there is a gourmet break in France that will suit.

The **Go Learn To** cookery courses offer short breaks or week-long holidays to suit your taste in Provence, Bordeaux, Lyon, Gascony, La Rochelle, Brittany and the Loire Valley. They provide cookery courses in stunning château settings, as well as more specialized courses in Paris, such as cheese and wine pairing and wine tasting.

Petra Carter, chef and food writer, shows food lovers how to rustle up a menu based on whatever looks great in the market that day, as well as how to prepare foolproof fish recipes and duck confit. These cookery courses, which take place near Nîmes in the Languedoc area, combine fun with practical tips, and include waterside picnics and visits to saltpans, olive presses, beekeepers and local markets. There are also tutored wine tastings.

Budding culinary stars might want to head to Paris and Alain Ducasse's **Ecole de Cuisine**, which organizes both cooking and wine courses. It offers day and evening courses, held in an ultra-modern, professionally equipped kitchen. Also in Paris is the **Ecole Ritz Escoffier**, which holds workshops, for both adults and children, at the Ritz Hotel. Lessons last from an hour to half a day and cover themes such as chocolate or making the perfect pastry.

Oenophiles, on the other hand, might like to join the **French Wine Explorers**, who offer tours around vineyards. Alternatively, arranging wine classes via the French tourist office can be an excellent idea. **French Wine Adventures** offers a range of wine tours – day courses, walking tours, play winemaker for a day – in the Bordeaux wine regions of Saint-Emilion, Bergerac and Médoc.

Arts and Crafts

France is a top choice for creative people looking to get away from it all and to express themselves in beautiful surroundings. Whether your preferred method of expression is scribbling in a notebook by yourself on the banks of a river, or perfecting your pastel technique in an art master class, there is an outlet for you somewhere in France.

Adam Cope Painting Holidays offers painting courses in several historic sites in the Dordogne, including a 17th-century abbey and an 18th-century château. Adam Cope provides personal instruction and caters to all levels of ability. It is possible to hire paints on the courses.

Martine Vaugel, winner of the International Rodin prize, is the founder of the Loire Valley's **Vaugel Sculpture Studio**, which offers foundation and advanced portrait, standing and reclining figure courses ranging from one week to two months.

Those with a passion for seeing life through a lens are well catered for with photography courses by **Graham and Belinda Berry** at their farmhouse in the Lot, southwest France. Courses suitable for all ages and abilities are offered here.

DIRECTORY

Specialist Holidays

French Institute
17 Queensberry Place, London SW7 2DT, United Kingdom.
Tel 020 7871 3515.
W institut-francais.org.uk

Union REMPART
1 rue des Guillemites, 75004 Paris.
Tel 01 42 71 96 55.
W rempart.com

Golf

American Golf Academy
Tel 06 81 54 96 42.
W american-golf-academy.com

Evian Championship Golf Course
South Shore Lake Geneva, 74500 Evian.
Tel 04 50 26 85 00.
W evianresort.com

Fédération Française de Golf
68 rue Anatole France, 92300 Levallois Perret.
Tel 01 41 49 77 00.
W ffgolf.org

Golf Hotel Grenoble Charmeil
38210 Saint Quentin sur Isère. **Tel** 04 76 93 67 28.
W golfhotel charmeil.com

Hotel de Mougins
205 av du Golf, 06250 Mougins. **Tel** 04 92 92 17 07. **W hotel-de-mougins.com**

St-Malo Golf and Country Club
Domaine de St-Yvieux, 35540 Le Tronchet.
Tel 02 99 58 96 69.
W saintmalogolf.com

Hiking

Fédération Française de Randonnée Pédestre
64 rue du Dessous des Berges, 75013 Paris.
Tel 01 44 89 93 90.
W ffrandonnee.fr

Cycling

CTC
Parklands, Railton Road, Guildford, Surrey GU2 9JX, United Kingdom. **Tel** 0148 3238 301. **W ctc.org.uk**

Duvine Adventures
W duvine.com

Fédération Française de Cyclisme
1 rue Laurent Fignon, CS 40 100, 78180 Montigny le Bretonneux. **W ffc.fr**

Velo Echappe
W veloechappe.com

Voies Vertes
W voiesvertes.com

Horse Riding

A La Carte Sportive
W carte-sportive-com.iowners.net

Cheval et Châteaux
W cheval-et-chateaux.com

Ride in France
W rideinfrance.com

DIRECTORY

Mountain Sports

Féderation Française de la Montagne et de l'Escalade
8–10 quai de la Marne, 75019 Paris.
Tel 01 40 18 75 50.
W ffme.fr

Skiing

For information on the different resorts, visit the following websites:

La Clusaz
W laclusaz.com

Courchevel
W courchevel.com

Flaine
W flaine.com

Megève
W megeve.com

Les Menuires
W lesmenuires.com

Méribel
W meribel.net

Les Trois Vallées
W les3vallees.com

Val Thorens
W valthorens.com

Aeronautical Sports

Ballon de Paris
Parc André-Citroën, 75015 Paris.
Tel 01 44 26 20 00.
W ballondeparis.com

Fédération Française de Vol Libre
4 rue de Suisse, 06000 Nice. **Tel** 04 97 03 82 82.
W federation.ffvl.fr

Fédération Nationale Aéronautique
155 av Wagram, 75017 Paris.
Tel 01 44 29 92 00.
W ff-aero.fr

France Montgolfières
Tel 03 80 97 38 61.
W franceballoons.com

Water Sports

Fédération Française de Canoë-Kayak
87 quai de la Marne, 94340 Joinville-le-Pont.
Tel 01 45 11 08 50.
W ffck.org

Fédération Française d'Études et de Sports Sous-Marins
W ffessm.fr

Fédération Française de Voile
17 rue Henri Bocquillon, 75015 Paris. **Tel** 01 45 58 75 75. **W ffcv.org**

Hossegor Tourist Office
166 av de la Gare, BP 6, 40150 Hossegor.
Tel 05 58 41 79 00.
W hossegor.fr

Lacanau Tourist Office
Pl de l'Europe, 33680 Lacanau. **Tel** 05 56 03 21 01. **W medoc-atlantique.com**

Sunsail
W sunsail.com

Wissant Tourist Office
Pl de la Mairie, 62179 Wissant. **Tel** 03 21 82 48 00.
W terredes2caps.fr

Naturism

Fédération Française de Naturisme
W ffn-naturisme.com

Spa Holidays

Algotherm Thalassotherapy Spa
3 rue Sem, 14800 Deauville.
Tel 02 31 87 72 00.
W algotherm.fr

Les Celestins Vichy
111 bd des Etats-Unis, 03200 Vichy.
Tel 04 70 30 82 82.
W vichy-spa-hotel.fr

Evian-les-Bains
Rive Sud du Lac de Génève, 74501 Evian-les-Bains. **Tel** 04 50 26 85 00.
W evianresort.com

Hotel Four Seasons George V
31 av George V, 75008 Paris. **Tel** 01 49 52 70 00.
W fourseasons.com

Hotel Meurice
228 rue de Rivoli, 75001 Paris.
Tel 01 44 58 10 10.
W lemeurice.com

Hôtel Thalasso Sofitel (Quiberon)
Pointe de Goulvars, BP 10802 Quiberon Cedex, 56178 Quiberon.
Tel 02 97 50 20 00.
W sofitel-quiberon-thalassa.com

Le Mas Candille
Bd Clément Rebuffel, 06250 Mougins.
Tel 04 92 28 43 43.
W lemascandille.com

Les Sources de Caudalie
Chemin de Smith Haut Lafitte, 33650 Bordeaux–Martillac.
Tel 05 57 83 83 83.
W sources-caudalie.com

Terre Blanche Hôtel Spa Golf Resort
Domaine de Terre Blanche, 83440 Tourrettes, Var.
Tel 04 94 39 90 00.
W terre-blanche.com

Yoga

Domaine de la Grausse
09420 Clermont la Grausse, Ariège.
Tel 05 61 66 30 53.
W yogafrance.com

Manolaya Yoga Centre
FFPY 39 rue de la Bonneterie, 84000 Avignon. **Tel** 04 90 82 10 52. **W manolaya.org**

Les Passeroses
Le Bas Metraud, 16190 Nonac. **Tel** 05 45 21 51 74.
W passeroses.com

Sivananda Ashram Yoga Group
Neuville aux Bois, Loiret 45170. **Tel** 02 38 91 88 82. **W sivananda.org**

Gourmet

Ecole de Cuisine
64 rue du Ranelagh, 75016 Paris.
Tel 01 44 90 91 00.
W ecolecuisine-alainducasse.com

Ecole Ritz Escoffier
Tel 01 44 16 30 50.
W ritzescoffier.com

French Wine Adventures
Tel 05 53 22 72 71.
W frenchwine adventures.com

French Wine Explorers
W wine-tours-france.com

Go Learn To
Tel 020 8144 5990 (UK).
W http://euro.golearnto.com

Petra Carter
Place Albert 1er, 30700 Uzès.
Tel 07 77 23 41 57.
W petracarter.com

Arts and Crafts

Adam Cope Painting Holidays
Tel 05 53 01 22 91.
W artists-atelier.com

Graham and Belinda Berry
46800 Montcuq.
Tel 05 65 31 49 72.
W imagefrance.co.uk

Vaugel Sculpture Studio
2 rue Petit Anjou, Les Cerqueux Sous Passavant, 49310 Vihiers.
Tel 02 41 59 54 14.
W vaugel sculpture.com

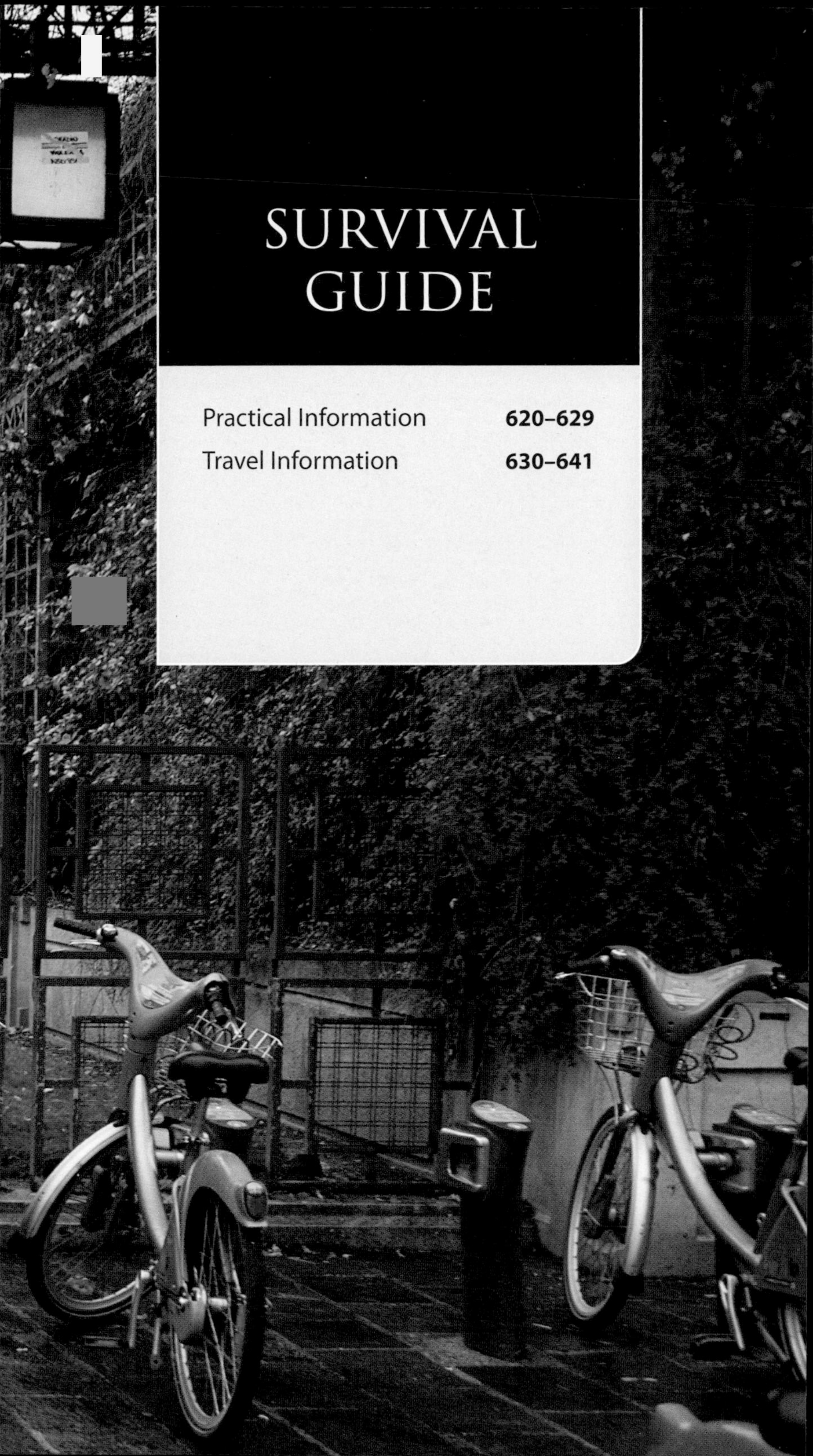

SURVIVAL GUIDE

PRACTICAL INFORMATION

France is justifiably proud of its many attractions, for which it has excellent tourist information facilities. Both in France and abroad, French government tourist offices are an invaluable source of reference for practical aspects of your stay. Most towns and large villages have a tourist information office; the relevant address, telephone number and website (if available) are provided for each town and area listed in this guide. Domestic tourism in France creates peak holiday migration periods, especially between 14 July and 31 August. Consequently, the hotel and restaurant trades are seasonal. A little forward planning will allow you to avoid the pitfalls of seasonal closure.

Visas and Passports

Citizens of EU countries, apart from the UK and Ireland, can enter France with a national identity card. Visitors from the UK, Ireland, the US, Canada, Australia and New Zealand need a full passport. Tourist trips may last up to 3 months; after this a *carte de séjour* (residency permit) is required. Like most EU countries (but not the UK and Ireland), France is part of the Schengen agreement for shared border controls. If you enter the Schengen area through a member country, you are free to cross into all member countries within your 90-day stay.

Non-EU nationals who wish to work or study in France, or stay longer than three months, should obtain a visa from a French consulate in their home country. For more information, check the website of your French embassy and your own country's foreign office.

Travel Safety Advice

Visitors can get up-to-date travel safety information from the **Foreign and Commonwealth Office** in the UK, the **State Department** in the US and the **Department of Foreign Affairs and Trade** in Australia.

Customs Information

EU residents are allowed to carry any amount of goods between EU countries without paying customs duties, as long as the goods are for personal use. Among the limits generally accepted as being for personal use are 800 cigarettes, 90 litres of wine and 110 litres of beer.

Visitors from outside the EU can reclaim sales tax *(TVA)* on many French goods, if more than €175 is spent in one shop in one day. To claim the tax back you must get a *détaxe* form from the store and take your goods out of the EU within three months. Present the receipt at customs when leaving the country, and mail the stamped receipt as instructed. The refund will then be sent to you or credited to your bank card. There are *détaxe* desks at all main airports and in big stores. Full information is available from the **Centre des Renseignements des Douanes**.

Tourist office in Bagnoles de l'Orne in Normandy

Tourist Information

All cities, towns and many villages have *offices de tourisme*, which provide invaluable free maps and information on local attractions and accommodation. Tourist offices often produce useful guides covering walking and cycling routes, bike hire, local gastronomy, traditional farm produce and more. Some regional and *département* offices also offer well-priced hotel and tour packages, and many city offices have organized imaginative guided tours and themed routes.

Before travelling to France, you can get basic orientation information and advice from France's official tourist website **Atout France** or from the French government tourist office in your country. For in-depth regional planning, it is best to use the websites of the relevant Regional Tourist Boards *(Comité Régional du Tourisme)* or those of the many *départements (Comités Départementaux du Tourisme)*. The latter provide a valuable range of detailed information. Nearly all websites are available in English. Links to these sites can be found on the Atout France website.

Admission Charges

Most museums and monuments in France charge an entry fee, usually from €2 to €10. There are often family discounts, and those under 26 years old with an EU passport have free access to permanent exhibitions at state-owned sights.

Several multi-entry schemes are available that reduce costs if you plan to visit a number of sights. Foremost, the Paris Museum Pass gives unlimited entry to over 60 museums and monuments in and around Paris for either 2, 4 or 6 days. It can be bought in advance online (www.parismuseumpass.com). Other places have local schemes, which often include unlimited use of local transport. Check local tourism websites to see what is available.

◀ Parked bikes, part of the Vélib' bicycle-sharing scheme in Paris

The Arc de Triomphe du Carrousel and the Musée du Louvre in Paris

Opening Hours

This guide lists which days of the week sights are open. National museums and sights normally close on Tuesdays, with a few exceptions that close on Mondays. Generally, the larger museums and sights are open from 9am or 10am to 6pm, sometimes with one late evening a week, often Thursday. Note that smaller museums and churches may close from 12:30pm to 2pm.

Opening times can also vary considerably by season, especially for country châteaux, estates and gardens. Many are open daily in the peak July to August holiday season and then close completely from November to March, or are only open at weekends. Most sights are closed on Christmas Day and New Year's Day.

See page 604 for details on opening hours for shops; page 626 for banks; and pages 572–3 for restaurants.

Taxes and Tipping

A service charge of 10 to 20 per cent is included on all restaurant bills, and it is customary to round up the bill by a few euros in a restaurant, or a few cents in a café, especially if the service has been good. In grander restaurants, an extra tip of 5–10 per cent is the norm.

For taxi drivers, the usual tipping rate is around 10 per cent. For hotel porters, it is common to tip around €1–€2.

Travellers with Special Needs

France is working hard to improve access to all its services. There are disabled parking spaces in many streets and all public car parks. These can be used free of charge with a European Blue Badge. SNCF (French railways) has introduced the *Accès Plus* scheme, through which wheelchair users and others with mobility problems can book ahead to guarantee a space and free assistance. For information, go to the "Everyday Life" *(Vie Pratique)* section on the SNCF website and look under Services + *(see p634)*.

In Paris, some buses, some RER lines and one Métro line (no. 14) are wheelchair-accessible *(see pp640–41)*. By law, all taxis must carry wheelchair users for no extra charge *(see p640)*.

Much has been done to improve access to attractions, but access to smaller historic houses and country châteaux can be difficult at times. The blue *Tourisme & Handicap* label indicates attractions, hotels, restaurants and other facilities that meet full disabled access criteria. Many hotels and *chambres d'hôtes* (bed and breakfasts) have adapted rooms, and major booking agencies such as Logis de France or Gîtes de France indicate this on their websites.

For information on disabled facilities in France, the best resource is the **Association des Paralysés de France** (APF), which produces an annual *Guide Vacances* holiday booklet. The **Infomobi** website also has comprehensive information on transport services for the disabled in and around Paris. Both these resources are in French and in English. Further information in English can be found on the Atout France website.

Travelling with Children

Families travelling in France benefit from a range of cost-cutting discounts, including reduced or free admission to attractions for children. Those under 4 travel free on most public transport, and youngsters aged 4 to 11 (4 to 9 in Paris) travel half-price.

Some of the big French hotel chains (notably Novotel) specialize in catering for families, while many small country hotels and *chambres d'hôtes* have cost-efficient family rooms *(chambres familiales)*. If you base yourself in one area for two days or more, a self-contained *gîte*, with several rooms and a kitchen, can offer exceptional value for money *(see p551)*.

Virtually all French restaurants welcome children, and many have a children's menu *(menu d'enfants)* for €8–€12.

The Atout France website has information on attractions throughout France, while local tourism websites list regional-specific family attractions and activities. For more ideas, consult websites such as **France for Families** and **Kids in Tow**.

The Château de Versailles has excellent disabled access

Senior Travellers

Senior visitors to France do not enjoy reduced admission fees at national museums and monuments, although some privately owned châteaux and attractions do offer lower prices for older people. Discounted travel on public transport is only available with multi-journey passes issued by some cities, and the SNCF *Carte Senior* for the over-60s *(see p634)*. However, these cards are not much use for short visits, as you'll only notice the discount if you make several journeys on each system. Rail passes *(see p634)* bought in advance outside France can be better value.

Student Information

Students aged under 26 with a valid **International Student Identity Card** (ISIC) benefit from many discounts, as well as those available to everyone in France aged 25 or under. The Centre d'Information et de Documentation Jeunesse will provide you with further information (www.cidj.com).

Gay and Lesbian Travellers

France has prominent gay and lesbian communities that are becoming ever more part of the cultural mainstream. The Marais district of Paris is the country's foremost "gay village", but there are gay clubs and services all over the capital. There are gay communities in many other cities, especially in Toulouse, Nantes, Montpellier and Nice. Tune into Radio FG (98.2 MHz) or consult listings in ***Têtu*** magazine for a wide range of gay-friendly information. For further help, contact **Centre LGBT** in Paris.

Travelling on a Budget

How much you spend on a holiday in France will vary enormously depending on what you do. However, in general, two people staying at a basic hotel (an average of €60 for a double room), eating both lunch and dinner in restaurants, visiting a few attractions and using public transport can roughly expect to spend €160 per day in most parts of France, or €80 each.

Staying in Paris, the Cóte d'Azur and other fashionable resorts is expensive, but less-visited rural regions such as Normandy, inland Brittany and Lorraine can be more affordable. Travelling in peak season (July–mid-September) will also be costly with high hotel rates, particularly in the most popular regions. December through to March, the winter sports season, can also be pricey, particularly in the Alps. If you want to keep costs down it is best to travel during the low season, when hotel prices are much cheaper. City hotels, however, can be more reasonable between July and August, when most French

International Student Identity Card

people head for the country.

Staying in a *chambre d'hôte* (bed and breakfast) is a good alternative to costly hotels. Traditionally, these are located in the countryside but they are now popping up in towns and the average price for a comfortable double room is around €40 including breakfast. Another option is a *gîte*, which offers self-catering facilities, though these usually require a minimum stay of a weekend or a week.

When dining, opt for a set menu – ordering from the à la carte menu will be far more expensive. Taking your main meal at midday rather than in the evening will mean you can make the most of the best-value set menus or *formules*. To keep costs down when sightseeing, opt for a City Pass that gives unlimited travel on local transport as well as entry to local monuments *(see p641)*. If you intend to rent a car, book it in advance through an internet rental agency for the best rates.

French Time

France is one hour ahead of Greenwich Mean Time (GMT) or British Summer Time (BST).

Waiting to travel at Marseille Gare St-Charles train station

Electrical Adaptors

The voltage in France is 220 volts. Plugs are the standard type used in most of Europe with two round pins, or three for applications that need to be earthed. Many hotels offer built-in adaptors for shavers.

Conversion Chart

Imperial to metric
1 inch = 2.54 centimetres
1 foot = 30 centimetres
1 mile = 1.6 kilometres
1 ounce = 28 grams
1 pound = 454 grams
1 pint = 0.6 litre
1 gallon = 4.6 litres

Metric to imperial
1 millimetre = 0.04 inch
1 centimetre = 0.4 inch
1 metre = 3 feet 3 inches
1 kilometre = 0.6 mile
1 gram = 0.04 ounce
1 kilogram = 2.2 pounds
1 litre = 1.8 pints

Queuing for the Eiffel Tower

Responsible Travel

In France, as in many other countries, there has been a rapid growth in environmental awareness. **Echoway** and the **Association Française d'Ecotourisme** are two leading French ecotourism organizations, encouraging heightened awareness of responsible travel. **Mountain Riders** promotes sustainable winter tourism in the Alps, providing information on how to get to the mountains by public transport and arranging group walks to clean up mountain pistes each spring.

France has a long-running rural tourism network, with farmhouse accommodation available through the central Gîtes de France agency *(see p551)*. There are also smaller organizations with a more defined ecological stance, such as **Accueil Paysan**, which is a network of small-scale farmers practising low-impact, sustainable agriculture. Another alternative to staying in a hotel is camping, and there are over 11,000 fully equipped campsites across the country to choose from *(see p552)*.

Information on local green tourism (*tourisme vert* or *eco*) initiatives and activities can be found through local tourist offices. Many towns have weekly markets selling only organic and traditional produce (usually called a *marché bio*), which allow visitors to give back to the local community. Marketdays have been provided throughout the guide.

DIRECTORY

Embassies

Australia
4 rue Jean Rey, 75015 Paris. **Map** 6 D3. **Tel** 01 40 59 33 00. **W france.embassy.gov.au**

Canada
35 av Montaigne, 75008 Paris. **Map** 6 F1. **Tel** 01 44 43 29 00. **W canadainternational. gc.ca/france**

United Kingdom
35 rue du Faubourg-St-Honoré, 75383 Paris. **Map** 3 C5. **Tel** 01 44 51 31 00. **W ukinfrance.fco.gov.uk**

United States
2 av Gabriel, 75008 Paris. **Map** 3 A5. **Tel** 01 43 12 22 22. **W france.usembassy.gov**

Travel Safety Advice

Australia
Department of Foreign Affairs and Trade
W dfat.gov.au
W smartraveller.gov.au

United Kingdom
Foreign and Commonwealth Office
W gov.uk/foreign-travel-advice

United States
Department of State
W travel.state.gov

Tourist Offices

Atout France
W atout-france.fr

Australia
Level 13, 25 Bligh St, Sydney NSW 2000.
Tel (2) 9210 5400.
W au.france.fr

Paris Convention and Visitors Bureau
25 rue des Pyramides, 75001 Paris.
Tel 01 49 52 42 63.
W parisinfo.com

United Kingdom
Lincoln House, 300 High Holborn, London WC1V 7JH.
Tel 020 7061 6600.
W uk.france.fr

United States
825 Third Ave, 29th Floor, NY 10022.
Tel (1) 212 838 7800.
W us.france.fr

Customs Information

Centre des Renseignements des Douanes
Tel 08 11 20 44 44.
W douane.gouv.fr

Gay and Lesbian Travellers

Centre LGBT
63 rue Beaubourg, 75003 Paris.
Tel 01 43 57 21 47.

Têtu
W tetu.com

Special Needs

APF
W apf.asso.fr

Infomobi
W infomobi.com

Tourisme et Handicaps
W tourisme-handicaps.org

Families and Students

France for Families
W franceforfamilies.com

International Student Identity Card (ISIC)
W isic.org
W isiccard.com

Kids in Tow
W kidsintow.co.uk

Responsible Travel

Accueil Paysan
Tel 04 76 43 44 83.
W accueil-paysan.com

Association Française d'Ecotourisme
W ecotourisme.info

Echoway
W echoway.org

Mountain Riders
W mountain-riders.org

Personal Security and Health

On the whole France is a safe place for visitors, but it is always a good idea to take the normal precautions of looking after your possessions and avoiding unfamiliar or unfrequented residential urban areas after dark. If you fall ill during your stay, pharmacies generally offer good advice, while the emergency services can be contacted for any serious medical problems. Consulates and consular departments *(see p623)* at your embassy can also provide assistance in an emergency.

Gendarmes

Police

Violent crime is not a major problem in France, but, as in any country, it is advisable to be on your guard against petty theft, especially in cities. If you are robbed, lose any property or are the victim of any other type of crime, report the incident as soon as possible at the nearest *commissariat de police* (police station). In an emergency, dialling 17 will also connect you to the police department, but you will still have to go to a station to make a statement. In small towns and villages, crime is reported to the *gendarmerie*, the force mainly responsible for rural policing. The *mairie* (town hall) is also a good place to go for help, but this will only be open during office hours.

At all police stations you will be required to make a statement, called a *PV* or *procès verbal*, listing any lost or stolen items. You will need your passport and, if relevant, your vehicle papers. It is important to keep a copy of your police statement for your insurance claim.

Lost and Stolen Property

The likelihood, and impact, of street theft can be considerably reduced by a few simple precautions. In the first instance, ensure that all possessions are covered by a comprehensive travel insurance policy before arrival. Once in France, avoid risky city neighbourhoods, and beware of pickpockets, especially on the Paris Métro during rush hour (particularly just as the carriage doors are closing). When you sit at a pavement café table, always keep your bag within reach and in sight, preferably on your lap or on the table, and never leave it on the ground or hanging on the back of a chair. Keep bags zipped up and held close to you when walking along, and never leave luggage unattended at train stations or other travel centres. Keep valuables securely concealed and only carry with you as much cash as you think you will need for the day.

For lost or stolen property, it may be worth returning to the station where you reported the incident to check if the police have retrieved some of the items. In addition, all French town halls have a *Bureau d'Objets Trouvés* (lost property office), although they are often inefficient and finding items can take time. Lost property offices can also be found at larger train stations, which will be open during office hours.

If your passport is lost or stolen, notify your consulate immediately *(see p623)*. The loss of credit or debit cards should also be reported as soon as possible to your bank to avoid fraudulent use.

What to Be Aware Of

Isolated terrorist incidents over the past few years have led to an increased police presence. Be sure to carry a photo ID with you, avoid carrying large bags and suitcases to public buildings, and be prepared for your bags to be searched upon entering museums, theatres, large shops and public buildings.

Travel Insurance

All travellers in France should have a comprehensive travel insurance policy providing adequate cover for any eventuality, including potential medical and legal expenses, theft, lost luggage and other personal property, accidents, travel delays and the option of immediate repatriation by air in the event of a major medical emergency. Winter sports are not covered by standard travel policies, so if you are planning to ski or to undertake any other adventure sports in France, you will need to pay an additional premium to ensure you are protected. All insurance policies should come with a 24-hour emergency number in case of need.

In an Emergency

The phone number for **all emergency services** is 112, but in practice it is often quicker to call the relevant authority direct on their traditional two-digit numbers. In a medical emergency, for an **ambulance**, call the **Service d'Aide Médicale Urgence (SAMU)**. However, it can sometimes be faster to call the **fire service** – **Sapeurs**

DIRECTORY

Emergency Numbers

All Emergency Services
Tel 112.

Ambulance (SAMU)
Tel 15.

Fire (Sapeurs Pompiers)
Tel 18.

Police and Gendarmerie
Tel 17.

Pompiers, who also offer first aid and can take you to the nearest hospital. This is particularly true in rural areas, where the fire station is likely to be much closer than the ambulance service based in town. The paramedics are called *secouristes*.

Hospitals and Pharmacies

All European Union nationals holding a European Health Insurance Card (EHIC) are entitled to use the French national health service. However, under the French system patients must pay for all treatments and then reclaim most of the cost from the health authorities. Therefore, non-French EU nationals who use health services in France will need to ensure they keep the statement of costs (*feuille de soins*) that is provided by the doctor or hospital. This should include stickers for any prescription drugs, which must be stuck onto the statement by the pharmacist once you have made your purchase. Around 80 per cent of the cost can be claimed back by following the instructions provided with your EHIC card. This can be a time-consuming process, and it can often be simpler to use private travel insurance. Non-EU nationals must have full private medical insurance while in France and pay for services in the same way, claiming their costs back in full from their insurance company.

Well-equipped public hospitals can be found throughout France. In all towns and cities there are hospitals with general casualty/emergency departments (called *urgences* or *service des urgences*) that can deal with immediate medical problems. If your hotel cannot direct you to one, call the SAMU or fire service. Should you require an English-speaking doctor, your consulate should be able to recommend one in the area, and in Paris and some other cities in France, there are both American and British private hospitals (these do not have emergency or *urgences* facilities). Pharmacies, identified by an illuminated green cross sign, are plentiful and easy to find. French pharmacists are highly trained and can diagnose minor health problems and suggest appropriate treatments. When one is closed, a card in the window will give details of the nearest *pharmacie de garde* that is open on Sundays or during the night.

Police car

Fire engine

Ambulance

Natural Hazards

Forest fires are a major risk in many parts of France. High winds can mean fires spread rapidly in winter as well as in summer, so be vigilant about putting out all campfires and cigarette butts. Keep well away from any area where there is a fire, as its direction can change quickly.

Before exploring any of the country's seven national parks or its regional nature parks (*parcs naturels*), visit the relevant park information centre to check the regulations and recommendations that apply within the area, and take care to observe them. When walking in mountains or sailing, inform the relevant authority – such as a park information centre or a harbourmaster – of your intended route and when you expect to return. Never try to walk in remote mountain areas or across tidal marshes without an experienced guide, or against local advice.

Fire hazard poster

During the hunting season (Sep–Feb and especially Sundays) dress in visible colours when out walking and avoid areas where hunters are staked out in hides *(see p615)*.

Safety on Beaches

Throughout France, there are many good family beaches where bathing is rarely dangerous. Many beaches are guarded in summer by lifeguards *(sauveteurs)* – always heed their instructions and only swim in supervised areas. Also look out for the system of coloured flags, indicating whether it is safe to swim. Green flags mean bathing is safe; orange flags warn that bathing may be dangerous and that only the part of the beach marked out by flags is guarded. Swimming outside this area is therefore not recommended. Red flags indicate dangerous conditions (high waves, shifting sands, strong undercurrents), so all bathing is forbidden. Many beaches also display blue flags, which are used throughout the European Union as a sign of cleanliness.

Banking and Local Currency

Banks usually offer the best rates of exchange. Cash can be changed at banks and main post offices. The easiest method for obtaining local currency is by using a debit card or credit card to withdraw cash from an ATM. Bureaux de change can be found at airports, large railway stations, in some international hotels and shops and in the centre of large cities, but they have variable rates and charges, and often charge a high commission for transactions.

Using Banks

Currencies other than euros are generally not accepted in France. Most banks will exchange foreign currency, but the commission rates vary, so it is worth looking around to make sure you get the best deal. Virtually all bank branches have ATMs (called *distributeurs* or *points argent* in French), which accept major credit and debit cards. Most ATMs give instructions in several European languages.

Banking Hours

In Paris, and many other cities, banks are generally open from 9am or 10am to 5pm Monday to Friday, with some branches open on Saturdays. Outside large cities banks are usually closed on Mondays and generally open from 8am or 9am until 12:30pm, and from 2pm to 5pm Tuesday to Friday and 8am or 9am until 12:30pm on Saturday. There are, however, many variations between banks, and individual branches. All banks close on Sundays and public holidays, and many also close at noon on the working day before a holiday.

Credit and debit card reader requiring you to enter your PIN

Credit and Debit Cards

Major credit cards such as **Visa** (called Carte Bleue in France) and **MasterCard** and debit cards, such as Switch, Maestro or Cirrus, are widely used. American Express credit cards are less widely accepted in France. Some smaller establishments do not take cards or will do so only if you spend a certain amount of money. Many credit card companies charge a sizeable fee for every transaction.

A convenient way to access local currency is to withdraw it from an ATM with a debit card. There is a transaction fee so it costs less to take out a sizeable sum each time rather than make many small withdrawals. If an ATM is not working, you can also withdraw cash on major credit cards at the foreign counter of a bank. The bank may need to obtain telephone authorization for such withdrawals first.

Pre-Paid Currency Cards

Pre-paid currency cards, such as those offered by **FairFX**, are more economical than credit and debit cards and are widely accepted in France. You can use them to withdraw cash at an ATM and pay for goods and services. You can load up your card with credit ahead of your trip, and top it up online or by phone while in France. Currency cards are often linked to Visa or MasterCard so you can use them anywhere you would normally use a credit or debit card. Some currency card providers charge a fee to top up your card and for ATM cash withdrawals but this is much lower than for a standard credit card.

ATM in Paris

DIRECTORY

Foreign Banks

Barclays
24bis av de l'Opéra, 75001 Paris. **Map** 8 E1. **Tel** 08 10 06 06 60 or 01 44 86 00 00.
W barclays.fr

HSBC
103 av des Champs-Elysées, 75008 Paris. **Map** 2 E4.
Tel 08 10 24 68 10 or 08 10 83 84 85.
W hsbc.fr

Bureaux de Change

Travelex

Paris
125 av des Champs-Elysées, 75008. **Map** 2 E4.
Tel 01 47 20 25 14.
W travelex.fr

Lille
69 rue Faidherbe, 59000.

Lyon
Gare de Lyon-Part-Dieu, bd Marius Vivier Merle, 69003.

Nice
13 av Thiers, 06000.

Lost Credit Cards

MasterCard
Tel 08 00 90 13 87.

Visa
Tel 08 00 90 11 79.

Pre-Paid Currency Cards

FairFX
Tel 020 7107 1206.
W fairfx.com

The Euro

France was one of the 12 countries taking the euro (€) in 2002, with the original currency, the franc, phased out on the 17 February 2002.

EU members using the euro as sole official currency are known as the Eurozone. Several EU members have either opted out or have not met the conditions for adopting the single currency.

Euro notes are identical throughout the Eurozone countries, each one including designs of fictional monuments and architectural structures, and the 12 stars of the EU. The coins, however, have one side identical (the value side), and one side with an image unique to each country. Both notes and coins are exchangeable in any of the participating Eurozone countries.

Banknotes

Euro banknotes have seven denominations. The €5 note (grey in colour) is the smallest, followed by the €10 note (pink), €20 note (blue), €50 note (orange), €100 note (green), €200 note (yellow) and €500 note (purple). All notes show the stars of the European Union.

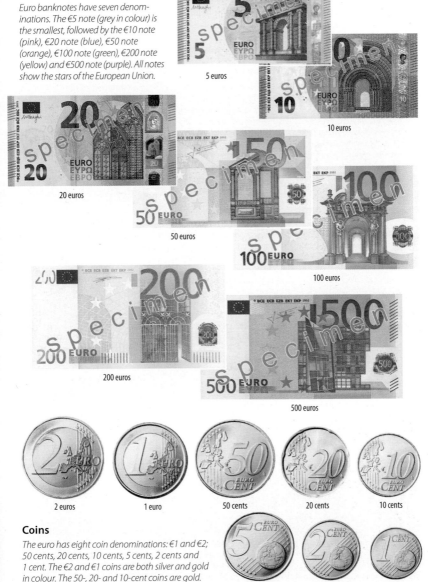

5 euros

10 euros

20 euros

50 euros

100 euros

200 euros

500 euros

2 euros

1 euro

50 cents

20 cents

10 cents

Coins

The euro has eight coin denominations: €1 and €2; 50 cents, 20 cents, 10 cents, 5 cents, 2 cents and 1 cent. The €2 and €1 coins are both silver and gold in colour. The 50-, 20- and 10-cent coins are gold. The 5-, 2- and 1-cent coins are bronze.

5 cents

2 cents

1 cent

Communications and Media

France has world-class telecommunications. Many cities and venues offer free public Wi-Fi. Phone booths have given way to affordable prepaid SIM cards, with 3G and 4G coverage available even in the Paris Metro. With many competing providers, prices for internet and phone services are competitive. Post offices (bureaux des postes), identified by the blue-on-yellow La Poste sign, are your best bet for sending items nationally or worldwide. The French generally speak more English than they let on, but the service industry is better than ever at communicating with English-speakers. Publications, TV and radio in foreign languages can be found easily in major towns.

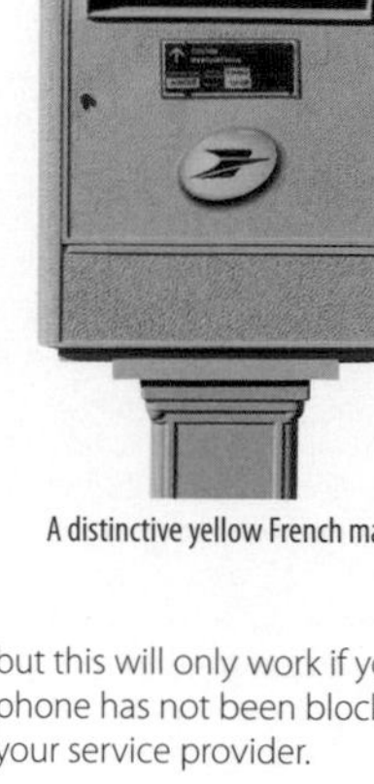

A distinctive yellow French mailbox

Local and International Phone Calls

All French telephone numbers have ten digits, and you must key in all the digits, even if you are in the same area. In landline numbers the first two digits indicate the region: 01 is for Paris and the Ile-de-France; 02, the northwest; 03, the northeast; 04, the southeast; and 05, the south-west. French mobile phone numbers begin with 06, and 08 indicates a special rate number. All 0800 numbers are free. For landline numbers, cheap rates operate on evenings, weekends and public holidays. It is best to avoid making calls from hotels, as most add hefty surcharges.

To call France from abroad, dial 00 33 and omit the initial zero from the 10-digit French number. You cannot call French 08 numbers from outside France.

To call abroad from France, dial 00 and then the country code (Australia 61, USA and Canada 1, Irish Republic 353, New Zealand 64 and UK 44).

Mobile Phones

Mobile phone coverage is generally good throughout France, although signals may be weak in some mountain areas. French mobiles use the European-standard 900 and 1900 MHz frequencies, so UK mobiles work if they have a roaming facility enabled. North American mobile phones will only operate in France if they are tri- or quad-band. Always check roaming charges with your service provider before travelling, as making and receiving calls can be very expensive. Some companies offer "packages" for foreign calls and these can work out cheaper.

If you expect to use your phone frequently, it can be more economical to buy a pay-as-you-go French mobile from one of the main local providers such as **Orange France**, **Bouygues Télécom**, **SFR** and **Free**. All four companies have shops in most towns. You can also insert a local SIM card into your own phone, but this will only work if your phone has not been blocked by your service provider.

Tourists using smartphones at the Colonnes de Buren, Palais Royal in Paris

Public Telephones

With the rise in the use of mobile phones, there are now very few pay phones *(cabines téléphoniques)*, and few of these accept coins. Many phones now accept credit cards (with a PIN number), but for some you will need to use a phone card *(télécarte)*. Sold in *tabacs*, post offices, train stations and some newsagents, cards are available for 50 or 120 telephone units, and are simple to use. For calls abroad, international code cards are available at the Travelex bureaux de change *(see p626)*.

The cheapest way to phone abroad is to connect to Wi-Fi (for free) and use an internet calling app such as WhatsApp or Skype.

Internet Access

The internet is widely used in France, but internet cafés have diminished in number. There are usually a few Taxiphone internet cafés offering computers with cheap Wi-Fi in most cities and resorts, but in small towns and rural areas they can be hard to find. For mobile phone, tablet and laptop users there are free Wi-Fi hot spots in many Métro stations, public libraries and other locations in Paris and other major cities. Many hotels and even *chambres d'hôtes* now offer Wi-Fi connections, but check that these are free.

Most hotels use one of several subscription services such as Orange France and **Meteor**, with which you buy a certain amount of time-credit and are then given an access code. Any time-credit remaining can be used anywhere that uses the same service.

French Wi-Fi servers often use different frequencies to those in the UK and North America, so you may need to manually search for the network (for more details, see the Orange Wi-Fi website). If you need to use a cable connection, note that the French modem socket is incompatible with US and UK plugs. Adaptors are available, but it is often cheaper and easier to buy a French modem lead.

Postal Services

The postal service in France is fast and usually reliable. There are post offices in most towns, and there are large main offices in all cities. Postage stamps *(timbres)* can be bought at post offices individually or in a *carnet* of seven or ten, although the most convenient place to buy stamps is often at a *tabac*, where phone cards can also be purchased.

Post offices usually open 9am–5pm Mon–Fri, often with a break for lunch, and 9am–noon on Saturdays. Post offices in towns and cities are best avoided when they first open, as this is when they are at their busiest.

Letters are posted in yellow mailboxes, which often have separate slots for post within the town you are in, within the *département* and for other destinations *(autres destinations)*. There are eight different price zones for international mail. Information on mail services is provided on the **La Poste** website.

Newspapers and Magazines

Newspapers and magazines can be bought at newsagents *(maisons de la presse)* or news-stands *(kiosques)*. Regional newspapers tend to be more popular than the Paris-based national papers, such as the conservative *Le Figaro*, weighty *Le Monde* or leftist *Libération*. The daily *International Herald Tribune* can be found in Paris and throughout France. Other foreign newspapers are also often available on the day of publication in resorts and large cities.

The weekly listings magazines *Pariscope* (Thursday) and *L'Officiel des Spectacles* (Wednesday) give the latest on entertainment news in Paris. *Les Inrockuptibles* has information on current music, film and the other arts from all over France. Many smaller cities have their own listings magazines, usually in French and often free, which can generally be found at tourist offices.

TV and Radio

All French television networks use Digital Video Broadcasting (DVB). There are 18 free channels, including the major national channels TF1 and France 2. Canal Plus (or Canal +), a subscription-only channel, offers a broad mix of programmes including live sports and films in English with French subtitles. A film shown in its original language is listed as *VO (Version Originale)*; a film dubbed into French is indicated as *VF (Version Française)*. Most hotels subscribe to Canal +, and many also have cable and satellite TV, including English-language stations such as CNN, MTV, Sky, BBC World and the English version of the round-the-clock French news service France24.

It is easy to pick up UK radio stations in France, including Radio 4 (198 long wave). BBC World Service broadcasts through the night on the same wavelength. Voice of America can be found at 90.5, 98.8 and 102.4 FM. Radio France International (738 AM) gives daily news in English from 3–4pm.

La Poste road sign

Newspapers sold in France

DIRECTORY

Telephone and Internet Services

Bouygues Télécom
Tel 1064 (from a landline).
W bouyguestelecom.fr

Free
W free.fr

Meteor
W meteornetworks.com

Orange France
Tel 0810 555 421.
W orange.fr
W orange-wifi.com

SFR
Tel 1026 (from a landline phone in France).
W sfr.fr

Postal Services

La Poste
W laposte.fr

Useful Telephone Numbers and Codes

- **Directory enquiries** 118 712.
- **International directory enquiries** 118 700.
- **France Telecom/Orange** 0800 36 47 75; 0969 363 900 (for English).
- **Free, reduced and premium numbers** 0800; 0810, 0820, 0825 (free and reduced rate); 0890, 0891, 0892 (premium rate).
- **In case of emergencies** 17.

TRAVEL INFORMATION

France enjoys sophisticated air, road and rail travel. Direct flights from all over the world serve Paris and some regional airports. Paris is the hub of a vast internal rail network and of Europe's high-speed train network, with the Eurostar to London, Thalys to Brussels and TGVs to Geneva and other destinations. Motorways cross into all surrounding countries including, via the Eurotunnel, the UK. France is also served by frequent Channel and Mediterranean ferries.

Getting to or from France on the national carrier, Air France

Arriving by Air

France is served by nearly all international airlines. Most long-haul flights arrive at Paris Charles de Gaulle airport, but there are flights from Europe and North Africa to many other airports around the country.

Airlines with regular flights between the UK and France include **British Airways**, **Air France** and low-cost airlines such as **Flybe**, **Jet2**, **Ryanair** and **easyJet**. From North America there are direct flights to Paris from about 20 cities, mainly on **Air Canada**, **American Airlines**, **Delta**, **United** and **Air France**. **Qantas** provides connecting flights from Australia and New Zealand.

Paris Airports

Paris's Charles de Gaulle airport (CDG), about 30 km from the city, is the main hub airport in France. Access to central Paris is by RER line B from CDG2, which takes 40 minutes to Gare du Nord and 45 minutes to Châtelet-Les Halles. Regular bus services run from the airport to different parts of Paris, and to Disneyland® Paris theme park. Air France buses run to the Arc de Triomphe and western Paris, and to Montparnasse; each journey takes about 45 minutes. RATP buses (Roissybus) depart every 20 minutes for L'Opéra and take about 50 minutes. Taxi fares are fixed from CDG to the Right Bank (€50) and Left Bank (€55) for up to four people.

Paris's other main airport, Orly, in the south of the city, serves primarily domestic and short-haul international flights. Shuttle buses link the airport with RER line C at Pont de Rungis and an automatic train, Orlyval, links the airport with RER line B at Antony, from where trains run to Châtelet-Les Halles in 35 minutes. Air France buses for central Paris depart every 30 minutes; RATP Orlybus runs to Denfert-Rochereau Métro; and the Jetbus connects Orly to Châtelet-Les Halles, departing every 15–20 minutes. Taxi fares from Orly to the Left Bank are €30 and €35 to the Right Bank.

Arriving by Sea

Several regular ferry services operate between the UK and Ireland and France. Dover–Calais is the fastest route: **P&O Ferries** has up to 25 crossings daily, with a journey time of 90 minutes or less. **DFDS Seaways** runs from Dover to Dunkerque in about 2 hours and has some of the lowest fares. It also has crossings between Newhaven and Dieppe (about 4 hrs), and between Dover and Calais or Dunkerque. The biggest operator in the western Channel is **Brittany Ferries**, which sails from Portsmouth to Caen (7 hrs overnight), Poole to Cherbourg (6 hrs overnight), Portsmouth to St-Malo (10 hrs overnight), Plymouth to Roscoff (8 hrs overnight), and between Cork and Roscoff (14 hrs). From April/May to September/October, Brittany Ferries also runs high-speed services on the Poole–Cherbourg and Portsmouth–Cherbourg routes (4 hrs 30 mins). **Condor Ferries** sail from Portsmouth to Cherbourg in 5 hours (July–September only) and

Plying the Mediterranean with SNCM Ferryterranée

from Poole and Weymouth to St-Malo via Jersey or Guernsey (May–September only).

Irish Ferries run between Rosslare and Cherbourg (17 hrs overnight) from January to December, and to Roscoff (15 hrs 30 mins overnight) from mid-May to September. **Maritima Ferries** run from a range of European ports *(see p635)*.

Arriving by Train

There are at least 20 **Eurostar** trains daily between London St Pancras and the Gare du Nord in Paris. The journey via the Channel Tunnel takes 2 hrs 15 mins. Several trains also stop at Ebbsfleet or Ashford in Kent, Calais–Frethun, Lille (1 hr 30 mins from London) and Disneyland® Paris.

Paris and its six main stations are the great hub of the French rail network. Travelling from Belgium, Holland and north Germany, you arrive at the Gare du Nord; from other parts of Germany you come into the Gare de l'Est. Trains from Switzerland and Italy arrive at the Gare de Lyon. From Spain you come into the Gare d'Austerlitz. Outside Paris, other major rail hubs include Lille, Tours, Bordeaux and Lyon. For more information on French rail services and travelling to France by train, see pp632–4.

EURO TUNNEL

Eurotunnel logo

Arriving by Road

Passengers from the UK can travel to France with their vehicle either by ferry or on the **Eurotunnel** shuttle through the Channel Tunnel. Eurotunnel runs at least four trains an hour during the day, and the trip takes about 35 minutes. Fares compete with those of the ferry companies, and similarly vary by season, day and time of travel. For Eurotunnel crossings, it is possible to turn up and wait for the next available space.

Coach travel is a good-value alternative, and **Eurolines** runs three to five departures daily from Victoria Coach Station in London to Bagnolet in eastern Paris. Coaches also run from London and other parts of the UK to Lille, Lyon, Marseille and several other French towns and cities. The SNCF-run **Ouigo** coach service offers low-cost bus travel within France and to cities in other countries.

Green Travel

Travelling in France without flying or driving is easier than in many countries thanks to the high quality of public transport, particularly the SNCF rail network. There are daily train services from across Europe, ferries to the UK, Ireland and Mediterranean destinations, and the Eurostar connection with London.

The French government has introduced an "Ecomobility" programme, which aims to make it easier to transfer from trains to local buses, bicycles or other non-car forms of transport. This includes public cycle schemes such as the *Vélib'* in Paris and similar bike-sharing initiatives in other cities *(see p641)*. Many regions have also developed **Voies Vertes**, long-distance paths for cycling or walking, such as the one along the Loire from Orléans to St-Nazaire.

DIRECTORY

Arriving by Air

Air Canada
Tel 01 888 247 2262 (Canada), 0825 880 881 (France).
W **aircanada.com**

Air France
Tel 01 800 667 2747 (France). W **airfrance.com**

American Airlines
Tel 01 800 433 7300 (USA), 0821 980 999 (France). W **aa.com**

British Airways
Tel 0844 493 0787 (UK), 0825 825 400 (France).
W **britishairways.com**

Delta
Tel 01 800 221 1212 (USA), 08 11 64 00 05 (France). W **delta.com**

easyJet
Tel 0330 3655 0000 (UK), 0820 420 315 (France).
W **easyjet.com**

Flybe
W **flybe.com**

Jet2
Tel 0333 300 0404 (UK), 0821 230 203 (France).
W **jet2.com**

Qantas
Tel 13 13 13 (Australia), 01 57 32 92 83 (France).
W **qantas.com**

Ryanair
Tel 0871 246 000 (UK), 0892 562 150 (France).
W **ryanair.com**

United
Tel 01 800 864 8331 (USA), 01 71 23 03 35 (France).
W **united.com**

Arriving by Sea

Brittany Ferries
W **brittany-ferries.com**

Condor Ferries
W **condorferries.co.uk**

DFDS Seaways
W **dfdsseaways.co.uk**
W **norfolkline.com**

Irish Ferries
W **irishferries.com**

P&O Ferries
W **poferries.com**

Maritima Ferries
W **ferries.co.uk/maritima_ferries.html**

Arriving by Train

See also pp632–4

Eurostar
Tel 08705 186 186 (UK), 0892 35 35 39 (France).
W **eurostar.com**

Arriving by Road

Eurolines
Tel 0871 781 8181 (UK), 0892 899 091 (France).
W **eurolines.co.uk**

Eurotunnel
Tel 08443 35 35 35 (UK), 0810 630 304 (France).
W **eurotunnel.com**

Ouigo
W **ouigo.com**

Green Travel

Train+Bicycle Travel
W **velo.sncf.com**

Voies Vertes
W **voiesvertes.com**

Travelling by Train

The French state railway, the Société Nationale des Chemins de Fer (**SNCF**), runs Europe's most comprehensive national rail network. Its services include high-speed, long-distance TGVs and mainline expresses, overnight sleepers, AutoTrain and rural branch lines that reach every corner of the country. Lines closed for economic reasons are replaced by SNCF's modern buses, which are free to Rail Pass holders. Travel off the main lines can be slow, though some cross-country journeys are quicker, if you change trains in Paris.

Travelling around France by Train

France has always been known for the punctuality of its trains, and has maintained a high level of investment in the state-owned rail system, **SNCF**. The pride of the SNCF is its TGV high-speed train, with journey times such as Lille–Lyon or Paris–Marseille in just 3 hours. In addition, frequent, fast and comfortable mainline express trains provide a comprehensive city-to-city service, while regional lines provide connections to smaller towns and villages. SNCF is also the largest bus operator in France, filling in the gaps where railway lines have been closed.

Sleeper trains are a convenient way to travel long distances at night, and motorists can travel with their cars on **AutoTrain** trains. Most (but not all) long-distance trains have restaurant cars.

Further information on French railways is provided on the main SNCF website *(see p634)*, where reservations can also be made. To book a long-distance train from abroad, visit the **Voyages SNCF** website. **Rail Europe** also offers a comprehensive information and booking service for travel throughout Europe. For useful links and an invaluable guide to every aspect of using French and other European railways, visit **The Man in Seat 61** website.

RER

Symbol for Paris suburban trains

Local and Scenic Railways

Alongside the national rail network, there are several special railways that operate around France. On Corsica, the **Chemins de Fer de la Corse** has narrow-gauge lines between Calvi, Bastia and Ajaccio. Particularly spectacular is the rail trip along the north-west coast between L'Ile-Rousse and Calvi. In summer, old-style *trains touristiques* run on this and other lines. In Provence, the privately run **Chemins de Fer de Provence** runs the *Train des Pignes* over a magnificent 150-km (90-mile) mountain route from Nice to Digne-les-Bains. SNCF also runs many more *trains touristiques* on particularly scenic sections of its regional network. These are usually in mountainous areas during the winter months and in summer on the coast and in the countryside. *Gentiane Bleu* trains run from Dijon to the winter snows in the Jura, and the *Train des Merveilles* runs from Nice into the Alps at Tende. For a guide to all these routes, visit www.sncf.com/fr/trains/trains-touristiques. Several privately or locally owned rail lines around France are kept going by enthusiasts, who offer excursions for part of the year, often using steam trains. The *Chemin de Fer de la Baie de la Somme* travels around the Somme Bay in Picardy and the *Chemin de Fer Touristique du Tarn* operates in the Tarn hills near Albi. Nearly all of these companies are members of the **UNECTO** association.

The train to Le Montenvers is a particularly scenic route

Types of Train

SNCF trains are divided into several types. TGV (*Train à Grande Vitesse*) trains are the flagships of the network, travelling on specially built track at around 300 kph (186 mph). There are four main TGV route networks; to the north, west, east and southeast from Paris, with additional hubs at Lille, Lyon, Bordeaux and Marseille. In some places, TGVs have separate stations built outside town centres. The trains have first- and second-class carriages, and some of them offer internet access. Seat reservations are obligatory for all TGV trains: tickets can be bought at stations until shortly before departure time, or booked ahead online.

Within the TGV network there are several international

services, including Eurostar, linking France with the UK; Thalys, which links stations in France with Belgium, Holland and Germany; Lyria, serving Switzerland; and TGV and ITALO, which run TGV services to the main cities in Italy, and a conventional train from Paris to Rome. Non-TGV international trains also operate, notably the nightly Elipsos from Paris to Madrid and Barcelona.

Intercités and Transilien trains are conventional long-distance express trains with modern carriages. Reservations are obligatory for all long-distance trains and can be made through Rail Europe or SNCF.

The AutoTrain allows drivers to cut out long distances by travelling overnight with their car on the same train. Those using the service from the UK should take the Eurostar to reach Paris first. The AutoTrain runs to twelve destinations in the south of France including Nice, Narbonne, Avignon, Lyon and Bordeaux.

The TGV, with its distinctive-looking "nose"

TER trains are regional services that usually stop at every station. Reservations are not required, although tickets can be purchased in advance. Route maps and information (in French only) for each region are available at stations and on the TER website *(see p634)*. Transilien is the TER network for the Ile-de-France around Paris, and is integrated with the RER suburban trains and the Métro.

TGV Rail Service

Trains à Grande Vitesse, or high-speed trains, travel at speeds up to 300 kph (186 mph). There are four routes: TGV Nord from Paris Gare du Nord, TGV Atlantique from Paris Gare Montparnasse, TGV Sud-Est from Paris Gare de Lyon and TGV Est from Paris Gare de l'Est.

Key

High-speed lines

Other lines

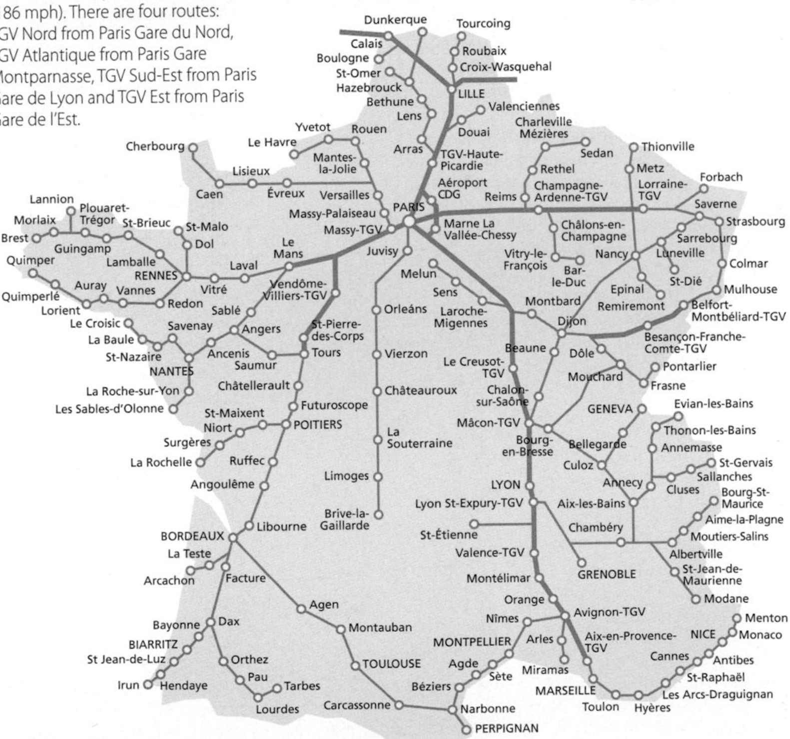

The automatic ticket machines at the Gare de Lyon in Paris

Fares and Passes

Fare rates vary according to the type of train. For all trains that can be booked online (TGV, Transilien, Eurostar), there are two or three basic fare rates for each class. The cheapest tickets are called Prems, which must be booked well in advance and cannot be altered after payment. On most TER and some Transilien trains fares are cheaper at off-peak times *(périodes bleus)*; peak times *(périodes blanches)* are 5–10am Monday and 3–8pm Friday and Sunday.

SNCF sells several travel cards that give fare reductions. Examples are *Carte Weekend*, giving 25% off weekend travel, *Carte Jeune* for those aged 12–27, *Carte Senior* for over-60s, *Carte Escapades* for frequent travellers and *Carte Enfant* + for parents with children under the age of 12. Further details are available on the SNCF website.

For visitors intending to make several train journeys around France, it is worth investing in a multi-journey rail pass, which can only be bought outside the country. The **Interrail** pass, for UK and other European residents, is valid for several European countries, giving unlimited travel for 3, 4, 6 or 8 days (not necessarily consecutively) within one month. Visitors from outside Europe can buy a France Rail Pass, permitting 3 to 9 days of unlimited travel within one month, or a **Eurail** Select Pass that covers France and neighbouring countries.
Be aware that some trains, including the TGV, charge additional supplements, which are not included in the price. For more information, visit the Rail Europe website.

Booking Tickets

Train tickets can be bought at any SNCF station and by phone or online through SNCF's free app. At most stations, there are both staffed counters and automatic ticket machines *(billetteries automatiques)*, which accept cash or credit cards and have instructions in English. Tickets for trains that require a reservation (TGV) can be bought up to 90 days in advance and up until 5 minutes before departure. Tickets bought in advance can be collected from the station, or sent to your address.

From outside France, you can book TGV and Intercité tickets through www.voyages-sncf.com (the website is in multiple languages), although it can be easier to use Rail Europe. Travellers with mobility problems can arrange assistance through the *Accès Plus* programme; more information is available online or from Atout France *(see pp620–23)*.

Note that before any train journey in France, you must validate your ticket in a *composteur* machine *(below)*.

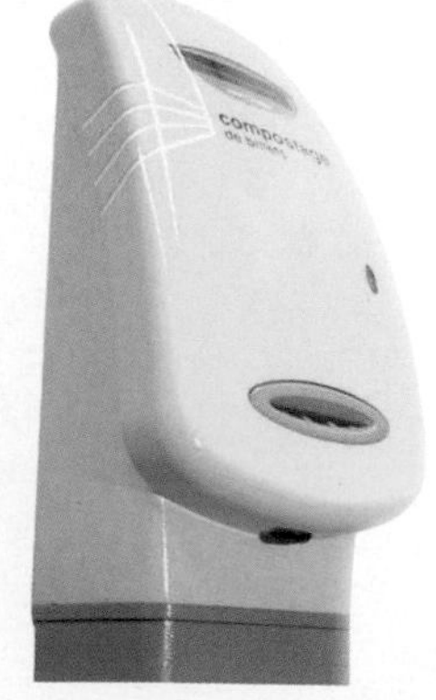

Timetables

French railway timetables change twice a year, in May and September, and all of them can be consulted on the SNCF website. Stations have free regional TER timetables available and information on the TGV network. Other free leaflets provide information on topics such as travelling with children, reduced fares and travel for the disabled.

DIRECTORY

Rail Information

AutoTrain
W autotrain.voyages-sncf.com

Eurail
W eurail.com

Interrail
W rail.cc

The Man in Seat 61
W seat61.com

Rail Europe
W raileurope.com

SNCF
W sncf.com

TER
W sncf.com/en/trains/ter

Voyages SNCF
W voyages-sncf.com

Local and Scenic Railways

Chemins de Fer de la Corse
W train-corse.com

Chemins de Fer de Provence
W trainprovence.com

UNECTO
W unecto.fr

Composteur Machine

Yellow *composteur* machines (left) are located in station halls and at the head of each platform. You must validate passes by inserting tickets and reservations separately, with the printed side up. The *composteur* will punch your ticket and print the time and date on the back. A penalty may be imposed by the inspector on the train if you fail to do this.

Travelling by Boat

With both Mediterranean and Atlantic coastlines, France offers excellent opportunities for sailing and has very good facilities. Inland, there is an extensive network of rivers, canals and other waterways. Cruising through them is an ideal way to discover some of the country's most charming countryside. Frequent scheduled ferries also connect mainland France to Corsica and other parts of the Mediterranean as well as to the British Channel Islands off Normandy.

Boats moored along the Canal du Midi, Roussillon

Travelling by Ferry

Car ferries sail to Corsica from Marseille, Nice and Toulon, the main operators being **Maritima Ferries** and **Corsica Ferries**. **La Méridionale** sails between Corsica and Sardinia, and **Moby Lines** also connects Corsica with Livorno and Genoa in mainland Italy. Regular ferries also connect France and North Africa; Maritima Ferries runs to Algeria and Tunisia, while **Aferry** goes to Morocco and Italy; it also has a luxury service from Sète to Morocco.

In the Atlantic, **Manche-Iles Express** and **Compagnie Corsaire** sail from St-Malo and the Normandy ports of Granville, Barneville-Carteret and Diélette to the British Channel Islands. For a guide to all European ferry services, visit www.ferrylines.com.

Sailing in France

France has excellent sailing facilities, with marinas all around its coast. On the Atlantic coast, well-equipped ports include Honfleur and St-Vaast-la-Hougue in Normandy, St-Malo and Pleneuf-St-André in Brittany and La Rochelle and Arcachon on the west coast. Among the best in the Mediterranean are St-Cyprien near the Spanish border, Antibes on the Côte d'Azur and the small harbours of Corsica. Boats for charter or short-term hire are available at most marinas and information on rules and permits is available from the **Ministère de l'Ecologie**. The **Fédération Française de Voile** provides updates on sailing conditions.

Canal and River Trips

There are many options for exploring French waterways, from short boat trips to cruises of several days. The official guide to the system is provided by **Voies Navigables de France**. Many companies offer cruises around France, among the best of which are **En Péniche**, which uses traditional barges or *peniches*; **Locaboat** and **En-Bateau Tourisme Fluvial**. For narrowboats on the Canal du Midi, try **Minervois Cruisers**.

Short excursions are popular around the Marais Poitevin wetlands between La Rochelle and Poitiers, and along the Canal de Bourgogne from Dijon. **Best of Perigord** runs trips along the Dordogne in traditional *gabarre* boats. For rides on the River Seine in Paris see p641.

DIRECTORY

Travelling by Ferry

Aferry
Tel 09 70 80 90 18. W **aferry.fr**

Compagnie Corsaire
Tel 0825 138 100.
W **compagniecorsaire.com**

Corsica Ferries
Tel 0825 095 095.
W **corsica-ferries.fr**

Manche-Iles Express
Tel 0825 133 050 (in France), 015 34 88 07 56 (in Jersey).
W **manche-iles-express.com**

Maritima Ferries
Tel 0844 815 7785.
W **ferries.co.uk/maritima_ferries.html**

La Méridionale
Tel 0970 83 20 20.
W **lameridionale.fr**

Moby Lines
Tel 00 49 (0)611 14020.
W **mobylines.fr**

Sailing in France

Fédération Française de Voile
W **ffvoile.fr**

Ministère de l'Ecologie
W **developpement-durable.gouv.fr**

Canal and River Trips

Best of Perigord
Tel 06 44 06 83 48.
W **best-of-perigord.tm.fr**

En-Bateau Tourisme Fluvial
Tel 04 67 13 19 62.
W **en-bateau.com**

En Péniche
Tel 04 67 13 19 62.
W **en-peniche.com**

Locaboat
Tel 03 86 91 72 72.
W **locaboat.com**

Minervois Cruisers
Tel 01926 811 842 (in UK).
W **minervoiscruisers.com**

Voies Navigables de France
W **vnf.fr**

On the Road

France's network of modern motorways (*autoroutes*) allows quick and easy access to all parts of the country. However, you can save money on tolls and explore France in a more leisurely way by using some of the other high-quality roads that dissect the country. This section outlines both alternatives and gives instructions on how to use motorway tollbooths *(péage)* and French parking meters (*horodateurs*), as well as some of the rules governing driving in France. There are also tips on how to get weather and traffic forecasts, where to hire a car and how to get the best road maps.

Motorway and main road signs

What to Take

Effective insurance is essential when taking a car to France. All car insurance policies in the EU automatically include minimum third-party insurance cover, which is valid in any EU country. However, the extent of cover provided beyond the legal minimum varies between insurance companies, so it is best to check your policy before you travel, and, if necessary, procure additional cover. For holders of fully comprehensive car insurance, most companies provide full European cover for a small extra premium; some do not charge for this, but still require you to notify them before travelling. It is also advisable to have breakdown cover with one of the Europe-wide networks with English-speaking phone lines.

While driving in France you must carry in the car your driving licence, passport, the vehicle registration document and a certificate of insurance. You must also have a set of spare light bulbs, at least one red warning triangle and a luminous reflecting jacket to be worn if you ever have to stop on a motorway because of a breakdown or other emergency. You can be fined if you are stopped by the police and do not have this equipment. The car's country of registration should be displayed on a sticker or as part of the registration plate, and right-hand-drive cars need headlamp deflectors for driving on the right – kits are available at most ports.

Buying Petrol

All fuel stations have unleaded petrol and diesel fuel (*gazole* or *gas-oil*, or a high-grade *gas-oil* +). Many stations also have LPG (*GPL*). The cheapest places are attached to big supermarkets, and many major service stations have 24-hour pumps, with payment by credit card.

Rules of the Road

Wearing seatbelts, in the front and back of the car, is compulsory in France, as is the use of booster seats for children under 10. It is illegal to use a mobile phone while driving, even if it's on hands-free mode. Dipped headlights must be used in poor visibility, and motorcyclists must have dipped headlights lit at all times. Unless road signs indicate otherwise, *Priorité à droite* means that you must give way to any vehicle joining the road from the right except on roundabouts. Flashing headlights mean that the driver is claiming the right of way. For further details, consult **AA** or **RAC** websites *(see p639)*.

Speed Limits and Fines

Speed limits in France are as follows:

- On *autoroutes*: 130 kph (80 mph); 110 kph (68 mph) when it rains.
- On dual carriageways: 110 kph (68 mph); 90–100 kph (56–62 mph) when it rains.
- On other roads: 90 kph (56 mph); 80 kph (49 mph) when it rains.
- In towns and villages: 50 kph (31 mph).

There are also lower speed limits on all roads for vehicles towing a trailer or caravan.

On-the-spot fines are levied for speeding, not stopping at a Stop sign, for overtaking where forbidden and exceeding the speed limit by over 40 kph (25 mph). Driving with over 0.05 per cent alcohol in the blood is illegal.

Motorways

Most motorways in France are toll roads (*autoroutes à péage*). The **Societé d'Autoroutes** website *(see p639)* lists the rates charged for each journey. There are also toll-free autoroutes, notably those around big cities such as Paris (A3 and A86) and Lille, and some cross-country stretches such as the A84 from Caen to Rennes, and the A75 south of Clermont-Ferrand.

A sign at a gas pump points to *GPL* (LPG) or *gazole* (petrol)

The scenic route around Mont Cenis lake

Much of the *autoroute* network includes rest areas, petrol stations every 40 km (25 miles) and emergency phones every 2 km (1 mile).

Other Roads

RN (*Route Nationale*) roads are the main alternative to motorways for long-distance trips. They are often far more scenic, but can be more congested. To get really off the beaten track, travel by D (*départementale*) roads, which snake around the countryside. Look out for **Bis/Bison Futé** signs, which indicate quieter, alternative routes.

Try to avoid travelling at the French holiday rush periods, known as *grands départs*. The worst times are weekends in mid-July, and the beginning and end of August.

Certain signs are particularly useful to know when driving in and out of towns. Follow *Centre Ville* signs for the town centre and *Toutes Directions* (all routes) to take you out of the centre to where you can find ongoing routes. If your destination is not signposted, follow *Autres Directions* (other directions).

Scenic Routes

France's dense web of *Routes Nationales* and D roads weave through some of the country's most gorgeous scenery. The most celebrated roads are in mountain regions, such as the Col du Galibier road over the Alps east of Grenoble (N91, then D902), but there are many others throughout the country. Some hug the coast, such as the roads along the Côte d'Azur or the rugged coasts of Brittany and Normandy. Information on these *routes touristiques* is available from tourist offices *(see p620)*.

Road Conditions

The French Highway Authorities' *Bison Futé* website *(see p639)* provides essential information for driving in France, with details of weather conditions, winter driving requirements and roadworks. Check also www.autoroutes.fr for motorway driving.

Motoring organizations such as the AA and RAC sell tailor-made route-planning services, giving scenic options and road conditions *(see p639)*.

Using the Autoroute Toll

Collect a ticket from the tollbooth and keep it safe until you reach an exit toll, where you will be charged according to the distance travelled and type of vehicle used. To pay at small tolls, just throw your coins into the large receptacle.

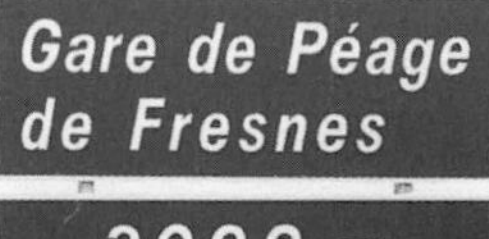

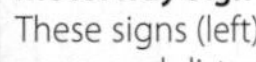

Motorway Sign
These signs (left) indicate the name and distance to the next tollbooth. They are usually blue and white; some show the tariff rates for cars, motorbikes, trucks and caravans.

Tollbooth with Attendant
When you hand in your ticket at a manned tollbooth, the attendant will tell you the cost of your journey on the *autoroute* and the price will be displayed. You can pay with coins, notes, credit cards or with a cheque in euros. A receipt can be issued on request.

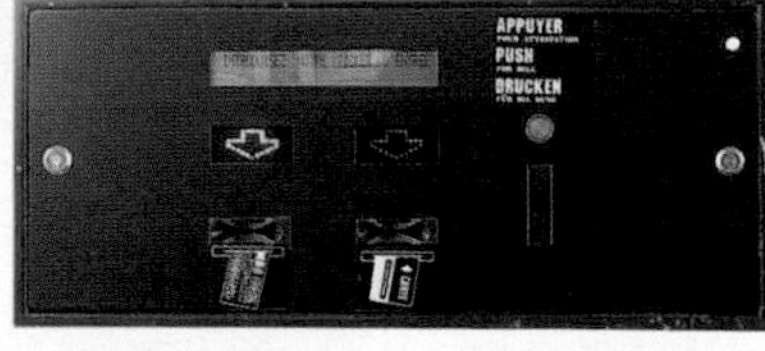

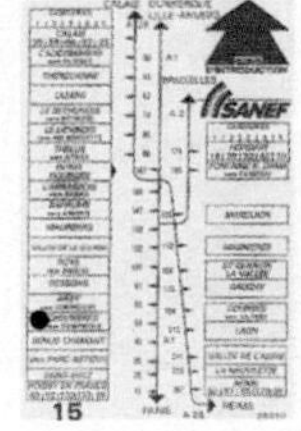

Automatic Machine
On reaching the exit toll, insert your ticket into the machine and the price of your journey will be displayed in euros. You can pay either with coins or by credit card. The machine will give change and can issue a receipt.

Parking

Parking regulations vary from town to town, but most cities have street pay-and-display machines *(horodateurs)*, with spaces marked out in blue. Some machines accept a parking payment card, sold at *tabacs*. Parking is normally limited to 2 hours. Charges are relatively low, and in most provincial towns parking is free between noon and 1:30pm. In narrow streets, parking may be confined to one side of the street and this can alternate at different times of the month.

Finding a parking space in larger cities, especially in Paris, can be difficult and it is often easier to use a car park. These are well indicated by a large "P" sign, accompanied by the word *libre* to indicate that there are spaces available.

Car Hire

All the main international car-hire companies operate in France, as well as local French-based companies such as **ADA** and **Rentacar**, which often have very competitive prices. You will nearly always get the best rates by booking a car in advance through one of the internet car-rental booking services including **Auto Europe** or **Autos Abroad**.

Requirements for car hire vary, but in general you must be over 21 and have held a driving licence for at least a year. You will need to present your licence, passport and a credit card against a deposit.

The price quoted should include all taxes and unlimited mileage. All rental contracts include basic third-party insurance, and some companies also include comprehensive insurance. Extras such as car seats, snow chains or an automatic car should be indicated when booking. Most car hires offer GPS devices, which makes navigating the French roads easier.

Before you drive away, check the general condition of the car and also ensure it has a set of spare bulbs, a warning triangle and a luminous jacket, which are all legal requirements in France *(see p636)*.

Maps

Each chapter in this guide begins with a map of the region showing all the sights and information on getting around. As additional maps, the excellent **Michelin** Tourist and Motoring Atlas at a scale of 1:200,000 is the most comprehensive driving map available. The red-cover Michelin maps of the whole of France (scale 1:1,000,000) are useful for planning trips, as are the regional maps with orange covers (scale 1:200,000). Larger-scale Michelin maps with green covers are only for certain parts of France such as Paris and the Côte d'Azur.

The **Institut Géographique National** (IGN), the equivalent of the British Ordnance Survey, produces high-quality maps in different scales. Particularly useful are their *Cartes de Randonnée* (scale 1:25,000), an excellent series of walking maps covering every part of the country. Also recommended, are the **Blay Foldex** town maps.

In France, all newsstands and petrol stations stock maps and most tourist offices provide good free maps. In the UK, **Stanfords** is one of the best places to look for a full selection of French maps.

Eurolines coaches at Porte Bagnolet bus station in Paris

Travelling by Coach

The French railway is so fast and reliable that there is not much demand for long-distance coaches and they tend to only operate in areas with poor train services.

Eurolines offers a wide range of low-priced international services, many of which make stops within France. These services are centred on the Porte de Bagnolet bus station in Paris (Métro Galliéni).

Transdev runs an extensive network of coaches that cover the Ile-de-France, and **Lignes d'Azur** provides a good service along the Côte d'Azur. **OuiGo** is the SNCF's low-cost bus service providing trips for as little as €10.

Local buses are definitely an important means of transport, particularly in rural areas. These run in and out of villages from the *gare routière* (bus station), which is often located next to the SNCF train station of the main town of each *département* or area. Buses run mostly at peak times to take people to and from work and school.

Taxis

There are taxi services in every part of France, although in rural areas you will normally have to book a cab by phone.

Mountain cyclists in the Alps

Hotels, bars and restaurants will have the numbers of local taxis. Otherwise, in towns look for a taxi rank *(station de taxi)* outside railway stations, airports or in the town centre.

All taxis must use meters *(compteurs)*, but prices do vary from one region to another. In general, the pick-up charge should be about €2 plus 50 cents or more per kilometre (half mile). It is often possible to agree a fixed price for a long journey. For city taxis, see pp640–41.

Cycling

Cycling is extremely popular in France and facilities are steadily improving as part of the government-backed "Eco-mobility" scheme *(see p631)*. Several long-distance **Voies Vertes** footpaths and cycle tracks have been created, and more are being established. Every local tourist office has a leaflet on nearby *véloroutes*, and many have developed their own schemes, such as the network of cycle routes around the main Loire Valley châteaux *(La Loire à Vélo)*. Details are available from local tourist offices and *département* websites.

Bicycles can be taken on nearly all **SNCF** trains, and on some routes you can reserve a rental bike at your destination station when booking a train ticket. There are also cycle hire shops in nearly every town with standard and mountain bikes *(VTT)* for rent at reasonable prices. Tourist offices can advise on local companies.

More information on cycling in France can be found on the Atout France website and through the **Fédération Française de Cyclisme** (in French only). Most cities offer rental cycling schemes *(see p641)*.

Hitchhiking

It is not easy to get around France by hitchhiking, and it is not advisable to try either. There is, however, a safe car-sharing *(co-voiturage)* scheme called BlaBlaCar (www.blablacar.fr), which has branches in many towns and through which you can set up lifts at reasonable rates.

DIRECTORY

General Motoring Information

AA
Tel 08 00 88 77 55 (from abroad).
W theaa.com

Bison Futé
W bison-fute.gouv.fr

RAC
Tel 0330 159 1111.
W rac.co.uk

Societé d'Autoroutes
W autoroutes.fr

Zagaz
W zagaz.com (for fuel price guide in French).

Car Hire

ADA
Tel 08 99 46 46 36.
W ada.fr

Autos Abroad
Tel 0844 826 6536 (UK).
W autosabroad.com

Auto Europe
Tel 1 888 223 5555 (USA & Canada). **W autoeurope.com**

Avis
Tel 0821 230 760 (France), 0808 284 0014 (UK).
W avis.co.uk

Budget
Tel 0825 003 564 (France), 0844 544 3455 (UK).
W budget.com

Europcar
Tel 0825 358 358 (France), 0871 384 0235 (UK).
W europcar.co.uk

Hertz
Tel 01 41 91 95 25 (France), 020 7026 0077 (UK).
W hertz.com

National/Citer
Tel 0800 131 211 (France), 0800 121 8303 (UK).
W nationalcar.com

Rentacar
Tel 0891 700 200.
W rentacar.fr

Maps

Blay Foldex
W blayfoldex.com

Institut Géographique National
W ign.fr

Michelin
W viamichelin.fr

Stanfords
12–14 Long Acre, London WC2E 9LP.
Tel 020 7836 1321.
W stanfords.co.uk

Coach Travel

Eurolines
Tel 0892 899 091.
W eurolines.fr

Lignes d'Azur
W lignesdazur.com

OuiGo
W ouigo.com

Transdev
W transdev.com

Cycling

Fédération Française de Cyclisme
Tel 08 11 04 05 55.
W ffc.fr

SNCF
W velo.sncf.com (for train and bicycle travel).

Voies Vertes
W voiesvertes.com

Travelling within Cities

The charming centres of France's cities are best enjoyed on foot. If, however, you need to cover a fair amount of ground in a day, it is best to use the excellent range of public transport available. Paris and many other cities have tram and underground rail networks, often integrated with local train and bus services, and efforts have been made to create user-friendly ticketing systems. France has led the world in encouraging urban cycle use as an alternative to the car, with easy-access bike-hire schemes. In each city, local tourist offices will provide full information on services, including free maps.

Marseille tram travelling along boulevard Longchamp

Paris Métro, RER and Tram

The **RATP** operates 14 Métro underground train lines. The Métro is the most convenient way to get around the city, and you are never far from a station in central Paris. Each line can be identified by its colour and number. The direction the train is travelling in is indicated by the name of the station on the front of the train – this is always the last station on the route, so it's worth checking the Métro map before boarding. Trains run frequently on each line from 5:20am to 1:20am Monday to Thursday and till 2am on Friday and Saturday.

The RER commuter trains complement the Métro and run across Paris and the suburbs. There are five lines (A–E). The most useful for visitors are B3 from Charles de Gaulle airport; A4 to Disneyland® Paris Resort; and C5 to Versailles.

The tramway lines most useful for visitors are from Gare de St-Denis to Noisy-le-Sec; La Défense to Porte de Versailles; and Pont du Garigliano to Porte d'Ivry.

Other Métro and Tram Systems

The cities of **Lyon**, **Marseille**, **Toulouse**, **Lille** and **Rennes** all have Métro systems. The Lille Métro serves the whole conurbation known as Lille-Métropole, including towns such as Roubaix and Tourcoing. All Métros connect with SNCF railways at main stations.

Rouen's two-line Métro is actually made up of overground trams (light rail lines) that connect the city to the outer suburbs. Some 22 other cities around France use trams as well as local buses, and Paris too has some suburban tram lines that connect with the Métro and RER.

Buses

Every city has local buses. In Paris, RATP buses provide cheap opportunities for sightseeing. Throughout France, most routes operate from around 6am to midnight; routes and times are indicated at bus stops. Most French cities also have several night bus routes, and in Paris and the Ile-de-France, 42 Noctilien bus routes operate throughout the night, passing the main railway stations. A fast-growing number of buses in Paris and other cities have wheelchair ramps. On all French city buses, you must board at the front of the bus, and get off through the middle or rear doors. Tickets can be bought from the driver or in advance from a range of outlets, which saves time when boarding.

Local Trains

Regional TER lines *(see p633)* are operated by the SNCF and are well integrated with local transport around cities. In some cases, tickets are interchangeable. Around Paris, the SNCF Transilien lines form a third level of rail services with the Métro and RER.

Taxis

In Paris and most other cities taxis have a light on top of the car, which is white when the taxi is free, and orange (or just switched off) when it is taken. Paris taxi fares are more expensive between 5pm and 10am, Monday to Saturday, and all day Sunday and holidays, and cost more for any journey outside central Paris (limited by, but including, the boulevard Périphérique). Many taxis take credit cards, but often only for fares over €15. At busy times the best places to find taxis in Paris are taxi ranks *(stations de taxis)* marked with a blue "T" sign. Ranks are found at major road junctions and train stations. Though taxis are operated by several companies, **Paris Taxis** provides a single number to phone for them in Paris. All taxis in France are required to carry wheelchair users for no extra charge, but in the Paris region **Taxis G7** provide a specialized service for passengers with mobility problems.

In other cities taxis are similarly operated by several companies. Taxi ranks are found at airports, most train stations and around city centres. Otherwise, tourist offices and hotels can provide you with local firm numbers.

Taking a bicycle from one of the Vélib' stands in Paris

Cycling

Great efforts are underway in French cities to encourage town cycling. On Sundays, some major streets are closed to traffic to make way for cyclists and roller-bladers. Paris city council has a world-leading pro-cycling programme, and there are now over 700 km (435 miles) of cycle routes. The centrepiece of the programme is the **Vélib'** scheme, where you can pick up a basic bike at any one of hundreds of Vélib' stations around Paris and leave it at another. To do this you must purchase a Vélib' card, which is available for a day or a week and can be bought from machines at the bike racks, or by annual subscription. Other cities run similar bike-sharing schemes under different names (**Vélo'V** in Lyon, **Le Vélo** in Marseille, **Vélobleu** in Nice and **Vélopop** in Avignon). Tourist offices will have full information on them.

Tickets

In Paris, RATP T-tickets are valid for city buses, the Métro, the tramway and the RER. Tickets are available singly or for lower prices in carnets (books) of 10 and can be bought at Métro and RER stations, the airports, tourist offices and *tabacs*. Single tickets can also be bought on board buses but they are not valid for other forms of transport. Don't forget to validate your ticket.

An alternative aimed at tourists is the ParisVisite card, which gives unlimited travel on all systems for 1, 2, 3 or 5 days, as well as discounted admission fees to sights. The card is sold at Métro, RER and train stations, as well as at tourist offices or online.

Nearly all larger cities offer some kind of city pass for visitors, giving unlimited travel and other advantages for one or more days. Inquire at tourist offices for local schemes.

Cruise boats plying the River Seine

Seine Cruises

A boat trip on the Seine is one of the classic ways to see Paris. The long-running **Bateaux-Mouches**, **Bateaux Parisiens** and **Vedettes du Pont-Neuf** offer traditional cruises along the river with multilingual commentary. The **Batobus** is a more flexible alternative, allowing you to hop on and off as many times as you want during the day. Another option is to see a more intimate side of Paris with a cruise along the St-Martin canal. Full information is available from tourist offices.

DIRECTORY

Transport Authorities

Lille – Transpole
W **transpole.fr**

Lyon – TCL
Tel 04 26 10 12 12.
W **tcl.fr**

Marseille – Le Pilote/RTM
Tel 08 10 00 13 26.
W **lepilote.com**

Paris – RATP
Tel 3246. W **ratp.fr**

Rennes – STAR
Tel 08 11 55 55 35 or 09 70 82 18 00. W **star.fr**

Rouen – TCAR
Tel 02 35 52 52 52. W **tcar.fr**

Toulouse – Tisséo
Tel 05 61 41 70 70. W **tisseo.fr**

Taxis

Paris Taxis
W **taxis-paris.fr**

Taxis G7
Tel 3607. W **taxisg7.fr**

Cycling Schemes

Vélib' (Paris)
Tel 01 30 79 79 30.
W **velib.paris.fr**

Le Vélo (Marseille)
Tel 01 30 79 29 13.
W **levelo-mpm.fr**

Vélobleu (Nice)
Tel 04 93 72 06 06.
W **velobleu.org**

Vélopop (Avignon)
Tel 08 10 45 64 56.
W **velopop.fr**

Velo'V (Lyon)
Tel 01 30 79 33 40.
W **velov.grandlyon.com**

Seine Cruises

Bateaux-Mouches
Tel 01 42 25 96 10.
W **bateaux-mouches.fr**

Bateaux Parisiens
Tel 08 25 01 01 01.
W **bateauxparisiens.com**

Batobus
Tel 01 76 64 79 12.
W **batobus.com**

Vedettes du Pont-Neuf
Tel 01 46 33 98 38.
W **vedettesdupontneuf.com**

General Index

Page numbers in **bold** refer to main entries.

A

B

I

M

N

Y

Z

Acknowledgments

Dorling Kindersley would like to thank the following people, whose contributions and assistance have made the preparation of this book possible.

Main Contributors
John Ardagh, Rosemary Bailey, Judith Fayard, Lisa Gerard-Sharp, Robert Harneis, Alister Kershaw, Alec Lobrano, Anthony Roberts, Alan Tillier, Nigel Tisdall.

Contributors and Consultants
John Ardagh is a writer and broadcaster, and author of many books on France, among them *France Today* and *Writers' France*.

Rosemary Bailey has written and edited several guides to regional France, including *Burgundy*, the *Loire Valley* and the *Côte d'Azur*.

Alexandra Boyle is a writer and editor based in England and France.

Elsie Burch Donald, editor and writer, is the author of *The French Farmhouse*.

David Burnie B.Sc. has written over 30 books on natural sciences, including *How Nature Works*.

Judith Fayard, an American based in Paris, was Paris bureau chief for *Life* magazine for 10 years, and is now European editor of *Town & Country*. She contributes to various publications, including the *Wall Street Journal*.

Lisa Gerard-Sharp is a broadcaster and author of several regional guides to France and Italy.

Robert Harneis is editorial correspondent for the English-language newspaper *French News*.

Colin Jones is Professor of History at Exeter University. His books include *The Longman Companion to the French Revolution* and *The Cambridge Illustrated History of France*.

Alister Kershaw is an Australian writer and broadcaster who lives in the Loire Valley.

Alec Lobrano is an American writer, based in Paris. He is the European editor of *Departures* magazine and contributes to *International Herald Tribune, Los Angeles Times* and *The Independent*.

Anthony Roberts is a writer and translator who lives in Gascony and contributes to various publications including *The Times, World of Interiors* and *Architectural Digest*.

Anthony Rose is the wine correspondent of *The Independent* and co-author of the *Grapevine*.

Jane Sigal is the author of two books on French food, *Normandy Gastronomique* and *Backroom Bistros, Farmhouse Fare*.

The late Alan Tillier was the main contributor to the *Eyewitness Guide to Paris*. He lived in Paris from the 1960s until 2004 and was correspondent for the *International Herald Tribune, Newsweek* and *The Times*.

Nigel Tisdall is a travel writer and author of guides to Brittany and Normandy.

Patricia Wells is food critic of the *International Herald Tribune* and author of the *Food Lovers' Guide to Paris* and the *Food Lovers' Guide to France*.

Additional Contributors
Nathalie Boyer, Caroline Bugler, Ann Cremin, Jan Dodd, Bill Echikson, Robin Gauldie, Adrian Gilbert, Peter Graham, Marion Kaplan, Jim Keeble, Alexandra Kennedy, Rolli Lucarotti, Fred Mawer, Lyn Parry, Andrew Sanger, Katherine Spenley, Clive Unger-Hamilton, Roger Williams.

Additional Photography
Jo Craig, Andy Crawford, Michael Crockett, Mike Dunning, Philip Enticknap, Lydia Evans, Philippe Giraud, Steve Gorton, Alison Harris, John Heseltine, Roger Hilton, Andrew Holligan, Paul Kenwood, Oliver Knight, Eric Meacher, Neil Mersh, Roger Moss, Robert O'Dea, Ian O'Leary, Rough Guides: Marc Dubin, Jules Selmes, Tony Souter, Alan Williams, Peter Wilson.

Additional Illustrations
Dinwiddie Maclaren, John Fox, Nick Gibbard, Paul Guest, Stephen Gyapay, Kevin Jones Associates, Chris Orr, Robbie Polley, Sue Sharples.

Additional Cartography
Colourmap Scanning Limited; Contour Publishing; Cosmographics; European Map Graphics; Meteo-France. Street Finder maps: ERAMaptec Ltd (Dublin), adapted with permission from original survey and mapping by Shobunsha (Japan).

Cartographic Research
Rachel Hawtin (Lovell Johns); James Mills-Hicks, Jennifer Skelley, Peter Winfield, Claudine Zarte (Dorling Kindersley Cartography).

Revisions Team
Peter Adams, Azeem Alam, Michelle Arness Frederic, Elizabeth Ayre, Laetitia Benloulou, Steve Bere, Kate Berens, Sonal Bhatt, Uma Bhattacharya, Hilary Bird, Anna Brooke, Arwen Burnett, Cate Craker, Maggie Crowley, Alison Culliford, Lisa Davidson, Simon Davis, Emer FitzGerald, Helen Foulkes, Fay Franklin, Tom Fraser, Kyra Freestar, Anna Freiberger, Rhiannon Furbear, Catherine Gauthier, Camilla Gersh, Eric Gibory, Emily Green, Vinod Harish, Robert Harneis, Elaine Harries, Victoria Heyworth-Dunne, Paul Hines, Nicholas Inman, Rosa Jackson, Sarah Jackson-Lambert, Stuart James, Laura Jones, Nancy Jones, Bharti Karakoti, Sumita Khatwani, Kim Laidlaw Adrey, Cécile Landau, Kathryn Lane, Maite Lantaron, Delphine Lawrance, Jude Ledger, Colette Levitt, Jason Little, Siri Lowe, Francesca Machiavelli, Carly Madden, Hayley Maher, Nicola Malone, Lesley McCave, Alison McGill, Ella Milroy, Jason Mitchell, Casper Morris, Claire Naylor, George Nimmo, Malcolm Parchment, Lyn Parry, Helen Partington, Shirin Patel, Susie Peachey, Alice Peebles, Clare Peel, Alice Pennington-Mellor, Marianne Petrou, Bryan Pirolli, Pollyanna Poulter, Pete Quinlan, Salim Qurashi, Rada Radojicic, Akshay Rana, Marisa Renzullo, Philippa Richmond, Nick Rider, Ellen Root, Sands Publishing Solutions, Baishakhee Sengupta, Shailesh Sharma, Kunal Singh, Rituraj Singh, Shruti Singhi, Cathy Skipper, Jaynan Spengler, Niamh Smith, Joanna Stenlake, Andrew Szudek, Hollie Teague, Priyanka Thakur, Helen Townsend, Victoria Trott, Nikky Twyman, Conrad van Dyck, Vinita Venugopal, Dora Whitaker, Fiona Wild, Nicholas Wood, Sophie Wright, Irina Zarb.

Special Assistance
Mme Jassinger, French Embassy Press Department; Peter Mills, Christine Lagardère, French Railways Ltd.

Photographic Reference
Altitude, Paris; Sea and See, Paris; Editions Combier, Maçon; Thomas d'Hoste, Paris.

Photography Permissions
Dorling Kindersley would like to thank the following for their assistance and kind permission to photograph at their establishments: The Caisse Nationale des Monuments Historiques et des Sites; M A Leonetti, the Abbey of Mont St-Michel; Chartres Cathedral; M Voisin, Château de Chenonceau; M P Mistral, Cité de Carcassonne; M D Vingtain, Palais des Papes, Avignon; Château de Fontainebleau; Amiens Cathedral; Conques Abbey; Fontenay Abbey; Moissac Abbey; Vézelay Abbey; Reims Cathedral and all the other churches, museums, hotels, restaurants, shops, galleries and sights too numerous to thank individually.

Picture Credits
a = above; b = below/bottom; c = centre; f = far; l = left; r = right; t = top.

Works of art have been reproduced with the permission of the following copyright holders; ©ADAGP, Paris and DACS, London 2011: 33ca, 33crb, 67tl, 68–9, 69tl (d), 94tc, 97cra, 97cb, 97bl, 97br, 103tr, 217bc, 355t, 339br, 486tc, 512ca, 526b, 528bc, 528br; ©ARS, NY and DACS, London 2011: 96c; ©DACS, London 2011: 97tc, 385br, 426t; Artwork and photograph © Succession H. Matisse/ DACS 2015: 33bl, 96bl, 530br; © Succession Picasso/DACS, London 2011: 92cl, 94br, 477t, 525tr.

Photos achieved with the assistance of the EPPV and the CSI: 140–41; Photo of Euro Disneyland® Park and the Euro Disneyland Paris® 182crb; The characters, architectural works and trademarks are the property of The Walt Disney Company. All rights reserved; Courtesy of the Maison Victor Hugo, Ville de Paris: 95cra; Musée National des Châteaux de Malmaison et Bois-Préau: 177br; Musée de Montmartre, Paris: 136cb.

The publisher would like to thank the following individuals, companies and picture libraries for permission to reproduce their photographs:
123RF.com Philippe Halle 620c, Ostill 108, Pedro Antonio Salaverría Calahorra 464tr, Wallace Weeks 386cr.
Le 36, Amboise: 586bc.
Alamy Stock Photo: AF archive 72clb; age fotostock 422tl, 553tc; amana images inc. 468–9; Jon Arnold Images Ltd 272; Arterra Picture Library 439cl; Andy Arthur 424bc; Martin Bache 98; Sébastien Baussais 626tr; Tibor Bognar 213tr; Josse Christophel 501br; Chronicle 247bl; Directphoto.org 621br; dpa picture alliance 438tl; David R. Frazier Photolibrary, Inc 624cla; FORGET Patrick/ SAGAPHOTO.COM 587tr; David Giral 137tc; Bjorn Grotting 440cb; guichaoua 205cl; Cris Haigh 481b; Philippe Hays 627cb; Chris Hellier 533br; Hemis 53tl, 79cr, 122clb, 139br, 183b, 196, 273bc, 278tr, 374br, 408, 420cr, 520cr, 594tl, 600bc; Iconotec 285tc; imageBROKER 545tr; Images & Stories 22; incamerastock 250; INTERFOTO 405br; Eric James 437br; Brian Jannsen 222; Joy 174; Neil Juggins 634tl, Michael Juno 243c; Justin Kase Zfivez 625tr; Valerijs Kostreckis 120; LOOK Die Bildagentur der Fotografen GmbH 536; London Entertainment 524br; mauritius images GmbH 496t; mcx images 376; George Munday 497bl; nagelstock.com 502; nobleIMAGES 460–61; North Wind Picture Archives 285bc; Peter Noyce FRA 595tr; James Osmond Photography 452; a la poste 628tr, 622b; Prisma Bildagentur AG 133; SFL Choice 430; robertharding 436tr; Craig Roberts 276bc; SAGAPHOTO.COM/FORGET Patrick 603tc; Shawshots 325ca, 325cb; SOTK2011 68clb; Antony SOUTER 571bl; Jack Sullivan 625cra; travelbild.com 527b; F. Vrouenraths (Spain) 464cla; **Alpine Garden Society/Christopher Grey-Wilson**: 464bc, 464br; **Agence Photo Aquitaine**: D Lelann 425tc; **Ancient Art and Architecture Collection**: 51crb, 54ca, 54cb, 61clb, 256–7b, 339bl, 386tl, 442crb; **Photo AKG, Berlin**: 49cra, 50bl, 59crb, 406tr, 407br; **Archives Photographiques, Paris/DACS**: 426t; by kind permission of **www.artinswfrance.com**: 612bc; **L'Arnsbourg:** 582tl; **Atelier Brancusi/Centre Georges Pompidou, Paris**: Bernard Prerost 97br; **Atelier du Regard/A Allemand**: 446cl, 446cr, 446br; **L'Axel**: 579bc. **La Bastide de Voulonne:** 570tc; **Hostellerie Berard**: 612cla; **Bibliothèque Nationale, Dijon**: 53cb; **F Blackburn**: 465bl; **Le Bouclier d'Or:** 558tl; **Gerard Boullay/Photola**: 91bl, 91cra; **Brasserie Bofinger:** 578tc; **Bridgeman Art Library**: Albright Knox Art Gallery, Buffalo, New York 279br; Anthony Crane Collection 215br; Bibliothèque Nationale, Paris 54cr–55cl, 57crb, 73bl; British Library, London 56bl, 72br, 296c, 297br, 297tl; Bonhams, London 63tc; Château de Versailles, France 73tr; Christie's, London 33ca, 517b; Giraudon 33tl, 32cla, 60cr–61cl, 61tl, 63tl, 73bc, 185br, 338cl, 347c, 369tl; Guildhall Library, Corporation of London 421c; Index 476br; Kress Collection, Washington D C 297bl; Lauros-Giraudon 73br; Musée des Beaux-Arts, Quimper 247cr; Musée Condé, Chantilly 61tr, 72bl, 73tc, 73tl, 73cb, 208tr, 297c; Musée d'Orsay, Paris 32bl; Musée du Quai Branly, Paris 116cb; Paul Bremen Collection 259tc; Sotheby's New York 59tl; V&A Museum, London 342crb; Walters Art Gallery, Baltimore, Maryland 360tl; **Buerehiesel:** 583bc; **Bureau Alain Ducasse:** 602tr. **Cafe du Palais:** 581br; **Campagne, Campagne**: 354tl; C. Guy 329t; Lara 195cr; B. Lichtstein 221br, 328clb; Pyszel 194bl; **CNMHS, Paris/DACS**: Longchamps Delehaye 217cla; **Hôtel Caron de Beaumarchais:** 554bc; **Centre Georges Pompidou**: **Cephas**: 42crb; Stuart Boreham 264–5; Hervé Champollion 326tr, 338tr, 354crb; Mick Rock 402cla, 475t, 522–3; **Le Chabichou:** 593br; **Hostellerie du Chapeau Rouge:** 589tc; **Champagne Billecart-Salmon:** 193cr; **Jean Loup Charmet**: 51cb, 54br, 56clb, 66cl, 66clb, 67tl, 67ca, 68bl, 68br, 69crb, 218br, 269crb, 347br, 365c, 405cr, 479t, 511cr, **Château de Barive:** 557tc; **Château des Brottiéres:** 561br; **Château de La Liquière:** 474ca; **Château d'Ygrande:** 564tl; **Château Margaux:** 30crb, 30br; **Cité des Sciences et L'industrie**: Michel Lamoureux 140ca; NASA/ESA 140tr, 141br; Sylvain Sonnet 140clb; **Collection CDT Gard**: 329bl; **CDT Lot**: 443br; **Corbis**: Stuart Black/Robert Harding World Imagery 13bl; Guillaume Bonn 26tl; Gary Braasch 473c; Joel Damase/Photononstop 318–19; Leroy Francis/Hemis 414–15; Owen Franken 16bc; Frumm John/Hemis 238–9; Ray Juno 12cla, Patrice Latron 240cla, 636br; Leemage 8–9; Douglas Pearson 396–7; People Avenue/Pool 535tc; Reuters 609tl; Robert Harding World Imagery/Charles Bowman 637tl; Jean-Daniel Sudres/Hemis 597tc; Russel Wong 40cr; Jim Zuckerman 186–7; **Depositphotos Inc:** Picturereflex 398cl; **E. Donard:** 39c, 39clb, 39bc; **Editions D'Art Daniel Derveaux**: 404cr–405cl; **Photo Daspet, Avignon**: 508bl; **Doherty**: 249tc; **Domaine de la Courtade**: 475cr; **Domaine des Hauts de Loire:** 588bc; **Domaine Sarda Malet:** 474cb; **Domaine Tempier:** 475cl; **Dreamstime.com:** Adeliepenguin 15bc; Sibel Aisha 179bl; Steve Allen 509tl, 517tl; Americanspirit 526tr; Auris 189cr; Ihar Balaikin 78; Bargotiphotography 525br; Michal Bednarek 516tl; Philip Bird 398bl; Bjulien03 432cl; Lesley De Boelpaep 388tl; Flaviu Boerescu 330; Ryhor Bruyeu 534tr; Olga Buiacova 525cl; Bunyos 520tl; Julia Burlachenko 394b; Byelikova 489tc; Musat Christian 327tc; Ciolca 476cl; Claudio Giovanni Colombo 13tr, 356; Demid 497cr; Dennis Dolkens 11tc; Pierre Jean Durieu 491tl; Elenaphotos 327c; Elena Elisseeva 240bl, 263br; Erdalakan 72cl; Steve Estvanik 441crb; Eugenesergeev 547tl; Eyewave 29tl; Henri Faure 391br; Prochasson Frederic 4cb; Janos Gaspar 29bc; Radu Razvan Gheorghe 15tc, 41bl; Rostislav Glinsky 530tr; Gynane 290; Hornet83 384cl; Ifeelstock 73crb; Sergey Kelin 84; Veniamin Kraskov 534cl; Mihai-bogdan Lazar 10bc; Rozenn Leard 434tc; Rainer Lesniewski 26b; Neil Letson 471t; Lev Levin 292br; Elisa Locci 28clb; Frank Lukasseck 542–3; Madrabothair 471bl; Denis Makarenko 524br; Tomas Marek 4c; Marekusz 463tr; Zdeněk Matyáš 29c, 479bl; Milosk50 426bc; Minacarson 79bl, 628bl; Oleg Mitiukhin 392cl; Radovan Mlatec 182c; Martin Molcan 16tl, 522–3; Enrico Morando 327tr; Moskwa 134tr; Roland Nagy 12bc; Nexus7 132; Fabio Nodari 2–3; Odrachenko 29crb; Olegmit 355t; Olgacov 638bl; Andrey Omelyanchuk 143bl; Palaine 17cl; Patrickwang 1c; Petr 122cl; Photoprofi30 507bc; Photowitch 29cr; Patrick Poendl 287tl; Beatrice Preve 327bl; 480; Ondřej Prosický 375br; Richair 630cla; Ricok 28cla; Rndmst 544t; Guy Rouget 28tr; Sam74100 518brl; Richard Semik 29tr, 29bl, 210; Jose I. Soto 264–5; Stevanzz 534br; Timothy Stirling 548–9; Takepicsforfun 234cl; Tehnik83 524tl; Anibal Trejo 443tr; Tupungato 74–5; Vlastas 234tr; Viachaslau Zhukau 43b; **Alain Ducasse Entreprise:** 572cra.**Editions Tallandier**: 46, 48cb, 51tl, 52br, 52br–53bl, 55tl, 55cb, 56cl, 57tr, 58br, 62clb, 62bl, 62cr–63cl,

63crb, 63bc, 65tr, 65crb, 65br, 67bl, 67bc, 68cla, 68crb, 69tc, 69cra; **L'Ermitage Hotel:** 565bc; **Estaminet T'Kasteel Hof:** 580tl; **ET Archive**: 304bl; Cathedral Treasury, Aachen 4tr; 52cla; Musée Carnavalet, Paris 65tl; Museum of Fine Arts, Lausanne 59br; Musée d'Orsay, Paris 65cra; Musée de Versailles 60bl; 303bl; National Gallery, Scotland 62br; V&A Museum, London 57tl; 347bl; **European Commission**: 679; **Mary Evans Picture Library**: 50br, 54bl, 55c, 57br, 60cla, 62c, 66bc, 67cr, 67br, 69br, 117clb, 181cb, 187c, 195tc, 201bc, 295br, 297tr, 305bl, 370b, 459tr, 477br; Explorer 35br; **La Ferme aux Grives:** 595bc; Xavier Boymond 573tr; **Festival d'Avignon**: Marc Chaumeil 608cl; **Festival International du Film de la Rochelle**: 608br; **Fleur de Sel:** 562bc; **Foundation Royaumont**: J Johnson 176tl; **Fotolia:** Paula Kirsch 14bl.**Georges Blanc:** 591tr; **Getty Images:** AFP/Jean Ayissi 641tl; De Agostini Picture Library 488t; Andia 363cr; Christophel Fine Art 56bc, 304br; Soltan Frédéric 72-73c; Historical Picture Archive 69tl; Hulton Archive 195br; Glenn Van Der Knijff 529cr; Leemage / Photo Josse 69c; MIGUEL MEDINA 73ca; Manfred Mehlig 632bl; National Geographic/Ed George 635cla; Panoramic Images 155br; Sergio Pitamitz 641bl; David Pollack 70bc, 362bc; Pascal Preti 618–19; Peter Scholey 621tl; Stringer 72bc; Stringer/John Chillingworth 520bc; Stringer/London Express 70crb; Stringer/Thurston Hopkins 305br; swim ink 2 llc 478tr; UniversalImagesGroup 58clb; WireImage/Tony Barson 71bc; **Giraudon, Paris**: 32cla, 21cb, 33cra, 33crb, 50cla, 52clb, 53tl, 54cl, 56cr–57cl, 60clb, 62cl, 64cl, 64cr–65cl, 337br, 351br, 373br, 495cb MS Nero Ell pt.2 fol. 20V0; Lauros-Giraudon 48bc, 49tc, 49crb, 49cb, 49br, 51ca, 53tr, 55crb, 59cl, 64clb, 64br–65bl, 495cl; Musée d'Art Moderne, Paris 32cb; Musée de Beaux-Arts, Quimper 32cl; **Le Grand Véfour:** 576bl; **Ronald Grant Archive**: 70clb. **La Halle Saint Pierre:** *Untitled* Stavroula Feleggakis 137br; **Sonia Halliday Photographs**: Laura Lushington 313cla; **Robert Harding Picture Library**: 34bl, 41tr, 43tr, 43clb, 47cb, 116br, 247tr, 326bl, 326br, 327br, 353tr, 404cla, 441cr, 465tr, 493bc; C Bowman 456tc; Explorer, Paris 71br, 105bl, 366tl, 375cra, 464cb, 465tl, 488bl, 613bl, 639tl; Robert Francis 28bl; D Hughes 396–7; Peter Langer 419tc; W Rawlings 53br, 71tl, 241tl, 260bc; A.Wolfitt 30tr; **Hemispheres Images:** Hervé Hughes 263br; **John Heseltine**: 143c; **Honfleur, Musée Boudin**: 266bl; **Hotel le Mas Trilles:** *596tc;* Stavroula Feleggakis 137br; **David Hughes**: 371t, 371b; **L'Huitrière:** 574tr; **Hôtel Imperator:** 569br; **Jacana**: JM Labat 465bc; **Le Jardin Gourmand**: 575tr, 589tl; **Restaurant Patrick Jeffroy:** 585bl; **Trevor Jones**: 208bl; **Louis XV Monaco:** Bernard Touillon 602br; **Magnum Photos ltd**: 25c; Bruno Barbey 24br, 35tr, 40bl; R Capa 476tr; P Halsman 529bl; **La Maison d'Olivier Leflaive:** 590bl; **Manoir du Vaumadeuc:** 560tr; **The Mansell Collection**: 35tl, 286t, 299br, 463bc; **Hotel Marotte:** 556bl; **Le Marquière:** 599bx; **Mas Daumas Gassac:** 474cr; **Michel Bras:** Aragorn agence de communication 592tr; **John Miller**: 228bl, 340tr, 411br; **Montpellier Danse Festival**: 609br; **Musée de l'Annonciade, St-Tropez**: 528tr; **Musée d'Art Moderne et Contemporain de Strasbourg**: Edith Rodeghiero 235tl; **Musée des Beaux-Arts, Carcassonne**: 493tl; **Musée des Beaux-Arts, Dijon**: 347tl; **Musée des Beaux-Arts de Lyon**: 385cra, 385c, 385br; **Musée de la Civilisation Gallo-Romaine, Lyon**: 51cr, 382clb; **Musée Courbet**: Pierre Guénat 355br; **Musée Departmental Breton, Quimper**: 278clb; **Musée Flaubert, Rouen**: 269bl; **Museum National d'Histoire Naturelle, Paris**: 142c; **Musée National d'Art Moderne, Paris**: 96clb, 97tc, 97cra, 97cb, 339br; **Musée Réattu, Arles**: M Lacanaud 512ca; **Cliché Musée de Sens/J P Elie**: 334tl; **Musée Toulouse-Lautrec, Albi**: 448bc; **Network Photographers**: Barry Lewis 342t; Rapho/Mark Buscail 613tc; Rapho/De Sazo 613br; **Hôtel Normandy Barrière:** 559bc; **Office de Tourisme de Dijon:** Musée Magnin 345fcr; **Orient-Express Hotels Trains & Cruises**: 552tl; Hotel du Palais 568tl; **OTC Marseille:** 638tl, 640cla; **Photos Editions Combier, Mâcon**: 207tc; **Photolibrary**: Jean-Marc Romain 625cr, Widmann Widmann/F1 Online 626bl; **Pictures Colour Library**: 406crb, 430, 670–71; **Le Pirate:** 603br; **Michel le Poer Trench**: 34br; Bernard Prerost 97b; **Le Pont de l'Ouysse:** 567tc; **Popperfoto:** 255cr; **La Poste:** 629bl; **Les Pres d'Eugenie**: Tim Clinch 566bc; **Pyrenees Magazine/DR**: 404bl; **Reims Tourisme:** Carmen Moya 214tl, 214cr; **Rennes Tourisme:** Jose Mouret 288bl; **Restaurant de La Tour d'Argent:** 574br; **Réunion des Musées Nationaux**: Musée des Antiquités Nationales 407cr; Musée Guimet 115tl; Musée du Louvre 61ca, 105bl, 106cla, 106bl, 106br, 107tl, 107c, 107bc; Musée Picasso 92cl, 94br, 477tr; Musée de Versailles 183tl; **RF Reynolds**: 249bc; **M Reynard:** 674b; **Rocamadour**: 441tr; **Roger-Viollet**: 117cla; **Réunion des Musées Nationaux**: *Le Duo* (1937) by Georges Braque, Collections du Centre Pompidou, Musée Nationaux d'Art Moderne, 97cra; **Le Sin:** 598tc; **Sipa Press**: 136bl; **Photo SNCM/Southern Ferries**: 630br; **SNCF – Société National des Chemins de Fer:** 634bc, Fabbro & Levesque 633tr; **Spectrum Colour Library**: P Thompson 253br; **Frank Spooner Pictures**: Simon 71ca; 71crb; **STA Travel Group:** 674tr; **Tony Stone Images**: 326c; **SuperStock:** age fotostock/J.D. Dallet 425bl; Hemis.fr 596bl; Hemis.fr/ SUDRES Jean-Daniel 441bc; **Sygma**: 535t; C de Bare 40cr; L'Illustration 112tl; T Prat 440cl; L de Raemy 70br; **Telarci:** 53cr; **Les Terraillers:** 601tl; **Tourist Office Semur-en-Auxois**: 339tr; **Les Ursulines Hotel**: Gourmet restaurant 574tl. **Jean Vertut**: 48br–49bl; **La Villa:** U Callelu 603tl; **Visual Arts Library**: 33cr; **O. Zimmerman/Musée d'Unterlinden 6800 Colmar**: 231tl.

Front Endpaper: **Alamy Images:** Jon Arnold Images Ltd Ltl; Hemis Rtl, Lcl; incamerastock Ltc; Brian Jannsen Rtr; LOOK Die Bildagentur der Fotografen GmbH Rbr; mcx images Rcrb; nagelstock.com Rcb; James Osmond Photography Lbl; SFL Choice Lbc; **Dreamstime.com:** Flaviu Boerescu Rca; Claudio Giovanni Colombo Rcr; Gynane Lc; Beatrice Preve Rbl; Joern Rynio Rcra; Richard Semik Rtc.

Back Endpaper: **Alamy Images:** Martin Bache Rtc; Valerijis Kostreckis Lbc; **Dreamstimecom:** Sergey Kelin Rtr; Luciano Mortula Lclb.

Cover: Front and spine – **4Corners:** Olimpio Fantuz; Back – **Dreamstime.com:** Elena Duvernay.

Phrase Book

In Emergency

Help!	**Au secours!**	oh se**koor**
Stop!	**Arrêtez!**	aret-**ay**
Call a doctor!	**Appelez un médecin!**	apuh-**lay** uñ med**sañ**
Call an ambulance!	**Appelez une ambulance!**	apuh-**lay** oon oñboo-**loñs**
Call the police!	**Appelez la police!**	apuh-**lay** lah poh-**lees**
Call the fire department!	**Appelez les pompiers!**	apuh-lay leh poñ-**peeyay**
Where is the nearest telephone?	**Où est le téléphone le plus proche?**	oo ay luh tehleh**fon** luh ploo **prosh**
Where is the nearest hospital?	**Où est l'hôpital le plus proche?**	oo ay l'**opee**tal luh ploo **prosh**

Communication Essentials

Yes	**Oui**	wee
No	**Non**	noñ
Please	**S'il vous plaît**	seel voo **play**
Thank you	**Merci**	mer-**see**
Excuse me	**Excusez-moi**	exkoo-**zay** mwah
Hello	**Bonjour**	boñ**zhoor**
Goodbye	**Au revoir**	oh ruh-**vwar**
Good night	**Bonsoir**	boñ-**swar**
Morning	**Le matin**	ma**tañ**
Afternoon	**L'après-midi**	l'apreh-**meedee**
Evening	**Le soir**	swar
Yesterday	**Hier**	ee**yehr**
Today	**Aujourd'hui**	oh-zhoor-**dwee**
Tomorrow	**Demain**	duh**mañ**
Here	**Ici**	ee-**see**
There	**Là**	lah
What?	**Quel, quelle?**	kel, kel
When?	**Quand?**	koñ
Why?	**Pourquoi?**	poor-**kwah**
Where?	**Où?**	oo

Useful Phrases

How are you?	**Comment allez-vous?**	kom-moñ tal**ay voo**
Very well, thank you.	**Très bien, merci.**	treh byañ, mer-**see**
Pleased to meet you.	**Enchanté de faire votre connaissance.**	oñshoñ-**tay** duh fehr votr kon-ay-**sans**
See you soon.	**A bientôt.**	byañ-**toh**
That's fine	**Voilà qui est parfait**	vwalah kee ay par**fay**
Where is/are...?	**Où est/sont...?**	oo ay/soñ
How far is it to...?	**Combien de kilomètres d'ici à...?**	kom-**byañ** duh keelo-**metr** d'ee-**see** ah
Which way to...?	**Quelle est la direction pour...?**	kel ay lah **deer**-ek-**syoñ** poor
Do you speak English?	**Parlez-vous anglais?**	par-**lay** voo oñg-**lay**
I don't understand.	**Je ne comprends pas.**	zhuh nuh kom-**proñ** pah
Could you speak slowly, please?	**Pouvez-vous parler moins vite, s'il vous plaît?**	poo-**vay** voo par-**lay** mwa**ñ** veet, seel voo play
I'm sorry.	**Excusez-moi.**	exkoo-**zay** mwah

Useful Words

big	**grand**	groñ
small	**petit**	puh-**tee**
hot	**chaud**	show
cold	**froid**	frwah
good	**bon**	boñ
bad	**mauvais**	moh-**veh**
enough	**assez**	as**say**
well	**bien**	byañ
open	**ouvert**	oo-**ver**
closed	**fermé**	fer-**meh**
left	**gauche**	gohsh
right	**droit**	drwah
straight ahead	**tout droit**	too drwah
near	**près**	preh
far	**loin**	lwañ
up	**en haut**	oñ **oh**
down	**en bas**	oñ **bah**
early	**de bonne heure**	duh bon **urr**
late	**en retard**	oñ ruh-**tar**
entrance	**l'entrée**	l'on-**tray**
exit	**la sortie**	sor-**tee**
toilet	**les toilettes, les WC**	**twah**-let, vay-**see**
free, unoccupied	**libre**	leebr
free, no charge	**gratuit**	grah-**twee**

Making a Telephone Call

I'd like to make a long-distance call.	**Je voudrais faire un interurbain.**	zhuh **voo**-dreh fehr uñ añter-**oor**bañ
I'd like to make a collect call.	**Je voudrais faire une communication PCV.**	zhuh voo**dreh** fehr oon ko**moo**nikah-**syoñ** peh-seh-veh
I'll try again later.	**Je rappelerai plus tard.**	zhuh rapel-**eray** ploo tar
Can I leave a message?	**Est-ce que je peux laisser un message?**	es-**keh** zhuh puh leh-**say** uñ meh**sazh**
Hold on.	**Ne quittez pas, s'il vous plaît.**	nuh kee-**tay** pah seel voo play
Could you speak up a little, please?	**Pouvez-vous parler un peu plus fort?**	poo-**vay** voo par-**lay** uñ puh ploo for
local call	**la communication locale**	komoonikah-**syoñ** low-**kal**

Shopping

How much does this cost?	**C'est combien s'il vous plaît?**	say kom-**byañ** seel voo play
I would like...	**Je voudrais...**	zhuh voo-**dray**
Do you have?	**Est-ce que vous avez?**	es-**kuh** voo zav**ay**
I'm just looking.	**Je regarde seulement.**	zhuh ruh**gar** suhl**moñ**
Do you take credit cards?	**Est-ce que vous acceptez les cartes de crédit?**	es-**kuh** voo zaksept-**ay** leh kart duh kreh-**dee**
Do you take travellers' cheques?	**Est-ce que vous acceptez les chèques de voyage?**	es-**kuh** voo zaksept-**ay** leh shek duh vwa**yazh**
What time do you open?	**A quelle heure vous êtes ouvert?**	ah kel urr voo zet oo-**ver**
What time do you close?	**A quelle heure vous êtes fermé?**	ah kel urr voo zet fer-**may**
This one.	**Celui-ci.**	suhl-wee-**see**
That one.	**Celui-là.**	suhl-wee-**lah**
expensive	**cher**	shehr
cheap	**pas cher, bon marché**	pah shehr, boñ mar-**shay**
size, clothes	**la taille**	tye
size, shoes	**la pointure**	pwañ-**tur**
white	**blanc**	bloñ
black	**noir**	nwahr
red	**rouge**	roozh
yellow	**jaune**	zhohwn
green	**vert**	vehr
blue	**bleu**	bluh

Types of Shops

antiques shop	**le magasin d'antiquités**	maga-**zañ** d'oñteekee-**tay**
bakery	**la boulangerie**	booloñ-**zhuree**
bank	**la banque**	boñk
bookshop	**la librairie**	lee-**brehree**
butcher	**la boucherie**	boo-**shehree**
cake shop	**la pâtisserie**	patee-**sree**
cheese shop	**la fromagerie**	fromazh-**ree**
chemist	**la pharmacie**	farmah-**see**
dairy	**la crémerie**	krem-**ree**
department store	**le grand magasin**	groñ maga-**zañ**
delicatessen	**la charcuterie**	sharkoot-**ree**
fish seller	**la poissonnerie**	pwasson-**ree**
gift shop	**le magasin de cadeaux**	maga-**zañ** duh ka**doh**
greengrocer	**le marchand de légumes**	mar-**shoñ** duh lay-**goom**
grocery	**l'alimentation**	alee-moñta-**syoñ**
hairdresser	**le coiffeur**	kwa**fuhr**
market	**le marché**	marsh-**ay**
newsstand	**le magasin de journaux**	maga-**zañ** duh zhoor-**no**
post office	**la poste, le bureau de poste, le PTT**	pohst, boo**roh** duh pohst, peh-teh-teh
shoe shop	**le magasin de chaussures**	maga-**zañ** duh show-**soor**
supermarket	**le supermarché**	soo pehr-**marshay**
tobacconist	**le tabac**	tabah
travel agent	**l'agence de voyages**	**l'az**hoñs duh vwa**yazh**

Sightseeing

abbey	**l'abbaye**	l'abay-**ee**
art gallery	**la galerie d'art**	galer-**ree** dart
bus station	**la gare routière**	gahr roo-tee-**yehr**

cathedral	**la cathédrale**	katay-**dral**
church	**l'église**	ayg**leez**
garden	**le jardin**	zhar-**dañ**
library	**la bibliothèque**	beeb**leeo**-tek
museum	**le musée**	moo-**zay**
tourist information office	**les renseignements touristiques, le syndicat d'initiative**	roñsayn-**moñ** too-rees-**teek**, sandee-ka d'eenee-sya**teev**
town hall	**l'hôtel de ville**	oh**tel** duh veel
train station	**la gare (SNCF)**	gahr (es-en-say-ef)
private mansion	**l'hôtel particulier**	oh**tel** partikoo-**lyay**
closed for public holiday	**fermeture jour fériée**	fehrmeh-**tur** zhoor fehree-**ay**

Staying in a Hotel

Do you have a vacant room?	**Est-ce que vous avez une chambre?**	es-kuh voo-**zavay** oon shambr
double room, with double bed	**la chambre à deux personnes, avec un grand lit**	shambr ah duh pehr-**son**, avek un groñ lee
twin room	**la chambre à deux lits**	shambr ah duh lee
single room	**la chambre à une personne**	shambr ah oon pehr-**son**
room with a bath, shower	**la chambre avec salle de bains, une douche**	shambr avek sal duh bañ, oon doosh
porter	**le garçon**	gar-**soñ**
key	**la clef**	klay
I have a reservation.	**J'ai fait une réservation.**	zhay fay oon rayzehrva-**syoñ**

Eating Out

Have you got a table?	**Avez-vous une table libre?**	avay-**voo** oon tahbl leebr
I want to reserve a table	**Je voudrais réserver une table.**	zhuh voo-**dray** rayzehr-**vay** oon tahbl
The bill, please.	**L'addition, s'il vous plaît.**	l'adee-**syoñ** seel voo **play**
I am a vegetarian.	**Je suis végétarien.**	zhuh swee vezhay-**tehryañ**
Waitress/ waiter	**Madame, Mademoiselle/ Monsieur**	mah-**dam**, mah-demwah**zel**/ muh-**syuh**
menu	**le menu, la carte**	men-**oo**, kart
fixed-price menu	**le menu à prix fixe**	men-**oo** ah pree feeks
cover charge	**le couvert**	koo-**vehr**
wine list	**la carte des vins**	**kart**-deh vañ
glass	**le verre**	vehr
bottle	**la bouteille**	boo-**tay**
knife	**le couteau**	koo-**toh**
fork	**la fourchette**	for-**shet**
spoon	**la cuillère**	kwee-**yehr**
breakfast	**le petit déjeuner**	puh-**tee** deh-**zhuh-nay**
lunch	**le déjeuner**	deh-**zhuh-nay**
dinner	**le dîner**	dee-**nay**
main course	**le plat principal**	plah prañsee-**pal**
appetizer, first course	**l'entrée, le hors d'oeuvre**	oñ-**tray**, or-duhvr
dish of the day	**le plat du jour**	plah doo zhoor
wine bar	**le bar à vin**	bar ah vañ
café	**le café**	ka-**fay**
rare	**saignant**	**say**-noñ
medium	**à point**	ah **pwañ**
well done	**bien cuit**	byañ **kwee**

Menu Decoder

l'agneau	an**yoh**	lamb
l'ail	eye	garlic
la banane	ba**nan**	banana
le beurre	burr	butter
la bière, bière à la pression	bee-**yehr**, bee-**yehr** ah lah pres-**syoñ**	beer draught beer
le bifteck, le steack	beef-**tek**, stek	steak
le boeuf	buhf	beef
bouilli	boo-**yee**	boiled
le café	kah-**fay**	coffee
le canard	ka**nar**	duck
le chocolat	**shoko**-lah	chocolate
le citron	see-**troñ**	lemon
le citron pressé	see-**troñ** press-**eh**	fresh lemon juice
les crevettes	kruh-**vet**	prawns
les crustacés	**kroos**-ta-**say**	shellfish
cuit au four	kweet oh foor	baked
le dessert	deh-**ser**	dessert
l'eau minérale	oh **meeney**-ral	mineral water
les escargots	es-kar-**goh**	snails
les frites	freet	chips
le fromage	from-**azh**	cheese
le fruit frais	frwee freh	fresh fruit
les fruits de mer	frwee duh mer	seafood
le gâteau	gah-**toh**	cake
la glace	glas	ice, ice cream
grillé	gree-**yay**	grilled
le homard	om**ahr**	lobster
l'huile	weel	oil
le jambon	zhoñ-**boñ**	ham
le lait	leh	milk
les légumes	lay-**goom**	vegetables
la moutarde	moo-**tard**	mustard
l'oeuf	uf	egg
les oignons	zon**yoñ**	onions
les olives	zo**leev**	olives
l'orange	oroñzh	orange
l'orange pressée	oroñzh press-**eh**	fresh orange juice
le pain	pan	bread
le petit pain	puh-**tee** pañ	roll
poché	posh-**ay**	poached
le poisson	pwah-**ssoñ**	fish
le poivre	pwavr	pepper
la pomme	pom	apple
les pommes de terre	pom-duh **tehr**	potatoes
le porc	por	pork
le potage	poh-**tazh**	soup
le poulet	poo-**lay**	chicken
le riz	ree	rice
rôti	row-**tee**	roast
la sauce	sohs	sauce
la saucisse	soh**sees**	sausage, fresh
sec	sek	dry
le sel	sel	salt
la soupe	soop	soup
le sucre	sookr	sugar
le thé	tay	tea
la viande	vee-**yand**	meat
le vin blanc	vañ **bloñ**	white wine
le vin rouge	vañ **roozh**	red wine
le vinaigre	vee**naygr**	vinegar

Numbers

0	**zéro**	zeh-**roh**
1	**un, une**	uñ, oon
2	**deux**	duh
3	**trois**	trwah
4	**quatre**	katr
5	**cinq**	sañk
6	**six**	sees
7	**sept**	set
8	**huit**	weet
9	**neuf**	nerf
10	**dix**	dees
11	**onze**	oñz
12	**douze**	dooz
13	**treize**	trehz
14	**quatorze**	ka**torz**
15	**quinze**	kañz
16	**seize**	sehz
17	**dix-sept**	dees-**set**
18	**dix-huit**	dees-**weet**
19	**dix-neuf**	dees-**nerf**
20	**vingt**	vañ
30	**trente**	tront
40	**quarante**	kar**oñt**
50	**cinquante**	sañk**oñt**
60	**soixante**	swas**oñt**
70	**soixante-dix**	swasoñt-**dees**
80	**quatre-vingts**	katr-**vañ**
90	**quatre-vingt-dix**	katr-vañ-**dees**
100	**cent**	soñ
1,000	**mille**	meel

Time

one minute	**une minute**	oon mee-**noot**
one hour	**une heure**	oon urr
half an hour	**une demi-heure**	oon **duh-mee** urr
Monday	**lundi**	luñ-**dee**
Tuesday	**mardi**	mar-**dee**
Wednesday	**mercredi**	mehrkruh-**dee**
Thursday	**jeudi**	zhuh-**dee**
Friday	**vendredi**	voñdruh-**dee**
Saturday	**samedi**	sam-**dee**
Sunday	**dimanche**	dee-**moñsh**

Central Paris

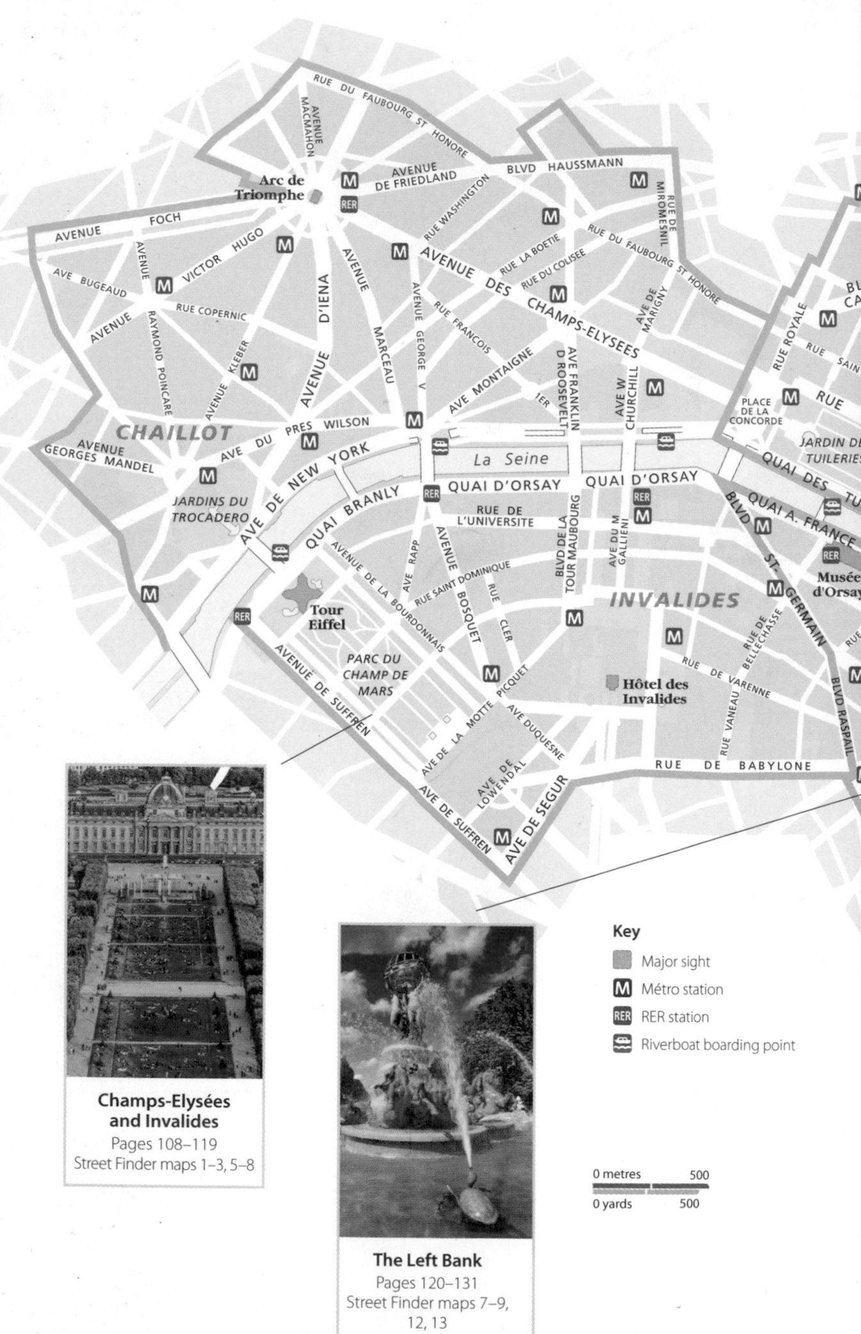

Champs-Elysées and Invalides
Pages 108–119
Street Finder maps 1–3, 5–8

The Left Bank
Pages 120–131
Street Finder maps 7–9, 12, 13